British Master Tax Guide
2016–17

British Master Tax Guide
2016–17

Wolters Kluwer

© 2016 Wolters Kluwer (UK) Limited

Wolters Kluwer
145 London Road
Kingston upon Thames KT2 6SR
United Kingdom
Telephone: (0) 844 561 8166
Facsimile: +44 (0) 208 247 2637
E-mail: uk-customer.services@wolterskluwer.com
Website: www.wolterskluwer.co.uk

ISBN 978-1-78540-278-4

British Library Cataloguing-in-Publication Data

A catalogue record for this book is available from the British Library.

Typeset by Innodata
Printed in Spain by Rotabook, S.L.

About the authors

Sarah Arnold FCA CTA is an independent tax consultant who provides specialist tax advice via her own tax consultancy to fellow professionals providing tax and accountancy services. She additionally contributes to a number of CCH publications, including the *British Tax Reporter,* the *Weekly Tax News,* the *Red & Green* legislation volumes and *Hardman's Tax Rates & Tables.*

Sarah Laing CTA has been writing professionally since joining CCH Editions in 1998 as a Senior Technical Editor, contributing to a range of highly regarded publications including the *British Tax Reporter, Taxes – the Weekly Tax News*, the *Red & Green* legislation volumes, *Hardman's, International Tax Agreements* and many others. She became a Publishing Manager for the tax and accounting portfolio in 2001, and later went on to help run CCH Seminars (including ABG Courses and Conferences). Sarah originally worked for the Inland Revenue in Newbury and Swindon Tax Offices, before moving out into practice in 1991. She has worked for both small and big five firms, and now works as a freelance author providing technical writing services for the tax and accountancy profession.

Lakshmi Narain LLM MSc FCA CTA (Fellow) is Chairman of the South Wales Branch of the Chartered Institute of Taxation and a member of the Property Taxes Subcommittee of the Chartered Institute of Taxation. Lakshmi was the chairman of the Stamp Taxes Practitioners Group from its formation in 2004–2007 was the Adviser to the Finance Committee and a member of the Technical Experts Group advising the Welsh Government on the introduction of the Land Transaction Tax. Lakshmi writes and lectures extensively on tax matters.

Paul Seal FCA CTA (Fellow), TEP is a sole practitioner specialising in tax issues through his own practice and for a number of other firms. He is senior tutor for the Society of Trust and Estate Practitioners for the England and Wales examination on taxation of trusts and estates, an author of a number of publications on taxation matters and an occasional contributor to the professional press. He is a Board member, as World Wide Treasurer, for the Society of Trust and Estate Practitioners.

Michael Steed MA (Cantab) CTA (Fellow), ATT (Fellow), MAAT, trained and qualified with Coopers & Lybrand (now PwC). VAT is one of Michael's lead areas and he has advised a wide range of businesses on VAT matters over the last 25 years. Michael is a senior tax consultant in Kaplan's Leadership and Professional Development team. He is the current President of the ATT.

Preface

The *British Master Tax Guide 2016–17* is designed primarily to assist practitioners in understanding tax liabilities and entitlements for the tax year 2015–16. It is written not only to answer those questions which arise in the preparation of tax returns for the year, but also to provide information on the tax consequences flowing from decisions and transactions faced by taxpayers. The Guide also provides a concise but clear guide to tax for students and others who come to the subject for the first time.

The Guide has 12 chapters. The first chapter provides key dates, rates and other information collated in a user-friendly section. The second chapter provides a brief overview of the tax system. The third details the charge to income tax and includes full details of all the reliefs and deductions available. Similar treatments of National Insurance contributions, corporation tax, etc. follow. At the beginning of the book, there is a *What's New* section which highlights key changes since the last edition. Each chapter begins with a *Key Points* section. '*What's New*' gives a concise listing of new developments in that particular area since last year whilst '*Key Points*' is a concise listing of the major issues in that area.

The Guide explains the rules affecting everyday business and personal tax issues in the simplest possible way. Examples are included throughout which illustrate the text and show how these rules apply. There are also extensive links to the in-depth commentary which can be found in CCH's *Tax Reporter, VAT Reporter, NIC Reporter* and *SDLT Reporter*. The Guide rests on the firm foundation of legislation, statements of practice, extra-statutory concessions and other non-statutory sources, and decisions of the courts; references to which are included on separate lines at the end of each paragraph for easy reference.

The text is fully updated for *Finance Act* 2016 and all other relevant legislation, case law, HMRC statements of practice and extra-statutory concessions. Proposed future changes are included to the extent that details have been released at the date of publication.

An exhaustive case table, legislation finding list and topic index facilitate access to the Guide.

November 2016

What's new?

Overview

206: Wales Bill 2016–17 introduced to Parliament on 7 June 2016.

206: The *Tax Collection and Management (Wales) Act* 2016 received Royal Assent on 25 April 2016.

212: Directive 2016/881 of 25 May 2016 amending Directive 2011/16/EU as regards mandatory automatic exchange of information in the field of taxation.

Income tax

242: Rate of income tax for 2016–17 per *Finance Act* 2016, including new savings nil rate (personal savings allowance) and new dividend nil rate (dividend allowance).

265: Restriction on travel expenses for workers providing services through intermediaries from 6 April 2016 per *Finance Act* 2016.

286; 420: Taxation of sporting testimonials and limited exemption from 6 April 2017 (*Finance Act* 2016).

288; 312: *Finance Act* 2016 clarifies the concept of 'fair bargain' not applicable to certain benefits.

383; 390: Statutory exemption for trivial benefits in kind per *Finance Act* 2016.

402: Cars: appropriate percentage for 2019–20 and subsequent tax years (*Finance Act* 2016).

402: Diesel supplement for company car tax retained until April 2021 (*Finance Act* 2016).

474: Reduction in lifetime allowance to £1m from April 2016 (*Finance Act* 2016).

571: *Stayton* [2016] TC 05104: purchase and resale of property not an adventure in the nature of trade.

626: Charge on trading income received in money's worth from 16 March 2016 (*Finance Act* 2016).

942: Extension of farmers averaging period from two to five years from 2016–17 (*Finance Act* 2016).

985: Dividends received by relevant property trusts from 6 April 2016 taxed at 38.1% following the changes to dividend taxation; the £5,000 exemption will not be available but the full 38.1% can enter the tax pool.

987: For 2016–17 (only), if the only income received by trustees is savings interest where the aggregate gross is less than £500 and the tax less than £100, a tax return need not be completed but note receiving any dividend income puts the trust outside the 'concession'; income distribution taxation is unaffected.

1006: Dividends received by interest in possession trusts taxed at 7.5%; the £5,000 exemption will not be available.

1031: Dividends received by estates in administration taxed at 7.5%; the £5,000 exemption will not be available.

1031: For 2016–17 (only), if the only income received by an estate in administration is savings interest where the aggregate gross is less than £500 and the tax less than £100, a tax return need not be completed by the executors but note receiving any dividend income places the estate outside the 'concession'.

1200: Charge on property income received in money's worth from 16 March 2016 (*Finance Act* 2016).

1210: Abolition of wear and tear allowance and renewals allowance for furnished lettings and introduction of new allowance from 6 April 2016 per *Finance Act* 2016.

1350: Dividend tax rates and new dividend nil rate (dividend allowance) from April 2016 (*Finance Act* 2016).

1352: TAAR for distributions in a winding up from April 2016 (*Finance Act* 2016).

1372: Automatic deduction of 20% income tax by banks and building societies ceased from April 2016 per *Finance Act* 2016.

1412: Amendments to disguised investment management fees and carried interest rules from 6 April 2016 (*Finance Act* 2016).

1420; 1422: Amendments to transactions in securities anti-avoidance rules from 6 April 2016 (*Finance Act* 2016).

1851; 1852: Personal allowances for 2016–17 and 2017–18 (*Finance Act* 2016).

1883: Relief for peer-to-peer investments from April 2016 (*Finance Act* 2016).

1921: New power to amend legislation in relation to individual savings accounts of deceased investors per *Finance Act* 2016.

1921: Amendments to ISA rules by SI 2016/364.

1932: Exclusion of energy-generation activities as qualifying activities for Venture Capital Schemes from 6 April 2016 (*Finance Act* 2016).

2225: Time limits for self-assessments clarified (*Finance Act* 2016).

2328: Simple income tax assessments from 15 September 2016 (Royal Assent of *Finance Act* 2016).

2387: Construction Industry Scheme Compliance Test simplified by SI 2016/404.

NICs

2502: Further review by OTS on alignment of income tax and National Insurance contributions.

2676: Confirmed abolition of Class 2 National Insurance from April 2018 (Budget 2016).

2780: Three-day easement for PAYE and NIC penalties to continue for 2016–17.

Corporation tax

3000: Dividend tax credit abolished from 6 April 2016.

3000: Possible further reduction of CT rates.

3015: Anti-avoidance legislation following the publication of certain action points from the BEPS project.

3015: Anti-avoidance legislation targeting offshore dealers and developers of UK property.

3060: Update on consultation on tax deductibility of corporate interest.

3100: Proposed CT rate from April 2020.

3100: Changes made to the Patent Box regime in the *Finance Act* 2016.

3152: Transactions for money's worth – *Finance Act* 2016 changes.

3158: Changes to relief for wear and tear and replacement of domestic items.

3164: Loan relationships and derivatives changes – *Finance Act* 2016 changes.

3171: Update on deductibility of corporate interest expense.

3330: Proposal to restrict carry forward of losses from April 2017.

3370: *Leekes v HMRC* released 12 July 2016.

4040: Change to tax rate on loans to participators.

4080: Impact of the removal of the small companies' rate of corporation tax.

4390: Publication of tax strategy statement.

Capital allowances

4640: Updated energy technology list (for enhanced capital allowances on energy saving plant and machinery) published 7 September 2016.

4645: Updated water technology list (for enhanced capital allowances on environmentally beneficial plant and machinery) published June 2016.

4648: New areas designated by SI 2016/751 as designated assisted areas for the purposes of enterprise zones first-year allowances.

4648: Enhanced capital allowances (ECAs) in enterprise zones to be made available for eight years following establishment of the site as an ECA site (*Finance Act* 2016).

4650: extension of 100% first year allowances for very low CO2 emission cars to April 2021 announced at Budget 2016.

Capital gains tax

5090: Negligible value securities list updated 24 June 2016.

5294: Retrospective amendments to entrepreneurs' relief restriction on goodwill transferred to a related party from 3 December 2014 (*Finance Act* 2016).

5294: Retrospective amendments to definitions of 'trading company' and 'trading group' for entrepreneurs' relief purposes from 18 March 2015 (*Finance Act* 2016).

5295: *Castledine* [2016] TC 04930 decision released 1 March 2016 and *McQuillan* [2016] TC 05074 decision released 5 May 2016.

5298: Retrospective amendments to conditions to be satisfied for an associated disposal to qualify for entrepreneurs' relief from 18 March 2015 (*Finance Act* 2016).

5310ff.: New relief for investors extends 10% rate of tax to disposals of certain qualifying shares issued on or after 6 April 2016 and held for three years (*Finance Act* 2016).

5410; 5415; 5697: Reduction in rates of capital gains tax from 6 April 2016 (*Finance Act* 2016).

5710: All non-dom reforms to be legislated for in Finance Bill 2017 (Budget 2016).

5817: Charge to capital gains tax on carried interest determined under legislative test from 6 April 2016 (*Finance Act* 2016).

5929A: Lifetime limit of £100,000 on CGT exempt gains on the disposal of shares acquired under employee shareholder agreements entered into after 16 March 2016 and amendments to rules relating to share reorganisation provisions (*Finance Act* 2016).

6428A: Prescribed circumstances under which a person not required to submit an NRCGT return may submit an elective NRCGT return (*Finance Act* 2016).

6470: Payment of capital gains tax on residential property disposals from April 2019 per Autumn Statement 2015.

Inheritance tax

Proposals to be introduced in Finance Bill 2017 to make individuals who have been UK resident for 15 out of the previous 20 years to be deemed domicile *for all tax purposes* with effect from 6 April 2017. This will replace the 17 out of 20 year rule which currently applies but only to IHT.

Proposals included in *Finance Act* 2016, s. 93 to give an additional nil rate band from 6 April 2017 that will be available to help those who wish to pass on to their children their home tax free. There will also be provisions to allow tracing of funds, where an individual has sold their home (or downsized), so released on or after 8 July 2015 (see 7193).

Proposals to be enacted to make all UK residential property, owned by non-domiciles, subject to UK IHT, no matter how that property is owned. This is clearly a logical extension of the ATED rules (see 6550).

Value Added Tax

8222: In the Pre-Brexit negotiations, David Cameron was able to get the EU to agree to a zero-rating of women's sanitary products from a date to be agreed.

8365: Following Tribunal decisions in respect of the appropriate rate for mechanical engineers under the Flat Rate Scheme, HMRC have softened their stance and have produced a new edition of the Flat Rate Scheme Public Notice.

SDLT

9070: From 1 April 2016, FA 2016 introduces a new higher rate of SDLT for second homes and residential properties purchased in companies.

9070: HMRC have published guidance on the application of the SDLT higher rates.

9070: The SDLT rates for mixed and commercial properties have been moved onto the same progressive system as residential properties from the same date.

Other Indirect Taxes

9500: The revised customs code – the Union Customs Code (UCC) is now in force together with its Implementing Regulations and Delegated Regulations from 1 May 2016. This is a European-wide computer-based movement control system, that will control the import and export of goods in and out of the EU. The EU Commission has committed to implementing electronic customs in the EU and to replace the hybrid system of part-paper and part-electronic systems with a totally electronic customs regime.

HMRC have published detailed guidance on the operation of the UCC in May 2016 and this can be found at www.gov.uk/guidance/introduction-ofthe-union-customs-code-ucc.

9580: HMRC have published guidance (Notice 3001) which explains the legal basis and generic requirements of the Customs Special Procedures under the Union Customs Code (UCC).

9690: There are new rates of Gaming Duty from 1 April 2016.

9710: There are new rates of alcoholic liquor duties from 21 March 2016.

9720: Tobacco duties have been raised from 16 March 2016.

9730: The main rates of hydrocarbon oils duties remain frozen.

9760: There are new rates for Air Passenger Duty from 1 April 2016.

9800: HMRC have introduced a new standard rate of 10% for Insurance Premium Tax from 1 October 2016.

Dealing with HMRC

11914: *National Crime Agency, ex parte a taxpayer* [2016] TC 05191 decision released 3 June 2016.

11930: Extension of data gathering powers under FA 2011, Sch. 23 and clarification of procedure for administering penalties for non-compliance with data-holder notices (*Finance Act* 2016).

11932: New powers to obtain information about certain tax advantages and publish state aid information (*Finance Act* 2016).

12000: Offshore tax errors, etc.: publishing details of deliberate tax defaulters (*Finance Act* 2016).

12024; 12129; 12202: Increased minimum penalties (after mitigation) for offshore matters and new disclosure requirement to obtain mitigation (*Finance Act* 2016).

12252: New asset based penalties for offshore inaccuracies and failures penalty (*Finance Act* 2016).

12255: New penalty for enabling offshore tax evasion (*Finance Act* 2016).

12260: Offences relating to offshore income, assets and activities (*Finance Act* 2016).

12420: New GAAR penalty and changes to GAAR procedure from Royal Assent of *Finance Act* 2016.

12422: Factsheet CC/FS30a Tax avoidance schemes – penalties for follower notices published.

12424: New threshold for promoters of tax avoidance schemes from 15 September 2016 (Royal Assent of *Finance Act* 2016).

12424A: New regime for serial avoiders from 6 April 2017 per *Finance Act* 2016.

12440: Online complaints form for income tax (Self-assessment and PAYE) launched.

Sarah Arnold, Paul Seal, Lakshmi Narain and Michael Steed

November 2016

Contents

Contents

Contents

Key Data

PRINCIPLES OF INCOME TAX

1 Income tax rates: 2016–17

(FA 2015, s. 4; FA 2016, s. 1; ITA 2007, s. 6–15)

(Tax reporter: 148-075ff.)

UK rates (England, Wales and Northern Ireland): 2016–17

	Taxable income band £	Tax rate[1] %	Tax on band £
Basic rate	1–32,000	20	6,400
Higher rate	32,001–150,000	40	47,200
Additional rate	Over 150,000	45	
Starting rate for savings income	1–5,000	0	

Starting rate for savings income[2]	0% up to starting rate limit
Rate on non dividend savings income	0% on savings income charged at the savings nil rate[2]
	20% up to basic rate limit
	40% up to higher rate limit
	45% thereafter
Dividend nil rate[4]	0% on first £5,000 dividends
Dividend ordinary rate	7.5%[4] up to basic rate limit
Dividend upper rate	32.5%[4] up to higher rate limit
Dividend additional rate	38.1%[4] above higher rate limit
Trust rate	45%[3]
Dividend trust rate	38.1%[3]

Notes

[1] Income tax lock: F(No. 2)A 2015, s. 1 sets a ceiling for the main rates of income tax at 20%, 40% and 45% respectively for tax years beginning on or after 18 November 2015 (Royal Assent) but before the date of the first parliamentary general election after that day.

[2] The 'starting rate for savings' is available for savings income only. If an individual's taxable non-savings income (i.e. after deduction of their personal allowance) exceeds the starting rate, then

the starting rate is not available and an individual's savings income is chargeable at the basic, higher or additional rate (as would otherwise apply). From 6 April 2016, a new savings allowance is available to individuals with savings income, 'the savings nil rate'. The savings allowance is £1,000 for basic rate taxpayers, £500 for higher rate taxpayers and £nil for additional rate taxpayers. Savings income within the savings allowance is chargeable at the savings nil rate 0% (ITA 2007, s. 12A and 12B). The 'savings nil rate' is available in addition to the 'starting rate for savings' (where this is available) on savings income above the starting rate limit.

(3) The special trust rates do not apply to the first £1,000 slice of the 'trust rate income'. Instead, the normal income tax rates (currently the basic rate and dividend ordinary rate) apply as appropriate (ITA 2007, s. 491(1)–(3)).

(4) From April 2016, the dividend tax credit was abolished and replaced with a £5,000 tax-free dividend allowance. The allowance operates as a 0% tax rate in place of the dividend ordinary rate, dividend upper rate or dividend additional rate as would otherwise apply on the first £5,000 of an individual's dividend income (ITA 2007, s. 13A).

2 Scottish income tax rates: 2016–17

(Scotland Act 1998; ITA 2007, s. 6A and 11A)

(Tax Reporter: 148-160)

UK rate for England, Wales and Northern Ireland	Taxable income band £	UK rate paid in Scotland %	Scottish rate(1) %	Total rate for Scottish taxpayers %
Basic rate 20%	1–32,000	10	10	20
Higher rate 40%	32,001–150,000	30	10	40
Additional rate 45%	Over £150,000	35	10	45

Note
(1) Rate based on draft Scottish Budget 2016–17 delivered to Parliament on 16 December 2015.

3 Income tax rates: 2015–16

(FA 2014, s. 2; ITA 2007, s. 6–15)

(Tax reporter: 148-075ff.)

2015–16

	Taxable income band £	Tax rate %	Tax on band £
Basic rate	1–31,785	20	6,357
Higher rate	31,786–150,000	40	47,286
Additional rate	Over 150,000	45	

Rate on non dividend savings income	0% up to £5,000[1]
	20% up to basic rate limit
	40% up to higher rate limit
	45% thereafter
Dividend ordinary rate (effective rate with tax credit)	10% up to basic rate limit 0%
Dividend upper rate (effective rate with tax credit)	32.5% up to higher rate limit 25%
Dividend additional rate (effective rate with tax credit)	37.5% above higher rate limit 30.6%
Trust rate	45%[2]
Dividend trust rate	37.5%[2]

Notes

[1] The starting rate is available for savings income only. If an individual's taxable non-savings income (i.e. after deduction of their personal allowance) exceeds the starting rate limit, then the starting rate is not available.

[2] The special trust rates do not apply to the first £1,000 slice of the 'trust rate income'. Instead, the normal income tax rates (currently the basic rate and dividend ordinary rate) apply as appropriate (ITA 2007, s. 491(1)–(3)).

4 Income tax rates: 2014–15

(FA 2014, s. 1; ITA 2007, s. 6–15)

(Tax Reporter: 148-075ff.)

	Taxable income band £	Tax rate %	Tax on band £
Basic rate	1–31,865	20	6,373
Higher rate	31,866–150,000	40	47,254
Additional rate	Over 150,000	45	

Rate on non dividend savings income	10% up to £2,880[1]
	20% up to basic rate limit
	40% up to higher rate limit
	45% thereafter
Dividend ordinary rate (effective rate with tax credit)	10% up to basic rate limit 0%
Dividend upper rate (effective rate with tax credit)	32.5% up to higher rate limit 25%

Dividend additional rate (effective rate with tax credit)	37.5% above higher rate limit 30.6%
Trust rate	45%[2]
Dividend trust rate	37.5%[2]

Notes

[1] A 10% starting rate applies to the first £2,880 of non-dividend savings income. The starting rate does not apply if non-savings income exceeds the personal allowance plus £2,880.

[2] The special trust rates do not apply to the first £1,000 slice of the 'trust rate income'. Instead, the normal income tax rates (currently the basic rate and dividend ordinary rate) apply as appropriate (ITA 2007, s. 491(1)–(3)).

5 Personal allowances and reliefs

(ITA 2007, s. 35–46)

(Tax Reporter: 155-000ff.)

From 6 April 2016, there is one income tax personal allowance of £11,000 (2016–17) regardless of an individual's date of birth.

For tax years up to 2012–13, higher (age-related) allowances were available for individuals attaining 'age 65–74' or age '75 and over' in the tax year. These allowances were frozen at 2012–13 rates and phased out between 2013–14 and 2015–16 as the basic personal allowance caught up with the frozen amounts of the former allowances.

From 6 April 2016, a personal savings allowance is available for up to £1,000 of a basic rate taxpayer's savings income and up to £500 of a higher rate taxpayer's savings income each year. The personal savings allowance is not available to additional rate taxpayers. Automatic deduction of 20% income tax by banks and building societies on non-ISA savings also ceased from the same date (amendments by FA 2016, s. 39–41 and Sch. 6).

Existing legislation within ITA 2007 requires the Government to increase personal allowances and rate limits (except the £150,000 higher rate limit, £100,000 personal allowance income limit) by the annual percentage increase in the consumer prices index (CPI) for the year to September preceding the new tax year (indexation). Amounts determined by the annual indexation order may be overridden by provision in a Finance Act.

However, once the personal allowance has reached £12,500, it will be uprated in line with the national minimum wage (NMW) (and existing indexation provisions will no longer apply) ensuring that anyone on the NMW working 30 hours per week or less, does not pay income tax (ITA 2007, s. 57A, 57(8)).

6 Transferable tax allowances for married couples

(ITA 2007, Pt. 3, Ch. 3A)

(Tax Reporter: 156-725)

From the 2015–16 tax year, a spouse or civil partner who is not liable to income tax because their income is below their personal allowance or who is liable to income tax at the basic rate, dividend ordinary rate or the starting rate for savings may elect to transfer a portion of their personal allowance to their spouse or civil partner (effectively 10% of the personal allowance), with a corresponding reduction to the transferring spouse's personal allowance. Only a spouse or civil partner who is liable to income tax at the basic rate, dividend ordinary rate or the starting rate for savings can receive the transferred personal allowance, which is given effect as a reduction to the recipient's income tax liability at the basic rate of tax. Married couples or civil partners entitled to claim the married couple's allowance are not entitled to make a transfer.

Income tax reliefs	2016–17 £	2015–16 £	2014–15 £
Personal allowance[1]			
All ages	11,000	—	—
– born after 5 April 1948	—	—	10,000
– born after 5 April 1938	—	10,600	—
– born after 5 April 1938 but before 6 April 1948	—	—	10,500
– born before 6 April 1938	—	10,660	10,660
Marriage allowance	1,100	1,060	—
Married couple's allowance[2][3]			
– born before 6 April 1935 and age 75 & over	8,355	8,355	8,165
– minimum amount of allowance	3,220	3,220	3,140
Maximum income before abatement of:			
– personal allowance	100,000	100,000	100,000
– reliefs for older taxpayers	27,700	27,000	27,000
Abatement Income ceilings Personal allowance: (basic)	122,000	121,200	120,000
Single (age personal allowance)			
– born after 5 April 1938 but before 6 April 1948	—	—	28,000
– born before 6 April 1938	—	27,820	28,320

Income tax reliefs	2016–17 £	2015–16 £	2014–15 £
Married couples allowance (only)	37,970	37,970	37,050
Married (age personal allowance and MCA)			
– relevant partner born after 5 April 1938 but before 6 April 1948	—	—	38,050
– relevant partner born before 6 April 1938	—	38,090	38,370
Blind persons allowance	2,290	2,290	2,230
Dividend allowance[5]	5,000	2,230	2,160
Personal savings allowance[6]			
Basic rate taxpayers	1,000	—	—
Higher rate taxpayers	500	—	—
Life assurance relief (policies issued before 14 March 1984)[4]	—	—	12.5% of premiums
'Rent-a-room' limit	7,500	4,250	4,250

Notes

[1] From April 2010, the personal allowance is gradually withdrawn for income over £100,000 at a rate of £1 of allowance lost for every £2 over £100,000 until it is completely removed (ITA 2007, s. 35–37).

[2] Relief is given as a tax reduction at a rate of 10%.

[3] The married couple's allowance is available only where at least one partner reached the age of 65 before 6 April 2000, i.e. was born before 6 April 1935. That partner will have become 75 at some point during 2009–10 and therefore will be entitled to the higher amount of the allowance for that tax year and subsequent tax years, i.e. for those aged 75 or over.

[4] By relief at source. Abolished for payments becoming due and payable on or after 6 April 2015, and payments becoming due and payable before 6 April 2015 but actually paid on or after 6 July 2015 (FA 2012, s. 227 and Sch. 39, para. 23).

[5] From 6 April 2016, a 0% rate of tax (the dividend nil rate) applies to the first £5,000 of dividend income received (ITA 2007, s. 13A).

[6] From 6 April 2016, a new 0% rate of tax applies to an individual's savings income (the savings nil rate or savings allowance). The savings nil rate applies to the first £1,000 of a basic rate taxpayer's savings income, or the first £500 of a higher rate taxpayer's savings income. The savings nil rate is not available to additional rate taxpayers (ITA 2007, s. 12A and 12B).

COMPANY CARS

7 Car benefits: relevant thresholds

(ITEPA 2003, s. 139)

(Tax Reporter: 415-050ff.)

The benefit is calculated as a percentage of the list price of the car appropriate to the level of the car's CO_2 emissions. The 'appropriate percentage' depends upon whether the car was first registered on or after

1st January 1998 and whether it has a CO_2 emissions figure or is a diesel car. Relevant percentages are set out below:

For cars registered on or after 1 January 1998 (with CO_2 emissions figures)

CO_2 emissions	2014–15	2015–16	2016–17	2017–18[3]	2018–19[3]	2019–20[4]
50g/km or below[2]	5%[2]	5%	7%	9%	13%	16%
51–75g/km		9%	11%	13%	16%	19%
Above 75g/km up to relevant threshold	11%	13%	15%	17%	19%	22%
Equal to relevant threshold[1]	12%	14%	16%	18%	20%	23%
Above relevant threshold:						
Increase per 5g/km[1]	1%	1%	1%	1%	1%	1%
Up to maximum	35%	37%	37%	37%	37%	37%
Diesel supplement[5]	3%	3%	3%	3%	3%	3%

Notes

[1] Where CO_2 emissions are not a multiple of five, round down to the nearest multiple of five.

[2] If a car cannot emit CO_2 by being driven, the appropriate percentage is 0% until 5 April 2015 (when the five year exemption for zero carbon cars ends).

[3] In both 2017–18 and 2018–19, the appropriate percentage of list price subject to tax will increase by two percentage points for cars emitting more than 75g/km CO_2, to a maximum of 37%. In 2017–18, there will be a four percentage point differential between the 0–50 and 51–75g/km CO_2 bands and between the 51–75 and 76–94g/km CO_2 bands. In 2018–19, this differential will reduce to three percentage points (FA 2015, s. 7 and 8).

[4] In 2019–20, the appropriate percentage of list price subject to tax will increase by three percentage points for cars emitting more than 75g/km CO_2, to a maximum of 37%. There will be a three-percentage point differential between the 0–50 and 51–75g/km CO_2 bands FA 2016, s. 8.

[5] All diesel cars are currently subject to a 3% addition (but subject to the absolute cap). The 3% diesel supplement was due to be abolished from 2016–17 (FA 2014, s. 24), however, FA 2016, s. 10 retains the diesel supplement in company car tax.

The relevant threshold is as follows:

Year	Relevant threshold
2016–17	95g/km
2013–14 to 2015–16	95g/km
2012–13	100g/km

Cars registered on or after 1 January 1998 without CO_2 emissions, or cars first registered before 1 January 1998

	2014–15 Registered		2015–16 Registered		2016–17	2017-18[3]	2018-19[4]	2019-20[5]
	on or after 01/01/1998	before 01/01/1998	on or after 01/01/1998	before 01/01/1998				
Cylinder capacity of car with internal combustion engine in cubic centimetres								
● 1,400 or less	15%	15%	15%	15%	16%	18%	20%	23%
● More than 1,400 but not more than 2,000	25%	22%	25%	22%	27%	29%	31%	34%
● More than 2,000	35%	32%	37%	32%	37%	37%	37%	37%
Cars without an internal combustion engine								
● Zero-emission cars registered on or after 1 January 1998	0%[1]	—	5%	—	7%	9%	13%	16%
● Any other case	35%	32%	37%	32%	37%	37%	37%	37%
Diesel supplement	3%	N/A	3%	N/A	3%	3%	3%	3%

Notes

(1) If emissions are zero when driven, the appropriate percentage is zero until 5 April 2015.

(2) All diesel cars registered on or after 1 January 1998 are currently subject to a 3% addition (but subject to the absolute cap). The 3% diesel supplement was due to be abolished from 2016–17 (FA 2014, s. 24), however, FA 2016, s. 10 retains the diesel supplement in company car tax.

(3) Rates per FA 2015, s. 7 (amending ITEPA 2003, s. 140 and 142).

(4) Rates per FA 2015, s. 8 (amending ITEPA 2003, s. 140 and 142).

(5) Rates per FA 2016, s. 8 (amending ITEPA 2003, s. 140 and 142)

8 Car benefits: table of percentages

Table of taxable percentages

(ITEPA 2003, s. 139)

(Tax Reporter: 415-720)

CO₂ emissions	Appropriate percentage						
	2013–14[1]	2014–15[1]	2015–16[1][2]	2016–17[1]	2017–18[1][2]	2018–19[1][2]	2019–20[1][3]
0	0	0	5	7	9	13	16
1–50	5	5					
51–75			9	11	13	16	19
76–94	10	11	13	15	17	19	22
95–99	11	12	14	16	18	20	23
100–104	12	13	15	17	19	21	24
105–109	13	14	16	18	20	22	25
110–114	14	15	17	19	21	23	26
115–119	15	16	18	20	22	24	27
120–124	16	17	19	21	23	25	28
125–129	17	18	20	22	24	26	29
130–134	18	19	21	23	25	27	30
135–139	19	20	22	24	26	28	31
140–144	20	21	23	25	27	29	32
145–149	21	22	24	26	28	30	33
150–154	22	23	25	27	29	31	34
155–159	23	24	26	28	30	32	35
160–164	24	25	27	29	31	33	36
165–169	25	26	28	30	32	34	
170–174	26	27	29	31	33	35	
175–179	27	28	30	32	34	36	
180–184	28	29	31	33	35		
185–189	29	30	32	34	36		
190–194	30	31	33	35			37
195–199	31	32	34	36			
200–204	32	33	35			37	
205–209	33	34	36		37		
210–214	34			37			
215–219	35	35	37				
220+							

Notes

[1] All diesel cars are subject to a 3% loading, but not to take the maximum figure above 35% for years up to including 2014–15 and 37% for 2015–16. The 3% diesel supplement was due to be abolished from 2016–17 (FA 2014, s. 24), however, FA 2016, s. 10 retains the diesel supplement in company car tax.

(2) In both 2017–18 and 2018–19, the appropriate percentage of list price subject to tax will increase by two percentage points for cars emitting more than 75g/km CO_2, to a maximum of 37%. In 2017–18, there will be a four-percentage point differential between the 0–50 and 51–75g/km CO_2 bands and between the 51–75 and 76–94g/km CO_2 bands.

In 2018–19, this differential will reduce to three percentage points (FA 2015, s. 7 and 8).

(3) In 2019–20, the appropriate percentage of list price subject to tax will increase by three percentage points for cars emitting more than 75g/km CO_2, to a maximum of 37%. There will be a three-percentage point differential between the 0–50 and 51–75g/km CO_2 bands (FA 2016, s. 8).

9 Diesel cars: loading of appropriate percentage

(ITEPA 2003, s. 141)

(Tax Reporter: 415-740)

Most diesel cars have an appropriate percentage that is three points higher than an equivalent petrol car (but still subject to a 37% overall cap).

The 3% diesel supplement was due to be abolished from 6 April 2016 (FA 2014, s. 24), however, FA 2016, s. 10 retains the diesel supplement in company car tax. Further provisions to remove the diesel supplement are expected to be made in a future Finance Bill, with effect from 6 April 2021.

Cars that do not meet the Euro IV emissions standard

These cars are subject to the three point loading in all cases.

Cars that do meet the Euro IV emissions standard

The following table shows whether or not a 3% loading is needed for diesel cars meeting the Euro IV emissions standard:

Tax year	Car first registered by 31 December 2005	Car first registered from 1 January 2006
2011–12 to 5 April 2016	3% loading applies	3% loading applies
2006–07 to 2010–11	No loading	3% loading applies

10 Ultra-low emission cars

(ITEPA 2003, s. 139)

(Tax Reporter: 415-750)

A reduced appropriate percentage of 5% applied, from 6 April 2010 for five years, for company cars with an approved CO_2 emissions figure not exceeding 75g per kilometre. Diesel cars were still subject to the appropriate 3% loading.

From April 2015, the first-year exemption for ultra-low emission cars ended with two new bands introduced for cars emitting 0–50g/km and 51–75g/km: see section 5.

11 Zero emission cars

(ITEPA 2003, s. 140)

(Tax Reporter: 415-760ff.)

From 6 April 2010 to 5 April 2015, there was a zero tax charge for cars producing no emissions when driven (e.g. electric cars).

For rates from 6 April 2015, see section 5.

Battery electric cars had an appropriate percentage of 9% from 6 April 2006 to 5 April 2010.

FUEL FOR COMPANY CARS

12 Fuel benefit charges

(ITEPA 2003, s. 150)

(Tax Reporter: 416-000ff.)

The additional taxable benefit of free fuel provided for a company car is calculated using the same CO_2 percentages as are used for calculating the company car charge.

The CO_2 percentage figure is applied to a fixed amount in accordance with the following table:

Tax year	£
2016–17	22,200
2015–16	22,100
2014–15	21,700
2013–14	21,100
2012–13	20,200
2011–12	18,800

The fuel benefit is reduced to nil if the employee is required to make good the full cost of all fuel provided for private use, and does so.

A proportionate reduction is made where the company car is only available for part of the year, where car fuel ceases to be provided part-way through the year, or where the benefit of the company car is shared.

13 Fuel types

Employers must notify HMRC of the type of fuel (or other power) used by an employer provided car by entering the appropriate 'key letter' on the forms P11D and P46(Car). The key letters in use for P11D reporting and form P46(Car) in respect of periods post 6 April 2011 are as follows:

Key letter	Fuel or power type description
A	All other cars
D	Diesel (all Euro standards)
E	Zero emission, including electric

14 Advisory fuel rates for company cars

(Tax Reporter: 416-040)

HMRC publish rates that can be used by employers wishing to pay their employees the cost of fuel for business journeys in company cars (or, where the employer initially pays for all fuel, for reimbursement of private mileage by company car drivers to their employers). Passenger payments may be made for company cars as for private cars. Petrol hybrid cars are treated as petrol cars for this purpose.

In a change of policy announced in May 2011, HMRC now review the rates four times a year – on 1 March, 1 June, 1 September and 1 December. For one month from the date of change, employers may use either the previous or new current rates, as they choose.

	Cost per mile		
Engine size	**Petrol**	**Diesel**	**LPG**
Rates applying from 1 September 2016			
1400cc or less	11p	—	7p
1600cc or less	—	9p	—
1401cc to 2000cc	13p	—	9p
1601cc to 2000cc	—	11p	—
Over 2000cc	20p	13p	13p

Engine size	Cost per mile		
	Petrol	Diesel	LPG
Rates applying from 1 June 2016			
1400cc or less	10p	—	7p
1600cc or less	—	9p	—
1401cc to 2000cc	13p	—	9p
1601cc to 2000cc	—	10p	—
Over 2000cc	20p	12p	13p
Rates applying from 1 March 2016			
1400cc or less	10p	—	7p
1600cc or less	—	8p	—
1401cc to 2000cc	12p	—	8p
1601cc to 2000cc	—	10p	—
Over 2000cc	19p	11p	13p
Rates applying from 1 December 2015			
1400cc or less	11p	—	7p
1600cc or less	—	9p	—
1401cc to 2000cc	13p	—	9p
1601cc to 2000cc	—	11p	—
Over 2000cc	20p	13p	13p
Rates applying from 1 September 2015			
1400cc or less	11p	—	7p
1600cc or less	—	9p	—
1401cc to 2000cc	14p	—	9p
1601cc to 2000cc	—	11p	—
Over 2000cc	21p	13p	14p
Rates applying from 1 June 2015			
1400cc or less	12p	—	8p
1600cc or less	—	10p	—
1401cc to 2000cc	14p	—	9p
1601cc to 2000cc	—	12p	—
Over 2000cc	21p	14p	14p
Rates applying from 1 March 2015			
1400cc or less	11p	—	8p
1600cc or less	—	9p	—
1401cc to 2000cc	13p	—	10p
1601cc to 2000cc	—	11p	—
Over 2000cc	20p	14p	14p

Engine size	Cost per mile		
	Petrol	Diesel	LPG
Rates applying from 1 December 2014			
1400cc or less	13p	—	9p
1600cc or less	—	11p	—
1401cc to 2000cc	16p	—	11p
1601cc to 2000cc	—	13p	—
Over 2000cc	23p	16p	16p
Rates applying from 1 September 2014			
1400cc or less	14p	—	9p
1600cc or less	—	11p	—
1401cc to 2000cc	16p	—	11p
1601cc to 2000cc	—	13p	—
Over 2000cc	24p	17p	16p
Rates applying from 1 June 2014			
1400cc or less	14p	—	9p
1600cc or less	—	12p	—
1401cc to 2000cc	16p	—	11p
1601cc to 2000cc	—	14p	—
Over 2000cc	24p	17p	16p
Rates applying from 1 March 2014			
1400cc or less	14p	—	9p
1600cc or less	—	12p	—
1401cc to 2000cc	16p	—	11p
1601cc to 2000cc	—	14p	—
Over 2000cc	24p	17p	17p

COMPANY VANS

15   Van benefits

(ITEPA 2003, s. 114, 154–164)

(Tax Reporter: 416-200ff.)

	£
2016–17	3,170
2015–16	3,150
2014–15	3,090
2013–14 (from April 2007)	3,000

But nil if:

(1)   the restricted private use conditions are met (available and used only for ordinary commuting and business travel);

(2)   private use in the tax year is insignificant; or

(3)   (from 6 April 2010 to 5 April 2015) the van cannot produce any CO_2 emissions under any circumstances by being driven (e.g. an electric van).

Zero-emission vans

For tax years 2010–11 to 2014–15, the cash equivalent of the benefit of a van was nil if the van could not produce any CO_2 emissions under any circumstances by being driven (e.g. an electric van). From 2015–16, the charge for zero-emission vans is calculated as the 'relevant percentage' per the table below of the main rate as per the table above.

Tax Year	Appropriate percentage[1]
2015–16	20%
2016–17	20%
2017–18	20%
2018–19	40%
2019–20	60%
2020–21	80%
2021–22	90%

Notes

[1] *Finance Act* 2016 extends the van benefit charge support for zero-emission vans so that from 6 April 2016, the charge will be 20% of the main rate in 2016–17 and 2017–18 and will then increase on a tapered basis to 5 April 2022. Previously announced rates were due to increase to 40%, 60%, 80% and 90% in each of tax years 2016–17 to 2019–20 respectively.

16   Fuel for company vans

(ITEPA 2003, s. 160ff.)

(Tax Reporter: 416-200ff.)

Tax Year	£
2016–17	568
2015–16	594
2014–15	581
2013–14	564
2012–13	550
2011–12	550

But nil if:

(1) the restricted private use conditions are met (available and used only for ordinary commuting and business travel);
(2) private use in the tax year is insignificant; or
(3) (from 6 April 2010 to 5 April 2015) the van cannot produce any CO_2 emissions by being driven.

PRIVATE VEHICLES

17 Mileage allowance payments

(ITEPA 2003, s. 230)

(Tax Reporter: 432-100ff.)

Statutory rates are set for mileage allowance payments. An employer may, of course, reimburse business mileage driven in a privately-owned car at more or less than the statutory rates but any excess is taxable. Any shortfall is tax deductible and the employee may claim relief accordingly. The rates were amended from 6 April 2011.

Kind of vehicle	Rate per mile from 6 April 2011
Car or van	45p for the first 10,000 miles 25p after that
Motorcycle	24p
Cycle	20p

18 Passenger payments

(ITEPA 2003, s. 233)

(Tax Reporter: 432-150)

No liability to income tax arises in respect of an approved passenger payment made to an employee for a car or a van, whether the vehicle is privately owned or provided by the employer. The approved amount is 5p per passenger mile.

BUSINESS PROFITS

19 Cash basis for small businesses

(ITTOIA 2005, Pt. 2, Ch. 3A)

(Tax Reporter: 206-481ff.)

From April 2013 (with effect for the tax year 2013–14 and subsequent tax years), eligible businesses may elect to calculate their profits on the cash basis instead of in accordance with generally accepted accountancy principles. The cash basis is optional but circumstances under which a business can leave the scheme are limited (businesses must continue to use the scheme until their circumstances change so that the cash basis is no longer suitable for them). Under the scheme, businesses calculate their taxable income by taking business income received in a year and deducting business expenses paid in a year. This means they do not need to adjust for debtors, creditors and stock, and generally do not have to distinguish between revenue and capital expenditure. Capital allowances remain available for expenditure on cars only. Businesses using the cash basis do not have to use the simplified flat rate expenses for their cars.

Eligible barristers are able to choose either to use the new cash basis and simplified expenses or the accruals basis. The existing cash basis arrangement for barristers is withdrawn except for barristers already using it, for the remainder of their qualifying period.

	Relevant max. Joining [2] £	Leaving Threshold [2] £
From 1 April 2016		
Standard	83,000	
Recipients of Universal credit[1]	166,000	166,000
2015–16		
Standard	82,000	
Recipients of Universal credit[1]	164,000	164,000
2014–15		
Standard	81,000	
Recipients of Universal credit[1]	162,000	162,000
2013–14		
Standard	79,000	
Recipients of Universal credit[1]	158,000	158,000

Notes

[1] Recipients of universal credit must use the cash basis for income assessment for UC purposes.

[2] Joining and leaving thresholds are determined by reference to the VAT registration threshold (in place at the end of the tax year) and twice the VAT registration threshold respectively.

Excluded persons:

- Companies
- Limited liability partnerships
- Partnerships with a non-individual partner during the basis period
- Lloyd's underwriters
- Farming businesses with a herd basis election in effect for the tax year
- Farming and creative businesses with a profits averaging election in effect for the tax year
- Businesses that have claimed business premises renovation allowances within the previous seven years (ending immediately before the basis period)
- Businesses that carry on a mineral extraction trade during the basis period for the tax year
- Businesses that still own an asset in respect of which research and development capital allowances have been claimed (at any time)

20   Trade profits: deductions allowable at a fixed rate

(ITTOIA 2005, Pt. 2, Ch. 5A)

(Tax Reporter: 208–380)

From April 2013 (with effect for the tax year 2013–14 and subsequent tax years), unincorporated businesses will be entitled to use flat rates to calculate certain types of expenses rather than having to calculate actual amounts.

Expense	From 6 April 2013
Expenditure on vehicles	
Car or goods vehicle	
– first 10,000 miles	£0.45/mile
– above 10,000 miles	£0.25/mile
Motorcycle	£0.24/mile
	Rate per Month £
Use of home for business[1]	
25–50 hours per month	10.00
51–100 hours per month	18.00
101 hours or more per month	26.00
Or claim allowable portion of actual costs	

Expense	From 6 April 2013
Premises used both as home and business premises(2)	
Disallowance (for personal element of expenses)	350.00
1 occupant using premises as a home	500.00
2 occupants using premises as a home	650.00
3 or more occupants using premises as a home	
Or identify allowable portion of actual costs	

Notes

(1) Deduction is given for each month or part of a month in relation to the number of hours spent wholly and exclusively on work done by the person in their home wholly and exclusively for the purposes of the trade (ITTOIA 2005, s. 94H).

(2) Available for premises which are mainly used for the purposes of carrying on the trade but also used by the person as a home. Instead of apportioning expenses between business and personal use, a deduction may be claimed for the full expense minus the relevant flat rate non business use amount (ITTOIA 2005, s. 94I).

ADMINISTRATION

21 Submission dates for 2016–17 personal tax returns

(TMA 1970, s. 8)

(Tax Reporter: 180-125)

Taxes Management Act 1970, s. 8 contains provisions concerning submission dates for returns issued on or after 6 April 2017 which relate to 2016–17, as follows:

- paper returns (whether or not HMRC is to calculate the tax liability) must be filed by 31 October 2017; and
- online returns must be filed by 31 January 2018.

There are the following exceptions:

Circumstances	Filing date(1)
Return issued after 31 July 2017 but before 31 October 2017	Three months from the date of issue (paper returns); 31 January 2018 (online returns)
Return issued after 31 October 2017	Three months from date of issue
Taxpayer wishes underpayment (below £3,000) to be coded out under PAYE in a subsequent year (paper returns)	31 October 2017

Taxpayer wishes underpayment (below £3,000) to be coded out under PAYE in a subsequent year (online returns)	30 December 2017

Notes

(1) The time allowed for making a self-assessment when HMRC have served a notice to file a return is four years after the end of the tax year to which it relates (TMA 1970, s. 34A, as inserted by FA 2016, s. 168, with effect from 15 September 2016).

Withdrawing a notice to file a self assessment return

(TMA 1970, s. 8B and 12AAA)

With effect in respect of returns for the tax year 2012–13 and subsequent tax years, HMRC will withdraw a notice to file a return, on request or otherwise, where they agree a self assessment return is not required and cancel any late filing penalty already issued in respect of the outstanding return. A notice may only be withdrawn within the period of two years beginning with the end of the relevant year of assessment or period in respect of which the return is required or, in exceptional circumstances, such extended period as HMRC may agree.

Simple assessment

Finance Act 2016 provides a new power to allow HMRC to make an assessment of an individual's income tax or capital gains tax liability without them first being required to complete a self-assessment return where it has sufficient information about that individual to make the assessment. This measure will have effect in relation to the 2016–17 tax year and subsequent years (TMA 1970, s. 28H–28J and 59BA, as inserted by FA 2016, s. 167 and Sch. 23).

22 Payment dates: 2016–17

(TMA 1970, s. 59A, 59B)

(Tax Reporter: 182-725ff.)

Tax is paid on 31 January next following the year of assessment as a single sum covering capital gains tax and income tax on all sources. Interim payments on account may be required. No interim payments are required if:

- the tax paid by assessment was less than £1,000; or
- more than 80% of the tax due the previous year was collected at source.

A payment on account can never exceed 50% of the net tax for the preceding year, even though it may already be clear, at the time the payments are made, that the actual liability for the year will exceed that for the preceding year. Net tax is the excess of assessed tax over tax deducted at source (incl. tax credits on dividends for tax years up to 2015-16). For 2016–17, the following due dates apply:

First interim payment	31 January 2017
Second interim payment	31 July 2017
Final balancing payment	31 January 2018
Simple assessment[(1)]	31 January 2018

Note

[(1)] If a return is not issued until after 31 October 2017 and the taxpayer has notified chargeability by 5 October 2017, the due date for the final payment becomes three months from the issue of the return (TMA 1970, s. 59B).

The due date for income tax and capital gains tax payable under a 'simple assessment' (from 2016–17) is three months after the day on which the simple assessment notice was given if given after 31 October following the year of assessment and otherwise on 31 January next following the year of assessment (TMA 1970, s. 59BA).

23 Main penalty provisions: 2015–16

Offence	Penalty[(1)(2)]
Late return for 2010–11 and later years (FA 2009, Sch. 55; Tax Reporter: 181-500)[(3)]	
Failure to submit by the filing date (by 31 October 2017 for 2016–17 paper return; by 31 January 2018 for 2016–17 online return)	£100
Failure continues three months after the filing date (1 February 2018 for 2016–17 paper returns; 1 May 2018 for 2016–17 online returns) by HMRC notice	£10 per day for a period up to 90 days beginning with the date specified in the notice (maximum £900)
Failure still continues six months after the filing date (1 May 2018 for 2016–17 paper return; 1 August 2018 for 2016–17 online return)	The greater of £300 or 5% of the liability to tax shown by the return
Failure still continues after 12 months (1 November 2018 for 2016–17 paper return; 1 February 2019 for 2016–17 online return)	greater of relevant percentage of liability shown by the return and £300

Offence	Penalty[(1)(2)]		
	Relevant percentage		
	Category 1[(6)]	Category 2	Category 3
• withholding information deliberate and concealed	100%	150%	200%
• withholding information deliberate but not concealed	70%	105%	140%
• any other case	5%	5%	5%
Reductions for disclosure (maximum reduction weighted according to quality of disclosure determined as: • 30% for telling, • 40% for helping and • 30% for giving access)	Standard penalty	Prompted disclosure Minimum	Unprompted disclosure Minimum
	70%	35%	20%
	105%	52.5%	30%
	140%	70%	40%
	100%	50%	30%
	150%	75%	45%
	200%	100%	60%

Failure to notify chargeability For failures after 1 April 2010 (FA 2008, Sch. 41)	Percentage of potential lost revenue				
	Category 1[(6)]	Category 2		Category 3	
• failure deliberate and concealed	100%	150%		200%	
• failure deliberate but not concealed	70%	105%		140%	
• any other case	30%	45%		60%	
Reductions for disclosure (maximum reduction weighted according to quality of disclosure determined as: 30% for telling, 40% for helping and 30% for giving access)	Standard penalty	Prompted disclosure Minimum[(4)]		Unprompted disclosure Minimum[(4)]	
		Case A	Case B	Case A	Case B
	30%	10%	20%	0%	10%
	45%	15%	30%	0%	15%
	60%	20%	40%	0%	20%
	70%	35%		20%	
	105%	52.5%		30%	
	140%	70%		40%	
	100%	50%		30%	
	150%	75%		45%	
	200%	100%		60%	

Failure to keep and retain tax records (TMA 1970, s. 12B; Tax Reporter: 181-900)	Up to £3,000 per year of assessment
False statements to reduce interim payments (TMA 1970, s. 59A[(5)]; Tax Reporter: 182-725)	Up to the difference between the amount correctly due and the amount paid

Offence	Penalty[1][2]		
Failure to comply with an information notice (FA 2008, Sch. 36, para. 39 and 40; Tax Reporter: 186-550ff.)			
• standard amount	£300		
• continued failure	daily penalty of £60		
Tax-related penalty where significant tax is at risk (FA 2008, Sch. 36, para. 50)	tax geared amount decided by Upper Tribunal		
Inaccurate information/documents in complying with an information notice (FA 2008, Sch. 36) Inaccuracy careless or deliberate	Up to £3,000 for each inaccuracy		
Errors in returns			
Errors in returns for periods starting 1 April 2008 where return is filed on or after 1 April 2009 (FA 2007, Sch. 24; Tax Reporter: 184-850)[5]	Percentage of potential lost revenue		
	Category 1[6]	Category 2	Category 3
• careless action	30%	45%	60%
• deliberate but not concealed action	70%	105%	140%
• deliberate and concealed action	100%	150%	200%
Reductions for disclosure (maximum reduction weighted according to quality of disclosure determined as:	Standard penalty	Prompted disclosure Minimum	Unprompted disclosure Minimum
	30%	15%	0%
• 30% for telling,	45%	22.5%	0%
• 40% for helping and	60%	30%	0%
• 30% for giving access)	70%	35%	20%
	105%	52.5%	30%
	140%	70%	40%
	100%	50%	30%
	150%	75%	45%
	200%	100%	60%

Offence	Penalty[1][2]
Offshore asset moves (FA 2015, Sch. 21) Additional penalty for offshore asset moves from specified territory[7] to non-specified territory on or after 26 March 2015 following an original deliberate failure penalty under: FA 2007, Sch. 24, para. 1; FA 2008, Sch. 41, para. 1; or FA 2009, Sch. 55, para. 6.	50% of the original penalty

Notes

[1] Interest is charged on penalties not paid when due. The due date is 30 days after the notice of determination of the penalty is issued.

[2] Defences of 'reasonable excuse' or 'special circumstances' may be available.

[3] Late return penalties are cumulative, e.g. for a return six months late, there are two penalties.

[4] The case A minimum applies if HMRC become aware of the failure less than 12 months after the time when the tax first becomes unpaid by reason of the failure, otherwise the case B minimum applies.

[5] No penalty for inaccuracies that occur despite taking reasonable care.

[6] FA 2015, s. 120 and Sch. 20 introduces a new category of penalty, category 0, from a date to be appointed. The new category of penalty will carry the lowest level of penalty equivalent to those currently in category 1 (i.e. 30%, 70% and 100%) and the penalty percentages for category 1 penalties will be increased to 37.5%, 87.5% and 125% respectively.

[7] See below for table of specified territories.

[8] Finance Act 2016 contains the following changes:

- a new criminal offence that removes the need to prove intent for the most serious cases of failing to declare offshore income and gains (TMA 1970, s. 106B–106H, as inserted by FA 2016, s. 166, with effect from a date to be appointed by Treasury Order);
- increased civil penalties for deliberate offshore tax evasion, (amendments by FA 2016, s. 163 and Sch. 21, with effect from a date to be appointed by Treasury Order);
- a new penalty linked to the value of the asset on which tax was evaded (FA 2016, s. 165 and Sch. 22, with effect from a date to be appointed by Treasury order);
- civil penalties for those who enable offshore tax evasion, including public naming of those who have enabled the evasion (FA 2016, s. 162 and Sch. 20, with effect from a date to be appointed by Treasury Order);
- increased public naming of tax evaders (FA 2009, s. 94, as amended by FA 2016, s. 164, with effect from a date to be appointed by Treasury order).
- a new regime of warnings and escalating sanctions for those who persistently engage in tax avoidance schemes which HMRC defeat. Following the first defeat of a tax avoidance scheme, HMRC will place the taxpayer on a warning for five years. If the taxpayer uses any further schemes while under warning which HMRC defeats, the rate of penalty will be 20% for the first defeat, 40% for the second defeat and 60% for the third defeat. If HMRC defeat three tax avoidance schemes while the taxpayer is on warning, the taxpayer's details can be published. If three avoidance schemes which exploit reliefs are used while under warning and HMRC defeat them, the taxpayer will be denied further benefit of reliefs until the warning period expires. The regime comes into effect on 6 April 2017 (FA 2016, s. 159 and Sch. 18); and
- a new penalty of 60% of tax due to be charged in all cases successfully tackled by the GAAR (FA 2013, s. 212A and Sch. 43C, as inserted by FA 2016, s. 158, with effect from 15 September 2016).

Offshore penalties – territory categories

The table below shows which territories are classified in 'category 1' and 'category 3' for the purposes of penalties for offshore non-compliance.

Territories not listed here (other than the UK) are in 'category 2'. Penalties for domestic (UK) matters fall into category 1.

Territories are allocated into one of the categories depending upon the level of information exchange arrangements with the UK, with category 1 territories having the highest level of information sharing arrangements so penalties are the same as for penalties involving domestic matters, whereas territories in categories 2 and 3 have correspondingly poorer information exchange arrangements.

A new category of territory, category 0, is prospectively introduced by FA 2015, s. 120 and Sch. 20, with effect from a date to be appointed. The new category of penalty will apply to overseas territories making information exchange arrangements with the UK that meet the new Common Reporting Standard. It is envisaged that most or all territories currently in category 1 will, over time, make arrangements so as to fall within category 0 (FA 2015, Sch. 20).

Category 1	Category 3[1]
Anguilla	Albania
Aruba	Algeria
Australia	Andorra
Belgium	Bonaire, Sint Eustatius and Saba
Bulgaria	Brazil
Canada	Cameroon
Cayman Islands	Cape Verde
Cyprus	Colombia
Czech Republic	Congo, Republic of the
Denmark (not including Faroe Islands and Greenland which are in category 2)	Cook Islands
	Costa Rica
	Curacao
Estonia	Cuba
Finland	Democratic People's Republic of Korea
France	
Germany	Dominican Republic
Greece	Ecuador
Guernsey (includes Alderney and Sark)	El Salvador
	Gabon
Hungary	Guatemala
Ireland	Honduras
Isle of Man	Iran
Italy	Iraq
Japan	Jamaica
Korea, South	

Key Data

Category 1	Category 3[1]
Latvia	Kyrgyzstan
Lithuania	Lebanon
Malta	Macau (China and Hong Kong are in category 2)
Montserrat	
Netherlands (not including Bonaire, Sint Eustatius and Saba)	Marshall Islands
	Micronesia, Federated States of
New Zealand (not including Tokelau)	Monaco
Norway	Nauru
Poland	Nicaragua
Portugal (includes Madeira and the Azores)	Niue
	Palau
Romania	Panama
Slovakia	Paraguay
Slovenia	Peru
Spain (includes the Canary Islands and other overseas territories of Spain)	Seychelles
	Sint Maarten
Sweden	Suriname
Switzerland (from 24 July 2013)	Syria
	Tokelau
United States of America (not including overseas territories and possessions of the United States of America which are in category 2)	Tonga
	Trinidad and Tobago
	United Arab Emirates
	Uruguay

Notes

[1] Before 24 July 2013, category 3 territories included additionally:
- Antigua and Barbuda
- Armenia
- Bahrain
- Barbados
- Belize
- Dominica
- Grenada
- Mauritius
- Saint Kitts and Nevis
- Saint Lucia
- Saint Vincent and the Grenadines
- San Marino

Offshore asset moves penalties: specified territories

(SI 2015/866)

Albania	Andorra	Anguilla	Antigua and Barbuda
Argentina	Aruba	Australia	Austria
The Bahamas	Barbados	Belgium	Belize
Bermuda	Brazil	British Virgin Islands	Brunei Darussalam
Bulgaria	Canada	Cayman Islands	Chile
China	Colombia	Costa Rica	Croatia
Curaçao	Cyprus	Czech Republic	Denmark
Dominica	Estonia	Faroe Islands	Finland
France	Germany	Gibraltar	Greece
Greenland	Grenada	Guernsey	Hong Kong
Hungary	Iceland	India	Indonesia
Ireland	Isle of Man	Israel	Italy
Japan	Jersey	Korea (South)	Latvia
Liechtenstein	Lithuania	Luxembourg	Macau
Malaysia	Malta	Marshall Islands	Mauritius
Mexico	Monaco	Montserrat	Netherlands (including Bonaire, Sint Eustatius and Saba)
New Zealand (not including Tokelau)	Niue	Norway	Poland
Portugal	Qatar	Romania	Russia
Saint Kitts and Nevis	Saint Lucia	Saint Vincent and the Grenadines	Samoa
San Marino	Saudi Arabia	Seychelles	Singapore
Sint Maarten	Slovak Republic	Slovenia	South Africa
Spain	Sweden	Switzerland	Trinidad and Tobago
Turkey	Turks and Caicos Islands	United Arab Emirates	United States of America (not including overseas territories and possessions)
Uruguay			

24 Penalties for late payment of tax: 2016–17

(FA 2009, Sch. 56)

(Tax Reporter: 182-875)

A new penalty regime for late payments under income tax self assessment was introduced by FA 2009, Sch. 56. This applies from 6 April 2011 to payments for the tax year 2010–11 and later years.

Tax overdue	Penalty
30 days	5% of tax overdue
6 months	further 5% of tax overdue
12 months	further 5% of tax overdue

These penalties will be issued automatically and are in addition to the interest that will be charges on all outstanding amounts, including unpaid penalties, until payment is received.

Penalties apply to:

- final tax payments on self-assessments (this includes any amounts due as interim payments which remain unpaid);
- tax on inspector's amendments to a self-assessment made during or as a result of an audit; and
- discovery assessments.

25 Rates of interest

(FA 2009, s. 101–102; SI 2011/2446)

(Tax Reporter: ¶182-925; ¶182-975)

The following table gives the rates of interest applicable in recent years.

Period	Late payment %	Repayment %
23 August 2016	2.75	0.50
29 Sept. 2009 to 22 Aug. 2016	3.00	0.50

Notes

(1) SI 2011/2446 sets the interest rates for the purposes of s. 101 and 102 at the Bank of England base rate plus 2.5% and minus 1% respectively. Changes in interest rates announced in Bank of England Monetary Policy Committee meetings take effect from the 13th working day following the meeting and apply in respect of interest running from before that date as well as interest running from on or after that date.

(2) Tax-related judgment debts: the Government will set the rate of interest which applies on taxation-related debts payable under a court judgment or order by HMRC to a rate equal to the Bank of England base rate plus 2%. The Government will also apply the late payment interest rate of 3% to taxation-related debts owed to HMRC under a court judgment or order. These changes will apply to new and pre-existing judgments and orders in respect of interest accruing on and after 8 July 2015 (F(No. 2)A 2015, s. 52).

NIC

26   Class 1 NIC: 2016–17

(SSCBA 1992, s. 8-9; SI 2001/1004, reg. 10-11 and 131; NICA 2014, s. 1)

Class 1 contributions

Class 1 primary (employee) contributions 2016–17	
Lower earnings limit (LEL)[4]	£112 weekly £486[2] monthly £5,824[2] yearly
Primary threshold (PT)[4]	£155 weekly £672[3] monthly £8,060[3] yearly
Upper earnings limit (UEL)	£815 weekly £3,532[3] monthly £42,385[3] yearly
Rate on earnings up to PT[1]	0%
Rate	12% on £155.01 to £827 weekly 2% on excess over £827 weekly
Reduced rate	5.85% on £155.01 to £827 weekly 2% on excess over £827

Notes

[1] No national insurance contributions (NICs) are actually payable but a notional Class 1 NIC is deemed to have been paid in respect of earnings between the LEL and PT to protect contributory benefit entitlement.

[2] Monthly and annual LEL and UAP figures are calculated as per SI 2001/1004, reg. 11.

[3] Monthly and annual PT and UEL figures are prescribed by SI 2001/1004, reg. 11 and amended by Statutory Instrument.

[4] These thresholds are uprated by CPI.

Class 1 primary (employee) contributions 2016–17	
Secondary earnings threshold (ST)[4]	£156 weekly £676[1] monthly £8,112[1] yearly
Upper secondary threshold (UST) for under 21s[2]	£827 weekly £3,583[1] monthly £43,000[1] yearly
Apprentice upper secondary threshold (AUST) for under 25s[3]	£827 weekly £3,583[1] monthly £43,000[1] yearly
Rate	13.8% on earnings above ST/UST(2)/AUST[3]
Employment allowance[5]	£3,000 per year, per employer

Notes

(1) Monthly and annual ST and UST figures are prescribed by SI 2001/1004, reg. 11 and amended by Statutory Instrument. Rates for 2016-17 figures have yet to be specified and the amounts shown are calculated amounts (by reference to prior year equivalents) and may be subject to change.

(2) Upper secondary threshold (UST) introduced from April 2015 for employees under the age of 21. The rate of secondary NICs for employees under the age of 21 on earnings between the ST and UST will be 0%.

(3) Apprentice upper secondary threshold (AUST) introduced from April 2016. The rate of secondary NICs for employees under the age of 21 on earnings between the ST and AUST will be 0%.

(4) The weekly secondary threshold is uprated by CPI.

(5) From April 2016, companies where the director is the sole employee will no longer be able to claim the allowance (NICA 2014, s. 2(4A)).

27   Class 1 NIC: 2015–16

(NIC Reporter: ¶305-575ff.)

Class 1 contributions

Class 1 primary (employee) contributions 2015–16	
Lower earnings limit (LEL)(4)	£112 weekly £486(2) monthly £5,824(2) yearly
Primary threshold (PT)(4)	£155 weekly £672(3) monthly £8,060(3) yearly
Upper earnings limit (UEL)	£815 weekly £3,532(3) monthly £42,385(3) yearly
Upper accruals point (UAP)	£770 weekly £3,337(2) monthly £40,040(2) yearly
Rate on earnings up to PT(1)	0%
Not contracted out rate	12% on £155.01 to £815 weekly 2% on excess over £815 weekly
Contracted-out rate	10.6% on £155.01 to £770 weekly 12% on £770.01 to £815 weekly 2% on excess over £815 weekly
Reduced rate	5.85% on £155.01 to £815 weekly 2% on excess over £815 (no rebate even if contracted out)

Notes

(1) Earnings from the LEL, up to and including the PT, count towards the employee's basic state pension, even though no contributions are paid on those earnings. Similarly, earnings between the LEL and the PT count towards the employee's entitlement to certain benefits including the second state pension (S2P). Employees in contracted-out employment earn no S2P rights and receive a rebate of contributions of 1.4%. This applies from the LEL to the UAP, so earnings from LEL to PT attract a 'negative' contribution of 1.4% and the rate for earnings from PT to UAP becomes 10.6%. Earnings from UAP to UEL are subject to the main not contracted-out rate.

(2) Monthly and annual LEL and UAP figures are calculated as per SI 2001/1004, reg. 11.

(3) Monthly and annual PT and UEL figures are prescribed by SI 2001/1004, reg. 11 and amended by Statutory Instrument.

(4) These thresholds are uprated by CPI.

Class 1 secondary (employer) contributions 2015–16	
Secondary earnings threshold (ST)(4)	£156 weekly £676(2) monthly £8,112(2) yearly
Upper secondary threshold (UST) for U21's(3)	£815 weekly £3,532 monthly £42,385 yearly
Not contracted out rate	13.8% on earnings above ST
Contracted-out rate(1)	10.4% for salary related (COSR) on earnings from ST to UAP (plus 3.4% rebate for earnings from LEL to ST), then 13.8% above UAP
Employment allowance(5)	£2,000 per year, per employer

Notes

(1) Although employer contributions do not per se give any benefit entitlements, earnings between the LEL and ST are those classed as relevant for S2P. Employers with contracted-out occupational pension schemes receive a rebate of contributions
for scheme members of 3.4% (COSR). This applies from the LEL to the UAP, so earnings from LEL to ST attract a 'negative' contribution and the rate for earnings from ST to UAP is reduced as shown.

(2) Monthly and annual ST figures are prescribed by SI 2001/1004, reg. 11 and amended by Statutory Instrument.

(3) Upper secondary threshold (UST) introduced from April 2015 for employees under the age of 21. The rate of secondary NICs for employees under the age of 21 on earnings between the ST and UST will be 0%.

(4) The weekly secondary threshold is uprated by RPI.

(5) From April 2015, the allowance is extended to care and support workers (NICA 2014, s. 2(3A)).

28 Class 1 NIC: 2014–15

(NIC Reporter: ¶305-575ff.)

Class 1 contributions

Class 1 primary (employee) contributions 2014–15	
Lower earnings limit (LEL)	£111 weekly £481(2) monthly £5,772(2) yearly
Primary threshold (PT)	£153 weekly £663(3) monthly £7,956(3) yearly
Upper earnings limit (UEL)	£805 weekly £3,489(3) monthly £41,865(3) yearly

Class 1 primary (employee) contributions 2014–15	
Upper accruals point (UAP)	£770 weekly
	£3,337[2] monthly
	£40,040[2] yearly
Rate on earnings up to PT[1]	0%
Not contracted out rate	12% on £153.01 to £805 weekly
	2% on excess over £805 weekly
Contracted-out rate	10.6% on £153.01 to £770 weekly
	12% on £770.01 to £805 weekly
	2% on excess over £805 weekly
Reduced rate	5.85% on £153.01 to £805 weekly
	2% on excess over £805 (no rebate even if contracted out)

Notes

[1] Earnings from the LEL, up to and including the PT, count towards the employee's basic state pension, even though no contributions are paid on those earnings. Similarly, earnings between the LEL and the PT count towards the employee's entitlement to certain benefits including the second state pension (S2P). Employees in contracted-out employment earn no S2P rights and receive a rebate of contributions of 1.4%. This applies from the LEL to the UAP, so earnings from LEL to PT attract a 'negative' contribution of 1.4% and the rate for earnings from PT to UAP becomes 10.6%. Earnings from UAP to UEL are subject to the main not contracted-out rate.

[2] Monthly and annual LEL and UAP figures are calculated as per SI 2001/1004, reg. 11.

[3] Monthly and annual PT and UEL figures are prescribed by SI 2001/1004, reg. 11 and amended by Statutory Instrument.

Class 1 secondary (employer) contributions 2014–15	
Secondary earnings threshold (ST)	£153 weekly
	£663[2] monthly
	£7,956[2] yearly
Not contracted out rate	13.8% on earnings above ST
Contracted-out rate[1]	10.4% for salary related (COSR) on earnings from ST to UAP (plus 3.4% rebate for earnings from LEL to ST), then 13.8% above UAP
Employment allowance	£2,000 per year, per employer)

Notes

[1] Although employer contributions do not per se give any benefit entitlements, earnings between the LEL and ST are those classed as relevant for S2P. Employers with contracted-out occupational pension schemes receive a rebate of contributions for scheme members of 3.4% (COSR). This applies from the LEL to the UAP, so earnings from LEL to ST attract a 'negative' contribution and the rate for earnings from ST to UAP is reduced as shown.

[2] Monthly and annual ST figures are prescribed by SI 2001/1004, reg. 11 and amended by Statutory Instrument.

29   Class 1A contributions

(SSCBA 1992, s. 10)

(NIC Reporter: ¶310-000ff.)

From 2016–17, employers (but not employees) pay NIC on an annual basis on benefits in kind provided to all employees (other than lower paid ministers of religion). Prior to 5 April 2016 (since 6 April 2000), NICs were payable only on benefi ts provided to employees earning at a rate of £8,500 p.a. or more or to directors (SSCBA 1992, s. 10). Contributions for the year are due by 19 July following the end of the tax year to which they relate (22 July for electronic payment). Rates applying are always the full Class 1 secondary (employer) rate for each year, as follows:

Period	%
2011–12 to 2016–17	13.8

30   Class 1B contributions

(SSCBA 1992, s. 10A)

Class 1B contributions are payable by employers on the amount of earnings in a PAYE settlement agreement (PSA) that are chargeable to Class 1 or Class 1A NICs, together with the total amount of income tax payable under the agreement (SSCBA 1992, s. 10A). Class 1B contributions are charged at the same rate as Class 1A contributions (see above) and are payable by 19 October after the end of the tax year to which the PSA applies (22 October for electronic payment).

31   Class 2 contributions

(SSCBA 1992, s. 11)

Class 2 contributions are paid at a flat rate by a self-employed person. From 2015–16, the contributions are collected through self-assessment alongside income tax and Class 4 contributions and only those with profits at or above the small profits threshold (SPT) are liable to Class 2 NICs. Prior to 2015–16, a person had to pay Class 2 NICs unless he had applied for and been granted exception because his earnings were below the small earnings exception (SEE) limit. Persons with profits below the small profits threshold (or who were previously granted exception for earnings below the SEE limit) can (could) still pay voluntary contributions in order to protect entitlement to contributory benefits.

Rates and SEE limit

Tax year	Rate £	Share fishermen £	Volunteer development workers £	Small profits threshold[2] £
	Weekly contribution rate[1]			
2016–17	2.80	3.45	5.60	5,965
2015–16	2.80	3.45	5.60	5,965
2014–15	2.75	3.40	5.55	5,885
2013–14	2.70	3.35	5.45	5,725
2012–13	2.65	3.30	5.35	5,595
2011–12	2.50	3.15	5.10	5,315

Notes

[1] These rates are uprated by CPI.

[2] The 'small profits threshold' replaced the 'small earnings exception' from 6 April 2015. This threshold is uprated by CPI.

32 Class 3 contributions

(SSCBA 1992, s. 13)

(NIC Reporter: ¶320-000ff.)

Class 3 contributions are paid voluntarily by persons not liable for contributions, or who have been excepted from Class 2 contributions, or whose contribution record is insufficient to qualify for benefits (i.e. Class 3 contributions allow people to fill gaps in their contributions record for basic state pension purposes). They are paid at a flat rate. Class 3 contributions may not be paid where an individuals earnings factor (earnings on which primary class 1 or class 2 contributions have been paid) equals or exceeds the qualifying limit for the year.

Rate and earnings factor

Tax year	Weekly contribution rate[1] £	Earnings factor for each contribution in col. 2 £
2016–17	14.10	112.00
2015–16	14.10	112.00
2014–15	13.90	111.00
2013–14	13.55	109.00
2012–13	13.25	107.00
2011–12	12.60	102.00

Note

[1] Rate is uprated by CPI.

33 Class 3A contributions

(SSCBA 1992, s. 14A–14C; PA 2014, Sch. 15, para. 4; SI 2014/3240)

(NIC Reporter: ¶321-500)

From 12 October 2015 until 5 April 2017, existing pensioners and those reaching state pension age before 6 April 2016 have the opportunity to gain additional state pension by paying Class 3A voluntary National Insurance contributions. There are two conditions:

- contributors must have entitlement to a UK state pension; and
- contributors must reach state pension age before 6 April 2016.

The measure is in addition to Class 3 voluntary contributions (see above).

The amount of a Class 3A contribution needed to obtain a unit of additional pension is determined by reference to the age of the person who is paying the contribution per the table below. Where a person had not reached state pension age on the date of payment but would do so before 6 April 2016, the amount of contribution needed to obtain a unit of additional pension is the amount that would be needed if the person had reached pensionable age.

The maximum number of units of additional pension that a person can obtain is 25 and each unit is equivalent to £1 per week of additional pension (i.e. a maximum of £25 per week of additional pension can be acquired).

A cooling-off period of 90 days applies for the contributor to apply for a repayment, beginning with the date of payment.

Age at payment date (12 October 2015 to 5 April 2017)	Rate for each additional pension unit of £1 per week £	Age at payment date (12 October 2015 to 5 April 2017)	Rate for each additional pension unit of £1 per week £
62 (women only)	956	82	484
63 (women only)	934	83	454
64 (women only)	913	84	424
65	890	85	394
66	871	86	366
67	847	87	339
68	827	88	314

69	801	89	291
70	779	90	270
71	761	91	251
72	738	92	232
73	719	93	216
74	694	94	200
75	674	95	185
76	646	96	172
77	625	97	159
78	596	98	148
79	574	99	137
80	544	100	127
81	514	—	—

34   Class 4 contributions

(SSCBA 1992, s. 15)

(NIC Reporter: ¶317-650ff.)

Self-employed people whose profits or gains are over a certain amount have to pay Class 4 contributions as well as Class 2 contributions. These contributions are earnings-related and paid at a main rate on trading profits (earnings) between the lower and upper annual limits (which are the same as the Class 1 earnings threshold and upper earnings limit), with an additional 2% on profits above the upper limit since 6 April 2011.

Tax year	Rate on profits between upper and lower limits %	Annual lower profits limit[1] £	Annual upper profits limit £	Rate on profits in excess of upper limit %	Maximum contribution £
2016–17	9	8,060	43,000	2	unlimited
2015–16	9	8,060	42,385	2	unlimited
2014–15	9	7,956	41,865	2	unlimited
2013–14	9	7,755	41,450	2	unlimited
2012–13	9	7,605	42,475	2	unlimited
2011–12	9	7,225	42,475	2	unlimited

Note
[1] This threshold is uprated by CPI.

CORPORATION TAX

35 Rates of corporation tax

(Tax Reporter: 704-000ff.)

Rates from financial year 2015

Financial year[1]	Main rate[2][4]	Main ring fence profits rate[3]	Small ring fence profits rate[3]	Special IP rate[5]	Diverted profits rate[6]
		%	%	%	%
	%				
2016	20	30	19	10	25
2015	20	30	19	10	25

Notes

[1] A financial year begins on 1 April and ends on 31 March. The financial year 2016 began on 1 April 2016 and will end on 31 March 2017.

[2] F(No.2)A 2015, s. 7 sets the main rate of corporation tax for the financial years 2017, 2018 and 2019 at 19%. FA 2016, s. 46 reduces the rate set by F(No.2)A 2015 for financial year 2020 from 18% to 17%.

[3] The Small ring fence profits rate applies to profits falling below the lower limit of £300,000 and the main ring fence rate applies otherwise. However, where ring fence profits exceed the lower limit of £300,000 but do not exceed the upper limit of £1,500,000, the amount of corporation tax (calculated at the main rates) is reduced by an amount equal to:

$$R \times (U\text{-}A) \times \frac{N}{A}$$

Where:

R   is the marginal relief fraction of 11/400ths

U   is the upper limit of £1,500,000

A   is the amount of the augmented profits (CTA 2010, s. 279G), and

N   is the amount of the taxable total profits.

The lower and upper limits are reduced proportionally for accounting periods of less than 12 months; and where a company has one or more related 51% group companies by dividing the limits by one plus the number of those related 51% group companies.

(CTA 2010, Ch. 3A)

[4] Special rules apply to companies in liquidation and administration (CTA 2010, s. 628 and 630) and to open-ended investment companies and authorised unit trusts (CTA 2010, s. 614 and 618).

[5] For accounting periods beginning on or after 1 April 2013, qualifying companies may elect that relevant intellectual property profits of a trade are chargeable at a lower rate of corporation tax (CTA 2010, s. 357A).

[6] From 1 April 2015, diverted profits tax is charged at a rate of 25% where multinational companies use artificial arrangements to divert profits overseas in order to avoid UK tax (FA 2015, Pt. 3);

Rates to financial year 2014

Financial year[1][2]	Main rate %[2][3]	Small profits rate %[2][3]	Limit for small profits rate (lower limit) £[2][4]	Limit for marginal relief (upper limit) £[2][4]	Standard fraction for marginal relief[2][3]	Special IP rate[5] %
2014	21	20	300,000	1,500,000	1/400	10
2013	23	20	300,000	1,500,000	3/400	10
2012	24	20	300,000	1,500,000	1/100	—
2011	26	20	300,000	1,500,000	3/200	—

Notes

[1] A financial year begins on 1 April and ends on 31 March. The financial year 2014 began on 1 April 2014 and ended on 31 March 2015.

[2] The small profits rate for non-ring fence profits was abolished with effect for the financial year 2015 and subsequent financial years (*Finance Act* 2014).

[3] 'Close investment holding companies' did not receive the benefit of the small profits rate or of marginal relief and so were taxable entirely at the main rate regardless of the level of their profits (former CTA 2010, s. 18).

For companies with ring fence profits, the rates are as above except that:

● the small profits rate of tax is 19% and the standard fraction is 11/400; and

● for financial years 2008 to 2015 the main rate is 30%.

Special rules applied to companies in liquidation and administration (CTA 2010, s. 628 and s. 630) and to open-ended investment companies and authorised unit trusts (CTA 2010, s. 614 and s. 618).

[4] The lower and upper limits for the small profits rate and marginal relief were reduced proportionally:

● for accounting periods of less than 12 months; and

● in the case of associated companies, by dividing the limits by the total number of associated companies (CTA 2010, s. 24).

[5] For accounting periods beginning on or after 1 April 2013, qualifying companies may elect that relevant intellectual property profits of a trade are chargeable at a lower rate of corporation tax (CTA 2010, s. 357A).

Effective marginal rates to financial year 2014

For marginal relief and marginal starting rate relief, there is an effective rate of tax in the margin, i.e. between the lower and upper limits given for each in the preceding table, which *exceeds* the main rate. These marginal rates are not prescribed by statute, but are derived from the appropriate corporation tax rates and fractions. The applicable rates are as follows.

Financial year	Marginal rate %
2014	21.25
2013	23.75
2012	25.00
2011	27.50

Marginal relief

(CTA 2010, s. 19)

(Tax Reporter: 704-200)

$$\text{Deduction} = (\text{Upper Limit} - \text{Augmented Profits}) \times \frac{\text{Taxable Total Profits}}{\text{Augmented Profits}} \times \text{Standard Fraction}$$

'Augmented Profits' (formerly 'Profits') means a company's taxable total profits *plus* franked investment income *excluding* franked investment income received from companies in the same group (CTA 2010, s. 32). Distributions are treated as coming from within the group if they are received from a company which is either a 51% subsidiary or a consortium company (the recipient being a member of the consortium).

'Franked investment income' means a distribution in respect of which the company is entitled to a tax credit (CTA 2010, s. 1126). This includes a distribution which is exempt for the purposes of CTA 2009, Pt. 9A (CTA 2010, s. 1109).

'Taxable Total Profits' (formerly 'Basic Profits') means profits as finally computed for corporation tax purposes (CTA 2010, s. 4(2)).

Charge on loan to participators

(CTA 2010, s. 455)

(Tax Reporter: 776-900ff.)

Loans and benefits conferred	Rate
On or after 6 April 2016	32.5%[1]
Pre 5 April 2016	25.00%

Note

[1] Finance Act 2016 amends existing legislation to set the rate as such percentage as corresponds to the dividend upper rate specified in ITA 2007, s. 8(2) for the tax year in which the loan or advance is made.

The charge itself is separate from other liabilities, being treated as if it were an amount of corporation tax chargeable on the company. *Finance Act* 2016 amends existing legislation so that a tax charge is not applied to loans or advances made by close companies to charity trustees for charitable purposes. The amendments apply to qualifying loans or advances that are made on or after 25 November 2015 (CTA 2010, s. 456(2A)).

RETAIL PRICES INDEX

36   Retail prices index

The Retail Prices Index (RPI), issued by the Office for National Statistics, is used to calculate the indexation allowance for the purposes of calculating capital gains on corporation tax. (Since April 1998, the indexation allowance has ceased to be available when calculating gains liable to capital gains tax.) Certain personal and other reliefs are also linked to RPI subject to Parliament determining otherwise, although since April 2011, the Consumer Price Index (CPI) has been used for the indexation of benefits, tax credits and public service pensions. Historically, the RPI was used for indexation of pensions and state benefits.

With effect from February 1987 the reference date to which the price level in each subsequent month is related was changed from 'January 1974 = 100' to 'January 1987 = 100'.

Movements in the RPI in the months after January 1987 are calculated with reference to January 1987 = 100. (With a base of January 1974 = 100, January 1987's RPI was 394.5). A new formula was provided by the then Department of Employment for calculating movements in the index over periods which span January 1987:

> 'The index for the later month (January 1987 = 100) is multiplied by the index for January 1987 (January 1974 = 100) and divided by the index for the earlier month (January 1974 = 100). 100 is subtracted to give the percentage change between the two months.'

CCH has prepared the following table in accordance with this formula:

	1982	1983	1984	1985	1986	1987	1988	1989	1990	1991
Jan.		82.61	86.84	91.20	96.25	100.0	103.3	111.0	119.5	130.2
Feb.		82.97	87.20	91.94	96.60	100.4	103.7	111.8	120.2	130.9
March	79.44	83.12	87.48	92.80	96.73	100.6	104.1	112.3	121.4	131.4
April	81.04	84.28	88.64	94.78	97.67	101.8	105.8	114.3	125.1	133.1
May	81.62	84.64	88.97	95.21	97.85	101.9	106.2	115.0	126.2	133.5
June	81.85	84.84	89.20	95.41	97.79	101.9	106.6	115.4	126.7	134.1
July	81.88	85.30	89.10	95.23	97.52	101.8	106.7	115.5	126.8	133.8

	1982	1983	1984	1985	1986	1987	1988	1989	1990	1991
Aug.	81.90	85.68	89.94	95.49	97.82	102.1	107.9	115.8	128.1	134.1
Sept.	81.85	86.06	90.11	95.44	98.30	102.4	108.4	116.6	129.3	134.6
Oct.	82.26	86.36	90.67	95.59	98.45	102.9	109.5	117.5	130.3	135.1
Nov.	82.66	86.67	90.95	95.92	99.29	103.4	110.0	118.5	130.0	135.6
Dec.	82.51	86.89	90.87	96.05	99.62	103.3	110.3	118.8	129.9	135.7

	1992	1993	1994	1995	1996	1997	1998	1999	2000	2001
Jan.	135.6	137.9	141.3	146.0	150.2	154.4	159.5	163.4	166.6	171.1
Feb.	136.3	138.8	142.1	146.9	150.9	155.0	160.3	163.7	167.5	172.0
March	136.7	139.3	142.5	147.5	151.5	155.4	160.8	164.1	168.4	172.2
April	138.8	140.6	144.2	149.0	152.6	156.3	162.6	165.2	170.1	173.1
May	139.3	141.1	144.7	149.6	152.9	156.9	163.5	165.6	170.7	174.2
June	139.3	141.0	144.7	149.8	153.0	157.5	163.4	165.6	171.1	174.4
July	138.8	140.7	144.0	149.1	152.4	157.5	163.0	165.1	170.5	173.3
Aug.	138.9	141.3	144.7	149.9	153.1	158.5	163.7	165.5	170.5	174.0
Sept.	139.4	141.9	145.0	150.6	153.8	159.3	164.4	166.2	171.7	174.6
Oct.	139.9	141.8	145.2	149.8	153.8	159.5	164.5	166.5	171.6	174.3
Nov.	139.7	141.6	145.3	149.8	153.9	159.6	164.4	166.7	172.1	173.6
Dec.	139.2	141.9	146.0	150.7	154.4	160.0	164.4	167.3	172.2	173.4

	2002	2003	2004	2005	2006	2007	2008	2009	2010	2011
Jan.	173.3	178.4	183.1	188.9	193.4	201.6	209.8	210.1	217.9	229.0
Feb.	173.8	179.3	183.8	189.6	194.2	203.1	211.4	211.4	219.2	231.3
March	174.5	179.9	184.6	190.5	195.0	204.4	212.1	211.3	220.7	232.5
April	175.7	181.2	185.7	191.6	196.5	205.4	214.0	211.5	222.8	234.4
May	176.2	181.5	186.5	192.0	197.7	206.2	215.1	212.8	223.6	235.2
June	176.2	181.3	186.8	192.2	198.5	207.3	216.8	213.4	224.1	235.2
July	175.9	181.3	186.8	192.2	198.5	206.1	216.5	213.4	223.6	234.7
Aug.	176.4	181.6	187.4	192.6	199.2	207.3	217.2	214.4	224.5	236.1
Sept.	177.6	182.5	188.1	193.1	200.1	208.0	218.4	215.3	225.3	237.9
Oct.	177.9	182.6	188.6	193.3	200.4	208.9	217.7	216.0	225.8	238.0
Nov.	178.2	182.7	189.0	193.6	201.1	209.7	216.0	216.6	226.8	238.5
Dec.	178.5	183.5	189.9	194.1	202.7	210.9	212.9	218.0	228.4	239.4

	2012	2013	2014	2015	2016	2017	2018	2019	2020	2021
Jan.	238.0	245.8	252.6	255.4	258.8					
Feb.	239.9	247.6	254.2	256.7	260.0					
March	240.8	248.7	254.8	257.1	261.1					
April	242.5	249.5	255.7	258.0	261.4					
May	242.4	250.0	255.9	258.5	262.1					
June	241.8	249.7	255.9	258.9	263.1					
July	242.1	249.7	256.0	258.6	263.4					
Aug.	243.0	251.0	257.0	259.8	264.4					
Sept.	244.2	251.9	257.6	259.6	264.9					
Oct.	245.6	251.9	257.7	259.5						
Nov.	245.6	252.1	257.1	259.8						
Dec.	246.8	253.4	257.5	260.6						

CAPITAL ALLOWANCES

37 Plant and machinery: annual investment allowances

(CAA 2001, s. 51A)

(Tax Reporter: 236-400ff.)

	Maximum (£)
1 January 2016	200,000
1/6 April 2014 to 31 December 2015	500,000[1]
1 January 2013 to 31 March/5 April 2014	250,000[1]
1/6 April 2012 to 31 December 2012	25,000
1/6 April 2010 to 31 March/5 April 2012	100,000

Note

[1] Temporary increase in the annual investment allowance initially for the period of two years beginning with 1 January 2013 (FA 2013, s. 7 and Sch. 1) was extended to 31 December 2015 (and increased to £500,000) by FA 2014, s. 10 and Sch. 2.

This figure is adjusted pro rata for chargeable periods shorter or longer than one year.

Where a chargeable period spans the above dates of change (i.e. 1/6 April 2014 or 1 January 2016), the maximum AIA is calculated by splitting the chargeable period into separate periods falling before and after each of the dates of change. Transitional rules are then applied to determine the maximum AIA available in respect of the total chargeable period and the maximum AIA that may be allocated against qualifying expenditure incurred in each of the separate periods (FA 2014, Sch. 2; FA 2013, Sch. 1; FA 2011, s. 11).

Groups of companies, companies and qualifying activities carried on by individuals or partnerships, under common control which share premises and carry on similar activities are entitled to a single annual investment allowance only.

38 Plant and machinery: 100% first-year allowances

(CAA 2001, s. 52)

(Tax Reporter: 237-000ff.)

Subject to the general exclusions, full 100% allowances are available for the following types of expenditure incurred by a business of any size. If full FYAs are not claimed, WDA is normally available on a reducing balance basis.

Nature of expenditure	Authority (CAA 2001)	Notes
Energy-saving plant or machinery	s. 45A–45C	Loss-making companies may claim tax rebate[1][2] (CAA 2001, Sch. A1)
Cars with very low CO_2 emissions	s. 45D	On expenditure incurred until 31 March 2018 (as extended from 31 March 2015 and to be further extended to April 2021 (Budget 2016)).
Zero-emission goods vehicles	s. 45DA	On expenditure incurred before 1 April 2018 (corporation tax) or 6 April 2018 (income tax) (as extended from 31 March or 5 April 2015).
Plant or machinery for certain refuelling stations	s. 45E	On expenditure incurred until 31 March 2018 (for both corporation tax and income tax) (as extended from 31 March 2015).
Plant or machinery (other than a long life asset) for use by a company wholly in a ring fence trade	s. 45F	
Environmentally beneficial plant or machinery	s. 45H–45J	Loss-making companies may claim tax rebate[2]
Expenditure on plant and machinery for use in designated assisted areas	s. 45K–45N	Initially due to end on 31 March 2017 but extended to 31 March 2020

Notes

[1] FYAs are not available on expenditure incurred on or after 1 April 2012 (corporation tax) or 6 April 2012 (income tax) on plant or machinery to generate renewable electricity or heat where tariff payments are received under the Feed-in Tariff or Renewable Heat Incentive schemes. In the case of expenditure incurred on a combined heat and power system, this restriction applies from 1 April 2014 (corporation tax) or 6 April 2014 (income tax). FYAs granted in respect of expenditure incurred from April 2012 (or April 2014 for CHP installations) will be withdrawn if FIT or RHI tariffs are paid subsequently (CAA 2001, s. 45AA).

[2] First year tax credits, for companies surrendering losses attributable to their expenditure on designated energy-saving or environmentally beneficial plant or machinery has been extended for a further five years until 31 March 2018 (SI 2013/464).

39   Plant and machinery: writing-down allowances

(CAA 2001, s. 56)

(Tax Reporter: 238-050ff.)

	Standard rate (%)	Special rate (%)
From April 2012	18	8
April 2008 to April 2012	20	10

Note

Different rules apply for certain cars.

WDA for small pools

Main pool or special rate pool only where tax written down value brought forward plus expenditure added to the pool during the period minus disposal receipts deducted from the pool during the period totals less than or equal to £1,000 (apportioned for periods of more or less than one year), an allowance may be claimed for the former amount in place of the standard rates above (CAA 2001, s. 56A).

Pooling

Expenditure is allocated to the main pool unless it is allocated to either a single asset pool or single class pool. Single asset and single class pools are as follows:

Single asset pools

- Short life asset (CAA 2001, s. 86)
- Ship (CAA 2001, s. 127)
- Assets with partial non qualifying use (CAA 2001, 206)
- Expenditure in relation to which a partial depreciation subsidy is received (CAA 2001, s. 211)
- Contribution allowances: plant and machinery (CAA 2001, s. 538)

Single class pools

- Special rate expenditure (see below) (CAA 2001, s. 104A)
- Overseas leasing (CAA 2001, s. 107)

Special rate expenditure

Expenditure	Incurred on or after	Provision
Thermal insulation of buildings	1 April 2008 (corporation tax) or 6 April 2008 (income tax)	CAA 2001, s. 28
Integral features	1 April 2008 (corporation tax) or 6 April 2008 (income tax)	CAA 2001, s. 33A
Long life asset expenditure	26 November 1996, or 1st January 2001 in pursuance of a contract entered into before 26 November 1996 or incurred before 26 November 1996 but allocated to a pool in a chargeable period beginning on or after that date	CAA 2001, Ch. 10

Expenditure	Incurred on or after	Provision
Cars (excluding main rate cars (first registered before 1 March 2001, cars with low CO_2 emissions, electrically-propelled cars))	1 April 2009 (corporation tax) or 6 April 2009 (income tax)	CAA 2001, s. 104AA
Provision of cushion gas	1 April 2010	CAA 2001, s. 70J(7)
Solar panels	1 April 2012 (corporation tax) or 6 April 2012 (income tax)	CAA 2001, s. 104A(1)(g)

40 Plant and machinery: allowances for cars

(CAA 2001, s. 104A and 104AA)

(Tax Reporter: 238-500ff.)

		CO_2 emissions		
	2018-19 to 2020-21[1]	**2015–16 to 2017–18**	**2013–14 & 2014–15**	**2012–13 (from 2009–10)**
100% FYAs (CAA 2001, s. 45D)	50g/km or less	75g/km or less	95g/km or less	110g/km or less
Main rate pool (18%)	Over 50g/km up to 110g/km	Over 75g/km up to 130g/km	Over 95g/km up to 130g/km	Over 110g/km up to 160g/km
Special rate pool (8%)	Over 110g/km	Over 130g/km	Over 130g/km	Over 160g/km

Note

[1]   Rates announced at Budget 2016.

Cars with private use go to a single asset pool but still with WDA as above, but then adjusted for private use percentage.

Cars acquired before April 2009

(Former CAA 2001, s. 74ff.)

(Tax Reporter: 238-880)

Under rules which applied until April 2009, cars costing more than £12,000 were allocated to a single asset pool and had the annual WDA capped at

£3,000. The £3,000 restriction continued for cars owned at April 2009 until the car was disposed of, or if it was still owned on the first day of the first chargeable period beginning on or after 1 April 2014 (corporation tax) or 6 April 2014 (income tax) ('the third relevant date'), then any unrelieved old expenditure was carried forward to the main plant and machinery pool at that time (whatever the level of vehicle emissions).

41 Other allowances

Allowance	Date expenditure incurred (from)	Initial allowance (%)	WDA (%)	CAA 2001	Tax Reporter
Business premises renovation(3)	11 April 2007 (to 31 March or 5 April 2017)	100	25	s. 360A	252-500
[Flat conversion(1)]	[11 May 2001 (to 31 March or 5 April 2013)]	[100]	[25]	[former s. 393A]	254-000
Mineral extraction(4)	1 April 1986	–	25	s. 394	255-500
Research and development	6 November 1962	100	–	s. 437	256-000
Know-how(2)	1 April 1986	–	25	s. 452	257-000
Patents(2)	1 April 1986	–	25	s. 464	257-500
Dredging	6 November 1962	–	4	s. 484	258-000
Assured tenancy	10 March 1982 (to 31 March 1992)	–	4	s. 490	258-500

Notes

(1) Flat conversion allowances are abolished in respect of expenditure incurred on or after 1 April 2013 for corporation tax purposes and 6 April 2013 for income tax purposes (FA 2012, s. 227 and Sch. 39, paras. 36 and 37). The entitlement to claim writing-down allowances on any residual expenditure is also withdrawn from that date.

(2) Capital allowances for know-how and patents still apply for income tax but were replaced for most corporation tax purposes by the intangible assets regime with effect from 1 April 2002.

(3) With effect from 1/6 April 2014, *Finance Act* 2014 amended CAA 2001, Pt. 3A to: specify qualifying expenditure for BPRA; prevent claims where another form of State aid has or will be received on the same investment project; introduce a time limit for works to be completed after expenditure has been incurred (and relief claimed) of 36 months (otherwise relief is withdrawn and the expenditure is treated as incurred when the works are provided); and reduce the period in which balancing adjustments must be made if certain events occur from seven years to five years.

(4) With effect in relation to claims made on or after 1 April 2014 (corporation tax) or 6 April 2014 (income tax) the treatment of MEAs is aligned with the existing principles for plant and machinery allowances and a mineral extraction trade for the purposes of MEAs must consist of activity within the charge to UK tax. *Finance Act* 2014 also amends the legislation to confirm that activity of an exempt foreign permanent establishment (FPE) is treated as a separate mineral extraction trade for the purposes of MEAs and to confirm that notional allowances will be given automatically in calculating the profits or losses of the exempt FPE as if the exempt FPE were within the charge to UK tax (with effect in relation to elections under CTA 2009, s. 18A which are to have effect on or after 1 April 2014). With effect from 17 July 2014, expenditure incurred on seeking planning permission qualifies as expenditure on mineral exploration and access whether the planning permission is successful or not. Previously, where planning permission was granted, the expenditure was treated as acquiring a mineral asset and eligible for relief at the lower rate of 10%.

CAPITAL GAINS TAX

42 Rates, annual exemption, chattel exemption

(TCGA 1992, s. 3, 4 and 262)

(Tax Reporter: 500-220, 509-050, 535-100)

Tax year	Gains eligible for:		Individuals		Trustees and PRs	
	Entrepreneurs' relief	Investors' relief[3]	Main rates[1]	Residential property/ carried interest[2]	Main rate	Residential property/ carried interest[2]
2016–17	10	[10]	10/20	18/28	20	28
2015–16	10	–	18/28	18/28	28	28
2014–15	10	–	18/28	18/28	28	28
2013–14	10	–	18/28	18/28	28	28
2012–13	10	–	18/28	18/28	28	28

Note

[1] For disposals on or after 6 April 2016, the chargeable gains arising from those disposals are aggregated with the individual's taxable income and to the extent that the aggregate falls above the threshold of the income tax basic rate, capital gains tax is charged at 20% (previously 28%) (taking the chargeable gains as being the highest part of that aggregate). If the aggregate falls below the threshold, the capital gains tax rate is 10% (previously 18%). (TCGA 1992, s. 4, as amended by FA 2016, s. 83).

[2] Gains accruing on the disposal of interests in residential properties that do not qualify for private residence relief and carried interest remain chargeable at the 18% and 28% rates as applicable for disposals before 6 April 2016 (TCGA 1992, s. 4, as amended by FA 2016, s. 83).

[3] Finance Act 2016 introduces a new relief for investors in unlisted trading companies. The relief applies a lower (10%) rate of capital gains tax on disposals of qualifying holdings (of newly issued shares purchased on or after 17 March 2016), providing they are held for a minimum of three years from 6 April 2016 (meaning that effectively, the relief will not be available until 2019–20). (TCGA 1992, Pt. 5, Ch. 5).

Exemptions

Tax year	Annual exempt amount[1]		Chattel exemption (max sale proceeds)[4] £
	Individuals, PRs[2], trusts for mentally disabled £	Other trusts[3] £	
2016–17	11,100	5,500	6,000
2015–16	11,100	5,550	6,000
2014–15	11,000	5,500	6,000
2013–14	10,900	5,450	6,000
2012–13	10,600	5,300	6,000
2011–12	10,600	5,300	6,000

Notes

(1) The annual exempt amount is increased annually, unless Parliament determines otherwise, by reference to the increase in CPI (from 2013–14, previously by reference to RPI).

(2) For year of death and next two years in the case of personal representatives (PRs) of deceased persons.

(3) Multiple trusts created by the same settlor; each attracts relief equal to the annual amount divided by the number of such trusts (subject to a minimum of 10% of the full amount).

(4) Where disposal proceeds exceed the exemption limit, marginal relief restricts any chargeable gain to 5/3 of the excess. Where there is a loss and the proceeds are less than £6,000 the proceeds are deemed to be £6,000.

43   Entrepreneurs' relief and Investors' relief

Entrepreneurs' relief and Investors' relief

(TCGA 1992, s. 169H–169S; and Pt. 5, Ch. 5 (as inserted by FA 2016, s. 87 and Sch. 14))

(Tax Reporter: 572-500ff.)

Chargeable gains arising on disposals of qualifying business assets on or after 23 June 2010 are charged to tax at a rate of 10%.

Period	Lifetime limit for entrepreneurs[1]	Lifetime limit for investors[2]
From 2019–20		10,000,000
From 6 April 2011	1,00,00,000	–

Notes

(1) The limit is a lifetime limits applying to disposals on or after 6 April 2008. Transitional provisions allow relief to be claimed in certain circumstances where gains deferred from disposals made on or before 5 April 2008 subsequently become chargeable (FA 2008, Sch. 3, para. 7 and 8).

(2) Finance Act 2016 introduces a new relief for investors in unlisted trading companies. The relief applies a lower (10%) rate of capital gains tax on disposals of qualifying holdings (of newly issued shares purchased on or after 17 March 2016), providing they are held for a minimum of three years from 6 April 2016 (meaning that effectively, the relief will not be available until 2019–20). The relief issubject to a separate lifetime limit of £10m of gains. (TCGA 1992, Pt. 5, Ch. 5).

44   Other exemptions and reliefs

EMI shares

(TCGA 1992, s. 169I(7A)–(7R))

(Tax Reporter: ¶572-950)

With effect in relation to disposals on or after 6 April 2013 of shares acquired pursuant to the exercise of a qualifying EMI option, entrepreneur's relief will be available in respect of the disposal notwithstanding that the 'personal company' requirement (>5% holding) may not be satisfied. To qualify, the shares must be:

- acquired since 6 April 2012;
- disposed of at least one year after the grant of the option; and
- the individual must have been an employee of the company, or a company in the same trading group, throughout the one year period ending with the disposal.

Employee shareholder status

(TCGA 1992, s. 236B–236G)

(Tax Reporter: 565-050)

Period	Gains exemption[1] £	Lifetime limit[2] £
From 17 March 2016	50,000	100,000
From 1 September 2013	50,000	–

Note

[1] Gains on the disposal of up to £50,000 worth of shares (based on acquisition value) are exempt from capital gains tax. Where a particular acquisition of shares causes the £50,000 limit to be breached, the remainder of the £50,000 limit is applied against the total value of the particular share acquisition and only that portion of the total number of shares acquired by the particular acquisition will be exempt from capital gains tax. The capital gains tax exemption is not available if the shareholder or connected person has a material interest (25% or more) in the company or parent undertaking. Normal share pooling and share identification rules do not apply to exempt employee shareholder shares.

[2] *Finance Act* 2016 introduces a lifetime limit of £100,000 in respect of capital gains tax exempt gains arising on employee shareholder shares. The limit will apply to employee shareholder shares issued as consideration for entering into employee shareholder agreements from midnight at the end of 16 March 2016. Any past or future gains, realised or unrealised, on employee shareholder shares that were issued in respect of employee shareholder agreements made before midnight at the end of 16 March 2016 will not count towards the limit (TCGA 1992, s. 236B).

Employee-ownership trusts

(TCGA 1992, s. 236H–236U)

(Tax Reporter: ¶361-400ff.)

From 6 April 2014, disposals of shares to a trust with specific characteristics which benefits all employees of a company (or a group) may be wholly relieved from capital gains tax if certain criteria are met. The relief requirements are:

- **the trading requirement:** the company whose shares are disposed of must be a trading company, or the parent company of a trading group;
- **the all-employee benefit requirement:** the trust which acquires the shares must operate for the benefit all employees;

- **the controlling interest requirement:** the trust must have a controlling interest in the company at the end of the tax year, which it did not have at the start of that year;
- **the limited participation requirement:** certain participators must be excluded from being beneficiaries of the trust; and
- neither the claimant (nor anyone connected with him) has previously received relief on the same company's (or any group company's) shares.

The relief operates by disapplying TCGA 1992, s. 17(1) (market value disposals) and treats the disposal (and acquisition by the trustees) as a no gain, no loss disposal. The relief is available on disposals which take place in a single tax year; disposals may be made by more than one person, and can be of any number of shares. Where a disqualifying event (broadly, the relief requirements cease to be met) occurs in the following tax year, any relief given is withdrawn and where a disqualifying event occurs in any later tax year, this triggers a deemed disposal and reacquisition at market value by the trustees.

Rollover relief

(TCGA 1992, s. 152)

(Tax Reporter: 570-100)

To qualify for rollover relief, an asset must fall within one of the 'relevant classes of assets' and the reinvestment must generally take place within the period from 12 months before to three years after the disposal of the old asset. Classes of assets qualifying for relief are as follows, but see TCGA 1992, s. 156ZB for the interaction of this section with the corporation tax rules for gains and losses on intangible fixed assets:
- land and buildings occupied and used exclusively for the purposes of a trade;
- fixed plant or machinery (not forming part of a building);
- ships, aircraft, hovercraft;
- satellites, space stations and spacecraft (including launch vehicles);
- goodwill;
- milk quotas and potato quotas, ewe and suckler cow premium quotas, fish quotas;
- entitlements under the single farm payments scheme;
- entitlements under the basic payment scheme (with effect in relation to disposals of old assets or acquisitions of new assets on or after 20 December 2013); and
- Lloyd's members' syndicate rights and assets treated as acquired by members.

Private residence relief

(TCGA 1992, s. 222)

(Tax Reporter: 540-000)

Relief is given on gains arising on the disposal of a dwelling house and on land enjoyed with the residence as it's garden or grounds (up to the permitted area of half a hectare, or more if required for the reasonable enjoyment of the property).

Gains are time apportioned across the period of ownership between periods of occupation (including deemed occupation) and other periods, with relief being available against the portion of the gain attributable to periods of occupation. The final period of ownership is always eligible for relief, provided the property was at some time the only or main residence. For disposals on or after 6 April 2014, the final period exemption applies to the last 18 months of ownership (previously, 36 months) except for individuals who are disabled or in a care home and with no other property who continue to get a 36 month final period exemption.

Where a residence is let during a period of non occupation, relief is available on the portion of the gain attributable to the let period up to £40,000.

Enterprise investment scheme

(TCGA 1992, s. 150A and Sch. 5B)

(Tax Reporter: 564-400ff. and 568-000)

A disposal of shares on which income tax relief has not been withdrawn is exempt from capital gains tax; losses arising are eligible for relief in the normal way, but the base cost is treated as reduced by any EIS income tax relief which has been given and not withdrawn.

Reinvestment relief is available for gains on assets where the disposal proceeds are reinvested in new EIS shares.

Gains that are eligible for entrepreneurs' rellef and deferred into investment under the enterprise investment scheme on or after 3 December 2014 will benefit from entrepreneurs' relief when the gain is realised.

Seed enterprise investment scheme

(TCGA 1992, Sch. 5BB)

(Tax Reporter: 568-500)

Disposal relief

The exemption from capital gains applies where SEIS shares are held for more than three years from their issue. Losses are eligible for relief in the normal way but the base cost is treated as reduced by any SEIS income tax relief which has been given and not withdrawn.

Reinvestment relief

For 2012–13, initially a re-investment exemption is available in respect of a gain arising on the disposal of any asset to the extent that the individual makes a qualifying investment under SEIS in the same tax year. *Finance Act* 2013 extended the relief and *Finance Act* 2014 made it permanent. Capital gains reinvestment relief is subject to the £100,000 annual investment limit which applies for income tax relief.

Relevant year[1]	Relevant percentage[2]
2016–17	50%
2013–14 to 2015–16	50%
2012–13	100%

Notes

[1] The relevant year is year in which the investor is eligible for and makes a claim for SEIS income tax relief in respect of an amount subscribed for an issue of shares which must be the same tax year as the disposal of the asset and year in which the chargeable gain accrues.

[2] The relevant percentage of the 'available SEIS expenditure' is to be set against a corresponding amount of the original gain. The 'available SEIS expenditure' is the amount specified in the claim (provided that the amount has not been previously set against a gain) but cannot exceed the amount of the gain which remains unmatched after any previous claims or claims under the EIS deferral relief. To the extent that the gain is matched with the relevant percentage of the amount subscribed, it is not a chargeable gain.

Investment in social enterprises

(TCGA 1992, s. 255A–255E, Sch. 8B)

(Tax Reporter: 569-300ff.)

Disposal relief

The disposal relief provides an exemption from capital gains tax in respect of the disposal of an investment where the investor has received income tax relief (which has not subsequently been withdrawn) on the cost of the investment, and the investment is disposed of after it has been held for at least three years. However, if no claim to income tax relief is made, then any subsequent disposal of the investment will not qualify for exemption from capital gains tax.

Deferral relief

The deferral relief enables the payment of tax on a capital gain to be deferred where the gain is reinvested in shares or debt investments which also qualify for SITR income tax relief. It is not, however, necessary for the investor to have made a claim for SITR income tax relief. The gain can arise from the disposal of any kind of asset, but must arise in the period from 6 April 2014 to 5 April 2019. The SITR qualifying investment must be made in the period one year before or three years after the gain arose. There is no minimum period for which the investment must be held; the deferred capital gain is brought back into charge whenever the investment is disposed of or the social enterprise ceases to meet the requirements of the scheme, but if an amount equal to the gain is once more invested in shares or debt investments which also qualify for SITR income tax relief then the gain may be held over again.

Gains that are eligible for entrepreneurs' relief and deferred into investment under the enterprise investment scheme on or after 3 December 2014 will benefit from entrepreneurs' relief when the gain is realised.

Charities

(CTA 2010, s. 466ff.; TCGA 1992, s. 256, 257; ITA 2007, s. 518ff.)

(Tax Reporter: 815-440)

The gains of charities are not taxable provided they are applicable, and applied, for charitable purposes only. The legislation is designed to charge charities to tax on the amount of their income and gains that has not been invested, lent or spent in an approved way.

A charge to capital gains tax arises if a charity ceases to be a charity, when there is a deemed sale and reacquisition of the trust property by the trustees at market value.

Gifts to the nation

(TCGA 1992, s. 258; FA 2012, Sch. 14)

(Tax Reporter: ¶535-620)

Gains arising on gifts of pre-eminent property to be held for the benefit of the public or the nation are not chargeable to capital gains tax.

For the tax year 2012–13 and subsequent tax years, a reduction in income tax and/or capital gains tax is available where an individual makes a gift of pre-eminent property to be held for the benefit of the public or the nation. The tax reduction is 30% of the value of the gift. A gift offer must be made and registered in accordance with the scheme and relief is available against the individual's liability for the year in which the gift offer is registered and/or any of the succeeding four tax years.

Pre-eminent property includes any picture, print, book, manuscript, work of art, scientific object or other thing that is pre-eminent for its national, scientific, historic or artistic interest, collections of such items and any object kept in a significant building where it is desirable that it remain associated with the building.

Disincorporation relief

(FA 2013, s. 58–60; TCGA 1992, s. 162B and 162C; CTA 2009, s. 849A)

Disincorporation relief is a form of roll-over or deferral relief which allows a company to transfer certain assets to its shareholders who continue the business in an unincorporated form. The assets are deemed to be transferred at below market value so that no corporation tax charge arises to the company, although shareholders may still be liable to income tax or capital gains tax on the transfer of assets to them by the company. Shareholders will be liable to capital gains tax, as usual, on a future sale of the assets, for which purpose the assets are treated as having been acquired at the reduced transfer value.

The relief applies in relation to a 'qualifying transfer' of a business with a disposal date falling within the period of five years beginning 1 April 2013. A qualifying transfer is one which meets the following conditions:
- the business must be transferred as a going concern;
- the business must be transferred together with all the assets of the business or together with all the assets of the business apart from cash;
- the total market value of the 'qualifying assets' at the time of the transfer must not be more than £100,000;

- the shareholders that the business is transferred to must be individuals; and
- those shareholders must have held shares in the company throughout the 12 months before the transfer.

Qualifying assets are interests in land (other than land held as trading stock) and goodwill. Special rules apply to determine the transfer value of any post-FA 2002 goodwill.

A claim for Disincorporation Relief must be made jointly by the company and all the shareholders to whom the business is transferred. The claim must be made within two years of the business transfer date.

INHERITANCE TAX

45   Rates of tax

(IHTA 1984, s. 7 and Sch. 1)

(Tax Reporter: 607-000; 624-000)

From 15 March 1988

	Gross rate of tax
Lifetime transfers	
Gross transfers up to cumulative limit	Nil
Gross transfers over cumulative limit	20%
Grossing-up fraction	$1/_4$
Death transfers	
Gross transfers up to cumulative limit	Nil
Gross transfers over cumulative limit	40%
Grossing-up fraction	$2/_3$
Reduced rate[1]	36%

Note

[1] For deaths occurring on or after 6 April 2012, a reduced rate of inheritance tax of 36% applies where 10% or more of a deceased person's net estate (after deducting IHT exemptions, reliefs and the nil-rate band) is left to charity. To determine whether the lower rate will apply, the estate is broken down into three components (with the nil rate band apportioned): the survivorship component (property passing automatically to the survivor), the settled property component (settled property in which the deceased held an interest in possession) and the general component (all other property excluding gifts with reservation of benefit to which the lower rate cannot apply). The 10% test is applied to each component separately and the lower rate applied to those components which satisfy the 10% test. An election to merge components of the estate and apply the 10% test in aggregate is possible, as is an election to opt out of the lower rate for one or more components of the estate. Both elections must be made within two years of the date of death and may be withdrawn within two years and one month of the date of death.

46 Cumulative chargeable transfers limit

(IHTA 1984, s. 7 and Sch. 1)

Transfers from 15 March 1988

Period	Cumulative chargeable transfers limit[1] £
2016–17 [2]	325,000
2009–10 to 2015–16	325,000

Notes

[1] *Finance Act* 2008, s. 10 and Sch. 4 allow a claim to be made to transfer any unused nil-rate band of the first deceased spouse or civil partner to the estate of their surviving spouse or civil partner who dies on or after 9 October 2007.

[2] *Finance Act* 2010, s. 8 froze the nil rate band at £325,000 for tax years 2012–13 to 2014–15. *Finance Act* 2014, Sch. 25, para. 2 extends the freeze for a further three years from 2015–16 until 2017–18 and F(No. 2)A 2015, s. 10 further extends the freeze until April 2021.

47 Residence nil-rate band

(IHTA 1984, s. 8D–8M)

Year	Residential enhancement £
2017–18	100,000
2018–19	125,000
2019–20	150,000
2020–21	175,000

Note

[1] For deaths on or after 6 April 2017, an additional nil-rate band is available when a residence is passed on death to direct descendants. Amounts are set for years 2017–18 to 2020–21 as per the table above and the amount will then increase in line with CPI from 2021–22 onwards. Any unused nil-rate band will be transferred to a surviving spouse or civil partner. It will also be available when a person downsizes or ceases to own a home on or after 8 July 2015 and assets of an equivalent value, up to the value of the additional nil-rate band, are passed on death to direct descendants. There will also be a tapered withdrawal of the additional nil-rate band for estates with a net value of more than £2m. This will be at a withdrawal rate of £1 for every £2 over this threshold (IHTA 1984, s. 8D–8M, as amended by FA 2016, s. 93 and Sch. 15).

48 Annual and small gift exemption

(IHTA 1984, s. 19 and 20)

(Tax Reporter: 643-200 and 643-700)

	On or after 6 April 1981 £
Annual	3,000
Small gift (to the same person)	250

49 Gifts in consideration of marriage/civil partnership

(IHTA 1984, s. 22)

(Tax Reporter: 644-450)

Donor	Exemption limit £
Parent of party to the marriage/civil partnership	5,000
Remote ancestor of party to the marriage/civil partnership	2,500
Party to the marriage/civil partnership	2,500
Any other person	1,000

50 Transfers by UK-domiciled spouse/civil partner to non-UK domiciled spouse/civil partner

(IHTA 1984, s. 18)

(Tax Reporter: 644-900)

Transfer on or after	Exemption limit £
6 April 2013	325,000[1]
9 March 1982	55,000

Notes

[1] *Finance Act* 2013 increased the lifetime limit on the amount that can be transferred exempt from IHT to a spouse or civil partner domiciled outside the UK to the exemption limit at the time of the transfer per IHTA 1984, Sch. 1 (the nil rate band).

Election to be treated as domiciled in UK

(IHTA 1984, s. 267ZA–267ZB)

(Tax Reporter: 684-575)

A person who is not domiciled in the UK but who is, or has been married to, or in a civil partnership with, someone who is domiciled in the UK can elect to be treated as domiciled in the UK for the purposes of inheritance tax. There are two types of elections:

1. A lifetime election by the non domiciled individual who is at any time on or after 6 April 2013 and during the period of seven years ending with the date of the election married to or in a civil partnership with a UK domiciled individual.

2. A death election by the personal representatives of a deceased person who was at any time on or after 6 April 2013, and during the period of seven years ending with the date of death themselves domiciled in the UK and married to or in a civil partnership with a non domiciled person who is, by virtue of the election, to be treated as domiciled in the UK.

The election is irrevocable but ceases to have effect if the individual is not resident in the UK for income tax purposes for four successive tax years. The election must be in writing and in the case of a death election made within two years of the date of death. The election cannot relate back to before 6 April 2013, or more than seven years before either the election is made or the date of death and any date the election relates back to must be a date when the individual was married, or in a civil partnership, and either the individual or their spouse (as the case may be) was UK domiciled on that date.

51   Agricultural and business property relief

(IHTA 1984, s. 103ff. and 115ff.)

(Tax Reporter: 664-000 and 658-000)

Type of relief	Rate of relief for disposals on or after 6/4/96 %
Agricultural property[1][2]	
Vacant possession or right to obtain it within 12 months	100
Tenanted land with vacant a possession value	100
Entitled to 50% relief at 9 March 1981 and not since able to obtain vacant possession	100
Agricultural land let on or after 1 September 1995	100
Other circumstances	50
Business property	
Nature of property	
Business or interest in business	100
Controlling shareholding in quoted company	50
Controlling shareholding in unquoted[3]company	100
Settled property used in life tenant's business	100/50[4]
Shareholding in unquoted[3] company: more than 25% interest	100
Minority shareholding in unquoted[3]company: 25% or less	100
Land, buildings, machinery or plant used by transferor's company or partnership	50

Notes

[1] *Finance Act* 2009, s. 122 extends agricultural property relief to property in the European Economic Area. Inheritance Tax due or paid on or after 23 April 2003 in relation to agricultural property located in a qualifying EEA state at the time of the chargeable event will become eligible for relief.

[2] From 6 April 1995, short rotation coppice is regarded as agricultural property.

[3] With effect from 10 March 1992, 'unquoted' means shares not quoted on a recognised stock exchange and therefore includes shares dealt in on the Unlisted Securities Market (USM) or Alternative Investment Market (AIM).

[4] The higher rate applies if the settled property is transferred along with business itself.

52 Quick succession relief

(IHTA 1984, s. 141)

(Tax Reporter: 627-400)

Years between transfers		Percentage applied to formula below
More than	Not more than	
0	1	100
1	2	80
2	3	60
3	4	40
4	5	20

Formula

$$\text{Tax charge on earlier transfer} \times \frac{\text{Increase in transferee's estate}}{\text{Diminution in transferor's estate}}$$

53 Fall in value relief

(IHTA 1984, s. 179, 191 and 197A)

(Tax Reporter: 627-900)

Type of property	Period after death
Quoted securities sold	One year
Qualifying investments[1]	One year
Interests in land – deaths after 15 March 1990	Four years

Notes

[1] Qualifying investments means shares or securities which are quoted at the date of death in question, holdings in a unit trust which at that date is an authorised unit trust, shares in an open-ended investment company and shares in any common investment fund established under the *Administration of Justice Act* 1982, s. 42.

54 Taper relief

(IHTA 1984, s. 7(4))

(Tax Reporter: 611-400)

Years between gift and death		Percentage of full tax charge at death – rates actually due
More than	Not more than	%
3	4	80
4	5	60
5	6	40
6	7	20

VALUE ADDED TAX

55 Rates

(VATA 1994, s. 2)

(VAT Reporter: 18-014)

Period of application	Standard rate[1] %	VAT fraction %	Reduced rate[1] %	VAT fraction %
From 4 January 2011	20	1/6	5.0	1/21
1 January 2010 to 3 January 2011	17.5	7/47	5.0	1/21

Notes

[1] VAT lock: F(No. 2)A 2015, s. 2 sets a ceiling on the standard and reduced rates of VAT at 20% and 5% respectively, for the period beginning with 18 November 2015 and ending immediately before the date of the first Parliamentary general election after that day (the 'VAT lock period').

[2] Supplies of fuel and power for domestic, residential and charity non-business use and certain other supplies are charged at 5% (VATA 1994, Sch. 7A).

[3] Imports of certain works of art, antiques and collectors' items are charged at an effective rate of 5% from 27 July 1999 (VATA 1994, s. 21(4)–(6)).

[4] The zero rate has applied from 1 April 1973 to date.

56 Registration limits

(1) Taxable supplies in the UK

(VATA 1994, Sch. 1; Notice 700/1)

(VAT Reporter: 43-025)

Period of application	Past turnover 1 year £	Future turnover 30 days £	Unless turnover for next year will not exceed £
From 1/4/16	83,000	83,000	81,000
1/4/15–31/3/16	82,000	82,000	80,000
1/4/14–31/3/15	81,000	81,000	79,000
1/4/13–31/3/14	79,000	79,000	77,000
1/4/12–31/3/13	77,000	77,000	75,000
1/4/11–31/3/12	73,000	73,000	71,000

Notes

Taxable supplies at both the zero rate and positive rates are included in the above limits.

All of a person's taxable supplies are considered, because it is 'persons' not 'businesses' who can or must register.

If a person took over a business as a 'going concern', he is deemed to have made the vendor's supplies for the purposes of registration.

These limits are exclusive of VAT, as VAT is not chargeable unless a person is registered or liable to be registered.

The limit which applies for a particular past period is that which is in force at the end of the period.

There are two alternative tests of the liability to notify HMRC of a person's liability to register as a result of making taxable supplies:

(1)   past 12 months turnover limit; and

(2)   future 30 days turnover limit. Registration is required if there are reasonable grounds for believing that the value of taxable supplies in a period of 30 days will exceed the limit. This limit is the same as that for the past 12 months, but applies to 30 days from any time.

The following are excluded from the supplies for the purpose of applying the registration limits:

(1)   the value of capital supplies (other than of land); and

(2)   any taxable supplies which would not be taxable supplies apart from VATA 1994, s. 7(4), which concerns removal of goods to the UK.

Any supplies made at a previous time when the person was registered are disregarded if all necessary information was given to HMRC when the earlier registration was cancelled.

(2) Supplies from other member states (distance selling into the UK)

(VATA 1994, Sch. 2; Notice 700/1)

(VAT Reporter: 43-030)

Period of application	Cumulative relevant supplies from 1 January in year to any day in same year £
From 1/1/93 (VATA 1994, Sch. 2; Notice 700/1).	70,000

Generally, the value of relevant supplies is of those made by persons in other member states to non-taxable persons in the UK.

If certain goods, which are subject to excise duty, are removed to the UK, the person who removes the goods is liable to register in the UK because all such goods must be taxed in the country of destination. There is no de minimis limit.

(3) Acquisitions from other member states

(VATA 1994, Sch. 3; Notice 700/1)

(VAT Reporter: 43-035)

Period of application	Cumulative relevant supplies from 1 January in year to any day in same year £
From 1/4/16	83,000
1/4/15–31/3/16	82,000
1/4/14–31/3/15	81,000
1/4/13–31/3/14	79,000
1/4/12–31/3/13	77,000
1/4/11–31/3/12	73,000

Future prospects rule: a person is also liable to register at any time if there are reasonable grounds for believing that the value of his relevant acquisitions in the period of 30 days then beginning will exceed the given limit. This limit is the same as that for the period starting on 1 January above.

(4) Assets supplied in the UK by overseas persons

(VATA 1994, Sch. 3A; Notice 700/1)

(VAT Reporter: 43-045)

From 21 March 2000, any person without an establishment in the UK making or intending to make 'relevant supplies' must VAT register, regardless of the value of those supplies.

'Relevant supplies' are taxable supplies of goods, including capital assets, in the UK where the supplier has recovered UK VAT under:

- Directive 2008/9 for a person in a member state as regards VAT incurred in another member state; or
- Directive 86/560 (the thirteenth VAT directive) for claimants established outside the member states.

This applies where:

- the supplier (or his predecessor in business) was charged VAT on the purchase of the goods, or on anything incorporated in them, and has either claimed it back or intends to do so; or
- the VAT being claimed back was VAT paid on the import of goods into the UK.

(5) Electronic, telecommunication and broadcasting services

(VATA 1994, Sch. 3B and 3BA; Notice 700/1)

(VAT Reporter: 43-047)

A person can register if he makes or intends to make qualifying supplies, i.e. electronically supplied services to a person who belongs in the UK or another member state and who receives such services otherwise than for business purposes. The person who registers must have neither a business establishment nor a fixed establishment in the UK or in another member state in relation to any supply. Generally, the person must also be neither registered nor required to be registered for VAT in the UK or the Isle of Man or, under equivalent legislation, in another member state.

Digital services in the EU from 1 January 2015 (VAT MOSS)

From 1 January 2015, there are new place of supply rules for VAT on the supply of digital services by businesses to consumers in the EU. VAT on digital services will be paid in the consumer's country, not the supplier's country. It will be charged at the rate that applies in the consumer's country. Suppliers of digital services to EU consumers can either:

- register for VAT in each EU country; or
- register to use the VAT Mini One Stop Shop (VAT MOSS) online service.

VAT MOSS enables businesses to account for the VAT due on business-to-consumer (B2C) sales in other EU countries by submitting a single quarterly return and payment to HMRC. HMRC will send an electronic copy of the appropriate part of the return, and any payment, to each relevant country's tax authority.

(6) Non-established taxable persons

(VATA 1994, Sch. 1A Notice 700/1)

(VAT Reporter: 43-049)

From 1 December 2012, if a person makes taxable supplies in the UK but has no establishment there, he must register for VAT regardless of the value of such supplies. Thus, non-UK established taxable persons (NETPs) no longer benefit from the UK VAT registration threshold.

A NETP is any person not normally resident in the UK, does not have a UK establishment and, in the case of a company, is not incorporated here.

57 Input tax and mileage allowances (advisory fuel rates)

SI 2005/3290

(VAT Reporter: 19-071)

An employer can reclaim the VAT incurred by employees on fuel costs that are reimbursed by the employer on the basis of cost or via a mileage allowance. VAT can only be reclaimed by an employer on fuel which is used in the course of the business to make taxable supplies. However, the key practical change is that employers must obtain and retain a valid VAT invoice to support the reclaim. Generally, a retailer's invoice (also known as a 'less-detailed invoice') should suffice, because the amount of fuel that is purchased by an employee in a single supply is likely to be within the VAT-inclusive limit of £250 for a retailer's invoice.

Generally, the invoiced amount does not match the input tax claim for the fuel in any one claim period and invoices may concern more than one period. For example, if fuel is purchased towards the end of a period, it may not be fully used until a subsequent period. An invoice may cover more than one claim and this needs to be taken into account when checking the evidence to support claims. Another possible reason why the invoiced amount does not match the claim is that often some of the fuel is used by the employee for private journeys. Generally, the VAT can be reclaimed if the invoice(s) are for sufficient fuel to cover the claimed mileage, and cover the relevant period. Strictly, a claim cannot be supported by an invoice that is dated after the dates covered by the claim.

HMRC publish 'advisory fuel rates' to determine the business fuel cost, but rates set by recognised motoring agencies, such as the RAC and the AA, are usually acceptable. HMRC first published the rates in 2002 (www. gov.uk/advisory-fuel-rates-when-you-can-use-them).

Transition to revised 'advisory fuel rate': one-month rule

For one month from the date of change, employers may use either the previous or new current rates, as they choose.

Key Data

Engine size	Rate per mile		
	Petrol	**Diesel**	**LPG**
For journeys from 1 September 2016			
1400cc or less	11p	9p	7p
1401cc to 1600cc	13p	9p	9p
1601cc to 2000cc	13p	11p	9p
Over 2000cc	20p	13p	13p
For journeys from 1 June 2016			
1400cc or less	10p	9p	7p
1401cc to 1600cc	13p	9p	9p
1601cc to 2000cc	13p	10p	9p
Over 2000cc	20p	12p	13p
For journeys from 1 March 2016			
1400cc or less	10p	8p	7p
1401cc to 1600cc	12p	8p	8p
1601cc to 2000cc	12p	10p	8p
Over 2000cc	19p	11p	13p
For journeys from 1 December 2015			
1400cc or less	11p	9p	7p
1401cc to 1600cc	13p	9p	9p
1601cc to 2000cc	13p	11p	9p
Over 2000cc	20p	13p	13p
For journeys from 1 September 2015			
1400cc or less	11p	9p	7p
1401cc to 1600cc	14p	9p	9p
1601cc to 2000cc	14p	11p	9p
Over 2000cc	21p	13p	14p
For journeys from 1 June 2015			
1400cc or less	12p	10p	8p
1401cc to 1600cc	14p	10p	9p
1601cc to 2000cc	14p	12p	9p
Over 2000cc	21p	14p	14p
For journeys from 1 March 2015			
1400cc or less	11p	9p	8p
1401cc to 1600cc	13p	9p	10p
1601cc to 2000cc	13p	11p	10p
Over 2000cc	20p	14p	14p
For journeys from 1 December 2014			
1400cc or less	13p	11p	9p
1401cc to 1600cc	16p	11p	11p
1601cc to 2000cc	16p	13p	11p
Over 2000cc	23p	16p	16p

Engine size	Rate per mile		
	Petrol	**Diesel**	**LPG**
For journeys from 1 September 2014			
1400cc or less	14p	11p	9p
1401cc to 1600cc	16p	11p	11p
1601cc to 2000cc	16p	13p	11p
Over 2000cc	24p	17p	16p
For journeys from 1 June 2014			
1400cc or less	14p	12p	9p
1401cc to 1600cc	16p	12p	11p
1601cc to 2000cc	16p	14p	11p
Over 2000cc	24p	17p	16p
For journeys from 1 March 2014			
1400cc or less	14p	12p	9p
1401cc to 1600cc	16p	12p	11p
1601cc to 2000cc	16p	14p	11p
Over 2000cc	24p	17p	17p

58   VAT on private fuel (scale charges)

(VATA 1994, Sch. 6, para. B1; SI 2013/2911; Notice 700/64)

(VAT Reporter: 18-320ff.)

From 1 May 2016

Fuel scale charges for 12-month period

CO_2 band	VAT fuel scale charge, 12 month period £	VAT on 12 month charge £	VAT exclusive 12 month charge £
120 or less	467.00	77.83	389.17
125	699.00	116.50	582.50
130	747.00	124.50	622.50
135	792.00	132.00	660.00
140	841.00	140.17	700.83
145	886.00	147.67	738.33
150	934.00	155.67	778.33
155	979.00	163.17	815.83
160	1028.00	171.33	856.67
165	1073.00	178.83	894.17
170	1121.00	186.83	934.17

CO$_2$ band	VAT fuel scale charge, 12 month period £	VAT on 12 month charge £	VAT exclusive 12 month charge £
175	1166.00	194.33	971.67
180	1214.00	202.33	1011.67
185	1259.00	209.83	1049.17
190	1308.00	218.00	1090.00
195	1353.00	225.50	1127.50
200	1401.00	233.50	1167.50
205	1446.00	241.00	1205.00
210	1495.00	249.17	1245.83
215	1540.00	256.67	1283.33
220	1588.00	264.67	1323.33
225 or more	1633.00	272.17	1360.83

Fuel scale charges for 3-month period

CO$_2$ band	VAT fuel scale charge, 3 month period £	VAT on 3 month charge £	VAT exclusive 3 month charge £
120 or less	116.00	19.33	96.67
125	175.00	29.17	145.83
130	186.00	31.00	155.00
135	197.00	32.83	164.17
140	209.00	34.83	174.17
145	221.00	36.83	184.17
150	233.00	38.83	194.17
155	245.00	40.83	204.17
160	256.00	42.67	213.33
165	268.00	44.67	223.33
170	279.00	46.50	232.50
175	291.00	48.50	242.50
180	303.00	50.50	252.50
185	314.00	52.33	261.67
190	326.00	54.33	271.67
195	338.00	56.33	281.67
200	350.00	58.33	291.67
205	362.00	60.33	301.67

CO_2 band	VAT fuel scale charge, 3 month period £	VAT on 3 month charge £	VAT exclusive 3 month charge £
210	373.00	62.17	310.83
215	384.00	64.00	320.00
220	396.00	66.00	330.00
225 or more	408.00	68.00	340.00

Fuel scale charges for 1-month period

CO_2 band	VAT fuel scale charge, 1 month period £	VAT on 1 month charge £	VAT exclusive 1 month charge £
120 or less	38.00	6.33	31.67
125	58.00	9.67	48.33
130	61.00	10.17	50.83
135	65.00	10.83	54.17
140	69.00	11.50	57.50
145	73.00	12.17	60.83
150	77.00	12.83	64.17
155	81.00	13.50	67.50
160	85.00	14.17	70.83
165	89.00	14.83	74.17
170	92.00	15.33	76.67
175	96.00	16.00	80.00
180	101.00	16.83	84.17
185	104.00	17.33	86.67
190	108.00	18.00	90.00
195	112.00	18.67	93.33
200	116.00	19.33	96.67
205	120.00	20.00	100.00
210	123.00	20.50	102.50
215	128.00	21.33	106.67
220	132.00	22.00	110.00
225 or more	135.00	22.50	112.50

1 May 2015 to 30 April 2016

Fuel scale charges for 12-month period

CO_2 band	VAT fuel scale charge, 12-month period, £	VAT on 12-month charge, £	VAT exclusive 12-month charge, £
120 or less	536.00	89.33	446.67
125	802.00	133.67	668.33
130	857.00	142.83	714.17
135	909.00	151.50	757.50
140	965.00	160.83	804.17
145	1,016.00	169.33	846.67
150	1,072.00	178.67	893.33
155	1,123.00	187.17	935.83
160	1,179.00	196.50	982.50
165	1,231.00	205.17	1,025.83
170	1,286.00	214.33	1,071.67
175	1,338.00	223.00	1,115.00
180	1,393.00	232.17	1,160.83
185	1,445.00	240.83	1,204.17
190	1,501.00	250.17	1,250.83
195	1,552.00	258.67	1,293.33
200	1,608.00	268.00	1,340.00
205	1,660.00	276.67	1,383.33
210	1,715.00	285.83	1,429.17
215	1,767.00	294.50	1,472.50
220	1,822.00	303.67	1,518.33
225 or more	1,874.00	312.33	1,561.67

Fuel scale charges for 3-month period

CO_2 band	VAT fuel scale charge, 3-month period, £	VAT on 3-month charge, £	VAT exclusive 3-month charge, £
120 or less	133.00	22.17	110.83
125	200.00	33.33	166.67
130	213.00	35.50	177.50
135	227.00	37.83	189.17

CO$_2$ band	VAT fuel scale charge, 3-month period, £	VAT on 3-month charge, £	VAT exclusive 3-month charge, £
140	240.00	40.00	200.00
145	254.00	42.33	211.67
150	267.00	44.50	222.50
155	281.00	46.83	234.17
160	294.00	49.00	245.00
165	308.00	51.33	256.67
170	320.00	53.33	266.67
175	334.00	55.67	278.33
180	347.00	57.83	289.17
185	361.00	60.17	300.83
190	374.00	62.33	311.67
195	388.00	64.67	323.33
200	401.00	66.83	334.17
205	415.00	69.17	345.83
210	428.00	71.33	356.67
215	441.00	73.50	367.50
220	455.00	75.83	379.17
225 or more	468.00	78.00	390.00

Fuel scale charges for 1-month period

CO$_2$ band	VAT fuel scale charge, 1-month period, £	VAT on 1-month charge, £	VAT exclusive 1-month charge, £
120 or less	44.00	7.33	36.67
125	66.00	11.00	55.00
130	70.00	11.67	58.33
135	75.00	12.50	62.50
140	80.00	13.33	66.67
145	84.00	14.00	70.00
150	88.00	14.67	73.33
155	93.00	15.50	77.50
160	97.00	16.17	80.83
165	102.00	17.00	85.00
170	106.00	17.67	88.33

CO$_2$ band	VAT fuel scale charge, 1-month period, £	VAT on 1-month charge, £	VAT exclusive 1-month charge, £
175	111.00	18.50	92.50
180	115.00	19.17	95.83
185	119.00	19.83	99.17
190	124.00	20.67	103.33
195	129.00	21.50	107.50
200	133.00	22.17	110.83
205	138.00	23.00	115.00
210	142.00	23.67	118.33
215	146.00	24.33	121.67
220	151.00	25.17	125.83
225 or more	155.00	25.83	129.17

1 May 2014 to 30 April 2015

Fuel scale charges for the 12-month period

CO$_2$ band	VAT fuel scale charge 12-month period £	VAT on 12-month charge £	VAT exclusive 12-month charge £
120 or less	627.00	104.50	522.50
125	939.00	156.50	782.50
130	1,004.00	167.33	836.67
135	1,064.00	177.33	886.67
140	1,129.00	188.17	940.83
145	1,190.00	198.33	991.67
150	1,255.00	209.17	1,045.83
155	1,315.00	219.17	1,095.83
160	1,381.00	230.17	1,150.83
165	1,441.00	240.17	1,200.83
170	1,506.00	251.00	1,255.00
175	1,567.00	261.17	1,305.83
180	1,632.00	272.00	1,360.00
185	1,692.00	282.00	1,410.00
190	1,757.00	292.83	1,464.17
195	1,818.00	303.00	1,515.00

CO_2 band	VAT fuel scale charge 12-month period £	VAT on 12-month charge £	VAT exclusive 12-month charge £
200	1,883.00	313.83	1,569.17
205	1,943.00	323.83	1,619.17
210	2,008.00	334.67	1,673.33
215	2,069.00	344.83	1,724.17
220	2,134.00	355.67	1,778.33
225 or more	2,194.00	365.67	1,828.33

Fuel scale charges for the 3-month period

CO_2 band	VAT fuel scale charge 3-month period £	VAT on 3-month charge £	VAT exclusive 3-month charge £
120 or less	156.00	26.00	130.00
125	234.00	39.00	195.00
130	251.00	41.83	209.17
135	266.00	44.33	221.67
140	282.00	47.00	235.00
145	297.00	49.50	247.50
150	313.00	52.17	260.83
155	328.00	54.67	273.33
160	345.00	57.50	287.50
165	360.00	60.00	300.00
170	376.00	62.67	313.33
175	391.00	65.17	325.83
180	408.00	68.00	340.00
185	423.00	70.50	352.50
190	439.00	73.17	365.83
195	454.00	75.67	378.33
200	470.00	78.33	391.67
205	485.00	80.83	404.17
210	502.00	83.67	418.33
215	517.00	86.17	430.83
220	533.00	88.83	444.17
225 or more	548.00	91.33	456.67

Fuel scale charges for the 1-month period

CO_2 band	VAT fuel scale charge 1-month period £	VAT on 1-month charge £	VAT exclusive 1-month charge £
120 or less	52.00	8.67	43.33
125	78.00	13.00	65.00
130	83.00	13.83	69.17
135	88.00	14.67	73.33
140	94.00	15.67	78.33
145	99.00	16.50	82.50
150	104.00	17.33	86.67
155	109.00	18.17	90.83
160	115.00	19.17	95.83
165	120.00	20.00	100.00
170	125.00	20.83	104.17
175	130.00	21.67	108.33
180	136.00	22.67	113.33
185	141.00	23.50	117.50
190	146.00	24.33	121.67
195	151.00	25.17	125.83
200	156.00	26.00	130.00
205	161.00	26.83	134.17
210	167.00	27.83	139.17
215	172.00	28.67	143.33
220	177.00	29.50	147.50
225 or more	182.00	30.33	151.67

STAMP DUTIES

Note: See section 69 for rates applicable in Scotland from 1 April 2015.

59 Stamp duty land tax rates

Applies to contracts entered into (or varied) after 10 July 2003 and completed after 30 November 2003 and to leases granted after that date.

SDLT also applies to transfers of an interest in land into or out of a partnership, and to an acquisition of an interest in a partnership where the partnership property includes an interest in land (from 22 July 2004). From 19 July 2006, SDLT additionally applies to transfers of partnership interests but only where the sole or main activity of the partnership is investing or dealing in interests in land.

SDLT: residential property rates

(FA 2003, s. 55; SDLTA 2015)

(SDLT Reporter: 50–105; 50–106)

Rate on portion of value above threshold

Period	Band £	Rate %	Additional property rate %
On or after 1 April 2016	0–125,000	0	%
	125,001–250,000	2	3
	250,001–925,000	5	5
	925,001–1,500,000	10	8
	1,500,001 and over	12	13
	Over 500,000	15[(1)(2)(3)(4)]	15
On or after 4 December 2014	0–125,000	0	–
	125,001–250,000	2	–
	250,001–925,000	5	–
	925,001–1,500,000	10	–
	1,500,001 and over	12	–
	Over 500,000	15[(1)(2)(3)]	–

Rate on entire property value

Period	Band £	Rate %
20 March 2014 to 3 December 2014	0–125,000	0
	125,001–250,000	1
	250,001–500,000	3
	500,001–1,000,000	4
	1,000,001–2,000,000	5
	Over 2,000,000	7
	Over 500,000	15[(1)(2)(3)]

Period	Band	Rate
22 March 2012 to 19 March 2014	0–125,000	0
	125,001–250,000	1
	250,001–500,000	3
	500,001–1,000,000	4
	1,000,001–2,000,000	5
	Over 2,000,000	7
	Over 2,000,000	15[1][2][3]
6 April 2011 to 21 March 2012	0–125,000	0
	125,001–250,000	1
	250,001–500,000	3
	500,001–1,000,000	4
	Over 1,000,000	5

Notes

[1] The 15% rate applies if the property is acquired by certain non-natural persons (e.g. companies, partnerships with corporate members and collective investment schemes) with effect from 21 March 2012. *Finance Act* 2014 reduces the threshold from £2m to £500,000 where the effective date is on or after 20 March 2014 with the £2m threshold continuing to apply, subject to exceptions, where contracts were entered into before that date.

[2] *Finance Act* 2013 introduced a number of reliefs to reduce the 15% rate to 7% with effect in relation to transactions with an effective date on or after 17 July 2013 (Royal Assent). The reliefs will broadly match those where there is relief against the annual tax on enveloped dwellings. However, these SDLT reliefs will apply only if the property continues to satisfy the qualifying conditions throughout the following three years, otherwise, additional SDLT will become payable.

[3] *Finance Act* 2013 introduced legislation to reform the stamp duty land tax rules for 'transfer of rights' with effect from 17 July 2013 (Royal Assent).

[4] Reliefs available from the 15% higher rate of SDLT extended to equity release schemes (home reversion plans), property development activities and properties occupied by employees from 1 April 2016 (FA 2003, Sch. 4A, as amended by FA 2016, s. 129–131).

[5] From 1 April 2016, higher rates of stamp duty land tax apply to purchases of additional residential properties, such as second homes and buy-to-let properties in England, Wales and Northern Ireland. Purchasers have 36 months to claim a refund of the higher rates if they buy a new main residence before disposing of their previous main residence. Purchasers also have 36 months between selling a main residence and replacing it with another without having to pay the higher rates. A share (of up to 50%) in a property which has been inherited within the 36 months prior to a transaction will not be considered as an additional property when applying the higher rates (FA 2003, s. 55 and Sch. 4ZA, as amended and inserted by FA 2016, s. 128).

SDLT: non-residential or mixed property rates

(FA 2003, s. 55)

(SDLT Reporter: 50–110)

Rate on portion of value above threshold

Period	Band £	Rate %
On or after 17 March 2016[1]	0–150,000	0
	150,001–250,000	2
	Over 250,000	5

Note

(1) Where contracts have been exchanged but transactions have not completed before 17 March 2016 purchasers will have a choice of whether the old or new structure and rates apply. (FA 2016, s. 127(13)–(14)).

Rate on entire property value

Period	Band £	Rate %
6 April 2011 to 16 March 2016	0–150,000	0
	150,001–250,000	1
	250,001–500,000	3
	Over 500,000	4

Duty on premium is the same as for transfers of land (except special rules apply for premium where rent exceeds £1,000 annually (£600 annually before 12 March 2008)

Finance Act 2013 simplifies reporting requirements that apply when a lease continues after the expiry of its fixed term and where an agreement for the lease is substantially performed before the actual lease is granted and abolishes the rules on abnormal rent increases with effect from 17 July 2013 (Royal Assent).

SDLT: lease rental rates

(FA 2003, Sch. 5)

(SDLT Reporter: 60-405)

Residential

Period	Rate %	Net present value of rent £
From 1 January 2010	0	0–125,000
	1	Over 125,000

Non-residential (on portion of value above threshold)

Period	Rate %	Net present value of rent £
On or after 17 March 2016	0	0–150,000
	1	150001–5,000,000
	2	Over 5,000,000
From 1 January 2010	0	0–150,000
	1	150001–5,000,000

60 Stamp duty rates

Conveyance or transfer on sale of shares and securities

(FA 1999, Sch. 13, para. 3, FA 1986, s. 67(3))

Instrument[1][2][3][4][5]	Rate of tax %
Stock transfer	0.5
Conversion of shares into depositary receipts	1.5
Take overs and mergers	0.5
Purchase by company of own shares	0.5
Letters of allotment	0.5

Notes

[1] Stamp duty is rounded up to the nearest multiple of £5 (FA 1999, s. 112).

[2] Loan capital is generally exempt from transfer on sale duty subject to specific exclusions (designed to prevent exemption applying to quasi-equity securities) (FA 1986, s. 79).

[3] Stamp duty is not chargeable on a transfer of stock or marketable securities where the amount or value of the consideration for the sale is £1,000 or under, and the instrument is certified at £1,000 (with effect in relation to instruments executed on or after 13 March 2008 and not stamped before 19 March 2008) (FA 1999, Sch. 13, para. 1(3A)).

[4] From 28 April 2014, transfers of securities admitted to trading on recognised growth markets are exempt from stamp duty (Finance Act 2014, Sch. 24).

[5] Shares transferred to a clearance service or depositary receipt issuer as a result of the exercise of an option will now be charged the 1.5% higher rate of stamp duty based on either their market value or the option strike price, whichever is higher. This will prevent avoidance using 'Deep in the Money Options' (DITMOs), which are options with a strike price significantly below (for call options) or above (for put options) market value. Share transfers made other than to a clearance service or depositary receipt system as a result of exercising an option will be unaffected. The change will apply to options exercised on or after 23 March 2016 which were entered into on or after 25 November 2015. (FA 1986, s. 67 and 70, as amended by FA 2016, s. 138).

61 Stamp duty reserve tax rates

(FA 1986, s. 87, 93 and 96)

Principal charge

Subject matter of charge	Rate of tax %
Agreements to transfer chargeable securities[1] for money or money's worth	0.5
Renounceable letters of allotment	0.5
Shares converted into depositary receipts[2][4]	1.5
Chargeable securities[1] put into clearance system[2][4]	1.5

Note

[1] Chargeable securities = stocks, shares, loan capital, units under unit trust scheme (FA 1986, s. 99(3)). From 28 April 2014, the definition of chargeable securities for SDRT purposes excludes securities admitted to trading on a recognised growth market (FA 1986, s. 99(4A) and 99A).

(2) Following the European Court of Justice judgement in *HSBC Holdings Ltd and Vidacos Nominees v Commissioners for HM Revenue & Customs*, HMRC accept that Article 11(a) of Council Directive 69/335/EEC of 17 July 1969 concerning indirect taxes on the raising of capital, as amended by Council Directive 85/303/EEC of 10 June 1985 (now Council Directive 2008/7/EC) ('the EC Capital Directive') must be interpreted as meaning that it prohibits the levying of a duty such as the charge to SDRT imposed by FA 1986, s. 96 on the issue of shares to a depositary receipt issuer or a clearance service located within the European Union.

(3) From 30 March 2014, the stamp duty reserve tax charge for which fund managers are liable when investors surrender their units in UK unit trust schemes or shares in UK OEICs is abolished. Previously, the charge was at the 0.5% rate. Non pro-rata in specie redemptions remain subject to the principle SDRT charge (FA 2014, s. 114).

(4) Shares transferred to a clearance service or depositary receipt issuer as a result of the exercise of an option will now be charged the 1.5% higher rate of stamp duty based on either their market value or the option strike price, whichever is higher. This will prevent avoidance using 'Deep in the Money Options' (DITMOs), which are options with a strike price signifi cantly below (for call options) or above (for put options) market value. Share transfers made other than to a clearance service or depositary receipt system as a result of exercising an option will be unaffected. The change will apply to options exercised on or after 23 March 2016 which were entered into on or after 25 November 2015 (FA 1986, s. 93 and 96, as amended by FA 2016, s. 139).

INSURANCE PREMIUM TAX

62 Rates

(FA 1994, Pt. III; Notice IPT 1; HMRC 'Insurance premium tax' manual)

Insurance premium tax (IPT) is imposed on certain insurance premiums where the risk is located in the UK.

Period of application	Standard rate[1] %	Higher rate[2] %
From 1 October 2016[3]	10.0	20.0
From 1 November 2015	9.5	20.0
From 4 January 2011	6.0	20.0

Notes

[1] Rate increase to 9.5% with effect in relation to premiums received on or after 1 November 2015. For insurers using the special accounting scheme, there will be a four-month concessionary period that will begin on 1 November 2015 and end on 29 February 2016, during which premiums received that relate to policies entered into before 1 November 2015 will continue to be liable to IPT at 6%. From 1 March 2016, all premiums received by insurers will be taxed at the new rate of 9.5%, regardless of when the policy was entered into.

[2] From 1 August 1998, the higher rate applies to all travel insurance.

[3] Standard rate of IPT increased from 9.5% to 10% with effect from 1 October 2016, with an exception for those insurers who use a special accounting scheme rather than the cash receipt method. The exception operates to require the new standard rate to be applied by them only to premiums received on or after 1 February 2017, where the premium relates to risks covered by the terms of a contract entered into before 1 October 2016 (FA 2016, s. 141).

LANDFILL TAX

Note: See section 70 for rates applicable in Scotland from 1 April 2015.

63 Rates

(FA 1996, s. 42; Notices LFT 1; HMRC 'Landfill tax' manual)

Landfill tax was introduced on 1 October 1996 and is collected from landfill site operators.

Landfill tax aims to encourage diversion of waste disposal from landfill sites.

Type of waste	Rate (per tonne) £
Inactive waste liable to lower rate	
From 1 April 2018	2.80[2]
From 1 April 2017	2.70[1]
From 1 April 2016	2.65
1 April 2015 to 31 March 2016	2.60
1 April 2008 to 31 March 2015	2.50
1 October 1996 to 31 March 2008	2.00

Type of waste	Rate (per tonne) £
Active waste liable to standard rate	
From 1 April 2018	88.95[2]
From 1 April 2017	86.10[1]
From 1 April 2016	84.40
1 April 2015 to 31 March 2016	82.60
1 April 2014 to 31 March 2015	80.00
1 April 2013 to 31 March 2014	72.00
1 April 2012 to 31 March 2013	64.00
1 April 2011 to 31 March 2012	56.00

Note

[1] Rates set by FA 2016, s. 142.

[2] Rates set by FA 2016, s. 143.

AGGREGATES LEVY

64 Rates

(FA 2001, s. 16; Notices AGL 1 and AGL 2; HMRC 'Aggregates levy' manual)

Aggregates levy seeks to incorporate the environmental costs imposed by aggregates extraction into the price of virgin aggregate, and to encourage the use of alternative materials such as wastes from construction and demolition.

Generally, 'aggregate' is rock, gravel or sand and whatever occurs or is mixed with it as well as, in certain circumstances, spoil, offcuts and by-products.

Period of application	Rate (per tonne) £
From 1 April 2016	2.00
1 April 2009 to 31 March 2016	2.00

CLIMATE CHANGE LEVY

65 Rates 2016–17
(FA 2000, Sch. 6, para. 42)

Commodity	Rates from 1 April 2016	Reduced rate for holders of a CCA
Electricity	£0.00559 per kilowatt hour	10%
Natural gas	£0.00195 per kilowatt hour	35%
Liquefied petroleum gas	£0.01251 per kilogram	35%
Any other taxable commodity	£0.01526 per kilogram	35%

Note

[1] Climate change levy (CCL) exemption for renewably sourced electricity abolished from 1 August 2015 (FA 2000, Sch. 6, para. 19(3)(za)), subject to a transitional period for suppliers to claim the CCL exemption on any renewable electricity that was generated before that date. Finance Act 2016 legislates for an end date to the transitional period of 31 March 2018 (FA 2000, Sch. 6, para. 19(1), as amended and prospectively repealed by FA 2016, s. 144).

66 Rates 2015–16

(FA 2000, Sch. 6, para. 42)

Commodity	Rates from 1 April 2015	Reduced rate for holders of a CCA
Electricity	£0.00554 per kilowatt hour	10%
Natural gas	£0.00193 per kilowatt hour	35%
Liquefied petroleum gas	£0.01240 per kilogram	35%
Any other taxable commodity	£0.01512 per kilogram	35%

Note

(1) Climate change levy (CCL) exemption for renewably sourced electricity abolished from 1 August 2015 (FA 2000, Sch. 6, para. 19(3)(za)), subject to a transitional period for suppliers to claim the CCL exemption on any renewable electricity that was generated before that date.

67 Rates 2014–15

(FA 2000, Sch. 6, para. 42)

Taxable commodity supplied	Unit	Rate from 1 April 2014		
		Rate	Reduction on main commodity rate for holders of a CCA	Lower rate when used in approved metal recycling process
Electricity	per kWh	£0.00541	10%	20% of full electricity rate
Natural gas	per kWh	£0.00188	35%	20% of main gas rate
Liquefied petroleum gas and other gaseous hydrocarbons in a liquid state	per kilogram(1)	£0.01210	35%	20% of main LPG etc rate
Any other taxable commodity	per kilogram	£0.01476	35%	20% of rate for other taxable commodities

Note

(1) For CCL purposes, the conversion rate of 2,000 litres per tonne is to be used when converting litres of butane and propane to kilograms.

68 Carbon price support (CPS) rates

(FA 2000, Sch. 6)

CPS rates of CCL	2016–17 [to 2018–19][1]	2015–16	2014–15	2013–14
Natural gas (£ per kilowatt hour)	0.00331	0.00334	0.00175	0.00091
LPG (£ per kilogram)	0.05280	0.05307	0.02822	0.01460
Coal and other taxable solid fossil fuels (£ per gross gigajoule)	1.54790	1.56860	0.81906	0.44264

Note

[1] Rates per *Finance Act* 2014. At Budget 2016, the Government confirmed, as previously announced, that it will continue to cap CPS rates until 31 March 2019.

AIR PASSENGER DUTY

69 Rates

(FA 1994, s. 30)

	Air passenger duty rates from 1 April 2015[1][4]								
Band (approximate distance in miles from London)	Reduced rate (lowest class of travel)			Standard rate (other than lowest class of travel)[2]			Higher rate[3]		
	From 1 April 2015	From 1 April 2016	From 1 April 2017[5]	From 1 April 2015	From 1 April 2016	From 1 April 2017[5]	From 1 April 2015	From 1 April 2016	From 1 April 2017[5]
	£	£	£	£	£	£	£	£	£
Band A (0–2,000 miles)	13	13	13	26	26	26	78	78	78
Band B (Over 2,000 miles)	71	73	75	142	146	150	426	438	450

Notes:

[1] From 1 April 2015, the number of destination bands was reduced from four to two by merging the former bands B, C and D and the higher rates that apply to aircraft with an authorised take off weight of 20 tonnes or more and with fewer than 19 seats was increased to six times the reduced rate (previously twice the standard rate).

[2] If any class of travel provides a seat pitch in excess of 1.016 metres (40 inches) the standard rate is the minimum rate that applies.

[3] The higher rate applies to flights aboard aircraft of 20 tonnes and above with fewer than 19 seats.

[4] From 1 May 2015, economy tickets for children under 12 are exempt from the reduced rate of APD. The exemption was extended to include children under 16 from 1 March 2016 (FA 1994, s. 31 as amended by FA 2015, s. 57).

[5] Rates announced at Budget 2016 (Finance Bill 2017).

Key Data

Air Passenger Duty Rates[1][2]								
Bands (approximate distance in miles from the UK)	**Reduced rate (lowest class of travel)**			**Standard rate (other than the lowest class of travel)[3]**			**Higher rate[4]**	
From	**1 April 2012 £**	**1 April 2013 £**	**1 April 2014 £**	**1 April 2012 £**	**1 April 2013 £**	**1 April 2014 £**	**1 April 2013 £**	**1 April 2014 £**
Band A (0–2000 miles)	13	13	13	26	26	26	52	52
Band B (2001–4000 miles)	65	67	69	130	134	138	268	276
Band C (4001–6000 miles)	81	83	85	162	166	170	332	340
Band D (over 6000 miles)	92	94	97	184	188	194	376	388

Notes:

[1] From 1 April 2013, APD has applied to all flights aboard aircraft 5.7 tonnes and above.

[2] From 1 January 2013, the rates for direct long-haul flights from NI were devolved to the Northern Ireland Executive, and set at £0. Direct long haul journeys from NI are those where the first part of the journey is to a destination outside Band A.

[3] If any class of travel provides a seat pitch in excess of 1.016m (40 inches), the standard rate is the minimum rate that applies.

[4] The higher rate applies to flights aboard aircraft of 20 tonnes and above with fewer than 19 seats.

VEHICLE EXCISE DUTY

70   Rates

Rates: General

(VERA 1994, Sch. 1, Pt. 1)

VED bands and rates for cars and vans registered before 1 March 2001 (pre-graduated VED)

Engine size	2016-17 £	2015–16 £	2014–15 £	2013–14 £
1549cc and below	145	145	145	140
Above 1549cc	235	230	230	225

Rates: Light passenger vehicles: graduated rates of duty
(VERA 1994, Sch. 1, Pt. 1A)

VED band	CO_2 emissions (g/km)	2016–17 Standard rate[1] £	2016–17 First year rate[1] £	2015–16 Standard rate[1] £	2015–16 First year rate[1] £	2014–15 Standard rate[1] £	2014–15 First year rate[1] £	2013–14 Standard rate[1] £	2013–14 First year rate[1] £
A	Up to 100	0	0	0	0	0	0	0	0
B	101–110	20	0	20	0	20	0	20	0
C	111–120	30	0	30	0	30	0	30	0
D	121–130	110	0	110	0	110	0	105	0
E	131–140	130	130	130	130	130	130	125	125
F	141–150	145	145	145	145	145	145	140	140
G	151–165	185	185	180	180	180	180	175	175
H	166–175	210	300	205	295	205	290	200	285
I	176–185	230	355	225	350	225	345	220	335
J	186–200	270	500	265	490	265	485	260	475
K[2]	201–225	295	650	290	640	285	635	280	620
L	226–255	500	885	490	870	485	860	475	840
M	Over 255	515	1120	505	1,100	500	1,090	490	1,065

Notes

[1] Alternative fuel discount 2010–11 onwards: £10 for all cars.

[2] Includes cars emitting over 225g/km registered before 23 March 2006.

Rates: Light goods vehicles

(VERA 1994, Sch. 1, Pt. 1B)

VED bands and rates for vans registered on or after 1 March 2001

Vehicle registration date	2016–17 £	2015–16 £	2014–15 £	2013–14 £
Early Euro 4 and Euro 5 compliant vans	140	140	140	140
All other vans	230	225	225	220

Rates: Motorcycles

(VERA 1994, Sch. 1, Pt. II)

VED bands and rates for motorcycles

Engine size	2016–17 £	2015–16 £	2014–15 £	2013–14 £
Not over 150cc	17	17	17	17
151cc and 400cc	39	38	38	37
401cc to 600c	60	59	58	57
Over 600cc	82	81	80	78

VED bands and rates for motor tricycles

Engine size	2016–17 £	2015–16 £	2014–15 £	2013–14 £
Not over 150cc	17	17	17	17
All other tricycles	82	81	80	78

Rates: Trade licences

(VERA 1994, s. 13)

VED bands and rates for trade licences

Vehicle type	2016–17 £	2015–16 £	2014–15 £	2013–14 £
Available for all vehicles	165	165	165	165
Available only for bicycles and tricycles (weighing no more than 450kg without a sidecar)	82	81	80	78

SCOTTISH DEVOLVED TAXES

Note: See section 1 for Scottish rates of income tax from 2016–17.

Land and Buildings Transaction Tax (LBTT)

71   LBTT rates from 1 April 2015

(Land and Buildings Transaction Tax (Scotland) Act 2013; SSI 2015/126)

The Scottish LBTR has a progressive rate structure, which means that the rates shown in the table below are marginal rates, payable on the portion of the total value which falls within each band. Tax bands and percentage tax rates are set by order of the Scottish Ministers.

Residential transactions		Non-residential transactions		Non-residential leases	
	Rate %		Rate %		Rate %
Up to £145,000	nil	Up to £150,000	nil	Up to £150,000	nil
£145,001 to £250,000	2.0	£150,001 to £350,000	3.0	Over £150,000	1.0
£250,001 to £325,000	5.0	Over £350,000	4.5		
£325,001 to £750,000	10.0				
Over £750,000	12.0				

Note

As part of the Scottish Government's 2016–17 Draft Budget delivered to Parliament on 16 December 2015, the Finance Secretary proposed that LBTT rates would remain the same for 2016–17 but additional residential properties, such as buy to let or second homes, will be subject to a new LBTT supplement from 1 April 2016.

Scottish Landfill Tax

72   SLT rates from 1 April 2015

(Landfill Tax (Scotland) Act 2014; SSI 2016/93 and SSI 2016/94)

Rates are specified by order of the Scottish Ministers.

	Standard rate (per tonne) £	Lower rate (per tonne) £	Scottish Landfill Communities Fund Credit rate %
From 1 April 2016	84.40	2.65	5.6
From 1 April 2015	82.60	2.60	5.6

Overview

KEY POINTS

- Taxes may be direct or indirect.

- Direct taxes include income tax (see 240ff.), corporation tax (see 3000ff.), capital gains tax (see 5000ff.) and inheritance tax (see 6505ff.).

- Indirect taxes include VAT (see 7700ff.), stamp duty land tax (see 9050ff.), stamp duty (see 10100), stamp duty reserve tax (see 10150ff.), customs duties (see 9500ff.), excise duties (see 9650ff.), air passenger duty (see 9760ff.), insurance premium tax (see 9800ff.), landfill tax (see 9950), climate change levy (see 10020), aggregates levy (see 10040) and council tax (see 10050ff.).

- Tax law is derived from various sources – Acts of Parliament (primary legislation) (see 209); orders and regulations, usually made by statutory instrument (secondary legislation) (see 211); European legislation (see 212) and case law (see 214).

- Interpretation of tax law is aided by various non-statutory sources, including statements of practice, Extra-statutory Concessions, departmental leaflets and online guidance, HMRC interpretations and decision and internal guidance manuals (see 213).

- Tax law distinguishes between items of an income nature and of a capital nature (see 217).

- Income and capital gains tax are charged by reference to a year of assessment (or tax year) which runs from 6 April to the following 5 April (see 216).

- Corporation tax is charged by reference to financial years. A financial year runs from 1 April to the following 31 March (see 216).

- Income tax is a tax on profits or gains of an income nature (see 219).

- Capital gains tax is a tax on chargeable gains resulting from chargeable disposals (see 219 and 5000ff.).

- Corporation tax is a tax on profits, including income and capital gains, of a company (see 219 and 3000ff.).

- Inheritance tax is a tax on transfers of value made by individuals, executors and trustees (see 219 and 6505ff.).

A brief history of taxation

200 The introduction of income tax

In order to help finance the Napoleonic wars, the then prime minister, William Pitt, introduced income tax as a temporary measure. Income taxation, however, brought with it the necessity that the taxpayer must reveal his income. This was most unpopular and when the then prime minister, Henry Addington, re-introduced income tax in 1803, he chose a method of classifying income by its source and charged each source of income separately under a Schedule. Using this method, a taxpayer's total income could not be ascertained without assessing and computing his income under each source or Schedule.

Income tax was last introduced by Sir Robert Peel in 1842 as a three-year temporary measure, but it has been with us ever since. There have been four consolidations since 1842, in the *Income Tax Acts* 1918 and 1952 and in the *Income and Corporation Taxes Acts* 1970 and 1988.

The Tax Law Rewrite Project was commissioned with the task of rewriting tax legislation into a more logical and 'user-friendly' format. The publication of the *Income Tax (Earnings and Pensions) Act* 2003 (ITEPA 2003) covers income from employments, pensions and social security benefits. The *Income Tax (Trading and Other Income) Act* 2005 (ITTOIA 2005) covers income from trades, professions and vocations, income from property, savings income and investments.

In 1970, for the first time, the consolidating statute was entitled the 'Income and Corporation Taxes Act'. Its subsequent counterpart was the *Income and Corporation Taxes Act* 1988. Latterly, however, as the legislation was rewritten, it was decided to separate once more the income tax and corporation tax legislation. Thus, there is now an *Income Tax Act* 2007 (ITA 2007), as well as a *Corporation Tax Act* 2009 (CTA 2009), a secondary *Corporation Tax Act* 2010 (CTA 2010) and the *Taxation (International and Other Provisions) Act* 2010 (TIOPA 2010).

Tax Reporter: ¶102-000

201 The National Insurance Scheme

The National Insurance Scheme first came into effect in 1948. It was based on proposals made in a government report on Social Insurances and Allied Services – the so-called 'Beveridge Report'. The original plan was for flat-rate contributions to be paid into the scheme so that flat-rate benefits could be paid out. Graduated pension arrangements were grafted onto the scheme in 1959, so that employees were required to contribute an amount based on a percentage of their earnings in return for enhanced pensions. In 1975, the rules were consolidated into a single scheme, which forms the crux of the National Insurance regime as it is today.

As indicated above, the original principle was that all benefits were contributory. Since the introduction of the scheme, there has been increasing divergence of the contributions side from the benefits side, so that in recent times, benefits far outpace contributions. Indeed, there have been an increasing number of non-contributory benefits for which entitlement does not depend upon an individual having contributed to the fund.

202   The addition of taxation on capital gains

Any system of taxation that failed to tax capital profits or gains would effectively be providing an open invitation to avoid tax. A taxpayer would simply devote more time to the making of capital profits to avoid liability to tax. It is, therefore, not surprising that capital gains are now taxed. It was not, however, until 1962 that a tax on short-term capital gains was introduced. This taxed gains on land made within three years of acquisition and all other gains made within six months of acquisition. The gain was treated as unearned income and taxed under former Sch. D, Case VI.

In 1965, capital gains tax (CGT) was introduced which taxed capital gains not already covered by the short-term capital gains legislation. In 1971, the Government abolished income tax on short-term capital gains, and CGT became the only tax on capital gains.

The statutory provisions relating to CGT are now to be found in the *Taxation of Chargeable Gains Act* 1992, subject to amendment or supplementation by subsequent Finance Acts. This 1992 Act includes provisions relating to the taxation of chargeable gains by way of corporation tax as well as CGT. It should be noted that there are still some capital receipts that fall to be taxed as income, e.g. lease premiums and reverse premiums (see 1260 and 1290).

Until 1985, gains from development land were taxed separately from capital gains. The last of this series of taxes, development land tax, was imposed from 1976 until its abolition in the Budget of 19 March 1985. Its rationale was to tax any gain over and above the current use value of the land at an appreciably higher rate than the CGT rate (then 30%). At the time of its abolition in 1985, development land tax was charged at 60%.

For the early part of its history, CGT was charged at a significantly lower rate than the higher rates of income tax. This encouraged the proliferation of sophisticated devices whereby an income profit could be 'turned into' a capital gain (e.g. 'bond washing'). The scope for this kind of fiscal alchemy was reduced, but not eliminated, by anti-avoidance legislation such as the accrued income scheme (1985: see 1378). Only when, in 1988, CGT rates were aligned with the basic and higher rates of income tax, and capital gains became taxed as the highest part of a taxpayer's income, did this kind of anti-avoidance lose much of its purpose. From 1999–2000, CGT rates were aligned with those for savings income so that gains in excess of the annual exempt amount were charged at 20% where the gains when added to total income were below the basic rate limit and 40% where they exceeded that limit. From 6 April 2008, CGT was payable at a flat rate of 18% (see 5410). In the June 2010 Budget, it was announced that a higher rate of tax was to be immediately introduced to reduce the gap between the existing 18% rate and the higher rates of income tax. Accordingly, a higher rate of 28% was introduced and applied in respect of disposals on or after 23 June 2010. The 28% rate replaced the 18% rate in respect of trustees and personal representatives and for individuals it applied in addition to the 18% rate; the actual rate applicable will be determined by the aggregate of the individual's taxable income and chargeable gains. In the March 2016 Budget, the rates were again cut in order to ensure that companies have the opportunity to access the capital needed to grow and create jobs as well as to promote a strong investment culture in the next generation. From 6 April 2016, there are two main rates of capital gains tax of 10% and 20% replacing the previous 18% and 28% rates, however, the 18% and 28% rates continue to apply for gains on residential property and carried interest. In addition, a special 10% rate applies to gains eligible for entrepreneurs' relief and, effectively, from the tax year 2019–20, the 10% rate will also be available to gains eligible for the new investors' relief introduced by *Finance Act* 2016.

Tax Reporter: ¶102-450

203   History of taxation on death

The notion of taxing a deceased person's estate is a long-standing one in the UK tax system. As a deceased's personal representatives are obliged to gather in all the property formerly belonging to him, the administration of an estate represents an ideal tax point.

The value attributable to the personal property comprised in an estate has been taxable since 1694, and from 1894, with the introduction of estate duty, broadly speaking, the entire estate of a deceased person has been subject to tax. Further, from 1965–1971, death was also the occasion of a charge to capital gains tax (CGT).

Estate duty was abolished upon the introduction of capital transfer tax (CTT) in 1975. Whilst CTT preserved the notion of taxing the estate of the deceased, it additionally introduced the novel concept of charging lifetime transfers of wealth cumulatively to tax. However, since *Finance Act* 1986, CTT has itself been replaced by inheritance tax, which retains the principal features of CTT but is confined in its operation to the taxation of deceased persons' estates, transfers of capital made within seven years of death, and lifetime transfers into certain settlements. The inheritance tax represents in many ways a return to the estate duty system. The statutory provisions relating to inheritance tax are to be found in the *Inheritance Tax Act* 1984 (previously known as the *Capital Transfer Tax Act* 1984) as amended and supplemented by subsequent Finance Acts.

Tax Reporter: ¶600-000

204   Development of the taxation of companies

The *Joint Stock Companies Act* 1844 heralded the first of the statutory registered companies. This was superseded by the former *Companies Act* 1985 and now the *Companies Act* 2006. Notwithstanding this, no separate code of taxation for companies appeared until 1965 when corporation tax was introduced (although companies were previously subject to income tax and profits tax). The *Income and Corporation Taxes Act* 1988, as amended and supplemented, principally by parts of the Finance Acts receiving Royal Assent between 1988 and 1996, embodied the main corporation tax provisions.

Most of the provisions applying for corporation tax purposes have now been rewritten by the *Corporation Tax Act* 2009 and the *Corporation Tax Act* 2010. Many provisions dealing with international matters have been rewritten by the *Taxation (International and Other Provisions) Act* 2010. The enactment of the *Corporation Tax Act* 2010 and the *Taxation (International and Other Provisions) Act* 2010 effectively brought the Tax Law Rewrite Project to an end (see 200).

Tax Reporter: ¶102-400

205   The introduction of VAT

The UK joined what was then the European Economic Community in 1973. The treaty establishing the Community stated that one of its aims was the harmonisation of turnover taxes of member states. As a result, member states were encouraged to adopt a broadly common tax on value added. The UK's obligations in this respect were met with the introduction of VAT in 1973.

There have been a number of attempts to further harmonise the taxes that were introduced in each of the member states, but there remain considerable divergences, both in rates and in those items that are subject to charge.

Indirect Tax Reporter: ¶1-100

206 Devolution of powers to Scotland, Wales and Northern Ireland

In September 1997, referendums were held in Scotland and Wales, and a majority of voters chose to establish a Scottish Parliament and a National Assembly for Wales. In Northern Ireland, devolution was a key part of the agreement, sometimes referred to as the Good Friday Agreement or the Belfast Agreement, supported by voters in a referendum in May 1998.

Following this public endorsement, Parliament passed three devolution Acts: the *Scotland Act* 1998 (as amended by the *Scotland Act* 2012); the *Northern Ireland Act* 1998; and the *Government of Wales Act* 1998 (which was later effectively superseded by the *Government of Wales Act* 2006). These Acts established the three devolved legislatures, which were given some power previously held at Westminster.

Northern Ireland

The Northern Ireland devolution settlement gives legislative control over certain matters (known as 'transferred matters') to the Northern Ireland Assembly. In the main, these are in the economic and social field. The NI Assembly may also in principle legislate in respect of 'reserved' category matters subject to various consents. Matters of national importance which, in the normal course of events, it is expected will remain the responsibility of HM Government and Westminster, are known as 'excepted matters', and the NI Assembly does not have competence to legislate on these.

On 26 March 2015, the *Corporation Tax (Northern Ireland) Act* 2015 received Royal Assent. The Act makes provision for devolution of tax powers to the NI Assembly which should allow Northern Ireland to set its own rate of corporation tax for certain trading profits from April 2017.

Scotland

The *Scotland Act* 1998 does not specify which matters are devolved to the Scottish Parliament, rather it specifies those matters that are reserved to the UK Parliament and those matters not reserved are devolved to the Scottish Parliament. The *Scotland Act* 1998, Pt. IV also introduced a tax-varying power to enable the Scottish Parliament to vary the rate of income tax levied on the income of Scottish taxpayers by up to 3%. However, this power was never been used and has now been replaced with a new power to set a Scottish rate of income tax (SRIT) by the *Scotland Act* 2012.

The *Scotland Act* 2012 amended the *Scotland Act* 1998 to fully devolve the power to raise taxes on land transactions and on waste disposal to landfill which took effect from 1 April 2015, and since then, the existing stamp duty land tax and landfill tax do not apply in Scotland. The Act also provides powers for new taxes to be created in Scotland and for additional taxes to be devolved.

Further powers are devolved via the *Scotland Act* 2016 which received Royal Assent on 23 March 2016. The *Scotland Act* 2016 is an enabling Act and the majority of the provisions in the Act set out the powers that are being transferred to the Scottish Parliament and or the Scottish Ministers. In particular, the Scotland Act amends sections of the *Scotland Act* 1998 and rebalances the devolved and reserved responsibilities between the administrations. The Act also includes provisions which set out the constitutional relationship of the Scottish Parliament and Scottish Government within the United Kingdom's constitutional arrangements. It does not amend this relationship.

The Act also provides the structure within which the Scottish Parliament may legislate to set the rates of income tax and the limits at which these are paid for the non-savings and non-dividend income of Scottish taxpayers, replacing the power of the Scottish Parliament to set, by resolution, a single Scottish rate of income tax, enabling it to instead set a basic rate and any other rates of income tax; makes provision for Scotland to control the first ten percentage points of the standard rate of VAT receipts and first two and a half percentage points of the reduced rate of VAT receipts; and provides that air passenger duty and aggregates levy will be fully devolved taxes.

The devolved taxes are collected by Revenue Scotland, Scotland's tax authority which started accepting returns and collecting taxes from 1 April 2015. Revenue Scotland was established by the *Revenue Scotland and Tax Powers Act* 2014 (RSTPA 2014) which received Royal Assent on 24 September 2014 and came into force on 1 April 2015 (to the extent not already in force). RSTPA 2014 provides for the general functions and responsibilities of Revenue Scotland, including the use and protection of taxpayer and other information, the self-assessment system, checking of tax returns, claims for repayment of tax, investigatory powers, penalties and interest, debt enforcement and the review, mediation and appeal of decisions. The Act further establishes the Scottish Tax Tribunals (the First-tier Tribunal for Scotland and the Upper Tribunal for Scotland) to exercise functions in relation to devolved taxes and puts in place a general anti avoidance rule.

The *Tribunals (Scotland) Act* 2014, which received Royal Assent on 15 April 2014 (and came into force on 1 April 2015 (so far as not already in force), establishes the First-tier Tribunal for Scotland and the Upper Tribunal for *Scotland and the Scottish Tribunals (Eligibility for Appointment) Regulations* 2015 (SSI 2015/381) set eligibility criteria for appointments as legal members of the First-tier Tribunal for Scotland and Upper Tribunal for Scotland. They also provide eligibility criteria for appointment of ordinary members of the First-tier Tribunal.

Wales

The *Government of Wales Act* (GoWA) 2006 enables the Welsh Assembly to legislate in relation to the subjects listed under the 20 headings (as qualified by certain exceptions and restrictions) which cover the delivery of local services, education and training, fire and rescue services, health services, highways and transport, housing, local government, social welfare, planning (except major energy infrastructure) and water supplies, agriculture, fisheries, forestry, culture, including the Welsh language and ancient monuments, economic development and the environment.

The *Wales Act* 2014, which received Royal Assent on 19 December 2014, makes further provisions including about the setting by the Assembly of rates of income tax to be paid by Welsh taxpayers and about the devolution of taxation powers to the assembly. The Act also provides for the Assembly to decide to trigger a referendum so that people in Wales can decide whether some of their income tax should be devolved, specifies taxes on land transactions and on disposals of waste to landfill as devolved taxes and makes provisions allowing the Assembly to bring in its own land transaction tax and its own tax on disposals of waste to landfill, as well as providing for additional taxes to be devolved to the assembly by Order in Council.

On 10 February 2015, Welsh Government published a consultation document on the structure and rates for a new land transaction tax (LTT) to replace stamp duty in Wales in April 2018. The consultation closed on 6 May 2015. A summary of responses was published in September 2015 and is available at www.gov.wales/docs/caecd/consultation/150915-ltt-responses-en.pdf.

On 27 February 2015, new devolved powers for Wales were announced under the St David's Day Agreement and a command paper published setting out, in particular, a new model of devolution for Wales. A reserved powers model (as for Scotland) where the default position is that everything is devolved except those things that are reserved by Westminster will replace the existing model which specifies which matters are devolved.

The Wales Bill 2016–17 was introduced to Parliament on 7 June 2016 and sets out in detail how the Government plans to deliver the St David's Day commitments including creating a new Welsh devolution system, moving to a reserved powers model similar to the one which currently operates in Scotland. The Bill also devolves important new powers over energy, transport and local government and Assembly elections and provides greater powers for the Assembly over its own affairs including the ability to change its name.

The *Tax Collection and Management (Wales) Act* 2016 received Royal Assent on 25 April 2016 and establishes the Welsh Revenue Authority

(WRA) and makes provision about its organisation and main functions (which will be the collection and management of devolved taxes). The Act also confers powers and duties on the WRA (and corresponding duties and rights on taxpayers and others) in relation to the submission of returns and the carrying out of enquiries and assessments; provides civil investigation and enforcement powers including powers allowing the WRA to require information and documents and to access and inspect premises and other property; provides for penalties and interest to be payable by taxpayers in certain circumstances; provides for rights for taxpayers to request internal reviews of certain WRA decisions and to appeal to the First-tier Tribunal against such decisions, and confers criminal enforcement powers on the WRA.

Tax Reporter: ¶102-900ff.

The sources of tax law

208 The legality of taxation

For the levying of taxes to be legal, they must have the authority of Parliament. The Bill of Rights of 1688 states (in olde English!) that 'levying moneys for or to the use of the Crowne by preference of prerogative without grant of parliament … is illegale'. Similar provision is made in Scotland by the Claim of Right 1689. It follows then that there is no such thing as a common law tax (though 'cheating the Revenue' is a common law crime).

Tax Reporter: ¶103-000

209 Acts of Parliament

The various taxation provisions are made known to us primarily through statutes. The more important ones are the *Corporation Tax Act* 2009, the *Corporation Tax Act* 2010, the *Taxation (International and Other Provisions) Act* 2010, the *Taxation of Chargeable Gains Act* 1992, the *Inheritance Tax Act* 1984, the *Value Added Tax Act* 1994, the *Social Security Contributions and Benefits Act* 1992, the *Income Tax (Earnings and Pensions) Act* 2003, the *Income Tax (Trading and Other Income) Act* 2005 and the *Income Tax Act* 2007. The *Taxes Management Act* 1970, the *Customs and Excise Management Act* 1979 and the *Social Security Administration Act* 1992 regulate the institutions involved in the imposing and collecting of the main taxes, and the *Capital Allowances Act* 2001 the granting of capital allowances. In some parts, Customs and Excise leaflets go further than providing a useful explanation of the views of Customs and actually have the effect of law: particular examples of this are the parts of Notice 700 (*The VAT guide*) which relate to the records to be retained by traders, and the booklets concerning retail schemes and second-hand goods schemes. Other legislative sources include statutory instruments, made by government departments under the authority of 'enabling' Acts of Parliament, and European Community legislation.

The *Commissioners for Revenue and Customs Act* 2005 provided the legal basis for the integrated department, Her Majesty's Revenue and Customs (HMRC), and the independent prosecutions office, Revenue and Customs Prosecutions Office.

Income tax is perhaps unusual in that it has to be imposed year-by-year by way of a Finance Act (though the legislation authorises the continuity of operation of the administrative machinery). Such Finance Acts also make amendment to the other main statutes and provide additional rules to implement government policy changes or to target avoidance. Social security changes are also made by statutes other than the annual Finance Act.

Statute entrusts HMRC with the 'care and management' of income tax, corporation tax and CGT.

Legislation: TMA 1970, s. 1(1); ICTA 1988, s. 820

Tax Reporter: ¶103-050

210 Provisional collection of taxes

Parliament imposes income tax separately for each year of assessment (tax year) by passing the yearly Finance Act. The legislation provides that the Income Tax Acts' provisions continue to apply in a new tax year despite the fact that the Finance Act may not have, as yet, been given Royal Assent. The *Income and Corporation Taxes Act* 1988, s. 820 does not impose the tax or allow deductions without the Finance Act being in force but allows the continuity of the administration connected with the Acts to continue.

The Finance Bill does not normally receive the Royal Assent until the middle of July after the beginning of the tax year on 6 April, which means that a vacuum is created when there is no provision authorising payment or deductions of tax. Therefore, at the conclusion of the Budget debate, the House of Commons passes resolutions declaring that they are to have statutory effect under the *Provisional Collection of Taxes Act* 1968. This states that income tax which was in force in the previous financial year is to be renewed, reimposed or any income tax in force at present is to be varied, abolished or repealed. The resolutions may make changes to the previous year's income tax before being reimposed. The 1968 Act also applies to corporation tax, petroleum revenue tax, stamp duty reserve tax, certain VAT provisions, and duties of customs and excise (there is no similar requirement in relation to NIC).

The resolutions then have the same effect as would an Act of Parliament. This statutory effect is for a limited period only however. The House of Commons must give a Bill, which includes provisions that will achieve what the resolutions provide, a second reading within 30 sitting days or the resolutions lose their effect. If the provisions in the Bill that support the resolutions are rejected during the passage of the Bill, or an Act is passed giving effect to the provisions, or Parliament is dissolved or prorogued, the statutory effect of the resolutions is lost.

To allow employers time to update their payroll systems following a March Budget, no change as a result of the statutory indexation of income tax rates and allowances needs to be made for PAYE purposes until after 17 May in the relevant tax year.

Legislation: ICTA 1988, s. 820

Tax Reporter: ¶103-150

211 Regulations, orders, statutory instruments

Finance legislation in recent times increasingly contains provisions which empower administrative bodies to make 'secondary' legislation, and prescribes the purpose and extent of their powers to do so. The Treasury and HMRC are empowered to make orders or regulations, usually by means of statutory instrument or – in the case of double taxation treaties – the sovereign is empowered to make an Order in Council. The legislation provides for control of statutory instruments by Parliament by either requiring approval of the draft by the House of Commons before they are made or by making them subject to annulment by resolution of the House of Commons (or either House).

Legislation: TIOPA 2010, s. 2

Tax Reporter: ¶103-500

212 European Community legislation

The UK became a member of what is now the European Union by virtue of the Treaty of Accession of 1972, and the *European Communities Act* 1972, which incorporates the treaties establishing the Communities into UK law. There are three types of European Community legislation:

- *Regulations* of the Council of Ministers and the Commission are directly applicable in member states and do not depend for their enforcement on the passing of national legislation. In the UK, they have direct effect.

- *Directives* are generally binding but require to be separately enacted within member states. In the UK, this is done either by Act of Parliament or by subordinate legislation.

- *Decisions* are addressed to individual member states and are binding on them alone (e.g. those authorising derogations in the UK from the sixth VAT directive).

Most EC taxation law is concerned with VAT and duties of customs and excise: the UK law on VAT derives from EC law, notably Council Directive 2006/112 on the common system of value added tax (formerly the sixth directive on VAT). Note, however:

- Directive 2011/16/EU on 'administrative cooperation in the field of taxation and repealing Directive 77/799/EEC' which provides for mutual assistance between the Revenue authorities of member states with a view to preventing international tax evasion and avoidance. The directive establishes all the necessary procedures for better cooperation between tax administrations in the European Union – such as exchanges of information on request, spontaneous exchanges, automatic exchanges, participation in administrative enquiries, simultaneous controls and notifications to each other of tax decisions. It also provided for the necessary practical tools such as a secure electronic system for the information exchange. This directive was amended by extending the cooperation between tax authorities to automatic exchange of financial account information (Council Directive 2014/107/EU) and cross-border tax rulings and advance pricing arrangements (Council Directive of 8 December 2015) and more recently, by Directive 2016/881 of 25 May 2016. Directive 2016/881 builds on 2015 OECD recommendations to address tax base erosion and profit shifting (BEPS) by implementing the OECD's anti-BEPS action 13, on country-by-country reporting by multinationals (covering groups of companies with a total consolidated group revenue of at least €750m).

- Directive 2009/133 (the Mergers directive) and Directive 2011/96 (the EU Parent Subsidiary directive) on the tax treatment of cross-border mergers and payment of dividends by subsidiaries to parent companies in different member states; and

- Directive 2003/49/EC (the Interest and Royalties directive) 'on a common system of taxation applicable to interest and royalty payments made between associated companies of different member states' which provides that interest and royalty payments shall be exempt from tax in the member state where the payments arise, provided the beneficial owner of the interest or royalties is a company of another member state or a permanent establishment of such a company which is itself situated in a member state.

In addition, the convention on the elimination of double taxation in connection with the adjustment of profits of associated enterprises (Convention 90/436 of 23 July 1990), which seeks to address transfer pricing issues, has been ratified, and entered into force on 1 January 1995.

Former Directives:

Directive 2003/48/EC (the Savings directive) on the 'taxation of savings income in the form of interest payments' was repealed by Council Directive (EU) 2015/2060 of 10 November 2015, with effect from 1 January 2016 (subject to certain transitional provisions). The directive previously (since 2005) allowed tax administrations better access to information on private savers by providing for reporting by businesses and public bodies who paid interest to, or collected interest on behalf of, EU-resident individuals of details of the payments and the payees to the tax authorities. The EU Savings Directive also required that information relating to residents of another member state be passed on to the authorities in that state. Repeal of the directive followed a strengthening of measures to prevent tax evasion which led to a significant overlap with other legislation in the field and the directive was accordingly repealed in order to eliminate the overlap.

Legislation: ECA 1972, s. 2; Council Directive 2006/112 (28 November 2006, OJ 2006 L347/1)

Tax Reporter: ¶103-800

213   Non-legislative sources

HMRC often issue statements in which they make known their views on the correct interpretation of statute, or the way in which they propose to apply certain rules. In addition, they may announce a relaxation in their approach to a particular statutory provision, where to adhere strictly to it would cause undue administrative difficulties, or hardship to the taxpayer. Such statements of practice and Extra-statutory Concessions (ESCs) lack the force of law and do not affect a taxpayer's rights on appeal. However, a taxpayer may rely on those concessions except where an attempt is made to use them for the purpose of tax avoidance. Customs concessions are generally limited in number and scope and do not carry the same weight.

The House of Lords' decision in the *Wilkinson* case clarified the scope of HMRC's administrative discretion to make concessions that depart from the strict statutory position. HMRC are therefore reviewing its concessions and those that are considered to be beyond the scope of HMRC's discretion are either being legislated to preserve their effect or withdrawn. HMRC have powers to give statutory effect to concessions (FA 2008,

s. 160). A list of current and obsolete Extra-statutory Concessions can be found in HMRC publications 'VAT Notice 48: Extra-statutory Concessions' (detailing Customs and Excise concessions) and 'Extra-statutory Concessions: ex-Inland Revenue' (detailing Inland Revenue concessions), which were last updated on 21 May 2015 and 13 April 2015 respectively. Both publications can be found at www.gov.uk/government/collections/extra-statutory-concessions.

Departmental press releases are also a useful source of information on topical issues: the intention to legislate is often announced in a press release, and it is established practice to bring a law into force retrospectively from the date on which the intention to legislate is so announced. Press releases are also the medium for announcing new ESCs or statements of practice.

Interpretations of various points of tax law are often published in the HMRC Brief. Such interpretations are qualified by an important caveat that particular cases may turn on their own facts or context, and that there may be circumstances where the interpretation would not apply. In addition, there may be circumstances in which the board would find it necessary to argue for a different interpretation in appeal proceedings. HMRC Brief also contains articles which give an insight into the thinking of HMRC head office specialists.

In a further step towards greater openness, the HMRC internal guidance manuals are now freely available.

Proposals for future tax legislation on difficult or controversial matters are increasingly set out in consultative documents.

Legislation: *Enactment of Extra-Statutory Concessions Order* 2009 (SI 2009/730); *Enactment of Extra-Statutory Concessions Order* 2010 (SI 2010/157); *Enactment of Extra-Statutory Concessions Order* 2011 (SI 2011/1037); *Enactment of Extra-Statutory Concessions Order* 2012 (SI 2012/266); *Enactment of Extra-Statutory Concessions Order* 2013 (SI 2013/234); *Enactment of Extra-Statutory Concessions Order* 2014 (SI 2014/211)

Other Material: Extra-statutory Concessions: www.gov.uk/government/collections/extra-statutory-concessions; www.gov.uk/government/publications/extra-statutory-concessions-ex-inland-revenue#history

Tax Reporter: ¶103-520

214 The function of the courts

Hand-in-hand with the growth of statute, law on taxation has gone the need for its interpretation.

By 1805, the administration had taken broadly the form in which it was to remain, with the general commissioners responsible for appeals rather than assessments (which were the province of the surveyors and assessors), the special commissioners as a central overseeing body, and the additional commissioners (who were abolished many years ago) for commercial assessments. It was not until 1874, that the right of further appeal from the commissioners to the High Court was established, and since then, the judiciary has played an important part in the interpretation of tax law as the legislature in its inception. In the 1920s, the function of the general commissioners became confined to the hearing of local appeals, and the whole of revenue administration at the local level was handed over to the inspectors and collectors of taxes.

In April 2009, a unified appeals system was introduced. The system abolished the General and Special Commissioners and established a tribunal divided into two tiers: the First-tier Tribunal and the Upper Tribunal. The bulk of appeals are to be heard by the First-tier Tribunal, with the Upper Tribunal exercising an appellate function (and hearing complex tax cases). Each tier is also divided into 'Chambers', depending on the field of expertise.

In 2014, the First-tier Tribunal for Scotland and Upper Tribunal for Scotland were established by the *Tribunals (Scotland) Act* 2014 and the *Revenue Scotland and Tax Powers Act* 2014. The Scottish Tribunals were constituted on 1 April 2015 and operate in parallel with the existing tribunals exercising functions in relation to devolved taxes.

Legislation: *Tribunals, Courts and Enforcement Act* 2007; *Tribunals (Scotland) Act* 2014; *Revenue Scotland and Tax Powers Act* 2014

Tax Reporter: ¶102-850

215 Interpretation or construction

The fact that tax is a statutory creature (see 208) and the ability of the courts only to hear appeals based upon an error of law (see 214) means that they will, in most cases, find it necessary to construe the words of the statute to ascertain their applicability to the facts in question. All statutes are subject to certain rules of interpretation, but whereas with non-fiscal legislation the courts may resolve any absurdity by looking at the spirit and intendment of the Act, they are more reluctant to do so with fiscal legislation. In 1970, Lord Donovan outlined the rules governing the interpretation of tax legislation:

> 'First, the words are to be given their ordinary meaning. They are not to be given some other meaning simply because their object is to frustrate legitimate tax avoidance devices. As Turner J. said in his (albeit dissenting) judgment in

> *Marx* v. *Inland Revenue Commissioners* ... moral precepts are not applicable to the interpretation of revenue statutes.
>
> Secondly, '... one has to look merely at what is clearly said. There is no room for any intendment. There is no equity about a tax. There is no presumption as to a tax. Nothing is to be read in, nothing is to be implied. One can only look fairly at the language used': *per* Rowlatt J. in *Cape Brandy Syndicate* v. *Inland Revenue Commissioners* ... (approved by Viscount Simons L.C. in *Canadian Eagle Oil Co. Ltd.* v. *The King* ...)
>
> Thirdly, the object of the construction of a statute being to ascertain the will of the legislature, it may be presumed that neither injustice nor absurdity was intended. If therefore a literal interpretation would produce such a result, and the language admits of an interpretation which would avoid it, then such an interpretation may be adopted ...
>
> Fourthly, the history of an enactment and the reasons which led to its being passed may be used as an aid to its construction.'

Therefore, if the words are ambiguous, the taxpayer is entitled to the benefit of the doubt but if there is no ambiguity, the words must take their natural meaning however great the hardship to the taxpayer.

In a later House of Lords case, some attention was focused on the general principles of construing fiscal legislation in the light of tax avoidance schemes. Lord Steyn indicated that an approach that followed a narrow, literalistic interpretation of such statute was outmoded when he said:

> 'During the last 30 years there has been a shift away from literalist to purposive methods of construction. Where there is no obvious meaning of a statutory provision the modern emphasis is on a contextual approach designed to identify the purpose of a statute and to give effect to it. But under the influence of the narrow *Duke of Westminster* doctrine tax law remained remarkably resistant to the new non formalist methods of interpretation ... Tax law was by and large left behind as some island of literal interpretation ... the intellectual breakthrough came in 1981 in *Ramsay*, and notably in Lord Wilberforce's seminal speech ... It marked the rejection by the House [of Lords] of pure literalism in the interpretation of tax statutes'

The House of Lords has decided that Parliamentary material (in that case, *Hansard*) may, in limited circumstances, be used to ascertain the *intention* of Parliament when enacting legislation. A majority of the House held that, subject to the question of Parliamentary privilege, the rule excluding reference to *Hansard* should be relaxed where:

- legislation was ambiguous or obscure, or led to absurdity;

- the material relied on consisted of statements by a minister or other promoter of a Bill, together with any other Parliamentary material necessary to understand such statements and their effect;

- the statements relied on were clear.

The UK law on VAT derives from EC law, notably Council Directive 2006/112 on the common system of value added tax (formerly the sixth directive on VAT). Under the Treaty of Rome, the government is obliged to enact the UK law in such a way as to implement the provisions contained in the European directives and regulations. Consequently, it is sometimes possible to refer to the EC legislation for guidance on the interpretation of the UK law. Furthermore, if the UK law fails to implement the EC law, the citizen is entitled to rely on the EC law where it has direct effect in the UK.

Legislation: Council Directive 2006/112 (28 November 2006, OJ 2006 L347/1)

Cases: *IR Commrs v Hinchy* [1960] AC 748; *Mangin v IR Commrs* [1971] AC 739; *Pepper (HMIT) v Hart* [1992] BTC 591; *IR Commrs v McGuckian* [1997] BTC 346

Tax Reporter: ¶104-000

216 Tax periods

Liability to both CGT and income tax is in respect of a 'year of assessment' (or 'tax year'), beginning on 6 April and ending on 5 April in the following year. Liability to corporation tax, however, is in respect of a 'financial year' (see 3030), which begins on 1 April and ends on 31 March in the following year. While liability arises by reference to a 'year of assessment' or a 'financial year', it does not necessarily follow that it is the income or gain made during those periods that is taxed. Where income or gain is taxed in the year of assessment or financial year in which it arises, tax is said to be calculated on a 'current year' basis.

For VAT, a trader is normally required to make VAT returns and provisional attributions of input tax for each prescribed accounting period (VAT return period: see 8454), and then review this for his VAT tax year, i.e. a period of 12 months ending on 31 March, 30 April or 31 May, depending upon the business' VAT accounting period.

Class 1, Class 2 and Class 3 National Insurance contribution are recorded for the purposes of computing benefit entitlement on the basis of years ending on 5 April, although (unlike income tax) NICs of those classes do not arise on an annual or annualised basis and liability within each tax year is calculated by reference to earnings paid in an earnings period for Class 1, and by reference to contribution weeks for Class 2 and Class 3; contributions of Class 1A arise on an annual basis while Class 4 contribution liability is linked to tax liability on income arising from a trade, profession or vocation.

Legislation: ITA 2007, s. 4(3), (5); CTA 2010, s. 1119 and Sch. 1, para. 248, 689(3); *Value Added Tax Regulations* 1995 (SI 1995/2518), reg. 99(3)

Tax Reporter: ¶102-000

217 Income or capital

Tax law generally makes a distinction between capital and income items when analysing receipts and expenditure. This distinction was more important in the days when income tax was calculated at progressive rates while capital gains were taxed at a flat rate of 30%. In general, a sum which is derived from the sale of a capital item will not give rise to an income receipt but it does not follow that what is a capital expense to one party is necessarily a capital receipt to the other party.

Example

X owns a factory, manufacturing toys. He sells his factory to Y who deals in buying and selling commercial properties. In X's hands the receipt is capital; in Y's hands the expense is an income (or revenue) expense. Capital items include any profit-making apparatus of the business. For further details of the distinction, see 630.

The Tax Acts give no general definition of income, but a receipt, to be taxable, must fall within one of the heads of charge listed in the Acts if it is to be charged to income tax or corporation tax as income. Income is taxed according to the source from which it arises: e.g. the profits of a trade are taxed under the special rules of CTA 2010, Pt. 2 in the case of corporation tax and ITTOIA 2005, Pt. 2 in the case of income tax. The source of income must, as a general rule, exist in the year in which the income arose.

Example

A taxpayer (an individual) who is not domiciled in the UK and who receives bank interest in Jersey could close the account and remit the interest to the UK in the financial year after the one in which the interest arose and that interest would not be taxable. The reason is that, for non-domiciliaries, liability may be calculated using the remittance basis and in the tax year in which the liability arose the source, i.e. the bank account, had ceased to exist.

Tax Reporter: ¶106-000

General principles of direct taxation

219   Liability to tax

Income tax is a tax on profits or gains of an income nature. It is therefore necessary to distinguish them from gains of a capital nature (see 630). The Taxes Acts do not define either income or capital.

Capital gains tax is a tax on certain gains of a capital nature. Broadly, it seeks to tax chargeable gains resulting from chargeable disposals of chargeable assets by chargeable persons.

Corporation tax is a tax on profits, including income and chargeable gains.

Inheritance tax is altogether different and applies to transfers of value.

In general, a sum received from the sale of a capital item will be a capital sum and will not attract income taxation. Capital items are defined widely and include such things as contracts under which the business operates to make profits, know-how and any other profit-making apparatus of the business.

In general, the basic liability to tax is in each case given without reference to the circumstances of the person concerned. The scope of charge is then limited in certain cases. However, there is also a generally accepted principle that the extent of a territory's taxation should not exceed its national boundaries – this is generally determined by 'residence', 'ordinary residence' (until 5 April 2013 – see 224ff.) and 'domicile' (see 227) or the location of the 'source' of income or gains (see 220). Where the rules of other territories also impose tax in accordance with this principle relief may be provided to limit any double taxation.

Tax Reporter: ¶106-000

220   The source doctrine

Income profits are charged by reference to their source. For a receipt to be taxable it must have a source under the provisions of one of the Taxes Acts. If it has not, it will not be taxable. Moreover, the source must normally be in existence at the time when liability arises. Sources outside the UK may be subject to separate rules of calculation.

Capital taxation is also determined in part by the location of assets or property.

Tax Reporter: ¶103-000

221 Form and substance

The words of a taxing statute must clearly lay the burden of tax upon the taxpayer. If they do not, the taxpayer will not be taxed purely because it was the intention of the legislature that the taxpayer be taxed. It is, however, up to the court to decide upon the legal rights of the parties and in doing so they will not be influenced by nomenclature. Where the transactions are a sham or constitute a blatant scheme for tax avoidance, the court may decide to look at their substance or end result to determine how they should be taxed.

Cases starting with *WT Ramsay Ltd v IR Commrs* [1982] AC 300 and *Furniss (HMIT) v Dawson* [1984] BTC 71 have established that where there:

- is a *pre-ordained series* of transactions or *single composite* transaction;
- are steps inserted with no commercial purpose other than the avoidance of tax,

the court may ignore the inserted steps and tax the transaction, or series of transactions, accordingly.

Transactions regarded as a sham

Only bona fide transactions are to be taken into account for tax purposes, 'shams' being ignored. An avoidance scheme in pursuance of which a chain of companies was set up and the declaration of a dividend out of capital reserve which was created by the passing of a sum of money along the chain and the creation of an alleged dealing loss of £3m (approximately) was held not to be trading. These cases set the scene for the later development of the *Furniss v Dawson* doctrine.

Cases: *Johnson v Jewitt (HMIT)* (1961) 40 TC 231; *WT Ramsay Ltd v IR Commrs* [1982] AC 300 and *Furniss (HMIT) v Dawson* [1984] BTC 71

Tax Reporter: ¶104-450

222 Methods of collecting tax

There are two methods of collecting tax. The first is by direct assessment. This is done by HMRC assessing the amount that the taxpayer is liable to pay, or by the taxpayer producing a self-assessment.

The second method is by deduction of tax at source by the person who makes the payment to the taxpayer. In principle, the payer then sends that deducted tax to HMRC.

Tax Reporter: ¶187-995

223 Grossing up

Income may be received which has already had tax deducted from it at source, i.e. before it is received. Where this is done, a calculation must be made to ascertain the gross figure which forms part of the taxpayer's total income. The process of calculating this gross figure is called 'grossing up'. The calculation is as follows:

- Multiply the net amount received by the grossing-up fraction.

- The grossing-up fraction is 100 divided by (100 less the rate of tax).

Example

If £160 is received after the basic rate income tax of 20% has been deducted, the grossed-up figure is as follows:

$$£160 \times \frac{100}{100 - 20}$$

$$£160 \times \frac{100}{80} = £200$$

Therefore £200 is the grossed-up figure.

Example

If £160 is received after income tax of 40% has been deducted, the grossed-up figure is as follows:

$$£160 \times \frac{100}{100 - 40}$$

$$£160 \times \frac{100}{60} = £266.67$$

Therefore £266.67 is the grossed-up figure.

A special grossing up process is required for inheritance tax. Tax in respect of a disposition made by a transferor which is chargeable is calculated by reference to the reduction in value of his estate. If he also agrees to pay any tax due, the reduction in his estate is that much greater. A complex grossing up of the value of the disposition is required (see 6620).

Tax Reporter: ¶117-000ff.

224 Residence of individuals

From 6 April 2013, a new statutory residence test (SRT) applies to determine the residence of an individual for tax purposes. This is designed to provide clear rules, providing greater certainty and clarity for taxpayers.

The test of 'residence' historically, not being founded in statute, has derived from cases decided by the courts. On top of this, HMRC have long since set out their own views and approach to matters of residence (and 'ordinary residence'), contained in their published booklets (currently HMRC booklet RDR1: *Residence, domicile and the remittance basis*, formerly HMRC 6).

These two source materials – case law and HMRC practice – have not proved entirely satisfactory. Many of the cases on the subject were decided a considerable time ago, and do not reflect modern work or lifestyle patterns. In addition, some recent cases, in particular, the *Gaines-Cooper* case showed it is probably fair to say that there had been a widespread element of misunderstanding as to the application of certain provisions in former booklet IR 20.

Further guidance was included in former HMRC 6, in the light of that case, regarding individuals leaving the UK to take up permanent or indefinite residence abroad. This emphasised the significance, in the context of the test of residence, or of 'ceasing to be UK-resident', of the individual's continuing family, business and social connections, if there were such, in or with the UK.

The statutory residence test was enacted in *Finance Act* 2013, and is effective for the 2013–14 and subsequent tax years. The test applies for the purposes of income tax, capital gains tax, and, 'so far as the residence status of individuals is relevant to them', inheritance tax and corporation tax. Full guidance on the statutory residence test can be found in the HMRC guidance RDR1: *Residence, domicile and the remittance basis* and RDR3: *Statutory Residence Test (SRT)*.

The basic rule is that an individual (P) is resident in the UK for a tax year (year X) if:

(a) the automatic residence test is met for that year; or

(b) the sufficient ties test is met for that year.

If neither of those tests is met for the year, P is not resident in the UK for that year.

As regards (a), the 'automatic residence test' is met for year X if P meets:

(i)   at least one of the automatic UK tests; and

(ii) none of the automatic overseas tests.

In practice, these rules can be applied in the following order:

- consider whether P spent more than 183 days in the UK in the tax year – if so, then P is UK resident for the year, if not;

- consider whether any of the automatic overseas tests are met for the year – if so, then P is not resident for the year;

- if none of the automatic overseas tests are met, consider whether any of the remaining automatic UK tests are met for the year – if so, then P is UK resident for the year;

- if none of the automatic overseas tests, and none of the automatic UK tests, are met for the year, move to consider whether the 'sufficient ties' test is met for the year – if so, P is resident; if not, P is not resident.

The relevant tests are set out below.

Automatic overseas test

There are five automatic overseas tests and if an individual (P) meets the conditions of any one of these tests, they are automatically non-resident. The tests are:

(1) that P was resident in the UK for one or more of the three previous tax years and spends fewer than 16 days in the UK in the current tax year;

(2) that P was not resident in the UK for any of the previous three tax years and spends fewer than 46 days in the UK in the current tax year;

(3) P worked full-time overseas over the tax year without any significant breaks during the tax year from overseas work, and:

    (a) spent fewer than 91 days in the UK in the tax year; and

    (b) the number of days in the tax year on which P worked for more than three hours in the UK is less than 31;

(4) that P died in the current year having spent fewer than 46 days in the UK during that year and:

    (a) P was not resident in the UK in the two preceding tax years; or

    (b) P was not resident in the UK in the preceding tax year and the tax year before that was a split year by virtue of Case 1, 2 or 3; or

(5) that P died in the current year would meet the third automatic overseas test for the current year considering only the period until P's death and:

(a) P was not resident in the UK for the two preceding tax years because P met the third automatic overseas test for each of those years; or

(b) not resident in the UK in the preceding tax year because P met the third automatic overseas test for that year and the tax year before that was a split year by virtue of Case 1 (leaves UK for full-time work overseas).

Automatic UK test

An individual (P) who does not meet any of the automatic overseas tests will be automatically UK resident if they meet any of the four automatic UK tests. The tests are:

(1) P spends at least 183 days in the UK during the tax year;

(2) that there is a period of more than 90 days, part of which falls within the tax year, when P has a home in the UK, and no home overseas (disregarding any home at which they are present for fewer than 30 days in the tax year);

(3) that in the current tax year, P works full-time in the UK; or

(4) that P dies in the current year having been UK resident for each of the three preceding tax years by virtue of meeting one of the automatic UK tests (and none of the automatic overseas tests), and:

(a) the tax year before P died was not a split year (assuming the year in which P died was a year of non-residence);

(b) when P died, P had his/her home in the UK, or if P had more than one home, at least one of them was in the UK; and

(c) if P had a home or homes overseas during all or part of the tax year, P did not spend a sufficient amount of time (at least 30 days) in the overseas home(s) in the tax year.

Sufficient ties test

An individual who meets none of the automatic overseas tests and none of the automatic UK tests will need to look at the sufficient ties test. This test compares the number of days spent in the UK against a small number of connection factors (ties) as follows:

- UK-resident family;

- substantive UK employment (including self-employment);

- available accommodation in the UK;

- more than 90 days spent in the UK in either or both of the previous two tax years;

- a country tie (but only if individual resident in one or more three previous tax years).

Days spent in the UK during the tax year	Number of ties that are sufficient	
	Not resident in previous three tax years	**Resident in any of the previous three tax years**
More than 15 but not more than 45	[Automatic overseas test is satisfied]	At least four
More than 45 but not more than 90	All four	At least three
More than 90 but not more than 120	At least three	At least two
More than 120	At least two	At least one

Family tie

Either:

- individual has a UK-resident spouse (unless separated), or partner (if living together as husband and wife or civil partners); or

- individual has a UK-resident child under 18 years old (unless spends fewer than 61 days with the child in the tax year).

(An individual will not be considered to have a family tie with a child who is UK resident and under 18 years who is in full-time education and would not be a UK resident if the time spent in full-time education were disregarded and the child spends fewer than 21 days in the UK outside term time (half-term counts as term time)).

Work tie

Individual does more than three hours of work (employed or self employed) a day in the UK on at least 40 days in that year (whether continuously or intermittently). (NB. Special rules apply to determine what constitutes three-hours work for workers on board a vehicle, aircraft or ship.)

Accommodation tie

Individual has a place to live in the UK (including a home, holiday home, temporary retreat of other accommodation) that is:

- available for a continuous period of 91 days or more during the year;

- the individual spends one or more nights there during the year; or

- if it is at the home of a close relative (parent, grandparent, sibling, child or grandchild over 18 years old), the individual spends 16 or more nights there during the year.

90-day tie

Individual spends more than 90 days (counting midnights) in the UK in either or both of the previous two tax years.

Country tie

Applicable only where 'resident' in any of previous three tax years.

An individual has a country tie for the tax year if the UK is the country in which they were present at midnight for the greatest number of days in that tax year.

If the number of days an individual is present in a country at midnight is the same for two or more countries in a tax year, and one of those countries is the UK, then the individual will have a country tie for that tax year if that is the greatest number of days spent in any country in that tax year.

Split tax year treatment

Under the SRT, an individual is either UK resident or non-UK resident for a full tax year and at all times in that tax year. However, if during a year that individual either starts to live or work abroad or comes from abroad to live or work in the UK, the tax year will be split into two parts if their circumstances meet specific criteria (see below):

- a UK part for which they are charged to UK tax as a UK resident; and

- an overseas part for which, for most purposes, they are charged to UK tax as a non-UK resident.

The taxpayer must be UK resident for a tax year under the SRT to meet the criteria for split year treatment for that year. They will not meet the split year criteria for a tax year for which they are non-UK resident under the SRT.

Split year treatment in the context of the SRT applies only to an individual in his or her individual capacity. It does not apply to individuals acting as personal representatives. It applies in a limited way to individuals acting as trustee of a settlement in determining the trustees' residence status:

- if the individual becomes or ceases to be a trustee of the settlement during the tax year; and

- provided that the period they are a trustee falls within the overseas part of the tax year for that individual.

Split year treatment will not affect whether the individual is regarded as UK resident for the purposes of any double taxation arrangement.

Specified criteria

There are eight sets of circumstances which enable an individual to qualify for split year treatment. Where an individual's circumstances fall into more than one, the cases must be considered in the following priority order to determine which case applies:

- where an individual falls within two or more of Cases 1–3, Case 1 has priority over Cases 2 and 3, and Case 2 has priority over Case 3;

- where an individual falls within two of more of Cases 4–8; the case with the earliest split year date takes priority as between Cases 5 and 6, and also as between Case 7 (but not 6) and 5; where two or all of Cases 4, 5 and 8 (but not 6 or 7) applies, the case or cases with the only (or earlier) split year date takes priority. (For these purposes, the split year date is the final day of the overseas part of the year for that Case.)

Leaving the UK

Case 1: Starting full-time work overseas

The individual must be:

- UK resident for the tax year in question and the previous tax year (whether or not it was a split year);

- not resident for the following tax year by meeting the third automatic overseas test (works full-time overseas); and

- satisfy the overseas work criteria during the relevant period from first starting to work overseas to the end of the tax year.

An individual satisfies the overseas work criteria if they work full-time overseas without significant break, do not work for more than three hours in the UK on more than the permitted limit of days during that period and spend no more than the permitted limit of days in the UK during that period.

Case 2: The partner of someone starting full-time work overseas

The individual's partner meets the conditions for Case 1 split year treatment for that year or the previous year and the individual moves overseas so that they can continue to live with their partner while they are working overseas. The individual must also:

- be UK resident for the tax year in question and the previous tax year (whether or not it was a split year);

- be non-UK resident for the tax year following the tax year being considered for split year treatment;

- have a partner whose circumstances fall within Case 1 for the tax year or the previous tax year who the individual has been living together with in the UK either at some point in the tax year or the previous tax year;

and in the period from leaving the UK until the end of the tax year:

- have no home in the UK, or if there are homes in both the UK and overseas spend the greater part of the time living in the overseas home; and
- spend no more than the permitted limit of days in the UK.

Case 3: Ceasing to have a home in the UK

The individual leaves the UK and ceases to have a UK home. The individual must:

- be UK resident in the tax year in question and the previous tax year (whether or not it was a split year);
- be non-UK resident for the following tax year;
- have one or more homes in the UK at the start of the tax year and at some point in the year cease to have any home in the UK for the rest of the tax year.

The individual must also spend fewer than 16 days in the UK from ceasing to have a home there and establish a sufficient link with an overseas country by either becoming tax resident there within six months, or being present there at the end of each day for six months, or by having their only home (or all homes if more than one) there.

Coming to the UK

Case 4: Starting to have a home in the UK only

The individual was not resident in the previous tax year and did not have their only home (or all of their homes if more than one) in the UK at the start of the tax year but there comes a day in the tax year when that ceases to be the case and for the rest of the tax year the individual has their only (or all) homes in the UK. The individual must also not fall to be resident by virtue of the sufficient ties during the non-resident part of the tax year (which is determined by proportionately reducing the numbers of days spent in the UK for the part of the year to which test is applied).

Case 5: Starting full-time work in the UK

The individual starts to work full-time in the UK and meets the third automatic UK test over a period of 365 days. If there is more than one such period, then the UK part of the year will run from the beginning of the first such period. The individual must also be:

- be UK resident in the tax year;

- be non-UK resident for the previous tax year; and

- not meet the sufficient ties test for the part of the tax year prior to first meeting the third automatic UK test.

Again, when considering the sufficient ties test, the day count limits in the UK ties tables are reduced proportionately for the part of the year to which the test is applied.

Case 6: Ceasing full-time work overseas

The individual was non-UK resident in the previous tax year by virtue of working full-time overseas and ceases to work full-time overseas in the tax year to which split year treatment applies. The individual must:

- be UK resident for the tax year in question;

- have been not UK resident for the tax year before the year in question by virtue of either satisfying the third automatic overseas test for that year or, if the year was 2012–13, working full-time overseas for the whole of the tax year under the rules in force prior to the Statutory Residence Test, see HMRC 6;

- have been UK resident for one or more of the four tax years immediately preceding that year (i.e. the four years before the year in which the individual was not UK resident under the previous bullet point);

- be UK resident in the tax year following the year in question (whether or not it is a split year); and

- satisfy the overseas work criteria for a relevant period beginning with the first day of the tax year and ending on the last day of overseas work (i.e. works full time overseas without significant break, does not work for more than three hours in the UK on more than the permitted limit of days during that period and spends no more than the permitted limit of days in the UK during that period).

Case 7: The partner of someone ceasing full-time work overseas

The individual has been living abroad with their partner while the partner was in full-time employment overseas, and, on their partner stopping working overseas, the individual accompanies them in returning or relocating to the UK. The individual must also:

- be UK resident for the tax year and have been not resident in the UK for the previous tax year;

- have a partner whose circumstances fall within the criteria for Case 6 split year treatment, either in the tax year in question or in the previous tax year;

- be resident in the UK for the following tax year;

and, in the part of the year before the deemed arrival day:

- have no home in the UK at any time or if there are homes in both the UK and overseas spend the greater part of the time living in the overseas home; and

- not exceed the permitted limit of days spent in the UK.

The deemed arrival day is the later of the first day of the UK part of the tax year for the partner under Case 6, or the date of moving to the UK.

Case 8: Starting to have a home in the UK

The individual was not resident in the UK for the previous year and had no home in the UK at the start of the tax year but at some point during the tax year starts to have a home in the UK and from then on has a home in the UK for the rest of that year and the whole of the next tax year. The individual must also not fall to be resident by virtue of the sufficient ties during the non-resident part of the tax year (which is determined by proportionately reducing the numbers of days spent in the UK for the part of the year to which test is applied) and must be UK resident for the following tax year (which must not be a split year).

Abolition of the 'ordinary residence' test

The concept of ordinary residence for tax purposes has been abolished for tax years from 2013–14 onwards.

Transitional provisions apply, however, to ensure that those who currently benefit from being not ordinarily resident will continue to be able to enjoy such treatment, for a maximum of two complete tax years.

Overseas workday relief

Overseas workday relief (OWR), refers to the relief granted to certain resident, but non-UK domiciled individuals, with an employment duties of which are carried out partly in the UK and partly overseas. If the relevant conditions are met, the earnings which relate to the duties performed overseas are only taxable on the remittance basis. If not remitted, they are not taxable – this is the OWR.

The concept of OWR is retained, but has been put onto a statutory footing in a simplified way to provide certainty, but which is necessarily different from the current regime.

OWR is available to all non-UK domiciled individuals who arrive in the UK after 5 April 2013 having been non-UK resident for the previous three years. It is available for the whole of the tax year that the individual becomes resident in the UK (or for the UK part of the year if that year is a split year) and for the two tax years following.

There are no restrictions on the relief being available when an individual decides to buy a property in the UK or takes any other steps that would suggest a more permanent connection to the UK.

Legislation: TCGA 1992, s. 9(3); ITEPA 2003; ITA 2007, s. 829, 831; FA 2008, s. 24; FA 2013, s. 218 and Sch. 45, s. 219 and Sch. 46

Cases: *R (on the application of Davies) v R & C Commrs; R (on the application of Gaines-Cooper) v R & C Commrs* [2011] BTC 610; *R & C Commrs v Grace* [2009] EWCA Civ 1082; *Levene v IR Commrs* [1928] AC 217; *Wilkie v IR Commrs* [1952] Ch 153

Website: HMRC guidance on SRT:

www.hmrc.gov.uk/international/rdr3.pdf; HMRC guidance RDR1: *Residence, domicile and the remittance basis*: www.hmrc.gov.uk/cnr/rdr1.pdf

Tax Reporter: ¶199-000

225   Residence of companies

Company residence is important because a UK-resident company is taxed on its worldwide profits, whereas a non-resident company is taxed generally only on profits arising from its operations in the UK (see 3015).

Three rules apply in determining if a company is resident in the UK for corporation tax purposes:

* the incorporation rule whereby a company which is incorporated in the UK is UK resident;

* the case law rule whereby a company which has its central management and control in the UK is UK resident; and

* the tie-breaker rule whereby a company which is treated as non-UK resident by any double taxation arrangements is non-UK resident for corporation tax purposes despite the application of the incorporation or case law rules.

European Companies (or Societas Europaea, SEs) and European Co-operative Societies (or Societas Co-operative Europaea, SCEs) will be regarded as UK resident for tax purposes if they transfer their registered office from another EU member state to the UK. Any other place given by rule of law is to be disregarded in determining their residence status. In addition, they will not cease to be regarded as UK resident merely because of a subsequent transfer of their registered office out of the UK.

Any liabilities or obligations which arise under self-assessment will continue to apply where a UK-resident company ceases to be resident as a direct consequence of the formation of an SE by a merger of companies, whether or not the UK company ceases to exist; where it does cease to exist, those liabilities and responsibilities will fall on the SE. Similar provisions apply if an SE transfers its registered office outside the UK (and ceases to be UK resident) in respect of liabilities before then.

A company which is resident in the UK is liable to corporation tax on its worldwide profits. A company which is not resident in the UK is liable to corporation tax only if it trades in the UK through a permanent establishment. A non-resident company not trading in the UK through a PE/branch or agency is not liable to corporation tax but, generally, such a company is assessed to income tax on income arising from sources within the UK.

Where a non-resident company receives any payment from which income tax has been deducted, it may set the amount of income tax deducted against any assessment for corporation tax on that income. The company is not entitled to a repayment of income tax until the assessment for the accounting period is finally determined and a repayment appears due. Where the non-resident company is an overseas life insurance company, only a limited amount of the income tax is available for set-off.

Special provisions apply to certain foreign subsidiaries of UK-resident companies, such subsidiaries being referred to in the legislation as 'controlled foreign companies' (see 4150).

There are also special provisions which apply to the foreign element of certain companies and their funds. In general, such companies are subject to corporation tax rather than income tax and the special provisions relate to the corporation tax charge rather than the rare circumstances in which a company is subject to income tax, although in some cases the provisions apply in respect of all revenue taxes.

Legislation: F(No. 2)A 2005, s. 61; CTA 2009, s. 14–18

Cases: *De Beers Consolidated Mines Ltd v Howe* [1906] AC 455; *Unit Construction Co Ltd v Bullock* [1960] AC 351

Other Material: SP 1/90, *Company residence*

Tax Reporter: ¶764-000

227 Domicile

Domicile is important largely for inheritance tax purposes whereas CGT and income tax are founded mainly on residence. Domicile is where the individual has a settled intention permanently to reside. Everybody must have a domicile, one cannot be without one and a person can only be domiciled in one place at any one time.

Under English law, a person has either a domicile of origin, a domicile of dependency, or a domicile of choice. Until 1 January 1974, the domicile of a married woman was dependent on her husband; thereafter, a married woman is capable of having a separate domicile.

(1) Domicile of origin

Domicile of origin follows that of the father or, if illegitimate, that of the mother and will, in the case of adults, apply in the absence of a domicile of choice. The domicile of a minor is dependent on that of the father if legitimate, and on the mother if illegitimate, and will change according to whether the parent acquires a new domicile of choice.

(2) Domicile of choice

At the age of 16, an individual acquires the right to a domicile of choice. To establish a domicile of choice, there must be evidence of fact and intention. The required fact would be habitual residence in the country where it is alleged that the domicile is established, and the required intention would be the intention to abandon the domicile of origin and establish a permanent home in the country of choice. In one case, the taxpayer, with a domicile of origin in the UK, failed to establish a domicile of choice in Guernsey when she remained in the UK during school and university terms to complete her education. Until a domicile of choice is established, the domicile of origin continues. Once a domicile of choice is abandoned, the domicile of origin is revived and continues until another domicile of choice is established.

(3) Domicile by operation of law

For any given purpose, a person may be considered to be domiciled in the UK irrespective of domicile under general law. There is a deemed domicile provision in relation to inheritance tax (see 6540).

Domicile for tax purposes of overseas electors

In order to determine a person's domicile for inheritance tax, income tax or CGT purposes on or after 6 April 1996 (or for the purposes of the deemed domicile rule, considered at 6540, on or after 6 April 1993), any action taken by a person in becoming an overseas elector or voting in an overseas election is disregarded. This rule applies unless the taxpayer in question wishes such an action to be taken into account.

Companies' domicile

A company's domicile is its country of registration.

Domicile reform

Summer Budget 2015 announced a number of changes in respect of domicile.

- Abolishing non-domicile status for long domicile residents for the purposes of the remittance basis of taxation and the point at which an individual is classed as deemed domicile for inheritance tax purposes will be brought forward to 15 out of 20 years; from April 2017, anyone who has been resident in the UK for more than 15 of the past 20 years will be deemed domicile for all tax purposes.

- Eligibility of non-domicile status for UK born individuals – from April 2017, individuals born in the UK to parents who are domiciled here, will no longer be able to claim non-domicile status whilst they are resident in the UK.

- UK residential property of non-domiciles, including non-domiciles who are not UK resident, will be subject to inheritance tax from April 2017.

All non-dom reforms are to be legislated for in Finance Bill 2017 (Budget 2016).

Legislation: FA 1996, s. 200

Cases: *Gasque v IR Commrs* [1940] 2 KB 80; *Re Clore (dec'd)* [1984] BTC 8,101; *Plummer v IR Commrs* [1987] BTC 543

Other Material: RDR1: *Residence, domicile and the remittance basis*: www.gov.uk/government/publications/residence-domicile-and-remittance-basis-rules-uk-tax-liability

Tax Reporter: ¶199-520ff.

228   Taxation of spouses

A husband and wife are treated as independent taxpayers. This applies for income tax and CGT; it has always been the case for inheritance tax. This independent treatment affects a number of reliefs but principally 'personal allowances' (see 1850ff.) and the 'annual exemption' applying to CGT (see 6150). Transfers between spouses are generally on a no gain/no loss basis for CGT purposes and are exempt from inheritance tax (see 5500 and 7192). There are a number of other CGT provisions relating to spouses (see 5460ff.).

Jointly held property

If, after 1989–90, a husband and his wife who is 'living with' him (see 1862) are beneficially entitled to income from property held in their names, they will be treated as entitled to it in equal shares unless they make a joint declaration (on form 17) to the contrary. The declaration has effect in relation to income arising on or after its date; however, a declaration made before 6 June 1990 also had retrospective effect. The declaration is ineffective if:

- notice of it is not given to the officer (on form 17) within 60 days of its making; or

- the spouses' interests in the property do not correspond to their interests in the income.

Once validly made, the declaration continues in effect unless and until the spouses' interests in either the income or capital cease to accord with the declaration.

From 6 April 2004, distributions (usually dividends) from jointly owned shares in close companies are no longer automatically split 50/50 between husband and wife but are taxed according to the actual proportions of ownership and entitlement to the income.

Gains are apportioned according to the beneficial interests of the spouses at the date of disposal; if the split is unclear, HMRC will usually accept that it is in equal shares. However, where a declaration is made for income tax HMRC will presume that the same split applies for CGT (see 5502).

In one case, the taxpayer had instructed the Department of Social Security to pay his retirement pension into his wife's bank account and claimed that, since he had not received the income, he was not liable to pay tax on it. A special commissioner held that the taxpayer had not disclaimed his pension into his wife's bank account; he had assigned it to his wife, and in so doing he exercised dominion over it by directing to whom it should be paid.

Legislation: ITA 2007, s. 836 and 837

Cases: *Meredith-Hardy v McLellan (HMIT)* (1995) Sp C 42; *Koshal* [2013] TC 02806

Tax Reporter: ¶504-100

229 Taxation of infants

There is a statutory duty on 'every person ... who is chargeable' to income tax or CGT for a particular tax year and who has not received a notice to make a return of his total income and gains (see 2200) to give notice of his chargeability to HMRC not later than six months after the end of that year. 'Every person ... chargeable' includes a child under the age of 18: in effect the obligation to make a return in respect of non-settled property will fall upon the child's parent or guardian (see 987).

Cases: *R v Newmarket Income Tax Commrs, ex parte Huxley* (1916) 7 TC 49

Tax Reporter: ¶134-150

230 Same-sex couples

The *Civil Partnership Act* 2004 (CPA 2004), which gives legal recognition to same-sex couples, became law in November 2004 and came into effect on 5 December 2005. Broadly, the Act allows same-sex couples to make a formal legal commitment to each other by entering into a civil partnership through a registration process. A range of important rights and responsibilities flows from this, including legal rights and protections. One of the key taxation areas that is affected by this legislation is inheritance tax where transfers between partners are now exempt.

In addition, only one property owned by a couple who are civil partners, whether that property is owned solely or jointly, may be treated as the principal private residence of either of them at any time for the purposes of capital gains tax private residence relief (see 6220). Transfers of assets between civil partners living together will be on a no-gain-no-loss basis for CGT purposes.

Legislation relating to all areas of taxation, social security benefits and NICs has been amended to reflect the introduction of CPA 2004. Broadly, references to husband, wife, ex-husband, ex-wife, spouse, ex-spouse, surviving spouse, widow and widower include civil partner, former civil partner and surviving civil partner under the terms of CPA 2004. References to 'step' relations and 'in-laws' are also to be interpreted to include relationships arising from a civil partnership.

The *Marriage (Same Sex Couples) Act* 2013 makes provision for the lawful marriage of same sex couples in England and Wales. Previously, a legal marriage could only take place between a man and a woman. The majority of the Act including provisions extending lawful marriage to same sex couples was brought into force on 13 March 2014 with the first same sex marriages taking place on 29 March 2014. A same sex marriage is an alternative to a civil partnership which continues to be available, although the Act contains provisions enabling the conversion of a civil partnership into a marriage (under s. 9 of the Act), with effect from 30 June 2014.

Schedule 3 of the Act (interpretation of legislation) provides that in existing England and Wales legislation, references to marriage, a married couple and a person who is married are to be read as including a reference to marriages of same sex couples and in new England and Wales legislation, the term husband includes a man married to another man, wife includes a woman married to another woman (and widower and widow are similarly defined). New legislation is defined as legislation passed after the end of the 2013–14 Parliamentary Session, or in the case of England and Wales legislation that is subordinate legislation, legislation made after 17 July 2013 (Royal Assent).

Other Material: *Tax Bulletin*, Issue 80, December 2005

Tax Reporter: ¶134-350

Income tax

KEY POINTS

- Income tax is a charge on receipts, profits or gains (see 240).

- There are four main rates of income tax – the starting rate (which applies to savings income only), the basic rate, the higher rate, and the additional rate – special rates apply to dividends (see Key Data).

- From 6 April 2016, there is also a dividend nil rate for the first £5,000 of dividend income ('the dividend allowance') and a savings nil rate for basic rate and higher rate taxpayers for the first £1,000 and £500 of savings income respectively ('the savings allowance').

- Tax is collected either by direct assessment or by deduction at source (see 2381ff.).

- Income from employment, pensions and social security is dealt with under the provisions of ITEPA 2003 (see 250ff.).

- Benefits in kind are taxable on all employees irrespective of their level of earnings following the abolition of the £8,500 threshold for certain benefits from 2016–17 (see 312ff.).

- Profits from trades, professions and vocations are taxed under ITTOIA 2005 (see 555ff.).

- Under self-assessment, income tax is charged directly on the partners in a partnership (see 750ff.).

- Special rules apply to certain categories of taxpayers, including charities (see 900ff.), farmers and market gardeners (see 940ff.); mining concerns (see 960ff.) and Lloyd's underwriters (see 970ff.).

- Special rules apply to tax the income of trusts and deceased person's estates (see 985ff.).

- Income from property is taxed under the tax on property income rules of ITTOIA 2005 (see 1200ff.).

- Foreign income may be taxable in the UK, depending on the recipient's residence and domicile status. Relief is available to prevent double taxation (see 1550ff.).

- There are various deductions and reliefs to which an individual may be entitled in computing his or her income tax liability (see 1840ff.).

- Allowable business expenses are taken into account in computing taxable business income (see 2050ff.).

- Depreciation is not an allowable expense in computing tax profits, instead capital allowances (effectively depreciation for tax purposes) may be available (see 4520ff.).

- Under the self-assessment regime, taxpayers can work out their own tax and pay the tax due by the payment date. HMRC will work out the tax for those taxpayers not wishing to perform their own calculation provided the return is submitted by 31 October.

General framework of income tax

240   Introduction to income tax

Income tax is a tax on income, but also on some capital receipts.

The taxation of employment income is generally charged under the provisions of ITEPA 2003.

The *Income Tax Act* 2007 came into force on 6 April 2007. The Act covers basic provisions about the charge to income tax, income tax rates, the calculation of income tax liability, and personal reliefs; various specific reliefs (including relief for losses, the enterprise investment scheme, venture capital trusts, community investment tax relief, interest paid, gift aid and gifts of assets to charities); specific rules about trusts, deduction of tax at source, manufactured payments and repos, the accrued income scheme and tax avoidance; and general income tax definitions.

The *Income Tax (Trading and Other Income) Act* 2005 (ITTOIA 2005) took effect from 6 April 2005. The Act covers the taxation of trading, property, savings and investment and miscellaneous income.

Certain persons are exempt from all taxes on income and gains, while some are specifically exempt from income tax. Certain income is also exempt from income tax.

Legislation: ITEPA 2003; ITTOIA 2005; ITA 2007

Cases: *Salisbury House Estate Ltd v Fry* [1930] AC 432; *Mitchell and Edon v Ross* [1962] AC 813

Tax Reporter: ¶100-900

242   Rates of income tax

There are three main rates of income tax. For 2016–17, these are:

- the basic rate – 20%;

- the higher rate – 40%; and

- the additional rate – 45%

(FA 2016, s. 1).

Income tax is charged at the basic rate on an individual's income up to the basic rate limit (ITA 2007, s. 10(2)). For 2016–17, the basic rate limit is £32,000, rising to £33,500 for 2017–18 (FA 2015, s. 4(1)(b) (as amended by FA 2016, s. 2(1))).

Income tax is charged at the higher rate on an individual's income above the basic rate limit (ITA 2007, s. 10(3)) up to the higher rate limit of £150,000 (ITA 2007, s. 10(5A). The 'higher rate threshold' (the rate at which an individual entitled to a full basic personal allowance will start to pay tax at the higher rate) is, therefore, £43,000 for 2016–17.

The additional rate applies to taxable income above £150,000.

The rates of income tax are determined by Parliament for the tax year, however, a ceiling applies by virtue of F(No.2)A 2015, s. 1 (income tax lock) which provides that rates shall not exceed 20% (basic rate), 40% (higher rate) or 45% (additional rate) for the remainder of the current Parliament.

Certain types of income are charged at their own particular rates. Those rates are:

- the starting rate for savings income and the savings nil rate;

- the dividend nil rate, the dividend ordinary rate, the dividend upper rate and the dividend additional rate; and

- the trust rate and dividend trust rate.

Rates on savings income

There is a 0% starting rate for savings income up to £5,000 (ITA 2007, s. 12). The rate applies on so much of an individual's income up to £5,000 as is savings income. The starting rate is only available if an individual's non-savings income (NSI) (earned income, trading income, property income, trust income but excluding dividend income) is less than their personal allowance plus £5,000. If, however, after taking the personal allowance off NSI, the amount taxable is more than £5,000, none of their savings income will be taxed at the 0% starting rate. Instead, the savings income will be taxed at the savings nil rate to the extent that this is available (see below), at 20% to the extent the savings income falls within the basic rate income band (up to the basic rate limit (see above)), at the higher rate of 40% to the extent that the savings income falls above the basic rate income band but below the higher rate limit (or additional rate threshold (see above)) and at additional rate where savings income falls above the higher rate limit.

Finance Act 2016 introduces a savings nil rate (the savings allowance) with effect from 6 April 2016. The savings nil rate is available for up to £1,000 of a basic rate taxpayer's savings income and up to £500 of a higher rate taxpayer's savings income each year. The savings nil rate is not available for additional rate taxpayers.

The savings nil rate is applied in addition to the starting rate for savings, where this is available (see above), to so much of the individual's savings income as exceeds the starting rate for savings, or where the starting rate for savings is not available (if the individuals NSI exceeds £5,000), the savings nil rate applies to the first £500 or £1,000 of savings income (ITA 2007, s. 12A).

Rates on dividend income

Finance Act 2016 introduces a new dividend nil rate (the dividend allowance) which applies to the first £5,000 of an individual's dividend income from 2016–17 (ITA 2007, s. 8(1A) and 13A. Also from 6 April 2016, the dividend tax credit is abolished (*Finance Act* 2016, s. 5 and Sch. 1).

Dividends above £5,000 are charged to tax at the dividend ordinary rate of 7.5% (from 6 April 2016, previously, 10%) to the extent that dividend income falls within the individual's basic rate income band (below the basic rate limit), at the dividend higher rate of 37.5% to the extent that the dividend income falls above the individual's basic rate income band but below the higher rate and at the dividend upper rate of 38.1% to the extent that the dividend income falls above the higher rate limit (see above) (ITA 2007, s. 8).

The 'dividend allowance' does not reduce the individual's total income for tax purposes and dividends within the allowance still count towards the basic or higher rate tax bands. Effectively, the dividend nil rate is substituted for the 7.5%, 37.5% or 38.1% rate(s) that would otherwise apply to the first £5,000 of dividend income (ITA 2007, s. 13A).

See further commentary on taxation of dividend income at 1350ff.

Trust and dividend trust rates

For 2016–17, the trust rate is 45% and the dividend trust rate is 38.1% (ITA 2007, s. 9). Previously, the dividend trust rate was 37.5%. For further commentary on the taxation of trust income trusts, see 985ff.

Savings and dividend income treated as highest part of total income

Where a person has more than one type of income, ITA 2007, s. 16 sets out rules to determine the rate at which income is charged on savings and dividend income. If a person has savings income but no dividend income, the savings income is treated as the highest part of the person's total income (ITA 2007, s. 16(3)). If a person has both savings and dividend income, the savings and dividend income are together treated as the highest part of the person's total income, but the dividend income is treated as the top slice of that part (ITA 2007, s. 16(5)). If a person's income is regarded as being in layers, the dividend income is the top layer, savings income the middle and non-savings income (e.g. employment income, trading income, property income) is the bottom layer.

Scottish rate of income tax

The *Scotland Act* (SCA) 2012 introduces a new power to set a Scottish rate of income tax (SCA 1998, Pt. 4, Ch. 2), with effect for the tax year 2016–17 and subsequent tax years and repeals the previous tax-varying power which had never been used. SCA 1998, s. 80C enables the Scottish Parliament to levy a Scottish rate of income tax to be used for the purpose of calculating the rates of income tax to be paid by Scottish taxpayers. The Scottish rate of income tax is 10% from 6 April 2016, however, Scottish taxpayers continue to pay the same tax as the rest of the UK because the Scottish rate (of 10%) is added to the UK main rates (20%, 40% and 45%) minus 10 percentage points.

The *Scotland Act* 2016 prospectively amends the power to set a Scottish rate of income tax under SCA 1998, s. 80C to enable the Scottish Parliament to set instead a Scottish basic rate, a Scottish higher rate and a Scottish additional rate of income tax (ITA 2007, s. 11A). The Scottish basic, higher and additional rates of income tax will only apply to non-savings, non-dividend income of those defined as 'Scottish taxpayers' (ITA 2007, s. 11A, 13).

Finance Act 2016 further prospectively amends ITA 2007 to separates the rates that apply to savings income from the main rates of income tax and to create a default rate of income tax on 'non-savings, non-dividends' income (i.e. employment income, pension income, property income and trading income) that will apply to, but is not limited to, trustees and non-resident taxpayers. The measure will take effect from the first tax year for which the Scottish Government can set Scottish rates of income tax (anticipated to be the tax year 2017–18). In April 2017, the UK Government will devolve the power to set the rates and thresholds that apply to the 'non-savings, non-dividends' income of individuals resident in Scotland to the Scottish Government.

244 Pro forma income tax computation

The amount of a person's income to which the income tax rates are to be applied is generally known as 'taxable income'.

Taxable income is statutory 'total income' less amounts *deductible from* total income, as opposed to amounts *deductible in computing* total income.

To find a person's ('the taxpayer') liability to income tax for a tax year, the following steps are applied:

Step 1 – Identify the amounts of income on which the taxpayer is charged to income tax for the tax year. The sum of those amounts is 'total income'. Each of those amounts is a 'component' of total income.

Step 2 – Deduct from the components the amount of any relief (subject to certain restrictions, under a provision listed below) to which the taxpayer is entitled for the tax year. The sum of the amounts of the components left after this step is 'net income'.

Step 3 – Deduct from the amounts of the components left after Step 2 any allowances to which the taxpayer is entitled for the tax year

At Steps 2 and 3, the reliefs and allowances are deducted in the way which will result in the greatest reduction in the taxpayer's liability to income tax (ITA 2007, s. 25(2)).

Step 4 – Calculate tax at each applicable rate on the amounts of the components left after Step 3 (see Key Data for rates).

Step 5 – Add together the amounts of tax calculated at Step 4.

Step 6 – Deduct from the amount of tax calculated at Step 5 any tax reductions to which the taxpayer is entitled for the tax year (under a provision listed below).

Step 7 – Add to the amount of tax left after Step 6 any amounts of tax for which the taxpayer is liable for the tax year under any provision listed below.

The result is the taxpayer's liability to income tax for the tax year.

Reliefs

If the taxpayer is an individual, the provisions referred to at Step 2 above are (subject to certain restrictions) broadly as follows:

(a) early trade losses relief;

(b) share loss relief;

(c) gifts of shares, securities and real property to charities, etc.;

(d) payments to trade unions or police organisations;

(e) pension schemes: relief under net pay arrangement: excess relief;

(f) pension schemes: relief on making of claim;

(g) trade loss reliefs: against general income; carry-forward loss relief; terminal loss relief; and post-cessation relief;

(h) property reliefs: carry-forward; against general income; and post-cessation;

(i) employment loss relief against general income;

(j) loss relief against miscellaneous income;

(k) interest payments and annual payments;

(l) manufactured dividends on UK shares: payments by non-companies; manufactured interest on UK securities: payments not otherwise deductible;

(m) plant and machinery allowances in a case where the allowance is to be given effect under CAA 2001, s. 258 (special leasing of plant and machinery);

(n) patent allowances in a case where the allowance is to be given effect under CAA 2001, s. 479 (persons having qualifying non-trade expenditure);

(o) deduction for liabilities related to former employment;

(p) strips of government securities: relief for losses;

(q) listed securities held since 26 March 2003: relief for losses: persons other than trustees); and

(r) relief for patent expenses.

From 6 April 2013, a cap applies to certain previously unlimited income tax reliefs that may be deducted from income under Step 2 above. The cap is set at £50,000 or 25% of income, whichever is greater. The reliefs affected by the cap are as follows:

(a) trade loss relief against general income (ITA 2007, s. 64);

(b) early trade losses relief (ITA 2007, s. 72);

(c)   post-cessation relief (ITA 2007, s. 96);

(d)   property loss relief against general income (ITA 2007, s. 120);

(e)   post-cessation property relief (ITA 2007, s. 125);

(f)   employment loss relief against general income (ITA 2007, s. 128);

(g)   share loss relief (ITA 2007, Pt. 4, Ch. 6);

(h)   relief for interest payments (ITA 2007, Pt. 8, Ch. 1);

(i)   deduction for liabilities relating to former employment (ITEPA 2003, s. 555);

(j)   relief for losses on strips of government securities (ITTOIA 2005, s. 446); and

(k)   relief for losses on listed securities held since 26 March 2003 (persons other than trustees) (ITTOIA 2005, s. 454(4)).

Tax reductions

If the taxpayer is an individual, the provisions referred to at Step 6 above are broadly as follows:

(a)   tax reductions for married couples and civil partners;

(b)   transferable tax allowance for married couples and civil partners;

(c)   EIS relief;

(d)   SEIS relief;

(e)   relief for social investments;

(f)   VCT relief;

(g)   community investment tax relief;

(h)   relief for non-deductible interest on loan to invest in partnership with residential property business;

(i)   qualifying maintenance payments;

(j)   spreading of patent royalty receipts;

(k)   relief for interest on loan to buy life annuity;

(l)   relief at source: additional relief (FA 2004, s. 192);

(m)   property business: relief for non-deductible costs of a dwelling-related loan;

(n)   top slicing relief;

(o)   relief for deficiencies;

(p)   double taxation relief;

(q) relief for foreign tax where no double taxation arrangements;

(r) relief for qualifying distribution after linked non-qualifying distribution; and

(s) relief where foreign estates have borne UK income tax.

Tax reductions are deducted in the order which will result in the greatest reduction in the taxpayer's liability to income tax for the tax year.

If the taxpayer is an individual, the provisions referred to at Step 7 above are broadly as follows:

(a) Gift Aid: charge to tax;

(b) tainted Gift Aid donations: charge to tax;

(c) tainted charity donations by trustees: charge to tax;

(d) high income child benefit charge;

(e) pension schemes: the short service refund lump sum charge;

(f) pension schemes: the serious ill-health lump sum charge;

(g) pension schemes: the special lump sum death benefits charge;

(h) pension schemes: the unauthorised payments charge;

(i) pension schemes: the unauthorised payments surcharge;

(j) pension schemes: the lifetime allowance charge;

(k) pension schemes: the annual allowance charge; and

(l) social security pension lump sum.

Legislation: ITA 2007, s. 23, 24, 25, 26–30

Tax Reporter: ¶148-400

Employees and the charge on employment income

Introduction: scope of the charge on employment income

250 The charge on employment income

Income tax is generally charged under *Income Tax (Earnings and Pensions) Act* 2003 (ITEPA 2003). The charge applies in respect of:

- emoluments from any office or employment (see 252ff.);

- pensions;

- other income directed to be charged under the charge on employment income, e.g. certain social security benefits (see 365ff.), certain contributions by employers to retirement benefit schemes (see 430ff.) and certain termination payments (see 438ff.).

Income tax is generally charged on a receipts basis rather than on earnings.

It is generally accepted that liability falls on the holder of the office or employment and that it is not possible to assign the right to income to avoid that liability. Although distinction perhaps needs to be drawn between the income and any underlying right, a taxpayer's instructions, say, for payment of his state retirement pension into his wife's bank account does not amount to a disclaimer of the pension, which remains taxable on him.

Legislation: ITEPA 2003, s. 6(1), 7(2), (3), 10(2)

Cases: *Dewar v IR Commrs* [1935] 2 KB 351; *Meredith-Hardy v McLellan* (1995) Sp C 42

Tax Reporter: ¶405-000

252 The meaning of 'office'

An 'office' (see 250) has been judicially described as:

> 'a subsisting, permanent, substantive position, which had an existence independent of the person who filled it, which went on and was filled in succession by successive holders ...'

Company directors are the most numerous examples of office holders.

However, a rigid requirement that the office be permanent is no longer appropriate, nor is it vouched by any decided case, and continuity need not be regarded as an absolute qualification. Although an office is often associated with some constituent instrument (creating and defining it but more than a job description), or some degree of public relevance and formality of appointment, none of these is essential.

The question whether a person is the holder of an office is a mixed question of fact and law, involving the application of the facts as found to the proper legal meaning of the word 'office' in the charge on employment income (see 250).

Cases: *Great Western Railway Co v Bater* [1922] 2 AC 1; *Edwards (HMIT) v Clinch* [1982] BTC 109; *McMenamin (HMIT) v Diggles* [1991] BTC 218

Tax Reporter: ¶400-020

253   Employed or self-employed?

Employees are taxed under entirely different provisions from those which tax the self-employed. It is therefore necessary to distinguish an employment from a trade, profession or vocation.

In deciding whether a contract of service exists, all the relevant facts are looked at and weighed in the balance. Some of the more obvious facts are as follows.

For employment	Against employment
Control by another over the manner in which the work is performed.	No control by another over the manner in which the work is done.
The person performing the work is restricted from delegating his work to another.	The person performing the work is free to delegate his duties to another.
The person performing the work does not bear the losses nor keep the profits.	The person performing the work bears the losses and keeps the profits.
Tax and National Insurance contributions are withheld by the person for whom the work is done.	No tax or National Insurance contributions are withheld from payments.
The parties agree employment.	The parties agree self-employment.
The person for whom the work is done provides the tools and equipment.	The person performing the work provides his own tools.
The person for whom the work is done lays down regular and defined hours of work.	The person performing the work is free to decide when he wishes to work.
The person for whom the work is done cannot withhold payment.	The person for whom the work is done is free to withhold payment until the work is performed as agreed.
The person for whom the work is done can dismiss.	The person for whom the work is done cannot dismiss the worker or cancel the work once the work is agreed, without compensation.
The person for whom the work is done has an obligation to provide work and to pay the 'employee' when no work is available.	There is no obligation to provide the 'employee' with work, or to pay him when no work is available.

Individually, the above points do not prove the existence or otherwise of a contract of employment. The HMRC website gives useful guidance on what HMRC regard as important criteria. However, they are points which influence the decision whether such a contract exists. The list is not exhaustive, and any fact which appears relevant in a particular case is taken into account and considered. The important factor is the actual performance of the contract.

Legislation: ITEPA 2003, s. 4

Cases: *Davies (HMIT) v Braithwaite* [1931] 2 KB 628; *Ready Mixed Concrete (South East) Ltd v Minister of Pensions and National Insurance* [1968] 2 QB 497; *Market Investigations Ltd v Minister of Social Security* [1969] 2 QB 173; *Fall (HMIT) v Hitchen* [1973] 1 WLR 286; *Warner Holidays v Secretary of State for Social Services* [1983] ICR 440; *Walls v Sinnett (HMIT)* [1987] BTC 206; *Sidey v Phillips (HMIT)* [1987] BTC 121; *Andrews v King (HMIT)* [1991] BTC 338; *Hall (HMIT) v Lorimer* [1993] BTC 473; *Sherburn Aero Club Ltd* [2009] TC 00006 *Athenaeum Club* [2010] TC 00341

Tax Reporter: ¶400-010

260 Agency workers

In the Autumn Statement 2013, the Government announced a consultation on onshore agencies. The consultation sought to address 'false self employment' and strengthen existing agency legislation to require agencies to operate PAYE and NIC correctly. *Finance Act* 2014 subsequently introduced a tighter regime for agency workers under Pt. 2, Ch. 7.

For periods from 6 April 2014, ITEPA 2003, s. 44 applies if:

(a) an individual ('the worker') personally provides services (which are not excluded services) to another person ('the client');

(b) there is a contract between:

(i) the client or a person connected with the client;

(ii) a person other than the worker, the client or a person connected with the client (the agency); and

(c) under or in consequence of that contract:

(i) the services are provided; or

(ii) the client or any person connected with the client pays, or otherwise provides consideration, for the services.

However, the section won't apply if:

(a) it is shown that the manner in which the worker provides the services is not subject to (or to the right of) supervision, direction or control by any person; or

(b) remuneration receivable by the worker in consequence of providing the services constitutes employment income of the worker apart from this Ch. 7.

Effect where section does apply

Where s. 44 does apply:

(a) the worker is to be treated for income tax purposes as holding an employment with the agency, the duties of which consist of the services the worker provides to the client; and

(b) all remuneration receivable by the worker (from any person) in consequence of providing the services is to be treated for income tax purposes as earnings from that employment,

but this is subject to cases involving fraudulent documents.

Fraudulent documents

The tax treatment immediately above does not apply in relation to services, the worker provides to the client after a fraudulent document is provided in the circumstances specified below, but instead:

(i) the worker is to be treated for income tax purposes as holding an employment with the client or (as the case may be) with the relevant person, the duties of which consist of the services; and

(ii) all remuneration receivable by the worker (from any person) in consequence of providing the services is to be treated for income tax purposes as earnings from that employment.

The relevant circumstances are if (whether before or after the worker begins to provide the services):

– the client provides the agency with a fraudulent document which is intended to constitute evidence that, by virtue of s. 44(2)(a), s. 44 does not or will not apply

– a relevant person provides the agency with a fraudulent document which is intended to constitute evidence that, by virtue of subs. (2)(b), this section does not or will not apply.

For these purposes, 'relevant person' means a person, other than the client, the worker or a person connected with the client or with the agency:

– who is resident, or has a place of business, in the United Kingdom; and

– is party to a contract with the agency or a person connected with the agency, under or in consequence of which:

(i) the services are provided; or

(ii) agency, or a person connected with the agency, makes payments in respect of the services.

Income tax

PAYE

The PAYE rules in ITEPA 2003, Pt. 11, Ch. 3 (PAYE: special types of payer or payee) are also amended, to provide that the agency is the deemed employer, and that either the agency, or any 'intermediary' of the agency (under s. 687), or any other person who makes payment to the worker (such other person being deemed to be an intermediary of the agency) is required to operate PAYE.

Anti-avoidance

The *Income Tax (Earnings and Pensions) Act* 2003, s. 46A (anti-avoidance) applies if:

(a) an individual ('W') personally provides services (which are not excluded services) to another person ('C');

(b) a third person ('A') enters into arrangements the main purpose, or one of the main purposes, of which is to secure that the services are not treated for income tax purposes under s. 44 as duties of an employment held by W with A, and

(c) but for this section, s. 44 would not apply in relation to the services.

The reference to 'arrangements' includes 'any scheme, transaction or series of transactions, agreement or understanding, whether or not legally enforceable, and any associated operations'.

Where s. 46A applies then, subject to s. 44(2), s. 44 applies in relation to the services, and for these purposes:

(i) W is to be treated as being the worker;

(ii) C is to be treated as being the client;

(iii) A is to be treated as being the agency; and

(iv) s. 44 has effect as if subs. (4)–(6) of that section were omitted.

Legislation: ITEPA 2003, s. 44, 46A; FA 2014, s. 16;

Cases: *Brady (HMIT) v Hart (trading as Jaclyn Model Agency)* [1985] BTC 373; *Bhadra v Ellam (HMIT)* [1988] BTC 25; *Talentcore Ltd (t/a Team Spirits) v R & C Commrs* [2011] UKUT 423 (TCC); *Oziegbe* [2014] TC 03733; *Thoene* [2016] TC 05207

Tax Reporter: ¶407-500

265 Personal service companies

From 6 April 2000, anti-avoidance provisions apply to prevent workers avoiding tax and National Insurance contributions (NICs) (see 2530) by offering their services through an intermediary, such as a personal service company. The legislation is widely referred to as the IR 35 rules after the number of the 1999 Budget press release in which they were first announced. To assist workers in determining whether they are within the scope of the rules, HMRC will provide an opinion on a contract if submitted together with any relevant details of recent engagements. Details of this service are given on the HMRC website.

Income received by domestic workers, including nannies and butlers, in respect of services provided via an intermediary, are also caught by the intermediaries legislation.

The IR35 legislation was tightened from 6 April 2013 and this will have an impact on individuals who hold an office (an executive or non-executive director) on the board of a company and are paid via a personal service company (PSC). Historically, there was a view that income received by a PSC did not fall within the IR35 legislation and was therefore not treated as employment income subject to PAYE. Broadly, the changes from 6 April 2013 brought individuals who hold an office through a PSC within the scope of the IR35 legislation. So, from 6 April 2013, any payment to a PSC from a third party for the provision of an individual as an 'office holder' will be deemed to be employment income whether the PSC or the individual is registered as the office holder or the engager. This means that HMRC can invoke IR35 and seek recovery of tax under PAYE from the PSC when PAYE has not already been applied. This places office holders in the same position as contractors and other workers that currently have to apply IR35.

Following consultation published at Summer Budget 2015, *Finance Act* 2016 introduces legislation to restrict access to relief for home to work travel and subsistence where a worker:

- personally provides services to another person;

- is employed through an employment intermediary;

- is under (the right of) the supervision, direction or control of any person, in the manner in which they undertake their work;

- (ITEPA 2003, s. 339A, 688B; SI 2003/2682, Ch. 3B).

Broadly, the 'IR35' rules provide that:

(1) where an individual ('the worker') personally performs, or has an obligation personally to perform, services for the purposes of a business carried on by another person ('the client');

(2) the performance of those services by the worker is referable to arrangements involving a third party, rather than referable to a contract between the client and the worker; and

(3) the circumstances are such that, where the services to be performed by the worker under a contract between him and the client, he would be regarded as employed in the employed earner's employment by the client,

then the relevant payments and benefits are treated as emoluments paid to the worker in respect of his or her employment. These rules apply irrespective of whether the client is a person with whom the worker holds any office or employment. Under the rules, a deemed salary payment, subject to tax under PAYE, may fall to be made to the worker on 5 April at the end of the tax year. The tax and NICs due on this deemed payment must be accounted for by 19 April.

To ascertain whether a deemed salary payment falls to be made, and the extent of any such payment, the following procedure should be followed.

Step 1

Find the total amount of all payments and other benefits received by the intermediary in the year in respect of the relevant engagements and reduce that figure by 5%.

Step 2

Add to the result of Step 1 the amount of any 'payments and benefits' received by the worker (or the worker's family: ITEPA 2003 s. 61(3)(b)) in respect of 'relevant engagements' during the tax year, from any person other than the intermediary, where such amounts are not chargeable to income tax as employment income and would be so chargeable if the worker were employed by the client.

This rule ensures that any amounts paid directly to the worker as part of an arrangement to avoid the application of these provisions is caught.

Step 3

Deduct the amount of any expenses met in the year by the intermediary, or met by the worker and reimbursed by the intermediary, that would have been deductible from the emoluments of the employment if the client had employed the worker and the expenses had been met by the worker out of those emoluments. Where the intermediary provides a vehicle for the worker, deduct any mileage allowance that would have been available had the worker been directly employed and provided their own vehicle.

If the result of applying Step 3, or at any later point, is nil or a negative amount, there is no deemed employment payment. Neither, by implication, is there a deductible deemed amount.

Step 4

Deduct the amount of any capital allowances in respect of expenditure incurred by the intermediary that could have been claimed by the worker had he been employed by the client and had incurred the expenditure.

Step 5

Deduct any contributions made in that year for the benefit of the worker by the intermediary to an approved retirement benefit scheme or personal pension plan that if made by an employer for the benefit of an employee would not be chargeable to income tax as income of the employee.

Step 6

Deduct the amount of any employer's NIC paid by the intermediary for the year in respect of the worker.

Step 7

Deduct the amount of any payments and benefits received in the year by the worker from the intermediary:

(a) in respect of which the worker is chargeable to income tax as employment income; and

(b) which do not represent items in respect of which a deduction was made under step 3.

If the result at this point is nil or a negative amount, there is no deemed charge on employment income.

Step 8

Assume that the result of Step 7 represents an amount together with employer's National Insurance contributions on it, and deduct what (on that assumption) would be the amount of those contributions. The result of this 'netting down' is the deemed employment payment.

Example

Zeus and Hera, a married couple, provide consultancy services through a limited company in which they own all the shares. The company's normal accounting date is 31 March. During the tax year ended 5 April 2013, a detailed review of the contracts on which Zeus worked indicates that four out of five could be regarded as 'relevant engagements'. A similar review of Hera's work indicated that two out of four were 'relevant engagements'. The amounts received by the company in respect of these engagements amounted to £60,000 for Zeus' engagements and £40,000 for Hera's. Receipts from

---

non-relevant engagement activity were £35,000. Zeus and Hera have each received salary payments of £25,000 during the year. Zeus and Hera also both have company cars, with a scale charge for private usage of £5,000 each for the year. A summary of the details taken from the company's accounts and returns shows:

Expense	Zeus	Hera	Notes
Salary paid in year	£25,000	£25,000	Paid during year ended 5 April 2013
Motor car – scale charge	£5,000	£5,000	
	£30,000	£30,000	
Employer's Class 1 contributions	£2,400	£2,400	Paid/provided for year ended 5 April 2013
Employer's Class 1A contributions	£690	£690	Paid/provided for year ended 5 April 2013
Travel and subsistence (all allowable)	£9,000	£4,000	Paid during year ended 5 April 2013
Employer's pension scheme contributions	£3,000	£3,000	Paid during year ended 5 April 2013

The computation of the deemed payment/attributable earnings for the year to 5 April 2013 (2012–13) will be as follows:

Step		Zeus £	Hera £	Notes
Step 1	Receipts from relevant engagements	60,000	40,000	
	Less: 5%	(3,000)	(2,000)	
		57,000	38,000	
Step 2	*Add:* other receipts – *not applicable*	–	–	
Step 3	*Less:* allowable expenses			
	• Travel and subsistence	(9,000)	(4,000)	
		48,000	34,000	
Step 4	*Less:* capital allowance – *Not applicable*	–	–	
Step 5	*Less:* employer's pension contributions	(3,000)	(3,000)	
		45,000	31,000	
Step 6	*Less:* employer's NIC paid – Class 1	(2,400)	(2,400)	(a)
	– Class 1A	(690)	(690)	(b)
		41,910	27,910	

Step		Zeus	Hera	Notes
		£	£	
Step 7	*Less:* salary and benefits paid in year	(30,000)	(30,000)	
	Gross deemed amount	11,910	(2,090)	(c)
Step 8	Calculate deemed payment and NIC thereon		*No deemed*	
	• deemed payment 100/113.8 × £11,910 =	10,465	*payment*	(d)
	• employer's NIC 13.8/100 × £10,465 =	1,444		(e)
		11,909		
Step 9	Deemed payment/attributable earnings – treated as paid 5 April 2013 for all PAYE purposes.	10,465		(f)

Notes

(a) Assumes a rate for employer's Class 1 contributions of 13.8% and a threshold of £7,605.

(b) Assumes a rate for employer's Class 1A contributions of 13.8%.

(c) The amount of £11,910 represents the amount of the deemed payment inclusive of employer's Class 1 NICs; the negative result for Hera indicates that there is no deemed amount for the year.

(d) £11,910 is the gross amount of the deemed payment, therefore it represents 113.8% of the deemed payment/attributable earnings (assuming a rate of 13.8% for employer's NICs).

(e) The amount of employer's NIC calculated by this process is payable by the intermediary along with other PAYE liabilities by 19 April 2013.

(f) The amount of the deemed payment (£10,465) is treated for income tax purposes including PAYE as if paid on 5 April 2013; the company must calculate the amount of income due on such a payment and account for it along with the company's other PAYE obligations (including the calculated employer's NIC) by 19 April 2013.

The calculation of the deemed employment payment is made for each tax year in isolation. It follows that if income is taxed as an element in the deemed employment payment in one tax year, and is paid out as taxable earnings in a later tax year, no credit will be given for the tax previously charged under IR35, and the income will be taxed twice. To escape this trap, income which has been taxed under IR35 should be paid out by way of dividend rather than earnings, and relief should be claimed under ITEPA 2003, s. 58.

An IR35 calculator is available on HMRC website (see link below).

Legislation: FA 2000, s. 60 and Sch. 12; ITEPA 2003, Pt. 2, Ch. 8

Cases: *Island Consultants Ltd v R & C Commrs* (2007) Sp C 618; *Jones v Garnett (HMIT)* [2007] UKHL 35; *Dragonfly Consulting Ltd v R & C Commrs* [2008] EWHC 2113 (Ch); *Autoclenz Ltd v Belcher* [2009] EWCA Civ 1046; *Primary Path Ltd v R & C Commrs* [2011] TC 01306; *Slush Puppies Ltd* [2012] TC 02042; *EMS (Independent Accident Management Services) Ltd* [2014] TC 04006

Other Material: IR35: find out if it applies: www.gov.uk/ir35-find-out-if-it-applies; www.gov.uk/guidance/hmrc-tools-and-calculators#ir35-working-through-an-intermediary

Tax Reporter: ¶407-600

267 Managed service companies

Dividend (and indeed any other non-employment) income is deemed to be employment income where individuals provide their services through managed service companies (MSCs) and their income is not already treated as employment income. This means MSCs have to operate and account for PAYE tax and NICs on all payments that individuals receive for services provided through the MSC. If the MSC does not pay the tax and NICs, HMRC will be able to recover them from others, principally the MSC's director and the person who provided the company and management services for the company to the individual.

Broadly, MSCs are personal service companies, often referred to as 'managed personal service companies' or 'composites'.

In a composite company scheme before the FA 2007 changes led to their virtual disappearance, several (typically ten to 20) otherwise unrelated workers were made worker-shareholders of the company. The size of the company was restricted to ensure that profits did not exceed the threshold for the small companies' rate of corporation tax. Each worker usually held a different class of share in the company. This enabled the company to pay different rates of dividend to each worker, and in practice the dividend received would be directly related to the company's income from the end client for work undertaken by that worker.

In a managed personal service company (MPSC) scheme, in contrast to a composite company, there was only one worker per company structure. The MSC scheme provider performed similar functions for MPSCs as for composite companies – it usually provided a director and exercised financial and management control of the company (e.g. operating the bank account, invoicing, preparing accounts and tax returns, etc. leaving the worker simply to provide the service to the end user), typically performing this function for many MPSCs.

The MSC was used to save both tax and NICs. Many contractors working through MSCs had a company paying them a salary of around £5,000, to use up their personal allowance and earn them a deemed contribution record. Because the company typically took on numerous short-term contracts in different places, the worker was also able to claim tax and NIC-free home-to-work travel expenses, as each location was a temporary workplace for that employment. The company paid corporation tax at former 19% on the profit (after deducting the scheme provider's charges), and paid out the net by way of dividend. To the extent that the worker was a basic rate taxpayer, there was no further tax to pay, and for higher rate earners the effective tax rate was only 25% on the dividend received. Crucially, dividends are classed as investment income, not earnings, so NIC liability did not arise.

HMRC believed that most of these MSC schemes involved working arrangements that fell foul of the IR35 rules (see 265), but when faced with nearly a quarter of a million such companies HMRC's compliance teams could not cope with challenging them. Some of the workers were from overseas and had left the UK by the time questions could be asked of their companies, and others simply put their companies into liquidation in order to avoid being challenged.

The anti-avoidance provisions introduced by FA 2007 did not try to change the status of the workers, who are always employees and/or directors and therefore 'employed earners'. Instead, they deem any non-employment payments (in effect, dividends) made by a MSC to be earnings for NIC and PAYE purposes. Unlike IR35, the rules create the liability at the time of payment, not at the end of the tax year. Note that the PAYE liability was backdated to 6 April 2007, but the NIC regulations could not be laid before Royal Assent to the Act, so they applied only from 6 August 2007.

They also solve the problem of runaway workers and liquidated employers by creating transfer of debt rules that enable HMRC to pursue the scheme providers for any unpaid liabilities. It is hardly surprising that MSC schemes closed down quickly when their liabilities were no longer avoidable (or indeed easy to evade for the unscrupulous).

Legislation: ITEPA 2003, s. 61A–61J, 688A; FA 2007, Sch. 3; *Income Tax (Pay as You Earn) (Amendment No. 3) Regulations* 2007 (SI 2007/2296); *Income Tax (Pay as You Earn) (Amendment No. 2) Regulations* 2007 (SI 2007/2069); *Social Security (Contributions) (Amendment No. 5) Regulations* 2007 (SI 2007/2068); *Social Security Contributions (Managed Service Companies) Regulations* 2007 (SI 2007/2070); *Social Security Contributions and Benefits Act 1992 (Modification of Section 4A) Order* 2007 (SI 2007/2071)

Case: *Christianuyi Ltd* [2016] TC 05045

Other Material: HMRC: *MSC Guidance: Chapter 9 and Section 688A ITEPA and Transfer of Debt: MSCs*

Tax Reporter: ¶408-550

Taxable earnings

273   Taxable earnings

Under the provisions of ITEPA 2003, the charge to tax on employment income is a charge to tax on general earnings and specific employment income. 'Taxable earnings' and 'taxable specific income' are two labels used to identify income at various stages from which it arises to when it becomes chargeable to tax in a particular tax year.

Legislation: ITEPA 2003, s. 10(2)

Cases: *Hochstrasser (HMIT) v Mayes* [1960] AC 376; *Pritchard (HMIT) v Arundale* [1972] Ch 229; *Hamblett v Godfrey (HMIT)* [1987] BTC 83; *Shilton v Wilmshurst (HMIT)* [1991] BTC 66; *Mairs (HMIT) v Haughey* [1993] BTC 339; *Wilcock (HMIT) v Eve* [1994] BTC 490

Tax Reporter: ¶416-000

274   Earnings

'Earnings' means:

* any salary, wages or fee;
* any gratuity or other profit or incidental benefit of any kind obtained by the employee if it is money or money's worth; or
* anything else that constitutes an emolument of the employment.

'Money's worth' means something that is of direct monetary value to the employee, or capable of being converted into money or something of direct monetary value to the employee.

The most obvious forms of earnings arising from an office or employment are the salary, wages, fees or commissions payable, in cash or by cheque. Other receipts or non-cash benefits in kind may be directly regarded as emoluments and therefore taxable; particular regard should be given to:

* gifts, awards and prizes (see 285);
* rewards for future services;

- restrictive covenants (see 283);

- contractual entitlement (see 277);

- receipts from third parties (see 284 and 285);

- tips (see 285);

- non-cash benefits (see 288);

- reductions in wages in return for benefits (see 279); and

- discharging an obligation of the employee (see 292).

As far as non-cash benefits in kind are concerned, from 2016–17, all benefits are taxable irrespective of the level of an individual's earnings; previously, certain benefits were treated as emoluments for employees earning at a rate of £8,500 a year or more (including benefits in kind and expenses not covered by a dispensation) and for directors (see 382ff.) only.

For the treatment of reimbursed expenses and round-sum allowances, see 322.

A receipt that is remuneration for future services may be taxable despite the element of non-recurrence or the fact that the employee did not expect it (see 285).

Payments made to induce a person to enter into employment are taxable if they represent an advance of salary.

Legislation: ITEPA 2003, s. 62

Cases: *Jarrold (HMIT) v Boustead* (1964) 41 TC 701; *Riley (HMIT) v Coglan* (1967) 44 TC 481; *Pritchard (HMIT) v Arundale* (1971) 47 TC 680; *Glantre Engineering Ltd v Goodhand (HMIT)* [1982] BTC 396; *O'Leary v McKinlay (HMIT)* [1991] BTC 37; *R & C Commrs v PA Holdings Ltd* [2011] BTC 705

Tax Reporter: ¶412-020

277   Contractual entitlement

The fact that an employee is contractually entitled to a payment is not conclusive in establishing that the payment was either taxable or non-taxable.

See further 284 and 285.

Cases: *Denny v Reed (HMIT)* (1933) 18 TC 254; *Jarrold (HMIT) v Boustead* [1964] 1 WLR 1357

Tax Reporter: ¶412-400

279   Reductions in wages in return for benefits

A salary sacrifice arrangement is an agreement between an employer and an employee to change the terms of the employment contract to reduce the employee's entitlement to cash pay. This sacrifice of cash entitlement is usually made in return for some form of non-cash benefit. Salary sacrifice can be financially beneficial for both employer and employee. For example, when part of an employee's remuneration shifts from cash – on which tax and National Insurance contributions are due – to non-cash benefits that are wholly or partially exempt.

From 6 April 2016, *Finance Act* 2015 introduced a new exemption for expenses which are paid or reimbursed by an employer where the employee would be due a deduction under ITEPA 2003, Pt. 5, Ch. 2 or 5 (see 1990A). It also provides an exemption in respect of benefits treated as earnings under the benefits code for which there is a deductible amount under ITEPA 2003, Ch. 3 (see 383A). Neither of these exemptions apply if the payment or benefit is provided as part of a relevant salary sacrifice arrangement. This is to prevent the new exemption being exploited in conjunction with salary sacrifice arrangements and used to reduce liability to NIC.

Legislation: ITEPA 2003, Pt. 4, Ch. 7A

Case: *Heaton (HMIT) v Bell* [1970] AC 728

Tax Reporter: ¶412-900

283   Restrictive covenants

The provisions relating to the taxation of payments for entering into restrictive covenants currently apply where an individual holds, has held or is about to hold an office or employment, and he gives in connection with his holding of the employment an undertaking the tenor or effect of which is to restrict him in the conduct of his activities. It is immaterial that the undertaking may be qualified, or even unenforceable.

In the situations above, any payment made in respect of the undertaking, or its total or partial fulfilment, either to the individual or to any other person, which would not otherwise be treated as an emolument of the office or employment (see 273), is so treated, and tax under the charge on employment income is chargeable for the tax year in which it is paid.

The circumstances in which HMRC do not charge tax under the above provisions in respect of certain undertakings made by individuals under a financial settlement when their employment is terminated are set out in a statement of practice. The statement makes it clear that where sums are paid in settlement of financial claims relating to the employment which the employee could have pursued in law, and the employee accepts that the sums payable satisfy claims and legal rights to which he may be entitled under the terms of his employment or statutory provisions, then a charge does not arise. However, a charge under that provision may arise where an agreement contains specific provisions as to the employee's conduct or activities which involve an undertaking going beyond the settlement of existing claims and rights which he may have against the employer.

Payments caught by the charge are deductible by the employer (see 2030).

Legislation: ITEPA 2003, s. 225, 226

Case: *Vaughan-Neil v IR Commrs* [1979] 1 WLR 1283

Other Material: SP 3/96, *Sections 225–226 ITEPA 2003: Termination payments made in settlement of employment claims*

Tax Reporter: ¶423-500

284   Receipts from third parties

The legislation now found in ITEPA 2003, Pt. 7A (employment income provided through third parties) and commonly referred to as the 'disguised remuneration' provisions was first announced in the Budget of 24 March 2010 in the following terms:

> 'The government will be taking action to prevent attempts to avoid tax and NICs through the use of employee benefit trusts and other arrangements to disguise payments of remuneration and intends to introduce anti-avoidance legislation to take effect from 6 April 2011.'

In the Emergency Budget on 22 June 2010, the then new coalition government confirmed its intention to bring forward the new legislation and confirmed also that employer-financed retirement benefit schemes (EFRBS) would come within the scope of the measures. Draft legislation and explanatory notes were then published on 9 December 2010. As can be seen from the above announcement, one of the main targets of the disguised remuneration provisions was the use of employee benefit trusts to defer or avoid income tax liabilities for employees. The purpose of an employee benefit trust is generally to provide employees and directors with specific kinds of benefit such as loans, shares in their employing company, pensions and other retirement benefits, accident benefits or health care benefits, but HMRC had become increasingly concerned by perceived widespread abuse of such trusts, in particular the use of employee benefit trusts where the employee was paid a relatively small amount by way of salary but then granted a loan that may never be repaid. Of necessity, the legislation to prevent such abuse had to be both complex and wide-ranging, but much concern was expressed, when the draft legislation was published, by certain professional bodies and other interested parties, that many 'innocent' arrangements could fall within the provisions. Despite the draftsman's attempts to exclude such arrangements from the scope of the provisions, there is still the possibility of unintended consequences. This is because of the way that the legislation has been drafted, i.e. all encompassing, but subject to numerous specific exclusions.

In summary, the disguised remuneration provisions impose an income tax charge where:

- there are arrangements (known as 'relevant arrangements') which are in essence for rewards or loans to be provided to past, present or future employees and various other associated persons;

- a 'relevant third party' takes a 'relevant step'; and

- it is reasonable to suppose that the relevant step is taken pursuant to the arrangements, or that there is some other connection between the relevant step and the arrangements.

A 'relevant third party' includes any other person, other than the employer, but will also include the employer if it is acting as trustee. The exclusion for employers extends to companies in the same group as the employer, again, unless acting as trustee.

A 'relevant step' is any of the three following activities:

- the earmarking of a sum of money, or an asset, by a relevant third party, with a view to taking another relevant step in the future;

- the making available of an asset to a relevant person in a way that is substantially the same as if the asset had been transferred.

A charge under these provisions arises when a relevant step is taken (not when anybody actually benefits). The value of the relevant step counts as employment income in the hands of the employee (under PAYE). That value is taken to be:

- where the relevant step involves a loan or cash payment, the amount of the loan or cash payment; and

- where no money is directly involved, the market value of the asset which is the subject of the relevant step.

Entertainment provided by a third party to employees is not taxable on the employees (see 383).

For the tax treatment of gifts and tips, etc. see 285.

Legislation: ITEPA 2003, Pt. 7A

Cases: *Blakiston v Cooper* (1909) 5 TC 347; *Moorhouse (HMIT) v Dooland* (1954) 36 TC 1; *Wright v Boyce (HMIT)* (1958) 38 TC 160

Tax Reporter: ¶412-310

285 Gifts, awards, prizes and tips

A gift received from an employer or third party by an employee is not automatically tax-free. It is taxable if it is received as a reward for services past, present or future (or simply, if it is provided by reason of the individual's employment by way of voucher, see 318 and 382). Some factors of relevance in deciding whether a voluntary payment, benefit or perquisite may escape tax are as follows.

- Whether, from the recipient's standpoint, it accrues to him as a reward for services.

- If his contract of employment entitles him to receive the payment, there is a strong ground for holding that it accrues by virtue of the employment and is therefore remuneration.

- The fact that a voluntary payment is of a periodic or recurrent character affords a further, though less cogent, ground for the same conclusion.

- If it is made in circumstances which show it is given by way of a present or testimonial on grounds personal to the recipient (e.g. a collection made for a vicar of a given parish because he is so poor), then the proper conclusion is likely to be that it is not a reward for services and is therefore not taxable (but see 286 and 420 re sporting testimonials).

Awards made under most staff suggestion schemes are tax free (ITEPA 2003, s. 321 and 322).

Long service awards

Tax is not charged in respect of certain awards made to directors and employees as testimonials to mark long service. Such awards must take the form of tangible articles or shares in an employing company (or another group company), costing the company up to £50 per year of service; the recipient must have completed at least 20 years' service and have had no similar award within the previous ten years.

Taxed award schemes

Employers who provide non-cash incentive awards and prizes (e.g. cameras or holidays), and most of those who provide such prizes for employees of third parties, can operate HMRC's 'taxed award scheme'. Such schemes:

- allow the provider of the incentive to pay the tax due on the award, so that the incentive for the recipient is not blunted by having to pay tax on it; and

- provide an economical means of collecting the tax due (in bulk, instead of from individual recipients).

Before an incentive campaign begins, the provider enters into a contract with HMRC's *Incentive Award Unit* (for the address and contact details, see HMRC *Employment Income Manual* at EIM11240) to pay the tax on the total value of the awards to be made. The provider can pay tax at different rates: there are separate contracts for different rate schemes.

The amount of the tax payable is worked out on the grossed-up value (see 223) of the award to the recipient. Providers must give recipients details of the tax paid so that they can complete their tax returns, or claim repayment if appropriate. Providers give HMRC details of recipients so that any higher-rate tax can be collected.

Most awards under taxed award schemes are suitable for inclusion in a PAYE settlement agreement (see 2356) instead of a taxed award scheme. However, a third party who provides awards to the employees of another and who wishes to pay the employees' tax bill must use a taxed award scheme.

An information pack on the scheme can be obtained from the Incentive Award Unit.

Christmas parties and gifts provided by third parties

Gifts made by a third party to any employee are not taxable provided the cost does not exceed £250 in any tax year: if the cost is, say, £251, all of the £251 is assessable. The same concession allows employers to provide one or more annual events at a cost of up to £150 per head without the employees incurring tax liability in respect of the benefit.

Tips and service charges

Tips are generally part of an employee's taxable income in the same way as his other earnings (see 284). However, not all employees return full details of the tips they receive. Therefore, HMRC may estimate the tips earned on the basis of the facts available to ensure that the correct amount of tax is paid. Before doing this, HMRC establish first who is in a position to receive them. Wherever possible they negotiate agreed figures with the employees concerned or with their representative where large numbers are employed at any one establishment.

For the PAYE position in relation to tips, see 2384.

Legislation: ITEPA 2003, s. 264 (Annual parties and functions), 270 and 324 (Small gifts from third parties), 323 (Long service awards), 703 (PAYE settlement agreements)

Cases: *Reed (HMIT) v Seymour* (1927) 11 TC 625; *Calvert (HMIT) v Wainwright* (1947) 27 TC 475; *Moorhouse (HMIT) v Dooland* (1954) 36 TC 1; *Ball (HMIT) v Johnson* (1971) 47 TC 155; *Moore v Griffiths (HMIT)* (1972) 48 TC 338; *Wicks v Firth (HMIT)* [1982] BTC 402

Tax Reporter: ¶412-600

286 Sporting testimonials

Some professional sportsmen, such as footballers and cricketers, receive money from testimonial matches.

The money usually comes from a public collection at that particular match, the player concerned usually receiving the gate money less expenses.

From 6 April 2017, all income from sporting testimonials is subject to income tax. A one-off exemption from income tax of £100,000 applies for income which is neither contractual nor customary (ITEPA 2003, s. 226E and 306B, as inserted by *Finance Act* 2016).

The charge to income tax and limited exemption apply with effect in relation to a sporting testimonial payment made out of money raised by a sporting testimonial where the sporting testimonial was made public on or after 25 November 2015, and the payment is made out of money raised by one or more relevant events or activities which take place on or after 6 April 2017. This means that for a testimonial year announced on or after 25 November 2015 with events taking place, say, between September 2016 and September 2017, only the payments from events taking place after 5 April 2017 can be taken into account for the exemption to apply. The payments for events taking place before 6 April 2017 will not be subject to the charge to tax under s. 226E.

For payments prior to 6 April 2017, where there was either a contractual right or a customary expectation that an employee who is or has been a sportsperson receives a sporting testimonial, the income fell within the charge to tax as earnings under ITEPA 2003, s. 62 and liable to Class 1 NICs no matter who arranged the testimonial. However, by concession (within HMRC guidance), where there was no entitlement to the testimonial match, and no custom existed in respect of it, then the proceeds were not earnings within ITEPA 2003, s. 62 and the guidance suggested that this would usually be the case where the match was organised by a testimonial committee independent of the club.

Legislation: ITEPA 2003, s. 226E, 306B

288 Non-cash benefits

Most non-cash benefits are charged to tax under the benefits code as set out in ITEPA 2003, Pt. 3, Ch. 2–11. From 2016–17, the benefits code applies equally to all employees irrespective of their level of earnings (previously, only certain chapters applied to employees earning less than £8,500 p.a., see 312).

However, to the extent that any benefit in kind is not chargeable under the benefits code (where for tax years up to 2015–16, an employee was a lower paid employee), a charge can/could still arise under the general charge on employment income provisions as earnings in money or money's worth (see 274).

'Money's worth' means those things that can be converted into money by the employee.

The taxable amount is the amount of money into which the employee can lawfully convert the benefit, whether or not he actually does so. It follows that if a restriction is placed upon the use of the benefit by the employer so that the employee cannot convert it into money without being in breach of the condition, he is not taxed on it, provided the restriction is not a sham, e.g. the gift to the employee could only be sold to a scrap merchant. Speaking of the position of employees earning at a rate of less than £8,500 p.a., Lord Reid declared in a House of Lords case:

> 'In my judgment the recipient of a perquisite other than a sum of money can be assessed and can only be assessed, on the amount of money which he could have obtained by some lawful means by the use or in place of the perquisite.
>
> I say by lawful means because I see no ground for HMRC being entitled to disregard a genuine condition restricting the recipient's right to use or dispose of the perquisite. But of course if any restrictive condition is a sham or inserted simply to defeat the claims of HMRC it can be disregarded.'

Payment in the form of a tradable asset is a payment by the employer for the purposes of PAYE (see 2384).

Interaction between earnings charge and benefits code

As a general rule, where a benefit may be taxed both as earnings and as an amount treated as earnings under the benefits code, it is taxed first as earnings on the basis of its realisable value and then, if the cost to the provider exceeds this amount, the excess is taxable under the benefits code (ITEPA 2003, s. 64(1) and (2)), subject to special rules if the benefit is living accommodation.

Concept of a 'fair bargain'

Something which is a 'fair bargain' between the employer and the employee is not a 'benefit'. Fair bargain applies where an employee has received goods or services from their employer at exactly the same cost, terms and conditions as a member of the public or other independent third party dealing with the employer on an arms-length basis. When this occurs, there is no benefit in kind. However, Government's policy intention is that the principle of 'fair bargain' does not apply to benefits chargeable to income tax within ITEPA 2003, Pt. 3, Ch. 3–9 because, for those benefits, the amount of the taxable benefit is calculated by reference to the specific charging rules and any payments made by the employee are deducted from that charge. *Finance Act* 2016 contains provisions to put beyond doubt that the fair bargain principle does not apply to benefits within ITEPA 2003, Pt. 3, Ch. 3–9 (which covers beneficial loans, employer-provided living accommodation, and company cars and vans).

Legislation: ITEPA 2003, s. 62, 64

Cases: *Laidler v Perry (HMIT)* (1965) 42 TC 351; *Heaton (HMIT) v Bell* (1969) 46 TC 211

Tax Reporter: ¶412-850

292   Discharging an employee's obligation: pecuniary liabilities

As noted at 288, a benefit is charged as earnings if it is money or money's worth, which includes things that are of direct monetary value to the employee.

Where an employer discharges a debt owed by an employee to a third party, the employer's payment is of direct monetary value to the employee because he no longer has to pay the third party. This is known as the pecuniary liability principle because the employer bears the employee's pecuniary liability. The payment by the employer counts as money's worth under ITEPA 2003, s. 62 and will be taxed as earnings if it comes from the employment. The employee is taxable on the cost to the employer.

The same principle applies where the employer releases the employee from an obligation owed to the employer. If the employer discharges a debt of the employee in respect of something from which the employee is entitled to an exemption, such as living accommodation (see exceptions to charge in 314), those exceptions still apply and the employee is only charged, at the cost to the employer, on payments to which the exemption does not apply.

Example 1

In order to induce the employee to stay in the house in which he was living, the company paid his various outgoings. It was held that he was correctly assessed on an amount equal to the cost to the employer of discharging the employee's debts.

Example 2

An employee agreed with her employer that, while she was away from work on a nine-month course of study, her employer would advance to her, on loan, the pay that she would have earned had she been working. The arrangement was that the loan need not be repaid if she remained with her employer for a further 18 months upon her return. She did so. The loan was cancelled and it was held that she had been correctly assessed on the amount of the loan.

Cases: *Nicoll (HMIT) v Austin* (1935) 19 TC 531; *Clayton (HMIT) v Gothorp* (1971) 47 TC 168; *Richardson (HMIT) v Worrall* [1985] BTC 508; *Willey* [2016] TC 04913

Tax Reporter: ¶412-140

293   Medical treatment and insurance

If an employee or director undergoes medical treatment or diagnosis and the employer reimburses the employee, or settles his personal medical bill, the amount reimbursed, etc. is taxable (see 292). See below regarding a new exemption for recommended medical insurance (as introduced in *Finance Act* 2014).

However, if the employer contracts direct with the provider of the medical services, the cash equivalent of the benefit is the cost incurred by the employer in providing the treatment, less any amount which the employee or director makes good (see 388).

However, there is no such benefit where:

- the employee is provided with medical treatment outside the UK (including in-patient treatment); and

- the need for the treatment arises while the employee is outside the UK for the purpose of performing the duties of his employment.

'Medical treatment' includes all forms of treatment for, and all procedures for diagnosing, any physical or mental ailment, infirmity or defect.

One health screening and one medical check-up per employee per year may be treated as exempt from the charge to income tax and NICs.

For tax years up to and including 2015–16, no taxable benefit arose for lower paid employees (see 382ff.), as conversion into cash was not possible (see 288).

Recommended medical treatment

From 1 January 2015, a tax and NIC-free exemption allows employers to meet the cost of recommended medical treatment for employees, up to an annual cap of £500 per employee. Medical treatment will be 'recommended' where it is provided in accordance with a recommendation from an occupational health service in order to help an employee return to work after a period of absence due to ill-health or injury.

Medical insurance

Employers commonly contribute to medical insurance schemes for their employees. Members of the employee's family or household are sometimes covered. Any premium paid by the employer in respect of a policy under which the *employer* is the insured person is not a benefit chargeable on the employee.

However, a premium paid by the employer in respect of a policy under which the *employee* (or a member of his family or household) is the insured person, less any part of the premium which the employee makes good (see 388), constitutes a chargeable benefit. (For tax years up to and including 2015–16, the benefit was not taxable for a lower paid employee, as conversion into cash was not possible: see 288.) However, there is no such taxable benefit where the employee, etc. is provided with medical treatment outside the UK and the need for it arises while the employee is outside the UK for the purpose of performing the duties of his employment.

Legislation: ITEPA 2003, s. 325; FA 2014, s. 12; *Income Tax (Recommended Medical Treatment) Regulations* 2014 (SI 2014/3227); *Income Tax (Exemption of Minor Benefits) (Revocation) Regulations* 2009 (SI 2009/695)

Other Material: Revenue Interpretation, Inland Revenue *Tax Bulletin*, May 1993, p. 74

Tax Reporter: ¶437-900

294 Sickness, maternity, paternity, adoption and disability payments

Employees are taxed under the charge on employment income provisions of ITEPA 2003 on sick pay or disability pay (paid to them or to members of their family or household) where such payments have been arranged with the employer. Statutory maternity pay (SMP), ordinary statutory paternity pay (OSPP), additional statutory paternity pay (ASPP) (from 3 April 2011); statutory adoption pay (SAP) and statutory sick pay (SSP) paid by the employer are also taxable under these charging provisions.

Legislation: ITEPA 2003, s. 221, 660

Tax Reporter: ¶420-050

298 Relocation expenses and benefits

Certain relocation expenses and benefits paid on behalf of, reimbursed to, or provided for employees who are obliged to move with their job or in order to start a new job are exempt from tax.

Specified costs incurred in the tax year of the move or the following tax year are exempt up to a limit of £8,000. Eligible benefits include those in respect of disposal, acquisition and the new residence itself (or abortive acquisition), transport of belongings, travelling and subsistence. PAYE need not be applied to relocation packages, even if the £8,000 limit is exceeded – the benefits will instead be reported in the P11D (or P9D). If HMRC are satisfied that flat rate allowances do no more than reimburse employees' eligible expenses, they may be paid gross in similar fashion. Strictly, an interest-free bridging loan is not an eligible expense but, if the rest of the employee's relocation package does not use up the £8,000 exemption the balance can be converted into a number of days' relief by which the income tax charge on the beneficial loan (see 406) is reduced. Relief for international travel continues to be available under other provisions (see 1574).

For guaranteed selling price schemes operated by employers in respect of employees' homes, see 388.

Legislation: ITEPA 2003, Pt. 4, Ch. 7

Tax Reporter: ¶433-850

302 Incidental overnight expenses

To reduce the burden on employers of identifying and reporting to HMRC what would otherwise be taxable expenses, certain minor personal expenditure are exempt from tax. The exemption applies to amounts of personal expenditure up to £5 per night in the UK and £10 for each night overseas. If this limit is exceeded, the whole amount is taxable. Thus, in most cases, it is still necessary to analyse the receipts submitted with employees' expenses claims. This is unfortunate, given that one of the stated purposes of the legislation was to reduce such compliance costs. Incidental overnight expenses paid to an employee who is away from home on a training course may be paid tax-free to the same extent as those paid when an employee is away on business.

Legislation: ITEPA 2003, s. 240 and 241

Other Material: HMRC *Employment Income Manual* EIM02710ff.

Tax Reporter: ¶432-900

304   Work-related training

Certain work-related training may be provided free of tax. The exemption applies both to that funded by an employer and that funded by a third party.

To qualify for the exemption, the training must be 'work-related'. This covers any training course or other activity designed to impart, instil, improve or reinforce any knowledge or skills or personal qualities which are, or are likely to be useful to the employee in performing the duties of any 'relevant employments' or which will qualify or better qualify the employee to undertake any relevant employment or such charitable or voluntary activities which could be undertaken in connection with the relevant employment. An employment is a 'relevant employment' if it is the employee's current job or a job which he is to hold with his employer or a person 'connected' with his employer.

The expenditure covered by the exemption is limited to the cost of providing the training plus any 'related costs', such as the cost associated with an assessment or obtaining a qualification.

A number of specific exclusions from the exemption ensure that it is restricted to genuine work-related training. For example, the exemption is unavailable to the extent that the 'training' is actually for recreation, entertainment, reward or offered as an inducement. Activity which is partly work-related training and partly recreation is apportioned.

The transfer of assets under the guise of work-related training is also excluded from the exemption, except where, for example, an employee is provided with stationery, books or other written material, audio or video tapes and compact or floppy disks as part of the work-related training.

Incidental overnight expenses in connection with the training are tax-free to the same degree as those paid to an employee away on a business trip (see 302).

Legislation: ITEPA 2003, s. 240, 250

Tax Reporter: ¶433-500

308 Miscellaneous exemptions and concessions

The following do not constitute taxable earnings for employees or directors:

- employers' contributions to approved retirement benefit schemes, etc. or personal pension schemes;
- priority share allocations (see 438);
- cash in lieu of miners' free coal, or the free coal itself;
- awards in respect of long-service or staff suggestions (see 285);
- limited exemption for sporting testimonials (see 286);
- financial assistance, etc. for travel either: from home to work for the severely disabled; or when public transport is disrupted; or when employees are occasionally required to work until at least 9 p.m.; or for offshore oil and gas, etc. workers travelling to and from the mainland (see 1580 and 1994); or for members of the armed forces (see 318); or for additional travelling and subsistence costs for 'away' jobs, etc. (see 2000);
- clergymen's reimbursed/settled council tax (or other statutory amounts) if the premises belong to the charity or organisation, etc. and lower-paid clergymen's reimbursed/settled heating, cleaning or similar expenses;
- costs either reimbursed, etc. in respect of work-related training (see 304) or incurred by an employer with a view to retraining present or past employees (see 2065);
- scholarship income, including certain payments for attending sandwich courses; sponsorship by the Home Office for training as a trainee probation officer on a two-year postgraduate course was, in one case, held to be within this exemption;
- a pension, lump sum, etc. to be given on an employee's death or retirement to a member of his family or household and pensions in respect of awards of the Victoria Cross or various other medals, etc.;
- grants or resettlement payments, etc. made to individuals ceasing to be MPs or MEPs;

- free or subsidised canteen meals (see 412);

- employer-provided workplace nurseries (see 409);

- vouchers exchangeable for the use of sports or recreational facilities (see 318);

- small gifts by third parties (see 285);

- employers' expenditure on certain social events (see 285);

- incidental overnight expenses of up to £5 per night in the UK, or £10 per night outside the UK paid by the employer (see 302);

- mobile telephones (see 415);

- the provision of routine health checks (see 293);

- uniforms provided as a necessary part of employment duties;

- works bus services (see 417);

- the provision of certain computer equipment for use by the employee (see 416);

- provision of cycles and cyclists' safety equipment (see 418);

- small amounts of private use of items provided by the employer for use in the employee's work (see 396); and

- contributions by employers towards additional household costs incurred by employees who work some or all of the time at home. For payments of up to £4 per week, no supporting evidence is required to obtain the income tax exemption. For payments of more than £4 per week, supporting evidence is required (see 383).

See also 383.

Legislation: ITEPA 2003, s. 242, 243, 244, 290, 291, 306, 306B, 307, 320, 638

Tax Reporter: ¶437-450

Benefits

312 All-employee charge on benefits

From 6 April 2016, all benefits dealt with by specific legislation are taxable (or exempt), irrespective of the level of earnings of the employee or office holder. This does not affect the charge under general provisions where benefits can be directly regarded as earnings (see 273ff.).

For tax years up to and including 2015–16, only certain benefits were taxable (or exempt) on all employees regardless of their level of earnings. Other specific provisions applied only to benefits received by employees earning £8,500 p.a. or more (P11D employees) and directors (see 382ff.). The relevant parts of the benefits code which applied only to P11D employees and which did not apply to employees earning less that £8,500 p.a. were as follows:

ITEPA 2003, Pt. 3:

- Ch. 3 (taxable benefits: expenses payments);
- Ch. 6 (taxable benefits: cars, vans and related benefits);
- Ch. 7 (taxable benefits: loans);
- Ch. 10 (taxable benefits: residual liability to charge).

A charge could, however, still arise for lower paid employees on any benefit in kind which constituted earnings in 'money's worth' (of direct monetary value to the employee) (see 288).

As noted at 288, something which is a 'fair bargain' between the employer and the employee is not a 'benefit'. However, government's policy intention is that the principle of 'fair bargain' does not apply to benefits chargeable to income tax within ITEPA 2003, Pt. 3, Ch. 3–9 because, for those benefits, the amount of the taxable benefit is calculated by reference to the specific charging rules and any payments made by the employee are deducted from that charge. *Finance Act* 2016 clarifies that the concept of 'fair bargain' does not apply to certain taxable benefits in kind where the charge is based on tax rules specifying how the cash equivalent of that benefit should be calculated, including beneficial loans, employer-provided living accommodation, and company cars and vans.

Legislation: ITEPA 2003, Pt. 3

314 Living accommodation

A director or employee, or a member of his family or household (see 386) who is provided with accommodation, such as a company house or flat, rent-free or at a nominal rent, is generally liable to tax on it under the provisions of ITEPA 2003, Pt. 3, Ch. 5 (irrespective of his rate of pay). The main charge is based on the greater of the 'annual value' and rent paid by the 'person providing the accommodation' less, in either case, any sums made good by the employee. The 'annual value' is usually the gross rateable value of the property, adjusted for Scottish property, but is the open market rental for property outside the UK or property rented from a connected person.

Note that the charge is avoided if the employee pays rent of an amount at least equal to the benefit otherwise computed under these provisions.

Where a property is provided as living accommodation to more than one employee or director in the same period, the amounts chargeable on each is reduced so that the total does not exceed the amount which would have been chargeable had the property been provided as living accommodation to a single employee.

The concept of 'fair bargain' (see 288) does not apply to employer-provided living accommodation (ITEPA 2003, s. 97(1A)).

Exceptions

There is no charge to tax in the following circumstances.

- It is necessary for the proper performance of the employee's duties that he resides in the accommodation. It must be the nature of the duties of his employment that make it necessary for him to reside there (e.g. a lighthouse keeper) and not just a condition imposed by his employer. This exception, sometimes called 'representative occupation', does not apply to directors.

- The accommodation is provided for the better performance of the duties of his employment, and his is one of the kinds of employment in the case of which it is customary for employers to provide living accommodation for employees: e.g. hostel wardens. In deciding whether the practice is customary, statistical evidence, the time for which the practice has continued and whether it is generally accepted are factors to be considered. This exception does not apply to directors.

- There being a special threat to his security, special security arrangements are in force and he resides in the accommodation as part of those arrangements, e.g. the prime minister's occupation of 10 Downing Street.

- The employer is an individual and the accommodation is provided in the normal course of his domestic, family or personal relationships, e.g. to a domestic servant.

- The accommodation is provided by a local authority (see 5800) on terms no more favourable than those on other accommodation it provides, e.g. a council house for a council employee.

- The accommodation is provided temporarily by way of subsistence for an MP, member of the Scottish Parliament or the devolved assemblies for Wales and Northern Ireland, or other person holding an office or position within the *Ministerial and other Salaries Act* 1975, or to a member of that person's family or household.

Expensive accommodation

In addition to the standard charge above, there is a further charge where the cost to the employer exceeds £75,000. Here, the charge is the excess multiplied by the 'official rate of interest' (at the beginning of the tax year: see 406) less any excess rent. HMRC do not seek an additional charge under these provisions where the main charge is calculated on the basis of the market rental.

The cost is the actual cost to the employer, not the value of the property when it is occupied by the employee except, broadly, where the employer owned the property throughout the six years ending with the employee's first occupation. Each property can be considered separately for the purposes of the £75,000 test.

In ascertaining the cost of providing the accommodation, any improvement expenditure must be added to the acquisition cost. From this may be deducted any sums reimbursed by the tenant. The figure in respect of excess rent is the amount by which the rent paid by the employee is greater than the value to him of the accommodation as determined under the general charge (i.e. 'annual value').

Example

Sam, on 6 April 2003, took up residence in a house provided by his employer. His employer bought the property in July 1997 for £300,000 and installed a sauna at a further cost of £10,000. Sam pays rent that is £5,000 in excess of the annual value.

Thus the cost of provision is £300,000 + £10,000 = £310,000.

As the official rate of interest on 6 April 2016 is 3.0%, the additional charge for 2016–17 is £2,050 ((£310,000 − 75,000) × 3.0%) − £5,000).

A charge may also arise in respect of other expenses connected with the accommodation, e.g. rates, heating, provision of furniture, etc. (see 398).

Legislation: ITEPA 2003, Pt. 3, Ch. 5, s. 108; *Taxes (Interest Rate) (Amendment) Regulations* 2015 (SI 2015/411)

Cases: *Vertigan v Brady (HMIT)* [1988] BTC 99; *Stones v Hall (HMIT)* [1988] BTC 323; *Tennant v Smith* [1892] AC 150

Other Material: ESC A56, *Benefits in kind; the tax treatment of accommodation in Scotland provided for employees*

Tax Reporter: ¶414-500

318   Vouchers and credit cards

Where a voucher other than a 'cash voucher' (see 320) is provided for an employee by reason of his employment, there is generally a charge on the employee (although some exemptions apply – for example where the voucher is for the provision of a benefit that would, if provided directly, be tax-free). It may arise in the tax year in which the expense is incurred or the voucher is received or used but it is reduced by amounts the employee reimburses or amounts deductible if the employee had incurred the expense himself.

A benefit received by an employee (whatever his annual pay) through the use of a credit card or credit-token is also taxed as an emolument. It arises in the tax year in which the card or token is used but it is reduced by amounts deductible if the employee had incurred the expense himself or amounts he reimburses. The definition of 'credit-token' refers to a card, token, document or other thing given to a person by another person who undertakes:

- that on the production of it (whether or not some other action is also required) he will supply money, goods and services (or any of them) on credit; or

- that where, on the production of it to a third party (whether or not some other action is also required), the third party supplies money, goods and services (or any of them), he will pay the third party for them (whether or not taking any discount or commission).

In either case, the liability of the employee will be the cost to the employer (or other person bearing the cost) of providing the voucher, token and goods/services obtained. If, as a result of its use, the user obtains money or goods which are tradable (or the voucher itself is tradable), the appropriate amounts are also brought within the PAYE scheme (see 2384); if the employee does not reimburse the tax to the employer within 30 days of the deemed payment in point, that tax is treated as an additional PAYE income of the employee.

Use of a credit token or voucher by a relation of the employee is treated as if it were use by the employee.

Exclusions

The rules do not apply where a voucher or credit-token is exchangeable for the right to make use of most types of in-house (or shared-employer) sporting or recreational facilities or is provided by a person other than the employer to obtain alternative entertainment for the employee. Nor are they applicable where a voucher or token is used to provide parking (including parking for cycles and motor cycles) at or near the workplace. There are also exemptions for certain travel vouchers, warrants for particular journeys and allowances and payments for travel or leave by members of the armed forces. There is no charge on certain meal vouchers (see 412 and 2000). See also 302 regarding incidental overnight expenses.

HMRC have the power to make regulations to remove from a tax charge a voucher or credit token used to provide an otherwise tax-exempt employee benefit.

Legislation: *Finance Act* 2006, s. 63; ITEPA 2003, Pt. 3, Ch. 4

Other Material: SP 6/85, *Incentive awards*

Tax Reporter: ¶433-800

320 Cash vouchers

A 'cash voucher' is a document or stamp exchangeable for a sum of money not substantially less than its cost of provision where the sum for which it is exchangeable would have been chargeable to tax if received directly, i.e. where it is not a gift or otherwise exempt.

Cash obtained by virtue of cash vouchers given by employers to their employees would generally be chargeable to tax as emoluments under the charge on employment income provisions (ITEPA 2003) (see 274). However, this rule is overridden by a provision treating as emoluments the amounts for which they are capable of being exchanged, unless they are paid under approved schemes. Such vouchers are also generally within the PAYE system (see 2384); if the employee does not reimburse the tax to the employer within 30 days of the deemed payment in point, that tax is treated as an additional emoluments of the employment.

Legislation: ITEPA 2003, Pt. 3, Ch. 4

321 Employee liability and indemnity insurance

In certain circumstances employees are entitled to a deduction for the costs of meeting or defending claims to do with liabilities arising out of their work, or insuring against those costs; equally, no tax liability arises on the employee when such costs are met by the employer. The deduction is available provided expenditure relates to a 'qualifying liability' (broadly an act or omission of a person in the capacity of office holder or employee, or a claim in respect of such an act or omission, but not including any deduction where it would be illegal for the employer to insure against them), or where a premium relates to a 'qualifying contract of insurance' (which is widely defined). A similar relief is available in respect of expenditure defrayed by former employees which occurred in the year in which the employment ceased, or in the following six years, and where the payment would have been allowable as above but for the fact that the employment ceased.

No deduction is allowed for a payment which is made in pursuance of arrangements. The main purpose, or one of the main purposes, of which is the avoidance of tax.

Normal rules apply to the timing of relief. Generally, relief is available in the year in which the payment is made against the emoluments of that year for the employment in respect of which the payment arises. In relation to ex-employees, relief reduces the employee's total income of the year (and, if that income is insufficient, his excess chargeable gains over allowable losses for that year).

Legislation: ITEPA 2003, s. 346

Tax Reporter: ¶457-000

322   Reimbursed expenses and round-sum allowances

The reimbursement of an expense incurred in the performance of an employee's duties is not generally regarded as a perquisite or other amount which would fall within the meaning of the term 'emoluments' (see 274).

If, however, the amount reimbursed to the employee is excessive, the excess could be regarded as emoluments and taxable as such. Further, any round-sum allowance made 'by reason of employment' (see 273) to cover expenses incurred, or to be incurred, is generally regarded as an emolument rather than a reimbursement of actual expenses on the facts of each case. There will be exceptions to this rule on specific facts (see 302 regarding incidental overnight expenditure). Further, where an individual receives an allowance in respect of duties performed outside his controlled duties as an employee, it may not be 'for acting as an employee'.

HMRC have introduced a set of benchmark scale rates that employers can use to make certain day subsistence payments free of tax and National Insurance contributions to employees who incur allowable business travel expenses.

Contributions by an employer of up to £4 per week towards additional household costs incurred by employees working at home may be paid tax free (see 383).

Expenses payments made by the employer which would not otherwise be chargeable to tax are treated as emoluments and are assessable on all employees from 6 April 2016 (previously, assessable on employees earning over £8,500 or more per year (see 382)).

There are special exemptions for payments in respect of travel assistance during strikes or for the disabled (see 308), of pure training (see 304) or retraining (of the sort set out at 2065), of subsistence (see 2000), of rates but probably not council tax for certain employer-provided accommodation and of special allowances or expenses for civil servants abroad, armed forces, reserve or auxiliary forces and clergymen.

From 6 April 2016, a specific exemption applies for tax deductible benefits (see 383A). Previously, where any amount is treated as taxable emoluments, an employee could claim a deduction to the extent that his expenses have been incurred wholly, exclusively and necessarily in the performance of his duties.

Cases: *Owen v Pook (HMIT)* [1970] AC 244; *Donnelly (HMIT) v Williamson* [1982] BTC 11

Other Material: HMRC *Employment Income Manual* EIM05230

P11D Employees and Directors

382   Charge on expenses and cash equivalent of benefits

From 6 April 2016, the £8,500 threshold for determining whether employees pay income tax on all of their benefits in kind and expenses is abolished. All employees are now subject to income tax on benefits in kind and expenses.

For tax years up to and including 2015–16, certain benefits were charged only on directors (see 312) and 'employees earning at the rate of £8,500 p.a. or more' known as 'P11D employees' (from the end-of-year return form which employers must send to HMRC) (see 312).

From 6 April 2016, a statutory exemption allows employers to identify and treat certain low value benefits in kind provided to employees as 'trivial' (see further 383).

Expenses and benefits given to an employee are deemed to be provided by reason of his or her employment. The measure of the taxable benefit is its cash equivalent value. Unless the value is determined by a specific statutory provision (see 383) for those benefits where specific charging provisions exist, the cash equivalent value is determined in accordance with the general charging provisions; the cash equivalent value being the cost to the employer of providing the benefit, less any amount made good by the employee (see further 388).

Legislation: ITEPA 2003, s. 70–72

Other Material: Booklet 480, *Expenses and benefits: a tax guide*: www.gov.uk/government/publications/480-expenses-and-benefits-a-tax-guide

Tax Reporter: ¶412-850

383   Exceptions from the general charge

Specific charging provisions

Certain benefits are specifically charged under provisions separate from the general benefits charge (and until 5 April 2016 were charged only on a director or P11D employee (see 384 and 386)). The provisions prescribe the calculation to be applied in determining the cash equivalent value of the benefit. For example, special rules apply to:

- employer-provided vans (see 400), cars and petrol (see 402 and 403);
- mileage allowances (see 405);
- beneficial loans (see 406);
- directors' tax paid by employers (see 407);
- scholarships (see 408); and
- shares acquired at an undervalue (see 410).

Exemptions

Certain benefits are exempt from the general benefits charge altogether. For example:

- mobile telephones, subject to certain conditions (see 415);
- employer-provided and supported bus services (see 417);
- most in-house sporting or recreational facilities (including shared-employer facilities). The exemption for the tax charge on subsidised meals (see 412) and recreational benefits is extended to persons other than employees who work on the premises of an employer who provides such benefits for their employees;
- accommodation provided on the employer's premises for the employee to enable him to carry out his duties;
- the giving of a lump sum pension or gratuity on the death or retirement of the employee;
- the provision of canteen meals to all staff (see 412);
- medical treatment or insurance provided in respect of an overseas business trip (see 293);

- entertainment and hospitality provided by third parties otherwise than in consideration of specific services;

- workplace nurseries (see 409);

- car, motor cycle and cycle parking facilities at or near the workplace;

- bicycles and cycling safety equipment provided for employees' commuting journeys (see 418);

- certain incidental overnight expenses (see 302);

- security assets and services (see 2008);

- contributions by employers towards additional household costs incurred by employees who work some or all of the time at home. For payments of up to £4 per week, no supporting evidence is required to obtain the income tax exemption. For payments of more than £4 per week, supporting evidence is required; and

- pensions advice and information provided, on behalf of employers, to employees of up to £150 per employee per year.

Trivial benefits

Finance Act 2016 introduces a new statutory exemption for trivial benefits in kind costing less than £50 with effect for the tax year 2016–17 and subsequent tax years (see 390).

Legislation: ITEPA 2003, s. 237, 240, 241, 265, 307, 313, 317(1), 325, 718

Other Material: HMRC Booklet 480, *Expenses and benefits: a tax guide*: www.gov.uk/government/publications/480-expenses-and-benefits-a-tax-guide

Tax Reporter: ¶432-000

383A   Exemption for benefits

From 6 April 2016, *Finance Act* 2015 introduced an exemption for benefits in kind (including vouchers and credit tokens) which the employee would otherwise have been entitled to a deduction for under ITEPA 2003, Pt. 5, Ch. 3:

- an amount equal to the benefit would be allowed as a deduction from the employee's earnings under ITEPA 2003, Pt. 5, Ch. 3; and

- the benefit is not provided pursuant to relevant salary sacrifice arrangements.

The exemption does not apply to benefits in kind which are given as part of arrangements that reduce the amount of general earnings or specific employment income of the employee subject to tax and National Insurance contributions where one of the main purposes of the arrangement is to avoid tax or National Insurance contributions.

Legislation: ITEPA 2003, s. 289D(2)

Tax Reporter: 413-235

384   Meaning of 'director' (tax years up to 2015–16)

For the purposes of the charge to tax on directors and 'higher paid' employees only in respect of certain benefits for tax years up to 2015–16, a 'director' was a member of the board of directors or similar body, or if the company's affairs were managed by one person, that person. If the company's affairs were managed by the members themselves, a member was a director for tax purposes. In addition, any person upon whose instructions the directors of the company were accustomed to act was also a director, but there was an exception made for solicitors and other professional advisers who advised the company in their professional capacity. They were not treated as directors by doing so.

A person was not treated as a director if:

(1)   his total emoluments from the company were at the rate of £8,500 or more (see 386);

(2)   he had no 'material interest' in the company, and either:

    (a)   he was a 'full-time working director'; or

    (b)   the company was non-profit making (i.e. it is not a trading company and does not hold investments) or was established for purely charitable purposes.

Broadly, a person had a material interest for present purposes if he, alone or with any associate(s), beneficially owns or was able to control more than 5% of the ordinary share capital of the company or on the company's liquidation would be entitled to more than 5% of its assets.

Legislation: ITEPA 2003, s. 67, former s. 216(3), 223(8)

Tax Reporter: ¶413-000

386 Whether employee earns at the rate of £8,500 p.a. or more (tax years up to 2015–16)

For tax years up to 2015–16, in determining whether the £8,500 threshold (see 382) was reached (and thus whether an employee was within the benefit regime applying to P11D employees and directors), the following items were included in the calculation unless they were covered by a dispensation:

- emoluments chargeable under the charge on employment income provisions;

- payments by way of expenses;

- benefits chargeable on P11D employees and directors;

- living accommodation provided by the employer;

- amounts chargeable in respect of cash and credit tokens; and

- tax accounted for by the employer (because PAYE could not be applied) and not reimbursed by the employee.

However, the calculation was performed *before* the deduction of expenses other than:

- contributions to a superannuation scheme in respect of which the individual was entitled to tax relief as an expense;

- contributions to an approved payroll giving scheme.

Example

Ruby is paid £5,000 a year. She is also provided with a company car, the cash equivalent value of which is £3,500. Her employer also provides private medical insurance, the cost of which is £300 a year. Ruby meets expenses of £225 from her emoluments that are deductible for tax purposes and contributes £100 to an approved payroll giving scheme.

For the purposes of determining whether Ruby is a P11D employee, she has emoluments of:

	£
Salary	5,000
Add: car	3,500
private medical insurance	300
	8,800
Less: contribution to approved payroll giving scheme	(100)
	8,700

> Ruby's emoluments exceed the £8,500. For the purposes of this calculation her deductible expenses of £225 are not taken into account.

Note that the £8,500 threshold that determines whether employees pay income tax on all of their benefits in kind and expenses is to be abolished from 6 April 2016.

Legislation: ITEPA 2003, s. 66(4), former s. 216(1)–(4), 217(1), 218(1), (3), (4), 219(5), (6)

Tax Reporter: ¶419-600

388   General charge on benefits

Unless a benefit is covered by a specific provision that dictates how the cash equivalent of the benefit is to be calculated, for tax purposes, the measure of a benefit provided to an employee or a director is its cash equivalent value as calculated in accordance with the general charging provision as follows:

	£
Cost to employer	x
Less: amount made good by employee	(x)
Cash equivalent value	x

> **Example**
>
> As a reward for meeting her sales targets, Polly's employer gives her a luxury hamper. The hamper cost £300. Polly makes no contribution towards the cost. The cash equivalent value of the benefit is thus the cost to Polly's employer of providing the hamper, i.e. £300.

Where the benefit comprises facilities shared between the person to whom the benefit is provided and others (e.g. cheap school fees for a child of a teacher at an independent school) only the additional direct costs (or 'marginal costs') are taken into account in calculating the cash equivalent and not the total cost of providing the facilities which might include a rateable proportion of overheads and other expenses.

VAT

Where the cost to the employer includes VAT, the cash equivalent of the benefit is computed using the VAT-inclusive cost, even if the VAT element is subsequently recovered by the employer.

Legislation: ITEPA 2003, s. 201–203

Cases: *Mairs (HMIT) v Haughey* [1992] BTC 373; *Pepper (HMIT) v Hart* [1992] BTC 591; *R & C Commrs v Apollo Fuels Ltd* [2014] BTC 510

Other Material: Booklet 480; *Expenses and benefits: a tax guide*

Tax Reporter: ¶412-850

390   Trivial benefits

A statutory exemption for trivial benefits in kind costing less than £50 was introduced by *Finance Act* 2016, with effect for the tax year 2016–17 and subsequent tax years.

ITEPA 2003, s. 323A–323C provides a statutory definition of a trivial benefits in kind (BiK) eligible for the exemption. The exemption sets out a number of conditions that must be met for a BiK to be exempt, including an upper limit per individual BiK of £50. Qualifying trivial BiKs provided to directors and other office holders of close companies will be subject to an annual cap of £300. Where the director's or other office holder's family or household member is also an employee of the company, they will be subject to a £300 cap in their own right.

Prior to 6 April 2016, there was no de minimis level below which tax was not chargeable on benefits in kind or expenses payments. Certain benefits might be exempted by statutory instrument but they were very specific and therefore of limited practical application. HMRC instructions to staff stated (at EIM21860) that the lack of any general exemption:

> 'does not mean that you should insist that every trivial benefit should be included on a form P11D or included in a PAYE Settlement Agreement (PSA), irrespective of the administrative burdens on both the employer and the Inland Revenue in handling P11Ds and PSAs.'

Guidance to HMRC officers encouraged them to:

> 'strike a balance between sensible practical administration of the tax system and the need to deter employers from providing what is in reality part of the remuneration of their employees in a form that seeks to exploit that practical administration.'

Legislation: ITEPA 2003, s. 210(1), 210(2), 266(4), 266(5), 323A–323C

Tax Reporter: ¶432-050

394   Assets transferred

Where an asset is transferred to an employee or director, several factors need to be taken into account in determining the cash equivalent value of the resultant benefit.

Asset transferred to employee/director before it has depreciated

Where the asset is transferred to an employee or a director (or for tax years up to and including 2015–16, an employee earning £8,500 or more or a director), the cash equivalent will depend on whether the asset has been used or depreciated at the time of transfer and whether it has previously been placed at the employee or director's disposal.

In the situation that an asset is transferred before it has been used or has depreciated, the cash equivalent value is the greater of the:

- cost of providing the asset; or

- its second-hand value,

less any amount made good by the employee.

Asset transferred to an employee or director after it has depreciated or has been used

Where an asset is transferred to an employee or director (or for tax years up to and including 2015–16, an employee earning £8,500 or more or a director) after it has been used or has depreciated, the cash equivalent value of the resultant benefit is the market value of the asset at the date of transfer less any amount made good by the employee.

Asset transferred after being made previously available to the employee/director

It may be the case that the asset is lent to the employee/director (or for tax years up to and including 2015–16, an employee earning £8,500 or more or a director) before being transferred to him or her. In this situation, the cash equivalent value of the resultant benefit is the higher of:

- the market value at the date of transfer; and

- the market value when the asset was first made available for use by the employee/director, less any amounts charged in respect of that benefit,

less any amounts made good by the employee/director.

P9D employees (tax years up to and including 2015–16)

If the asset was transferred to a P9D employee, or a member of his or her family or household, the basic rule was that the employee was taxed on the second-hand value of the asset, less any amount made good by the employee.

From 6 April 2005, no tax charge arises where employees/directors buy computers or bicycles from their employer, provided that the bicycle or computer has previously been loaned to them or to another employee, and that they pay market value (see 394).

Legislation: ITEPA 2003, s. 203(2), (3), 206, 208; FA 2005, s. 16 and 17

Tax Reporter: ¶437-950

396   Assets placed at employee's disposal

Where an asset is placed at the disposal of an employee or a director (or for tax years up to and including 2015–16, an employee earning £8,500 or more or a director) for his or her private use, the cash equivalent value of the resultant benefit is the higher of:

- 20% of the market value of the asset when it was first made available for use by an employee; and

- the annual rent or hire charge of the asset,

plus any costs incurred in the tax year less in association with the provision of the asset, less any amount made good by the employee.

Example

David's employer lent him a fridge and a freezer for his personal use. The assets were first made available in 2004 when they had market values of £400 and £600 respectively. In 2016–17, David's employer pays for an annual service contract covering both appliances. The contract costs £100. David makes no contribution towards the costs.

The taxable benefit charged on David in 2016–17 is £300, calculated as follows:

	£	£
Fridge – higher of		
• 20% market value when first made available (20% × £400)	80	
• annual hire/rent	Nil	
		80

Freezer – higher of		
• 20% market value when first made available (20% × £600)	120	
• annual hire/rent	Nil	
		120
		200
Add: associated costs		100
		300
Less: amount made good by employee		(Nil)
Cash equivalent value		300

It should be noted that the charge arises where the asset is *available* for private use, even if no actual private use takes place.

If the asset is land, the annual value is the amount that the land would reasonably be expected to produce on a yearly letting.

For the position where ownership of the asset is transferred to an employee having been previously placed at his disposal, see 394.

Incidental private use

No charge arises in respect of incidental private use of assets which are used by the employee in performing the duties of his or her employment. For the exemption to be in point, the private use must not be 'significant'.

However, the exemption will not extend to small amounts of private use of certain high value assets (the assets in question to be specified by a Treasury Order).

Legislation: FA 2000, s. 57 and Sch. 10; ITEPA 2003, s. 203(2), (3), 205, 206, 207(1), 316

Case: *Rockall* [2014] TC 03767

Tax Reporter: ¶413-500

398   Living accommodation and related expenses

The provision of living accommodation is and has always been a taxable benefit whatever the recipient's rate of pay; however, there are exceptions to the charge (see 314).

Where an employee or a director (or for tax years up to and including 2015–16, an employee earning £8,500 or more or a director) has the running expenses of his accommodation paid by his employer, that will constitute a benefit chargeable to tax in accordance with the general charging provisions (see 388). However, the amount of the charge is partially exempt from tax where the employee qualifies for a job-related exemption (see 314). The partial exemption reduces what would otherwise be a charge on the full cost of the provision of such expenses as lighting, heating, repairs, cleaning, maintenance, and decoration to an amount not exceeding 10% of the emoluments of the employee, less any amount paid by the employee for them; 'emoluments' for these purposes means the employee's total emoluments, including any emoluments of any employment with an associated company, but after making certain deductions.

Legislation: ITEPA 2003, s. 99(1), (2), 100, 314, 315

Tax Reporter: ¶414-500

400   Vans used by employees

Where a company van is available for the private use of an employee or a director (or for tax years up to and including 2015–16, an employee earning £8,500 or more or a director) a taxable benefit arises. The tax treatment of vans provided by the employer currently works on the basis of a fixed charge per van, irrespective of the cost of the van. As such, the legislation concerning vans is simpler than that governing the taxation of company cars. The concept of 'fair bargain' (see 288) does not apply to employer-provided vans or the related fuel benefit (ITEPA 2003, s. 114(1A) (as inserted by *Finance Act* 2016, with effect for the tax year 2016–17 and subsequent tax years)).

There is no tax charge if the van is not in fact used for private purposes. From 6 April 2014, any payments required by the employer as a contribution for private use of a car or van needs to be made before the end of the tax year in which the private use was undertaken in order to qualify for a reduction in the cash equivalent of the benefit.

For those who are liable to tax on the provision of a company van, the taxable benefit is a fixed amount of £3,170 from 6 April 2016, but a reduction may be made if there is shared use of the van, there is a period in the year during which the van is not available for private use, or the employee makes contributions for private use of the van.

There is no fuel benefit where the benefit of the van itself is exempt. In other cases, the taxable cash equivalent of free fuel is £598 per year from 6 April 2016.

Zero emission vans

From 2015–16, a taxable benefit arises in relation to zero emissions employer-provided vans (previously no benefit charge arose for such vans). See key data for table of rates.

Shared vans

Changed rules for shared vans were introduced from 6 April 2005, representing a considerable simplification of the previous position.

The current rules apply where a van is made available by the same employer to more than one employee, and where both employees may use the van for private purposes.

The taxable benefit is first calculated in accordance with normal principles. A reduction is then given for any periods during which the van is unavailable. To recognise that the benefit of the van is shared between more than one employee, a further reduction is then made 'on a just and reasonable basis'. Discretion as to what is just and reasonable will presumably be left to employers unless HMRC suspect deliberate manipulation of the rules. Subject to the following paragraph, use by all employees is included in the calculation, even if an individual is not in fact chargeable to tax on the van benefit because he earns less than £8,500 – still possible, in theory at least, for a part-time worker.

For tax years up to and including 2015–16, a complication arose where two employees who share a van were members of the same family or household. Suppose, for example, that they had equal use of a van, with unrestricted private use. The overall taxable benefit would be £3,150 (2015–16 rate) and in the ordinary way this might therefore be split £1,575 to each. However, if one of the two was in lower-paid employment (broadly, earning less than £8,500 per year), then he or she might escape any tax liability on the van. In that case, the other member of the same family or household would still pay tax on the full value of £3,150.

Example

John is sole shareholder of his own building company. He drives a van and uses it for both private and business purposes. John employs his 17-year-old son, Steve, in the business, paying him £5,000 per year for ten hours per week. Steve is also allowed to drive the vehicle and father and son make roughly equal use of the van overall, in each case with unrestricted private use.

For 2015–16, the overall taxable benefit is £3,150. In the ordinary way, this might therefore be split £1,575 to each. However, as Steve is in lower-paid employment, he would escape any tax liability on the van. In this case, his private use is ignored and John will pay tax on the full value of £3,150.

This anti-avoidance rule did not apply where the two employees were unconnected.

Example

Pete is employed as an electrician in Luton. His employer provides him with a van which he uses every day for work. Pete is allowed to use the van for private journeys within Bedfordshire, though he has to ask for permission if he wants to take the van outside the county. For 2016–17, Pete's taxable benefit for the van is £3,170. Unless Pete pays for all his private fuel he will also incur a fuel scale charge of £598 in 2016–17.

Example

Bob works as a plumber. He is provided with a van which is kept full of tools and plumbing accessories. Bob is allowed to take the van home at the end of each day but is strictly forbidden to make any other private use. The insurance of the van reflects these conditions.

Bob meets the restricted private use condition as the only permitted private use is for ordinary commuting. His taxable benefit is therefore nil.

Example

Jack is director of a company that imports fruit and vegetables. He works almost entirely from the warehouse. Jack has a luxury car at home, but on advice from his accountant, he uses an (expensive) van for commuting to and from work, a round trip of 40 miles. The company pays for all expenses, including fuel. Nobody else drives the van. Jack tells his accountant that he almost never uses the van for purposes other than commuting to and from work.

Jack will pay tax on a benefit of £3,170. A fuel scale charge of £598 also applies for 2016–17. The fact that Jack may make occasional private use of the van for other purposes is not the main problem – other private use is not fatal as long as it is insignificant. However, it is clear on these facts that the van is not being made available mainly for the purposes of business travel. It therefore fails the second leg of the restricted private use condition. It also appears on these facts that there may be no formal restriction in place to prevent other private use.

Legislation: ITEPA 2003, s. 114, 115, 155, 157, 161, 169A; FA 2014, s. 25; *Van Benefit and Car and Van Fuel Benefit Order* 2014 (SI 2014/2896)

Other Material: Booklet 480, *Expenses and benefits: a tax guide*: www.gov.uk/government/publications/480-expenses-and-benefits-a-tax-guide

Tax Reporter: ¶416-200

402 Company cars

A company car tax charge will arise if three conditions are all met:

- first, a car is made available to an employee or a member of the employee's family or household;
- second, the car is so available by reason of the employment.
- finally, it is available for the employee's or member's private use.

If these conditions are met, the cash equivalent of the benefit of the car is treated as earnings.

No benefit arises where a car is provided to an employee in lower-paid employment.

If an employee is given the choice between a car and a cash alternative, the employee is taxed on whichever is chosen

The concept of 'fair bargain' (see 288) does not apply to employer-provided cars (ITEPA 2003, s. 114(1A) (as inserted by *Finance Act* 2016, with effect for the tax year 2016–17 and subsequent tax years)).

Tax charge

The company car tax charge is based on a percentage of the car's price, graduated according to carbon dioxide emission levels. The charge usually lies between 7% (for small, fuel efficient/low emissions cars) and 37% (for high pollution cars).

For 2016–17, the rates applicable are 7% for CO_2 emissions of 50g/km or below, 11% for CO_2 emissions of 51–75g/km, 15% for CO_2 emissions above 75g/km up to the relevant threshold (95g/km for 2016–17); 16% for CO_2 emissions equal to the relevant threshold (rounding down to the nearest five below applies if the emissions figure is not divisible by five).

If emissions exceed the relevant threshold for the year, the threshold percentage is increased by one percentage point for each 5g/km by which emissions exceed the relevant threshold for the year to a maximum of 37%. Rounding applies.

In both 2017–18 and 2018–19, the appropriate percentage of list price subject to tax will increase by two percentage points for cars emitting more than 75g/km CO_2, to a maximum of 37%. In 2017–18, there will be a four percentage point differential between the 0–50 and 51–75g/km CO_2 bands and between the 51–75 and 76–94g/km CO_2 bands. In 2018–19, this differential will reduce to three percentage points (FA 2015, s. 7 and 8).

Income tax

In 2019–20, the appropriate percentage of list price subject to tax will increase by three percentage points for cars emitting more than 75g/km CO_2, to a maximum of 37%. There will be a three-percentage point differential between the 0–50 and 51–75g/km CO_2 bands (FA 2016, s. 8).

The resulting appropriate percentage is subject to the normal diesel adjustment if appropriate (see below).

Example

A petrol car with a CO_2 figure of just 50g/km is provided as a company car. The appropriate percentage for 2016–17 is 7%. On the basis of the legislation as it currently stands, the 7% figure will be 9% from 6 April 2017.

Cars with emissions limits at or above the relevant threshold

For these cars, any emissions figure that is not divisible by five is rounded down to the nearest number that is so divisible. For cars with an emissions figure equal to the relevant threshold, the appropriate percentage is 16% for 2016–17, which is referred to in the legislation as 'the threshold percentage'. In practice, because of rounding, this percentage applies to petrol cars with emissions of between 95 and 99g/km inclusive for the year 2016–17. The threshold percentage of 16% is increased by 1% for each additional five grams per kilometre, first rounding down any amounts not divisible by five. Once more, this is subject to the diesel adjustment if appropriate.

Example

A petrol car with a CO_2 figure of 118g/km is provided as a company car. The figure of 118 is rounded down to 115 and the appropriate percentage for 2016–17 is 20%, rising to 22% from April 2017.

Contribution for private use

From 6 April 2014, any payments required by the employer as a contribution for private use of a car or van needs to be made before the end of the tax year in which the private use was undertaken in order to qualify for a reduction in the cash equivalent of the benefit.

Appropriate percentage: diesel cars

The rules for petrol cars apply equally to diesel cars, but the latter are then subject to further adjustment.

For cars that are 'propelled solely by diesel', a supplement of 3% is normally added to the figure produced by following the principles described above, though the maximum cannot rise above 35% for years up to and including 2014–15 and 37% for 2015–16 and 2016–17. The reasoning for this differential for diesel cars was explained in a Budget press release of 21 March 2000, as follows:

> 'Diesel cars emit less CO_2 than petrol cars and so will be taxed on a lower percentage of the car's price if the charge was based purely on CO_2 emissions. This tax advantage is unwarranted, however, as diesel cars emit greater quantities than petrol cars of the two local air pollutants of most concern (particulates and oxides of nitrogen), and are expected to continue to do so even with the introduction of tighter vehicle emission standards.'

The 3% diesel supplement was due to be abolished from 6 April 2016, however, legislation in *Finance Act* 2016 retains the diesel supplement in company car tax. Further provisions to remove the diesel supplement, are currently expected to be made in a future Finance Bill, with effect from 6 April 2021.

Zero emission cars

From 6 April 2010 to 5 April 2015, there was a zero tax charge for cars producing no emissions when driven (e.g. electric cars).

From 6 April 2016, the percentage for cars producing no emissions when driven (e.g. electric cars) is 7%, rising to 9% for 2017–18 and 13% for 2018–19 (FA 2016, s. 9).

Legislation: ITEPA 2003, Pt. 3, Ch. 6; FA 2012, s. 17 ; FA 2014, s. 24, 25

Cases: *Gurney (HMIT) v Richards* [1989] BTC 326; *Brown v Ware (HMIT)* (1995) Sp C 29; *IR Commrs v Quigley* [1995] BTC 356; *R & C Commrs v Apollo Fuels Ltd* [2014] BTC 510;; *Fowler* [2016] TC 05095

Other Material: Booklet 480, *Expenses and benefits: a tax guide*: www.gov.uk/government/publications/480-expenses-and-benefits-a-tax-guide

Tax Reporter: ¶415-050

403 Fuel benefits

The taxable benefit arising where an employer provides an employee with free fuel for private motoring in a company car is linked to the level of the car's carbon dioxide emissions, providing symmetry with the regime that has applied since 6 April 2002 to tax the benefit derived from the private use of a company car. For 2003–04 and subsequent tax years, the cash equivalent of the benefit of free fuel will be found by applying the percentage figure used in the car benefit calculation to an amount set by the Treasury. This amount is £22,200 for 2016–17.

The annual charge may be apportioned where free fuel is withdrawn part way through the tax year, provided that it is not reintroduced before the end of the tax year.

The concept of 'fair bargain' (see 288) does not apply to employer-provided fuel (ITEPA 2003, s. 114(1A) (as inserted by *Finance Act* 2016, with effect for the tax year 2016–17 and subsequent tax years)).

Legislation: ITEPA 2003, s. 149–153

Other Material: Booklet 480, *Expenses and benefits: a tax guide*; 490, *Employee travel, a tax and NICs guide*

Tax Reporter: ¶416-000

405 Mileage allowances

Employers are required to use HMRC's system for working out and reporting any taxable part of payments made to employees for the expenses of business travel in privately owned cars, vans, motorcycles and cycles. There is a tax-free approved amount that employers can pay to employees using their own vehicles for business travel. If an employer pays more than the approved amount, the excess will be charged to tax. Employers will need to include the excess when completing form P11D (or P9D). The tax-free approved amount is expressed in terms of pence per mile. For current rates, see Key Data.

Passenger payments

Passenger payments up to the approved rate for business travel (see Key Data) may be made to an employee for carrying passengers in his/her own car or van or in the company's car or van.

Legislation: *Approved Mileage Allowance Payments (Rates) Regulations* 2011 (SI 2011/896)

Case: *R & C Commrs v Cheshire Employer and Skills Development Ltd (formerly Total People Ltd)* [2011] BTC 1,832

Other Material: Booklet 480, *Employer's Further Guide to PAYE and NICs*

Tax Reporter: ¶432-100

406 Beneficial loans

Where a low-interest or interest-free loan is made to an employee or to a director (for tax years up to and including 2015–16, an employee earning £8,500 or more or a director), a tax charge arises on the cash equivalent of the benefit of the loan, with allowance for any potential relief in respect of interest paid on certain loans. Similarly, where a loan to such an individual is written off (whether or not a 'soft loan' and whether or not a 'qualifying loan'), the amount written off is treated as a taxable emolument unless the write-off occurs on death. The concept of 'fair bargain' (see 288) does not apply to employer-provided fuel (ITEPA 2003, s. 114(1A) (as inserted by *Finance Act* 2016, with effect for the tax year 2016–17 and subsequent tax years)).

Loans by a close company to one of its directors may in some cases be aggregated for the purposes of determining the interest paid and the benefit so arising; before 1996–97, this applied to many more cases of loans between the same borrower and lender.

Before 1995–96, any loan which replaced a beneficial loan was treated as the original loan. From 6 April 1995, the replacement loan is not automatically a beneficial loan, but the same tests apply to determine whether the replacement is a beneficial loan. The effect of this is to remove an obstacle to the provision of replacement loans to employees. An employer who wishes to stop providing cheap or interest-free loans to employees can now transfer the loans to a subsidiary of a commercial lender set up for the purpose without the loans automatically becoming taxable. Under the old rules, the loans would have been treated as beneficial loans even if the subsidiary made commercial loans to the general public, but this is not now the case.

The exemption from the charge to tax on beneficial loans applying to loans made to employees on the same terms as to members of the public ('ordinary commercial loans') is widened from 6 April 2000 to include loans to employees that are varied to bring them onto ordinary commercial terms. Also from 6 April 2000, the exemption is extended to cover lending by an employer who supplies goods or services on credit. For years prior to 2000–01, the exemption applied only to loans made by the employer in the ordinary course of his business, which includes lending money. This extension ensures that employees receiving the same credit arrangements as other customers, for example payment in arrears for gas and electricity, are not inadvertently caught by the beneficial loan provisions.

In relation to arrangements entered into on or after 22 March 2006, cheap loans provided by employers to their employees which do not involve the payment of interest are taxed in the same way as conventional employee loans, i.e. on the difference between the interest (or its equivalent) payable by the employee and the amount of interest that would be payable at the official rate.

A loan made to an employee's spouse or civil partner , his spouse's or civil partner's parents, grandparents, children, grandchildren, brothers, sisters, or their spouses or civil partners, is treated as if it were made to the employee unless he can show that he received no benefit from it.

Loans made in the normal course of domestic, family or personal relationships are exempt from the soft loan provisions including personal loans within families where the employer is a close company. Loans which employers provide to employees on the same terms as loans they make to the public are similarly exempt.

Small loans

An exemption applies to remove certain small loans from the beneficial loans provisions. All soft loans may be omitted if they total £10,000 or less; failing this, all non-qualifying loans (such as season ticket loans) may be disregarded if they total £10,000 or less.

If the original loan is replaced by another loan from the same employment (an 'employment-related loan'), or replaced by a non-employment-related loan, which in turn is replaced by an employment-related loan, then the loans are all treated, for the purposes of averaging, as the same loan. This seeks to prevent exploitation of the part months which may occur at the beginning or end of each of the various loans.

The current £10,000 exemption threshold on employment-related loans applies from 6 April 2014. Prior to 6 April 2014, the limit was £5,000.

Taxable amount in respect of beneficial loans

There are alternative methods for determining the cash equivalent of beneficial loans. The standard method is that the average amount of the loan which is outstanding at either end of the tax year is multiplied by the average official rate of interest for the year in question (see the Key Data section) and there is then subtracted the interest actually paid (the cash equivalent of any loan which is not outstanding for the whole of the tax year is reduced by a proportionate amount and there are special rules for multiple loans). The alternative method may be employed if the inspector requires or if the taxpayer elects for it: this uses a daily basis of calculation. The Treasury is able to set a lower official rate (see Key Data again) for loans in a foreign currency where interest rates are significantly lower than in the UK.

Example 1

George's employer makes him a loan interest-free. The balance outstanding at 5 April 2015 is £20,000. He repays £6,000 on 15 January 2016 so that the balance on 5 April 2016 is £4,000. Assume the official rate of interest in force is 4%.

Standard method

$$\frac{(£20,000 + £4,000)}{2} \times 4.0\% = \qquad £480$$

Alternative method   £

£20,000 × $^{284}/_{365}$ × 4.0%   622

£4,000 × $^{81}/_{365}$ × 4.0%   36

                                                                               658

Beneficial loans where all the interest qualifies for tax relief are exempted from charge.

Legislation: ITEPA 2003, s. 173–191; *Finance Act* 2006, s. 97; *Finance Act* 2014, s. 22; *Taxes (Interest Rate) (Amendment) Regulations* 2015 (SI 2015/411)

Cases: *Euro Fire Ltd v Davison (HMIT); Hill v Davison (HMIT)* [1997] BTC 191; *Harvey v Williams (HMIT) (No. 2)* (1998) Sp C 168; *West (HMIT) v O'Neill; West (HMIT) v Crossland* [1999] BTC 32; *Grant v Watton (HMIT)* [1999] BTC 85

Other Material: SP 7/79, *Benefits in kind – cheap loans – advances for expenses*; Booklet 480, *Expenses and benefits: a tax guide*

Tax Reporter: ¶417-000

407   Director's tax paid by employer

Where a person is employed as a 'director' (see 384) of a company and the company fails to deduct tax under PAYE from his emoluments but accounts to HMRC for the tax, any tax for which the director does not reimburse the company is treated as a benefit received by the director and is chargeable as an emolument of his employment.

Legislation: ITEPA 2003, s. 223

Tax Reporter: ¶420-100

408 Scholarships

It is not unusual for employers to offer, as incentives to attract employees, scholarships for the education of employees' children. Except as noted below, any scholarship payments made to a child of a 'director' (see 384) or to the child of an 'employee (for tax years up to and including 2015–16, earning at a rate of £8,500 p.a. or more') (see 386) are taxed as benefits in kind where they are made as a result of 'arrangements entered into by an employer, or a connected person'.

The charge arises in accordance with the general charging provisions (see 382).

Scholarships not affected

For the general exemption from tax for scholarship income, see 308.

The charging provisions do not apply to scholarships awarded out of a fund or under a scheme where 75% or more of the scholarships (by value) go to scholars otherwise than by reason of their parents' employment, i.e. not more than 25% of payments are made for children of directors or higher-paid employees by reason of their employment. The 25% test excludes from the charge to tax only those awards where the connection between the award and the parent's employment is purely fortuitous.

Legislation: ITEPA 2003, s. 211–215

Other Material: SP 4/86, *Scholarship and apprenticeship schemes at universities and technical colleges*; Booklet 480, *Expenses and benefits: a tax guide*

Tax Reporter: ¶419-150

409 Employer-provided childcare

In certain circumstances, employers may meet the cost of childcare for the children of employees without triggering any tax liability for those employees. There are, in fact, two different forms of exemption for childcare costs. These are referred to (here, as in the legislation) as 'employer-provided care' and as 'other care'. The first of these offers unrestricted relief but is subject to much tighter conditions regarding the involvement of the employer.

The relief for the costs of 'other care' is of much wider application but offers a more restricted level of relief. This is discussed in detail below. The key features of this newer relief may be summarised as follows:

- up to £55 per week per employee may be paid by the employer free of tax and all NIC, either directly to a childcare provider or by way of voucher;

- no tax relief is due if the employer pays a cash allowance to the employee or settles the employee's personal liability for childcare costs;

- if an employer pays more than £55 per week, the excess will be taxable but the first £55 will still qualify for relief if the necessary conditions are met;

- relief for certain higher earners is restricted from April 2011 (see below);

- no relief is due for the costs of school fees or for unapproved childcare; and

- various restrictions apply, especially where care is provided by somebody connected with the child.

Employers may well wish to implement a salary sacrifice scheme, i.e. offering the benefit of childcare in return for a reduction in the current salary level (or possibly in return for forgoing a pay increase). The implementation of a salary sacrifice scheme need not be unduly onerous but it is important to ensure that care is taken with the paperwork so as to achieve the right end result.

A statutory exemption applies to remove from the charge to tax employer-provided childcare in a workplace nursery or similar facility. The exemption to tax applies if the following conditions are satisfied:

- the employee has 'parental responsibility' for the child or resides with it or, being the employee's child or stepchild, he maintains it at his expense;

- the care is provided on premises that are not wholly or mainly used as a private dwelling;

- *either* the care is provided on premises which are made available by the employer alone *or* the care is provided under arrangements made by persons who include the employer and which make him at least partly responsible for financing and managing the care provision; *and*

- in a case where 'the registration requirement applies, it is met'.

The registration requirement applies where either the premises or the carer must be registered under various care statutes and the requirement is met if the premises or person are so registered.

According to HMRC, to satisfy the condition that the care must be provided under arrangements which make the employer at least partly responsible for financing and managing the care provision (see above), the employer's role must be a real one which renders him accountable for his actions if things go wrong.

'Parental responsibility' means all the rights, duties, powers, responsibilities and authority which by law a child's parent has in relation to the child and his property.

'Care' means any form of care or supervised activity, provided on a regular or an irregular basis, but does not extend to supervised activity primarily provided for educational purposes.

For the purposes of the exemption, a 'child' is someone under the age of 18.

Other childcare

The more popular exemption for childcare prevents a tax charge where the employer meets certain other childcare costs (i.e. where that care is not organised by the employer). In essence, employers may now contribute up to £55 per week, plus certain voucher administration costs, for registered childcare.

The scheme limits relief to £55 for each week for which care is provided for a child and the relevant conditions are met. A week begins on whichever day starts the tax year. As if 6 April in a particular year falls on a Tuesday, for example, weeks for that year each begin on a Tuesday. There will always be 53 such weeks in any tax year, the final week being either one or two days. No tax-free payment may be made, however, if no care is provided in the week in question – for example, during a family holiday when the child is with the parent.

Booklet 480 states that 'if childcare vouchers are provided monthly, the equivalent monthly exemption is £243' so the monthly figure is based on 53 rather than 52 weeks.

The relief is limited to £55 per week per employer per employee. In other words, if a mother has two children, her employer can only contribute up to £55 per week, not up to £110. However, if the father also works, then his employer can also contribute up to £55 per week if he or she is also operating such a scheme. Indeed, even if there is only one child, each parent's employer may contribute up to £55.

The limit may be amended without new primary legislation.

Restrictions from April 2011
From April 2011, tax relief was restricted to basic rate only for all new recipients of childcare vouchers, or directly contracted childcare. The

weekly cap is £55 for an employee paying tax at no more than the basic rate, £28 for one paying at the higher (40%) rate, and £22 for an individual paying at the additional (50%) rate. The changes did not affect care provided directly by the employer (e.g. on the employer's own premises). The purpose of the change was to even out the amount of tax saving available for all employees regardless of the tax rate that the individual pays. The changes meant that anyone who joined an employer supported childcare scheme from 6 April 2011 will receive the same level of income tax exemption, which is approximately £11 per week.

Restrictions from April 2013

From 6 April 2013, the weekly amount of tax and NIC-free qualifying childcare payments that an employee earning over £150,000 p.a. can receive increased from £22 per week to £25 per week. This change is designed to ensure that the benefit of childcare vouchers remains unaffected by the reduction in the additional tax rate from 50% to 45% from that date. There are no changes for employees with earnings below this figure.

Payments for care: vouchers

Where care is provided by way of voucher, the same £55 limit applies per employee, and any amount paid by way of voucher is taken into account to restrict tax relief for any other form of payment. It will be possible, however, to pay by voucher one week and by other means the next (but not to have a mixed payment for the same week). See below regarding voucher administration costs.

Childcare vouchers exceeding £55 per week will be taxable and liable to Class 1 National Insurance contributions, as will vouchers used for 'informal' care (per Employer's Bulletin, February 2004). HMRC have specifically confirmed, however, that employees do not have to use the vouchers in the week or month in which they are provided but may save them up, for example to meet higher childcare costs during the school holidays (booklet E18, at page seven).

In addition to the £55 per week, an exemption is given for voucher administration costs. These are defined as the difference between the cost of providing the vouchers and the value of childcare provision that may be obtained by using the voucher.

HMRC recognise that employers may either administer a voucher scheme themselves or may engage an external voucher provider to do so. Either way, the employer remains responsible for the correct operation of PAYE.

Existing tax and NIC reliefs will be withdrawn from employees and employers where the employee enters a childcare voucher or directly contracted childcare scheme (see below) after the new scheme has come into force, however, as part of the transition to tax-free childcare, employer-supported childcare will remain open to new entrants until April 2018 (Budget 2016).

Childcare accounts

The *Childcare Payments Act* 2014 introduces a new scheme which provides financial support to help working families with the cost of childcare. Once the scheme is implemented, the Government will make a top-up payment of £2 for every £8 which a person pays towards childcare. Government support will be capped at a maximum of £4,000 in the case of a disabled child and £2,000 in the case of any other child, per year, although there will be no restriction on the number of children for whom support is available. The scheme will be managed by HMRC and the Government is due to be launched in 2017, initially by way of a trial period running from 14 November 2016–15 May 2017 (SI 2016/1083).

A person will be eligible to receive government support (referred to as a 'top-up payment') if they meet the eligibility conditions; provide information to demonstrate their eligibility in a declaration to HMRC, and HMRC agree, based on that information, that they are eligible; have a child who qualifies for support (broadly, a child under the age of 12 years old, or if disabled, 17 years old); have opened a childcare account in accordance with the scheme; and they, or another person, pay money into the childcare account.

A top-up payment made into a childcare account is not to be regarded as income of the account holder for the purposes of the Income Tax Acts (CPA 2014, s. 66).

Support through tax credits and universal credits

For parents who currently receive childcare support through tax credits and in due course Universal Credit, the Government will increase childcare support to improve work incentives and ensure that it is worthwhile to work up to full-time hours for low and middle income parents. An additional £200m of support will be provided within Universal Credit, which is equivalent to covering 85% of childcare costs for households qualifying for the Universal Credit childcare element where the lone parent or both earners in a couple pay income tax. The details of how to provide this support will be determined as part of the consultation on the scheme for parents not in receipt of Universal Credit, to ensure the two schemes operate effectively together.

The £200m Universal Credit offer is planned to be phased in from April 2016 as childcare support moves from tax credits into Universal Credit and will be funded from within social security budgets at the time.

Legislation: ITEPA 2003, s. 318 and 318A; FA 2011, s. 35 and Sch. 8; *Income Tax (Qualifying Child Care) Regulations* 2008 (SI 2008/2170); *Employer Supported Childcare (Relevant Earnings and Excluded Amounts) Regulations* 2011 (SI 2011/1798); *Universal Credit (Transitional Provisions) Regulations* 2013 (SI 2013/386); *Universal Credit Regulations* 2013 (SI 2013/376); *Universal Credit and Miscellaneous Amendments Regulations* 2015 (SI 2015/1754); *Childcare Payments Act 2014 (Amendment) Regulations* 2015 (SI 2015/537); *Childcare Payments Regulations* 2015 (SI 2015/522); *Childcare Payments (Eligibility) Regulations* 2015 (SI 2015/448); *Income Tax (Qualifying Child Care) Regulations* 2015 (SI 2015/346)

Other Material: HMRC Technical Note (www.hmrc.gov.uk/employers/employersupportedchildcare.pdf); HMRC information (www.hmrc.gov.uk/childcare): *Employer supported childcare short guide for small and medium businesses*; *Childcare tax and National Insurance contributions – employers' factsheet*; Questions and answers on changes from 6 April 2011: www.hmrc.gov.uk/thelibrary/esc-qa.htm; *How you can help your employees with childcare*: www.hmrc.gov.uk/helpsheets/e18.pdf; Inland Revenue *Tax Bulletin*, Issue 34, April 1998; Booklet 480, *Expenses and benefits: a tax guide*

Tax Reporter: ¶434-500; ¶490-670

410 Shares acquired at undervalue

Acquisition of the shares

Where, under an opportunity 'available by reason of his employment', an employee or director acquires shares at less than their market value when fully paid, or without payment at all, the difference between market value and the amount paid by the employee is treated as a notional loan to him, unless the benefit is otherwise charged to tax (as it often is: see 431). Any payment subsequently made by the employee will reduce the notional outstanding loan. The loan will cease to exist when the shares are fully paid or when the employee dies. In the meantime, the loan is taxed year by year or on other termination (see 406).

Disposal of the shares

Where the employee or director disposes of the beneficial interest in the shares or he is released from his obligation to pay for them or the debt is written off, etc. the amount so written off (the corresponding amount of the loan) is treated as an emolument of the employee's employment and is taxable (see 406).

A disposal by the director or employee of the shares, at more than their market value, results in the excess over market value being treated as an emolument of the employee's employment. A disposal on death is excluded but a disposal after leaving the job still attracts the charge to tax.

Application of provisions

The above provisions apply to shares acquired by persons who are (or are about to be) employed as employees or directors (or for tax years up to and including 2015–16, an employee earning £8,500 or more or a director), and those 'connected with' them (see 1260). The provisions do not apply to 'approved profit-sharing schemes', while there are interaction rules with charges for 'approved share option schemes' (see 434).

Legislation: ITEPA 2003, s. 192–197

Case: *IR Commrs v Herd* [1993] BTC 245

412   Provision of subsidised meals

The provision by employers of meals in a canteen in which meals are provided for staff generally is exempted from the charge on directors and employees (or for tax years up to and including 2015–16, an employee earning £8,500 or more or a director). By concession, tax is not charged on such meals, or on the use of any ticket or token to obtain such meals, if the meals are provided on a reasonable scale and either:

- all employees may obtain free or subsidised meals on a reasonable scale, whether on the employer's premises or elsewhere; or

- the employer provides free or subsidised meal vouchers for staff for whom meals are not provided.

The concession does not apply, in the case of a hotel, catering or similar business, to free or subsidised meals provided for its employees in a restaurant or dining room at a time when meals are being served to the public, unless part of it is designated as being for the use of staff only.

The former exemption relating to the provision of cyclists' breakfasts was removed from April 2013.

Legislation: ITEPA 2003, s. 266, 317; *Income Tax (Exemption of Minor Benefits) Regulations* 2002 (SI 2002/205)

415   Mobile telephones

An employer-provided mobile telephone (including one mounted in a car, van or heavier commercial vehicle) which is used for private calls is exempted from any income tax charge in accordance with the general charging provision (see 382).

A 'mobile telephone' is one not physically connected to a land line (including a car telephone), but not telepoint telephones or cordless extensions to domestic telephones. HMRC accept that smartphones satisfy the conditions to qualify as 'mobile phones'.

From 6 April 2006, this exemption applies where only one mobile phone or similar device is lent to an employee but it must not be lent to his or her family or household. If the phone was first made available to the employee or member of his or her household before 6 April 2006, no charge arises. No charge will be due where provision of the phone is facilitated by the use of a voucher or credit token. For years prior to 1999–2000, a standard charge of £200 per phone applied.

Legislation: FA 2006, s. 60; ITEPA 2003, s. 319

Other Material: HMRC Brief 02/12

416 Computer equipment

Prior to 6 April 2006, the first £500 of the annual benefit in kind of a computer borrowed from an employer was exempted. From 2006–07 onwards, this exemption has been removed. Equipment first made available to the employee, or his or her family, before 6 April 2006 is unaffected by the change.

Legislation: FA 1999, s. 45; FA 2004, s. 79; FA 2005, s. 17; FA 2006, s. 61

417 Works bus services

Any benefits attributable to an employee as a result of an employer either directly providing a works bus service or subsidising, in any way, a public transport bus service, are exempt from the general benefit-in-kind charge (see 382). Where such a benefit is made available through a ticket or voucher, any charge under the non-cash voucher rules is also exempted.

To qualify for this exemption for a works bus service, the buses used must have a seating capacity of 12 or more (a 'large' bus) and the facility must be available to employees generally. However, to make it easier for smaller employers to offer such a service, the exemption allows the service to be provided by means of a minibus, which has a seating capacity of at least nine but not more than 12 seats. To ensure that safety is not compromised by unscrupulous employers squeezing additional seats into vehicles such as people carriers to bring them within the definition of 'minibus', the exemption will only apply to vehicles originally constructed to carry nine or more seats.

Where a subsidy is provided to a bus service operator, the fares paid by employees must not be lower than non-employee passengers' fares. The exemption only extends to bus services that convey employees on 'qualifying journeys'; these are trips between:

- an employee's home and workplace; or

- one workplace and another.

However, employees may benefit from lower fares without a benefit arising, so long as the service is a local stopping service. The definition of a qualifying journey includes the situation where the bus is used for only part of the journey to work.

Legislation: ITEPA 2003, s. 242; FA 1999, s. 45

Other material: Employer-supported local bus service – FAQs: www. hmrc.gov.uk/thelibrary/local-bus-faqs.pdf

418   Bicycles and cycling safety equipment

The benefit of bicycles and cycling safety equipment provided by employers to employees for their commuting journey is exempt from the general benefit-in-kind charge (see 382).

No tax charge arises where employees buy bicycles from their employer, provided that the bicycle has previously been loaned to them or to another employee, and that they pay market value.

Legislation: FA 1999, s. 50; ITEPA 2003, s. 244; FA 2005, s. 16 and 17

419   Eye tests and spectacles

The provision by an employer of eyecare tests and/or corrective spectacles for VDU users is exempt from 2006–07 onwards. The exemption applies irrespective of whether the costs are paid directly, reimbursed or provided by means of a voucher.

There are two conditions that must be met. Condition A is that the provision of the test or appliances is required by the *Health and Safety at Work, etc. Act* 1974. Condition B is that tests and glasses are made available generally to employees working with VDUs.

Legislation: ITEPA 2003, s. 320A

420 Sporting testimonials: limited exemption

From 6 April 2017, all income from sporting testimonials is subject to income tax. A one-off exemption from income tax of £100,000 applies for income which is neither contractual nor customary (ITEPA 2003, s. 226E and 306B, as inserted by *Finance Act* 2016). Prior to 6 April 2017, income from sporting testimonials where there was no entitlement to the testimonial and no custom existed in respect of it was not treated as earnings within ITEPA 2003, s. 62 by HMRC concession (within HMRC guidance). The amendments by *Finance Act* 2016 are to put the treatment of sporting testimonials beyond doubt and take effect in relation to a sporting testimonial payment made out of money raised by a sporting testimonial where the sporting testimonial was made public on or after 25 November 2015, and the payment is made out of money raised by one or more relevant events or activities which take place on or after 6 April 2017. This means that for a testimonial year announced on or after 25 November 2015 with events taking place, say, between September 2016 and September 2017, only the payments from events taking place after 5 April 2017 can be taken into account for the exemption to apply. The payments for events taking place before 6 April 2017 will not be subject to the charge to tax under s. 226E. See also 286.

Legislation: ITEPA 2003, s. 226E, 306B

Termination payments

422 Nature and treatment of termination payments

Whether a payment made to a director or employee on the termination of his office or employment is taxable depends on whether the payment was made by way of reward for services (see 273), or whether it is made to compensate the employee, etc. for the loss of his rights in respect of his employment, etc. It is only the former which is taxable on general principles (though those payments which escape tax on general principles are usually now caught in part by specific provisions: see 424). It is now accepted that genuine non-statutory redundancy payments are not within the former, even if they form part of an employee's terms of employment.

Similar arguments apply to partial termination payments by way of a reduction in duties or the emoluments therefrom. Payments made for such a reduction are generally taxable. However, payments have escaped the general principle where they related to compensation for giving up certain financial advantages which would have accrued and commutation of pension rights. Payment under a termination clause agreed following a move between subsidiaries, resented by the director but enforced by the parent company, has been held to be an emolument rather than damages.

Payments in lieu of notice

The term 'payment in lieu of notice' (PILON) is not a tax term and may be used to describe a number of differing payments made on termination of employment. The exact nature of the payment, rather than the label ascribed to it, will determine the tax consequences. The following table summaries the tax position for various payments commonly described as PILONs.

Nature of payment	Tax implications
Notice is given but not worked commonly referred to as 'gardening leave'), salary for the notice period being paid as a lump sum	There is no payment in lieu. The salary payment is taxed as normal under ITEPA 2003, s. 6(1)
Contractual arrangements provide for PILON to be paid as an alternative to notice	The PILON replaces the salary that would have been payable had proper notice been given. It is a chargeable emolument under ITEPA 2003, s. 6(1)
Employer and employee agree at the time of termination that the employment is to be terminated without proper notice, but on making of a PILON	No contractual PILON. Payment is a termination payment chargeable under ITEPA 2003, s. 401
Contractual arrangements do not provide for a PILON. The employer terminates the contract and tenders a PILON	No contractual PILON. Payment represents liquidated damages and is taxed under ITEPA 2003, s. 401

Where a professional person also holds an office and is paid compensation in respect of its termination, that payment is assessable under the charge on employment income provisions and not under the charge on business profits provisions.

Statutory redundancy payments and similar 'employer's payments' are exempt from tax under the charge on employment income provisions.

'Outplacement counselling' and related fees or travelling expenses are also, for most employees and office holders, exempt from tax to the extent that they are provided in the UK.

Legislation: ITEPA 2003, s. 309, 310

Cases: *Moorthy* [2014] TC 03952; *Devaraj* [2014] TC 03834; *Clinton* [2010] TC 00278; *Cornell v R & C Commrs* [2009] TC 00108; *SCA Packaging Ltd v R & C Commrs* [2007] EWHC 270 (Ch); *Brander & Ors v R & C Commrs* (2007) Sp C 610; *EMI Group Electronics Ltd v Coldicott (HMIT)* [1999] BTC 294; *Antelope v Ellis (HMIT)* (1995) Sp C 41; *Mairs (HMIT) v Haughey* [1993] BTC 339; *IR Commrs v Brander & Cruickshank* [1971] 1 WLR 212; *Dale (HMIT) v de Soissons* (1950) 32 TC 126; *Wales (HMIT) v Tilley* [1942] 2 KB 169; *Cameron v Prendergast (HMIT)* [1940] AC 549; *Hunter (HMIT) v Dewhurst* (1932) 16 TC 605; *Phillips* [2016] TC 04950

Other Material: SP 1/94, Non-statutory lump sum redundancy payments

Tax Reporter: ¶437-000

424 Tax treatment of termination payments

To the extent that a termination payment exceeds £30,000, payments and other 'benefits' which are not otherwise chargeable to tax (see 426) are specifically charged under the charge on employment income provisions if they are received in connection with:

- the termination of a person's office or employment; or

- any change in its duties or emoluments.

This had the effect that, technically, some benefits that would have been exempt if provided in connection with continuing employment, could be taxed in connection with a termination or change of duties.

Tax Reporter: ¶437-000

426 Termination settlement agreements

Payments and benefits under a termination settlement agreement are taxable for the year in which they are received, rather than (as previously) being treated as income of the year of termination or change.

For these purposes, 'benefit' includes anything which, if received for performing the duties of the employment, would be (apart from any exemption):

- an emolument of the employment (see 273ff.); or

- taxable as an emolument of the employment (see 312 and 382ff.).

A cash benefit is treated as received:

- when payment is made of or on account of the benefit; or
- the recipient becomes entitled to require payment of or on account of the benefit.

A non-cash benefit is treated as received when it is used or enjoyed.

The rules apply to all payments and other benefits received directly or indirectly in consideration or in consequence of, or otherwise in connection with, the termination or change:

(1) by the employee or former employee;

(2) by the spouse or civil partner, or any relative or dependant of the employee or former employee; or

(3) by the personal representatives of the former employee.

A payment or other benefit which is provided on behalf, or to the order, of the employee or former employee is treated as received by the employee or former employee.

The following are excluded from charge.

(1) Payments, etc. made on account of injury to or 'disability' of the employee, or where termination of employment is as a consequence of the employee's death. A 'disability' can be caused by a slow deterioration in mental or physical health, as well as a sudden affliction.

(2) Terminal grants, gratuities or other lump sums paid to members of the armed forces.

(3) Benefits under pension schemes run by the government of an overseas Commonwealth territory, or compensation for career loss, interruption of service or disturbance made in connection with any constitutional change in such a territory to a person who, before the change, was employed in the territory's public service (this effectively re-enacts previous provisions).

Application of £30,000 threshold

The application of the £30,000 threshold is as follows:

(1) payments and benefits in respect of different employments with the same or an 'associated' employer are aggregated;

(2) if the payments, etc. are received in different tax years, the £30,000 is set against payments, etc. received in earlier years before those of earlier later years (thus reflecting that payments, etc. are now chargeable as they are received); and

(3)   within any particular tax year, any outstanding exemption is allocated first to cash benefits as they are received, any balance at the end of the year being set against the aggregate value of non-cash benefits received in the year.

Exclusion or reduction of charge in case of foreign service

Relief is available in respect of payments in relation to 'foreign service'. Full exemption continues to be given from the charge where the period of foreign service meets one of three tests.

Where there has been foreign service but on a scale insufficient to qualify for exemption as above, the charge is proportionately reduced (as previously). However, a taxpayer is not entitled to this relief in so far as the relief, together with any personal relief allowed to him, would reduce the income on which he is chargeable below the amount of income tax which he is entitled:

(1)   to charge against any other person; or

(2)   to deduct from any payment he is liable to make.

Valuation of benefits

The amount of a payment or other benefit is:

(1)   in the case of a cash benefit, the amount received; and

(2)   in the case of a non-cash benefit, the 'cash equivalent' of the benefit.

The 'cash equivalent' of a non-cash benefit is whichever is the greater of:

(1)   the amount which would be chargeable to tax if the benefit were an emolument of the employment chargeable to tax under ITEPA 2003 (see 250) (which would catch a benefit which has risen in value since acquisition); or

(2)   the cash equivalent of benefits under non-approved pension schemes (see 422), which largely follows the counterpart rules for employee benefits (see 382).

Notional interest treated as paid if amount charged in respect of beneficial loan

Where a person is taxable under the present provisions on the cash equivalent of a beneficial loan, relief is given which mirrors that available to employees for 'notional interest' payable on a beneficial loan that attracts interest relief (see 406).

Giving effect to the charge to tax

Tax under the present provisions is charged on the employee or former employee, whether or not he or she is the recipient of the payment or other benefit. After the death of the employee or former employee, any outstanding charge is attached to his or her estate (as previously).

Reporting requirements

Employers must provide a report by the 6 July after the tax year in which any termination award is made. (This relaxes the previous requirement of a report within 30 days of the tax year end.)

For more details of the rules concerning ex gratia payments, see 422.

Legislation: ITEPA 2003, s. 401–404; *Income Tax (Pay As You Earn) Regulations* 2003 (SI 2003/2682); *The Tax and Civil Partnership Regulations* 2005 (SI 2005/3229)

Cases: *Colquhoun* [2010] TC 00348; *Moorthy v R & C Commrs* [2016] BTC 501; *Gedir* [2016] TC 04974; *Tottenham Hotspur Ltd* [2016] TC 05143

Tax Reporter: ¶437-000

428   The treatment of damages

An employee may commence or threaten legal proceedings for wrongful dismissal or breach of contract. Any payment made in settlement of such a claim is treated as a payment in compensation for loss of office and is chargeable as a specific termination payment, and the usual exemptions apply to it where appropriate (see 424).

Damages for wrongful dismissal or for breach of contract are to put the innocent party in the same position that he would have been in had the contract been carried out. In most instances, the employee would have been liable to tax on the payment. A deduction can accordingly be made to allow for tax from such payments so that the employee is in no better position than he would have been in had there been no breach of contract. This is known as the rule in *Gourley's* case.

Limitations to the Gourley rule

The following limitations to the *Gourley* rule should be noted:

- income tax is only deducted if such tax would have been deducted had there not been a breach of contract; and

- the damages, etc. themselves must not be the subject of a charge to tax.

In the case of damages for wrongful dismissal and breach of contract, the taxpayer would have paid tax on the payments as wages or salary if there had been no breach of contract, but such damages are charged to tax allowing the first £30,000 to be tax-free (see 424). The excess over £30,000, therefore, does not fall within the *Gourley* rule, whereas the first £30,000 does.

Case: *British Transport Commission v Gourley* [1956] AC 185

Tax Reporter: ¶437-000

Employee share schemes

430   Share incentives generally

All shares and securities acquired in connection with an employment come within the scope of the employment-related securities regime, including shares acquired by directors or employees on the formation of a company. The rules also extend to rights or opportunities to acquire securities, and to benefits in connection with shares and securities that are not otherwise chargeable to tax. They cover cases where the securities, or opportunities or rights to acquire the securities, are provided by a person other than the employer, and where the securities are not directly received by the employee.

In general, the treatment of remuneration received through shares and other forms of security follows the main principle that applies to other forms of remuneration such as cash and benefits. That principle is to charge to income tax and National Insurance contributions (NICs) the value that the employee receives as reward for his services at the time he has access to that value.

In deciding whether the employee has received reward for services in connection with securities, it is necessary to look at the extent to which, if at all, the employee has given consideration other than services. If, for example, the employee has paid the full market value for a simple share received from his or her employer, then there will be no employment reward and no charge to income tax and NICs on acquisition of the share. Any future normal commercial growth in the value of the share is within the capital gains tax regime.

Similarly, if an employee is given a free share as a reward for services, and pays income tax and NICs on the full value of that share, then the employee is exposed to exactly the same potential financial loss if the venture fails as he or she would have been having risked his or her own funds from the outset. Future normal commercial growth in value of such a security is also within the capital gains regime.

In more complex situations, the employee may receive a share as a reward for services, with the acquisition structured so that the value is acquired at some future point, contingent on some future event or condition being fulfilled and as a reward for future services. This right or opportunity is not dissimilar to a share option. When that opportunity crystallises and the employee receives the benefit of that value, then the rules also tax that benefit.

An employee who acquires shares at less than market value under an opportunity available by reason of his employment may be treated as if his employer has lent him that amount interest-free (see 410) (before 6 April 2016, this charge would apply only to employees earning over £8,500 per year and directors).

It is probably worth highlighting here that FA 2013 provided for a new capital gains tax exemption for shares received through the adoption of 'employee shareholder'. Such shares are those acquired by the new category of 'employee shareholder', introduced by the *Growth and Infrastructure Act* 2013. The new legislation applies from 1 September 2013. Broadly, the exemption will be available on shares received with an 'unrestricted' market value between £2,000 and £50,000, subject to various stipulations, including a 'material interest' threshold (see 441).

Relief for National Insurance contributions on share option gains is dealt with at 2568.

Relief is given in respect of CGT for amounts charged to income under these provisions (see 5925).

Legislation: FA 2003, s. 140, Sch. 23; ITEPA 2003, s. 471–487; *Finance Act 2013, Schedule 23 (Employee Shareholder Shares) (Appointed Day) Order* 2013 (SI 2013/1755)

Cases: *Abbott v Philbin (HMIT)* [1961] AC 352; *Ball (HMIT) v Phillips* [1990] BTC 470; *Hunt (HMIT) v Murphy* [1992] BTC 28; *Tailor* [2013] TC 02614

Other Material: HMRC *Employee Share Schemes Manual*; *Tax Bulletin*, Special Edition (May 2005)

Tax Reporter: ¶464-000

431 Unapproved schemes

It is possible to do almost anything with an unapproved scheme, always provided that any company law or regulatory requirements are complied with. The attraction to employers is the complete flexibility to create their own rules. Such schemes may for example embody the use of growth shares (including by means of so-called JSOPs ('Joint Share Ownership Plans')).

Whilst this flexibility all sounds very attractive, there is a downside, namely, the tax liabilities that the employee may or will suffer on acquisition of the shares, exercising options or receiving any other benefit. Employees will pay tax at their highest marginal income tax rate, often through PAYE. For the employer, there could be a National Insurance charge at the full employer rate (currently 13.8%). In addition, a NIC charge of up to 12% may impact on employees, albeit at a much lower rate (2%) for those on higher salaries.

Unapproved share schemes may take various forms, including unapproved share option schemes and share incentives. Employees and officers may be offered the opportunity to acquire shares in their capacity as employees and officers, such incentives including:

- formal incentive schemes, such as employee benefit trusts;
- individual service agreements;
- pre-emption rights, especially in the case of directors;
- flotations or public offers;
- management buy-outs; or
- one-off offers to individuals or groups of individuals.

Also falling under the heading of unapproved schemes are (for example) the following:

- share acquisitions at an undervalue;
- participation in public offers;
- share sales at an overvalue;
- conditional acquisition of shares;
- acquisition of convertible shares; and
- lifting of restrictions on shares, growth in value of shares in dependent subsidiaries and shares providing special benefits.

Although unapproved schemes do not have the tax advantages associated with the approved schemes, they are useful in some circumstances. Because they do not need to meet the stringent conditions for HMRC approval, they are more flexible in their application and can be better tailored to the needs of the organisation. They are often used where the company wishes to reward selected employees only and where this is not possible within the confines of an approved scheme. Unapproved schemes are often cheaper and quicker to set up and there is no approval process that has to be undertaken.

Legislation: ITEPA 2003, Pt. 7, Ch. 1–5

432   Key tax charges in employee shares

Where a participating employee exercises an option under an approved scheme, there will always be a charge to income tax on exercise. There is no exception to this rule. The income tax charge is calculated as follows:

Value of shares at date of exercise	x
Less: Cost of shares	(x)
Charge at date of grant (if any)	(x)
Taxable income	x

The grant of an option by an employer to an employee is a disposal of an asset by the employer (the option itself) and an acquisition of that asset by the employee at that time. Where the grant of the option is in recognition of past, present or future office or employment services, which would be the case where the obtaining of the option was by reason of holding the office or employment as a director or an employee, the market value rule that would apply is disapplied in determining the employer's disposal proceeds of the option (and the employee's cost of acquiring the option) for capital gains tax purposes. Therefore, the gain realised by the employer on the grant of the option is computed as follows:

(1)   actual consideration received for granting the option; *less*

(2)   the cost of providing the option (if any).

When the option is exercised by the employee, the grant and exercise of the option become a single transaction. Thus, at the time of exercising the option, the grant of the option ceases to be a disposal by the employer, or an acquisition by the employee, of an asset. Any capital gains tax paid in respect of the grant of the option is set off or refunded. It should be noted that the cessation of the option on its exercise does not amount to a disposal of the option by the holder (i.e. employee).

Where an employee is granted an option to acquire shares in his employer or some related company, there are potential income tax charges:

- on the grant of an option under an approved company share option plan where any amount paid for the grant plus the amounts payable to acquire the shares is less than the market value of the shares at the date of the grant. The granting of any other employment-related options does not give rise to an income tax charge;

- on the exercise of the option, where the market value of the shares acquired exceeds the amount paid for them. The employee must be UK resident at the time the option was granted.

An income tax charge may also arise where an option is assigned or surrendered without being exercised.

The market value rule

Where the option is granted over shares which are already in existence (i.e. they are currently held by another shareholder or some form of trust), the disposal of the shares on the exercise of the option and the corresponding acquisition by the employee would normally fall within TCGA 1992, s. 17 because the option would have been granted in recognition of the employee's services and as a result the consideration for both the disposal and acquisition would be the market value of the shares at that time. However, following the decision in *Mansworth v Jelley* [2003] BTC 3, the market value rule does not apply. Instead, the consideration for the disposal and acquisition will be the actual exercise price.

The *Mansworth v Jelley* case concerned the amount which should be taken as the 'cost' of the shares acquired under an option granted to an employee. Mr Jelley was non-resident when the options were granted although resident when they were exercised. Therefore, there was no income tax charge, which would otherwise have been treated as part of his cost for CGT purposes. That being the case, his cost would have been merely the amount paid to acquire the shares on the exercise of the option, so that the whole of his profit would have been liable to CGT. However, a vital point (and one overlooked by many, including HMRC) was that the shares he received were already in existence (probably held by some form of trust) and so he could argue successfully that the market value rule in TCGA 1992, s. 17 applied because his acquisition was a transaction not at arm's length and/or was in recognition of his services as an employee. So his base cost was the market value of the shares when he acquired them, which being the same as the sale proceeds, meant that there was no capital gain and the whole of his profit escaped tax. TCGA 1992, s. 144A was introduced with effect from 10 April 2003 to deny the use of the market value rule in circumstances where assets are acquired as a result of the exercise of an option.

(If the shares acquired by Mr Jelley had been issued to him by the company, the market value rule could not have applied as this requires the transaction to be both an acquisition and a disposal and the company does not make a disposal when it issues shares.)

Computation of gains or losses

The current position is therefore that if the employee subsequently disposes of shares which were acquired on the exercise of the option, then, regardless of whether those shares were in existence prior to his acquisition, the gain or loss on that disposal is computed as follows:

(1) disposal proceeds; *less*

(2) the actual consideration paid for the shares on exercise of the option; *less*

(3) any amount(s) charged to income tax as a result of being granted the option or the acquisition of the shares.

Example

An employee pays £100 for the granting of an unapproved share option to buy 1,000 shares in his employer at £1 each. At the time of the grant of the option, the shares are worth £5 each. When the employee exercises the option, the shares are worth £10 each. A year later, the employee sells the shares for £15,000.

The employee is not subject to income tax in respect of the benefit on the grant of the option (i.e. on the gain of £3,900, being £5,000 less £1,000 less £100). When he exercises the option, the gain charged to income tax is £8,900 (namely, £10,000, less £1,000, less £100). On the sale of the shares, he realises a chargeable gain of £5,100 (namely, £15,000, less £1,000, less £8,900).

Shares acquired by the exercise of options prior to 10 April 2003

It is theoretically possible (but highly improbable) that taxpayers still hold shares which were acquired before 10 April 2003 by the exercise of employment-related options. Following the decision not to appeal against the Court of Appeal's ruling in *Mansworth v Jelley*, HMRC issued a technical note which advised that in all cases where shares were acquired on the exercise of an option prior to 10 April 2003, the gain or loss on the subsequent disposal of the shares was to be computed by deducting from the sale proceeds:

- the market value of the shares at the time the option was exercised; *plus*

- any amount chargeable to income tax on the exercise of that option.

This advice was heavily criticised at the time. In particular, Counsel for Mr Jelley described the guidance as 'incomplete and seriously muddled'. HMRC had overlooked two key aspects of the case:

(1) the market value rule cannot apply where the shares were issued by the company to the employee. That rule does not apply unless there is both an acquisition and a disposal and the company does not make a disposal when it issues shares;

(2) the income tax charge is treated as a element of the acquisition cost under TCGA 1992, s. 38, but, if the market value rule applies, s. 38 is displaced. The two are thus incompatible.

It took six years before HMRC admitted that the guidance they had issued in 2003 was incorrect (HMRC Brief 30/09, issued on 12 May 2009). It accepted that, where the market value rule applied, that was the full measure of the acquisition cost; it was not to be augmented by the amount of any income tax charge.

This 'new understanding' was to be applied to cases where there was an open enquiry.

The *Mansworth* case only affects unapproved share option schemes and EMIs. It does not affect the treatment of gains arising under SAYE option schemes or CSOPs.

Legislation: TMA 1970, s. 33 and 43; FA 2006, s. 92

Case: *Mansworth (HMIT) v Jelley* [2002] BTC 270

Tax Reporter: ¶465-000

433   Restricted securities

'Restricted securities' are, as the name suggests, those that are acquired by employees and have restrictions attaching to them. These restrictions might commonly include a prohibition on selling or transferring the securities other than in specified circumstances, and a positive requirement to sell (or in some circumstances forfeit) the securities on termination of employment. Not every 'restriction' though will be a relevant restriction for the purposes of the legislation governing restricted securities.

Restricted securities originally became popular because they could provide two separate benefits. First, they could act as a kind of handcuff on employees who realised that they had assets of considerable value in a growing market, and would be reluctant to lose them by leaving the company. Second, they were carefully structured to take full advantage of the relevant tax legislation: the concept being that securities subject to certain restrictions had a value or worthless than those without restrictions, and hence, produced a lower (or eliminated any) income tax charge on acquisition by the employee; but that on a subsequent sale of the company, those restrictions effectively fell away, such that the employee, as a selling shareholder, could enjoy his full pro-rata share of the entire sale proceeds.

It was as a reaction to the potential tax advantages of restricted securities that the legislation was tightened up in 2003. *Finance Act* 2003 provisions, embodied in ITEPA 2003, enacted a new regime for 'restricted securities'. In part, this replaced the 'conditional shares' regime that was then in place, and which HMRC have clearly concluded was not serving its purpose.

Where income tax is charged under the rules for restricted securities in ITEPA 2003, Pt. 7, Ch. 2, TCGA 1992, s. 120 provides that the amount chargeable to tax will form part of the base cost for capital gains tax purposes on a subsequent disposal of the shares.

The specific legislation relating to restricted securities is in ITEPA 2003, s. 422ff. This needs to be read in particular with the more general rules in ITEPA 2003, s. 417ff., and (with respect to PAYE) in s. 698ff. For market value definitions, see TCGA 1992, Pt. VIII.

The legislation in this area has been criticised, in the Supreme Court case of *Grays Timber Products Ltd v R & C Commrs* [2010] BTC 112, for its lack of coherence – in the sense that it seeks to apply the statutory 'market value' definition in the TCGA 1992 to securities subject to restrictions that are personal to the employee.

The current legislation applies to all securities acquired by an employee on or after 16 April 2003, but does not apply to those acquired before that date. The latter are still governed by the old rules (including those for 'conditional shares' in place up to April 2003).

Legislation: ITEPA 2003, s. 435–446

Case: *Cyclops Electronics Ltd* [2016] TC 05237

Tax Reporter: ¶474-500

434 Tax-advantaged share option schemes

To encourage share ownership, successive governments have introduced various tax-advantaged share option schemes (generally referred to as 'approved' schemes). Provided that certain conditions are met normally, there is no charge to income tax under general principles on the grant or exercise, etc. of an option (see 431) where shares are acquired under an approved share option scheme.

From 6 April 2014, taxpayers must register all existing and new employee share schemes and arrangements online. They must also self-certify that any tax advantaged schemes meet certain requirements. Registration and self-certification had to be completed by 7 July 2015 in order for tax advantages to apply for (and, it would seem therefore, in respect of awards made in) tax year 2014–15.

HMRC will no longer approve any new tax advantaged schemes (these will be subject to self-certification above). Companies will be able to apply for a 'non-statutory clearance' from HMRC.

From April 2015, taxpayers must file all information returns online. Automatic penalties will apply for late filing. HMRC no longer send a notice to file or reminder. Schemes previously approved lost their tax advantages where they had not registered by 6 July 2015.

For details of the various tax-approved schemes, see 435ff.

Tax Reporter: ¶465-500

435   Company share option schemes

The company share option plan (CSOP) is one of the tax-advantaged share incentive schemes available to companies. It is a 'discretionary', as distinct from an 'all-employee', type of scheme. The employer company or group can therefore decide precisely which of its employees and/or directors are to be invited to participate (so long as any such individual will meet the eligibility criteria).

The value of shares for which a person may hold options under any approved scheme established by his employer or any associated company is limited to £30,000.

In the case though of smaller companies seeking to provide a share incentive to management, the £30,000 limit is not necessarily an impediment. Here, the principal difficulties which in many cases have precluded use of a CSOP have been the requirements that, first, generally prohibit the placing of restrictions on scheme shares and, second, stipulate that the company over whose shares options are to be granted must not be under the 'control' of another company.

These two requirements have, for example, generally precluded private equity groups from employing CSOPs in their investee companies. In addition, the rule that any exercise of options within three years from the date of grant normally incurs income tax treatment for the exercising employee, rather than capital gains tax treatment, has been a discouraging factor too.

The above landscape is however now changing, in two principal respects, following a review of the various tax-advantaged share schemes undertaken by the Office of Tax Simplification (OTS) during 2012. Broadly, provisions included in FA 2013, which took effect from 17 July 2013, remove the former prohibitions on the use of certain 'restricted' shares, and provide that no income tax liability will arise where share options are exercised within three years from grant under a CSOP scheme, following the making of a general offer to acquire the relevant company by way of a qualifying (and cash, or cash and other assets) takeover. These two changes will undoubtedly allow CSOP schemes to be adopted and utilised in a wider range of cases than hitherto. For those companies that do not qualify to use the enterprise management incentives (EMI) scheme (see 437), it might repay considering whether a CSOP could be a way forward. It is conceivable that the CSOP could enjoy something of a resurrection at least. However, it should be noted that the prohibition on 'control', referred to above, does remain in place.

The share price must be specified at the time the option is granted and must not be manifestly less than their market value at that time.

Following the Autumn Statement in December 2012, the Government announced various changes to the four tax-advantaged share schemes. These resulted from an earlier review and consultation process. In relation to CSOPs, FA 2013 therefore includes changes:

- to simplify and harmonise the 'retirement' rules that apply to give favourable tax treatment;

- to simplify the CSOP rules that govern when those leaving employment can qualify for favourable tax treatment as 'good leavers'. Where options are exercised within three years from grant, but in connection with the employment ceasing by virtue of a TUPE transfer, or the employer company ceasing to be an 'associated' company (for example, on being sold off), such favourable tax treatment will remain available to the exercising option holder;

- so that no income tax liability will arise where share options are exercised within three years from grant under a CSOP scheme following the making of a general offer to acquire the relevant company by way of a qualifying (and cash, or cash and other assets) takeover;

- to raise the 'material interest' threshold for CSOP schemes from 25% to 30%; and

- to remove the former prohibitions on the use of certain 'restricted shares'.

These changes have effect from the date of Royal Assent to FA 2013 (17 July 2013).

HMRC's *Employment-Related Shares and Securities Bulletin* 7 (issued March 2013) confirmed that CSOP scheme documents that are amended solely to reflect the new legislation above, will not require approval, notwithstanding there may be alterations to a 'key feature' of the scheme.

The procedure for obtaining approval is substantially the same as that for approved savings-related share option schemes.

Legislation: ITEPA 2003, Pt. 7, Ch. 7, Sch. 3, para. 46, Sch. 4, para. 34

Cases: *Reed International plc v IR Commrs* [1995] BTC 373; *IR Commrs v Eurocopy plc* [1991] BTC 459

Website: www.gov.uk/tax-employee-share-schemes

Tax Reporter: ¶467-000

436   Savings-related share options (SAYE)

Tax-advantaged savings-related share option schemes are generally known as 'SAYE share option schemes'. As with other approved schemes, their approved status confers certain tax advantages.

Generally, no income tax liability arises on the grant of the options or upon their exercise (provided three years have elapsed), but see below regarding FA 2013 changes where there is a general offer to acquire the relevant company, by way of a qualifying (and cash, or cash and other assets) takeover. SAYE options can be exercised where an employee loses their job as a result of injury, disability, redundancy or retirement, or following a move between associated companies (usually after restructuring).

Under a SAYE scheme, the employee commits to save a fixed amount each month for five years. The minimum monthly contribution is £10 and the maximum is currently £500 (£250 prior to 6 April 2014). Any return from the plan will be free from tax. A bonus is paid if the savings are not encashed at the end of the five years and are allowed to accumulate for a further two years. A decision needs to be taken at the outset as to whether the amount payable on the exercise of the option should take account of the bonus.

Simple interest is paid on uncompleted contracts repaid after one year. Contributions and bonuses repaid between years five and seven attract compound interest.

Capital gains tax only is charged on an eventual disposal of the shares. However, the employee's acquisition value is the amount that he pays under the option and not the market value of the shares at that time.

Following the Autumn Statement in December 2012, the Government announced various changes to the four tax-advantaged share schemes. These resulted from an earlier review and consultation process. In relation to SAYE schemes, FA 2013 therefore includes changes:

- to simplify and harmonise the 'retirement' rules that apply to give favourable tax treatment;

- to simplify the SAYE rules that govern when those leaving employment can qualify for favourable tax treatment as 'good leavers'. Where options are exercised within three years from grant, but in connection with the employment ceasing by virtue of a TUPE transfer, or the employer company ceasing to be an 'associated' company (for example, on being sold off), such favourable tax treatment will remain available to the exercising option holder;

- so that no income tax liability will arise where share options are exercised within three years from grant under a SAYE scheme following the making of, a general offer to acquire the relevant company, by way of a qualifying (and cash, or cash and other assets) takeover;

- to remove the 'no material interest' requirement for SAYE schemes;

- to remove the former prohibitions on the use of certain 'restricted shares'.

These changes have effect from the date of Royal Assent to FA 2013 (17 July 2013).

HMRC's *Employment-Related Shares and Securities Bulletin* 7 (issued March 2013) confirmed that SAYE scheme documents that are amended solely to reflect the new legislation above, will not require approval, notwithstanding there may be alterations to a 'key feature' of the scheme.

Legislation: ITEPA 2003, Pt. 7, Ch. 7, Sch. 3, 4

Other Material: www.gov.uk/tax-employee-share-schemes

Tax Reporter: ¶470-000

437 Enterprise management incentives

In nine cases out of ten, if a company qualifies for the selective enterprise management incentives (EMI) scheme, and takes the project to fruition, it will end up implementing that scheme. This is due to a combination of great flexibility and particularly attractive tax breaks for employees.

EMI schemes benefit from the relatively low rates of capital gains tax, compared with up to 47% combined for income tax and NIC. Further, those employees holding sufficient shares to qualify for entrepreneurs' relief (at least 5% of the ordinary shares and voting rights), may enjoy a 10% rate chargeable on the first £10m of lifetime gains.

The Government's proposal to enhance the EMI scheme in relation to CGT entrepreneurs' relief was enacted by FA 2013. Broadly, gains on the disposal of shares acquired through the exercise of EMI options on or after 6 April 2013 (with a further rule for certain disposals within the 2012–13 tax year), may benefit from two changes to the CGT entrepreneurs' relief rules, specific to EMI options:

- the individual no longer has to meet the 'personal company' requirement (the requirement to hold a minimum 5% of ordinary share capital and of voting rights), invariably a hurdle that many EMI option holders find difficult to satisfy; and

- the minimum 12-month ownership period runs from the date of EMI option grant and not from the date of acquisition of the shares.

The major factors that might prevent qualification for EMIs are:

- the working hours requirement;

- the gross assets limit for the company or group of £30m;

- the restrictive qualification with regard to trading which eliminates, among others, property developers and accountants; and

- the individual limit on shares under option at any time, which currently stands at £250,000, having increased from £120,000 from 16 June 2012.

With effect from 21 July 2008, an additional limit on the number of employees was imposed. This prevented companies or groups with 250 or more employees from participating.

There is also an overall limit of £3m on the total value of shares that can be held under option at any time for each company (or group), although it is highly unlikely in practice that this will stop any but a handful of companies that might be interested in implementing an EMI scheme.

From 17 July 2013, the time within which EMI options may be exercised following a 'disqualifying event', and retain their favourable tax treatment was extended from 40 to 90 days.

These are simple, flexible option arrangements that almost allow the company to draw up its own arrangements in an atmosphere of complete freedom. Options can be offered at any price and with an exercise date that could be as soon as the next week, should that prove attractive. Further, the arrangements are administratively simple as there is no need to obtain HMRC approval in advance of commencing an agreement.

This means that, at least in theory, a company could draw up an agreement and put an EMI scheme into place on the day that they first thought of it. In practice, it is at least advisable to obtain both an agreed share valuation and clearance that the company is a qualifying company with HMRC before embarking.

Obviously, it is important to remember that formal agreement documentation is required.

Legislation: ITEPA 2003, s. 527–541; FA 2014, Sch. 37, para. 22(1); FA 2013, s. 14 and Sch. 2; FA 2000, s. 62 and Sch. 14; *Finance Act 2014, Schedule 37, Paragraph 22 (Commencement) Order* 2014 (SI 2014/2461); *Finance Act 2013, Schedule 2, Paragraph 31 (Enterprise Management Incentives) (Appointed Day) Order* 2013 (SI 2013/2796); *Income Tax (Limits for Enterprise Management Incentives) Order* 2012 (SI 2012/1360)

Other Material: Tax and employee shares schemes: www.gov.uk/tax-employee-share-schemes

Tax Reporter: ¶466-000

438 Priority share allocations for employees

Where a company makes a public offer of shares, employees are often given priority rights so that if the offer is over-subscribed, the employees will receive either their full allocation or where there is a scaling-down more shares than a member of the public who subscribed for the same number; without special provision, a tax charge could arise (see 430). There are two possible charges: the benefit of priority and the discount.

No taxable benefit accrues from such a share allocation where the offer is at a fixed price or by tender, the employees or directors are entitled to a priority allocation at the fixed price or at the lowest price successfully tendered, and not more than 10% of the shares on offer are subject to employee/director priority. Further, all the persons entitled to the priority allocation must be so entitled 'on similar terms', though discrimination according to pay level, length of service, etc. is allowed. In relation to offers made after 25 July 1990, the 'similar terms' test is not failed where persons who are not directors or employees of the company have a smaller entitlement to shares in the company than those who are, if:

- those who are not employees, etc. are nonetheless entitled, by reason of their employment and in priority to the public, to share allocations in another company which are offered to the public at the same time; and

- the total entitlement of each of those persons is on a par with the entitlement of comparable employees, etc. of the first-mentioned company.

From 16 January 1991, the discount is not covered by the above exemption to the extent that it exceeds a 'registrant discount', i.e. one which is available to directors/employees but which is also available (or for which a suitable alternative is offered) to those individual members of the public who are allocated at least 40% of the rest of the shares.

The condition that a maximum of 10% of the shares offered can be subject to employee/director priority is also modified where the offer to the public is part of an arrangement which includes other offers of shares of the same class in the same company or is made after 15 January 1991 and is part of an offer to the public consisting of a package of shares in two or more companies where employees/directors are entitled to shares in just one (or some) of them. Where there is such an arrangement and employee/director priority applies only to one of those offers, the percentage limit above is both 10% of all the shares and 40% of the shares subject to that offer; in the case of the packaged, multi-company offer, the limit is 10% of each share on offer.

Legislation: ITEPA 2003, Pt. 7, Ch. 10

Tax Reporter: ¶472-360

439 Share incentive plans

Employees can be awarded shares in a tax and NIC-efficient fashion through the means of a share incentive plan. The plan which is an all-employee scheme and which replaced approved profit-sharing schemes has the following key features:

- employers can give employees up to £3,600 (£3,000 prior to 6 April 2014) of shares each year, free of tax and National Insurance;

- some or all of the shares can be awarded to employees for reaching performance targets;

- employees will be able to buy partnership shares out of their pre-tax salary, to a maximum of £1,800 (£1,500 prior to 6 April 2014), free of tax and National Insurance; and

- employees can match partnership shares by giving employees up to two free shares for each partnership share that they buy.

Following the Autumn Statement in December 2012, the Government announced various changes to the four tax-advantaged share schemes.

These resulted from an earlier review and consultation process. In relation to SIPs, FA 2013 therefore includes changes:

- to simplify and harmonise the 'retirement' rules that apply to give favourable tax treatment. In addition, the rules that prohibit the forfeiture of free and matching SIP shares on retirement will continue in relation to shares awarded before 17 July 2013, but as modified by this change;

- so that no income tax liability will arise where shares are withdrawn from a SIP in order to accept a general offer to acquire the relevant company, by way of a qualifying (and cash, or cash and other assets) takeover;

- to remove the 'no material interest' requirement for SIP schemes;

- to remove the former prohibitions on the use of certain 'restricted shares';

- to revise, and give greater flexibility in, the valuation method for determining the number of shares awarded to an employee under a SIP, when applying money deducted in an accumulation period for purchases of 'partnership shares';

- to remove the £1,500 limit on reinvestment of dividends, and the three-year time limit for reinvestment. SIP schemes approved before 17 July 2013, and whose scheme rules provide for reinvestment of dividend shares, will be treated as if such modifications had been made; and

- to remove the requirement for a SIP trust instrument to include provision in relation to the acquisition by the SIP trustees of shares from qualifying ESOTs (Employee Share Ownership Trusts).

These changes took effect from the date of Royal Assent to FA 2013 (17 July 2013), save that the SIP dividend reinvestment rule applies for tax year 2013–14, from 6 April 2013.

HMRC's *Employment-Related Shares and Securities Bulletin* 7 (issued March 2013) confirmed that SIP scheme documents that are amended solely to reflect the new legislation above, will not require approval, notwithstanding there may be alterations to a 'key feature' of the scheme.

Legislation: ITEPA 2003, Pt. 7, Ch. 6 and Sch. 2

Other Material: Tax and employee shares schemes: www.gov.uk/tax-employee-share-schemes

Tax Reporter: ¶468-000

440 Research institution spin out companies

Where the method by which employees share in the rewards of the exploitation of their own intellectual property is via shares in a so-called 'spin out' company, from 2 December 2004, the tax charge on the employee will no longer depend on the value of that property at the time of transfer. The purpose of this rule is intended to encourage the formation of such companies by institutions such as universities, health trusts and the like.

Legislation: FA 2005, s. 20; ITEPA 2003, s. 451

Tax Reporter: ¶471-020

441 Employee shareholder shares

Finance Act 2013 contains provisions, which came into effect from 1 September 2013, dealing with the taxation of 'Employee Shareholder Shares'. Such shares are those acquired by the new category of 'employee shareholder', introduced by the *Growth and Infrastructure Act* 2013.

'Employee shareholder' is a new status for employment law purposes, under which an individual who is or becomes an employee gives up certain employment law rights that would otherwise be available or accrue to the individual, in return for the receipt of shares in the employer or employer parent company. Such parcel of shares must have a market value, on acquisition, of not less than £2,000, and in that case (and subject to meeting the qualifying conditions generally, see further below) will carry with them certain tax advantages. It seems possible that this new category of shareholding will most commonly find use in certain 'growth companies'. Such companies, and perhaps too the type of individual who is interested in working for them, may be attracted to the scheme.

Definition of 'employee shareholder'

This is found in the *Employment Rights Act* 1996 (ERA 1996), s. 205A, inserted by the *Growth and Infrastructure Act* 2013, s. 31.

An individual who is or becomes an employee of a company is an 'employee shareholder' if:

(a) the company and the individual agree that the individual is to be an employee shareholder;

(b) in consideration of that agreement, the company issues or allots to the individual fully paid up shares in the company, or procures the issue or allotment to the individual of fully paid up shares in its parent undertaking, which have a value, on the day of issue or allotment, of no less than £2,000;

(c) the company gives the individual a written statement of the particulars of the status of employee shareholder and of the rights which attach to the shares referred to in paragraph (b); and

(d) the individual gives no consideration other than by entering into the agreement.

The written statement in (c) above must contain the ten items of information set out in the ERA 1996, s. 205A(5). These items include whether any voting or dividend rights, or rights to participate in the distribution of surplus assets on a winding up, attach to the employee shares; whether the employee shares are redeemable and, if they are, at whose option; whether the employee shares are subject to restrictions on transferability and, if so, what those restrictions are; and whether the employee shares are subject to 'drag-along' or 'tag-along' rights and, if they are, the effect of the shares being so subject.

For the above purposes:

(i) 'company' means a company or overseas company (within the meaning, in each case, of the *Companies Act* 2006) which has a share capital, or a European Public Limited-Liability Company (or Societas Europa) within the meaning of Council Regulation 2157/2001/EC of 8 October 2001 on the Statute for a European Company;

(ii) 'parent undertaking' has the same meaning as in the *Companies Act* 2006;

(iii) the 'value' of shares is a reference to their 'market value', within the meaning of TCGA 1992, s. 272 and 273.

Employee must have prior independent advice

Agreement between a company and an individual that the individual is to become an employee shareholder is of no effect unless, before the agreement is made:

- the individual, having been given the statement referred to in (c) above, receives advice from a relevant independent adviser as to the terms and effect of the proposed agreement; and

- seven days have passed since the day on which the individual receives the advice.

The term 'relevant independent adviser' has the meaning it has for the purposes of ERA 1996, s. 203(3)(c), and includes a qualified lawyer and certain certified trade union and advice centre individuals.

The *Employment Rights Act* 1996, s. 205A(7) stipulates that any reasonable costs incurred by the individual in obtaining the advice (whether or not the individual becomes an employee shareholder) which would, but for this subsection, have to be met by the individual are instead to be met by the company.

Employment law rights surrendered

The employment law rights which the employee gives up by becoming an employee shareholder as above are:

(a)   the right to make an application under ERA 1996, s. 63D (request to undertake study or training);

(b)   the right to make an application under ERA 1996, s. 80F (request for flexible working), but see further at ERA 1996, s. 205A(8);

(c)   the right under ERA 1996, s. 94 not to be unfairly dismissed, but see further at ERA 1996, s. 205A(9) and (10); and

(d)   the right under ERA 1996, s. 135 to a redundancy payment.

In addition, the period of notice that an employee must give of her intention to return to work following maternity leave (and corresponding provision for adoption leave) is increased from eight to 16 weeks; and in the case of an employee's notice of intention to return to work following additional paternity leave, increased from six to 16 weeks.

Tax on acquisition

From 1 September 2013, ITEPA 2003, s. 226A (Amount treated as earnings) applies 'if shares having a market value of no less than £2,000 are acquired by an employee in consideration of an employee shareholder agreement'. An 'employee shareholder agreement' means an agreement by virtue of which an employee is an 'employee shareholder' under ERA 1996, s. 205A (see above). In that case, and provided the shares are not acquired pursuant to an employment-related securities option, an amount is to be treated as earnings from the employment in respect of the acquisition, for the tax year in which the shares are acquired, in accordance with s. 226A(2). Shares are 'acquired' by an employee 'if the employee becomes beneficially entitled to them'.

The amount treated as earnings is:

$$MV - P$$

where:

(a)   MV is an amount equal to the market value of the shares;

(b)   P is any payment the employee is treated as making for the shares under ITEPA 2003, s. 226B.

But if P exceeds MV, the amount is nil.

'Market value' has the meaning it has under TCGA 1992, Pt. VIII; and the market value of shares is their market value on the day on which they are acquired.

For the purposes, however, of ascertaining if shares have a market value of no less than £2,000, such market value is to be determined ignoring:

- any election under ITEPA 2003, s. 431 (election for market value of restricted shares to be calculated as if not restricted); and

- s. 437 (market value of convertible securities to be determined as if not convertible).

But if the £2,000 threshold test is satisfied, then for the purposes of determining the amount treated as earnings under s. 226A, the market value of the shares (MV in the formula) is then ascertained in the normal way, and so for example taking account of any s. 431 election (thus, disregarding any relevant restrictions (or relevant specified restriction)), or of the rule in s. 437 (thus, determining market value of convertible securities as if they were not).

Tax on events or circumstances during ownership

Although employee shareholder shares are charged to income tax on acquisition under a new, separate charging provision, such shares are 'employment-related securities' for the purposes of ITEPA 2003, Pt. 7, and so subject generally to the provisions of that Part. Such provisions can operate to impose income tax charges on certain events or circumstances occurring during the employee's ownership of shares.

Finance Act 2013 inserted amendments into Pt. 7 to ensure that these charging provisions marry up with the amount of any income tax charge incurred on acquisition of shares under s. 226A. Thus, in particular, any amount treated as earnings under s. 226A is a 'deductible amount' for the purposes of calculating:

(a) the amount of any charge on a chargeable event under Pt. 7, Ch. 2 (restricted securities);

(b) the amount of any notional loan under Pt. 7, Ch. 3C (securities acquired for less than market value).

Tax on disposal

The principal tax advantage afforded to the owner of employee shareholder shares is the exemption from capital gains tax, on disposal of the shares.

Subject to one other legislative change specific to employee shareholder shares – for certain company purchases of own shares, below – there are no other specific provisions enacted in relation to the disposal of such shares. Accordingly, employee shareholder shares remain subject to those provisions in ITEPA 2003, Pt. 7 that can apply to generate an income tax charge on a disposal of employment-related securities. These include in particular (but are not limited to) charging provisions under:

(a) Pt. 7, Ch. 2 (restricted securities);

(b) Pt. 7, Ch. 3 (convertible securities); and

(c) Pt. 7, Ch. 3D (securities disposed of for more than market value).

Legislation: FA 2013, s. 55 and Sch. 23; *Finance Act 2013, Schedule 23 (Employee Shareholder Shares) (Appointed Day) Order* 2013 (SI 2013/1755)

Other Material: Employee shareholders: www.gov.uk/employee-shareholders

Tax Reporter: ¶471-500

Pensions

450 Introduction

6 April 2006 was the effective date of a major reform of the taxation treatment of pension schemes. From that date, a single unified tax regime applies in place of the eight previous regimes. This regime applies to all types of schemes and to all members of those schemes, regardless of when they joined. Under the unified regime, there are no limits on the amount that an individual can save in a registered pension scheme. However, there are limits on the amount of pension savings that qualify for tax relief.

Legislation: FA 2004, Pt. 4

Tax Reporter: ¶375-250

Types of pension schemes

452 Introduction

Although there is now one universal tax regime for pensions, some pension arrangements still continue to be affected by older legislation and therefore it is important to have an understanding of these issues and how they affect an individual's retirement planning.

Whilst legislation lays down the legal parameters with which schemes must operate, it is important to remember that particular schemes may apply more restrictive rules to the benefits they provide.

There are two main generic types of pension scheme:

(1) Occupational schemes;

(2) Personal schemes.

Tax Reporter: ¶375-250

454 Types of Occupational or Company-sponsored Pension Schemes

Final Salary Scheme

These are also known as 'defined benefit' schemes. They are established by companies to provide retirement benefits for their employees based on salary and length of pensionable service. They are normally regarded as the gold standard for pensions, despite the high profile failure of some schemes, since the employee is guaranteed a certain level of retirement income irrespective of investment performance, and this will increase in retirement (see section on pension increases). Although employees may be required to make contributions, the employer is required to underwrite benefits.

Changes in legal solvency criteria and past stock market declines have put financial pressure on many final salary schemes and increased the level of contributions required which, in turn, has led many employers to seek to wind up their final salary schemes and to switch to alternative arrangements. Clients who have the chance to join a final salary scheme should almost certainly do so, although it may be wise to check the solvency position if personal contributions are required. The benefits are based on the length of a member's pensionable service and their final pensionable salary. A common basis is an initial retirement benefit of one-sixtieth of final pensionable pay for each year of service. Part of this can be commuted for a tax free Pension Commencement Lump Sum. Other rates, such as one-eightieth may also be used, in which case the tax-free Pension Commencement Lump Sum may be additional. Schemes may be contributory or non-contributory. If a scheme is contributory, members will be required to pay a percentage of their salary to the scheme.

Career Average Scheme

These schemes are a 'paired-down' final salary scheme and are becoming increasingly popular as employers try to find a middle ground between maintaining the defined benefit scheme whilst controlling the costs of funding it. At the point of retirement, the pay that the individual has earned in each year will take inflation into account, and then be aggregated. The total will then be divided by the number of years service to provide the 'average' pay, on which the pension will then be based.

Money Purchase Scheme

Also known technically as 'defined contribution' schemes, these depend on investment performance and annuity rates at retirement to determine the final pension payable. The employer and, normally, the employee contribute a percentage of salary into a pension fund for the employee, which hopefully accumulates over time. This money purchase scheme can either be trust based with trustees to look after scheme members' interests, or can be a group personal pension or stakeholder arrangement. Employees who are offered the opportunity to join an occupational or company-sponsored arrangement should usually do so, not only to obtain the benefit of any employer contribution, but also because the charges are generally lower than a scheme organised by the individual.

Contracted-out Pension Schemes

Occupational schemes can either be contracted in, or out, of the State Second Pension (previously State Earnings Related Pension Scheme). See section on contracting-out.

Additional Voluntary Contribution (AVC) Schemes

Members of occupational schemes who wish to make additional contributions in order to enhance their final retirement benefits would normally have done so into an AVC scheme. Benefits are usually based on a money purchase arrangement, although some public sector schemes may provide additional years of pensionable service.

The maximum contribution that members could make prior 6 April 2006 was 15% of total remuneration. So, if the main scheme required contributions of 9%, this only allowed AVC contributions of 6%. This has now changed (see section on maximum contributions) but many individuals may not be aware that they can make increased contributions.

Free Standing Additional Voluntary Contributions (FSAVC) Schemes

Where the individual wished to make private arrangements, for example because the investment options under the AVC were limited, this could be done through FSAVCs. The same contribution limits applied to FSAVCs, except that if the total annual contributions were £2,400 p.a. or less, then no formal test for excessive benefits was necessary. In many cases this set the actual amount of the contribution for the sake of simplicity.

Before 6 April 2001, it was not possible for a member of an occupational pension scheme to contribute to a personal pension. However, since the introduction of stakeholder pensions from 6 April 2001 a member of an occupational pension scheme who earned less than £30,000 gross p.a. could also contribute to a stakeholder pension as long as HMRC contribution limits were not exceeded, and £3,600 in any case. From 6 April 2006, this earnings restriction has been removed (see section on annual allowance). The charges under stakeholder pension plans are likely to be less than those of an FSAVC, and individuals may wish to review this aspect.

Section 32 Policy

This is a policy that can be used to take a transfer from an occupational pension scheme. Although the structural differences between occupational and personal pension regimes have been removed, a s. 32 policy can be appropriate where a transfer from an occupational pension is required while maintaining enhanced benefits.

Executive Pension Schemes

These are plans set up for directors or senior employees. Benefits are provided on a money purchase basis.

Small Self-Administered Pension Schemes (SSAS)

A SSAS is a pooled executive pension plan. For a scheme to qualify as a SSAS, it must abide by the following:

(1) Have no more than 11 active members, of whom at least one must:

    (a) be a controlling director;

    (b) have been a controlling director in the last 10 years; or

    (c) be closely related to:

- another member of the scheme;

- a trustee of the scheme;

- a partner (if the sponsoring company is a partnership); or

- a person who is, or at any time has been in the last 10 years, a controlling director (if the sponsoring employer is a company).

(2) Not have all the assets invested only in insurance policies.

SSASs were popular because they offered the opportunity of wide investment options and in particular the possibility to purchase property. They have therefore been ideal for directors who wish to purchase the company's premises.

They are still popular in some quarters because they permit a loan-back to the company, subject to certain restrictions. However, most of the special features of a SSAS have been removed by the new pension regime.

Funded Unapproved Retirement Benefit Schemes (FURBS)

These arrangements were introduced to provide additional retirement benefits for some employees whose earnings were in excess of the pensionable limit. Although their relevance diminished with the introduction in 2006 of the generous annual allowance and the fairly restrictive Lifetime Allowance, were they saw a resurgence following the anti-forestalling rules from 22 April 2009. FURBS are an individual trust based arrangement between the employee and the employer with the employer acting as the trustee. The contributions do not benefit from tax relief, but there is no limit to the benefits payable, and if required, the entire fund accumulated prior to 6 April 2006 could be taken on retirement as a tax-free lump sum. HMRC now refer to FURBS as Employer-Financed Retirement Benefits Schemes (EFRBS).

Issues surrounding Employer-Financed Retirement Benefits Schemes (EFRBS)

The term Employer Financed Retirement Benefit Scheme (EFRBS) was introduced by the *Finance Act* 2004; this amongst other things amended the definition of the previously used terminology: 'non-approved' schemes (outlined in *Income Tax Earnings and Pensions Act* 2003). Non-approved was the collective pre-A day term used for Funded Unapproved Retirement Benefits (FURBS) and Unfunded Unapproved Retirement Benefits Schemes (UURBS) and all such schemes became EFRBS with effect from 6 April 2006. HMRC must be notified within three months of an EFRBS commencing and by 7 July following the tax year any benefit is provided.

There are special transitional rules for non-approved schemes as the tax position of an EFRBS is markedly different to non-approved schemes.

An EFRBS is an arrangement entered into by an employee and an employer to provide relevant benefits. Relevant benefits are any lump sum, gratuity or other benefit (including non-cash benefits) paid in respect of:

- retirement or death;
- anticipation of retirement;

- after retirement or death in connection with past service;

- anticipation or connection with a change in the nature of the employee's service; or

- a result of a pension sharing order.

Benefits can be constructed either on a money purchase or final salary basis. Regardless of how benefits are accrued under an EFRBS, currently they do not count towards the Annual Allowance and Lifetime Allowance as EFRBS are not registered pension schemes (this may be subject to legislative change).

EFRBS can be both funded and unfunded; however, if unfunded there is an obvious lack of security (**note:** any provision of security/insurance on an unfunded arrangement will give rise to a benefit kind charge on the employee equal to the cost of provision). EFRBS are also not subject to the contribution and investment restrictions which apply to registered pension schemes, providing greater flexibility in design.

The advantages of an Employer-Financed Retirement Benefits Scheme have been undermined by the introduction in *Finance Act* 2011 of an income tax charge on third-party arrangements used by employers to provide a reward to employees. This charge will affect any reward, recognition or loan provided by an employer to an employee in connection with their employment. The charge will be based on the full value of the benefit. In particular, the income tax charge will apply to third-party arrangements which are provide in addition to, in replacement of, registered pension schemes. This means that the legislation includes EFRBS.

Unfunded Unapproved Retirement Benefit Schemes (UURBS)

These arrangements are a means that some employers used to enhance a selected individual's occupational pension scheme. As with FURBS, they were an individual trust-based arrangement between the employee and the employer with the employer acting as the trustee. They differ in that no contributions were actually made at the time to provide the future retirement benefits, which meant that the employee had no tax liability for any employer contributions. However, there is also no guarantee that a pension will be paid in the future. As with FURBS, the pension promise can be exchanged for a lump sum instead. HMRC now refer to UURBS as an Employer-Financed Retirement Benefits Scheme (EFRBS). They are subject to the same new restrictions mentioned above.

456 Types of Personal Pension Schemes

Individuals who are either self-employed, not employed, whose employer does not offer occupational pension arrangements, or who simply wish to establish a private pension scheme (which may be additional to an occupational one) will do so through either a personal or a stakeholder pension plan. These are invariably money purchase schemes in which contributions accrue in selected fund(s) and are subsequently converted into retirement benefits in the future. There are three main personal schemes: retirement annuities, personal pensions, and stakeholder pensions.

Retirement Annuities

Also known as s. 226 contracts, these were the precursor to personal pensions, which were introduced in July 1988. Contributions can continue to be made to these policies, but no new plans can be established.

Personal Pension Plans

These were introduced in July 1988. They are usually offered by life offices, and have a range of charging structures. The investment options are set by the life office although many now have a range of external funds links.

There are a number of features that can apply to these policies of which professional advisers need to be aware.

(1) Although many of these are written under a master trust with a nomination of beneficiary form, this is not necessarily the most inheritance tax efficient solution. Consideration should be given to using a spousal bypass trust as an alternative to the nomination form.

(2) Many older policies are still invested in with-profits, which may no longer be optimal.

(3) Some early personal pensions were written with a fixed guaranteed annuity rate. Although the terms of the annuity can be inflexible, the rate is generally very attractive compared with what is currently available.

(4) Some of these old funds also have a guaranteed annual interest rate, which can be beneficial during market downturns.

(5) Both the Myners Report in 2001 and the Sandler Report in 2002 highlighted that asset allocation decisions can be critical determinants of investment performance. It is therefore vital that this aspect of a client's pensions is properly assessed. Investment management issues are covered later in this chapter.

Stakeholder Pension Plans

Stakeholder pensions were introduced from 6 April 2001. They were an attempt by the Government to introduce low cost, simple pension plans in which the charges that could be levied were controlled. At first, no initial charges could be taken and the maximum annual management charge (AMC) was restricted to 1%. Whilst no initial charge can still be taken, the maximum AMC for individuals who join a stakeholder pension scheme on or after 6 April 2005 is now 1.5% for the first 10 years, reducing to 1% thereafter if the individual remains in the scheme. Other mandatory standards required to qualify as a stakeholder pension are that:

- the scheme cannot charge for transfers into or out; and
- the scheme must accept contributions of as low as £20.

There are a number of features that can apply to these policies of which professional advisers need to be aware.

(1) The earlier schemes had very limited investment options. There may be an opportunity to improve this choice.

(2) As the funds increase over time, the issue of asset allocation becomes increasingly important and a balance needs to be struck between cost and investment risk.

Group Stakeholder Pension Plans

Since 6 April 2001, all employers have been required to provide access to a workplace stakeholder pension scheme unless they meet one of the following exemptions.

(1) They employ fewer than five people. Part-time and non-permanent (i.e. agency) employees have to be included in this total.

(2) All employees are offered access to an occupational scheme that they can join within 12 months of commencing employment.

(3) The company has established a group personal pension scheme that meets the following requirements:

   (a) all relevant employees are eligible to join;

   (b) the company makes employer contributions of a minimum 3% of basic salary to the personal pension;

   (c) the pension scheme is not permitted to impose penalties on those who cease contributions or who transfer to a different arrangement;

   (d) if requested, the company will deduct employees' contributions at source and pay them direct to the scheme.

(4) The company has a restricted membership occupational scheme, but offers the remainder of the workforce the opportunity of joining a group personal pension scheme, which meets the conditions described above.

National Employment Savings Trust (NEST)

The Government introduced new responsibilities for both employers and employees from 2012 aimed at encouraging greater private pension saving via the workplace. These changes include the introduction of a new type of multi-employer national pension scheme. Originally, these were referred to as 'Personal Accounts' but have now been renamed 'National Employment Savings Trust' (NEST). They are available for use by employers who do not have, or choose not to use, any existing pension schemes to meet the new obligations.

Employers have a duty to automatically enrol their eligible employees into a good quality workplace pension scheme.

Employers also have a duty to provide a minimum contribution, and employees have to make mandatory contributions; unless they opt-out of pension provision.

Self Invested Personal Pension (SIPP)

A SIPP is simply a personal pension arrangement that allows investors maximum flexibility in the choice of the underlying investments. It is a registered pension scheme for the purposes of the *Finance Act* 2004, s. 150 and it is now a financial product regulated by the Financial Services Authority. The following table shows the permitted range of investments within SIPPs. This is not exhaustive, but includes the most common assets that are held:

Stocks & Shares	Cash Deposits	Discretionary Management
Internal Life Office insured funds	Corporate Bonds	OEICS, Unit Trusts and Investment Trusts
Commercial Property & Land	Fixed Interest/Gilts	Futures and Options

There are now (post 6 April 06) new rules governing the level of borrowing in respect of a SIPP. A member can now borrow up to 50% of the value of the SIPP, with the most popular reason being for commercial property purchase.

Tax relief on pension contributions

467 Introduction

There are three methods by which a member can receive tax relief for contributions:

- relief at source;
- net pay arrangements; and
- relief on making a claim.

The member cannot choose how the relief is given. The mechanism for giving relief depends on the method that the pension scheme is allowed to operate under the legislation. The 'default' method is relief at source (FA 2004, s. 191(2)) and the other methods are only permitted if certain conditions are satisfied.

Tax Reporter: ¶376-000

471 Contributions and tax relief

The rules on contributions and tax relief have been changed a number of times over recent years.

There is no limit on the amount that an individual can contribute to a registered pension scheme each year. However, there is a limit on the amount of those contributions which are eligible for tax relief. The maximum amount of relievable contributions in any year is the amount of the individual's relevant UK earnings that are chargeable to income tax for that year.

Where those earnings are less than the 'basic amount' of £3,600, the maximum amount of relievable contributions is increased to that amount. However, in such a case, relief is only to be given by means of relief at source. (FA 2004, s. 190(2)–(4), 191(7)). The basic amount may be changed by Treasury order.

Certain contributions do not count towards the annual limit set out above. Where an employer recovers from an employee minimum contributions paid by that employer under the *Pensions Act* 1993, s. 8(3) (or Northern Ireland equivalent) that amount does not count towards the limit on tax relief. Relief is always given on these amounts, regardless of whether tax relief has already been given on contributions to the annual limit. This means that it is possible for tax relief to be given in a year on more than 100% of UK relevant earnings.

473 Annual allowance

A charge to income tax, known as the annual allowance charge, arises where the total pension input for a tax year in respect of a member of one or more registered pension schemes exceeds the annual allowance for that year (FA 2004, s. 227(1)). The charge also applies, with modification, in the case of certain non-UK pension schemes. The amount of the annual allowance for 2016–17 is £40,000.

FA 2004, s. 228ZA provides for a tapered reduction of the annual allowance for 'high-income individuals', with effect for tax year 2016–17 and subsequent years. The taper works by reducing the annual allowance for the year by an amount given by the following formula (which, given the annual allowance for 2016–17 will be £40,000, has the effect of reducing the allowance by £1 for every £2 by which income exceeds £150,000):

$$(T - £150,000) \times (A - £10,000/£60,000)$$

Where T is the individual's adjusted income for the year and A is the annual allowance for the year.

The amount of the reduction is rounded down to the nearest £1.

As the annual allowance cannot be reduced below £10,000 (FA 2004, s. 228ZA(1), (2)), if adjusted income exceeds £210,000 for 2016–17 the annual allowance will be £10,000.

An individual is a 'high-income individual' if:

- his adjusted income for the tax year exceeds £150,000; and

- his threshold income for the tax year exceeds £150,000 less the annual allowance specified for the tax year (as the annual allowance for 2016–17 is £40,000, threshold income will have to exceed £110,000).

The annual allowance charge is levied on so much of the 'total pension input amount' as exceeds the annual allowance for that year. This excess is not treated as income for any purposes of the Tax Acts (FA 2004, s. 227(4), (5)). However, the charge is amended where the individual meets the 'flexible drawdown conditions'.

From 2011–12 onwards, the rate of tax to be charged on the excess is to be the 'appropriate rate'; that is, the rate or rates which would be charged on the excess if it was to be added to the individual's 'reduced net income' for the tax year concerned. That figure is the sum calculated at Step 3 of the prescribed method of calculating income tax liabilities. Any increase in the basic rate or higher rate bands due to pension contributions made under deduction of tax or gift aid payments is also taken into account for this purpose.

Liability for the annual allowance charge normally falls on the member but, in certain circumstances, some part may fall on the scheme administrator.

Total pension input amount

This is the aggregate of the pension input amounts in respect of each arrangement relating to the individual under a registered pension scheme. The pension input amount depends on the nature of the arrangements. However, no pension input amount is taken into account if, before the end of the tax year, the individual either dies or satisfies the following 'severe ill-health condition':

- he becomes entitled to all his benefits under the scheme as a result of evidence from a registered medical practitioner that his health is such that he is unlikely to be able to carry on in gainful employment;
- he becomes entitled to a serious ill-health lump sum; or
- he is a member of the armed forces entitled to a tax-exempt wounds and disability pension.

Carry-forward of allowance (to years 2011–12 onwards)

Where the annual allowance for a tax year exceeds the pension input amount for that year, a limited form of carry-forward is available. Where, in a 'current year' (being 2011–12 or subsequent years), there is an excess of pension input amount over the annual allowance, that allowance may be increased by the 'unused' annual allowance of the three immediately preceding years.

An amount of annual allowance is 'unused' to the extent that, ignoring the effect of any carry-forward, it exceeds the pension input amount for that year and, where that excess arises in the penultimate or the antepenultimate year to the current year, that excess has not been 'used up'. An excess is 'used up' if there is an excess of pension input amount for an 'intervening year' (i.e. one between the year in which the excess arose and the 'current year') and that excess has been used under these provisions to reduce an annual allowance charge for that intervening year.

For any part of a year's annual allowance to be available for carry-forward, the individual must have been a member of a registered pension scheme at some time in that year, even if there were no pension input amounts for that year.

Where unused annual allowance is brought forward to a current year, it is regarded as being set against the current year's pension inputs on a 'first-in, first-out basis', i.e. the allowance for earlier years is used in priority to that for later years.

No claim is required; the carry-forward is mandatory. As a result, unused annual allowance is automatically set off against the next available year's pension input amount.

Legislation: FA 2004, s. 227, 228ZA; *Finance Act 2004 (Registered Pension Schemes and Annual Allowance Charge) (Amendment) Order 2015 (SI 2015/80)*

Tax Reporter: ¶386-000

474   Lifetime allowance

As well as controlling pension contributions through tax reliefs, the total amount that can be accumulated, without penalties, in pension funds is restricted by the 'lifetime allowance'. The lifetime allowance is £1m for 2016–17. Any amounts in excess of the lifetime allowance when benefits are taken will be subject to a tax charge, the amount depending upon how the surplus is taken. There is a lifetime allowance charge of 25% on funds in excess of the lifetime allowance which are used to provide a pension. If funds in excess of the lifetime allowance are taken as a lump sum, there is a lifetime allowance charge (FA 2004, s. 215). Historically, this charge has been 55%. However, from April 2015, people aged 55 and over will only pay their marginal rate of income tax on anything they withdraw from their defined contribution pension.

The lifetime allowance was reduced to £1m for 2016–17 and 2017–18, by *Finance Act* 2016 (previously £1.25m). *Finance Act* 2016 also provides a requirement for the Treasury to make regulations before the start of tax year 2018–19 and each subsequent tax year, specifying the amount of the standard lifetime allowance for the year. The allowance will be increased by CPI (rounded up to the nearest £100) where the CPI for the year to the previous September is higher than it was 12 months earlier, otherwise, the allowance will remain the same as for the previous tax year (FA 2004, s. 218(2A)–(2D)). Transitional protection for pension rights already over £1m has also been introduced alongside this reduction to ensure the change is not retrospective by way of two transitional protections 'fixed protection 2016' and 'individual protection 2016', which also take effect from 6 April 2016. Individuals with fixed protection 2016 have a lifetime allowance of the greater of £1.25m and the standard lifetime allowance and individuals with individual protection 2016 will have a lifetime allowance of the greater of the value of their pension savings at 5 April 2016, subject to an overall maximum of £1.25m, and the standard lifetime allowance (FA 2016, Sch. 4).

Legislation: FA 2004, s. 218; FA 2016, Sch. 4

Tax Reporter: ¶384-000

475 Lump sums

Subject to the scheme rules, it is possible to take 25% tax-free cash from all pension arrangements.

Withdrawals in excess of the 25% limit are charged to tax. With the remainder, there are four options:

- those aged 55 and over who have overall pension savings of less than £30,000 (£18,000 prior to 27 March 2014) can take them all in one lump sum (this is known as trivial commutation);

- a 'capped drawdown' pension allows investors to take income from their pension, but there is a maximum amount that can be withdrawn each year (150% of an equivalent annuity from 27 March 2014, 120% prior to that date);

- with 'flexible drawdown' there's no limit on the amount that can be drawn from the pot each year, but the investor must have a guaranteed income of more than £12,000 per year (£20,000 prior to 27 March 2014) in retirement;

- purchasing an annuity where a fixed sum of money is paid each year.

Regardless of total pension wealth, those aged 60 or over can take any pot worth less than £10,000 as a lump sum (£2,000 prior to 27 March 2014), as this classifies as a 'small pot'. From 27 March 2014, the number of personal pension pots that can be taken as a lump sum under the small pot rules has been increased from two to three.

From April 2015, from age 55, whatever the size of a person's defined contribution pension pot, they will be able to take it how they want, subject to their marginal rate of income tax in that year. 25% of the pot will remain tax-free.

There will be more flexibility. People who continue to want the security of an annuity will be able to purchase one and people who want greater control over their finances can drawdown their pension as they see fit. Those who want to keep their pension invested and drawdown from it over time will be able to do so.

Legislation: FA 2004, Sch. 29

Tax Reporter: ¶378-500

Business income

550 Profits from trades, professions and vocations – liability

Profits arising from a trade, profession or vocation are taxed under the provisions of the *Income Tax (Trading and Other Income) Act* 2005 (ITTOIA 2005).

If a proprietor of a business wishes to show that he is not the person who carries on the trade and is not entitled to the profits, he has to prove that they accrue to someone else.

Legislation: ITTOIA 2005, s. 5

Case: *Alongi v IR Commrs* [1991] BTC 353

Tax Reporter: ¶200-000

Trades

555 Introduction to meaning of 'trade'

The word 'trade' is incompletely defined in the legislation. 'Trade', it is stated, includes 'every trade, manufacture, adventure or concern in the nature of a trade': without a definition of 'trade', this is of limited assistance. The only thing to do, as Lord Denning MR once declared, is to look at the usual characteristics of a trade and see how the transaction under consideration measures up to them. While some activities are deemed to be trades by statute (see 556) for the most part, decided cases must be studied, to distinguish the borderline between trading and other activities: most of such cases fit easily within one or more of the 'badges of trade' (see 560).

The term 'trade' is defined in ITA 2007, s. 989 as including 'any venture in the nature of trade'.

Entertainers

Until 5 April 2014, some entertainers who were treated as self-employed for income tax purposes are nevertheless subject to National Insurance liabilities as if they were employees, a position somewhat enforced by the case of *ITV Services Ltd* and upheld by the Upper Tribunal. For these purposes, an entertainer is a person employed (but in this context, the word means 'engaged') 'as an actor, singer or musician, or in any similar performing capacity' (SI 1978/1689, reg. 1(2)).

From 6 April 2014, the former legislation has been removed so that entertainers will now, by default, be treated as self-employed for National Insurance purposes and (subject to normal minimum National Insurance thresholds) be liable to Class 2 and 4 National Insurance contributions on their earnings (see 2520 for further details).

Legislation: ITA 2007, s. 989

Cases: *JP Harrison (Watford) Ltd v Griffiths (HMIT)* (1962) 40 TC 281; *ITV Services Ltd v R & C Commrs* [2012] BTC 1,561; *McMorris* [2015] TC 04204

Other material: National Insurance – Changes for entertainers from 6 April 2014

Tax Reporter: ¶200-500

556 Statutory trades

1 Farming and market gardening (except woodlands)

All 'farming' and 'market gardening' in the UK, and the occupation of other UK land (except woodlands) managed on a commercial basis with a view to profits, are treated as a trade, the profits from which are taxed under ITTOIA 2005 (see further 940ff.).

2 Woodlands

Profits from occupying land which comprises 'woodlands or is being prepared for use for forestry purposes' are not taxable under ITTOIA 2005 as being profits from the 'commercial occupation of land' (see above).

Timber merchants are taxed on their profits under ITTOIA 2005 on general principles.

Legislation: ITTOIA 2005, s. 9–16

Case: *Jaggers (t/a Shide Trees) v Ellis (HMIT)* [1997] BTC 571

Tax Reporter: ¶200-500

558 Trade v investment

The holding of an asset would seem to require that it be either an investment (whether as a capital asset of a business or otherwise) or an item of trading stock; the term investment in this sense does not imply any overwhelming desire to make a profit (see also 571). Lord Wilberforce said in a House of Lords case:

'What I think is not possible is for an asset to be both trading stock and permanent investment at the same time, nor to possess an indeterminate status – neither trading stock nor permanent asset. It must be one or the other, even though, and this seems to be legitimate and intelligible, the [taxpayer] in whatever character it acquires the asset, may reserve an intention to change its character.'

In the case, properties acquired by a group for retention were sold on the liquidation of the group and the decision to liquidate did not turn capital profits into trading profits.

Where a person buys an article or item for investment rather than trade, the following factors are usually present.

- A feeling on his part that he will enjoy the possession or use of the item purchased, apart from the pleasure he will feel at its increase in value.

- An intention to keep the article or item for a reasonable time. What is considered to be a reasonable time? The buyer must keep the item for long enough to make it clear that he did have the feeling mentioned above. However, a resale by the buyer almost immediately will not necessarily mean that he is trading if he has a good reason to sell (see 570).

A gain made from the sale of assets held for investment may give rise to a charge under the CGT provisions (see 5000ff.) but is not subject to income tax (see further the 'badges of trade' at 560).

Cases: *Simmons (as liquidator of Lionel Simmons Properties) v IR Commrs* [1980] 1 WLR 1196; *Klrkby v Hughes (HMI I)* [1993] BTC 52; *Koenigsberger v Mellor (HMIT)* [1995] BTC 292; *Ali* [2016] TC 04816

Other Material: SP 03/02, *Tax treatment of transactions in financial futures and options*; SP 01/01, *Treatment of investment managers and their overseas clients* (revised 20 July 2007)

Tax Reporter: ¶200-575

560   The 'badges of trade'

To find the characteristics of a trade it is helpful to look at the case law in some detail. In order to make the matter a little easier, the principles were categorised within six badges or identifying features of trading by the (Radcliffe) Royal Commission on the Taxation of Profits and Income in 1954 (Cmd. 9474). The categories are subject-matter (see 562), period of ownership (see 564), frequency of the transactions (see 566), supplementary work (see 568), circumstances responsible for sale (see 570) and motive (see 571). In 1986, Browne-Wilkinson V-C has enumerated slightly different badges, though he has subsequently redefined his entire approach to the consideration of trading (see 555).

Case: *Marson (HMIT) v Morton* [1986] BTC 377

Tax Reporter: ¶200-600

562 Badge of trade: subject-matter

The Radcliffe Report (see 560) states:

> 'While almost any form of property can be acquired to be dealt in, those forms of property, such as commodities or manufactured articles, which are normally the subject of trading, are only very exceptionally the subject of investment. Again property which does not yield to its owner an income or personal enjoyment merely by virtue of its ownership is more likely to have been acquired with the object of a deal than property that does'

In one case, a merchant in agricultural machinery was offered 44m yards of aircraft linen which he bought and sold at a considerable profit. To do so, he found it necessary to set up a business to handle sales of it to the public. Because of the nature of the subject-matter involved (and admittedly because he had set up a business to sell it), the court held that the resale of the aircraft linen was a trading transaction.

In another case, a money-lender on business abroad bought 1m rolls of toilet paper. He sold the toilet paper to a single purchaser on his return to the UK and made a profit of £10,000. The Court of Session, in holding that the taxpayer was engaged in an adventure in the nature of a trade, said that he:

> 'made himself liable for the purchase of this vast quantity of toilet paper obviously for no other conceivable purpose than that of reselling it at a profit.'

In another Court of Session case, a woodcutter who had never previously traded in whisky bought three lots of it and sold them two years later at a profit. The court said the nature of the transaction is important. Some things are bought for pleasure, but not vats of whisky. The size of the transaction also is important. A very large transaction can be evidence that the taxpayer never intended to keep the asset.

Cases: *Martin v Lowry (HMIT)* [1927] AC 312; *Rutledge v IR Commrs* (1929) 14 TC 490; *IR Commrs v Fraser* (1942) 24 TC 498

Tax Reporter: ¶200-600

564 Badge of trade: period of ownership

The Radcliffe Report (see 560) states:

> 'Generally speaking, property meant to be dealt in is realised within a short time after acquisition. But there may be exceptions to this as a universal rule'

A case which demonstrates this concerned a taxpayer who was in a position to purchase land at a favourable price. However, he could not raise a loan. To get over this problem, he contracted to sell the land to a purchaser, at a profit, before he had contracted to buy it. It was this fact that persuaded the High Court to hold the transaction to be an adventure in the nature of trade.

The knowledge alone that a purchase will increase in value is insufficient evidence upon which to find that a transaction is in the nature of trade. Many people buy things to keep and enjoy but at the same time they know that they will increase in value and may be sold at a profit. Where, however, the resale at a profit appears to be the only reason for the purchase, the inference drawn will be that the taxpayer is trading.

In another case, a farmer bought two fields and sold one with planning permission nine months later. He repeated this a few months later with the second field. In holding that he was liable to tax under former Sch. D, Case I, the High Court said the motive for resale was important. A taxpayer may unexpectedly be offered money but a quick resale always invites close scrutiny of the transaction.

Cases: *Turner v Last (HMIT)* (1965) 42 TC 517; *Johnston (HMIT) v Heath* [1970] 1 WLR 1567

Tax Reporter: ¶200-600

566 Badge of trade: the frequency of the transactions

The Radcliffe Report (see 560) states:

> 'If realisations of the same sort of property occur in succession over a period of years or there are several such realisations at about the same date a presumption arises that there has been dealing in respect of each'

This statement is well illustrated by a case where a taxpayer started a driving school and later sold it at a profit. He then set up and sold some 30 driving schools. The High Court held that the sales which followed the first had tainted the first, so that it too was a trading transaction. This does not mean that a single transaction cannot be a trading transaction (see 562). It would appear that there may not have been, initially, any intention to sell the first driving school from the outset but the subsequent sales led the court to believe that there must have been.

In another case, a taxpayer bought and resold a spinning mill. Then, in partnership with friends, he repeated the transaction four times. The High Court said that one transaction does not usually give rise to a finding of trading but systematic repetition raises an inference of trading.

Another case concerned a mathematician with £100,000, who wanted to produce £7,000 per year. He went to auctions and bought up endowment policies on other people's lives to produce the income. The Court of Appeal said that it was not necessary to buy and sell to be trading. Because of the huge number of policies or the frequency of the transactions, the court held him to be trading.

An isolated transaction involving the purchase, development, and resale of land may not be regarded as trading where the development is a subsidiary purpose of the acquisition and sale.

Cases: *Pickford v Quirke (HMIT) (1927) 13 TC 251; Barry v Cordy (HMIT) (1946) 28 TC 250; Leach v Pogson (HMIT) (1962) 40 TC 585; Kirkham v Williams (HMIT) [1991] BTC 196*

Tax Reporter: ¶200-600

568   Badge of trade: supplementary work

The Radcliffe Report (see 560) states:

> 'If the property is worked up in any way during the ownership so as to bring it into a more marketable condition, or if any special exertions are made to find or attract purchasers, such as the opening of an office or large-scale advertising, there is some evidence of dealing. For when there is an organised effort to obtain profits there is a source of taxable income. But if nothing at all is done, the suggestion tends the other way'

A number of cases illustrate this point. In one such case, a ship repairer, a blacksmith and an employee of a fish salesman bought a cargo ship and converted it into a steam drifter which was then sold at a profit. They had never done this sort of work before nor were they connected persons. Lord President Clyde said that this was more than just a purchase and resale. They had actually spent money on making the asset something else. The court held the venture to be a trading transaction.

In another case, the taxpayers were members of different firms. They bought three lots of brandy, shipped it to London where it was blended, mixed and packaged before being sold by the taxpayers. This required expertise. The Court of Appeal held this to be trading.

The supplementary work must change the asset

To polish, clean or otherwise prepare an asset for sale so that it will attract the best price will not be considered to be trading. In one case, a taxpayer bought two metal stills. Having carried out considerable work on the stills consisting mainly of removing a sticky glue from them, he then sold them individually to each of two companies which he controlled. The Court of Appeal declined to disturb the general commissioners' finding of fact that he was not trading. The courts will not disturb a finding of fact by the commissioners if it was one which there was evidence to support, notwithstanding that a different body of commissioners might have reached a different finding on the same evidence.

In another case, a grocer and newsagent who lived over his shop noticed a house for sale. He went to the auction, bought it on impulse, and then decided that he did not want to live in the house. He then obtained planning permission for the land and sold it at a vast profit. The Crown conceded that the original purchase of the house as a residence was not in the course of trade. Taking steps to enhance its value did not make him a trader. However, it should be noted that the Court of Appeal also said that improving land often indicates trading, particularly where the taxpayer's business is connected with land.

Cases: *Cape Brandy Syndicate v IR Commrs* [1921] 2 KB 403; *IR Commrs v Livingstone* (1926) 11 TC 538; *Jenkinson (HMIT) v Freedland* (1961) 39 TC 636; *Taylor v Good (HMIT)* [1974] 1 WLR 556

Tax Reporter: ¶200-600

570   Badge of trade: circumstances responsible for sale

A quick resale leads to an inference of trading, but if the asset is sold in response to 'a sudden emergency or opportunity calling for ready money, that negatives the idea that any plan of dealing prompted the original purchase' (Radcliffe Report: see 560).

In one case, the taxpayer built 2,500 houses. Some were for letting and some for resale. The letting business started losing money and the taxpayer decided to sell the letting houses. The High Court said this was a forced sale and was not trading.

Case: *West v Phillips (HMIT)* (1958) 38 TC 203

Tax Reporter: ¶200-600

571   Badge of trade: motive

The taxpayer's motive was considered to be a significant factor by the Radcliffe Report (see 560).

Where there is clear evidence upon which it can be decided whether a taxpayer is trading, the taxpayer's motive is irrelevant. However, where the evidence is ambiguous, the taxpayer's motive can be considered. A clear intention to buy and resell quickly at a profit will be taken to be trading if in fact the taxpayer does resell quickly. A desire to make a profit is not, *per se*, sufficient evidence to support a finding of trading. It is clear that a desire to make a profit is uppermost in the minds of all who buy for investment. But where that desire is not coupled with an intention to hold the item as one would hold an investment, it will assist in a finding of trading.

The question of motive becomes more important where the taxpayer buys for investment and quickly thereafter changes his mind and decides to sell, or where he buys with the sole intention of reselling the asset at a profit but then realises that he likes the asset and decides to keep it for the enjoyment he derives from it. Providing that there is clear evidence that the asset was bought for investment, a quick resale will not make the transaction an adventure in the nature of trade (see 570). The reason for sale will rather be looked upon as an unforeseen contingency. To be unexpectedly offered a good price for the asset could be an unforeseen contingency, but enjoyment derived from an expectation of price rise will not assist in a finding that the asset is held for investment.

If a decision is made by the taxpayer shortly after the purchase to retain an asset (which was bought with the intention of reselling it at a profit) because he enjoys using or having it (apart from the enjoyment derived from a knowledge that the asset is increasing in value), then clearly when he later comes to sell it he will not be held to be trading. If, on the other hand, the taxpayer intends to sell as soon as possible, but cannot find a buyer for a considerable time, he is much more likely to be considered to be trading. In one case, the Court of Session, in deciding that very question, decided that the taxpayer was not trading. The taxpayer had bought four houses with a view to resale and had instructed his agents to sell whenever a suitable opportunity arose. He sold them three years later. Lord Keith said that the intention to resell some day at a profit is not in itself sufficient to attract tax.

The FTT case of *Stayton* [2016] TC 05104 concerned a taxpayer who bought a property and began renovating it with the intention of moving in to it as her main home, but who after a dispute with a neighbour instead downgraded the renovation work to minimise costs and maximise profit and then sold the property. The FTT rejected the taxpayer's assertions that she had been trading as a property developer. The FTT considered that based on case law:

- normally a taxpayer who acquires a single property without the intention of trading in that property is not engaged in an adventure in the nature of a trade; and

- it was possible for intentions to change, so that there was 'supervening trading', but that would be unusual in the case of land unless there was a pre-existing trade of dealing in land into which the asset was subsumed.

The FTT found that there was no supervening trading from the date of her change of intention to live in the property. The taxpayer did not have a trading intention at any time, and when she decided to renovate the property to sell rather than to live in she had no more involvement with the property's development than she had had previously.

In another case, the Court of Appeal said that in addition to bearing badges of trade, a trading transaction must have a commercial purpose: if the sole purpose of the transaction was to obtain a fiscal advantage, it was impossible to postulate the existence of any commercial purpose. However, the House of Lords has effectively refuted this view, implying that the decision pertained to the fact that a transaction whose effect was fiscal alchemy was not trading (see 555). In the Court of Appeal case, the issue was whether the company was trading when it assumed liability for the risk of foreign exchange losses from another company in the same group. The object was to convert capital losses to revenue losses which could then be set off against trading profits. The court held that the company was not trading in respect of these transactions. They had no commercial justification in the group context.

Cases: *IR Commrs v Reinhold* (1953) 34 TC 389; *Overseas Containers (Finance) Ltd v Stoker (HMIT)* [1989] BTC 153; *Ensign Tankers (Leasing) Ltd v Stokes (HMIT)* [1992] BTC 110; *Stayton* [2016] TC 05104; *Gray* [2016] TC 05151

Tax Reporter: ¶200-600

572 Mutual trading

It is a basic rule that:

> 'No man ... can trade with himself [or] make ... taxable profit by dealing with himself.'

In other words, a person's taxable profits must derive from sources outside himself.

The 'mutuality' principle has been ascribed to this rule and is a principle which has been developed by the courts over a long period. For mutuality to apply, there must be a class of contributors to a common fund, all of who are entitled to participate in the surplus. Where all the participators in the surplus are contributors to the common fund, then the participators are trading mutually and any surplus made from the venture is not assessable. A distribution of fund assets on its dissolution may give rise to a taxable receipt on the contributor.

Outsiders

Where the mutual trade has dealings with outsiders and those dealings produce profits, then those profits are assessable under ITTOIA 2005. This point is demonstrated by a case where the members of a golf club paid an annual subscription and were allowed to use the facilities of the club. Non-members were allowed to use the facilities upon the payment of green fees. The High Court held that profits made from the green fees were assessable under former Sch. D, Case I. A Revenue 'interpretation' (see HMRC *Business Income Manual* BIM24215) reiterates this view and adds that even where visitors become 'temporary members' of a golf club, the income received from their use of the club's facilities is taken into account for tax purposes unless their rights are the same as those of full members (e.g. including a right to vote at meetings and generally to exercise control over the running of the club).

Liabilities and rights

There must be a balance between the amount which the member contributes to the fund and that which he draws from it.

In one case, hotel owners paid more in membership fees to a club so that their guests could use club facilities. The Privy Council held that the hotel owners were trading with the club because they contributed a great deal more than other members but received the same benefits in return.

However, a special commissioner has held that equality of rights was not an essential requirement. A club had two classes of membership: 'ordinary' and 'associate'. Associate members were non-voting, were not involved in the management of the club's affairs and were not entitled to a share in the club's assets on dissolution. The mutual trading exemption applied to surpluses in respect of business with both classes.

Legislation: ITTOIA 2005, s. 104

Cases: *Dublin Corporation v M'Adam* (1887) 2 TC 387; *Carlisle and Silloth Golf Club v Smith (HMIT)* [1913] 3 KB 75; *Fletcher v Jamaica*

Income Tax Commissioner [1972] AC 414; *Westbourne Supporters of Glentoran Football Club v Brennan (HMIT)* (1995) Sp C 22

Tax Reporter: ¶203-750

573 Illegal trading

Whilst there are conflicting dicta on the matter, it now seems clear that the profits of an illegal trade are taxable. Profits obtained from shipping whisky to the US during prohibition have been held taxable, as have profits from illegal wagering contracts. The profits of prostitution have also been held to be trading income.

Cases: *Lindsay v IR Commrs* (1932) 18 TC 43; *Partridge v Mallandaine* (1886) 18 QBD 276; *IR Commrs v Aken* [1990] BTC 352

Tax Reporter: ¶200-925

574 The realisation of trade assets

Where a trade goes into liquidation, the mere realisation of assets after discontinuance of the trade will not constitute trading if it is incidental to the liquidation. A whisky broker who was compelled to discontinue trading due to ill health and sold his business and whisky to another person has been held not to be trading.

However, it is possible for the realisation of assets to be trading. In one case, two wine and spirit merchants sent a letter to customers explaining that they were about to retire and asking if they wished to buy stock. The process of discontinuance took about one year during which time stock was still being bought in to fulfil contracts of sale agreed previously. The House of Lords said that they were trading.

The executors of a sole trader are normally not regarded as trading. However, if they go beyond what is necessary for prudent winding up of the estate they can be found to be trading. The executor of a deceased partner does not become a partner. However, should the executor associate himself with the surviving partners in trading activities, he may be treated as trading in partnership with them.

Cases: *J & R O'Kane & Co v IR Commrs* (1922) 22 TC 303; *Marshall's Exors v Joly (HMIT)* (1936) 20 TC 256; *Newbarns Syndicate v Hay (HMIT)* (1939) 22 TC 461; *IR Commrs v Nelson* (1939) 12 TC 716; *Pattullo's Trustees v IR Commrs* (1955) 36 TC 87

Tax Reporter: ¶202-500

Professions and vocations

584 Introduction to the meaning of profession or vocation

The same problem presents itself in defining 'profession or vocation' with respect to the charge of business income (see 550) as is found with 'trade' (see 560). There is no definition in statute. In practice, there is no need to distinguish between professions (see 586) and vocations (see 587).

Tax Reporter: ¶200-550

586 'Profession'

A 'profession' involves work requiring purely intellectual skill or manual labour dependent upon purely intellectual skill. However, while the activities of a person may on the above tests amount to a profession, he may still be employed. If so, his emoluments are taxed under ITEPA 2003 and not under ITTOIA 2005 (see 253). An example of this would be a barrister employed by a company.

Legislation: ITTOIA 2005, s. 5

Cases: *IR Commrs v Maxse* [1919] 1 KB 647; *Billam v Griffith* (1941) 23 TC 757; *Hobbs v Hussey* (HMIT)(1942) 24 TC 153

Tax Reporter: ¶200-550

587 'Vocation'

In a case concerning partners who went to the races as bookmakers and punters, it was said that the term 'vocation' is analogous to calling: the way in which a man passes his life.

In another case, the taxpayer's sole means of livelihood was betting on horses which he did from a private residence with bookmakers at starting prices. The High Court held that the profits were not assessable. This was not a vocation: the taxpayer was simply addicted to betting.

Legislation: ITTOIA 2005, s. 5

Cases: *Partridge v Mallandaine* (1886) 18 QBD 276; *Graham v Green (HMIT)* [1925] 2 KB 37; *Graham v Arnott* (1941) 24 TC 157

Tax Reporter: ¶200-550

Annual profits from business

588   Calculation of taxable business profits

Once it is established that a person is engaged in a trade, profession or vocation (see 555 and 584ff.), his 'annual profits' must be ascertained because it is only these which are liable to income tax (see 550).

Unless there is an explicit provision otherwise:

- statutory references to 'receipts' and 'expenses' are to be taken as items brought into account as credits and debits in computing profits, there being no implication thereby that any amount is actually received or paid; and

- the rules used to compute profits for trades, professions and vocations must be used to compute losses.

Legislation: ITTOIA 2005, s. 26(1)–(2), 27(1)–(3)

Tax Reporter: ¶205-000

589   Cash basis for small businesses

From 6 April 2013 onwards, individuals (whether carrying on a trade or profession as a self-employed sole trader, or in partnership with other individuals) may use a voluntary simplified cash basis for income tax and simplified arrangements for certain expenses. Qualifying small businesses can now choose to be taxed on the basis of the cash that passes through their books, rather than being asked to spend their time doing calculations designed for big businesses.

The rules allow cash basis accounting for small self-employed businesses that have an income of up to the current VAT registration threshold in force for a particular year. Participation in the scheme may continue until receipts reach twice the VAT registration ceiling.

General partnerships may use the cash basis as long as the partnership meets the receipts and other entry criteria, the partners are all individuals, and either there is no individual treated as controlling the partnership, or any such individual would be eligible to use the cash basis if they were conducting the business as a sole trader.

Generally, an individual who undertakes (whether as a sole trader or a partner) more than one unincorporated trading or professional business, will only be eligible for the cash basis if all those businesses are also eligible for, and use, the cash basis. Additionally, any subsequent use of the 'ordinary' rules for any of those business should have the effect of precluding eligibility for the cash basis for all such businesses. This is because simultaneous use of two different regimes would cut across the simplification benefits of the cash basis.

An exception would be where an individual is a partner in a partnership that they do not control that uses the ordinary rules. So, for example, a partner in a large professional partnership would be eligible to use the cash basis in respect of any separate unincorporated businesses they conduct as a sole trader as long as those businesses meet the eligibility criteria.

The cash basis is available to foreign resident individuals, to the extent that they carry on a trade, profession or vocation in the UK, providing that the other eligibility criteria are met.

The cash basis operates by reference to the basis period for the tax year. This means small businesses can calculate their taxable income for the tax year by adding or subtracting:

- receipts in connection with the business received in the tax year;
- payments made in the tax year to cover allowable expenses;
- amounts allowed for simplified expenses, subject to certain restrictions.

There is no requirement to apply generally accepted accounting practice (GAAP) or calculate profits/losses.

Once a business is using the cash basis, it can only leave the scheme if either they are no longer eligible or there has been a 'change in commercial circumstances which means that the cash basis is no longer appropriate'.

Under the scheme, losses cannot be carried back or set off sideways.

Transitional rules apply to a business entering or leaving the cash basis to ensure that:

- receipts are taxed once and only once;
- payments are deducted once and only once; and
- people leaving the cash basis can spread any adjustment income over the following six tax years.

The legislation to ensure that receipts are taxed once and only once and payments are deducted once and only once is that which already applies where a trader changes the basis on which their trading profits are calculated for tax purposes.

Legislation: FA 2013, s. 17 and 18, Sch. 4 and 5

Tax Reporter: ¶205-000; ¶206-481; ¶208-380

602 Timing and nature of business results

A person's annual profits from business (see 588ff.) are computed in accordance with generally accepted accounting practice ('GAAP'), unless they have opted for the cash basis (see 589). His gross profit is the difference between sales made (whether or not he has received cash) and the cost of purchases (purchases adjusted for opening and closing stock, etc.: see 652). To obtain net taxable profits, add to gross profit other 'chargeable trading receipts' (see 626ff.) and deduct 'allowable revenue expenses' (see 2050ff.) incurred (whether or not paid). Where a customer does not pay this will give rise to a bad debt in due course (see 2059).

Trading income is taxable when the trader has fulfilled all conditions necessary to earn it.

Cases: *Eckel v Board of Inland Revenue (Trinidad and Tobago)* [1989] BTC 94

Tax Reporter: ¶210-700

Chargeable business receipts

626 Extent to which business receipts are chargeable

For businesses who have not opted to use the cash basis (see 589), all trading-related receipts count in the computation of 'chargeable business income' unless they fall into one of the following categories:

- income arising from outside the scope of the taxpayer's trade, profession or vocation (see 628);
- capital receipts (see 630);
- receipts already taxable by deduction at source (see 635).

Trading income received in non-monetary form is also fully brought into account in calculating taxable trading profits for income tax purposes by the insertion of ITTOIA 2005, s. 28A by *Finance Act* 2016, with effect from Budget 2016 in relation to trading transactions occurring on or after 16 March 2015.

There are also various types of receipt for which specific rules have developed either through the courts or by way of statute. In particular, adjustments may be made for undervalue sales, etc. (see 636), certain windfall gains (see 640 and 642) and the eventual recovery of bad debts (see 648). There are also rules affecting foreign exchange gains.

Legislation: ITTOIA 2005, s. 28A and Pt. 2, Ch. 3

Tax Reporter: ¶220-000

628 Income outside the scope of the taxpayer's business

Profits from activities outside the taxpayer's trade, profession or vocation do not give rise to a charge to tax as a profit of the trade, etc.

Income from investments held by a trader is prima facie investment income, but may in certain circumstances be brought into account as a trading receipt. Whether it may or may not be so treated depends on the nature of the trade. Decided cases show that the nature of the trade must be such that it can fairly be said that the making and holding of investments at interest is an integral part of the trade.

A person's exploitation of anything produced in the course of his profession cannot be regarded as outside its scope.

Receipts arising outside the scope of the taxpayer's existing trade, whilst not being receipts from that trade, may nevertheless be regarded as the receipts of another (i.e. different) trade or may simply constitute capital receipts (see 5000ff.). Motor mileage allowances for volunteer services are, in the case of taxi drivers and the like, trading receipts as they are received in connection with the taxpayer's trade.

Cases: *Scott (HMIT) v Ricketts* [1967] 1 WLR 828; *Simpson (HMIT) v John Reynolds & Co (Insurances) Ltd* [1975] 1 WLR 617; *Wain v Cameron (HMIT)* [1995] BTC 299; *Nuclear-Electric plc v Bradley (HMIT)* [1996] BTC 165

Tax Reporter: ¶220-000

630 Distinguishing capital and revenue receipts

For businesses who have not opted to use the cash basis (see 589), revenue receipts need to be distinguished from capital receipts, because it is normally only revenue receipts which are chargeable to income tax. Gains from capital receipts normally attract capital gains tax (CGT). However, the equalisation of income tax and CGT rates (see 5000) greatly reduces the importance of the distinction.

What is income and what is capital is a question of law, rather than a question of fact. However, the question has to be answered in the light of all the circumstances, and the weight to be given to a particular circumstance depends on common sense, rather than any single legal principle.

There are two well-known tests for distinguishing a revenue receipt from a capital one, though both of them are of limited value, as will be shown further in this paragraph. The first test is to distinguish receipts which relate to assets which form part of the permanent structure of the business. An example of this would be machinery, the sale of which would give rise to a capital receipt.

The second test is to distinguish between circulating and fixed capital. A fixed capital asset is retained in the business with the object of making profits. An example of this would again be machinery. Circulating capital, on the other hand, is acquired to be used or sold. An example would be the raw materials used in the business.

While the above two tests are of some help, they do not resolve all the problems. What is established is that certain types of receipts will be treated in a particular way. The position is summarised in the table below.

Capital	Revenue
Receipts from sale of business assets	*Payments in lieu of trading receipts*
Sale of fixed assets is a capital receipt, although a profit on the sale of trading stock constitutes an income receipt	Including:
Receipts for the sale or destruction of the taxpayer's profit-making apparatus	• agreed damages for loss of profits arising from delay in repairs
Receipts in return for restrictive convenants	• damages in excess of repair costs to cover lost profits
Payments received in return for the sterilisation of assets are capital receipts, although treatment of lump sums for 'exclusivity agreements' depends on purpose of payment	• compensation for increased revenue expenditure
One-off receipts	• damages for negligence of agents resulting in a trading loss
A one-off receipt strongly, but not conclusively suggests a capital receipt	• rebates against price due for goods supplied
	Recurring receipts
	Recurring receipts are more likely to be revenue receipts

Legislation: ITTOIA 2005, s. 105, 207

Cases: *Total Mauritius Ltd v Mauritius Revenue Authority* [2011] UKPC 39; *Glenboig Union Fireclay Co Ltd v IR Commrs* (1921) 12 TC 427; *Burmah Steam Ship Co Ltd v IR Commrs* (1930) 16 TC 67; *Van den Berghs Ltd v Clark (HMIT)* [1935] AC 431; *Kelsall Parsons & Co v IR Commrs* (1938) 21 TC 608; *Thompson (HMIT) v Magnesium Elektron Ltd* (1943) 26 TC 1; *Barr, Crombie & Co Ltd v IR Commrs* (1945) 26 TC 406; *Davies (HMIT) v Shell Company of China Ltd* (1951) 32 TC 133; *Orchard Wine and Spirit Co v Loynes (HMIT)* (1952) 33 TC 97; *Higgs (HMIT) v Olivier* [1952] Ch 311; *Evans Medical Supplies Ltd v Moriarty*

(HMIT) [1957] 1 WLR 288; *Jeffrey (HMIT) v Rolls-Royce Ltd* [1962] 1 WLR 425; *London and Thames Haven Oil Wharves Ltd v Attwooll (HMIT)* [1967] Ch 772; *Murray (HMIT) v Imperial Chemical Industries Ltd* [1967] Ch 1038; *Ryan (HMIT) v Crabtree Denims Ltd* [1987] BTC 289; *Donald Fisher (Ealing) Ltd v Spencer (HMIT)* [1989] BTC 112; *Deeny v Gooda Walker Ltd (in vol liq)* [1996] BTC 144; *Tanfield Ltd v Carr (HMIT)* (1999) Sp C 200

Tax Reporter: ¶220-000

633 Taxation of 'know-how' sales

A trader's receipts from the sale of know-how are nowadays only treated as capital receipts if the sale accompanied the sale of part or all of his business and if he and the buyer do not elect otherwise. Non-traders' receipts from know-how sales may attract income tax under ITTOIA 2005. 'Know-how' is orthodoxly defined.

These rules will not apply to businesses using the cash basis (see 589).

Legislation: ITTOIA 2005, s. 192–195

Tax Reporter: ¶221-500

635 Business receipts already taxable by deduction at source

Since the provisions under which earnings from employment, etc. and trading income is charged to tax are mutually exclusive (see 240), it is clear that the same income must not be taxed twice. Any sum received under deduction of tax is therefore not included in a trading computation.

Tax Reporter: ¶220-000

636 Dispositions at an undervalue and stock taken for own use

A trader could reduce his profits and as a consequence his liability to tax by selling his stock at less than it is worth or by giving it away. This would benefit somebody else at his expense. However, if he does so, for tax purposes he must bring into his accounts a figure representing the market value of the goods sold. The authority for this is the case of *Sharkey v Wernher*. Lady Wernher owned a stud farm, the profits of which were assessed under former Sch. D, Case I. She also owned racing stables. At the racing stables, she trained horses which she had bred at the stud farm. The racing stables were a hobby; thus any profit was not assessable and any loss not allowable. She transferred five horses from the stud farm to the racing stables. It was admitted that some figure had to be entered in the accounts of the farm to represent the disposition of trading stock but it was contended that the appropriate figure was the cost of breeding the horses rather than their market value. The House of Lords decided that the correct figure was the market value of the horses transferred.

The effect of Sharkey v Wernher

The rule in *Sharkey v Wernher* not only means that it is possible for a trader to trade with himself (e.g. a grocer who supplied his family with goods off the shelf of his shop would be required to enter market value in his books as if he had made the same profit on their sale as he would have done had he sold them to the public), but that he must enter the market value in his books if he throws the stock away.

Further, the rule affects both the accounts of the disponor and the accounts of the recipient of those goods. The recipient of goods given gratuitously to him must enter the market value of those goods in his books and cannot value his stock at nil.

The *Sharkey v Wernher* rule applies to most non-commercial disposals of trading stock. It follows from the necessity that there be a disposal of trading stock that the rule is confined to taxpayers who are assessed on an earnings basis.

It also follows that the rule does not apply to services given without payment (e.g. by a professional person). The reason is that there is no disposal of trading stock. In one case, an author assigned the copyright in a book to his father. HMRC sought to assess the author on the market value of the book. The Court of Appeal held that the rule in *Sharkey v Wernher* did not apply, even though the expenses of writing the book had been allowed in his accounts.

Note that rules will not be applicable to businesses using the cash basis from 6 April 2013 (see 589).

There are special statutory rules in relation to bodies of persons, e.g. partnerships or companies.

Gifts of equipment made to schools and other institutions

The rule in *Sharkey v Wernher* does not apply to gifts, made after 18 March 1991 to educational institutions designated in regulations made by the various Secretaries of State for Education and Science, etc. of equipment manufactured, sold or used in the course of the taxpayer's trade. The long list of qualifying establishments includes local education authority-maintained schools in England, Wales and Northern Ireland, grant-maintained schools, independent schools administered by educational charities, public and self-governing schools (in Scotland), universities, and most other higher education establishments.

The above relief has effectively been extended to all charitable causes on or after 27 July 1999.

Legislation: ITTOIA 2005, s. 107–110; *Taxes (Relief for Gifts) (Designated Educational Establishments) Regulations (Northern Ireland) 1992 (SI 1992/109)*

Cases: *Sharkey (HMIT) v Wernher* [1956] AC 58; *Petrotim Securities Ltd v Ayres (HMIT)* [1964] 1 WLR 190; *Ridge Securities Ltd v IR Commrs* [1964] 1 WLR 479; *Mason (HMIT) v Innes* [1967] Ch 1079

640   Ex gratia business receipts

Sometimes receipts take on the appearance of gifts. That is, they are made without legal obligation. Such receipts may escape income tax (see 628) if the following conditions are met:

- the payment must be unsolicited and unexpected;
- if a business connection existed between the donor and recipient then this must have ended before the voluntary payment is made;
- the payment must not be for past services;
- the payment must not be a retainer or an advance payment for further services;
- the payment must not be compensation for loss of business.

If the payment is merely to supplement the trader's income, then it will not escape income tax.

Cases: *Simpson (HMIT) v John Reynolds & Co (Insurances) Ltd* [1975] 1 WLR 617; *IR Commrs v Falkirk Ice Rink Ltd* (1975) 51 TC 42

Tax Reporter: ¶220-000

642   Deposits and unclaimed money

Where a trader receives money from or on behalf of a customer which the trader is supposed to repay and the customer neglects to claim it, the unclaimed money is not a trading receipt. The money never belonged to the trader, was never part of his income and cannot subsequently become so.

However, sometimes the money becomes the trader's by operation of law (as in relation to unclaimed surpluses on a pawnbroker's sale of unredeemed pledges) and in such cases it may be held to be a trading receipt. If the payment was strictly a deposit (i.e. it goes towards the cost of whatever is ordered), then this is a trading receipt even though whatever was ordered was not collected.

Cases: *Morley (HMIT) v Tattersall* (1938) 22 TC 51; *Jay's the Jewellers Ltd v IR Commrs* (1947) 29 TC 274; *Elson (HMIT) v Prices Tailors Ltd* [1963] 1 WLR 287

Tax Reporter: ¶220-050

646 Stock lending

Stock lending transactions take place when a person lends securities (stocks and shares) in circumstances which involve his parting with the legal interest in them, and is repaid in securities of the same type. As a general principle, stock lending is governed by commercial accountancy principles. These ensure that, in computing trading profits, transfers under stock lending arrangements are ignored whatever the purpose of the loan, as in the parallel case of sale and repurchase arrangements ('repo') with which the tax treatment of stock lending is now broadly aligned.

There are two exceptions. First, anti-avoidance rules are necessary to prevent stock lending being used to switch dividend income from one person to another for tax reasons. This is done by deeming manufactured dividend payments to be made in any case where stock lending arrangements do not provide for such payments to be made.

Second, stock lending arrangements may not require the borrower to pay to the lender amounts representing any interest or dividends arising on the borrowed stock. Without anti-avoidance provisions, the legislation would deem a manufactured dividend payment to be made for tax purposes. The borrower would gain relief for, and the lender would be taxable on, the deemed payment. But if the lender was, for example, not resident, then a tax advantage would be obtained. The legislation therefore prevents the stock borrower from gaining a tax deduction for the deemed payment. The rule only applies where no representative payment is made. It does not affect arrangements where representative payments are actually made.

Legislation: ITA 2007, s. 596; TCGA 1992, s. 271(9); FA 1997, Sch. 10

648 Debts: release or receipt after write off

If a trade debt is incurred and the creditor later releases the debt (otherwise than under a 'voluntary arrangement' under the *Insolvency Act* 1986 after 29 November 1993), then the debtor has in fact made a profit which is taxable on release.

Note that without a formal release from the debt, the amount is not taxable under the statute. However, it is HMRC's view that, with effect for accounting periods that start from 1 January 2002 onwards, normal accounting practice should determine the tax treatment of debts that are written off, but not formally released. Accordingly, if the debtor writes the amount back to the profit and loss account, there is no need for a tax adjustment, and it will therefore be taxed.

Example

John owes Thomas £100. Thomas later releases John from the debt. John has therefore made a profit of £100 which is taxable in the period of release.

If a trader eventually receives more than he *originally* estimated he would, then the excess must be related back and the accounts of that period should be reopened. This rule only applies to receipts which are analogous to trade debts.

Example

Peter agrees to supply Ian with goods at a price to be agreed under a certain formula. The agreement is made in 2014. Peter enters a notional price into his books for 2016–17. He is assessed to tax on this notional figure in 2016–17. Subsequently under the formula for ascertaining the price he receives more than the notional amount that he entered in his books and on which he was taxed. The difference between the notional price and the actual price has to be entered into his books for 2016–17 as a trading receipt on which he will be taxed. This will obviously involve reopening his accounts for that year.

If, however, after a debt is written off for tax purposes (or a specific provision is made against it), a trader recovers the amount, it will be treated as a receipt of the trade on receipt.

Legislation: ITTOIA 2005, s. 97

Case: *Bristow (HMIT) v William Dickinson & Co Ltd* (1946) 27 TC 157

Tax Reporter: ¶223-100

Trading stock and work in progress

652   Valuation of stock in trade in continuing business

Stock in trade is that portion of the goods purchased for resale by a trader but which is not yet sold and can include such things as contracts and land. At any given time, a trader may have goods which are ready for sale and he may have some which are in the process of being made ready; these items are known as work in progress – both are also generally classed as stock.

From 12 March 2008, a long established rule, which has effect where goods are appropriated into or from trading stock other than by way of trade, has been put on a statutory footing. In such circumstances, the profits of the trade for tax purposes should be adjusted to replace the cost of the stock or the actual proceeds with their market value.

Since taxable profits from business are computed in accordance with generally accepted accounting principles, the cost of sales (deducted from turnover to produce gross profit) is calculated by reference to movements in stock, i.e. in very broad terms:

gross profit = turnover − (purchases + opening stock − closing stock)

so that stock directly affects taxable profit. Where a property development company carries forward interest as part of work in progress in the balance sheet, no trading deduction can be claimed until it is effectively charged as part of the cost of sales; conversely, no adjustment need be made to reflect any disallowance until that time (allowance as a charge on income is unaffected, relief being given when the interest is paid).

Stock is valued at the end of each period of account for tax purposes at the lower of cost or market value. The trader may value each item of stock individually at the lower of cost or market value. As stock normally increases in value it is usual to value it at cost price, thus reducing the trader's profit. However, if items of stock decrease in value, then obviously market value will be used. If someone donates stock to a trader to start him in business, then the trader may bring in that stock at market value.

Example

Roger, a grocer, is set up in his business by Jack who provides all of Roger's stock. If Roger put down in his accounts no value for his opening stock, then his profits would be extremely high when he came to enter the sale price in his books. HMRC allow the trader in these circumstances to value his opening stock at open market value. This will naturally mean lower profits and a lower liability to tax than if he had brought in the opening stock at cost, which was free.

An element of prudence has to be balanced with a degree of expectation. Lord Pearson has said:

'that the correct principle is that goods should not be written down price unless there really is a loss actual or prospective. So long as the fall in prevailing prices is only such as to reduce prospective profit, the initial valuation at cost should be retained.'

Example of trading accounts

Trading account for the year ended 30 June 2015

	£	£
Sales		105,000
Less: cost of goods sold–		
stock on hand 1 July 2014	20,000	
purchases	80,000	
	100,000	
Less: stock on hand at 30 June 2015	(30,000)	
		(70,000)
Gross profit for the year ended 30 June 2015		35,000

Trading account for the year ended 30 June 2016

	£	£
Sales		170,000
Less: cost of goods sold–		
stock on hand 1 July 2015	30,000	
purchases	120,000	
	150,000	
Less: stock on hand at 30 June 2016	(20,000)	
		(130,000)
Gross profit for the year ended 30 June 2016		40,000

No general rule can be laid down for valuing work in progress for tax purposes. The method used will depend on which is best fitted to the trade in question.

There are particular problems in relation to farmers (see 940ff.).

Long-term contracts

HMRC now accept that there is no longer a tax rule which denies provisions for anticipated losses or expenses. This means in particular that accurate provisions for foreseen losses on long-term contracts (e.g. in the construction industry) made in accordance with correct accounting practice will be tax deductible. A statement of practice on the subject has accordingly been withdrawn.

Market value of stock

Market value is taken to be that market in which the trader would normally sell his stock, be it wholesale or retail.

Cost price of stock

Identification of stock

Quite often stock is mixed and stored together so that it is impossible to tell the cost price of each particular item.

Example

A coal merchant buys five tons of coal at £30 per ton in August 2015 and ten tons of coal at £35 per ton in September 2015. All the coal is stored together so there is no indication what part of the stock cost £30 per ton and what cost £35 per ton.

In practice, HMRC accept all those methods recognised by the accountancy profession so long as they do not violate the taxing statutes.

The answer usually adopted and generally accepted by the courts to this problem is known as first-in, first-out (FIFO). This means that the first to be sold will be considered to be the first acquired. Thus, in the above example, the first five tons of coal sold by the trader will be brought into his trading accounts at £30 per ton.

The opposite method known as last-in, first-out (LIFO) has been rejected by the courts as unsuitable for tax purposes.

Another method commonly used for valuing stock at cost is the 'average cost' method. The average cost of the stock is arrived at by adding together all the stock and dividing this into the total price paid for all that stock.

Example

A coal merchant buys four tons of coal at £25 per ton and four tons of coal at £15 per ton and ten tons of coal at £20 per ton. He has bought 18 tons at a total cost of £360. If the cost of £360 is divided by the amount 18 tons, the average cost of £20 per ton is arrived at.

Other methods which are used and accepted by HMRC are the 'adjusted selling price' method and the 'standard cost' method. The 'adjusted selling price' is used when it is impractical to value such items at cost individually. In this case, the cost price is taken to be the selling price less the normal mark up. This applies only where the selling prices are full selling prices.

This is not normally the position, so HMRC accept value as marked prices less the normal mark up. This 'adjusted selling price' method is quite often used by the department stores.

The 'standard cost' method is a method whereby a standard price is chosen by the trader to be the cost price of his stock. However, this will not be accepted by HMRC unless the standard chosen closely reflects the current market value.

There is also the base stock method of valuation which assumes the necessity for a minimum or basic amount of stock which is necessary for the operation of the business. The base stock is valued at cost as at the date of the manufacturing process to which it relates and quantities in excess of the base stock are valued by some other method. This method is not accepted by HMRC for tax purposes.

Attribution of overheads

There are two accepted methods in arriving at cost.

- The 'direct cost' method which only takes account of the actual cost of the labour and materials used.

- The 'on cost' method or 'indirect cost' method which also takes account of the general overheads, e.g. heating, lighting, etc.

Legislation: FA 2008, s. 37

Cases: *Kelsall Parsons & Co v IR Commrs* (1938) 21 TC 608; *IR Commrs v Cock Russell & Co Ltd* (1949) 29 TC 387; *Rellim Ltd v Vise (HMIT)* (1951) 32 TC 254; *Minister of National Revenue v Anaconda American Brass Ltd* [1956] AC 85; *Duple Motor Bodies Ltd v Ostime (HMIT)* [1961] 1 WLR 739; *BSC Footwear Ltd v Ridgway (HMIT)* [1972] AC 544; *Symons (HMIT) v Weeks* [1983] BTC 18

Tax Reporter: ¶224-000

654 Change from one valid method to another

According to a statement of practice (which was withdrawn on 20 July 1999), when a change is made from one valid method of stock valuation to another (see 652), the opening stocks figure in the year of change must remain the same as the closing figure for the preceding year. Thus a tax-free uplift cannot be obtained where the opening stocks of one year exceed those of the previous year. See also 636 and 660.

Cases: *Pearce (HMIT) v Woodall-Duckham Ltd* (1978) 51 TC 271; *R v IR Commrs, ex parte SG Warburg & Co Ltd* [1994] BTC 201

Tax Reporter: ¶224-900

660 Stock valuation on discontinuance of trade

Where the cash basis is not being used (see 589) and a trade is discontinued or, except as noted below, is deemed discontinued (see 675ff.), any trading stock belonging to the trade at the time of discontinuance must be valued at market value at discontinuance.

However, if:

- the stock is sold to a UK trader; *and*

- the cost of it is deductible in computing the new trader's profits,

then the value of the stock will be taken to be the price the trader paid for it. For sales taking place after 24 July 2002, it is possible to make a just and reasonable apportionment of the consideration received where stock is transferred along with other assets.

Example of rule

Ten years ago Rupert, an art dealer, bought a painting for £2,000. He does not keep it on open display (or if he does he prices it much too highly). He now ceases to trade, with the painting unsold and worth an estimated £22,000. He cannot avoid income tax by bringing the painting into his final accounts at cost and later selling it privately for £25,000. £22,000 is the figure which he will bring into his final accounts.

Example of exception

Sebastian discontinues in trade. He sells his stock to an unconnected UK trader, Max, who enters the cost of this stock in his books as a deduction. Sebastian can enter into his accounts the price Max paid for his stock. Usually this exception will make very little difference to the basic rule of valuing at market value on discontinuance, since most traders will want to sell their goods at market value.

Where the transferor and transferee are 'connected', the arm's length price rather than the actual transfer price (subject to the possibility of a joint election made by the parties in certain circumstances) is to be used for the valuation of the stock transferred.

If a sole trader dies and, as a result, the trade is discontinued, stock will be valued in the normal way, at the lower of cost price or market value.

The above provisions (with the exception of the 'new rules' relating to transfer of stock on a discontinuance) apply to work in progress of professions and vocations with the proviso that the excess of the market value or sale price of the work in progress over cost can be taxed as a post-cessation receipt. However, an election to do this must be made within 12 months of discontinuance.

Example

Robert, an architect, discontinues his profession. The value of his work in progress at discontinuance is taken to be the amount it would have realised if sold on the open market at the discontinuance.

Any dispute concerning such transfer between trades, professions or vocations is dealt with in the same way as an appeal.

Where a person within the cash basis (see 589) permanently ceases to carry on a trade in a tax year, the value of any trading stock is to be determined on a 'just and reasonable basis'.

Legislation: ITTOIA 2005, s. 173–186

Tax Reporter: ¶225-600

Whether continuance of trade

675   Assessing beginning and cessation of trade

It is important for tax purposes to know when a trade has commenced and when it has ceased. On a discontinuance, trading stock may have to be uplifted to market value (see 660). Relief for trading losses depends upon a continuing trade (see 2104ff.).

It is usually quite clear when a trade commences though care must be taken to distinguish between trading and investment or other activities (see 555ff.) and between trading activity and preparation for trading activity. This is of less importance since 1980, when pre-trading expenditure became allowable as a trading loss on the day when the trade actually starts (see 2101).

In one case, the directors of a company between June and October arranged for premises and plant and for the supply of trading stock. They engaged a works manager in August and work commenced in October. It was held that the trade commenced in October and that the activity before October was preparation for trading activity.

However, it is not always clear when a trade has ceased. In particular, an existing trade may have continued as the same trade notwithstanding that it has:

- expanded or contracted (see 677);

- ceased temporarily (see 678);

- changed ownership by way of succession (see 752).

The Court of Session has indicated that, in respect of the transfer of a business to a company, a farming business is capable of being moved from one piece of land to another without being brought to an end. All farming businesses carried on by one person are treated as one trade (see 940).

Cases: *Birmingham & District Cattle By-Products Co Ltd v IR Commrs* (1919) 12 TC 92; *Gordon v IR Commrs; IR Commrs v Gordon* [1991] BTC 130

677 Expansion or contraction of trade and continuing trade

Where a trader expands or reduces the scope of his trade this will not necessarily be regarded as either, in the former case, the commencement of a new trade or, in the latter case, as a discontinuance of the trade (but see 752 on successions).

Example 1

A trader who has two shops selling sports goods decides to open a third shop also selling sports goods. This will not generally be regarded as the commencement of a new business.

Example 2

A trader has five shops all selling wine. He decides to close one of them. This will not generally be regarded as the cessation of a business.

It should be noted that any expansion of trade should be of the same nature as the previous trade.

It is a question of fact in each case whether a trade has been expanded or a new trade commenced (or a succession has taken place). An illustrative case, showing current thinking, involved taxpayers who had carried on the business of a fish and chip shop for a number of years. They bought an existing fish and chip shop business five miles away. Immediately on acquiring the new shop, the taxpayers changed its name and ran the business in their own style with their daughter in charge. The High Court upheld the general commissioners' right to reject HMRC's analysis of the facts that the second business was the same as before: they found that the taxpayers had not succeeded to that business but expanded their own trade into new premises.

Income tax

Generally, losses of an existing business can be brought forward from previous years and set off against the profits of the acquired business by virtue of the nature of relief for losses in respect of any trade (see 2104ff.).

Case: *Maidment (HMIT) v Kibby* [1993] BTC 291

678   Trade ceased temporarily

A business may have a slack period in which little or no work can be done. This may involve closing the business down. If the same business is reactivated at a later date, then it will not usually be regarded as permanently discontinued and/or as the commencement of a new business (see 675), but it is all a question of degree. The reactivated business must be substantially the same as before.

Partnerships

750   Partnerships: general

The existence of a partnership is a question of fact. What is agreed between the parties is not conclusive of its existence; neither is the existence of a partnership agreement. For taxation purposes, a partnership is a trade or profession carried on by two or more persons jointly and a limited partnership is a partnership for tax purposes.

There are some differences in law between English and Scottish partnerships. For example, although a partnership is a legal person in Scotland, in England and Wales it is the individual members of a partnership who are trading and not the partnership itself.

However, for taxation purposes provisions generally apply to partnerships in the UK irrespective of their form. Income tax in respect of partners chargeable thereto has historically been assessed jointly in the name of the partnership. Under self-assessment income tax is assessed directly on the partners. Partners chargeable to corporation tax have always been assessed directly (see 762).

Legislation: *Partnership Act* 1890, s. 4(2); ITTOIA 2005, s. 848

Cases: *Morden Rigg & Co and R B Eskrigge & Co v Monks* (1923) 8 TC 450; *Dickenson v Gross (HMIT)* (1927) 11 TC 614

Other Material: *Business Brief* 30/04, 19 November 2004, 'VAT and partnership "shares"'

Tax Reporter: ¶286-000

751   Limited liability partnerships

Where a limited liability partnership (LLP) carries on a trade, profession or other business with a view to profit:

- all the activities of the partnership are treated as carried on in partnership by its members (rather than by the partnership as such);

- anything done by, or in relation to the partnership for the purposes of, or in connection with, any of its activities is treated as done by, to or in relation to the members as partners; and

- the property of the partnership is treated as held by the members as partnership property.

This treatment applies where the LLP is no longer trading with a view to profit and the cessation is temporary. Where there is a permanent cessation, the above treatment applies in the period of winding up provided that the winding up is not for reasons connected with the avoidance of tax, nor is it unreasonably prolonged. However, this treatment ceases on the appointment of a liquidator or, if earlier, the making of a winding up order by the court.

The following changes, which took effect from 6 April 2014, were introduced to prevent tax loss:

- disguising employment relationships through limited liability partnerships; and

- certain arrangements involving allocation of profits and losses among partnership members.

Broadly, the changes affect Limited Liability Partnership (LLP) members who work for LLPs on terms that HMRC view as 'tantamount to employment' (i.e. disguised employment).

The new rules, designed to counter avoidance of tax, only apply to individuals that are members of LLPs, and to fall within the rules they have to satisfy three conditions (A–C) as follows:

Condition A is that there are 'relevant arrangements' in place for the individual to perform services as a member of the LLP. 'Relevant arrangements' means arrangements under which amounts are to be, or may be, payable by the LLP in respect of the individual's performance of services for the partnership in his capacity as a member of the partnership. The condition will be met if it is reasonable to expect that at least 80% of the total amount payable by the LLP in respect of the individual's performance, during the relevant period of services for the partnership in the individual's capacity as a member of the partnership, will be disguised salary.

An amount will be treated as 'disguised salary' if it:

(a)　is fixed;

(b)　is variable, but is varied without reference to the overall amount of the profits or losses of the LLP; or

(c)　is not, in practice, affected by the overall amount of those profits or losses.

In many cases, this will not lead to any difficulties as partners in an LLP will be remunerated by reference to the overall profits available.

Condition B is that the person concerned does not have significant influence over the affairs of the partnership.

Condition C is that the person's partnership capital is less than 25% of the amount of reasonable expected disguised salary for the tax year. In other words, the person concerned has to have at stake capital of at least one quarter of their partnership income to avoid satisfying this test. The partnership capital is determined on 6 April 2014 or at the date of appointment of the partner and then at the beginning of each subsequent tax year or whenever the partnership sharing arrangements change.

If a person satisfies all three conditions above, then that person is taxed as if they were an employee of the partnership, although their wider legal status as a member of the LLP is not changed.

Legislation: ITTOIA 2005, s. 863; FA 2014, s. 74 and Sch. 17

Tax Reporter: ¶292-400

752　Membership changes

Under the self-assessment regime as it applies to partnerships (see 750), a change in the personnel carrying on a partnership business triggers provisions treating the business as permanently discontinued at the date of the change and a new business as having commenced if none of the original partners continues to carry on the business thereafter.

Where a partner joins or leaves a partnership, the commencement and cessation rules apply to him individually. A sole trader who takes on a partner is treated as continuing to trade, and the partner is treated as commencing to trade. Conversely, when a business goes from a partnership to a sole trader, the latter is treated as continuing and the other partner(s) as ceasing. If partners dissolve the partnership but each continues with part of the business, the partnership business ceases and the commencement provisions apply to the businesses run by the ex-partners.

A change in the personal representatives or trustees who carry on a trade is not treated as a discontinuance.

Legislation: ITTOIA 2005, s. 246

Other Material: SP 9/86, *Partnership mergers and demergers*

Tax Reporter: ¶287-650

754 Partners' salaries and interest on capital

In England and Wales (unlike Scotland), a partnership is not a legal entity. Thus, a partnership cannot enter into a contract of employment with an equity partner and such a partner cannot be the employee of the remaining partners – the same person cannot be both master and servant.

If, therefore, an equity partner is, by virtue of the terms of the agreement of partnership, entitled to salary or wages, he is merely entitled to an allocation of profits before the general division among the partners. This compares with some salaried partners who, by the nature of the particular arrangement in point, are more akin to employees.

The tax consequences of the legal position that equity partners' salaries are not deductible in arriving at the net partnership income (or net partnership loss) poses no problem where the adding back of salaries results in the individual interests of both partners in the net income or net loss showing either a surplus or a deficiency.

Example 1

Alex and Ben are in partnership. Alex is the only active partner and receives a salary of £20,000 p.a. as manager. The profits and losses (calculated after deducting Alex's salary) are to be shared equally. Profits of £15,000 are made in the basis year after deducting Alex's salary.

	£
Partnership profit (after Alex's salary deducted)	15,000
Add: Alex's salary	20,000
Assessable income	35,000

Allocation of assessment:	£	
Alex: salary	20,000	
plus 50% of balance (£15,000)		7,500
		27,500
Ben: 50% of balance (£15,000)		7,500
Total		35,000

Example 2

Charlie and David are partners in a firm. The partnership agreement provides for salaries to be paid as follows:

Charlie = £10,000

David = £5,000

Profits or losses remaining after an allowance for the salaries has been made are shared equally between Charlie and David. The firm makes a loss in a tax year of £20,000 after the salaries have been deducted. The tax-allowable loss is restricted to:

	£	£
Partnership loss		(20,000)
Less: Charlie's salary	10,000	
David's salary	5,000	
		15,000
Tax loss		(5,000)
Allocation of loss:	£	£
Charlie: salary		10,000
Less: 50% of loss of 20,000		(10,000)
		–
David: salary		5,000
Less: 50% of loss of 20,000		(10,000)
		(5,000)
Total		(5,000)

However, it is in cases where the distribution between the partners in accordance with the partnership agreement results in a surplus for one partner and a deficiency for the other that problems arise.

The basic position can be summarised as follows:

- Where, before taking partners' salaries into account, there is a *net partnership income* for tax purposes, the partner whose entitlement (including salary) shows a surplus is taxed on the whole of the net partnership income; no loss for tax purposes is allowable to the other partner.

- Where, before taking partners' salaries into account, there is a *net partnership loss*, the partner whose entitlement (including salary) shows a deficiency is entitled to the whole of the net partnership loss; no amount is assessable to the other partner.

Interest on capital

Interest paid to a partner on capital which he contributes to the partnership is likewise not an allowable expense but rather an allocation of profit. However, a partner who makes, for the purpose of the partnership, any actual payment or advance beyond the amount of capital which he has agreed to contribute is entitled (in the absence of a contrary agreement) to simple interest at 5% p.a. Such interest constitutes an allowable expense of the partnership and attracts an income tax charge (see 1366ff.).

Legislation: *Partnership Act* 1890, s. 24(3)

Case: *Heastie (HMIT) v Veitch & Co* (1933) 18 TC 305

Tax Reporter: ¶287-200

756   Partnership income

Partnership income is apportioned according to the shares current in the tax year even though, before self-assessment, the assessment may be based on profits of an earlier period. Salaries paid to partners and interest on capital contributed by partners are deducted from the partnership profits before the shares of each partner are ascertained (see 754). Where a partnership involves a company, slightly different rules apply (see 762).

Other income of a trading partnership is computed as if the partnership were a UK-resident individual, and allocated according to sharing ratios in the period covered by the computation. This is achieved by treating such income as if it were profits, gains or losses of a trade or profession. If the other income is untaxed, then, for basis periods purposes, all sources of untaxed income are pooled and treated as arising from a separate deemed trade.

HMRC have clarified the treatment of partnership income from jointly owned property. Consider two individuals carrying on business in partnership with land-owning and trading activities arranged such that:

- the partnership business comprises both a business trading income source and a property income source: the income from the property income source will be assessable using the basis periods that apply for the business trading income source;

- there are two separate businesses and two separate partnerships, albeit partnerships between the same two individuals: the income from the property source will be assessable on a tax year basis;

- the letting income is not ancillary to the trading partnership source, and the letting activity cannot be described as the carrying on of a business: the income arising is not assessable as partnership income and each share will be assessable as the personal income of the individuals.

A partner cannot assign his income to another person for tax purposes.

Legislation: ITTOIA 2005, s. 851(1)–(2), 854–855

Cases: *Hadlee v Commr of Inland Revenue (New Zealand)* [1993] BTC 133

Tax Reporter: ¶287-000

759 Transactions between the partnership and individual partners

Transactions between the partnership and an individual partner are subject to transfer pricing rules. The actual sale proceeds or actual purchase price as appropriate may be adjusted so as to prevent the avoidance of UK tax; thus sales at an overvalue or undervalue may be prevented. The provisions may apply where the buyer or seller is a body of persons, including a partnership, and there is common control with the other party – in the case of a partnership control is determined by reference to a right to more than 50% of the assets or income (for details of the anti-avoidance provision).

Transfers of trading stock may fall within the above provisions or may alternatively be subject to further provisions (see 636).

Assets owned by an individual partner but used in the partnership trade may attract capital allowances on general principles or, in the case of machinery or plant, by statute.

Legislation: CAA 2001, s. 264; ITA 2007, s. 995

Tax Reporter: ¶287-000

762 Partnerships with company members

A company may be a member of a partnership, with other companies and/ or with one or more individuals. Where a partnership involves a company, the general rules for computing income profits and losses are modified, as set out below.

In the case of partnership trading income, profits ('profits' does not here include chargeable gains) and losses are computed as if the partnership were a UK-resident company (except in the case of a corporate partner which is a company resident outside the UK). This is in order to ascertain the corporation tax liability of the company partner. However, although tax is computed applying corporation tax principles (with reference to accounting periods), initially distributions are ignored and no adjustment is made for capital allowances and charges; also, no deduction is made in any accounting period for losses incurred in an earlier accounting period.

A change in the persons carrying on a trade is treated as a transfer of the trade to a different company if a company continues to be a member of the partnership but is not also a company which was a partner before the change. Thus, a transfer of the trade might give rise to balancing charges in relation to capital allowances. A company's share in the profits and losses of any accounting period is calculated according to its entitlement during that period. Corporation tax is charged as if that share was derived from a trade carried on by the company alone in its corresponding accounting period or periods.

In many cases, the corporate member of the partnership will perform few, if any, duties but will nevertheless be allocated a substantial proportion of the profits. HMRC see this as tax avoidance on the basis that profits parked in the company are only charged to corporation tax at 20%, in contrast to the much higher rates of income tax and National Insurance contributions applicable to the profits allocated to individual partners. To counter this perceived avoidance, from 6 April 2014 (subject to certain anti-avoidance rules, which came into force on 5 December 2013), HMRC have the legislative facility to allocate the profits of a partnership to the individual members, replacing any allocation to non-individual partners.

Legislation: CTA 2009, s. 77(5), 1262 FA 2014, s. 74 and Sch. 17

Case: *Ensign Tankers (Leasing) Ltd v Stokes (HMIT)* [1992] BTC 110; *Hamilton & Kinneil (Archerfield Ltd)* [2014] TC 03485

Tax Reporter: ¶291-150

764   Partnership retirement annuities

In some cases, agreements to pay partnership annuities to retired partners might constitute 'settlements' and thus be caught by the anti-avoidance provisions discussed at 1070ff. Normally, however, they will not be settlements, having been made for full consideration.

Tax Reporter: ¶287-000

766   General partnership losses

As with profits, partnership losses are divided among partners according to their respective shares. For losses generally, see 2104ff..

Briefly, a partner is entitled to loss relief, for his share of the partnership loss, against other income of the same tax year and against any income of the following year (in so far as relief has not already been given) if he is still a partner in the firm.

However, loss relief available to non-active general partners and non-active members of limited liability partnerships are restricted. Broadly, the amount which may be given otherwise than against income consisting of profits arising from the trade only to the extent that:

- the amount given; or

- the aggregate amount,

does not exceed the amount of the individual's contribution to the trade at the end of the tax year in question.

A loss (in so far as relief has not already been given) may be carried forward by the partner and set against his share of the profits of the trade, etc. for subsequent years (see 2107).

Each partner may choose whether he prefers the former ('carry-across') relief or 'carry-forward' relief. The calculation of the two reliefs may vary where partnership profit-sharing ratios are changed because for carry-across relief (where the loss is generally treated as arising in the tax year in which the accounting period ends), the relevant profit-sharing ratio is that existing during *the tax year* in which the accounting period ends. For carry-forward relief, the relevant profit-sharing ratio is that existing during *the accounting period* in which the loss arose.

Upon the death or retirement of a partner, losses which have not been relieved cannot be carried forward. However, the relief described in 2122 (carry-back of terminal losses) may apply in such cases.

Terminal loss relief applies on a permanent discontinuance of a trade, etc. which includes a deemed discontinuance on a change in partners (see 752). A person who continues to be a partner after the deemed discontinuance is not entitled to terminal loss relief (though he continues to be entitled to carry forward his losses).

Relief for losses in the early years of a trade may be available (see 2119).

Limited recourse or non-repayable loans, or other reimbursable amounts are excluded from being treated for tax purposes as part of the partner's contribution to a trade, thereby preventing that partner from benefiting from loss relief in excess of the actual amounts lost or at risk. The rules apply to individual partners in limited partnerships, limited liability partnerships, partners who spend less than ten hours per week actively carrying on a partnership trade, and any partners who have claimed film-related losses.

Legislation: ITA 2007, s. 110; *Partnerships (Restrictions on Contributions to a Trade) Regulations* 2005 (SI 2005/2017)

Tax Reporter: ¶287-600

767   Limited partnership losses

A limited partnership is one in which one or more members have limited liability provided that at least one member has unlimited liability.

When a limited partnership makes a trading loss, the partners are entitled to make a claim for relief from income tax in the same way as a partner in an ordinary partnership (see 766). The limited partner's share of the loss is restricted to the amount of his capital contribution. Only that amount can be set off against his other income. The restriction applies to both individual and company partners. It applies not only to limited partners in partnerships restricted under the *Limited Partnership Act* 1907 but also to persons participating in other joint venture arrangements where the liability is limited in a similar way by contract, agreement or guarantee or by the laws of other countries. Any balance of a limited partner's share of the partnership loss which cannot be relieved against other income because of this restriction may be carried forward and set against the limited partner's share of any future profits from the partnership.

See 766 regarding a restriction for loss relief available to non-active members of partnerships.

Legislation: ITA 2007, s. 56, 104, 110

Case: *Reed (HMIT) v Young* [1986] BTC 242

Tax Reporter: ¶292-000

768   Personal reliefs: partnerships

Partners may claim 'personal reliefs' (see 1850) according to their respective shares and interests. Any partner's personal reliefs may be set off against the share of tax attributed to him. Any excess of allowances over tax due on his partnership share can be set off against any other income that he might have.

Legislation: ITA 2007, Part 3

Tax Reporter: ¶286-350

800 European Economic Interest Groupings (EEIGs)

The tax regime for European Economic Interest Groupings (EEIGs) broadly provides that:

- any trade or profession carried on by an EEIG is treated as carried on in partnership by the members of the grouping (any member's share of UK trading operations of a group managed and controlled abroad being chargeable in the same way as a non-resident trading in the UK); and

- disposals of assets by an EEIG are treated for tax purposes as disposals by members of the grouping of their shares of the assets concerned;

and income tax or corporation tax, as the case may be, is then charged if appropriate on the profits and gains attributed to the separate members of the grouping.

Legislation: ITA 2007, s. 842 and Sch. 1

Tax Reporter: ¶772-200

Special taxpayers

Charities

900 Special treatment for charities

Charities are favourably treated for tax purposes. A 'charity' is defined as 'any body of persons or trust established for charitable purposes only'. Whether a purpose is charitable is a question largely answered by case law and reference should be made to one of the standard textbooks. A training and enterprise council (or TEC, donations to which may be deductible: see 2056) has been held not to be a charity.

A revised definition for tax purposes of charities and other organisations entitled to UK charity tax reliefs applies from 1 April 2010. One condition that must be satisfied to fall within the revised definition is that the managers of the body are 'fit and proper persons' to be its managers.

In the Autumn Statement 2013, the Government announced that legislation would be brought forward to prevent charities being set up to avoid tax following consultation with the sector. HMRC have developed two alternative legislative approaches to implement the Autumn Statement announcement. Following informal consultation, HMRC published a discussion paper seeking feedback to the two approaches. Based on responses to that discussion paper and engagement with the sector, the Government decided not to legislate in Finance Bill 2014. Feedback confirmed that the two approaches outlined in the paper would have a disproportionate and unacceptable effect upon the charity sector and legitimate donors. Possible damage to innocent charities and existing and new HMRC controls mean that changing the law is not justified at this point.

HMRC already have a wide range of tools available to tackle avoidance and have recently had considerable success in the courts in challenging certain schemes. HMRC believe that recent changes in powers such as the General Anti-Abuse Rule (GAAR), the fit and proper person test for charities, and the new accelerated payments regime, will provide additional deterrence.

The British Museum, the Natural History Museum, the Historic Buildings and Monument Commission and the National Heritage Memorial Fund enjoy the same exemptions available to charities generally.

A gain is not a chargeable gain (and, therefore, not liable to CGT) if it accrues to a charity and is applicable and applied for charitable purposes (see 6189). For the inheritance tax exemption for gifts to charities, see 7195. For covenanted payments to charity, see 1073.

Gift aid small donations scheme

The *Small Charitable Donations Act* 2012 received Royal Assent on 19 December 2012. The Act legislated the gift aid small donations scheme (GASDS) announced at Budget 2011 and the changes have been implemented from 6 April 2013.

GASDS allows eligible charities and community amateur sports clubs to claim gift aid style top-up payments on small cash donations without requiring the donor to provide a gift aid declaration.

Legislation: ITTOIA 2005, s. 108(4), 878(1); FA 2010, Sch. 6; *Taxes (Definition of Charity) (Relevant Territories) (Amendment) Regulations* 2014 (SI 2014/1807); *Finance Act 2010, Schedule 6, Part 1 (Further Consequential and Incidental Provision etc) Order* 2012 (SI 2012/735); *Finance Act 2010, Schedule 6, Part 2 (Commencement) Order* 2012 (SI 2012/736)

Cases: *IR Commrs v Oldham Training and Enterprise Council* [1996] BTC 539

Other Material: Charity tax relief model declaration: www.gov.uk/government/publications/charity-tax-relief-model-declaration; Claim tax back on donations using Charities Online: www.gov.uk/claim-tax-back-on-donations-using-charities-online

Tax Reporter: ¶815-000

901 Exemptions for charities' trading or investment income

Charities benefit from a number of exemptions in relation to their trading and investment income. These are summarised below.

Rents

Exemption is given, upon a claim being made, from income tax in respect of the rents or other receipts from land vested in trustees for charitable purposes, so far as the rents are applied to charitable purposes only.

Interest, annuities, dividends

Charities are exempt from tax in respect of:

- yearly interest or other annual payments or equivalent foreign income (see 1366ff.); or

- any chargeable distribution or equivalent foreign income.

The amount of tax credit attaching to distributions by UK companies was 10% until 5 April 2016. From 6 April 2016, the dividend tax credit was abolished by *Finance Act* 2016. Prior to 6 April 2016, in general, all entitlement to payment of tax credits had been removed, other than tax credits payable under double taxation agreements.

Income from trade

Prior to 22 March 2006, charities were exempt from income tax under ITTOIA 2005 in respect of trading income if the profits were applied solely for the purposes of the charity and either:

- the trade was exercised in the course of the actual carrying out of a primary purpose of the charity (e.g. school education); or

- the work in connection with the trade was mainly carried out by beneficiaries of the charity. The Court of Session has held that an association, whose object was to promote and conduct concerts, etc. was exempt from tax on its income from admission charges to its musical festival: the competitors were the beneficiaries of the charity and they did the most essential part of the work in conducting the festival.

For chargeable periods commencing on or after 22 March 2006 (FA 2006, s. 56), this relief is extended to charities where the trade is undertaken only partly for the primary (charitable) purposes, or is only carried out by the beneficiaries of the charity. From that date, relief will be given on the profits that can be reasonably attributed to the part of the trade carried on for the primary purpose or to the part carried out by the beneficiaries.

From 6 April 2000, for charitable trusts, and for accounting periods beginning on or after 1 April 2000 in relation to charities that are companies, the exemption for a charities trading income is widened to encompass small trades, provided that the following conditions are met:

- the income must be applied solely for the purposes of the charity; and

- the gross income (before expenses) must be within the limits of the greater of £5,000 and whichever is the lesser of £50,000 and 25% of the charity's income.

The condition is met if at the beginning of the period the charity had a reasonable expectation that its gross income would be within the limit. Where the period in question is less than 12 months, the £5,000 and £50,000 limits are reduced proportionately.

The extension of the relief introduced by FA 2006 (see above) will particularly help charities where more than 10% of their trading activity is not attributable to their primary charitable purpose. Where charities operate a small trade not for the primary purpose of the charity, they may continue to obtain relief under the exemption for small trades.

Universities

The Financial Secretary to the Treasury has commented on Revenue discussions with university representatives on the tax treatment of consultancy earnings, holiday lettings and conference facilities:

> 'The Inland Revenue has explained that universities are entitled to the same tax exemptions as other charities. Trading profits are exempt only where the trade is exercised in the course of the actual carrying out of a primary purpose of the charity, or where the work in connection with the trade is mainly carried out by beneficiaries of the charity. Profits from other trading activities are likely to be taxable, in the same way as for other traders. The outcome in each case depends on its particular facts.'

Trading activities for charitable purposes

Profits of bazaars, jumble sales and similar activities arranged by voluntary organisations to raise funds for charity are usually exempt from tax provided a range of conditions are met.

Covenanted payments from associated trading companies

Where the trade is carried on by a company whose shares are held by the charity, any profits from the trade are exempt from tax if the company covenants to make payments to the charity equal to its profits. HMRC have confirmed that this arrangement will not constitute a tax ineffective 'scheme' within *Furniss v Dawson*.

Lottery income

Profits accruing to a charity from a lottery are exempt from tax, provided that they are applied solely to the charity's purposes and the lottery is promoted in accordance with the *Lotteries and Amusements Act* 1976, s. 3 or 5, or the corresponding Northern Ireland legislation.

Legislation: FA 1989, s. 59; F(No. 2)A 1992, s. 28; FA 1993, s. 80; F(No. 2)A 1997, s. 28, 35; FA 2000, s. 46; ITTOIA 2005, s. 385(1), 397(1), (6); FA 2006, s. 56; ITA 2007, s. 529

Cases: *IR Commrs v Glasgow Musical Festival Association* (1926) 11 TC 154; *IR Commrs v National Book League* [1957] Ch 488; *Furniss (HMIT) v Dawson* [1984] BTC 71; *Guild (as trustees of the William Muir (Bond 9) Ltd Employees' Share Scheme) v IR Commrs* [1993] BTC 267; *Siri Ltd* [2011] UKFTT 794 (TC); [2011] TC 01630; ; ; ;

Tax Reporter: ¶815-300

902   Charitable donations by individuals: gift aid

A specific relief, 'gift aid', is available to individuals in respect of certain single gifts in money to charities (relief for covenanted payments is available under other provisions: see 1073 and 1840). Gifts are made net of basic rate tax, which charities reclaim from HMRC; higher-rate relief is also available to donors.

Gift aid and small donations scheme payments can be claimed online.

The GADs scheme includes donations by Crown servants, members of the UK armed forces serving overseas, foreign donors and donors who pay capital gains tax and who pay tax at below the basic rate.

For the gift to 'charity' (see 900), to be a 'qualifying donation', it must constitute a sum of money; and:

- be subject to no repayment condition;

- not fall within the payroll deduction scheme (see 904);

- not be conditional on or associated with, or part of an arrangement involving, the acquisition of property by the charity, otherwise than by way of gift, from the donor or a person 'connected with' him (see 1260).

A qualifying donation is to be treated as paid after deduction of basic rate tax and the individual's basic rate limit is to be increased by the amount of the donation grossed up at the basic rate for the year in which it is made (ITA 2007, s. 414(2), 415). Because the basic rate band for the year is increased by the grossed-up amount of the donation, a donor liable at the higher rate gets relief on the grossed-up amount of the donation, at the difference between the higher rate and basic rate.

To the extent that the gross donation is not matched by the donor's taxable income, the donor is assessable and chargeable with basic rate tax. However, if HMRC find that a non-taxpayer's donation has been included in a gift aid claim from a charity, they pursue the charity for the shortfall rather than the donor.

Relief for gift aid payments may be set against the previous year's liability. An election for this must be made on or before the date the tax return for the previous year is delivered, but in any case no later than the 31 January filing date. There must be enough income and gains in the previous year to cover the donation. The election does not affect the position of the recipient.

Charities are not required to send donors a written record of an oral declaration providing certain conditions are met.

Certain heritage and conservation charities may offer free admission in return for a donation without the admission counting as a benefit for gift aid purposes. This exemption was extended from 6 April 2006 to any type of charity that grants the right to pay to view its property. However, if a donation is made instead of paying an admission charge, gift aid will only apply to the whole of the gift if:

- the right of admission is for an unrestricted number of visits over a period of at least one year; or

- the right of admission is for less than one year but the gift is at least 10% more than the amount any member of the public would have to pay for the same right of admission. If there is not a comparable admission ticket, the value of the right of admission will count towards the benefit limit for gift aid purposes (25% of the donation, up to a maximum of £250 in any year).

The effect is that charities can no longer simply reclassify admission fees as donations subject to gift aid.

Where an individual makes a donation to a charity and receives the right of admission in consequence, the right of admission is, in restricted circumstances, disregarded as a benefit to the donor in determining whether the donation is eligible for gift aid relief.

In the charity's hands, a qualifying donation is treated as an annual payment from which basic rate tax has been deducted, thus entitling the charity to reclaim that tax from HMRC provided certain procedures have been followed (see 901).

Legislation: ITA 2007, Pt. 8, Ch. 2; FA 2008, s. 53

Case: *LCC v Attorney-General* (1900) 4 TC 265

Other Material: Claiming a top-up payment on small charitable donations: www.gov.uk/claiming-a-top-up-payment-on-small-charitable-donations

Tax Reporter: ¶815-330

903   Gifts to the nation

A scheme designed to encourage taxpayers to donate pre-eminent objects, or collections of objects, to the nation was introduced with effect from 1 April 2012. Under the scheme, the objects may be loaned or given to appropriate institutions including certain charities and accredited museums for safe keeping and to provide public access. In return, donors will receive a reduction in their UK tax liability based on a percentage of the value of the object they are donating.

A potential donor will offer to give a pre-eminent object (or collection of objects) to the nation with a self-assessed valuation of the object. It is a condition of the new reliefs that the gift is made in accordance with a scheme (the 'Cultural Goods Scheme') administered by the Arts Council. A panel of experts will consider the offer and, if it considers the object is pre-eminent and should be accepted, the panel will agree the value of the object with the donor. If the donor decides to proceed based on that valuation they will receive a tax reduction as a fixed percentage of the object's agreed value. The fixed percentage will be 30% for individuals (20% for companies). Individuals will be able to spread the tax reduction forward across a period of up to five years starting with the tax year in which the object is offered. The donor will specify in advance how the tax reduction is to be used. Gifts made under the scheme are not chargeable gains for capital gains tax purposes. The item donated will not regarded as remitted to the UK under ITA 2007, s. 809Y(1) for the purposes of the remittance basis rules.

Legislation: FA 2012, s. 49 and Sch. 14; *Finance Act 2012, Sch. 14 (Appointed Day) Order* 2013 (SI 2013/587)

Other material: Guidance on Cultural Goods Scheme: www.artscouncil. org.uk/media/uploads/pdf/DCMS_Guidance_15_March.pdf

Tax Reporter: ¶716-685

904   Gifts of shares and securities, etc. to charities

Tax relief is available for gifts of qualifying investments to a charity.

Where the donor is an individual, he or she will benefit from an income tax deduction for the full market value of the qualifying investment at the date of the gift, plus incidental expenses of transfer, less any consideration or benefit received. This relief is in addition to capital gains tax relief available for gifts of shares, securities and other assets to a charity.

Qualifying investments

The following constitute qualifying investments:

- shares or securities that are listed or dealt in on a recognised stock exchange;

- units in an authorised unit trust;

- shares in an open-ended investment company;

- an interest in an offshore fund; and

- from April 2002, a freehold interest or leasehold interest in land and buildings in the UK.

The relief

The amount of relief (known as the 'relevant amount') is, in the case of a gift, the market value at the time of the disposal. Where the disposal is at an undervalue, the relevant amount is the difference between the market value at the date of the disposal and the amount of value of any consideration received. In the hands of the charity, the base cost of the investment for capital gains tax purposes is reduced by the relevant amount, or to nil if the relevant amount exceeds the base cost. Incidental costs of disposal are taken into account in computing the relevant amount where the disposal is at an undervalue, although the base cost is not reduced for such incidental expenses.

Legislation: ITA 2007, Pt. 8, Ch. 3

Tax Reporter: ¶116-000

905 Payroll deduction scheme donations

Under the payroll deduction scheme, an employee's donation to 'charity' (900) from his pay-packet, subject to an annual limit, attracts tax relief. Relief is available where:

- an employee suffers deduction of tax under PAYE;

- the employer operates an approved scheme for the deduction of charitable donations;

- the employee authorises the employer to make the deductions;

- the employer pays the deducted sums to an approved agent;

- the approved agent pays the deducted sums to a charity or charities; and

- the sums deducted constitute gifts from the employee to the charity and are not paid under a covenant.

The deduction of a donation to charity under the scheme occurs before PAYE is applied, thus giving relief by means of a 'net pay' arrangement.

There are regulations under which payroll deduction schemes are approved.

For relief for expenses incurred by the employer, see 2030.

Legislation: FA 2003, s. 146; FA 2000, s. 38; ITEPA 2003, s. 713; *Charitable Deductions (Approved Schemes) (Amendment) Regulations* 2014 (SI 2014/584); *Charitable Deductions (Approved Schemes) Regulations* 1986 (SI 1986/2211)

Tax Reporter: ¶457-700

906 Community amateur sports clubs

Amateur sports clubs that register as community amateur sports clubs (CASCs) are given various tax reliefs and exemptions similar to those given to a charity.

From 1 April 2015, CASCs are exempt from corporation tax if their trading income is less than £50,000 or where their gross property income is less than £30,000. CASCs which do not exceed these thresholds do not have to complete an annual tax return. In addition, there is no longer a limit on the amount of trading income at can be earned from members. The new income condition means that CASCs cannot earn more than £100,000 a year from trading with non-members and/or property income.

From 1 April 2015, CASCs can pay players as long as they do not pay more than £10,000 in total to all their players in a single year and there are new limits on fees and costs associated with membership.

A CASC is treated as a charity for the purpose of gift aid donations by individuals (see 902), although membership fees may not be treated as gifts. The CASC will be able to reclaim basic rate tax on donations. The treatment of a CASC as a charity also means that gifts and bequests to it are free of IHT (see 7195) and exempt from CGT (see 6189). Relief is also available on gifts from businesses (see 636) and for gifts of plant and machinery.

CASCs wishing to claim a repayment from HMRC should use Revenue form R68 (CASC).

Small local sports clubs

There is a cap on membership costs, which means that any club charging more than £31 a week (£1,612 a year) for members will not qualify for the relief. Any club charging more than £10 per week will have to offer alternatives such as special discounts for those who cannot afford membership. Clubs can pay expenses for some matches and tours where players take part in and promote the club's sport. At least 50% of a club's members must participate in sport at the club.

Legislation: FA 2004, s. 56; *Community Amateur Sports Clubs (Exemptions) Order* 2014 (SI 2014/3327); *Community Amateur Sports Clubs Regulations* 2015 (SI 2015/725)

Other Material: Community amateur sports clubs: detailed guidance notes: www.gov.uk/government/publications/community-amateur-sports-clubs-detailed-guidance-notes

Tax Reporter: ¶806-310

907 Large charities with non-qualifying expenditure: restricted exemptions

The tax exemptions available to a charity (see 901) are restricted if, in its chargeable period:

- its 'relevant income and gains' exceeded its 'qualifying expenditure'; and

- it incurred non-qualifying expenditure.

'Relevant income and gains' means income otherwise so exempted from tax and income taxable notwithstanding those provisions, taken together with capital gains exempted from CGT (see 5800) and gains which are chargeable notwithstanding that exemption.

'Qualifying expenditure' means any expenditure made for charitable purposes only and includes qualifying investments and qualifying loans. Payment made to overseas bodies is not qualifying expenditure unless the charity concerned has taken such steps as may be reasonable to ensure that the payment is applied for charitable purposes.

Where the conditions above are met, exemption from tax is not available in respect of so much of the excess of relevant income and gains over qualifying expenditure as does not exceed the non-qualifying expenditure.

Where, in a chargeable period, the sum of qualifying and non-qualifying expenditure exceeds the relevant income and gains of that period, some or all of the excess may be carried back and treated as the non-qualifying expenditure of an earlier period.

Where a charity's own exemption from tax is limited by these rules, higher rate tax relief for covenantors will be similarly restricted (see 1073 and 1840).

Legislation: ITA 2007, Pt. 10; ITTOIA 2005, s. 878(1)

Tax Reporter: ¶815-300

909   Grants paid by one charity to another

A sum received by a charity by way of a grant from another charity is chargeable to income tax as income of the payee charity, but is treated as if it were an annual payment thereby eligible for exemption from tax if applied for charitable purposes (see 901).

Legislation: ITA 2007, s. 523

Tax Reporter: ¶815-300

911   Covenanted payments by subsidiary to parent

Where a subsidiary company pays a covenanted sum to its parent charity, such a sum must be paid under deduction of income tax if the payer company is to treat the sum so paid as a charge on income. The parent charity may reclaim the tax so paid provided it satisfies the conditions for exemption from income tax.

Tax Reporter: ¶815-300

913 Substantial donors

Rules up to 31 March 2011

Additional restrictions have been placed on transactions that can take place on or after 22 March 2006 (unless a contract was entered into earlier), between a charity and its substantial donors without the charity's tax relief being restricted.

Broadly, an individual or a company will be treated as a 'substantial donor' if they give the charity £25,000 or more in any 12-month period, or £100,000 over a six-month period, both for the chargeable period in which they exceed these limits and the following five chargeable periods. The limits apply only to amounts on which tax relief has been claimed.

The 'substantial donor' rules apply to various specified transactions unless the transaction is otherwise exempt, or where HMRC are satisfied that a charity has engaged in it for genuine commercial reasons, or on terms that are no less beneficial to the charity than those that might be expected of an identical arm's length transaction, so long as the transaction is not part of an arrangement for the avoidance of tax.

The rules do not apply to a disposal at less than market value by a substantial donor to a charity to which the 'gifts of shares, securities and real property to charity' rules (see 903), or the capital gains 'gifts to charities' (see 6189) rules apply.

Where a charity takes part in any one of the specified transactions that are not otherwise exempt, any payments made by the charity in connection with the transaction will be treated as non-charitable expenditure. Where the transaction is not on arm's length terms, any difference between the actual terms and arm's length terms, so far as it favours the substantial donor, will be treated as non-charitable expenditure and the charity will have its tax relief restricted.

Changes from 1 April 2011

Finance Act 2011 introduced new rules that deny tax relief on donations only where the donor is party to arrangements, the main purpose or one of the main purposes of which is to obtain an advantage for the donor or a connected person, directly or indirectly, from the charity (known as 'tainted donations'). The legislation has effect in relation to charity donations made on or after 1 April 2011 irrespective of when the arrangements were entered into. The previous legislation ceased to have effect in respect of donations received on or after 1 April 2011. Under the revised rules, there are no thresholds on the size of a donation that must be exceeded before the legislation can apply and consequently the concept of a 'substantial donor' has subsequently disappeared. Another key change in approach is that where a donation is deemed tainted under the revised rules, tax relief is denied and the donor (as opposed to the charity) will be the primary target for recovery of any relief that, under these rules, should not have been given.

Legislation: ITA 2007, Sch. 2, para. 105 and 106; FA 2011, s. 27 and Sch. 3

Tax Reporter: ¶815-660

923 Scientific research associations

The exemptions applying to charities, the procedures for reclaiming tax deducted at source, the treatment of tax credits associated with dividends from UK companies and HMRC's information powers (see 901) also apply to certain scientific research associations. The exemptions are available where:

- the object of an association is 'scientific research' which may lead to or facilitate an extension of any class or classes of trade approved by the Department of Trade and Industry; and

- the memorandum of association or other similar instrument regulating the functions of the association precludes the direct or indirect payment, or transfer, to any of its members of any of its income or property by way of dividend, gift, bonus, etc. (except for reasonable payment for goods, labour, services, or reasonable interest or rent).

Legislation: CTA 2010, s. 469

Other Material: ESC C31, *Scientific research associations*

Tax Reporter: ¶806-300

Farming concerns and market gardeners

940 Farming concerns and market gardeners: introduction

All farming and market gardening in the UK is treated as the carrying on of a trade (or part of a trade) chargeable under ITTOIA 2005, s. 9.

'Farming' consists of occupying land for the purposes of husbandry but excluding market gardening. 'Market gardening' consists of occupying land (other than for the growth of hops) as a nursery or garden for the sale of produce.

Share farming

'Share farming' is a method of farming where the owner or tenant of farm land (the landowner) enters into a contract with a working farmer (the share farmer). Typically:

- the landowner provides the farm land and buildings, fixed equipment and machinery, major maintenance of the buildings and his expertise;

- the share farmer provides labour, field and mobile machinery and his expertise;

- other costs such as seed, fertilisers and feed are shared. If there is a livestock enterprise, then ownership of the animals is shared on the basis that each party owns a share in each animal;

- each party is rewarded by a share in the produce of the farm which he is free to sell as he likes; and

- each party produces his own accounts and is responsible for his own tax and VAT returns.

HMRC consider that both parties to a genuine share farming agreement are carrying on a 'farming' business for tax purposes.

Grants to farmers

Payments to taxpayers by way of grants cause difficulty and general rules are problematic since it is the precise purpose of the grant in each case which is critical – however, some guidance is available as set out below.

- Amounts received by farmers to make good a possible loss or temporary loss of income are generally taxable as income. Hence, the first premium under the EC Dairy Herd Conversion Scheme has been treated as taxable under former Sch. D, Case I, where it was held that under the scheme taxpayers gave up the right to continue producing milk for supply and sale but neither lost nor surrendered any capital assets (the conversion premium was for expected loss during the exchange from dairy cows to beef cattle which would be taxable if received). HMRC have confirmed that a payment of superlevy made after a farmer has exceeded his milk quota is an allowable trading deduction.

- Aid under the Oilseeds Support Scheme 1992 is generally to be treated as a subsidy towards the selling price; hence, accounts should recognise the payments as income for tax purposes at the time the crop is sold and, if best estimates are used until final figures are available, the inspector may decide to agree the computation and adjust the amount in the following period.

All farming by same person to be treated as one trade

All farming (but not market gardening) carried on by one person (or partnership or body of persons) is treated as one trade. Thus, a farming company which bought one farm in Scotland and soon after sold a farm in England was (being engaged in a continuous trade) entitled to carry forward losses and unused capital allowances from the English farming business to the Scottish one.

Legislation: ITTOIA 2005, s. 9–11

Cases: *Bispham (HMIT) v Eardiston Farming Co (1919) Ltd* [1962] 1 WLR 616; *IR Commrs v Biggar* [1982] BTC 332

Tax Reporter: ¶270-500

942   Relief for fluctuating profits from farming

Because personal reliefs which are unused in one tax year cannot be carried forward or backward to another tax year (see 1850), and because of the progressive nature of income tax liability, a person who earns, say, £40,000 in one tax year and £10,000 in the next pays more income tax than a similarly placed person who earns £25,000 in each of two succeeding tax years. Special relief is accordingly available to individuals and partnerships engaged in a 'farming or market gardening business' (see 940) to take account of fluctuating profits.

Farming, for these purposes, includes the intensive rearing of livestock or fish on a commercial basis for the production of food for human consumption.

The relief

For 2016–17 and subsequent years, individuals carrying on qualifying trades will be able to claim to average trading profits for income tax purposes over two or five consecutive tax years. Previously averaging over only two years was possible.

Two-year averaging

From 2016–17, full two-year averaging relief will be available where the profits of one year are 75% or less of the profits of the other year. Previously, full averaging applied only where profits of one of the tax years were less than 70% of profits for the other year or where profits of one (but not both) of the tax years were nil.

Marginal relief

For tax years prior to 2016–17, where lower profits were between 70% and 75% of higher profits, the profits of each year could be adjusted by an amount calculated as follows:

$$(D \times 3) - (P \times 0.75)$$

where:

D   is the difference between the relevant profits of the two years; and

P   is the relevant profits of the tax year of which those profits are higher.

Marginal relief is removed by *Finance Act* 2016, with effect where the latest year is 2016–17 (and subsequent tax years).

Five-year averaging

For 2016–17 and subsequent years, individuals will be able to claim to average trading profits for income tax purposes over five consecutive tax years where the 'volatility' condition is met.

The volatility condition is that:

(a) one of the following is less than 75% of the other:
  (i)   the average of the relevant profits of the first four tax years to which the claim relates;
  (ii) the relevant profits of the last of the tax years to which the claim relates; or

(b) the relevant profits of one or more (but not all) of the five tax years to which the claim relates are nil.

(ITTOIA 2005, s. 222A, as inserted by *Finance Act* 2016, with effect from the tax year 2016–17 (meaning that a five-year averaging claim with 2016–17 as the final year would involve averaging the profits of the years 2012–13 to 2016–17).)

A year in which a loss is incurred is, for the purposes of the relief, deemed to be a year of nil profit. Loss relief is, nevertheless, still available.

The introduction of self-assessment changed the method of dealing with capital allowances in the computation of profits, and consequently, it also changes the measure of profits to be used in an averaging claim. For trades which commenced on or after 6 April 1994 regardless of the years covered by the claim, and for other trades where the claim is for 1996–97 and 1997–98 or a later pair of years, 'profits' for the purpose of averaging are the net trading profits *after* the deduction or addition of capital allowances and balancing charges.

In either case, the profits to be taken are the profits before any deduction for losses.

A claim for the relief must be made in writing within two years of the end of the second tax year to which the claim relates. Under self-assessment, the claim is to be related to the later year, with any necessary adjustments in respect of the earlier year being given in the later year (see 2336).

The average profits for the second year can provide the basis for averaging the profits for years two and three.

Example

Andrew, a farmer, has profits as follows:

Year 1 £30,000

Year 2 £10,000

Andrew claims the relief.

His profits for each of Year 1 and Year 2 will be deemed to be:

$$\frac{£30,000 + £10,000}{2} = £20,000$$

The profits in Year 3 are £10,000. Andrew again claims relief. His profits for Years 2 and 3 will each be adjusted to:

$$\frac{£20,000 + £10,000}{2} = £15,000$$

A claim for relief cannot be made for a year of commencement or discontinuance. If a person has made a claim for profits averaging in relation to a tax year, they are not able to use the cash basis (see 589) for that tax year.

Legislation: ITTOIA 2005, s. 221–225

Cases: *Donaghy v R & C Commrs* [2012] BTC 1,601

Tax Reporter: ¶272-300

944   Restriction of loss relief for farming

In general, any loss incurred in 'farming or market gardening' (see 940) is unavailable for loss relief by offset against general income (see 2110ff.) if in each of the prior five years a loss was incurred (disregarding capital allowances) in carrying on that trade, i.e. losses can only be relieved against general income for five years. The restriction also applies to capital allowances related to the loss.

Legislation: ITA 2007, s. 67

Tax Reporter: ¶272-850

946 Treatment of livestock, tillages and harvested crops

The treatment and valuation of stock-in-trade is a particular problem for farmers. This applies to livestock, tillages, harvested crops, etc. As a general rule, animals kept for farming are treated as trading stock; however, animals are not so treated where the farmer makes an election for 'the herd basis' (see below). A number of long-standing practices were called into question by HMRC, their views being set out in a business economic note (BEN 19) issued in April 1993. HMRC later commented on their revised practice in ascertaining the cost of harvested crops (from 85% of market value to 75% thereof) and clarified further the areas in which they expected changes to valuation methods: full waygoing valuations, dilapidations reserves, certificates under the 1942 NFU arrangement and production animals taken at cull value.

The herd basis

Where animals are treated as part of the trading stock, payments and receipts for animals bought and sold are dealt with in the accounts in the usual way. Trading stock will have to be revalued at the end of the period of account. However, where an election for the herd basis is made, the initial cost of the herd, and of any animal added to the herd which is not a replacement animal, is not deducted in the accounts as an expense and the value of the herd is not brought into account.

Generally, where an animal is sold, or dies, and is replaced, the proceeds of sale are included as a trading receipt and the cost of the replacement animal is deductible as an expense. It is not always clear whether the acquisition of one animal is necessarily a 'replacement' for another. HMRC have confirmed that inspectors will accept that replacement treatment is applied where an animal is brought into the herd within 12 months of the corresponding disposal. If the interval is longer than 12 months, replacement treatment may be accepted if the facts of the case support it.

Where at least 20% of the herd is sold within a 12-month period, and is not replaced within five years, any profit or loss is treated as a capital profit or loss. However, no chargeable gain will accrue on disposal as animals are wasting assets which are tangible moveable property (see 5330).

An election for the herd basis can only be made in relation to 'production herds': i.e. herds of animals of the same species kept wholly or mainly for the sake of the products which they produce for the farmer to sell, e.g. dairy herds. An election must be made in writing and must specify the class of herds to which it relates. An election is irrevocable and normally must be made within two years of the end of the first chargeable period for which the farmer is chargeable under ITTOIA 2005, or is given relief for trading losses against general income. In commencement cases, the time-limit is extended to two years after the end of the first period of account if that is later.

The herd basis extends to cases where several farmers hold shares in one animal for the purposes of a herd, or in animals forming part of a herd.

Where there is a change in any of the persons carrying on the farming trade, HMRC's view is that the herd basis election made by the old 'farmer' ceases and the new 'farmer' can decide whether to make a fresh election.

Capital allowances cannot be claimed in respect of animals in respect of whom the herd basis is used to compute profits. If a person has made an election under the herd basis rules in relation to a tax year they are not able to use the cash basis (see 589) for that tax year.

Example

Farmer Brown buys a herd of cows for £1,000. He elects for the herd basis to apply. There is therefore no tax relief in respect of the initial cost of £1,000, either as revenue or capital.

The next year, he sells two cows for £150 and buys two more for £130. He is therefore assessable on the difference of £20 as a trading receipt.

In the following year, he retires and sells his whole herd for £1,200. This receipt is not subject to tax.

Legislation: ITTOIA 2005, Pt. 2, Ch. 8

Tax Reporter: ¶271-000

Mining concerns

960 Mining concerns identified for tax purposes

Receipts derived from the exploitation of minerals in land raise difficulties in terms of their taxation. The minerals themselves clearly represent a capital asset to their owner. As they are removed, his asset diminishes. The royalties he receives in respect of such removal, however, have the quality of income. Thus, in such circumstances, the owner of mineral bearing land who allows the minerals to be removed in return for royalties may find himself in the unfortunate position of not only having his capital diminished, but also of paying income tax upon the proceeds derived from that diminution.

Such a system can mitigate against the exploitation of mineral bearing land, especially when the top rate of income tax is higher than the top rate of capital gains tax. In consequence, for mineral royalties received before 6 April 2013, there are provisions designed to render the exploitation of minerals more attractive to the owner of such land from a tax viewpoint. Broadly speaking, the owner of mineral bearing land who receives mineral rents or royalties is charged in respect of those royalties partly to income tax and partly to capital gains tax (ITTOIA 2005, s. 157).

From 6 April 2013, the relief has been repealed by FA 2012, s. 227 and Sch. 39, para. 43. This is because the Government no longer feels the relief is necessary and is part of the drive to simplify the UK tax system. Therefore, from 6 April 2013, all mineral royalties received will be subject to income tax in full.

Legislation: ITTOIA 2005, s. 157

Tax Reporter: ¶265-500

Lloyd's underwriters

970   Lloyd's underwriters: introduction

An applicant may be elected as an underwriting member of Lloyd's from 1 January in a calendar year. Groups of members get together to form syndicates to provide insurance. Each member is known as a Name and each syndicate is run by a managing agent. It became possible to admit corporate members from 1 January 1994.

Each Name underwrites a risk with unlimited liability but is not held responsible for the whole of the syndicate's debts.

A Name may be a working Name, i.e. one who works full-time in the ambit of Lloyd's, or may be purely an investor who delegates responsibility for investment, etc. to an underwriting agent. A Name will often be a member of several syndicates and will have a members' agent to look after his various interests. The Corporation of Lloyd's or the syndicate managers hold the Name's investments as bare trustees.

A Name does not receive any distribution profits from the syndicate during the first three calendar years – each trading account remains open for at least three years. The syndicate draws up accounts to 31 December each year and the accounts are not finalised (remain open) for a further two years, when any outstanding claims are valued and reinsured.

The taxation of Lloyd's underwriters was reformed retrospectively for most purposes (for years after 1991–92) but not for profits or losses in respect of ancillary trust funds arising before 6 April 1993, nor in relation to the deemed disposal and reacquisition of assets in the premiums trust fund for the underwriting year (calendar year) 1993.

Under self-assessment, profits are assessed in the tax year corresponding to that in which the results are declared and distributed. For example, the 2012 account closed on 31 December 2012 and the results are declared in 2015. As the underwriting year 2015, the year in which the results are declared, corresponds to the tax year 2015–16, the profits of the 2012 account are assessed in 2015–16. This basis of assessment is known as the 'distribution year basis'.

Profits from underwriting business are chargeable as trading profits and are earned income Underwriting losses can be set off in the same way as trading losses.

Assets in premiums trust funds are treated as acquired and disposed of each underwriting year, with the exception of certain UK securities where an exemption applies for particular non-resident holders.

Gains or losses on the disposal of assets in funds other than a premiums trust fund or the new special reserve fund continue to be subject to CGT and are not brought within the computation of trading profits.

Distributions relating to assets held in a corporate member's ancillary trust fund, or employed by it in its underwriting business are to be included in its trading profits, without taking into account the associated tax credit.

Relief for payments ('reinsurance to close' premiums) which one syndicate makes to its successor to take over its outstanding liabilities is available to the extent that the payments are fair and reasonable having regard to the liabilities transferred.

Rules give relief for payments and charge receipts in respect of loss insurance and of the new Lloyd's High Level Stop Loss Fund; relief is also provided for payments made to transfer to someone else a member's rights and liabilities in respect of business he has underwritten – a 'quota share contract'.

The final tax year of a member's underwriting business is generally that in which his deposit at Lloyd's is repaid, subject, in cases of death, to the final year not being later than the year in which the underwriter dies.

Amendments were made, from 1 January 2006 for corporation tax and 6 April 2006 for income tax, to the powers for making regulations relating to Lloyd's underwriters. Broadly, FA 1993, Sch. 19 was repealed and future legislation will be made by Statutory Instrument. This allows for greater flexibility when amending and modernising the current procedures by, for example, allowing for electronic filing of syndicate returns and by applying self-assessment principles to the determination of syndicate profits. (Lloyd's managing agents are required to make returns to HMRC of syndicate profits and losses, computed for tax purposes.) If an individual has been a Lloyd's underwriter at any time during the basis period for a tax year, they are not able to use the cash basis (see 589) for that tax year.

Legislation: FA 1993, s. 176

Tax Reporter: ¶275-000

972 Requirements as to special reserve funds

A special reserve fund is made up of funds set aside each year by a Lloyd's Name out of his profits to meet potential future liabilities (see 970).

Tax deductibility is available for up to 50% of a member's profits transferred to an approved reserve each year subject to an overall fund value limit of 50% of the member's overall premium limit. Income and gains on assets within the fund will be free of tax. Withdrawals from the fund will be required, notably, to meet losses and where the member ceases underwriting, and will be treated as trading income.

Where the funds are released after trading has ceased, from 31 December 1999, all sums released from the special reserve fund, including accumulated profits to the date of disposal, are brought into charge.

Legislation: FA 1993, s. 175, Sch. 20; *Lloyd's Underwriters (Equalisation Reserves) (Tax) Regulations* 2009 (SI 2009/2039); *Lloyd's Underwriters (Special Reserve Fund) Regulations* 1999 (SI 1999/3308); *Lloyd's Underwriters (Special Reserve Fund) Regulations* 1995 (SI 1995/353)

Tax Reporter: ¶276-200

974 Payment of tax by Lloyd's underwriters' agents

Since syndicate profits are assessed for the tax year corresponding to the underwriting year in which the profits are declared, modifications of the self-assessment rules are not required. For example, profits for the 2012 underwriting account are declared in 2015, corresponding to the tax year

2015–16. Under self-assessment, tax is payable on the same dates as are for other trades generally, i.e. for 2015–16 (2012 underwriting account), tax on syndicate income falls due on 31 January 2016, 31 July 2016 and 31 January 2017.

Legislation: FA 1993, s. 173, 182 and Sch. 19; *Lloyd's Underwriters (Tax) Regulations* 1995 (SI 1995/351)

Case: *Blackburn (HMIT) v Keeling*

Tax Reporter: ¶276-600

Income of trusts and deceased persons' estates

985 Operation of trusts

The question 'what is a trust?' is a matter of general trust law. Briefly, a 'trust' is an obligation imposed on trustees (who may be individuals or corporate bodies) to hold and deal with property, that has been transferred to them, in particular ways (which will usually be specified in a trust deed) for the benefit of specified persons, or a class of beneficiaries or, if charitable, for particular purposes. The person providing the trust property (the settlor) may be among the beneficiaries; however, in most circumstances, having the settlor as a beneficiary will result in severe taxation disadvantages.

A 'settlement' is, basically, a trust which creates successive interests in trust property. Such interests may be of income or capital, as between those with a life interest or remaindermen. Normally, life interests have a right to income but not capital whereas a remainderman has the absolute right to receive the capital of the trust to use as they think fit. There may not be a life interest or other interest in possession, e.g. a discretionary trust.

From 6 April 2006, 'settled property' is defined as any property held in trust other than property held as nominee, bare trustee for a person absolutely entitled, an infant or disabled person. References in the legislation to a settlement are construed as references to settled property and the meaning of settlement is determined by case law. This measure aligns what is treated as a settlement for the general purposes of income tax and tax on chargeable gains (see also 1071 for further commentary on the definitions of settlor and settlement contained in *Finance Act* 2006).

Trustees are liable to income tax on the income of the trust on an annual basis as the income is receivable (as with other taxable persons) so are generally required to complete a tax return.

Some trusts, where an interest in possession exists and all the trust income is directly paid to the beneficiary, technically known as mandating the income, will not have to return the same income on the trust return because the beneficiary includes the income on his return; however only the trust can return transactions liable to CGT.

Where income is actually received by the trustees and then paid to a beneficiary, the trustees have to provide a certificate, a form R185, to the beneficiary which allows them to complete their own return. Where the trust is interest in possession, the R185 will show income subject only to the basic rates of tax (2016–17, 2015–16 and 2014–15 – 20% for savings or other income or 7.5% for dividends for 2016–17, 10% previously) which matches the tax paid by the trustees.

If the trust is discretionary, the income distributed carries a 45% tax credit (2013–14 to 2016–17) (2012–13 – 50%) whereas the underlying income suffers tax at 38.1% on dividends (2016–17) (2013–14 to 2014–15 – 37.5%) and 45% on everything else (2012–13 – 50% and 42.5% respectively) so there is the possibility of a mismatch between the tax certified on income distributions and the tax paid by the trustees; if that occurs, the trustees will have to pay any shortfall between the tax paid and the tax certified to HMRC.

Different formats of R185 are available on HMRC's website for the different types of trust and estate income.

For the incidence of CGT on trusts and settlements, see 5550ff. For the incidence of inheritance tax on trusts and settlements, see 6880ff.

There were proposals from the European Commission for a public register of trusts open to public scrutiny, that would have included disclosure of the trust assets, disclosure of the trust deed and other documents including the letter of wishes but as at February 2016 that possibility is not currently being pursued although there remain some in Europe who would wish that it were so. Company information is in the public domain, with new legislation to increase company disclosure as to beneficial ownership in respect of persons with significant control (PSC) registers where every company must have in place an appropriate register by 30 June 2016 and update it on an annual basis but where a trust owns a company disclosure will only extend to the name of the trust, not the underlying beneficiaries.

Guidance was published on the Department for Business, Innovation and Skills website on 15 February 2016 and should be required reading for all who are involved in managing trusts. The guidance contains the following:

'If an individual has significant influence or control over the activities of a trust or firm, which would be a PSC of the company if it were an individual, then you should enter that person's details on the PSC register. If a registrable relevant legal entity (RLE) controls the trust or firm then its details must be entered on the PSC register. If a legal entity which is not an RLE controls the trust or firm, then you should continue to explore the ownership chain until you have identified an individual or registrable RLE with majority ownership of that legal entity, or are confident none exists. [...] If someone other than the trustees, such as the settlor or beneficiary of the trust, or partners has the right to exercise significant influence or control over the trust or firm, then they would also be shown on the register [...].'

Reasons for creating a trust

Since time immemorial trusts have often been formed to avoid some unpleasant consequence, and non-tax reasons must not be forgotten; indeed, in many cases, the non-tax purposes will be the primary driver. Often trusts are created because an individual wants to save tax, by giving some assets away, but is uncertain as to the persons who should receive those assets, or knows who they want to benefit but are uncertain if that individual is currently sufficiently mature to look after the assets properly.

In modern marriages, there is often concern with children from a previous marriage that if assets are left to a surviving spouse absolutely that in due course they will not do the right thing and only benefit their own family. This could result in assets being diverted away from the children of the deceased; a trust can achieve the appropriate result. Using a trust allows both flexibility and certainty as to whom or when the assets are transferred absolutely. Trusts and tax planning have a long history; in medieval times, they were used to avoid feudal dues.

These days, there are many reasons for establishing a trust over property, including mitigation of tax. For example, a trust may be set up to save income tax. A settlor, whose income is taxed at the higher rate, could transfer the income-producing capital to trustees. They would hold it for beneficiaries taxed at lower rates or who could then offset their personal allowances or other reliefs against income received from the trust.

Currently, the main tax reason for creating many trusts is to pass property on during the lifetime of the settlor to trustees for beneficiaries to reduce the burden of inheritance tax on death. Trusts preserve maximum flexibility over the ultimate destination of the property. By making a gift into trust (whether during lifetime or by will), the settlor can achieve these objectives as well as securing the inheritance tax advantages that would apply to an outright gift. However, as a result of *Finance Act* 2006 changes, almost all trusts established on or after 22 March 2006 will suffer an IHT charge at commencement, as well as ten yearly periodic charges, if the taxable value of assets transferred into trust exceeds the available balance of the settlor's nil rate band.

The usual IHT rules apply to assets transferred into trust. Agricultural Property Relief (APR) and Business Property Relief (BPR) will reduce the taxable value transferred but the IHT position will only be confirmed once the settlor has survived seven years.

Example

Lee transfers shares in Lee Trading Limited worth £350,000 into trust but because the shares are eligible for BPR the taxable value is nil.

Example

Laura transfers farmland worth £500,000 into trust; again the taxable value is nil because the farmland is eligible for APR.

Where the assets to be transferred into trust are non-business, then before 22 March 2006, the potential settlor had to use a discretionary trust because then that was the only type of trust that allowed CGT holdover relief on non-business assets. Following *Finance Act* 2006 changes, CGT holdover relief is now available on transfers of non-business assets into most types of trust. This is because almost all transfers into trust are now potentially chargeable to IHT on establishment; the fact that the taxable value is nil, as in the Lee and Laura examples above, or the transferred value is less than the settlor's nil rate band does not make any difference (transferable nil rate band does not count for this purpose as it is only available on death). Holdover relief under TCGA 1992, s. 260 is available on transfers into most types of trust on or after 22 March 2006.

This means that a potential settlor of non-business assets can now choose the type of trust that best suits their planning objectives rather than being forced to use a discretionary trust.

Trusts are frequently set up for purposes other than tax mitigation and may be used:

- to hold property for those who cannot manage their affairs, such as minors or mentally incapacitated persons;

- to hold property for persons in succession as when property is left to A for life thereafter to B;

- to protect spendthrifts from themselves (a very Victorian concept);

- to preserve maximum flexibility in the event of unforeseeable circumstances. The discretionary trust is the ideal vehicle to achieve this objective;

- to benefit charity.

In some cases, trusts represent a convenient legal regime for certain activities (e.g. pension funds and unit trusts). In other cases, trusts may be imposed by law. This happens when, for example, a person dies intestate and property passes to minors under the intestacy law.

How to create a trust

A trust may be established by a settlor during lifetime ('inter vivos') or by will, or it may arise automatically if someone dies intestate (i.e. without making a will).

An inter vivos trust may be oral (exceptionally rare but often a recipe for confusion) but it is eminently desirable to set out all the necessary provisions in a formal deed. Indeed, if the trust property comprises land, it is generally the case that the trust must be evidenced in writing. A will must be in writing and satisfy certain other formalities as to execution unless made by a person on active service in the armed forces, or a mariner or seaman at sea.

The creation of trusts by deed or will is generally the province of lawyers and advice must be taken.

In particular, it is essential that the trust document should set out in full everything that is required. Once it is executed, a trust may not be altered unless the trustees have been given powers of variation. This is unlike a contract where the parties are free to agree to subsequent changes. A will can always be changed at any time before death provided the necessary formalities as to execution are observed. Even after death, a deed of variation, formally a deed of family arrangement, may be effective for capital gains tax and inheritance tax but not income tax if the variation is from a parent to the benefit of their minor children where the income remains taxed on the parent even though the capital has been moved on.

The *Trustee Act* 1925 and *Trusts of Land and Appointment of Trustees Act* 1996 apply, unless and except to the extent that the trust instrument provides to the contrary. These Acts contain a number of useful automatic provisions. The trust document does not need to set out these provisions specifically unless variations are to be made. Other Acts and case law provide a general framework but considerable thought must be given to the contents of the document. For example, it is usual to provide very wide powers of investment. Unless this was done, trustees could otherwise invest only in investments authorised by the *Trustee Investments Act* 1961. These investment powers have been extended by the *Trustee Act* 2000 so that, for example, trustees may proceed with an investment without taking advice where they judge this a reasonable course of action.

In setting up a trust, there must be what are commonly called three certainties:

(1) the certainty of words;

(2) the certainty of subject matter; and

(3) the certainty of objects of the trust.

If the trust fails in these certainties, it will not be effective under trust law and, as a result, may not achieve the desired tax savings.

Trust documentation

Since 6 April 1991, HMRC do not ask for a copy of trust documents. Instead, they rely on information shown by trustees, settlors and beneficiaries in their annual tax returns or repayment claims. When a new trust is created, trustees need to complete a form 41G (Trust), which is available to download from HMRC website, which gives basic factual information about the identities of the trustees and settlor and whether the trustees can accumulate income or distribute it at their discretion. That will procure a self-assessment UTR for the trust and ensure HMRC issue annual tax returns. The 41G (Trust) needs to be submitted by 5 October following the end of the tax year in which the trust was established but only if income or gains arose in that tax year.

If neither income nor gains immediately arise, there is no need to advise HMRC of the establishment of the trust until income or gains arise when the obligation would then be to tell HMRC by 5 October following the end of the tax year in which a taxable event occurred. This change does not alter the examination of deeds for inheritance tax purposes by the Capital Taxes Offices.

HMRC will seek further information only where necessary, and only exceptionally will they ask to see trust deeds, wills or other documents. That may happen if, for example, there are queries with a tax return or repayment claim, or if the taxpayer is unsure of the effect of the document and the issue cannot be resolved in some other way. Part of the usual self-assessment process.

Trust provisions

Beneficial interests

Analysis and classification of the particular type of beneficial interest is essential for tax purposes. This is discussed in more detail in the sections dealing with each tax.

When a trust is set up, the tax consequences of the precise beneficial interests created must be borne in mind.

(1) Income or capital: a beneficiary may only have an interest in income. A life interest is usually a right to receive income for life or for a set period although it can extend to use of assets, such as occupation of a property, during the lifetime of the beneficiary. An annuity might be given. This is a right to receive specified periodical payments for a specified period that could be for life. A beneficiary may only have an interest in capital. This would be where, for example, property is left to A for life and thereafter to B. B has an interest in the trust capital but can only take that capital when A dies.

(2) In possession or in remainder or reversion: this is where property is held on trust for A for life and then for B. A has an 'interest in possession' which has been described as a present right of enjoyment. B has an 'interest in remainder' which is deferred until after A's death. This is sometimes called a 'reversionary interest'. B would be known as a 'remainderman' or 'reversioner'.

(3) Vested or contingent: where property is held on trust for A for life, the remainder to such of the children of A as attain the age of 21, A has a vested interest. A does not need to satisfy any conditions to be entitled to it: A's children have contingent interests. Each child's interest will only become vested if and when they reach 21 years of age.

(4) Determinable and defeasible: if property is held on trust for A (a widow) until she remarries, A's interest is determinable because she is only entitled to enjoy it until she remarries. An interest is defeasible if, though vested, it can subsequently be lost. This would be the case if, for example, property is held for the children of A if they attain 18. If no child reaches 18, the trust would fail because there would be no certainty of objects. This is why many trust deeds leave the funds to a charity if all else fails. The charity has a vested interest but one which will be defeated if any child of A attains 18. Its interest will be in possession if in the meanwhile it is entitled to the income ('the intermediate income') but in remainder if the income goes to A's children. Often, the vested interest of a beneficiary is defeasible because the trustees have a power of appointment enabling them to pay income or capital to another beneficiary.

(5) Mere *spes*: a beneficiary under a discretionary trust has a mere *spes* (a Latin word meaning hope). Unless and until the trustees decide to pay something, income or capital, the beneficiary is entitled to nothing. Trustees of such a trust therefore enjoy enormous flexibility. They can usually accumulate income for the period permitted by law and are not bound to know who has a vested interest in capital until the end of the maximum period permitted by law. They are

also usually given wide powers to change the nature of the trust, particularly the beneficial interests, and an absolute discretion over who amongst the class of beneficiaries may receive income and capital and in what shares although the exercise of discretion must be exercised in a reasonable manner.

Trusts and powers

A *trust* is mandatory. If the trustees fail in their duty, the courts will enforce it at the request of any beneficiary. A *power* is discretionary. Trustees may choose whether or not to exercise a power and if they decide not to, the courts will not compel them to do so.

It is often important to determine whether a provision is a *trust* or a *power*. A trust to distribute income with a power to accumulate means that income must be paid out unless all the trustees agree to accumulate it. A trust to accumulate income with power to distribute it means that one trustee can insist income be accumulated. There must be unanimity between the trustees. The distinction between a trust to sell with a power to retain, and a power of sale in relation to trust property, is similar, but the importance of a trust for sale has declined following the *Trusts of Land and Appointment of Trustees Act* 1996.

Trustees, particularly of discretionary trusts, are often given powers of appointment. These are powers to alter the beneficial interests in income and capital by taking these away from one beneficiary, or class, and giving them to another. Such powers may permit the creation of new trusts, sub-trusts, alterations to the size of particular shares, and distributions to other trusts, even foreign trusts.

Accumulations and perpetuity

The rules concerning accumulations and perpetuity had long been the subject of debate and were reformed by the *Perpetuities and Accumulations Act* 2009 which came into effect 6 April 2010. However, the main change is to the law relating to perpetuities; in general, the rules against excessive accumulations for charities remains unchanged at 21 years because accumulation would affect a charity's primary purpose of assisting the community.

The current rules apply to documents executed on or after 6 April 2010 but there is provision for pre-6 April 2010 trusts to opt into the current regime. For trusts operating under the old rules, the law did not permit trust income to be accumulated indefinitely (whether under a trust or power). It laid down six maximum periods, the most common of which was the period of 21 years from the date of the deed for a lifetime settlement or from the date of death for a will trust.

Income tax

In addition, income could be accumulated during the minority of any minor beneficiary.

Once the permitted accumulation period had expired, the income must be distributed.

The property comprised in the trust fund has to become vested in a beneficiary or beneficiaries within the 'perpetuity period', i.e. the maximum period permitted by law. The law's intention is to prevent a settlor from tying up property in trust for generations without any limit. For trusts governed by the pre-6 April 2010 rules, property must vest within the lifetime of a living person plus 21 years, or, if specifically chosen, within a period of up to 80 years, from the date when the settlement commenced. For trusts governed by the post-5 April 2010 rules, the maximum permitted period is 125 years. The settlor must choose the period required. Some trusts, such as charitable trusts and pension funds, are exempt from the perpetuity rule.

If, at the outset, it seems possible that some interests may not vest within the perpetuity period, it is permitted to wait-and-see for a period which is broadly similar to the perpetuity period. If an interest vests within the wait-and-see period, the trusts are valid.

For trusts governed by the *Perpetuities and Accumulations Act* 2009, there is a single period of 125 years during which, if desired income can be accumulated but at the end of that period the assets would have to vest in a beneficiary.

Power of maintenance

Under the *Trustee Act* 1925, trustees have a power to pay or apply income to or for the maintenance, education or benefit of a beneficiary who is an unmarried minor (under the age of 18) but must otherwise accumulate it. It is essential that the gift should 'carry the intermediate income' and that the settlor should not exclude this section of the Act unless similar trusts are set out in the settlement document. Most trusts allow this part of the *Trustee Act* 1925 to be implied, though many vary its terms slightly. They may, for example, enable the trustees to exercise their discretion subjectively, as they may think fit, rather than objectively. Provided the trustees do not act unreasonably, a subjective discretion is less open to challenge than an objective requirement on the basis an objective test will require guidelines which can then either be seen to apply or not.

This section of the *Trustee Act* 1925 (s. 31) should be expressed to apply whether the minor's beneficial interest is vested or contingent. It has two main effects:

(1) During minority, the trustees have discretion to pay the income out for the maintenance, education or benefit of a beneficiary, but otherwise they must accumulate it.

(2) When the minor attains 18, or marries earlier, they must pay income from then on until the beneficiary's interest vests, is defeated or the beneficiary dies. Accumulations of income not paid out during minority will go to the beneficiary if the interest vests on attaining 18 but, if not, they are added to capital. As a result, the accumulations would only pass to the beneficiary if the beneficiary attains a vested interest in capital. Such a vesting of capital would arise, for example, where the beneficiary attains 25 in a trust contingent on attaining 25.

A minor who marries under 18 is treated as ceasing to be a minor at marriage but pre-1970 trusts will have 21 as the relevant age (the then age of majority).

Power of advancement

The *Trustee Act* 1925, s. 32 allows trustees to advance 50% of the prospective share of capital to any beneficiary. Most modern trust documents vary this to 100%. It is a type of special power that is exercisable by a trustee resolution and is read into every trust unless excluded. If a beneficiary's interest is defeated, the advance does not have to be repaid but it is taken into account on final distribution.

Legislation: *Trustee Act* 1925, s. 31, 32; *Finance Act* 2006, s. 88, 89 and Sch. 12 and 13

Case: *Sinclair v Lee* [1993] Ch 497

Tax Reporter: ¶350-000 and ¶354-300

Trustees' income tax position

987   Trustees generally

The provisions of tax legislation frequently refer to 'the person' or 'any person'. 'Person' is defined in the *Interpretation Act* 1978 as including a body of persons. It follows that such provisions are able to cover trustees of a settlement, as well as individuals.

Where a valid trust has been created and trustees receive income from the settled property on trusts, other than bare trusts, the trustees are chargeable to income tax in respect of that income in accordance with the rules applicable to the income. The basis of this is that the trustees either receive or are entitled to this income (and in most cases both receive and are entitled to the income) and hence are, for example, within the charging provisions in respect of:

- trading profits;
- property business profits;
- interest;
- dividend and dividend related income; and
- miscellaneous income.

Trustees are treated as a deemed single person, distinct from the actual persons who are (from time to time) the trustees of the settlement, who are jointly (but not jointly and severally), entitled to the settled property. They are liable to income tax on income arising from the settled property independently of the settlor and the beneficiaries. Where different trust assets are held by different persons, then (unless a sub-fund election is in place) all such persons are treated as one.

A sub-fund election allows part of the trust, which may already be independently administered, to be taxed independently of the trust of which it was previously a part. A sub-fund election should not be made lightly; it triggers a CGT charge on the sub-fund assets (unless holdover under TCGA 1992, s 165 is available) and in addition there is then an additional settlement to be taken into account for the purposes of dividing both the CGT Annual Exempt Amount and the income tax £1,000 standard rate band.

Changes of the individual trustees are ignored. Thus, if a sole trustee carries on a trade within the trust, then his resignation as trustee and the substitution of another individual in his stead does not give rise to a cessation and recommencement of that trade.

Tax may be assessed and charged on and in the name of any one or more of 'the relevant trustees', i.e. the trustees to whom the income arises and any subsequent trustees of the settlement.

Trustees are not 'individuals' and are accordingly not entitled to personal allowances or other reliefs which are only available to individuals; nor are they subject to progressive rates of tax (see, however, 989 in respect of the 'trust' rates of tax on income which is accumulated or paid at the trustees' discretion) or charges that only apply to individuals such as Class 4 NIC on business profits.

In an interest in possession (IIP) settlement, the trustees are liable to tax at the basic rates on any income received (thus, for 2015–16 and earlier years, 10% on dividends but covered by the non-refundable tax credit and 20% on everything else). For 2016–17, interest in possession trustees will pay tax at 7.5% on dividends (the position on income otherwise taxable at 20% is unchanged). Trustees should consider whether they should mandate the income to the beneficiary (who, in any event, is entitled to the income) to avoid having to complete a return. That will then allow the life tenant full use of the £5,000 dividend 0% band with the result that possible repayment claims can be avoided. Many IIP trustees already mandate the income; this change may encourage many more to do so.

The HMRC April 2016 Trusts and Estates Newsletter introduced a concession for trustees for 2016–17 (only) that allows trustees not to have to complete a tax return if the only income received is savings interest where the aggregate gross interest is less than £500 and the tax liability less than £100. Any distribution, would be taxed in the normal way. In reality is this concession of any practical use? Many trusts will receive both dividends and interest so it would seem that trusts in 2016–17 receiving (say) dividends of £100 and savings interest of £300 will have to make a return.

Double taxation agreements

Trustees are regarded as a deemed 'person' and not as individuals. Any provision in a double tax agreement which is applicable to a 'body of persons' is potentially applicable to trustees. It is necessary, therefore, to look at any relevant double taxation agreement to see whether this overrides the domestic law in relation to their tax residence. Where, by application of their domestic laws, the two parties to the agreement would regard the settlement as being resident in both countries for the same year, the agreement will specify which of the two shall be treated as the residence of the trust and relief within the agreement will be available to the trustees against liabilities arising in the other country.

Trustees' management expenses

Because the charge to income tax is on income received by the trustees, the expenses of the trustees in administering the trust are not generally deductible. The measure of the income is in accordance with the normal rules. However, the trust rates charged on discretionary trusts are not charged on that part of the income of such a trust which is used to defray appropriate trust management expenses (see 991). The trust income that is used to pay the expenses is only liable at the usual basic rates of income tax (see 989).

Following the *Peter Clay* case, HMRC updated their guidance on trust management expenses; see HMRC *Trusts, Settlements and Estates Manual* 8000–8790. In particular, apportionment of expenses between income and capital may be permitted provided the trustees have sufficient information to justify the proposition that the part apportioned to income was incurred solely for income purposes. As with any self-assessment issue, no query arises until HMRC seek justification for the claimed deduction. A blanket 50% claim against income every year is unlikely to be appropriate. In addition, apportionment must follow the basis upon which charges are calculated.

So, for example, Stockbroker fees are unlikely to be apportioned because they usually charge a composite fee to cover fund management, both income and capital; the charge will not vary whatever results the Stockbroker achieves so cannot be said to be 'wholly and exclusively' for either income or capital purposes.

Income charged on settlor

Income of a settlement is treated as income of the settlor if he or his spouse retains any interest in the trust property or if the income is paid or can be paid, or applied for the benefit of his minor unmarried child. In addition, capital sums paid to the settlor may be treated as his income to the extent that it falls within the amount of income available up to the end of the year of payment. This circumstance would arise if a parent varied a will to redirect their inheritance to a trust for their minor children.

Under current rules, where a parent settles funds for the benefit of their minor children, unless the amount of income received by the trust is below the de minimis limit of £100 per parent per child (ITTOIA 2005, s. 629–632), all income arising on the settlement, where the settlement was made after 9 March 1999 is assessable on the parent who made the settlement. Accordingly, in general, under current rules establishing an income producing settlement for the benefit of minor children is an unattractive proposition.

The position was different for settlements created before 9 March 1999 where, provided the income is not distributed, it is not assessed on the settlor parent; that position continues today for such settlements. If, however, capital is added to a pre-9 March 1999 settlement, then any income that arises on the added capital is then taxable on the settlor parent in exactly the same way as income arising on a settlement created on or after 9 March 1999; even if that income is not paid out.

If the settlement can invest in non-income producing assets, then the parental settlement rules can be avoided. Equally, the charge on parents can be avoided provided the income, as of right, belongs to the child. Because the child is under 18, it cannot be paid out to them because, until they are 18, they cannot give a valid receipt. However, that means that when the child becomes 18 they have an absolute right to have the income paid out to them. That is likely to raise the traditional concerns that parents and grandparents have about allowing individuals who they still regard as children access to either income or capital at an age where they may not be fully responsible.

Where a tax repayment is available to the settlor, where the income is assessable on him, because his lower rate band and personal allowances are not absorbed by other income, that repayment must be paid to the trustees or the person entitled to the income under the terms of the settlement (see 990).

Further, the income treated as belonging to the settlor is income before deduction of any trust expenses. Therefore, the R185 issued by the trustees to the settlor should show the income assessable at the rate at which tax was deducted at source, without allowance for expenses not the reduced income that would have been assessable at the special trust rates.

Where income arising in a settlement is treated as the settlor's income, he should complete the Trusts page T1, boxes 7–14 after reviewing the guidance in Helpsheet HS 270.

Trustees acting for incapacitated persons

The trustee, guardian, tutor, etc. of any incapacitated person is in a special position. He is assessable and chargeable to income tax to the extent that the incapacitated person would be charged and assessed. This is so where the trustee, etc. has the direction, control or management of the property of the incapacitated person, whether or not that person resides in the UK.

A special tax regime applies (from 6 April 2004) for certain trusts with vulnerable beneficiaries. Such trusts and beneficiaries can elect into the regime and, where a claim for special tax treatment is made for a tax year, no more tax will be payable in respect of the relevant income and gains of the trust for that year than would be paid had the income and gains accrued directly to the beneficiary.

Income and gains arising from the property held on qualifying trusts for the benefit of a vulnerable person is eligible for the alternative tax treatment. The special treatment does not apply in cases where the settlor is regarded as having an interest in the property from which the qualifying trust income arose.

Broadly, the amount of income tax relief under this regime is the difference between two amounts. The first of those amounts is what (were it not for the special rules) the income tax liability of the trustees would be in respect of the qualifying trusts income for the tax year. The second amount is the amount of tax to which the vulnerable person would be liable if the qualifying trusts income were that person's own income.

For details on the special CGT treatment available, see 5595.

Legislation: FA 1989, s. 151(4); ITA 2007, s. 474

Cases: *Williams v Singer* [1921] 1 AC 65; *Reid's Trustees v IR Commrs* (1929) 14 TC 512; *Dawson v IR Commrs* [1989] BTC 200; *Aikin v Macdonald's Trustees* (1894) 3 TC 306; *Trustees of the Peter Clay Discretionary Trust v R & C Commrs* [2009] BTC 50

Other Material: HMRC *Trusts, Settlements and Estates Manual* 8000–8790

Tax Reporter: ¶350-100

989   Rate of tax for discretionary trusts

Special rates of tax (termed the 'trust rate' and the 'dividend trust rate') are levied on settlement income which is either accumulated or is payable at the discretion of the trustees or of some other person and is not within one of a narrow group of exclusions.

The relevant tax rate for dividends for 2016–17 will be 38.1%, in line with the highest rate of tax on dividends on individuals on the dividend as received. The trust rate for 2016–17 remains at 45%. For 2015–16 and 2014–15, the trust rate was 45% and the dividend trust rate was 37.5%. For 2010–11 to 2012–13, the rates were 50% and 42.5% respectively. In 2009–10, the trust rate was 40% and the dividend trust rate was 32.5%.

Income which is excluded from the charge comprises:

- income which, before it is distributed, is the income, as of right, of someone other than the trustees (e.g. the settlor);

- income from property that is held for a superannuation fund relating to an undertaking carried on outside the UK and not held as a member of a property investment LLP; and

- income from a 'relevant housing body', e.g. a local authority, social landlord, charitable housing trust, etc. From that date, the exclusion was extended to cover private landlords as well.

However, there are 11 categories of receipt which are charged at the special trust rates, that within category 1 (see below) is charged at the dividend trust rate whilst the remainder are charged at the trust rate irrespective of the type of trust. The specified categories are:

(1) an amount received or receivable on a company's purchase of own shares (including a redemption or repayment of shares) or on the purchase of rights to acquire such shares;

(2) amounts chargeable under the accrued income scheme;

(3) offshore income gains;

(4) deemed income arising to an employee share ownership trust;

(5) amounts treated as receipts of a property business (lease premiums, etc.);

(6) profits from deeply discounted securities;

(7) chargeable event gains on life assurance policies, other than policies held on charitable trusts;

(8) profits arising from transactions in deposits;

(9) profits on disposals of futures and options involving guaranteed returns, except where the profits are chargeable on the settlor, or where the profits arise to charitable trustees or those of a superannuation fund;

(10) amounts received in respect of sales of foreign dividend coupons; and

(11) deemed income arising under the anti-avoidance provisions for transactions in land.

For the purposes of the special trust rates, personal representatives are not 'trustees'. However, where personal representatives pay (on or before the completion of the administration of the estate) a sum which represents income that has arisen during the period of administration to trustees of a will trust (who are commonly the same individuals as the personal representatives), this sum is treated as income of the trustees; and if this income is to be accumulated or payable at their discretion, it attracts a charge to income tax at the special rate. Where this happens, the sum is treated as having borne tax at the applicable rate for grossing up basic amounts of estate income.

Relief for the first slice of trust rate income

From 2005–06 onwards, the special trust rates do not apply to the first slice of the 'trust rate income', i.e. the income which would have otherwise attracted tax at the special trust rates (it is therefore the income remaining after any allowable trustees' expenses have been deducted). Instead, the normal income tax rates (currently, the 20% basic rate and 7.5% dividend ordinary rate) apply as appropriate.

For 2006–07 onwards, the first slice is the first £1,000 divided between the number of continuing trusts set up by a settlor subject to a maximum of five. In 2005–06, it only applied to the first £500 but this was available to every trust.

This relief is applied to the first or lowest slice of the 'trust rate income', where dividend income is taken as the higher slice of that income after income chargeable at the basic rate. For years 2005–06 to 2007–08 inclusive, there were both the lower rate and the savings rate to contend with and the order of set off was that a source of income suffering a higher rate of tax, interest in preference to dividends, in priority to that bearing a lower rate was allocated to the standard rate band.

For 2006–07 onwards, where the same person is the settlor in respect of more than one current settlement, the standard rate band is divided equally between those settlements. However, the minimum band available to any settlement is £200. Where there is more than one settlor in respect of a settlement, the available band is found by calculating it for each settlor separately and then taking the lowest figure, but again subject to a £200 de minimis.

Where trustees make discretionary distributions to beneficiaries which are then their income for tax purposes, the distributions 2015–16 and 2014–15 are treated as an amount from which tax payable at the 45% trust rate has been deducted (in 2012–13, 50%). Trustees have to have paid sufficient income tax to cover the amount of that deemed deduction, which is available as a tax credit to the beneficiary, and is disclosed as such on the form R185 (Trust Income), otherwise additional tax becomes payable.

Income tax paid by the trustees at the trust rate or dividend trust rate (less the 10% non-repayable dividend tax credit up to 5 April 2016) goes into the 'tax pool'. From 6 April 2016, the full 38.1% tax charged enters the tax pool. This pool can be used to cover the amount of the deemed deduction, with the trustees paying any additional tax to cover a shortfall. Any tax charged at the basic rate (but not at the dividend ordinary rate) as a result of the relief for the first slice of trust rate income can be added to the tax pool and can be used to cover the amount of the deemed deduction. However, it will be seen that effectively the relief from using the standard rate band restricts the amount of tax going into the tax pool and, where all discretionary income is distributed, there will be an additional tax levied on the trustees.

HMRC initially announced that only 30.6% of the 38.1% dividend tax could enter the tax pool (mirroring the position before 6 April 2016 where only 27.5% of the 37.5% tax entered the tax pool) which would have had the consequent result that any 7.5% dividend tax within the standard rate band would also not enter the tax pool. However, it is understood *Finance Act* 2016 was amended to ensure that for 2016–17 onwards, all dividend tax can enter the tax pool.

Note that with effect from 6 April 2016, dividend tax credits are abolished and dividends received by individuals would, if they were basic rate taxpayers, be subject to tax at 7.5% (above a £5,000 dividend nil rate amount) with consequent increases for higher rate and additional rate taxpayers. The draft legislation governing the removal of dividend tax credits and introduction of the dividend nil rate amount is included in *Finance Act* 2016. The relevant tax rate for dividends for 2016–17 will be 38.1%, in line with the highest rate of tax on dividends on individuals on the dividend as received.

Legislation: F(No. 2)A 1997, s. 31–33 and Sch. 4, para. 16, Sch. 6, para. 11; FA 2004, s. 29; FA 2005, s. 14; ITA 2007, s. 479–487; FA 2009, s. 6(4)

Case: *Carver v Duncan (HMIT); Bosanquet v Allen (HMIT)* [1985] BTC 248

Tax Reporter: ¶351-100

990 Treatment of tax refunds received by settlors

In some settlor interested trusts, the trust pays income tax at trust rates but the settlor also has to put that same income on their own tax return and can then claim credit for the tax paid by the trust. Thus, a settlor may obtain a refund if their tax rates are lower than the trust rates.

The *Income Tax (Trading and Other Income) Act* 2005, s. 646 requires settlors to repay to the trust any repayments of tax in respect of any 'allowance or relief' in relation to trust income although this was always the legal position. For 2010–2011 onwards, s. 646 is extended to all repayments or reductions of tax obtained by settlors in relation to such trust income. But when the settlor transfers the refund to the trust, this is not a transfer of value and so no IHT charge will arise. The legislation refers to 'repayments' but this includes a credit that may simply reduce the balancing payment. Settlors will therefore have to undertake a supplementary calculation to calculate their notional liability if the trust income and tax credit were ignored.

Example

Alan, in 2016–17, received a salary of £18,000 on which tax deducted was £2,300, net rental income of £4,000 and deemed income from a settlor interested trust of £2,000 which carries a tax credit (at 45%) of £1,636. Alan was not required to make payments on account in 2016–17.

Alan's actual tax position is as follows.

	Gross £	Tax £
Salary	18,000	2,300
Rental income	4,000	–
Settlor interested income	3,636	1,636
	25,636	3,936
Less: Personal Allowance	(11,000)	
	14,363	

Tax due at 20% = £2,927 so a refund of £1,009.

Alan's tax position ignoring the settlor interested trust income would be as follows.

	Gross £	Tax £
Salary	18,000	2,300
Rental income	4,000	–
	22,000	2,300
Less: Personal Allowance	(10,000)	
	11,000	

Tax due at 20% = £2,200 so refund of £100.

There is a difference of £909 (refund of £1,009 and refund of £100) between the two calculations. This is the amount Alan should pay over to the trustees. This is not directly an income tax issue. The consequence of a settlor receiving a refund of tax is that the trust fund is diluted (because the trust paid too much tax) so a transfer is required to maintain the integrity of the trust fund.

There is no tax penalty for non-compliance but if trustees take no action to recover the tax that should be refunded other beneficiaries might pursue the trustees for failing to deal with matters properly. The purpose of the rule is to ensure that any payment from the settlor to a trust in these circumstances is not an IHT event.

If a settlor cannot work out the amount of 'repayment' that has to be made to the trustees, they can apply to HMRC for a certificate showing the reduction in liability deriving from the tax credit on income treated as belonging to them. To obtain the certificate, the settlor must submit a copy of form R185 (Settlor) or such other notification of income and tax paid by the trustees to the settlor as exists, presumably a letter from the trustees will suffice. HMRC, if the application is made by the trustees, must take care not to divulge details of the settlor's other income without the consent of the settlor and, equally, the certificate cannot be issued until the settlor's tax return for the relevant year has been processed.

Legislation: ITTOIA 2005, s. 646

Tax Reporter: ¶357-350

991 Payments under discretionary trusts

Income received by a discretionary trust is liable to tax at the rate applicable to trusts and, for 2007–08 onwards, is subject to a standard rate band of £1,000 (see 989). This income is assessed for the year in which it arises. If the income is not distributed until a later year, when the rate of tax credit on the distribution has increased, then the trustees may be liable to make an additional payment of tax, effectively representing the difference in rates if they have not paid enough tax to cover the tax certified on the income distribution.

In managing the tax affairs of a discretionary trust, the trustees need to keep a memorandum of all the real tax paid by the trust; that is the total tax liability of the trust less any 10% credit on dividends (up to 5 April 2016). This is known as the tax pool. They then deduct from the total real tax paid any tax that has been certified on income distributions. If at the end of a particular tax year there remains a positive balance, then that balance is simply carried forward to the next tax year and the process repeated. If there is a negative balance, then that negative balance has to be paid over to HMRC with the self-assessment balancing payment.

Examples

The Elroy Discretionary trust was established in 2016–17 and paid total tax of £6,600. The trustees made an income distribution of £5,000, requiring a tax credit of £4,090 so there is a balance to carry forward at 6 April 2017 of £2,510.

The Sadie Discretionary trust was established in 2016–17 and paid total tax of £5,500. The trustees made an income distribution of £7,000, requiring a tax credit of £5,727 so there is a deficit at 6 April 2017 of £227. This has to be paid over to HMRC on 31 January 2018 and there is a balance to carry forward at 6 April 2017 of £0.

Discretionary payments by trustees are treated as income of the payee, received net after the rate applicable to trusts. The tax certified is deducted from the tax pool and only if the certified tax exceeds the tax pool balance is it immediately assessable on the trustees.

Any payment of deficit on tax pool is paid as part of the balancing payment on 31 January following the end of the tax year. As this is income tax, tax certified on an income distribution, it also impacts upon the payments on account for the next year. Thus if the trust's normal liability for 2015–16 were £6,000 and the deficit on tax pool were £4,000, each payment on account for 2016–17 would normally be expected to be £5,000.

Legislation: F(No. 2)A 1997, s. 20, Sch. 4, para. 15; FA 2004, s. 29; FA 2006, Sch. 12 and 13; ITA 2007, s. 499–503

Case: *Stevenson (HMIT) v Wishart* [1987] BTC 283

Tax Reporter: ¶354-800

993   Trustees' remuneration

Some trust instruments specify a fixed remuneration to which trustees are entitled. This remuneration is regarded as an annual payment under ITTOIA 2005 (see 1366ff.).

Cases: *Jones v Wright* (1927) 13 TC 221; *Baxendale (HMIT) v Murphy* [1924] 2 KB 494

Tax Reporter: ¶351-950

Tax position of the beneficiary

1001   General

The gross equivalent of the income received from a settlement is treated as part of the total income of the recipient for the tax year in which it is actually received, if paid at the discretion of the trustees, or if the beneficiary has an interest in possession in the year in which it arises. Credit for tax deducted by the trustees is given to the beneficiary, who may use the tax credit shown on the certificate R185 supplied to him to satisfy his own liability to income tax. The beneficiary is responsible for any tax liability in excess of that shown on the certificate or can claim repayment where his own tax liability on the income from the trust is less than that on the certificate.

Under English law, a beneficiary with an interest in possession in a trust is treated as entitled to the income of the trust as it arises, but this is not the position under Scots law. In order that beneficiaries under Scottish trusts should not be put at a disadvantage compared with their English counterparts, and that they should be able to enjoy the benefit of the lower rates on interest and dividends where appropriate, the rights of a beneficiary under a UK-resident trust subject to Scots law are, from 1993–94, deemed to include the same right to income as under English law.

Bare trustees for minor or incapacitated person

A trustee having the direction, control or management of property held on bare trusts for a minor is assessable and chargeable to income tax in respect of income arising from that property. The quantum of the liability is calculated as if the income arose directly to the minor himself and no regard is taken of the personal circumstances of the individual trustee. It is thus possible for the trustee to claim repayment of income tax by reference to the personal allowance available to the minor.

The trustee of a minor is also subject to any liability to higher rates of tax, calculated with respect to the total income of that minor. Furthermore, in relation to such a charge, a trustee is answerable for all matters required to be done by the Income Tax Acts for assessment and payment of income tax on behalf of the minor. However, the trustee in this situation may retain out of money coming into his hands sufficient to reimburse him for the tax charged and he is entitled to an indemnity in respect of payments made in pursuance of the Taxes Acts. The above provisions also apply to incapacitated persons.

Further, where the beneficial owner is a minor, his parent, guardian (or, in Scotland before 25 September 1991, his tutor) is liable, not only for tax levied in respect of the minor's income but also in respect of any payment arising from neglect or refusal to pay that tax. He is therefore liable to pay any appropriate interest or penalties. A parent, etc. is similarly indemnified as against the minor in respect of all sums so paid. These provisions only apply if the income arises from property which is held on bare trusts.

Nominees or bare trustees for a person sui juris

Where the beneficial owner of the property that gives rise to the income is sui juris (i.e. of full age and legal capacity), the provisions of TMA 1970, s. 72 (see above) have no application. The general rule is that the bare trustee or nominee is ignored and the income taxed on the beneficial owner.

Legislation: TMA 1970, s. 72, 73

Cases: *Hamilton-Russell's Executors v IR Commrs* (1943) 25 TC 200; *Corbett v IR Commrs* [1938] 1 KB 567

Tax Reporter: ¶350-250 and ¶350-300

1003 Income applied for trust beneficiary's benefit

Income arising from pre-9 March 1999 settlements distributed to a minor beneficiary, as well as income arising on post-9 March 1999, trusts is treated as the beneficiary's income in the year of receipt. The beneficiary is treated as having received the grossed up amount (see 991). However, in most cases, the income is then treated as that of the settlor and not of the beneficiary (e.g. where the beneficiary is an infant child of the settlor – see 1075). In 2016–17, the relevant rates are 45%/38.1%. The trust was liable in 2015–16 and 2014–15 to the 45/37.5% tax rates (2012–13 – 50/42.5% tax rates) so if the settlor is liable to higher rate tax, no extra tax will be due (but see 990 of the consequence of a settlor receiving a refund because they are taxed at a lower rate of tax than the trust).

The following payments by trustees have been held to be income of the beneficiary:

- the payment of rates in respect of a house which a beneficiary was entitled to occupy under the terms of a settlement; and

- the payment of outgoings in respect of a mansion (which the beneficiary was entitled 'to occupy, use and enjoy'), the expenses of keeping up the mansion as a residence, and the expenses of maintaining game for sport.

Cases: *Drummond v Collins* [1915] AC 1011; *Sutton v IR Commrs* (1929) 14 TC 662; *IR Commrs v Miller* [1930] AC 222

Tax Reporter: ¶353-200

1005 Payments to trust beneficiaries out of capital

Whether or not a payment is treated as having been made out of trust income or capital is usually of significance only if the beneficiary is entitled absolutely to both income and capital of the trust fund. In such a case, payments to the beneficiary out of income retain their income character whilst payments to the beneficiary out of capital retain their character as capital. In other cases, it is the character of the payments in the hands of the beneficiary which is important. Capital can be taxed as income if it replaces or substitutes for an income obligation.

Example

Henry, the testator, directs trustees to pay his widow £4,000 out of income of the trust fund and, where the income is not sufficient to meet this obligation, the trustees are to raise and pay the balance out of capital. The top-up payments out of capital are annual payments charged under ITTOIA 2005 (see 1366) and are part of the widow's total income.

Cases: *Brodie's Will Trustees v IR Commrs* (1933) 17 TC 432; *Stevenson (HMIT) v Wishart* [1987] BTC 283

Tax Reporter: ¶353-150

1006   Non-discretionary trusts

Non-discretionary trusts

Tax law regards the beneficiary of a trust with an interest in possession, as owning the income from the trust as it arises. This is typically the position of a life tenant who is a beneficiary entitled to income for life.

From 6 April 1993, UK and overseas dividend income was chargeable at the lower rate of 20% and from 6 April 1996, savings income was also chargeable at that rate. From 6 April 1999, dividends are charged at the rate of 10% (until 5 April 2016). From 2016–17 onwards, dividends will be taxed at 7.5% unless mandated to the beneficiary. The trustees will account for tax at basic rate on all other non-dividend investment income. The question then arises whether the beneficiary is liable to higher rates or has available reliefs that give a repayment of tax.

Effectively, the beneficiary of a fixed interest trust can, unlike the trustees, obtain relief for administration expenses, but only at the higher rate. Trust expenses are set first against dividend income, then savings income and then other income when calculating the income available for distribution to the beneficiary in order to preserve repayable tax credits.

To the extent that the beneficiary's income is liable to tax at the higher or additional rates, there will be a further income tax liability on the beneficiary in 2016–17, 2015–16 and 2014–15 of either 20% (40 − 20) or 25% (45 − 20) on non-dividend savings income. In effect, the beneficiary is treated as if receiving the savings income direct (2012–13 of either 20% (40 − 20) or 30% (50 − 20)).

Example

Trustees receive income in 2016–17 of £1,000 rent (net of expenses), dividends of £1000 and interest of £500. They pay expenses relating to income of £200. The beneficiary (B) has a life interest. If the beneficiary's top slice of income is within the basic rate tax band, no relief is given for expenses but there will be no further income tax on the income:

	Income received	Tax credit/ tax deducted	Gross income
	£	£	£
Property income	800	200	1,000
Interest	400	100	500
Dividends	925	75	1,000
	2,125	375	2,500

If B is liable to tax at the higher rates of 40% or 45%, there will be a further liability to income tax over and above that paid by the trustees. Also, relief will be given to expenses but only for the excess liability and first against dividend income.

	Income received	Tax credit/ tax deducted	Gross income
	£	£	£
Dividends	925	75	1,000
Expenses	(200)	(16)	(216)
	725	59	784
Property income	800	200	1,000
Interest	400	100	500
	1,925	359	2,284

For calculating the additional liability if it is all taxed within the 40% band, £1,500 will be taxed at 40% with a tax credit of £300 and £784 will be taxed at 32.5% with a tax credit of £59. In either instance, the dividend income will be the highest slice of taxed income. If both types of income were within the 45% band, then £1,500 would be taxed at 45%, with a tax credit of £300, and £778 at 38.1%, with a tax credit of £59.

With effect from 6 April 2016, dividend tax credits are abolished and dividends received by individuals would, if they were basic rate taxpayers, be subject to tax at 7.5% (above a £5,000 dividend nil rate amount) with a rate of 32.5% for higher rate and 38.1% for additional rate taxpayers. The legislation governing the removal of dividend tax credits and introduction of the dividend nil rate amount is included in *Finance Act* 2016.

Discretionary trusts

Sums paid to beneficiaries under discretionary trusts are paid at the exercise of the trustees' discretion and are taxable on the beneficiary on the basis of receipt of the income, because there is no entitlement until the trustees agree to make the payment.

A beneficiary who receives income in 2016–17 is treated as receiving an amount from which tax has been deducted at 45% (since 2013–14, 2011–12 and 2012–13 at 50%) and is taxable on the gross (with a credit for the tax withheld).

Where the income is paid by a UK-resident trustee, tax at the rate applicable to trusts will have been deducted from the income and accounted for on payments from trusts where there is discretion as to payment or a power to accumulate. In either case, trust income received by a beneficiary and which has borne tax is the income of the beneficiary, grossed up to take account of the tax.

Example

David, a beneficiary of the Ward Discretionary Trust, receives trust income of £1,500 in 2015–16. The income has borne tax at 45% (the rate applicable to trusts). David is treated as having received £2,727 (£1,500 grossed up at 45%). In making his tax return, David is entitled to a tax credit of £1,227 (£2,727 − £1,500). Where the beneficiary's total income brings him into higher rates, then no further tax will be due on the trust income received but if the beneficiary is only liable to 40% a refund will arise.

Trust income received by children of a settlor

Under current rules where a parent settles funds for the benefit of their minor children, then unless the amount of income received by the trust is below the de minimis limit of £100 per parent per child (ITTOIA 2005, s. 629–632), all income arising on the settlement where the settlement was made on or after 9 March 1999 is assessable on the parent who made the settlement. Accordingly, in general, establishing an income producing settlement for the benefit of minor children is an unattractive proposition.

The position is different for settlements created before 9 March 1999 where, provided the income is not distributed, it is not assessed on the settlor parent; that position continues today for such settlements. If, however, capital is added to a pre-9 March 1999 settlement, then any income that arises on the added capital is taxable on the settlor parent in exactly the same way as income arising on a settlement created on or after 9 March 1999 even if that income is not paid out.

If the settlement can invest in non-income producing assets, the parental settlement rules can be avoided. Equally, the charge on parents could be avoided provided the income, as of right, belonged to the child. Because the child is under 18, it cannot be paid out to them because, until they are 18, they cannot give a valid receipt. However, that would mean that when the child becomes 18 that they have an absolute right to have the income paid out to them. That is likely to raise the traditional concerns that parents and grandparents have about allowing individuals who they still regard as children access to either income or capital at an age where they may not be fully responsible.

It should also be noted that for 2006–07 onwards, a standard-rate band of £1,000 (2005–06 – £500) applies to all trusts paying tax at the 'rate applicable to trusts', so that trusts with small amounts of taxed income will have no further liability and potentially no obligation to submit a self-assessment return if the amount of income received annually by the trust does not exceed this threshold. Not submitting a return would require HMRC not to issue a notice requiring a return.

Trust income received by grandchildren of a settlor

The following examples consider a grandfather setting up a trust for grandchildren, so the parental settlor problems are avoided but which illustrate the tax issues that arise. They would equally apply to a case where the beneficiaries are not the minor children of the settlor. These issues continue on the basis that the rates of tax paid by trustees, particularly on dividend income, are lower than the rate of tax that has to be certified on distributions.

Example 1

Andrew settles shares on discretionary trusts for his grandchildren, giving the trustees power to accumulate the income for 21 years. The trustees receive £9,000 of dividends from UK companies in 2016–17. The tax position of the trustees is as follows:

	£
Dividends received	9,000
Tax credit	
Income of trustees	9,000
Less trust taxation (1,000 at 7.5% + 8,000 at 38.1%)	(3,123)
Available for distribution (and distributed)	5,877
Tax due from trustees	3,123

The trustees decide to distribute £5,877 net to Andrew's ten-year-old granddaughter Martha, who has no other income, because that is what is in the bank. This is treated as a payment net of tax at the trust rate of 45%.

	£
Paid to Martha	5,877
Gross up (× $^{100}/_{55}$)	10,681
Tax due from trustees	
Tax certified by trustees	1,685
Less: tax paid by trustees	(3,123)
Tax payable on distribution	1,685

Unless the trustees have an additional £1,685 which they can apply to meet the tax liabilities, they will only be able to pay out part of the net dividends, that is £817. This figure will represent £6,940 of gross income in Martha's hands. The trustees' liability on that distribution becomes £3,123, which is satisfied by the £3,123 tax paid on the receipt of the dividend.

Example 2

Martha will be entitled to a repayable tax credit on the trust distribution. If she has no other income for 2016–17, her tax position will be as follows. The first column assumes that the trustees are able to meet the additional tax pool deficit out of other funds while the second column assumes that they cannot.

	£	£
Martha's tax:		
Gross income	10,685	6,940
Less: personal allowance	(11,000)	(11,000)
Taxable income	Nil	Nil
Income tax		
	Nil	Nil
Less: paid by trustees (45% tax credit)	(4,808)	(3,123)
Repayment due to Martha	4,808	3,123

If Martha had owned the shares outright, as a basic rate taxpayer she would have received £9,000 with a tax liability of £300. She will actually receive either £10,685 (£5,500 distribution plus £4,808 tax repayment), if the trustees have other assets out of which they can pay the tax, or £6,940 (£3,817 plus £3,123) if the distribution has to cover the trustees' tax liabilities. A very wide range of return but there are often non tax reasons why a discretionary trust is the chosen inheritance vehicle; perhaps the additional tax is the proper price to pay for protecting the capital.

Benefits in kind

Beneficiaries of UK trusts are not taxed on benefits in kind (e.g. the notional value of the right to occupy rent-free accommodation owned by the trustees). There is no charge comparable to that which applies to benefits from an employment. Payment of rates and other outgoings would be taxable in the same way as a cash payment. Such a payments merely represent an indirect payment of income to a beneficiary.

Capital payments taxed as income

In principle, payments of capital to beneficiaries are not taxable as income in the recipient's hands though they may give rise to a liability to CGT or inheritance tax within the trust. Where a capital payment is made to the settlor it may be taxed as income.

Where a beneficiary is entitled only to capital, it is unlikely that HMRC will seek to tax capital distributions as income but problems arise where the beneficiary is or may also be entitled to income. Examples include the situation where:

(1) a life tenant is entitled to the income of the trust for life but the trustees may have power to appoint capital to him or her. This is now very common;

(2) a beneficiary under a discretionary trust may be eligible to receive either income or capital, subject to the trustees exercising their discretion in the beneficiary's favour;

(3) a minor beneficiary is usually in the position that the trustees have discretion to pay sums for maintenance during minority but must accumulate the balance.

If capital payments are made to a life tenant under a power to augment income or defray living expenses, they will be liable to income tax (in exactly the same way as an income distribution).

In other cases, this is less likely if the payments are not regular or if the purpose is to meet a 'capital' commitment such as the purchase of a house or car or to set up in business. Regular payments of capital by standing order every month to the same beneficiary is likely to be classified as income. If this might become an issue, careful attention to trustee minutes and varying the amounts and recipients may help to retain the payment's character as capital.

Payments to minors from accumulated income in a trust set up by their parents will be taxed as the income of their parents (see above) but otherwise payments out of accumulated income are capital, unless made for an income purpose. Often, accumulated income will specifically be added to capital but this does not alter the tax treatment in the hands of the recipient.

Payment of school fees causes particular difficulty. HMRC treat each case on its special facts. The most that can be said is that payment of a composition fee, pre-payment of several years fees in advance, may well be treated as capital but payments of fees on a term-by-term basis could well be taxed as income (regular payments having the character of income).

Loans by trustees are not generally liable to income tax. Trustees, of discretionary trusts, must be careful if they make a loan to the settlor or his or her spouse or repay a loan made by either of them. Such a transaction could cause the settlor to be liable to income tax on the amount lent or repaid up to the amount of accumulated trust income or, as to any excess, future trust income, not otherwise distributed to beneficiaries, of the next ten years.

A payment by way of a loan or repayment of a loan by a company in which the trustees own shares is also caught under these rules if within five years before or after it, there is an associated payment by the trustees to the company (e.g. a loan or subscription for shares).

Liability to income tax is not affected by the fact that the trustees charge the payment to capital rather than income. The important point is the nature of the receipt in the recipient's hands. If the payment is to maintain a particular historical income level or has the character of income purposes, then it is treated as income. A single lump sum is likely to be of capital whereas a succession of smaller payments income.

It should not be automatically assumed that income tax treatment is unfavourable. If beneficiaries are liable to rates of tax lower than those borne by the trustees, trustees will be able to make distributions without further income tax liability and the beneficiary may even be eligible to make repayment claims. This may be preferable to making distributions of capital involving possible CGT or inheritance tax liabilities. However, capital payments treated as income, as with all other income payments, require a tax credit which is, in turn, deducted from the tax pool (see 991). If the consequence is that the balance on tax pool becomes a negative, then extra tax has, in turn, to be paid over to HMRC.

Tax Reporter: ¶351-100

1007   Treatment of trust beneficiary's income

A beneficiary's share (as grossed up: see 210) of the income of a trust fund forms part of his total income (see 244) in the tax year in which it arises. The income is from the trust and not from the underlying property;

hence, except in relation to discretionary trusts (see below), the grossing up process is at the *basic rates* by virtue of the deduction at source being under the normal rules for payments out of profits chargeable to income tax, etc. in the hands of the trustees (see 1368 and 1370).

Example

In 2016–17, Dwight is entitled to a personal allowance of £11,000 (see 1851). His only income is taxable trading income of £14,000 and trust income of £3,000 (received under deduction of basic rate income tax). His total income is thus £17,750 (i.e. £14,000 + (£3,000 × $^{100}/_{80}$)) and his tax liability should be £1,350 (i.e. 20% × (£17,750 − £11,000)). As Dwight has already suffered £750 by deduction, he must pay the balance of £600 to HMRC.

Although trustees are not entitled to deduct management expenses in calculating the trust's tax liability (see 987), such expenses are deductible in ascertaining the beneficiary's income.

A discretionary beneficiary who receives, as income, payments from a trust is treated as receiving an amount net of a rate equivalent to the rate applicable to trusts for the year of payment (see 991).

Case: *Macfarlane v IR Commrs* (1929) 14 TC 532

Tax Reporter: ¶353-200

1009　Claims in respect of trust beneficiaries' income

Claims on behalf of incapacitated persons are made by the trustees. In other cases, claims must be made by the beneficiary in receipt of income. Claims for repayment relating to trust income which forms part of the beneficiary's total income as it arises must be made, after 1 April 2010, and subject to some transitional measures within four years of the end of the tax year in which the income arises. Those transitional rules are no longer applicable.

Tax Reporter: ¶353-200

1010　Trusts with vulnerable beneficiary

On 6 April 2004, a special tax regime for certain trusts with vulnerable beneficiaries began. Under the provisions, certain trusts and beneficiaries are able to elect into the regime and, where a claim for special tax treatment is made for a tax year, no more tax will be payable in respect of the relevant income and gains of the trust for that year than would be paid had the income and gains accrued directly to the beneficiary.

Income and gains arising from the property held on qualifying trusts for the benefit of a vulnerable person are eligible for the new tax treatment. The special treatment does not apply in cases where the settlor is regarded as having an interest in the property from which the qualifying trust's income arose.

Broadly, the amount of income tax relief under the new regime is the difference between two amounts. The first of those amounts is what (were it not for these rules) the income tax liability of the trustees would be in respect of the qualifying trusts income for the tax year. The second amount is the amount of tax to which the vulnerable person would be liable if the qualifying trust income were that person's own income.

With regards to CGT, the special capital gains tax treatment applies in relation to chargeable gains arising to the trustees of a settlement if the following conditions are met in relation to the tax year in question:

- chargeable gains ('qualifying trusts gains') arise in the tax year to the trustees on the disposal of settled property held on qualifying trusts for the benefit of a vulnerable person;

- the trustees would be chargeable to CGT in respect of those gains were it not for the application of the new rules in FA 2005, Ch. 4, Pt. 2;

- the trustees are resident or ordinarily resident in the UK during any part of the tax year; and

- the trustees make a claim for special tax treatment for the tax year.

Under the rules, the trustees' liability to CGT for the tax year will be reduced by an amount determined by using a formula set out in the legislation. Broadly, the amount is equal to the difference between two amounts. The first amount is the CGT liability that the trustees would have in respect of the qualifying trusts gains were it not for the new regime contained in FA 2005. The second quantity is the amount of tax to which the vulnerable person would be liable to under the new rules, subject to making certain assumptions, in relation to the qualifying trusts gains.

Once an election is made (within 22 months of the end of the tax year to which it is to apply), it is then applied on a year by year basis. The self-assessment return asks whether a relevant vulnerable beneficiary election has been made and whether the trustees wish it to apply for the particular year.

Legislation: FA 2005, s. 23–45 and Sch. 1

Other Material: *Tax Bulletin*, Issue 78, August 2005 (Changes to the taxation of trusts introduced by *Finance Act* 2005)

Estates of deceased persons

1030   Death, personal representatives and administration period

When a person dies, his property passes to his personal representatives, i.e. either executors appointed by his will or administrators of his estate appointed by the court. Personal representatives are liable for any tax liability of the deceased to the extent that there are sufficient assets of the deceased coming into their hands to meet the debt. Any one or more of several personal representatives is assessable and chargeable in respect of estate income. A personal representative who neglects or refuses to pay may be proceeded against as any other defaulter; but the personal representative may deduct any payments of tax made out of the assets of the deceased.

A personal representative may also be assessed to tax in respect of income (and chargeable gains) accruing to the deceased but not assessed on him. The enquiry process must begin within three years ten months of the end of the tax year in which the deceased died. It is accepted by HMRC that, as a consequence of the *Human Rights Act* 1998, executors and personal representatives cannot be charged penalties where extra tax arises.

A specific legatee is generally entitled to the income from the property in point from the date of the testator's death, while a general legatee may only be entitled to interest in respect of the value of the property and then only from a given date (see 1038). A residuary legatee has no interest in any particular asset of the estate until the residue has been ascertained. So far as not covered by specific legacies therefore, the income of the estate is the income of the personal representatives (though by special provision payments to residuary legatees are to be treated as their income: see 1032 and 1034). If the personal representatives appropriate specific assets to a residuary beneficiary, during the administration period, the appropriated asset is deemed to attract the beneficiary's share of estate income that has arisen up to the date of appropriation up to the value of the appropriated asset.

Example

The executors of Peter appropriate a piano, with a value of £3,000 to Sally, a one-third beneficiary; the net estate income actually received up to the date of appropriation, comprised bank interest of £6,000 net of which Sally's share is £2,000 (because she is a one-third beneficiary). She must receive an R185 showing £2,000 net income when the piano is made over to her.

Any charge on the personal representatives is at the basic rate. The income is computed in the usual way appropriate to the source of income and the appropriate reliefs and deductions are taken into account. When certain payments and deemed payments are added to the aggregate income of estates, they are treated as made after deduction of tax at the appropriate rate. The payments affected include certain chargeable event gains which arise to personal representatives in connection with certain life annuities and policies.

Payments to beneficiaries of estates in administration which are funded out of:

- *non*-qualifying distributions and are received after 1 July 1997; or

- distributions received after 1998–99,

are treated as made under deduction of non-repayable lower rate, etc. tax. Without this change, such payments would be treated as paid under deduction of repayable tax. The change ensures that beneficiaries are taxed in the same way as if they had received the distribution direct.

Personal representatives cannot utilise personal reliefs against estate income nor are administration expenses deductible in computing tax payable. However, personal reliefs to which the deceased was entitled can be used by his personal representatives against income of the deceased.

Example

Trevor, the testator, dies unmarried on 10 July 2016. Trevor's executors are entitled to set off his full personal allowance of £11,000 for 2016–17 (see 1851) against his income tax liability for that year.

When the administration of the estate is complete, the personal representatives hold the property as trustees until such time as the property vests in the beneficiaries or in other trustees, and 987ff. will apply to the income arising from the estate.

All personal representatives are treated as UK resident where any personal representative is so resident provided that the deceased was resident, (until 5 April 2013) ordinarily resident or domiciled in the UK (see 213ff.) at his death.

In the final period from 6 April to death, executors previously had the choice of either submitting a self-assessment return or following the simplified R27 procedure. If the executors wanted to submit a manual return before the current year return is available from HMRC's website they should download the previous year's return and amend to the relevant year. Note in *Taylor (Executor of Taylor, Dec'd)* [2013] TC 02866, an executor completed an R27. HMRC then issued a repayment which the executor disputed. He appealed but this was rejected. The calculation HMRC prepared, following submission of an R27, was not a formal assessment so because it was not an assessment there were no grounds for appeal.

The distinction is important. If within an estate there are matters which are capable of alternative interpretation, then submit a formal tax return would seem the better option in order to preserve the right of appeal. That advice remains good following the withdrawal of form R27. Only assessments made following submission of a return are capable of challenge.

HMRC no longer issue forms R27. Instead, PAYE cases should get refunds automatically and self-assessment cases would be issued with tailored letters only requiring directly relevant information. Anecdotal evidence thus far suggests the transition is less than smooth.

UK and foreign estates

A foreign estate is one which is not a UK estate. A 'UK estate' is defined as an estate, the income of which comprises only income which either:

* has borne UK income tax by deduction; or

* is directly assessable to UK income tax on the personal representatives.

To be a UK estate, the personal representatives must not be entitled to claim exemption from UK income tax (in respect of any part of the income of the estate) by reason of their residence or (until 5 April 2013) ordinary residence outside the UK.

Note however that Finance Bill 2017 will include legislation to make individuals who have been UK resident for 15 out of the previous 20 years deemed to be UK domiciled for all tax purposes. Currently, deemed domicile only applies for IHT purposes with income tax and CGT on worldwide income being avoided provided the relevant individual pays an appropriate annual fee. Finance Bill 2017 amendments will take effect from 6 April 2017.

Legislation: TMA 1970, s. 40, 74; ITTOIA 2005, s. 651, 680

Cases: *R v Income Tax Acts Special Purposes Commrs, ex parte Dr Barnardo's Homes* (1921) 7 TC 646; *Taylor (Executor of Taylor, Dec'd)* [2013] TC 02866

Tax Reporter: ¶362-000

1031 The administration period

This is the period between the date of death of a deceased and the completion of the administration of the estate, which takes place when all the debts and legacies have been paid or provided for and the residue of the estate is ascertained and can be distributed either outright to beneficiaries or to the trustees of any continuing trust.

Excepted estates

To simplify the administration of smaller estates, executors do not need to file accounts where the estate does not exceed a prescribed limit. See the Key Data section regarding present and past prescribed limits.

Executors or administrators of straightforward smaller estates ('excepted estates') do not have to deliver an account to HMRC. For valid excepted estates, personal representatives obtain a grant of representation simply by swearing a revised form of oath for the Probate Registry that the various criteria have been satisfied. However, HMRC have 35 days from the making of the first full grant to the deceased to call for an account and does so in about 2% of cases.

An estate qualifies as excepted only where:

* the deceased died domiciled in the UK;

* the total gross value of the estate before deduction of any debts, together with the value of any gifts as mentioned below, does not exceed the prescribed annual limit, currently £325,000;

* the gross value of the estate is less than £1,000,000 and the net chargeable value is less than the IHT threshold after deducting the spouse/charity exemptions (only). Where any of the value of an estate relates to joint property passing by survivorship, it is the value of the deceased's beneficial interest in that property which counts for the purposes of the prescribed limit (£325,000 from 6 April 2009);

* any estate assets situated outside the UK have a total value of not more than £100,000;

* if there are trust interests, then unless the property passes either to a spouse or civil partner or charity, the trust interests must only consist of a single trust with a value of less than £150,000;

* any taxable lifetime transfers made within seven years of the deceased's death consisted only of cash, quoted shares or quoted securities with a total gross value not exceeding the prescribed limit, currently £150,000. In determining if the £150,000 limit is satisfied where transfers in excess of £3,000 have been made in any particular tax year which would otherwise be exempt as gifts out of income, then for the purposes of deciding if the £150,000 limit has been breached then such gifts are treated, for this purpose only, as taxable;

* no gifts with reservation apply to the estate; and

* no IHT charge arises on alternatively secured pensions under IHTA 1984, s. 151A–C.

Income tax

In relation to a death that occurs after 5 April 2010 in establishing if no tax is due on an estate, to determine if it is exempt or excepted, then a transferrable nil rate band from a former spouse or civil partner can be taken into account but only if a full nil rate band is available from a single person. Achieving the equivalent of a full nil rate band from a series of former spouses or partners would not allow the excepted estate rules to be used.

The excepted estates procedure does not apply where the deceased had:

- within seven years of the death made a chargeable or potentially exempt transfer other than transfers of cash, etc.;

- made a gift with reservation of benefit which either continued until death or ceased within seven years before the death;

- enjoyed an interest in possession in settled property at, or within seven years before, the death except in the circumstances indicated above.

The excepted estates rules do not apply, even if they otherwise would, because the value of the estate and lifetime transfers is less than £1,000,000 and the value is less than the nil-rate band £325,000 if there are no transfers to a spouse, civil partner or charity. This change applies to deaths on or after 1 March 2011 by virtue of the *Inheritance Tax (Delivery of Accounts) (Excepted Estates) (Amendment) Regulations* 2011 (SI 2011/214), reg. 4(3)(f).

Personal representatives are required to include details of the transfers made by the deceased within seven years preceding death. This is, of course, unless the estate is an excepted estate.

The excepted estate rules as currently stated represent a revenue risk to HMRC in that the effective limit is the current nil-rate band although for deaths between 6 April and 6 August in any tax year the nil-rate band taken into account is that for the previous tax year (if there was a change). Previously, the excepted estate limit was below the nil-rate band limit so for estates on the margin the loss of revenue risk for marginal under valuations was limited; now for an estate right on the margin an under value, or omitted transaction, of £1,000 represents a tax loss of £400. It is therefore unsurprising that the March 2011 Regulations indicated above are seeking to allow review of perceived loopholes. This is particularly so in relation to gifts out of income where HMRC are known to have concerns that the relief may be open to abuse.

Income tax and capital gains tax

Personal representatives are either executors or administrators. They administer the estate. They collect income in and are liable to pay the tax on it but generally only have to pay at the basic rate. This income is then attributed to the beneficiaries.

Payments to beneficiaries out of estates funded by dividend income are treated as made after deduction of a non-refundable tax credit of 10% and then taxed on the recipient as if they had received the dividend.

A beneficiary entitled to a specific legacy under the will is taxable on the income arising from it from the date of death unless the executors have to use the income to pay debts. This is because usually the specific legacy beneficiary has an absolute right to both the asset and the income from that asset. Personal representatives should advise the specific legacy beneficiary every tax year on the basis of the arisen income. Residuary beneficiaries are taxed on estate income on the basis of what they receive. There is no adjustment to the actual income of each tax year of the administration period. This is to ensure finality of an individual's tax affairs which is a key element of self-assessment. Under the position that existed before self-assessment, once an estate was finalised, the income of that estate was allocated to each tax year (with assessments) as it arose even if, as was sometimes the case, an estate took 15 years to finalise!

Accordingly now, any income not previously paid out is assessable on the residuary beneficiary in the tax year when the estate is finalised (residue ascertained). Thus, if an estate was finalised in February 2016 but the final payments were not actually made until April 2016, the balance of income would be assessable in 2015–16, the date matters were finalised. Beneficiaries are liable to any higher rate tax that is due as the executors will only have borne tax at basic rate or the 7.5% dividend ordinary rate (10% for dividends until 5 April 2016). A beneficiary may be entitled to a repayment of tax treated as borne by the executors.

Note that with effect from 6 April 2016, dividend tax credits are abolished and dividends received by individuals would, if they were basic rate taxpayers, be subject to tax at 7.5% (above a £5,000 dividend nil rate amount) with consequent increases for higher rate and additional rate taxpayers. The legislation governing the removal of dividend tax credits and introduction of the dividend nil rate amount is included in *Finance Act* 2016. The consequence of this change is that executors in 2016–17 will now have a liability to tax on dividends of 7.5% whereas, up to 5 April 2016, the non-repayable dividend tax credit satisfied any liability the executors would otherwise have had. This change will increase the complexity of the administration period because executors will have to pay tax over to HMRC, on dividends and bank interest both of which are from 6 April 2016 received gross, often of trivial amounts. Unlike interest in possession trustees, executors are unable to mandate the income to a beneficiary and avoid having to account for any tax otherwise due.

The HMRC April 2016 Trusts and Estates Newsletter introduced a concession for executors for 2016–17 (only) that allows executors not to have to complete a tax return if the only income received in the administration period is savings interest where the aggregate gross interest is less than £500 and the tax liability less than £100. Any interest received by the beneficiary, on distribution, would be taxed in the normal way. In reality is this concession of any practical use? Most estates will receive dividends as well as interest so it would seem that estates in 2016–17 receiving (say) dividends of £30 and savings interest of £40 with an aggregate tax liability of £12.25 will have to make a return.

In the early stages of an administration, it may be difficult for the executors to know the level of future costs, although tax on gross income like rents should be readily ascertainable, and therefore how much of the income they can distribute to beneficiaries. Reserves against contingent or unascertained costs may mean that further distributions are made in a later tax year. This may also happen if fresh income sources come to light after initial distributions.

Where a beneficiary has a right to income only, any distributions are taxed in the tax year they are received, but if any 'excess' arising from income reserved against possible costs is then due at the end of the administration period and taxed in the year the administration is completed. It is not possible under self-assessment to reopen the beneficiary's tax affairs for previous years in these circumstances.

Where a beneficiary is absolutely entitled to part or the whole of the residuary estate, the due share of income is calculated and matched against payments made. In this connection, the term 'payment' extends to cover any assets that are transferred in part satisfaction of their entitlement. Where an asset is transferred, that transfer is deemed to include a beneficiary's proportionate share of income up to the value of the asset transferred calculated to the date of transfer of the asset. Any excess of entitlement is carried forward and added to the entitlement for the succeeding year, so it is available for matching against payments (or asset transfers) in that year. Only payments (or asset transfers) that exceed the total income entitlement, up to and including the year in which the payment is made, escape income tax at this stage. This procedure applies for all years, and any final balance is paid at the end of the administration period and taxed as the beneficiary's income in the tax year the administration period ceased, even if the remaining income is paid in a later tax year.

Example

In the estate of A, who died in April 2013, there were two residuary beneficiaries – T and S; net bank interest of £400 was received in 2013–14, £600 in 2014–15 and £700 in 2015–16, a total of £1,700. All the interest was credited on 31 January in each year. The estate was wound up on 31 January 2016.

A bicycle with a value of £1,000 was transferred to beneficiary T on 31 March 2015. Up to that date, the estate had received £1,000 of net income of which T's entitlement is 50% so the transferred bicycle also requires an R185 for £500 net to be prepared for 2014–15.

T will receive a second R185 for £350 for 2015–16. If a card table with a value of £300 was transferred to S on 31 March 2015, they would receive an R185 in 2014–15 for £300 with the surplus income share of £200 being carried forward and added to the 2014–15 income share so S then receives a further R185 for £550 in 2015–16.

Both beneficiaries receive R185s for the same total but the tax years vary because the interim distributions to them also varied.

Personal representatives should consider if they need to pay income out on an annual basis if the payment of income as a single payment might take the beneficiary into higher rates with potential exposure to self-assessment. If the income can be paid out over the administration period and the beneficiary remains a basic rate taxpayer throughout, then an advantage may be obtained. This may be more important where estate income may cause the withdrawal of child benefit from higher rate taxpayers with incomes in excess of £50,000 from January 2013. Although there is a form of tapering relief, allowing some retention of child benefit where the individual's income is below above £50,000 but £60,000, this would still effectively result in double taxation. Higher rates of tax on estate income coupled with child benefit clawback.

There are techniques to allow an individual who accidentally falls into higher rates to reduce their income. These generally require either payment of additional pension contributions, in the year of assessment only, or charitable donations, either in the year of assessment or the next tax year. Where charitable donations are made in the subsequent tax year, they must be paid, and an election made to carry the donation back to the previous tax year before the tax return for that previous year is submitted.

Example

Pete's income is always just below the higher rate margin, his accountant organises it that way, but in March 2016, he received an unexpected legacy including estate income, which took him into higher rate tax. In May 2016, he makes a charitable donation that brings his income back below the higher rates threshold; in July 2016, he writes to HMRC to make the claim to carry back and in October 2016, his tax return is submitted. He satisfies the carry back requirements.

Where a deed of variation is put into effect, provided the original beneficiary who had an absolute interest had received no payment from the estate, all the income received belongs to the new beneficiary because they actually receive the income.

For gains arising on disposals occurring on or before 22 June 2010, personal representatives were liable to CGT at the rate of 18%. Where disposals occur on or after 23 June 2010, the rate is 28% until 6 April 2016 when a lower rate of 20% is introduced for gains other than 'upper rate gains' (residential property/carried interest) for which the rate remains at 28% (*Finance Act* 2016). Personal representatives can claim the same annual exempt amount for the year of death and the next two tax years only.

On death, a deceased's assets are deemed to be disposed of and re-acquired at market value but without chargeable gain or allowable loss. In effect, the base cost for the personal representatives is the market value at death, on which IHT was paid. If these assets are distributed in kind, a beneficiary inherits the assets at market value at death. This is then the beneficiary's base cost. This differs from the position of interest in possession trusts where there is a capital gain on a beneficiary obtaining the asset.

Sometimes, the income distribution to a beneficiary includes income that was accrued at the date of death where IHT was then paid on the accrued value. If the beneficiary is a higher rate taxpayer, then relief is available under ITTOIA 2005, s. 669 on the part of their share of the income that was subject to IHT. In order to calculate the relief, establish the proportion of the beneficiary's distribution that was subject to IHT, multiply that figure by the IHT estate rate and then gross up at the rate appropriate to the income. The resulting figure is then deducted from the gross income shown on the R185 and the net figure is taxed.

> **Example**
>
> Angela received an R185 from her brother's estate showing bank interest of £1,000 gross (£800 + tax credit of £200). Of this, £200 (net) was accrued at death and IHT paid. The estate IHT rate was 20%. Thus, the amount eligible for relief is £200 × 20% = £40 × 100/80 = £50. So the taxable amount is £950.

There is no box on the self-assessment return to allow this relief to be claimed, partly because it is rarely claimed (usually the amounts involved are ludicrously small), so an affected taxpayer needs to show the net figure (£950 in the above example) in the relevant return box and refer to what they have done in any available white space. Thus, the result of the calculations in Angela's case, as a 40% taxpayer, is that she saves £10. Some might speculate what the cost to the estate was to provide information to allow that reduction.

1032   Income of person with limited interest in residue

Special provisions apply to persons with limited interests in the residue of the whole or part of an estate during the administration period (or part of it) (see 1030).

A person is deemed to have a limited interest if he does not have an absolute interest and the income of the residue (or part of it) would be properly payable to him, or directly or indirectly paid for his benefit, if the residue had been ascertained at the commencement of the administration period. A life interest is a limited interest.

Any underpayment of income in the administration period in respect of a limited interest is deemed to have been paid as income in the tax year in which the sum was paid, or the year in which the administration period ceased if earlier. Where the sum is paid in respect of a limited interest which has ceased during the administration, the sum paid after the interest has ceased is similarly deemed to have been paid in the last tax year in which the interest subsisted. So even if the income is paid in a later tax year, the executors would still have to prepare an R185 for the year in which the income should have been paid. Personal representatives may be treated as residuary beneficiaries in such a way that the deemed income forms part of the estate of a second deceased person. The legislation also caters for discretionary payments.

In the case of a 'UK estate' (see 1030), the personal representatives will have paid tax at basic or dividend rates and any sum paid to a beneficiary is treated as a net amount after the application of the appropriate rate. Payments are made first out of payments bearing basic tax and there are provisions for effecting a reasonable apportionment of amounts between persons with different interests (see 1030).

Example

In the estate of B, who died May 2015, there were two equal residuary beneficiaries – Q and R and in 2015–16 dividends of £1,000 and net bank interest of £500 was received. If a payment of £600 was made to Q on 5 April 2016, it would comprise £250 net bank interest and £350 of dividends. The £150 of unpaid dividends (on the basis a 50% share equals £500) is carried forward to 2016–17 to be included in future distributions.

In the case of a 'foreign estate' (see 1030), the sum paid is treated as gross income chargeable under ITTOIA 2005, Pt. 5, Ch. 6 with a possible proportionate reduction on proof of tax deduction in respect of the aggregate income of the estate.

In respect of discretionary payments out of income, beneficiaries are treated as receiving income on which tax has been paid at the basic rate or, in the case of payments routed through trustees, at the rate applicable to trusts.

A residuary beneficiary who is neither resident nor ordinarily resident in the UK may claim to have his income from an estate in the course of administration treated as if it had arisen directly to him, so that he will not be liable to tax on, for example, foreign source income of the estate. The claim is conditional upon the personal representatives complying with their obligations to submit returns.

On the completion of the administration of an estate, where an amount remains payable in respect of a limited interest, the amount is deemed to have been paid as income for the tax year in which the administration period ends; if the sum is deemed to be paid in respect of an interest which ceased before the end of the administration period, then it is deemed to have been paid in respect of the last tax year in which that interest subsisted.

Because of the finality that is a key element of the self-assessment regime, it is unusual for adjustments to be made to assessments already made on the beneficiary during the administration period. Any required adjustments may be made within three years of 31 January following the end of the tax year in which administration of that estate was completed. Where a beneficiary is entitled to a specific asset, which produces income, if the executors held that income back, for example, in order to determine if the estate were solvent, then when the income is ultimately paid, the beneficiary can require the assessments for earlier years to be reopened to allow the income to be assessed in the years it arose. This is in accordance with *IR Commrs v Hawley* (1927) 13 TC 327. Adjusting earlier years in this way may expose the beneficiary to the usual self-assessment interest and late payment surcharges. This occurrence is understood to be extremely rare and HMRC will consider favourably any claim to reduce the otherwise automatic surcharges on the basis the beneficiary did not know, when they completed their tax return, the quantum of income that would be received.

Legislation: ITTOIA 2005, Pt. 5, Ch. 6

Case: *IR Commrs v Hawley* (1927) 13 TC 327

Other Material: ESC A14, *Deceased person's estate: residuary income received during the administration period*

Tax Reporter: ¶364-600

1034　Income of person with absolute interest in residue

A person is deemed to have an absolute interest if and so long as the capital of the residue (or of the relevant part) would, if the residue had been ascertained, be properly payable to him or, directly or indirectly, payable for his benefit.

A person entitled to an absolute interest may receive payments during the administration period of either income or capital and these have to be distinguished for estate accounting purposes but if income has arisen in the administration period, before a capital payment is made, the capital payment is deemed to include the beneficiary's share of income up to the date of payment. See 'In the estate of A' example in 1031. This is done by first calculating the residuary income during such part of the administration period in which the beneficiary had an absolute interest.

The 'residuary income' is ascertained by deducting from the income of the estate for that year:

- annual interest, annuities or other annual payments for that year which are a charge on residue (see below), except for any interest, etc. which is allowable in computing the income of the estate;
- management expenses (unless allowable in computing the aggregate income of the estate) which, in the absence of any express provision in a will, are properly chargeable to income;
- the income of the estate to which any person is specifically entitled as a devisee or legatee.

There is available to the beneficiary a reduction in residuary income by way of relief for higher rate tax purposes where accrued income has also been included in the value of the estate for inheritance tax purposes;

the reduction is the grossed-up value (see 1031) of inheritance tax attributable to the accrued income net of accrued liabilities. This relief cannot be adjusted, on the R185, by the personal representatives but has to be claimed by the beneficiary. In the great majority of cases, the relief is disappointingly modest and inevitably will cost the executors more to calculate that the achieved tax reduction

The importance of calculating the residuary income to disclose it on form R185 lies in the fact that any sum paid during the administration period in respect of the absolute interest is deemed to have been paid as income to the extent that it does not exceed the residuary income for that year (less basic rate tax for that year in the case of a UK estate). Personal representatives may be treated as residuary beneficiaries in such a way that the deemed income then forms part of the estate of a second deceased person. The legislation caters for successive absolute interests and discretionary payments.

Where any deductions exceed the amount of residuary income, the excess may be carried forward and treated as an amount to be deducted from the aggregate income of the estate for the following year.

Example

In the estate of C, who died June 2015, in 2015–16, there was bank interest of £400 net and dividends of £600 received.

- If the management expenses were £300, the residuary income would be £400 bank interest and £300 dividends.

- If the management expenses were £700, the residuary income would be £300 bank interest and £nil dividends.

- If the management expenses were £1,200, the residuary income would be £nil bank interest and £nil dividends but £200 of management expenses are then carried forward to set against 2016–17 income on the same basis, i.e. first against dividends.

The effect of the allocation basis is to try to preserve repayable basic rate tax at the expense of non repayable dividend tax credit (until 5 April 2016).

In the case of a 'UK estate' (see 1030), the sum deemed to have been paid as income includes the amount by which the aggregated income entitlement of the person for the tax year exceeds the aggregate of all the sums which have been paid (as income) to that person in respect of that absolute interest. It is, therefore, grossed up (see 210) at the basic, lower or dividend rate (see 1030) in force for the year of payment; payments are made first out of payments bearing tax at basic rate and there are provisions for effecting a reasonable apportioning of amounts between persons with different interests. Where the dividend rate applies, the income is then taxable in the hands of the beneficiary (or intermediate trustees) at that rate as the top slice of income. In the case of a 'foreign estate' (see 1030), the amount paid is treated as gross income with a possible proportionate reduction on proof of tax deduction in respect of the aggregate income of the estate.

Example

In the estate of D in 2015–16, there is income potentially distributable to beneficiary P, calculated as above, of £500 net bank interest and £900 dividends. If a payment of £1,000 were made, it would comprise £500 net bank interest and £500 dividends with the balance of £400 dividends being carried forward to the next tax year.

The 2016–17 change that results in a tax charge on dividends from an estate is causing some difficulty. In 2015–16 (and earlier years), executors would pass the non-repayable 10% dividend tax credit to beneficiaries. Income distributions must carry the tax credit of the year of distribution so the possibility is that an estate distribution in 2016–17 of dividend income received in 2015–16 could carry a repayable tax credit where no tax was actually paid. It is understood HMRC are reviewing the R185 (Estate) for distributions in 2016–17 and later years to require executors to divide dividend income distributions into those relating to 2015–16 and earlier (which will carry a 7.5% non-repayable tax credit) and dividend distributions for 2016–17 (onwards) which will carry a 7.5% repayable tax credit. Guidance will be issued in due course.

Example

The estate of John received distributable dividends of £100 in the year to 5 April 2016 and £200 in the year to 5 April 2017 (where the executors will pay 7.5% tax). If there is only a single-residuary beneficiary the R185 would show dividends as follows:

From 2015–16 income of £100 with non-repayable tax credit £9

From 2016–17 income of £185 with repayable tax credit £15

A residuary beneficiary who is neither resident nor ordinarily resident (ordinarily resident applying only up to 5 April 2013) in the UK may claim to have his income from an estate in the course of administration treated as if it had arisen directly to him, so that he will not be liable to tax on, for example, foreign source income of the estate. The claim is conditional upon the personal representatives complying with their obligations to submit returns.

Because of the finality that is a key element of the self-assessment regime, it is unusual for adjustments to be made to assessments already made during the administration period. The circumstances discussed above which allow reallocation to the tax years the income was received are unusual. Any required adjustments may be made within three years of 31 January following the end of the tax year in which administration of that estate was completed.

Charges on residue

'Charges' on residue means the following liabilities (to the extent that the liabilities fall ultimately on residue) properly payable out of the estate and interest payable in respect of those liabilities:

- funeral, testamentary and administration expenses and debts;

- general legacies, demonstrative legacies, annuities and any sum payable out of residue under an intestacy;

- any other liabilities of the personal representatives;

- (relating to Scotland only) any sums required to meet claims in respect of legal rights by the surviving spouse or children.

Thus, for example, interest payable in respect of a general legacy is a charge on residue and is not taken into account in calculating residuary income, it does not reduce residuary income. In Scotland, sums required to meet certain claims by a surviving spouse or child are also charges on residue.

Legislation: ITTOIA 2005, Pt. 5, Ch. 6

Other Material: ESC A14, *Deceased person's estate: residuary income received during the administration period*; former ESC A13, *Administration of estates: beneficences of income received during the administration period*

Tax Reporter: ¶364-800

1038 Income of legatees and annuitants

In the case of a specific legacy, the legatee is entitled to the income (subject to a contrary provision in the will which would be unusual) from the relevant property from the date of the testator's death. The income from the property, therefore, forms part of the legatee's total income as it arises, notwithstanding the general charge on the personal representatives (see 1030).

In the case of a general legacy, the legatee is entitled to interest calculated in accordance with Practice Direction 40A, para. 15 which states interest shall be allowed on legacies at the basic rate payable for the time being on funds in court or at such other rate as the court shall direct, beginning one year after the testator's death. The current basic rate is 0.3%. If the legacy is an immediate one, the interest is generally payable (subject to any contrary provision in the will which might also specify the relevant interest rate) only after the end of the executor's year. Such interest is charged to tax under ITTOIA 2005 (former Sch. D, Case III) (see 1366) as part of the legatee's total income. However, a legatee may refuse to accept payment of the interest and in such instances the interest is only treated as his income if there is identifiable income which he can claim, e.g. from a fund set aside to meet the legacy.

In general, an annuitant is not entitled to the capital value of his annuity though he is entitled to have a fund set aside to secure the annuity. The first instalment of the annuity is payable only at the end of the executor's year but (subject to a contrary intention) the annuity runs from the testator's death and forms part of the annuitant's total income from that date. In modern wills, the use of annuities is rare and has a more Victorian flavour of support for family retainers.

In some cases, and in particular where the estate is insufficient to provide an annuity fund and also to pay the pecuniary legacies in full, the annuitant is entitled to the actuarial value of his annuity (duly abated, if necessary). This is regarded as a capital payment and is not included in the annuitant's total income. Thus, payments made in respect of an annuity are regarded as capital payments where the payments are made before it is discovered that the income of the estate is insufficient to pay the annuity in full.

References in a will or codicil to payments by reference to the former 'surtax' and 'standard rate' (now long gone) are treated as if they were references to higher rate(s) and basic rate.

Cases: *IR Commrs v Hawley* [1928] 1 KB 578; *Dewar v IR Commrs* [1935] 2 KB 351; *IR Commrs v Lady Castlemaine* (1943) 25 TC 408; *Spens v IR Commrs* [1970] 1 WLR 1173

Tax Reporter: ¶365-250

Settlements: anti-avoidance

Settlements and the transfer of income

1070 Avoidance of tax on income using settlements

There are specific anti-avoidance provisions designed to prevent higher-rate taxpayers reducing their liability to tax by giving away the right to receive income. 'Settlements' (see 1071) have often been used by taxpayers to alienate, or transfer to another, a portion of their income. Basically, the theoretical possibilities have been as set out below.

- S transfers to B a portion of his income each year (an 'income settlement'). If the obligation to B is a legally binding one, then, ignoring the special provisions relating to such 'settlements', the payments to B would be a 'charge' on the income of S. He would retain basic rate tax and would escape liability to tax at the higher rate. B may be entitled to reclaim the whole or part of the basic rate tax deducted depending on his personal tax liability.

- S transfers capital to trustees to hold for the benefit of B (a 'capital settlement'). Ignoring the special provisions, this would effectively divest S of any tax liability on the income derived from that capital.

The provisions prevent certain 'settlements' being effective at all for the purpose of taxes on income whilst other provisions only prevent certain settlements being effective for the purpose of the 'settlor' avoiding higher rate tax. In the latter case, the beneficiary retains the right to make a claim for repayment of basic rate tax in appropriate circumstances. These provisions affect only the tax treatment of the settlement income and not any rights or obligations under the general law.

The use of the settlement provisions to counteract income shifting is still a live issue and was further considered in *Donovan* [2014] TC 03188 in a case with complicated facts with multiple dividend waivers in both directions (but with the fatal flaw that unless the husbands waived their entitlement to dividends, there were insufficient reserves to allow the dividends that were actually paid to be paid) ultimately resulting in monies being transferred to wives. The consequence was that the transferred dividends were then assessed on the husbands to the extent they did not represent the normal proportionate share that the wives would have expected from their shareholding without waiver.

Cases: *Bird v R & C Commrs* (2008) Sp C 720; *Donovan* [2014] TC 03188

Tax Reporter: ¶350-000

1071 Meaning of 'settlement' and 'settlor' for income tax

In general terms, a 'settlement' is the creation of a trust with successive interests; but, for the purposes of the income tax anti-avoidance provisions (see 1070), 'settlement' is much more widely defined to include any disposition, trust, covenant, agreement or arrangement.

From 6 April 2006, 'settled property' is redefined as any property held in trust other than property held as nominee, bare trustee for a person absolutely entitled, an infant or disabled person. References in the legislation to a settlement are construed as references to settled property and the meaning of settlement is determined by case law. This measure effectively aligns what is treated as a settlement for the general purposes of income tax and tax on chargeable gains. The effect is that income tax will be charged on income arising to the trustees of a 'settlement' with the definition of settlement being derived from existing trust law and case law, and 'settled property' being defined in the tax legislation. The existing definition of settlement in ITTOIA 2005, s. 620 still applies for the purposes of the settlements anti-avoidance legislation.

'Settlor'

A 'settlor' is any person who makes a settlement. He is deemed to have made a settlement if he makes or enters into the settlement directly or indirectly and, in particular, if:

* he has directly or indirectly provided or undertaken to provide funds for the purpose of the settlement; or

* he has made a reciprocal arrangement with any other person for that other person to make or enter into the settlement.

Finance Act 2006 inserted ICTA 1988, s. 685B for income tax purposes to define a settlor. This is based on the wider definition in the settlements anti-avoidance legislation. The measure is effective from 6 April 2006 and affects settlements whenever created. A person is a settlor in relation to a settlement if it was made (or treated as made) by that person directly or indirectly or if it arose on his or her death. A settlor of property means that which is settled or derived from settled property and a person is treated as having made a settlement if he or she has provided (or undertaken to do so) property directly or indirectly for the settlement. If A enters into a settlement where there are reciprocal arrangements with B, B is treated as the settlor for these purposes.

Finance Act 2006 also inserted ICTA 1988, s. 685C which takes effect from 6 April 2006 in relation to settlements whenever created. The new section identifies the settlor where there is a transfer of property between settlements made for no consideration or less than full consideration. Where property is disposed of from settlement 1 and acquired by settlement 2 (even if in a different form), the settlor(s) of settlement 1 will be treated as the settlor(s) of settlement 2 unless the transfer occurs because of a will variation.

Finance Act 2006 also contains a measure to identify the settlor in relation to will and intestacy variations occurring on or after 6 April 2006 regardless of the deceased's date of death. The measure applies where there is a variation in accordance with TCGA 1992, s. 62(6) and property which was not settled property under the will becomes settled. In this case, a person mentioned in the group below is treated as having made the settlement and providing the property for it:

- a person who immediately before the variation was entitled to the property, or to property from which it derives, absolutely as legatee (as defined);

- a person who would have become entitled to the property, or to property from which it derives, absolutely as legatee but for the variation;

- a person who immediately before the variation would have been entitled to the property, or to property from which it derives, absolutely as legatee but for being an infant or other person under a disability; and

- a person who would, but for the variation, have become entitled to the property, or to property from which it derives, absolutely as legatee if he had not been an infant or other person under a disability.

If property would have been comprised in a settlement as a result of the deceased's will but the effect of the variation is that it becomes comprised in another settlement, the deceased will be treated as the settlor. He or she will also be the settlor if an existing settlement of which the deceased was settlor becomes comprised in another settlement. In both cases, the deceased is treated as having made the settlement immediately before his or her death unless the settlement arose on the person's death.

Legislation: *Finance Act* 2006, s. 88, 89 and Sch. 12 and 13; ITTOIA 2005, s. 620(1)–(3)

Cases: *Yates (HMIT) v Starkey* [1951] Ch 465; *Crossland (HMIT) v Hawkins* [1961] Ch 537; *IR Commrs v Mills* [1975] AC 38; *IR Commrs v Plummer* [1980] AC 896; *IR Commrs v Levy* [1982] BTC 235; *Harvey (HMIT) v Sivyer* [1985] BTC 410; *Butler (HMIT) v Wildin* [1988] BTC 475

Tax Reporter: ¶350-000

1073 Payments to charity

Charitable covenants are exempt from the provisions treating income of settlements in which the settlor retains an interest as the settlor's income. However, charitable covenants are only effective for tax purposes if the covenant was made before 6 April 2000 but covenants so made before that date continue to be effective.

Payments to charity remain a relatively efficient form of giving since the payer is often eligible for higher rate relief (see 1840).

A 'covenanted payment to charity' is defined as a payment made under a covenant which:

- is not made in consideration of money or money's worth (but rights of admission to view wildlife or property held by a charity do not count as consideration: see 901);

- is in favour of a body of persons or a trust established for charitable purposes;

- requires the annual payments to be made for a period which may exceed three years; and

- is not capable of earlier termination without the consent of the persons for the time being entitled to the payments.

Companies, as well as individuals, can take advantage of these provisions (covenanted donations to charity being charges on income).

Charities receiving covenanted payments may generally reclaim the tax deducted from HMRC (see 901), but now any payment under a covenant must be accompanied by a gift aid declaration so current practice would suggest that the use of covenants is now largely obsolete.

For one-off charitable payments under the gift aid scheme, see 902.

Legislation: ITTOIA 2005, s. 627(2), 727(1), Sch. 2, para. 132(1)–(2);

Case: *Racal Group Services Ltd v Ashmore* [1995] BTC 406

Tax Reporter: ¶350-000

Settlements on children

1075　Payments to minor unmarried children of settlor

If a settlement is not caught by the provisions outlined at 1078, but income from it is paid during the settlor's lifetime to or for the benefit of a minor unmarried child of the settlor, that income is treated for all tax purposes as the settlor's income for the tax year in which it is so paid. A 'minor' is defined as a person under 18 years of age, and a 'child' as including a stepchild and an illegitimate child, while references in this provision to payments include payments in money or money's worth.

Where there is accumulated income in the settlement, any kind of payment to a minor unmarried child of the settlor is treated as a payment of income to the extent that it matches available retained or accumulated income. 'Available retained or accumulated income' is the total income that has arisen under the settlement since it began, excluding:

- income treated as income of the settlor or a beneficiary;

- income paid to or for the benefit of a beneficiary other than a minor unmarried child of the settlor, whether as income or as capital; and

- income applied in defraying expenses of the trustees which were properly chargeable to income, notwithstanding any express provision of the trust.

Where an offshore income gain accrues to a bare trustee or nominee for a minor beneficiary, the gain is treated, for the purposes of the charge on offshore income gains, as income paid to the beneficiary. Accordingly, if the beneficiary is a minor unmarried child of the settlor, the gain is converted into income chargeable on the settlor.

Income of no more than £100 paid to a minor unmarried child of the settlor in any tax year is not treated as that of the settlor.

1999 changes

Where a trust is set up after 8 March 1999 by parents on behalf of minor unmarried children which, for tax purposes, is treated as a bare trust because the children are entitled to the income and capital of the trust, any income arising from the trust, whether paid for the child's benefit or accumulated, is taxed as the parents' income; likewise, the income from new funds added to existing trusts after that date. However, the charge does not apply where the total income from all settlements by the same parent for the same child does not exceed £100 in any tax year.

Legislation: ITTOIA 2005, s. 629–632

Tax Reporter: ¶355-600

1077   Maintenance payments to children

An arrangement whereby a divorced or separated parent undertakes to maintain his minor child is still treated as a 'settlement' and no tax relief is available.

Legislation: ITTOIA 2005, s. 727–730, Sch. 2, para. 146

Cases: *Sherdley v Sherdley* [1987] BTC 273; *Harvey (HMIT) v Sivyer* [1985] BTC 410; *Morley-Clarke v Jones (HMIT)* [1985] BTC 460

Other Material: *Practice Direction* [1983] 1 WLR 800

Tax Reporter: ¶350-000

Benefit retained by settlor

1078   Settlor retaining an interest

The rules on revocable settlements and settlements where the settlor retains an interest were recast for years after 1994–95. The rules are not restricted to undistributed income and they apply to all settlements whenever made.

The basic rule is that during the settlor's lifetime, settlement income is to be treated as income of the settlor for all tax purposes unless it arises from property in which the settlor has no interest. The question whether the settlor has an interest in any property is addressed by the provisions which follow.

A settlor has an interest in settled property if there is any possibility of the property or any 'derived property' being paid to the settlor, or the settlor's spouse, or applied for their benefit in any circumstances whatever. The term 'derived property', in relation to the settled property, is given a specific, if wide, definition. It can mean any of the following:

- income from the settled property;

- other property 'directly or indirectly representing the proceeds of' the settled property;

- other property 'directly or indirectly representing the proceeds of' the income of the settled property;

- income from such proceeds.

Where the settled property or derived property cannot be paid to the settlor or his spouse while someone else is alive unless that person becomes bankrupt or assigns or charges his interest, the settlor will not be regarded as having an interest while that person is under the age of 25. Furthermore, there are four circumstances in which property may become payable to the settlor or his spouse without triggering a charge on the settlor:

- the bankruptcy of a possible beneficiary;

- a possible beneficiary assigning or charging his beneficial interest;

- in the case of a marriage settlement, the death of both parties to the marriage and all or any of the children of the marriage;

- the death of a child of the settlor who had become beneficially entitled to the property or any derived property on or before the age of 25.

If property is payable to a possible future spouse, a separated spouse or a widow or widower of the settlor, the settlement income is not caught by these provisions. This is a relaxation of the former rule that income from settlements which can benefit a future spouse of the settlor is deemed to be income of the settlor for tax purposes. A separation must be by court order or by separation agreement, or take place in such circumstances that the separation is likely to be permanent.

The following do not constitute a settlement for the purposes of these provisions:

- an outright gift between spouses (but see below);
- an irrevocable allocation of pension rights between spouses under a relevant statutory scheme;
- income from settlements made by one party to a marriage to provide for the other party following a divorce or annulment, or a separation pursuant to a court order, a separation agreement or in such circumstances that the separation is likely to be permanent;
- annual payments made by an individual for bona fide commercial reasons in connection with his trade, profession or vocation; and
- covenanted payments to charity.

The outright gift exclusion does not apply to the following:

- a gift which does not carry a right to the whole of the income from the gifted property;
- a gift which consists wholly or substantially of a right to income;
- a gift which is subject to conditions; and
- a gift the subject-matter of which, or any derived property from which, will or may become payable to or applicable for the benefit of the donor in any circumstances whatever.

Legislation: ITTOIA 2005, s. 622–627

Tax Reporter: ¶355-000

1081   Nature of charge and other provisions

Tax chargeable on the settlor is treated as the highest part of the settlor's income barring termination payments and gains on chargeable events associated with certain policies. The same deductions and reliefs are available to the settlor as if the income treated as his had actually been received by him.

Adjustments between settlor and trustees

A settlor who pays tax is entitled to recover the tax paid from the trustees or from any person to whom the income is payable under the settlement, and as conclusive evidence of payment of tax he may require HMRC to certify the amount of income charged to tax, and the amount of tax paid. Conversely, a person who receives a repayment of tax in excess of his entitlement must repay the excess to the trustee or the appropriate beneficiary. Any question as to the amount of such a payment, or as to any apportionment where more than one beneficiary is entitled, is to be decided by the tribunal, whose decision is final.

Settlements by two or more settlors

Where there is more than one settlor, the code applies separately to each settlor as if he were the only settlor in relation to the property or income originating from him. Payments of income to a minor unmarried child of the settlor are only taken into account, in relation to each settlor, to the extent that they emanate from income originating from that settlor, and other such payments to the extent that they represent retained or accumulated income which has originated from that settlor.

'Property originating from a settlor' is property which that settlor has provided for the settlement, and property representing it or accumulated income from it, including an apportioned part of any property which represents both it and other property. 'Income originating from a settlor' includes both income from property which originates from the settlor, and income which the settlor has provided. A settlor is treated as providing property or income which has been provided by another person under reciprocal arrangements with the settlor, but not property which the settlor has provided under reciprocal arrangements with another person.

Power to obtain information

HMRC have wide powers to obtain information from any party to a settlement. Any notice requiring such information must give the recipient at least 28 days in which to respond.

Legislation: ITTOIA 2005, s. 619–648

Tax Reporter: ¶356-000

Capital sums paid to settlor

1097   Capital sums paid by trustee to settlor as income

'Capital sums' (see below) paid directly or indirectly by the trustees of a 'settlement' (see 1071) to the settlor are treated as the income of the settlor (for all income tax purposes), except to the extent that the payment exceeds the amount of 'income available' up to the end of that tax year. Where the capital sum does exceed the income available, the excess is treated as the income of the settlor for following years to the extent that the payment does not fall within the amount of income available up to the end of the year of payment, but does fall within the amount of income available up to the end of the following ten years.

'Income available' is, basically, the aggregate of undistributed income arising in the year in question and in any previous year, less:

- capital payments already treated as the settlor's income;

- settlement income which is treated as the settlor's income under the provisions outlined at 1075 and 1078; and

- basic rate tax on undistributed income not otherwise treated as the settlor's income.

Example

In May 2013, Stuart (the settlor), receives a capital payment of £100,000. The undistributed income of the settlement is as follows:

	£
2013–14	20,000
2014–15	30,000
2015–16	40,000
2016–17	50,000

There is no undistributed income for 2012–13 or earlier years.

The sum of £100,000 is treated as Stuart's income in the following amounts and tax years:

	£
2013–14	20,000
2014–15	30,000
2015–16	40,000
2016–17	10,000
	100,000

Capital sums

A 'capital sum' is:

- any loan (see below) or repayment of a loan; and

- any other sum not paid as income and which is not paid for full consideration in money or money's worth.

Certain sums (which would not otherwise be so treated) are treated as capital sums paid to the settlor by the trustees of a settlement. These are sums which:

- are paid by the trustees to a third party at the settlor's direction or because of the assignment by him of his right to receive it; or

- are otherwise paid or applied by them for the benefit of the settlor.

A capital sum is paid to the settlor if it is paid directly or indirectly to the settlor, the settlor's spouse, or jointly to the settlor (or his or her spouse) and another person.

Loans

If the capital sum paid to the settlor (or spouse, etc.) is a loan only, then no part of the loan is treated by these provisions as the settlor's income for any tax year after that in which the loan is wholly repaid.

Deemed tax deduction

Any sum treated by these provisions as the income of the settlor is treated as income grossed up at the basic rate of tax applicable to the year of payment.

Income tax is chargeable under ITTOIA 2005 and the settlor is entitled to set off against that tax the lesser of:

- basic rate tax for that year on the amount treated as his income; or

- the tax charged.

Legislation: ITTOIA 2005, s. 622, 633(1)–(5)

Tax Reporter: ¶358-000

1098   Capital sums paid by company connected with settlement as income

Capital sums (see 1097) paid to a settlor by a company connected with a settlement which also receives an associated payment from the trustees of the settlement are treated in the same way as amounts paid direct by the trustees (see 1097); the onus is on the settlor receiving such a sum and on the trustees to show that there was no associated payment. An 'associated payment' is, broadly, any payment or transfer at an undervalue within five years either side or any capital sum; a company is 'connected with a settlement' if it is a close company (or would be if UK-resident) and the trustees are participators or is controlled by such a company. There are certain exemptions for short-term (less than 12-month) loans.

A capital sum to which this provision applies is treated as having been paid to the settlor in the year of payment to the extent that the sum falls within the total of associated payments made up to the end of the year in which they are made. To the extent that the capital sum is not treated as paid to the settlor in the year of payment, it is treated as having been paid to the settlor in the following year (so long as it falls within the total of associated payments to the end of that year) and so on for each subsequent year.

Legislation: ITTOIA 2005, s. 641

Tax Reporter: ¶358-200

Maintenance funds for historic buildings

1103 Election for maintenance fund for historic buildings to avoid income charges on settlor

The trustees of a maintenance fund for historic buildings (see 7040ff.) may elect for the exclusion of certain settlement provisions in relation to any tax year, or part. If they do so:

- income arising in that year from property comprised in the settlement which would otherwise be treated as the income of the settlor (see 1070ff.) is not so treated; and

- sums applied in that year out of the property in the settlement for the maintenance, repair or preservation of, or making provisions for public access to, qualifying property (see 7349) are not treated as the income of the settlor if they otherwise would have been so treated by the provisions outlined at 1097, or because the settlor has an interest in the property (see 1078ff.).

Also, where gains arising under the settlement would otherwise have been deemed to be the settlor's gains for the purpose of applying the settlor's rates to non-discretionary trusts, that rule will not apply where an election is in force.

If a settlement relates partly to historic buildings, etc. and partly to other property, it is treated as two separate settlements.

The election must be made within one year of 31 January following the end of the tax year to which it relates; before self-assessment, two years from the end of the tax year).

Income of the settled property which is treated as the income of the settlor (see 1070ff.) and is applied in reimbursing the settlor for expenditure incurred in the maintenance, repair, etc. of qualifying property is not to be treated as reducing deductible expenditure, in computing the profits of the trade, where the settlor is carrying on the trade of showing his property.

Legislation: ITA 2007, s. 507–510

Tax Reporter: ¶351-500

1104 Exit charge where property leaves maintenance fund for historic buildings

Where property (whether capital or income) comprised in a maintenance, fund is applied for any purpose other than the maintenance, repair or preservation of the heritage property, or for the benefit of a heritage body or charity (see 7198), an exit charge arises on the whole of the income which has not been so applied, and which has arisen either since the last such exit charge, or since the settlement began. The rate of charge is equivalent to the higher rate of tax for the tax year during which the charge arises, reduced by the rate applicable to trusts (see 989) for the year. The charge is in addition to any tax otherwise chargeable but does not apply to income deemed to be that of the settlor (see 1070ff.).

The exit charge also bites where any property leaves the settlement and devolves otherwise than on a heritage body or charity, or where the Treasury direction confirming the maintenance fund's privileged status (see 7371) ceases to have effect. However, it does not apply if property is simply transferred from one maintenance fund to another.

Legislation: ITA 2007, s. 512

Tax Reporter: ¶351-500

Income from property

Income from land and buildings

1200 Taxation of income from land

Income from property is taxed under the provisions of the *Income Tax (Trading and Other Income) Act* 2005 (ITTOIA 2005).

Income tax and corporation tax under ITTOIA 2005 are charged on any business which exploits rights over land in the UK to produce rents or other receipts. Moreover, to the extent that any transaction is entered into for exploiting, as a source of rents or other receipts, any such estate, etc. the transaction is deemed to have been entered into in the course of such a business. Thus, a 'receipt' (see below) from a one-off or casual letting which may lack the degree of organisation usually associated with a business may be chargeable.

Receipts, in relation to any land, include:

- any payment for a licence to occupy or otherwise to use any land or in respect of exercising any other right over the land; and

- rental charges, ground annuals and (in Scotland) feu duties, and any other annual payments reserved in respect of, or charged on or issuing out of, the land.

From 16 March 2016 (transactions entered into on or after), income received in non-monetary form is also fully brought into account in calculating taxable property income (ITTOIA 2005, s. 28A as applied by ITTOIA 2005, s. 272).

Excluded from the charge are profits:

- charged to tax by virtue of the provisions outlined at 940, 962 and 2059, respectively relating to farming and market gardening, mines, quarries and similar concerns, rents from mines, etc. or rent from electric line wayleaves;

- from letting tied premises, the rent from which is deemed to be a trading receipt (see 556).

Rents for 'caravans' confined to use at a single UK location and for permanently moored houseboats come within the property business income tax charge. 'Caravan', for this purpose, broadly means any structure designed or adapted for human habitation which is capable of being moved. Sums payable, or valuable consideration provided, by a tenant or licensee for the use of furniture also come within the rules, unless they constitute receipts of a trade which consists in, or involves, the making available of furniture for use in premises (including caravans and houseboats).

'Land' includes buildings and other structures, land covered with water, and any estate, interest, easement, servitude or right in or over land.

For rent a room relief, see 1254.

Legislation: *Caravan Sites and Control of Development Act* 1960, s. 29(1); *Interpretation Act* 1978, Sch. 1; FA 1998, s. 38 and Sch. 5; ITTOIA 2005, s. 264

Other Material: HMRC *Property Income Manual*

Tax Reporter: ¶300-000

1205 Chargeable persons

Under ITTOIA 2005, it is the person who is receiving or entitled to the income from the property who is charged to tax. It is important to note that beneficial entitlement may be unnecessary as far as, for example, an estate agent or other agent in receipt of such property is concerned.

Legislation: ITTOIA 2005, s. 271

Tax Reporter: ¶304-160

1210 Computational rules

Income tax under ITTOIA 2005 is computed on the full amount of the profits arising in the tax year.

Subject to any express contrary rules, such profits are computed as if the trading income deductions rules were, in general, applicable (see 2008).

From 6 April 2016, *Finance Act* 2016 repealed the 10% wear and tear allowance and renewals allowance previously available in respect of furnished lettings and instead introduced a deduction for capital expenditure incurred by a lessor on replacing furnishings, appliances and kitchenware provided for the use of a lessee in a dwelling house. The deduction is available in respect of expenditure incurred on or after 6 April 2016 and is given for the expenditure when calculating the profits of the property business.

Apportionment of rents on sale of land

Where, on disposal, a rental payment is apportioned between the vendor and purchaser, the income is split between the parties, and the party with no interest in the land at the time the amount was due is deemed to have received his share at the date by reference to which the apportionment is made.

Legislation: ITTOIA 2005, s. 264, 270(1), 272(2), 275(2)–(3), 320–321

Tax Reporter: ¶300-000

1254   Rent a room scheme

In relation to people who let furnished rooms in their homes, there is a 'rent a room' relief. The relief applies to owner occupiers and tenants. Gross annual rents which do not exceed £7,500 are exempt from income tax; those who receive gross annual rents in excess of £7,500 can choose between paying tax on the excess (but forgoing relief for allowable expenses) or on the actual profit in the usual way. If someone else receives income in such circumstances when the property is the individual's only or main residence, the individual's rent a room limit is reduced by half to £3,750.

The annual tax free limit was increased to £7,500 from April 2016 (previously, £4,250).

Example 1

Lenny lets furnished accommodation in his house for £185 a week (£9,620 a year). As he incurs expenses of £2,000, his profit is £7,620. The amount of gross rent he receives (£9,620) exceeds the basic limit (£7,500) by £2,120. Lenny will be taxed on the profits derived from the let in the normal way (i.e. on £7,620). But if he makes the alternative basis election, he will only be taxed on £2,120.

Example 2

Lara lets furnished accommodation in her house, and provides meals, cleaning and a laundry service, for £185 a week (£9,620 a year). As she incurs expenses of £8,000, her profit is £1,620. The amount of gross rent she receives (£9,620) exceeds the basic limit (£7,500) by £2,120. Lara will be taxed on the profits derived from the let in the normal way (i.e. on £1,620). Were she to make the alternative basis election, she would be taxed on £2,120.

Legislation: ITTOIA 2005, Pt. 7, Ch. 1

Tax Reporter: ¶303-000

1255 Furnished holiday letting income

The letting of furnished holiday accommodation constitutes a property income business and the basis period rules, as well as most of the business income rules for calculating profits (see 2050ff.), accordingly apply. However, the letting of furnished holiday accommodation is treated in an especially beneficial way, i.e. as a trade.

All the commercial lettings of furnished holiday accommodation made by a particular person or partnership are treated as one trade. The profit or loss has to be calculated, in practice, separately from other property income business profits and losses in order to see whether advantage can be taken of the above benefits. However, any overall profit is included in the general property income business result, as is any loss unless used separately against other income.

Although the special regime applies to furnished holiday lettings in both the UK and the EEA (excluding the UK), they are to be treated as two separate property businesses. Legislation effective from 6 April 2011 contains parallel provisions for each type of business and the results of each will need to be separately calculated.

Benefits of furnished holiday lettings

The main benefits for the taxpayer of treatment as a trader are as follows:

* up to 5 April 2011, losses were not restricted to property business income but could be set against general income (see below) or capital gains (see 2116);

* capital allowances are available for expenditure on plant and machinery acquired for purposes of the letting;

* CGT rollover reliefs are available, where applicable and subject to the usual rules; likewise, relief for gifts of business assets and in respect of loans to traders (see 6305);

* the income qualifies as earned income for pension contribution purposes.

It should nevertheless be noted that the 'rent a room' exemption (see 1254) may prove more advantageous to the taxpayer.

Conditions to be satisfied

The above treatment applies only where there is a 'commercial letting' of 'furnished holiday accommodation' in the UK or in the European Economic Area, excluding the UK.

Income tax

'Commercial letting'

'Commercial letting' requires that the property be let:

(1) on a commercial basis; and

(2) with a view to the realisation of 'profits'.

'Profits' here means the 'commercial', not the 'tax adjusted', profit.

It should be noted that HMRC take the view that the required income profit motive may be displaced where the taxpayer's motive is the acquisition of a second, or retirement, home, or securing a long-term capital profit on disposing of the property. Claimants may also fail the above requirements where the size of the mortgage used to purchase the property is so large that the projected profitability is jeopardised or the commercial credibility of the scheme as a whole is, consequently, questionable even though individual lettings are on a commercial basis. In such cases, HMRC expect a written business plan to be prepared, with credible figures.

Where the taxpayer seeks relief for losses in the early years of a trade (see 2119), there is an additional, *objective*, condition that profits could reasonably be expected to be realised in the year of the loss or within a reasonable time thereafter. HMRC's view is that this test must be considered for each year for which relief is claimed and that it is necessary to look at the year of the loss and whatever, on the facts, is a reasonable time thereafter. And they dissent from a special commissioner's view that this relief is available so long as profits may be expected not later than a reasonable time after the end of the statutory four-year period:

> 'We consider that 'reasonable time' depends on the facts and, particularly, the nature of the loss making activity. In general, our view is that this should be a fairly short period. But, in the context of capital intensive activities, such as furnished holiday lettings, we would normally expect there to be a reasonable and realistic expectation of profits emerging within five years from the date of the commencement of the activities.'

'Furnished holiday accommodation'

Accommodation is 'furnished holiday accommodation' if:

- the person entitled to the use of the accommodation is also, in connection with that use, entitled to the use of furniture (note that there is nothing in the legislation specifying a minimum amount of furniture); and

- the accommodation is 'qualifying holiday accommodation'.

There is no restriction to particular kinds of accommodation and so houses, flats, caravans or other types of accommodation will all potentially qualify.

Accommodation that is let during a tax year is 'qualifying holiday accommodation' if certain conditions regarding the availability, the letting and the pattern of occupation are met:

(1) 'the availability condition': the accommodation must be available for commercial letting to the public generally as holiday accommodation for a minimum number of days during the 'relevant period'. Where the 'relevant period' is a tax year from 2012–13 onwards or begins on or after 6 April 2012, the requirement is 210 days. For relevant periods which are tax years up to and including 2011–12 or which begin before 6 April 2012, the requirement was 140 days;

(2) 'the letting condition': the accommodation must actually be commercially let as holiday accommodation for a minimum number of days during the 'relevant period'. Where the 'relevant period' is a tax year from 2012–13 onwards or begins on or after 6 April 2012, the requirement is 105 days. For relevant periods which are tax years up to and including 2011–12 or which begin before 6 April 2012, the requirement was 70 days; and

(3) the 'pattern of occupation condition': during the 'relevant period', there must not be more than 155 days falling in 'periods of longer term occupation'.

A 'period of longer term occupation' is a continuous period of more than 31 days during which the accommodation is in the same occupation, unless there are abnormal circumstances. No guidance is provided for the exclusion to the rule on continuous occupation, otherwise than in circumstances that are not normal. There is no guidance on what constitutes 'not normal', but it is likely that this will cover unexpected situations such as where a tenant exceeds the 31-day limit due to illness.

As far as the letting condition is concerned, a period of longer-term occupation will not (unless covered by the exception for abnormal situations) count as letting for holiday accommodation.

Every furnished property must meet all the conditions in order to be treated as qualifying holiday accommodation. However, where a business comprises two or more properties of which some qualify under the letting condition and others do not, a claim can be made to average the lettings. From 2010–11 onwards, where properties which have previously met the letting condition, fail it in the following year or two despite a genuine intention on the part of the taxpayer to meet that condition, an election may be made to treat that property as qualifying holiday accommodation.

The three conditions referred to above must be met during the 'relevant period'. There are three possible 12-month periods that may count as 'relevant periods', depending on whether the furnished letting is starting, ceasing or continuing (ITTOIA 2005, s. 324). The relevant period, in relation to accommodation let in a tax year, will be one of the following:

- *starting*: the relevant period is 12 months beginning on the first day of the tax year on which it is let as furnished accommodation (in a case where it was not let as furnished accommodation in the previous tax year);

- *ceasing*: the relevant period is the 12 months ending with the last day in the tax year under consideration on which it is let as furnished accommodation (in a case where it was let as furnished accommodation in the previous tax year but is not let as furnished accommodation in the next tax year); or

- *continuing*: if neither of the above apply, then the 'relevant period' is the tax year itself.

Furnished holiday letting losses

Years 2011–12 onwards

Relief for losses generated by a furnished holiday lettings business may only be used to carry forward against profits of subsequent tax years arising from the same business in which the loss arose. Consequently the profits and losses of a UK business and an EEA business need to be calculated separately.

Years up to and including 2010–11

For these years, the regime was more generous in that relief could also be claimed:

- against general income for the year of the loss and/or the immediately preceding year;

- against capital gains;

- as terminal loss relief.

The only restriction was that no claim could be made to set losses of the early years of a business against general income of previous years.

Legislation: FA 2011, s. 52 and Sch. 14; ITTOIA 2005, s. 323–326

Cases: *Walls v Livesey (HMIT)* (1995) Sp C 4; *Brown v Richardson (HMIT)* (1997) Sp C 129; *Pawson (dec'd)* [2012] TC 01748; *Nott* [2016] TC 04897

Tax Reporter: ¶303-100

1260 Treatment of lease premiums as rent

The legislation relating to lease premiums, etc. is largely unchanged by the introduction of the rules relating to property income businesses (see 1200ff.), with amendments being made to include references to the new system.

Premiums in respect of leases of more than 50 years' duration are charged to CGT. Grants, variations, surrenders and other lump sum payments in respect of leases which do not exceed 50 years are charged partly to CGT and partly to income tax under the property income provisions (see 1264, 1268 and 1270); such 'short leases' are also potentially subject to charges under ITTOIA 2005 in the case of a sale with a right to reconveyance or leaseback (see 1274 and 1276) or of a profit on sale (see 1278). The duration of a lease is determined by reference to certain specific principles (see 1262).

A 'lease' includes an agreement for a lease as well as any tenancy, but does not include a mortgage. A 'premium' includes:

'any like sum, whether payable to the immediate or a superior landlord or to a person connected [see below] with the immediate or a superior landlord.'

'Connected persons' in relation to an individual are his spouse or relative (i.e. brother, sister, ancestor or lineal descendant), or his relatives' spouses, or trustees of a settlement of which he (or an individual connected with him) is the settlor, or a partner or a partner's spouse or relative, or a company of which he, or he and persons connected with him, have control.

Legislation: ITTOIA 2005, s. 306–307, 364, 878–879

Tax Reporter: ¶300-115

1262 The duration of a lease

There are rules for determining the duration of a 'lease' (see 1260), as follows.

- Where the terms of the lease or any other circumstances render it unlikely that the lease will continue beyond a date falling before the expiry of the term of the lease and the premium was not substantially greater than it would have been (on certain specified assumptions) had the term been one expiring on that date, the duration of the lease is calculated to that earlier date.

- Where there is provision for the extension of the lease beyond a given date by notice given by the tenant, account may be taken of any circumstances making it likely that the lease will be so extended.

- Where the tenant, or a person connected with him, is, or may become, entitled to a further lease or the grant of a further lease (whenever commencing) on the same premises, or on premises including the whole or part of the same premises, the term of the lease may be treated as not expiring before the term of the further lease.

In applying the above it is assumed that all parties concerned act as they would act if they were at arm's length and that, where an unusual benefit is conferred by the lease, the benefit would not have been conferred had the lease been for a period ending on the likely date of determination, rather than on the actual date. The likely date of determination is in most cases the end of the period of the lease. An unusual benefit would be any benefit other than the right to enjoy the beneficial occupation of the premises or the right to receive a reasonable commercial rent in respect of them.

Where a premium is paid for the grant of a lease of less than 50 years, this is generally treated as being an income payment for tax purposes (as opposed to a capital payment). This may also be the case in some situations where the term of the lease is more than 50 years and there are rules designed to prevent leases being artificially extended beyond 50 years by landlords to avoid the tax charge. The legislation also treats work required to be carried out by a tenant as a premium in certain circumstances. In relation to leases granted on or after 6 April 2013 (1 April 2013 for companies), relief is no longer available to a trader or intermediate landlord who pays a lease premium on a lease that is only deemed to be short because of the operation of 'Rule 1' in CTA 2009, s. 243.

Legislation: ITTOIA 2005, s. 303–305; FA 2013, s. 75 and Sch. 28

Tax Reporter: ¶300-115

1264 Short leases: portion of premium treated as rent

Premiums arising on the grant of 'leases' (see 1260) which do not exceed 50 years are taxed as part income (i.e. deemed rentals) and part capital gain (for the meaning of 'premium', see 1260; for the duration of a lease, see 1262). To ascertain what part of the premium falls to be taxed as income and what part is the capital element, a formula exists by which the appropriate part of the premium to be charged to income tax can be ascertained, i.e. the amount of the premium minus one-fiftieth of that amount for each complete period of 12 months (other than the first) in the duration of the lease.

Example

Anna grants Emma a lease for $21^1/_2$ years for a premium of £10,000.

	£
Premium	10,000
Less: (21 − 1) × 2% × £10,000	(4,000)
Amount assessable under ITTOIA 2005	6,000

The part of the premium chargeable is taxable in full in the chargeable period in which the lease is granted.

Where provision is made in the lease for the tenant to carry out work instead of paying a premium, the amount by which the landlord's estate has been increased in value by the provision requiring the work to be done is treated as a premium. However, if the work is of a type which, if the landlord and not the tenant were obliged to carry it out, would be deductible from the rent under general rules or as an expense of a property income business, the rule does not apply.

A complex form of relief may also be available (and continues to be available in the case of a property income business), if the premium arises on the grant of a sub-lease out of a head lease in respect of which a charge under these provisions has previously been made; also if a charge would have been made except for any exemption from tax); similarly, relief may be available if the previous charge arose as a result of the grant of a lease at undervalue (see 1278).

Where it appears to an inspector that the amount chargeable affects the tax liability of any other person, he may notify those other persons of the amount he proposes to charge. All parties may then object if they so wish and the amount will be determined by the tribunal as if it were an appeal.

The various payments under the present provisions are taxable in full in the chargeable period in which payment is received.

In general, the whole of a discounted premium is taxable in the relevant chargeable period. However, there is a relief where a premium is payable by instalments: originally, a taxpayer who satisfied HMRC that he would otherwise suffer undue hardship could elect to pay the tax chargeable by such instalments as HMRC might allow over a period not exceeding eight years. As this did not fit with self-assessment, the income or corporation tax payer now has the option to pay tax by instalments over the eight-year period.

Legislation: ITTOIA 2005, s. 277–279

Tax Reporter: ¶300-120

1268   Short leases: lump-sum rents and surrender payments

Where, under the terms subject to which a 'lease' (see 1260) is granted, a sum becomes payable by the tenant in lieu of the whole or part of the rent for any period, that sum is deemed to be a premium and a notional rent arises when it becomes payable by the tenant. The lump sum or premium is treated as relating only to the period of the lease for which the payment was made in lieu of rent. The sum may thus be taxable to the extent which applies in relation to premiums generally under short leases (see 1264).

Example

A landlord grants a lease of 31 years. The lease provides that the landlord can demand a lump sum after ten years of £40,000 in lieu of rent for the remainder of the lease. The £40,000 is deemed to be a premium payable for a lease of 21 years (31 − 10).

Where, under the terms subject to which a lease is granted, a sum becomes payable by the tenant as consideration for the surrender of the lease (brought to an end by an agreement between landlord and tenant), that sum is deemed to be a premium and a notional rent arises when it becomes payable by the tenant. The premium is taken to be paid in consideration of the lease from the date of commencement to the date of surrender. The sum may thus be taxable to the extent which applies in relation to premiums generally under short leases (see 1264). If, however, surrender is agreed between landlord and tenant after the lease has commenced, the above provision will not apply and CGT only will be chargeable on the surrender payment.

Example

The landlord grants a lease for 31 years with a surrender clause and the tenant surrenders in accordance with the clause after ten years for the stipulated figure of £20,000. The £20,000 is treated as a premium applicable to the duration of the lease from commencement to surrender (i.e. ten years).

Legislation: ITTOIA 2005, 279–280

Tax Reporter: ¶300-130

1270   Short leases: payments to waive or vary the terms of the lease as income

Where a sum becomes payable by the tenant, otherwise than by way of rent, in consideration for a variation of any term of the 'lease' (see 1260), that sum is deemed to be a premium in the year when the contract providing for the variation or waiver was entered into. The sum may thus be taxable to the extent which applies in relation to premiums generally under short leases (see 1264). The premium is treated as attributable to the period during which the waiver or variation is to have effect, i.e. the duration of the lease to which the variation or waiver applied. (Payments in point paid to a person other than the landlord are assessable only if paid to a person who in relation to the landlord is a 'connected person'.

Example

The landlord grants a lease of 31 years. Under the provisions in the lease, the tenant has an option to take a further term provided he observes all the conditions of the lease. If the tenant fails to do so after ten years have elapsed but then pays the landlord £10,000 to waive his (the landlord's) right to object to a further term being taken, that £10,000 would be treated as a premium attributable to that period of the lease over which the variation or waiver occurred, i.e. 21 years.

Legislation: ITTOIA 2005, s. 313(5)

Case: *Banning v Wright (HMIT)* [1972] 1 WLR 972

Tax Reporter: ¶300-140

1274   Short leases: sale proceeds as income where right of reconveyance

In addition to the anti-avoidance provisions relating to the duration of the lease (the lease term for tax purposes being determined in a specific way: see 1262), there are also provisions designed to prevent specific avoidance schemes in connection with leasebacks (see 1276) or reconveyances (see below).

Where the terms subject to which an estate or interest in land is sold provide that it shall be, or may be required to be, reconveyed at a future date to the vendor or a person 'connected' with him, the vendor may be chargeable to tax under ITTOIA 2005 (or the sum may be treated as received as income of a property income business). The charge is on any amount by which the price at which the estate or interest is sold exceeds the price at which it is to be reconveyed, or, if the earliest date at which in accordance with those terms it would fall to be reconveyed is a date two years or more after the sale it is discounted in accordance with the provisions taking only a portion of premiums as income (see 1264).

Where the terms of the sale do not stipulate a date for reconveyance and the price varies with the date of reconveyance, the price of the reconveyance is taken to be the lowest possible under the terms of the sale. The vendor may reclaim (up to six years after the reconveyance) that amount of the tax assessed on him which exceeds the amount which would have been assessed had the date been treated as the date fixed by the terms of sale.

Where it appears to an inspector that the amount chargeable affects the tax liability of any other person, he may notify those other persons of the amount he proposes to charge; all parties may then object if they so wish and the amount will be determined by the tribunal as if it were an appeal.

Legislation: ITTOIA 2005, s. 284, 286

Tax Reporter: ¶300-160

1276 Short leases: sale and leaseback income charges

In addition to the anti-avoidance provisions which deal with the duration of the lease (the lease term for tax purposes being determined in a specific way: see 1262) and those which deal with the sale of land with the right to reconveyance (see 1274), the legislation deals with ascertaining the charge to tax where land is sold and the agreement contains a provision for its lease back to the vendor or a person connected with him (rather than a reconveyance as such).

The amount of the premium payable on the grant of the lease plus the value at the date of sale of the right to purchase the reversion when the lease is granted is taken to be the reconveyance price for the purposes of the rules set out in 1274. The date of reconveyance is deemed to be the date of the grant of the lease.

Example

A landlord sells the property to the tenant for £30,000 but the agreement gives the landlord the right to take a 999-year lease for £15,000 after ten years.

If the value of the reversion was £500, the landlord would be charged as follows:

£30,000 − (£15,000 + £500) = £14,500 over ten years, discounted in accordance with the provisions treating only a portion of any premium as income (see 1264).

This type of transaction is frequently used, not as a means of avoidance, but as a bona fide commercial method to finance the development of land; therefore, an express proviso excludes situations where the lease is granted and begins to run within one month after the sale.

The amount deemed to have been received is taken into account in computing the property business profits in the period in which the estate or interest is 'sold'. The estate or interest is treated as 'sold' when any of the following occurs:

(1) an unconditional contract for its sale is entered into;

(2) a conditional contract for its sale becomes unconditional; or

(3) an option or right of pre-emption is exercised requiring the vendor to enter into an unconditional contract for its sale.

Where it appears to an inspector that the amount chargeable affects the tax liability of any other person, he may notify those other persons of the amount he proposes to charge; all parties may then object if they so wish and the amount will be determined by the tribunal as if it were an appeal.

Legislation: ITTOIA 2005, s. 285–286, 301–302

Tax Reporter: ¶304-600

1278 Short leases: premium foregone treated as income

Where a lease of not more than 50 years (see 1262) is granted at less than its market value, the difference between the amount for which it was granted and the market value of the lease is called 'the amount foregone'.

On a subsequent first assignment of the lease by the tenant, any consideration over and above the premium on the grant of the undervalued lease, is chargeable to income tax under ITTOIA 2005 in the assignor's hands. The amount so chargeable is limited by the 'amount foregone' and is discounted in accordance with the provisions treating only a portion of any premium as income (see 1264) as if it had arisen on the original grant of the lease. The balance of the 'amount foregone' is carried forward to subsequent assignments until used up: at each stage the relevant excess is the excess of consideration for the assignment in question over the consideration previously given.

The amount of any 'excess' is taken into account in computing property income profits in the period in which the payment is due.

Because future assignees of the lease may not know if the lease has been previously granted at an undervalue, the grantor or any assignor or assignee of the lease may submit a statement to HMRC showing whether or not a charge to tax arises and the inspector must, if he is satisfied with the accuracy of the statement, certify its accuracy.

Where it appears to an inspector that the amount chargeable affects the tax liability of any other person, he may notify those other persons of the amount he proposes to charge; all parties may then object if they so wish and the amount will be determined by the tribunal as if it were an appeal.

Legislation: ITTOIA 2005, s. 282–283, 300

Tax Reporter: ¶300-110

1290   Reverse premiums

Reverse premiums are the sums landlords pay to induce potential tenants to take a lease and are taxable as revenue receipts. However, the charge to tax does not apply to a premium to which the recipient was entitled immediately before that date, arrangements made on or after that date being ignored for this purpose.

Inducements

The legislation taxes 'a payment or other benefit by way of inducement'. Such an inducement may take the form of a cash payment by the landlords, a period of rent-free occupation, a contribution to the tenant's costs or the assumption by landlord of the tenant's liabilities. However, not all such inducements are caught by the rules. The following table summarises those inducements that are taxable under the reverse premium provision and those that are not.

Taxable	Non-taxable
• Cash payments • Contributions towards specified tenant's costs, e.g. relocation costs, start-up costs or fitting-out costs • Sums paid to third parties to meet obligations of the tenant, e.g. rent to a landlord due under an old lease or a capital sum to terminate such a lease • An effective payment of cash by other means, e.g. the landlord writing off a sum owed by the tenant	• The grant of a rent-free period of occupation • The replacement by agreement of an existing rent with a lower rent because market conditions have made the original rent onerous • A new lease by agreement without an onerous condition present in former lease

Broadly, inducements are caught if they involve the laying out of money. Benefits representing amounts foregone or deferred are not generally caught as they do not involve an outlay.

Tax treatment of receipts by way of reverse premiums

For tax purposes, a reverse premium is treated as a revenue receipt taxable under ITTOIA 2005.

The timing of the charge generally follows accepted principles of commercial accounting, the broad effect of which is to spread the reverse premium over the period of the lease, or to the first rent review, whichever is the shorter. See, however, the anti-avoidance provision below.

Arrangements not at arm's length

An anti-avoidance provision aims at preventing the exploitation of timing differences by the grant of a lease to a connected person on clearly uncommercial terms (e.g. a 25-year lease with no rent review clause).

Exclusions

The above provisions do not apply to a payment or benefit:

- if or to the extent that it is taken into account under the capital allowances provision relating to subsidies, contributions, etc. to reduce the recipient's expenditure qualifying for allowances (see 2336);

- received in connection with a relevant transaction where the person entering into the transaction is an individual and the transaction relates to premises occupied or to be occupied as his only or main residence; or

- to the extent that it is consideration for the transfer of an estate or interest in land which constitutes the sale in a 'sale and leaseback transaction' as described in ITA 2007, Pt. 12A, Ch. 1.

Legislation: ITTOIA 2005, s. 311, Sch. 2, para. 28, 72, 99, 101–103

Cases: *Commr of Inland Revenue (New Zealand) v McKenzies (NZ) Ltd* [1988] 2 NZLR 736; *Commr of Inland Revenue (New Zealand) v Wattie* [1998] BTC 438

Tax Reporter: ¶300-190

1300   Transactions in land: anti-avoidance

Transactions designed to avoid tax on the sale of land by direct or indirect means are taxed as income under ITTOIA 2005. Some of the transactions caught are normal developments of land. To the extent that capital gains are now taxed at income tax rates in the case of individuals and the full corporation tax rate in the case of companies, the importance of the provisions is diminished.

The provisions are nevertheless very wide in scope, applying to all persons (which include companies and unincorporated bodies), whether or not resident in the UK. However, the land in question (or part of it) must be situated in the UK for the provisions to apply.

These provisions apply wherever:

- land, or any property deriving its value from land (including shares in a land-owning company), is acquired with the sole or main object of realising a gain from disposing of the land;

- land is held as trading stock; or
- land is developed with the sole or main object of realising a gain from disposing of the land when developed,

and any gain of a capital nature is obtained from the disposal of the land, by the person acquiring, holding or developing the land, or by any 'connected person' or, where any arrangement or scheme is effected in respect of the land which enables a gain to be realised by any indirect method, or by any series of transactions, by any person who is a party to, or concerned in, the arrangement or scheme, and whether any such person obtains the gain for himself or for any other person.

Supplementary provisions ensure that the rules apply to many transactions whereby a person indirectly benefits, though where one person is assessed to tax in respect of consideration receivable by another person, there is a right of recovery. However, the operation of the provisions is restricted where a company holds land as trading stock, or where a company owns 90% or more of the ordinary share capital (directly or indirectly) of another company which holds land as trading stock, and there is a disposal of shares in either the land trading company or the holding company, and all the land so held is disposed of in the normal course of trade by the company which held it, and all the opportunity of profit or gain in respect of the land arises to that company.

Adjustments have been upheld in respect of:

- the grant by trustees of a lease of land to a developer, with a clause ensuring that the premium payable should be linked with the prices obtained from the sale of the underleases following the redevelopment of the land;
- the sale of properties through the medium of Bahamian companies.

HMRC are given powers to obtain such information as they think necessary for these purposes. Conversely, the taxpayer can apply for advance clearance or can request confirmation after the fact that HMRC will not challenge any transaction.

Legislation: ITA 2007, Pt. 13, Ch. 3

Cases: *Page (HMIT) v Lowther* [1983] BTC 394; *Sugarwhite v Budd (HMIT)* [1988] BTC 189

Tax Reporter: ¶304-000

1305   Rent factoring

Rent factoring is the sale of the right to receive rents. The right to receive rents over a period of time is valuable, but a business may prefer to realise that value upfront, rather than over the period of the lease. The right to receive the rents is therefore sold for a lump sum that realises most of the value but which also allows the purchaser, usually a bank or other finance house, to make a commercial profit from the receipt of the rents over time.

In some circumstances, the lump sum may be taxable as income but the transactions could be structured so that the lump sum would not be brought into charge as income of the seller (i.e. a capital sum). Where the lump sum is capital, it could effectively escape taxation, either because of costs that could reduce the gain to nil (or nearly so) or because of the availability of capital losses.

This type of tax avoidance was addressed by *Finance Act* 2004 by ensuring that, where the right to receive all or part of the rental stream arising from a lease of plant and machinery is sold or otherwise transferred to another person, the proceeds are brought into charge as income if they would not otherwise be brought into account as income.

Tax Reporter: ¶300-042

1320   Real estate investment trusts

The regime for Real Estate Investment Trusts ('UK-REITs' and 'Group REITs') took effect from 1 January 2007. It is part of a trend in various countries, including the USA, Germany, Japan and Australia, to encourage property investment by offering a fund in which investors can buy shares or units, and which is 'look-through' for taxation purposes – the liability falling not on the fund but on the investor.

UK-REITs must be publicly listed on a stock exchange, so that the method of investment is to purchase shares in the open market.

The legislation provides an alternative taxation treatment for listed companies that invest substantially in real property held as part of a property rental business. To comply with the conditions laid down, such a company must distribute at least 90% of its profits from its property rental business each year.

The alternative taxation treatment on offer consists of exemption from corporation tax for the investing company, in so far as it carries on a property rental business that meets the conditions; instead, liability to income tax or corporation tax falls on the shareholder in respect of the distributions from the UK-REIT that they receive. This replaces the normal UK taxation regime whereby the company to which the profits accrue is charged to corporation tax on them, and the shareholder then receives a dividend which may or may not in practice give rise to a further liability to tax.

A company that meets the conditions may give notice to enter the UK-REIT regime for any accounting period commencing on or after 1 January 2007. A new accounting period starts on entry into the regime. Tax penalties may arise if the company leaves the regime before ten years have expired.

There are conditions that the company's property rental business, the income arising from that business, and the company itself must meet if the notice given is to be valid. Failure to meet these and other conditions or requirements of the regime once the UK-REIT is in existence can lead to a tax charge or cessation of UK-REIT status. The Group REIT regime, and the regime for joint ventures, also contain special rules. Directors and advisers should in particular be aware of the increased accounting requirements for Group REITs, and for single company UK-REITs that have a 40% interest in a joint venture company.

A number of compliance rules are framed so as to ensure that a 'minor or inadvertent' breach of the rules will not result in UK-REIT status being invalid. Some rules are of an 'x strikes and you're out' nature, intended to enable a company or group that takes its responsibilities seriously to survive without harm in spite of the occasional breach. Major breaches, on the other hand, can result in UK-REIT status being denied from the start, or from the beginning of an accounting period that ended some time ago. The risks arising from this need no emphasis.

With the introduction of the UK-REIT regime, the legislation relating to housing investment trusts was repealed.

Legislation: FA 2006, Pt. 4

Tax Reporter: ¶300-020

Investment income

Dividends and unit trust income receivable

1350   Dividends receivable

Prior to 6 April 2016, where a company made a 'qualifying distribution' to an individual shareholder who was resident in the UK, he generally received a tax credit. He was treated as if he received an amount of income equal to the cash amount (or value) plus the tax credit; such credit then reduced his income tax liability for the relevant year in which the distribution is made. By this method, the tax paid by the company on its income is partially imputed to the shareholder.

Given that the rate of corporation tax has fallen significantly since the system of tax credits on dividends was designed over 40 years ago, the Government believed that the dividend tax credit was an arcane and complex feature of the tax system. Therefore from April 2016, the dividend tax credit was abolished and partially compensated for with the introduction of dividend nil rate (dividend allowance) of £5,000 a year.

Special rates of income tax apply to dividend income. These rates are known as the dividend nil rate (from 6 April 2016), the dividend ordinary, the dividend upper rate and (since 6 April 2010) the dividend additional rate. The charge to tax at the dividend rates is subject to any other provisions of the Income Tax Acts that provide for income to be charged at different rates of income tax in some circumstances.

Dividend nil rate (dividend allowance)

Finance Act 2016 introduces a new 0% rate of tax for dividend income, called 'the dividend nil rate', with effect from 6 April 2016.

Where an individual receives dividend income that would otherwise be chargeable at the dividend ordinary, upper or additional rate, and the income is less than or equal to £5,000, the dividend nil rate will apply to all of the dividend income. Where the dividend income is above £5,000, the lowest part of the dividend income will be chargeable at 0%, and anything received above £5,000 is taxed at the rate that would apply to that amount if the dividend nil rate did not exist.

Dividend ordinary rate

As far as individuals are concerned, income tax is charged at the dividend ordinary rate on an individual's dividend income which would otherwise be charged to income tax at the basic rate (or, previously, the starting rate) and which is not relevant foreign income charged on the remittance basis.

Income tax is also charged at the dividend ordinary rate on the dividend income of persons other than individuals which would otherwise be charged at the basic rate and which is not relevant foreign income, unless the income in question is charged at another rate by other provisions of the Income Tax Acts, e.g. the certain trustees and unauthorised unit trusts.

Income tax

The dividend ordinary rate is set at 7.5% from 2016–17, previously, 10%. For tax years up to and including 2015–16, as dividends and distributions from UK companies carried a tax credit equal to 10% of the aggregate value of the dividend and the tax credit itself, no additional tax was due on this category of income which fell within the basic rate limit.

Dividend upper rate

Individuals are charged to income tax at the dividend upper rate on dividend income which would otherwise be chargeable at the higher rate of tax. The dividend upper rate is set at 32.5%. For tax years up to and including 2015–16, the tax credit attaching to dividends and distributions from UK companies was set against the tax charged at the dividend upper rate. The dividend upper rate does not apply to relevant foreign income charged in accordance with ITTOIA 2005, s. 832.

Dividend additional rate

Individuals are charged to income tax at the dividend additional rate on dividend income which would otherwise be chargeable at the additional rate of tax. The dividend additional rate is set at 38.1% from 2016–17, previously, 37.5% (unchanged from 2014–15). For tax years up to and including 2015–16, the tax credit attaching to dividends and distributions from UK companies was set against the tax charged at the dividend additional rate.

The dividend additional rate does not apply to relevant foreign income charged in accordance with ITTOIA 2005, s. 832.

Dividend income

The dividend rates apply to dividend income. Dividend income comprises:

- dividends and distributions from UK companies;

- dividends and 'relevant foreign distributions' from non-UK resident companies. A relevant foreign distribution is a distribution, other than a dividend, corresponding to taxable distributions from UK companies;

- stock dividends from UK-resident companies; or

- the release of a loan to a participator in a close company.

Example 1

Martha is a non-taxpayer. She receives a dividend of £1,000 in 2016–17. The dividend falls within the dividend nil rate (dividend allowance) and is not taxable.

Example 2

Ellie receives a dividend of £10,000 in 2016–17. She has other income of £10,500. She has taxable income of £9,500 (£10,500 + £10,000) – personal allowance of £11,000). £5,000 of the dividend falls within the dividend nil rate (dividend allowance) and is not taxable. The remaining £4,500 is taxable at 7.5%. The tax on the dividend is £337.50.

Example 3

George receives a dividend of £20,000 in 2016–17. He has other income of £30,000. His taxable income is £39,000 (£30,000 + £20,000 – personal allowance of £11,000). The basic rate limit is £32,000 of which £19,000 is used by other income (offsetting the personal allowance against other income first), therefore, of the £20,000 dividend, £13,000 falls within the basic rate band and £7,000 within the higher rate band. The dividend nil rate is applied against £5,000 of the basic rate band dividend income leaving £8,000 taxable at 7.5%. The £7,000 dividend falling within the higher rate band is taxable at 32.5%. The tax on the dividend is £2,875 (£8,000 × 7.5% + £7,000 × 32.5%).

Example 4

Hannah earns £300,000 in 2016–17. She also receives a dividend of £6,000. The dividend nil rate is applied against the first £5,000 of dividend income and the remaining £1,000 is treated as the top slice of her income, being taxed at the rate of 38.1%. Additional tax payable in respect of the dividend is £381.

Legislation: ITA 2007, s. 13; ITTOIA 2005, Pt. 4, Ch. 3

Tax Reporter: ¶328-000

1352 Distributions in a winding up

Finance Act 2016 introduces a targeted anti-avoidance rule (TAAR) that will apply to certain company distributions in respect of share capital in a winding up. The TAAR will treat the distribution from a winding up as if it were a distribution chargeable to income tax (rather than capital gains tax) where certain conditions are met. The TAAR will apply to distributions made on or after 6 April 2016.

The conditions that will trigger the TAAR are:

(1) the company is a close company or has been a close company at some point in the two years prior to the winding up;

(2) the person who receives the distribution is involved with carrying on a trade or activity similar to that carried on by the company being wound up;

(3) it is reasonable to assume that the winding up forms part of arrangements designed to reduce the person's income tax liability.

An exemption will apply in respect of distributions received which are a repayment of share capital originally subscribed or where the distribution comprises only shares in a subsidiary of the wound up company as with a 'liquidation de-merger'.

Finance Act 2016 further introduces mirror image legislation in respect of distributions in respect of shares from a non-UK resident company (treating the non-UK resident company as close if it would have been close had it been resident in the UK).

Legislation: ITTOIA 2005, s. 396B, 404A

1358   Unit trust income receivable

The tax treatment of income arising in respect of investment through a unit trust depends upon whether the trust is authorised. Authorised unit trusts are generally treated as companies subject to corporation tax while unauthorised unit trusts are treated as trusts subject to income tax.

Income from underlying investments made through authorised unit trusts are effectively treated as those of the trustees rather than of the ultimate investors (the precise way in which effect is given to this differs depending upon the circumstances, as noted below). There is a deemed 'full-payout' of scheme income. The scheme may distinguish in its accounts whether amounts are to be paid out wholly as dividends (and in part as FIDs if desired) or wholly as yearly interest; non-resident investors can register to receive such interest without deduction of tax where it derives from eligible assets (for special provisions for corporate recipients, see 3027).

For unauthorised unit trusts, unit holders are liable to tax on amounts which are paid out or reinvested in the fund for their benefit, those amounts being treated as reaching unit holders with basic rate tax having been deducted by the trustees.

(Investment trusts are companies whose distributions are taxable in the usual manner: see 1350.)

Legislation: ITTOIA 2005, s. 372–381; *Authorised Investment Funds (Tax) Regulations* 2006 (SI 2006/964); *Authorised Investment Funds (Tax) (Amendment) Regulations* 2009 (SI 2009/2036)

Tax Reporter: ¶328-000

Interest, annuities and other annual payments

1366   The income charge on annual payments, including interest

The following items are charged to tax under ITTOIA 2005.

- Any interest of money, whether yearly or otherwise, or any 'annuity' (see 1396) or other 'annual payment' (see below and 1398), whether such payment is payable within or out of the UK, either as a charge on any property of the person paying the same by virtue of any deed or will or otherwise, or as a reservation out of it, or as a personal debt or obligation by virtue of any contract. This applies whether it is received and payable half-yearly or at any shorter or more distant periods, but excludes any payment chargeable under the tax on property income rules. The Court of Appeal has held that interest credited to the taxpayer's account but retained by the bank as security for a debt was taxable as interest to which the taxpayer was entitled: although he never received the interest, he received the benefit of it since his liability for the debt was reduced. Investors in certain unit trusts are deemed to receive interest (see 1358).

- All discounts (see 1400).

- Income from securities bearing interest payable out of the public revenue (including those which the Treasury has directed are gross payment securities).

There are certain exempt forms of interest, such as that on certain National Savings and ISAs (see 1372 and 1921). Interest on compensation paid in respect of certain mis-sold personal pensions, buy-out contracts and retirement annuity contracts is also exempt.

Generally, certain annual payments made by an individual, that individual's personal representative or a Scottish partnership involving an individual are not taxable if they fall due after 14 March 1988. Specifically excluded from this exemption (and therefore still within the charge to tax) are the following:

- payments of interest;

- payments made for bona fide commercial reasons in connection with the individual's trade, profession or vocation;

- certain payments for non-taxable consideration; and

- certain maintenance payments (see 1404).

Other exempt annual payments include benefits paid under certain 'self-contained' insurance policies to those who make arrangements to protect themselves from financial losses caused by accident, sickness, disability, infirmity or unemployment, or from the cost of long-term care. Benefits received under employers' group policies and passed on to an employee are also exempt if and to the extent that the employee has contributed to the premiums. Benefits are not exempt where they fall to be taken into account in computing the insured's trading or similar profits, or where the insured person was entitled to deduct the premiums in the computation of his income tax liability. (HMRC treat benefits paid under insurance policies taken out by medical practitioners in respect of locum and fixed practice expenses in the event of the policyholder's incapacity or illness as taxable professional receipts, and the premiums as deductible.)

Certain other income is specifically directed to be charged under ITTOIA 2005: e.g. certain rents, interest paid by registered industrial and provident societies, loans against life assurance policies (see 1465), and under-deductions from payments made before passing of the annual Finance Act.

Legislation: ITA 2007, s. 7, 12, 16, 18

Case: *Peracha v Miley (HMIT)* [1990] BTC 406

Tax Reporter: ¶327-000

1368   Gross or net: payments out of profits or gains brought into the charge to income tax

Subject to the important exceptions noted below, where an 'annuity' (see 1396) is paid, or an 'annual payment' (see 1398) is made, in a tax year when the payer has sufficient income chargeable to income tax to match the gross payment, the payer has a right to deduct a sum equal to basic rate income tax thereon. That deducted sum is treated as income tax paid by the payee. The payment, less tax, fully discharges the payer's obligation to the payee. The computation of the payee's total income must include the gross amount of the payment, i.e. the amount actually received plus the amount of the tax deducted by the payer. The payee usually receives a certificate showing the relevant amounts and may otherwise demand one.

The payer's taxable income includes the amount which he is liable to pay to the payee. The payer therefore compensates himself by keeping the tax he has deducted from the payment made to the payee. Personal allowances are available to the payer as though his income excluded the gross amount of the payment made to the payee (see 1850).

Although the payer's taxable income includes an amount equivalent to the payments, such profits are generally taxable only at the lower or basic rate, i.e. the payments attract higher rate relief.

A tenant who fails to deduct tax from rent paid to a non-resident landlord may not be able to set off the amount which should have been deducted against subsequent payments. This contrasts with views expressed in relation to the requirement that tax must be deducted when amounts are paid out of funds not chargeable to income tax (see 1370).

Legislation: ITTOIA 2005, s. 727–729 and Sch. 2, para. 147

Cases: *IR Commrs v Crawley* [1987] BTC 112; *Tenbry Investments Ltd v Peugeot Talbot Motor Co Ltd* [1992] BTC 547

1370   Gross or net: payments made out of profits or gains which are not brought into the charge to income tax

Subject to the important exceptions noted in 1368, where an 'annuity' (see 1396) or 'annual payment' (see 1398) (other than interest) is paid in a tax year when the payer lacks sufficient taxable income fully to match the gross payment, the payer must deduct income tax from the payment and to account to HMRC for it. The deduction is made at the basic rate. The payment, less basic rate tax, made to the payee discharges the payer's obligation to the payee. The payee usually receives a certificate showing the relevant amounts and may otherwise demand one.

Where a payment is made in a later tax year than that in which it fell due, an allowance is made where the payment, if made on the due date, could have been paid wholly or partly out of taxed income.

All chargeable profits must be exhausted before it can be said that the payment is made other than out of profits or gains brought into the charge to tax.

Legislation: ITA 2007, Pt. 15; FA 2004, Pt. 3, Ch. 6; EC Directive 90/435

Cases: *Taylor v Taylor* [1938] 1 KB 320; *Johnson v Johnson* [1946] P 205; *Tenbry Investments Ltd v Peugeot Talbot Motor Co Ltd* [1992] BTC 547

Other Material: ESC A16, *Annual payments (other than interest) paid out of income not brought into charge to income tax*

1372   Gross or net: interest

Investments with banks and building societies

From 6 April 2016, *Finance Act* 2016 removes the requirement upon deposit-takers (such as banks), building societies and other institutions to deduct sums representing income tax from the interest or other returns they pay on certain savings, investments and alternative finance arrangements. The changes have effect in relation to interest paid or credited on and after 6 April 2016.

Prior to 6 April 2016, in respect of interest on most deposits made by individuals with savings institutions, the bank, building society, etc. was obliged to deduct and account for basic rate tax (at 20%). The tax deducted was repayable where appropriate, though non-taxpayers could complete a certificate permitting gross payment. The payee usually received a certificate showing the relevant amounts and could otherwise demand one.

The scheme applied in principle to any building society or any person who received deposits in the course of business as a prescribed deposit-taker.

For tax years up to and including 2015–16, interest could be paid gross to investors in the following circumstances:

- on payments to tax-exempt charities (see 900 and 901);

- on payments to companies (including unincorporated associations such as clubs or societies), local authorities and health service bodies;

- on payments to the trustees of unit trust schemes;

- on certificates of deposit (including paperless ('dematerialised') certificates) and sterling or foreign currency time deposits providing that the loan is not less than £50,000 and is repayable within five years;

- on general client deposit accounts;

- on accounts held at overseas branches of UK and foreign banks and building societies; and

- under 'repos' (see 1378).

Distributions and interest in respect of quoted securities issued by building societies are subject to a direct tax deduction requirement equivalent to that for non-bank interest (see below) rather than the above scheme (interest payable by a deposit-taker on any security may fall directly within such non-bank regime on definitional grounds, although generally covered by the exclusions); this does not apply to certain certificates of deposit issued in paperless ('dematerialised') form, which are 'gross payments' under the scheme. This duty to deduct continues unaffected by the *Finance Act* 2016 changes and the removal of the requirement upon deposit-takers and building societies to deduct income tax on interest or other returns.

Non-taxpayers (for tax years up to and including 2015–16)

Non-taxpayers could complete a certificate claiming gross payment in order to avoid having income tax deducted at source. If a building society incorporated, the registration was carried forward. Gross interest registration forms could be signed by a parent, spouse or civil partner, son or daughter of a mentally incapacitated person; a receiver or other person appointed by the court to manage the affairs of such a person can also register on their behalf. The TaxBack pages of the HMRC website (www. hmrc.gov.uk/taxback/index.htm), also explained some important points and contained a copy of the relevant form (R85):

- a parent or guardian could register a child's account if the child's total income is expected to be below the tax threshold, although registration was not possible if interest of £100 or more arises on money provided by either parent;

- a separate form needed to be completed for each account;

- completed forms needed to be taken to the bank, building society, etc. which would make the necessary arrangements;

- each joint holder who did not expect to be taxable was required to complete a form and where, say, two individuals had a joint account and only one of them expected to be a non-taxpayer, the institution could offer to pay gross interest on the non-taxpayer's share of the interest (where tax was deducted, it was reclaimable).

There was a maximum penalty of £3,000 for a person making a false declaration in order to receive gross interest or failing to notify the institution of becoming liable to tax. HMRC have indicated that the penalty would not be applied where taxpayers have acted in good faith; in these cases, an assessment, or coding adjustment, would be made to collect any tax which was due.

People claiming a repayment of the tax deducted from bank and building society interest did not need to wait until the end of the tax year, so long as the amount at stake was £50 or more. Those who were entitled to self-certify could obtain repayment of tax previously deducted in the same year by completing R85 and submitting it to the bank, building society, etc. (although not all payers would agree to this).

Client moneys (for tax years up to and including 2015-16)

Tax on dividends paid gross by building societies and payments representing interest in respect of a general client account, paid gross by a bank, etc. or building society by virtue of being exempt from the basic rate deduction requirements, was not generally pursued from non-residents (see 1366). The following HMRC-approved aide-memoire dealt with the tax treatment of interest received on clients' money in most normal situations.

Aide-memoire of normal situations prior to 6 April 2016

Type of account	*Payment of interest by bank or building society*	*Consequences*
A Designated – where subject to tax deduction.	Net	Pay net to client, who gets basic rate tax credit. No further tax deductions for non-residents (unless the solicitor is assessable as an agent).
B Designated – where paid gross (client money generally).	Gross	Pay gross to client who is assessable on payment as gross income. No deduction of tax for non-residents (unless the solicitor is assessable as agent).
C Bank and building society general client account deposit – always paid gross (client money generally and stake money).	Gross	Pay gross to client who in turn is assessable on payment as gross income; in practice solicitor assessed on net interest after setting-off this payment. No deduction of tax for non-residents.

Interest paid by and to companies

Where annual interest is paid by a company, a partnership of which a company is a member, or any person to another person whose usual place of abode is outside the UK, the payer must deduct income tax. However, there is no such obligation in the case of certain specified payments, including payments to a person within the charge to corporation tax in respect of interest on an advance from a bank. Where interest is paid to a company within the charge to corporation tax, the receipt is taxed under the loan relationships provisions. If the loan relationship is for trade purposes, yearly interest received will be a credit which falls to be taxed as part of the company's profit. However, the obligation to deduct income tax remains.

Gilt interest

Interest received on gilt-edged securities, where taxable, is charged under ITTOIA 2005.

For companies interest on certain gilt-edged, securities may be paid without deduction of tax.

Legislation: ITA 2007, s. 892, 893; FA 1998, s. 37; F(No. 2)A 1997, s. 37; TMA 1970, s. 99A; *Income Tax (Deposit-takers and Building Societies) (Interest Payments) (Amendment) Regulations* 2015 (SI 2015/653); *Income Tax (Gilt-Edged Securities) (Gross Payments of Interest) Regulations* 1995 (SI 1995/2934); *Income Tax (Deposit-Takers) (Interest Payments) Regulations* 1990 (SI 1990/2232), reg. 1–9

1374   Non-bank interest

Where 'yearly interest' (see 2089) is chargeable to tax and is paid:

- otherwise than in a fiduciary or representative capacity, by a company or local authority;
- by or on behalf of a partnership of which a company is a member; or
- by a person to another person whose usual place of abode is outside the UK (other than to a UK branch outside the scope of any treaty exemption),

then the person by or through whom the payment is made must, on making the payment, deduct out of it a sum representing the amount of basic rate income tax thereon in force for that year. This does not apply to certain interest including the following:

- interest payable in the UK on an advance from a bank carrying on a genuine banking business in the UK (this can include UK branches of overseas banks); or
- interest paid by such a bank in the ordinary course of that business.

Accordingly, in the above two cases the payment is made without deduction of income tax. Where tax is deducted, the payee usually receives a certificate showing the relevant amounts and may otherwise demand one.

Annual interest paid after 8 October 1991 is eligible for gross payment if the terms and conditions of the borrowing (whether for capital or revenue purposes) are broadly the same as those offered by the other UK banks on comparable borrowings; however, interest on certain loans, relating to the capital structure of a bank is to be treated as subject to withholding.

Where tax is deducted on making the payment, the payer must deliver up that tax to HMRC. Until the rate has been fixed for any tax year, tax is accounted for at the rate applicable in the previous year (though Budget resolutions are usually made in sufficient time for them to be applied); where the rate falls, any over-deduction must be made good either by payment or by adjustment of the following interest payment. Where agreements refer to amounts less tax or of fixed net amount, they are taken to refer to the gross amount if no deduction is required.

Subject to special provisions for interest on quoted Eurobonds, public revenue dividends (see 1402) and foreign dividends (see 1654), other types of interest, whether yearly or 'short', are paid gross without any deduction being made by the payer.

Except in relation to certain of the special provisions, above, the requirements are apparently unaffected by an EC Council directive dealing with abolition of withholding taxes on interest and royalty payments made between parent companies and subsidiaries in different member states.

Legislation: ITA 2007, s. 874–879; *Provisional Collection of Taxes Act* 1968, s. 2; EC Directive 90/435

Other Material: SP 4/96, *Income tax: interest paid in the ordinary course of business*

Tax Reporter: ¶327-000

1375 Gross or net: manufactured dividends or interest

Manufactured payments are made by one party to a transaction in securities to a second party. They take the place of 'real' payments of interest or dividends that the second party would have received but for the transaction. They arise in a variety of situations, but in particular when stock is lent or sold under a repurchase agreement. From 1 July 1997, the previous complex legislation concerning manufactured dividends was replaced by simplified provisions. Regulations about manufactured interest and dividends provide detailed rules about how the tax due each quarter from those involved is to be accounted for (see below).

Manufactured interest on UK securities

Manufactured interest is any payment by one of the parties to a contract (or other arrangement) for the transfer of UK securities to the other party, which represents a periodical payment of interest on those securities. In relation to the manufacturer, the interest is treated for tax purposes as if it were an annual payment to the recipient, but is neither annual interest nor an amount payable wholly out of profits or gains brought into charge for income tax purposes. The manufacturer is liable to make an annual return of such payments.

A payer who is resident and trading in the UK should deduct tax from the payment at the lower rate, unless the payment relates to either manufactured gilt interest or other interest which is normally paid gross.

The gross amount of the payment is deductible in computing the amount of his profits for tax purposes and in the recipient's hands the manufactured interest is treated as if it were real taxed interest. However, if the payer is not resident and trading in the UK, the recipient must account for income tax of an amount equal to that which the payer would have had to deduct had he been resident and trading in the UK.

The interest manufacturer must provide a tax voucher to the recipient showing the gross and net amounts of the manufactured interest, the tax deducted and the date of payment.

Accounting for tax

The machinery for collecting income tax on company payments applies, with modifications, to payments of manufactured interest on UK securities received by UK-resident companies (or non-resident companies which receive such payments for the purposes of a trade carried on by them in the UK through a branch or agency) from non-resident interest manufacturers. The recipient companies (or any person claiming title through them) are treated as if the payment received had borne income tax by deduction. Provision is made for liability for tax in circumstances where the interest manufacturer in question is in receipt of the real interest of which the manufactured interest is representative.

Manufactured interest on gilts

Tax does not have to be deducted from manufactured interest on gilt and certain other securities, either by the manufacturer or the recipient.

Manufactured dividends on UK equities

A manufactured dividend paid by a UK-resident company is treated in the same way as its real counterpart, subject to treatment as a dividend (with a responsibility to account for ACT until its abolition from 6 April 1999: see 3000). In all other cases, an amount equivalent to the ACT which would have been due had the payer been a UK-resident company must be paid over to HMRC. This should be paid by the manufacturer, if he has a presence in the UK, or the recipient.

In either case, the payer must provide a voucher to the recipient in the same way as if the manufactured payment were a real dividend. The voucher should show the amount of the manufactured dividend, the date of payment and the amount of tax credit to which the recipient is entitled.

Provided that the dividend manufacturer is UK-resident and is not a company, the amount of the manufactured dividend actually paid, together with an amount equal to the notional ACT, is allowed as a deduction in computing profits for income tax. However, where the payer is a non-resident company, no deduction is allowed.

Accounting for tax

Provision is made for accounting for tax in relation to manufactured dividends on UK equities other than manufactured dividends paid by UK-resident companies. The tax accounted for on manufactured dividends on UK equities by UK branches of non-resident companies can be set off against corporation tax on their profits.

Manufactured dividends representative of foreign income dividends

A manufactured overseas dividend is a payment, representative of an overseas dividend, made by one party to a transfer of overseas securities to the other. The payment was treated as a foreign income dividend (see 1350) made by the manufacturer until 5 April 1999 (when the foreign income dividend scheme was abolished). The manufacturer was not liable to account for ACT on it.

The recipient of a manufactured overseas dividend was treated for tax purposes as having received a foreign income dividend. He too was not liable to account for ACT on the amount received.

Where the dividend manufacturer was UK-resident and not a company, he was entitled to deduct, in computing his profits for tax purposes, an amount equivalent to the net manufactured payment made. He could not deduct an amount equal to the notional ACT on the payment.

The payer had to provide a tax voucher to the recipient in the same way as if the payment had been a real foreign income dividend. The voucher showed the amount of the manufactured dividend, the date of payment and the fact that the dividend carried no entitlement to a tax credit, etc.

Stock lending and deemed manufactured payments

From 1 July 1997, the legislation relating to transfers of equities under approved stock lending arrangements (see 646) was repealed, as was legislation relating to the tax treatment of interest earned on cash collateral provided in connection with certain stock lending arrangements, and stock lending does not give rise to an income tax charge. (Similar changes have been made to the CGT rules.) As there are now no restrictions on terms under which stock lending is carried out, anti-avoidance legislation prevents stock lending being used to switch dividend income from one person to another for tax reasons. If a stock lending arrangement does not provide for manufactured payments to be made, then such payments are deemed to have been made stock lending arrangements.

Sale and repurchase of securities: deemed manufactured payments

Price adjustments made in lieu of 'manufactured payments' under agreements for the sale and repurchase of securities are treated in the same way as actual manufactured payments.

Manufactured dividends after 6 April 1999

As a consequence of the abolition of the requirement to account for advance corporation tax (ACT) on actual distributions with effect from 6 April 1999 (see 1350), it is confirmed that ACT will not have to be provided for on manufactured dividends either.

Unallowable purpose provision

Finance Act 2004 introduced an 'unallowable purpose' rule for manufactured payments. It applies only where the manufactured payment is made by a company. Broadly, 'relevant tax relief' is restricted where that relief is attributable to manufactured payments made by a company in pursuance of arrangements having an unallowable purpose. The restriction applies only to the extent that, on a just and reasonable basis, the relief is attributable to the unallowable purpose. However, before the new rule can apply the following conditions must be met:

- a company must make, or be deemed to make, a manufactured payment in pursuance of arrangements to which it is party; and

- the arrangements, or any transaction entered into in pursuance of them, must have an unallowable purpose.

Arrangements have an unallowable purpose at any time where the purposes for which the company is party to the arrangements or to any transaction in pursuance of them or to any related transaction include a purpose which is not amongst the business or other commercial purposes of the company. The business or commercial purposes of a company are defined to exclude the purpose of any part of its activities which is outside the scope of corporation tax. Tax avoidance is an unallowable purpose if it is the main or one of the main purposes for which the company is party to the arrangements. Tax avoidance means a purpose that consists in securing a tax advantage for the manufacturer or any other person. Where the relevant conditions are met, then relevant tax relief attributable to the manufactured payment is disallowed on a just and reasonable basis. The restriction can apply only to the company that makes the payment. It follows that where that person would not otherwise receive relief for the payment, for instance because it is representative of a dividend on UK equities and the manufacturer is not within the scope of ITTOIA 2005, s. 366(1) then the rule can have no effect.

The rule will not operate where any relief for the manufactured payment could be restricted under the existing unallowable purpose rule in the loan relationships legislation. For accounting periods starting on or after 1 April 2004, the new management expense rules contain an unallowable purpose rule. Again, the new manufactured payments rule will not apply where relief is restricted under this provision.

Relevant tax relief is any of the following:

- any deduction in computing profits or gains for the purposes of corporation tax;
- any deduction against total profits;
- any debit brought into account under the loan relationship provisions; and
- the surrender of any amount by way of group relief.

The basic rule is that the new rules apply to all manufactured payments made on or after 2 July 2004, subject to certain transitional provisions.

Legislation: FA 1997, Sch. 10; FA 2004, s. 136, 137; *Manufactured Interest (Tax) Regulations* 1997 (SI 1997/992); *Manufactured Dividends (Tax) Regulations* 1997 (SI 1997/993)

Tax Reporter: ¶327-000

1376 Interest on damages

Where the courts award interest on damages or debts, the position appears to be that, except as noted below, if the interest is paid for more than one year it is yearly interest upon which tax must be paid (see 1366). The fact that the payee's tax rate may be affected because the interest is paid to him all in one year is irrelevant. If the person paying the interest is an individual, he must pay the interest as a gross sum and the payee will be responsible for the tax. But if the payer is a company or a local authority, tax must be deducted from the payment before it is made (see 1372).

Interest on damages for personal injuries are excluded from the above and are exempt if awarded by a UK court. (This extends to foreign court awards if the interest is exempt from tax in the appropriate territory.) Where such damages are paid by way of an annuity, the sum paid is, after 1 May 1995, to be paid without deduction of tax. This also applies to criminal injuries compensation paid after 8 November 1995 by way of an annuity.

Legislation: ITTOIA 2005, s. 731–734

1377   Interest on overpaid student loan repayments

Borrowers will start making loan repayments under the income-contingent student loans scheme from April 2000. For borrowers paying tax under PAYE, HMRC will collect the repayments, based on income, from their employers. A borrower who, at the end of the loan, turns out to have paid too much will get a refund with interest which will be tax-free.

Legislation: ITTOIA 2005, s. 753

1378   'Bondwashing': accrued income scheme on purchase/sale of interest on securities

Interest or dividends on stocks and shares do not become 'income' until they become due and payable. No apportionment of interest which actually becomes due and payable is made over the period in respect of which it is paid. Certain anti-avoidance provisions have been introduced to prevent the avoidance of tax by broadly purchasing shares or securities just after a dividend or interest has been paid and selling them just before a dividend or interest becoming due, or by sale and repurchase around a dividend or interest payment.

Sale and repurchase of securities

Sale and repurchase transactions (REPOs) involve the sale for cash and repurchase of the same or similar securities by the 'original holder' at a repurchase price fixed at the time of the original transfer to the 'interim holder'. Any fluctuations in market value are therefore borne by the original holder, who must repurchase the securities at a fixed price. The difference between the sale and repurchase price of securities (the price differential) is treated as interest on the recipient for the purposes of the Taxes Acts. (Correspondingly, the payer can treat the difference between purchase and repurchase prices as an interest expense for tax purposes.)

Securities covered by the accrued income scheme (below) are excluded from these provisions but may, instead, be subject to similar rules within the manufactured payment regime (see 1375).

Transfer of interest

Where the owner of a security transfers only the right to receive the interest from it, the interest is deemed to be that of the owner of the security for tax purposes.

Accrued income scheme

If the owner of securities sells them just before a certain date (fixed by the stock exchange), he will not be entitled to that year's interest on them. The new owner will receive it. This is called selling 'cum dividend' or 'cum interest'. If the securities are sold after that date, the original owner will remain entitled to that year's interest despite the fact that the securities have been transferred to a new owner. This is called selling 'ex dividend' or 'ex interest'.

Under the 'accrued income scheme', where securities are transferred, accrued interest reflected in the value of the securities is taxed separately as income at the lower rate (10% for 2005–06), instead of the basic rate, of tax from 1998–99 though not for trustees or taxpayers liable at the higher rate. The seller is treated as entitled to the proportion of interest which has accrued since the last interest payment. The purchaser is entitled to relief of the same amount. Where securities are sold ex dividend the tax charge falls on the transferee, in respect of interest attributable to the remainder of the interest period.

If the amounts to which a person is treated as entitled in a particular period exceed the amounts of relief, he is charged to income tax on the difference. If the relief exceeds the amount of deemed interest, the taxpayer is entitled to an allowance. The sale and repurchase of securities can, in certain REPO arrangements, be excluded from the application of the accrued income scheme.

The scheme does not apply where the seller:

- carries on a trade and the sale is taken into account in computing his trading profits;
- did not hold securities with a nominal value exceeding £5,000 during the tax year in which the interest period ends (this limit applies to husband and wife jointly);
- was neither resident nor ordinarily resident in the UK during any part of the period in question; or
- is taxed on the interest under manufactured payment rules (see 1375).

Special provisions may apply in relation to securities held by a company associated with the issuer, so as to establish both a time and a method for determining the quantum of chargeable income deemed to arise in relation to such debts (see 3027).

Purchase and sale of securities

Special provisions apply where there is a purchase of securities by a person (called the first buyer) and then a subsequent sale by him, the result of which being that the interest becoming payable in respect of those securities is received by the first buyer.

These provisions vary according to whether the first buyer is a dealer in securities and whether he is entitled to exemptions. Dealers are discouraged from buying and selling securities in this way by reducing the amount which they can deduct for tax purposes in respect of the accrued dividend and, from 2 July 1997, requiring them to include all distributions from such securities in the calculation of trading profit. Market makers are exempt from these anti-bondwashing provisions, and they do not apply in the case of certain REPO agreements. Relief extends to all principal traders on LIFFE, in relation to hedging transactions and transactions entered into as a result of the exercise of options.

The charge will not generally arise if the period between the purchase and sale is more than six months or, in the case of most options, one month.

Interest payable under REPOs after 30 July 1997 does not trigger the above provisions.

The accrued income scheme (above) generally takes precedence over the above provisions, so that securities acquired by the first buyer after 27 February 1986 are covered by that scheme.

Legislation: ITTOIA 2005, s. 151–154; *Income Tax (Dealers in Securities) Regulations* 1992 (SI 1992/568)

1395 Securities issued in tranches: additional returns

Where securities of a given class are not all issued at the same time, but in stages ('tranches') any additional return paid to the second or subsequent issue to compensate for the fact that interest is accruing on the earlier issue(s) is treated as interest.

The deemed interest in point will then be chargeable to tax in the same way as actual interest (see 1366).

Legislation: ITA 2007, s. 845

1396 Annuities

An annuity is *always* an annual payment, but *not all* annual payments are annuities. Annuities usually comprise income bought from insurance companies.

Annuities are specifically included within the charge to tax in respect of annual payments (see 1366).

An annuity has been described as income purchased with a sum of money when the capital has gone and has ceased to exist, the principal having been converted into an annuity.

Debts paid by instalments are not annuities because liability for the capital sum remains.

A purchased life annuity (see 1898) is actuarially dissected into non-taxable capital and taxable income elements, the income element being received net of basic rate income tax; the mortality tables have been revised with effect where the first payment begins to accrue on or after 1 March 1992.

Annuities from FSAVC schemes

A flaw in the original legislation has meant that pensions paid as a result of free-standing additional voluntary contribution (FSAVC) retirement schemes could be taxable in the same manner as purchased annuities above: i.e. with a non-taxable capital element. However, the intention was that annuities from FSAVC schemes should be taxed in full in the same way as other pensions for which tax relief has been given for the contributions, and the legislation has accordingly been amended to achieve this. The amendment is deemed to have always applied.

Legislation: ITTOIA 2005, s. 717–724

Case: *Lady Foley v Fletcher* (1858) 28 LJ Exch 100

Tax Reporter: ¶345-000

1398   Annual payments

The charge to tax as income on annual payments refers to any interest, annuity or other annual payment (see 1366). In general, those annual payments other than interest or annuities in point are those which are construed along the same lines as interest and annuities. However, decided cases indicate that annual payments must be:

- capable of continuing for more than one year;
- payable under a binding legal obligation;
- of an income nature; and
- subject to the provision of permitted benefits by charities (see 901), pure income profit in the hands of the recipient.

Tax Reporter: ¶346-200

1400   Discounts generally

Where a bill or promissory note is bought by someone before it matures, the price the buyer will pay for it will be less than the value of it on maturity. The profit the buyer will make on maturity is called a discount (see 1366) unless it is a trading profit.

In one case, the Court of Appeal said that trustees had acquired a promissory note before maturity at less than its face value. On maturity, they had made a profit which was a plain case of a discount received on a discounting transaction. Whether a receipt was of an income or capital nature was dependent on the facts. In the present case, the only proper conclusion was that the excess received was of an income nature, and so it was chargeable under former Sch. D, Case III as a discount.

There are special rules for certain securities issued at a large discount (see 1401).

Case: *Ditchfield (HMIT) v Sharp* [1983] BTC 360

1401   Securities with significant discounts

Background

As part of the reform of provisions dealing with corporate debt or 'loan relationships', the income tax treatment of securities issued at a significant discount became divorced from that applicable for corporation tax. From 1996–97, a charge to income tax is made in respect of relevant discounted securities (RDSs) with the abolition altogether of provisions relating to deep discount securities and deep gain securities (including qualifying convertible securities and qualifying indexed securities).

Relevant discounted securities

An income tax charge arises on sale, exchange, gift, redemption, conversion or death by reference to the proceeds (or deemed proceeds) less acquisition cost and incidental costs. A RDS is, subject to specific exclusions, any security issued at a deep gain, i.e. more than one-half of 1% of the redemption price for each year of the security's life (or 15% for a security with a life of more than 30 years).

Example

Dickens plc issues a security on 1 January 2015 at 80 for redemption on 31 December 2019 at 100.

Discount is $((100 - 80)/100) \times 100 = 20$.

This is more than 0.5×5, so the security is an RDS.

Each of the following is expressly not an RDS:

- shares;

- unstripped gilts;

- life assurance policies;

- capital redemption policies;

- securities issued under the same prospectus where the preponderance of the securities so issued are not RDSs;

- 'excluded indexed securities', i.e. chargeable assets for which the redemption value is found by increasing its issue price in the same proportion as the change in value of specified assets or an index over them (excluding the RPI).

A loss may be set against other income for the tax year on the making of a claim within one year of 31 January next following the year of loss, i.e. some 22 months. Allowable incidental costs can increase a loss but cannot turn a profit into a loss. There are special rules for losses of trusts, pension funds and charities.

Market value is substituted on a transfer between connected persons, for a consideration not in money or money's worth or not at arm's length.

There are special rules for securities issued in separate tranches and for gilt strips.

The definition of a 'relevant discounted security' has been amended to block an avoidance device that relied on a weakness in the previous definition. The defining test now applies to the discount at maturity, and at any occasion on which the security may be redeemed (except for redemptions triggered by a default, which is unlikely to happen).

This applies to:

- any transfer of a security on or after 15 February 1999; or

- any occasion on or after 15 February 1999 on which the holder of a security becomes entitled to any payment on its redemption.

Legislation: FA 1999, s. 65

Tax Reporter: ¶346-200

1402 Investment in public funds

The rules relating to the deduction of tax in respect of public revenue dividends (i.e. any income paid in respect of securities which is paid out of the UK public revenue except interest on local authority stock) are in ITA 2007, Pt. 15, Ch. 5: in particular, s. 892, which provides that:

'The person by or through whom the payment is made must, on making the payment, deduct from it a sum representing income tax on it at the savings rate in force for the tax year in which it is made.'

Legislation: ITA 2007, Pt. 15, Ch. 5

1404   Maintenance receivable on separation and divorce

Following separation or divorce, maintenance payment arrangements are often made between the spouses. Most maintenance payments are periodical payments which would fall to be taxed in the same way as other annual payments (see 1398). However, there are special rules for certain types of payment.

Voluntary payments have never been taxable for the recipient.

Legally binding payments, whether under a court order or an agreement, are not taxable if they fall due after 14 March 1988 unless they are made in pursuance of 'existing obligations' at that date. From 6 April 2000, this is also the case in relation to arrangements made prior to 15 March 1988.

Legislation: ITTOIA 2005, s. 727(1)

Case: *Morley-Clarke v Jones (HMIT)* [1985] BTC 460

Tax Reporter: ¶115-660

1406   Patent royalties

Patent royalties may be annual payments (see 1398) as well as trade or professional receipts. UK patents only last 20 years and are, therefore, wasting assets.

A UK resident who sells patent rights for a capital sum is charged to income tax on the receipt on the net proceeds. An election may be made either for such a sum to be chargeable only in the period of receipt (e.g. where the sale is at a loss) or for spreading of the sum over six years. Under self-assessment, such an election must be made to HMRC in writing before the first anniversary of 31 January following the tax year of receipt or payment. Previously, it had to be made within two years of the chargeable period in which the amount was received or paid, as the case might be.

A non-UK resident who sells UK rights for a capital sum is charged to income tax, but the purchaser will deduct tax from the payment and account for it to HMRC (see 1683); this is subject to relief under any double taxation agreement (see 1780).

Legislation: ITTOIA 2005, s. 587–590; *Patents Act* 1977, s. 25

Tax Reporter: ¶115-900

1408 'Tax-free' arrangements for making annual payments

Where an 'annual payment' (see 1398) is expressed to be made free of tax, it is in fact made after tax where a deduction should have been made (see 1368).

The usual way of clarifying the situation is to use the formula 'the payment of such an amount as shall, after the deduction of basic rate income tax for the time being in force, bear the sum of £x p.a. in the payee's hands'. Such a formula is typical, for example, in deeds of covenant.

If the payee is liable to the higher rate of tax, he will bear this without recourse to the payer, and if the payee is not liable to income tax, he can claim repayment without having to account to the payer for the tax reclaimed. The gross amount of the payment will vary only with a variation in the rate of basic rate tax (see Key Data section for details).

Annuities under wills

An arrangement to pay an 'annuity' (see 1396) free of tax constitutes an arrangement to pay an amount which, after basic rate tax has been deducted from it, leaves the desired amount in the hands of the payee. The payee is then liable for any higher rate tax which may be due on the payment. Where a payment under a will is directed to be paid free of tax, the direction is treated as one to pay an amount which leaves the amount directed to be paid to the payee, in the payee's hands, after basic rate tax has been deducted from it. In addition, for the payment to be tax-free, the payee will have to be indemnified for any excess tax that he may have to bear because he is a higher rate taxpayer.

Thus, an arrangement to pay an annuity free of tax is void, but this does not apply to a direction under a will though the effect is essentially the same for a basic rate taxpayer.

Legislation: TMA 1970, s. 106(2)

Case: *Re Pettit* [1922] 2 Ch 765

1410   Child Trust Fund

Until August 2010, all children born since September 2002 received an initial government voucher worth at least £250, with those from low-income families receiving an additional £250 paid directly into their accounts, making £500 in total. However, government contributions to CTFs were reduced to a basic £50 from August 2010 and ceased completely from 1 January 2011.

A further universal payment of £250 has formerly been made to the child at age seven, with children from low-income families receiving £500. However, such contributions ceased with effect from August 2010.

With regards to tax, there will be no tax to pay on the income or gains arising on the monies in the account, provided the person entitled to the fund is UK resident at the time the fund is paid out. This makes CTFs an attractive and tax-efficient way of saving for parents and carers wondering how they will ever be able to afford seemingly ever-increasing educational fees.

From April 2015, parents and guardians are allowed to transfer CTFs to Junior ISAs.

The annual subscription limit for Junior ISAs and Child Trust Funds is £4,080 for 2016–17.

HMRC have launched a consultation seeking views on the potential consequences of removing the legislative requirement that stakeholder child trust fund (CTF) accounts should be subject to 'lifestyling'. Around three quarters of CTFs held are stakeholder accounts. These are stocks and shares accounts containing 'stakeholder' features and protections set out in legislation. One such feature is the requirement that stakeholder CTFs must usually be subject to 'lifestyling' – a process designed to manage risk and volatility in account investments as the CTF approaches maturity. Currently, unless the registered contact for the account (usually the parent of the account holder) has instructed otherwise, the process of lifestyling a stakeholder CTF must have started by the time the account holder reaches 15. This means that CTF providers should start lifestyling some of their accounts by 2017–18 at the latest. The consultation will gather views and evidence about the costs and benefits of lifestyling for CTF account holders and providers. It also seeks views on the potential consequences of removing the requirement that stakeholder CTFs should be subject to lifestyling.

Legislation: *Child Trust Funds Regulations* 2004 (SI 2004/1450, as variously amended).

1412 Disguised investment management fees and carried interest

Managers of investment funds are rewarded in a variety of ways. Management fees are charged to tax as income, and legislation in FA 2015 was introduced to ensure that fee income could not be disguised as a form of capital receipt ('DMF rules') (ITA 2007, Pt. 13, Ch. 5E).

The income tax charge applies from 6 April 2015, in respect of disguised fees arising on or after that date, whenever the arrangements were entered into and applies to certain fees or other sums paid to investment managers and to sums paid through structures involving partnerships, unless they are already charged to income tax as employment income or brought into account in calculating profits.

Finance Act 2016 makes further changes to the DMF rules to ensure they apply to individuals who have performed or will, in the future, perform investment management services (i.e. there is no requirement that the individual performs investment management services in the year in which the sums arise); to remove the requirement for a partnership in the arrangements (e.g. to be present in the investment scheme or management structure) as was a condition of the rules as originally introduced, and to make clear that the DMF rules apply to sums arising from any investment scheme, not just a scheme in respect of which an individual performs investment management services.

Carried interest

Managers also receive performance-based rewards, sometimes known as 'carried interest'. 'Carried interest' is a form of performance linked reward, contingent upon the assets in the fund making a specified level of return over the life of the fund, and is specifically excluded from the income tax charge under ITA 2007, Pt. 13, Ch. 5E. Sums allocated to an individual in satisfaction of carried interest are treated, for tax purposes, as though the individual had carried out the transactions which gave rise to the sums and accordingly, may be chargeable to income tax or capital gains tax.

Prior to 6 April 2016, the test as to whether a sum is chargeable to income tax or capital gains tax has been based on case law and centred around the so-called 'badges of trade'. The case law underlying this test has mainly considered trades connected with areas such as manufacturing and retail with the result that the test is more difficult to apply to a business such as asset management. Accordingly, from 6 April 2016, *Finance Act* 2016 introduces a legislative test to determine whether performance-based rewards (or 'carried interest') paid to asset managers should be taxed as income or as chargeable gains. (ITA 2007, Pt. 13, Ch. 5F)

Tax treatment under the new rules will be determined by testing the average period for which the fund holds assets. All returns which are not subject to capital gains tax will be chargeable to income tax and Class 4 National Insurance contributions as trading profits.

ITA 2007, Pt. 13, Ch. 5F provides broadly, that where an individual performs investment management services for a collective investment scheme, then any sum of carried interest arising from that fund will only be eligible for capital gains tax treatment if the fund holds investments, on average, for at least four years. Partial capital gains tax treatment will be available where the average holding period is between three and four years. Where the average hold period is below three years, all sums of carried interest arising to the individual – however structured – will be charged to tax and NICs as trading profits. The provisions apply to sums of carried interest arising on or after 6 April 2016.

Finance Act 2016 also makes provision that where an individual first comes into the UK having performed *pre-arrival services* in the UK, the carried interest referable to those services is treated as profits of a distinct and separate trade carried on by the individual meaning that if the manager is domiciled outside the UK, he or she will be potentially able to access the remittance basis in relation to profits of the pre-arrival trade.

Legislation: ITA 2007, Pt. 13, Ch. 5E, Ch. 5F

Tax Reporter: ¶131-000ff.

Transactions in securities: anti-avoidance

1416   Introduction

The provisions aimed at cancelling tax advantages obtained through 'transactions in securities' were first introduced in 1960. At that time, there was no tax on capital profits and therefore if company profits could be extracted in a capital form, rather than as dividends, a significant income tax saving could be achieved. For example, the owners of a company with undistributed profits could sell their shares at a price which reflected those profits and pay no tax.

If the sale was to a dealer in securities, the dealer would extract the profits by way of a large dividend and then sell the company on at a loss which was set against the dividend income, resulting in a repayment of the tax which was, in those days, deducted from the dividend. This was termed 'dividend-stripping'. Even with the introduction of capital gains tax in 1965, it was still advantageous to realise a capital profit rather than receive the same amount as income.

To counter such transactions and others which sought to extract profits from companies in capital form, legislation was introduced by *Finance Act* 1960 which allowed for counteraction to be taken to cancel out the tax advantage arising from the transaction. These provisions have been largely unchanged over the years until they were rewritten, for income tax purposes, in the *Income Tax Act* 2007, which introduced cosmetic changes in terminology. (The original provisions in the *Income and Corporation Taxes Act* 1988 were then only applicable to companies and have recently been rewritten and incorporated into the *Corporation Tax Act* 2010).

Following an 'Anti-avoidance Simplification Review' launched at the time of the 2007 Pre-Budget Report and a public consultation exercise in 2009, *Finance Act* 2010 has redrafted the income tax provisions in respect of income tax advantages obtained on or after 24 March 2010. It is claimed that the new provisions are simpler and ensure that 'all relevant transactions that involve tax avoidance are within its scope.'

Legislation: ITA 2007, Pt. 13, Ch. 1

Case: *Griffiths v JP Harrison (Watford) Ltd* [1963] AC 1

Tax Reporter: ¶339-300

1420 Transactions within the scope of the legislation from 24 March 2010

The provisions which enable HMRC to take counteraction against income tax advantages obtained as a consequence of one or more transactions in securities apply where:

- the individual is a party to one or more transactions in securities;

- either Condition A or Condition B is satisfied (see below);

- the individual's main purpose (or one of his main purposes) in being a party to any one of the transactions is to obtain an income tax advantage; and

- that purpose is actually fulfilled in that an income tax advantage is obtained as a consequence of the transaction or the combined effect of the transactions.

However, an overriding protection from counteraction applies where there is a 'fundamental change in ownership'.

From 6 April 2016, ITA 2007, s. 684 is amended by *Finance Act* 2016 so as to consider 'the purpose of the transactions' in place of 'the purpose of a person being party to a transaction' and extended so as to apply also to a tax advantage obtained by any person, not just the person who is a party to the transaction. *Finance Act* 2016 also clarifies that a repayment of share capital or share premium is a transaction in securities and also extends the definition of transaction in securities to include a distribution in respect of securities in a winding up (ITA 2007, s. 684(2)(e) and (f)).

Condition A

This condition is satisfied where:

(1) as a result of the transaction in securities, or as a result of any one or more of a number of such transactions;

(2) the individual (or, from 6 April 2016, a relevant person) receives 'relevant consideration' on which he is not liable to income tax and which is received in connection with:

  (a) the distribution, transfer or realisation of assets of a close company;

  (b) a close company applying its assets in discharging liabilities; or

  (c) a transfer of assets between close companies, whether directly or indirectly. (Where this relates to share capital (other than redeemable capital), Condition A only applies so far as the share capital is repaid. For this purpose, any distribution made on a winding-up or dissolution of a company is to be regarded as a repayment of share capital.)

Relevant person

For the purposes of the amendments applied by *Finance Act* 2016 from 6 April 2016, a relevant person means the party to the transaction, or any person other than the party to the transaction who obtains a tax advantage as a consequence of the transaction or the combined effect of the transactions (ITA 2007, s. 685(3A)).

Condition B

This condition is satisfied where:

(1) the individual (or, from 6 April 2016, a relevant person) receives 'relevant consideration' on which he is not liable to income tax and the consideration is received in connection with the transaction in securities or any one or more of a number of such transactions. (Note that Condition A requires the consideration to be received as a result of the transaction, whereas Condition B only requires the receipt of the consideration to be in connection with the transaction); and

(2) two or more close companies are concerned in the transactions in question.

Income tax

Where a transaction in securities relates to a transfer of share capital (other than redeemable capital), Condition B only applies so far as the share capital is repaid. For this purpose, any distribution made on a winding up or dissolution of a company is to be regarded as a repayment of share capital.

Relevant person

For the purposes of the amendments applied by *Finance Act* 2016 from 6 April 2016, a relevant person means the party to the transaction, or any person other than the party to the transaction who obtains a tax advantage as a consequence of the transaction or the combined effect of the transactions (ITA 2007, s. 685(3A)).

Relevant consideration

The definition of relevant consideration varies according to its context.

In Condition A where the consideration is received in connection with either a close company disposing of assets or using them to discharge liabilities, it is consideration which:

- is or represents the value of assets which can be distributed as a dividend or assets which could have been distributed but for some action taken by the company;
- is received in respect of the company's future receipts; or
- is or represents the value of the company's trading stock.

Where Condition A applies because of a transfer of assets between close companies or where Condition B applies, 'relevant consideration' is that which consists of any share capital or security issued by a close company which is or represents the value of assets which:

- can be distributed as a dividend or which could have been so distributed but for some action taken by the company;
- are trading stock of the company.

Fundamental changes in ownership

An income tax advantage is not liable to counteraction where the individual (or, from 6 April 2016, the party) held shares (or an interest in shares) in a close company immediately before the transaction in securities (or the first in a number of such transactions) and there has been a 'fundamental change in ownership'. This is intended to take bona fide commercial sales of companies outside the remit of these provisions and no doubt to cut out the desire on the part of tax advisers to apply for clearance applications in such cases.

Transactions occurring on or after 6 April 2016

Amendments by *Finance Act* 2016 change the way that the 'fundamental change of ownership' rule applies. The new rule considers what the original shareholders of the company still hold after the transaction or transactions, rather than considering the new ownership structure. The new rule provides that there will be a fundamental change of ownership where the original shareholder or original shareholders taken together with any associate or associates:

- do not directly or indirectly hold more than 25% of the ordinary share capital of the close company;

- do not directly or indirectly hold shares in the close company carrying an entitlement to more than 25% of the distributions which may be made by the close company; and

- do not directly or indirectly hold shares in the close company carrying more than 25% of the total voting rights in the close company.

(ITA 2007, s. 685(2)–(5)).

Transactions occurring before 6 April 2016

For a fundamental change in ownership to occur, three conditions need to be satisfied for a period of two years from the date of the transaction in securities (or the first in a number of such transactions). These are that, as a result of the transaction(s):

(1) at least 75% of the ordinary shares are beneficially held by a person or persons who are not connected to the individual and who have not been connected within the two years ending when the transaction (or the first transaction) takes place;

(2) those shares carry the right to at least 75% of the dividends which might be paid by the company; and

(3) those shares also carry at least 75% of the voting rights in the company

In effect, this means a normal sale to unconnected persons. There is, however, a slight problem in the wording in that this 75% holding by unconnected persons has to arise 'as a result of the transaction in securities'. No protection seems to be afforded where these conditions are already satisfied before the transaction. An individual holding, say, 20% of the ordinary shares in a close company would not necessarily be connected with the other shareholders (unless they were his relatives or companies under his control). If that company had distributable reserves but had never paid a dividend, the sale of his shares would not be a fundamental change in ownership and the exemption would be of no use to him. (He may nevertheless seek advance clearance, perhaps on the grounds that his main objective was to realise his investment rather than obtain an income tax advantage.)

A further limitation on this exclusion is the insistence that the remaining shareholders are not connected with the individual vendor. Given that this legislation is now aimed at close companies and that the vast majority of such companies are family owned, this exclusion can never apply in respect of transfers of shares within a family (gifts excluded). It would only be of use where the whole of the share capital is sold to an outsider. In all other cases an advance clearance application will be necessary.

Legislation: ITA 2007, Pt.13, Ch. 1

Tax Reporter: ¶339-750

1422 Meaning of 'tax advantage'

From 24 March 2010, an income tax advantage is obtained where the income tax which would be payable by the individual (or, from 6 April 2016, a person) in respect of the 'relevant consideration' if it was treated as a distribution, exceeds the amount of any capital gains payable in respect of it.

In arriving at this notional income tax liability, the relevant consideration is limited to the maximum amount which could have been payable to the person (or, from 6 April 2016, an associate of the person) as a dividend. Thus, if the relevant consideration exceeds the company's distributable profits, the notional income tax liability is restricted to tax on the amount which could have been paid as a dividend under company law.

The amount of the income tax advantage is the excess of the notional income tax liability over any capital gains tax payable in respect of the relevant consideration.

Even if it has been established that an income tax advantage has been obtained, from 24 March 2010, it must also be established that the individual's main purpose, or one of his main purposes, in being a party to the transaction in securities or any transaction in a series of transactions in securities (or from 6 April 2016, the main purpose of the transaction(s)), is to obtain that advantage (see 1420).

Legislation: ITA 2007, s. 687

Cases: *Marwood Homes Ltd v IR Commrs* (1996) Sp C 106; *IR Commrs v Universities Superannuation Scheme Ltd* [1997] BTC 3; *Grogan v R & C Commrs* [2009] TC 00187

Tax Reporter: ¶339-550

1426 Clearance procedure: tax advantage from transactions in securities

A procedure exists for advance clearance of transactions in which there is a potential tax advantage which may be challenged by HMRC (see 1416). Where the taxpayer provides HMRC with details of the transactions concerned, HMRC must either give or refuse clearance, or request further details, within 30 days.

HMRC will only refuse clearance where they would actually take action to cancel the tax advantage.

Legislation: ITA 2007, s. 701

Tax Reporter: ¶340-700

Life policies, life annuities and capital redemption policies

1460 Gains on life assurance policies, investment bonds, etc.

Because insurance policies can be used as investment vehicles, a profit may be able to be obtained in excess of the premiums paid. That is a capital profit rather than income. However, that profit represents an accumulation of income generated by the investment of premiums by the insurance company, therefore, the profit is brought into charge to income tax, rather than capital gains tax.

See further 1465ff.

Tax Reporter: ¶343-050

1465 Chargeable events

The profit is deemed to arise on the happening of a chargeable event, basically when value is received, or deemed to be received, from the policy. As the profit will have arisen over a period of years, a form of 'top-slicing' relief is available to mitigate the effects of all the profit being taxed in one year.

The chargeable event regime applies to:

- policies issued in respect of life insurance contracts;
- contracts for life annuities; and
- capital redemption policies (the statutory definition of a capital redemption policy is not helpful; it merely tells us that it is a contract

issued in the course of a capital redemption business (ITTOIA 2005, s. 473(2)). Such a business is defined elsewhere as effecting contracts, on an actuarial basis, which provide for a specified payments to be made at some future date or over a future period in return for one or more fixed payments (FA 2012, s. 56(3)),

where they were effected on or after 20 March 1968.

However, where a life insurance contract was made before that date but the terms varied afterwards so as to increase the benefits secured or to extend the term of the insurance, it was treated as being within the scope of the regime. Nevertheless, a variation made before the end of 1968 was ignored if it was only made to conform with the qualifying conditions for endowment policies and it varied a policy previously conforming except for the amount guaranteed on death and no increase was made in the premiums payable under the policy.

Certain policies are specifically excluded from the scope of the charge, whilst other policies are subject to special rules, in particular what are termed 'qualifying policies', personal portfolio bonds, foreign policies and certain older policies.

The regime as originally implemented applies to each individual policy or contract and provides that the amount of a gain that may be liable to income tax is the difference between the value of benefits paid from a policy and the total of premiums paid into the policy and certain gains arising earlier in the life of a policy. However, in order to counter exploitation by the use of 'cluster policies', policies and contracts issued or varied on or after 21 March 2012 which are 'connected' with each other are to be treated as a single policy or contract.

Other qualifying conditions are specific to the type of policy concerned, for example:

- foreign policies;
- whole of life policies;
- term insurance policies;
- endowment policies; and
- whole of life and term assurance policies taken out on or after 1 April 1976 subject to additional conditions .

Finance Act 2013 amended the definition of qualifying policy to exclude policies taken out on or after 21 March 2012 where the premiums exceed an annual limit of £3,600. The logic behind this proposal is that, because there is no restriction on the amount of premiums which can be paid in to qualifying policies, they can be used to avoid higher and additional rate tax on the resulting profit generated from those premiums. Restricting the premiums in this way would thereby restrict the amount of tax-free profit which could be received on maturity or surrender, etc. For HMRC guidance, see the HMRC website at www.hmrc.gov.uk/news/life-insurance-policies-faqs.pdf

Legislation: ITTOIA 2005, s. 473–526

Other Material: www.hmrc.gov.uk/news/life-ins-policy-faqs.pdf

Tax Reporter: ¶343-500

1482 Non-resident life assurance policyholders

For policies issued in respect of contracts made on or after 6 April 2013, FA 2013, s. 24 and Sch. 8 introduced a time-apportionment relief to recognise periods of non-UK residence during the period the policy has run, regardless of the issuer of the policy. Originally, such relief only applied where the gain arose from a foreign life or capital redemption policy.

Relief will now be available where the individual is on a gain from a life or capital redemption policy, wherever issued and there are one or more days during the policy period on which he is both non-resident and on which he satisfies at least one of the three conditions (i.e. he is the beneficial owner, the settlor of the trust which holds the rights under the policy or the rights secure his debts). The days in the policy period on which he satisfies any one of those three conditions is termed the 'material interest period'. In addition, and where there has been an assignment between spouses or civil partners before the chargeable event, the material interest period includes so much of the policy period before the assignment during which the assign or met any of those three conditions. The relief is given by reducing the gain by the fraction representing the number of days of non-residence in the material interest period over the total number of days in the material interest period.

Where the gain arises on a policy issued in substitution for an earlier policy, the policy period is regarded as beginning on the issue of that earlier policy and, if that earlier policy was itself a substitute, from the date of the even earlier policy and so on.

Deceased policy holders

The relief is also extended to gains arising to the personal representatives of a deceased policy holder, and to gains arising to trustees in respect of a deceased settlor, on a similar basis as for individual.

The previous prohibition on relief where the policy was held by non-resident trustees or a foreign institution was repealed from 6 April 2013.

Transitional provisions

The new relief will also apply in respect of contracts made before 6 April 2013, where, after that date:

- the policy/contract is varied to increase the benefits secured;
- the individual (or the deceased) becomes entitled to a share in the rights under the policy/contract as the result of an assignment (whether for consideration or not); or
- some or all of the rights under the policy/contract become held as security for a debt of the individual (or the deceased)

Legislation: ITTOIA 2005, s. 528

Other Material: ESC C33: *Non residents and gains on life insurance policies*

Tax Reporter: ¶344-440

1485   Personal portfolio bonds

Following a 1997 decision, a charge to tax has been imposed on 'personal portfolio bonds'. Such a bond is a policy of life assurance where the assets backing the policy and giving rise to the benefits under the policy are personal to the individual policy holder, who may have significant control over those assets. Such policies retain many of the benefits of direct investment, while the policy holder is able to defer taxation of investment income and gains by choosing the date of surrender, or to escape taxation altogether by becoming non-resident before the policy is surrendered.

Legislation: ITTOIA 2005, 526(1)–(2); FA 1998, s. 89; *Personal Portfolio Bonds (Tax) Regulations* 1999 (SI 1999/1029)

Case: *IR Commrs v Willoughby* [1997] BTC 393

Tax Reporter: ¶343-600

1495   Accident insurance policies

Subject to certain conditions, exemption from income tax is provided for benefits paid under insurance policies to those who make arrangements to protect themselves financially in the event of accident, sickness, disability, infirmity or unemployment. The benefits covered will include those paid under some kinds of long-term care insurance. Where an employer has taken out a group policy to meet the cost of sick pay for his employees, benefits received under the policy and passed on to an employee are also exempt if and to the extent that the employee has contributed to the premiums.

Other Material: SP 6/92, *Accident insurance policies: chargeable events and gains on policies of life insurance*

Tax Reporter: ¶133-150

Foreign income and double taxation

1550　Introduction to foreign income

The tax treatment of income derived from overseas sources, or of income arising in the UK to someone from abroad, often depends on whether the person liable to tax is resident, (until 5 April 2013) ordinarily resident or domiciled in the UK. These terms are explained in more detail in 224, 226 and 227ff. Double tax relief (see 1780ff.) might apply in cases of income having a foreign source and in cases of dual residence, where the UK and another jurisdiction both claim taxing rights under their domestic fiscal regimes.

Non-resident partners

In the case of a partnership, under self-assessment, a non-resident's share of partnership profits is treated as arising from a trade carried on in the UK by the non-resident partner alone. Equivalent provisions for non-resident companies which are members of partnerships ensure that corporate partners only pay UK tax on their share of partnership profits arising in the UK. The non-resident company's share is treated as arising from a trade carried on by it through a UK branch or agency.

Legislation: ITTOIA 2005, s. 857–858

Other Material: RDR1: *Residence, domicile and the remittance basis*

Tax Reporter: ¶288-500

Employees' foreign income

1560　The charge to tax on foreign income

In general, whether income arising from an employment is subject to tax depends upon the 'residence' (see 224) and (until 5 April 2013) 'ordinary residence' of the taxpayer (see 1572). 'Domicile' is important in so far as emoluments may then become foreign emoluments eligible for relief (see below).

The place of performance of duties is also critical. For a discussion of incidental duties, see 1572. Where duties are ordinarily performed in the UK, emoluments during any absence from employment are related to UK duties unless, but for that absence, they would have been emoluments for duties performed outside the UK; an airline pilot's rest days were not attributable to duties performed outside the UK – in order to bring himself within the exception, the taxpayer would have to show that had he worked on those days his actual duties would have been performed outside the UK and it did not matter that most of his time was spent on duties abroad.

Except in relation to such foreign emoluments as are mentioned above, any person who is resident in the UK is liable to income tax on the whole of his earnings wherever earned and irrespective of whether they are remitted to the UK. The taxpayer may be entitled to a special deduction where his duties are carried out wholly or partly outside the UK (see below) and in many cases double taxation relief will apply (see 1780ff.).

An employee resident in the UK is liable to tax on earnings from duties performed in the UK, under ITEPA 2003, s. 25 and 26.

The relative levels of the emoluments received here and abroad may not reflect the relative duties performed here and abroad. The split may be made simply to suit the employee's convenience and there may be scope for tax planning in this area. He may, therefore, be remitting to the UK emoluments received abroad but attributable to the UK duties. Each case must be studied on its facts.

HMRC will accept that the total emoluments may be apportioned between UK and overseas duties on the basis of working days, unless there are special circumstances.

An employee who is not resident in the UK is only liable to tax on earnings from duties performed in the UK, under ITEPA 2003, s. 27.

A person may be entitled to a deduction from his earnings where the earnings from his employment are 'foreign emoluments'. Foreign emoluments are the earnings of a person who is:

- not 'domiciled' (see 227) in the UK; and

- the earnings are derived from an office or employment which is with an employer who is not 'resident' (see 224 and 225) in the UK or the Republic of Ireland.

Basis of charge

Emoluments are taxed in the year in which they are received, rather than earned. However, liability to the charge depends on residence and/or ordinary residence in the tax year in which the emoluments are earned.

Example 1

A bonus of £5,000 earned in 2015–16 when the employee was resident in the UK is chargeable to UK income tax and will be assessed for 2016–17 when it is received even if, following a move abroad, the employee is not resident in 2016–17.

Example 2

In the converse situation, an overseas resident who comes to work in the UK and is resident here in 2016–17 is not chargeable on a bonus received in 2016–17 but earned in 2015–16 when he was not resident here.

The charge to income tax remains fundamentally the same, with the same available deductions (see below).

Available deductions

There is a 100% deduction for seafarers' earnings derived from duties performed abroad where there is a 'qualifying period' consisting of at least 365 days (see 1567).

Other deductions, in respect of expenses, etc. are generally available in the same way irrespective of residence, ordinary residence or domicile (see 1990).

Legislation: ITEPA 2003, s. 38

Cases: *Langley v R & C Commrs* (2007) Sp C 642; *Leonard v Blanchard (HMIT)* [1993] BTC 138

Other Material: SP 1/09, *Employees resident but not ordinarily resident in the UK: general earnings chargeable under sections 15 and 26 Income Tax (Earnings and Pensions) Act 2003 (ITEPA) and application of the mixed fund rule under sections 809Q onwards of the Income Tax Act 2007 (ITA)*; RDR1: *Residence, domicile and the remittance basis*

Tax Reporter: ¶199-000

1567   Foreign earnings deduction for seafarers

The 100% deduction in determining the foreign earnings which are brought into charge to income tax (see 1560) was withdrawn for all office holders, and for all employees except seafarers, with effect from 17 March 1998. The definition of seafarers has also been clarified to exclude explicitly those employed on offshore installations for oil or gas exploration or extraction. FED now remains available only to the parts of the shipping sector for whom it was intended.

The foreign earnings deduction is thus unavailable to non-seafarers for emoluments attributable to 'qualifying periods' (see below) beginning on or after 17 March 1998, or to emoluments attributable to qualifying periods beginning before that date but received thereafter. The deduction remains available for emoluments attributable to qualifying periods beginning before 17 March 1998 and received before that date. For such relief, there must still be a full qualifying period, but part of it can fall after that date.

The deduction is calculated by reference to emoluments for the qualifying period *after* allowing such deductions as pension contributions, expenses and capital allowances.

To qualify for the 100% deduction, the duties of the employment must be:

• performed wholly or partly outside the UK; and

• performed in the course of a qualifying period consisting of at least 365 days, falling wholly or partly in any tax year.

For this purpose, seamen (and, before the deduction's withdrawal, aircrew) are generally treated as performing their duties abroad where the voyage (or journey) or any part of it begins or ends outside the UK; this applies notwithstanding the provision which treats such duties as performed in the UK for most purposes (see 1572). The days which a seafarer can spend in the UK as part of a qualifying period of absence are 183 days or one-half of the total days.

From 6 April 2011, the seafarers' earnings deduction is extended so that seafarers resident in the EU or EEA can also claim the deduction on their earnings as a seafarer where those earnings are liable to UK income tax.

Where duties of the employment are performed partly outside the UK, the earnings subject to the deduction are determined on a reasonable basis (see also 1578).

The European Commission has requested the UK to change its income tax provisions that allow a tax deduction for the earnings of seafarers who are resident in the UK but do not allow the same deduction for seafarers who are not resident in the UK.

Where a period of leave immediately follows a qualifying period, the earnings attributable to that leave generally qualify for the 100% deduction (such period not being part of a qualifying period: see below).

A 'qualifying period'

A 'qualifying period' is a period of consecutive days which consists of days of absence from the UK. The qualifying period need not coincide with a complete tax year in order to take advantage of the deduction.

The date of departure from the UK counts as a day of absence (the test being whether an individual is present in the UK at midnight on a particular day); the date of arrival does not. Days spent abroad on holiday can be included towards the 365-day period.

For seafarers who have previously been resident in the UK and who return to the UK following a period of absence abroad during which they have not been resident or ordinarily resident in the UK, such absences are not taken into account when calculating the qualifying period.

Legislation: FA 1998, s. 63; ITEPA 2003, s. 378; FA 2004, s. 136

Cases: *Robins (HMIT) v Durkin* [1988] BTC 195; *Torr v R & C Commrs and related appeals* (2008) Sp C 679; *Spowage v R & C Commrs* [2009] TC 00110; *R (on the application of Cameron) v R & C Commrs* [2012] EWHC 1174 (Admin)

Other Material: HMRC Brief 10/12; SP 18/91

Tax Reporter: ¶488-500

1572   Incidental duties: employments partly overseas

Duties performed in the UK which are merely incidental to duties performed abroad are treated as if they were performed abroad.

For the purpose of the 100% deduction for seafarers (see 1567), incidental duties performed abroad are treated as performed in the UK where the duties of the employment are in substance performed in the UK.

Whether duties performed in the UK are 'incidental duties' is a question of fact. It is the nature of the duties which is the most significant factor, but the time spent on such duties is also a factor to be taken into account.

The following duties appear to be regarded as incidental or not incidental to duties performed abroad (see booklet RDR1).

Not incidental	Incidental
(1) *Directors' meetings*	(1) *Overseas representative*
A company director, usually working abroad, attends directors' meetings in the UK.	An overseas representative of a UK employer comes to the UK to report to the employer or receive fresh instructions.
(2) *Three months or more*	(2) *Training*
Duties performed for an aggregate period of three months or more.	An overseas employee visiting the UK for a training period not exceeding three months in a year and where no productive work is done by him in that time.

Legislation: ITEPA 2003, s. 39(1), (2), 341(6), (7), 376(4), (5)

Case: *Robson v Dixon (HMIT)* [1972] 1 WLR 1493

Other Material: RDR1: *Residence, domicile and the remittance basis*

Tax Reporter: ¶293-400

1574 Travel expenses: employees' overseas duties

Deductible travel expenses for tax purposes are travel where the expenses would have been deductible when calculating earnings from employment and the travel would have fallen under the following categories:

- the travel expenses were necessarily incurred on travelling in performance of the duties of the employment;
- the travel was required for necessary attendance in the performance of the duties of the employment;
- the travel was travel between employments where the duties are performed abroad; or
- the expenses would have been deductible when calculating the profits of a trade.

Travel to or from a temporary workplace whilst working full-time overseas

An employee who:

- works full time overseas;
- has a permanent workplace overseas; and
- occasionally travels to a temporary workplace in the UK,

may claim the cost of travelling between their home overseas and the temporary workplace in the UK, which means that the time spent travelling is treated as time spent working.

Legislation: ITEPA 2003, s. 341, 342, 373, 374

Other Material: RDR1: *Residence, domicile and the remittance basis*

Tax Reporter: ¶199-000

1578   More than one job: tax avoidance through overseas earnings

Special provisions apply where the employee has two or more employments. These provisions are largely designed to prevent the 'loading' of earnings onto the overseas employment in order to avoid tax.

Where the duties of an employment and any associated employment (see below) are wholly performed abroad, the deductions referred to above will apply to all the earnings of the employment.

The 100% deduction for seafarers and the deduction relating to 'foreign emoluments' (see 1567) apply to only a proportion of the earnings from the employment abroad where the duties of the employment or any associated employment are *not* performed wholly outside the UK. That proportion is one which is shown by the employee to be reasonable having regard to the nature of the duties and the time devoted to them within the UK and abroad and other relevant circumstances.

An employment is an 'associated employment' of another employment for these purposes if they are with the same person or with persons associated with each other. A company is associated with another if one of them has control of the other or both are under the control of the same person or persons. An individual or partnership is associated with another person (whether or not a company) if one of them has control of the other or both are under the control of the same person or persons.

Legislation: ITEPA 2003, s. 23(3), 24, 329(1), 331(2)

Other Material: RDR1: *Residence, domicile and the remittance basis*

Tax Reporter: ¶199-000

1580   Special employees with foreign income

Diplomats

Diplomats and diplomatic staff are entitled to a number of exemptions from tax.

Visiting forces

Emoluments paid by the government of any designated country (basically, countries which are members of NATO are exempt from income tax where they are paid to a member of a visiting force of the designated country and that person is not a British citizen, a British Dependent Territories citizen or a British Overseas citizen.

Crown servants

The duties of Crown servants are, in general, treated as being performed in the UK. This is so where the duties are of a public nature and the emoluments are paid out of the public revenue of the UK or of Northern Ireland. The nature of the Civil Service and its duties are prima facie public. By concession, tax is not charged in the case of unestablished staff engaged locally if they are non-UK resident and are paid less than London staff.

Allowances given to any Crown servant representing compensation for the extra cost of having to live abroad in order to perform their duties are not regarded as income. Such allowances are not, therefore, liable to tax. To qualify for the exemption, the allowances must be certified by the Minister for the Civil Service as representing such compensation.

Oil rig workers

UK territorial waters are generally considered to be 12 nautical miles. The territorial sea is deemed to be part of the UK for the purposes of income, capital gains and corporation taxes.

The UK is also extended to certain parts of the continental shelf for tax purposes. Any earnings from an employment in connection with exploration or exploitation activities are treated as earnings for duties performed in the UK. This is so where the earnings are in respect of duties performed in an area of the continental shelf designated by Order in Council under the *Continental Shelf Act* 1964, s. 1(7). A non-UK resident company operating in such an area must make tax deductions under the PAYE system from employees' emoluments if the company has a 'tax presence' in the UK.

The benefit of free transportation of offshore oil and gas rig workers to and from the mainland, and of necessary overnight accommodation near the mainland departure point, are not charged to income tax.

Legislation: ITEPA 2003, s. 28, 299, 305; *Territorial Sea Act* 1987, s. 1; *Diplomatic Privileges Act* 1964; *Visiting Forces (Income Tax and Death Duties) (Designation) Order* 1964 (SI 1964/924); *Visiting Forces and Allied Headquarters (Income Tax and Death Duties) (Designation) Order* 1961 (SI 1961/580)

Cases: *Clark (HMIT) v Oceanic Contractors Inc* [1982] BTC 417; *Graham v White (HMIT)* [1972] 1 WLR 874

Tax Reporter: ¶199-000

1583   'Golden handshakes' where foreign service

Compensation payments made to employees for loss of office, etc. are wholly exempt from tax where the duties of the employment included 'foreign service'. Foreign service is such service during which the employee was not resident in the UK or else the emoluments of the service qualify for the 100% deduction (see 1567).

If the employee has been in foreign service, but this is insufficient to give full exemption from tax, part of the golden handshake may still be non-taxable. The amount which is not taxable will depend on the length of the foreign service in relation to the total length of service.

The foreign service, in general, must comprise one of the following:

* three-quarters of the whole period of service;

* the last ten years where the period of service exceeded ten years; or

* where the period of service exceeded 20 years, one-half of that period, including any ten of the last 20 years.

Legislation: FA 1998, Sch. 9

1585   Personal reliefs for non-residents

Non-UK residents are not entitled to 'personal reliefs' (see 1850ff.) except where the individual is:

* a national of a state within the European Economic Area (EEA), which comprises all EU states plus Norway, Iceland and Liechtenstein[1];

* a person who is or has been a Crown servant;

Note

[1] FA 2009, s. 5 and Sch. 1 withdrew the entitlement to personal allowances and reliefs for commonwealth citizens with effect from 6 April 2010.

- a widow (or from 1990–91, a widower) of a Crown servant;
- a missionary;
- a person in the service of a British protectorate;
- a resident of the Isle of Man or Channel Islands;
- a person who has been resident in the UK but is now resident abroad for the sake of his health or the health of a member of his family who resides with him.

In the above cases, the non-resident is entitled to the personal reliefs to which residents are entitled.

Most Hong Kong residents who were British Dependent Territories citizens were expected to have registered as British Nationals (Overseas) by 1 July 1997, when the Hong Kong Special Administrative Region came into existence, and therefore continue to be entitled to UK personal reliefs from that date. Of those not registering, only those who are citizens of other Commonwealth countries and/or the EEA will continue to benefit from the reliefs.

To ensure compliance with certain aspects of the *Human Rights Act* 1998, from 6 April 2010, entitlement for non-resident individuals who previously qualified for UK personal tax allowances and reliefs *solely* by virtue of being a Commonwealth citizen was withdrawn. Most individuals affected are still able to benefit through other means such as Double Taxation Treaties.

Legislation: FA 2009, s. 5; ITA 2007, s. 35

Other Material: RDR1: *Residence, domicile and the remittance basis*

Tax Reporter: ¶158-000

Remittance of income

1600   Importance of remittances

In most cases it is unimportant whether income of a person subject to UK tax arising abroad is remitted or sent back to the UK. In the majority of cases, income is taxed on an 'arising basis'. However, in some situations, income is only charged to UK tax if received in the UK.

Income falling within ITTOIA 2005 is usually charged on an arising basis; but the remittance basis may apply where the resident taxpayer is not domiciled in the UK or is a Commonwealth (including a British) citizen (or citizen of the Republic of Ireland). In the case of any income liable to tax on a remittance basis, tax is charged on the amount received in the UK on a current year basis.

Income falling within ITEPA 2003 is charged to tax on a remittance basis. Such income comprises emoluments of a person resident in the UK (see 224) derived from duties performed abroad.

It is not always easy to ascertain if amounts have been remitted to the UK (see 1603). Emoluments are treated as received in the UK if they are paid, used or enjoyed in the UK, or transmitted or brought to the UK; amounts treated as remitted which are not directly received are sometimes known as 'constructive remittances'.

Income received in a tax year after the source of the income has ceased to exist is not taxable on the remittance basis so long as the remittance is not in the same tax year.

No loss can ever arise on income taxed on the remittance basis.

Legislation: ITEPA 2003, s. 33

Case: *Joffe v Thain (HMIT)* (1956) 36 TC 199

Other Material: RDR1: *Residence, domicile and the remittance basis*

Tax Reporter: ¶199-620

1603   Whether income remitted to UK

Income considered as remitted to the UK need not necessarily be paid to the taxpayer (for the definition of remittance in relation to emoluments, see 1600); but income which is properly alienated abroad to another person is not regarded as remitted to the UK by the original owner if the new owner sends that money to the UK.

It is sometimes difficult to distinguish between income and capital, but, in general, the proceeds of investments purchased abroad with income that would be taxable if remitted are liable to tax as income if those proceeds are themselves remitted.

The fact that sums remitted are derived from a bank overdraft is not in itself sufficient to establish that the remittance is out of capital.

However, investments purchased out of income before taking up residence in the UK may be realised and the money remitted without liability.

Cases: *Walsh v Randall (HMIT)* (1940) 23 TC 55; *Carter (HMIT) v Sharon* (1936) 20 TC 229; *Timpson's Exors v Yerbury (HMIT)* [1936] 1 KB 645;

Fellowes-Gordon v IR Commrs (1935) 19 TC 683; *Kneen (HMIT) v Martin* [1935] 1 KB 499

Other Material: RDR1: *Residence, domicile and the remittance basis*

Tax Reporter: ¶199-620

1605   Delayed remittances

Difficulties may arise where income is liable to tax only when remitted to the UK (see 1600) if the taxpayer is prevented from remitting the income until some later stage when rates of tax may be higher. Relief can be obtained on making a claim. For the relief to apply, the taxpayer must:

- have been prevented from transferring the income to the UK, either by the laws of that territory or any executive action of its government or by the impossibility of obtaining foreign currency in that territory; and

- have used reasonable endeavour to transfer the income.

Legislation: ITEPA 2003, s. 35–37

Other Material: RDR1: *Residence, domicile and the remittance basis*

1607   Unremittable overseas income

Persons (including companies) who are liable to tax on their overseas income wherever it arises are (for example, because of foreign exchange controls) sometimes unable to remit the income to the UK. This can cause hardship in some cases. In certain circumstances, therefore, the overseas income will not be taken into account in assessing that person to tax.

Unremittable overseas income is the income arising abroad which:

- a person is prevented from transferring to the UK, either by the laws of that territory or any executive action of its government or by the impossibility of obtaining foreign currency in that territory;

- the person has used reasonable endeavour to transfer; and

- that person has not realised in some other currency which he is not prevented from transferring to the UK.

To take advantage of this relief, a claim must be made not later than the first anniversary of the 31 January from the end of the tax year (or, in the case of companies, two years from the end of the accounting period) in which the income arises. The relief will be given only as long as the three conditions above continue to be satisfied, i.e. the tax liability is only postponed, not removed.

Any appeal against an assessment where these provisions apply is to be made to the tribunal.

Legislation: ITTOIA 2005, s. 841–845

Other Material: RDR1: *Residence, domicile and the remittance basis*

Tax Reporter: ¶293-300

Trades, professions and vocations: foreign income

1620 Charge on foreign income from trade, profession or vocation

Income of a UK resident derived from a trade, profession or vocation (see 550ff.) which is carried on wholly abroad is liable to tax only if it was remitted to the UK where he is:

- not domiciled in the UK (see 227); or

- a Commonwealth (including a British) citizen or a citizen of the Republic of Ireland and is not (until 5 April 2013) 'ordinarily resident' (see 226) in the UK.

For whether income is remitted, see 1603.

In all other cases, the income of a resident is liable to tax whether or not the income is remitted. Income arising in the Republic of Ireland is treated as if it arose in the UK but is nevertheless entitled to the same deductions (and subject to the same limitation of reliefs) as apply to trades, etc. carried on abroad.

The income of a non-resident derived from a trade carried on wholly abroad is not liable to tax. However, a non-resident trading in the UK through a branch or agency is liable to tax on consequent profits (see 1622).

For double tax relief, see 1780ff..

Legislation: ITTOIA 2005, s 7(4); *Income Tax (Removal of Ordinary Residence) Order* 2014 (SI 2014/3062)

Tax Reporter: ¶293-000

1622 Trading in the UK

A 'non-UK resident' (see 224) trading in the UK is only liable to UK tax where he is trading through a branch or agency.

What constitutes a trade is dealt with at 555ff. Whether a person is trading in the UK through a branch or agency is a question of fact, but the distinction has to be made between trading with the UK and trading in the UK: soliciting orders in the UK will not by itself constitute trading in the UK. An important factor is whether the contract for sale or supply of services was made abroad, but the contract may not be conclusive.

Cases: *Firestone Tyre and Rubber Co Ltd v Lewellin (HMIT)* [1957] 1 WLR 464; *FL Smidth & Co v Greenwood* (1922) 8 TC 193; *Grainger & Son v Gough* [1896] AC 325

Tax Reporter: ¶293-350

1623   Business investment relief

Finance Act 2012 introduced a new business investment relief for individuals who are eligible to be taxed on the remittance basis. The relief allows such individuals to bring foreign income and gains to the UK tax free for the purposes of making a qualifying investment. If the investment subsequently ceases to qualify for the relief, the foreign income and gains will become taxable unless the investor takes certain mitigation steps within a specified period known as the grace period. In certain circumstances, HMRC may extend that grace period.

Legislation: FA 2012,   Sch. 12;   *Business   Investment   Relief Regulations* 2012 (SI 2012/1898)

1624   UK resident trading wholly abroad

An individual who is resident in the UK and carries on a trade, profession or vocation wholly abroad, either alone or in partnership, is liable to tax on all his income from such a trade. The income is assessed on a current year basis. Losses, etc. can only be set off against the income of that or another overseas source, foreign emoluments, other overseas income (see 1654ff.) and certain pensions (see 1640 and 1642).

However, a person who is not domiciled in the UK or else is a Commonwealth (including a British) citizen (or a citizen of the Republic of Ireland) who is not ordinarily resident in the UK is liable only on a remittance basis (see 1600).

Legislation: ITTOIA 2005, s. 7, 19, 227

Tax Reporter: ¶293-150

1625   Expenses connected with foreign trades

Special rules apply to travel expenses and board and lodging expenses incurred by an individual taxpayer whose trade, profession or vocation is carried on wholly outside the UK, and who has failed to satisfy HMRC that he is not domiciled here or else, being a Commonwealth (including a British) citizen (or a citizen of the Republic of Ireland) here.

Where the rules apply, the travel and board and lodging expenses are to be treated as deductible provided that the taxpayer's absence from the UK is wholly and exclusively for the purpose of performing the function of the foreign trade.

In certain conditions, travel expenses of the taxpayer's spouse or civil partner and any child of his are deductible.

Travel between foreign trades is also deductible, subject to conditions.

Legislation: ITTOIA 2005, s. 92–94

Tax Reporter: ¶293-400

1630   Non-resident entertainers and sportsmen

There is a system of withholding basic rate income tax from payments made to visiting, non-resident entertainers and sports personalities (see 1673). Except where the activity in point is performed in the course of an office or employment, it is treated as if it were a trade, profession or vocation exercised in the UK and the income from it plus payments connected with it are chargeable on a current year basis; it is stated that regulations dealing with the system generally can provide specifically for losses and reliefs.

Legislation: ITTOIA 2005, s. 13–14

Tax Reporter: ¶293-550

Foreign pensions

1640   Foreign pensions

Generally, pensions of UK residents are assessed to tax under the charge on employment income provisions, but in the case of foreign pensions the assessment is under the income from foreign possessions rules. These are pensions which:

- are paid by or on behalf of a person outside the UK; *and*
- are not pensions charged to income tax in respect of overseas public service (see 1642).

If a foreign pension or increase is granted retrospectively and the pension is chargeable to tax on an arising basis, the full amount of the award, including arrears, is assessable in one sum. However, where it is to the taxpayer's advantage, the tax is calculated as if the arrears (after making the deduction mentioned below) arose in the years to which they relate.

A pension or annual payment paid by or on behalf of an employer outside the UK to an ex-employee (or his widow, child, relative or dependant) is assessed under the income on foreign possessions rules even if paid voluntarily.

Foreign pensions paid to a UK resident are only liable to tax if remitted to the UK where the person entitled to the pension is:

- not 'domiciled' in the UK (see 227); or
- a Commonwealth (including a British) citizen or a citizen of the Republic of Ireland.

In most other cases, the pension is liable to tax whether or not it is remitted. Pensions which have their source abroad and are not taxed on a remittance basis are eligible for a 10% deduction. Pensions arising in the Republic of Ireland are treated as if they arose in the UK, but nevertheless attract the 10% deduction unless the pensioner is either not domiciled in the UK or a Commonwealth (including a British) or Irish citizen. Pensions payable under German or Austrian law in compensation to victims of Nazi persecution are exempt from income tax altogether.

Cases: *Albon v IR Commrs* [1999] BTC 138; *Aspin v Estill (HMIT)* [1987] BTC 553

Tax Reporter: ¶375-450

1642 Pensions from overseas public service

Certain overseas public service pensions and annuities paid to UK residents are assessed on a current year basis, but nevertheless attract a 10% deduction. These are pensions which are:

(1) payable in the UK;

(2) so payable through any public department, officer or agent of the government of any country forming part of the British dominions or any country mentioned in the *British Nationality Act* 1981, Sch. 3 or any British protectorate;

(3) paid to a person (or his widow, child, relative or dependant) who has been employed in the service of the Crown or in the service of such a territory as in (2) above; and

(4) paid in respect of that service.

This provision does not apply where the payment is out of the public revenue of the UK or of Northern Ireland.

Legislation: ITEPA 2003, s. 615

Tax Reporter: ¶375-450

Foreign investment income

1650   UK government securities: foreign income

An exemption from tax applies to UK government securities issued by the Treasury with a condition that the interest is not liable to tax where evidence is provided that the beneficial ownership of the securities is in a person not ordinarily resident in the UK though other conditions may be imposed – often termed FOTRA securities since they are free of tax to residents abroad.

The number of securities which are exempt varies with the redemption of old securities and the issue of new securities (the list current at any time may be obtained from FICO (International)). The income will not be exempt where, by any provision of the Tax Acts, it is deemed to be the income of any other person who is ordinarily resident in the UK. Special regard must be had to the anti-avoidance provisions concerning the transfer of assets by virtue of which income becomes payable to persons abroad (see 1700).

Banks and approved stockbroking firms can obtain block exemption from income tax on behalf of various overseas customers, irrespective of whether the relevant securities have been held for at least two dividend dates.

A non-resident who is trading in the UK would ordinarily be exempt where the interest forms part of the trading receipts; but in all cases to date, except with regard to the $3^1/_2$% War Loan, the Treasury has modified the exemption so as not to apply to trades or businesses carried on in the UK.

Special rules apply to non-resident banks, insurance companies and dealers in securities carrying on business in the UK.

Legislation: ITTOIA 2005, s. 73, 714, 716; FA 1996, Sch. 28

1652   Foreign government securities: foreign income

From 1996–97, overseas public revenue dividends fall within the ambit of provisions relating to 'foreign dividends' (see 1654).

Previously, although deduction of tax under Sch. C was broadly cast so as to apply to almost anyone in the UK handling such dividends, exemptions were provided in relation to securities held in a recognised clearing system or on proof that the person owning the securities, and entitled to the proceeds, was not resident in the UK.

1654   Foreign dividends

Whether a dividend emanates from a foreign possession depends upon the residence of the company.

From 1993–94, the foreign dividends above are generally charged at the same rate of income tax as UK dividends (see 1350).

Paying and collecting agents

Foreign dividends can be subject to a form of tax deduction or payment on account of the person entitled to them. The rules for UK paying agents and collecting agents were replaced in 1996. Foreign dividends now encompass overseas public revenue dividends (see formerly 1652). The replacement of the old rules involves little substantive change, but rather a reorganisation of the rules together with the codification (in some instances through regulations) of existing administrative practice.

Three requirements have to be met before a receipt becomes subject to the collecting agent rules:

(1)   a person of a specified type (bank, coupon dealer or person acting in the course of a trade or profession – including acting as a custodian of holdings – but not someone merely clearing a cheque);

(2)   performs a relevant function;

(3)   as a result of which he receives or otherwise realises the value of foreign dividends or quoted Eurobond interest (a 'relevant receipt').

Income tax deducted or to be accounted for is due and payable to HMRC 14 days after the end of the month in which the 'chargeable date' falls, i.e. the date on which the foreign dividends or quoted Eurobond interest obtained by a collecting agent are paid or the date on which the collecting agent sells or otherwise realises coupons for them.

For 2000–01 and with deemed effect for 1999–2000, the rate of income tax deducted by paying and collecting agents in relation to foreign income dividends is 10%.

Legislation: FA 2000, s. 111; FA 1996, Sch. 7; *Income Tax (Paying and Collecting Agents) Regulations* 1996 (SI 1996/1780); *Income Tax (Interest on Quoted Eurobonds) Regulations* 1996 (SI 1996/1779); EC Directive 90/435

Case: *Bradbury v English Sewing Cotton Co Ltd* [1923] AC 744

1656 Local authority securities in foreign currency

Interest on certain securities quoted in foreign currencies is paid without deduction of income tax and, so long as the beneficial owner is not resident in the UK, is exempt from income tax (but not corporation tax). Such securities are those issued by local authorities and statutory corporations which are the subject of a Treasury direction.

Legislation: ITTOIA 2005, s. 755–756

Tax Reporter: ¶132-900

1658 Annual interest as foreign income

Income from foreign 'securities' is charged under ITTOIA 2005 (former Sch. D, Case IV). Deep discounts on certain securities are specifically charged under this head (see 1401).

The person by or through whom a payment is made of annual interest of money chargeable to tax must deduct lower rate income tax (basic rate tax before 1996–97) before making the payment if the payment is to a person whose usual place of abode is outside the UK (see 1372). The tax deducted must be accounted for to HMRC. An exemption is provided for interest paid to non-resident holders of quoted Eurobonds held in a recognised clearing system (Euroclear, CEDEL, First Chicago Clearing Centre).

For provisions requiring paying or collecting agents for foreign interest to deduct tax, see 1654.

Where interest is paid gross to a non-resident (notably in the case of certain bank and building society interest: see 1372), HMRC will not pursue the income tax liability unless the person is chargeable in the name of a trustee, agent or branch in the UK (see 1672).

1660   Rent from properties outside the UK

Rent and other receipts from properties outside the UK are charged to tax under ITTOIA 2005. The profits or losses are normally calculated in the same way as those of a property income business (see 1200ff.). However, the property income business approach does not apply where the taxpayer is entitled to the benefit of the remittance basis (see below).

All businesses and transactions carried on or entered into by a person or partnership are treated as a single business (an 'overseas property business'). However, separate computations may be necessary for tax credit relief purposes where there are properties in different countries (see 1780ff.).

Where a person carries on a business of letting property situated in the UK and an overseas property business, the two businesses are treated separately. The special provisions relating to relief in respect of certain travel connected with foreign trades (see 1625), and furnished holiday lettings (see 1255) are disregarded in computing the profit or loss of an overseas property business.

> **Example**
>
> David travels to Tuscany and spends two weeks redecorating the villa which he lets to holidaymakers. The following week he goes on a walking holiday in the area. None of his travel costs are tax deductible (see 2020 and 2056).

Losses from overseas property business

Except for losses of a trade, etc. carried on wholly abroad, before 1998–99 there was no provision for relief for foreign income losses. However, deficiencies from overseas lettings could be carried forward and set off against future income from the same property. Currently, as all overseas lettings are treated as a single business (see above), excess expenditure on one such letting is automatically set against surplus receipts from other such lettings. Any overall loss can only be carried forward and set against future foreign rental business profits. See further 2030.

Remittance basis

The remittance basis (see 1600) may apply to rental income from overseas lettings where the taxpayer:

- is not 'domiciled in the UK' (see 227); or

- is a Commonwealth (including a British) citizen, or a citizen of the Republic of Ireland.

Legislation: ITTOIA 2005, s. 261, 265–365

Tax Reporter: ¶300-020

1663 Annual payments as foreign income

The remittance basis (see 1600) may apply to annual payments and similar income from foreign possessions where the taxpayer is not 'domiciled in the UK' (see 227) or in certain cases before 6 April 2013, is not 'ordinarily resident in the UK' (see 216). In other cases, such income is charged on an arising basis (i.e. on the full amount of the income arising).

Exempt annual payments include benefits paid under certain 'self-contained' insurance policies to those who make arrangements to protect themselves from financial losses caused by accident, sickness, disability, infirmity or unemployment, or from the cost of long-term care.

Legislation: ITTOIA 2005, s. 227, 229, 269, 610–617, Sch. 1, para. 606–607, 609

Tax Reporter: ¶346-700

1664 EU Savings Directive

Directive 2003/48/EC on the 'taxation of savings income in the form of interest payments' was adopted by the Council on 3 June 2003 and entered into force on 1 July 2005. It was repealed by Council Directive (EU) 2015/2060 of 10 November 2015, with effect from 1 January 2016 (subject to certain transitional provisions), follows a strengthening of measures to prevent tax evasion which had resulted in a significant overlap with other legislation in this field. The repeal eliminates that overlap.

It directed each member state to introduce legislation requiring businesses and public bodies established in that state (referred to as 'paying agents') who pay interest to, or collect interest on behalf of, EU-resident individuals, to report details of the payments and the payees to the tax authorities (art. 8). The directive also required that information relating to residents of another member state be passed on to the authorities in that state (art. 9). A paying agent was obliged to establish the identity and state of residence of the beneficial owner of the interest and in particular where there was evidence to suggest that the recipient was not the beneficial owner. Rules were provided setting out the minimum steps the agent was required to take to establish the identity and residence position of the beneficial owner (art. 2 and 3). Where the contractual relationship between the paying agent and the beneficial owner was established before 1 January 2004, the agent was to establish the owner's identity and residence position by reference to information at its disposal and with regard to the existing anti-money laundering legislation in force in its state of establishment implementing Directive 91/308/EEC (art. 2(a), 3(a)). Where the contractual relationship was established on or after 1 January 2004, or, where no contractual relationship existed, transactions taking place after that date, the agent had to establish identity and state of residence by reference to the owner's name, address and 'tax identification number' (if one existed) obtained from a passport, official identity card or 'any other documentary proof of identity presented by the beneficial owner' (art. 2(b), 3(b)). Member states were required to adopt the legislation necessary to implement the terms of the Directive by 1 January 2004 with a view to bringing it into force from 1 January 2005 (art. 17). However, the Council, using its powers under art. 17(3), decided to defer the start date to 1 July 2005, as it did not consider that the conditions set out in art. 17 for the Directive to come into force would be satisfied by the original date.

Legislation: FA 2003, s. 199; *Reporting of Savings Income Information (Amendment) Regulations* 2005 (SI 2005/1539); *Reporting of Savings Income Information Regulations* 2003 (SI 2003/3297)

Tax Reporter: ¶103-835

Assessment and collection of tax on foreign income

1670 PAYE and payment of tax on employees' foreign income

Tax will often be deducted by the employer under the PAYE system in respect of employees' earnings (see 2384). Entitlement to deductions will be taken account of as far as possible in the PAYE codings. However, this is not always possible: an employee working and paid abroad by a foreign employer may be directly assessed. HMRC will generally make an estimated assessment and tax will be collected in four equal instalments.

A non-UK resident company operating in a designated area of the continental shelf must operate the PAYE system if it has a 'taxable presence' in the UK.

Legislation: *Income Tax (Pay As You Earn) Regulations* 2003 (SI 2003/2682)

Case: *Clark (HMIT) v Oceanic Contractors Inc* [1982] BTC 417

Tax Reporter: ¶493-000

1671   Income from property assessments on non-residents

Income tax of persons normally living abroad arising from property in the UK is charged by way of deduction at source by the agent for the property or, where there is no agent, from the tenant, with a final settling-up with the non-resident under self-assessment. Tenants who pay rent of £100 or less per week do not have to operate the scheme unless asked to do so by HMRC. Non-residents may apply to HMRC for approval to receive their UK property income with no tax deducted provided:

- their UK tax affairs are up to date;

- they have never had any obligations in relation to UK tax; or

- they do not expect to be liable to UK income tax;

and they undertake to comply with all their UK tax obligations in the future. The regulations also set out details of annual information returns to be made by letting agents and tenants who have to operate the scheme, as well as other information to be supplied to HMRC on request. Landlords are non-residents for the purposes of the scheme if they have a usual place of abode outside the UK.

Legislation: ITA 2007, s. 971; *Taxation of Income from Land (Non-residents) Regulations* 1995 (SI 1995/2902)

Tax Reporter: ¶300-020

1672   Non-residents trading through UK representatives

Where a non-resident is carrying on a trade, profession or vocation in the UK, via a branch or agency, the UK branch or agent is treated as the non-resident's 'UK representative' in respect of:

- trading income arising directly or indirectly to the non-resident through the branch or agency;

- income from property or rights relating to the branch or agency;

- gains of the non-resident chargeable by virtue of TCGA 1992, s. 10 (essentially, gains on disposals of assets of the branch or agency).

Where the non-resident ceases to conduct a UK trade through the branch or agency, that branch etc. will continue to be the UK representative in relation to taxable sums which have already arisen. A UK representative is a legal entity distinct from the non-resident.

Where the branch or agency consists of a partnership, it is the partnership which is the UK representative, not any individual partner.

Where a non-resident trading in the UK through a branch or agency trades in partnership with others (i.e. the non-resident is a non-resident partner), the trade carried on by the branch or agency is treated as including the 'deemed trade' from which the non-resident's share of partnership profits is treated as deriving. In addition, if one of the non-resident's partners is a UK resident, the 'deemed trade' is treated as carried on in the UK by the partnership. The effects of this are that the partnership itself will be treated as the non-resident's UK representative and the UK partners will be jointly liable for the tax on the non-resident's share of the profits.

'Branch or agency' is defined as 'any factorship, agency, receivership, branch or management'.

Legislation: ITA 2007, s. 835C–835F

Other Material: SP 15/91, *The treatment of investment managers and their overseas clients*

Tax Reporter: ¶135-600

1673 Payment of tax by foreign entertainers and sportsmen

Where a payment is made in respect of an appearance by a non-resident entertainer or sportsman in the UK, the payer must deduct tax at the basic rate. This rule does not apply if:

- the payment is below £1,000;
- the recipient has agreed a lower or nil rate of withholding tax with HMRC.

Regulations give definitions of 'entertainers' and 'sportsmen', and detail the activities covered by the rules, the types of income subject to withholding, the deduction of expenses and the administration arrangements in connection with the procedure. The rules apply to fees and prize money, and also to associated income from advertising, sponsorship and endorsements. The deduction at source cannot be avoided by directing payment to a third party.

Tax is assessed on a current-year basis (see 1630).

Legislation: ITTOIA 2005, s. 13–14; *Income Tax (Entertainers and Sportsmen) Regulations* 1987 (SI 1987/530)

Tax Reporter: ¶293-550

1674   Returns for foreign secondees

An employer must, if required so to do, prepare and deliver to HMRC a return relating to persons who are or have been employed by him. Where a person performs the duties of an office or employment in the UK for a continuous period of at least 30 days and the employment is with a non-UK resident but the duties are performed for the benefit of a UK resident (or person carrying on a trade, profession or vocation in the UK), then the person benefiting from those services may be required to make a return of the name and address of the 'employee'.

Legislation: FA 1974, s. 24

Tax Reporter: ¶170-100

Intellectual property royalties as foreign income

1680   Copyright royalties as foreign income

Certain copyright or design royalties paid to an owner of the copyright, etc. who does not usually live in the UK are to be paid after deducting income tax at the basic rate. The tax retained must be accounted for to HMRC.

The amount of the payment of royalties can be reduced by any agent's commission before deducting income tax if the royalties are paid through an agent resident in the UK and he is entitled, as against the owner of the copyright, etc. to deduct commission. Copyright royalties include authors' public lending rights and the rules relating to returns and penalties for failure to deliver a return in respect of fees, commissions, etc. also apply accordingly.

Legislation: ITA 2007, s. 906, 907(1)

1683   Patent right disposals: foreign income

Basic rate income tax is deducted in accordance with the usual mechanism for deducting basic rate tax at source (see 1370) from the proceeds of sale of any UK patent by a non-resident and the proceeds (consisting wholly or partly of a capital sum but net of any capital cost attributable) are taxed on a current year basis. The seller can elect to have the proceeds of sale (net of any acquisition cost) treated as the income of the year of receipt and of the five succeeding years as if one-sixth was received in each tax year.

Legislation: ITTOIA 2005, s. 587–599

Transfer of income/assets abroad

1700 Deemed income where transferor receives benefit of transfer abroad

Overseas income of a person who is 'resident' (see 224) and 'domiciled' (see 227) abroad is not liable to tax in the UK. Special anti-avoidance provisions prevent an individual (or his spouse/civil partner) who is resident in the UK from obtaining a tax advantage by transferring his assets abroad in such a way that the income is paid to persons who are resident or domiciled abroad but is in some manner still enjoyed by the resident himself.

The income of any such transfer is regarded as that of the individual making the transfer where he has power to enjoy the income and, in particular, where:

- the income is used for his benefit;

- the income increases the value of any assets held by or for him;

- he receives or is entitled to receive any benefit out of that income or money which represents that income;

- he may become entitled to enjoy the income through the exercise of any power (e.g. where he is a member of a class of beneficiaries who may be entitled to income if a power within the trust is exercised); or

- he is able directly or indirectly to control the way the income is applied (a right to direct investments is not included, nor a power of appointment in connection with capital payments.

A transferor is also liable to tax on the income of the assets transferred if he is entitled to receive any capital sum the payment of which is in any way connected with the transfer. 'Capital sum' means:

- any sum paid or payable as a loan or repayment of a loan; and

- any other sum which is not income and which is not paid for full consideration in money or money's worth.

Any sum which a third person becomes entitled to receive is treated as a capital sum to which an individual becomes entitled if the third person's entitlement is at the individual's direction or is because of an assignment by the individual of his right to receive it.

Income is not treated as an individual's for any tax year merely because he has received a loan if the loan is wholly repaid before the beginning of that year.

An individual who is domiciled abroad is not liable to tax on income deemed to be his if it in fact had been his income and he would not have been liable to tax on it by reason of his domicile (this prevents these anti-avoidance provisions disrupting the normal operation of the remittance basis applying to non-domiciliaries: see 1600ff.).

Legislation: ITA 2007, Part 13, Ch. 2

Cases: *Lord Vestey's Exors v IR Commrs* (1949) 31 TC 1; *Vestey v IR Commrs* [1980] AC 1148; *IR Commrs v Brackett* [1986] BTC 415; *IR Commrs v Willoughby* [1997] BTC 393; *IR Commrs v Botnar* [1999] BTC 267

Tax Reporter: ¶129-700

1701   Deemed income where non-transferor receives benefit from transfer abroad

Anti-avoidance provisions dealing with the transfer of income-producing assets abroad generally charge only the transferor (see 1700). Additional provisions attack non-transferors who receive a similar benefit.

They apply where assets are transferred abroad (where the purpose or one of the purposes is to avoid tax) and:

- income becomes payable to a person 'resident' (see 224) or 'domiciled' (see 227) outside the UK; *and*

- an individual (until 5 April 2013)'ordinarily resident' (see 226) in the UK (and who is not the original transferor) receives a benefit out of the assets transferred.

The amount of the benefit is treated as the income of the recipient and charged to UK tax accordingly, and he is liable to income tax upon it in the year of receipt. This is so long as the amount received is not more than the relevant amount of income from the transferred assets which can be used for his benefit.

The relevant amount of income is the income up to and including the tax year in which the benefit is received. Any part of the benefit received which exceeds this relevant amount of income is taxed as the income of the next or subsequent years when it is covered by income which can be used for his benefit.

No income is to be taken into account more than once in charging tax under these provisions. HMRC have a discretion to apportion the income as it considers just and reasonable where there is more than one person liable under these provisions, including those charging the transferor (see 1700). The tribunal has jurisdiction to review such a decision.

An individual who is domiciled abroad is not liable to tax on income deemed to be his if in fact it had been his income and he would not have been liable to tax on it by reason of his domicile (this prevents these anti-avoidance provisions disrupting the normal operation of the remittance basis applying to non-domiciliaries; see 1600ff.).

Legislation: ITA 2007, Pt. 13, Ch. 2

Case: *A beneficiary v IR Commrs* (1999) Sp C 190

Tax Reporter: ¶129-700

Double tax relief

1780   Tax treaties

The UK has concluded a large number of tax treaties with other countries to avoid international double taxation and to prevent fiscal evasion. Tax treaties covering all usual areas of possible double taxation (comprehensive agreements) have been made. A list of all current and pending Tax Treaties can be found on the HMRC website.

Legislation: TIOPA 2010, Pt. 2; Convention 90/436

Tax Reporter: ¶170-050

1783   Types of double tax relief

There are different kinds of relief from double taxation.

- *Relief by treaty exemption* – certain categories of income are exempted from tax in whole or in part in one or other of the countries which are parties to the 'double taxation agreement' or 'double tax treaty' (see 1780).

- *Relief by treaty credit* – tax charged in one country may be available as a credit in the other.

- *Unilateral relief* – where there is no provision for double taxation relief, any foreign tax paid may nevertheless be available as a credit in calculating UK tax.

- *Relief by deduction* – the taxpayer can treat the foreign tax paid as a deduction from his taxable income (for example, the foreign tax suffered may be 'inadmissible' for credit relief: see 1789).

The provision made for double tax relief also apply to capital gains and chargeable gains of companies.

Whether HMRC will admit a foreign tax for unilateral double taxation relief in relation to business profits is determined by examining the tax within its legislative context in the foreign territory and deciding whether it serves the same function as income tax and corporation tax serve in the UK in relation to such profits (see 1789).

For the calculation and effect of the available relief, see 1789 and 1792.

Effect must be given to agreements, decisions or opinions in connection with transfer pricing made in accordance with the arbitration convention (see 1780) whether by assessment or discharge or repayment of tax.

Legislation: TCGA 1992, s. 277(1); TIOPA 2010, Pt. 2

Tax Reporter: ¶170-150

1786   Model treaty provisions as typically used in the UK

Two chief methods of relieving double taxation are adopted in 'tax treaties' (see 1780). First, taxing rights over certain classes of income are reserved entirely to the country of residence of the person deriving the income. Second, all other income may be taxed (in some cases, only to a limited extent) by the country of origin of that income; if the country of residence of the recipient also taxes that income, it must grant a credit against its tax for the tax levied by the country of origin (see 1783).

Many tax treaties are based on the 1977 or 1992 Model Convention published by the Organisation for Economic Co-operation and Development. They usually provide that a national from one territory should not be treated more harshly than a national from the other territory (a 'non-discrimination clause'; though the EC Treaty (formerly known as the Treaty of Rome) requires similar treatment within the EC, as noted at 1780): the matter in point must fall within the provision for the reliefs effected by arrangements agreed with foreign governments.

Some of the usual exemption provisions of treaties are noted below, but it is emphasised that each treaty must be looked at individually for its specific provisions.

Business profits

The profits of any business carried on by a resident of country A is taxable only in country A unless the business is carried on in country B through a permanent establishment (a fixed place of business, e.g. a branch, office, factory or mine) in country B. Where this is the case, the profits of the business are taxable in country B, but only to the extent that those profits are attributable to the permanent establishment.

Shipping, inland waterways and air transport

Profits from the operation of ships, aircraft or inland waterways transport are taxable only in the country in which the place of effective management of the relevant enterprise is situated.

Interest, dividends, royalties, non-government pensions

Interest, dividends, patent and copyright royalties, and non-government pensions are often taxable only in the country of residence or are taxed at a reduced rate in the other country. Prior to 6 April 2016, recipients of dividends were often entitled to a proportion of the tax credit to which a UK-resident would have been entitled (see 1350). Where a tax credit on a dividend was to be determined subject to a deduction based on the aggregate of the dividend plus the tax credit, the deduction was calculated on the gross amount of the dividend and the tax credit, without any allowance for the deduction itself.

Professional services

The income of a person in respect of professional services is generally only taxable in the country in which he is resident, unless he has a fixed base regularly available to him in the other country for the purpose of providing his services. However, actors, musicians and athletes are generally liable to tax in both countries.

Salaries and wages

Most salaries and wages are generally taxable only in the country of residence unless the employment is exercised in the other country, in which case income derived from such employment is also taxable in the other country. However, usually the treaty will contain a provision that the salary, etc. is only taxable in the country of residence if:

- the taxpayer is present in the other country for an aggregate period not exceeding 183 days in the relevant tax year;

- the salary, etc. is paid by, or on behalf of, an employer who is not resident in the other country; and

- the payments are not borne by a permanent establishment which the employer has in the other country.

However, actors, musicians and athletes are generally liable to tax in the country in which they perform.

Government salaries and pensions

Government pensions, salaries, etc. are generally taxable only in the country responsible for paying the pensions, salaries, etc. However, the income is only taxable in the other country if the services are rendered in that country and the taxpayer is resident in, or is a citizen of, that country.

Students

Students temporarily abroad for the purposes of education are generally not taxable on their grants and other income reasonably necessary for maintenance and education.

Teachers

A resident of country A who visits country B for the purpose of teaching is usually exempt from tax in country B on the income derived from his teaching. The normal proviso is that the period of temporary residence in country B does not exceed two years.

Personal allowances and reliefs

Many double tax agreements provide that individuals who are resident in country A are entitled to the same personal allowances, reliefs, and deductions for the purposes of tax in country B as subjects of country B who are not resident in that country.

Often the double taxation agreement will exclude entitlement to the personal allowances, etc. where the income consists solely of dividends, interest or royalties.

Legislation: TIOPA 2010, Pt. 2

Cases: *Strojírny Prostějov, a.s. and ACO Industries Tábor s.r.o. v Odvolací finanční ředitelst* (Cases C-53/13 and C-80/13)

Tax Reporter: ¶170-300

1789   Effect of exemptions under double tax treaties

If a double tax treaty provides an exemption from tax or a partial exemption from tax in a particular territory (see 1783), the amount in respect of which tax is exempt may nonetheless be brought fully into account in the UK – there is very little relief for 'tax spared' in the other territory, except in the case of transfers of foreign branches of UK-resident companies between EC member states (see below) and in the case of certain interest.

There is an element of tax sparing provided by virtue of EC provisions. A UK-resident company transferring a foreign branch activity between EC member states may be exempt from tax in the territory in which the branch subsisted (in accordance with the mergers directive); chargeable gains in respect of the transfer may be netted with allowable losses and the resultant taxable amount may be subject to double tax relief on the basis of the tax which would have been payable but for the exemption.

Non-resident companies carrying on business in the UK are unable to claim relief for losses incurred as a result of the exemption of dividends, interest or royalty income under a double taxation convention. For accounting periods beginning before 30 November 1993, the restriction applied only to dividends and interest received by non-residents carrying on business as a bank, insurance company or dealer in securities.

Legislation: TIOPA 2010, Pt. 2; EC Directive 90/434

Tax Reporter: ¶170-750

1792   Calculation of double tax credit relief available

In many cases, double tax agreements provide that where there is no deduction or exemption from UK tax, credit is to be given for any foreign tax which is paid and which corresponds to income tax whilst similar credit is given by 'unilateral relief' (see 1783); this reduces the amount of UK tax chargeable except in certain cases where a non-resident company is connected with a state or province of a foreign territory which operates a 'unitary tax' regime. In general, a claim for relief by way of credit for foreign tax must be made within the period ending five years from 31 January following the end of the tax year within which the income falls to be charged to tax (before self-assessment, a period of six full years). For tax spared when a UK-resident company transfers a foreign branch activity between EC member states, see 1789.

From 17 March 1998, taxpayers who have claimed relief for foreign tax must notify HMRC if there is an adjustment to the amount of foreign tax and the relief claimed has become excessive as a consequence. This requirement clarifies taxpayers' obligations under self-assessment.

For trades, professions and vocations, there are special rules relating to the years of commencement and cessation.

An overseas dividend manufacturer may have his right to double tax relief restricted, in particular, in respect of tax credits on overseas dividends received when the tax credits have been offset against tax due on manufactured overseas dividends paid or when the overseas dividends have been effectively paid on to a non-resident (see 1375).

Where no credit is allowable, the foreign tax may be deducted (see 1794). A person may elect that any treaty provision giving credit is ignored.

Where transitional rules apply to average (or scale down) profits or income under self-assessment, double tax relief may be treated similarly.

Thin capitalisation

Some treaties contain thin capitalisation provisions, restricting relief or exemption where the size of loans is greater than would be expected between unrelated parties (or their terms are more beneficial to the lender). In this regard, it is specifically provided that, for interest paid after 14 May 1992, account should be taken in the UK of whether the loan would have been made at all, whether it would have been of such size and whether the rate and other terms would have been of that order. HMRC have confirmed that the absence of cross-default and cross-guarantee provisions, etc. in an intra-group loan will not be taken into account as regards the terms on which a loan is made.

Finance Act 2004 introduces measures to merge the current thin capitalisation requirements and subsume them within the general transfer pricing rules. The new rules will end transfer pricing and thin capitalisation requirements for small and medium-sized enterprises in most circumstances from 1 April 2004.

Legislation: FA 2004, s. 30–37 and Sch. 5; TIOPA 2010, Pt. 2

Cases: *Yates (HMIT) v GCA International Ltd (formerly Gaffney Cline and Associates Ltd)* [1991] BTC 107

Other Material: SP 7/91, *Double taxation relief: business profits: unilateral relief*; TAX 5/93

Tax Reporter: ¶171-350

1794   Foreign tax as an expense

If no credit is allowable (or taken: see 1792), the foreign tax may be deducted so that only the net income is charged to UK tax.

Legislation: TIOPA 2010, s. 112

Tax Reporter: ¶171-350

Reliefs and deductions for income tax

Nature of income tax reliefs and deductions

1840   Types of income tax relief or deduction

There are various tax reductions and reliefs to which an individual is entitled or which are available for the purposes of income tax generally. These can be categorised as items which:

- produce income which is exempt from tax, such as investments in individual savings accounts and personal pension schemes;

- are deductible in computing income from a particular source or offset against income from a particular source, such as employment expenses (see 1990) and business expenses (see 2050);

- can be offset against total income, such as with certain losses, and the personal allowance; and

- give rise to credits against tax (known as 'income tax reductions': see below).

Offsets against total income

There are a number of personal reliefs from income tax available to individuals, depending on their circumstances; there are also a number of loss reliefs which are given in respect of an amount of income equal to any loss. In general, deductions may be set off against total income in the way which is most favourable to the taxpayer. However, personal reliefs are deducted after other deductions: thus to the extent that other deductions claimed reduce taxable income, personal reliefs may be lost (see example at 2113).

The amount of each personal relief is determined for each tax year. From 1994–95, the personal allowance, the blind person's allowance and life assurance premium relief are obtained by deducting set amounts from or offsetting them against an individual's total income, depending on his circumstances; other allowances are given by income tax reduction, as set out below (for eligibility, see 1850; for amounts, see 56). (NB. Life assurance premium relief was abolished for payments becoming due and payable on or after 6 April 2015 and payments becoming due and payable before that date but actually paid on or after 6 July 2015 (FA 2012, s. 227 and Sch. 39, para. 23).)

For reliefs for business losses against general income, see 2110ff. and 2119.

Income tax reductions

Double tax relief has always been available in suitable circumstances by way of credit against tax otherwise payable (see 1792).

Basic rate tax on the following amounts has also been relieved in this manner:

- enterprise investment scheme (see 1930ff.) – although the rate of relief was increased to 30% with effect from 6 April 2011;

- medical insurance premiums relief;

- qualifying maintenance payments (see 1882);

- married couple's allowance, additional personal allowance and widow's bereavement allowance (see 1851ff.).

An effective order of offset is given by the amounts respectively taken into account before any particular reduction is determined (see 244).

From 2000–01, the married couple's allowance was withdrawn for most couples (see 1853ff.), the additional personal allowance was totally withdrawn and the widow's bereavement allowance was withdrawn for new claimants.

Legislation: ITA 2007, s. 23, 900; ITTOIA 2005, s. 727(1); FA 1996, s. 147

Tax Reporter: ¶154-000.

1843 Claims for income tax reliefs and deductions

Deductions are usually given automatically. Reliefs and allowances generally have to be claimed by the taxpayer (see 2336).

If no specific time-limit is provided, a claim for relief must generally be made within four years from the end of the tax year to which it relates (see 2339).

Tax Reporter: ¶184-200

Payable tax credits

1845 Introduction to tax credits

Tax credits come in a variety of forms. Some are true tax credits – that is to say they may only be used to reduce an amount of tax that is due. If no tax is due, they are lost. The relief under the Enterprise Investment Scheme falls into this category (subject to a limited carry-back facility – see 1934). The tax credits brought in to replace social security benefit payments (working tax credit and child tax credit are different in character. They are 'payable' tax credits, and do not have to be covered by a comparable tax liability. Indeed, they are not actually set against an income tax liability, but are paid out directly by HMRC.

From 5 December 2005, the *Civil Partnerships Act* 2004 came into effect and ensures that same-sex couples are now treated in the same way as husband and wife couples.

Overview of tax credits

Very broadly, the WTC is payable to people in low-paid work, and the CTC to people with children, whether in work or not.

Tax credits are payable in full to people on income support or income-based jobseeker's allowance, or those whose income is very low. The maximum amount is then tapered away (currently at 41%) as income rises. While the WTC minus the childcare element disappears fairly low down the income distribution, the childcare element and the CTC is retained as the claimants' income rises – and when the level of benefit finally dwindles away, there is still universal, tax-free, child benefit, although this is subject to the high income child benefit charge from 7 January 2013.

Tax credits have to be claimed. Any claim can be backdated by up to one month provided the conditions for entitlement are satisfied during the intervening period. Credits are awarded for a tax year, from 6 April to the following 5 April. If however a claim is made part-way through the year, the award period starts with the date of claim, subject to backdating. Certain changes in claimants' personal circumstances will also entitle HMRC to bring the award to an immediate end.

The claimant's entitlement is assessed, initially, on the basis of the previous tax year's income, and current circumstances. At the end of the award period, the claimant's entitlement is adjusted to reflect the actual income of that period. If the claimant's income has fallen, more credit will be due. If it has risen by more than £2,500 above the level at which it was originally assessed, an overpayment may have arisen, which is recoverable at the discretion of HMRC.

The system can also recognise changes in a claimant's personal or financial circumstances during the year. Certain changes in circumstances have to be notified to HMRC within one month, but many do not. Changes in income do not have to be notified as they are reflected in the year-end 'reconciliation'. Any change that increases a claimant's award, if notified, can be backdated by one month, but no more. A penalty of up to £300 may be imposed for failing to notify HMRC regarding a change in circumstances.

The calculation of a tax credit award is a complicated process. First, a claimant's circumstances are reviewed to find out which of several elements of the WTC and CTC they are entitled to. Then those elements are added together to reach the 'maximum' credit. The result is then tapered away as the claimant's income rises above a fixed threshold.

Neither tax credit, nor child benefit, is counted as taxable income.

A claim to tax credits may be made by an individual, a couple, or a polygamous unit. A claim is a 'joint claim' if made by a couple, or the members of a polygamous unit, and a 'single claim' if made by a single person. If a member of a couple or a polygamous unit wishes to make a claim, it must be a joint claim. In any case, every claimant, whether claiming singly or jointly, must be over 16 years of age, and be 'in the UK'.

Residence for tax credits purposes is different from the income tax concept. The statutory requirement for claimants to be 'in the United Kingdom' was expanded in SI 2003/654 on which the *Tax Credits Technical Manual* (TCTM) is regarded by HMRC as an authoritative commentary. Broadly, a person who is not 'ordinarily resident' in the UK is regarded as not in the UK for this purpose; but HMRC take the view that 'ordinary residence' here has a different meaning from 'ordinary residence' for income tax. However, as will be seen, some anomalous situations arise as a result of the peculiar set of rules. Practitioners will need to be wary of potential clashes between the two systems, and should be particularly alert to HMRC's declared readiness to change its mind on a person's residence status. Note also that although the concept of ordinary residence was abolished for income tax purposes from 6 April 2013, it continues to apply for tax credits purposes.

SI 2014/1511 applies from 1 July 2014 and implements a three month residence qualification, with some exceptions, to be satisfied by people who arrive in the UK before they are able to access Child Benefit or Child Tax Credit awards.

Note that the Universal Credit is being phased in and will replace income-based Jobseeker's Allowance, income-related Employment and Support Allowance, Income Support, Child Tax Credits, Working Tax Credits, and Housing Benefit.

Legislation: *Tax Credits Act 2002; Tax Credits (Residence) Regulations 2003 (SI 2003/654); Child Benefit (General) and the Tax Credits (Residence) (Amendment) Regulations 2014 (SI 2014/1511); Tax Credits Act 2002 (Commencement and Transitional Provisions) (Partial*

Revocation) Order 2014 (SI 2014/1848); *Universal Credit (Transitional Provisions) (Amendment) Regulations* 2014 (SI 2014/1626)

Tax Reporter: ¶164-000

1846   Working Tax Credit

The basic element of WTC

Before April 2012, couples responsible for children, with one partner working at least 16 hours a week could claim working tax credit. From 6 April 2012, the rules for couples with children have changed. Single people who are responsible for children (for example single parents) are not affected by the new rules. From 6 April 2012, a couple with children usually need to jointly work at least 24 hours a week to qualify. This means:

- if they both work, joint weekly hours must be at least 24, with one party working at least 16 hours a week;

- if only one party works, that person must be working at least 24 hours a week.

If neither of these apply, payments of WTC will have ceased from 6 April 2012. However, there are some exceptions to the rules (see the GOV.UK website at www.gov.uk/working-tax-credit/eligibility).

Other elements of WTC

Provided they are eligible for the basic element of WTC, claimants to WTC may be entitled to various other elements, based on their circumstances (for a table of the amounts of these elements, see the Key Data section):

- A second adult element. This is automatic where a joint claim to WTC is made.

- A lone parent element, where a single claim is made and the claimant is responsible for a child or children.

- A 30 hour element. This is designed to encourage those with a disability, or families with children, to move to full-time work. Couples with children will be entitled to it if one of the couple works at least 30 hours a week, or if they jointly work 30 hours a week, provided that one of them works at least 16 hours. Note that, for the purposes of claiming the child care element of WTC (see below) both partners in a couple must work for at least 16 hours a week.

- A disability element. Joint claimants may each claim this if they both qualify.

- A severe disability element. Joint claimants may each claim this if they both qualify.

The child care element

Families are eligible for the child care element where a lone parent or both partners in a couple work. It is paid directly to the main carer by HMRC, either weekly or four-weekly at the claimant's choice. It is worth up to 70% of qualifying childcare costs, although a maximum limit to those costs is set (see the Key Data section for a table showing the maximum costs). Child care costs are calculated on the basis of the average weekly cost, either using the four weeks immediately prior to the claim, or, in the case of monthly payments, multiplying by 12 and dividing by 52.

The childcare provider must be registered with Ofsted to allow the claimant to get tax credits help for childcare costs. Foster carers who work as childminders will have to officially register with Ofsted.

Any 'relevant' change in child care costs must be reported to HMRC. A relevant change occurs where:

- there is any change in the child care provided; or

- there is an increase or decrease in child care costs of £10 a week or more for a four-week period.

The four-week rule is designed to prevent the need to notify one-off variations. Where the changed sum is paid in each of the four weeks, the need to notify is triggered.

When a relevant change occurs, the child care element of WTC must be recalculated. It is important to note that where child care costs decrease, and therefore less WTC is due, the recalculation will be made from the week following the four-week period of the change. Where costs increase, so that more WTC is due, the recalculation is made from the later of:

- the first day of the week in which the change occurred; and

- the first day of the week in which falls the date three months prior to the change being notified to HMRC.

Hence, there is the possibility of obtaining the increase from the first day of the four-week period (any decrease begins from the end of the four-week period) – but any delay in notification of more than one month will mean a loss of credit.

Legislation: *Tax Credits Up-rating Regulations* 2015 (SI 2015/451)

Other Material: Leaflet WTC2: *A Guide to child tax credit and working tax credits*; Leaflet WTC6: *Child Tax Credit and Working Tax Credit – Other types of help you may be able to get*

Tax Reporter: ¶164-000

1847   Child tax credit

Child tax credit (CTC) can be claimed by people who are responsible for one or more children or qualifying young persons. It is immaterial whether the claimant is in work. In that respect, CTC differs from the child elements of the former working families' tax credit (WFTC) which were only available where the claimant, or claimant's partner, was in work.

Child tax credit is available to a lone parent, a couple, or the members of a polygamous unit. It is sufficient if responsibility for the child or young person rests with just one of the members of a couple or polygamous unit.

In simple terms, a child is defined as being under the age of 16, while a qualifying young person is one between the ages of 16 and 20 who is receiving full-time education or training; but there is much more to the definitions than that.

Elements of CTC

Unlike working tax credit, which has six elements, CTC has only two – the family element and the individual element – but the regulations prescribe different rates for each element depending on the circumstances of the children.

The maximum rate of CTC is worked out by aggregating each of the elements to which the claimant is, or joint claimants are, entitled, at the appropriate rate. A joint claim can be made by a couple, or by a polygamous unit.

Legislation: *Tax Credits (Miscellaneous Amendments) (No. 2) Regulations* 2008 (SI 2008/2169); *Child Tax Credit Regulations* 2002 (SI 2002/2007); *Child Benefit and Tax Credits Up-rating Order* 2015 (SI 2015/567)

Other Material: Leaflet WTC2: *A Guide to child tax credit and working tax credits*; Leaflet WTC6: *Child Tax Credit and Working Tax Credit – Other types of help you may be able to get*

Tax Reporter: ¶165-000

1848   Calculating the tax credit

An award of tax credit lasts for a tax year, and this may have to be divided into 'relevant periods'. A relevant period is a part of the period of award (i.e. the tax year) where there is no change to the elements of WTC which the claimant is entitled to, and no relevant change in child care costs or arrangements (see 1849). Thus, a fluctuation in income does not trigger a new relevant period, but changes in circumstances (such as a material change in working hours) do. It follows that if there is no change in circumstances during the tax year, then the relevant period is the whole tax year.

Note that there is an extended definition of 'relevant period' where both WTC and CTC are claimed (see below).

The general method of calculation is to compute the maximum that can be claimed, and then to reduce this figure if income exceeds the threshold (see Key Data).

Income for tax credit purposes

'Income' is the gross income (i.e. before tax and NIC) of the claimant or, in the case of a joint claim, of the couple for a tax year. This is deemed to include 'notional' income – items which would otherwise be capital, like stock dividends, and items which are treated for tax purposes as the individual's income, like trust income where the settlor retains an interest, or payments to unmarried minor children. There are anti-avoidance provisions to ensure that income is not artificially reduced so as to increase credit entitlement.

Income for tax credit purposes is arrived at in a series of steps, as follows.

Step one

Add together:

- pension income;
- investment income;
- property income;
- foreign income; and
- notional income.

Each of these items is subject to complex definition in regulations. HMRC have given detailed guidance in the notes accompanying claim forms.

Income tax

If the sum of these items is £300 or less, it is treated as nil. If it is more than £300, only the excess is carried forward to the next stages in the computation.

Step two

Add together:

- employment income;

- social security income;

- student income (grants); and

- miscellaneous income not taxed under any other provisions.

Once again, these items are subject to detailed regulations, but there is extensive guidance available in the notes accompanying claim forms.

Step three

Add together the results of steps one and two.

Step four

Calculate trading income/loss. Add the income or deduct the loss from the result of step three.

Deductions

In calculating income for tax credit purposes, the following may be deducted:

- any banking charge or commission for conversion of income into sterling;

- charitable donations under the gift aid scheme; and

- the gross amount of any contributions to an occupational pension scheme, a personal pension scheme (including a stakeholder plan) or a retirement annuity plan.

Legislation: *Tax Credits (Definition and Calculation of Income) Regulations 2002 (SI 2002/2006); Tax Credits (Income Thresholds and Determination of Rates) Regulations 2002 (SI 2002/2008)*

Tax Reporter: ¶165-500

1849 Making and adjusting claims

Initial claims to WTC and CTC are based on current circumstances and the previous tax year's income. On the basis of this information, HMRC will make an initial decision as to the award of tax credit. HMRC are empowered to require what further information or evidence they need for this decision from the claimant(s) or from an employer.

It is possible for intermediaries such as the citizens advice bureau to act on behalf of an individual in cases concerning both tax credits and child benefits. In order for the intermediary to be recognised by HMRC, a form TC689 must be completed by both the individual concerned and the target intermediary.

Claims may be backdated for up to one month.

An appeal may be brought against HMRC's initial decision on the award of tax credit.

Adjustments to claims during the period of award

Claims to WTC and CTC will run for 12 months unless there is a change in circumstances or income. The system provides for adjustments to be made during the year. Tax credit awards can be affected by:

- changes in the adults heading a household;

- changes in the circumstances giving entitlement to tax credits or the various elements of those tax credits; or

- changes in income.

Changes in circumstances

There are two changes of circumstance where it is compulsory to inform HMRC:

- Changes in the adults heading a household. This is because an award of tax credit is made to a household based on the income of those adults. Any change signifies the end of that particular claim.

- Use of qualifying child care changes or the weekly cost varies by £10 or more (see 1846).

Changes should be notified to HMRC within one month.

Apart from these mandatory notifications, it is up to the claimant whether to tell HMRC about changes in their circumstances during the year that increase or reduce entitlement to tax credit. Provided notification is within one month of the change, increased entitlement will run from the date of that change – otherwise, the increased entitlement will run from the date of notification (thus, missing this deadline will result in a loss of some of the tax credit that would have been due for the year). It should be noted that changes reducing entitlement always run from the date of that change, so significant overpayments may be run up if HMRC are not informed.

Changes in income

HMRC will respond to all notifications of a decrease in income (and thus an increase in tax credit due) during the year. However, if the claimant does not inform HMRC during the year, no credit is lost – the change will form part of the end-of-year adjustment.

From April 2012, there is an income fall disregard of £2,500. From April 2013, there is also an income rise disregard of £5,000. Changes falling within these boundaries do not need to be notified to HMRC. From April 2016, the rise disregard is reduced from £5,000 to £2,500.

Example

Stephen is a lone parent who works full-time and has one child. In 2013–14, he earned £8,000. At the start of 2014–15, he gets a better job and expects to earn £11,500.

Stephen's rise in income of £3,500 is above the £2,500 disregard, and will thus reduce his entitlement to tax credit. He does not have to inform HMRC, but if he does not, he will be faced with the recovery of any overpayment for 2014–15 during 2015–16. His entitlement to tax credit for 2014–15 will be calculated as if his income were £9,000 (£11,500 − £2,500). However, for 2015–16, entitlement will be based on the actual income of 2014–15, i.e. £11,500.

An appeal may be brought against HMRC's decision to adjust an award of tax credit.

Finalising claims

At the end of the year a renewal form will be issued by HMRC. The renewal form asks for confirmation of circumstances and income (or an estimate of income) for the year just finished so that HMRC may finalise the claim for that year. It also provides the basis for the next year's claim. Whilst HMRC are awaiting the return of the renewal form, the existing level of credit will continue.

Claimants must normally respond to the renewal notice by 6 July following the year end.

Thus, the year end sees HMRC having to make adjustments to the amount of credit paid out during the year. If credit has been underpaid, HMRC will make a single payment of the amount they owe.

Claimants who have been overpaid tax credits may have their tax credits award reduced to repay outstanding debts from previous claims. Depending on a person's circumstances, outstanding overpayments may be from one or more previous awards. A revised award notice will be issued to the claimant before recovery of overpayments starts and HMRC will continue to collect the money owed until it has been repaid in full. HMRC will apply a different rate of recovery depending on a household's circumstances and income. Those on lowest incomes will have their debt repayments spread over a longer time frame. The maximum recovery rate is 25% of current payments. However, households with a limited income who are receiving a maximum tax credits award may only experience a 10% reduction in payments.

HMRC's 'finalising' decision on a claim may be appealed.

Legislation: *Tax Credits Act* 2002; *Working Tax Credit (Entitlement and Maximum Rate) (Amendment) Regulations* 2010 (SI 2010/918); *Tax Credits (Claims and Notifications) (Amendment) Regulations* 2015 (SI 2015/669); *Tax Credits Up-rating Regulations* 2015 (SI 2015/451); *Tax Credits (Provision of Information) (Functions Relating to Health) Regulations* 2003 (SI 2003/731); *Tax Credits (Polygamous Marriages) Regulations* 2003 (SI 2003/742); *Tax Credits (Claims and Notifications) Regulations* 2002 (SI 2002/2014); *Tax Credits (Appeals) (No. 2) Regulations* 2002 (SI 2002/3196); *The Social Security Commissioners (Procedure) (Tax Credits Appeals) Regulations* 2002 (SI 2002/3237)

Tax Reporter: ¶164-000

Personal reliefs

1850   Nature of personal reliefs

The various personal reliefs are available to UK residents and, in certain cases, non-residents (see 1585). Personal reliefs cannot be carried forward or backwards to other tax years. For interaction with other reliefs and deductions, see 1840.

The personal allowance, the blind person's allowance and former life assurance premium relief are obtained by deducting set amounts from or offsetting them against an individual's total income (see 1851, 1878 and 1880, respectively).

The necessary claims are normally made in the tax return in respect of the previous year's income. For the time-limit for claims, see 1843.

Legislation: ITA 2007, Pt. 3

Tax Reporter: ¶154-000

1851   Personal allowance

Every individual, irrespective of sex and marital status, who is liable to income tax is entitled to a personal allowance of £11,000 for 2016–17 (rising to £11,500 for 2017–18). For a table of recent allowances, see the Key Data section. The individual may deduct this amount from his total income, along with any other deductions to which he may be entitled, and will then be taxed on the remainder. If the individual earns less than the personal allowance to which he is entitled for that year, he will not be liable to income tax.

Example 1

In 2016–17, Amanda's only taxable income comprises business profits of £12,220. She is a single woman aged 35.

	£
Earnings	12,220
Less: personal allowance	(11,000)
Taxable income	1,220
Tax on £1,220 @ 20%	244

Example 2

In 2016–17, Bella's only income comprises earnings of £5,500. Since this figure is less than the personal allowance of £11,000, she will not have to pay any income tax.

The necessary claim is normally made in the tax return in respect of the previous year's income (see 1850).

Existing legislation within ITA 2007 requires the Government to increase personal allowances and rate limits (except the £150,000 higher rate limit, the £100,000 personal allowance income limit and, since 2013–14, the higher age-related personal allowances) by the annual percentage increase in the Consumer Prices Index (CPI) for the year to September preceding the new tax year (indexation). Amounts determined by the annual indexation order may be overridden by provision in a Finance Act.

However, once the personal allowance has reached £12,500, it will be uprated in line with the National Minimum Wage (NMW) (and existing indexation provisions will no longer apply), ensuring that anyone on the NMW working 30 hours per week or less does not pay income tax (ITA 2007, s. 57A, 57(8)).

Transferable tax allowances for married couples and civil partners

From 2015–16, spouses and civil partners are able to transfer part of their income tax personal allowance (the 'transferable amount') to their spouse or civil partner where neither is a higher or additional rate taxpayer.

The transferable amount is set at £1,100 for 2016–17 (£1,060 for 2015–16), at 10% of the standard personal allowance (under ITA 2007, s. 35(1)) for the tax year.

ITA 2007, s. 55A provides that the transferred allowance is given as a deduction from an individual's income tax liability (step 6 of ITA 2007, s. 23).

Legislation: ITA 2007, s. 23, 35, 57, 57A; FA 2014, s. 1, 2, 11; FA 2015, s. 3; *Income Tax (Indexation) Order* 2013 (SI 2013/3088)

Other Material: SP 2/03; SP 1/05

Tax Reporter: ¶155-000

1852   Reduced personal allowance for those with income exceeding £100,000

The basic personal allowance is restricted for any individual whose adjusted net income exceeds £100,000 in any tax year from 2010–11 onwards. Specifically, the allowance is reduced by half of the excess, rounding up the remaining allowance as necessary.

Example

John has an adjusted net income of £105,127 in 2016–17. His income thus exceeds £100,000 by £5,127. Half of £5,127 is £2,563.50. The personal allowance of £11,000 is therefore reduced to £8,436.50, which is rounded up to £8,437. John's adjusted personal allowance for the year is therefore £8,437.

Legislation: ITA 2007, s. 35(2)

Other guidance: *Adjusted net income*: www.gov.uk/adjusted-net-income

Tax Reporter: ¶155-050

1852A   Higher 'age-related' personal allowances for tax years up to 2015–16

For tax years up to 2012–13, higher (age-related) allowances were available for individuals attaining 'age 65–74' or age '75 and over' in the tax year. These allowances were frozen at 2012–13 rates and phased out between 2013–14 and 2015–16 as the basic personal allowance caught up with the frozen amounts of the former allowances.

2013–14 and 2014–15

From 2013–14 onwards, turning age 65 (or age 75) during the tax year would no longer trigger entitlement to a higher category of allowance. Those higher allowances continued to be available but only to those individuals who had already attained age 65 (or age 75) by 5 April 2013.

- Individuals who had yet to reach age 65 by 5 April 2013 were born after 5 April 1948, therefore, the basic category of allowance for age under 65 was renamed accordingly.

- Individuals who had attained age 65 but not age 75 by 5 April 2013 were born after 5 April 1938 but before 6 April 1948 and the age 65–74 category of allowance was renamed accordingly.

- Individuals who had attained age 75 by 5 April 2013 were born before 6 April 1938 and the age 75 or over category of allowance was renamed accordingly.

2015–16

For 2015–16 onwards, the higher category of allowance for those 'born after 5 April 1938 but before 6 April 1948' (i.e. individuals who had triggered entitlement to the aged '65–74' allowance by 2012–13) was removed from statute as the basic personal allowance had surpassed it. Effectively, that category and the category for individuals born after 5 April 1948 (formerly under 65) were merged.

- Individuals who were either 'aged under 65' or 'aged 65–74' as at 5 April 2013 were born after 5 April 1938 and were entitled to the same personal allowance, which was correspondingly re-entitled as the 'personal allowance for those born after 5 April 1938', with effect for the tax year 2015–16.

- The category 'born before 6 April 1938' (the former 'aged 75 and over' category) remained.

2016–17

By 2016–17, the basic personal allowance has been set an amount higher than the one remaining category of age allowance ('born before 6 April 1938', formerly 'age 75 and over') and accordingly, that category has also been withdrawn.

From 2016–17, there is only one category of personal allowance irrespective of age.

The personal allowance is available to reduce or extinguish taxable income. Any unused allowance cannot be carried forward or back. From 2015–16 onwards, a portion of an individual's unused personal allowance can be transferred to their spouses or civil partners in certain circumstances, but otherwise, the personal allowance cannot be surrendered to another taxpayer. Thus, any personal allowance which cannot be transferred or used in the tax year to which it relates is wasted.

Legislation: ITA 2007, Pt. 3, Ch. 3

Tax Reporter: ¶156-000

1853   Tax reductions for married couples and civil partners generally

Married couples, and for 2005–06 onwards, civil partners are entitled to a tax reduction where a party to the marriage or civil partnership was born before 6 April 1935. The tax reduction, originally called the married couple's allowance (a term retained in the legislation) was extended to civil partners by amendments made to the *Tax and Civil Partnership Regulations* 2005. However, where, after 5 April 2008, the individual is either not ordinarily resident or not domiciled and makes a claim for the remittance basis of taxation to apply to his foreign income or gains, he is not entitled to the tax reduction.

The legislation retains one set of provisions for marriages entered into prior to 5 December 2005 with separate provisions for marriages and civil partnerships entered into on or after that date. The two sets of provisions are intended to operate in the same way except that, under the rules applying to unions on or after 5 December 2005, it is the spouse or civil partner with the higher income who is entitled to claim, rather than the husband. A couple who married prior to 5 December 2005 can elect for the new rules (i.e. those applying to post-5 December 2005 unions) to apply to them.

In past years, there was a differential rate of allowance for those aged 75 or more at any time in the tax year. However, as the allowance is only available where at least one party to the relationship was born before 6 April 1935, it now follows that at least one party will by definition be 75 or more during the tax year. The fixed allowance for 2016–17 is £8,355 (and 2015–16). See key data for rates for earlier years.

The relief can be transferred between parties to the marriage or civil partnership in certain cases, provided that the necessary election has been made.

Income tax

Unlike the personal allowance, the married couple's allowance is not given as a deduction from total income. Instead, relief is allowed at the rate of 10% of the amount of the allowance by means of a reduction in the claimant's income tax liability.

The tax reduction is given at Step 6 of the income tax liability calculation.

Abatement

The married couple's allowance is subject to abatement where the claimant's 'adjusted net income' exceeds the income limit of £27,700 for 2016–17 (and 2015–16). It is always the claimant's income that determines the level of abatement (if any). This is so even if it is the other spouse or civil partner's age that has given entitlement to the higher level of relief. However, the married couple's allowance is only subject to restriction once the claimant's personal allowance has first been reduced to the standard level. The abatement process cannot reduce the married couple's allowance below a specified minimum amount. For 2016–17 (and 2015–16), that amount is £3,220. Any abatement utilised in reducing the claimant's personal allowance cannot also be used to reduce age-related married couple's allowance.

Election to transfer relief

In respect of couples who married before 5 December 2005, the married couple's allowance was allocated to the husband in the first instance. For those marrying or entering into a civil partnership on or after that date, the allowance is given initially to the spouse or civil partner with the highest income for the year. Married couples who married before 5 December 2005 may nevertheless elect to come within the new rules.

However, it is possible for the spouse or civil partner who would not otherwise be entitled to claim the allowance to make a unilateral election to claim a tax reduction of one-half of the minimum amount (ITA 2007, s. 47(1)). The election can only be made if that individual meets the following conditions:

- he or she has made an election that is in force for the tax year;
- makes a claim; and
- meets the residence requirement.

The effect of such an election is that the allowance due to the other spouse or civil partner is reduced by one-half of the minimum amount.

Example

Chris and John form a civil partnership in January 2011. John was born in 1932 and Chris was born in 1937. John is the civil partner with the highest income. For 2016–17, his income is £18,000. Chris unilaterally elects for one-half of the minimum amount of the allowance.

For 2016–17, Chris is entitled to an income tax reduction of 10% of £1,610 (being one-half of the minimum amount for that year of £3,220).

John is entitled to an income tax reduction of 10% of £6,745, being the allowance of £8,355 he would have been entitled to in the absence of an election, less the £1,610 transferred to Chris.

Joint claim for transfer of the entire minimum amount

The entire minimum allowance (£3,220 for 2016–17 and 2015–16) can be transferred to the other spouse or civil partner if a joint election is made. This is an all or nothing claim, no other permutations are possible (except where relief is unused).

For such a transfer to be made, the following conditions must be met:

- the parties to the marriage or civil partnership have made a joint election which is in force for the tax year;

- the individual who would not otherwise be entitled to the allowance makes a claim; and

- that person meets the requirements of the residence condition.

The effect of the election is that the minimum amount is transferred to the wife or lower earning partner (as applicable depending on the date of the union). That partner is then entitled to a tax reduction of 10% of the minimum amount. The allowance available to the husband or higher earning partner, as applicable, is reduced by the minimum amount.

Example

Albert and Flo got married on 1 January 2009. Albert was born in 1932 and Flo was born in 1937. For that tax year, Flo is the higher earning spouse, with income of £17,000.

Flo is entitled to claim a tax reduction in respect of the married couple's allowance as Albert was born before 6 April 1935 (both Albert and Flo were born before 6 April 1938). The allowance is £8,355 for 2016–17. As Flo's income is below the adjusted income limit, the allowance is not abated.

A joint election is in force for 2016–17 to transfer the minimum amount to Albert.

> The effect of the election is that Albert is entitled to a tax reduction of 10% of £3,220 for 2016–17 and Flo is entitled to a tax reduction of 10% of £5,135 (being the allowance of £8,355, less the minimum amount of £3,220).

Election for partial transfer for back of relief

Where a joint election has been made to transfer the minimum amount of the allowance to the wife or lower income partner (as applicable depending on the date of the union), the individual originally entitled to the allowance can make a unilateral election to reclaim one-half of the minimum amount (ITA 2007, s. 49). The effect is that the wife or lower income partner is entitled only to one-half of the minimum amount. The minimum amount is effectively shared between the partners in the same way as if the wife or lower income partner had made a unilateral election for one-half of the minimum amount.

Example

Louisa and Mathilda form a civil partnership on 1 April 2010. They were both born before 6 April 1935. For 2016–17, they are entitled to the tax reduction for married couples and civil partners. They can claim the reduction in respect of the allowance of £8,355.

Mathilda has the higher income and is entitled to claim the reduction. Her income is £18,000, so the allowance is not abated.

They jointly elect for Lousia to be entitled to a tax reduction in respect of the minimum amount.

Mathilda then reclaims one-half of the minimum amount.

The net effect is that Louisa is entitled to a tax reduction of 10% of £1,610 (being one-half of the minimum amount of 2016–17) and Mathilda is entitled to a tax reduction of 10% of £6,745 (being the original allowance of £8,355 less one-half of the minimum amount transferred to Louisa).

Procedure for making elections

Elections have to be made either before the start of the first tax year to be covered by the claim (ITA 2007, s. 50(2)).

An election may be made during the first year for which it is to be in force provided:

- it is made within the first 30 days of that tax year and the intention to make the election has been notified to HMRC before the start of the year; or

- that is the year in which the marriage or civil partnership takes place.

Once made, elections remain in force until they are withdrawn. The election can be withdrawn by a notice given by the individual or individuals by whom the election was made. The withdrawal must be given to HMRC in writing (ITA 2007, s. 50(5)(a), (6)). The withdrawal does not have effect until the tax year after the one in which the notice is given. Therefore, if an election is not required for a tax year, it must be withdrawn before the start of that year.

An election can also be withdrawn by the making of a new election to transfer all or part of the minimum amount (ITA 2007, s. 50(5)(b)).

Two other circumstances which can cause these elections to cease are:

- if the spouse or civil partner died, the election ceases in the tax year in which death occurred;
- if the couple or civil partners separate, any election ceases to have effect in the following tax year, unless they were reconciled, which would restore the original election back into force.

Practical considerations

Because for marriages and civil partnerships entered into on or after 5 December 2005, the entitlement to the allowance in any year goes to the spouse or civil partner with the highest income, it would seem that an election under ITA 2007, s. 45 to transfer one-half of the minimum allowance to the other partner must lapse automatically if the spouse/civil partner making the unilateral election in year 1 becomes the one with the highest income in year 2. This is because the election is to be made by the spouse/civil partner who is not entitled to the allowance. If in year 2 the spouse/civil partner who made the election in year 1 now becomes entitled to the allowance in his or her own right, then he or she cannot make such an election for year 2.

A further complication can arise both with elections and with the withdrawal of elections already in force. Because they have to be made before the start of the tax year concerned, the partners may not know which has the higher income and, if they wish to share the minimum amount, which partner needs to make the election in order to claim the tax reduction in respect of it.

However, as for post-5 December 2005 unions, it is the highest income partner who can claim the tax reduction, this will ensure that overall, the couple achieve the best possible use of the tax reduction.

Legislation: ITA 2007, s. 42; *Tax and Civil Partnership Regulations* 2005 (SI 2005/3229)

Cases: *Rignell (HMIT) v Andrews* [1990] BTC 306; *Nabi v Heaton (HMIT)* [1983] BTC 359

Other guidance: *Adjusted net income*: www.gov.uk/adjusted-net-income

Tax Reporter: ¶156-000

1854   Transfer of unused allowance

Where the primary claimant is unable to take advantage of the full income tax reduction to which he or she is entitled (either because there is no income tax liability for the year, or because the reduction was reduced to the amount which reduced any liability to nil), the unused part of the allowance can be transferred to the claimant's spouse or, from 2005–06, civil partner, provided that the primary claimant gives notice to the inspector, the spouse/civil partner makes a claim and meets the residence requirement.

Likewise, where the spouse or civil partner is unable to utilise fully any married couple's allowance to which he or she may have been entitled by virtue of an election under ITA 2007, s. 45 or 46, the unused reduction could be transferred back to the primary claimant, provided the spouse/ civil partner gives notice to the inspector and the primary claimant makes a claim.

The amount of unused relief which can be transferred in these situations is the excess of the tax reduction to which the surrendering spouse/civil partner is entitled over their 'comparative tax liability'. This is the amount of their liability after Step 6 in the prescribed method of calculating an individual's income tax, taking into account the reduction in married couples allowance which is required to keep in charge sufficient tax to satisfy gift aid payments but without any deduction for double taxation relief.

To be effective, notices to transfer unused relief or to transfer back unused relief must be given not later than four years after the end of the tax year to which they relate. The notice must be given in the form required by HMRC and once made cannot be withdrawn.

Legislation: ITA 2007, s. 51, 52, 53

Tax Reporter: ¶156-200

1856   Allowance for the year of marriage/civil partnership

In the year in which the marriage or civil partnership takes place, if the claimant has not previously been entitled to the allowance for that year, the allowance is reduced by one-twelfth for each tax month (i.e. a month beginning on the sixth and ending on the following fifth) of that year ending before the date of marriage/civil partnership ceremony.

The minimum amount is also reduced by one-twelfth for each tax month ending before the month in which the marriage took place or the civil partnership was formed.

If the individual had previously been married or in a civil partnership in the same tax year and qualified for the married couples allowance in that same year in respect of the former relationship, the reduction in the allowance only applies to the extent that it is available in relation to the subsequent marriage or civil partnership. However, an individual is not entitled to more than one tax reduction for a tax year irrespective of whether the individual is party to more than one marriage or civil partnership in that year.

The monthly reduction does not apply where a couple 'permanently' separated in one tax year but are reconciled in a subsequent tax year; the reduction only applies where a marriage or civil partnership takes place.

Legislation: ITA 2007, s. 54, 55

Tax Reporter: ¶156-300

1862   Allowance for the year of separation

A married couple or civil partners are treated for income tax purposes as 'living together' unless:

- they have been separated by a court order or by deed of separation; or

- they are in fact separated in such circumstances that the separation is likely to be permanent.

If a married couple or civil partners claim to be separated but still live together in the same house, HMRC will usually treat them as not separated for income tax purposes. However, where separate households have been set up and the couple (or at least one of them) show that they intended to break their ties, HMRC would treat the couple as separated from the date of the separate households (HMRC Manual, Relief, RE 1065; see also *Holmes v Mitchell (HMIT)* [1991] BTC 28). In practice, HMRC would look for 'the same degree of separation within the household as there would be if one of them had left home'. They would look at factors such as:

- how the accommodation has been divided between the parties;

- arrangements for sharing the kitchen, bathroom and similar facilities;

- whether the parties share meals, do their own laundry, cooking, shopping and cleaning, etc. maintain their own bank accounts, and what the arrangements are for meeting household expenses;

- whether there is any contact between the parties, or how they avoid contact;

- whether maintenance is paid; and

- where the parties are divorced or the civil partnership dissolved, whether the grounds for divorce/dissolution included separation, and if so whether for two or five years.

Where a couple are living separately because of illness, work, old age, immigration difficulties or imprisonment, HMRC will usually treat them as still living together unless there is a clear intent to end the marriage/civil partnership (HMRC Manual, Independent Taxation Handbook, IN 346).

When a married couple or civil partnership first separate, they should advise their tax office on form 41 (SEP). The full married couple's allowance remains available for that year. There is no reduction similar to that made in the year of the marriage or civil partnership ceremony took place

During the tax year in which the couple separate, the married couple's allowance is allocated in accordance with any elections/claims which were in force for that year.

Legislation: ITA 2007, s. 1011

Tax Reporter: ¶156-400

1864   Annulment, death, divorce and dissolution

Annulment

A man did not lose the married couple's allowance in respect of years during which the parties lived together before the date of the final decree declaring the marriage void (*Dodworth (HMIT) v Dale* (1936) 20 TC 285). The same principle should apply where a civil partnership is annulled.

Death

Spouse or civil partner's death

A spouse or civil partner's death does not reduce the claimant's married couple's allowance for the tax year of death (i.e. there is no reduction similar to that made in the year of marriage or civil partnership). If the deceased was entitled to one-half or all the married couple's allowance, his or her executors can give notice that any of the allowance for the tax year of death, which could not be used against his or her income tax liability, be transferred back to the claimant.

Claimant's death

A deceased claimant's executors could request that any of the married couple's allowance for the year of death which could not be used against his income be transferred to his surviving spouse or civil partner (*Independent Taxation Manual* IN492). (The legislation contained no provision to require them to do this in the event of their neglect or refusal). Any election to transfer half or all of the married couple's allowance to a spouse or civil partner will be effectively nullified in the year of the claimant's death. All allowances so transferred will revert to the claimant's estate in the year of his death. Any balance of allowance that could not be used by the claimant's estate is automatically transferred to his widow.

Divorce/dissolution

The married couple's allowance is only due for a tax year at any time during which the couple were married or civil partners and living together.

Divorce or the dissolving of a civil partnership may usually be preceded by separation, the implications of which on the availability of the married couple's allowance are discussed above. It is separation rather than divorce or dissolution itself which will trigger the loss of the married couple's allowance.

Tax Reporter: ¶156-500

1878   Blind person's allowance

An allowance of £2,290 for 2016–17 (and 2015–16) is available to a person who proves that he is a registered blind person for all or part of a tax year. For the amount of the allowance for recent years, see Key Data.

A person who becomes entitled to the blind person's allowance by being registered blind will also be granted the allowance for the previous tax year, if, at the end of that year, he had obtained proof of blindness subsequently used to qualify for registration. This concession is intended to prevent people losing the allowance because of delays in the registration process.

Where a blind person is unable to utilise the whole of the allowance because of an insufficiency of income, any excess may be transferred to his or her spouse, or, from 2005–06 onwards, his or her civil partner. The spouse or civil partner must be living with the claimant for the whole or any part of the tax year, and, for new claimants after 6 April 2007, that spouse or civil partner must satisfy the residence condition (ITA 2007, s. 56). Where a claimant was entitled to the allowance before 6 April 2007, the residence condition did not have to be satisfied until the start of the 2009–10 tax year.

Prior to the introduction of the *Income Tax Act* 2007, it was possible for the allowance to be transferred to a non-resident spouse or civil partner who was a commonwealth citizen or an EEA national, which is not one of the qualifying residence conditions now specified in ITA 2007, s. 56. That ability has now been restricted to cases where the claimant is also non-resident and able to claim personal allowances as a commonwealth citizen or EEA national.

In determining whether the individual has any unused allowance, all other deductions are required to be made in priority to the allowance, except:

- enterprise investment scheme relief; and

- relief for contributions paid to certain occupational pension schemes or into personal pension schemes.

Before these transfer provisions can apply, the person entitled to the allowance must have made an election to that effect, not later than four years from the end of the tax year to which it relates, the reduced time limit applying from 1 April 2010. Such an election, which is irrevocable, also operates as a notice under ITA 2007, s. 51 (transfer of married couple's allowance).

A registered blind person means a person registered as blind under the *National Assistance Act* 1948 or Northern Ireland counterpart.

Legislation: ITA 2007, s. 38–40

Tax Reporter: ¶157-000

1879 Qualifying care relief

A measure of tax relief is given to individuals who provide qualifying care (formerly, foster-care services) and who might be considered to be carrying on a trade, profession or vocation). The relief formerly given to foster carers was extended from April 2010 so that the relief is now available to 'qualifying shared lives carers'. As part of this change, 'foster care relief' was renamed 'qualifying care relief'.

For an individual whose receipts from providing the care do not exceed a given threshold, a complete exemption is given from income tax on those receipts.

Individuals with a higher level of receipts can elect for an alternative (simplified) method of calculating the taxable profits of their trade, profession or vocation. Special rules are then needed if accounts are not drawn up to 5 April each year. Special rules are also required to ensure that the capital allowances rules integrate fairly with the qualifying care relief.

From 6 April 2010, an upper limit of three (the 'placement cap') is imposed on the total number of 'shared lives placements' that the carers in a household can provide simultaneously before they cease to qualify for qualifying care relief. The loss of relief applies if the placement cap is exceeded for any residences used by the individual to provide the care from which qualifying care receipts are derived. The placement cap applies if, at any given time during the relevant period, shared lives care is provided in the residence for more than three people in total (whether or not by the individual in question). In relation to any given residence, the relevant period is the period for which the residence is the individual's only or main residence during the income period for the receipts. Where there is more than one carer in the household, the cap applies to the total number of shared lives placements provided by all those carers. Foster care placements are not counted as shared lives care placements. If the placement cap is exceeded, the qualifying care relief will not be available in respect of shared lives care but will continue to be available for foster care. A group of siblings placed in the same household will count as one shared lives placement for the purpose of the placement cap, however many siblings are in fact placed within the household.

Individual's limit

The individual's limit, used to determine whether there is to be any tax liability, consists of two elements:

- the fixed amount for the tax year (currently £10,000) (or, in certain circumstances, the individual's share of that amount); and

- the amount per adult or child for the tax year. The amount per child is currently £200 per week for a child who has not yet reached his or her 11th birthday, and £250 per week for an older child or an adult. The £250 starts to apply from the week in which the child reaches 11. A week is a seven-day period starting on a Monday.

Legislation: ITTOIA 2005, Pt. 7, Ch. 2, *Qualifying Care Relief (Specified Social Care Schemes) Order* 2011 (SI 2011/712)

Tax Reporter: ¶281-800

1880   Life assurance premium relief

Life insurance premium relief was withdrawn in respect of premiums due and payable on or after 6 April 2015 and premiums payable before that date but actually paid after 5 July 2015. Life assurance premium relief ('LAPR') has been abolished for policies issued after 13 March 1984. Prior to 2015–16 (for insurances made before 13 March 1984), taxpayers were entitled to relief on 12.5% of the premiums paid on qualifying policies (subject to a limit on premiums of £1,500 p.a. or one-sixth of the individual's total income for the tax year if greater). The insurance had to be on the taxpayer's life, or that of his/her spouse and relief was available regardless of which spouse paid the premium. Relief continued after divorce in respect of premiums paid by one party on the other's life if they were married when the policy was taken out but were divorced after 5 April 1979. This treatment extended to premiums paid by a divorced person on a policy taken out before the marriage. The person paying the premium had to be 'resident in the UK' (see 224) when the payment was made and the payment had to be made to a UK company or a UK branch of an overseas company.

Relief was also available for certain payments made to secure a deferred annuity for any widow, widower or child of the claimant after death.

Legislation: ITA 2007, Pt. 8, Ch. 6; FA 2012, s. 227 and Sch. 39, para. 23

Tax Reporter: ¶343-000

1882   Relief for maintenance payments

This relief is of limited, and diminishing, relevance as it is only available where one of the parties to the agreement under which the payments are made was born before 6 April 1935.

Where applicable, the relief is given as a tax reduction at Step 6 of the income tax calculation prescribed by ITA 2007, s. 23 at the rate of 10% of the amount of the payments but capped at the minimum amount of the married couples allowance prescribed by ITA 2007, s. 43. For 2015–16, this amount is £3,220 and thus the maximum tax reduction is £322. Payments are made gross, without any deduction of tax.

There are two categories of payment which rank as qualifying maintenance payments:

- payments for the benefit of former or separated spouses and civil partners; or

- payments in respect of children.

Legislation: ITA 2007, Pt. 8, Ch. 5

Tax Reporter: ¶115-650

1883 Relief for peer to peer investments

Finance Act 2016 introduces a new relief to allow individuals investing in certain P2P loans to set the losses they incur, from loans which default, against income that they receive from other P2P loans when considering their savings income for tax purposes.

This will be achieved by introducing a new tax relief against P2P income in ITA 2007, Pt. 8. The relief will automatically apply from 6 April 2016 to set bad debts arising on eligible P2P loans against interest received in the same tax year from other eligible P2P loans made using the same P2P platform.

In the case of bad debts arising on eligible P2P loans between 6 April 2015 and 5 April 2016, investors in P2P loans will be able to make a claim to set those losses against interest received in the same tax year from any other eligible P2P loans. From 6 April 2016, investors in P2P loans will also be able to make claims to set bad debts in excess of the interest that they receive during the tax year on eligible loans made using the same platform sideways, or to carry them forward:

- excess bad debts arising on eligible P2P loans made through one platform will be available to set against interest received from other eligible P2P loans made through other platforms;

- excess bad debts arising on eligible P2P loans in one tax year will be available to set against interest received in the next four tax years from other eligible P2P loans.

Legislation: ITA 2007, Pt. 8, Ch. 1A

Relief for interest payments

1884 Nature of relief against income tax for interest payments

Income tax relief (at various effective rates) is available for an interest payment if it relates to one of the specified categories of loan, below.

Relief is not granted in the following circumstances:

- where interest is paid on an overdraft or under credit card arrangements;

- where interest is paid at a rate greater than a reasonable commercial rate (in which case the excess is ineligible for relief);

- where the main benefit of the arrangement is the reduction of tax;

- where relief is sought by a company within the charge to corporation tax.

Interest paid as a revenue rather than capital item on money borrowed wholly and exclusively for the purposes of a trade, profession or vocation is not subject to the foregoing restrictions (see 2050ff.). There are provisions intended to prevent any double deductions for interest.

Categories of qualifying loan

Interest relief is available on loans applied for the following purposes:

- to purchase machinery and plant (see 1886);
- in acquiring an interest in a close company (see 1888);
- in acquiring an interest in a co-operative (see 1890);
- in acquiring shares in an employee-controlled company (see 1892);
- in acquiring an interest in a partnership (see 1894);
- to pay inheritance tax (see 1896);
- to purchase a life annuity where the borrower is 65 years old or more (see 1898).

The giving of credit to a purchaser under any sale is treated as the making of a loan to defray money applied by him in making the purchase.

Where only part of a loan satisfies the conditions for interest relief, only a proportion of the interest will be eligible for relief. That proportion is one which is equal to the proportion of the loan fulfilling those conditions at the time the money is applied.

Full interest relief is generally available on a joint loan to a husband and wife (or between civil partners) where only one of them satisfies the qualifying conditions as respects investment in a close company or partnership and that spouse (or civil partner) makes the payments or they are made out of a joint account.

Form of relief

Relief generally takes the form of a deduction from or offset against total income in respect of the interest paid. However, if relief is not available at source, relief for interest on a loan to purchase a life annuity is given by way of a reduction in the income tax otherwise payable, though the rate of relief in this case remains the basic rate; an effective order of offset of reliefs (see 244) is provided (for relief at source, see 1898). Any necessary apportionment of the interest where a loan is used the purpose of purchasing such annuity and for other qualifying purposes is made on a specified basis.

Where an individual would obtain relief in respect of interest on a loan but the loan is on preferential terms and is obtained by reason of his employment, no taxable benefit ultimately arises (the benefit is effectively offset by relief for the deemed interest) (see 406).

Indirect recoveries of capital

If at any time after the application of the proceeds of the loan, the borrower has recovered capital from the close company, employee-controlled company, co-operative or partnership (but does not use it in repayment of the loan) he is treated as repaying the loan (in whole or in part) so that the interest eligible for relief, and payable for any period after capital is recovered, is reduced by an amount equal to the interest on the capital recovered.

The borrower is treated as having recovered capital if he receives consideration for the sale, exchange or assignment of his ordinary shares in the close company or of his shares in the co-operative or of his interest in the partnership. Capital is deemed to have been recovered if the company, etc. repays the loan or the partnership returns capital to the borrower. HMRC's view is that the conversion of loan stock into ordinary shares is an assignment of the loan stock to the company (in exchange for shares), so that relief ceases.

Claim for relief

As a general rule, a claim (see 1843) must be made for interest relief. The person making the claim must supply the inspector with a written statement from the lender which contains the following information:

- the date when the debt was incurred;
- the amount of the debt when incurred;
- the interest paid in the tax year for which the claim is made; and
- the name and address of the debtor.

Local authorities and building societies (or companies carrying out similar business) are excluded from this requirement. HMRC forms can be used but are not required.

Legislation: ITA 2007, s. 383

1886 Interest on loan to buy machinery or plant

Interest attracts income tax relief (see 1884) where it is paid by an individual member of a partnership to buy machinery or plant if the partnership is entitled to capital allowances in respect of that machinery, etc.

An employee or director is entitled to such interest relief if he is entitled to a capital allowance (or would be so entitled but for some contribution made by his employer) for machinery or plant belonging to him and used for the purposes of his office or employment (e.g. a car: see 1997).

In cases both of partnerships and employments, the relief is available for interest payable up to three years from the end of the tax year in which the debt was incurred.

Where the plant or machinery is used only partly for the purposes of the trade, etc. or the employment, then a just and reasonable apportionment is made of the interest eligible for relief.

Legislation: ITA 2007, s. 388–391

Tax Reporter: ¶115-200

1888   Interest on loan to invest in a close company

Interest paid on a loan made to an individual may be eligible for income tax relief (see 1884) if the money is borrowed:

(1)   to acquire ordinary shares of a qualifying 'close company';

(2)   in making a loan to a qualifying close company where the loan is used wholly and exclusively for the business of the company or of any associated qualifying close company; or

(3)   in satisfying an earlier loan which would have qualified for interest relief.

A close company is a qualifying close company if it falls within one of the types of company excluded from being a close investment-holding company. Note that for 2014–15 onwards, the definition of a close company is extended to include a company which is resident in an EEA state other than the UK and, if it were UK resident, would be a close company.

Relief will generally be denied unless either of the conditions set out below is satisfied. However, the following points should be noted:

- HMRC are willing to allow relief for interest, following a reorganisation involving an exchange of shares after the loan proceeds are applied, provided the conditions for relief would have been met had the loan been a new loan taken out to invest in the new business entity; and

- relief has been allowed where taxpayers borrowed money to buy shares in a close company formed to put into effect a management buyout, even though the company had not started trading when the loans were taken out: the High Court said that if a loan was made and shares subscribed to enable a company to acquire a business, it could be said that the company existed for the purpose of carrying on that business and that the acquisition of the business was the means by which that purpose was to be achieved and not an end in itself (*Lord (HMIT) v Tustain* [1993] BTC 447).

1 Investors with a 'material interest'

The company must be a qualifying close company at the time the interest is paid and the borrower must have a material interest in the company. Basically, an individual has a material interest if he, alone or with any associate(s), owns beneficially or is able to control more than 5% of the ordinary share capital of the company or would be entitled to more than 5% of the assets on a winding up, etc. (for accounting periods beginning before 1 April 1989: 5% of the apportionable income). As well as holding a material interest, the claimant must also show that he has not recovered any capital from the company apart from any amount taken into account in reducing the interest eligible for relief (see 1884). If the company exists wholly or mainly to hold investments or other property, the borrower must not use property held by the company as a residence unless he has spent the majority of his time in the management or conduct of the company's business or that of an associated company.

Note that the definition of 'associate' for the purpose of establishing a material interest prevents the personal shares of other trust beneficiaries being aggregated with those of the participator. The effect is that close company interest relief is not available where a material interest has been artificially created by a token trust holding.

2 Investors managing the company

At the time the interest is paid, the company must be a qualifying close company and the borrower must hold shares of the company. Up to the date of the interest payment, the borrower must have worked for the majority of his time in the management or conduct of the company or of an associated company. He must also show that he has not recovered any capital up to the time interest is paid apart from any amount taken into account in reducing the interest eligible for relief (see 1884).

Relief in respect of shares acquired is denied if the acquirer or his spouse claims EIS relief in respect of them. Relief continues to be denied whatever relief is claimed under the *new* EIS (which combines the old EIS relief with reinvestment relief for CGT: see 1930).

Legislation: ITA 2007, s. 392–395; FA 2014, s. 13

Other Material: ESC A43, *Interest relief: investments in partnerships, co-operatives, close companies, and employee-controlled companies;*

SP 3/78, *Close companies: income tax relief for interest on loans applied in acquiring an interest in a close company*

Tax Reporter: ¶115-200

1890 Interest on loan to invest in a co-operative

A co-operative is a common ownership enterprise or a co-operative enterprise as defined in the *Industrial Common Ownership Act* 1976, s. 2.

Interest paid by an individual (the borrower) on a loan to buy shares in a co-operative or its subsidiary may be eligible for income tax relief (see 1884) if the loan is made after 10 March 1981 and at the time the interest is paid, the co-operative continues to be a co-operative; the borrower must for the greater part of his time have been an employee of the co-operative or its subsidiary from the time the loan is applied to the time of the interest payments. He must also show that he has not recovered any capital from the co-operative before the interest payment except for any amount taken into account in reducing the interest eligible for relief (see 1884).

Legislation: ITA 2007, s. 401

Tax Reporter: ¶115-350

1892 Interest on loan to invest in an employee-controlled company

Interest may be eligible for income tax relief (see 1884) if it is paid on a loan made to an individual to acquire ordinary shares in an employee-controlled company or to pay off another loan which would have qualified for interest relief.

Conditions for relief

Relief will only be given if the following conditions are satisfied:

(1) the company must be (from the date on which the shares are acquired to the date on which interest is paid):

    (a) an unquoted company that is resident in the UK or, from 2014–15 onwards, another EEA state and is not resident outside the European Economic Area; and

    (b) a trading company or the holding company of a trading company,

(2) the shares must be acquired before, or not later than 12 months after, the date on which the company first becomes an employee-controlled company;

(3)   during the tax year in which the interest is paid, the company must either:

    (a)   first become an employee-controlled company; or

    (b)   be employee-controlled throughout a period of at least nine months;

(4)   the individual must be a full-time employee of the company from the date of buying the shares to the date on which the interest is paid. Relief will continue to be given for interest paid up to 12 months after the taxpayer has ceased to be a full-time employee;

(5)   the taxpayer must not have recovered any capital from the company unless that amount is treated as a repayment of the loan in whole or in part (see 1884).

What is an employee-controlled company?

A company is an employee-controlled company at any time when at least 50%:

- of the issued ordinary share capital of the company; and

- of the voting power in the company,

is beneficially owned by persons who are full-time employees of the company.

Where an individual owns beneficially more than 10% of the issued ordinary share capital or controls more than 10% of the voting power in the company, the excess over 10% is not regarded as being owned by a full-time employee.

Legislation: ITA 2007, s. 396; FA 2014, s. 14

Tax Reporter: ¶115-400

1894   Interest on loan to invest in partnership

Interest on a loan to an individual attracts income tax relief (see 1884) if the loan is used to defray money applied in the following ways:

- to purchase a share in a partnership;

- to contribute capital to a partnership, or advance money to it, where it is used wholly for the purposes of the business carried on by the partnership; or

- to pay off another loan interest on which would have been eligible for relief.

The individual must be a member of the partnership but not a limited partner throughout the period from the application of the loan until the interest is paid. He must also show that, up to the date interest is paid, he has not recovered any capital from the partnership apart from any amount taken into account in reducing the interest eligible for relief (see 1884).

Interest may also be eligible for relief if a loan is used by a partner to buy land occupied by the partnership.

Restriction on relief for loan to invest in property partnership

From 6 April 2017, a similar restriction to that outlined at 2029 applies in relation to loans for investing in partnerships where the partnership carries on a property business and generates income from residential dwellings. Loan interest relief will be restricted for tax years 2017–18 to 2019–20 and a tax reduction is given instead in respect of the non-deductible amount. For the tax year 2020–21 and subsequent tax years, no relief will be available and instead a tax reduction will be available for non-deductible qualifying interest payments.

The restriction

The amount of (restricted) relief available is as follows:

- 2017–18 – 75% of the amount of relief that would be given apart from the restriction;
- 2018–19 – 50% of the amount of relief that would be given apart from the restriction;
- 2019–20 – 25% of the amount of relief that would be given apart from the restriction;
- 2020–21 – no relief available.

The tax reduction

If for a tax year an individual would be given relief for an amount ('the relievable amount') by ITA 2007, s. 383(1) but for the restriction applied by ITA 2007, s. 399A, the individual is entitled to relief for the tax year in respect of that amount, calculated as:

BR × the relievable amount

where BR is the basic rate of income tax for the year.

Legislation: ITA 2007, s. 398–400

Tax Reporter: ¶115-450; ¶115-460; ¶115-875; ¶115-880; ¶300-350; ¶300-360

1896   Interest on loan to pay inheritance tax

Interest on a loan made to personal representatives of a deceased person attracts income tax relief (see 1884) if the loan is applied either:

- to pay, before the grant of representation, inheritance tax on the deceased's personal estate; or

- to pay off another loan, interest on which would be eligible for relief as above.

Only interest paid in the first year of the making of the original loan is eligible for relief.

Where, in the year interest is paid, income is insufficient for full relief to be given, relief may be given against income of preceding tax years (taking the earliest year first) and, if still unrelieved, relief may be given against income of succeeding tax years.

Legislation: ITA 2007, s. 403–405

Tax Reporter: ¶115-550

1898   Interest on loan to purchase life annuity

Life annuities are sold by specialist plan providers and normally form part of a home income plan. Interest paid on a loan to purchase a life annuity attracts income tax relief (see 1884) if the following conditions are satisfied:

(1) the loan must have been made before 9 March 1999;

(2) the loan must be made as part of a scheme under which at least 90% of the loan is applied in purchasing a life annuity ending with the death of the borrower or the survivor of the borrower and two or more annuitants;

(3) at the time the loan is made, the borrower and any other annuitant must be at least 65 years old;

(4) the loan must be secured on land in the UK or Republic of Ireland and the borrower, or one of the annuitants, must own an estate or interest in that land;

(5) for any loan made after 26 March 1974, the annuitant must use the land on which the loan is secured as his only or main residence at the time the interest is paid, or within 12 months of leaving the property, must intend to dispose of it, and take steps actually to do so; and

(6) the interest must be payable by the borrower or by one of the annuitants.

In respect of payments of interest made after 6 April 2000, relief is fixed at 23% (the basic rate of tax in 1999–2000), rather than being linked to the prevailing basic rate of tax. Similarly, the ceiling for loans is fixed at £30,000 and is not reset annually.

As regards (1) above, a loan made on or after 9 March 1999 may be treated as made before that date if it is made in pursuance of an offer in writing made by the lender before that date. This ensures that anyone who was in the process of taking out a loan on that date and whose application was well advanced will still be entitled to relief.

As regards (5) above, with effect from 27 July 1999, these conditions are relaxed and the borrower will no longer lose relief simply because he stops using, as his only or main residence, the property on which the loan is secured. This change ensures that a borrower can move, say, into a nursing home, without losing relief.

Also, borrowers are able to move house or remortgage without moving (for example, to obtain a lower interest rate, or to increase the size of the loan) without losing their existing relief. A new loan made after 26 July 1999 qualifies for relief if either:

- it is applied wholly in paying off the old (qualifying) loan; or

- if only partially applied in paying off the old loan, not less than nine-tenths of the new part is applied to the purchase of a qualifying annuity.

Interest on a loan made after 26 March 1974 only attracts relief on an amount up to the 'qualifying maximum' – for recent years, the figure has been £30,000; if interest is payable by two or more persons, interest payable by each is eligible for relief on a proportion of the total eligible interest.

Tax relief for interest payments on loans within these provisions is given in most cases through MIRAS, i.e. *basic* rate tax is to be deducted and retained by the borrower from the interest payments before the payments are made.

Legislation: ITA 2007, s. 385

Tax Reporter: ¶115-600

1921 Individual savings accounts

Individual savings accounts (ISAs) are stand-alone savings products which started on 6 April 1999. Interest, dividends and capital gains held within ISAs are not liable to income tax or CGT.

An ISA can be made up of an investment in cash, or investments like stocks and shares or insurance. Individual savers are able to invest in two separate ISAs in any one tax year: one cash ISA and one stocks and shares ISA.

All individuals resident in the UK for tax purposes and are aged 18 or over have the same opportunity to subscribe to the new account, and husbands and wives each have their own annual limit.

The annual subscription limit is £15,240 (since 6 April 2015).

Previously, up to one-half of the annual allowance could be saved in cash with one provider. The remainder could be invested in stocks and shares with either the same or a different provider. From 1 July 2014, the restriction that only 50% of the overall subscription limit may be invested in a cash ISA was removed. Legislation has also been introduced to allow transfers to be made from a stocks and shares account to a cash account.

The annual ISA limits usually increase annually in line with inflation, measured initially by reference to the Retail Prices Index at September of the previous year, and rounded up to the nearest multiple of £120. However, from 2012–13 onwards, inflation is measured by the Consumer Prices Index. In the event that inflation is zero, the previous limits would be unchanged.

Junior ISAs became available from 1 November 2011. The maximum annual subscription for 2016–17 is £4,080. Investments may be made in any combination of qualifying cash or stocks and shares investments. Withdrawals are not permitted until the named child has reached the age of 18, except in cases of terminal illness. Prior to April 2015, only those who did not hold a Child Trust Fund (CTF) account could hold a Junior ISA. However, from April 2015, it is now possible to transfer CTF accounts to Junior ISAs.

Flexible ISAs

From 6 April 2016, savers can replace cash they have withdrawn from their ISA account earlier in a tax year, without this replacement counting towards the annual maximum savings limit (amendments by SI 2016/16). Replacement subscriptions may also be made using certain types of shares (amendments by SI 2016/364).

Accounts of deceased investors

Since 6 April 2015, the surviving spouses or civil partners of ISA savers are entitled to an additional ISA allowance, equal to the value held in ISA when the deceased saver died. *Finance Act* 2016 introduces further legislation which will allow regulations to be made by HM Treasury to provide that individual savings accounts can retain their tax-advantaged status following the death of the account holder. The Government has announced that it intends to use the powers within this clause to amend SI 1998/1870 during 2016–17, following consultation.

Help-to-buy ISAs

Help-to-buy ISAs, available from 1 December 2015, are designed to help first-time buyers to save up to £200 a month towards their first home. Investors will receive £50 from the government for every £200 saved, up to a maximum of £3,000. This means that the maximum that can be saved in a help-to-buy ISA is £12,000. The government bonus is added to this amount, so total savings towards the property purchase can be up to £15,000.

Accounts are limited to one per person rather than one per home, which means that those buying together can both receive a government bonus. A couple will be entitled to hold an ISA each, meaning that a total of £24,000 could be built up across two accounts. With the addition of the government bonus, a total of £30,000 can be built up by a couple under the scheme.

An initial deposit of £1,200 may be made into the account, in addition to regular monthly savings limits. This initial deposit also qualifies for the 25% boost from the government.

The minimum bonus payable by the government will be £400 and the maximum £3,000 per person.

The bonus can be claimed once savings have reached the minimum amount of £1,600. Under the scheme, it will take investors just over four and a half years to qualify for maximum bonus of £3,000, if desired.

Help-to-buy ISAs are available to individuals aged 16 and over. The bonus will only be available to first-time buyers purchasing UK properties.

New accounts will be available for four years, but once opened, there will be no limit on how long an account can be held.

The bonus will be paid when the property is purchased. It will be available on home purchases of up to £450,000 in London and up to £250,000 outside London.

There are certain restrictions under the new scheme, including:

- help-to-buy ISAs cannot be used if the property is to be rented out;
- purchases of overseas property do not qualify under the scheme;

- only one help-to-buy ISA may be held by an individual; and

- investors cannot open a help-to-buy ISA and a normal cash ISA in the same tax year.

Innovative finance ISA

From 6 April 2016, a new ISA was introduced to allow individuals to use some (or all) of their annual ISA investment allowance to lend funds through the growing Peer-to-Peer lending market, whilst receiving tax-free interest and capital gains (amendments by SI 2016/364).

Legislation: ITTOIA 2005, s. 697; FA 2011, s. 40; *Individual Savings Account (Amendment No. 3) Regulations* 2015 (SI 2015/941); *Child Trust Funds (Amendment No. 2) Regulations* 2015 (SI 2015/876); *Individual Savings Account (Amendment) Regulations* 2015 (SI 2015/608); *Individual Savings Account (Amendment No. 2) Regulations* 2014 (SI 2014/1450); *Individual Savings Account (Amendment) Regulations* 2014 (SI 2014/654); *Individual Savings Account (Amendment) (No. 2) Regulations* 2012 (SI 2012/1871); *Individual Savings Account (Amendment No. 2) Regulations* 2011 (SI 2011/1780); *Individual Savings Account (Amendment) Regulations* 2013 (SI 2013/267); *Individual Savings Account Regulations* 1998 (SI 1998/1870)

Other material: Government homeowner website: www.ownyourhome. gov.uk

Tax Reporter: ¶315-000

Enterprise investment scheme

1930   Introduction

The enterprise investment scheme (EIS) was introduced to encourage new equity investment in trading companies by providing tax incentives to investors. These incentives take the form of an income tax reduction, a capital gains tax exemption and a capital gains tax deferral (see 5923).

Any company which carries on a qualifying activity wholly or mainly in the UK can issue shares under the EIS. A qualifying activity comprises the carrying on of a qualifying trade, the preparation for carrying on such a trade or the research and development for use in such a trade. There is no requirement for the company to be incorporated here. Additionally, any investor with a UK tax liability qualifies for EIS relief regardless of whether he is UK-resident. Both of these measures were designed to help to attract foreign investors into the UK.

The range of qualifying trades in which a company wishing to issue EIS shares may engage is strictly prescribed. Prohibited activities include those such as dealing in goods (other than wholesale and retail distribution), leasing, receipt of royalties and licence fees, property development, shipbuilding, production of coal and steel, the operation of hotels, nursing homes and residential care homes and the provision of legal and accounting services.

Various anti-avoidance measures exist to counter attempts to protect the investor from risk and to prevent him from realising value from the company as a result of his investment. These measures will result in the withdrawal or reduction of relief.

Finance (No. 2) Act 2015 made a number of changes to EIS, SEIS and VCT schemes, with effect from 18 November 2015 (except where stated otherwise) but subject to state aid approval, including:

- introducing a requirement that all investors are 'independent' from the company at the time of the first share issue (excluding any connection by virtue of holding 'founder shares' or shares subscribed for under the EIS, SEIS or SITR rules);

- introducing a cap on the total amount of investment a company may receive through the EIS and VCT of £20m for knowledge intensive companies, and £12m for other qualifying companies;

- with effect in relation to shares issued on or after 6 April 2015, removing the requirement that the company must have to have spent 70% of any SEIS funds already raised;

- introducing a requirement that all investments are made with the intention to grow and develop a business;

- introducing new rules to prevent EIS funds being used to acquire existing businesses regardless of whether it is through share purchase or asset purchase;

- introducing new qualifying criteria to limit relief to investment in companies that meet certain conditions demonstrating that they are 'knowledge intensive' companies within ten years of their first commercial sale, and other qualifying companies within seven years of their first commercial sale (except where the investment represents more than 50% of turnover averaged over the preceding five years); and

- increasing the employee limit for knowledge intensive companies to 500 employees.

Finance (No. 2) Act 2015 also included legislation placing a time limit on the availability of relief: only shares issued before 6 April 2025 will be eligible for relief (ITA 2007, s. 157(1)(aa)). However, the Treasury retain the power to amend the end date (s. 157(1A)).

The prescribed periods

The legislation lays down a number of conditions relating to the investor, the issuing company and the 'relevant shares' which must be satisfied for certain periods. In addition, relief, once given, may be withdrawn or reduced on the occurrence of certain events with those periods.

There are three periods prescribed, all of which terminate immediately before the 'termination date' relating to the share issue, which is the third anniversary of the issue (ITA 2007, s. 256). The periods differ only in their start dates, which are:

- Period A: either the incorporation of the company or a date two years before the share issue;

- Period B: the share issue;

- Period C: 12 months before the share issue.

Income tax relief

An investor obtains income tax relief for EIS investments at the 'EIS Rate' of 30% from 6 April 2011 (20% prior to April 2011), on the amount of his investment in eligible shares in the tax year, subject to the current overall limit. He may make a claim for relief in respect of some or all of the shares included in the issue. The overall limit for investment was increased to £1m with effect from 6 April 2012.

The relief is given by means of a reduction in his income tax liability at Stage 6 of the prescribed method of calculation. That reduction cannot reduce the liability to less than nil. In other words, it cannot create a repayment.

Where there is more than one tax reduction to be made at Step 6 for a tax year, a prescribed order of priority is set out.

Carry-back relief

Subject to the overall maximum relief allowable for any year, an individual may claim relief in one tax year for amounts invested in qualifying shares in the immediately following year.

For 2009–10 onwards, the whole of the following year's qualifying investment can be carried back to the extent that the total relief claimed in the earlier year does not exceed the current investment limit. Thus an investment in 2014–15 can be carried back to 2013–14.

Eligibility for income tax relief

Relief is available in respect of an amount subscribed for shares in the issuing company where:

- 'relevant shares' are issued to the individual;

- he is a 'qualifying investor' in relation to those shares;

- the issuing company is a 'qualifying company';

- the shares are issued in order to raise money for a qualifying business activity and the funds raised are so employed; and

- the amounts subscribed in the tax year at least total £500 (unless the subscription is made via an approved investment fund).

Pre-arranged exits

In relation to shares issued after 1 July 1997, relief cannot be given where, at the time of an investment, certain exit arrangements are in place which guarantee the investor a way of disposing of the shares at the end of the qualifying period, effectively turning the whole investment into a low-risk venture. Broadly, relief is denied where the terms of the issue include, or there already exist at the time of issue, arrangements for repurchasing or exchanging the shares, ceasing the trade, disposing of assets of the company or otherwise providing some form of protection or guarantee for the investor.

Legislation: ITA 2007, Pt. 5; FA 2011, s. 42; FA 2012, Sch. 7; ; *Finance Act 2008, Section 31 (Specified Tax Year) Order* 2008 (SI 2008/3165); *Finance Act 2011, Section 42 (Appointed Day) Order* 2011 (SI 2011/2459); *Finance Act 2011, Section 42 (Appointed Day) Order* 2011 (SI 2011/2459); *Finance Act 2012 (Enterprise Investment Scheme) (Appointed Day) Order* 2012 (SI 2012/1896)

Case: *Taylor* [2009] TC 00277

Other Material: SP 6/98, *Enterprise investment scheme, venture capital trusts, capital gains tax reinvestment relief and business expansion scheme: loans to investors*; HMRC website: www.hmrc.gov.uk/eis/index. htm

Tax Reporter: ¶323-000

1932   Individuals, companies and activities qualifying for EIS relief

Qualifying investors

There is no requirement for an investor to be resident or ordinarily resident in the UK. However there is little point in investing under the EIS unless the individual has a UK income tax liability against which relief can be set.

There are three requirements that an investor must satisfy:

- he must not be 'connected with the issuing company';

- no 'linked loan' must be made to the investor or his associates by any person at any time in Period A (see 1930);

- he must subscribe for the shares for genuine commercial reasons and not as part of some scheme or arrangement which has a main purpose of avoiding tax.

The investor and directors may not be connected with the company during the relevant period. The relevant period begins two years before the EIS shares are issued and ends immediately before the termination date. The termination period is the third anniversary of the later of the share issue date and the trade commencement date (i.e. where the trade for which the shares were issued had begun after the share issue date).

A person is 'connected with' the company if he is (or an associate of his is) in relation to that company or any 51% subsidiary of it:

- a partner;

- an employee;

- a director who receives or becomes entitled to a payment which does not fall within a given list of bona fide commercial payments unless he was unconnected with the company before his investment and he receives remuneration commensurate with his duties as director;

- a person who controls it (see 4265) or who is entitled to over 30% of the company's assets available for distribution to its equity holders on a winding-up or any person with, or entitled to acquire, over 30% of the issued share capital, loan capital or voting power in the company.

An individual will not fail to qualify for relief solely because he or she (or any associate) held any subscriber shares at a time when the company in question had not yet begun to carry on any trade or business, and had not yet begun to make any preparations for doing so.

Qualifying company

To obtain EIS relief, the individual must invest wholly in cash in a qualifying company. A 'qualifying company' is one which is, throughout the period beginning on the share issue date and ending on the third anniversary of the later of the share issue date and the trade commencement date (i.e. where the trade for which the shares were issued had commenced after the share issue date):

- an unquoted company which is not controlled by another company or persons connected with such other company, so that companies dealt in on the Unlisted Securities Market are excluded from the scheme;

- in existence largely to carry on one or more qualifying trades or to be the holding company (and/or funding company) of one or more qualifying subsidiaries;

- qualifying companies must have fewer than 250 employees (from April 2012, prior to then the limit was 50 employees) at the date on which the relevant shares or securities are issued.

Prior to 6 April 2011, the EIS regime, in a bid to attract foreign investors to the UK, only required the trade, or the research and development to be carried out 'wholly or mainly in the United Kingdom'.

A company can be a qualifying subsidiary of an EIS company if it is a 51% subsidiary (except a property management subsidiary or a subsidiary which carries on the trade, or research and development, in question – these have to be 90% subsidiaries).

From 19 July 2007, an investment limit applies to a company raising money under the EIS. For an 'investment' to qualify for relief, the company (or group of companies) must have raised no more than £2m under any or all of the venture capital schemes (EIS, CVS, VCT) in the 12 months ending on the date of the relevant investment. If the limit is exceeded, none of the shares or securities within the issue that causes the condition to be breached will qualify for relief under the EIS or CVS, or rank as a qualifying holding for a VCT. *Finance Act* 2012 increased this limit to £5m, in respect of shares issued on or after 6 April 2012.

In respect of shares issued on or after 6 April 2011, the requirement is that, at that time, the issuing company is not 'in difficulty'. This term is defined as meaning that it would be reasonable to assume that the relevant company would be regarded as in difficulty under the European Commission's Community Guidelines on State Aid for Rescuing and Restructuring Firms in Difficulty (2004/C 244/02) (ITA 2007, s. 180B). These guidelines regard a firm as being 'in difficulty' where it is unable, whether through its own resources or with the funds which it is able to obtain from its owners/shareholders or creditors, to stem losses which, without outside intervention by the public authorities, will almost certainly condemn it to going out of business in the short or medium term.

A company ceases to satisfy the conditions for being a qualifying company when it ceases to trade or is wound-up or dissolved unless for bona fide commercial reasons resulting in the distribution of its assets to members within a specified time. If such a bona fide winding-up is initiated as promptly as circumstances permit, HMRC will ignore any short gap between the cessation of trading and the passing of the winding-up resolution. The appointment of an administrative receiver has no effect on the company's status.

Unquoted status

A fundamental condition of EIS was that the EIS company must be unquoted when it issues the shares and remain unquoted for three full years after the issue. For shares issued on or after 7 March 2001 (2001 Budget day), this requirement is replaced with conditions that only apply when the EIS shares are issued. These conditions are:

(1) the EIS company is unquoted; and

(2) no arrangements exist for either:

  (a) the company to become unquoted; or

  (b) it to become a subsidiary of a company which has plans to become unquoted.

The company will not lose its unquoted status if its shares are listed on an unrecognised exchange (such as the AIM – alternative investment market) which then becomes recognised after the EIS shares are issued.

Gross assets test

A gross assets test applies in order to confine EIS relief to investment in smaller companies. The issuing company's assets (together with the assets of all other companies, if any, in the company's group) must not exceed £15m (from April 2012; prior to then the limit was £7m) immediately before the issue of shares, and must not exceed £16m (from April 2012; prior to then the limit was £8m) immediately afterwards.

Qualifying activities

A 'qualifying business activity' is:

(1) either:

  (a) the carrying on of an existing qualifying trade at the date the relevant shares are issued, by either the issuing company or any qualifying 90% subsidiary; or

(b) preparing to carry on a qualifying trade which is intended to be carried on by the issuing company or its qualifying 90% subsidiary and that intention is fulfilled within two years of the issue of the relevant shares.

(2) research and development activity carried on by the issuing company or its qualifying 90% subsidiary at the time of the share issue (or which is commenced immediately after the issue) which, at that date, is intended to result in either:

(a) the derivation of a qualifying trade which, at the time of the share issue, is intended to be carried on by the company or any qualifying subsidiary; or

(b) a benefit to an existing qualifying trade being carried on by the issuing company or a qualifying 90% subsidiary.

In respect of shares issued prior to 6 April 2011, the trade, intended trade or the research and development had to be carried on wholly or mainly in the UK.

For these purposes, any activities carried on by a company before it became a qualifying 90% subsidiary of the issuing company is ignored and references to such a subsidiary include companies already in existence or still to be incorporated which will become qualifying 90% subsidiaries in the future.

Qualifying trade

A 'qualifying trade' is one which is not excluded by statute. The trade must be carried on a commercial basis with an intention to realise profits. With the exception of certain research and development activities and short-term ship chartering, it excludes banking, insurance, money lending, debt factoring, hire-purchase financing or other financial services, leasing or receiving royalties or licence fees, providing legal or accounting services, dealing in shares, commodities, securities, financial instruments, futures, land or goods (except in the course of an ordinary trade of wholesale and retail distribution) providing facilities for a trade (other than carried on by its parent) controlled by the same person and consisting of excluded trades and (after 16 March 1998) property development, farming and market gardening, forestry activities and timber production, operating and managing hotels and comparable establishments, or property used as such, and operating or managing nursing or residential care homes, or property used as such. From 2008–09, excluded activities also include shipbuilding and coal and steel production. The Treasury can amend the list of disqualified activities by order.

Finance Act 2016 amends the excluded activities lists, with effect from 6 April 2016, so that any company whose trade consists substantially of energy generation activities (including the production of gas or other fuel) will be unable to use the venture capital schemes.

In relation to those companies carrying out research and development within the scope of the relief, 'research and development' is limited to any activity which is intended to result in a patentable invention (within the meaning of the *Patents Act* 1977) or in a computer program. The fact that the company's income is substantially from royalties or licence fees will not exclude it from qualification, provided that those royalties or fees are attributable to research and development activities and provided that such activities are continued during the period in question.

The activity of electricity generation which receives Feed-in Tariffs or other subsidies is an excluded activity, where the commercial generation did not begin before 6 April 2012 and the shares were issued on or after 23 March 2011.

Using the money raised: time-limit

Prior to 22 April 2009, the legislation specified that 80% of the monies raised from an EIS share issue must be used within 12 months of the share issue (or within 12 months of the commencement of trading if later). The remaining 20% of the monies raised had to be used within the later of 24 months of the share issue or the commencement of trading. However, FA 2009 relaxed this time-limit, so that all money raised by the issue of shares must be wholly employed in a qualifying activity within two years of the EIS share issue, or (if later) within two years of the qualifying activity commencing. The use to which the monies raised must be put, within the specified time-limit, is a 'qualifying business activity'.

These conditions are not treated as failed if some of the funds are applied for a non-qualifying purpose provided the amount so used is 'not significant'. No guidance is given regarding the meaning of 'not significant', but in other contexts a proportion may be regarded as 'significant' once it exceeds 5%. In the absence of detailed guidance, this level could probably be argued as being the measure of a significant amount.

In *Forthright (Wales) Ltd v HMIT*, the company was formed to take over an existing business (FMS) which provided management services to an accountancy firm. The monies obtained on the issue of shares (nearly £300,000) were used to settle liabilities taken over from FMS and to pay dividends to its shareholders, some of whom were employees of the company who had agreed to be remunerated by way of dividend. It was held that the payments of FMS's liabilities and dividends to investors (as opposed to employees) using money raised by the share issue did not employ the money wholly for the purposes of the (otherwise) qualifying trade. The dividends paid to employees who had agreed to be paid through dividends rather than wages were found to be made for the purposes of the trade. The payments of the former trader's liabilities and significant dividends (30% of the total) to non-employee investors were not made for the purposes of the company's trade and so the claim for EIS relief failed (at the commissioners and High Court).

Legislation: FA 2007, s. 51 and Sch. 16; ITA 2007, Pt 5; FA 2008, s. 31, 32 and Sch. 11; FA 2009, Sch. 55; FA 2012, s. 39 and Sch. 7; *Finance Act 2012 (Enterprise Investment Scheme) (Appointed Day) Order* 2012 (SI 2012/1896)

Case: *Bell* [2016] TC 04969

Other Material: HMRC Brief 77/09

Tax Reporter: ¶323-000

1934   Scope of EIS relief available

Relief under the EIS is available where an individual who qualifies for the relief subscribes for eligible shares in a suitable company, provided the money raised is employed by the company within a specified time. For discussion of whether an individual qualifies for relief, the suitability of a company and the time period involved, see 1932. For claims, see 1936.

Eligible shares are new ordinary shares which, throughout the period beginning with the date on which they are issued and ending immediately before the termination date for those shares, carry no present or future preferential right to be redeemed. The termination date is the third anniversary of the later of the share issue date and the trade commencement date (i.e. where the trade for which the shares were issued had begun after the share issue date).

Prior to 2009–10 and subject to the overall investment limit, an individual could claim relief in one tax year (say, 2008–09) for one-half of any amount invested in qualifying shares before 6 October in the following year (i.e. before 6 October 2009). The maximum amount that an investor could request to carry back in this way was £50,000. FA 2009 extended the carry-back period so that for 2009–10 onwards, investors may carry back the full amount subscribed for shares (subject to the EIS qualifying limit). The amount of the subscription carried back is treated as though it related to a share issue made in the previous tax year.

The minimum investment required to attract EIS relief is £500, except in the case of purchases by 'approved investment funds' (see 1946).

Relief for any tax year is attributed pro rata to shares subscribed for (or treated as subscribed for) in that year, treating any bonus issue as if it were in the same year as the original investment; a withdrawal of relief is treated in a similar way.

Any gain on disposal of EIS shares is generally exempt but, where a loss arises, that loss is effectively reduced by the amount of income tax relief given (see 5925). An individual may claim income tax relief for any loss if he would have satisfied the necessary conditions had the investee company been a qualifying trading company.

Legislation: FA 2009, Sch. 55; ITA 2007, Pt 5

Tax Reporter: ¶323-000

1936   Claiming EIS income tax relief

To obtain EIS relief, an investor must submit a claim:

- not before the qualifying activity has been carried on for four months; and

- no later than the fifth anniversary of the 31 January following the tax year in which the shares were issued.

However, a claim can be made if the company concerned commences the qualifying business activities but is wound up, or dissolved without winding up, before the end of the four-month period, provided the winding up/dissolution is for bona fide commercial reasons and not as part of a scheme or arrangement in which one of the main purposes is to avoid tax. Similarly if, having commenced the activities, the issuing or any other company goes into administration or receivership within four months, a claim may still be made.

Legislation: ITA 2007, s. 158(1), 176, 202

Tax Reporter: ¶323-100

1938   Withdrawal of EIS relief: general

'EIS relief' (see 1930) will generally be withdrawn by assessment for the tax year for which the relief was given if it is subsequently found that it was not due. Except in the case of fraudulent or negligent conduct, no such withdrawal will be made:

- by reason of any event occurring after the taxpayer has disposed of all the shares (unless he remains connected) or after his death;

- because the company is not a qualifying company, unless the company has notified the inspector that this is the case and he has informed the company that, as a result, relief obtained by any individual was not due; or

• more than six years after the tax year in which the event occurs or, if later, in which the funds must be employed.

Withdrawals may be made by reference to a number of events, including sale (see 1939), receipt of value from the company (1940) and replacement capital (see 1942). There are provisions requiring the investor, the company and, in some cases, other persons to notify HMRC within 60 days if the conditions for relief cease to be satisfied; HMRC also have other information gathering powers in this respect.

There are rules determining the date from which interest on overdue tax will run in respect of additional tax resulting from a withdrawal.

Legislation: ITA 2007, s. 234, 235

Tax Reporter: ¶323-650

1939 Withdrawal of EIS relief: disposal of shares

Where, following receipt of 'EIS relief' (see 1930), a shareholder sells the shares at an arm's length price (or the shares become subject to a call or put option) within the relevant period, relief will be withdrawn on a first-in/first-out (FIFO) basis by reference to the amount which he receives for their sale; if such a sale is not at arm's length, his whole relief for those shares will be withdrawn. This does not apply to a disposal to one's spouse if they are living together at that time; the transferee spouse then steps into the shoes of the transferor.

The relevant period begins on the share issue date and ends immediately before the termination date. The termination date is the third anniversary of the later of the share issue date and the trade commencement trade (i.e. the trade for which the shares were issued began after the share issue date).

For the nature of any withdrawal, see 1938.

Legislation: ITA 2007, s. 209–212

Tax Reporter: ¶323-650

1940 Withdrawal of EIS relief: members receiving value from the company

Where, for the purposes of 'EIS relief' (see 1930), an individual subscribes for eligible shares in a company and receives any value from the company (or a 51% subsidiary of it) at any time in the 'period of restriction', the amount of the relief to which he is entitled in respect of those shares will be reduced by reference to the value received; reasonable directors' remuneration is excluded.

The period of restriction begins 12 months before the issue of the shares and ends immediately before the termination date. The termination date is the third anniversary of the later of the share issue date and the trade commencement date (i.e. where the trade for which the shares were issued had begun after the date the shares were issued).

For this purpose, an individual also receives value if any person connected with the company (see 1932) either purchases any of its share capital or securities which belong to the individual or pays him for giving up any right in relation to any of the company's share capital or securities.

Equally, where a shareholder other than a claimant receives value from the company, by way of a repayment, redemption or repurchase of capital, every individual who qualified for relief is subject to a proportionate clawback.

For the nature of any withdrawal, see 1938.

Legislation: ITA 2007, s. 213–223

Tax Reporter: ¶323-850

1942 Withdrawal of EIS relief: replacement capital

A taxpayer will not be granted 'EIS relief' (see 1930) where he has an opportunity to receive back from someone other than the company the 'additional' capital he has subscribed, as set out below (as regards value received from the company, see 1940). The company itself is not disqualified and so new investors can obtain relief for additional capital subscribed for shares in that company.

As a general rule, an individual is not entitled to relief where at any time in the 'relevant period' (i.e. the period beginning on the share issue date and ending on the termination date, which is the third anniversary of the later of the date of the share issue and the date of the commencement of the trade for which the shares were issued) – or, in the case of certain directors, at any time before the termination date – the company or its subsidiary takes over a trade or trade assets and either:

- the individual had more than a 50% interest in the previous trade and has a similar interest in the new trade; or

- the individual 'controlling' (see 4265) the company also controlled another company which previously carried on the trade.

There are various definitions which apply for this purpose and the concept is extended to situations in which the company takes over another company. For the nature of any withdrawal, see 1938.

Legislation: ITA 2007, s. 224–234

Tax Reporter: ¶324-050

1946 Approved EIS investment funds

An individual investor may obtain 'EIS relief' (see 1930) where an approved investment fund invests on his behalf in a number of qualifying companies (see 1932). HMRC have full power to approve the investment and must be satisfied that the managers of the fund are reputable and capable of handling the necessary administration. Since 15 March 1988, relief has been granted when the fund closes rather than the date the share issue is made, provided 90% of the individual's subscription has been invested within six months of the fund closure.

Legislation: ITA 2007, s. 250(3), 251(1), (2)

Tax Reporter: ¶325-350

Venture capital trusts

1950 Overview of VCTs

A 'venture capital trust' (VCT) is essentially a specific type of investment trust which invests in unquoted trading companies. Individual investors in VCTs receive various tax incentives:

- the rate of income tax relief on qualifying investments is 30%;

- the maximum amount invested for which tax reliefs can be obtained is £200,000 per tax year;

- exemption from income tax on distributions paid by VCTs (see 1956);

- prior to 2004–05, deferral of CGT on a chargeable gain from the disposal of an asset where the gain is invested in new VCT shares. From 6 April 2004, it is no longer possible to defer CGT by reinvesting gains in VCT shares (see 5925); and

- exemption from CGT on the disposal of ordinary shares in VCTs, whether or not they were new shares when acquired (see 5925).

In respect of shares or securities issue by the relevant company on or after 6 April 2011, the requirement is that the company has had a 'permanent establishment' in the UK continuously since the issue of the relevant holding.

VCTs are exempt from corporation tax on any capital gain arising on disposal of their investments.

A VCT is defined as a company which is not close and which has obtained HMRC's approval, satisfying the conditions below; the grant of approval can be made retrospective to the date of the application.

Finance (No. 2) Act 2015 introduced a number of changes to the VCT rules, with effect from 18 November 2015 (except where stated otherwise) but subject to state aid approval, including:

- introducing two extra conditions a company must meet in order to be approved as, and retain its status as, a VCT: 'the permitted maximum age condition' and 'the no business acquisition condition';

- introducing two extra limits an investee company must meet if a VCT is to make an investment in that company. As well as meeting the total annual investment limit of £5m, the relevant company must also meet a total (lifetime) investment limit of £20m for knowledge-intensive companies and £12m for other companies as at the date the VCT invests in it and, in certain circumstances, that limit must not be breached for the following five years;

- introducing new qualifying criteria to limit relief to investment in companies that meet certain conditions demonstrating that they are 'knowledge intensive' companies within ten years of their first commercial sale, and other qualifying companies within seven years of their first commercial sale (except where the investment represents more than 50% of turnover averaged over the preceding five years);

- introducing a requirement that all investments are made with the intention to grow and develop a business;

- introduce new rules to prevent VCT funds being used to acquire existing businesses, including extending the prohibition on management buyouts and share acquisitions to VCT non-qualifying holdings and VCT funds raised pre-2012, and preventing money raised through VCT from being used to make acquisitions of existing business regardless of whether it is through share purchase or asset purchase;

- with effect in relation to shares issued on or after 6 April 2015, removing the requirement that the company must have to have spent 70% of any SEIS funds already raised; and

- increasing the employee limit for knowledge intensive companies to 500 employees.

Finance (No. 2) Act 2015 also includes legislation placing a time limit on the availability of relief: only shares issued before 6 April 2025 will be eligible for relief (ITA 2007, s. 261(3)(za)). However, the Treasury retain the power to amend the end date (s. 261(5)).

Conditions to be satisfied

The conditions which a company must satisfy (in its most recent complete accounting period and in the accounting period during which the application for approval as a VCT is made) are as follows:

(1) the company's ordinary share capital has been admitted to trading on an EU-regulated market. Prior to 6 April 2011, the requirement was that the shares had been listed in the Official UK List of the Stock Exchange;

(2) the company's income has been wholly or mainly derived from shares or securities;

(3) the company has not retained more than 15% of the income it derived from shares or securities;

(4) no holding in any company, other than another VCT (or a company which would qualify as a VCT if its ordinary shares were listed in the Official List of the Stock Exchange) amounts to more than 15% of the company's investments;

(5) at least 70% (by value) of its investments has been in shares or securities in 'qualifying holdings';

(6) at least 70% of the qualifying holdings has been in holdings of 'eligible shares'. Prior to 6 April 2011, the percentage required was 30%. Transitional provisions apply where shares in relevant companies were issued before 6 April 2011 or were acquired with money raised before that date.

Provisional approval

For approval to be granted, the conditions set out above must be met in the company's most recent complete accounting period. In addition, HMRC must also be satisfied that the conditions will be met in the accounting period during which the application for approval as a VCT is made.

If all the conditions are not satisfied for the company's most recent complete accounting period, HMRC may nevertheless grant provisional approval to a company, if they are satisfied that:

•   if any condition other than (5) or (6) above is not met, it will be met in the accounting period in which the application is made, or in the following accounting period;

- if condition (5) and/or (6) is not met, it will be met in an accounting period of the company beginning within three years of the date on which approval is given, or, if approval is given retrospectively, within three years of the time at which approval takes effect; and

- any condition which will be met within the timescales outlined above will then continue to be met throughout subsequent accounting periods.

Where these conditions do not prove to be met, the provisional approval will be withdrawn and the company will be treated as never having been approved.

Withdrawal of approval

HMRC may, at any time, withdraw approval of a company as a VCT if they believe that the necessary conditions were not fulfilled at the time of granting of approval. Equally, approval may be withdrawn if:

- HMRC had given approval on the basis that a condition would be met in an accounting period, but the condition was not then met;

- the company failed to meet any necessary conditions or regulations within the three-year period referred to above; or

- the company failed to meet the appropriate conditions in its most recent complete accounting period, or in the current one, but approval will not be withdrawn for this reason if the failure was anticipated at the time of the granting of provisional approval.

Withdrawal of approval will normally take effect at the time when the notice of withdrawal is given to the company. However, the withdrawal of provisional approval may, if the conditions were never completely satisfied, take effect as if the provisional approval had never been given.

Any assessment consequential on withdrawn approval may be made within three years of the date on which the notice of withdrawal is given, regardless of the normal rules on time limits.

Merger and winding up

Finance Act 2002 gives authority to the Treasury to make regulations to ensure that approval continues when a VCT is being wound up or when it merges with another VCT. Thus, tax reliefs for investors will be preserved. Furthermore, some of the capital raised as part of a merger from a new issue of shares, which would normally be used to acquire more shares in unquoted trading companies, can be used to repay investors who wish to realise their investment. This applies to a winding up or merger after 16 April 2002.

Approval should not be withdrawn where there has been a merger of VCTs, and the return of capital is in respect of new shares issued on or after 6 April 2014 which correspond to old shares in the merging companies that had been issued before 6 April 2014. For the purposes of this rule, the specified period in respect of those new shares runs from the date when the old shares were issued.

Legislation: ITA 2007, Pt. 6; FA 2008, s. 32 and Sch. 11; FA 2012, s. 40 and Sch. 8; FA 2014, s. 53 and Sch. 10; *Venture Capital Trust (Winding up and Mergers) (Tax) (Amendment) Regulations* 2015 (SI 2015/361); *Venture Capital Trust (Amendment) Regulations* 2014 (SI 2014/1929); *Finance Act 2012 (Venture Capital Trusts) (Appointed Day) Order* 2012 (SI 2012/1901); *Venture Capital Trust (Winding up and Mergers) (Tax) (Amendment) Regulations* 2011 (SI 2011/660)

Tax Reporter: ¶326-280

1952 'Qualifying holding'

In order for a VCT's investment in another company (a 'relevant holding' in a 'relevant company') to be a qualifying holding for the purposes gaining HMRC's approval (Conditions 5 and 6; see 1950), a number of requirements must be satisfied in relation to the relevant holding and the relevant company. In addition, the relevant holding must comprise shares or securities which were issued by the relevant company to the VCT, which has held those shares ever since.

The requirements, all of which need to be satisfied if a holding in a relevant company is to be a qualifying holding, are:

- the UK permanent establishment requirement which applies in respect of shares, etc. issued on or after 6 April 2011;
- the financial health requirement which also applies in respect of shares, etc. issued on or after 6 April 2011;
- the maximum qualifying investment requirement ;
- the no guaranteed loan requirement;
- the proportion of eligible shares requirement;
- the qualifying activity requirement;
- the Annual Maximum Amount Raised Requirement ;
- the use of money raised requirement;
- the relevant company's activity requirement;
- the unquoted status requirement;
- the control and independence requirement;

- the gross assets requirement;

- the number of employees requirement;

- the qualifying subsidiaries requirement; and

- the property managing subsidiaries requirement.

Legislation: ITA 2007, Pt. 6, Ch. 4; FA 2007, s. 51 and Sch. 16; FA 2009, Sch. 55; FA 2012, s. 40 and Sch. 8

Tax Reporter: ¶326-380

1954   Relief from income tax on investment

Entitlement to claim relief

Individuals will have relief from income tax on dividends from VCTs in respect of investments of up to £200,000 per year for 2004–05 onwards. In relation to shares issued after 6 April 2000 but prior to 6 April 2006, the minimum period is three years. From 6 April 2006, investors must hold their shares for a minimum of five years to qualify for income tax relief.

Relief will be given to an individual on an amount equal to his subscription, on his own behalf, for shares in a VCT, but no relief will be available for any amount so subscribed, which is in excess of £200,000. The individual must be aged 18 or over at the time of issue of the shares.

The maximum relief which can be given will be an amount which reduces the individual's liability to nil, and in determining an individual's liability this relief will be given before any reliefs given by way of an income tax reduction.

No relief will be given if the circumstances are such that any relief, which might previously have been given, would have had cause to be withdrawn and relief will not be available unless the shares were both issued and subscribed for (for bona fide commercial purposes, and not as part of any tax avoidance scheme). Tax relief is also denied in certain circumstances in which the issue of shares is related to the making of loans, or any equivalent act such as the giving of credit or the assignment of a debt. A statement of practice sets out the application of these rules.

Loss of investment relief

If investment relief has been given to an individual, it will be lost in whole or in part if the individual disposes of the shares in the VCT within the period of five years (i.e. for shares issued after 5 April 2006, otherwise the period is three years) beginning with the issue of those shares to that individual. If the original subscriber makes a disposal to his or her spouse, then the spouse is treated as if he or she was the original subscriber for the shares.

If the disposal within the five-year time limit (three-year time limit for shares issued before 6 April 2006) is by way of a bargain not at arm's length, then the relief is withdrawn in full, but if the disposal is at arm's length, then the amount of relief withdrawn is based on the consideration for the disposal.

Specific rules apply where it is necessary to identify which shares have been disposed of. If a VCT loses its approved status, then any person holding shares in that VCT is deemed to have disposed of them immediately before that time, and not at arm's length, with the result that all the relief previously granted will be withdrawn.

Assessment on withdrawal or reduction of relief

If relief, once given, needs to be withdrawn, it will be withdrawn by way of an assessment for the tax year in respect of which the relief to be withdrawn was originally given. The assessment may be made at any time not more than six years after the end of that tax year. No assessment will be made to withdraw or reduce relief as a result of an event occurring after the subscriber's death.

Provision of information

An individual investor should inform the inspector within 60 days, if he becomes aware of an event which would cause his relief to be reduced or withdrawn. Equally, an inspector may require an individual to supply any information (within a period of not less than 60 days) which the officer believes may be reasonably required regarding an event which may cause relief to be reduced or withdrawn. An officer may, without breaching confidentiality, inform a VCT that relief given by reference to a number or proportion of its shares has been given or claimed under these provisions.

Legislation: ITA 2007, Pt. 6, Ch. 2; FA 2014, Sch. 10, para. 1

Tax Reporter: ¶326-010

1956 Exemption from income tax on distributions

'Qualifying investor' and 'relevant distribution'

If a qualifying investor (see below) becomes beneficially entitled to a relevant distribution (see below) of a VCT, then the distribution is not regarded as income for any income tax purposes.

A qualifying investor is an individual aged 18 or over who is beneficially entitled to the distribution, either because he holds the shares in respect of which the distribution is made, or because the shares are held by a nominee of his (including the trustees of a bare trust of which the individual is the only beneficiary).

A relevant distribution, as regards a company which is a VCT, is one consisting of a dividend paid in respect of ordinary shares (i.e. shares forming part of the company's ordinary share capital) where the shares:

- were acquired by the person to whom the distribution is made at a time when the company was a VCT; and

- are not shares in excess of the permitted maximum (see below) for any year of investment.

A dividend is excluded from being a relevant distribution if it is paid in respect of profits or gains arising in an accounting period at the end of which the company was not a VCT. In addition, in relation to shares acquired on or after 9 March 1999, the shares must have been acquired for bona fide commercial purposes, and not part of a tax avoidance scheme.

Meaning of 'permitted maximum'

If an individual acquires, directly or via a nominee (see above), ordinary shares in a VCT, for bona fide commercial purposes (i.e. not as part of a tax avoidance scheme), he may so acquire shares to the value of £200,000 without exceeding the permitted maximum. The 'value' of shares acquired is taken to be market value as at the time of acquisition.

If the investor acquires new shares in a VCT in exchange for shares in another VCT (which were originally acquired in whole or in part within the permitted maximum for the year), then the value of the new shares is ignored in calculating the permitted maximum for the year in which the new shares were acquired. However, the new shares still qualify for distribution relief, with the proviso that if only part of the original shares qualified for such relief, then a similar part of the new shares continue so to qualify.

Where shares are acquired in excess of the permitted maximum, specific rules apply, broadly, to give relief on the first £200,000 worth acquired in any year. This would appear to mean that the shares on which tax relief on distributions is given may not be the same shares on which tax relief on investment (see 1954) is given. If an investor acquires *existing* shares for £30,000 and, later in the same year, subscribes for £200,000 worth of *new* shares, then tax relief on distributions will be given on the £30,000 existing shares and the first £170,000 new shares. However, tax relief on investment will be given on the £200,000 new shares subscribed for.

Legislation: FA 2007, s. 51 and Sch. 16; ITA 2007, Pt. 6

Tax Reporter: ¶326-080ff.

Social investment tax relief

1958 Introduction

Finance Act 2014 introduced tax relief to individual investors who invest in new shares or new qualifying debt investments in qualifying social enterprises, and who have a UK tax liability against which to set the relief although investors need not be UK resident. The Social Investment Tax Relief (SITR) legislation applies for investments made on or after 6 April 2014.

The income and capital gains tax reliefs are available to individual investors who invest in new shares or new qualifying debt investments in qualifying social enterprises on or after 6 April 2014 but before 6 April 2019, although this later date can be extended by Treasury order.

The investment must be held for a period of three years from the date the investment is made for relief to be retained. If it is disposed of within that three year period, or if any of the qualifying conditions cease to be met during that period, relief will be withdrawn or reduced.

Relief is available at 30% of the amount invested, on a maximum annual investment of £1,000,000. The relief is given by way of a reduction of tax liability, providing there is sufficient tax liability which to set it. A claim to relief can be made up to five years after the 31 January following the tax year in which the investment was made.

Example

Alex invests £150,000 in 2016–17 in SITR qualifying shares. The SITR relief available is £45,000 (£150,000 × 30%). His tax liability for the year before SITR relief is £55,000 which he can reduce to £10,000 as a result of his investment.

Example

Sam invests £300,000 in 2016–17 in SITR qualifying debt. The SITR relief available is £90,000. His tax liability for the year before SITR is £70,000. Sam can reduce his tax bill to nil as a result of his SITR investment, but loses the rest of the relief available.

There is a carry-back facility which allows all or part of the amount invested in one tax year to be treated as though the investment had been made in the preceding tax year. This is subject to the overriding limit for each year. There is no SITR for a year earlier than 2014–15.

Legislation: FA 2014, s. 57 and Sch. 9; ITA 2007, Pt. 5B

Other material: Government factsheet: *Social investment tax relief:* www. gov.uk/government/publications/social-investment-tax-relief-factsheet/ social-investment-tax-relief; www.hmrc.gov.uk/sitr/index.htm.

Community investment tax relief

1960   Introduction

Community investment tax relief was introduced by FA 2002, but much of the detail is dealt with in regulations. The legislation applies to investments made on or after 17 January 2002. Claims to relief may be made from 23 January 2003 onwards.

The scheme borrows much from the Enterprise Investment Scheme (EIS) with the position of the SME company in that scheme being taken by an accredited Community Development Finance Institution (CDFI). The investment in the CDFI may be in the form of a loan, shares or securities held for a five-year period.

The investor, which may be a company, bank or an individual, can claim tax relief of up to 25% of the amount invested once a tax relief certificate has been issued by the CDFI, but the tax relief must be spread over the five-year term of the investment giving only 5% tax relief per year. The tax relief reduces the investor's tax liability, and is limited by the amount of that liability. If the investor receives any significant value from the CDFI within a six-year period starting one year before the date of the investment, the tax relief is withdrawn.

Legislation: ITA 2007, Pt. 7

Tax Reporter: ¶325-000

1962   Conditions of investment

A number of conditions surround the CDFI, the investor and the type of investment.

Conditions for the CDFI

The objective of a CDFI must be to provide finance and financial advice to enterprises for disadvantaged communities, which include enterprises in disadvantaged areas and enterprises for disadvantaged groups.

The enterprises in which the CDFI may invest must be SMEs but they do not need to be incorporated. The finance provided by the CDFI to the SME must be in the form of a loan or equity investment, or a combination of the two. There are restrictions on property investment by the CDFI.

There will be two types of CDFI: those which invest only directly in enterprises for disadvantaged communities, known as 'retail' CDFIs, and those 'wholesale' CDFI bodies which invest in other CDFIs as well as directly in the community enterprises.

Conditions for the investor

An investor in the CDFI may be an individual, a partner, a company or a bank, but in each case the investor or any person connected with him, must not control the CDFI at any time during the five years immediately following the investment date.

Conditions for the investment

The investment in the CDFI can be in the form of a loan, shares or securities, all of which have particular conditions attached. However, any investment in a CDFI can only qualify for tax relief under this scheme if there are no arrangements made to reduce the risk of that investment, such as a guarantee or insurance. Such prohibited arrangements do not include not normal commercial arrangements which may be undertaken by a bank when lending as part of its business, such as a charge on property taken as security for a loan, or foreign currency hedging contracts.

Loans

The investment in the CDFI may be in the form of a loan that is either drawn down by the CDFI in full on the investment date, or is drawn down in stages over a period of up to 18 months after the investment date. Tax relief will only be given on the capital balance of the loan that has been drawn-down, (see tax relief below).

The loan must not be convertible into shares or securities that have rights to allow redemption within five years of the investment date, but the loan may be repayable in stages as follows:

- nothing repayable in the first two years after investment;

- in the third year, up to 25% of the capital outstanding after two years;

- in the fourth year, up to 50% of the outstanding loan;

- in the fifth year, up to 75% of the outstanding loan.

These percentages may be altered by regulation.

Shares or securities

Any shares or securities received as part of an investment in a CDFI under this scheme must be subscribed for in cash and fully paid up on the date of the investment. They must also not have any rights to allow redemption within five years, or conversion into a loan or other shares or securities which could be redeemed within five years of the investment date. The shares or securities must not be jointly subscribed for, as the investor must be the sole beneficial owner of the shares at the date of the investment.

No tax avoidance motive

The standard anti-avoidance clause applies such that any investment will not receive tax relief if the main purpose of any scheme or arrangement under which the investment is made is the avoidance of tax.

Legislation: FA 2014, s. 35; FA 2008, s. 54; ITA 2007, Pt. 7

Tax Reporter: ¶325-000

1964   The tax relief

Tax relief under this scheme must be claimed on an annual basis at the rate of 5% of the 'invested amount' (see below) for the tax year (or accounting period for a corporate investor) in which the investment date falls and the four subsequent tax years (or accounting periods). If the investment was by way of a loan the 'invested amount' will not necessarily be the amount of the loan made available at the beginning of the five-year investment period, (see below). The tax relief due under this scheme is a tax reducer rather than an allowance, so it cannot reduce the taxpayer's tax liability below zero.

The investor must receive a tax relief certificate from the CDFI before claiming any tax relief in respect of the investment.

Tax relief for shares and securities

For shares and securities, the invested amount will normally be the amount subscribed for in cash. However, where the investor has received a significant receipt of value (see below) which does not exceed the permitted levels, the invested amount is treated as being reduced by the amount of value received.

Tax relief for loans

As an investment made as a loan may be drawn-down over an 18-month period and repaid in stages, (see conditions for the investment above) the 'invested amount' for the tax years or accounting periods corresponding to the five-year investment period is determined according to the average balance of the loan in the relevant 12-month investment period as follows:

Tax Year or accounting period:	Relevant investment period:	Invested amount calculated as:
1. In which the investment was made.	12 months from the date of investment.	The average capital balance, calculated on a daily basis in the relevant period of investment.
2. In which the first anniversary of the investment date falls.	12 months from 1st anniversary of date of investment.	The average capital balance, calculated on a daily basis in the relevant period of investment.
3, 4 or 5: In which the 2nd, 3rd or 4th anniversary of the investment date falls.	12 months from the anniversary of the investment date falling in the tax year or accounting period.	The average capital balance, calculated on a daily basis in the relevant period of investment, but subject to restriction.

If the amount of the loan is increased during the third, fourth or fifth years of the investment period, the 'invested amount' is restricted to the average capital balance of the last six months of the second year of the five-year investment period. This ensures that tax relief is only given for loan capital which was made available from the start of the investment period, and drawn-down within 18 months of the investment date.

Example

S made a loan of £100,000 on 30 June Year 1 to an accredited CDFI, which is repayable at the rate of £10,000 per year from 30 June Year 3. The relevant investment period for each tax year runs from 30 June to 29 June. The tax relief due for each relevant investment period is calculated as follows:

Relevant investment period	Average capital balance of loan in the relevant investment period	Tax relief due at 5% of capital balance in the relevant investment period
1	£100,000	£5,000
2	£100,000	£5,000
3	£90,000	£4,500
4	£80,000	£4,000
5	£70,000	£3,500

If S advanced a further £50,000 on 30 June Year 4, the capital balance for the year to 30 June Year 5 would be £130,000 but the tax relief due for Year 5 would be:

5% × £100,000 = £5,000

The 'invested amount' is restricted to the amount of the average capital balance between 1 January and 29 June Year 3.

Order of set-off

The tax relief given under this scheme is only available after any relief due under the EIS, VCT scheme and corporate venturing relief has been taken, and before any double taxation relief due. Individuals must also retain sufficient income tax to cover any gift aid donations made.

Legislation: ITA 2007, Pt. 7, Ch. 5

Tax Reporter: ¶325-100

1966 Withdrawal or reduction of tax relief

When tax relief under this scheme must be reduced due say to a sale of the investment (see below), or it is found not to be due, the tax relief will be clawed back by way of an assessment. However, no tax relief will be clawed back if the event triggering the tax relief reduction occurs after the investor's death.

Example

P Ltd has a calendar accounting period and subscribed for £80,000 worth of shares in an accredited CDFI on 1 March 2003. It sold shares for £20,000 on the open market on 1 September 2007. The qualifying date for 2007 is 1 March 2008. The tax relief due is calculated as follows:

Year	Tax relief first claimed	Claw-back of tax relief
2003	5% × £80,000 = £4,000	5% × 20,000 = 1,000
2004	5% × £80,000 = £4,000	5% × 20,000 = 1,000
2005	5% × £80,000 = £4,000	5% × 20,000 = 1,000
2006	5% × £80,000 = £4,000	5% × 20,000 = 1,000
2007	Nil	No tax relief due as shares have been sold by the qualifying date.

Receipt of value

The receipt of value rules try to ensure that the funds invested in the CDFI cannot be returned to the investor in another guise either shortly before the investment date, or during the five-year investment period.

The investor will suffer a reduction or complete withdrawal of the tax relief given under this scheme if he (or a person connected with him) receives an amount that is not of 'insignificant value' (broadly less than £1,000 or insignificant compared with the investment) from the CDFI (or a person connected with it) during the restricted period. The restricted period is the period of six years beginning exactly one year before the investment date. Certain payments are excluded from this including the payment of dividends or other distributions (provided they do not exceed a normal return), and the discharge of an ordinary trade debt, where the credit given is not more than six months.

If the investment in the CDFI was as shares or securities, the investor is permitted to receive some value (ignoring insignificant amounts) from the CDFI before his tax relief is reduced. The permitted levels of receipts are as follows:

- Before the 3rd anniversary of the investment date: up to 25% of the invested capital;

- Before the 4th anniversary of the investment date: up to 50% of the invested capital;

- Before the 5th anniversary of the investment date: up to 75% of the invested capital.

If the value received exceeds these permitted levels, all the tax relief in respect of the investment must be withdrawn.

If the value received is significant but does not exceed these permitted levels, the 'invested amount' is treated as reduced by the value received, in respect of the tax year or accounting period in which the value was received and any later periods.

If the investment in the CDFI was a loan, the receipt of value is treated as being a repayment of the loan made at the beginning of the year in which the value was received. However, if the value was received in the first 24 months of the period of restriction, the deemed loan repayment is treated as being made on the investment date.

Multiple investments

If the investor has made more than one investment in the CDFI and receives a receipt of value within the period of restriction, the receipt of value is allocated against those investments in proportion to the relative value of each investment in the year the receipt of value is received.

Loss of accreditation

If the CDFI losses its accreditation during the five-year investment period the investor will also lose its tax relief.

Investor becomes accredited

If the investor body becomes an accredited CDFI it will lose any further tax relief due on investments it has made under this scheme.

Early loan repayment

An investment in a CDFI made in the form of a loan may be partially repaid within the five-year investment period within prescribed limits. If the loan repayments exceed those limits by more than £1,000, or by an amount that is significant compared to the average capital balance of the relevant year of the investment period, all of the tax relief must be withdrawn.

Disposal of investment

Generally, if an investor disposes of all or part of his investment in a CDFI within the five-year investment period, he will lose all the tax relief due on that investment unless the disposal falls within one of the following circumstances:

- as part of the winding up or dissolving of the CDFI;
- as a deemed disposal the investment becomes of negligible value or is lost completely;
- the disposal is made after the CDFI has lost its accreditation; or
- sale of shares or securities as part of an arms-length bargain.

Where the shares or securities are sold, the tax relief due is reduced by 5% of the sale proceeds. If the shares are sold at book profit, 5% of the proceeds will be more than the tax relief due so all the tax relief must be withdrawn. If the tax relief attributed to the shares is less than 5% of the invested amount, say because the tax relief has been limited by the total tax liability of the investor, the reduction in the tax relief due to a sale is also proportionately reduced.

Example

P Ltd has a calendar accounting period and subscribed for £80,000 worth of shares in an accredited CDFI on 1 March 2003. It sold those shares for £20,000 on the open market on 1 September 2007. The qualifying date for 2007 is 1 March 2008. the tax relief due is calculated as follows:

Year	Tax relief first claimed	Claw-back of tax relief
2003	5% × £80,000 = £4,000	5% × 20,000 = 1,000
2004	5% × £80,000 = £4,000	5% × 20,000 = 1,000
2005	5% × £80,000 = £4,000	5% × 20,000 = 1,000
2006	5% × £80,000 = £4,000	5% × 20,000 = 1,000
2007	Nil	No tax relief due as shares have been sold by the qualifying date.

When an investor disposes of his shares or securities in a CDFI, the normal pool rules do not apply. The shares or securities are treated as being disposed of on a first in first out basis.

Legislation: ITA 2007, Pt. 7, Ch. 6; FA 2002, Sch. 26, Pt. 6

Tax Reporter: ¶325-000

1968 Information requirements

If an investor disposes of his investment in the CDFI within the five-year investment period or receives a loan repayment or receipt of value that would create a claw-back or restriction of his tax relief under this scheme, he must inform HMRC of the circumstances within the following deadlines:

- *For individuals*: by 31 January following the end of the tax year in which the event occurred;

- *For companies*: within 12 months of the end of the accounting period in which the event occurred.

If a person connected to the investor receives value from the CDFI, the investor must inform HMRC within 60 days of becoming aware of the event.

Legislation: ITA 2007, Pt. 7, Ch. 7

Tax Reporter: ¶325-000

Employees' and directors' expenses

1990   Extent of employees' deductions

Employees and directors are charged to tax on all their 'emoluments' (see 250ff.). The legislation allows a few special deductions but, apart from these, relief for necessary expenses is only given where the money is expended wholly, exclusively and necessarily in the performance of the employee's duties.

See further 1992 and 1994.

Legislation: ITEPA 2003, s. 327

Tax Reporter: ¶454-000

1990A   Exemption for paid or reimbursed expenses

From 6 April 2016, the dispensation regime (see 1991) was replaced with an exemption for reimbursed expenses and benefits (ITEPA 2003, Pt. 4, Ch. 7A). The exemption applies to expense payments and benefits in kind provided to employees where the employees would have been eligible for tax relief had they paid for the expenses themselves. Employers will also be able to reimburse employees at a scale rate rather than reimbursing the employee for the expense actually incurred. The exemption does not apply where the benefits or expenses are provided in connection with salary sacrifice arrangements.

To qualify for the exemption:

Paid or reimbursed expenses

- an amount equal to or exceeding the amount paid or reimbursed must be allowed as a deduction under ITEPA 2003, Pt. 5, Ch. 2 or 5 from the employee's earnings in respect of the expenses; and

- the payment or reimbursement is not provided pursuant to relevant salary sacrifice arrangements.

Scale rate payments

- the amount must be calculated and paid or reimbursed in an approved way;
- the payment or reimbursement must not be provided pursuant to relevant salary sacrifice arrangements;
- the payer or another person operates a system for checking:
  - (a) that the employee is, or employees are, in fact incurring and paying amounts in respect of expenses of the same kind;
  - (b) that a deduction would be allowed under ITEPA 2003, Pt. 5, Ch. 2 or 5, in respect of the amounts; and
- neither the payer nor any other person operating the system knows or suspects, or could reasonably be expected to know or suspect:
  - (a) that the employee has not incurred and paid an amount in respect of the expenses; or
  - (b) that a deduction from the employee's earnings would not be allowed under ITEPA 2003, Pt. 5, Ch. 2 or 5 in respect of the amount.

A sum is calculated and paid or reimbursed in an approved way if:

(a) it is calculated and paid or reimbursed in accordance with regulations made by HMRC; or

(b) it is calculated and paid or reimbursed in accordance with an approval given by HMRC (bespoke scale rate payments).

The exemption does not apply to expenses payments which are given as part of arrangements that reduce the amount of general earnings or specific employment income of the employee subject to tax and National Insurance contributions where one of the main purposes of the arrangement is to avoid tax or National Insurance contributions.

Legislation: ITEPA 2003, Pt. 4, Ch. 7A; SI 2015/1948

Tax Reporter: ¶413-235

1991   Dispensations

The dispensation regime was abolished from 6 April 2016 and replaced with a tax exemption for paid and reimbursed expenses (see 1990A) (although HMRC retain the powers to revoke dispensations issued prior to April 2016).

For tax years up to and including 2015–16, in cases where the employer satisfied the inspector that his arrangements for paying expenses to employees were adequately controlled and the amounts would be fully covered by an expenses deduction, the inspector could give a dispensation. The effect of this was that the PAYE procedure would not apply to the expenses for which the dispensation has been given.

Dispensations were not given for 'round-sum' expense allowances nor where such action would allow an employee to escape the implications of various chargeable benefit-in-kind provisions (see 382).

An application for a dispensation had to be made on form P11DX.

Dispensations given by HMRC also counted for National Insurance contributions (NICs).

Legislation: ITEPA 2003, s. 65 and Sch. 7, para. 15; FA 2015, s. 11 and 12

1992   Deductibility of employees' general expenses

For an employee or director to be allowed a particular deduction, the following conditions must be satisfied:

- the employee, etc. must be obliged to incur and pay the expense as holder of the employment; and

- the expense must be wholly, exclusively and necessarily incurred in the performance of those duties (see 1990).

'Wholly and exclusively'

Wholly and exclusively means that there cannot be any dual purpose in incurring the expenditure. Thus, expenditure which is partly incurred for personal purposes (e.g. on food or clothing) will be disallowed. However, HMRC may sometimes allow a proportionate part of the expenditure. See further 2010 and 2056.

Necessarily

The test for deduction of expenses under ITEPA 2003 is stricter than that applying for Sch. D purposes in that the expense must be necessarily incurred, as well as wholly and exclusively so. Thus, the fact that an expense was wholly and exclusively incurred in the performance of the duties will not be sufficient to support a claim for relief if it were not also necessary that the employee incurred the expense.

The courts have interpreted this very narrowly. For instance, it has been held that an expense must be one that each and every holder of the office would incur, not peculiar to the circumstances of any particular incumbent.

In the performance of the duties of the employment

In the performance of the duties means that any expenses incurred before the employee's duties commence or after they terminate will not be allowed as a deduction. Thus, the expense of obtaining a job or a job qualification is not usually deductible.

Expenditure incurred by an employee to qualify himself, or to keep himself qualified, to perform the duties of the employment – such as expenditure by a professional person in keeping himself informed of developments in his professional field – would not be incurred in the performance of his duties in the statutory sense. It appears that it is irrelevant whether the actions might be regarded as necessary.

For travelling, etc. expenses, see 1994.

Legislation: ITEPA 2003, s. 336

Cases: *R & C Commrs v Decadt*; *Brown v Bullock (HMIT)* (1961) 40 TC 1; *Smith (HMIT) v Abbott* [1994] BTC 66; *Fitzpatrick v IR Commrs (No. 2)* [1994] BTC 66; *Baird v Williams (HMIT)* [1999] BTC 228; *R & C Commrs v Banerjee* [2010] BTC 662; *Huhtala v R & C Commrs* [2011] UKUT 419 (TCC)

Tax Reporter: ¶453-200

1994   Employees' deductible travelling expenses

The tax treatment of employees' and directors' travelling and subsistence expenses was modernised and simplified from 6 April 1998.

Benchmark rates

Employers can use HMRC benchmark rates to make certain day subsistence payments free of tax and NICs to employees who incur allowable business travel expenses (see www.hmrc.gov.uk/employers/wwsr-bench.pdf). Employers do not have to use the rates. They can reimburse their employees' actual expenditure or apply to HMRC to agree a scale rate appropriate for their business needs in a dispensation.

HMRC have published benchmark worldwide subsistence rates, effective from 1 October 2014, that employers can use to reimburse accommodation and subsistence expenses incurred by employees who have to travel outside the UK. The benchmark rates are intended to represent the accommodation and subsistence expenses that employees incur during a period spent in a foreign country and do not cover incidental, allowable expenses that employees may incur en route, such as the taxi fare to the airport in the UK, which should be reimbursed separately. The worldwide

subsistence rates effective from 1 October 2014 are available at www.
gov.uk/government/uploads/system/uploads/attachment_data/file/
359797/2014_Worldwide_subsistence_rates.pdf.

Qualifying travelling expenses

'Qualifying travelling expenses' are now deductible from emoluments
(see 1990). These are:

(1) amounts necessarily expended on travelling in the performance of
     the duties of the employment, etc.; or

(2) other expenses of travelling which:

     (a) are attributable to the employee's, etc. necessary attendance at
          any place in performing the duties of the employment, etc.; and

     (b) are not expenses of 'ordinary commuting' or 'private travel'
          (see below).

HMRC regard 'travelling expenses' as including subsistence costs
attributable to the journey in question.

Travel between group companies

Expenses of travel between places where duties are carried out for
different offices or employments under or with companies in the same
group are treated as necessarily expended in performing the duties to be
performed at the destination.

Ordinary commuting and private travel

'Ordinary commuting' means travel between:

(1) the employee's home;

(2) a place that is not a 'workplace' in relation to the employment;

(3) and a place which is a 'permanent workplace' in relation to the
     employment.

'Private travel' means travel between:

(1) the employee's home and a place that is not a workplace in relation
     to the employment; or

(2) between two places neither of which is a workplace in relation to the
     employment.

'Workplace' means a place at which the employee's attendance is
necessary in performing the duties of the employment.

Travel between any two places which is for practical purposes substantially ordinary commuting or private travel is treated as ordinary commuting or private travel.

Permanent and temporary workplaces

For the purposes of (3) above, and subject to what follows below, 'permanent workplace' means a place which the employee regularly attends in performing the duties of the employment, and which is not a 'temporary workplace'. A 'temporary workplace' means a place which the employee attends in performing the duties of the employment for the purpose of performing a task of limited duration or for some other temporary purpose (see further below).

The 24-month rule and fixed term appointments

A place is not regarded as a temporary workplace if the employee's attendance is in the course of a 'period of continuous work' at that place:

(1) lasting more than 24 months; or

(2) comprising all or almost all of the period for which the employee is likely to hold the employment,

or if the employee's attendance is at a time when it is reasonable to assume that it will be in the course of such a period.

A 'period of continuous work' at a place is a period over which, looking at the whole period and considering all the employment duties, the employment duties fall to be performed to a significant extent at that place.

Where there is a change, or a contemplated change, in the place at which the employment duties are to be carried out, the change is ignored if it does not have any substantial effect on the employee's journey or on the expenses of travelling.

Depots and bases

A place which the employee regularly attends in performing employment duties is treated as a *permanent* workplace if it is either:

(1) the base from which the employment duties are performed; or

(2) the place at which the tasks to be carried out in performing the employment duties.

Area-based employees

An employee is treated as having a permanent workplace consisting of an area if all the following conditions are met:

(1) the employment duties are defined by reference to an area (whether or not they also require attendance at places outside the area);

(2) in performing the employment duties the employee attends different places within the area;

(3) none of the places which he or she attends in performing the employment duties is a permanent workplace; and

(4) applying para. 4 and 5 above to the area as if it were a place, the area meets the conditions for being a permanent workplace.

Example

An employee's return journey from home to his permanent workplace costs him £7. No relief has ever been available for this expenditure.

The employee makes an occasional journey from home to a temporary workplace which costs £15 return. Relief is available for the full cost of the journey: £15.

Concessions in relation to the following should also be noted.

- Financial assistance (including subsistence), etc. when public transport is disrupted.

- Financial assistance, etc. for home-to-work travel for the severely disabled.

- Offshore oil and gas, etc. workers' travel to and from the mainland (see 1580).

- Payments for employees' late-night journeys home. An employee's late-night taxi fares home which are reimbursed by the employer may be income tax-free where the employee is occasionally required to work late, but those occasions are neither regular nor frequent. 'Late' means after 9 p.m. The term 'regular' means following a predictable pattern in the normal course of employment. The exemption will therefore not apply to, for example, bar staff who regularly work until after 11 p.m., or a cashier who must work late every Friday night to deal with the week's takings.

- Employers may pay tax free (from 9 March 1999) for alternative transport to get car sharers home when exceptional circumstances, such as a domestic emergency, mean that the normal car sharing arrangements unavoidably break down. The concession aims to help employers promote car-sharing arrangements by their employees.

The last two concessions apply to a maximum of 60 journeys in a tax year.

See also 302 (incidental overnight expenses); 318 (members of the armed forces); 405 (mileage allowances); 2000 (subsistence costs).

Legislation: ITEPA 2003, s. 245–248, 337–342

Other Material: HMRC Brief 24/09

Tax Reporter: ¶454-000

1997 Machinery and plant allowances

Employees and directors may be entitled to capital allowances in respect of machinery or plant which is 'necessarily' provided for use in the performance of their duties.

However, in relation to an employee, etc. who uses his own 'mechanically propelled road vehicle' (or cycle, from 1999–2000) for work, only part of the capital expenditure on which was incurred for work purposes, the vehicle need *not* have been necessarily provided for use in the performance of his duties.

An employee's entitlement to balancing allowances (e.g. on leaving employment) is limited to a fraction (A/B) of the excess of 'qualifying expenditure' over 'disposal value', 'A' being the number of tax years for which he has claimed allowances, and 'B' being the number of tax years for which allowances fall to be made to him. Thus, if an employee chooses not to claim allowances in a period in which he is entitled to them, for instance because his income is insufficient to absorb them, his entitlement to balancing allowances is proportionately reduced, so that he cannot recoup the lost writing-down allowances at the end of his employment, or when the car ceases to belong to him.

See also 1886 (interest on loans to buy machinery).

Legislation: CAA 2001, s. 15(1), 36 and 262; FA 1999, s. 50

Case: *White v Higginbottom* [1983] BTC 46

Tax Reporter: ¶237-000

1998 Allowable accommodation and residence expenses of employees

Like most expenses other than qualifying travelling expenses (see 1992 and 1994), accommodation expenses, to be deductible, must be incurred wholly, exclusively and necessarily in the performance of an employee's or director's duties. Everyone has to live somewhere, so if an individual chooses to live a great distance from his place of work and stays at a hotel during the working week, he will be unable to deduct the hotel expenses.

Example 1

Sue has jobs with two completely separate companies, one in London, and the other in Birmingham. She lives in London, but on those days when she works in Birmingham she stays in a hotel. The expenses of living in the hotel would not be deductible.

Example 2

Teresa has a job in London and is occasionally required to go to Liverpool on business. She stays in a hotel when in Liverpool. The hotel expenses in this case are deductible.

The cost of providing personal accommodation for employees by employers will form part of that employee's taxable emoluments whether or not it is deducted from that employee's wages or salary (see 314).

Employees required to work from home are permitted to deduct a proportion of many costs attributable to the property, including council tax.

Other Material: *Tax Bulletin*, Issue 69, October 2005 (homeworking expenses)

Tax Reporter: ¶454-000

2000 Employees' subsistence costs

The expense of meals is rarely necessarily incurred in the performance of one's duties, as required for it to be allowable (see 1990). Even if the expense is necessarily incurred, it would be unusual to find that the expense was incurred wholly and exclusively in the performance of an employee's duties.

Deduction is currently allowed of obligatory travelling expenses attributable to an employee's necessary attendance at any place in performing his employment duties (and which are not expenses of ordinary commuting or private travel); such expenses include subsistence costs attributable to the journey in question (see 1994). See also 302 as regards incidental overnight expenses.

Working rule agreements

Working rule agreements drawn up between employers' federations and trade unions set out the terms and conditions of a large number of employees in the construction and allied industries. HMRC have agreed that some of the modest travel and subsistence allowances which employees receive under these agreements will not be taxed. However, the employees covered can still choose relief under the ordinary rules. If so, they are entitled to relief for the full cost of business journeys *less* the amount of tax-free allowance received.

Lorry drivers' meals

Where travelling itself is an essential feature of an employee's duties ('travelling appointments'), with the result that he has to spend money on meals in restaurants or cafés above what he would spend if he had a fixed place or area of work or were able to get home for meals, a deduction may be allowed for the extra expenses necessarily incurred in the performance of the duties.

Drivers who qualify for consideration under this heading are those who are engaged full-time in travelling in the performance of their duties. By this is meant employment as a driver throughout the full normal working hours of each day, except those days when the employee cannot work by reason of sickness or other reasonable cause, or which are holidays or rest days. Jobs which entail only incidental travelling are not regarded as 'travelling appointments'.

Even full-time drivers are excluded from consideration if they travel only in a limited area. This is because they incur no additional expenses when at work from one day to the next, as they have an established pattern of expenditure on meals in the same way as any other employee who has to work at a distance from home and who cannot return home for lunch.

HMRC require claimants to give full details of the nature of their duties in addition to providing evidence of the expenditure actually incurred. In practice, relief is not restricted by reference to amounts of expenditure saved by not having meals at home or a fixed place of work.

In addition, HMRC have agreed with the Road Haulage Association an overnight allowance tax-free without need for detailed bills and vouchers, but subject to production of documentary evidence that the taxpayer was absent from home overnight and based at a particular depot.

Legislation: ITEPA 2003, s. 89

Cases: *Williams* [2012] TC 02062; *Reiter* [2010] TC 00587

Tax Reporter: ¶455-000

2002 Employees' business entertaining

Usually, there are no allowable deductions for business entertainment expenses. However, if the expenses are met out of a sum provided by the employer for business entertainment and:

- that sum is included in the employee's emoluments; and

- that sum was disallowed in computing the profits or losses of the trade,

that sum may be deductible if it satisfies the 'wholly, exclusively and necessarily' test (see 1990).

Legislation: ITEPA 2003, s. 356 and 357

Tax Reporter: ¶455-200

2004 Fees and subscriptions to professional bodies

An employee or director may deduct an annual subscription paid to certain professional bodies and learned societies, etc. approved by HMRC. A lengthy list of approved bodies is published periodically by HMRC. It is available on the HMRC website at www.hmrc.gov.uk/list3/list3.htm.

From 6 April 2014, deductions can be made for trainee registration fees payable to bodies approved by the General Dental Council in respect of relevant specialist training and fees payable for entry or retention of a name on any register or list of veterinary nurses maintained by the Royal College of Veterinary Surgeons.

Fees and contributions are also deductible:

- in respect of the retention of a name in the Register of Architects;

- in respect of the retention of a name in the dentists' register or on a roll or record kept for a class of ancillary dental workers;

- in respect of the retention of a name in either of the registers of ophthalmic opticians or in the register of dispensing opticians;

- by a registered patent agent;

- in respect of the retention of a name in the register of pharmaceutical chemists;

- to the Compensation Fund or Guarantee Fund payable on the issue of a solicitor's practising certificate;

- by a registered veterinary surgeon or by a person registered in the Supplementary Veterinary Register.

Income tax

The above fees will be deductible if the fee is payable in respect of a registration (or retention of a name on a roll or record) or certificate which is a condition, or one of alternative conditions, of the performance of the duties of the office or employment.

HMRC generally permit relief for members of the ICAEW in respect of subscriptions to *Accountancy* on the basis that it is the official journal of the Institute and effectively part of the subscription to the Institute.

Entertainers' agency fees

In 1990, HMRC announced that actors and other performers engaged on standard Equity contracts would be moved from former Sch. D to Sch. E from 6 April 1990, unless their first appearance pre-dated 6 April 1987 (see 253). To secure engagements, most of such entertainers rely on theatrical agents, whose fees would be non-deductible under the strict rules of Sch. E (see 1990). However, from the same date actors, singers, musicians, dancers and theatrical artists may deduct from their chargeable emoluments fees, inclusive of VAT, paid to agents (including co-operative society arrangements), not exceeding $17\frac{1}{2}\%$ of their emoluments in any tax year.

Legislation: ITEPA 2003, s. 343–345; *Income Tax (Professional Fees) Order* 2014 (SI 2014/859)

Tax Reporter: ¶455-000

2006   Civil servants' expenses

Where persons such as civil servants are paid out of public funds, the Treasury will fix an amount representing the average amount spent wholly, exclusively and necessarily in the performance of their duties. The amount so fixed by the Treasury will then be deducted from salary when charging it to income tax. If a person actually has greater expenses than the amount fixed, he will be able to deduct the actual expenses incurred wholly, exclusively and necessarily in the performance of his duties.

Legislation: ITEPA 2003, s. 328–330, 368

Tax Reporter: ¶406-500

2008   Security assets and services

A deduction is allowed in respect of expenditure incurred or reimbursed by an employer on the provision of security assets and security services which improve personal security. The security asset or service must be provided for the employee to meet a special threat to his personal physical security which arises wholly or mainly by virtue of the particular employment concerned. HMRC have given such examples of qualifying security assets and services as alarm systems, bullet-resistant windows in houses, floodlighting and security guards.

Legislation: FA 1989, s. 50–52

Tax Reporter: ¶456-000

2010   Tools and special clothing allowance

In some cases, individuals will incur expenditure on the cost or upkeep of tools or special clothing necessary for work. By concession, HMRC give flat-rate allowances for most classes of trade, which have been agreed with the trade unions concerned, without enquiring what any individual employee has actually spent. A £60 allowance for fire fighters was agreed with fire service unions in 1994.

Further categories of allowance have been introduced for healthcare workers for 1998–99 onwards. Tax relief on between £45 and £110 per year will be available to certain employees who have to wear a uniform and are not provided with laundry services by their employers.

Legislation: ITEPA 2003, s. 367

Tax Reporter: ¶456-000

Property income deductions and losses

2020   Property business deductions

The profits of a property business are calculated in the same way as the profits of a trade, but are subject to certain limits (as set out in the table in ITTOIA 2005, s. 272). The following business deduction rules apply:

- business entertainment expenses;
- expenditure involving crime;
- redundancy payments;
- training courses for employees;

- counselling services for employees;
- consideration for restrictive undertakings;
- deductions on respect of certain emoluments;
- expenses connected with non-approved retirement benefit schemes;
- expenditure connected with providing security assets or services; and
- rules for computing profits and losses.

Legislation: ITTOIA 2005, s. 272, 274 and 275

Tax Reporter: ¶300-000

2022   Energy-saving items

Landlords may claim up to £1,500 per property per tax year for expenditure incurred in respect of energy-saving items (such as loft and cavity wall insulation, hot water system insulation, draught proofing and installation of floor insulation), where the expenditure is incurred in the course of a property income business. Where more than one person has an interest in the building concerned, the allowance may be apportioned accordingly.

From April 2007, the allowance is also available to corporate landlords who let residential properties.

Legislation: ITTOIA 2005, s. 312; FA 2004, s. 133; *Energy-Saving Items (Income Tax) Regulations* 2007 (SI 2007/3278)

2026   Maintenance funds for historic buildings

Adjustments are made where part of an estate is, or becomes, comprised in a maintenance fund for historic buildings, etc. This treatment has been modified for years after 1994–95, and from April 1998 for corporation tax purposes, to operate in the context of a property income business (see 1200ff.). Any excess expenditure remaining after relief is given under the provisions outlined at 2024 can be relieved as a property income business loss (see 2030).

The above provisions are to be repealed for income tax purposes from 6 April 2001 and for corporation tax purposes from 1 April 2001.

Legislation: FA 1998, s. 39; ICTA 1988, s. 27

Tax Reporter: ¶300-000

2028   Expenditure on making sea walls

Property income businesses may also attract an annual deduction for a twenty-first proportion of any expenditure on a wall or embankment erected to protect premises from the sea or a tidal river.

Legislation: ITTOIA 2005, s. 315–318

Tax Reporter: ¶300-000

2029   Relief for finance costs related to residential property businesses

From April 2017, per legislation introduced by *Finance (No. 2) Act* 2015, the amount of income tax relief certain landlords can obtain on residential property finance costs (such as mortgage interest) will move towards restriction to the basic rate of tax. The change is being phased in from 6 April 2017 over four years.

The restriction on the amount of deductible finance costs does *not* apply to property businesses carried on by companies otherwise than in a fiduciary or representative capacity. Furnished holiday lettings are excluded.

The legislation provides for a two-stage process: a restriction on the amount of deductible finance costs in calculating profits of the property business, and a new tax reduction (given to individuals and to trustees of certain settlements) for all such non-deductible finance costs.

A separate restriction applies, from April 2017, for investment loan interest in the case of property partnerships.

The restriction

Deductions for finance costs related to residential property will be restricted as follows:

(a) in 2017–18, the deduction from property income (as is currently allowed) will be restricted to 75% of the relevant finance costs (as to which, see further below);

(b) in 2018–19, restricted to 50% of such finance costs;

(c) in 2019–20, restricted to 25% of such finance costs; and

(d) from 2020–21, no such finance costs incurred by a landlord will be allowed as a deduction.

The tax reduction

In summary, individuals will be able to claim a tax reduction at step 6 in the calculation of income tax liability (see 244) on the portion of finance costs *not* deducted in calculating the profit, to be calculated as 20% of the lower of:

- the finance costs not deducted from income in the tax year (25% for 2017–18, 50% for 2018–19, 75% for 2019–20 and 100% thereafter);

- the profits of the property business in the tax year; or

- the total income (excluding savings income and dividend income) that exceeds the personal allowance and blind person's allowance in the tax year.

Any excess finance costs may be carried forward to following years if the tax reduction has been limited to 20% of the profits of the property business in the tax year.

Legislation: ITTOIA 2005, s. 272A–272B, 274A–274B; ITA 2007, s. 399A–399B

Tax Reporter: ¶300-350

2030 Property income business losses

Relief is provided for income tax losses arising in a property income business (see 1200) or an 'overseas property business' (see 1660).

Carry-forward relief

A loss sustained in a property income business is computed in the way in which property income profits are computed. Such a loss, sustained by an individual or partner in a tax year, is automatically carried forward to be set against the first available profits of that business. If those profits suffice to cover the loss, the taxpayer cannot opt to set off only part of the loss. If the business ceases with unrelieved losses, these cannot be carried forward to any new property income business subsequently set up.

Excess expenditure and interest

Unrelieved property income business excess expenditure and unrelieved furnished letting losses arising in years before 1995–96 are converted into losses to be set against the first available property income business profits after 1994–95. Similarly, where, on the change to the property income business rules, there is an excess of interest to be set against income from property which, but for the change, would have been carried forward against property income of a year or years after 1994–95, the unrelieved excess is converted into a loss to be set against the first available property income business profits after 1994–95.

Excess capital allowances

Where a taxpayer incurs a property income business loss, and:

- the capital allowances treated as expenses in computing the loss exceed the amount of any balancing charges treated as receipts in computing the loss; and/or

- the property income business has been carried on in relation to land which consists of or includes an agricultural estate to which allowable agricultural expenses, deducted in computing the loss, are attributable;

then the taxpayer may claim, in relation to the tax year of the loss or the following year, to have some or all of the capital allowances, or agricultural part of the loss, set against his *general* income. Before 1997–98, property income business losses attributable to excess capital allowances could not be set against other income of the same year.

Time-limit for claims

The above claim must be accompanied by all such amendments as may be needed of any self-assessment previously made by the claimant. The claim cannot be made after the end of 12 months from 31 January following the end of the year to which it relates.

Legislation: ITA 2007, s. 118–124; FA 1997, Sch. 15

Tax Reporter: ¶300-000

Business expenses and losses

2050 Extent of relief for business expenses and losses

Unless a business is using the cash basis (see 589), taxable business income is calculated by deducting *all allowable* expenses incurred in the income year from the total assessable income earned during that year (see 1850). Note that it is the gross receipts from a business activity that are brought in as assessable income, not the net profits or gains according to commercial principles.

Losses or outgoings of a capital nature, even though incurred in the course of producing assessable income, are not generally deductible. Expenses or losses of a private or domestic nature are not deductible at all.

As to the treatment of trading stock for tax accounting purposes, see 652ff.

The Taxes Acts seldom *expressly* allow deductible expenses, though it is provided that only deductions which are expressly enumerated in the Acts are allowable. The usual form is that the Acts set out what is disallowed, and by implication what is not disallowed is allowed (see 2059); however, certain transactions are effectively ignored, e.g. certain stock lending arrangements are ignored on both the expenditure and income sides (see 646).

In order to be allowable, an expense must normally be of a revenue nature (see 2053) and incurred wholly and exclusively for the purposes of the trade (see 2056).

Timing

Unless a business is using the new cash basis (see 589) from 2013–14, a long-established principle requires that, for tax purposes, expenditure should be taken into account when it is incurred (unless there is some overriding statutory provision or principle developed in the cases to the contrary).

There are special rules for spreading certain pension contributions (see 2062) and there is some uncertainty regarding lease rentals (see 2077).

Purely contingent liabilities cannot be recognised but statistical estimation of facts which had happened but were unknown does seem to be permissible. Hence, for example, the Privy Council has held that a figure for anticipated liability under warranties given with vehicles sold to remedy defects manifesting themselves within 12 months was deductible in computing profits.

Provisions for anticipated losses or expenses

A business makes a 'provision' where it expects to pay out money in the future and takes that probable expense into account when working out its current profits. The legislation requires a business to pay tax 'on the full amount of the profits or gains of the year of assessment' (no more and no less), and the courts until recently (see 2077) took the firm view that, for tax purposes, neither profit nor loss could be anticipated.

Legislation: ITTOIA 2005, s. 7(1), 200(4)

Cases: *Patel* [2015] TC 04225; *Herbert Smith v Honour (HMIT)* [1999] BTC 44; *Jenners, Princes Street Edinburgh Ltd v IR Commrs* (1998) Sp C 166; *Commr of Inland Revenue (New Zealand) v Mitsubishi Motors Ltd* [1996] BTC 398; *Gallagher v Jones (HMIT); Threlfall v Jones (HMIT)*

[1993] BTC 310; *BSC Footwear Ltd v Ridgway (HMIT)* [1972] AC 544; *Duple Motor Bodies Ltd v Ostime (HMIT)* [1961] 1 WLR 739

2053 Capital or revenue expenditure

Revenue expenditure is allowable as a business expense provided it is incurred 'wholly and exclusively for the purposes of the trade, etc.' (see 2056) and is not specifically disallowed in the Taxes Acts (see 2059). Usually, there is no problem in distinguishing between expenditure on revenue account and expenditure on capital account. Thus, the cost of purchasing (whether by a single payment or by way of instalments of the lump sum cost) business premises is capital expenditure, while rent paid for business premises is revenue expenditure, and the cost of alterations, additions, improvements or renovations is capital, while the cost of repairs is revenue.

There is clearly some overlap between the various 'tests' below which have been suggested by the courts.

Note that the capital versus revenue issue will not be the same for those businesses using the cash basis (see 589).

Fixed and circulating capital

Fixed capital and circulating capital should be distinguished. Fixed capital represents those assets which are retained and used in order to make profits, e.g. machinery used to make cars in a car factory is part of the fixed capital. Circulating capital on the other hand represents those assets which are bought and sold in the ordinary course of trade, e.g. machinery bought and sold by a trader in machinery is part of the circulating capital and the cost of it is deductible. In one case, £733,649 claimed as the cost of winding up a North Sea Oil operation was held to be a non-deductible capital expense as the cost related to the profit-making structure of the business, i.e. fixed capital.

The cost of 'creating, acquiring or enlarging the permanent ... structure of which the income is to be the produce or fruit' is of a capital nature, while 'the cost of earning that income itself or performing the income-earning operations' is a revenue expense. Applying these dicta, the Privy Council has held that interest paid by a Hong Kong development company on a loan obtained for a capital project was a payment on capital account, which was therefore not deductible from its taxable profits: the fact that interest is income in the recipient's hands and a recurring and periodic payment does not necessarily mean that it is a revenue expense.

With respect to operations after 6 April 1989, expenditure on making good landfill sites for waste disposal qualifies as a revenue deduction for persons holding disposal or waste management licences (unless capital allowances are available): expenditure on preparing a site is written off according to the proportion of site capacity filled with waste in the appropriate period, and expenditure on making good a site is allowed as a trading expense in the period in which it is paid. Site preparation expenditure includes costs incurred before the disposal licence is granted or in obtaining such licence. Authorisations for the disposal of radioactive waste are added to the lists of relevant licences for trades begun after 31 March 1993; relief for site preparation is also extended for such companies to any expenditure which is incurred before trading starts.

Enduring benefit

In difficult cases, the courts have held that, in the absence of special circumstances, expenditure is of a capital nature where it is made with a view to bringing into existence an asset or an advantage (tangible or intangible) for the enduring benefit of the trade or business.

One should perhaps look and see whether a capital asset is identifiable from the sum expended. The payment (to be of a capital nature) must be made for an enduring capital asset even if one of the advantages secured by the payment for the capital asset is an increased share in profits. The initial payment by a franchisee depends upon what it is for but, in HMRC's view, it is generally for substantial rights of an enduring nature to initiate or substantially extend a business and is together with any related professional fees; however, HMRC will accept that an appropriate part of the initial fee is for revenue items, such as stock or training of staff (not the franchisee), and hence allowable, where:

- the sum claimed in respect of revenue items fairly reflects the actual goods and services provided; and

- it is clear that those services are not separately charged for in the continuing fees.

Once-and-for-all expenditure on a capital asset

There has been distinguished as capital expenditure, 'once and for all expenditure on a capital asset to make it more advantageous'.

Preservation of trade

A payment to get rid of an obstacle to successful trading is a revenue and not a capital payment. However, the purpose of the taxpayer to preserve the trade is not determinative of the capital/income issue.

Software development costs

HMRC's view is that an in-house or contracted-out software project to ensure that existing computer systems could be adapted for the millennium would always be a revenue matter unless it was part of a major new project instituting other changes and the project was of a capital nature. Similarly, conversion-driven costs required in adapting computer systems for the euro are unlikely to be capital.

Legislation: ITTOIA 2005, s. 165–168

Cases: *Southern Counties Agricultural Trading Society v Blackler (HMIT)* (1999) Sp C 198; *Wharf Properties Ltd v Commr of Inland Revenue (Hong Kong)* [1997] BTC 173; *Croydon Hotel & Leisure Co v Bowen (HMIT)* (1996) Sp C 101; *Lawson (HMIT) v Johnson Matthey plc* [1992] BTC 324; *Rolfe (HMIT) v Wimpey Waste Management Ltd* [1989] BTC 191; *RTZ Oil & Gas Ltd v Elliss (HMIT)* [1987] BTC 359; *E Bott Ltd v Price (HMIT)* [1987] BTC 49; *Jeffs (HMIT) v Ringtons Ltd* [1985] BTC 585; *Whitehead (HMIT) v Tubbs (Elastics) Ltd* [1983] BTC 28; *Watney Combe Reid & Co Ltd v Pike (HMIT)* [1982] BTC 288; *Tucker (HMIT) v Granada Motorway Services Ltd* [1979] 1 WLR 683; *IR Commrs v Carron Co* (1968) 45 TC 18; *Commr of Taxes v Nchanga Consolidated Copper Mines Ltd* [1964] AC 948; *Anglo-Persian Oil Co Ltd v Dale (HMIT)* [1932] 1 KB 124; *Mallett (HMIT) v Staveley Coal and Iron Co Ltd* [1928] 2 KB 405; *British Insulated and Helsby Cables Ltd v Atherton (HMIT)* [1926] AC 205

Tax Reporter: ¶220-150

2056   Expenditure not wholly and exclusively for business

To be deductible as a business expense (see 2050) the expenditure must be wholly and exclusively laid out or expended for the purposes of the business. The word 'wholly' refers to the quantum, i.e. how much is referable to business purposes. Thus, if expenditure is not wholly referable to a business purpose, the excess will be disallowed as a deduction. The word 'exclusively' means that if the expenditure was partly laid out for business purposes and partly for personal purposes, then the expenditure will be disallowed as a deduction.

However, even if there is such a duality of purpose HMRC will often allow apportionment if *accurate* apportionment can be made. It should be noted that if the payment is solely for business purposes, then it will be deductible even if some private benefit is obtained by the taxpayer. Where a taxpayer runs his business from home, a proportionate part of his costs relating to the property will usually be allowed, including presumably council tax in the same way as for employees required to work from home; HMRC have ceased to apply the one-third rule of thumb for business use of a farmhouse (also reflected in a change to the CGT rules at 6244).

Note that the deductibility of expenditure issue will not be the same for those businesses using the cash basis (see 589).

Travelling expenses

Travelling expenses are not deductible unless they are wholly and exclusively for business purposes. HMRC by concession usually allow a proportionate part of the travelling expenses if there is duality of purpose (see above). Travelling expenses are allowed as a deduction where the taxpayer is travelling from one place of work to another in the course of his duties.

Where the cost of overnight accommodation is allowable as a business expense, HMRC accept reasonable claims for the cost of evening meals and breakfast (as substantiated by receipts or other records); in the case of long-distance self-employed lorry drivers, a deduction will be allowed whether such meals are taken as an adjunct to overnight accommodation or where they spend the night in their cabs.

Legislation: ITTOIA 2005, s. 34

Cases: *Huhtala v R & C Commrs* [2011] UKUT 419 (TCC); *McLaren v Mumford (HMIT)* [1996] BTC 490; *Redkite Ltd v Inspector of Taxes* (1996) Sp C 93; *MacKinlay (HMIT) v Arthur Young McClelland Moores & Co* [1989] BTC 587; *Mallalieu v Drummond (HMIT)* [1983] BTC 380; *Huntley* [2010] UKFTT 551 (TC); [2011] TC 00804

Tax Reporter: ¶208-000

2058 Deductions allowable at a fixed rate

From 2013–14, unincorporated businesses (more specifically self-employed individuals and partnerships where all the partners are individuals (ITTOIA 2005, s. 94C)) can choose to use any of the following 'simplified expenses' deductions when computing business profits:

- fixed allowances for business mileage (instead of deductions for actual expenditure incurred purchasing, maintaining and running vehicles, apportioned between business and private use) (ITTOIA 2005, s. 94Dff.);

- a flat rate to calculate expenses relating to business use of home (instead of deductions for expenditure incurred, apportioned between business and private use) (ITTOIA 2005, s. 94H); and

- a three-tier banded rate to calculate the adjustment of private use of business premises (instead of deductions for expenditure incurred, apportioned between business and private use) (ITTOIA 2005, s. 94I).

See key data tables for prescribed rates.

Legislation: ITTOIA 2005, Pt. 2, Ch. 5A

Tax Reporter: ¶208-380

2059 Statutory disallowances for business expenses

Expenditure not wholly and exclusively for trading purposes

See 2056.

Expenditure involving a criminal offence

Payments made as a result of blackmail or extortion, whether by terrorist groups or other criminals, or constituting the commission of a criminal offence (e.g. bribes), are disallowed.

Expenditure to maintain taxpayer or his family

No sum can be deducted in computing taxable business profits, in respect of any disbursements or expenses of maintenance of the taxpayer, his family or establishment, or any sums expended for any other domestic or private purposes distinct from business purposes.

Example

Alfie draws £150 a week from his business for personal expenditure. This will be disallowed as a deduction.

Rent for dwelling-house

The rent of a dwelling-house or domestic offices, or any part thereof, is not allowed as deduction, however, an allowance may be claimed for expenditure incurred in connection with a part of the taxpayer's home used for business purposes, for example as an office or a workshop. In practice, the deduction of a proportion of general expenditure, such as insurance or mortgage interest, is permitted.

From 2013–14, unincorporated businesses can choose to make a flat-rate deduction for use of home for business purposes instead of claiming deductions for actual expenditures incurred. These flat-rate allowances have been introduced as part of a set of simpler rules for some business expenses under the banner of 'simpler income tax for small businesses' (see 589).

> **Example**
>
> Alison rents premises for £120 per week. One-third of the premises is used as her office in the course of her business. One-third of the rent, i.e. £40, will be allowed as a deduction.

Repairs and alterations

While sums expended for repairing premises occupied, or for supplying, repairing or altering any implements, utensils or articles employed for business purposes are deductible, capital expenditure (e.g. on improving business premises) is disallowed.

> **Example 1**
>
> Brandon replaces the single glazing in his factory with double glazing. This will not be an allowable deduction since it is capital employed in improving the premises.

Deductions for expenditure on disrepair existing at the time of purchase may well be disallowed, though deduction for expenditure on deferred repairs (i.e. disrepair existing at the time of purchase but not dealt with for good reason) may be allowed if there is a good reason for deferral.

> **Example 2**
>
> Archie purchases a ship for his business. It is unseaworthy, which is reflected in the purchase price of £500,000. Archie spends £150,000 on making it seaworthy and uses it for two years when further repairs costing £200,000 are required due to deterioration over that period. The £150,000 spent making the ship into a profit-making asset will not be allowed as a deduction since it is regarded as capital expenditure as the asset was incapable of being used when acquired and the purchase price reflected this. However, the further repairs costing £200,000 will be allowed as a deduction since it is revenue expenditure.

Non-trading losses

Any losses not connected with or arising out of the business is not allowed as a deduction.

Capital withdrawn from, or employed in, the business

Any capital withdrawn from, or any sum employed or intended to be employed as capital in the business, is not allowed as a deduction. This, however, does not include interest.

Notional interest

Any interest which might have been made if any such sums withdrawn as capital (above) or expended on improvements to business premises (above) had been laid out at interest is not allowed as a deduction.

Example

Amelia decides to replace the single glazing in her factory with double glazing. This will not be an allowable deduction since it is capital employed in improving the premises. Amelia cannot claim that she could have invested the money used for double glazing and earned interest on it and therefore the interest forgone should be allowed as a deduction.

Debts

Any debts, except bad debts proved to be such, trade debts given up by a creditor as part of a formal voluntary arrangement under the *Insolvency Act* 1986 or a compromise with creditors under the *Companies Act* 2006, s. 895(1) and 896, and doubtful debts to the extent that they are respectively estimated to be bad, will be disallowed as a deduction in arriving at the profits of the year in which the debts become bad or doubtful; in the case of the bankruptcy or insolvency of a debtor, the amount which may reasonably be expected to be received on any such debt will be deemed to be the value thereof. If the debt is later paid, then it must be brought in as a trading receipt in the year in which it is paid (see 648).

Example

Annie, a trader, is owed money by Brenda for goods supplied in Year 1 and Annie decides to write the debt off as a bad debt. She is able to prove to HMRC that it is a bad debt and it is allowed as a deduction. However, in Year 5 Brenda pays the debt and Annie has to enter it into her books for that year as a receipt of her trade.

Relief is available for certain overseas trade debts. The legislation generally gives relief by deducting the appropriate amount from the trading profits of the 'accounting period' in which it is regarded as unremittable if it is outstanding for at least a year after the end of that period and meets certain general conditions. There are special provisions relating to companies holding debts with overseas governments.

A deduction may be permitted for a debt incurred in a prior trade proving to be irrecoverable after the deemed commencement of a new trade following a change in persons carrying it on, etc.

Average loss after adjustment

Any average loss beyond the actual amount of loss after adjustment will not be allowed as a deduction. This relates to marine, etc. insurance.

Insurance or indemnity

Any sum recoverable under an insurance or contract of indemnity will not be allowable as a deduction. HMRC treat benefits paid under insurance policies taken out by medical practitioners in respect of locum and fixed practice expenses in the event of the policyholder's incapacity or illness as taxable professional receipts, and the premiums as deductible.

Annuity or other annual payment

Any annuity or other annual payment (other than interest) payable out of profits will not be allowed as a deduction. This does not apply to payments made in earning profits but only to payments which are a charge on the profits and therefore paid under deduction of income tax.

Interest paid to non-residents

Any interest paid to a person not resident in the UK if and so far as it is interest at more than a reasonable commercial rate is not deductible (see further 2089).

Patent royalties

A royalty or other sum paid (under deduction of basic rate income tax: see 1368–1370) in respect of the user of a patent is disallowed as a deduction.

On the other hand, fees and expenses incurred in obtaining (or attempting to obtain) the grant of a patent, trade mark, etc. are allowable.

Mining rents and royalties

Any rent, royalty or other payment which, by ITTOIA 2005, s. 340 (in relation to payments made before 1 May 1995: see 962) or by ITTOIA 2005, s. 344, was subject to deduction of tax as if it were a royalty or other sum paid for the use of a patent, was disallowed as a deduction.

VAT penalties

The following are disallowed for all tax purposes:

(1) penalties under:

  (a) VATA 1994, s. 60–70 (see 8480ff.), FA 1994, s. 8–11 (excise); and

  (b) FA 1994, Sch. 7, para. 12–19 (insurance premium tax);

(2) interest under:

  (a) VATA 1994, s. 74 (see 8544); and

  (b) FA 1994, Sch. 7, para. 21 (insurance premium tax);

(3) surcharges under VATA 1994, s. 59 (see 8516).

As a corollary, any repayment supplement paid under VATA 1994, s. 79 (see 8522) is disregarded for all tax purposes.

Entertainment

Expenditure on business entertainment, including hospitality and most gifts, is disallowable unless provided in the ordinary course of the trade, profession or vocation (which is a trade, etc. relating to such activity) or for general advertising (though staff entertaining and certain promotional gifts are allowable: see 2080).

Legislation: ITTOIA 2005, s. 34, 35(1), 45–47, 55, 107–109

Cases: *Taylor v Clatworthy (HMIT)* (1996) Sp C 103; *Odeon Associated Theatres Ltd v Jones (HMIT)* [1973] Ch 288; *Law Shipping Co Ltd v IR Commrs* (1923) 12 TC 621

Tax Reporter: ¶207-200

2062 Payments for employees' benefit

The wages and salaries of employees are generally 'allowable business deductions' (see 2050) in the same way as other common payments made wholly and exclusively for the purposes of the business (see 2098). However, in the rare circumstances in which such amounts are not paid within the period of nine months from the end of the period of account, a deduction is denied until such emoluments are paid; special modifications apply to Lloyd's underwriters. Other payments made in connection with employees are set out below. See also 2065 (training costs).

Pension scheme contributions

Except as noted below, pension scheme contributions in respect of employees are generally allowable in the same way as pure wages.

Special contributions (as opposed to ordinary contributions) may have to be spread over a period depending upon the circumstances. The manner in which the Pension Schemes Office spreads such contributions was changed in August 1991, but later relaxed so as to allow the old rules to be used for accounting periods beginning before 1 September 1991 – the change involved spreading the whole contribution in accordance with the following table rather than spreading the excess over the normal level of contributions:

£0.5m to £1m	2 years
£1m to £2m	3 years
over £2m	4 years

The PSO's decision is not reviewable by the appeal tribunal.

An employer is only entitled to deduct payments to a non-approved retirement benefits scheme where, broadly, the employees who benefit are chargeable to income tax on the payments, though deductibility is to be determined on the general principles of business expenses (wholly and exclusively, etc.) or of investment companies' management expenses where payments or provisions are made in respect of the following (before 1996–97 relief was by concession):

(1) a superannuation fund accepted as a wholly overseas fund; or

(2) a retirement benefits scheme established outside the UK which is accepted as corresponding to an approved scheme, if the payments or provisions are made for the benefit of:

(a) employees who are in receipt of 'foreign emoluments'; or

(b) employees who are not resident in the UK whose duties are performed wholly outside the UK.

With effect from periods of account ending after 5 April 1993, tax relief is only due for sums actually paid by employers into occupational pension schemes and not for provisions or accruals in respect of such payments; payments which are spread forward are unaffected. No deduction can, in any event, be allowed for sums paid into schemes after 5 April 1993 to the extent that provisions in excess of contributions actually paid have already been allowed for tax purposes.

Compensation

A compensation payment to get rid of an unsuitable employee is allowable if it was necessary for the business and was made for that purpose. The payment would not be deductible if the trade were discontinued or if it were made to compensate for loss of office when the company was taken over. However, compensation payments on cessation of trading (or partial discontinuance) are allowable up to three times the statutory redundancy payment.

Payroll giving: administrative costs

The expenses which an employer incurs in operating a 'payroll giving scheme' (see 904) are normally deductible on general principles. Relief specifically extends to payments made to an agent approved by HMRC for the purposes of directing payments to appropriate beneficiaries.

Employee trusts and share schemes

The deductibility of sums paid into employee trust funds is ordinarily determined according to general principles; however, there are exceptions for pension schemes (see above), share option scheme costs and costs/contributions relating to profit-sharing schemes or employee share ownership trusts.

Restrictive covenants

Restrictive covenant payments caught by the provisions outlined at 283 are deductible as expenses of a trade, profession or vocation, and from the expenses of management of an investment company.

Redundancy

Redundancy payments are generally an allowable deduction either under general principles or specifically. If the right to a tax deduction depends on statute, relief is due for the period of account in which the payment is made, and where the payment is made after the discontinuance, it is regarded for this purpose as made on the last day on which the business is carried on.

Outplacement counselling

The costs of 'outplacement counselling', and related fees or travelling expenses, for redundant or potentially redundant employees are deductible, even if the redundancy arises out of the closing down of the business.

Benefits-in-kind

Benefit payments are usually deductible: i.e. expenditure which usually merely benefits the employee, e.g. for Christmas parties, is usually deductible since it fosters good industrial relations. This generally includes the situation in which an employer pays an employee's council tax.

National Insurance

Employers may deduct secondary Class 1, Class 1A and Class 1B National Insurance contributions when computing their taxable profits.

The employment allowance allows employers to make a reduction of up to £3,000 p.a. in secondary NIC payments against their employer PAYE NIC liabilities. Prior to 6 April 2016, the limit was £2,000 p.a. From April 2016, companies where the director is the sole employee are no longer be able to claim the employment allowance.

Legislation: ITTOIA 2005, s. 31, 35–36, 53, 69, 72–80, 865, 868, Sch. 1, para. 594(2)–594(3); FA 1999, s. 61; FA 1997, s. 65

Cases: *IR Commrs v Anglo Brewing Co Ltd* (1925) 12 TC 803; *B W Noble Ltd v Mitchell (HMIT)* (1927) 11 TC 372; *Kelsall (HMIT) v Investment Chartwork Ltd* [1994] BTC 16

Other Material: SP 11/81, *Additional redundancy payments*

2065   Staff training and development

The cost of general training and education in respect of the tasks and skills required of an employee to perform his duties are typically allowable as business expenses. Education of a special kind may be required in a particular trade and before 19 March 1991, employers could deduct payments made to provide special technical education necessary in a particular trade.

Where a business proprietor incurs costs in attending a training course, whether a deduction is available is largely a question of fact depending upon the course's purpose. If it is to extend or improve his or her professional knowledge or skills, it may well be capital expenditure and not deductible (see 2053); if it is to update his or her professional skills or knowledge, it would generally be of a revenue nature and therefore allowable if it met the 'wholly and exclusively test' (see 2056).

Where an employer incurs relevant expenditure in connection with a qualifying course of training for an employee or ex-employee, and it is undertaken with a view to retraining the employee for work of a nature not within the employer's requirements, the expenditure is nonetheless deductible as a 'business expense' (see 2050) by the employer, and the employee, etc. is not taxed on the expenditure. A training course qualifies if:

- it is designed to impart or improve skills or knowledge relevant to gainful employment or self-employment;

- it is entirely devoted to the teaching or practical application of the skills or knowledge;

- the duration does not exceed one year;

- all teaching takes place within the UK;

- the employee attends full-time;

- the employee has two years' service;

- it is available generally to employees (or a particular class of them) of that employer, and

a course is undertaken with a view to retraining if the employee commences the course whilst still employed or within one year of ceasing to be employed by the employer *and* he ceases to be employed within two years of the end of the course. Relevant expenses are:

- course fees;

- examination fees;

- cost of essential books;

- travelling expenses.

HMRC have outlined the circumstances in which expenditure by an employer on the training and development of employees may be disallowed either under the 'wholly and exclusively' rule (see 2056) or because for tax purposes it counts as capital (see 2053).

Legislation: ITTOIA 2005, s. 73–75, 107–108

Other Material: Inland Revenue *Tax Bulletin*, November 1991, p. 4, Issue 27, February 1997; Inland Revenue *Tax Bulletin*, Issue 64, April 2003

Tax Reporter: ¶208-850

2068 Legal and accountancy costs

Legal expenses are allowable as a 'business expense' (see 2050) where they relate to a revenue matter connected with the trade: e.g. allow legal expenses for recovering trade debts but not for recovering a loan to an employee. However, the legal cost of ascertaining or disputing profit is not strictly deductible, though in practice HMRC usually allow some deduction.

If the legal expenses are incurred in relation to a capital asset, then they are not deductible. Expenses on the redemption, repayment or purchase by a company of its own shares will generally be challenged by HMRC as capital rather than revenue under general principles (see 2053), as capital withdrawn (see 2059) or as failing the wholly and exclusively test (see 2056).

Accountancy expenses incurred in preparing accounts and agreeing tax liabilities are in practice normally deductible unless they relate to a tax investigation settlement (other than HMRC's in-depth examination of a particular year's accounts not resulting in penalties or interest nor in the adjustment of any other year's profits).

Accountancy expenses arising out of self-assessment enquiries

It is apparent that the above practice is incompatible with self-assessment procedures. HMRC have provided an interpretation of the current position which is as follows:

> 'Until such time as SP 16/91 is superseded the text below should be regarded as a statement of our practice, as it applies to self assessment enquiries.
>
> *Accountancy expenses arising out of self assessment enquiries*
>
> It is the practice to allow, in computing profits assessable under Case I and II of Schedule D, the normal accountancy expenses incurred in preparing accounts or accounts information and in assisting with the self assessment of tax liabilities.
>
> Additional accountancy expenses arising out of an enquiry into the accounts information in a particular year's return will not be allowed where the enquiry reveals discrepancies and additional liabilities for the year of enquiry, or any earlier year, which arise as a result of negligent or fraudulent conduct.
>
> Where, however, the enquiry results in no addition to profits, or an adjustment to the profits for the year of enquiry only and that adjustment does not arise as a result of negligent or fraudulent conduct, the additional accountancy expenses *will* be allowable.'

Case: *McKnight (HMIT) v Sheppard* [1999] BTC 236

Other Material: SP 16/91, *Accountancy expenses arising out of accounts investigation*; Revenue Interpretations, Inland Revenue *Tax Bulletin*, November 1991, p. 4, Issue 37, October 1998

Tax Reporter: ¶207-200

2071   Security assets or services for protecting proprietor

Revenue expenditure incurred in providing an individual with any security asset or service which meets a special threat to his personal physical security arising wholly or mainly by virtue of the particular business carried on by the taxpayer is deductible as a business expense (see 2050). HMRC have given such examples of security assets and services as alarm systems, bullet-resistant windows in houses and floodlighting. Expressly excluded as security assets are a car, ship, aircraft, dwelling or its appurtenant grounds. However, it does not prevent deductibility if the security asset becomes affixed to land or a dwelling.

If the security asset or service is not intended *solely* to improve personal physical security, a proportion of the expenditure is deductible.

If relief cannot be given against profits or gains the expenditure can be treated as capital expenditure for the purposes of capital allowances.

Legislation: ITTOIA 2005, s. 81

Tax Reporter: ¶208-800

2074   Payments to protect or obtain level of profits

Licences or rates have to be paid for whether or not a profit is made and are therefore deductible as a 'business expense' (see 2050), whereas the payment of income tax is not deductible since it is merely an application of the profits.

Payments made to safeguard future profits are deductible, such as payments to care for crops which will only yield a harvest several years in the future. A payment for a restrictive covenant not to compete with the company has been held to be capital. However, the deduction of payments to present or former employees for restrictive covenants entered into by them after 8 June 1988 is now permitted.

The costs of a campaign to safeguard against nationalisation of the taxpayer's industry have also been held to be deductible.

Indemnity insurance premiums can be relieved against a professional person's tax liability; after retirement, relief is limited to offset against post-cessation receipts (for the taxation of post-cessation receipts). From 1 October 1996, HMRC treat premiums paid under insurance policies taken out by medical practitioners in respect of locum and fixed practice expenses in the event of the policyholder's incapacity or illness as deductible (and the benefits as taxable professional receipts).

Income tax

Preservation of the level of profits should be contrasted with preservation of the trade itself. A payment to get rid of an obstacle to successful trading is a revenue and not a capital payment; however, the purpose of the taxpayer to preserve the trade may indicate that the payment is capital in nature (see 2053).

Legislation: ITTOIA 2005, s. 31, 69

Cases: *Vallambrosa Rubber Co v Farmer* (1910) 5 TC 529; *Anglo-Persian Oil Co Ltd v Dale (HMIT)* [1932] 1 KB 124; *Associated Portland Cement Manufacturers Ltd v Kerr (HMIT)* (1945) 27 TC 103; *Morgan (HMIT) v Tate & Lyle Ltd* (1954) 35 TC 367; *IR Commrs v Carron Co* (1968) 45 TC 18

2077   Lease rentals

Rental payments are generally allowable as a business expense if they satisfy the usual 'wholly and exclusively' test (see 2056). However, if there is any question that the payments do not in any period reflect the use of that item for that period relief may be restricted. A portion of any lease premium may be deductible as a deemed rental, the amount taxed as income of the recipient being spread over the term of the lease (see 1260).

Finance leases

HMRC have set out the way they treat rentals payable under finance leases entered into after 11 April 1991. (A 'finance lease' is different from an operating lease under which the lessee rents an asset for a fixed period which is generally well short of its full life. Under an ordinary finance lease, the lessor, commonly part of a banking group, buys a physical asset and leases it to someone who will use it. The rental payments from the lessee are generally such that the full cost of the asset, plus an amount equivalent to interest, are returned to the lessor. The terms of the lease are such that the lessee has all, or substantially all, of the benefits of outright ownership. A finance leasing arrangement thus resembles an ordinary loan with interest, which is how it is treated in companies' commercial accounts.)

SSAP 21 essentially requires a finance lease to be capitalised in the lessee's balance sheet as an asset with a corresponding creditor. Rentals payable are apportioned between the finance element, charged to the profit and loss account, and the capital repayment which reduces the outstanding liability. The asset is depreciated over the shorter of the lease term and its useful life.

Legislation: ITTOIA 2005, s. 60–64, 74–75

Cases: *Duple Motor Bodies Ltd v Ostime (HMIT)* [1961] 1 WLR 739; *Gallagher v Jones (HMIT); Threlfall v Jones (HMIT)* [1993] BTC 310

Other Material: SP 3/91, *Finance Lease rental payments*

2080 Payments to provide entertainment and promotional gifts

Expenditure on entertainment for trade purposes is disallowed (see 2059). However, provision for staff entertainment is allowed as a 'business expense' (see 2050). Reasonable entertainment expenses for overseas customers were allowed if provided by a UK trader but the relief has been withdrawn since 15 March 1988. Entertainment contracts already in existence on that date still qualify for relief.

Small gifts which conspicuously advertise the taxpayer's business and which are not food, drink, tobacco or gift tokens will be allowed as a deduction. A deduction is also allowed if the gifts are products of the taxpayer's trade: e.g. a manufacturer of plastic footballs who gives some away to promote his product will be allowed a deduction in respect of them.

Other expenditure on gifts is not regarded as within the statutory disallowance provided that:

(1) it satisfies the 'wholly and exclusively' test (see 2056);

(2) the gift is made for the benefit of a body or association of persons established for educational, cultural, religious, recreational or benevolent purposes, and the body or association is:

(a) local in relation to the donor's business activities; and

(b) not restricted to persons connected with the donor;

(3) the expenditure is reasonably small in relation to the scale of the donor's business.

The payment of an ordinary annual subscription to a local trade association by a non-member is similarly not regarded as a gift provided condition (1) is met.

For charitable donations, see also 902.

Legislation: ITTOIA 2005, s. 45(1) and 867(3)

Tax Reporter: ¶211-500

2083 Remuneration of employees seconded to charities

If an employer temporarily makes available to a charity or educational body the services of one of his employees, any expenditure incurred by the employer which is attributable to the employment of that person is deductible as a 'business expense' (see 2050) as if his services continue to be available to the employer whilst he is working for the charity. As a general guideline, the expenditure includes the employee's salary which the employer continues to pay.

Legislation: ITTOIA 2005, s. 31(1)–(3)

Tax Reporter: ¶213-950

2086 Contributions to local enterprise agencies

Contributions to 'local enterprise agencies', 'training and enterprise councils' and 'local enterprise companies' (from 1 April 1990) and 'business link organisations' (from 30 November 1993) are deductible so long as the person making them does not receive any specific benefit by doing so.

Legislation: ITTOIA 2005, s. 82–85; FA 2000, s. 88

2089 Interest and other costs of borrowing

Interest paid on loans to, or overdrafts of, a business is generally deductible as a 'business expense' (see 2050), under general principles, provided the interest is paid wholly and exclusively for the purposes of the business and at a reasonable rate of interest (see 2056 and 2059); in the case of companies, the interest must be 'short' rather than 'annual' (see below) or, broadly, be payable on an advance from a bank. There are certain additional requirements for income tax purposes in relation to payments to non-residents (see also 1884 and 2059). No deduction is allowed if the sole or main benefit to the payer from the transaction is a tax advantage.

It is not necessary for the loan to fall within one of the categories in respect of which an individual is permitted to deduct interest from total income, but interest which receives relief under those provisions may not also be deducted against business profits so as to give double relief.

No deduction is due if the loan effectively funds a proprietor's overdrawn current/capital account. In considering whether this is the case, accumulated realised profits must be distinguished from anticipated profits. A revaluation of business assets is therefore disregarded and the disallowance of the interest in point cannot be avoided by crediting the revaluation surplus to an overdrawn account.

Where a property development company charges disallowable interest to work in progress in accordance with 'correct' accounting practice, the interest need not be disallowed in the tax computation until it is effectively charged in the profits and loss account; conversely interest so charged is not allowable until it is similarly charged (see 652).

Note that for businesses using the cash basis (see 589), interest is limited to £500.

Incidental costs of business borrowings

Incidental costs of obtaining loan finance, such as fees, commissions, advertising and printing, are also specifically deductible in most cases. Such costs of taking out a life assurance policy as a pre-condition of receiving a loan would be included but the cost of the policy itself, i.e. the premiums, would, in HMRC's view be excluded. The deduction for incidental costs is given at the same time as any other deduction in computing profits for income tax purposes.

Yearly (annual) interest

The interest on loans capable of lasting longer than one year (whether or not they do in fact do so) is yearly interest and deciding whether interest is in fact 'yearly interest', regard is had to the loan agreement and the intention of the parties. A loan repayable on demand has been held to be an investment on which yearly interest was paid. Interest on an informal loan replacing an overdraft by a parent company to its subsidiary has also been held to be yearly interest.

Legislation: ITTOIA 2005, s. 52, 58, 362(1)–(2); CTA 2009, s. 131

Cases: *Minsham Properties Ltd v Price (HMIT)* [1990] BTC 528; *Cairns v MacDiarmid (HMIT)* [1983] BTC 188; *Corinthian Securities Ltd v Cato* (1969) 46 TC 93

Tax Reporter: ¶215-000

2092   Theft: business deductions

A deduction as a 'business expense' (see 2050) is allowed if an irrecoverable loss by theft occurs in the course of the trader's business. Petty theft by an assistant from a shop till would be in the course of the business, but large scale misappropriation by a director would not.

Case: *Bamford (HMIT) v ATA Advertising Ltd* (1972) 48 TC 359

2095 Expenditure on research and development

Revenue expenditure on research and development is specifically allowed as a deduction from profits.

The expenditure must be related to the trade carried on. Broadly, this means it must benefit the trade, of those employed in it. It must be undertaken by the trader or carried out on his behalf. Specifically, excluded is expenditure on obtaining rights connected with research and development.

Subject to broadly the same conditions, especially as to the relevance of the research to the trade carried on, payments to scientific research associations and universities, colleges or similar institutions is also deductible.

Legislation: ITTOIA 2005, s. 87–88

Tax Reporter: ¶256-000

2098 Miscellaneous business expenses: deductibility

A number of common items, such as stationery, utilities, postage, etc. are allowable deductions if used wholly and exclusively for business purposes (where used partly for business, a fraction of the expenses may be allowed).

2101 Pre-trading expenditure

Expenditure incurred by a person for business purposes before the business commences is treated for income tax purposes as a trading loss incurred on the day trading starts (for relief, see 2104); the expenditure must not be incurred more than seven years before trading commences and must be such that it would have been allowable had trading commenced (see 2050). The time period in point was five years for those who started to trade before 1 April 1993.

HMRC's view is that pre-trading expenditure does not include costs incurred by persons other than the eventual trader.

Legislation: ITTOIA 2005, s. 57

Tax Reporter: ¶208-300

2104   Business losses: meaning for income tax

Business losses occur where allowable expenses exceed taxable receipts, and they may be relieved for income tax purposes in a variety of ways.

Under self-assessment, capital allowances are generally deducted as if they were a trade expense in arriving at the trading result (see 2324).

Where a person has made annual payments out of profits which have not been charged to income tax (see 1368) and those payments are wholly and exclusively for the purposes of a trade, profession or vocation, then the amount on which tax has been accounted for (see 1370) is treated as a loss sustained in the trade, etc. for 'carry-forward relief' (see 2107).

Allowable interest (see 1884) which exceeds available income, if laid out or expended 'wholly and exclusively' (see 2056) for the business purposes, is treated as a loss for the purposes of 'carry-forward relief' (see 2107) or 'terminal loss relief' (see 2122).

There is an extended right of offset against general income for opening years' losses (see 2119).

Restriction on income tax reliefs (from 2013–14)

From 6 April 2013, a cap applies to certain previously unlimited income tax reliefs that may be deducted from income under ITA 2007, s. 24 (FA 2013, s. 16 and Sch. 3). The cap is set at £50,000 or 25% of income, whichever is greater. The reliefs affected by the cap are as follows:

- ITA 2007, s. 64 (trade loss relief against general income);

- ITA 2007, s. 72 (early trade losses relief);

- ITA 2007, s. 96 (post-cessation trade relief);

- ITA 2007, s. 120 (property loss relief against general income);

- ITA 2007, s. 125 (post-cessation property relief);

- ITA 2007, s. 128 (employment loss relief against general income);

- relief under ITA 2007, Pt. 4, Ch. 6 (share loss relief);

- relief under ITA 2007, Pt. 8, Ch. 1 (interest payments);

- ITEPA 2003, s. 555 (deduction for liabilities relating to former employment);

- ITTOIA 2005, s. 446 (strips of government securities: relief for losses); and

- ITTOIA 2005, s. 454(4) (listed securities held since 26 March 2003: relief for losses: persons other than trustees).

The limit does not apply to businesses using the cash basis (see 589) from 2013–14.

Restrictions on loss relief from 3 December 2014

Finance Act 2015 contains specific proposals designed to counter avoidance of income tax involving losses from miscellaneous transactions and limits the miscellaneous income against which a miscellaneous loss can be relieved. The changes denying loss relief where a miscellaneous loss, or miscellaneous income, arises as a result of relevant tax avoidance arrangements will have effect in relation to losses and income arising on and after 3 December 2014. The change limiting the deduction of miscellaneous losses to miscellaneous income of the same type will have effect for the tax year 2015–16 and subsequent years.

Legislation: ITA 2007, s. 88, 94

Tax Reporter: ¶260-000

2107 Business losses: income tax carry forward

Where a business 'loss' (see 2104) arises, relief may be obtained in some circumstances by carry forward against future income relating to the trade.

Where a person carrying on a business has suffered a loss therein which has not been wholly relieved under other provisions, he may make a claim (see 1843) that any of the unrelieved loss should be carried forward and set off against income from the same business in subsequent years: relief is given against the first subsequent tax year as far as possible and then against the next year, etc. indefinitely.

Under self-assessment, the relief is computed by reference to the same periods of account as profits from that source. The claims procedure is simple – there is only one claim, effective as regards the year of loss and this must be made within four years from the end of the tax year to which the loss relates (see 2339), i.e. the year of loss.

Relief claimed under this route cannot also be claimed under any other provision.

Business transferred to a company

Where an individual transfers his business to a company for shares in that company and the shares are held by that individual throughout the tax year, then he may claim (see 1843) that any unrelieved losses of his trade be carried forward and set against *any* income derived from the company (applicable equally to partnerships). Set-off must be primarily against earned income from the company, i.e. remuneration.

As with carry forward, generally, a deemed cessation on change in partners, etc. is effectively ignored.

Legislation: ITA 2007, s. 83, 86

Tax Reporter: ¶260-650

2110   Business losses: income tax offset against general income

Where any person sustains a 'loss' (see 2104) in any trade, profession, employment or vocation carried on by him either solely or in partnership, he may make a claim (see 1843) for relief from income tax against income for certain periods. This 'sideways relief' is an offset against his total income (see 244). Relief for limited partners is restricted (see 767). If the income is insufficient to set off the loss, then the outstanding loss may be carried forward (see 2107).

Any claim must be made by notice in writing given not later than 31 January which is 22 months after the end of the tax year in which the loss arose.

For late claims, see 2119.

A loss is not generally available for relief unless it is shown that, for the tax year in which the loss is claimed to have been sustained (i.e. at the end of that year or part), the trade was being carried on:

- on a commercial basis; and

- with a view to the realisation of profits in the trade (including a reasonable expectation thereof),

and, for this purpose, any cessation/recommencement deemed to have occurred before self-assessment on a change of partners is ignored.

Relief is also denied for a loss attributable to excess capital allowances on machinery, etc. let in the course of a part-time trade.

Farming and market gardening losses are often excluded if a loss was incurred in each of the prior five years (see 944).

Note that this paragraph will not apply to businesses using the new cash basis (see 589) from 2013–14.

Legislation: ITA 2007, s. 64–66

Cases: *Delian Enterprises (a partnership) v Ellis (HMIT)* (1999) Sp C 186; *Wannell v Rothwell (HMIT)* [1996] BTC 214; *Butt (HMIT) v Haxby* [1983] BTC 32; *Johnson* [2016] TC 04805; *Lucy* [2016] TC 04878

Tax Reporter: ¶260-100

2113   Offset against general income under self-assessment

Under self-assessment, relief may be given in respect of a person's business loss sustained for a tax year against income for the same year or income for the preceding year (apparently whether or not he carried on the business in that period); claims for current year losses take precedence over claims for losses carried back. A claim for carry-back is taken to relate to the later year (see 2336).

The amount of any loss for a tax year is calculated on the same basis as is income (i.e. subject to opening and closing year rules, in respect of a period of account ending in that year), but a loss which would fall into two periods is not included in the second of those periods.

Example

Steve, a single man, makes up his accounts to 31 December each year. He has the following results:

			£
Accounts for year ending	31/12/14	Profit	500
	31/12/15	Loss	5,000
	31/12/16	Profit	5,000

His other income consists of dividends as follows:

2014–15	Dividends	4,995 (net of 10% tax)
2015–16	Dividends	3,600 (net of 10% tax)
2016–17	Dividends	1,800 (no tax credit)

Loss for year		£
2013–14		3,750

Loss for year 2015–16 can be relieved under:

either ITA 2007, s. 64(2)(a) against net statutory income of the same year;

---

or ITA 2007, s. 64(2)(b) against net statutory income of the preceding year, to the extent that he does not relieve the income by a claim for current year offset in 2015–16;

or ITA 2007, s. 83 carried forward against trading profits of *same* trade:

Assuming he makes no other claims, the alternative ways of relieving the 2013–14 loss are:

	s. 64(2)(b)	ITA 2007 s. 64(2)(a)	s. 83
	2014–15	2015–16	2016–17
	£	£	£
Trading profit	500	–	5,000
Less: ITA 2007, s. 83	–	–	(3,750)
Net trading income	–	–	1,250
Dividends	5,550	4,000	1,800
Net statutory income	6,050	4,000	3,050
Less: ITA 2007, s. 64(2)(b)	(3,750)	–	–
ITA 2007, s. 64(2)(a)	–	(3,750)	–
	2,300	250	3,050
Personal allowance restricted to	(2,300)	(250)	(3,050)
Taxable income	Nil	Nil	Nil

In each case, part of the personal reliefs is lost. Here relief by way of carry forward seems best, in that the least amount of allowance is wasted.

Note that this paragraph does not apply to businesses using the cash basis, which took effect from 2013–14 (see 589).

Legislation: ITA 2007, s. 64

Tax Reporter: ¶260-100

2116   Business losses: income tax offset against chargeable gains

A 'business loss' (see 2104) may be offset against chargeable gains, whether arising on business or private assets.

The taxpayer may claim for the loss which exceeds general income in the same year against which a claim for offset could be made (see 2110ff.) to be offset against chargeable gains of the same year; if there is also insufficient general income in the following year to absorb the loss, the taxpayer may claim to set the excess loss against chargeable gains of that year. Once a claim for offset has been 'finally determined', the amount claimed is treated as an allowable loss and cannot be increased to take into account subsequent changes in circumstance: HMRC have indicated that the appropriate loss relief claim becomes final:

- 30 days after the inspector gives his decision on it;

- when, after an appeal, agreement is reached between the taxpayer and HMRC;

- when the tribunal determines an appeal; or

- when the courts decide an appeal,

and the point at which the inspector gives his decision would depend on the particular circumstances – for example, he could write agreeing the claim, or decide constructively by repaying tax, but any clear, unambiguous response of a positive nature would be regarded as constituting a determination. Claims are generally accepted even if not made (as strictly required) at the same time as claims for offset of trading losses against income.

The relief claimed may not exceed the amount on which the claimant would be chargeable to CGT, ignoring the annual exemption. Relief for capital losses in the same year is given in priority but relief for capital losses brought forward is not since the trading loss is treated as an allowable loss accruing in the year.

Example

Roger who has traded for many years as a builder, incurs a loss in the year ended 5 April 2016 of £16,200 (as adjusted). In the previous year, ended 5 April 2015, he has a trading profit of £10,000. In the year ended 5 April 2016, he has other income of £2,500 and net chargeable gains (on share disposals) of £8,600.

Roger is able to make a claim to set off £12,500 of the loss of the period ended 5 April 2016 against his general income. He can also claim to set off the remainder of the loss (£3,700) against the chargeable gains on the share disposal, though this may result in part of the benefit of the annual exemption being lost.

HMRC have provided some rules of thumb in determining the steps to go through in applying the relief:

(1) determine the 'relevant amount'. This is essentially the amount of unutilised trading loss available for relief under the present provision;

(2) then determine the 'maximum amount'. This is the amount on which the claimant would otherwise be chargeable to CGT for the year, ignoring the annual exempt amount;

(3) the 'maximum amount' is unaffected by a later reduction in the amount chargeable to CGT: for example, resulting from a rollover relief claim.

Note that this paragraph does not apply to businesses using the cash basis (see 589) from 2013–14.

Legislation: ITA 2007, s. 71

Tax Reporter: ¶260-300

2119 Business losses: income tax carry-back of losses in opening years

Where an individual carrying on a business sustains a 'loss' (see 2104) in:

- the tax year in which it is first carried on by him; or
- any of the next three tax years,

he may, by notice in writing given within one year of 31 January following the year of loss, make a claim for relief. A Revenue Interpretation sets out the circumstances in which late claims for the present relief (and for offset against general income, see 2110ff.) may be accepted. These are where the taxpayer or agent:

- had been misled by some relevant and uncorrected error on HMRC's part;
- had made an informal claim within the time-limit which fell short of a clear and unambiguous statement of what was being claimed but which he or she reasonably believed was an acceptable claim, and the need to formalise the claim was not, within the time-limit, pointed out by HMRC; or
- had effectively been prevented from making an in-date claim for reasons beyond his or her control.

Relief is given by carrying back that loss and setting it off against total income, being income for the three tax years last preceding that in which the loss is sustained, taking income for an earlier year before income for a later year. Under self-assessment, a claim for carry-back is treated as if it related to the later year (see 2336).

If relief has already been given for the loss, it cannot be claimed again.

Restrictions on relief are twofold:

- the trade must have been carried on throughout the period on a commercial basis and in such a way that profits in the trade could reasonably be expected to be realised in that period or within a reasonable time thereafter;

- relief is not given if at the time when the trade is first carried on by the trader he or she is married to and living with another individual who has previously carried on the trade and the loss is sustained in a tax year later than the third tax year after that in which the trade was first carried on by the other individual.

Example

Elaine was employed for many years; her last three years' taxable earnings were:

- 2012–13: £25,000

- 2013–14: £28,000

- 2014–15: £29,000

She left employment on 31 March 2015 and commenced as a sole trader on 1 July 2015, making up her first accounts to 30 June 2016 (and to 30 June thereafter). Her tax adjusted, trading loss for the 12 months to 30 June 2016 (including capital allowances) was £36,000. She has no other income sources apart from those indicated. Her trading activities are unlikely to show significant profits for several years. The claims available to her under s. 72 are as shown below.

(1) Determine the losses available £

   20015–16 (1 July 2015 – 5 April 2016) $^9/_{12}$ × £36,000 =   (27,000)

   2016–17 (1 July 2015 – 30 June 2016) £36,000 – £27,000 =   (9,000)

(2) The earliest year for carry-back is:

   (a) 2015–16 carry-back to 2012–13

   (b) 2016–17 carry-back to 2013–14

(3) *2012–13* £

		£	
	Income (Employment)	25,000	
	less		
	Loss of 2015–16	(25,000)	
		NIL	

2013–14		£	
	Income (Employment)	28,000	
	less		
	Loss of 2015–16	(2,000)	(27,000 – 25,000)
		26,000	
	Loss of 2016–17	9,000	
		17,000	

---

(4) *Loss of memorandum*

(a) loss of 2015–16	£27,000	
used 2012–13	(25,000)	
used 2013–14	(2,000)	
(b) loss of 2016–17	£9,000	
used 2013–14	(9,000)	

Note

Once a loss has been carried back three years under a s. 72 claim, any unused portion must be carried forward and set against income of the next year (as in the example, where £2,000 of loss unused in 2012–13 is carried forward to 2013–14) even if it results in other allowances (e.g. personal allowance) being wasted.

Alternative claims are available to Elaine should she wish to make them. For example, she could set the loss of 2015–16 (£27,000) against the income of 2014–15 (final year of employment; £29,000) using s. 64. Such a claim would have been advantageous if she had sufficient income in 2015–16 to make her liable at the higher rate. A claim under s. 72, to carry back the loss of 2016–17 (the second year of trade) would still have been possible if such a s. 64 claim had been made.

The relief is also available to partnerships. Any deemed cessation/ recommencement on a change in partners which is not a total change is ignored; under self-assessment, this becomes irrelevant since the deeming rule is repealed in such cases.

Note that this paragraph will not apply to businesses using the cash basis (see 589).

Legislation: ITA 2007, s. 72

Tax Reporter: ¶260-600

2122 Business losses: income tax carry-back of terminal losses

Where a loss is made in the final year of trading, i.e. the 12 months before the date of discontinuance, unless relief has already been given for that loss, it may be carried back and set against the profits of the same trade. Relief covers the year of cessation and the three previous years. Capital allowances are generally treated as trading deductions (see 2324) and are therefore automatically taken into account; before that, unrelieved capital allowances of the final 12 months may also be included in the claim. Relief is given as far as possible from the assessment for a later rather than an earlier year.

If the profits are insufficient for setting off the loss, then any interest or dividends arising in that year which would be trading receipts but for the fact that they have already been taxed will be treated as profits and relief will be given accordingly by repayment or otherwise.

Example

Gordon has traded for many years, normally preparing accounts to 30 September each year; he ceases trade on 30 April 2016 producing seven-month accounts to that date. Tax adjusted results (including capital allowance claims) for his final periods of trading are a profit of £12,000 for the 12 months ending 30 September 2015 and a loss of £3,500 for the seven months to cessation on 30 April 2016. He has transitional overlap profit relief of £1,000 available. His terminal loss is for the year 2016–17 and will be:

(1) *Loss arising in final year* (2016–17)   £

$\frac{1}{7}$ × (£3,500)   (500)

Overlap relief available   (1,000)

    (1,500)

(2) *Loss of preceding year* (beginning 12 months prior to cessation.)

Period 1/5/2015–5/4/2016   £

(a) 1/5/2015–30/09/2015 $\frac{5}{12}$ × £12,000 =   5,000

(b) 1/10/2015–5/4/2016 $\frac{6}{7}$ × (£3,500) =   (3,000)

    Profit   2,000

An overall profit is treated as a 'nil' loss   0

    (£1,500)

The terminal loss of 2016–17 is £1,500. It can be used against trading profits of 2016–17 (in this case there are none); then carried back to 2015–16 where the profit of £12,000 can be relieved. If the loss were greater than the 2015–16 profit further carry backs to 2014–15 and 2013–14 would be possible.

The loss of £3,000 which was aggregated computationally with profits for the period 1 May 2015 to 30 September 2015 is still available for relief against other income under ITA 2007, s. 64, since it has not been utilised in the terminal loss claim.

Legislation: ITA 2007, s. 89

Tax Reporter: ¶262-000

2128 Relief for post-cessation expenditure

A specific relief is available to individuals for certain types of post-cessation expenditure. These include expenses connected with remedying or paying compensation for defective work or supplies, collecting debts, and debts which go bad. Relief is given by way of a reduction of income (and, where appropriate, chargeable gains) for the tax year in which the expense is paid. Such expenditure must be incurred within seven years of the cessation of trade, and a claim for the relief must be made within 12 months from 31 January following the end of the tax year in which the payment is made (in line with other claims under self-assessment). If a claim is made, certain connected receipts (mainly to do with insurance receipts) are specified as being taxable under the existing post-cessation receipts legislation.

HMRC have stated their views of a number of issues in their *Tax Bulletin*. In particular, professional indemnity insurance premiums for work undertaken in the course of the business are now almost always allowable (this supersedes HMRC's earlier view). The new relief exists alongside the rules already on the statute book for post-cessation receipts and expenses. Those rules provide that any loss or expense which would have qualified as a trading deduction had the business not ceased is relieved against post-cessation receipts; however, where the deductions exceed the post-cessation receipts for a tax year, the excess can only be carried forward and relieved against any post-cessation receipts arising in later years. Where an expense qualifies for sideways relief under the new rules as well as for carry-forward under the provision described above, the new rules thus take priority.

Finance Act 2012 contained a measure designed to prevent post-cessation trade relief from being available where a payment or event for which relief is sought arises from relevant tax avoidance arrangements. The revised rules apply to events occurring on or after 13 March 2012.

Legislation: FA 2012, s. 9; ITTOIA 2005, s. 250, 349–352

Case: *Saheid* [2016] TC 04982

Tax Reporter: ¶262-750

Administration

Returns and information generally

2200   Notice of liability to income tax

Every person who is chargeable to income tax (or CGT) for any tax year and who has not received a notice requiring a tax return (see 2225) must notify HMRC that he is chargeable within six months after that year if he has not already been requested to make a tax return. However, the penalty only becomes due to the extent that he does not settle the liability by the following 31 January: i.e. there is a four-month period in which HMRC might issue an assessment on which he could pay the tax and avoid penalties.

The above notice must specify each separate source of income except sources excluded, broadly, by reference to deduction of tax at source where no liability will arise to a rate other than basic or lower rate. The notice must be given to an officer of the Board, and failure to give notice will render that person liable to a penalty not exceeding the tax due under late assessments, i.e. the taxpayer may end up paying double the tax due on undisclosed income.

A taxpayer will not generally be in a position to know by the end of the time-limit for notifying chargeability (5 October) whether a PAYE code change will be made to collect outstanding tax. HMRC will accept that an individual does not need to notify chargeability in respect of P11D items if he has received a copy of the P11D and is satisfied that it is correct and complete (and is not aware that it has not been submitted); he is not relieved of his responsibility to notify chargeability in relation to other items even if he is aware that the employer has submitted information in some form to HMRC.

Legislation: TMA 1970, s. 7

Other Material: SP 1/96, *Notification of chargeability to income tax and capital gains tax years 1995–96 onwards*

Tax Reporter: ¶180-325

2203 Return forms

A 'return' includes any statement or declaration under the Taxes Acts, but is generally taken to refer to the response to a statutory request by an inspector (or the Board) for information. HMRC may prescribe the format in which returns must be made and often issue specific forms. Computer-produced returns may be approved by HMRC in certain cases following written application.

A tax return is the term generally used to refer to the document issued by the tax inspector, instructing the person who receives it to furnish him with information about his (or, in certain cases, other persons') income for that year. It is delivered to the usual or last-known address of that person. Those who have property income or income from a trade, profession or vocation will have to complete an income tax return each year.

A HMRC statement clarifies the position regarding the use of schedules in making personal tax returns. Schedules (i.e. unofficial statements or forms) have always been acceptable as documents supporting entries in an official return form. HMRC will also accept returns where the declaration of accuracy and completeness on the official form is signed but which is otherwise answered generally by overall reference to attached schedules.

A return must in HMRC's view strictly be signed by the person liable to make it (see 2209). Signature by an attorney is accepted in cases of illness or old age if a copy of the general or enduring power has been sent to HMRC. Following an agreement with the Court of Protection, repayment claims for amounts less than £1,600 may be signed by the next of kin, provided the incapacitated person's income is less than £800 for claims of more than that amount.

Legislation: FA 1999, s. 133; TMA 1970, s. 115A, Sch. 3A

Other Material: SP 5/83, *Use of schedules in making personal tax returns*; SP 5/87, *Tax returns: the use of substitute forms*; SP 1/97

Tax Reporter: ¶180-000

2206   Internet filing

Individuals have been able to file their own self assessment (SA) tax returns directly with HMRC over a secure internet connection since July 2000. This service is known as Filing By Internet (FBI), to distinguish it from the Electronic Lodgement Service (ELS) which was only available to authorised agents to file their client's SA tax returns.

HMRC have now phased in the introduction of Real Time Information (RTI). Broadly, under RTI, information about tax and other deductions under the PAYE system are transmitted to HMRC by the employer every time an employee is paid. Under RTI, employers are no longer required to provide information to HMRC using forms P35 and P14 after the end of the tax year, or to send forms P45 or P46 to HMRC when employees start or leave a job (see 2241). Most employers were required to start using RTI from October 2013, however, a temporary relaxation of the rules allowed small businesses with less than 50 employees to delay full operation of RTI until 5 April 2014.

Legislation: FA 2003, s. 204; FA 2002, s. 135, 136; FA 2000, s. 143 and Sch. 38; *Income Tax (Pay As You Earn) (Amendment No. 2) Regulations* 2013 (SI 2013/2300); *Income Tax (Pay As You Earn) (Amendment) Regulations* 2013 (SI 2013/521); *Income Tax (Pay As You Earn) (Amendment) Regulations* 2010 (SI 2010/668); *Income Tax (Pay As You Earn) (Amendment No. 2) Regulations* 2009 (SI 2009/2029); *Income Tax (Pay As You Earn) Regulations* 2003 (SI 2003/2682), reg. 190, 209

Case: *ZXCV Ltd v R & C Commrs*(2008) Sp C 706

Tax Reporter: ¶180-020

2209   Persons liable to make returns

If income is received in any tax year, the person receiving that income, whether on his own behalf (individuals) or on behalf of others (trustees), must make a return. The persons who must make the returns include:

- individuals (see 2225);
- partnerships (see 2243);
- trustees (see 2249);
- personal representatives, e.g. executors (see 2246);
- EEIGs (see 2252); and
- agents (see 2255).

2212   Informing the authorities of a new business

Unlike some jurisdictions, an individual starting in business in the UK on their own account does not generally need permission to do so. Exceptions to this general principle apply when entry to the sector concerned is regulated, either by government (such as the medical profession) or by professional institutes.

When an individual begins to carry on a trade, he has a duty to inform HMRC that he is chargeable to income tax. Failure to do so will render him liable for a penalty of anything up to the amount of tax for which he is liable in respect of income from the relevant source for that year. This applies both where an assessment is made by an officer of HMRC and where there is a self-assessment, and is on the basis of the tax unpaid at the 31 January following the year of the failure.

Notification to HMRC will cover income tax, National Insurance contributions and VAT matters.

Legislation: TMA 1970, s. 7;   FA 2008, Sch. 41; *Social Security (Contributions) Regulations* 2001 (SI 2001/1004), reg. 87

Types of return

2222   System of returns and payment under self-assessment

The system of self-assessment normally requires returns from individuals, trustees, partnerships, etc. by 31 January following the tax year. Tax returns for 2007–08 onwards made on paper must be filed by 31 October. This date is the same for taxpayers who want HMRC to calculate their tax liability (30 September for earlier years). The present filing date of

31 January remains for returns filed online. HMRC have significant power to specify in the return form and in the accompanying guidance notes the necessary information, accounts and statements, which may need annual adjustment. They may also prescribe different return forms for different groups of taxpayers, and these may call for different information.

The return consists of a core section applying to all taxpayers, which is then customised by the addition of extra pages according to the taxpayer's known circumstances. It is up to the taxpayer to request supplementary pages if necessary.

Legislation: FA 2007, s. 88; TMA 1970, s. 8, 8A, 9, 12A, 113(1)

Tax Reporter: ¶180-025

2225 Personal returns

Individuals are to submit returns of income and capital gains when required by notice of an officer of the Board. This notice may also, within reason, require accounts, statements and documents relating to information contained in the return.

The self-assessment filing deadlines for returns are 31 October for paper returns and 31 January for online returns.

The amounts to be returned are net amounts: i.e. the amounts chargeable to income tax and CGT must take into account any claim or relief claimed in the return. Similarly, the amount payable by way of income tax must take into account tax deducted at source and tax credits on distributions received.

An individual's return is to include his share of any partnership income, losses, tax (i.e. tax deducted at source), tax credit or charge. These figures will be derived from the relevant partnership statement. A partnership statement is relevant if it is for a period which includes all or part of the tax year or its basis period. The requirement for a partnership statement is discussed at 2243.

Every return must include a declaration that the return made by the person is 'to the best of his knowledge correct and complete'.

For penalties in relation to failure to make the return or for submitting an incorrect return, see 12000ff.

Provisional figures

A late filing penalty may be levied where a return contains provisional figures if the taxpayer fails to take 'reasonable care' or if the taxpayer could have supplied the correct figures.

Amendment of self-assessment

Except when HMRC are formally investigating a return, the taxpayer has 12 months in which to amend it; HMRC may amend obvious errors. Such amendments do not preclude penalties being imposed for the incorrect completion of the original return.

Time limits for a self-assessment

Finance Act 2016 clarifies the time allowed for making a self-assessment when HMRC have served a notice to file a return is four years after the end of the tax year it relates to.

However, when HMRC issue a taxpayer with a notice to file within the four-year period, the taxpayer will always have three months to make and deliver their self-assessment. Time limits in relation to self-assessments made in response to determinations by HMRC will not be affected. The provision comes into force from 15 September 2016 (Royal Assent).

Legislation: TMA 1970, s. 8(1)–(2), 9(4)–(6)

Case: *Steedon v Carver* (1999) Sp C 212

Tax Reporter: ¶180-025

2234   Reporting benefits of certain employees and directors

The P11D (or for tax years up to and including 2015–16, form P9D for certain lower paid employees) is used to record the cash equivalents of benefits or expenses given to employees (for tax years up to and including 2015–16, who were paid at a rate of £8,500 or more (including benefits, etc.) or to directors (see 382ff.)). It is completed on a tax year basis (6 April to 5 April).

From 6 April 2016, an exemption applies for expenses and benefits that are tax deductible (see 383A and 1990A). For tax years up to and including 2015–16, the employee or director could claim that the benefit or expense was incurred wholly, exclusively and necessarily in the performance of his duties (see 1990).

Form P11D (P9D) must be submitted to HMRC, together with the employer's declaration and statutory Class 1A return, P11D(b), by 6 July after the end of the tax year to which they relate.

Under self-assessment, employees who are in employment on the last day of a tax year must be provided with a copy of the appropriate form by 6 July (i.e. within three months); employees who leave during the year can obtain a copy if they notify the employer.

Voluntary payrolling of benefits in kind

From April 2016, employers have the option to collect tax on benefits in kind through the payroll, a process known as payrolling (ITEPA 2003, s. 684 and SI 2003/2682, Pt. 3, Ch. 3A). Payrolling will be available for all benefits in kind, other than accommodation, beneficial loans, credit tokens and vouchers, with additional reporting requirements for employers payrolling cars to be introduced from April 2017.

Legislation: *Income Tax (Pay As You Earn) Regulations* 2003 (SI 2003/2682)

Tax Reporter: ¶495-010

2241　Real time information

Under Real Time Information (RTI), information about tax and other deductions under the PAYE system are transmitted to HMRC by the employer every time an employee is paid. Employers using RTI are no longer required to provide information to HMRC using forms P35 and P14 after the end of the tax year, or to send forms P45 or P46 to HMRC when employees start or leave a job. HMRC anticipate that over time, the new PAYE process will lead to more frequent updating of tax codes and less underpayments and overpayments being processed. The new system also supports the introduction of Universal Credit, an integrated working-age credit, which will replace income-related benefits and credits. It will give the Department for Work and Pensions (DWP) access to up-to-date information on a claimant's income from employment.

Most employers were required to start using RTI from October 2013, however, a temporary relaxation of the rules allowed small businesses with less than 50 employees to delay full operation of RTI until 5 April 2014.

Each time a payment is made to an employee, a Full Payment Submission (FPS) will be made to HMRC. The FPS includes:

- the amount paid to employees;

- income tax, NICs and other deductions, such as student loans; and

- details of new employees and employees who have left.

Details of all employees paid must be included in the FPS, including those who earn below the NICs lower earnings limit. There are other submissions employers may also make. These include:

- an Employer Alignment Submission (EAS) to align employee records with HMRC records before other information is submitted;

- a National Insurance Number Verification Request (NVR) to verify or obtain a National Insurance number for new employees;

- an Employer Payment Summary (EPS) to report a reduction in the amount paid to HMRC or if any employees have not been paid in a pay period; and

- an Earlier Year Update (EYU) to correct after 19 April any of the year to date totals submitted in the final FPS for the previous tax year. This only applies to RTI years and the first year an employer can use an EYU is 2012–2013.

RTI only affects the submission of PAYE information – payment arrangements will remain unchanged.

Penalties

From 6 October 2014, employers with 50 or more employees may be charged in-year penalties for failing to file PAYE submissions on time. Employers with fewer than 50 employees may be charged in-year penalties from 6 March 2015 onwards.

HMRC will apply penalties:

- where a Full Payment Submission (FPS) has not been filed on or before the date the employees were paid, or where the employer has not told HMRC why the submission is legitimately late by using the late reporting reason field; and

- where HMRC have not received the expected number of submissions from the employer.

Where employers believe they have a reasonable excuse for sending a return late, they will be able to appeal using HMRC's online appeals process for automated penalties.

Employers who do not need to submit an FPS because they did not pay any employees in a tax month must submit a nil Employer Payment Summary (EPS) by the 19th of the following tax month. Otherwise, it is likely that HMRC will assume that a submission has been missed and a late filing penalty will be issued. HMRC will charge one penalty for each tax month that the employer failed to file on time. However, they will not charge a penalty for the first month in each tax year where the employer failed to file on time (a maximum of 11 fixed penalties can be charged for late filing in a tax year).

A penalty will not be issued to a new employer if their first FPS is received within 30 days of making the first payment to their employee(s). But after that, normal penalties rules will apply if there is a failure to file on time. Employers with nine or fewer employees and who meet certain conditions can take advantage of a relaxation for 2014–15 and 2015–16 (see www. gov.uk/running-payroll/fps-after-payday). This allows them to report PAYE information about all their payments in a tax month on or before the last payday in that tax month.

The size of the late filing penalties depends on the number of employees within the PAYE scheme.

Number of employees	Amount of the monthly filing penalty per PAYE scheme
1 to 9	£100
10 to 49	£200
50 to 249	£300
250 or more	£400

Where a return is late for three months or more, HMRC may charge a further penalty of 5% of the tax/NICs that would have been paid if the information it provides had been sent on time. HMRC will apply this penalty only for the most serious and persistent failures.

Penalty notices will be issued quarterly at the end of July, October, January and April.

Legislation: *Income Tax (Pay As You Earn) Regulations* 2003 (SI 2003/2682); *Income Tax (Pay As You Earn) (Amendment No. 2) Regulations* 2013 (SI 2013/2300); *Income Tax (Pay As You Earn) (Amendment No. 3) Regulations* 2014 (SI 2014/2396); *Finance Act 2009, Schedule 55 (Penalties for failure to make returns) (Appointed Days and Consequential Provision) Order* 2014 (SI 2014/2395);

Case: *Thames & Newcastle Ltd* [2014] TC 03790

Other material: HMRC short guide to in-year late filing penalties: tinyurl. com/lqyf5rj; What happens if you don't report payroll information on time: www.gov.uk/what-happens-if-you-dont-report-payroll-information-on-time

Tax Reporter: ¶493-015

2243 Partnership return

Under self-assessment, a partnership return, made by a specified partner or his successor (or a person identified by a given rule), must include a statement of profits, the separate partners being treated as if their share of profits accrued directly to them from a sole trade. The partnership statement may be for the tax year as well as for the accounting period, and may include details of the allocation of consideration from the disposal of partnership property.

The filing deadline for returns is 31 October for paper returns and 31 January for online returns.

Every partnership return must, under self-assessment, include a partnership statement, showing partnership income (and gains) less charges and allocating the resulting amounts between the partners. Except when HMRC are formally investigating a statement, the partnership has 12 months in which to amend it; HMRC may amend obvious errors. (Such amendments do not preclude penalty charges being imposed for the incorrect completion of the original return.) Any amendment of the partnership statement will be reflected by HMRC in each of the partners' self-assessments.

The HMRC enquiry window into a return for a particular tax year will close one year after delivery of the return.

Following the completion of HMRC's enquiries, the officer of the Board will issue a closure notice. This will either make amendments to the return or state that no amendment is necessary. The taxpayer may appeal against any amendment the officer makes.

Legislation: TMA 1970, s. 12AA, 12AB, 12AC

Tax Reporter: ¶180-525

2246 Personal representatives' return

Personal representatives (executors and administrators) of a deceased person are required to return estate income and gains on the trusts and estates return. They are also liable for the tax chargeable on the deceased at death. HMRC will, on request, issue a tax return before the end of the tax year in which death occurred and give early confirmation if they do not intend to enquire into that return. Personal representatives can also request such confirmation at any time before the expiry of the normal time-limit.

Other Material: Inland Revenue press release, 4 April 1996

Tax Reporter: ¶180-600

2249 Trustees' returns

The requirements for returns by trustees under self-assessment resemble those for individuals: the time-limit is the same, as is the requirement to return net amounts and to include a self-assessment based on those amounts (see 2225).

Notices are given, by an officer of the Board, for the purposes of establishing the amounts in which the following persons are chargeable to income tax and CGT, and the amount payable by them by way of income tax:

- the 'relevant trustees' (see below);

- the settlor or settlors; and

- the beneficiary or beneficiaries.

Notices may be given to any relevant trustee, or separate notices given to each relevant trustee, or to such of the relevant trustees as the officer thinks fit.

'Relevant trustees' are:

- for the purpose of trust income, any person who was a trustee at or after the time when the income arose;

- for the purpose of trust gains, any person who was a trustee during or after the tax year in which the gain accrued.

The relevant trustees are liable for any tax which falls due as a result of the self-assessment included in the return.

In the absence of a return, an officer of the Board may determine the amount of the relevant trustees' liability (see 2327). Similarly, an assessment may be made on the relevant trustees where a loss of tax is discovered (see 2330).

Bare trusts under self-assessment

A 'bare trust' exists where the beneficial owner of the property held in trust is fully entitled to both the capital and the income from the property. Although the property is held in the trustee's name, the trustee has no discretion over what income to pay the beneficiary. The trustee is in effect a nominee in whose name the property is held. Trustees of such trusts are no longer expected to account for tax at the appropriate rate on income paid over to beneficiaries. Any income which is received gross by the trustees will be paid gross by them. In addition, trustees of bare trusts will not be required to complete self-assessment returns or make payments on account. (However, they are entitled, if they so wish, to make a self-assessment return of income (not capital gains) and to account for tax on it at the appropriate rate.) Beneficiaries must include income and gains from these trusts in their returns.

Legislation: TMA 1970, s. 7(9), 8A(1), (5), 118(1)

Tax Reporter: ¶180-600

2252   EEIG's return

If a European Economic Interest Grouping is registered in Great Britain or Northern Ireland, an inspector may require an individual to make a return. The individual in point is the manager or any manager or, if the manager is not an individual, any individual designated as the representative of the manager.

If the grouping is not so registered, the inspector may require any UK-resident member(s) or, if none, any member(s) to make a return. The return must include a declaration that, to the best of the maker's knowledge, it is correct and complete.

There are penalties on the grouping or members for failures to comply with the above.

Legislation: TMA 1970, s. 12A(8), 98B

Tax Reporter: ¶596-200

2255   Non-residents trading through UK representatives

In order to accommodate self-assessment, the regime for the taxation of non-residents trading through UK representatives (see 1672) was also modified for 1996–97 onwards (for corporation tax, from accounting periods beginning after 31 March 1996). In brief, the UK branch or agent is made jointly responsible with the non-resident trader for all that needs to be done in connection with self-assessment of the profits from or connected with the branch or agency.

Finance Act 2003 introduced a measure to change the term 'branch or agency' to 'permanent establishment' in relation to accounting periods beginning on or after 1 January 2003.

Legislation: FA 1995, s. 126(9), 127(19); FA 2003, s. 153

Tax Reporter: ¶765-100

2258 Returns of tax deducted from annual payments

A person who is required to deduct basic rate income tax from a payment must account for it to HMRC (see 1372).

Where such a payment is made and tax is deducted from it, the person receiving the payment will need to show that the tax has been paid if he is not liable to tax and wishes to reclaim the tax deducted. The R185 provides the necessary evidence. The payments covered are:

- certain interest;

- annuities;

- rents;

- royalties;

- payments from a trust (if it is not a discretionary trust R185E should be used).

Tax Reporter: ¶116-050

2261 Returns by banks and other payers of interest

Any bank and every person carrying on a trade who receives or retains money on which interest becomes payable without deduction of tax must make a return of interest paid if so required by notice from an inspector. The return must include:

- the names and addresses of persons to whom the interest is paid or credited; and

- the amount of interest (if the interest did not exceed a given level, it was ignored for this purpose during the existence of the arrangements before the basic rate of tax scheme: see 1372).

This only applies to money received or retained in the UK and, if the individual receiving the interest declares in writing that the person beneficially entitled to it is not ordinarily resident in the UK and asks for it to be left out of the return, then the person paying or crediting the interest will not be required to include it in any such return. A declaration of status to enable gross payment will often be sufficient as a declaration for this purpose also (see 1372).

Other payers

Similar provisions relate to the power of the inspector to call for information from other payers of interest without deduction of tax. This extends to individual payments rather than the more general requirement in relation to banks, etc.

Legislation: TMA 1970, s. 17, 18

Tax Reporter: ¶180-000

2264 Returns by persons of sundry payments

There are a number of returns which, albeit of a fairly rare nature, may be required by HMRC; these relate to the following:

(1) persons in receipt of taxable income belonging to another, as respects income in the three years before the notice;

(2) landlords in respect of the names and addresses of persons who have been lodgers or inmates;

(3) persons paying non-employee' fees, commissions, etc. for services or in respect of copyrights, designs, etc.;

(4) persons paying amounts for services of agency workers;

(5) payments in respect of grants, subsidies, licences or approvals in relation to public funds and licences;

(6) lessees, etc. in respect of lease terms;

(7) issuing houses, stockbrokers, etc. in relation to chargeable gains from share transactions entered into with other parties (see 6431).

The Court of Appeal has held that auctioneers who received the proceeds of sale on behalf of farmers selling livestock were obliged to provide details of farmers selling livestock at auction, including amounts of money received by the auctioneers on their behalf, information requested by HMRC in notices under (1) above. The court rejected the auctioneers' argument that the gross sums received on behalf of the farmers could not properly be described as 'profits or gains' within the legislation as that phrase denoted a net amount after deduction of appropriate expenditure.

Legislation: TMA 1970, s. 13, 14, 16, 16A, 18A, 19

Case: *Fawcett (HMIT) v Special Commrs and Lancaster Farmers Auction Mart Ltd* [1997] BTC 24

Assessments, determinations and claims generally

2324 Nature of assessments and determinations

Assessments other than self-assessments are generally made by an 'officer of the Board' or, in some specialised circumstances, by the Board (for assessments relating to a return, see 2327; for those relating to discovery, see 2330). Determinations apply to income tax and CGT only under self-assessment and are made by an officer of the Board where a taxpayer fails to submit his return on time (see 2327).

An assessment is made when a certificate recording its entry in the assessment book is signed but may be properly made where an inspector, etc. exercises his discretion to make it and calculates the amount but leaves another person to complete the administration.

A notice of assessment must be served on the person assessed. This may be done by delivering it to him, usually by post, or sending it to his usual or last-known place of residence, his place of business or employment.

Once an assessment has been served, it cannot be altered except on appeal. The burden is on the taxpayer to displace the assessment, not on the Crown to prove it.

The assessment becomes final unless an appeal is made in time; but the Board can 'vacate' an assessment, upon a claim, if there has been a double charge to tax.

The Board may also give relief, upon a claim, where an assessment or self-assessment has been excessive due to some error or mistake in a return or, under self-assessment, a partnership statement; in practice such 'overpayment relief' (formerly known as 'error or mistake relief') (see 2342) also applies to investigation settlements. HMRC will challenge an overpayment relief claim where a substantive point was 'squarely in issue' when a taxpayer agreed a computation with HMRC. Appeals against the Board's decision on such a claim lies to the First-tier Tribunal. Further appeal (to the High Court or, in Scotland, the Court of Session) is only allowed in respect of a point of law arising in connection with the computation of income or chargeable gains.

Under 'equitable liability', HMRC will also refrain from collecting the full amount legally due where HMRC's status as a preferred creditor puts other creditors at a disadvantage; under self-assessment it will be rare that the taxpayer misses an opportunity to displace an officer's determination, but HMRC will still consider applying equitable liability.

An assessment (or determination: see 2327) is not void by reason of mistake, defect or omission where in substance and effect it conforms with the Taxes Acts. So if, for example, the taxpayer's second forename were misspelt the assessment would stand. However, this provision does not justify HMRC treating an assessment for one year as an assessment for a different year where an error in dates is made.

Cumulative assessments are void. However, in a case where HMRC had claimed a cumulative sum in respect of assessments which should have been in the alternative but had corrected the error by amending the writ to include one assessment for each year, the taxpayer had no arguable defence to a summary judgment order for recovery of tax due to the Crown.

Income tax chargeable in respect of income arising to the trustees of a settlement, or to the personal representatives of a deceased person may be assessed and charged on any one or more of the 'relevant' (see 2249) trustees or personal representatives.

Legislation: TMA 1970, s. 30A(3), (4), 32–33A, 114, 115 and Sch. 1AB; FA 1989, s. 151; former TMA 1970, s. 29(5), (6)

Cases: *Honig v Sarsfield (HMIT)* [1986] BTC 205; *Brady (HMIT) v Group Lotus Car Companies plc* [1987] BTC 480; *Bird v IR Commrs; Breams Nominees Ltd v IR Commrs* [1988] BTC 164; *Baylis (HMIT) v Gregory* [1988] BTC 268; *Burford v Durkin (HMIT)* [1991] BTC 9; *IR Commrs v Wilkinson* [1992] BTC 297; *Eagerpath Ltd v Edwards (HMIT)* [1999] BTC 253; *Revell* [2016] TC 04887

Other Material: HMRC Brief 16/10; Report of the Parliamentary Commissioner for Administration: 2nd report, Session 1989–90, Selected Cases 1990, vol. 1, HC 151 at p. 51–62

Tax Reporter: ¶184-275

2327 Assessments and determinations relevant to returns

Apart from discovery assessments (see 2330), HMRC have powers to make estimated assessments or determinations by reference to the taxpayer's return (or his failure to make a return) or to adjust a taxpayer's self-assessment. For the nature of the assessment or determination, see 2324.

Self-assessment

Under self-assessment the duty of making assessments still generally falls on an officer of the Board of HM Revenue & Customs; however, the officer does not have to make an assessment if he accepts the taxpayer's own computation of his liability but, if he needs to do so, he can include income under every schedule in one assessment.

Enquiries

Indeed, the officer can enquire into aspects of the taxpayer's self-assessment and, if the taxpayer fails to amend the assessment to reflect the officer's opinion as to any discrepancy which will result in a loss of tax to the Crown, he can amend that assessment himself; on completion of his enquiries, the officer again has the chance to adjust the assessment to reflect final figures. Similar rules apply to enquiries into a partnership statement, amendments to which ripple through to the partners. If a taxpayer wishes to end the officer's enquiries, he can apply to the tribunal for a direction to that effect; this will not necessarily prevent the officer later making a discovery of further profits.

Determinations

Under self-assessment, an officer of the Board can also make a 'determination' of income or gains 'to the best of his information and belief' if the taxpayer fails to deliver the return on time; this does not relate to a partnership, since it is each partner who is responsible for the tax and the partnership return is entirely separate. It is assumed that these determinations will have many of the characteristics of best-of-judgment assessments (see below).

Legislation: TMA 1970, s. 28A–28C, 30A(1), (2), (5)

Cases: *Blackpool Marton Rotary Club v Martin (HMIT)* [1990] BTC 3; *Billows v Robinson (HMIT)* [1990] BTC 95; *Bi-Flex Caribbean Ltd v Board of Inland Revenue (Trinidad and Tobago)* [1990] BTC 452; *Montshiwa* [2015] TC 04701

Other Material: HMRC Brief 16/10

Tax Reporter: ¶184-275

2328　Simpler assessments

Finance Act 2016 provides a power to allow HMRC to make an assessment of an individual's income tax or capital gains tax liability without them first being required to complete a self-assessment return where it has sufficient information about that individual to make the assessment. Those individuals whose tax affairs are not straightforward or where HMRC do not have all the necessary information to calculate their tax liability will still be required to complete a tax return. This measure will have effect on and after 15 September 2016 (Royal Assent).

HMRC will be required to set out clearly how much is due and the information used when calculating the amount due. This will enable the individual to check whether the information used in the calculation is correct, including whether there are any omissions. If the individual disputes the amount due, they will be required to inform HMRC explaining why and provide necessary evidence. The requirement on individuals to report information to HMRC remains unless there is no further information than that used in the simple assessment. Where HMRC have issued an individual with a notice to file a return but then realise that a return is not necessary, they will be able to withdraw a notice where they intend to make a simple assessment instead.

2330   Assessments where loss of tax discovered

Whether under self-assessment or otherwise, if an HMRC officer or the Board itself 'discovers' that:

- any profits have not been assessed which should have been assessed;
- an assessment is or has become insufficient; or
- any relief given is or has become excessive,

the officer, etc. or the Board may make an assessment of an amount which it is felt should be charged. However, under self-assessment, no such assessment will be made if the taxpayer acted honestly (i.e. there was no careless or deliberate behaviour) and HMRC could reasonably have been expected to be aware of the deficiency when the officer concluded (or was treated as having concluded) his enquiries into the return nor if the return accorded with the basis prevailing at the time (or practice in relation thereto); notwithstanding the time-limit above, the assessment may be made at any time before HMRC's enquiries are treated as completed.

Under the self-assessment regime as it applies to partnerships, rules similar to those above apply in relation to a discovery in relation to the partnership statement (to be included with the partnership return), amendments to which ripple through to the partners.

An officer who discovers an error of substance in an assessment can correct the error by a further assessment. In the past, the question of what is meant by 'discover' has been debated at length but it is now clearly established that the word in this context broadly means 'to find out'. A discovery may be made even where the taxpayer has made a full disclosure and the officer or inspector was originally in error. However, in some cases, HMRC do forgo arrears of tax due to official error).

Once an assessment or additional assessment is made, either by agreement following an appeal or determined on appeal, the officer or inspector cannot make a new assessment on the same income for the same year even if he discovers a fresh point of law. In HMRC's view:

- if a point has been specifically agreed with HMRC or HMRC have agreed a computation containing a point which is both 'fundamental to the whole basis of the computation' and 'so fully described that its significance for the computation of the taxpayer's liability was clearly and immediately apparent', HMRC do not go back and raise a discovery assessment in respect of that point; by concession, this extends to cases where, even though there is no determination of an appeal or decision on a claim, the point relates to agreement of the final figures for assessment purposes;

- otherwise, by concession, HMRC regard themselves as bound by their acceptance of a computation (as respects a claim or the proper amount of the assessment) if the view of the point implicit in the computation was based on a full and accurate disclosure of all the relevant facts and was a tenable view.

HMRC may, in particular, make a discovery assessment where:

- '– profits or income have not earlier been charged to tax because of any form of fraudulent or negligent conduct;

- – the inspector has been misled or misinformed in any way about the particular matter at issue;

- – there is an arithmetical error in a computation which had not been spotted at the time agreement was reached, and which can be corrected by the making of an in date discovery assessment;

- – an error is made in accounts and computations which it cannot reasonably be alleged was correct or intended, e.g. the double deduction from taxable profits of a particular item (say group relief).'

However, the CIOT and ICAEW have obtained the opinion of leading counsel that the point at issue does not have to be fundamental to the agreement of the relevant figures provided that all such facts as it is reasonable to regard as relevant to considering the point at issue were disclosed and either:

- the particular point had previously been raised expressly by the inspector, the taxpayer or the taxpayer's agent; or

- the point was so clearly presented that 'an ordinarily competent inspector' would have, or ought to have, taken it into account.

HMRC guidance on the operation of discovery and disclosure under self-assessment makes it clear that where a taxpayer has made a self-assessment for the relevant chargeable period, HMRC can raise an assessment if there would otherwise be a loss of tax from the taxpayer's failure to make a complete disclosure of all the relevant facts relating to his liability to tax.

Statement of practice SP 01/06 sets out the circumstances in which HMRC will regard a taxpayer as having made full disclosure and gives assurance of finality in particular situations. The statement of practice confirms guidance issued to help taxpayers achieve finality when completing their returns and extends it to CTSA. The statement does not cover cases where a self assessment is insufficient due to careless or deliberate behaviour by or on behalf of the taxpayer.

An additional assessment is not precluded by an agreement between a taxpayer and HMRC, settling a dispute in respect of an earlier assessment, if the information on which the agreement was based was misleading or incorrect.

Legislation: TMA 1970, s. 29, 30B

Cases: *Hargreaves v R & C Commrs* [2014] BTC 526; *Pattullo* [2014] TC 03958; *Yip* [2014] TC 03981; *Key Recruitment (UK) Ltd* [2014] TC 03874; *Hankinson v R & C Commrs* [2011] EWCA Civ 1566; *Rouf v R & C Commrs* [2009] BTC 375; *Cenlon Finance Co Ltd v Ellwood (HMIT)* [1962] AC 782; *Scorer (HMIT) v Olin Energy Systems Ltd* [1985] BTC 181; *R v IR Commrs, ex parte Preston* [1985] BTC 208; *Coy v Kime (HMIT)* [1987] BTC 66; *Gray (HMIT) v Matheson* [1993] BTC 76; *Momin & Ors v R & C Commrs* [2008] BTC 623; *Burgess; Brimheath Developments Ltd v R & C Commrs* [2015] BTC 533; *Sanderson v R & C Commrs* [2016] BTC 3; *Thomas* [2016] TC 04921; *Ashcroft* [2016] TC 04962; *Bubb* [2016] TC 04992; *Ward* [2016] TC 04902; *Miesegaes* [2016] TC 05129; *Anderson* [2016] TC 05092; *Pattullo v R & C Commrs* [2016] BTC 510

Other Material: SP 01/06; SP 8/91 *Discovery assessments*; HMRC website www.hmrc.gov.uk/prosecutions/crim-inv-policy.htm

Tax Reporter: ¶184-280

2333 Time-limits for assessments

From 1 April 2010, the ordinary time-limit for making assessments reduced to four years after the end of the year of assessment.

There are a number of qualifications to the standard time-limit including:

(1) *Loss of tax brought about carelessly or deliberately.* Under self-assessment, an assessment on any person to make good loss of tax attributable to his careless or deliberate conduct or that of a person acting on his behalf may be made up to 31 January which is 20 years and ten months after the end of the tax year. In the case of partnerships, such an assessment may be made not only on the partner in default but on any of his individual co-partners. For the similar rules for corporation tax, see 4986. From 1 April 2010, the

former concept of 'fraudulent or negligent conduct' was replaced with the concept of a loss of tax brought about carelessly or deliberately. The time-limits under the revised legislation however, remain as above.

(2) *Personal representatives.* Under self-assessment, assessments on personal representatives in respect of income accruing to the deceased before his death cannot currently be made later than four years after the end of the year of assessment. See further 2246 .

Legislation: FA 2008, s. 118 and Sch. 39, para. 9; TMA 1970, s. 34, 36(1), (2), 40

Other Material: HMRC Brief 16/10

Tax Reporter: ¶184-375

2336 Nature of claims, elections and notices

Deductions are usually given automatically. Reliefs and allowances generally have to be claimed by the taxpayer in writing to HMRC; under self-assessment, most claims must, if possible, be made by way of inclusion in the tax return or an amendment to it and be quantified. Elections are generally treated in the same way but notices, originally within the scope of these provisions, are provided for in relation to each particular situation though notice generally means notice in writing.

Many of the rules relating to claims otherwise remain substantially the same under self-assessment:

- the claim may be made by a trustee, guardian, tutor or curator on behalf of an incapacitated taxpayer;
- if the claimant later discovers a mistake in his claim, a supplementary claim may be made within the time for making the original claim;
- where an assessment is adjusted in order to give effect to a claim, the assessment is not out of time if it is made within one year of the final determination of the claim.

Under self-assessment, claims for certain reliefs involving two or more years, for example loss carry-back, relief for fluctuating profits of farmers (see 942), carry-back of post-cessation receipts and spreading back payments – are effectively related to the later year so as to enable the earlier year's figures to be settled.

Those claims, elections and notices ('claims') which can be made under self-assessment otherwise than by way of the return and which do not relate to PAYE are subject to more stringent conditions than before that regime with regard to the matters set out below:

(1) Making of claims. The required form of claim will provide for the taxpayer to make a statutory declaration that it is correctly stated to the best of his information and belief. It may require a statement of the tax to be discharged or repaid (with documentary proof of payment in the latter case) and such information (being accounts, statements and documents) as is reasonably required to determine whether the claim is correct.

(2) Keeping and preserving records which may be required for the purposes of making a correct and complete claim.

(3) Amendment of claims. Except when HMRC are formally investigating a claim, the taxpayer has 12 months in which to amend it (HMRC may amend obvious errors).

(4) Power to enquire into claims. HMRC may give notice to the taxpayer at any time before the latest of the following:

(a) the first-quarter day falling more than 12 months after the claim is made (the quarter days are 31 January, 30 April, 31 July and 31 October);

(b) where the claim or amendment relates to a tax year, the period ending with the first anniversary of 31 January next following that year; or

(c) where the claim or amendment relates to a period other than a tax year, the period ending with the first anniversary of the end of that period.

(5) Power to call for documents for purposes of enquiries.

(6) Amendments of claims where enquiries made. Following the completion of HMRC's enquiries, the taxpayer has an opportunity to amend the claim within 30 days. HMRC have a further 30 days in which the claim can be amended. If a taxpayer wishes to end HMRC's enquiries, he can apply to the tribunal for a direction to that effect. HMRC have 30 days from any amendment to give effect to it and the taxpayer may, within that period, appeal against it. The tribunal may vary the amendment to the disadvantage of the taxpayer as well as to his advantage. HMRC again have 30 days in which to give effect to such variation.

However, various discretions have been removed. HMRC are no longer required to make a decision or take other action in relation to various provisions before an assessment can be made, the issues in point being reviewed in accordance with self-assessment procedures generally.

Legislation: ITTOIA 2005, s. 878(3); FA 1996, s. 130, 134; Sch. 20; ICTA 1988, s. 832(1); TMA 1970, s. 42(1)–(3), (5), 43A; Sch. 1A

Cases: *Savacentre Ltd v IR Commrs* [1995] BTC 365

Tax Reporter: ¶191-585

2339 Time-limits for claims

From 1 April 2010, the general time-limit for making claims is four years after the end of the year of assessment to which the claim relates.

For lists of time-limits for claims and elections for income tax, corporation tax and capital gains tax, please see the Key Data section.

Legislation: FA 2008, s. 118 and Sch. 39, para. 12; TMA 1970, s. 43(1)

Tax Reporter: ¶191-585

2342 Claims for relief for overpaid tax

Finance Act 2009, s. 100 and Sch. 52 provide for the modernisation of the error or mistake rules with effect for claims made on or after 1 April 2010. The *Taxes Management Act* 1970, Sch. 1AB contains provision for and in connection with claims for the recovery of overpaid income tax and capital gains tax. These new rules are referred to as 'Relief for overpayments' and replace the old 'error or mistake' provisions.

Where a taxpayer has paid tax which he believes not to be due, or where an assessment, determination or direction has been made but the taxpayer believes that tax is not due, he can make a claim for the tax to be repaid or for the assessment to be discharged. The claim must be made within four years from 31 January following the year to which the return relates, unless a notice requiring a return was sent later. In relation to a claim, the relevant tax year is:

(1) for claims made where tax has been overpaid as a result of a mistake in a return, the year to which the return relates (or if more than one, the first return); and

(2) otherwise, the tax year in respect of which the payment was made.

For claims made where an assessment, determination or direction has been made, the relevant tax year is the year to which the assessment, determination or direction relates.

Instances in which a claim cannot be made

(1) Where the amount paid, or to be paid, is excessive by reason of:

    (a) a mistake in a claim, election or a notice;

    (b) a mistake in making/giving, or not making/giving, a claim, election or notice;

    (c) a mistake in allocating expenditure to a pool, or in bringing a disposal value into account, for capital allowances purposes (see also HMRC Brief 12/09 for HMRC guidance on the interaction between error and mistake relief and claims for capital allowances); or

    (d) a mistake in making or not making an allocation of expenditure, or bringing into account or not bringing into account a disposal value, for capital allowances purposes.

(2) Where the taxpayer can take other action under the Income Tax Acts or Capital Gains Act in order to obtain relief.

(3) Where (2) above would apply had the relevant time limit not expired and where the taxpayer knew, or 'ought reasonably to have known', that such relief was available.

(4) Where the grounds for the claim have already been put to a court or tribunal or to HMRC in appealing against the amount determined by a tribunal.

(5) Where the taxpayer knew, or 'ought reasonably to have known' of the grounds for the claim before the latest of:

    (a) the date on which an appeal in the course of which the grounds could have been put forward was determined by a court or tribunal;

    (b) the date on which the taxpayer withdrew a relevant appeal to a court or tribunal; or

    (c) the end of the period in which the taxpayer was able to make a relevant appeal to a court or tribunal.

(6) Where the amount was paid, or is to be paid, as a result of proceedings brought by HMRC enforcing the payment or in accordance with an agreement between the taxpayer and HMRC settling such proceedings.

(7) Where the amount paid, or to be paid, is excessive by reason of a mistake in calculating the taxpayer's liability to income tax or capital gains (other than a mistake in a PAYE assessment of PAYE calculation), and the liability was calculated in accordance with the practice generally prevailing at the time.

Legislation: FA 2009, s. 100 and Sch. 52; TMA 1970, Sch. 1AB

Cases: *Test Claimants in the Franked Investment Income Group Litigation v IR Commrs* [2010] BTC 265

Other Material: HMRC Brief 22/10

Tax Reporter: ¶191-735

Payment and interest

2350   Methods of paying tax

HMRC accept payment of tax by a range of methods:

(1)   direct debit (if you are registered for self-assessment online);

(2)   internet or telephone banking;

(3)   with a debit or credit card issued by a UK card issuer using the BillPay service provided by Santander Corporate Banking (previously Alliance & Leicester Commercial Bank);

(4)   bank giro;

(5)   post office;

(6)   by post.

Credit card payments are subject to a transaction fee.

The BillPay service can be used to pay the following taxes:

- self-assessment;
- employers PAYE/NICS;
- VAT;
- corporation tax;
- stamp duty land tax;
- miscellaneous payments (only references beginning with 'X').

The web address for paying tax to HMRC over the internet with a debit or credit card is www.santanderbillpayment.co.uk/hmrc.

HMRC have requested agents to use the computer-printed payslip whenever possible if they choose to post their client's self-assessment payment to HMRC.

Legislation: *Fees for Payment of Taxes, etc. by Credit Card Regulations* 2016 (SI 2016/333)

Tax Reporter: ¶182-725

2353   Employers' payment of PAYE

In relation to PAYE, an employer is generally required to pay income tax deducted within 14 days of the end of every income tax month. Cleared payment must reach HMRC's bank account no later than 22nd of each month. However, where an employee receives a fixed salary or wage, HMRC can authorise the employer to deduct tax from each payment of emoluments by reference only to the amount of the payment (i.e. without regard to the cumulative emoluments and cumulative tax). In such a case, payment of tax deducted under PAYE is due quarterly (i.e. 19 July, 19 October, 19 January, 19 April).

Certain PAYE and other regular payments to HMRC may, if the employer so wishes, be made quarterly. The following conditions and procedures are relevant:

- the employer/contractor must reasonably believe that his average monthly payment due to HMRC for PAYE, NICs, and student loans recovered is £1,500;

- the decision to make quarterly payments can be made at any time in the year;

- any quarterly payments are for the quarters ending 5 July, 5 October, 5 January and 5 April and are payable within 14 days of the end of the quarter, i.e. by the nineteenth of these months;

- if the average monthly payments turn out to exceed the given limit in practice, the employer can continue to pay quarterly for the remainder of the tax year;

- a decision to pay quarterly only concerns the current tax year; a new decision must be taken at the start of the next tax year, based on a reasonable estimate of the average monthly payment for that tax year;

- employers need not notify HMRC of their decision to pay quarterly, unless the collector of taxes issues a reminder or demand; the collector will normally only issue reminders or demands to employers, who can pay quarterly, if no payment has been made by a quarter payment date;

- the starter pack for new employers will ask them to notify the collector if they have chosen to pay quarterly; and

- the payment books will have monthly pay slips; employers paying quarterly should use the pay slip for the last month in the quarter.

HMRC are able to offer the option of paying by direct debit for self-assessment tax payments, PAYE and corporation tax.

Legislation: *Income Tax (Pay As You Earn) Regulations* 2003 (SI 2003/2682)

Tax Reporter: ¶494-560

2356 PAYE settlement agreements

PAYE settlement agreements (PSAs) allow employers to account for any tax liability in respect of their employees on benefits and expense payments that are minor or irregular, or that are shared benefits on which it would be impractical to determine individual liability, in one lump sum. A statement of practice (SP 5/96) explains how PAYE settlement agreements operate.

National Insurance due in relation to items included with a PSA can be settled in a similar way to the tax by means of Class 1B contributions.

For interest on late payments, see 2368.

Legislation: ITEPA 2003, s. 703–707; *Income Tax (Pay As You Earn) Regulations* 2003 (SI 2003/2682)

Tax Reporter: ¶496-120

2359 Postponement of tax pending appeal

Where HMRC make an assessment, tax generally becomes due and payable on the date shown in the table at 58 despite an appeal by the taxpayer. However, if an application to postpone tax is also made by the taxpayer, some deferment in the due date may be obtained. The general rule is that an application to postpone payment must be made by a taxpayer within 30 days after the date of the issue of the notice of assessment. That 30-day period is extended if there is a change in the circumstances of the case as a result of which the appellant has grounds for believing that he is overcharged to tax by the assessment.

In appealing from the determination of the tribunal to the courts, tax must first be paid in accordance with that determination.

Legislation: TMA 1970, s. 55, 56(9)

Tax Reporter: ¶188-800

2362   Arrears of tax due to official error

In certain circumstances, by concession, arrears of tax are wholly or partly waived if the arrears have arisen due to official error in utilising the information supplied by the taxpayer (or in certain circumstances by an employer).

Other Material: ESC A19, *Giving up tax where there are Revenue delays in using information*

2365   Tax deposit certificates

A taxpayer may provide in advance for the payment of most taxes (except PAYE and corporation tax). This can be done by making deposits at any tax collecting office. The first payment must not be less than £2,000 and any subsequent deposit (which must not be less than £500) must maintain the total sum on deposit at or above £2,000.

The advantage in making such deposits lies partly in the fact that interest is paid by HMRC at attractive rates, although no interest is currently payable against deposits of less than £100,000. Full details of current rates and information on how to use certificates of tax deposit are on the HMRC website at www.hmrc.gov.uk/payinghmrc/cert-tax-deposit.htm.

Rates of interest in force at the date of deposit apply to the amount deposited for the first two years. Thereafter, the rates of interest are those applicable on the second and fourth anniversaries of the deposit. Interest is paid for a maximum of six years.

Deposits may be withdrawn for cash at any time in such order as the depositor requires. Generally, requests for withdrawal should be made to the Central Accounting Office.

Legislation: FA 1995, s. 157

Website: www.gov.uk/guidance/certificate-of-tax-deposit-scheme

Tax Reporter: ¶182-725

2368   Interest on overdue tax

Interest is charged on income tax (and CGT) which is overdue for payment.

Where tax is paid by cheque, the effective date of payment is the day when HMRC receive it. (The exception to this is where the payment is received by post following a day when the tax office is closed (for whatever reason), in which case the effective date of payment is the day the office was first closed. This means that payments received on Monday are treated as being made the previous Saturday.)

Where payment is made by electronic funds transfer (EFT), BACS or CHAPS, payment is treated as made one working day immediately before the date the value is received. Where payment is by Bank Giro or Giro Bank, it is treated as made three working days prior to the date of processing by HMRC.

Adjustments of interest charged may be made where a relief from tax is subsequently agreed.

Interest is chargeable on unpaid PAYE; before that date, interest could run only in respect of a formal determination on the employer.

For rates of interest and interest factor tables, see Key Data.

When interest starts to run

Interest runs on amounts due and payable under self-assessment from the 'relevant date' until the actual date of payment as follows:

- on the two required payments on account based on the previous year's assessment (adjusted to take into account any overpayment and, to the extent that the taxpayer has claimed a reduction, any underpayment), from 31 January in the tax year and 31 July immediately after the end of that year – the date they become due and payable;

- on the balance of the liability shown by any self-assessment, from 31 January which is ten months after the end of the tax year (or, where the individual gave notice of his liability to tax by 5 October following the end of the tax year but was not asked to make a return until after 31 October, three months after receiving the request) – the date it becomes due and payable; and

- in respect of additional tax resulting from an amendment of a self-assessment (whether or not it becomes due following a postponement application), the same day as in respect of the liability shown by the self-assessment (above) or, if later, 30 days after notice of the amendment is given (see 2327).

Discovery

If HMRC amend a return (see 2327) or discover further profits (see 2330), the increased amount is deemed always to have been the proper amount due, so interest will flow on that amount from the due date. Similar adjustments apply if the payments on account for the year affected by the discovery assessment also need adjustment: this will be the case where there has been a claim to reduce the amount of the payments on account.

Income tax

Legislation: FA 2009, s. 101–105 and Sch. 53; TMA 1970, 86, 91; *Income Tax (Sub-contractors in the Construction Industry) Regulations* 1993 (SI 1993/743), reg. 10(5); *Income Tax (Pay As You Earn) Regulations* 2003 (SI 2003/2682)

Case: *McMullan* [2010] TC 00305

Tax Reporter: ¶182-925

2371 Interest on overpaid income tax: 'repayment supplement'

There is provision for the payment of interest (also called repayment supplement) on delayed tax repayments which is free of all forms of tax. An overpayment of £10 or less will be informally adjusted unless the taxpayer requests otherwise.

Under self-assessment, the date varies according to the nature of the payment: essentially this allows for different due dates in respect of payments on account, a penalty or surcharge and other income tax – broadly, it is the date the tax is actually paid, even if this is earlier than the due date. Where a repayment is due to the taxpayer but HMRC commence an enquiry (see 2327), repayment is deferred until the enquiries have been completed but may, before then, be made on a provisional basis to the extent that the officer sees fit.

Interest is receivable on overpaid PAYE in certain circumstances.

A supplement will be added to tax repayments made to an individual for a tax year in which he or she is resident in an EU member state, other than the UK, on the same basis as applies to UK residents.

For rates of interest and interest factor tables, see Key Data.

Legislation: FA 2009, s. 101–105 and Sch. 54; TMA 1970, s. 59B(4A); *Income Tax (Pay As You Earn) Regulations* 2003 (SI 2003/2682)

Other Material: SP 6/95, *Legal entitlement and administrative practices*

Tax Reporter: ¶182-975

Collection

2381 Methods of collection

There are two basic methods of collecting tax:

- by direct assessment; and
- by deduction of tax at source.

Tax deduction at source is employed in relation to a number of sources of income, e.g. some annual payments (see 1368 to 1370), interest (see 1372), dividends, PAYE (see 2384), the subcontractors scheme (see 2387).

Tax Reporter: ¶187-995

2384 PAYE

The main method of collecting tax where emoluments are charged under the charge on income from employment provisions is by means of the pay as you earn ('PAYE') scheme. The scheme imposes upon the employer the duty to deduct tax from emoluments of his employees at the time when the emoluments are paid and to account for, and pay, the deductions to HMRC. The employer, in effect, acts as tax collector for HMRC. Failure to deduct tax may make the employer liable to pay the tax, and he may be subject to penalties. For the payment system, see 2353.

HMRC may collect debts owed through PAYE. From 3 October 2014, the maximum amount which may be collected through a PAYE code is £17,000 (increased from £3,000), using the following graduated scale:

Expected amount of PAYE income of employee in the tax year for which the code is determined	Total amount of debt that may be recovered from employee in that tax year
Less than £30,000	No more than £3,000
£30,000 or more but less than £40,000	No more than £5,000
£40,000 or more but less than £50,000	No more than £7,000
£50,000 or more but less than £60,000	No more than £9,000
£60,000 or more but less than £70,000	No more than £11,000
£70,000 or more but less than £80,000	No more than £13,000
£80,000 or more but less than £90,000	No more than £15,000
£90,000 or more	No more than £17,000

For PAYE purposes, an 'employer' includes any person paying emoluments or controlling/managing the worker. This might bring agency workers within its scope (see 260) and, even if a taxpayer pays a worker, control and management by another person (the principal employer) might make that person the deemed employer.

If tax should have been deducted by the employer under PAYE, in certain cases, HMRC may be unable to impose a charge directly on the employee.

Employers are not obliged to operate PAYE on cash payments to employees in respect of qualifying removal expenses which are taxable only because they exceed the £8,000 exemption (see 298). Retirement benefit scheme annuities and personal pension annuities are subject to PAYE.

Various indirect arrangements are treated as within the scope of PAYE and these include payments made by an intermediary, income in the form of a 'readily convertible asset' (e.g. gold bars, coffee beans, etc.), non-cash vouchers which are either exchangeable for tradeable assets or are themselves tradeable assets, credit-tokens to obtain money or tradeable assets, cash vouchers and payments of shares to employees (but not payments under approved share schemes); regulations may govern how employers are to account for PAYE on certain notional payments.

Tax codes

Briefly, the system operates to take account of a proportion of the employee's entitlement to reliefs and allowances when tax is deducted. This is done by providing the employer with a series of tables and by notifying him of the relevant code number applying to a particular employee. The tables set out the cumulative allowances and the cumulative tax applying to the employee.

Negative (or 'K') codes are designed to enable income tax on benefits in kind, where the value of the benefits exceeds the employee's personal allowances, to be collected through the PAYE system, rather than by assessment at the end of the tax year. The system contains an overriding limit on the amount of tax which may be deducted from a payment of emoluments so as to ensure that the tax liability does not exceed 50% of the employee's pay.

The system of coding is designed to allow to be taken into account the great variety of possible allowances and reliefs to which an employee might be entitled without actually informing the employer of the employee's reliefs' entitlement. Notice of the code determined by HMRC is given to the employer by a code authorisation and, if it differs from the code notified in the preceding year, the employee is also notified. The employee may appeal against such notice of coding.

The exact code depends on the employee's personal circumstances. Where these change during the year, the employee should inform HMRC so that his code can be altered accordingly.

The coding system can, of course, only approximate the tax position of each individual. An assessment might be used to make an adjustment at the end of the year (though in many cases there is no need for a formal assessment). If there has been an overpayment of tax, this is repaid by HMRC (subject to a de minimis limit: see 2371). Any underpayment of tax is usually taken into account in the following year's coding, a matter specifically incorporated into the self-assessment regime.

The code notified to the employer must be the one used by him. He must also keep records on a deductions working sheet regarding payments made to the employee, cumulative tax, etc. Where there is no code notification (e.g. in the case of a school-leaver who has not previously been employed), the emergency code must be used and HMRC informed under the real time information (RTI) system.

Joiners/leavers and casuals

When an employee leaves his employment, he is given a P45 by his employer which will show, inter alia, the last entries on the deductions working sheet kept by him. The form is handed to the departing employee's new employer which will enable him to make the correct tax deductions. There is the amount of £200 which:

- an employer may repay to a new employee, when making the first wage/salary payment, without reference to HMRC; and

- must be notified by the Department of Work and Pensions to HMRC (and which must not be repaid without his authority) as a repayment due to an unemployed person in receipt of social security benefits, some of which are taxable.

In the case of casual employees, where the PAYE system cannot be operated, HMRC may make an estimated assessment on the employee or else he may issue a deductions working sheet to the employee who then deducts tax from his emoluments (and pays it to HMRC) as if he were his own employer.

Troncs

Certain organised arrangements fall within the scope of the 'tronc' system which require PAYE to be deducted by the 'tronc master' (see 285). If the tronc master fails to do this, the responsibility falls on the principal employer. The Court of Appeal has held that the directors of a restaurant company who shared out the waiters' tips at the end of the week between themselves and the waiters were acting as officers of the company and the company was the person responsible for operating PAYE.

Note that in the case of Annabel's restaurant and nightclub, the Employment Appeal Tribunal held that tips and gratuities may not count towards a worker's earnings for the purposes of making wages meet the minimum wage payment requirement. Thus an employer must pay his staff the national minimum wage (NMW) regardless of the tips and gratuities they may receive. However, any tips paid through the employer's payroll will not be exempt and will count towards earnings for NMW purposes.

Student loans

Employers are responsible for collecting repayments of income contingent student loans through the PAYE system when notified by HMRC that repayments should be collected in respect of a particular employee. Broadly, deductions are made in respect of student loan repayment when a start notice (SL1) has been received from HMRC at the rate of 9% on income above the relevant threshold for the year (see key data). The repayments are determined for each pay period on a non-cumulative basis. Tables are provided in the annual pack, which can be used to determine the amount of the repayment to be deducted. The repayments deducted are paid over to HMRC with PAYE tax and National Insurance.

Legislation: FA 2009, s. 110 and Sch. 58; ITEPA 2003, 684–707; TMA 1970, s. 59A(10), 59B(8); *Income Tax (Pay As You Earn) Regulations* 2003 (SI 2003/2682); *Income Tax (Earnings and Pensions) Act 2003 (Section 684(3A)) Order* 2011 (SI 2011/1585); *Income Tax (Pay As You Earn) (Amendment) (No. 3) Regulations* 2011 (SI 2011/1584); *Finance Act 2009 (Consequential Amendments) Order* 2011 (SI 2011/1583); *Income Tax (Earnings and Pensions) Act 2003 (Section 684(3A)) Order* 2014 (SI 2014/2438)

Cases: *Andrews v King (HMIT)* [1991] BTC 338; *Figael Ltd v Fox (HMIT)* [1992] BTC 61; *Booth v Mirror Group Newspapers plc* [1992] BTC 455; *IR Commrs v Herd* [1993] BTC 245; *Stainer* [2016] TC 04924

Tax Reporter: ¶187-995

2387 Construction industry tax deduction scheme

The Construction Industry Scheme (CIS) first came into operation in 1971. However, extensive amendments were made in 1975 and full operation of the revised scheme commenced from 6 April 1977. Problems within the industry regarding the scheme continued to arise and led to certain changes contained in the Finance Acts 1995 and 1996. This was followed with major reform of the scheme from 6 April 2007.

Broadly, the CIS is a quasi PAYE system designed to counter tax evasion in the construction industry by imposing responsibility for making a deduction at source from payments made for labour services provided by self-employed building subcontractors and companies unless those persons have received prior certification from HMRC. The CIS, however, is not, and never has been, a system designed to replace the PAYE system with respect to the employees of firms in the construction industry. This is a common misconception brought about partly by the way in which HMRC have operated the scheme in practice. Nevertheless, since its inception, PAYE auditors have been charged with the responsibility for ensuring that the scheme is being operated properly by building contractors and many of the regulations providing the rules for operating the scheme have parallels within the PAYE regulations.

Following consultation during 2014, the Autumn Statement 2014 confirmed that the Government would implement a package of improvements to the CIS to reduce administrative burdens on construction businesses. The changes and their respective starting dates can be summarised as follows:

Measure	Effective from	Amending legislation
Removal of the statutory obligation to report nil CIS returns	6 April 2015	SI 2015/429
Easier access to gross payment status for joint ventures where one member already has gross payment status	6 April 2015	SI 2015/789
Earlier repayments in insolvency proceedings	6 April 2015	SI 2015/429
Reduction in the upper threshold for the turnover test from £200,000 to £100,000	6 April 2016	SI 2016/348
Simplification of the initial and annual compliance tests	6 April 2016	SI 2016/348
Mandatory online filing of CIS returns	6 April 2016	SI 2016/348
Mandatory online verification	6 April 2017	SI 2016/348

Main features

The main features of the current CIS scheme are as follows:

- contractors must check or 'verify' new subcontractors with HMRC;

- subcontractors are paid either net or gross, depending on their own circumstances, but it is HMRC who tell the contractor which treatment to use during verification;

- there is a higher rate tax deduction if a subcontractor cannot be 'matched' on the HMRC system. This rate applies until the subcontractor contacts HMRC and registers or sorts out any matching problem;

- there are no CIS annual returns under the scheme;

Income tax

- contractors are required to notify payments to subcontractors using HMRC's Real Time Information (RTI) system (see 2241); and

- new subcontractors are required to register with HMRC.

Employment status

Under the CIS, contractors must check or 'verify' new subcontractors with HMRC. Broadly, this means that HMRC will check the employment status of the subcontractor and ensure that he is properly registered for income tax and National Insurance contributions (NICs) purposes.

A worker's employment status, that is whether they are employed or self-employed, is not a matter of choice. Whether someone is employed or self-employed depends upon the terms and conditions of the relevant engagement. The tax and NICs rules do, however, contain some special rules that apply to certain categories of worker in certain circumstances. A worker's employment status will determine the charge to tax on income from that employment or self-employment. It will also determine the class of NICs, which are to be paid.

HMRC provide an 'Employment Status Indicator (ESI) Tool' on their website. Employers and contractors may use the tool to obtain a HMRC 'view' of the employment status of their workers. It should be noted that the tool will provide a general guide only which would not be binding on HMRC. To obtain a written 'opinion' of employment status in the construction industry the contractor will need to telephone the CIS Helpline on 0300 200 3210.

Payments to subcontractors

There are certain requirements that a contractor must fulfil before payments can be made to subcontractors.

Verification

Verification is the process HMRC use to make sure that subcontractors have the correct rate of deduction applied to their payments under the CIS. There are three main steps to the process:

- The contractor contacts HMRC with details of the subcontractor.

- HMRC check that the subcontractor is registered with them.

- HMRC tell the contractor what rate of deduction to apply, if any.

Before a contractor can make a payment for construction work to a subcontractor, they must decide whether they need to verify the subcontractor.

The general rule is that a contractor does not have to verify a subcontractor if they last included that subcontractor on a return in the current or two previous tax years.

If a contractor does not have to verify a subcontractor they must pay the subcontractor on the same basis as the last payment made to them. This means that if the subcontractor was last paid under the standard rate of deduction, the current payment must also be made under the standard rate of deduction. If the last payment was made gross, because a deduction was not required, the current payment must also be made gross.

Contractors must pay the amount deductible from payments to subcontractors to HMRC Accounts Office monthly. They must pay deductions due to be made in each tax month within 14 days of the end of that month or within 17 days where payment is made electronically, whether or not these deductions have actually been made. This means that where a required deduction has not actually been made from the subcontractor's payment, for whatever reason, the contractor is still responsible for paying that amount over to HMRC.

There are no annual returns within the CIS.

Registration

New subcontractors starting working in the construction industry on a self-employed basis should register for the CIS if they do not want deductions at the higher rate made from their payments.

HMRC will only authorise a contractor to make gross payments to a subcontractor where the following conditions are satisfied.

Tax will be deducted at the rate of 20% for registered subcontractors and at 30% if the subcontractor is not registered.

The business test

To satisfy this condition, the subcontractor must provide evidence that he is carrying on a business in the United Kingdom which:

(a) consists of or includes the carrying out of construction operations or the furnishing or arranging for the furnishing of labour in carrying out construction operations; and

(b) is, to a substantial extent, carried on by means of an account with a bank.

Income tax

Evidence prescribed to satisfy the business test is as follows:

- the business address;
- invoices, contracts or purchase orders for construction work carried out by the applicant;
- details of payments for construction work;
- the books and accounts of the business; and
- details of the business bank account, including bank statements.

The turnover test

The applicant must satisfy HMRC that in the year following the making of the application:

- as an individual, his net business turnover from construction work (that is, after the cost of any materials used to earn that income) is £30,000 a year or more; or
- as a partnership or company, the net business turnover from construction work (that is, after deducting the cost of any materials) is £30,000 a year or more multiplied by the number of partners or directors.

In the case of 'close companies' (broadly, companies controlled by five or fewer individuals), the figure will be multiplied by the number of individuals who are directors and/or shareholders. For a husband and wife team, for instance, it would be £60,000.

An alternative test for partnerships and companies is that the business has an annual net turnover from construction work (after deducting the cost of materials) of £200,000 or more.

The compliance test

The subcontractor must have met certain compliance requirements during the 'qualifying period' (the period of 12 months ending with the date of the application in question).

From 6 April 2016, this means complying with any obligations to file monthly returns in respect of the construction industry scheme, to file a self-assessment return or a corporation tax return and to have paid to HMRC the amounts which the applicant was liable to have deducted under FA 2004, s. 61 and under SI 2003/2682 (the PAYE Regulations) (amendments by SI 2016/404).

Previously, this meant he must have paid all tax liabilities, including any PAYE and subcontractor deductions, and submitted all tax returns on time.

HMRC will not accept an application from a subcontractor who brings his tax affairs up to date just prior to submitting that application. Having said that, regulations do allow applicants to pass the compliance test even though they have failed to pay their tax bill, or have paid late, provided that amount is small.

Legislation: FA 2004, s. 70 and 71; *Income Tax (Construction Industry Scheme) (Amendment) Regulations* 2015 (SI 2015/429); *Income Tax (Pay As You Earn) and the Income Tax (Construction Industry Scheme) (Amendment) Regulations* 2014 (SI 2014/472); *Income Tax (Construction Industry Scheme) (Amendment) Regulations* 2012 (SI 2012/820); *Finance (No. 3) Act 2010, Schedule 10 and the Finance Act 2009, Schedule 55 and Sections 101 to 103 (Appointed Day, etc) (Construction Industry Scheme) Order* 2011 (SI 2011/2391); *Finance Act 2009, Section 103 (Appointed Day) Order* 2011 (SI 2011/2401); *Finance Act 2004, Section 61(2), (Relevant Percentage) Order* 2007 (SI 2007/46); *Finance Act 2004, Section 77(1) and (7), (Appointed Day) Order* 2006 (SI 2006/3240); *Income Tax (Construction Industry Scheme) (Amendment) Regulations* 2010 (SI 2010/717); *Income Tax (Construction Industry Scheme) (Amendment) Regulations* 2009 (SI 2009/2030); *Income Tax (Construction Industry Scheme) Regulations* 2005 (SI 2005/2045), reg. 7, 27, 28

Cases: *Enderbey Properties Ltd* [2010] TC 00396; *Leeds Lifts Ltd* [2009] TC 00231; *Jonathan David Ltd* [2009] TC 00233; *A Longworth & Sons Ltd* [2009] TC 00230; *Mutch* [2009] TC 00232; *Munns* [2009] TC 00234; *Strongwork Construction Ltd* [2009] TC 00236; *Prior Roofing Ltd* [2009] TC 00246; *Ductaire Fabrication Ltd* [2009] TC 00288; *Castle Construction (Chesterfield) Ltd v R & C Commrs* [2008] Sp C 723; *Oriel Support Ltd v R & C Commrs* [2007] Sp C 615; *R & C Commrs v Smith* [2008] BTC 608; *Neil Martin Ltd v R & C Commrs* [2007] BTC 662; *Walker* [2016] TC 04911; *Mabe* [2016] TC 05098

Website: www.gov.uk/employment-status-indicator; www.gov.uk/topic/business-tax/construction-industry-scheme

Tax Reporter: ¶282-350

Recovery

2400   Choice of recovery methods

Unpaid tax may be recovered by the Crown in the following ways:

- direct from a taxpayer's bank account under the direct recovery of debts procedure (see 2402);

- by levying distress upon the lands or goods of the person in default (see 2403);

- by action to recover the debt through court proceedings (see 2406);

- by insolvency proceedings.

Outside debt collection agencies now assist HMRC with debt collection capacity. Contracts currently exist with various agencies, including:

- Advantis Credit Ltd;

- Apex Credit Management Ltd;

- Bluestone Credit Management Ltd (formerly named Close Credit Management Ltd);

- Commercial Credit Services Group;

- Credit Solutions Ltd;

- Direct Legal and Collections;

- Drydensfairfax solicitors;

- iQor Recovery Services Ltd; and

- Rossendales Ltd.

Before the debt is referred to a debt collection agency, HMRC will write to the debtor providing a final opportunity to pay or reach an agreement with the department.

Any amount mistakenly repaid (including by way of set-off or repayment supplement) by an assessment as if it were unpaid tax. Any such assessment must normally be made before the end of the later of the end of the accounting period following that in which the amount assessed was paid, or (if later) the date on which an enquiry into the relevant tax return is completed.

Special provisions ensure that tax not deducted from certain payments (notably wages and salaries) made by government departments, and not otherwise recoverable, can be obtained from them.

HMRC will consider all reasonable offers of payment of tax in arrears, including payment in instalments.

Legislation: TMA 1970, s. 30

Tax Reporter: ¶188-070

2402   Direct recovery of debts

Finance (No. 2) Act 2015 introduces a new power, with effect from 18 November 2015 (Royal Assent), to allow HMRC to recover debts due to them (including tax and tax credit debts) directly from the bank and building society accounts (including individual savings accounts) of debtors. This is also known as the Direct Recovery of Debts ('DRD'). This power can only be used to recover debts of more than £1,000, and is subject to a number of statutory safeguards, including a 30-day right of objection and a limit of £5,000 as the minimum amount. HMRC must always leave across a debtor's accounts more than the amount that has been recovered.

HMRC guidance is available at www.gov.uk/government/publications/ issue-briefing-direct-recovery-of-debts--2.

Legislation: F(No. 2)A 2015, s. 51 and Sch. 8

Other material: www.gov.uk/government/publications/issue-briefing-direct-recovery-of-debts--2

Tax Reporter: ¶188-070

2403   Distraint

The collector in England, Wales and Northern Ireland can distrain upon the land in respect of which tax is charged or upon the goods of any person charged where that person neglects or refuses to pay tax charged upon him and demanded from him. Interest on tax is treated as if it is tax charged, due and payable under the assessment; under self-assessment penalties and surcharges are also included. The distress levied by the collector may be sold by public auction and the costs and charges of distress may be retained by the collector from the proceeds.

The collector may break into premises in the daytime for the purpose of levying distress if he is in the possession of a warrant issued by a justice of the peace.

Similar provisions apply in Scotland as to recovering tax by poinding the goods of the defaulter.

Legislation: TMA 1970, s. 61, 63, 69

Tax Reporter: ¶188-095

2406   Court proceedings

Court proceedings to recover unpaid tax may be instituted in the magistrates' court (in England, Wales and Northern Ireland), the county court (or the sheriff court, in Scotland), or the High Court (the Court of Session sitting as the Court of Exchequer, in Scotland).

In certain cases an appeal can be lodged to the Court of Appeal in respect of county court proceedings for the recovery of tax. From 1 October 1991, leave of a Court of Appeal judge must be obtained if the value of the appeal is £5,000 or less.

Magistrates' court

Under self-assessment, tax which is due and payable and is less than £2,000 or, if payable by instalments or on account, where the sum due and payable in respect of any instalment or payment on account is less than £2,000, is recoverable summarily as a civil debt by proceedings in the magistrates' court commenced in the name of the collector.

Any tax due from one person to any one collector, and which is recoverable summarily, may be included in the same complaint, summons, order, warrant or other document required by law to be laid before the justices.

Under self-assessment, proceedings for the recovery of income tax charged may be brought in England and Wales at any time within one year from the time when the matter complained of arose (the usual time-limit for bringing summary proceedings is six months from the time that the tax became due).

County court and High Court

Where the amount of tax due and payable does not exceed the county court limit (or, in Scotland, the sheriff courts limit), it may be sued for as a debt due to the Crown. The action is brought in the name of the collector.

Tax may also be sued for and recovered in the High Court (or, in Scotland, the Court of Session) as a debt due to the Crown.

Proceedings for recovery of tax due to the Crown may be pursued under the Rules of the Supreme Court. In a case where HMRC had claimed a cumulative sum in respect of assessments which should have been in the alternative (see 2324) but had corrected the error by amending the writ to include one assessment for each year, the taxpayer had no arguable defence to such proceedings.

Legislation: TMA 1970, s. 65–68; *County Court Appeals Order* 1991 (SI 1991/1877); *Income Tax (Pay As You Earn) Regulations* 2003 (SI 2003/2682)

Case: *IR Commrs v Wilkinson* [1992] BTC 297

Tax Reporter: ¶188-120

2409   Evidence and pleadings

A written statement as to the wages, salaries, fees, and other earnings or amounts treated as earnings paid for any period to the person against whom proceedings are brought under TMA 1970, s. 65, 66 or 67, purporting to be signed by his employer for that period or by any responsible person in the employment of the employer, will be accepted prima facie as evidence that the wages, salaries, fees and other earnings or amounts treated as earnings therein stated to have been paid to the person charged have in fact been so paid.

Legislation: *Rules of the Supreme Court* 1965, O. 77, r. 6; *Limitation Act* 1980, s. 37(2)(a); TMA 1970, s. 70

Case: *Lord Advocate v Hepburn* [1990] BTC 250

Tax Reporter: ¶188-170

2412   Recovery of tax from unincorporated company

Tax may be recovered from the proper officer (i.e. treasurer or person acting as treasurer) of any unincorporated company (or a body corporate not incorporated in accordance with the law of the UK). That officer may retain out of any money coming into his hands on behalf of the company sufficient sums to pay that tax and, so far as the sums are insufficient to meet the liability, he is entitled to be indemnified by the company.

Legislation: TMA 1970, s. 108

Tax Reporter: ¶188-195

2415   Recovery from employees

If the employer does not deduct the full amount of tax due under the PAYE system (see 2384) and HMRC are of the opinion that an employee received his emoluments knowing that the employer wilfully failed to deduct the due amount of tax, the tax due can be recovered from the employee.

Legislation: *Income Tax (Pay As You Earn) Regulations* 2003 (SI 2003/2682), reg. 72

Cases: *Pawlowski v Dunnington* [1999] BTC 175; *Parmar* [2016] TC 04927

Tax Reporter: ¶494-500

NICs

Introduction to NICs

2500 The National Insurance scheme

The aim of the UK's National Insurance scheme is to protect members of the population of the nation who fall upon hard times. However, its resemblance to commercially-based insurance is limited in that only in part does it involve the payment of compulsory and voluntary contributions by people with some link to the UK (e.g. residence, presence, or habitual residence in the UK) to provide for certain state benefits. It is in reality a system of social insurance.

Social security forms represents the largest single class of government expenditure each year, but only around one-half of social security expenditure is financed by National Insurance contributions (NICs), the remainder being funded from general tax revenues.

National Insurance Fund

In reality, there is no insurance scheme in the accepted sense. There is a National Insurance Fund as a notionally separate entity within the government accounts, but it only ever contains enough money at any point to pay out benefits derived from it for between two and four months. In the main, it is a system of cross-generational transfer, in that contributions of the current working population are used mainly to pay current state pensions, the balance being used to fund other current benefits. The term contribution is, in effect, a euphemism for tax.

National Insurance contributions are thought by many to provide entitlement to care under the National Health Service (NHS), but in reality only a small proportion of National Insurance Fund income is transferred to the NHS. Most NHS funding comes from general taxation, and entitlement to health care does not depend on contributions paid.

National Insurance Contributions Office

As part of HM Revenue & Customs' (HMRC's) wider Service Delivery Team, NICO work closely with HMRC Local Services, Large Business Office, Share Pensions Savings Schemes Office and all the National Business Streams. It also has strong links with the Department for Work and Pensions (DWP). NICO maintains over 65m NIC accounts; updates over 40m individual NI accounts; processes more than 53m end of year notifications; deals with 1.4m employers, 3m self-employed and 5.7m personal pension accounts; collects around £100bn in NICs each year; and employs over 4,600 staff.

Governing legislation

The Acts

The law governing NICs is mainly contained in the *Social Security Contributions and Benefits Act* 1992 (SSCBA 1992), while provisions on the running of the scheme are set out in the *Social Security Administration Act* 1992 (SSAA 1992). Both of these Acts consolidate earlier legislation.

The *National Insurance Contributions Act* 2002 predominantly deals with increases in contributions applicable from 6 April 2003 to both primary and secondary Class 1 contributions and to Class 4 contribution levels.

The *National Insurance Contributions Act* 2006 contains provisions designed to ensure that all employers and employees pay the correct amount of tax and NICs, particularly in relation to schemes involving shares and securities.

The *National Insurance Contributions Act* 2008, which took effect from 21 July 2008, contains two substantive measures, namely the removal of the restriction on exercise of the delegated power to set the upper earnings limit for NICs, in order to allow that limit to be aligned with the point at which higher rate income tax becomes payable in the future; and the early introduction of the upper accrual point for state second pension that was included in the *Pensions Act* 2007, from 6 April 2009.

The *National Insurance Contributions Act* 2011 provided the necessary legislation to increase the main and additional rates of primary and secondary Class 1 and Class 4 NICs.

The *National Insurance Contributions Act* 2014 received Royal Assent on 13 March 2014. This Act makes provision for the new employment allowance, which took effect from 6 April 2014. It also makes provision for a reduction of secondary Class 1 NICs for certain age groups from 6 April 2014, makes certain changes to the Class 4 NIC rules governing partnerships.

The *National Insurance Contributions Act* 2015 received Royal Assent on 12 February 2015. The Act contains provisions in respect of zero-rate secondary Class 1 contributions for apprentices under 25; reform of Class 2 contributions; follower notices, accelerated payments and promoters of avoidance; categorisation of earners, anti-avoidance, etc. and other general provisions.

The *National Insurance Contributions (Rate Ceilings) Act* 2015 received Royal Assent on 17 December 2015. The Act provides that, for the duration of the current parliament, the rate of Class 1, 1A and 1B National Insurance contributions (NICs) paid by employees, employers and third parties will not exceed the current rates. In addition, the Act provides that the upper earnings limit (UEL) for Class 1 NICs should not exceed the higher rate threshold for income tax.

The Act sets the following ceilings:

- the main primary rate will not exceed 12% and the additional primary rate will not exceed 2%;

- the secondary contributions rate (paid by employers) will not exceed 13.8%; and

- the upper earnings limit specified in SSCBA 1992, s. 5(1) and SSCB(NI)A 1992 will not exceed the weekly equivalent of the proposed higher rate threshold for income tax purposes for the relevant tax year.

The provisions apply from 2016–17 until the tax year starting before the next general election.

The regulations

Numerous regulations have also been made under the two consolidation Acts and their predecessors to govern the payment of contributions and entitlement to benefits. The most important are the *Social Security (Contributions) Regulations* 2001 (SI 2001/1004) and the *Social Security (Categorisation of Earners) Regulations* 1978 (SI 1978/1689).

The *Civil Partnerships Act* 2004 came into effect from 5 December 2005, the main purpose of which is to give legal status to same-sex couples. As a result of this legislation, various statutory instruments have been laid for social security and National Insurance contributions purposes, so that same-sex couples are now treated as husband and wife couples for benefits and NIC purposes.

Cases

There are few judicial decisions dealing with the interpretation of the legislation governing NICs. However, some decided cases are of assistance in clarifying particular issues.

Official publications

In the commentary that follows, references are made to several official explanatory publications. Particularly, frequent references are made to booklet CWG2 *Employer's Further Guide to PAYE and NICs* (available from the employer's orderline (0300 123 1074) or from the employer's download page of HMRC's website (www.hmrc.gov.uk)).

HMRC's *National Insurance Manual* (www.hmrc.gov.uk/manuals/nimmanual/Index.htm) provides useful reference material. It is broken down into seven main sections, which follow the six classes of NICs plus a section dedicated to Special Cases.

Separate scheme for Northern Ireland

The Social Security Acts and regulations often refer to 'Great Britain'. A separate social security scheme exists for Northern Ireland, although following the consolidation of the Social Security regulations, the consolidated regulations (the *Social Security (Contributions) Regulations* 2001 (SI 2001/1004)) apply to both Great Britain and Northern Ireland but its rules on contribution liability are effectively identical to those in the rest of the UK.

Legislation: *Social Security Contributions (Transfer of Functions etc.) Act* 1999; *Social Security Contributions (Transfer of Functions etc.) Act 1999 (Commencement No. 1 and Transitional Provisions) Order* 1999 (SI 1999/527)

Liability to NICs

2502   Charge to NIC

Liability to National Insurance contributions (NICs) depends on the class of contributor into which the individual falls, i.e. whether an individual is employed or self-employed (see 253). In many cases, this will be obvious. At the margin, it is a question of law and is not determined merely from a job description or contract.

Between 19 October 2015 and 31 December 2015, the OTS ran a consultation entitled 'Key Questions on Income Tax & NICs' seeking evidence for a review of the potential for aligning more closely income tax (IT) with NICs. The consultation is available at www.gov.uk/government/consultations/key-questions-published-for-ots-review-on-itnics. In March 2016, the OTS published recommendations following the review which are available at www.gov.uk/government/publications/closer-alignment-of-income-tax-and-national-insurance-contributions. The Government has since commissioned two further reviews into the impact of proposed structural changes to NICs and that the OTS publish its findings in advance of Autumn Statement 2016. The Government will then respond in full on all the OTS's proposals to bring IT and NICs closer together.

2504   Categorisation of National Insurance contributors

The National Insurance Fund (see 2500) exists to pay the benefits specified under the *Social Security Contributions and Benefits Act* 1992,

Pt. II and to pay contributions towards the National Health Service. To enable the fund to pay benefits, contributions are paid by earners, employers and others.

Those paying contributions are further identified as being:

- employed earners;
- employers and other persons paying earnings;
- self-employed earners; and
- others paying voluntarily in order to provide or make up benefit entitlement.

An 'earner' may be employed or self-employed, since the term must be construed according to the definition of earnings, which includes any 'remuneration or profit derived from an employment' (see 2540ff.).

The term 'employment' includes any trade, business, profession, office or vocation, so contributions are potentially due in connection with any income derived from working, be it as an employee or as a self-employed person.

In order to establish whether a liability to NICs arises and, if so, to calculate that liability, it is first necessary to be able to determine the group or category into which an earner falls.

Classes of contributions

As noted above, liability depends on the class into which the individual falls. The classes are:

Class 1: earnings-related, primary contributions being payable by employed earners and secondary contributions being payable by employers and others paying earnings (see 2602ff.);

Class 1A: contributions payable annually by secondary contributors only, based on the cash equivalent value of taxable benefits in kind. Previously, the charge only applied in respect of employer-provided car and car fuel (see 2660ff.);

Class 1B: contributions paid by employers on the extension of PAYE settlement agreement principles to NICs (see 2670);

Class 2: flat rate, payable by self-employed earners (see 2676ff.);

Class 3: flat rate, payable voluntarily (to satisfy contribution requirements to certain long-term benefits) (see 2690ff.);

Class 3A: flat rates, payable voluntarily until 5 April 2017 by individuals reaching state pension age before 6 April 2016 (to gain additional state pension entitlement); and

Class 4: earnings-related, payable by self-employed earners (see 2700ff.).

As part of the planned reforms to tax administration, the Government has announced that it will abolish Class 2 NICs in the next parliament and will reform Class 4 NICs to introduce a new contributory benefit test.

An individual may be liable or entitled to pay more than one class of contribution. Various reliefs are also available where contributions are payable under certain combinations of classes (see 2720ff.).

Legislation: SSCBA 1992, s. 1(1), (2), (5), 2, 122

2506   The employed earner

Class 1 contributions are levied on the earnings of 'employed earners', i.e. persons gainfully employed in Great Britain either under a contract of service, or in an office with emoluments chargeable to income tax under the charge on employment income provisions of ITEPA 2003 (see 250ff.).

Remember that use of part-time labour can keep employees below lower earnings limits (LELs) so both employer and employee pay no NICs.

Legislation: SSCBA 1992, s. 2(1)(a)

2508   Office holders

The distinction between employment under a contract of service and employment in an office (see 2506) can be important. For example, certain company directors may receive fees as emoluments of the office but at the same time may be employees under a contract of service with an associated company, and since special rules apply to the calculation of the contribution liabilities of company directors (see 2622), it is important to know the true source of the individual's income.

An office has an existence independent of that of the person who occupies it at any particular time (see 252). No earnings-related contribution liability arises if the payment made to the office holder does not fall within the charge on employment income provisions of ITEPA 2003: for example, where the payment is made to a company director who is not resident in the UK and is paid only in respect of duties performed outside the UK.

The contributions legislation refers to *chargeable* emoluments, rather than simply charged under the provisions of the employment tax law. However, although a company auditor holds an office in relation to the company, for the sake of administrative convenience the strict legal position is not followed in relation either to income tax or NICs and, in practice, income tax under ITTOIA 2005 is charged on the profits of the profession and an auditor is treated as a self-employed earner for NIC purposes.

2510   Employed or self-employed?

Of vital significance to NICs is the distinction between a contract of service and a contract *for services*. While the former connotes an employer/employee relationship and, for NIC purposes, points clearly towards the existence of an employed earner, the latter is the legal relationship between an independent contractor and his customers.

The definition of 'contract of service', central to the distinction between employed and self-employed earners, is:

> 'any contract of service or apprenticeship whether written or oral and whether expressed or implied.'

This definition is equivalent to that used in employment protection law for the term 'contract of employment'. However, there are a number of situations in which a person is deemed by NIC regulations to fall into a category other than that into which he would normally fall, but it is generally the case that a person who falls to be treated as an employee for the purposes of NICs will equally be treated as an employee for the purposes of employment protection law, income tax law, and value added tax law.

The general discussion on employed or self-employed for income tax purposes is therefore also relevant to NICs (see 253).

Legislation: SSCBA 1992, s. 122

2512   The self-employed earner

A self-employed earner is any person who is gainfully employed in Great Britain other than in employed earner's employment.

There are a series of tests used to differentiate between employed and self-employed earners (see 2510). This does not, of course, mean that a particular individual may not be simultaneously employed and self-employed.

However, what is clear is that a self-employed individual can only be self-employed once. As an independent contractor, he may provide his services to numerous customers and the services provided need not be the same in each case. The only requirement of contribution law is that he be gainfully employed in Great Britain.

A person will fit these criteria if he holds himself out as being anxious to be employed for the purposes of gain, although until he in fact commences his trade, profession or vocation, he cannot be gainfully employed.

Whilst the charge to Class 2 contributions arises on a weekly basis in respect of any self-employed earner, it is insufficient to test the status of any particular individual on the basis of one week's activity or lack of activity. Inevitably, there are certain situations in which the motive and opportunity for gain are difficult to determine.

Although the individual concerned may not have a motive of gain in entering into an arrangement to provide services, nevertheless, where actual gain arises, he will be gainfully employed and will fall to be treated as a self-employed earner.

HMRC consider that sleeping and inactive limited partners are (and have in the past been) liable to pay Class 2 NICs as self-employed earners and Class 4 NICs in respect of their taxable profits. 'Inactive limited partners' are limited partners who take no active part in running the business. This view represents a change from that previously held by HMRC and the Department for Work and Pensions (DWP). Sleeping or inactive limited partners who have not paid Class 2 or Class 4 NICs for a past period will not be required by HMRC to pay those contributions. In relation to the payment of Class 2 NICs from 6 April 2013, sleeping and inactive limited partners must check their Class 2 NICs position and those who are not already paying Class 2 NICs as a result of being self-employed must advise HMRC of their self-employed status and arrange to pay NICs or seek exception/deferment, etc. according to their individual circumstances. Many sleeping and inactive limited partners will qualify under one of these exceptions but there is a need to ensure that the appropriate action has been taken.

From April 2015, regulations specify that inactive members of limited liability partnerships (LLPs) will be liable to pay Class 2 NICs in the same way as sleeping partners and inactive limited partners.

Legislation: SSCBA 1992, s. 2(1)(b); *Social Security Contributions (Limited Liability Partnership) (Amendment) Regulations* 2015 (SI 2015/607)

Cases: *Vandyk v Minister of Pensions and National Insurance* [1955] 1 QB 29; Decision M36 1953

Other guidance: HMRC guidance on sleeping and inactive limited partners: www.hmrc.gov.uk/news/sps-lps-announce.pdf; Class 2 National

Insurance contributions: inactive members of Limited Liability Partnerships (TIIN): http://tinyurl.com/q339too

2514 Decisions on status

Where persons paying or in receipt of earnings are in doubt about the class of National Insurance contributions (NICs) which they should be paying, they are advised to contact HMRC (see 2500) for advice. Such contact should be able to produce a firm decision, which will be binding in respect of both income tax and NICs, provided all relevant facts are disclosed.

Appeals against decisions

An appeal against a decision of HMRC as to whether a person is or was an earner and, if so, the category into which he is or was to be included, lies to the tribunal.

Legislation: *Social Security Contributions (Transfer of Functions etc.) Act* 1999, s. 11; *Social Security Contributions (Transfer of Functions etc.) Act 1999 (Commencement No. 1 and Transitional Provisions) Order* 1999 (SI 1999/527)

2516 Retrospective recategorisation

The National Insurance Contributions Office (NICO) (see 2500) will usually consider any categorisation question whenever an individual applies for Class 2 registration. Difficulties can arise where the individual's status is not clear-cut, since NICO must then make enquiry in an attempt to establish the facts of the employment relationship in question in order to collect the correct class of contribution. Such enquiries provide NICO with the opportunity to recategorise as employees other contributors in a similar relationship to the alleged employer.

Where incorrect categorisation is established, NICO insists on an immediate change to the correct class of contribution being implemented. The date of change could be effective from an earlier date. While the tax authorities, in the absence of fraud, are allowed to look back no more than six years, NICO is not subject to similar time limits.

The official practice in cases of retrospective recategorisation to Class 1 is as follows: any Class 2 contributions which the contributor has paid erroneously as a result of the change of status from self-employed to employed earner are reallocated as employee (primary) Class 1 contributions. Any balance of employee contributions due and any arrears of employer (secondary) contributions are generally requested from the employer. If the erroneous Class 2 contributions amount to more than the employee Class 1 contributions due, the excess is refundable. HMRC refund Class 4 contributions overpaid as a result of a change of status. Any Class 2 contributions paid in error may be reallocated as employee Class 1 contributions, but this is at the discretion of NICO.

On general principles, NICO cannot enforce collection for debts over six years old if they have not been deliberately concealed and are not acknowledged by the debtor.

All liabilities (after the set-off of any Class 2 contributions) fall to the account of the employer, since the regulations operate to prevent any recovery by the employer of employee (primary) contributions in respect of earlier tax years in this situation. The employer is made primarily liable whenever earnings are paid for the payment of Class 1 contributions, but is given a limited right of recovery against his employees in respect of the primary liability. Late recovery is allowed, but only:

- in respect of under-deductions in the current tax year;

- if those under-deductions were made by reason of an error made in good faith; *and*

- to the extent that the extra deduction in any earnings period does not exceed the employee contributions otherwise deductible.

Where recategorisation has taken place and the individual concerned has thereby been transferred into the category of self-employed earner after having paid Class 1 contributions, NICO's usual practice is to treat such recategorisation as having effect only from the date of the relevant decision. This effectively prevents any repayment claim in respect of Class 1 contributions paid, despite the fact that the individual has been found to have been self-employed during the period in question. However, the choice to make the change only prospectively rather than retrospectively may be challenged on those very grounds, and the question may even be taken as far as a decision by the Secretary of State under the procedure for the determination of questions.

There are special procedures when a formal decision is made by the Secretary of State resulting in the recategorisation of a contributor or when the High Court overturns such a status decision.

Legislation: SSCBA 1992, s. 19A; SSA 1998, s. 54; *Limitation Act* 1980; *Social Security (Contributions) Regulations* 2001 (SI 2001/1004), reg. 17, 51; *Social Security (Categorisation of Earners) Regulations* 1978 (SI 1978/1689), reg. 4; *Social Security (Categorisation of Earners) (Amendment) Regulations* 2012 (SI 2012/816)

2518 Categorisation regulations

The basics of identifying the employed earner and the self-employed earner are irrelevant where regulations specifically provide for earners to be put into one category. A number of specific types of employment (i.e. in the sense of employment both as an employed earner and as a self-employed earner) have been identified as causing particular problems or administrative difficulties. Regulations therefore change or fix the status of earners in each of the specified types of employment or even, in specified circumstances, provide that the employment in question shall be entirely disregarded (see 2520ff.).

Legislation: *Social Security (Categorisation of Earners) Regulations* 1978 (SI 1978/1689)

2520 Deemed employed earners

Earners in employments categorised as employed earners include the following:

- office cleaners, or those working in a similar capacity in any premises other than those used as a private dwelling-house;

- telephone kiosk cleaners, again excluding any who work on apparatus in premises used as a private dwelling-house;

- employment of a person by his or her spouse or civil partner for the purposes of the spouse's or civil partner's employment (which includes self-employment);

- employment as a minister of religion, not being employment under a contract of service or in an office within the charge on employment income provisions of ITEPA 2003. This rule is not applicable to ministers whose remuneration is not wholly or mainly stipend or salary, which means that, e.g. a Roman Catholic priest is not an employed earner, because his stipend is minimal; and

- employment via the agency of a third party. An employment is deemed to be employed earner's employment if the person concerned renders, or is obliged to render personal service and is subject to supervision, direction or control, or to the right of supervision, etc. as to the manner of the rendering of such service and he is supplied by or through some third person. Furthermore, for this rule to apply, the earnings paid must be paid by or through, or on the basis of accounts submitted by, the third person or in accordance with arrangements made with him, or payments other than to the person employed must be made by way of fees, commission, etc. which relate to the continued employment in that employment of the person in question. This rule specifically includes the possibility of a partnership supplying the services of one of its members, in which case the member concerned would be treated as an employed earner in relation to that employment. The deeming rule is expressed not to operate in respect of homeworkers or outworkers supplied through a third party, nor does it extend to persons employed as actors, singers, musicians or other entertainers, or as fashion, photographic or artists' models.

Formerly, lecturers, teachers, etc. employed at educational establishments were deemed employed earners. However, following a consultation in this area, the regulations in relation to such persons were repealed from 6 April 2012.

Regulations provide for the identification of the secondary contributor in relation to deemed Class 1 employments.

Entertainers

Historically, entertainers have generally been treated as employees for NIC purposes but as self-employed for income tax purposes (see 253). Having been advised that the NIC treatment was unsustainable and that entertainers should generally be regarded as self-employed, the former DSS made regulations, operative from 17 July 1998, that again required the majority of performers to be treated as employees for NIC purposes, whose earnings are liable to Class 1 contributions.

HMRC Brief 19/12 set out HMRC's position following the decision in the case of *ITV Services Ltd* at the Upper Tribunal. The case concerned the application of the *Social Security (Categorisation of Earners) Regulations* 1978 to payments made to actors engaged by ITV under specific contract types. The tribunal found against ITV and upheld the decision of the First-tier Tribunal that the actors' contracts provided for remuneration by way of salary and there was liability for Class 1 NICs under those regulations on all the remuneration payable under the contract types.

As a result of the decision on the *ITV Services Ltd* case, the system for NICs for freelance actors, musicians and performers has been reformed from 6 April 2014. Broadly, new legislations repealed the former 1978 Regulations. From that date, the previous law has been removed from the regulations and entertainers will by default (and subject to normal minimum national insurance thresholds) attract Class 2 and 4 NIC liabilities on their self-employed earnings.

Legislation: *Social Security (Categorisation of Earners) (Amendment) Regulations* 2014 (SI 2014/635); *Social Security (Categorisation of Earners) (Amendment) Regulations* 2012 (SI 2012/816)

Cases: *ITV Services v R & C Commrs* [2011] TC 00836; *ITV Services Ltd v R & C Commrs* [2013] BTC 633; [2013] EWCA Civ 867

Other Material: HMRC TIIN: *National Insurance – changes for entertainers from 6 April 2014*; HMRC Brief 35/13; HMRC Brief 19/12; HMRC Brief 10/11

2522   Deemed self-employment

The only persons who would normally be employed earners but who fall into the self-employed bracket are those employed other than through the agency of another as an examiner, moderator, or invigilator, etc., under a contract which is to be completed in less than 12 months, where the examination leads to a certificate, diploma, degree or professional qualification. (See further 2716.)

Legislation: *Social Security (Categorisation of Earners) Regulations* 1978 (SI 1978/1689), reg. 2(3)

Website: *National Insurance and Self-employed Entertainers – Summary of responses (23 October 2013)*: www.gov.uk/government/uploads/ system/uploads/attachment_data/file/251925/National_insurance_and_ self_employed_entertainers_-_response_document.pdf

2524   Deemed non-employment

Several types of employment are disregarded for NIC purposes. These include:

(1) employment by a close member of the family in a private dwelling house other than for the purposes of that family member's business;

(2) any employment by a spouse otherwise than for the purposes of the spouse's employment;

(3) any employment as a self-employed earner (including examiners, etc. deemed to be so: see 2522) where the earner is not ordinarily employed in such employment or employments. In practice, this is mainly taken to apply to those in an employed earner's employment who earn less than £800 per year from part-time self-employment but the limit has not been set by regulation, has remained unchanged since 1981–82 and as such is potentially open to challenge;

(4) employment for the purposes of any statutory election as a returning officer, etc. or any person employed by him;

(5) employment by visiting military forces, either as a member of those forces or as a civilian employee, except for civilians who are ordinarily resident (see 2550) in the UK; and

(6) employment as a member of any duly designated international headquarters or defence organisation, other than in the case of serving members of HM Forces or civilians ordinarily resident in the UK who are not members of the organisation's retirement scheme.

Legislation: *Social Security (Categorisation of Earners) Regulations* 1978 (SI 1978/1689)

2526 Personal service companies

In a bid to remove opportunities for the avoidance of Class 1 National Insurance contributions (NICs) by the use of intermediaries, such as service companies or partnerships, in circumstances where the worker would otherwise be an employee of the client, or the income would be the income from an office held by the worker, provisions were introduced that conferred wide ranging powers to make regulations to treat all money received by the intermediary in respect of a certain engagement, less certain deductions, as paid to the worker in a form subject to Class 1 NICs. The proposals, which are generally known as 'IR 35', came into force on 6 April 2000.

Broadly, the regulations provide that:

(1) where an individual ('the worker') personally performs, or has an obligation personally to perform, services for the purposes of a business carried on by another person ('the client');

(2) the performance of those services by the workers is referable to arrangements involving a third party, rather than referable to a contract between the client and the worker; and

(3) the circumstances are such that, were the services to be performed by the worker under a contract between him and the client, he would be regarded as employed in the employed earner's employment by the client,

then the relevant payments and benefits are treated as earnings paid to the worker in respect of the employed earner's employment. These rules apply irrespective of whether the client is a person with whom the worker holds any office or employment.

The effect is that the worker is treated as being employed by the intermediary in the employed earner's employed employment. He is deemed to have received a payment of his 'attributable earnings' (as calculated in accordance with the regulations) from the intermediary on 5 April in the tax year concerned. The worker's attributable earnings are aggregated with any other earnings paid to or for the benefit of him or her by the intermediary in the year concerned. The amount of earnings-related contributions is determined on the aggregate amount according to normal rules. The intermediary is be treated for those purposes as the secondary contributor.

It is not a requirement that a worker performs services for the purposes of the business, which means that the principal regulations (SI 2000/727) apply to all workers providing services through an intermediary.

Agency workers

Regulations came into force from 6 April 2014, which apply employer's and employee Class 1 NICs to workers who are engaged through an agency where the worker is subject to direction, control or supervision or a right of direction, control or supervision. The regulations also reformed the host employer rule and apply employer's Class 1 NICs to certain UK agencies who are involved in the supply of UK workers when the worker is engaged or employed outside of the UK.

Domestic workers

Domestic workers, such as nannies or butlers, who provide services through an intermediary (usually a service company), who would otherwise be directly employed by the person to whom they provide their services, but operate instead through an intermediary, such as a company, come within the personal services companies legislation.

Legislation: *Welfare Reform and Pensions Act* 1999, s. 75; *Social Security (Categorisation of Earners) (Amendment) Regulations* 2014 (SI 2014/635); *Social Security Contributions and Benefits Act 1992 (Modification of Section 4A) Order* 2003 (SI 2003/1874); *Social Security Contributions (Intermediaries) (Amendment) Regulations* 2003 (SI 2003/2079); *Social Security Contributions (Intermediaries) Regulations* 2000 (SI 2000/727); *Welfare Reform and Pensions Act 1999 (Commencement No. 2) Order* 1999 (SI 1999/3420)

Cases: *Cable & Wireless plc v Muscat* [2006] EWCA Civ 220; *Primary Path Ltd v R & C Commrs* [2011] TC 01306

Other Material: IR35: find out if it applies: www.gov.uk/ir35-find-out-if-it-applies

Social security benefits

2528   Types of social security benefit

Non-contributory benefits

National Insurance contributions (NICs) pay for only certain state benefits (see 2500). Many benefits are based on need or circumstantial conditions, with no link to past contributions paid. Instead they are based on some other link to the system, such as residence, and they are often subject to income limits or means testing. These non-contributory benefits are funded from general taxation and include:

- Attendance Allowance

- Back to Work Bonus

- Carer's Allowance (formerly Invalid Care Allowance)

- Child Benefit

- Child Tax Credit

- Christmas Bonus for pensioners

- Cold Weather Payments

- Community Care Grants

- Council Tax Benefit

- Disability Living Allowance

- Funeral Payment

- Guardian's Allowance

- Housing Benefit

- Income Support

- Industrial Injuries Benefits

- Jobseeker's Allowance (income-based)

- New Deal Payments

- Pension Credit

- Reduced Earnings Allowance

- Retirement Pension – Category D (paid to over-80s with inadequate contributory pensions)

- Severe Disablement Allowance

- Social Fund (grants, loans, payments)

- Vaccine Damage Payments
- War Pensions
- Winter Fuel payment and 80+ Annual Payment
- Working Tax Credit

Contributory benefits

The contributions paid by employees and their employers, the self-employed and voluntary contributors are used to pay for a series of short and long term benefits which are generally payable as of right to anyone with a qualifying contribution record. However, a number of extra qualifying circumstantial conditions limit entitlements in some cases even for those with full records.

Contributions, and earnings subject to contributions, are recorded on HMRC's National Insurance Recording System, Mark 2 (NIRS2) computer each year. In some circumstances, contributions or earnings are credited to a contributor's record. The amounts for each year are converted into an 'earnings factor', which forms the basis of entitlement to the following contributory benefits:

(1) Jobseeker's Allowance (contributions-based) (short-term);

(2) Incapacity Benefit:

    (a) short-term;

    (b) long-term;

(3) Maternity Allowance (a short-term benefit);

(4) Bereavement Benefits (long-term);

(5) Bereavement Payment (formerly Widow's Payment);

(6) Widowed Parent's (formerly Mother's) Allowance;

(7) Bereavement Allowance;

(8) Widow's Pension (or pension to surviving civil partner);

(9) Basic State Retirement Pension (a long-term benefit):

    (a) Category A, paid by virtue of the claimant's own contributions, and subject to additions;

    (b) Category B, paid by virtue of the contributions of a spouse or civil partner; and

(10) Child's Special Allowance (now obsolescent and paid only to existing claimants).

Note that contributions paid by employers (Class 1 secondary, Class 1A, Class 1B) and Class 4 contributions paid by the self-employed are irrelevant to benefit entitlements. Only Class 1 primary (main rate), Class 2 and Class 3 contributions count towards contribution records.

Legislation: SSCBA 1992, s. 20; *Social Security Revaluation of Earnings Factors Order* 2015 (SI 2015/187)

2530 The link between contribution classes and benefits

National Insurance contributions (NICs) are payable by the individuals who (or whose dependants) are to benefit and by employers. There are currently six classes of contribution, though Class 1 is split between employees (Class 1 primary) and employers (Class 1 secondary). The type of contribution payable (and the benefit entitlement available) depends on whether the contributor is in employment or is self-employed, or is contributing voluntarily:

- Class 1 secondary contributions and Class 1A contributions are payable by employers and certain others paying earnings to employees. They carry no benefit entitlement and could justifiably be described as payroll taxes to fund social security expenditure;

- Class 1B contributions (see 2670) give no entitlement to benefit, though it is understood there are plans to protect the position of those who may fail to qualify for statutory sick pay or statutory maternity pay as a result of their payment; and

- Class 4 contributions are payable by self-employed individuals on their trading profits taxable under ITTOIA 2005. They also carry no benefit entitlement.

The link between contributions and contributory benefits is based entirely on the other classes of contribution paid by individuals:

- Class 1 employee (primary) contributions at varying appropriate levels and for appropriate periods, can qualify the contributor for all contributory benefits (unless the contributor is a married woman or widow who decided before 11 May 1977 to forgo future benefit entitlement by electing to pay a reduced rate of contribution) and, indirectly, for SSP and SMP. Incapacity benefit does not depend solely on contribution conditions being satisfied. Long-term incapacity benefit becomes payable when entitlement to sickness benefit, or short-term incapacity benefit expires, which themselves may derive from contributions of this class on the expiry of entitlement to SSP. Importantly, employees who pay Class 1 contributions on earnings between set limits automatically qualify for the earnings-related component of the state pension. In return for paying lower contributions, they receive only the basic state pension;

- Class 2 contributions can qualify the self-employed contributor for all contributory benefits except contribution-based jobseeker's allowance and earnings-related state pension (though the basic state pension is still available). Class 2 contributions are also irrelevant to entitlement to SSP and SMP, as self-employed contributors claim instead incapacity benefit and maternity allowance; and

- Class 3 contributions can be paid voluntarily by certain individuals to enable them and their dependants to qualify for the basic long-term benefits (category A and B pensions, widow's payment, widowed mother's allowance, widow's pension), but nothing else.

- Class 3A contributions are payable voluntarily by individuals who reach state pension age before 6 April 2016 in order to increase state pension entitlement.

Contribution records

Contributory benefits are payable on the basis of the claimant having paid sufficient contributions in the relevant period, i.e. having a qualifying contribution record. For the long-term benefits, the claimant must have a qualifying contribution record for nine-tenths of his or her working life in order to obtain maximum entitlement. For short-term benefits, the period of qualification is limited to recent tax years.

The basic building blocks of the record are the contribution week and the lower earnings limit (LEL; see 2602). If an employed earner is paid earnings above the LEL in a week, he is liable to pay Class 1 contributions on those earnings and the week becomes a qualifying week. Following the introduction, from April 2000, of the threshold below which no primary Class 1 contributions are payable, an employee's entitlement to contributory benefits is maintained in respect of earnings from the LEL to the primary threshold by means of notional contributions at a zero-rate. If a Class 2 or Class 3 contribution is paid in respect of a week, it becomes a qualifying week and the earner is, broadly, treated as having paid contributions on earnings equal to the LEL. Similarly, certain individuals who do not actually pay contributions may in appropriate circumstances be credited with contributions or earnings to protect their future benefit entitlements (e.g. an unemployed person will pay no contributions during the period of interruption of employment, so his contribution record is generally protected for pension purposes by a credit). Such credits are also equivalent to Class 2 or Class 3 contributions in that they are deemed to represent contributions paid on earnings at the LEL.

Legislation: SSCBA 1992, s. 21

2532   Earnings factors

It is necessary to have a common unit of measure because NICs are paid at a number of rates and on different bases. They must therefore be converted to some common factor for comparison with the requirements for benefit entitlement. The common factor is the earnings factor, expressed as an amount of notional earnings for a tax year.

Legislation: SSCBA 1992, s. 22; *Social Security Revaluation of Earnings Factors Order* 2015 (SI 2015/187)

2534   Recording of contributions

Contributions are recorded against the contributor's computer record, using his or her National Insurance number as the key. They are recorded for tax years, and as it is the practice to update contribution rates with effect from 6 April each year, all contributions paid in any one year are calculated on the same basis.

Benefit years

Benefits are payable on the basis of benefit years rather than tax years. The benefit year runs from the first Sunday in January in any calendar year and ends with the Saturday before the same Sunday in the following year. The contribution conditions for benefits claimed or due in any particular benefit year refer to past tax years rather than benefit years. This has sound practical grounds, since the processing of contributions paid inevitably takes time. There is therefore a period of around nine months between the end of the tax year and the start of the next benefit year in which contribution returns can be collected, collated and processed into contribution records.

Legislation: SSCBA 1992, s. 21(6)

Earnings

2540   Definition of 'earnings' for NICs

Liability for National Insurance contributions (NICs) rests on the existence of an earner, who contributes to the National Insurance Fund an amount which is determined, directly or indirectly, by reference to his earnings.

For National Insurance purposes, 'earnings' include any remuneration or profit derived from an employment, while 'employment' includes any trade, business, profession, office or vocation, subject to a proviso that regulations may make exceptions to this definition in appropriate circumstances; for discussion of the terms remuneration and profit, see 2544. While the term is in principle all-embracing, regulations made under the 1992 Act make numerous amendments to the definition in specified circumstances with the result that the rules for employed and self-employed earners are very different.

Legislation: SSCBA 1992, s. 3, 122

2542 Earnings from self-employment

Earnings of individuals who are self-employed are relevant to Class 2 and Class 4 contributions. Earnings for Class 2 are accounts profits whilst earnings for Class 4 correspond closely with taxable profits: they determine the amount (within given limits) to which the appropriate percentage rate is applied for Class 4 purposes and the availability of an exception from the flat-rate Class 2 contributions.

Legislation: SSCBA 1992, s. 3, 122

2544 Remuneration or profit?

Earnings on which National Insurance contributions (NICs) are payable are defined by reference to remuneration or profit (see 2540). There is, in National Insurance law, no further general definition of 'remuneration' or 'profit', which therefore take their ordinary meaning.

When seeking to establish earnings for National Insurance purposes, it is necessary to consider the rewards paid for services under a contract of employment. The meaning of the term 'remuneration' was considered in a 1974 employment law case concerning redundancy pay. Although not directly relevant to NIC, the comments of sir John Donaldson are of persuasive authority in a NIC context. In that case, 'remuneration' was held to include any wage or salary, but to exclude any benefit in kind or amount paid by someone other than the employer. Additionally, expenses paid to the employee should be considered, with any payment which was a profit to the employee rather than reimbursement of an expense being included as remuneration.

The income tax equivalent of earnings is emoluments, which include 'all salaries, fees, wages, perquisites and profits whatsoever' (see 274) and which must be from the employment (see 273) before they may be taxed under the charge on employment income provisions of ITEPA 2003. There is clearly much in common between the two terms, but only the term emoluments has been subject to detailed judicial scrutiny.

Cash emoluments are taxable under the charge on employment income provisions of ITEPA 2003 and subject to the PAYE system of deduction at source. The equivalent collection mechanism is imported into Class 1 National Insurance law. However, this clearly does not extend to non-cash rewards. Where income tax law provides for non-cash items to be subject to PAYE, the terms are set out in primary legislation.

There are National Insurance provisions which specifically bring into charge certain payments which might be thought not to be earnings on basic principles, together with numerous further provisions to exclude from the definition other payments which would otherwise be caught as remuneration or profit.

Legislation: *Social Security (Contributions) Regulations* 2001 (SI 2001/1004)

Case: *S & U Stores Ltd v Wilkes* [1974] ICR 645

2546 Dividends

Unless NIC law specifically provides otherwise, basic principles of law will apply to determine whether a payment represents earnings for contribution purposes. The question is whether the payment under consideration is derived from an employment. Dividend income is, of course, derived not from employment but from the ownership of shares in a company and as such is free of NIC liability.

If a company declares a dividend to director-shareholders which is illegal (e.g. because there are insufficient distributable profits) or outside the terms of its articles of association, it may be officially argued that the payment must be derived from the employment and is therefore earnings. The validity of this argument is questionable.

2548 Rents

Where a director owns property used by the company, it is possible for the company to pay him a commercial rent for the use of that property. The income is derived not from the office or employment but from the ownership of the asset that the company uses, so the rents are not earnings for NIC purposes. However, tax complications must be borne in mind.

2550 Interest on directors' accounts NICs

A situation similar to that in relation to dividends (see 2546) occurs in respect of interest on current account balances. Because interest credited to a director on any balance standing to his credit in the company's books is derived from the lending of money rather than from the employment, such income is free of NIC liability.

2552   Calculation of earnings

Subject to exceptions outlined below, the amount of a person's earnings for Class 1 contribution purposes is to be calculated on the basis of his or her gross earnings from the employment or employments concerned. This is underlined in the official guidance, which devotes several pages to itemising for employers, whose responsibility it is to operate the Class 1 collection system, what is and is not included in 'gross pay', the term used in the guidance notes as a synonym for earnings. The term highlights the fact that employees' Class 1 contributions are, with only one exception (see 2584), collected at source from employees' pay by employers.

Furthermore, not all payments are automatically earnings for the purposes of NICs. Payments must be derived from the employment before they attract a Class 1 liability.

Unless contribution law dictates specifically how a particular type of payment is to be treated, it is necessary to examine the nature of the payment to an employee and ask whether it fits the criterion stated. Furthermore, it is important to note that the judicial definition (see 273) offers two alternatives, bringing into earnings not merely payments received by an employee in return for his acting as an employee, but also payments in return for his being an employee. While the first leg of this definition covers the common sense view of an employee being rewarded for services rendered or to be rendered, the second covers the less obvious position of employees who receive payments from their employer unrelated to the services they perform but which they would not have received had they not been employees.

Using the above principles, earnings will include the following items:

- wages, salaries, fees, overtime pay, bonuses, commission and so on;
- holiday pay;
- inducement payments (e.g. most 'golden hellos' or 'golden handcuffs');
- contractual maternity pay;
- statutory sick pay, statutory maternity pay, ordinary statutory paternity pay (OSPP), additional statutory paternity pay (ASPP) and statutory adoption pay.

Employment allowance

From April 2014, the new employment allowance potentially cut every employer's NIC payments by allowing businesses to offset up to £3,000 (2016–17, previously, £2,000) against their employer PAYE NIC liabilities (see 2062). From 6 April 2015, the employment allowance was extended to individuals who employ care and support workers.

From April 2016, companies where the director is the sole employee will no longer be able to claim the employment allowance (NICA 2014, s. 4(4A)).

For details of the treatment of specific payments that may be made to an employee, see 2564.

Legislation: *Employment Allowance (Care and Support Workers) Regulations* 2015 (SI 2015/578); *Social Security (Contributions) (Amendment No. 3) Regulations* 2013 (SI 2013/1907); *Social Security (Contributions) (Amendment No. 5) Regulations* 2006 (SI 2006/2829); *Social Security (Contributions) Regulations* 2001 (SI 2001/1004), reg. 24; *Social Security (Contributions and Credits) (Miscellaneous Amendments) Regulations* 1999 (SI 1999/568)

Case: *Key Recruitment (UK) Ltd* [2014] TC 03874

Other Material: Booklet CWG2, *Employer's further guide to PAYE and NICs*

2554 Timing of payment

Where in any tax week earnings are paid to or for the benefit of an earner in respect of any one employment of his which is employed earner's employment, a primary and secondary Class 1 contribution is payable (see 2602).

Payments made in advance

The most frequent problems with timing arise from payment in advance. The key factor to be considered is the unreserved entitlement to a payment. Where an employer takes on an employee on the basis that his salary will be paid monthly in arrears, but at the end of the first week lends the employee part of his first month's salary to tide him over until the first payroll run, no payment of earnings takes place, as the payment made is a loan. Until the employee has an unreserved entitlement to the first month's salary, the money in his hands is owed to the employer. Until it becomes his own money at the end of the month, it cannot be earnings for contribution purposes.

The position is, of course, the same in principle but quite different in effect if it is agreed between the employer and employee that salary will regularly be paid in advance: such advance payments are generally treated as normal pay.

2556 Apportionment of payments made for more than one earner

Payments made to or for the benefit of two or more earners may be apportioned, the aim being to strengthen provisions capturing vouchers (and certain payments into funded unapproved retirement benefit schemes (FURBS)).

Legislation: SSA 1998, s. 48

2558 Company directors

Special rules identify the earnings of company directors. Any payment made by a company to, or for the benefit of, any of its directors is treated as earnings if it is paid on account of or by way of an advance.

A company director is not usually entitled to remuneration until it has been voted to him by the members of the company. Such voting may, of course, take place in advance, or the director may be given a service contract which sets out a basis for his regular remuneration. This would mean that any amounts paid to him under normal circumstances would indeed be earnings for contribution purposes. However, where a company director draws cash from his business without the benefit of an agreed service contract or the advance voting of fees, he will effectively take a loan, albeit technically unauthorised, until such time as the members vote his remuneration.

For these purposes, directors include shadow directors, though a person is not to be treated as such by reason only that the directors act on advice given by him in his professional capacity.

It should be noted that no Class 1 liability arises on overdrawn accounts unless payments which caused the account to become overdrawn were made in anticipation of earnings. A liability would still arise:

- where payments are made on which PAYE tax has been assessed;

- where an agreement between the employer and the employee is in force providing for the payments to be made in anticipation of remuneration becoming due; or

- where shareholders have agreed that the director can make withdrawals from the account in anticipation of the voting of fees or remuneration.

Other Material: CWG2, *Employer's further guide to PAYE and NICs*

2560 Settlement of pecuniary liability

Where an employee incurs a personal liability to a supplier of goods or services, his liability to that supplier is usually measured in terms of money. For National Insurance contributions (NIC) purposes, as with income tax (292), if the employer pays the amount due by the employee to the creditor, the employer is effectively doing no more than give the employee cash with which he settles his debt. Where an employer contracts with a provider of goods and services, there is no Class 1 NIC liability (although a Class 1A liability may arise). However, if the contract is between the employee and the provider, a Class 1 NIC liability arises if the payment is made direct to the provider or payment is made or reimbursed direct to the employee.

In a typical small family company, the directors may routinely settle personal bills with a company cheque and charge the amount in question to a current or loan account. This should not present any difficulty if the account is in credit (i.e. the director has previously lent amounts to the company and has not at that point withdrawn them), but a liability to Class 1 contributions may well arise if the account is, or by virtue of the payment becomes, overdrawn.

The correct identification of earnings is perhaps best seen from an example.

Example

Chris is a director of and majority shareholder in his family company, Driver Ltd. He votes himself fees at the annual general meeting of the company, but does not draw a regular salary, preferring instead to take cash from his current account with the company as and when he needs it. It is understood by all the other directors and shareholders that this is the normal practice. Whatever is outstanding at the time of the annual general meeting is cleared by the annual voting of fees. At 6 April 2016, the balance on his current account stands at £1,000 in his favour.

On 1 May 2016, he asks the cashier to give him £5,000 in cash for personal expenditure and instructs him to charge it to his director's current account.

The first £1,000 drawn is, of course, no more than a withdrawal of money invested in the company by Chris. He probably does not regard the balance on his account as an investment as such, but the fact remains that the last fee-voting resolution led to a large credit (after deduction of PAYE and NICs) to Chris's current account and he chose at the time not to draw the cash to which he was entitled.

The balance of the withdrawal on 1 May is clearly an advance on fees to be voted at the next annual general meeting, so the payment of £4,000 represents a payment of earnings for NIC purposes (see 2558). The cashier must therefore account for Class 1 contributions on this sum in accordance with the normal rules for company directors.

> When Chris books his summer holiday, he gives the bill he has received to the cashier with the usual instruction to pay it and charge the amount to his current account. By this time, of course, his account is already overdrawn and the settlement of his personal pecuniary liability by the company simply increases the debit balance on his account. Once more, a payment of earnings has taken place which will lead to a Class 1 contribution liability.

Legislation: SSCBA 1992, s. 3(1), 6(1)

Other Material: CWG2, *Employer's further guide to PAYE and NICs*

2562   Waiver of earnings: NICs

The amount of a person's earnings are calculated on the basis of that person's gross earnings from the employment, unless specific provision is made to the contrary.

Hence, once earnings have been paid (i.e. actually paid by a transfer of cash or credited unconditionally to an account on which the director is free to draw), they remain earnings and any subsequent waiver or refund is not officially recognised. However, it is now fairly common for employees to make charitable donations via payroll giving schemes attracting income tax relief (see 904). However, there is no corresponding NIC relief. Consequently, the amount of the donation should be excluded from gross pay for PAYE purposes but not for NIC purposes.

However, as earnings do not arise until the earner becomes unconditionally entitled to them, if an employee agrees with his employer, *before* such unconditional entitlement arises, to waive any or all of his prospective earnings, it would seem that the creation of earnings liable to NIC liability is avoided.

Other Material: CWG2, *Employer's further guide to PAYE and NICs*

2564   Gross pay for NIC purposes

The following chart, based on the one that appears in CWG2, *Employer's further guide to PAYE and NICs*, indicates what should be included in gross pay for NIC purposes. It should be noted, however, where an item is not included in gross pay because it constitutes a payment in kind, although no Class 1 liability arises, there may be a Class 1A liability (see further 2650ff.). Where the position is particularly complex, a cross-reference is given to more detailed information included in the following paragraphs.

Type of payment	Include in gross pay for NIC purposes?
Car/van fuel supplied for private motoring when the fuel is supplied using your credit card, or garage account or an agency card	No, if the conditions outlined below for credit cards, charge cards and so on are satisfied, but there may be Class 1A liability – see 2650ff.
Car parking fees for **business related journeys** paid or reimbursed to employees	No
Cars or vans made available for private use	No but there may be Class 1A liability, see 2650ff.
Childcare vouchers	
• For people using a childcare voucher scheme before 6 April 2011, they can be included in a scheme and receive vouchers up to £55 a week if certain conditions were met	No, only any excess above £55 to be shown
• Where conditions were not met	Yes, the whole amount of all vouchers
• For people new to a childcare vouchers scheme from 6 April 2011 and conditions are met the amount available depends on the tax position of the individual	
– ordinary rate taxpayer	Yes, on any excess above £55 a week
– higher rate taxpayer	Yes, on any excess above £28 a week
– additional rate taxpayer	Yes, on any excess above £25 a week
• Where conditions are not met	Yes the whole amount of all vouchers
Christmas boxes in cash	Yes
Clothing or uniforms	
• clothing or uniforms provided by you	No but there may be a liability for Class 1A, see 2650ff.
• payments to employees for non-durable items such as tights or stockings	No but there may be a liability for Class 1A, see 2650ff.
• other payments to employees to purchase clothing or uniforms which can be worn at any time	Yes
• other payments to employees to purchase clothing or uniforms which can be worn only at work	No
Council tax on employee's living accommodation	
• employee provided with accommodation and the accommodation is within one of the categories where the value does not have to be included for tax purposes on form P9D or P11D	No
• all other circumstances	Yes

Type of payment	Include in gross pay for NIC purposes?
Credit card, charge cards and so on – employees use your card to purchase **goods or services bought on your behalf**	
• prior authority given by you to make the purchase **and** the employee explained in advance of the contract being made **and** the supplier accepted that the purchase was made on your behalf	No, but there may be a liability for Class 1A, see 2650ff.
• above condition not **fully** satisfied	Yes
Credit card, charge card and so on – employees use your card for expenditure **other than** goods or services bought on your behalf	
• payments relating to business expenses actually incurred	No
• readily convertible assets	See 2566
• any other payments not reimbursed to you	Yes at the date you decide not to seek reimbursement
Credit card reward payments made to employees for detecting and withdrawing lost or stolen cards:	
• made by you to your own employees	Yes
• made to your employees by a third party	No
Damages or similar payment made to an employee injured at work	
• there is a contractual liability to make it	Yes
• all other circumstances	No
Director's personal bills charged to loan account and so on	
• the transaction makes the account overdrawn (or more overdrawn) **and** it is normal practice for you to pay the director's earnings into the same account	Yes on the overdrawn (or additional overdrawn) amount
• all other circumstances	No
Director's remuneration, salary, bonuses, fees and so on, including any advance or anticipatory payments paid, voted or credited	Yes
Dividends from shares	No
Employee liability insurance – reimbursements of payments made by employees for insurance cover or uninsured liabilities (such as legal costs) for claims against the employee arising out of his or her work	No
Employment income provided through third parties – when taxable under 'disguised remuneration' rules in ITEPA 2003, Pt. 7A	Yes
Employment Tribunal Awards	See 2574

Type of payment	Include in gross pay for NIC purposes?
Eyecare vouchers to obtain:	
• an eyesight test	
• corrective appliance (for example, glasses or contact lenses) which the test shows are necessary where	
– the eyesight test is required under Health and Safety at Work Regulations and	No
– the eyesight test and corrective appliance are available generally to employees	
Expenses payments or reimbursements exempted from charge Expenses payments or reimbursements paid at an agreed scale rate are exempt from charge to tax	No
Guarantee payments under the *Employment Rights Act* 1996	Yes
Holiday pay	See 2578
Honoraria	Yes
Incentive awards	See 2586
Incidental overnight expenses (IOEs)	See 2584
Inducement payment such as 'golden hello' to recruit or retain employees	Yes
Insurance premiums for pension, annuities, or health cover and so on, **paid or reimbursed by you** where contract is between	
• you and the insurance provider	No, but there may be a liability for Class 1A, see 2650ff.
• employee and the insurance provider	Yes, see 2596
Loans	No, but there may be a liability for Class 1A, see 2650ff.
Loans written off	Yes at time of write off
Long service awards	
• Awards in the form of cash or cash vouchers	Yes
• Other awards	No, if they satisfy certain conditions
Lost time payments	
• payments made by a third party or by you on behalf of a third party	No
• all other circumstances	Yes
Maternity suspension payments made under the *Employment Rights Act* 1996 to an employee suspended from work on maternity grounds	Yes
Meal allowances and vouchers	
• cash payments for meals	Yes

Type of payment	Include in gross pay for NIC purposes?
• vouchers redeemable for food and drink or a cash alternative	Yes (see 2580)
• vouchers provided for food and drink provided on your business premises or any canteen where meals are generally provided for your staff	No
• vouchers redeemable for meals only	No
Medical suspension payments made under the *Employment Rights Act* 1996 to an employee suspended from work on medical grounds	Yes
Mobile phone vouchers to obtain one mobile phone for private use	No
Mortgage payments met directly by you for employees	
• mortgage provided by you or mortgage contract is between you and mortgagee	No, but there may be a liability for Class 1A, see 2650.
• mortgage contract is between employee and mortgagee	Yes
Parking fees at the normal place of employment paid for or reimbursed to employees	No
Payments in kind (but not readily convertible assets – see 2566)	
• which can be turned into cash **by surrender** such as Premium Bonds, and so on	Yes
• which can be turned into cash only **by sale** such as furniture, kitchen appliances, holidays and so on	No, but there may be a liability for Class 1A, see 2650ff.
Payments you make to an employee whilst he or she pursues a claim for **damages against a third party** for loss of earnings following an accident	
• employee must repay you, even if the claim for damages is unsuccessful	No
• employee not required to repay you	Yes, but if the employee later receives damages and repays you, NICs can be refunded
Pensions from:	
• registered pension schemes	No
• employer-financed retirement benefits schemes	No, if the payment satisfies certain conditions
Personal bills paid for goods and services supplied to employees, club memberships and so on	
• contract to supply goods and services is between you and the provider	No, but there may be a liability for Class 1A, see 2650ff.
• contract to supply goods and services is between the employee and the provider	
– payment made direct to the provider	Yes

Type of payment	Include in gross pay for NIC purposes?
– payment made or reimbursed direct to the employee	Yes
Phone calls and/or rental cost – Employer is the subscriber	No, but there may be a liability for Class 1A, see 2650ff.
Employee is the subscriber but, **employer meets the cost of calls and/or rental**:	
• phone used exclusively for business use	No
• phone used exclusively for private use	Yes
• phone used for both business and private use	Rental: yes – on the full amount of the
	Calls: yes – on the full amount of the cost of private calls. Any amount in respect of business calls, supported by appropriate evidence, can be excluded
Premiums for health cover, pensions, annuities and so on	See 'Insurance premiums' above
Prize money paid in cash to employees for competitions you run in connection with your business, which are not open to the public	Yes
Readily convertible assets: remuneration provided in non-cash form such as stocks and shares, gold bullion, commodities, fine wine and so on.	See 2566
Redundancy payments	See 2588
Relocation payments	See 2590
Retirement benefits schemes – payments you make into such schemes	
• Registered pension schemes	No
• Employer-financed schemes	No
Retirement benefits schemes – lump sum payments out of such schemes	
• Registered pension schemes	No
• Employer-financed retirement benefit schemes	No (provided certain conditions satisfied)
Round sum allowances	See 2592
Securities or interests in securities	See 'readily convertible assets'
Sickness, maternity and other absence from work payments	Yes
Statutory sick pay (SSP), statutory maternity pay (SMP), statutory adoption pay (SAP), statutory paternity pay (SPP), statutory shared parental pay (ShPP)	Yes
Stocks and shares	See 2566
Subscriptions or fees to professional bodies paid by you	

Type of payment	Include in gross pay for NIC purposes?
• are allowable tax deductions under ITEPA 2003, s. 343 and 344	No
• are not allowable tax deductions under ITEPA 2003, s. 343 and 344	Yes
Subscriptions or fees to professional bodies reimbursed by you which:	
• are allowable tax deductions under ITEPA 2003, s. 343 and 344	No
• are not allowable tax deductions under ITEPA 2003, s. 343 and 344	Yes
Suggestions schemes awards to employees	No, if the award satisfies the conditions for exemption from tax. If you make awards in the form of benefits, see 2650ff.
Third party payments made to your employees	See 2580
Tips and service charges	See 2594
Training – payments for such things as course fees, books and so on	
• training is work related or is encouraged or required by you in connection with the employment	No
• training is provided for an employee who is leaving to enable them to find alternative employment	See CWG2 (2016) page 95
• all other circumstances	Yes
Transport vouchers, such as season tickets and so on, provided for	
• employees of a passenger transport undertaking under arrangements in operation on 25 March 1982	No
• any other employee	Yes, see 2580
Travelling time payments	Yes
Trivial commutations from registered pension schemes	No
Vouchers which can be redeemed or exchanged for	
• both goods and cash or cash alone	Yes, see 2580
• goods alone (but not readily convertible assets)	Yes, see 2580
• use of sporting or recreational facilities	No
• readily convertible assets	See 2566
Wages, salaries, fees, overtime, bonuses, commission and so on	Yes

Note also that (from 6 April 2010) there is no liability to NICs for expenses paid for or reimbursed to ministers of religion in respect of heating, lighting, cleaning and gardening in connection with living accommodation provided with the employment.

Legislation: *Social Security (Contributions) Regulations* 2001 (SI 2001/1004), reg. 24, 25; *Social Security (Contributions) (Amendment No. 2) Regulations* 2010 (SI 2010/188); *Social Security Contributions (Decisions and Appeals) (Amendment) Regulations* 2015 (SI 2015/174)

Other Material: Booklet CWG2, *Employer's further guide to PAYE and NICs*

Website: www.gov.uk/government/publications/cwg2-further-guide-to-paye-and-national-insurance-contributions

2566 Readily convertible assets

Payments in the form of readily convertible assets must be included in gross pay for NIC purposes.

A 'readily convertible asset' is one which:

- is capable of being sold on a recognised investment exchange or London Bullion market (e.g. stocks, shares and other financial instruments, gold bullion, other precious metals, etc.);

- is a right over a money debt (e.g. trade debts assigned by an employer to an employee);

- is subject to a fiscal warehousing regime, such as a bonded warehouse;

- gives rise to a right to enable an employee to obtain money (e.g. an interest in a trust which comes to an end shortly after being assigned to an employee, resulting in an automatic right to cash);

- subject to trading arrangements, either at the time that the asset is provided or that come into existence shortly afterwards as a result of an arrangement or understanding (e.g. jewellery that can be sold either at the time of its provision or shortly afterwards in consequence of an arrangement or understanding existing at the time the jewellery was provided);

- is already owned by the employee and whose value is enhanced by the employer (e.g. the payment by the employer of an additional premium to an employee's life assurance policy, thereby greatly increasing its value).

The value that is included in gross pay is the 'best estimate' at the time the payment is paid or treated as paid. The payment is added to other payments made in the relevant earnings period and NIC worked out on the total in the normal way. The NIC liability arises at the same time as income tax is due under PAYE.

Cases: *R & C Commrs v Hyde Industrial Holdings Ltd* [2006] BTC 8,025; *EDI Services Ltd v R & C Commrs* (2006) Sp C 539

Other Material: Booklet CWG2, *Employer's further guide to PAYE and NICs*

Website: www.gov.uk/government/publications/cwg2-further-guide-to-paye-and-national-insurance-contributions

2568   Share options

National Insurance is payable by both employer and employee on the gains arising when share options granted after 5 April 1999 are exercised outside a HMRC-approved scheme (or are cancelled or assigned) and where the shares or the options are readily convertible into cash.

The employee is allowed to bear the employer's NIC on share option gains. Any employer's NIC paid by employees qualifies for relief against the share option. This may be achieved in one of two ways:

- the employer and employee agree that the employee bears some or all of the secondary NIC, the legal liability remaining with the employer and the employer recovering the sum from the employee; or

- the employer and employee jointly elect for some or all of the secondary NIC liability to be transferred to the employee, the employee assuming legal liability for NIC so transferred.

The *National Insurance Contributions Act* 2006 contains provisions designed to ensure that all employers and employees pay the correct amount of tax and NICs. The Act extended to NICs the avoidance disclosure rules that previously only applied to tax.

Legislation: *National Insurance Contributions Act* 2006; *Social Security Contributions (Share Options) Act* 2001; SSCBA 1992, Sch. 1, para. 3A, 3B; *Social Security Contributions (Share Options) Regulations* 2001 (SI 2001/1817)

Other Material: Booklet CWG2, *Employer's further guide to PAYE and NICs*; *Tax Bulletin*, Special Edition (May 2005)

Website: www.gov.uk/government/publications/cwg2-further-guide-to-paye-and-national-insurance-contributions

2570   Shares subject to forfeiture

Many companies offer their employees shares in the company they work for as part of their earnings. These shares often form part of a long-term investment plan (LTIP) and unconditional ownership of the shares is based on the employee satisfying relevant conditions (e.g. meeting performance targets).

With retrospective effect from 9 April 1998, if the shares are readily convertible assets and are not issued via a HMRC-approved scheme:

- there will normally be no National Insurance Contribution (NIC) liability when shares subject to forfeiture are first awarded; but

- there will be a liability based on the market value of the shares at the time when the risk of forfeiture is lifted, or, if sooner, when the shares are sold, less any consideration previously paid.

There will also be an NIC liability if the shares can still be subject to risk of forfeiture more than five years after they are first awarded. This is intended to stop NIC liability being postponed indefinitely but as most LTIPs run for five years or less, few employees will actually pay NICs when the shares are first awarded.

Legislation: *Social Security (Contributions) Regulations* 2001 (SI 2001/1004), reg. 22

Other Material: Booklet CWG2, *Employer's further guide to PAYE and NICs*

Website: www.gov.uk/government/publications/cwg2-further-guide-to-paye-and-national-insurance-contributions

2571 Employee shareholder shares

Finance Act 2013 contains provisions dealing with the taxation of 'Employee Shareholder Shares'. Such shares are those acquired by the new category of 'employee shareholder', introduced by the *Growth and Infrastructure Act* 2013.

'Employee shareholder' is a new status for employment law purposes, under which an individual who is or becomes an employee gives up certain employment law rights that would otherwise be available or accrue to the individual, in return for the receipt of shares in the employer or employer parent company. Such parcel of shares must have a market value, on acquisition, of not less than £2,000, and in that case (and subject to meeting the qualifying conditions generally) will carry with them certain tax advantages. The relevant legislation (both under the *Finance Act* 2013 and the *Growth and Infrastructure Act* 2013) took effect from 1 September 2013.

The NIC treatment of the shares received by employee shareholders follows the income tax treatment.

The cost of employer funded independent advice, which must be provided to individuals before they become employee shareholders, is disregarded from earnings for NIC purposes.

Legislation: *Employment Rights Act* 1996, s. 205A; *Finance Act* 2013, s. 55, Sch. 23; *Social Security (Contributions) (Amendment No. 3) Regulations* 2013 (SI 2013/1907)

2572   Convertible shares

Convertible shares are shares of a certain class which can subsequently convert into another class. For example, some have different voting or dividend rights. An employer may grant one class of share, which can then be converted to a more valuable class.

With retrospective effect from 9 April 1998, if such shares are not issued via an approved scheme and are readily-convertible assets, a NIC liability will arise on the gain from the conversion. Generally, the gain is the market value of the converted share less any consideration previously paid, and any NICs paid when the shares were first awarded.

These changes generally mirror tax changes introduced in 1998 (see 327) and have the effect that the amount on which NICs are due is the same as the amount on which tax is due.

Employees may be entitled to income tax relief where they agree to meet some or all of their employer's secondary National Insurance liability arising from restricted or convertible employment-related securities (see 324).

Legislation: FA 2004, s. 85 and Sch. 16; *Social Security (Contributions) Regulations* 2001 (SI 2001/1004)

Other Material: CWG2, *Employer's further guide to PAYE and NICs*

Website: www.gov.uk/government/publications/cwg2-further-guide-to-paye-and-national-insurance-contributions

2574   Employment tribunal awards

Where an NIC liability arises in respect of protective awards, an order for re-instatement or re-engagement or an order for continuation of employment required by an employment tribunal, the NIC liability should be based on the gross amount of the award, not the net amount payable.

If the tribunal decides that an employee was unfairly dismissed and the employer is ordered to re-employ the employee and pay arrears of pay, the award is liable to NIC. For NIC purposes, the payment of arrears is treated separately from other payments made at the same time. Where payment is made in a lump sum, the earnings period is the period covered by the award. If payment is made in instalments, the instalments must be added together and the NIC liability computed on the total amount. Again, the earnings period is the period of the award.

Where an employment tribunal orders that employment continues while a complaint of unfair dismissal is dealt with, the award attracts NIC. The earnings period is the period for which each payment which must be made under the order relates, or a week, if longer.

The tribunal may order the employer to pay wages for a certain time if it decides that the employer has broken some rules when making the employee redundant. This is known as a protective award, and is liable to NICs. Such payments are treated separately from other payments. The earnings period is the longer of the protected period, the part of the protected period to which the payment relates or a week.

Other Material: CWG2, *Employer's further guide to PAYE and NICs*

Website: www.gov.uk/government/publications/cwg2-further-guide-to-paye-and-national-insurance-contributions

2576   Payments or expenses covered by a dispensation

A dispensation is a notice sent by HMRC authorising the employer not to report on forms P11D the expenses and benefits specifically covered by the dispensation. Provided that the conditions under which the dispensation was granted are still valid, NICO accepts a dispensation as evidence that the payments which it covers are expenses incurred in carrying out employment and are not to be included in gross pay for NIC purposes.

Other Material: CWG2, *Employer's further guide to PAYE and NICs*

Website: www.gov.uk/government/publications/cwg2-further-guide-to-paye-and-national-insurance-contributions

2580   Non-cash vouchers

The computation of an employed earner's earnings for Class 1 NIC purposes includes payment made by non-cash vouchers, unless the vouchers are of a type specifically excluded by the legislation. The value of the voucher is the cost to the employer of providing that voucher.

Exemptions

The following types of vouchers are specifically exempt:

- transport vouchers provided for the employee of a passenger transport undertaking under arrangements in operation on 25 March 1982 where the employee is earning less than £8,500 a year;

- vouchers for leave travel facilities for members of the armed forces;

- vouchers for sporting and recreational facilities (subject to the same conditions applying for income tax exemption);

- vouchers for long service awards, provided that the cost of providing the voucher does not exceed £50 for each year of service and there has been no similar award in the previous ten years;

- vouchers for social functions organised for employees, provided that the cost of providing vouchers does not exceed £150 per head and the function is open to employees generally;

- vouchers for travel between home and work provided to a person with a severe and permanent disability who is unable to travel on public transport;

- childcare vouchers;

- from 6 April 2006, employees may receive up to £55 a week of childcare, tax and National Insurance free, where their employers contract with an approved childcarer or provide childcare vouchers for the purpose of paying an approved childcarer. For employees joining an employer-provided childcare scheme on or after 6 April 2011, the £55 a week limit is restricted for higher rate and additional rate taxpayers for both income tax and Class 1 NIC purposes. The weekly amount of tax and NIC-free qualifying childcare payments that an employee earning over £150,000 p.a. can receive increased from £22 per week to £25 per week from 6 April 2013. There is no change for employees with earnings below this figure (see 409);

- meal vouchers for meals provided on the employer's premises or in a canteen where meals are provided for staff generally;

- a voucher provided by a donor who is not the employer and is unconnected with allowing the employee to obtain goods, provided that the total of this and other vouchers provided by the donor does not exceed £150 per year and the voucher is not given in recognition of past or future services;

- from 6 April 2000, the provision of a non-cash voucher in respect of the private use of a car where such provision attracts a Class 1A liability;

- non-cash vouchers for mobile phones;

- non-cash vouchers for eye tests and also special corrective appliances such as glasses; and

- non-cash vouchers that can be used to obtain health screening or a medical check-up.

Voucher provided by third parties

From 6 April 2000, non-cash vouchers provided by a third party were removed from the Class 1 charge and brought within the scope of Class 1A.

Non-cash vouchers provided by employers remain within the scope of Class 1.

Legislation: FA 2004, s. 78 and Sch. 13; FA 2011, s. 35 and Sch. 8; *Social Security (Contributions) (Amendment No. 6) Regulations* 2007 (SI 2007/2091); *Social Security (Contributions) Regulations* 2001 (SI 2001/1004), reg. 24, 25, Sch. 3, Pt. V

Other Material: CWG2, *Employer's further guide to PAYE and NICs*

Website: www.gov.uk/government/publications/cwg2-further-guide-to-paye-and-national-insurance-contributions

2582   Retirement benefit schemes

No NIC liability arises in respect of an employer's contribution to a HMRC-registered retirement benefit scheme. Generally speaking, no NIC liability arises if there is no income tax liability.

However, contributions to a funded unapproved retirement benefits scheme (FURBS) attract NIC. Where there is a separate trust for each employee, the full amount paid into the FURBS on behalf of the employee must be included in his or her gross pay for NIC purposes.

In the event that there is a single trust fund, but each employee has a distinct and separate benefit share, the amount paid to secure the employee's separate benefit share should be included in his or her gross pay.

However, if there is a single trust fund and at the time payments into the fund are made, the trustees have no indication of the benefit to be received by each employee, the amount of the payment must be apportioned equally between the employees who are members of the scheme, the sum apportioned in this way being included in each employee's gross pay for NIC purposes.

Legislation: SSCBA 1992, s. 3(1), (2A), 6(1); SSA 1998, s. 48; *Social Security (Contributions) Regulations* 2001 (SI 2001/1004), reg. 25

Other Material: CWG2, *Employer's further guide to PAYE and NICs*

Website: www.gov.uk/government/publications/cwg2-further-guide-to-paye-and-national-insurance-contributions

2584 Incidental overnight expenses (IOEs)

No Class 1 NIC liability arises where an employer pays for incidental overnight expenses (IOEs) relating to a qualifying absence up to a maximum of £5 per night for stays within the UK and £10 per night for overnight stays outside of the UK. The NIC exemption mirrors that available for income tax purposes. Sums paid in excess of the tax-free limits must be included in gross pay.

Other Material: Booklet 480, *Expenses and benefits, a tax guide*, app. 8

Website: www.gov.uk/government/publications/480-expenses-and-benefits-a-tax-guide

2586 Prize incentive schemes

A prize incentive scheme is one where employees receive prizes or awards from either the employer or a third party. The awards may be made in cash or may be in the form of holidays, goods, vouchers, etc.

The extent to which an NIC liability exist depends on the nature of the award (see 2564). However, where the award is in a non-cash form, it should be noted that although a Class 1 liability may not arise, there may be a liability to Class 1A (see 2650ff.).

Where the award is made by way of a non-cash voucher, the rules described at 2580 are in point.

Other Material: CWG2, *Employer's further guide to PAYE and NICs*

Website: www.gov.uk/government/publications/cwg2-further-guide-to-paye-and-national-insurance-contributions

2588 Redundancy payments

No liability arises in respect of redundancy payments. The regulation does not specify that it covers only statutory redundancy pay. Since redundancy payments are really little more than compensation for the loss of rights in the employment, it would seem that any amount paid in excess of the statutory entitlement would also fall to be excluded from earnings. Before a payment is officially accepted as a redundancy payment, the following conditions must be met:

- the employee's contract has been terminated;

- the termination has occurred because of redundancy; and

- the payment is not being made for any reason other than redundancy.

For the redundancy to be officially regarded as a genuine redundancy, it must have arisen either because the employer ceased, or intends to cease, carrying on the business for the purpose of which, or the place in which, the employee was employed, or the requirements of the business have changed such that the employee's job is no longer needed.

Other Material: CWG2, *Employer's further guide to PAYE and NICs*

Website: www.gov.uk/government/publications/cwg2-further-guide-to-paye-and-national-insurance-contributions

2590   Relocation payments

All relocation allowances paid which qualify for income tax relief are excluded from gross pay, even if they exceed the £8,000 cap for tax. For NIC purposes, there is no time limit within which the payment of qualifying allowances must start being paid.

Where an employer pays an employee's council tax (e.g. because his old home stands empty for some time after he has relocated), this has traditionally been accepted as a business expense, though official guidance simply enjoins employers to seek advice on the Employer's Helpline (tel: 0300 200 3200).

Relocation allowances which are taxed through PAYE settlement agreements (see 2356) continue to be excluded from NIC liability (see 2676).

2592   Round sum allowances

An employer who pays a round sum allowance to an employee and who can identify specific and distinct business expenses can exclude these from gross pay for NIC purposes. If the employer cannot identify the business expense, the whole allowance is included in gross pay, regardless of whether an expense is actually incurred.

Legislation: *Social   Security   (Contributions)   Regulations* 1979 (SI 2001/1004), reg. 25

Other Material: CWG2, *Employer's further guide to PAYE and NICs*

Website: www.gov.uk/government/publications/cwg2-further-guide-to-paye-and-national-insurance-contributions

2594   Tips and service charges

The NIC position depends on the arrangements under which payments in respect of tips and service charges are made.

Tips and gratuities

The following flowchart taken from the *Employer's further guide to PAYE and NICs* (CWG2) summarises the NIC position as regards tips and gratuities.

Service charges

For NIC purposes, a service charge is any sum that a customer is required by management to pay for services. Where service charges are levied and the money is paid out to the employees, a Class 1 NIC liability arises, irrespective of who shares out the money. Payments in respect of service charges should be included in gross pay for NIC purposes.

Troncs

A tronc is a special arrangement used to pool and distribute tips. It is usually run by one of the employees referred to as a troncmaster and is generally run independently of the employer's influence.

The HMRC guidance: *Tips, Gratuities, Service Charges and PAYE* provides guidance for employers and troncmasters in the catering and service industries. It covers the treatment of tips and service charges for income tax, NICs, National Minimum Wage (NMW) and VAT purposes. The booklet was revised in February 2005 to clarify some aspects of the guidance but following legal advice HMRC found it necessary to withdraw that edition.

Payments of tips to the employee are liable for NICs if the employer makes the payment directly, or indirectly to the employee from sums previously paid to him; or allocates the tips directly or indirectly to his employees. Liability for NICs will always depend on the specific arrangements regarding the distribution of tips that are operated by individual employers. As regards NMW, provided the employer is not making the payment directly or indirectly to the employee from sums previously paid to him, or allocating the tips directly or indirectly to his employees, the tips are not liable for NICs. HMRC guidance advises that if the contract of employment indicates that the employee will be able to participate in the tronc, any payments made by the tronc are liable for NICs because they are contractual payments and therefore not gratuitous. HMRC now accept that these sorts of payments also fall to be disregarded from earnings and so are not liable for Class 1 NICs to the extent that the employer is not allocating, directly or indirectly, the tips.

Other Material: HMRC *Tax Bulletin*, Issue 82, April 2006; CWG2, *Employer's further guide to PAYE and NICs*

Website: *Employee gets tips, gratuities or service charges through a tronc:* www.gov.uk/employee-gets-tips-gratuities-or-service-charges-through-a-tronc

2596   Travel and subsistence

The changes to the income tax rules on employee travel and subsistence which apply from 6 April 1998 (see 1994) are also applicable to NICs from the same date. Broadly, in relation to business journeys made after 5 April 1998, reasonable travel and subsistence allowances paid to employees are excluded from 'earnings' attracting NICs.

Site-based employees

Reasonable costs paid by employers towards the costs of travel and/or subsistence of employees with no permanent workplace, may be excluded from gross pay.

Triangular travel

Where an employee with a normal, permanent place of work travels directly from his home to another temporary place of work, reasonable travel and subsistence expenses paid by the employer can be excluded in calculating gross pay for NIC purposes. Previously, the amount normally excluded from gross pay was the lesser of:

- the cost of travelling from the normal, permanent place of work to the temporary workplace; or

- the actual amounts of travelling costs incurred.

Home-to-work travel

The basic rule is that any reimbursement by an employer of home-to-work travel expenses to an employee is a payment of earnings for Class 1 purposes, though the rule is qualified in a number of respects.

Unexpected call-outs

If an employee is recalled to work unexpectedly (e.g. in the evening), reimbursement of the travelling expenses incurred is only a payment of earnings if the employee's conditions of service or employment require him to be on call.

Disabled employees

If the reimbursed employee is a disabled employee or trainee within the terms of the *Disabled Persons (Employment) Act* 1944, s. 15, or is a severely disabled person who cannot use public transport, travelling costs are NIC-free.

Temporary postings away from a permanent workplace

If an employee is temporarily sent to work somewhere other than his usual place of work for a period expected from the outset to be 24 months or less (12 months or less before 6 April 1998), the employer may pay travelling expenses free of contribution liability. If the absence lasts longer than 24 months, contributions should be paid once payments have been made for more than two years. If the posting is expected from the outset to last more than two years, all payments are liable to contributions from the start.

Employer contracts for the transport to be provided

If the employer contracts for the transport to be provided, the payment-in-kind rules exclude the payments made from earnings. This applies equally to, for example, season ticket purchases. However, a Class 1A liability may arise (see 2650ff.).

Payments to employees travelling abroad

Where employers pay the travelling expenses of employees travelling between the UK and an overseas employment, or mariners who work outside UK territorial waters, the payments may be excluded from earnings if those expenses are not taxable under the charge on employment income provisions of ITEPA 2003.

Armed forces operational allowance

From 1 April 2006, a non-taxable operational bonus may be paid to eligible service personnel deployed to specified operational locations. From 14 November 2006, regulations ensure that the operational allowance can also be paid to service personnel free of Class 1 NICs.

Late-night transport home

Late-night taxi, etc. fares home which are reimbursed rather than paid direct to the taxi company may be excluded from earnings (see further 1994).

Disruption of public transport

If public transport is disrupted by a strike or other industrial action, and employers reimburse employees with the cost of taxi or other fares or overnight accommodation near the place of work, such reimbursements are excluded from earnings.

Allowances for carrying passengers and equipment

Allowances paid to cover the additional expense of carrying passengers and/or equipment specifically related to the employment are excluded from gross pay.

Car parking costs and fines

Car parking costs may be excluded from earnings either entirely, if the employer contracts directly with the provider of the parking space, or at least in part if the employer reimburses parking fees incurred for business purposes. A record should be kept of individual items of expenditure. Parking fines paid for employees are stated specifically to constitute earnings to be included in gross pay.

Employers paying insurance

Where road fund licence, insurance premium, car servicing and AA/RAC, etc. membership are paid directly by the employer in respect of a vehicle which he owns, the payment-in-kind rule would normally operate to exclude payments from earnings for Class 1 purposes (although a Class 1A liability may arise). However, where the employer pays for these items in respect of the employee's own vehicle, the payments for these items must be included in the gross pay.

Legislation: *Social Security (Contributions) (Amendment No. 6) Regulations* 2006 (SI 2006/2924); *Social Security (Contributions) Regulations* 2001 (SI 2001/1004), Sch. 3

Case: *R & C Commrs v Cheshire Employer and Skills Development Ltd (formerly Total People Ltd)* [2011] BTC 1,832

Other Material: Booklet 490, *Employee travel – a tax and NICs guide for employers*; CWG2, *Employer's further guide to PAYE and NICs*

Website: www.gov.uk/government/publications/490-employee-travel-a-tax-and-nics-guide

2598   Pay in lieu of notice or remuneration

Pay in lieu of notice (PILON) and pay in lieu of remuneration (PILOR) are compensation payments made to employees whose contracts are terminated (i.e. breached) early or without notice, which covers three of the categories mentioned in the official guidance. Golden handshakes, etc. are no more than colloquial terms applied to any mixture of payments covering the termination of an employment, including redundancy, compensation and ex gratia elements. Since they derive from the termination of the employment rather than from the employee's acting as or being an employee, they could in principle be outside the definition of earnings. However, some contracts of employment make specific provision for such payments to be made. Where it is known from the commencement of an employment relationship that compensation will be paid to the employee in the event of breach by the employer, the contingent right to such compensation may form part of the consideration given by the employer as his half of the employment bargain. It is therefore quite clearly a payment of earnings when made.

Cases: *Du Cross v Ryall (HMIT)* (1935) 19 TC 444; *Dale v De Soissons* (1950) 32 TC 126; *Hochstrasser v Mayes* [1960] AC 376; *Delaney v Staples* [1992] 1 AC 687

Other Material: CWG2, *Employer's further guide to PAYE and NICs*

Website: www.gov.uk/government/publications/cwg2-further-guide-to-paye-and-national-insurance-contributions

Class 1 contributions

Class 1: Introduction and rates

2602   Nature of Class 1

Class 1 contributions are earnings-related and based on an employed earner's employment (see 2506). They are payable in two parts:

(1) *primary* contributions, payable by employed earners; and

(2) *secondary* contributions, payable by the employers of employed earners or, in certain circumstances, other persons paying earnings.

A primary Class 1 liability arises where in any tax week earnings are paid to or for the benefit of an earner in respect of any one employment of his which is employed earner's employment, and:

- he is over the age of 16; and

- the amount paid exceeds the primary threshold for Class 1 contributions in force for the year (or the prescribed equivalent in the case of earners paid otherwise than weekly).

A secondary Class 1 contribution is payable if the amount paid exceeds the secondary threshold.

The earnings on which contributions are payable are calculated or estimated in accordance with regulations, some of which provide for particular types of payment to be excluded from earnings in calculating liabilities (see 2540ff.).

Legislation: SSCBA 1992, s. 1(2), 5(1), 6(1); *Social Security (Contributions) (Amendment) Regulations* 2010 (SI 2010/834); *Social Security (Contributions) Regulations* 2001 (SI 2001/1004), reg. 11

2604 Primary (employee) Class 1 rate

Primary contributions at the rate of 12% are payable on earnings between the primary threshold and the upper earnings limit (UEL). A national zero-rate of contribution is payable on earnings that equal or exceed the lower earnings limit (LEL) but that do not reach the primary threshold. This is to preserve benefit entitlement for employees earning in excess of the LEL.

An additional 2% Class 1 NIC contribution is payable on earnings above the upper earnings limit.

Contracting out of SERPS is no longer possible since 6 April 2016 for salary-related occupational pensions schemes (COSR) and 5 April 2012 for money purchase schemes (COMPS), mixed benefit schemes (COMB) contracted-out on a defined contribution basis, appropriate personal pension schemes (APP) and APP stakeholder schemes. Employees previously contracting out of SERPS effectively paid a lower primary rate as a result of the contracting-out rebate (see 2608).

> **Example**
>
> With bonuses and commissions, Susan is paid £1,000 in a tax week. In 2016–17, she pays £84.10 ((12% × (£827 − £155)) + (2% × (£1,000 − £827)) and her employer pays £116.47 (13.8% × (£1,000 − £156)).

The *National Insurance Contributions (Rate Ceilings) Act* 2015 (NIC(RC)A 2015) sets a ceiling on the main and additional primary percentages, the secondary percentage and the UEL from 2016–17 until the tax year starting before the next general election. During this period, the main primary percentage will not be more than 12%; the additional primary percentage will not be more than 2%; the secondary percentage will not be more than 13.8%; and the UEL will not exceed the weekly equivalent of the higher rate threshold for that tax year as proposed in the pre-Budget proposals.

Legislation: SSCBA 1992, s. 8(1), (2); *Welfare Reform and Pensions Act* 1999, s. 73 and Sch. 9, para. 4; *National Insurance Contributions Act* 2002, s. 1; *Social Security (Contributions) (Amendment) Regulations* 2003 (SI 2003/193); *Social Security Contributions (Notional Payment of Primary Class 1 Contribution) Regulations* 2000 (SI 2000/747); *National Insurance Contributions (Rate Ceilings) Act* 2015

2606   Secondary (employer) Class 1 rate

The starting point for employer (secondary) Class 1 NICs is the secondary threshold which is aligned with the personal allowance for income tax. Employers of employees whose weekly earnings do not exceed the current 'earnings threshold' pay no (secondary) Class 1 NICs. Above that threshold, they pay NICs at 13.8%. There is no upper earnings limit for secondary Class 1 purposes.

The *National Insurance Contributions (Rate Ceilings) Act* 2015 (NIC(RC)A 2015) sets a ceiling on the main and additional primary percentages, the secondary percentage and the UEL from 2016–17 until the tax year starting before the next general election. During this period, the main primary percentage will not be more than 12%; the additional primary percentage will not be more than 2%; the secondary percentage will not be more than 13.8%; and the UEL will not exceed the weekly equivalent of the higher rate threshold for that tax year.

From April 2015, secondary Class 1 NICs have been abolished for under 21-year-old not earning more than the upper earnings limit (£43,000 a year or £827 a week for 2016–17). Employer NICs are liable as normal beyond the upper earnings limit. It applies equally to existing and new employees and does not affect the employee's entitlement to state pension.

From April 2016, employers of apprentices under the age of 25 will no longer be required to pay secondary Class 1 NICs on earnings up to the upper earnings limit for those employees (£43,000 a year or £827 a week for 2016–17). 'Apprentices' are prescribed by SI 2001/1004, reg. 154A (as inserted by SI 2016/117).

Legislation: SSCBA 1992, s. 9, 9A, 9B; *National Insurance Contributions Act* 2002, s. 2; *National Insurance Contributions (Rate Ceilings) Act* 2015; *Social Security (Contributions) Regulations* 2001 (SI 2001/1004), reg. 154A ; *Social Security (Contributions) (Amendment) Regulations* 2010 (SI 2010/834); *Social Security (Contributions) (Limits and Thresholds) (Amendment) Regulations* 2015 (SI 2015/577);

Other material: HMRC guidance on paying employer National Insurance contributions for apprentices under 25: www.gov.uk/government/publications/national-insurance-contributions-for-under-25s-employer-guide/paying-employer-national-insurance-contributions-for-apprentices-under-25

2608   Contracting-out

To tie in with the introduction of the new state pension from April 2016, the *Pensions Act* 2014, s. 24 and Sch. 13 provides for the abolition of contracted-out salary related (COSR) pension schemes from 6 April 2016. This means that employers and employees who were contracted out of SERPS pay the standard rate of Class 1 contributions instead of the contracted-out rate. Contracting out via money purchase pension arrangements was abolished in April 2012 under *Pensions Act* 2007, Sch. 4. Contracted-out money purchase (COMP) schemes and appropriate personal pension (APP) schemes simply became not contracted out in respect of contributions paid and benefits accruing from 6 April 2012.

Standard rate contributions buy entitlement to all contributory benefits. In the past, such contributions on earnings between the LEL and UEL gave entitlement to benefit from the state earnings related pension scheme (SERPS), but the arrival of the primary threshold (PT) and secondary threshold (ST) changed that. An employee who earns between the LEL and the PT pays no contributions (although he will be deemed to have paid contributions), but would nevertheless – at least until the introduction, in 2016, of the flat-rate state pension accrue entitlements to the State Second Pension, S2P, which replaced SERPS in April 2002.

However, the social security system (and the state pension scheme in particular) was originally attached to old mutual arrangements set-up, e.g. by guilds and friendly societies. When earnings-related contributions were introduced, it was recognised that there was already a significant body of contributors who had made private provision for their old age and who should therefore be given the chance to contract out of the state system. They were permitted to pay a reduced or 'rebated' NI contribution, but forfeited the right to an earnings-related component to the state pension, although they paid for and were entitled to the basic component of the state pension.

Under the regime until 6 April 2016, COSR schemes continued, but COMP and APP schemes became ordinary pension schemes with no impact on NI contribution rates. Until 5 April 2012, all employees who were members of registered occupational pension schemes or took out appropriate personal or stakeholder pensions could (but did not need to) contract out of S2P. From 2012, contracting out has only been possible in salary-related, 'defined benefit' or 'final salary' pension schemes, which have become increasingly rare.

The contribution reduction, known as the contracting-out rebate, applied until 5 April 2009 to earnings between the LEL and UEL (as was the case when SERPS was introduced in 1978), but this changed from 6 April 2009 (see below). A rebate was still due even where earnings fell below the ST, when no contributions were actually payable. This still applied in COSR employment until 6 April 2016 and meant that it was possible to have 'negative contributions', where earnings fall between the LEL and ST, or just above the ST, as a rebate would be due without a contribution liability.

From April 2009, the old structure was changed. The UEL was decoupled from the point at which S2P pension was capped, known as the upper accrual point (UAP). The UAP remained fixed at £770 per week until it was abolished, with the introduction of the new state pension from 6 April 2016. The UEL will be uprated by the Government each year (although, exceptionally, it fell in line with the 40% tax threshold in April 2011 and April 2012 and again in April 2013). The contracting-out rebate applied only to earnings up to the UAP. The aim was clearly to constrain the cost of the S2P state pension and to fund it by collecting extra contributions from higher earners without granting them further state pension entitlements.

The contracting-out arrangements are administered by what was Contracted-Out Employments Group (COEG) at NICEO in Newcastle, who provide advice and assistance to pension scheme providers and employers. The group was renamed National Insurance Services to Pensions Industry (NISPI), the name that has appeared in HMRC's employer guidance on contributions issued since 2003–04.

The contracted-out rebate

The rates so reduced were known as the contracted-out rates and the reduction was known as the contracted-out rebate. It was accounted for in one of two ways. In occupational schemes, both employer and employee were allowed to deduct the rebate from the contributions paid to HMRC each month, thus enabling them to pay the amount saved directly into the occupational scheme. Holders of personal pensions and their employers continued to pay the full not contracted-out rate of contribution, receiving the rebate directly into their policy by means of a payment from the National Insurance Contributions Office (see 2500) once year-end returns have been processed.

The rebate was 1.4% (from 6 April 2012) for employees for both COSR (salary related) and COMP (money purchase) schemes. As regards employers, the rebate was 3.4% (from 6 April 2012) for COSR schemes. The rebate for COMP schemes (1.4% in 2011–12) was abolished from 6 April 2012.

The rebate applies only to band earnings, since contributions on earnings up to the LEL count towards only the basic state retirement pension. Employers' contributions on earnings below the LEL and above the UEL are therefore due at the full rate.

Employers pay secondary contributions only on the earnings above the secondary (or employer's) threshold (see 2606). However, the NI rebate was still available in respect of all earnings between the lower earnings limit and the upper earnings limit, including those between the lower earnings limit and the secondary threshold on which no employer's NICs were payable. Employers operating contracted-out schemes were able to reduce their overall NIC liability to reflect the rebate applicable to the employer's contributions on earnings above the lower earnings limit and up to and including the secondary threshold.

The introduction of the primary threshold from 6 April 2000 (see 2604) introduced a further complication. As noted above, employees would not pay primary Class 1 contributions until their earnings reach the primary threshold. However, the employee's NI rebate remained payable in respect of earnings between the lower earnings limit and the upper earnings limit, including those above the lower earnings limit and up to an including the primary threshold. In the first instance, the rebate reduced total NICs payable by the employee. However, if the NIC payable by the employee was reduced to nil, the excess rebate was available for the employer to offset against his overall NIC bill. This is best illustrated by the following examples.

Example 1

From April 2015, Rupert earns £171 per week. He is a member of his employer's COSR scheme. In 2015–16, Rupert paid no primary contributions on earnings below £155 per week. On earnings between £155 and £171, he paid at the contracted-out rate of 10.6%, i.e. £1.70 per week (£16 × 10.6%). However, this was reduced by the rebate payable on earnings payable between the lower earnings limit and the primary threshold of 60 pence (£43 × 1.4%). Thus, Rupert's weekly NIC contributions were £1.10

Example 2

Zak earns £120 per week from April 2015. He is a member of his employer's COSR scheme. As his earnings are below the primary threshold, for 2015–16, Zak paid no primary NIC contributions. However, the NI rebate was available for earnings above the lower earnings limit (£112 for 2015–16) at Zak's actual earnings of £120 per week, amounting to 11 pence per week (£8 × 1.4%). As Zak's contributions were nil, this was available to reduce his employer's overall NIC bill.

Legislation: PSA 1993, s. 41; *Social Security (Contributions) (Limits and Thresholds) (Amendment) Regulations* 2015 (SI 2015/577); *Social Security (Reduced Rates of Class 1 Contributions, Rebates and Minimum Contributions) Order* 2006 (SI 2006/1009) (as amended by SI 2009/3094)

Earnings periods for class 1

2612   Earnings period

An 'earnings period' is a period to which earnings paid to or for the benefit of an employed earner are deemed to relate, irrespective of the period over which they were earned. Class 1 liability is calculated on the basis of the earnings paid in the earnings period and the limits applicable to that earnings period. No person may have more than one earnings period in respect of a single employment.

Employees paid at regular intervals

The majority of employees are paid a wage or salary at regular intervals of a week or a month. Where only a single regular payment pattern exists, except in the case of company directors in respect of whom special rules apply (see 2622), the earnings period equates with the pay interval, provided the interval is seven days or more (i.e. an employee who receives a weekly wage will have a weekly earnings period). The regular intervals need not be exactly equal, so payment on the last working day of each calendar month will satisfy this test, despite the fact that some months contain five weeks.

Where an employee (again, other than a company director) has more than one regular pay interval, special rules apply to identify the single earnings period on which liability is based. The earnings period is the *shorter* or *shortest* of those intervals, unless that interval is less than seven days. An employee in receipt of monthly salary, quarterly commission and annual bonus would therefore normally have a monthly earnings period, unless a written direction to the contrary is made by the National Insurance Contributions Office (NICO) (see 2500 and below).

An earnings period cannot be less than seven days in length and, if there is more than one such interval of less than seven days, the earnings period is set at a week. The same rule applies if there is more than one regular pay interval, one or more of which is less than seven days.

The first earnings period of the tax year

The first earnings period of the tax year begins on the first day of that year. For weekly-paid employees, the year may therefore contain *53* earnings weeks if they are paid on the first and last day of the year (or one of the last two days in a leap year). Similarly, an employee paid every four weeks may pay contributions on 56 weeks' earnings depending on how the payment dates fall. In such circumstances, NICO (see 2500) argues that no overpayment arises.

Payment intervals other than a week or month

If the regular payment interval is other than a week or month, the regular interval becomes the earnings period. The exact percentage method of calculation must also be used (see 2636).

Example

Nigel is paid every ten days.

Nigel has 37 earnings periods in a year (36 of ten days, one of five days), although he might be paid only 36 times.

Earnings limits and brackets are adjusted to match the length of the period by dividing each weekly bracket by seven and multiplying by the number of days in the regular interval.

Unusual circumstances

There are special rules for certain employment rights payments (see 2614). Official guidance sets out the earnings period rules in a number of unusual circumstances. NICO (see 2500) may sometimes direct that a particular earnings period should be used (see 2616).

Bonuses and commissions

Bonuses, commissions and suchlike are treated as part of the total pay at the time they are paid. If extra payments are made at a regular interval shorter than that for basic pay, the shorter period becomes the earnings period, but NICO (see 2500) can direct that the longer or longest interval be used if the greater part of earnings is paid at that interval, even if the structure of pay intervals was not intended as a method of avoiding contributions. If a second one-off payment is made after the normal rules have been applied to a first payment, the two payments must be aggregated within the earnings period to calculate the contribution rate. The deductions working sheet must be amended.

Legislation: *Social Security (Contributions) Regulations* 2001 (SI 2001/1004), reg. 1(2), 2, 3

Case: *Mehta* [2015] TC 04573

Other Material: CWG2, *Employer's further guide to PAYE and NICs*

2614   Earnings periods for employment rights payments

Payments made by employers to employees (other than directors) under the *Employment Rights Act* 1996, where the payments represent earnings, may have their own earnings period and are not in that case added to other payments of earnings made at the same time. These payments include:

- guarantee payments paid for weeks when there is no work – the normal earnings period rule applies;

- medical suspension payments paid for weeks when an employee is suspended on medical grounds – the normal earnings period rule applies;

- awards of arrears in cases of orders for reinstatement or re-engagement – the earnings period is the period for which arrears have to be paid under the order made by the industrial tribunal, or a week if longer;

- pay due following an order for the continuation of employment – the earnings period is the period covered by the order, or a week if longer; and

- pay due following a protective award – the earnings period is the longest of the protected periods stated in the award, the part of the protected period the sum is paid for, or a week.

2616   Official directions as to earnings periods

Manipulation of the earnings period rules (see 2612) by employers may lead to an official direction that a different earnings period should be used. Further, where the incidence of earnings-related contributions is avoided or reduced by means of irregular or unequal payments, counteracting directions may be given. However, any direction given may not be retrospective.

Legislation: *Social Security (Contributions) Regulations* 2001 (SI 2001/1004), reg. 3(2), 31

2618   Changes in normal pay days

Where a payment is not made on the usual day, it is treated as falling in the earnings period in which the usual day falls, unless that day falls in another tax year, in which case it is treated as made on the last day of the regular interval at which it is treated as paid in the same tax year. Thus a payment of salary always made on the last Friday in the month attracts a monthly earnings period. If the payment is exceptionally made on Thursday (e.g. before Good Friday), the change of pay day is irrelevant.

If two weeks' wages are paid together because an employee will be away on the next pay day, two earnings periods of a week are used. If the second of those weeks falls in the next tax year the earlier year's rates are used for that week but it is not aggregated with the payment in the last earnings period of the old year.

Two payments received in an earnings period

If an employee receives two payments in an earnings period because for example, the pay day is changed permanently or there is a change in week-in-hand arrangements, each payment has its own earnings period based on the regular interval.

Employer changes the earnings period

Where an employer changes the earnings period, the treatment depends on whether the new interval is shorter or longer:

- shorter interval (e.g. monthly paid becomes weekly paid) – contributions are worked out on payments made after the change completely separately using the new earnings period, even if the two earnings periods overlap; or

- longer interval (e.g. weekly paid becomes monthly paid) – contributions are worked out as above, unless payment has already been made at the old short interval in the first longer period, in which case all earnings are aggregated in the new period and the total contributions adjusted to take account of those already deducted.

Such a change from weekly to monthly pay often involves entry into a contracted-out occupational pension scheme. All payments made in the new earnings period are charged at the contracted-out rate.

Arrears of pay

Where arrears of pay are paid, the rates and limits applied are those of the earnings period in which payment takes place, not those of the period when earnings were earned.

Supplementary payments

Sometimes an employer makes a supplementary payment after the regular payment of wages or salary has been made but within the same earnings period. Contributions must be calculated on the total payment made in the period and the payroll records amended to show the increased contributions.

Legislation: *Social Security (Contributions) Regulations* 2001 (SI 2001/1004), reg. 7(1)–(3)

2620   Earnings periods for new and leaving employees

Difficulty or uncertainty is often caused when employments begin or end.

New employee

The first payment above the lower earnings limit (see 2602) gives rise to a contribution liability in respect of a new employee, but the earnings period is that which will apply for the future (e.g. a week or month), not the length of time between the date on which the employee joins and the date of payment, which may be only a few days.

In the First-tier Tribunal (FTT) case of *Mehta*, an employee began work at the beginning of February 1995 and should have been paid his basic salary for that month at the end of that month, but because his employer was unable to add him to its payroll system in time for this payment, the employer made a payment on account of his salary on 22 February 1995. When the employee was then paid at the end of March, he was paid his basic pay for February and March 1995, subject to a deduction for the amount previously paid on account. HMRC argued that the earlier payment came within the scope of the *Social Security (Contributions) Regulations* 1979 (SI 1979/591), reg. 6(1) (now *Social Security Contributions Regulations* 2001 (SI 2001/1004), reg. 7), as an advance payment and therefore the employer was not required to deduct NICs from the payment. The FTT found that reg. 6(1) was not on point because the payment was not made before it was due, it was made at the time the employee was due to be paid his basic pay for February 1995. Even if the FTT was wrong in this analysis, it found that the effect of reg. 6 would be that the payment made on 22 February 1995 would be treated as having been made on the 'regular' date on which it was due (presumably 28 February 1995).

Employee leaves

When an employee leaves, he may receive two or more payments together which would normally have been made at the regular interval. The normal earnings period applies to each such payment separately. Whether the earnings period rules apply to both employer and employee contributions, or to employer contributions only, usually depends on whether the employee who leaves is over pensionable age, since an individual over that age pays no primary contributions (see 2644).

Holiday pay

If holiday pay is paid with the last payment of wages or salary, the treatment depends on when the contract of service ends. If it ends on the day the employee leaves, both amounts are added together and treated as paid in one earnings period. In contrast, if the employee simply takes holiday while serving his notice, the whole amount is treated as holiday pay and effectively spread over the period of holiday.

Regular payments after leaving

If an employee continues to receive regular payments after leaving, contributions are due in the normal way, unless the payment is of a type specifically excluded from earnings (e.g. a pension).

One-off payments after leaving

Where an employee receives irregular or one-off payments after leaving, such as back-dated pay awards, holiday pay for a holiday not taken, or a retrospective bonus, a weekly earnings period applies.

Statutory maternity pay

Statutory maternity pay is often paid after an employee's contract of service has ended, since an employer usually has to pay the benefit even if the employee will not return to work for him after her maternity leave. If SMP is paid *in a lump sum*, the weekly earnings period applies to the payment, unless it is made with the last regular payment of wages, in which case the two sums are aggregated and the normal earnings period applied. If it is paid *at the same regular interval as were the earnings before the employee left*, the earnings period used during the period of employment applies. If payment is made *at different intervals from regular earnings*, the interval between payments is used.

Employee dies

No contribution liability arises in respect of payments made after the employee's death.

Case: *Mehta* [2015] TC 04573

2622 Directors

For ordinary employees, the earnings period is usually set by a person's regular pay interval or intervals (see 2612). Company directors are generally in a position to decide when and how they receive a payment of earnings, which potentially gives them the ability to avoid primary Class 1 contribution liability by astute use of the earnings period rules. For this reason, a director's earnings period is a tax year, even if he is paid, say, monthly or leaves during the year.

Newly-appointed directors

The only exception to the above rule is where a director is first appointed during the course of a tax year. In such an event, the earnings period is the period from the date of appointment to the end of the tax year, measured in weeks. The calculation of the earnings period includes the tax week of appointment, plus all remaining complete weeks in the tax year (i.e. week 53 is ignored for this purpose). This is known as the pro-rata earnings period.

Payments on account

Companies can save time and money by calculating directors' NICs in a similar way to other employees. Instead of paying very high levels of NICs on a short-term basis, directors who are paid regularly (e.g. directors who have contracts of service with their companies) can spread their contributions evenly throughout the tax year. The earnings period remains an annual earnings period, but contributions are made on account throughout the tax year.

Payments made in unusual circumstances

There are special earnings period rules where payments are made to directors in unusual circumstances:

Payments under the *Employment Rights Act* 1996	add any payments to other earnings from the company in the tax year of payment.
Payment to director for the period before appointment (i.e. for work as an employee)	use the earnings period which applies when the earnings are paid (i.e. the annual or pro-rata period).
Payment after resignation in respect of office previously held (even if the person is still an employee):	
• the same year	use annual or pro-rata earnings period for the year, adding payments to other earnings already paid.
• later tax year	separate from other earnings in the year, apply a separate annual earnings period and limits.

Directors include shadow directors, though a person is not to be treated as such by reason only that the directors act on advice given by him in his professional capacity.

Legislation: SSCBA 1992, s. 3(4), (5), 6A(2), (3), (6)

2624   COMPS and COSRS

Where earnings fall to be aggregated (see 2630ff.), the shortest earnings period in relation to a contracted-out money purchase (COMP) scheme employment takes priority over any relating to a contracted-out salary related (COSR) scheme. This benefits members of COMP schemes by maximising their potential benefits from both COMP schemes and COSR schemes.

Legislation: *Social Security (Contributions) Regulations* 2001 (SI 2001/1004), reg. 6(2)(b), (c)

Aggregation of earnings

2630   Aggregation: employees with more than one job

If an employee or director concurrently has more than one employment, it is a fundamental principle that contributions must be calculated separately for each.

The aggregation provisions

However, regulations contain aggregation provisions which lead in prescribed circumstances to different earnings being added together before contribution liabilities are calculated. The situations envisaged by the regulations are where earnings are paid in respect of different employments:

- under the same employer;

- with employers carrying on business in association (see below);

- with employers of whom only one is deemed by regulation to be the secondary contributor; or

- with employers of whom none is the secondary contributor because some other person is deemed by regulation to be the secondary contributor.

The main exception to these rules applies where it is not reasonably practicable to aggregate the earnings.

When employers are 'associated'

Employers are associated (see above) if they are carrying on business in association, which involves sharing profits or losses, or to a large extent sharing resources such as accommodation, equipment, personnel and customers, such that their fortunes are to some extent interdependent.

Mere constitutional links between two companies (e.g. a parent/subsidiary relationship) are irrelevant for this purpose unless the companies also fulfil the above criteria.

Class 1 maximum

The maximum amount that an employee is liable to pay in Class 1 contributions is equal to 53 weeks full contributions at the main rate (12% for 2011–12 onwards), plus 2% on all earnings above this sum. Where multiple jobs are held, the primary threshold applies to each employment. There continues to be no limit for the secondary contributor.

Deferment

If an employee receives two or more salaries or wages which are not aggregated, he may be eligible for deferment of contributions in one or more jobs (see 2724ff.).

Case: *Evans* [2012] TC 01973

2632   Not contracted out in all jobs

The following table summarises NICO's guidance on aggregation as set out in CWG2, *Employer's further guide to PAYE and NICs*.

Circumstances	Treatment
One payment of earnings for separate jobs with two or more employers.	If the employers are associated, the employer who pays the earnings accounts for contributions on all earnings and completes one P11 (Deductions Working Sheet); if the employers are independent, both account separately for contributions on earnings they pay and each completes a P11.
Employees with two or more jobs with the same employer (e.g. accounts clerk on the staff payroll but also weekly paid safety officer).	The employer must add all earnings together and use the shortest earnings period to calculate liability, keeping only one P11. If it is impracticable to do this, contributions are calculated and recorded separately.

Circumstances	Treatment
Employees with two or more jobs with different employers.	The normal rules apply to each employment separately, unless the employers trade in association. In that case, only one overall liability is calculated and recorded. The employers agree how their share of contributions is to be borne. Again, the impracticability exception may apply. If one of the employers is overseas and has no UK place of business, only employee contributions are due on any earnings from that employment. If the overseas employer has a UK place of business, aggregation may be necessary if two employers trade in association).

Legislation: SSCBA 1992, s. 6(4); *Social Security (Contributions) Regulations* 2001 (SI 2001/1004), reg. 15; *Social Security (Contributions) (Amendment No. 2) Regulations* 2014 (SI 2014/572)

Other Material: CWG2, *Employer's further guide to PAYE and NICs*

2634 Mixed employment

If all the employments of an earner are contracted-out, the normal aggregation rules as set out above apply. If, on the other hand, the employments under consideration are mixed, i.e. not-contracted-out and contracted-out, the earnings must be kept separate for the purposes of calculating liability. In the case of mixed employments, the procedure that is to be followed depends on whether or not the employee has an appropriate personal pension arrangement. Further refinements apply where the earnings relate to employments with mixed occupational pension schemes, where some may be salary-related and others money purchase.

The basic rule is that contributions are calculated by adding all earnings together and establishing the earnings limits for the common or shortest earnings period to establish whether contributions are due. Priority is given to the earnings period for the contracted-out earnings, but the procedure depends on the value of the contracted-out earnings. Detail guidance is given in Booklet CWG2, *Employer's further guide to PAYE and NICs* and on CWG1, *Employer's quick guide to PAYE and NICs*.

Legislation: SSCBA 1992, s. 6(4); *Social Security (Contributions) Regulations* 2001 (SI 2001/1004), reg. 15

2636   Class 1 calculation methods

The rates for calculating Class 1 liability are described at 2602ff. and a table of rates appears at 110.

There are two methods of calculating Class 1 liabilities, the exact percentage method and the tables method. Either may be used, but only one may be used in any single tax year in respect of any single employee, unless the National Insurance Contributions Office expressly permits a change. Permission is not required for a change resulting from a switch from a manual to a computerised payroll or vice versa.

Example

For 2016–17, the employee contributions due on weekly earnings of £165.20 are, on the exact basis, £1.22. Table A gives £1.26, because it is based on earnings of £165.50.

2638   Exact percentage method

The exact percentage method is the more accurate and is generally used by payroll software. It is provided that contributions are to be calculated separately at the appropriate rate and rounded to the nearest penny. This method *must* be used in certain specified circumstances, e.g. where earnings from two employments are aggregated and one of those employments is contracted-out while the other is not (see 2632).

Example 1

Ellen is paid weekly. She has not contracted out. For a particular week in 2016–17, her earnings are £1,000.

Primary contributions are payable on earnings between the primary threshold (£155 per week) and the upper earnings limit (£827 per week) at 12%, and on the excess over the upper earnings limit at 2%. Ellen thus pays primary contributions in respect of the week's earnings of £84.10.

Her employer pays secondary contributions on all earnings in excess of the secondary threshold (£156 per week), i.e. on earnings of £844, at a rate of 13.8%. The secondary liability is thus £116.47.

Example 2

Milo is paid monthly. He has not contracted out. For a particular month in 2016–17, he earns £2,000. His earnings do not exceed the upper earnings limit (£3,532 per month) and thus he pays primary contributions on all his earnings in excess of the primary threshold (£672 per month), i.e. £1,328 (£2,000 – £672), at a rate of 12%. His primary liability for that month's earnings is thus £159.36.

His employer pays secondary contributions on all his earnings above the secondary threshold (£676 per month), i.e. on earnings of £1,324. The secondary liability is thus £182.71 (£1,324 × 13.8%).

Example 3: contracting out (tax years up to and including 2015–16)

Patricia is paid weekly. She had contracted out and joined a contracted-out salary-related (COSR) pension scheme operated by her employer. For a particular week in 2015–16, her earnings were £1,000.

Primary contributions were payable at the contracted-out rate of 10.6% on earnings between the primary threshold (£155 per week) and the upper accrual point (£770 per week), at 12% on earnings between the upper accrual point and the upper earnings limit (£815 per week), and 2% on the excess earnings above the upper earnings limit, with a rebate payable of 1.4% on earnings between the lower earnings limit (£112 per week) and the primary threshold. Patricia therefore paid primary contributions of £73.65 ((£615 (£770 − £155) × 10.6%) + (£45 (£815 − £770) × 12%) + (£185 (£1,000 − £815) × 2%) − (£43 (£155 − £112) × 1.4%)) in respect of the week's earnings.

Secondary contributions were payable at the rate of 10.4% (13.8% less the rebate of 3.4% applying to COSR schemes) on earnings between the secondary earnings threshold (£156 per week) and the upper accrual point (£770 per week) and at a rate of 13.8% on earnings above the upper accrual point, with a rebate payable of 3.4% on earnings between the lower earnings limit (£112 per week) and the secondary earnings threshold. The secondary contributions payable were thus £94.09 ((£614 (£770 − £156) × 10.4%) + (£230 (£1,000 − £770) × 13.8%) − (£44 (£156 − £112) × 3.4%)).

2640   Tables method

The alternative method is the tables method, which relies on ready-reckoner tables in booklets prepared and distributed by HMRC each time rates change. The tables are issued as part of the employee's annual pack and can also be obtained from the employer's orderline (0300 123 1074) or downloaded from the employers' orderline download page of HMRC's website.

The contribution tables are divided into sections identified by letter. HMRC generally refer to these letters in order to identify the category of Class 1 contribution payable by an earner and his employer.

Table A

Table A, which appears in Booklet CA38 and covers full-rate contributions, is used for employees who are aged 21 or over (April 2015 onwards) and under state pension age **or** employees who are on approved apprenticeship scheme and over the age of 25.

Table B

Table B, which appears in CA41, is used for married women and widows who are:

- under state pension age; and
- who are entitled to pay employee's contributions at the reduced rate (see 2646).

The employer must have a valid certificate of election (CA4139 or CF383) or a valid certificate of reduced liability (CF380A) in respect of these women.

Table C

Table C, which appears in CA41 is used for employees who are state pension age or over, for whom a copy of either their birth certificate or passport is held as evidence of their date of birth.

Table H

Table H, which appears in CA38, is used for employees who are apprentices on an approved apprenticeship scheme and under the age of 25.

Table J

Table J, which appears in CA38, is used for all employees who are aged 21 or over, for whom a form CA2700 is held allowing them to defer payment of employee contributions at the full main percentage rate.

Table M

Table M, which appears in CA38, is used for all employees who are under the age of 21.

Table Z

Table Z, which appears in CA38, is used for all employees who are under the age of 21, for whom form CA2700 is held allowing them to defer payment of employee's NICs at the full main percentage rate.

2642 Company directors

HMRC allow alternative arrangements for the assessment and payment of NICs for company directors. Liability to NICs for company directors is calculated using an annual earnings basis. However, subject to the qualifying conditions set out below, payments on account of directors' NICs may be made during the year based on the actual intervals of payment, usually weekly or monthly, in the same way as for other employees.

The calculation

The following procedure can be applied to determine the contributions payable in respect of a director's earnings each time a payment is made.

Step 1

Use an annual or pro-rata annual earnings period to calculate NICs.

Step 2

Calculate NICs on total earnings paid to the director each time that a payments of earnings is made. When performing the calculation, all the director's earnings, including fees and bonuses should be included.

Step 3

Deduct the NICs already paid in the year, if any, to arrive at the contributions now due.

The calculation can be performed using the exact percentage method (see 2638 or by adapting the tables method (see 2640) as set out on CWG1 (*Employer's quick guide to PAYE and NICs*), card 13 and described below.

Using the monthly tables, the procedure is as follows:

Step 1

Divide the total earnings by 12. This gives average monthly earnings to date.

Step 2

Look at the relevant monthly table for the average monthly earnings.

Step 3

If the average monthly earnings are less than or equal to the primary threshold, no primary contributions are due. If it is more than the primary threshold, multiply the NICs figure given in the table by 12 to give the NICs due to date.

Step 4

Deduct NICs already paid, if any. This gives the NICs now payable.

Secondary contributions are calculated in a similar fashion, but with reference to the earnings threshold.

If the weekly tables are used, the same procedure is followed, except that in step 1 the earnings are divided by 52 not 12, in step 2, the relevant weekly table rather than the relevant monthly table is used and in step 3, the NICs figure taken from the table is multiplied by 52 not 12.

The tables method can also be adapted for a pro-rata annual earnings period.

Example

Chris is appointed to the board of Teachers Ltd in week 44 of the tax year. The primary threshold and upper earnings limit are calculated by multiplying the weekly values by nine, because the earnings period starts with the week of appointment.

In 2016–17, Chris will pay NIC at the main rate of 12% on his director's earnings between £1,395 (9 × £155) and £7,443 (9 × £827) and at the additional 2% rate on all earnings above £7,443 paid up to 5 April.

Alternative method

As noted at 2558, company directors may use the alternative arrangements to make payments on account of the annual liability based on the actual payment interval, as for other employees. Where the alternative arrangements are adopted, the directors contributions are calculated as for other employees, using either the exact percentage method (see 2638) or the tables method (see 2640). However, in month 12, it is necessary to compute the contributions for the year using and annual earnings period and deduct contributions paid on account to arrive at the month 12 figure.

Legislation: *Social Security (Contributions) Regulations* 2001 (SI 2001/1004), reg. 12(1), 12(2), 12(5)

Case: *Spring Salmon & Seafood Ltd* [2014] TC 04002

2644   Class 1 age limits

Class 1 liability does not begin to arise until the employed earner in question is over the age of 16. This is apparently linked to the statutory school leaving age, but it should be noted that children who stay on at school after that age are not automatically exempted from liability in respect of any earnings from weekend or evening employment.

Under 21s

From April 2015, secondary Class 1 NICs have been abolished for under 21-year-olds not earning more than the upper earnings limit (£43,000 a year or £827 a week for 2016–17). Employer NICs are calculated as normal beyond the upper earnings limit. It applies equally to existing and new employees and does not affect the employee's entitlement to the state pension.

Apprentices under 25

From April 2016, a zero rate of secondary Class 1 NICs applies for apprentices under the age of 25 on earnings between the secondary threshold and apprentice upper secondary threshold (£43,000 a year or £827 per week for 2016–17).

Persons over pensionable age

Liability for primary (but not secondary) contributions ceases, in principle, and subject to certain exceptions, when an employed earner reaches pensionable age. The liability rule applies where a payment of earnings takes place after the relevant birthday and is made on its normal due date. SSP paid to a woman over 60 constitutes earnings, but there is no primary contribution liability. To provide employers with the certainty that an employee is of pensionable age and that there is no requirement to deduct primary contributions, NICO will issue a certificate of age exemption (form CF4140 or CF384) on application by the employee on form CF13.

It should be noted that employers remain liable for secondary contributions in respect of employees who continue to work beyond pensionable age.

Legislation: SSCBA 1992, s. 6(1), (2), 122; *Social Security (Contributions) Regulations* 2001 (SI 2001/1004), reg. 7(1)(a), 28, 29

Other material: *Abolition of employers National Insurance contributions for the under 21s* (www.tinyurl.com/q5lsaag)

2646   Married women and widows: reduced rate elections

Prior to 12 May 1977, married women and widows were able to elect to pay reduced Class 1 contributions. Similarly, if self-employed they could elect to pay no Class 2 contributions (although Class 4 contributions remained payable).

Married women and widows who had reduced liability on 12 May 1977 can keep it unless:

- in the case of a married women, the marriage ends in divorce or is annulled;

- the marriage ends because the woman is widowed and she does not qualify for widow's benefits;

- widow's benefit ends, other than on re-marriage; or

- there has been no liability to pay NICs for two consecutive tax years after 5 April 1978 and the woman was not self-employed in those tax years.

Alternatively, a woman may decide to give up the right to reduced rate liability while reduced rate contributions are payable, the woman has no right to:

- retirement pension or other contributory benefits in respect of reduced Class 1 contributions;

- home protection responsibilities;

- pay voluntary contributions; and

- credits (except in the case of widows with reduced liability).

Employers should only deduct reduced rate contributions if the woman holds a certificate of election (form CA4139 or CF383).

Legislation: *Social Security (Contributions) Regulations* 2001 (SI 2001/1004), reg. 128(1), (2), 131–133

Cases: *Whittaker v R & C Commrs* (2006) Sp C 528; *Gutteridge v R & C Commrs* (2006) Sp C 534; *Morgan v R & C Commrs* (2008) Sp C 722; *Black* [2009] TC 00033; *Register* [2010] TC 00490; *Spraggs* [2011] TC 01193; *Franks* [2012] TC 02119; *Brown* [2013] TC 02705; *Humber* [2015] TC 04386

Class 1A contributions

2650   Nature of Class 1A contributions

Class 1A contributions were introduced with effect from 6 April 1991, the charge originally applying only where an income tax benefit arises (or, but for allowable deductions, would arise) on a director or P11D employee (see 386) in respect of private use of an employer-provided car and, where appropriate, fuel. However, from 6 April 2000, the Class 1A charge is widened to include most taxable benefits in kind (unless specifically exempted from the charge by the regulations). The liability for Class 1A contributions arises only in respect of the secondary contributor (i.e. the employer); there are no primary (employee) Class 1A contributions. The charge, based on the cash equivalent value of the benefit as calculated for tax purposes, is charged at the main secondary contributor rate.

The Class 1A contribution is based on tax years and is payable once annually after the end of the relevant tax year, on the basis of the cash equivalent value of the benefits as calculated for P11D purposes (see 2752).

Legislation: SSCBA 1992, s. 10

Other Material: CWG5, *Class 1A National Insurance contributions on Benefits in Kind*; CA 33, *Class 1A National Insurance contributions on car and fuel benefits*

2660   Liability for Class 1A contributions

Class 1A contributions are payable only by secondary contributors (usually employers), whereas the income tax charge on which they are based results in a liability only for the director or employee personally.

As far as benefits in kind are concerned, liability is based on fulfilling three conditions:

(1)   An employee is chargeable to income tax under ITEPA 2003 on an amount of general earnings from an employment.

(2)   That employment is both employed earner's employment (under social security law) and employment as a director or employee (i.e. within the benefits code in ITEPA 2003, Pt. 3, Ch. 2).

(3)   The general earnings in question are not already chargeable under Class 1.

No Class 1A liability arises if any benefit arising for tax purposes is offset by a corresponding deduction, for example, if the benefit was provided for use by the employee wholly, exclusively and necessarily in the performance of the duties of his employment or in the course of qualifying business travel.

Where a benefit attracts a liability to Class 1 (see 2602) or, because it has been included in a PAYE settlement agreement, to Class 1B (see 2670), no Class 1A charge will arise.

Employers may deduct Class 1A NICs when computing their taxable profits (see 2062).

For details of information requirements made of employers in relation to Class 1A, see 2738.

Legislation: SSCBA 1992, s. 10 (as substituted by the *Child Support, Social Security and Pensions Act* 2000, s. 75)

2662 Benefits in kind

The following table, which is adapted from CWG5, *Class 1A National Insurance Contributions on Benefits in Kind* summarises the liability arising in respect of the provision of benefits in kind.

Type of expense or benefit provided	Circumstances	Class 1 NICs due (include in gross pay)	Class 1A NICs due
Assets placed at the employee's disposal	provided for business use, and private use is insignificant	No	No
	provided for mixed business and private use	No	Yes
Assets transferred to the employee but not readily convertible assets	can be turned into cash only by sale, such as furniture, kitchen appliances, property and clothes	No	Yes
Car fuel for private motoring in a company car	Any means of supply or purchase – see booklet 480 for exceptions	No	Yes
Car/van fuel for private motoring in a privately owned car/van	supplied using a company credit card or garage account or agency card and the conditions described in booklet *CWG2* apply	No[2]	Yes
	from your own fuel pump	No	Yes
	Any other circumstances	Yes	No
Car parking facilities including motorcycles	at or near place of work	No	No
	elsewhere – unless the parking is part of a journey which is qualifying business travel	No	Yes
Car parking fees paid for or reimbursed to employee	at or near place of work	No	No
	for business-related journeys	No	No
	in all other circumstances	Yes	No
Cars made available for private use	See booklet 480	No	Yes

Type of expense or benefit provided	Circumstances	Class 1 NICs due (include in gross pay)	Class 1A NICs due
Childcare help (does not include vouchers – see separate entry below) provided by employer for children up to age 16 (excluding school fees – see separate entry on school fees)	Your contract with the provider:• value up to £55 per week (£243 per month) where the qualifying conditions are met	No	No
	value over £55 per week (£243 per month) where the qualifying conditions are met	No	Yes
	any amount not meeting the conditions (see footnote 3)	No	Yes
Childcare help provided by employer for children up to age 16	You provide a nursery at the workplace (or in a facility managed and financed by you)	No	No
	You reimburse the employee or provide additional salary to meet the cost of childcare	Yes	No
Christmas boxes	in cash	Yes	No
	in goods	No	Yes
Clothing (protective) or uniforms (may have a logo) which are necessary for work	all circumstances	No	No
Clothing or uniforms which can be worn at any time	provided by you see CWG2	No	Yes
	employee contracts[4]	Yes	No
Clothing (protective) or uniforms may have a logo which are necessary for work	all circumstances	No	No
Council tax	employee provided with accommodation which is within one of the categories where the value does not have to be included for tax purposes on form P11D, see CWG2	No	No
	all other circumstances	Yes	No
Credit cards, charge cards, employee uses your card to purchase	goods or services bought on your behalf and the conditions described in booklet CWG2 apply	No	No[2]
	items for the personal use of the employee	Yes	No

Type of expense or benefit provided	Circumstances	Class 1 NICs due (include in gross pay)	Class 1A NICs due
	items relating to specific and distinct business expenses actually incurred by the employee	No	No
Employee's liability insurance	see CWG2 for conditions	No	No
Entertaining clients expenses/allowances	all circumstances	No	No
Entertaining staff expenses/allowances	employer contracts[5]	No	Yes
	employee contracts[4]	Yes	No
Expenses and benefits covered by an exemption		No	No
Expenses not covered by an exemption	specific and distinct business expenses included in the payment	No	No
	any profit element in the payment	Yes	No
Eyecare test, or corrective appliance (e.g. glasses or contact lenses)	employer makes available generally to employees for whom tests and appliances are necessary under regulations made under the *Health and Safety at Work etc. Act* 1974	No	No
Eyecare voucher to obtain test or corrective appliance (e.g. glasses or contact lenses)	employer makes available generally to employees for whom tests and appliances are necessary under regulations made under the *Health and Safety at Work etc. Act* 1974	No	No
Food, groceries, farm produce	employer contracts[5]	No	Yes
	employee contracts[4]	Yes	No
Goods, such as TV, Furniture, etc. transferred to employee	employer contracts[5]	No	Yes
	employee contracts[4]	Yes	No
Holidays	employer contracts[5]	No	Yes
	holiday vouchers	Yes	No
	employee contracts[4]	Yes	No
Incidental overnight expenses	See para. 31 of CWG5 and booklet *480* for special conditions	No	No
Income tax paid	but not deducted from employee	Yes	No

Type of expense or benefit provided	Circumstances	Class 1 NICs due (include in gross pay)	Class 1A NICs due
	on notional payments not borne by employee within 90 days of receipt of each notional payment	Yes	No
Insurance premiums for pensions, annuities, etc. on the employee's death or retirement. See *CWG2* for exceptions	employee contracts[4]	Yes	No
Living accommodation provided by you	see booklet *CWG2* for special conditions	No	No
	in all other circumstances	No	Yes
Loans, beneficial arrangements	qualifying loans	No	No
	non-qualifying loans	No	Yes
Loans written off	at time you decide not to seek repayment	Yes	No
Long service Award	conditions of s. 323, ITEPA 2003 met	No	No
	above conditions not fully met	For the treatment applicable to NICs see the instructions under 'Staff suggestions' (para. 35 CWG5), which apply similarly for long service awards	
Meal vouchers	Vouchers redeemable for meals only (all values)	No	No
Meals provided by you	at canteen open to your staff generally or on your business premises on a reasonable scale and all employees may obtain free or subsidised meals as long as the meals are not provided in connection with salary sacrifice or flexible remuneration arrangements	No	No
	in all other circumstances	No	Yes
Medical, dental, etc. treatment or insurance to cover such treatment	employer contracts[5]	No	Yes
	employee contracts[4]	Yes	No
	outside the UK where the need for treatment arises while the employee is outside the UK working for you	No	No
Mobile phones provided by you	employer contracts[7]	No	No

Type of expense or benefit provided	Circumstances	Class 1 NICs due (include in gross pay)	Class 1A NICs due
Mobile phones costs of private calls	employer contracts[5]	No	No
	employee contracts[4]	Yes	No
Mobile phone vouchers provided by you	For use by employee to obtain one mobile phone for private use	No	No
Office accommodation, supplies/services used by employee in doing his/her work		No	No
Personal bills of the employee paid by you	employee contracts[4]	Yes	No
Phones you are the subscriber	Cost of rental, unless private use is not significant	No	Yes
	Cost of calls, unless private use is not significant	No	Yes
	Cost of all private calls is reimbursed by the employee	No	No
Phones your employee is the subscriber, and you meet the costs of calls and/or rental	Phone used exclusively for business	No	No
	Phone used exclusively for private use [4]	Yes	No
	Phone used for both business and private purposes	Rental – yes on the full amount of the rental	No
		Calls – yes on the full amount of the calls, but any amount for business calls, supported by evidence, can be excluded	No
Readily convertible assets (RCAs), securities or remuneration provided in non-cash form such as shares, share options, and commodities	see *CWG2* and para. 34, *CWG5* for detailed information	Yes	No
Relocation expenses/benefits	expenses which are not exempt[8]	Yes	No
	benefits which are not exempt and exempt expenses paid after the relevant day [9]	No	Yes
	exempt expenses/benefits of £8,000 or less[9]	No	No

Type of expense or benefit provided	Circumstances	Class 1 NICs due (include in gross pay)	Class 1A NICs due
	exempt expenses/benefits in excess of £8,000[9]	No	Yes
Retirement benefit schemes either registered schemes or employer-financed schemes	payments employer makes into such schemes	No	No
Round sum allowances	specific and distinct business expense identified	No	No
	profit element	Yes	No
Scholarships awarded to students because of their parent's employment	employer contracts[5]	No	Yes
	employee contracts[4]	Yes	No
School fees	employer contracts[5]	No	Yes
	employee contracts[4]	Yes	No
Securities or an interest in securities	See Readily Convertible Assets	—	—
Shares	See Readily Convertible Assets	—	—
Shares and share options not readily convertible assets		No	No
Social functions	conditions of ITEPA 2003, s. 264 are met	No	No
	any other type of function	No	Yes
Sporting or recreational facilities provided by you, for example, fishing and horse racing	conditions of ITEPA 2003, s. 261 are satisfied	No	No
	all other circumstances	No	Yes
Subscriptions, professional and fees which are allowable tax deductions under ITEPA 2003, s. 343 and 344	any circumstances	No	No
Subscriptions, professional & fees which are **not** allowable tax deductions under ITEPA 2003, s. 343 and 344	employer contracts[5]	No	Yes
	employee contracts[4]	Yes	No
Suggestion schemes awards to employees	conditions of ITEPA 2003, s. 321 met	No	No
	above conditions not fully met	See CWG5, para. 35	
Third party benefits/ payments		See CWG5, para. 36–42	

Type of expense or benefit provided	Circumstances	Class 1 NICs due (include in gross pay)	Class 1A NICs due
Training payments for course fees, books and so on	training is work-related or encouraged or required by employer in connection with the employment	No	No
	all other circumstances and employer contracts[5]	No	Yes
	all other circumstances and employee contracts[4]	Yes	No
Vans available for commuting and other private use	Other private use is more than insignificant	No	Yes
Van fuel provided for use in vans available for commuting and other private use	Any means of supply. Other private use is more than insignificant	No	Yes [11]
Vouchers	see booklet *CWG2* for exceptions	Yes	No

Notes

[1] Not in use

[2] Where an employee purchases goods or services including car fuel on employers behalf, and employer transfers ownership of these to the employee, Class 1A NICs will be due.

[3] Not in use

[4] Contract is between the employee and the provider. The employer pays the provider or reimburses the employee. Payments to the provider should be returned on the P11D as shown. Reimbursements to the employee are subject to PAYE and do not need to be returned on the P11D. These payments are simply meeting the employees debt and are therefore liable for Class 1 NICs.

[5] Contract is between you, the employer and the provider of the benefit.

[6] Specific and distinct business expenses may feature in a number of payments employers make to employees and should be recorded in the appropriate P11D section.

[7] There is no limit to the number of mobile phones that may be provided NICs free solely for business use and on which private use is not significant. Only one mobile phone per employee may be provided NICs free for private use. No mobile phone may be provided NICs free to a member of an employee's family or household. See *Employment Income Manual* EIM21778.

[8] Expenses which are not exempt are any expenses not included in the list of booklet 480 (2016). The employer will need to return on the P11D any amounts that the employee should have paid, but that the employer paid instead.

[9] Details of what constitutes exempt expenses and benefits are described in booklet 480 (2016).

[10] Round sum allowances may feature in a number of payments employers make to employees and should be recorded in the appropriate P11D section.

[11] Class 1A NICs are not due if the van:

- is available to the employee for business travel and commuting;
- is not used for any other private purpose except to an insignificant extent; and
- is available to the employee mainly for use for the employee's business travel.

The *Income Tax (Earnings and Pensions) Act* 2003, s. 320C provides an exemption from income tax of up to £500 per employee per tax year, where an employer funds recommended medical treatment, subject to certain conditions (see 293). Such payments are also exempt for NIC purposes from 1 January 2015.

Legislation: *Social Security (Contributions) (Amendment No. 6) Regulations* 2014 (SI 2014/3228)

2663 Cars

A car provided by reason of employment to a director or an employee (or for tax years up to 2015–16, employees earning at the rate of at least £8,500 p.a.), which is available for private use, attracts a Class 1A liability, as does the provision of any fuel for private use in such cars. There are special rules for Class 1A NICs for cars provided in unusual circumstances.

Detailed guidance on the Class 1A liability arising in respect of company cars and car fuel is given in HMRC booklet CA33, *Class 1A National Insurance contributions on car and fuel benefits*, available from the employer's orderline (0300 123 1074) or to download from the HMRC website.

In *Southern Aerial (Communications) Ltd*, Mr and Mrs Jones had structured their business so that their cars were provided by their partnership but via a recharge of costs from their company. The FTT held that the cars were provided by the company and, accordingly, by reason of the directors' employment and were, therefore, subject to Class 1A NICs.

More than one employment

A person may have two or more concurrent but independent employments: e.g. working four days per week for company C and one day per week for company D. If both C and D make available a company car *and* pay earnings, both have a Class 1A liability if the employee is a P11D employee (see 403). However, if C were to pay earnings but not provide a company car, while D paid no earnings whatsoever but made available a company car for private use, neither would have a Class 1A liability, provided it could be shown that the car was not made available by D by reason of the employment with C, and that the payment of salary by C was unconnected with the employment by D. However, it should be noted that a payment of £1 of earnings by D would make D liable to Class 1A contributions.

The key questions in identifying the person liable to pay the Class 1A contribution are:

- to which job does the provision of the car relate?
- who uses the car?
- who made the last payment of earnings to that person in the tax year in question?
- who was liable to pay the secondary Class 1 contribution on those earnings (or who would have been liable had they exceeded the primary threshold: see 2602)?

Where a person holds two or more employments and is provided with one car by virtue of both employments, whether under the same employer or different employers, the Class 1A charge is shared equally between the employers involved. It is irrelevant that the employee may cover 10,000 business miles on behalf of the first employer and only 5,000 on behalf of the second.

Shared cars

A shared car can be:

(1) a car made available for concurrent use by two or more employees by reason of their employment and available for use by both; or

(2) a car which is made available for private use to one employee by reason of two or more employed earners' employments with the same or different employers.

For (1), a Class 1A NIC liability arises in respect of each employee. For (2), each employment attracts a Class 1A NIC liability. If the two employments are with the same employer, the calculation will need to take into account any differences in the employee's conditions of employment in the separate employments.

Pooled cars

There is no tax charge on the benefit of a car if it is a pooled car used only for business purposes. Similarly, there is no liability to Class 1A NICs for that car or for fuel supplied for that car. There may however, be a liability for Class 1 NICs if a lump sum or mileage allowance is paid.

Legislation: *Social Security (Contributions) Regulations* 2001 (SI 2001/1004), reg. 34, 36

Cases: *Yum Yum Ltd* [2010] TC 00616; *Southern Aerial (Communications) Ltd* [2015] TC 04692

2664 Fuel provided for private purposes: Class 1A

Where in any tax year fuel is provided for private use by a director or employee, for Class 1A purposes, the amount of any cash equivalent taxable on the employee (see Key Data) is added to the cash equivalent of the benefit of the car. The contribution is calculated by applying the Class 1A percentage (see 2666) for the year of provision of the benefit to the total of the two figures.

If the full cost of private fuel is reimbursed by the employee, no Class 1A NICs are payable.

If the employer simply pays a round sum allowance which bears no relation to the actual expense incurred by the employee, the allowance should be included in gross pay and subjected to Class 1 contributions in the same way as a payment of wages or salary. In such a case, the employer does not provide free fuel for private motoring: the employee purchases the fuel personally out of net income. There is, accordingly, no liability to Class 1A contributions in respect of that employee.

Similarly, there is no question of a Class 1A liability arising in respect of fuel provided for private motoring in an employee's own car or in a van, lorry, etc. irrespective of the owner of the vehicle.

In *Southern Aerial (Communications) Ltd*, Mr and Mrs Jones has structured their business so that their cars were provided by their partnership. Although the FTT held that a car benefit arose (see 2663), as the fuel costs were paid for by the Jones through their partnership, there was no 'benefit' in economic terms and as this was an overriding requirement in ITEPA 2003, Pt. 3, there could be no fuel benefit within ITEPA 2003, s. 149.

Legislation: SSCBA 1992, s. 10

Case: *Southern Aerial (Communications) Ltd* [2015] TC 04692

2666 Calculating the Class 1A charge

Class 1A NICs are payable at a single rate applied to the cash equivalent of the benefit as calculated for income tax purposes. The single rate applicable is known as the Class 1A percentage and is equal to the main secondary contributor rate for Class 1 purposes (for a table of rates, see 110).

No reduction of the rate applies where the employment is contracted-out, or a reduced rate of Class 1 contribution applies for some other reason (e.g. where a married woman or widow pays at the reduced rate, or where the foreign-going rebate applies to a mariner's earnings).

Example 1

George's employer provides private medical insurance cover for George and his family. The contract is between the employer and the insurance company. For 2016–17, the cash equivalent of the benefit as calculated for income tax purposes is £900. A liability to Class 1A National Insurance arises in respect of the provision of the benefit. The liability, payable by the employer only, is £124.20 (£900 × 13.8%).

It should be noted, however, that if the contract had been between the employee and the insurer, and the employer had either made the payment on the employee's behalf or reimbursed the employee, the liability would have been to Class 1 rather than to Class 1A.

Example 2

Ruby is provided with a car by reason of her employment. The car is available for her private use throughout the tax year 2016–17.

The cash equivalent value of the benefit as calculated for income tax purposes (see 402) is £4,500. Class 1A contributions payable by Ruby's employer are £621 (£4,500 × 13.8%).

Example 3

Nigel is provided with fuel for private use in a company car provided by his employer. The fuel benefit for income tax purposes for 2016–17 is £2,592. Class 1A contributions payable by Nigel's employer are thus £357.70 (£2,592 × 13.8%).

Legislation: SSCBA 1992, s. 10

Class 1B contributions

2670 Nature of Class 1B contributions

PAYE settlement agreements (PSAs) allow employers to account for any NIC tax liability in respect of their employees on payments that are minor or irregular, or that are shared benefits on which it would be impractical to determine individual liability, in one lump sum (see 2356). Where an employer has a PSA with HMRC, he will be liable to Class 1B contributions (at the secondary rate – see 110) on the amount of the emoluments in the agreement that are chargeable to Class 1 or 1A contributions, together with the total amount of income tax payable under the agreement.

When Class 1B was introduced, ministers were concerned to ensure that the transfer of earnings out of Class 1 did not result in any loss of benefit entitlement for the workers concerned.

If the use of a PAYE settlement agreement (PSA) means that earnings drop below the LEL, it is possible that an employee could lose entitlement to SMP, SAP, SPP or SSP. Employers are required in such circumstances to recalculate earnings to include amounts in the PSA in respect of that employee. Where an amount is in the PSA because it is difficult to identify the recipients of the benefit, this will clearly be almost impossible to achieve. However, if the amount increases earnings to a level at which benefits become payable, the employee is treated as qualifying.

Example

Anna is a part-time barmaid. She earns £94 per week but the landlord also pays for a taxi home each night at a cost of £20 per week. He has several staff in this position and accounts for the tax through a PSA. Ignoring the PSA, Anna's earnings fall below the LEL so she would not qualify for SSP when she is unable to work through sickness. However, the landlord must include the amount paid for her taxis in assessing her average earnings for SSP, SMP and SAP purposes.

Legislation: SSA 1998, s. 53; *Social Security Act 1998 (Commencement No. 4) Regulations* 1999 (SI 1999/526)

Other Material: *PAYE settlement agreements*

2672 Calculating Class 1B contributions

Class 1B contributions are calculated on the value of the items included with the PAYE settlement agreement (PSA) that would otherwise have attracted a liability for Class 1 or 1A NICs and the total tax payable under the PSA. The Class 1B contributions due are at the secondary rate (see 110).

Example

Sunshine Ltd has a PSA in force for 2016–17. Tax payable under the agreement is £15,000. Included within the PSA are items to the value of £12,000 that would normally attract a Class 1 liability and items to the value of £30,000 that would normally attract a Class 1A liability.

The Class 1B liability is calculated as follows:

	£
Value of items that would normally attract a Class 1 liability	12,000
Add: value of items that would normally attract a Class 1A liability	30,000
Add: tax payable under the PSA	15,000
Value on which Class 1B contributions payable	57,000

Class 1B contributions payable are thus £7,866 (£57,000 × 13.8%).

Class 2 contributions

2676   Nature of Class 2 contributions

Class 2 contributions are payable at a flat weekly rate by every 'self-employed earner' (see 2512 and 2522) over the age of 16 and under pensionable age for any week during which he or she is such an earner. Special rates apply to share fishermen and volunteer development workers (see 2678). For a table of rates of Class 2 contributions, see Key Data.

A self-employed person who does not earn any income in any particular week (e.g. due to holidays) does not thereby cease to be self-employed, but a person who is not ordinarily self-employed will have no Class 2 liability provided his earnings from self-employment do not exceed an annual amount (see 2682).

For the methods of paying Class 2 contributions, see 2754.

At Spring Budget 2015, the Government announced its intention to abolish Class 2 NICs in the current Parliament. In December 2015, a consultation on abolishing Class 2 NICs and introducing a contributory benefit test into Class 4 NICs was opened and which closed for comment on 24 February 2016. The consultation is available at www. gov.uk/government/consultations/consultation-on-abolishing-class-2-national-insurance-and-introducing-a-contributory-benefit-test-to-class-4-national-insurance-for-the-self-employed. At Budget 2016, the Government confirmed that Class 2 NICs will be abolished from April 2018 (NICs Bill).

Legislation: SSCBA 1992, s. 1(2); *Social Security (Contributions) (Re-rating and National Insurance Funds Payments) Order* 2015 (SI 2015/588)

Other Material: CWL 1, *Starting your own business*; CF 10, *Self-employed people with small earnings*

2678   Calculation of Class 2 contributions

From 2015–16 onwards, the self-employed report their liability for Class 2 NICs through self assessment. Those that report profits below the small profits threshold (SPT), £5,965 for 2016–17, are not liable for Class 2 NICs, although they can pay voluntarily to protect their entitlement to contributory benefits. 'Profits' has the same meaning as applies for Class 4 NICs. The 'small profits threshold' replaced the 'small earnings exception' (see 2679) from 6 April 2015. This threshold is uprated by CPI.

Class 2 contributions are payable at a flat weekly rate.

A week is treated as falling wholly within the year in which it begins. In the past, if payment of Class 2 contributions was made at regular weekly intervals, it was possible in some years that 53 weekly contributions would be paid, since each year consists of 52 weeks and one or, in leap years, two days. If a year has 53 contribution weeks, this will be reflected in the NIC bills.

Class 2 and benefit claims

A Class 2 contribution paid will count towards the benefit entitlement of the individual concerned, but the benefits covered do not include contribution-based jobseeker's allowance or the earnings-related component of the state pension scheme (see 2530).

Share fishermen and volunteer development workers

Notwithstanding the above, regulations have been made to allow share fishermen and certain volunteer development workers to qualify for contribution-based jobseeker's allowance on the basis of Class 2 contributions payable at special rates (see 110 for a table of rates).

Residence conditions for Class 2 liability

No person is liable or entitled to pay contributions of any class unless he fulfils prescribed conditions of residence or presence in Great Britain (see 2802). Before a person may become liable to pay Class 2 contributions in respect of any particular week, he must be ordinarily resident (see 2806) in the UK or, if he is not so ordinarily resident, he must have been resident in the UK for at least 26 out of the preceding 52 contribution weeks. Before entitlement to pay a Class 2 contribution can arise for a self-employed earner, the earner in question must have been present in the UK in the week in respect of which the contribution is to be paid.

Legislation: SSCBA 1992, s. 11(1); *Social Security (Contributions) (Re-rating and National Insurance Funds Payments) Order* 2015 (SI 2015/588); *Social Security (Contributions) (Re-rating) Consequential Amendment Regulations* 2014 (SI 2014/634); *Social Security (Contributions) Regulations* 2001 (SI 2001/1004), reg. 125(c), 145(1)(c), (d), 149, 150

Other Material: *Share fisherman: Income Tax and National Insurance contributions*: www.gov.uk/share-fisherman-income-tax-and-national-insurance-contributions; *Share fisherman: tax budgeting scheme*: www.gov.uk/share-fisherman-tax-budgeting-scheme

2680 Incapacity: automatic exception from Class 2 liability

Automatic exception from Class 2 liability is granted to a self-employed earner for a week where certain conditions are fulfilled, though he may, if he wishes, pay the contribution, subject to certain restrictions, if he so wishes. Exception is mandatory in respect of a contribution week where the earner is:

- in receipt of sickness benefit, invalidity benefit or incapacity benefit in respect of the whole week;

- incapable of work throughout the whole week;

- in receipt of maternity allowance;

- detained in legal custody or imprisoned during the whole week; or

- in receipt of unemployability supplement or invalid care allowance.

Those provisions which refer to a whole contribution week mean a week which excludes Sunday or some other day which is excluded on religious grounds from the working week.

Legislation: *Social Security (Contributions) Regulations* 2001 (SI 2001/1004), reg. 43

2682 Small earnings exception from Class 2 liability – prior to 6 April 2015

Prior to 2015–16, a self-employed person could, on application and subject to conditions, be excepted from an otherwise unavoidable Class 2 liability for any period in which his earnings from self-employment were (or were treated as being) less than a specified amount. See Key Data for a table of specified amounts.

Approval of claim for small earnings exception

If the National Insurance Contributions Office (NICO) approved the application, it issued a certificate of exception, CF17, which stated the period of coverage, normally a tax year, or a period ending on 5 April if application was not made before the start of a tax year. The earner had to produce the certificate to any official on request.

If any of the conditions for the granting of exception were not, or ceased to be, fulfilled (e.g. the earner ceases to be a self-employed earner), the certificate became invalid at that time and the earner was required to notify NICO of the fact, which was achieved by completing a declaration on the certificate and returning it to NICO. Similarly, the earner was required to notify NICO in writing (in practice also by completing a declaration on the certificate itself) if he wished the certificate to be cancelled for whatever reason and the certificate ceased to have effect from a date specified by NICO.

Certificates could be renewed if the conditions of issue were still fulfilled and, indeed, NICO prompted any earner in possession of a certificate by forwarding a copy of booklet CA02 shortly before the old certificate expired. Certificates could cover three years from issue.

The granting of exception and the consequent non-payment of contributions could prejudice the earner's future benefit entitlement, which depends on the individual's contribution record.

Earnings for the purpose of small earnings exception

The key criterion for the availability of exception was the level of earnings. Earnings, in the context of the self-employed earner, meant net earnings from employment as a self-employed earner, which was officially interpreted as meaning profits calculated according to normal commercial accountancy principles such as would be shown in a profit and loss account, time apportioned to the relevant tax year. Total net earnings were to be arrived at by deducting from income business expenses incurred in the course of the self-employed activity, e.g. rent and rates, insurance, employees' wages, printing and stationery, repairs and postage. Furthermore, official guidance stated that the earner should make an allowance for depreciation of equipment such as a vehicle, if it was used for the business, and any stock taken for the earner's own use was to be taken into account as income. However, the guidance made it clear that no deduction was available in respect of income tax or Class 2 or Class 4 contribution liabilities.

Earnings from all sources as a self-employed earner had to be aggregated in arriving at a total to compare with the exception limit.

In looking at the likely level of earnings, NICO usually accepted the evidence of an income tax assessment, or the accounts for a period not yet agreed with the Revenue, or if neither was available, any evidence which the earner had to support his application, such as a record of business receipts and expenditure for the year.

Earnings which suffered Class 1 contributions, but were included in business profits (e.g. for sub-postmasters) could be excluded from the calculation of profit for the purposes of the small earnings exception.

Retrospective exception

Claims for retrospection may be made, in writing and with supporting evidence. Any application for exception must be made between 6 April following the end of the tax year and the following 31 December. As earnings are officially defined as profits as shown in the accounts for the year in question and expects those profits to be calculated on an actual basis (i.e. time-apportioned if the accounting year does not end on 5 April), many self-employed earners whose accounting year ends other than on 5 April find it impossible to make an application for a certificate. It is understood that local offices have been instructed to accept any reasonable evidence of profits in the period from the accounting year end to the following 5 April.

A retrospective claim may involve the contributor repaying benefits already claimed on the basis of those contributions. The repayment automatically excepts the earner from liability for the period covered by the repayment if the earner is not already excepted, and NICO must issue the appropriate certificate to that effect.

Legislation: SSCBA 1992, s. 11(4); *Social Security (Contributions) (Re-rating and National Insurance Funds Payments) Order* 2015 (SI 2015/588); *Social Security (Contributions) Regulations* 2001 (SI 2001/1004), reg. 44(4)–(6), 45(2), 46

2684 Married women and widows: Class 2

There is no separate rate or type of Class 2 contributions payable by married women or widows. However, where such earners are entitled by virtue of a reduced rate election made before 12 May 1977 (see 2646) not to participate in the NIC scheme, it is currently possible for them to elect not to pay Class 2 contributions.

Legislation: SSCBA 1992, s. 19(4); *Social Security (Contributions) Regulations* 2001 (SI 2001/1004), reg. 127(1)(b)

Class 3 contributions

2690 Nature of Class 3 (voluntary) contributions

Class 3 contributions are voluntary contributions. A person is never *liable* to pay Class 3 contributions, but he may be entitled to pay, to protect entitlement to widows' benefits and the basic retirement pension (see 2530). In certain limited cases involving overseas employment, voluntary Class 2 contributions may be paid as an alternative to Class 3 in order to protect entitlement to incapacity benefit and maternity allowance on the employee's return to the UK.

Class 3 contributions are flat-rate contributions. See 110 for a table of the rates applying.

Legislation: SSCBA 1992, s. 13(1), 14(1); *Social Security (Contributions) (Re-rating and National Insurance Funds Payments) Order* 2015 (SI 2015/588); *Social Security (Additional Class 3 National Insurance Contributions) (Amendment) Regulations* 2009 (SI 2009/659); *Social Security (Contributions) (Amendment No. 2) Regulations* 2008 (SI 2008/607); *Social Security (Contributions) Regulations* 2001 (SI 2001/1004), reg. 49, 126–139, 145

Other Material: CA5603, *To pay voluntary National Insurance contributions*

2692 Eligibility for Class 3 (voluntary) contributions

Class 3 contributions may be made by men and women under state pension age who satisfy the following conditions in respect of any tax year:

- the person is resident in the UK throughout the year;

- the person has arrived in the UK during the year and has been or is liable to pay Class 1 or Class 2 contributions in respect of an earlier period during that year;

- the person has arrived in the UK during the year and was either ordinarily resident (see 2806) in the UK throughout the year or became ordinarily resident during the course of it; and

- the person not being ordinarily resident in the UK has arrived during the year or the previous year and has been continuously present in the UK for 26 complete contribution weeks, entitlement where the arrival has been in the previous year arising only in respect of the next year.

No Class 3 contributions may be paid in respect of a contribution year if the individual has in any case satisfied certain contribution conditions by reference to Class 1 or Class 2.

Married women and widows with certificates of reduced liability following an election before 12 May 1977 (see 2646) (or under transitional provisions) cannot pay Class 3 contributions.

Case: *McPherson* [2014] TC 03456

Legislation: SSCBA 1992, s. 13(1), 14(1); *Social Security (Contributions) Regulations* 2001 (SI 2001/1004), reg. 49, 126–139, 145(1)(e)

2694   Is payment worthwhile?

The value of voluntary contributions will depend on a contributor's personal circumstances and attitude to investment return and risk.

With the basic state pension worth £115.95 per week in 2015–16 and pro-rata reductions for years with inadequate contribution records, the arithmetic for a single person should be fairly straightforward on one level.

The number of qualifying years required to qualify for a full basic state pension depends on age and whether the recipient is a man or a woman. Men born before 6 April 1945 usually need 44 qualifying years. Women born before 6 April 1950 usually need 39 qualifying years. Men born on or after 6 April 1945 need 30 qualifying years. Women born on or after 6 April 1950 need 30 qualifying years.

The Government's website (www.gov.uk) provides comprehensive information on pension planning and forecasting.

Case: *Clements v R & C Commrs* (2008) Sp C 677

Class 3A contributions

2696   Class 3A contributions liability

From October 2015, a new class of voluntary NICs (Class 3A) gives those who reach state pension age before 6 April 2016 (the date of the introduction of the single-tier pension) an opportunity to boost their Additional State Pension.

Legislation: *Pensions Act* 2014, s. 25 and Sch. 15; SSCBA 1992, s. 14A; *Social Security Class 3A Contributions (Units of Additional Pension) Regulations* 2014 (SI 2014/3240); *Social Security Class 3A Contributions (Amendment) Regulations* 2014 (SI 2014/2746)

Class 4 contributions

2700   Class 4 contributions liability

Class 4 contributions are profit-related and are payable by self-employed earners in addition to any Class 2 contribution liability (see 2676ff.). The Class 4 contribution liability arises in respect of tax years and is based on the earner's annual profits or gains immediately derived from the carrying on or exercise of one or more trades, professions or vocations, being profits or gains chargeable to tax under ITTOIA 2005 for the year of assessment corresponding to the tax year. Class 4 contributions do not count towards benefit entitlement (see 2530) but are nevertheless income of the National Insurance Fund used for the payment of benefits (see 2504).

At Spring Budget 2015, the Government announced its intention to reform Class 4 NICs to include a contributory benefit test. In December 2015, a consultation on abolishing Class 2 NICs and introducing a contributory benefit test into Class 4 NICs was opened and which closes for comment on 24 February 2016. The consultation is available at www.gov.uk/government/consultations/consultation-on-abolishing-class-2-national-insurance-and-introducing-a-contributory-benefit-test-to-class-4-national-insurance-for-the-self-employed.

Legislation: SSCBA 1992, s. 15(1)

Other Material: CWL 1, *Starting your own business*

2702 Exceptions from Class 4

The following categories of person may, on application, be excepted from Class 4 contributions:

- men aged 65 or over and women aged 60 or over at the beginning of the tax year (including people whose 60th/65th birthday falls on 6 April). However, a person reaching 60th/65th during the tax year is liable for Class 4 contributions up to the following 5 April;

- those who are non-resident in the UK for tax purposes during the tax year;

- in some cases, a trustee, executor or administrator;

- a diver or diving supervisor working in connection with exploration or exploitation activities on the UK continental shelf or in the UK territorial waters and whose earnings are taxed under ITTOIA 2005. (Such divers pay Class 1 contributions.)

HMRC consider that sleeping and inactive limited partners are (and have in the past been) liable to pay Class 2 NICs as self-employed earners and Class 4 NICs in respect of their taxable profits. 'Inactive limited partners' are limited partners who take no active part in running the business. This is a change of view from that previously held by HMRC and the Department for Work and Pensions (DWP). Sleeping or inactive limited partners who have not paid Class 2 or Class 4 NICs for a past period will not be required by HMRC to pay those contributions. In relation to the payment of Class 2 NICs from 6 April 2013, sleeping and inactive limited partners must check their Class 2 NICs position and those who are not already paying Class 2 NICs as a result of being self employed must advise HMRC of their self-employed status and arrange to pay NICs or seek exception/deferment, etc. according to their individual circumstances.

From April 2015, regulations specify that inactive members of limited liability partnerships (LLPs) will be liable to pay Class 2 NICs in the same way as sleeping partners and inactive limited partners.

It should be noted that exception is not automatic and must be applied for. The certificate should be requested before the start of the year to which it relates, but the National Insurance Contributions Office may accept a later application.

Legislation: SSCBA 1992, s. 1(6), 2(1)(b) and Sch. 2, para. 5; *Social Security (Contributions) Regulations* 2001 (SI 2001/1004), reg. 91(b), 92, 94, 97(5), 98; *Social Security Contributions (Limited Liability Partnership) (Amendment) Regulations* 2015 (SI 2015/607)

2706　Earnings for Class 4 purposes

The profits to which the specified percentage rate for Class 4 NICs is applied are closely related to the taxable profits.

The 'earnings' for Class 4 contributions purposes are defined as the profits or gains immediately derived from the carrying on of one or more trades, professions or vocations, being profits or gains chargeable to income tax under ITTOIA 2005 (for the income tax charge, see 550ff.). Furthermore, the charge is based on the full amount of such profits or gains, subject to deductions for allowances for capital expenditure (whether given by way of deduction from trading profits or by discharge or repayment of tax) available in respect of the activities of the trade, profession or vocation and to additions for any balancing charges arising. There is some relief for losses (see 2708).

'Immediately derived'

The term 'immediately derived' means that a contributor will not be liable to pay Class 4 contributions on profits or gains in the earning of which he was not personally involved. This covers the position of a sleeping partner, who is in reality no more than an investor in the business, supplying capital but taking no active part in the running of the business. Payment of a share of profits to a retired partner who provides no services, and the income of non-working Names at Lloyd's should also be covered by this rule.

Application of income tax basis of assessment

The basis of assessment adopted for income tax – including, before the introduction of self-assessment, opening and closing year rules – automatically applies for contribution purposes. It is also possible that the profits liable to Class 4 contributions will be affected by the use of the rule which allows farmers to average their year-on-year profits or by a change of accounting date, which allow HMRC to adjust the trading profits for more than one year.

Inapplicable income tax rules

Although, in principle, Class 4 contributions are levied on the taxable profits or gains from a trade, etc., it is important to distinguish those rules which apply for tax purposes but do not apply for Class 4 contribution purposes. The following are not deductible for Class 4 purposes:

- any personal allowance (see 1850ff.);

- deductions for personal pension premiums or retirement annuity premiums, etc.;

- interest paid in any tax year which falls under ITA 2007, s. 383 (see 1884);

- where a business charge exceeds available income in a year and an assessment has been raised on the person who paid the charge to collect the tax which he deducted at source in making the payment, such that the surplus is carried forward against the profits of a later year from the same trade as if it were a trading loss (though relief may be given differently: see 2710); and

- relief for excess interest payments laid out wholly and exclusively for the purposes of a trade, etc. by means of treating the excess as a loss available for carry-forward or carry-back under the terminal loss provisions (though relief may be given differently: see 2710).

The concessionary relief for self-employed doctors and dentists to qualify for relief in respect of contributions to the NHS superannuation scheme does not extend to Class 4 contributions, a special commissioner has held.

Partnerships

Partnerships present potential difficulties in the context of Class 4 contributions and specific provision is made in respect of the earnings of partners. Where a trade or profession is carried on by two or more persons jointly, the liability of any one of them in respect of Class 4 contributions is based on his share of the profits or gains of that trade or profession (bearing in mind that such profits must be immediately derived from that trade or profession) together with his share of the profits or gains of any other trade, etc. which he carries on. For 2014–15 onwards, new regulations provided for the deferment of the Class 4 NICs charge in respect of such profits and the imposition of the charge when those profits subsequently vest in individual partners. Deferment of Class 4 contributions is no longer possible (from 2015–16).

Legislation: SSCBA 1992, s. 15(1), Sch. 2; SI 2014/3196

Case: *Maher v IR Commrs* (1997) Sp C 111

2708 Loss relief

For the purposes of calculating the amount of profits or gains in respect of which Class 4 contributions are payable, relief is available under, and in the manner provided by, a number of provisions of the Taxes Acts, including the extension of offset to capital allowances:

- the set-off of trading losses against general income (see 2110; though relief is restricted for Class 4 contribution liability to losses arising from activities, the profits or gains of which would be brought into computation for the purposes of Class 4 contributions);

- the carry-forward of losses from trading not utilised under the aforementioned rules against future profits from the same trade (see 2107); and

- terminal loss relief (see 2122).

The rules of Class 4 loss relief are extended beyond certain of the restrictions imposed by income tax law. Where losses are carried forward for income tax purposes, they reduce profits from the same trade in a later period, thereby automatically reducing Class 4 profits in that same period. Similarly, where the terminal loss provisions apply, the relief is restricted for income tax purposes to a reduction in taxable profits from the same trade, which has retrospective effect on the assessment for the tax year affected and, again, automatically reduces the Class 4 profits for that year.

Where a trading loss is relieved by a claim to set it off against income other than that derived from a trade, for income tax purposes, the trading profits of other years would be unaffected and there would, in the absence of special provision, be no reduction in Class 4 contribution liabilities. Where a person claims and is allowed relief in respect of a loss in any relevant trade, profession or vocation against total income, rather than against the profits of the same trade, the deduction granted is to be treated as far as possible as reducing the profits or gains for that year of any relevant trade, profession or vocation.

Any excess of loss in that year is carried forward to reduce the first available profits or gains for later years, again from any relevant trade, etc., irrespective of whether a claim for a current year loss exists in those years.

Whether a trading loss is time-apportioned to tax years on the statutory basis or is claimed in full in the year in which the period-end falls on the concessionary basis, any amount which is set against non-trading income must be separately identified and claimed against other trading income in the same or a later year for Class 4 contribution purposes.

Legislation: SSCBA 1992, Sch. 2, para. 3

2710 Interest and annuity payments

Profits for Class 4 contribution purposes may be reduced by certain payments of interest for which income tax relief is, or can be, given (see 1884ff.). The deduction is available in the year in which payment is made to the extent that such interest has been paid and incurred wholly or exclusively for the purposes of any relevant trade, profession or vocation. Where the profits or gains of the tax year of payment are insufficient to allow relief in full, the payments are carried forward and deducted from, or set off against, the first available profits or gains of any subsequent year:

- It is irrelevant that the payment of interest may not be deductible for income tax purposes in that later year. The fact that the interest was incurred in respect of a relevant trade, profession or vocation is sufficient to create a deduction, which is carried forward until it has been fully utilised against profits.

- The deduction need not be given against the later income from the *same* trade, profession or vocation, since the Act refers to deduction from the profits or gains of any relevant trade, etc.

- Relief is not lost if the trade in which the loss arose ceases, provided there are earnings at some later point from some relevant trade, etc., since relief is carried forward without limit until it can be deducted.

Relief is also granted on the same basis as that applied to interest in respect of annuities (e.g. to retired partners) and other annual payments made under deduction of tax and wholly or exclusively for the purposes of the business.

Legislation: SSCBA 1992, Sch. 2, para. 3(5)

2712 Calculation of Class 4 liability

The calculation of liability to Class 4 contributions is based on limits and rates amended annually by statutory instrument, applied to a profit figure based closely, but not exactly, on that arrived at by applying the rules of ITTOIA 2005 income tax. Contributions are payable at a prescribed rate on so much of the relevant profits or gains as exceeds a specified lower annual limit. For a table of rates and limits, see 110.

Contributions are payable on earnings between the lower and upper limits and there is an extra 2% (1% prior to 6 April 2011) contribution on profits above the upper limit. Both the lower and upper limits for Class 4 purposes apply on an annual basis and are not time-apportioned if the trade is not carried on for a full year.

Example 1

Peter has earnings as calculated for Class 4 purposes of £18,000 in 2016–17. He is liable to pay Class 4 contributions on so much of his earnings as exceed the lower profit limit of £8,060 (i.e. £9,940 (£18,000 – £8,060)) at a rate of 9%. His Class 4 liability for 2016–17 is thus £894.60.

Example 2

Jerry has earnings as computed for Class 4 purposes of £47,000 in 2016–17. He is liable to pay Class 4 contributions in respect of those earnings falling between the lower and upper earnings limits, i.e. £34,940 (£43,000 – £8,060) at 9%, and at the rate of 2% of those earnings exceeding the upper earnings limit, i.e. £4,000 (£47,000 – £43,000). His Class 4 liability for 2016–17 is thus £3,224.60.

Legislation: SSCBA 1992, s. 15(3); SSAA 1992, s. 141(1), 143(1), (3), (4)(b)

2714   Deferment and annual maximum

For tax years up to 2014–15, where the National Insurance Contributions Office was satisfied that there is doubt as to the extent, if any, of an earner's liability to pay Class 4 contributions for a particular tax year (e.g. because of Class 1 liabilities), a certificate of deferment could be issued which deferred the collection of the Class 4 liability until a later date. It is no longer possible to defer Class 4 contributions (from 2015–16). From 2015–16 onwards, a repayment of Class 4 NICs must be claimed.

2716   Special Class 4 contributions

An examiner, moderator, invigilator, etc. (employed other than through the agency of another) who would normally be an employed earner is treated as a self-employed earner (see 2522). Such a person is liable to pay a 'special Class 4 contribution' where, in any tax year:

- he has earnings (disregarding the amount) which would otherwise be Class 1 earnings;

- the earnings are taxable (but not necessarily taxed) under ITEPA 2003; and

- his total earnings exceed a lower annual limit (which is in practice usually set at the same level as the limit for ordinary Class 4 purposes: see 2700).

The special contribution is calculated using the same basis as ordinary Class 4 contributions (see 2712) applied to the earnings calculated as if they were Class 1 earnings and rounded down to the nearest pound.

Although such special contributions resemble ordinary Class 4 contributions, they are collected directly by the National Insurance Contributions Office (NICO) (see 2500). NICO notifies the earner of the amount of special contributions due for any year and payment is due within 28 days from the receipt of the notice, unless a question is raised under the procedure outlined at 2770.

The employer of the contributor must record the earnings, category letter and the contributor's National Insurance number (which the contributor must disclose) on the deductions working sheet.

Legislation: SSCBA 1992, s. 18(1)(c); *Social Security (Contributions) Regulations* 2001 (SI 2001/1004), reg. 103–106

Interaction of NIC classes and annual maxima

2720   Need for NIC interaction rules

An individual can be liable to pay contributions in any year of Class 1, 2 and 4, e.g. because he has a job and also a part-time self-employed activity. He may also make voluntary contributions if necessary to make the year a qualifying year for benefit purposes. The rate of payment of each contribution is calculated initially without reference to any other class payable.

2722   Annual maximum amounts

Historically, the National Insurance system has worked on annual maximum amounts so that no employee ever paid more than the overall contribution limit based on the upper earnings limit. Legislation, which came into force on 6 April 2003, mimics this principle, but also provides for a charge of 2% (1% prior to 6 April 2011) on all earnings without limit.

The maximum contributions payable is now therefore a maximum with respect to a certain amount of earnings rather than an absolute maximum.

The maximum amount anyone is liable to pay in Class 1 contributions is equal to 53 weeks full contributions at the main rate of 12%, plus 2% on all earnings above this sum. However, where multiple jobs are held a primary weekly threshold will apply to each.

Legislation: *Social Security (Contributions) (Amendment) Regulations* 2003 (SI 2003/193); *Social Security (Contributions) (Amendment) Regulations* 2012 (SI 2012/573)

National Insurance: Deferment

2724   Class 1 deferment

Employees with more than one employment, who anticipate earning in excess of the upper earnings limit (UEL) in one, or in a number of employments, may apply to the National Insurance Contributions Office (NICO) for deferment of some of their contributions liability. Where permission is obtained, the employee will pay a reduced main employee rate of 2% on all earnings from the earnings threshold to the UEL and the additional employee rate of 2% on all earnings above the UEL in the deferred employments.

Where deferment is obtained, form CA2700 will be sent to the employers concerned authorising them to deduct primary NICs at a rate of 2% on all earnings above the earnings threshold. Employer's contributions will remain payable at the full standard rate.

Where there is a choice, standard rate employee Class 1 contribution liability will always be deferred, rather than contracted-out liability.

Any application for deferment should be made before the beginning of the tax year for which it is sought. An application form for deferment is contained within leaflet CA 72A, *Deferring employee Class 1 National Insurance contributions (NICs).*

Any employee Class 1 contributions which should have been paid but which, as a result of deferment, have not been paid, will be collected by direct assessment of the employed earner.

Example

Margaret has three non-executive directorships, with three independent companies: A, B and C generating income of £15,000, £16,000 and £17,000 per year respectively. She will have Class 1 earnings of £48,000, which is well above the UEL, but she will be unable to apply for deferment as she will only reach up to £33,000 of income from any two of the directorships (deferment will not be available if the annual maximum can only be reached by aggregating all contributions in all jobs). She will be obliged to pay full contributions in all jobs and make a refund claim after the year end.

She is then offered a further directorship by company D with a fee of £13,000. Taking the earnings from A, B and D together, Margaret will have total earnings above the UEL, so HMRC should grant deferment for the employment with C. Margaret will still have to apply for a refund if her total contributions exceed the annual maximum, after taking into account the fact that she will have been given the benefit of three primary thresholds when paying contributions via A, B and D.

Example

A company had an employee who advised that she was over 60 years old. The company asked her for an age exemption certificate, but she was unable to produce it, nor any other proof of her age. The payroll officer therefore used letter A to calculate her NIC liability. After a couple of months she left and she was given a form P45. However, the ex-employee later produced an exemption certificate and asked for a refund of her National Insurance payments. Is the company required to make the refund?

This will depend on whether or not the certificate was received in the same tax year as the payments. If the company received the certificate by 5 April, then it must repay the employee's contributions and adjust its monthly payments and year-end returns to account for the refund. If the certificate was received after 5 April, the company can make no adjustments and it is up to the employee to make an application to HMRC for a direct refund.

Legislation: SSCBA 1992, s. 19(1), (2); *Social Security (Contributions) Regulations* 2001 (SI 2001/1004), reg. 84, 85

Other Material: CA72A, *Deferring employee Class 1 National Insurance contributions (NICs)*

2726 Repayment

Where an individual has overpaid contributions, the order of repayment is:

(1) Class 4, both ordinary and special (see 2700 and 2716);

(2) primary Class 1 at married women's rate;

(3) Class 2;

(4) primary Class 1 at standard not contracted-out rate; and

(5) primary Class 1 at contracted-out rate.

However, this order is changed if the contributor concerned has a contracted-out personal pension plan or stakeholder personal pension plan, such that the order of the fourth and fifth items is reversed.

Legislation: *Social Security (Contributions) (Amendment No. 3) Regulations* 2010 (SI 2010/646); *Social Security (Contributions) Regulations* 2001 (SI 2001/1004), reg. 52(2), 100(1), 110(1)

Administration and payment of NICs

National Insurance returns and records

2736 Class 1 returns

Monthly recording

An employer must keep a P11 deductions working sheet (or computer equivalent) for each employee and record on it various information about the employee and the payments made.

Year-end reporting

Almost all employers are required to use Real Time Information (RTI). Broadly, under RTI, PAYE information is transmitted to HMRC by the employer every time an employee is paid. Under RTI, employers are no longer required to provide information to HMRC using forms P35 and P14 after the end of the tax year.

As stated above, under RTI, employers do not need to send an end-of-year return (P35s, P14s and P38As) to HMRC. Employers are however, required to provide each employee with a form P60 if the employee is in his employment on the last day of the year.

The contents of the P60 in relation to contributions for the year in question are specified in regulations.

Legislation: *Social Security (Contributions) (Amendment No. 4) Regulations* 2013 (SI 2013/2301)

Disclosure of NIC schemes

Certain NIC arrangements must be notified to HMRC. Broadly, the provisions for NICs correspond to the disclosure of information requirements for income tax purposes (see 12421).

Legislation: *Social Security Administration Act* 1992, s. 132A; *Social Security (Contributions) (Amendment) Regulations* 2014 (SI 2014/608); *National Insurance Contributions (Application of Part 7 of the Finance Act 2004) (Amendment) Regulations* 2013 (SI 2013/2600); *Social Security (Contributions) (Amendment No. 4) Regulations* 2010 (SI 2010/721); *Social Security (Contributions) (Amendment No. 4) Regulations* 2009 (SI 2009/2028); *National Insurance Contributions (Application of Part 7 of the Finance Act 2004) Regulations* 2007 (SI 2007/785); *Social Security (Contributions) Regulations* 2001 (SI 2001/1004), Sch. 4, para. 6; Sch. 4, para. 22; *Income Tax (Employments) Regulations* 1993 (SI 1993/744), reg. 43(1)

Other Material: *Disclosure of National Insurance Avoidance Schemes* (www.hmrc.gov.uk/aiu/avoidance-scheme.pdf)

2738 Class 1A information requirements

The employer will need to know the cash equivalent value of benefits provided, as calculated for income tax purposes and returned on forms P11D, to enable him to calculate the Class 1A liability (see 2650ff.).

Form P11D(b) is the statutory Class 1A return. It is due to HMRC no later than 6 July after the end of the tax year. The form contains boxes for the calculation of Class 1A NICs due and any adjustments which may be necessary to the total benefits figure shown as liable to Class 1A on the P11D.

As far as company cars are concerned, there is an onus of proof on the employer, as the contribution is his liability.

Legislation: SSCBA 1992, s. 10

Other Material: CWG5, *Class 1A National Insurance Contributions on Benefits in Kind*; www.gov.uk/government/publications/cwg5-class-1a-national-insurance-contributions-on-benefits-in-kind

2740 Class 1B reporting requirements

To calculate the amount of Class 1B contributions due in respect of a PAYE settlement agreement (PSA), records will need to be kept of:

- the overall cost of providing the benefits in question;

- the number of employees who received them;
- an indication of what rate of tax they pay;
- an indication which benefits and expenses give rise to a Class 1 or Class 1A liability; and
- the total tax payable under the PSA.

Other Material: *PAYE settlement agreements*

2742   Class 2 reporting requirements

From 6 April 2015, the principal reporting requirement relating to Class 2 contributions is the requirement to notify HMRC immediately, in writing or electronically, of the commencement or cessation of self-employment. Prior to 6 April 2015, it was the requirement to notify HMRC of the commencement or cessation of liability to Class 2 contributions.

For defaults prior to 6 April 2015, a penalty could be imposed for failing to notify HMRC when Class 2 NICs became payable.

Persons who have not previously notified NICO of their self-employment should complete and return to NICO CWF1.

Legislation: *Social Security (Contributions) Regulations* 2001 (SI 2001/1004), reg. 87, 88; *Social Security (Contributions) (Amendment No. 3) Regulations* 2009 (SI 2009/600)

2744   Class 3 reporting requirements

Since Class 3 contributions are voluntary contributions, there are no reporting requirements.

2746   Class 4 reporting requirements

Income tax information reporting requirements apply to anyone who is liable for Class 4 contributions (see 2200ff.).

Payment and collection of NICs

2750   Class 1 payment and collection

The secondary contributor (usually the employer: see 2602), as well as being liable for his own contributions, is liable, in the first instance, for the employee's primary contributions, on behalf of and to the exclusion of the earner. Any primary contributions paid by the secondary contributor are deemed to have been paid by the earner. However, the secondary contributor may recover the primary contributions by deduction from the earnings paid to the employed earner and in no other way, subject to conditions laid down by regulations.

Where earnings are subject to the aggregation rules, the secondary contributor may deduct primary contributions from any part or parts of those earnings.

When an employer makes an error in good faith which results in the under-deduction of primary contributions when earnings are paid, he is given a limited right to recoup that under-deduction from later payments of earnings within the same tax year. The maximum supplementary amount which may be deducted in each later period is an amount equal to the primary contributions otherwise due in respect of that later payment of earnings. Correction of past errors may not cross tax year-ends.

Employment allowance

From April 2014, the employment allowance is available and will potentially cut every employer's NIC payments by allowing businesses and charities to offset up to £3,000 for 2016–17 (£2,000 previously) against their employer PAYE NIC liabilities. To keep the process as simple as possible for employers, the employment allowance is delivered through standard payroll software and HMRC's Real Time Information (RTI) system. To claim the allowance, the employer will have to signify his intention to claim by completing the yes/no indicator just once. The employer will then offset the allowance against each monthly Class 1 secondary NICs payment that is due to be made to HMRC until the allowance is fully claimed or the tax year ends. For example, if employer Class 1 NICs are £1,200 each month, in April, the employment allowance used will be £1,200, £1,200 in May, and £600 in June, as the maximum is capped at £3,000. The following tax year, the allowance will be available as an offset against a Class 1 secondary NICs liability as it arises during the tax year.

From 6 April 2015, the employment allowance was extended to individuals who employ care and support workers.

From April 2016, companies where the director is the sole employee will no longer be able to claim the employment allowance (NICA 2014, s. 2(4A)).

The employment allowance applies per employer, regardless of how many PAYE schemes that employer chooses to operate, so each employer can only claim for one allowance. It is up to the employer which PAYE scheme to claim it against.

Legislation: *National Insurance Contributions Act* 2014; *Employment Allowance (Care and Support Workers) Regulations* 2015 (SI 2015/578)

Other Material: Employment Allowance: www.gov.uk/employment-allowance

Collection of Class 1 contributions with PAYE

The secondary contributor (i.e. usually the employer) is to pay, account for and recover Class 1 contributions in the same way as he pays, accounts for and recovers income tax deducted from emoluments under PAYE.

Payment of Class 1 contributions

Remittances of contributions, net of SSP and SMP recoveries, are generally made each month at the same time as any PAYE is remitted to the collector (i.e. within 14 days of the end of the tax period). Small employers can remit quarterly on or before 19 July, 19 October, 19 January and 19 April in respect of deductions in the quarter ended on the preceding fifth of the month. To qualify for this system, employers' average monthly remittances in the current year in respect of total deductions of PAYE, NICs and tax under the construction industry tax deduction scheme have to be less than £1,500. Quarterly payment may be chosen where the employer has reasonable grounds for believing that the £1,500 per month condition is met, or in the case of an employee who receives a fixed salary or wage, where the inspector of taxes has issued a week 1 or month 1 PAYE code.

Payment by cheque is treated as made on the day on which the cheque is received by the collector.

Legislation: SSCBA 1992, Sch. 1, para. 3, 6(1); *Social Security (Contributions) (Amendment No. 3) Regulations* 2012 (SI 2012/821); *Social Security (Contributions) (Amendment No. 4) Regulations* 2010 (SI 2010/721); *Social Security (Contributions) Regulations* 2001 (SI 2001/1004), reg. 67, 70, 86 and Sch. 4, para. 6–7, 10–11, 27–29

2752   Class 1A payment and collection

Class 1A contributions are payable by the secondary contributor to his or her PAYE reference at the Accounts Office by 19 July following the end of the tax year. Where payment is made other than by direct debit, a special Class 1A pay slip should be used.

Other Material: CA33, *Class 1A National Insurance contributions on car and fuel benefits*; CWG5, *Class 1A National Insurance Contributions on Benefits in Kind*

2754 Class 2 payment and collection

For 2015–16 onwards, the collection of Class 2 NICs is through self assessment, so that it can be collected alongside Class 4 NICs. Payments on account do not apply to Class 2 NICs, therefore full payment is to be made by the 31 January following the end of the relevant tax year, although regular monthly or weekly payments can be made in advance if preferred with the use of a Budget Payment Plan.

To ensure that people qualified to claim maternity allowance are not adversely affected by Class 2 NICs not being paid until the 31 January following the end of the relevant tax year from 2015–16, where a person who is either liable or entitled to pay Class 2 NICs, they can pay before the end of the tax year, even though liability to pay will not be established until the person's self assessment tax return is completed.

Deduction at source

Deduction of contributions at source from certain state benefits is sometimes possible. The benefits in point include war disablement pension.

Late payment

In *Hinton*, the FTT found that Mr Hinton was not entitled to make late payment of Class 2 or Class 3 NICs because his failure to pay was due to his ignorance or error caused by his failure to exercise due care and diligence.

Legislation: SSCBA 1992, Sch. 1, para. 10; *Social Security (Crediting and Treatment of Contributions, and National Insurance Numbers) (Amendment) Regulations* 2013 (SI 2013/3165); *Social Security (Contributions) Regulations* 2001 (SI 2001/1004), reg. 63A, 89, 90; *Social Security (Crediting and Treatment of Contributions, and National Insurance Number) Regulations* 2001 (SI 2001/769), reg. 10

Case: *Hinton* [2016] TC 04796

2756 Class 3 payment and collection

Since Class 3 contributions are voluntary contributions, there are less strict requirements for payment. The options are the quarterly bill or monthly direct debit, or single annual cheque.

Payment of Class 3 contributions is normally due on or before 5 April following the tax year in which the deficiency occurred, though six years may be allowed.

Late payment

In *Hinton*, the FTT found that Mr Hinton was not entitled to make late payment of Class 2 or Class 3 NICs because his failure to pay was due to his ignorance or error caused by his failure to exercise due care and diligence.

Legislation: *Social Security (Contributions) Regulations* 2001 (SI 2001/1004), reg. 89, 90(1)

Cases: *Hinton* [2016] TC 04796

Other Material: CA5603, *To pay voluntary National Insurance contributions*

2758   Class 4 payment and collection

Most Class 4 contributions are self-assessed in the same way as tax and collected by HMRC, together with income tax. Subject to specific exceptions, provisions as to assessment (see 2000ff.), collection (see 2381ff.), repayment (see 2371 and 2592), recovery (see 2400ff.) and penalties apply as they do to income tax.

Appeals

The appeals system applicable to income tax assessments now also extends to Class 4 contributions assessments, though the provisions of income tax law have no effect on determinations of questions arising in relation to certificates of exception or deferment, or in relation to special Class 4 contributions.

Partnership assessments

Where two or more persons are carrying on business in partnership, the assessment to both tax and NICs will usually be made as a joint assessment in the name of the partnership, though it is possible for each partner to be assessed separately.

HMRC will accept a spreadsheet from either the nominated partner or registered agent to register ten or more partners for self-assessment and National Insurance, preventing the need to complete individual forms SA401 and SA402 for each partner in the partnership. There are however strict rules for the format of the schedules and failure to adhere to the rules will result in the application being rejected and returned.

Construction industry tax deduction scheme

Deductions of income tax at source under the construction industry tax deduction scheme (see 2387) may exceed the subcontractor's final liability to income tax for a year (e.g. because of interest on borrowings or personal allowances). In such circumstances, the excess may be set off by HMRC against the subcontractor's liability for Class 4 contributions, up to the total of that liability for that year.

Legislation: SSCBA 1992, s. 15(2), 16(1), Sch. 2, para. 4(2), 8

2760 Repayment of Class 4 contributions

Excessive Class 4 contributions paid may be reallocated by the National Insurance Contributions Office as being on account of other contributions properly payable by the earner but they are otherwise repayable, provided they exceed the true liability by at least £0.50. The repayment must be claimed in the approved manner within:

(1) six years beginning with 6 April in the tax year following that in respect of which the payment was made where the application is in respect of any tax year ending before 6 April 1996;

(2) five years beginning with 1 February in the tax year following that in respect of which the payment was made where the application is in respect of any tax year beginning after 5 April 1996; or

(3) if later than (1) or (2), two years beginning with 6 April in the tax year following that in which the payment was made. The calculation is unaffected by a reduced rate election, even though no Class 2 contributions would in fact be payable.

Refunds of Class 4 contributions are not made automatically where they are due and a claim must be made by the taxpayer or his agent.

For the circumstances in which repayments will be made to subcontractors before the end of the tax year, see 2387.

Repayment supplement

Repayment supplement has applied to refunds of Class 4 contributions since 19 April 1993 at the same rate as applies to income tax refunds (see 2371).

Legislation: SSCBA 1992, Sch. 2, para. 6(1); SS(CP)A 1992, Sch. 4, para. 8; *Social Security (Contributions) Regulations* 2001 (SI 2001/1004), reg. 101–103

2762 Compliance checks

In recent years, significant changes have been made to the HMRC management of compliance checks across most taxes including income tax, capital gains tax, VAT, PAYE, the construction industry scheme and corporation tax. See 234 for commentary on the compliance regime.

NIC enforcement, penalties and interest

2770 Enforcement

A unified penalty regime now applies for errors in returns in relation to all the main taxes, including National Insurance contributions (see 11005).

Since 1 April 2009, HMRC have had powers to specify the records to be kept by particular types of business. In addition, HMRC have issued additional non-statutory guidance on the types of records that businesses are expected to maintain to satisfy the statutory requirements. Such powers apply equally to NICs as they do to the other main taxes (see 11400).

Legislation: *Social Security (Contributions) (Amendment No. 3) Regulations* 2014 (SI 2014/1016)

Case: *Williams* [2012] TC 01988

2780 NIC penalties

For many years, there were no penalties associated with NICs, other than those imposed by magistrates' or Crown Courts in the few cases where the DSS or Contributions Agency brought criminal proceedings against serious defaulters.

However, the Contributions Regulations were then amended to bring Class 1 returns into the penalty regime of TMA 1970, s. 98A. They were amended again from 6 April 2008 to incorporate the new tax-geared penalties for errors and inaccuracies set out in *Finance Act* 2007, Sch. 24, and once again under *Finance Act* 2009, s. 106 and Sch. 55 to update and harmonise the penalties for failure to make a return, although these latter provisions did not commence for PAYE and NIC until 6 October 2014 for existing employers with 50 or more employees and until 6 March 2015 for existing employers with fewer than 50 employees and new employers. Legislation in *Finance Act* 2013, s. 230 and Sch. 50 sets out a new model for late filing penalties for real time information (RTI). *Finance Act* 2009, s. 106 and Sch. 56 penalty or surcharge regime for late payment of PAYE and NICs, commenced on 6 April 2010, is almost a proxy for late payment interest and is discussed above.

This means, in effect, that there are, and still will be in future, automatic penalties for late and incorrect returns on the same basis as for PAYE.

Historically, late Class 1 annual returns attracted a penalty of £100 per 50 employees (or part) per month (or part) for the first 12 months of delay (e.g. if a return covering 51 employees arrived 32 days late, the penalty was £400). There were no penalties in 2013–14 for late FPS or EPS returns under RTI.

From 6 October 2014, for existing employers with 50 or more employees and from 6 March 2015 for existing employers with fewer than 50 employees and new employers, new *Finance Act* 2009, Sch. 55, para. 6B–6D as inserted by *Finance Act* 2013, Sch. 50, para. 6 introduce in-year penalties for an employer who fails to submit a monthly RTI return on or before the filing date as required by the legislation. Although in February 2015, HMRC announced that employers will not incur penalties for delays of up to three days. The three-day easement continues to apply for the 2016–17 tax year (as confirmed by HMRC in June 2016).

An employer will first be alerted to potential in-year penalties for late filing by Generic Notification Service (GNS) messages and then penalty notices will be sent by post each quarter at the end of July, October, January and April to show the penalty amount HMRC calculate as due for any filing failures during that quarter. Penalty notices can be appealed against if the employer thinks the notice is incorrect or there is a reasonable excuse for the failure. HMRC advise that the quickest way to do this is online by selecting the 'Appeal a Penalty' link from the employer's PAYE online account, but appeals can equally be made in writing. There will be no penalty for the first failure to submit a monthly return in any year and there is a maximum of one penalty per month even if more RTI returns are required and/or missed in one single month. HMRC will not issue a penalty to a new RTI employer if their first Full Payment Submission (FPS) is received within 30 days of making the first payment to their employee(s), but after that normal penalty rules apply. The penalty exception for the first filing failure in a year is disapplied in two instances:

(1) For RTI employers who at 6 October 2014 had less than 50 employees or new RTI employers (an employer issued with an employer's PAYE reference after 6 October 2014) for the period from 6 March 2015 to 5 April 2015. Therefore, if such an employer does not make a return on or before making the last relevant payment in the tax year 2014–15, he will be liable to a late filing penalty.

(2) For any tax year for which a RTI employer operates an annual PAYE scheme. Therefore, if such an employer fails to make the return in respect of that scheme or it is made late, he will be liable to a late filing penalty in respect of that return.

The amount of penalty is to be calculated according to the number of persons in the PAYE scheme so that employers with multiple schemes could be liable for more than one penalty per month. Where there are one to nine employees, the monthly filing penalty is £100, for 10–49 employees it is £200, for 50–249 employees it is £300, and for 250 or more employees, it is £400.

There will be penalties imposed under regulations for 'extended failures' (i.e. failures to file an RTI return which continue for longer than three months) and in these cases, HMRC may decide whether to impose a penalty for each default in the tax year or a global penalty but must give a warning notification to the employer before any penalty for extended failure may be issued. In either case, there will be a tax-geared penalty of 5% of the total tax and NIC liability. The HMRC Compliance Handbook advises that such penalties will only be charged in the most serious cases or where there have been persistent failures to file RTI returns.

A penalty of £500 for a late return for 2009–10 submitted by Hok Ltd was cancelled by the First-tier Tribunal as disproportionate in the circumstances. The company had only one employee during the year and had submitted a P45 when he left, which it regarded as sufficient notification to HMRC of the amounts that it had paid during the year. The Upper Tribunal reversed this decision as HMRC have acted within the statutory provisions. The Upper Tribunal ruled that the First-tier Tribunal have acted in excess of its jurisdiction by discharging the penalties on the grounds of fairness.

Prior to 2014–15, if any return was still outstanding after 12 months, the penalty was tax- and NIC-geared, up to 100% of the amount unpaid at the normal 19 April due date (which might, of course, have been nil if the contributions were paid on time but the returns were delayed).

The late filing penalty does not duplicate the PAYE late-filing penalty: only £100 per month is charged per 50 employees to cover both deductions.

Incorrect Class 1 returns made fraudulently or negligently (which effectively covers all incorrect returns) for years to 5 April 2008 may also be subject to a penalty of up to 100% of the NIC underpaid. Any such penalty is mitigable in the normal way, with discounts for disclosure, cooperation and size/gravity and it is sometimes possible to argue that the employer had a reasonable excuse for the failure.

Note that, although the Class 1 return will usually be part of the year-end PAYE reporting, the penalty may only be imposed once, rather than separately, for tax and NIC.

Cases: *Hok Ltd* [2011] TC 01286; *R & C Commrs v Hok Ltd* [2012] BTC 1,711

Legislation: *Social Security (Contributions) Regulations* 2001 (SI 2001/1004), Sch. 4, para. 22(7); *Finance Act 2009, Schedule 55 (Penalties for failure to make returns) (Appointed Days and Consequential Provision) Order* 2014 (SI 2013/2395); *Income Tax (Pay As You Earn) (Amendment No. 3) Regulations* 2014 (SI 2014/2396)

National Insurance: Foreign element

2800   Territorial scope of NICs and benefits

For the employee working overseas, it is important to know whether, if he is involved in an industrial accident while carrying out overseas duties, he is covered on repatriation to the UK or hospitalisation overseas for industrial injuries and invalidity benefits. By the same token, the responsible employer will wish to ensure that such cover is maintained. The employee who spends much of his working life overseas, but nevertheless intends throughout to retire to the UK, will wish to ensure that his retirement pension cover is being adequately maintained during his absence abroad.

For both employer and employee, it is obviously also very important to know how much continued social security cover is going to cost. For example:

- Is it necessary for the payment of Class 1 contributions to continue when an employee is sent to work overseas?

- Is there a liability to social security contributions or equivalent taxes in the host state?

- If overseas contributions are payable, what relief (if any) is available against UK liability? After all, income and corporation tax law provide for unilateral relief to prevent double taxation, so why should social security law be different?

- Are there any options as to the amount of cover which may be purchased?

Other important questions to consider are:

- Are there any steps which may be taken to mitigate liability, either in the host state or in the UK, or in both?

- If such steps are taken, what is the effect on benefit entitlement for the employees involved?

Given the wide range of types of social security provision around the world, it is critically important for an employer to be able to establish before posting an employee exactly how much will be payable in contributions and how much could potentially be received by his employees in benefits, both in the UK and overseas.

For these purposes, it is convenient to divide the nations of the world into three groups which match the three broad sets of rules which may apply to situations involving international movements of staff. These groups are, in suggested order of importance to UK employers:

- EEA member states;

- states with which the UK has concluded a reciprocal agreement on social security; and

- the rest of the world.

On 1 May 2010, rules were introduced for people moving around the European Union to work. European Union Regulation 883/2004 (amended by Regulation 988/2009) and Implementing Regulation 987/2009 co-ordinate all the social security systems of the member states. They change some of the UK's National Insurance contributions rules for people moving around the EEA and their employers. The rules largely replace similar Regulations 1408/71 and 574/72.

The rules were extended to Switzerland from 1 April 2012 and to Norway, Iceland and Liechtenstein from 1 June 2012. Prior to this, the UK continued to apply the existing rules in Regulation 1408/71 to these countries.

Legislation: *Recovery of Social Security Contributions Due in Other Member States Regulations* 2010 (SI 2010/926)

Other Material: Tax if you leave the UK to live abroad: www.gov.uk/tax-right-retire-abroad-return-to-uk

2802 National Insurance: cross-border implications generally

An understanding of the basic rules of the UK system as they apply in connection with most countries is fundamental. However, there are reliefs available under EEA provisions and reciprocal agreements (see 2544 and 2810).

Provision is made for exempting from paying UK contributions those persons who could make no call on the state for benefit.

An employed earner (i.e. potentially subject to Class 1 liability) is anyone who is gainfully employed *in Great Britain* (equivalent provisions apply in Northern Ireland) either under a contract of service, or in an office (including elective office) with emoluments chargeable to tax under the charge on employment income provisions of ITEPA 2003 (see 2506). However, no person is liable or entitled to pay contributions of any class on earnings of any kind unless he fulfils prescribed conditions of *residence* or *presence* in Great Britain. This applies to both employers and employees.

Anyone who falls to be categorised as an employed earner by reason of being gainfully employed in Great Britain is liable for employee Class 1 contributions in respect of the earnings from his employment if, at the time of his employment, he is:

- resident in Great Britain;

- present (or but for any temporary absence would be present) in Great Britain; or

- ordinarily resident in Great Britain (see 2814).

A person is employed in Great Britain if he works in Great Britain, irrespective of where he signed or otherwise entered into his contract of employment.

Legislation: SSCBA 1992, s. 1(6); *Social Security (Contributions) Regulations* 2001 (SI 2001/1004), reg. 145, 146

2804 Persons sent from abroad to work in the UK

Under the rule in 2802, an employee who visits the UK in the course of his employment potentially faces a contribution liability, however short the visit. Overseas directors of UK companies may, in certain cases, escape liability in respect of short visits, despite the fact that the board meets in the UK. Contributions may be avoided simply by ensuring that they fail to fulfil the specified conditions as to residence and presence. The directors in question are those UK company directors who are not ordinarily UK-resident.

The official view is as follows:

'At present, when a director is neither resident nor ordinarily resident in the United Kingdom, the Contributions Agency does not seek payment of Class 1 National Insurance contributions for employment in the United Kingdom as a director if;

(1) the only work they do in the UK is to attend board meetings; *and*

(2) either

    (a) they attend no more than 10 board meetings in a tax year, none of which lasts more than two days *or*

    (b) there is only one board meeting in a tax year and that meeting does not last more than two weeks.'

The rule may be automatically overridden by EEA regulations where they apply (e.g. where a French non-executive director attends four one-day quarterly board meetings of a UK company in the UK) or a reciprocal agreement applies.

Where an *employee* is not ordinarily resident (see 2814) in the UK, no Class 1 liability arises until a continuous period of 52 weeks of residence has elapsed beginning with the contribution week following the date of last entry into the UK. The conditions are that the employee:

• is not ordinarily employed in Great Britain; and

• the employment is mainly employment outside the UK by an employer whose place of business is outside the UK (whether or not he also has a place of business in the UK).

A 'place of business' is officially regarded as being any place from which a person can, as of right, conduct his business, or from which his agent has power to conduct business on his behalf. The premises of a UK subsidiary of an overseas parent company are not automatically a place of business of that parent. An employer who has no presence or place of business in the UK has no secondary Class 1 liability at any time, even when the initial period of 52 weeks has expired and the employee has become liable to primary contributions.

From 6 April 1994, a secondary liability has been imposed on UK host employers to which employees are seconded by overseas businesses with no UK presence, unless they are protected by treaty provisions.

Example

A Japanese employer seconds a member of staff to its UK subsidiary without his becoming an employee of the UK company. The UK subsidiary is responsible for secondary contributions in respect of the earnings of the employee, though only after the employee has lived in the UK for 52 continuous weeks.

2806 Persons sent from the UK to work abroad

Where a UK employer sends an employee to work overseas, UK Class 1 liability does not automatically cease immediately. Contributions continue to be due for 52 weeks on all of the employee's earnings from the employment if:

• the employer has a place of business in Great Britain (see 2804);

• the earner is ordinarily resident in Great Britain; and

• immediately before starting the employment abroad the employee was resident in Great Britain.

Ordinary residence

Official guidance is that a person is ordinarily resident in a particular country if he:

- normally lives there, apart from temporary or occasional absences; *and*

- has a settled and regular mode of life there.

It is also stated that a person may be ordinarily resident in:

- a place from which he is temporarily absent; *or*

- in some circumstances, two places at once.

Some of the factors which are considered in deciding whether a person is ordinarily resident in Great Britain are listed as follows:

Factor	Indication that you are
You return to the UK from time to time during the period of employment abroad.	Continued ordinary residence. The more frequent or the longer the returns, the stronger the indication that you are.
Visits to your family who have remained at your home in GB, or holidays spent at your home in GB.	Ordinarily resident.
Visits in connection with the overseas work, e.g. for briefing or training or to make a report.	Not such a strong indication that you are.
Partner and/or children are with you during your overseas employment.	Not ordinarily resident especially if you do not retain a home in GB or only make occasional visits to GB.
You maintain a home in GB during your absence.	Ordinarily resident.
Your home in GB is available for your use on your return.	Ordinarily resident, but if your house has been rented on a long let it is not a strong indication of ordinary residence.
You have lived in GB for a substantial period.	The longer the period, the stronger the indication that you are despite the period of employment abroad.
You will return to GB at the end of your employment abroad.	The earlier the return, the stronger the indication that you are.

Postings to associated companies

Where the person sent overseas is placed under contract to an overseas company, UK liability ceases at once, except on earnings paid under any continuing UK contract. Whether the UK contract ceases will depend on a number of factors:

- which company has the right to control the employee's work while he is overseas;

- which company has the right to suspend or dismiss the employee;

- whether the UK company is able to recall the employee at any time; and

- which company funds the employee's earnings.

Regard may also be had to continued membership of the employer's UK pension scheme, though this is not a decisive factor.

If an employee sent overseas in continuation of a UK employment and covered by the 52-week rule is transferred to another offshore posting with the same employer within the 52-week period, the Class 1 liability ceases, because the condition that the employee must be UK-resident immediately before starting the employment abroad (see above) is no longer fulfilled.

From 6 April 2010, NIC credits may be provided for the accompanying spouse or civil partner of a member of HM forces who is on an assignment outside the UK.

Legislation: *Social Security (Credits) (Amendment) Regulations* 2010 (SI 2010/385)

Cases: *Garland* [2011] TC 01135; *Garland v R & C Commrs* [2013] BTC 1,765; *McPherson* [2014] TC 03456; *Garland* [2015] TC 04594; *Edwards* [2016] TC 04933

Other Material: Tax if you leave the UK to live abroad: www.gov.uk/tax-right-retire-abroad-return-to-uk

2808 EEA regulations: National Insurance

General UK cross-border National Insurance rules (see 2802) may automatically be overridden in the case of EEA nationals transferred between member states, as they are subject to regulations on social security for migrant workers. These regulations have direct effect in all member states. The European Economic Area came into being on 1 January 1994, extending EU regulations on social security for migrant workers to the then EFTA countries which acceded to the EEA agreement (see below). For transfers before that date between the UK and non-EU states, the existing reciprocal agreements apply. The remaining notes below relate to transfers between EU/EEA states from 1 January 1994.

Employers must be aware that the definition of the territory of each state within the EEA may not be exactly as expected. For example, the UK excludes the Isle of Man and the Channel Islands, but includes Gibraltar. France includes its overseas departments but excludes Monaco, while Spain includes the Canary and Balearic Islands and two territories in North Africa, but excludes Andorra.

The reciprocal agreements on social security between the UK and Iceland, Norway, Sweden, Finland and Austria (these last three becoming members of the EU in any case on 1 January 1995) were superseded on 1 January 1994 by the EU regulations as a result of the European Economic Area Treaty. Liechtenstein also became a member of the EEA upon ratification, but it will not become party to the social security arrangements for some time, as it must first disentangle itself from the Swiss economy. Switzerland, the only EFTA country to vote against ratification of the EEA Treaty, will remain covered by a reciprocal agreement with the UK.

The regulations apply only to EU/EEA nationals, and each member state defines its nationals in its own terms. Some Channel Islanders and Manxmen with links to the UK are deemed to be EU nationals, but they are only affected by the EU regulations when moving between member states, not when moving to and from their home islands.

From 1 June 2012 EC Regulations 883/2004 and 987/2009 apply to Norway, Iceland and Liechtenstein. The new rules replace very similar Regulations 1408/71 and 574/72. Under both the old rules and the new rules, depending upon the circumstances of employment, it may be that an individual continues to pay UK NICs whilst abroad, or that they have to start paying contributions to the country they are in instead.

From 28 June 2012, new EU Regulation 465/2012 introduced a new 'Home Base' rule to EU Regulation 883/2004 for determining which member state aircrew and their employers will pay social security contributions to.

The basic premise of EEA law is that a worker pays social security contributions in the state in which he works. However, there are exceptions for temporary duties in other member states.

Short-term postings

Where an EU/EEA national employed in the UK by an undertaking to which he is normally attached is sent by the employer to work in, e.g. Germany, he may remain in the UK contribution scheme if:

- the period of employment in Germany is expected to be less than 12 months; and

- he is not being sent to replace another person whose tour of duty has ended.

This rule applies to any short-term secondment of an EU/EEA national between two member states. As a result of Decision 128 of the EU Administrative Commission on Social Security for Migrant Workers, it may even apply to staff recruited in one state for immediate posting to a second member state, provided the posting employer normally operates at least part of his business in the home state.

The competent authority in the state in which the transfer originates will issue a standard certificate (E101) which proves to the host country authorities that no contributions need be deducted there.

Where a person is recruited by a UK company in, for example Spain, for work in that country, the short-term secondment rule cannot apply and Spanish contributions will be due from the outset.

Similarly, where a person is transferred to another EU/EEA member state to work there for more than 12 months, liability will arise in the host state (unless the extension of postings or longer postings rules, below, apply) from the outset.

Extension of postings

The initial period of 12 months may be extended with the agreement of the host country's authorities by up to 12 further months provided that the extension beyond 12 months was genuinely a result of unexpected circumstances. The further certificate is the E102. Application is made by completing the E102 in quadruplicate and submitting it to the authorities.

Longer postings

In certain exceptional cases, it is possible to obtain the agreement of the authorities to an extension of an E101 certificate for up to five years or, even more exceptionally, longer. No time limit is specified, but a maximum of five years has become a de facto standard. The conditions are laid down in Decision 16 of the EU Administrative Commission on Social Security for Migrant Workers:

- the employee must have special knowledge or skills not available in the local labour market;
- the employer must have specific objectives in the other member state with which the employee is familiar;
- remaining in the home scheme is in the employee's best interests.

The individual's explicit consent is required before an extension may be issued.

The contractual link between posting employer and posted employee must be maintained throughout the secondment period, as specified in Decision 128.

Construction workers

Self-employed British construction workers are only eligible for E101 certificates (see above) if they have been self-employed in the UK for the majority of the 24 months before the E101 application.

Concurrent work in different member states

A person who is concurrently employed in two member states is subject to the legislation of the state in which he is habitually resident, if he carries out some of his duties there or he is attached to several undertakings or employers who have their registered offices or places of business in different member states. If he does no work in the state where he is habitually resident, he is subject to the legislation of the member state in whose territory is situated the registered office or place of business of his employer. If he has employers in different member states in these circumstances, there is no tie-breaker to settle where liability arises.

If a person is employed in one member state and self-employed in a second member state, he is generally subject to the legislation of the state in which he is in paid employment, though there are a number of exceptions.

Special provisions apply to mariners, staff engaged in international transport, civil servants and members of the armed forces.

Legislation: EC Regulation 1408/71, 574/72, 883/2004 and 987/2009

2810   Reciprocal agreements: National Insurance

The UK has entered into reciprocal agreements with many non-EEA states. Certain of those agreements deal only with reciprocity in benefit matters (e.g. Australia, New Zealand, Canada), though most deal also with the avoidance of dual liability for contributions. Some contribution arrangements cover only pension benefits (e.g. the UK–US agreement). Certain of the agreements cover only nationals of the contracting states while others cover any insured person.

In outline, the contributions articles of the agreements in force allow a similar form of temporary transfer relief to the EU regulations discussed above, though the 12-month limit varies. In the case of the UK–US agreement, for example, the period is five years, which may be extended for up to one further year. Again, standard certificates of coverage are issued to enable the host authorities to be satisfied that there is no host state liability.

2812 Overseas earnings

Two very important points must be made about the earnings of employees moving around the world with a continuing UK liability.

(1) As 'earnings' attracting Class 1 NICs include all remuneration or profit derived from the employment (see 2540ff.), any overseas allowances, educational allowances, disturbance payments, etc. must be treated as gross pay and NICs calculated.

(2) Nevertheless, certain allowances, etc. may be paid free of NIC liability. For example:

(a) where it can be shown that a business expense has actually been incurred in the course of the employment;

(b) in the case of income tax-free relocation allowances for employees moving abroad (see 298); or

(c) in the case of payments towards medical costs and expenses incurred by employees when carrying out overseas duties, and insurance against such costs.

2814 Cross-border movements: NI benefit entitlements

Absence from the UK need not necessarily prejudice future benefit entitlement, though this is a possibility about which employees should be warned. Benefit entitlement rests on the payment or credit of sufficient Class 1, Class 2 and/or Class 3 contributions in the relevant contribution year or years.

An employee may continue to pay Class 1 contributions while abroad. Short absences under a UK-based contract will generally lead to a liability under the 52-week rule, or the EU regulations may operate to create a liability. A reciprocal agreement may also permit the worker to be subject to a certificate of continuing liability in the UK while working abroad. UK benefit entitlement is maintained while Class 1 contributions are paid.

Where an employee pays overseas contributions, UK benefit cover may also be maintained by virtue of a reciprocal agreement or the EU regulations. Where no such cover is available, it is often possible for the employee to pay voluntary contributions in order to maintain UK coverage (see 2816).

2816 Voluntary contributions

If the employee is liable to pay UK contributions for the first 52 weeks of absence and then ceases to pay, his rights to all *short-term* benefits will be restored on his return to UK employment (provided that he remains with the same employer without a break in the employer-employee relationship). In that case, only Class 3 contributions may need to be paid in order to maintain entitlement to the UK basic state pension and widow's pension, i.e. the *long-term* contributory benefits.

If the employee is not abroad under the 52-week rule or covered by a treaty, he may lose both long *and* short-term benefit entitlement and should consider paying voluntary *Class 2* contributions during the last two complete tax years of his absence. These count for both basic state pension and all short-term contributory benefits except contribution-based jobseeker's allowance. However, the payment of such contributions is subject to certain restrictions.

If upon being posted, an employee has no 52-week continuing liability for UK Class 1 contributions, his benefit protection will cease on the date of his departure. If there is a possibility of UK benefits being needed in the future, he should be encouraged to obtain contribution protection by (where possible) voluntarily paying Class 2 or Class 3 contributions for the years he spends abroad.

The conditions for the voluntary payment of Class 2 contributions are that the employee concerned:

- was, immediately before he last left the UK, an employed or self-employed earner;

- has at some time in the past been resident in the UK for three continuous tax years or has paid contributions at basic level for each of any three past tax years; and

- is working overseas but had no continuing UK Class 1 liability on being posted there.

In November 2009, HMRC advised that non-residents whose previous application to pay voluntary Class 2 NICs was rejected because of their not being employed/self-employed 'immediately' before leaving the UK have a chance, if they wish, to resubmit their application for review. See the HMRC press release dated 25 November 2009 for further details.

The first condition need not be satisfied if an employee wishes to pay only voluntary Class 3 contributions, but that employee must still satisfy the second and third conditions.

The easiest way to pay voluntary contributions is by monthly direct debit (guidance and an application form are provided in leaflet CA04), but arrangements can be made for annual bills to be issued to employers who may pay as agents for their employees.

Most employees leave the UK in mid-year rather than on 6 April. If the employee pays Class 1 contributions for the part of the year before departure, there may be no need for voluntary contributions for the remainder of the year, as the Class 1 contributions paid for the part-year may make the year a qualifying year for benefit purposes. Similar considerations apply to the year of return. If the employee pays some, but insufficient, Class 1 contributions in a year, a deficiency notice is automatically issued after the end of the year, inviting payment of voluntary contributions by cheque. The employee needs therefore only to consider voluntary contributions for complete years of non-liability.

Legislation: *Social Security (Contributions) Regulations* 2001 (SI 2001/1004), reg. 146, 147

2818   SSP and SMP for posted workers

Because of regulations on benefits, employees working in EEA territories are entitled to statutory sick pay (SSP) and statutory maternity pay (SMP) on the same basis as if they were in the UK. With the abolition of the employers' SSP recovery from 6 April 1994, the SSP rule has become academic for those large employers who pay occupational sick pay at least equivalent to the SSP rate.

2820   Gurkhas

The earnings of members of the Brigade of Gurkhas from their duties performed overseas, which were previously exempt, are subject to UK income tax and NICs from 16 June 2006.

Legislation: ITEPA 2003, s. 28(5); *Social Security (Categorisation of Earners) (Amendment) Regulations* 2006 (SI 2006/1530)

Corporation tax

> • HMRC have various powers to ensure compliance with the corporation
>   tax regime and interest and penalties may be levied for overdue tax and
>   non-compliance (see 4300ff.). Significant changes have been made in
>   recent years as part of the harmonisation of tax administration.

Taxation of companies: General framework

3000   Introduction and background to corporation tax

Introduction of company taxation

Corporation tax was first imposed by *Finance Act* 1965 and separated
the tax liabilities of a company and its shareholders. Prior to 1965, there
was no general distinction between a company and any other person in
so much that all persons were subject to income tax.

The corporation tax system introduced in 1965 was a 'classical system'.
Under such a system, tax is levied at the level of the business entity
and when profits are withdrawn from it, usually by deduction at source
(withholding tax). Distributed profits are effectively taxed at a higher rate
than retained profits to encourage the company to reinvest profits in the
business.

Imputation system

Corporation tax was modified to the imputation system from 1 April 1973.

The salient features of the imputation system are that a company is
charged to corporation tax on all its profits, distributed and undistributed,
and income tax is not deducted at source from dividends paid to
shareholders.

Prior to April 1999, when a company made a qualifying distribution
(see 3915), it had to account to HMRC for advance corporation tax
(ACT) of an amount equal to a fraction of the distribution. This fraction
varied each year. The shareholder who received a distribution also had
imputed to him part of the tax payable by the company; this represented
a tax credit in his favour to satisfy his liability to income tax at the lower
rate.

A company was able to set off its ACT payments, up to a certain limit,
against its corporation tax bill and the resulting figure was payable by the
company as an amount sometimes referred to as mainstream corporation
tax (MCT).

Abolition of ACT

Advance corporation tax was abolished with effect for distributions made on or after 6 April 1999. A reduced imputation system remained with the continuation of an imputed tax credit but no actual tax needed to be accounted for.

From 6 April 1999, the amount of the tax credit attaching to distributions was 10% (matching the rate of tax on dividend income up to the basic rate limit).

From April 2016, the dividend tax credit was abolished and a new dividend tax allowance of £5,000 a year introduced. The impact on companies was the subject of consultation and no significant changes were made.

Tax devolution

The *Corporation Tax (Northern Ireland) Act* 2015 received Royal Assent on 26 March 2015 and provides for the devolution of tax powers to allow Northern Ireland to set its own rate of corporation tax from April 2017. Whilst the power to set the corporation tax rate over most trading profits is being devolved, it does not include taxation of non-trading profits such as income from property nor over a range of special trading activities. The power to determine the corporation tax base, including reliefs and allowances, will remain with the UK Parliament. The decision to leave the EU and the suggestion that the UK-wide standard rate of CT may be reduced even further from the proposed 17% (to a possible 15%) could have an impact on the timing and quantum of any proposed NI rate of CT.

Legislation: F(No. 2)A 1997, s. 30–33, 35, Sch. 4 and 5

Tax Reporter: ¶700-000

3005 The corporation tax legislation

The Tax Law Rewrite Project

Following the introduction of corporation tax in 1965, the legislation relating to income tax and corporation tax was consolidated in the *Income Tax and Corporation Taxes Act* 1970 and then later into the *Income and Corporation Taxes Act* 1988. Concerns about the complexity of tax law and the way it was written in the legislation led to the establishment of the Tax Law Rewrite Project (TLR Project). The principal focus of the project has been to rewrite the direct tax legislation in a way which is clearer and easier to understand, without making major changes to the legislation. This is achieved by using a more logical structure, shorter sentences, clearer signposts and grouping of similar rules together. Only minor changes are made to legislation, the changes that are made are to improve the rewritten legislation.

As part of the TLR Project, the provisions of the income tax code were rewritten in three acts: the *Income Tax (Earnings and Pensions) Act* 2003 (ITEPA 2003), the *Income Tax (Trading and Other Income) Act* 2005 (ITTOIA 2005) and the *Income Tax Act* 2007 (ITA 2007).

This left two separate sets of legislation based on income tax principles; the legislation in the rewritten style applying for income tax purposes and the old style legislation applying for corporation tax purposes. The separation of the two codes was completed when the *Corporation Tax Act* 2009 (CTA 2009) and *Corporation Tax Act* 2010 (CTA 2010) were enacted. The *Taxation (International and other Provisions) Act* 2010 (TIOPA 2010) also has effect for accounting periods ending on or after 1 April 2010 and contains the rewritten legislation on, in particular, transfer pricing, double tax relief for companies and the 2009 worldwide debt cap rules. Further legislation has been incorporated in CTA 2009, Pt. 9A, 15A and 15B; in CTA 2010, Pt. 8A, 14A, 17A, 21A, 21B and 21C; and in TIOPA 2010, Pt. 9A.

Corporation Tax Act 2009

The *Corporation Tax Act* 2009 (CTA 2009), which received Royal Assent on 26 March 2009, was the first of two Acts which rewrite the provisions of the tax code which apply to companies. It is the longest single Act to have been passed by Parliament and included 1,330 sections and four schedules. The act applies to accounting periods ending on or after 1 April 2009.

The *Corporation Tax Act* 2009 rewrote the charge to corporation tax and the primary corporation tax code used to compute the income of companies for corporation tax. The *Corporation Tax Act* 2009 removed the schedular system of taxing income, replacing it with the following main heads of charge:

- trading income;
- property income;
- loan relationships;
- intangible fixed assets;
- intellectual property; and
- miscellaneous income.

The *Corporation Tax Act* 2009 covers the charge to corporation tax, accounting periods, residence of companies, as well as those provisions which relate to trading income and income from other sources. The Act also contains those provisions necessary to calculate income from loan relationships, derivative contracts and intangible fixed assets. Also included in the act are those provisions which cover particular categories of expenditure including expenditure on research and development as well as film expenditure and remediation of contaminated land.

In common with the other rewritten legislation, CTA 2009 has not generally changed the law as a result of the rewriting of the legislation. Though there are over 100 minor changes to the legislation, they are designed to clarify the predecessor legislation and bring it in line with well-established practice. Schedule 2 of the Act provides for the continuity of the corporation code by stating that the repeal of provisions and their enactment in a rewritten form by CTA 2009 does not affect the continuity of the law, unless a change is made to the effect of the law by the Act. References to the new legislation should also be taken as references to the source legislation.

Corporation Tax Act 2010

The *Corporation Tax Act* 2010 is the second of two rewrite acts which address corporation tax. Whereas the first, CTA 2009, mainly rewrote the provisions dealing with the computation of a company's income, CTA 2010 is wider in application, rewriting the provisions dealing with:

- the calculation of corporation tax payable on a company's profits. This includes the renaming of the small companies' rate of corporation tax as the 'small profits rate' and the enactment of a number of Extra-statutory Concessions concerning the former small companies' rate;

- losses and reliefs, including group relief and charitable donations relief (which replaces the term 'charges on income');

- special types of business and company, including close companies and charitable companies;

- patent box;

- distributions; and

- tax avoidance including the transactions in securities rules.

The *Corporation Tax Act* 2010 has effect for accounting periods ending on or after 1 April 2010.

Election to use predecessor legislation

Although the changes to the law made by the Acts are minor, it is possible that a company could be adversely affected by one of those changes. Where this is the case with regard to a transaction that occurred before

1 April 2009 (for CTA 2009) or 1 April 2010 (for CTA 2010), provision is made for the company to elect for the consequences of a transaction for corporation tax purposes to be governed by the predecessor legislation. The election could only be made in respect of accounting periods which straddle 1 April 2009 (for CTA 2009) or 1 April 2010 (for CTA 2010). Such an election had to be made within two years of the accounting period concerned.

Taxation (International etc) Act 2010

The *Taxation (International and Other Provisions) Act* 2010 is the third and final of the rewrite acts. It was relatively short, comprising 382 sections (albeit with 11 schedules) and mops up the 'business' related issues and focuses on the international tax issues: Double Tax Relief, Transfer Pricing, Advance Pricing Agreements, Tax Arbitrage, Financing Costs and Income (the worldwide debt rules), Offshore Funds, and the CFC rules.

As with the CTA 2010, TIOPA 2010 has effect for accounting periods ending on or after 1 April 2010.

Legislation: CTA 2009, Sch. 2, para. 10; CTA 2010, Sch. 2, para. 10

Tax Reporter: ¶700-275

3010 Bodies liable to corporation tax

Corporation tax is charged on the profits of 'companies'.

A 'company' is any body corporate (e.g. a company incorporated under the *Companies Act* 2006 or predecessor Acts) or unincorporated association (e.g. a club or an authorised unit trust), but not a partnership, local authority or local authority association. Health service bodies are exempt from corporation tax.

There are three main types of incorporated company under the *Companies Act* 2006.

- A company formed so that, for example, a sole trader, family members or several partners can carry on a business and still retain control of its management and share any profits made, while separating the liability of the company from its members. The liability of such a 'private company' is limited by shares.

- A company formed to allow members of the public to invest in its profits without being involved in its management. The liability of such a 'public company' is limited by shares.

- A company formed for charitable, public or social purposes, which is limited by *guarantee*.

An incorporated company has a legal identity separate from that of its shareholders, with its own rights, powers, duties and liabilities, and is likewise a taxable entity distinct and separate from its shareholders.

Income tax and corporation tax cannot be charged on the same income or profits of a taxpayer. Any company paying corporation tax on its profits is not liable to suffer income tax on those profits.

Legislation: CTA 2009, s. 2, 3; CTA 2010, s. 1121

Tax Reporter: ¶700-550

The territorial scope of corporation tax

3015 Territorial scope of corporation tax

A UK-resident company is chargeable to corporation tax on all its profits wherever arising. However, with effect from 19 July 2011 a company has been able to elect for profits and losses from its permanent establishments (PEs) to be exempt from corporation tax. For commentary on the taxation of UK-resident companies with foreign PEs, see 3027.

A non-UK resident company is generally within the charge to corporation tax only if it carries on a trade in the UK through a UK permanent establishment. If a non-UK resident company does carry on a trade in the UK, it is chargeable to corporation tax on the profits attributable to the UK permanent establishment. Non-UK resident companies are liable to income tax on income from a UK source.

Anti-avoidance legislation in the form of the Diverted Profits Tax (DPT) will need to be considered where the structure may be considered to result in profits being diverted from the UK by, for example, avoiding creating a UK permanent establishment or the diversion of income intragroup (see www.gov.uk/government/uploads/system/uploads/attachment_data/file/422184/Diverted_Profits_Tax.pdf). Further anti-avoidance legislation is being introduced in consequence of the action points from the BEPS (tax base erosion and profit shifting) project – in particular, there are proposals to restrict relief for finance, to counter the use of hybrid structures and instruments and to impose withholding requirements on a broader range of royalty payments.

Changes have been made, effective from 5 July 2016, targeting offshore developers and dealers in UK land. This is achieved through a combination of amendments to CTA 2009, Pt. 5, recasting the legislation dealing with artificial transactions in land (CTA 2010, Pt. 18) and the introduction of a TAAR with effect from 16 March 2016.

Legislation: CTA 2009, s. 3, 5; FA 2015, Pt. 3; CTA 2009, Pt. 5

Tax Reporter: ¶764-000ff.

3020 Residence and companies

A company will be resident in the UK if it is incorporated in the UK or if it is centrally managed and controlled in the UK.

Incorporation

With effect from 14 March 1988, a company incorporated in the UK will be regarded as resident here. This rule has effect for companies incorporated before that date, from 14 March 1988 onwards. Where a company is given a different place of residence by a rule of law, it shall be ignored for the purpose of the incorporation rule.

This can clearly give rise to dual residence, as a company managed and controlled in another jurisdiction will also be UK resident if incorporated in the UK.

An important exception to the incorporation rule is provided by CTA 2009, s. 18 which was originally introduced in 1994. If a company is regarded as resident in another territory under the domestic law of that territory and also resident in the UK under UK tax legislation (e.g. by reason of being incorporated there) and there is a Double Taxation Agreement (DTA) between the UK and the other territory that includes a 'tie breaker' test and under the tie breaker test, the company is regarded as resident in the other territory (typically, under DTAs following the OECD model, because the 'effective management' of the company is exercised from the other territory), then the company will not be regarded as UK resident for UK tax purposes.

Central management and control

Prior to the statutory deeming provisions previously enacted in *Finance Act* 1988 (see under *Incorporation*, above) there was no statutory definition of residence for tax purposes. The test for residence developed by the courts and described below continues to apply where a company is incorporated outside the UK.

The courts determined in the early case of *Calcutta Jute Mills Co Ltd v Nicholson Ex D* that the test for residence was where the real business of the company is carried on, which is where its central management and control takes place. Several cases have been decided on this issue since then and the management and control criterion has stood the test of time.

The concept of central management and control is, in broad terms, directed at the highest level of control of the business of the company and can be distinguished from the place where the main operations of the business are to be found.

In the case of *De Beers Consolidated Mines Ltd v Howe* a South African company operating in South Africa but controlling its important affairs in the UK was held to be resident in the UK, where the Board meetings on important issues took place and where the majority of the Board were resident. Other decisions made in favour of HMRC on the same grounds include *New Zealand Shipping Co Ltd v Thew HL*; *American Thread Co v Joyce, HL*; *John Hood & Co Ltd v Magee KB*.

It is particularly difficult to apply the 'central management and control' test in the situation where a subsidiary company and its parent operate in different territories. In this situation, the parent will normally influence, to a greater or lesser extent, the actions of the subsidiary. Where that influence is exerted by the parent exercising the powers which a sole or majority shareholder has in general meetings of the subsidiary, for example to appoint and dismiss members of board of the subsidiary and to initiate or approve alterations to its financial structure, HMRC would not normally seek to argue that central management and control of the subsidiary is located where the parent company is resident. However, in cases where the parent usurps the functions of the board of the subsidiary or where that board merely rubber stamps the parent company's decisions without giving them any independent consideration of its own, HMRC draw the conclusion that the subsidiary has the same residence for tax purposes as its parent.

The case of *Wood v Holden* appeared in the Court of Appeal in January 2006. In this case, HMRC contended that a Dutch company used as part of sophisticated capital gains tax planning scheme, was resident in the UK. The CA stressed that the burden of proof was on HMRC to show that a company was UK resident and that HMRC in this case had not done so. The court held that the company's decisions, which were influenced by UK accountants, were made by the trust which was set up by the managing director of the company in the Netherlands, and that without those decisions having been made by the trust, the agreements that were the subject of the decisions would not have been entered into. There was no evidence produced by HMRC to show that the company was controlled otherwise than by the trust in the Netherlands, and that the meetings in which the transactions were approved were mere formalities.

In the case of *News Datacom Ltd v HMIT*, the special commissioners considered the existing line of authority and highlighted the tests distilled by Chadwick LJ in the Court of Appeal decision in *Wood v Holden*. No further tests were added to those that emerged from *Wood v Holden*, however, the special commissioners made it clear that in deciding where management and control is situated, there are two mutually exclusive categories to be considered.

Category 1

It must first be decided whether the functions of the constitutional organs have been usurped. If they have, then the case falls into the first category.

Category 2

Where this is not the case, i.e. where the functions are in fact carried out by those organs, it is essential to recognise the distinction between an outsider to those organs who influences the decisions of those organs, and one who dictates what those decisions should be.

In *News Datacom*, there was no usurpation of the Board of Directors and therefore the first category was not considered. In considering what the influence of outsiders to the constitutional organs were, the special commissioners found that any outside influence was exercised outside the UK, therefore the company could not be UK resident. Full consideration was found not to be required of the second category because the outside influence could only have made the company UK resident if it occurred in the UK.

It is therefore clear that the first thing to consider is whether the functions of the Board are actually carried out by the Board and not by some other person or persons. If some other person(s) carries out the functions of the Board, then the company will be resident where those functions are carried out. Where the functions of the Board are indeed carried out by the Board, the company will be resident where the functions of the board are carried out. In this case however, the role of outsiders who influence the decisions of the Board will also be examined, and if it transpires that there are outsiders who influence the Board to such an extent that it could be said that the Board are merely 'rubber stamping' decisions that have already been made elsewhere and by other people, then the company will be resident where the decisions are actually made.

In the more recent case of *Laerstate BV v R & C Commrs*, the First-tier Tax Tribunal found that a company incorporated in the Netherlands was centrally managed and controlled by its sole shareholder, and sometime director, in the UK. This does not mean to say that the existence of a dominant shareholder will always determine the residence of a company; it is still necessary to establish who exercises central management and control of the company and from where. The tribunal found that even where a majority shareholder instructs directors on how to act, and the directors consider those wishes and act on them, it will still be their decision: 'the borderline is between the directors making the decision and not making any decision at all'. Where directors engage in 'mindless signing', they can not be said to have made a decision and so can not be said to exercise central management and control.

SP 1/90 sets out the residence tests and HMRC's view of the test of management and control.

Legislation: CTA 2009, s. 14, 18, Sch. 2, Pt. 5

Cases: *Calcutta Jute Mills Co Ltd v Nicholson Ex D* (1876) 1 TC 83; *American Thread Co v Joyce, HL* (1913) 6 TC 163; *John Hood & Co Ltd v Magee KB* (1918) 7 TC 327; *New Zealand Shipping Co Ltd v Thew HL* (1922) 8 TC 208; *Unit Construction v Bullock* (1958) 38 TC 712; *Esquire Nominees Ltd v Commr of Taxation* (1971) 129 CLR 177; *Re Little Olympian Each Ways Ltd* [1995] 1 WLR 560; *Untelrab Ltd v McGregor; Unigate Guernsey Ltd McGregor* (1995) Sp C 55; *Wood v Holden (HMIT)* [2006] BTC 208; *News Datacom Ltd v HM Inspector of Taxes* (2006) Sp C 561; *Laerstate BV v R & C Commrs* [2009] TC 00162

Tax Reporter: ¶764-100ff.

3025 Permanent establishments

The concept of a 'permanent establishment' (PE) is much used in double taxation treaties. CTA 2010, Pt. 24, Ch. 2 provides a statutory definition for tax purposes which is intended to accord, in large part, with that in common use in the UK's tax treaties.

For corporation tax, a company has a PE in a territory if (and only if) either:

(1) it carries on business (wholly or partly) through a 'fixed place of business' in that territory; or

(2) there is an agent in the territory acting habitually on the company's behalf who is not acting in an independent capacity in the ordinary course of his own business.

However, it will not be treated as having a PE if the activities carried on are merely of a preparatory or auxiliary character (for example, storage, display, delivery operations or collecting information).

A 'fixed place of business' can include a number of possible types of establishment, but is not exclusively:

- a place of management;
- a branch;
- an office, factory or workshop;
- any project for construction or installation or building site;

- an installation or structure for the exploration of natural resources, as well as a mine, quarry, oil or gas well, or any other place where natural resources are extracted.

Case law has determined that a trade is carried on where its contracts are concluded (*Pommery & Greno v Apthope*) and 'where the operations take place from which the profits in substance arise' (*F L Smidth & Co v Greenwood*). In most cases, the substance of the business operations will be where the contracts are concluded.

The profits attributable to the PE comprise the following:

- trading income arising directly or indirectly through or from the permanent establishment;

- any income from property or rights used by, or held by or for the permanent establishment; and

- chargeable gains on the disposal of assets situated in the UK which are used for the purposes of the trade carried on though the permanent establishment.

For clarification, *Finance Act* 2003 inserted a new section and schedule which describe exactly what will be regarded as the chargeable profits of a PE of a non-resident company. Broadly, the profits attributable to the PE shall be those which it would have made had it been a separate entity dealing with the non-resident on arm's length terms – referred to as the 'separate enterprise principle'. Certain assumptions may be made in order to support this stand alone treatment, namely that:

- the PE shares the same credit rating as the non-resident company; and

- it has such equity and loan capital as would be expected given that treatment.

Expenses incurred, in the UK or elsewhere, for the purposes of the PE (whether reimbursed by the PE or not) will be allowable for corporation tax purposes on the same basis as a UK company. Certain costs are specifically disallowed or allowance for them is modified as follows:

(a) no relief is available for any payments akin to royalties made by the PE to another part of the non-resident for the use of intangible assets. However, a contribution towards the creation of such an asset may be deductible;

(b) unless the PE carries on a business as a bank, deposit-taker, money-lender, debt-factor or similar, or deals in commodity or financial futures, and pays interest, etc. in the ordinary course of that business, no deduction will be available for interest or other costs of finance made by the PE to another part of the non-resident; and

(c)   where the non-resident provides goods or services to the PE, they will be dealt with as an expense incurred by it for the PE (and hence allowable in calculating the chargeable profits of the PE, see above), except where they are goods or services that the non-resident supplies in the normal course of its own business. In that latter case, the stand alone 'separate enterprise principle' will apply in order to determine the amount deductible.

Legislation: CTA 2009, Pt. 2, Ch. 4; CTA 2010, Pt. 24, Ch. 2

Tax Reporter: ¶764-260ff.

3027   Foreign PEs of UK-resident companies

The general rule is that a UK-resident company is liable to corporation tax on its worldwide income including that earned through a foreign PE (see 3015). This is the case whether or not the income is remitted to the UK although relief is available where the company is unable to remit the overseas income.

Trading income and expenses relating to the PE are included within total trading income. However, where the trade is carried on 'wholly outside the UK', a trading loss relating to the PE can only be offset against future profits from that PE (see 3315 and 3320).

Credit relief is available where foreign tax has been suffered on the profits attributable to the PE, although only to the extent that the foreign tax does not exceed the corporation tax payable on those profits as determined for UK tax purposes (see 3130). Where the trade is controlled from the UK (i.e. it is not carried on wholly outside the UK), any unrelieved foreign tax can be carried forward and offset against corporation tax payable on the profits of the PE in future periods.

With effect from 19 July 2011, a company has been able to elect (under CTA 2009, s. 18A) for the profits and losses attributable to its PEs to be exempt from corporation tax. Once made, the election is irrevocable and applies with regard to all of the company's PE, current and future. Transitional provisions apply to restrict the application of the exemption where there are historic losses. Where this is the case, profits will be exempt once those losses have been fully matched with profits (either on a company basis or by reference to individual PEs where a streaming election has been made). An anti-avoidance rule applies to prevent profits which would otherwise remain within the charge to corporation tax from being diverted to an exempt foreign branch. Restrictions also apply with regard to small companies (in which case only profits and losses from certain types of territories, 'full-treaty territories', are subject to exemption) and close companies (in which case exemption is denied in respect of profits derived from chargeable gains).

The rules applying with regard to controlled foreign companies (CFCs) have been reformed by legislation included in *Finance Act* 2012 in respect of accounting periods beginning after 31 December 2012 (see 4180). The new (FA 2012) CFC regime also applies to branches where an election into the branch exemption regime has been made. Consequently, branch profits will be exempt only if the branch meets the lower level of tax test, in which case it will not fall within the CFC rules, or if an exemption under the CFC rules applies.

Legislation: CTA 2009, Pt. 2, Ch. 3A

Tax Reporter: ¶764-750ff.

3028   Diverted Profits Tax

With effect from 1 April 2015, *Finance Act* 2015 introduced the diverted profits tax (DPT) which is intended to counteract the diversion of profits from the UK both where a foreign company exploits the permanent establishment (PE) rules to avoid UK tax or where a UK company or a foreign company with a UK PE reduces UK tax through arrangements that lack economic substance.

There is an exemption from DPT for small and medium-sized businesses (based on the existing interpretation of the EU limits used in UK transfer pricing legislation). Further, there are further exemptions (for avoidance of UK permanent establishment cases) where either:

- total UK sales made by the group that are not within corporation tax are less than £10m p.a.; or

- UK expenses of the group are less than £1m p.a.

DPT applies at a rate of 25% to profits that are considered to have been artificially diverted from the UK but loan relationships (financing arrangements) and their derivatives are excluded from the scope of DPT.

DPT is distinct from corporation tax, and it has been suggested that it will fall outside the scope of the UK's existing bilateral tax treaties. HMRC have published guidance that includes a number of helpful examples at www.gov.uk/government/publications/diverted-profits-tax-guidance.

3029   Country by country reporting

Legislation allowing implementation of country by country reporting was enacted substantially unamended in *Finance Act* 2015, s. 122. Regulations are the subject of a consultation – these should be read in conjunction with the OECD's consolidated report on Action 13 of the BEPS action plan transfer pricing documentation and country-by-country reporting. Further information can be found at http://tinyurl.com/nrs8nry.

A requirement for large undertakings to publish information country by country, on profits or losses before tax, taxes on profits or losses and public subsidies received has been added to draft legislation currently being considered by MEPs. In addition, the European Parliament wants rules to enable shareholders to vote at least every three years on a listed company's remuneration policy for directors. Further information can be found at http://tinyurl.com/o2tvg7k.

3030 The charge to corporation tax

Corporation tax is an annual tax and is charged for each 'financial year'. A financial year is the period from 1 April to the following 31 March. Thus, the financial year 2015 started on 1 April 2015 and ends on 31 March 2016. Although corporation tax is charged for each financial year, it is computed and assessed by reference to a company's 'accounting periods' (see 3040) and then apportioned between the relevant financial years where the accounting period does not fall wholly within one financial year.

Corporation tax is charged on the profits of companies. The 'profits' means income and chargeable gains. For the rules for calculating income and chargeable gains, see 3050.

Companies within the charge to corporation tax (see 3015 for the territorial scope of UK corporation tax) are not chargeable to income tax or capital gains tax. A company's chargeable gains are, however, calculated in much the same way as for capital gains tax purposes (see 3400) but they are then chargeable to corporation tax (subject to the territorial scope limitations below).

A body is within the corporation tax charge if it has a source of income within the corporation tax charge. A source of income is within the corporation tax charge if corporation tax is chargeable on the income arising from it, or would be were there any such income. However, a non-resident company is only within the corporation tax charge if it trades in the UK through UK permanent establishment (see 3025).

A company may come within the corporation tax charge if it:

- acquires an appropriate source of income, not previously having had one; or

- becomes UK-resident while having an appropriate source of income.

Conversely, a company may cease to be within the corporation tax charge if it:

- ceases to have an appropriate source of income; or

- being non-resident ceases trading in the UK through a UK permanent establishment.

Legislation: CTA 2009, s. 2, 3, 4 and 8

Tax Reporter: ¶700-550ff.

3040 Accounting periods

Corporation tax is charged by reference to 'accounting periods'. Under the *Companies Act* 2006, a company is obliged to prepare accounts for each of its 'financial years', which are the periods between its accounting reference dates. A company's accounting financial years are normally 12 months in length but, confusingly, they are not always. Where a company changes its accounting reference date, the financial year can be as short as a few months or as long as 18 months. To prevent abuse and to create uniformity, tax legislation lays down certain rules to define what is an accounting period for tax purposes.

The *Corporation Tax Act* 2009, s. 9 states that an accounting period for corporation tax begins on one of the following occasions.

(1) Whenever the company first comes within the charge of UK corporation tax, perhaps by becoming UK resident, or by starting to trade, or acquiring a source of income.

(2) When an accounting period ends without the company ceasing to be within the charge to corporation tax.

The *Corporation Tax Act* 2009, s. 10 states that an accounting period ends on the earliest of the following occasions:

- 12 months after the accounting period started;

- an accounting date of the company (that is to say, the date to which the company makes up its accounts – which has been held to mean accounts made up on which the auditors have formally reported and which are laid before the company in general meeting – so, for example, drawing up management accounts will not bring the accounting period to an end);

- on the company beginning or ceasing to trade in respect of all of the trades carried on by it;

- the company beginning or ceasing to be resident in the UK;

- the company ceasing to be within the charge to corporation tax;

- on the company beginning or ceasing to be in administration; and

- the commencement of winding up of the company.

Example

Begonia Ltd was incorporated on 7 February 2013. It issued 50,000 ordinary shares on 25 April 2013 and most of the subscription moneys were placed in a bank deposit account on 29 April 2013. The company commenced trading on 1 July 2013 and registered to draw up its accounts to 31 December each year. Begonia Ltd's accounting periods would be as follows:

- 29 April 2013 to 30 June 2013: this period begins when Begonia Ltd acquires a source of income (the bank deposit account) and, in practice, would end on the day before trading commences;

- 1 July 2013 to 31 December 2013: this period starts on the day after the expiry of the previous period and ends on the date to which accounts are first drawn up; and thereafter

- a period ending on 31 December each year.

Where a company's financial year does not coincide with an accounting period, because, for example, the period of account exceeds 12 months, it will be necessary to allocate profits and losses between accounting periods. The general rule is that this is to be done on an actual basis with the exception of trading profits (before deduction of capital allowances), profits of a property business, management expenses and miscellaneous income which are to be allocated on a time basis.

Example

Amaryllis Ltd has traded for some years and accounts have previously been prepared annually to 31 March. As a result of being taken over, the company has prepared accounts for the 18-month period to 30 September 2015.

The following information has been extracted:

- Trading profits for the period, as adjusted for taxation purposes, but before capital allowances, were £137,250.

- The company is entitled to capital allowances on plant and machinery of £5,220 for the 12 months to 31 March 2015 and £2,750 for the six months to 30 September 2015.

- The accounts for the period showed the following investment income: Bank deposit interest (£1,530) and exempt dividends (£4,000).

- Interest of £18,000 was charged on a 12% £100,000 loan note issued for a £100,000 loan which was advanced to the company on 1 January 2007.

- The company covenanted to make an annual payment of £1,000 to Oxfam on 31 December each year. The first £1,000 was paid on 6 January 2013.

As the period of account exceeds 12 months, the company would have to prepare corporation tax computations for the following two accounting periods:

---

(1) 1 April 2014 to 31 March 2014 (12 months);

(2) 1 April 2015 to 30 September 2015 (6 months, ending on the date to which accounts are prepared).

Amaryllis Ltd

Corporation tax computation based on the accounts for the 18 months to 30 September 2015.

	1/4/14 to 31/3/15	1/4/15 to 30/9/15
	£	£
Adjusted trading profit	91,500	45,750
Capital allowances on plant	(5,220)	(2,750)
Trading profit	86,280	43,000
Less: current non-trading deficit	(10,980)	(5,490)
Profits before charges	75,300	37,510
Less: charges on income (gross):		
Gift Aid deduction	(1,000)	–
Profits chargeable to corporation tax	74,300	37,510

Current year non-trading deficit is made up as follows:

	£
Bank deposit interest income	1,530
12% loan note interest payable	(18,000)
	(16,470)

Legislation: CTA 2009, s. 9, 10, 52, 210, 1307, 1311; CTA 2010, s. 1119(1)

Tax Reporter: ¶700-800ff, ¶700-900

Computation of taxable profits

3050   Profits chargeable to corporation tax

Corporation tax is chargeable on the profits of a 'company' (see 3030).

Profits comprise the company's income and chargeable gains.

Legislation: CTA 2009, s. 2(1)

Tax Reporter: ¶700-550

3060 Computation of company's taxable profits

A company's taxable profits comprise its income and chargeable gains.

A company's taxable income and chargeable gains are computed in much the same way as those of an individual, using income tax and capital gains tax principles.

Corporation tax is payable on the total profits of a company for each of its 'accounting periods' (see 3040 above). The tax is calculated by apportioning the profits of those accounting periods so as to apply the tax rate for the relevant financial year (see 3100). Deductions can only be made in accordance with the Corporation Tax Acts (see also below). The rules relating to accounting years and corresponding years for individuals do not apply to companies.

Total profits are profits accruing to the company plus profits accruing for the benefit of the company under a trust or partnership and profits arising when the company is wound up.

Tax is strictly chargeable on every fraction of a pound, but in practice amounts chargeable are rounded down while tax is calculated to the nearest penny. Of particular relevance to companies is the willingness of HMRC to accept tax computations rounded to the nearest £1,000 in most cases where turnover exceeds £5m.

A pro forma corporation tax computation for accounting periods ending on or after 1 April 2009 would be as follows:

	£
Trading income	
Adjusted profits	X
Less: capital allowances	(X)
Net trading income	X
Property income	X
Net non-trading loan relationship credits	X
Net non-trading credits under derivative contracts	X
Net non-trading gains on intangible fixed assets	X
Profits from disposal of know-how or patent rights	X
Miscellaneous income	X
Gains on disposal of chargeable assets	X
	X
Less: amounts relieved by set off against total profits (e.g. trading losses of current accounting period, group relief, charitable donations relief, etc.)	X
Profits chargeable to corporation tax	X

In the above pro forma corporation tax computation it should be noted that credits arising on loan relationships or derivative contracts entered into by a company in the course of a trade continue to be brought into account for tax purposes as part of the trading profits. Similarly, credits arising under the intangible fixed asset code are brought into account as part of the trading profits to the extent that the intangible asset is held by the company for the purposes of its trade.

As implied above, the computation of trading profits for a company involves much the same principles as for an individual. The implications of receipt of certain foreign income and relief for unremittable foreign income are also relevant to companies in the same way as to individuals (see 1607 and 1650ff.). Payments, etc. constituting distributions to shareholders (see 3800) are not deductible in computing profits, and annual interest paid by companies is allowable, for accounting periods ending after 31 March 1996, in accordance with the rules for taxation of loan relationships (see 3164ff.).

If a corporate unit holder receives distributions from an authorised unit trust, various provisions govern the treatment of the distribution in the recipient's hands. The treatment broadly depends on the nature of the income (UK dividends, foreign income, or interest) out of which the distribution is made. Although a corporate unit holder will receive a single distribution, that distribution may consist of one or more elements of franked investment income (with a tax credit), unfranked income (with income tax deducted available for offset against corporation tax or repayment), a foreign income dividend (with a notional tax credit) or unfranked income (with notional income tax available for offset but not repayable). Alternatively, it might be received as interest under deduction of income tax.

Anti-avoidance rules generally apply irrespective of the nature of the taxpayer, though some measures are aimed purely at companies so that, for example, tax relief may be restricted where interest is paid by thinly capitalised companies, the profits of controlled foreign companies can in some situations be assessed on UK resident parent companies (see 4150ff.) and certain tax regimes that apply only for corporation tax purposes (e.g. those relating to loan relationships, derivatives, intangible fixed assets, R&D tax credits, groups of companies, corporate capital gains, etc.) have their own anti-avoidance provisions. There are also transfer pricing rules for certain transactions between affiliated companies, and other special provisions can apply to payments of rent and interest between affiliated companies.

Special rules apply in certain situations. There are rules for the taxation of 'loan relationships', i.e. interest and movements in value of debt which also incorporates the rules on foreign exchange gains and losses (see 3164ff.) applicable for accounting periods ending after 31 March 1996, intangible fixed assets (see 3179), reliefs for payments to employee share ownership trusts (see 3255) and rules giving a corporation tax deduction where shares are awarded to employees (see 3425). Special provisions apply to certain other types of company (see 4200ff.). Extensive provisions relating to the taxation of financial instruments held by companies for managing interest rate and currency risk apply in such a way that profits and losses on qualifying contracts are to be recognised for tax purposes as they accrue, and taxed or relieved as income receipts or deductions (see 3164).

A consultation was launched to examine ways to tackle base erosion profit shifting involving interest expense and comments invited by 14 January 2016. The consultation document summarises the key aspects of the OECD report on Action 4. Recommendations included the following:

- de minimis monetary threshold to remove low risk entities;

- a fixed ratio rule allowing an entity to deduct net interest expense up to a net interest/EBITDA ratio within a corridor of 10%–30%;

- a group ratio rule allowing an entity to deduct net interest expense up to its group's net interest/EBITDA ratio, where this is higher than the fixed ratio; and an option for a country to apply a different group ratio rule or no group ratio rule;

- rules to address volatility including carry forward of disallowed interest/ unused interest capacity and/or carry back of disallowed interest;

- public-benefit project exclusion;

- targeted rules to support general interest limitation rules and address specific risks; and

- specific rules to address issues raised by the banking and insurance sectors.

This has now moved further as the UK issued its own consultation document which is currently open for responses (www.gov.uk/government/ consultations/tax-deductibility-of-corporate-interest-expense/tax-deductibility-of-corporate-interest-expense-consultation).

Legislation: FA 2004, s. 207; CTA 2009, s. 5–8; CTA 2010, s. 4; *Authorised Investment Funds (Tax) Regulations* 2006 (SI 2006/964)

Tax Reporter: ¶700-550ff.

3070   Accounts or statements prepared in a foreign currency

The general rule is that a company's taxable profits and losses should be calculated in sterling. However, many companies have been required since the introduction of International Accounting Standards (IAS) on

1 January 2005 to prepare their accounts in a currency other than sterling and legislation now provides for companies in some circumstances to calculate their taxable profits and losses in a currency other than sterling. For accounting periods beginning after 31 December 2004, the position is as follows for companies who prepare their accounts in a currency other than sterling.

If the company is resident in the UK and in its accounts identifies sterling as its functional currency but (unusually) prepares its accounts in another currency, then the profits and losses of the company must be computed in sterling as if the company prepared its accounts in sterling. Situations like this are likely to be encountered rarely.

If the company is resident in the UK and prepares its accounts in one currency (other than sterling) and in those accounts it identifies another different currency (other than sterling) as its functional currency, then the profits and losses of the company must be computed in sterling by:

(a) computing those profits or losses in the functional currency as if the company prepared its accounts in that currency; and

(b) taking the sterling equivalent of those profits and losses by translating the amounts into sterling using the average exchange rate for the accounting period.

If the company, whether resident in the UK or not, prepares its accounts in accordance with generally accepted accounting practice in a currency other than sterling and neither of the two circumstances above apply, then the profits and losses of the company must be computed in sterling by:

(a) computing those profits and losses in the currency in which the accounts are prepared; and

(b) taking the sterling equivalent of those profits and losses by translating the amounts into sterling using the average exchange rate for the accounting period.

For the purposes of these rules, the functional currency is the currency of the primary economic environment in which the company operates. The above rules apply to the profits or losses of the company other than chargeable gains or allowable capital losses. For the purposes of corporation tax on chargeable gains (or allowable losses), the profits or losses always have to be computed in sterling. If the sale proceeds or cost of the relevant asset were in a currency other than sterling, they have to be translated into sterling using the spot rate on the date of the sale or purchase, as the case may be.

From January 2005, but with regard to accounting periods beginning before 29 December 2007 only, profits *and* losses calculations were always to be made using translation rates for the current period. This fixed the sterling amount of unutilised losses and other reliefs at that point (subject to a one-off adjustment to convert surplus management expenses, trading losses from an overseas property business and non-trading loan relationship deficits which were brought forward to the first period of account beginning after 31 December 2004).

For accounting periods beginning on or after 29 December 2007, subject to transitional arrangements, the general rule is that any losses carried forward to future accounting periods, or back to a previous accounting period, will be converted into sterling at the same exchange rates as the profits which they are offsetting. This removes significant exchange risk which all parties were exposed to under the previous rules. This was brought into sharp focus by the financial climate at the time and was of particular concern to foreign banks trading in the UK.

Companies can elect that the commencement date for the special rules applying to carried back and carried forward amounts is changed to 21 July 2009 (i.e. the new rules apply to accounting periods beginning on or after 21 July 2009). Such an election is irrevocable and must be made within 30 days of the beginning of the first accounting period beginning on or after 21 July 2009.

Legislation in FA 2013 amended CTA 2010 so that relevant companies are required to compute their chargeable gains and losses on disposals of shares in their functional currency (or for UK resident investment companies with a designated currency, that designated currency). Following consultation on the draft legislation, this measure was extended to also cover disposals of ships, aircraft and interests in shares. This measure has effect from 1 September 2013, in relation to disposals on or after that date.

Legislation: CTA 2010, Pt. 2, Ch. 4

Tax Reporter: ¶703-500ff.

3080　Priority of charge

Occasionally, there are difficulties in determining how and on what basis particular receipts are to be taxed. For accounting periods ended before 1 April 2009, HMRC have the power to direct what the basis of assessment should be in two sets of circumstances (former FA 1998, Sch. 18, para. 84):

- where amounts could be brought into charge either under Sch. D, Case I or alternatively Sch. D, Case III or Sch. D, Case V; and

- where amounts could be brought into charge either under the rules of Sch. D, Case I or under the 'I minus E basis' for companies carrying on life assurance (and annuity) business.

HMRC's determination on this matter was final and conclusive as regards the accounting period concerned.

For accounting periods ended on or after 1 April 2009, such issues are to be determined in accordance with the priority rules at CTA 2009, s. 287 and 982(1).

Legislation: CTA 2009, s. 287 and 982(1)

Tax Reporter: ¶812-000

Calculating the tax due

3100   The main rate of corporation tax

The basic rule is that corporation tax is charged at the main rate as set by Parliament for that financial year. The main rate of corporation tax for the financial year 2014 (the year beginning on 1 April 2014) was 21%. The corresponding figure for the financial year 2013 was 23%. The main rate of corporation tax for the financial year 2015 is 20%. Further changes have been announced so corporation tax rates will be reduced from the present rate of 20% to 19% with effect from 1 April 2017 and 17% with effect from 1 April 2020. There was a suggestion that rates may fall even further (to 15%) following the outcome of the referendum on 23 June.

A different rate applies with regard to North Sea Oil and Gas ring fence activities, and a special rate 45% is applied to restitution payments from 26 October 2015.

There were exceptions to the basic rule, most notably where a company had small profits; only companies with augmented profits in excess of the upper limit (see 3110) will pay corporation tax at the main rate (prior to 2015, when the rates are to be aligned). For commentary on the small profits rate, including on the meaning of 'augmented profits', see 3105.

A preferential regime for profits arising from patents, known as a Patent Box, applies from 2013. Briefly, a company will be able to elect for its profits from qualifying patents to be taxed at an effective rate of 10%, phased in over five years. Significant changes have been made to the Patent Box regime in the Finance Bill 2016 in order to ensure that it is compliant with proposals flowing from the BEP project.

For a table of corporation tax rates and limits, see the Key Data section.

Legislation: CTA 2010, s. 3(1), Pt. 8A; FA 2010, s. 2(2)(a); FA 2011, s. 5(2)(a)

Other Material: The June 2011 document *Consultation on the Patent Box* (see the HM Treasury website at www.hm-treasury.gov.uk/d/consult_patent_box.pdf)

Tax Reporter: ¶704-000

3105   Small profits rate

The small profits rate has for some time been 20%.

The small profits and the standard CT rates are, from 1 April 2015, aligned.

Legislation: CTA 2010, s. 18, 24, 32; FA 2011, s. 6(1)(a)

Tax Reporter: ¶704-200ff.

3110   Marginal relief

Until the rates of CT were aligned in 2015, there was a marginal relief on the corporation tax payable by a company whose profits exceed the lower limit (£300,000) but are less than the upper limit (£1,500,000); though again certain close investment-holding companies are excluded (see 4080). In these circumstances, the corporation tax payable at the main rate is reduced by reference to the following formula:

$$F \times (U - A) \times \frac{N}{A}$$

F   is the standard fraction;

U   is the upper limit;

A   is the profits chargeable to corporation tax, plus franked investment income ('augmented profits'); and

N   represents the basic profits, i.e. the profits chargeable to corporation tax,

the 'standard fraction' being the fraction determined by Parliament from time to time – for the financial year 2011 it is $^3/_{200}$. A different fraction applies with regard to North Sea Oil and Gas ring fence activities.

The lower and upper profit limits are reduced for accounting periods of less than 12 months and by reference to the number of associated companies (to be referred to as 'related 51% group companies' as a consequence of changes being made in *Finance Act* 2014 to deal with the alignment of the standard and small companies rates) (see 3115).

Corporation tax

For example, a nine months accounting period and three associated companies (i.e. four companies in total) gives:

$$M = £1,500,000 \times \frac{9}{12} \times \frac{1}{4}$$

$$= £281,250$$

The lower limit of £300,000 would similarly be reduced to £56,250.

If an accounting period straddles a change of tax rate at 31 March, profits must be apportioned between the financial years in order to apply the correct rate of tax. The relevant limits are time-apportioned as appropriate.

Example

For the year ended 31 August 2013, Axyd Ltd, which has no associated companies, has the following results:

	£
Profits chargeable to corporation tax ('basic profits' – 'N')	1,129,000
Franked investment income (gross) from unrelated companies	161,000
Augmented profits ('A') for the purpose of small profits rate	1,290,000

The corporation tax payable is calculated as follows:

	1/9/10 to 31/3/11 £	1/4/13 to 31/8/13 £
Upper profits limits:		
£1,500,000 × 7/12	875,000	
£1,500,000 × 5/12		625,000
Profits:		
£1,290,000 × 7/12	752,500	
£1,290,000 × 5/12		537,500
Corporation tax at full rate:		
28% × £1,129,000 × 7/12	184,403	
26% × £1,129,000 × 5/12		122,308
Deduct marginal relief:		
$(875,000 - 752,500) \times \dfrac{1,129,000}{1,290,000} \times \dfrac{7}{400}$	(1,876)	
$(625,000 - 537,500) \times \dfrac{1,129,000}{1,290,000} \times \dfrac{3}{200}$		(1,149)
	182,527	121,159
Corporation tax payable for year to 31/8/13	303,686	

The effective rate of tax in the margin

In effect, each additional £1 of profit over the lower limit is taxed at a marginal rate, which for the financial year 2013 is 23.75% until the upper limit marginal relief is reached. This is arrived at as follows:

	Profits	Tax
Lower limit when tax will be at 20% on	300,000	60,000
Upper limit for marginal relief £1,500,000 when tax will be at 23% on	1,500,000	345,000
Difference	1,200,000	285,000

As an extra £300,000 tax arises on an extra £1,200,000 of profit, the marginal rate is therefore:

$$\frac{285,000}{1,200,000} \times 100 = 23.75\%$$

For a list of marginal relief rates, see Key Data.

Legislation: CTA 2010, s. 19–24, 32

Tax Reporter: ¶704-300 and ¶704-350

3115   Associated companies

The basic rule is that a company is associated with another if one controls the other or if both are under common control. However, there are exemptions from this rule for dormant companies and certain non-trading holding companies (although not for non-resident companies). A company is associated with another in respect of an accounting period if it is associated with that company for any part of that accounting period. This rule has been amended to reflect the impact of the alignment of the standard and small company's tax rates from 2015. Thereafter the key link is in identifying the number of 'related 51% group companies'.

For this purpose, control has the same meaning as in the close company rules (see 4000). However, these rules are relaxed by statute where:

(1) there is no substantial commercial interdependence between the companies (see below);

(2) a non-close company holds fixed-rate preference shares in another company;

(3) a company is a loan creditor of another company;

(4) two companies are controlled by the same person who is a loan creditor of both; or

(5) two companies are controlled by the same person by virtue of rights and/or powers held in trust by that person.

All of the above were provided by concession (ESC C9) previously; the relaxation at (1) having been enacted, with some modifications, by FA 2011 and those at (2)–(5) having been enacted as part of the Tax Law Rewrite project.

With regard to the relaxation at (1) above, and with effect for accounting periods ending on or after 1 April 2011 (subject to transitional arrangements, see below), the requirement to take into account rights and powers held by other persons is relaxed where the companies are not substantially commercially interdependent. In determining if there is substantial commercial interdependence between two companies (A and B), the following factors should be taken into account:

- the degree to which the companies are financially interdependent. A and B will be financially interdependent if, in particular, one gives financial support to the other or each have a financial interest in the affairs of the same business;

- the degree to which the companies are economically interdependent. A and B will be economically interdependent if, in particular, they seek to realise the same economic objective, the activities of one benefit the other or they have common customers; and

- the degree to which the companies are organisationally interdependent. A and B will be organisationally interdependent if, in particular, they have or use common management, employees, premises or equipment

It should be noted that this relaxation applies with regard to all associates including the person's spouse and business partners. It is possible to elect to disapply the changes made by FA 2011 in respect of an accounting period which began before 1 April 2011 and ends on or after that date.

Legislation: CTA 2010, s. 25–30; FA 2011, s. 55; the *Corporation Tax Act 2010 (Factors Determining Substantial Commercial Interdependence) Order* 2011 (SI 2011/1784)

Tax Reporter: ¶704-500ff.

3125   Companies and income tax

Non-resident companies are chargeable to corporation tax only on the profits of a trade in the UK carried on through a UK permanent establishment. However, they are chargeable to income tax at the basic rate on other UK source income.

Apart from this, companies do not pay income tax. But they do have to deduct income tax from certain payments, and pass this tax on to HMRC. The tax is accounted for under a system of quarterly returns where income tax due to HMRC is set off against income tax suffered at source by the company. If at the end of its accounting period the company has suffered more deduction of tax on its income than it has deducted on payments, then it may set the excess against corporation tax due (or get a repayment if there is no CT liability).

The impact of the rules relating to deduction of tax has diminished considerably since 1 April 2001. From that date, the requirement to deduct tax on relevant payments between UK resident companies (or to non-UK companies carrying on a trade through a UK permanent establishment) is removed. For payments made after 30 September 2002, the list of recipients of gross payment is extended to include the manager of a personal equity plan or individual savings account; an institution which receives the payment in respect of a TESSA; and various tax-exempt bodies listed in ITA 2007, s. 936. From the same date, a company may pay royalties (but not interest) gross to a non-resident if it has a reasonable belief that the recipient is entitled to relief from UK tax on them under a double tax treaty. HMRC will collect the tax, plus interest, from the payer if this turns out to be incorrect. With regard to payments of annual or yearly interest by UK companies to non-resident lenders, from 1 September 2010 a Double Taxation Treaty Passport Scheme has been introduced under which an overseas corporate lender in a country with the UK has a double tax treaty that includes an interest article may apply for a 'Treaty Passport' from HMRC. If a Treaty Passport is granted by HMRC, the lender will notify the borrower of their passport holder status and the UK borrower then notifies HMRC within 30 days of the loan being taken out. HMRC will then issue a direction to the borrower to apply the lower rate of withholding tax (according to the relevant double tax treaty) on the payments of the interest.

In so far as they are not to other UK companies, payments from which tax must be deducted ('relevant payments') are:

(1) annuities and other annual payments (like deeds of covenant – although not for qualifying donations to charity, see 3230);

(2) patent royalties;

(3) annual interest paid (except to a bank carrying on business in the UK):

    (a) by a company; or

    (b) by a partnership which includes a company; or

    (c) to someone whose usual place of abode is outside the UK.

(4) copyright royalties paid to someone whose usual place of abode is outside the UK.

Tax is deducted at the basic rate apart from payments of interest before 6 April 2008, where tax is deducted at the lower rate. Where tax has been deducted from a payment, the recipient may demand a certificate of deduction of tax, showing the gross and net payment and the amount of tax deducted.

Tax deduction schemes also apply to the following in essentially the same way as for individuals:

- PAYE (see 2384);

- payments to subcontractors in the construction industry (see 2387);

- payments to non-UK resident entertainers and sportsmen (see 1673);

- public revenue dividends (see 1402 and 1652);

- foreign dividends (see 1654).

Legislation: ITA 2007, Pt. 15

Tax Reporter: ¶700-100 and ¶812-400

3130   Double tax relief

If income and gains are not exempted from tax in the UK (eg by the application of the distribution exemption provisions (see 3900) or the branch exemption regime (see 3027)), relief for foreign tax (known as 'double tax relief' (DTR)) is usually available in one of three forms:

(1) as a result of the operation of a double taxation agreement ('treaty relief');

(2) by way of 'unilateral relief'; or

(3) by deduction from profits taxable in the UK.

Where credit is claimed against UK tax for the foreign tax suffered (under (1) or (2) above), relief is capped at the amount of corporation tax payable. Unrelieved foreign tax in respect of a trade carried on through a PE, and managed at least in part in the UK, can be carried forward and offset against corporation tax payable on the profits of the PE in future periods.

Legislation: TIOPA 2010, Pt. 2

Tax Reporter: ¶765-500ff.

Income

3150 Introduction

The concept of income

Corporation tax is charged on the profits of companies, being their income and chargeable gains. It is therefore important to understand what constitutes income for these purposes.

Prior to the enactment of the *Corporation Tax Act* 2009, corporation tax was imposed on income computed according to income tax rules. For accounting periods ending on or after 1 April 2009, income is liable to corporation tax if it falls within one of the heads of charge laid out in CTA 2009 (see below). However, there is no general definition of 'income' in CTA 2009 or in any of the other Tax Acts. It is therefore necessary to rely on general principles. For example, the fundamental differences between income and capital have been much discussed by economists, capital often being likened to the tree or the land, and income to the fruit or the crop. There are also a number of things which are obviously income (e.g. business profits, interest and dividends), whilst there are also other things which are obviously not (e.g. a lump sum legacy and a prize).

In addition, there have been a large number of judicial decisions in regard to the question whether a particular item is 'income'. Although the courts have refrained from attempting to formulate any precise tests of general application, some general points arise. For example, income will usually have an element of periodicity, recurrence or regularity although it does not follow that an isolated payment could not be income. Also, the characterisation of a receipt or surplus as income is unaffected by the fact that the recipient is bound to use it in a particular way and cannot enjoy it as a profit in the ordinary sense.

In *Countrywide Estate Agents FS Ltd*, an up-front payment of £25m made in exchange for the company undertaking to use its position to introduce the third party's products to the customers of the group and held by the lower-tier tribunal to be revenue in nature and not, as the company had argued, a (capital) disposal of part of its goodwill.

As stated above, for accounting periods ending on or after 1 April 2009 income is liable to corporation tax if it falls within one of the heads of charge laid out in CTA 2009. This means that the charge to corporation tax on income is driven by the particular heads of the charge to corporation tax on income as set out in CTA 2009. The main heads of charge are as follows:

- trading income (see 3152);

- property income (see 3158);

- loan relationships (see 3164);

- intangible fixed assets (see 3179);

- intellectual property falling outside the intangible fixed asset regime; and

- miscellaneous income (e.g. past cessation receipts, non trading gains on intangible fixed assets, profits on disposal of know-how or patent rights, gains from artificial transactions in land etc.).

Case: *Countrywide Estate Agents FS Ltd* [2010] TC 00557

Tax Reporter: ¶701-200ff.

Restriction on deductions – rules applying generally

Restrictions are imposed on certain deductions. The restrictions apply to all income charged to corporation tax, including trading and property income, and also to expenses of management and expenses of companies with investment business. The restriction applies to the following expenses:

(1) remuneration not paid, broadly, within nine months of the end of the accounting period;

(2) contributions to an employee benefit trust (but see 3255 for details of a specific corporation tax deduction when benefits are provided out of the trust);

(3) business entertainment and gifts;

(4) annual payments;

(5) social security contributions (except employers' National Insurance contributions);

(6) penalties, interest and VAT surcharges;

(7) crime-related payments; and

(8) dividends and other distributions.

Legislation: CTA 2009, Pt. 20, Ch. 1

Tax Reporter: ¶703-200ff.

3152   Trading income

General Principles

The profits of a trade must be calculated for tax purposes in accordance with generally accepted accounting practice, subject to any adjustment required or authorised by law in calculating profits for corporation tax purposes. The starting point in calculating taxable business profit is therefore the profit and loss account. The profit and loss account and the balance sheet are part of the financial statements, or accounts that companies produce. The profit or loss of a trade consists of trading income less trading expenses.

The adjustments to the accounts profit (or loss) required or authorised by tax law typically include the following:

- a disallowance of expenses that are not incurred wholly and exclusively for the purposes of the trade (e.g. excessive director's remuneration, expenses incurred by one group company in respect of a trade carried on by another group company, expenses that have a dual purpose, payments made in connection with the discontinuance of the business, etc.);

- a disallowance of capital expenditure and the depreciation or amortisation of such expenditure (except in relation to certain intangible fixed assets – see 3179);

- a disallowance of the expenses for which a deduction is generally prohibited (see 3186 – for example, business entertaining, dividends and other distributions, etc.);

- a disallowance of expenditure which is specifically disallowed in computing trading profits, for example, a proportion of the hire costs of cars, patent royalties, etc.;

- the removal of expenditure or income which is dealt with for tax purposes otherwise than as part of trading profits (e.g. net non-trading credits or net non-trading debits on loan relationship or derivative instruments);

- a deduction for expenditure for which a specific deduction is allowed, for example, capital allowances, awards of shares to employees (see 3425), debts proving irrecoverable after a business discontinuance, certain pre-trading expenditure, a proportion of the premium paid in respect of a lease of property occupied for the purposes of the trade, gifts of medical supplies and equipment for humanitarian purposes;

- exclusion of income which is non taxable, for example, most company distributions received after 1 July 2009, capital receipts; and

- exclusion of income or expenses that are brought into account for tax purposes in a different accounting period than the one in which they are reflected in the accounts, for example, contributions to a pension scheme not paid during the accounting period, a general provision for bad debts, etc.

The rules for calculating trading income for corporation tax purposes, as contained in CTA 2009, Pt. 3, largely mirror those applying for income tax purposes (see 550ff.). The *Finance Act* 2016 (introducing ITTOIA 2005, s. 28A) contains legislation dealing with transactions involving 'money's worth' rather than money. It provides that: for the purpose of calculating the profits of the trade, an amount equal to the value of the money's worth is brought into account as a receipt if, had the transaction involved money, an amount would have been brought into account as a receipt in respect of it. A comprehensive example of the adjustments required to calculate trading profits can be found at 3154.

Post cessation receipts carry back

The *Income and Corporation Taxes Act* 1988 contained an election which allowed a post cessation receipt to be carried back to the date trade ceased. Unfortunately, this section was repealed by ITTOIA 2005. The *Corporation Tax Act* 2009 now reinstates the rule for corporation tax and allows the company to carry back the post cessation receipt.

The election is available where a company receives a post cessation receipt in an accounting period beginning not later than six years after the company ceased to carry on the trade. The effect of the election is to allow the company to have post cessation receipt carried back so that it is taxed as though it was received in the accounting period in which trade ceases. The election must be made within two years of the period beginning immediately after the accounting period in which the receipt is received.

The election may be useful where there are unrelieved trading losses.

Legislation: CTA 2009, Pt. 3 and s. 198–200

Tax Reporter: ¶707-000ff.

3154 Comprehensive example of adjustments to calculate taxable trading profits

A comprehensive example of the adjustments required to calculate trading profits follows.

Example

Acorus Ltd is a UK resident company which has traded as a manufacturer of gardening tools for many years. It has no associated companies. The company is a medium-sized company.

The company's summarised profit and loss account for the year ended 30 September 2013 showed the following:

	£	£
Sales		3,942,000
Less: cost of sales		(1,995,460)
Gross trading profit		1,946,540
Other income (note (a))		127,960
		2,074,500
Less:		
Rent and establishment costs	215,825	
Salaries and staff costs	535,900	
Directors' remuneration	135,400	
Pension contributions (note (b))	62,400	
Bad debts (note (c))	60,600	
Legal and professional costs (note (d))	12,000	
Audit and accountancy	60,000	
UK patent royalties	8,000	
Repairs and renewals (note (e))	27,400	
Depreciation (note (f))	428,000	
Sundries (note (g))	58,980	
Interest (note (h))	46,875	(1,651,380)
Profit before exceptional items		423,120
Less: exceptional items (note (i))		(471,000)
Loss before taxation		(47,880)

The following additional notes have been provided:

(a)   Other income

	£
Franked investment income	30,500
Proceeds from sale of know-how	76,460
Bank interest receivable	21,000
	127,960

(b)   Pension contributions of £45,000 were paid during the year to 30 September 2013.

(c) The bad debts account is analysed as follows:

	Dr £	Cr £
Balance at 1/10/12		
General provision	30,000	
Specific provision	23,000	
Profit and loss account	60,600	
Loss arising from staff pilferage		18,000
Balance at 30/9/13		
General provision		20,000
Specific provision		75,600
	113,600	113,600

(d) Legal and professional costs are analysed as follows:

	£
Company secretarial costs	6,000
Debt collection	1,750
Patent infringement claim work	1,200
Claim for unfair dismissal	700
Assignment of short lease	2,350
	12,000

(e) Repairs and renewals:

	£
Lorry park security fencing	2,050
Machinery protection guards	1,870
Factory storage shelving	13,230
General repairs provision	10,000
General factory maintenance (all allowable)	250
	27,400

(f) Depreciation is made up as follows:

	£
Owned assets	
Land and buildings	20,000
Plant and machinery	288,000
Finance lease assets	
Lorry fleet	120,000
	428,000

The company acquires all of its delivery lorries under finance leases. The lorries are depreciated at the rate of 25% with a full charge being made in the year of purchase and none in the year of disposal.

(g) Sundries are analysed as follows:

	£
Computer maintenance	16,600
Security costs	7,400
Damages paid to purchaser for supply of defective goods	4,000
Gift aid donation paid to BBC 'Children in Need' appeal	5,000
VAT serious misdeclaration penalty	3,600
Canteen expenses	21,700
Sundries (all allowable)	680
	58,980

(h) Interest is analysed as follows:

	£
Finance charge on finance leases	45,000
Loan stock interest accrued at 30/9/13	1,875
	46,875

(i) Exceptional items:

	£	£
Loan stock issue expenses		
Accountants' fees	50,000	
Solicitors' fees	25,000	
Bank guarantee charges	15,000	90,000
Rationalisation costs		
Cost of transferring equipment	25,000	
Redundancy costs		
Paid in period	96,000	
Provision for future redundancies at 30/9/13	180,000	
Provision for other closure costs at 30/9/13	80,000	381,000
		471,000

The company issued £100,000 10% loan stock on 20 July 2013. (The amount borrowed is to be used for capital investment in a new factory.)

The company has a constructive obligation to carry out the rationalisation programme, at 30 September 2013, having taken steps to move plant and notify its suppliers and customers. The rationalisation primarily relates to the closure of its Prunella Road factory. The provision for future redundancies at 30 September 2013 has been calculated by reference to the amounts due to the relevant employees who are to be made redundant on 31 October 2013. The provisions for redundancy and closure costs are validly made under FRS 12.

(j) The company can claim £55,185 in capital allowances.

Acorus Ltd's adjusted taxable trading profit and profit chargeable to corporation tax for the year ended 30 September 2013 is as follows:

	£	£
Loss before taxation		(47,880)
Add:		
Pension contributions charged	62,400	
Legal and professional costs – assignment of short lease	2,350	
Repairs and renewals (W2)	27,150	
Depreciation on 'owned' assets (£20,000 + £288,000)	308,000	
Sundries – VAT serious misdeclaration penalty	3,600	403,500
Less:		
Franked investment income	(30,500)	
Bank interest received	(21,000)	
Pension contributions paid	(45,000)	
Reduction in general provision for bad debts (£30,000 – £20,000) (W1)	(10,000)	
Capital allowances	(55,185)	(161,685)
Tax-adjusted trading profit		193,935
Non-trading loan relationship income		21,000
Profits chargeable to corporation tax		214,935

Workings and notes

W1 The loss arising from staff pilferage would be accepted as allowable as this would be an ordinary risk of the trade.

W2 Repairs and renewals

		Disallowable
	£	£
General repairs provision	10,000	10,000
Lorry park security fencing	2,050	2,050

Machinery protection guards	1,870	1,870
Factory storage shelving	13,230	13,230
General factory maintenance	250	
	27,400	27,150

W3   The company is obliged (constructively) to the closure of the factory and the redundancy programme. The redundancy cost provision (calculated accurately by reference to the relevant individual employees) and the provisions for other closure costs are made in accordance with FRS 12, and hence allowed for tax purposes.

3158   Property income

Rental and other income from the letting of UK land and (furnished and unfurnished) property is taxed as a single UK property business for corporation tax purposes. However, any property business income will generally be recognised as an investment activity. Capital allowances relating to the rental business are deducted as an allowable expense of the property business. Profits and losses from a property business are computed in the same way as for a trade. The results of the rental business are therefore calculated on an accruals basis in accordance with normal commercial accounting principles. Income from an overseas property is taxed as a single overseas property business on broadly the same basis as a UK property business (but separate from the single UK property letting business). Special rules apply with regard to furnished holiday lettings (see 1255).

Under the quasi-trading basis, relief is available for all expenses incurred wholly and exclusively for the purposes of the letting business. Certain statutory trading profit rules, including the disallowance of business entertaining and the timing of relief for unpaid remuneration (see 3186) also apply for rental business purposes. Premiums received are dealt with separately under the special rules which treat a proportion of the premium as income and a proportion as capital. Relief for bad or doubtful rental debts is based on trading profit principles. Expenses of a capital nature are not allowed. However, relief is available for the replacement of domestic items following the abolition of wear and tear allowance from April 2016. Provisions for future repairs are also not allowed. Legal and other fees for granting leases exceeding one year are disallowed as capital expenditure. Interest relating to the letting business is deducted under the loan relationship rules as a non-trade deduction (see 3164).

The rules for calculating income from a property business for corporation tax purposes, as contained in CTA 2009, Pt. 4, largely mirror those applying for income tax purposes (see 1200ff.).

Legislation: CTA 2009, Pt. 4

Tax Reporter: ¶711-000ff.

Loan relationships and derivative contracts

3164   Introduction and overview

All 'money debts' held and owed by companies which arise from the lending of money are known as 'loan relationships'. Profits and losses on such relationships are taxed or allowed, for corporation tax purposes, as income. Where the company is a party to the relationship for the purposes of its trade all profits, gains and losses are included in the calculation of its trading profit. In any other case, profits and gains are taxed as non-trading loan relationships and losses (called 'non-trading deficits') are set against non-trading loan relationship profits and gains in the same accounting period and any excess is relieved against specified profits of the company or of fellow group members. For accounting periods beginning on or after 1 October 2002, foreign exchange gains and losses on loan relationships and other transactions are included within these rules. Previously, these items were dealt with under FA 1993 foreign exchange legislation, now largely repealed. Also from 1 October 2002, derivative contracts are included within their own new provisions – which are very similar to the overall thrust of the loan relationships legislation. Like trading loan relationships, debits and credits on derivative contracts to which a company is a party for the purposes of its trade are included in the overall trading income result, whilst non-trading debits and credits are dealt with in a similar manner to non-trading debits and credits on loan relationships.

Overview of regime for taxation of loan relationships

To a very great extent, the treatment of corporate and government debt for corporation tax purposes follows the accounting treatment. It should be noted that a number of cases have now been heard where taxpayers have adopted tax avoidance structures. In *Vocalspruce Ltd v R & C Commrs* [2014] BTC 50), the Court of Appeal continuing the recent trend, upheld the decision of the Upper Tribunal, and found that a marketed tax avoidance scheme exploiting provisions in the loan relationships legislation and involving the capitalisation of the premium arising on the redemption of zero coupon loan notes in share premium account was ineffective.

A number of fundamental changes are being made to tighten up the rules. The proposals were not included in *Finance Act* 2015 but have been included in *Finance (No. 2) Act* 2015. In particular, changes are made providing:

- clarification, in respect of accounting periods commencing on or after 1 January 2016 of the relationship between tax and accounting – including removal of the 'fairly represent' requirement and basing the calculation of the taxable loan relationship profits solely on accounting entries in the income statement;

- introducing, from the date of Royal Assent, a new regime-wide anti-avoidance 'main purpose' rule for both loan relationships and derivative contracts;

- a new rule, from the date of Royal Assent, where loans are released in cases of debtor companies in 'financial distress';

- a range of updates to the rules on FOREX hedging, convertible instruments and property based derivatives will be introduced by regulations.

Further changes made in *Finance Act* 2016 to address situations where the interaction with accounting rules or other parts of the tax rules may lead to unintended consequences: specifically, in relation to interest-free loans and other loans on non-market terms and will have effect from 1 April 2016.

For the majority of companies which do not have complex borrowing or lending arrangements and are not attempting to exploit the loan relationship rules for tax avoidance, the legislation is simple to apply and is generally helpful. However, the rules behind the simple principle of taxing/relieving the profit and loss account entry are inevitably complex. They are found in CTA 2009, Pt. 5. The 'fairly represent' requirement has been the subject of litigation – see *GDF Suez Teeside Ltd* where the accounting treatment was overridden for tax purposes and replaced with a taxable credit based on the fair value of the debt claims.

Money debts

'Money' is defined to include money expressed in a currency other than sterling. A money debt is a debt settled in money, or by the transfer of a right to settlement under a debt which is a money debt. 'Money', which is not defined further, must be taken to have its ordinary meaning. It would not, therefore, include physical commodities or a barter arrangement. 'Debt' includes a debt the amount of which falls to be ascertained by reference to matters which vary from time to time.

A transaction for the lending of money

The rules provide the following guidance on the meaning of this term:

- where an instrument is issued to evidence any money debt, the debt is taken to have arisen from a transaction for the lending of money. This is intended to catch a situation where the original transaction is not one for the lending of money so the debt would not otherwise be a money debt arising from a transaction for the lending of money and bring the debt into the loan relationship provisions by virtue of the issue of the security. The instrument must be issued for the purpose of representing a security, and not simply documenting a transaction (such as a contract for a monthly service charge payable in arrears). An example would be a sale of shares in a company where the vendor receives part of the consideration in loan note;

- a debt arising from rights conferred by shares in a company does not arise from a transaction for the lending of money;

- 'loan' includes any advance of money.

According to the Revenue press release announcing the publication of the original draft legislation (REV 21 of 28 November 1995), a loan relationship would arise from any debt 'which, under general law, is a loan'. So any transaction which would generally be regarded as lending would qualify, e.g. unsecured loans, overdrafts, drawn-down credit facilities, in addition to all securitised debts. Neither the duration of the financing, nor the form of payment for the loan – interest, discount, premium, or any combination – is relevant. Finance leases are excluded for, whatever their economic character, they are not loans for legal purposes.

From 6 April 2005, references to loan relationships include references to 'alternative finance arrangements' for the taxation of lending under Shari'a law.

HMRC have confirmed that straightforward commercial contracts and invoices do not represent a security, and therefore, not a transaction of lending money. However, it would seem possible for such a transaction to become a transaction of lending – for example, where a debtor is granted extended time to pay.

Any instrument which represents a pure equity interest in a company cannot be a loan relationship. The reference to 'shares in a company' is qualified by CTA 2009, s. 476, in that the term 'share' is deemed to mean any share under which entitlement to receive distributions may arise. It must therefore be taken to include preference shares. Building society shares are not shares for this purpose (CTA 2009, s. 476) so debits and credits on those shares are taken into account under the loan relationship rules. Equity instruments which have some debt-like characteristics, such as convertibles, may rank as loan relationships but are subject to special rules.

The special commissioners have decided that, on the proper construction of the FA 1996 basis for the taxation of profits or losses arising from loan relationships, receipts from the making of contracts for financial futures by a number of life insurance companies were not subject to the loan relationship regime. Although tax considerations played a decisive part in the choice of structures, the transactions were genuine and not shams and the deliberate tax-efficient structuring of the business did not affect the commercial and legal characterisation of what was done (*HSBC Life (UK) Ltd v Stubbs (HMIT)* and related appeals). The mere economic equivalence of a transaction to a loan did not show that it was a loan. The authorities showed that the concept of 'loan' or 'lending' might vary from statute to statute if a particular meaning was adopted. By specifically referring to the concept of 'a transaction for the lending of money', CTA 2009, s. 302(1)(b) intended to confine a concept whose extent might otherwise be uncertain within well-known and ascertainable bounds. It was impossible to conclude that any of the parties to the transactions thought that they were lenders or borrowers, or that they intended that to be the case. They plainly intended to enter into the legal relationships which the documentation showed that they established, and they took care to enter the relationship of buyer and seller of financial futures and not that of lender and borrower. The fact that, in doing so, they were clearly anxious to fall within one tax regime rather than another was beside the point.

Relevant non-lending relationships

The application of the loan relationship legislation is extended by CTA 2009, s. 481 to money debts not arising from a transaction for the lending of money (referred to as a 'relevant non-lending relationship') where the debt is one:

(a) on which interest is payable (or receivable);

(b) on which a foreign exchange gain or loss arises;

(c) for creditor companies, in relation to which an impairment loss arises, or, with effect from 22 April 2009, where a release debit arises, in respect of a business payment;

(d) for debtor companies, from 22 April 2009, in relation to which a trading deduction or a UK or overseas property business deduction has been allowed to the company and which is released; or

(e) on which a discount arises to the company

In relation to (c) above, a business payment means a payment which, if it were paid, would fall to be brought into account for tax purposes as a receipt of a trade, UK property business or overseas property business. For example, a provision against trade debtors would fall into this category. As to the reasons for the extension in (d) above to some debtor company relationships from 22 April 2009, see below.

The loan relationship rules are extended to these type of non-lending relationships only in respect of the following matters:

(1) interest payable by or to the company;

(2) exchange gains and losses;

(3) for debts on which interest is payable to the company, profits (but not losses) on the sale of the right to the interest;

(4) for creditor companies, an impairment loss (and from 22 April 2009, release debits) in respect of a business payment and a credit in respect of the reversal of such an impairment loss;

(5) for debtor companies, from 22 April 2009, the release of a debt in relation to which a trading deduction, or a UK or overseas property business deduction has been allowed to the company;

(6) for creditor companies, the discount on the debt or an impairment loss in respect of the discount; and

(7) for creditor companies in relation to a debt from which a discount arises, the profit (but not the loss) on a disposal of the rights under the loan.

As to the reasons for the extension in (5) above to debtor companies from 22 April 2009 for the release of certain debts, see below.

An example of a relevant non-lending relationship would be consideration outstanding on the purchase of an asset (e.g. Co A is in the business of selling properties). Co B buys a property and fails to pay the consideration due to Co A. The amount outstanding did not arise from a transaction for the lending of money therefore there is no loan relationship. If Co B pays Co A interest on the amount outstanding, or Co A makes an impairment adjustment in respect of any of the amount outstanding, those debits and credits will be treated as loan relationship debits and credits in Co A, and the interest would be a loan relationship debit for B. If A was not in the business of selling properties but was, for example, disposing of its business premises, the interest would be a loan relationship credit for A but the impairment would not be an allowable debit since the impairment loss would not be in respect of a business payment.

Prior to 22 April 2009, there was an anomaly arising from a mismatch in treatment between the debtor and creditor company where a trade debt owed by a connected company was written off. The creditor company's position fell within the relevant non-lending relationship provisions above and so the release debit fell within the loan relationship rules and so no relief was available because of the connected party rules. However, prior to 22 April 2009 the release of the debt in the debtor company did not fall within the loan relationship rules (as it was not a relevant non-lending relationship prior to that date) and so the debtor company would have been taxable under CTA 2009, s. 94 on the release of the debt. From 22 April 2009, this anomaly has been removed by bringing the debtor company within the loan relationship rules in these circumstances so that the debtor does not need to bring in a taxable credit (if the creditor company is a connected company) because of the connected party rules.

Common instances where the tax treatment of loan relationships differs from the accounting treatment

The overall purpose of the recasting of the tax legislation dealing with loan relationships was to align the tax treatment with the accounting treatment. However, there are specific situations where the amounts brought into account for tax purposes differ from the amounts recorded in the company's profit and loss account. These include the following.

Late paid interest

A special rule applied for accounting periods beginning after 30 September 2002 but before 1 April 2009 (see below for the position for accounting periods beginning on or after 1 April 2009) where:

- the payer and the recipient of interest were connected (determined by a control test);

- the payer was a close company and the recipient was a participator, associate of a participator, or company controlled by a participator;

- the payer company had a major interest (40% or more) in the recipient company, or vice versa; or

- the recipient was a pension scheme and there was a connection between the paying company and the employer of the employees to whom the scheme related.

In these circumstances, if the creditor did not bring the corresponding credits for interest into account for corporation tax purposes, the debtor company's deduction for interest payable was deferred if it fails to pay the interest for more than 12 months after the end of the accounting period in which it accrued. The deduction was permitted only in the accounting period in which the company actually paid the interest. This applied, for example, where the connected lender was non-UK resident.

> **Example**
>
> Toad Rock Ltd owns High Rocks BV, a non-UK resident company. Toad Rock accrues interest annually on a loan from High Rocks in its accounting period ended 31 December 2005 but does not pay the interest until 28 February 2007. The deduction will be allowed in the period ended 31 December 2007.

Rulings of the European Court of Justice, however, raised concerns that this provision was not compatible with European law. To ensure that the law is compatible with European law, *Finance Act* 2009 amended the rule so that the accruals basis will apply unless the connected creditor company is resident or effectively managed in a 'non-qualifying territory'. Then the paid basis will apply. A territory is a non-qualifying territory for these purposes if it does not have a double tax agreement with the UK that includes a non-discrimination clause. Most tax havens will be non-qualifying territories.

The changes have effect for accounting periods beginning on or after 1 April 2009. As a transitional measure a company may elect that the amendment is not to have effect for the first accounting period beginning after that date. The election must be made on the corporation tax return for the accounting period which the election applies to. No election can be made for an accounting period after 31 March 2011.

Connected parties

Where the debtor company and the creditor company are connected, that is to say, one has control of the other:

- debits and credits in respect of the loan relationships have to be accounted for on an amortised cost basis; and
- debits and credits in relation to loans written off or released and debits in respect of impairment losses are not taken into account for tax purposes.

For the purposes of these connected party rules, 'control' is defined widely to include the power of a person to secure that the affairs of the company are conducted in accordance with his wishes. In *Fenlo Ltd v R & C Commrs*, the Special Commissioner decided that the terms of a debenture given to the lender charging the undertaking and assets of the borrower by way of security for the loan did not give the lender the power to secure that the affairs of the borrower were conducted in accordance with the lender's wishes and that the two companies were not therefore connected parties.

Loan relationship for unallowable purposes

Debits on loan relationships which have an unallowable purpose are not recognised for corporation tax purposes. In addition, any exchange gains on a loan relationship which has an unallowable purpose will similarly not be recognised. Where a loan relationship has an unallowable purpose, so much of the debits, and foreign exchange credits, on that loan relationship for the accounting period as are attributable, on a just and reasonable apportionment, to the unallowable purpose are left out of account. Debits on loans for unallowable purposes which are not brought into account (and thus are already refused relief as loan relationship debits) are similarly denied relief under any other corporation tax provisions in CTA 2009.

The test, which must be carried out for every accounting period during which the company is party to the loan relationship in question, is whether the purpose for which the company is a party to the loan relationship or enters into a related transaction in respect of that loan relationship (such as the disposal or release of a loan) is one 'which is not amongst the business or other commercial purposes of the company'.

In *Fidex Ltd v R & C Commrs* [2014] BTC 530, the Upper Tribunal allowed HMRC's appeal against the First-tier Tribunal's decision that the debit was not attributable to an unallowable purpose.

Credit not taxable on release of liability

In addition to the situation where the debtor and creditor are connected there are several circumstances listed at (1) to (4) below, where the release of a liability will not give rise to a taxable credit in the debtor company.

(1)   The release is part of a statutory insolvency arrangement.

(2)   The creditor company is in insolvent liquidation and immediately before it went into liquidation, the debtor and creditor were connected companies and they were not connected immediately after that time.

(3)   The relationship is not with a connected company but the debtor company is in insolvent liquidation.

(4)   The release is in consideration of, or of any entitlement to, shares forming part of the ordinary share capital of the debtor company.

Close company releasing loan to a participator

Where a close company makes a loan to an individual who is a participator and releases it, the recipient of the released loan is charged to income tax but is treated as having paid income tax at the dividend ordinary rate. As with the receipt of a dividend, there will be no further liability to income tax unless the participator is a higher rate taxpayer. The company will have a liability to corporation tax under CTA 2010, s. 455 at the time that the loan is made but this can be reclaimed once the loan is released or written off (or repaid). However, prior to 24 March 2010, for corporation tax purposes under the loan relationships rules a loan released will normally give rise to an expense recognised in the company's accounts and be allowable for corporation tax purposes (since, in particular, a participator who is an individual will not be a connected party for the purposes of determining whether an impairment loss is allowable). This position was changed with effect from 24 March 2010. Where a loan by a close company to a participator which gave rise to a charge to corporation tax under s. 455 is released or written off on or after 24 March 2010, the company is not entitled to a deduction under the loan relationship rules.

Deemed release where an impaired debt becomes held by connected party

There are two instances where there is a deemed release of a liability under a debtor loan relationship. Where these circumstances apply, the credit arising in the debtor company on the deemed release has to be brought into account for tax purposes.

The first instance applies where a company (C) acquires a debt from an unconnected creditor (T) and immediately after that acquisition C is connected with the debtor company (whether such connection arises by virtue of acquiring shares at the same time as the debt, or whether the debtor and C were previously connected) and the pre-acquisition carrying value of the debt (being the original amount of the liability in the accounts of the debtor due less any release by T) exceeds the consideration which C has paid for the debt. This would apply, for example, where a parent company acquires from a bank (for a consideration less than the face value of the loan) a loan made by the bank to a subsidiary company of the parent. In such circumstances, there is a deemed release of the debt in the amount of the excess, so that the difference between the face value of, and the amount actually paid for, the debt is treated as released and therefore constitutes a credit taxable on the debtor.

For acquisitions of debt after 14 October 2009, an exception to the deemed charge (referred to in the legislation as the 'corporate rescue exception') applies in the following circumstances:

- the acquisition by the new creditor is at arm's length;

- there has been a change in ownership of the debtor company in the period beginning one year before and ending 60 days after the acquisition of the debt;

- it is reasonable to assume that but for the change in ownership the debtor company would have become insolvent; and

- it is reasonable to assume that the new creditor would not have acquired the debt but for the change in ownership.

The second instance where a deemed release occurs is where the identity of the creditor remains the same, but the creditor changes from being unconnected to connected, in circumstances where the amount that would have been the carrying value of the loan relationship asset in the accounts of the creditor if a period of account had ended immediately prior to the companies becoming connected would have been adjusted for impairment. The deemed release is of an amount equal to the impairment adjustment that would have been made. This instance would occur, for example, if a parent company acquired the company that had previously made a loan to the parent company's subsidiary where the value of the debt had become impaired (for example, because the subsidiary was in financial difficulty).

Disguised interest

Finance Act 2009 makes changes to the loan relationship rules introducing a new comprehensive principle to tackle disguised interest.

Where a company is party to an arrangement which produces for the company a return in relation to any amount which is economically equivalent to interest, then the loan relationship rules apply as if the return were a profit arising to the company from a loan relationship. For this purpose, a return produced for a company by an arrangement in relation to any amount is 'economically equivalent to interest' if and only if:

(a) it is reasonable to assume that it is a return by reference to the time value of that amount of money;

(b) it is at a rate reasonably comparable to what is (in all the circumstances) a commercial rate of interest; and

(c) at the relevant time, there is no practical likelihood that it will cease to be produced in accordance with the arrangement unless the person by whom it falls to be produced is prevented (by reason of insolvency or otherwise).

There are three exclusions:

(1) where the return is otherwise taxable such as trading income, or under the fixed asset rules or under the derivative contracts rules;

(2) where the arrangements have no tax avoidance motive; or

(3) where the arrangements involve excluded shares such as certain group companies or companies that would be controlled foreign companies (CFCs) (see 4150) but for an exemption.

Corporation tax

Where there is no tax avoidance motive, a company can elect for the exclusion not to apply. The election must be made no later than the time when the arrangement begins to produce a return for the company, and is irrevocable.

The amendments made have effect in relation to any arrangement which produces for a company a return which is economically equivalent to interest if the company becomes a party to the arrangement on or after 22 April 2009.

Transitional arrangements apply in respect of existing arrangements in force as at 22 April 2009.

Derecognition

In certain circumstances, where a company holds a loan that is matched with another financial instrument issued by it, GAAP may permit or require the loan, or amounts arising in respect of it, not to be recognised in determining the company's accounting profits or losses for the period. For example, a company may have made a loan or hold securities from which it receives income in the form of interest, and issued fixed rate preference shares under which matching amounts are paid as dividends. While the interest income and dividend expense match each other economically, following the accounting treatment in such a case gives rise to a tax assymetry, since interest is normally fully taxable and the dividends are not deductible.

Legislation was first introduced in FA 2006 to counter the tax avoidance possibilities of this assymetry, and has been amended in subsequent Finance Acts as new schemes based on derecognition have come to light. Rather than continue to make additions to the legislation in response to new examples of such avoidance, the Government announced on 6 December 2010 that the legislative approach would be changed to create a general rule that taxable amounts arising on loan relationships and derivative contracts are to be computed as if all profits and losses on derecognised loan and other financial instruments were fully recognised for accounting purposes, where the company is party to tax avoidance arrangements. In addition, from 6 December 2010 a company is denied a tax deduction under the loan relationship rules for a loss on derecognition, where the company is party to tax avoidance arrangements. These new provisions take effect from 6 December 2010. The determination of the Upper Tribunal (UT) in *Greene King plc v R & C Commrs* should be noted for the approach taken to the accounting treatment. The UT agreed with an earlier decision by the First-tier Tribunal which had upheld HMRC's view that the taxpayer should de-recognise part of the value of the loans as required under FRS 5, Reporting the Substance of Transactions.

Legislation: CTA 2009, Pt. 5 and 6, s. 94 and 481

Cases: *HSBC Life (UK) Ltd v Stubbs (HMIT)* (2001) Sp C 295; *Fenlo Ltd v R & C Commrs* (2008) Sp C 714; *Greene King plc v R & C Commrs* [2014] BTC 515; *GDF Suez Teesside Ltd (Formerly Teesside Power Ltd)* [2015] TC 04590

Other Material: HMRC *Corporate Finance Manual* (CFM13420)

Tax Reporter: ¶717-000ff.

3168 Loan relationships – bringing amounts into account

For accounting periods beginning after 31 December 2004, debits and credits made in accordance with generally accepted accounting practice (GAAP) that are recognised in determining the company's profit or loss for the period are used to calculate a company's taxable income or deductions resulting from its loan relationships. For earlier accounting periods, the debits and credits were those made under 'authorised accounting methods'. Some debits and credits are disallowed, even though they fall to be made for the purposes of the company's accounts (see 3164 for common examples of this). Changes are being made in respect of accounting periods commencing on or after 1 January 2016 basing taxable amounts on those recognised only in profit or loss for accounting purposes.

Trading loan relationships

For any loan to which a company is a party for trading purposes:

- credits are treated as trading receipts; and

- debits are treated as deductible trading expenses.

The test of whether or not a company is party to a loan relationship for the purposes of its trade depends on whether the company is a creditor or debtor. As a debtor, it need only show that it took on the debt for the purposes of its trade: whether the loan represents a temporary facility or is part of the company's capital should be irrelevant. It should not matter whether the loan finances current or fixed assets.

A creditor, however, may only treat a loan as a trading loan if it made or acquired the loan 'in the course of activities forming an integral part of [its] trade'.

Non-trade loan relationships

Any loan which is not for a trading purpose will give rise to debits (i.e. losses) and credits (i.e. profits) which are called, respectively, 'non-trading debits' and 'non-trading credits'. In any accounting period, the treatment of these is respectively:

Corporation tax

- net non-trading credits (i.e. the aggregate of a company's non-trading credits, less the sum of all its non-trading debits, if any) are taxed as non-trading loan relationships; and

- net non-trading debits (i.e. the aggregate of a company's non-trading debits, less the sum of all its non-trading credits, if any) are relieved, as a 'non-trading deficit', under special rules outlined below.

Note that non-trading foreign exchange gains and losses are also dealt with under these loan relationship provisions for accounting periods ending after 31 March 1996.

Set off of non-trade deficits

To the extent that a non-trading deficit is not surrendered as group relief for a period, it can be used in any of the following ways, in this order:

(1) set against the company's total profits for the accounting period in which the deficit arises;

(2) to the extent not group relieved or set against profits of the same period, carried back and set against profits arising in earlier periods; or

(3) to the extent not used in any of the ways already mentioned, carried forward and set against non-trading profits arising in future periods to the extent that it is not used in any of the ways already mentioned.

Profits of the same period

Where a claim is made to set the deficit against profits arising in the same period, trading losses brought forward from earlier periods must be used in priority to the non-trading deficit. The non-trading deficits must be set off in priority to losses arising in that period from a UK property business, and in priority to losses arising from a trade in that period and in priority to non-trading deficits carried back from future accounting periods.

Example

For the two years ending 31 March 2013, S Ltd has the following results:

	2012	2013
	£	£
Trading profit/(loss)	80,000	(12,000)
Trading loss brought forward	(60,000)	–
Other income and gains	8,000	–
Loss on sale of fixed interest company debentures	(20,000)	–

A claim to set the entire non-trading deficit against trading profits for the deficit period would give rise to the following computation of profits for 2012:

	£	£
Trading	80,000	
Less: Trading loss brought forward	(60,000)	
Non-trading deficit	(20,000)	
		Nil
Other income and gains		8,000
Less: Trading loss carried back		(8,000)
Profits chargeable to corporation tax		Nil

Such a claim would leave the balance of the trading loss for the year to 31 March 2013 which could not be carried back – £4,000 – to be carried forward to later accounting periods. If the claim had been to set the non-trading deficit against other income and gains first, the result would have been the same.

Carry back claims

Where a carry back claim is made, the deficit can be set off against non-trading loan relationship profits arising in the period of 12 months preceding the beginning of the period in which the deficit arises. The non-trading loan relationship profits of the preceding period will first be reduced by the following in priority to the non-trading deficit carried back:

(1) relief in respect of losses or deficits incurred or treated as incurred in an accounting period before the period in which the deficit arose;

(2) charitable donations relief (previously charges on income) in relation to payments made wholly and exclusively for the purposes of the trade;

(3) where the company is a company with an investment business, priority will be given to capital allowances, management expenses, and charitable donations relief in relation to payments made wholly and exclusively for the purposes of the trade;

(4) trading losses of the same or a later period; and

(5) non-trading deficits of the preceding period.

Carry forward

To the extent not used in any of the ways already mentioned, excess non-trade deficits will be carried forward automatically and set against non-trading profits of future periods, however, the company can make a claim to exclude any amount of the deficits brought forward from being set off. Where such a claim is made, the deficit is treated as arising in the period in respect of which such a claim is made for the purpose of carry forward to the next period, such that a claim could be made for the deficit to be excluded from set off against non-trading profits in the following period, and so on, indefinitely.

Legislation: CTA 2009, s. 353, 471, 476 and 481; *Loan Relationships and Derivative Contracts (Exchange Gains and Losses using Fair Value Accounting) Regulations* 2005 (SI 2005/3422)

Case: *Nuclear Electric plc v Bradley* [1995] BTC 445

Tax Reporter: ¶717-200ff. and ¶717-600ff.

3171   Tax treatment of financing costs and income: debt cap

Finance Act 2009, Sch. 15 has introduced legislation aimed at preventing the use of interest deductions from eroding the UK corporation tax base, and is particularly aimed at upstream loans where a large group has either a UK or foreign parent. Schedule 15 has been rewritten as *Taxation (International and other Provisions) Act* 2010, Pt. 7 for accounting periods ending on or after 1 April 2010. The legislation itself applies to periods of account of a worldwide group that begin on or after 1 January 2010. A worldwide group is a large group which has at least one company which is UK tax resident. It includes a company which while not resident in the UK, carries on a trade in the UK through a permanent establishment. A group will be large where any member of the group has 250 or more employees or has both annual turnover of €50m or more and a balance sheet total of €43m or more (after aggregating the headcount, turnover and balance sheet totals of any partner or linked enterprises).

The broad effect of the new legislation is to restrict any tax deduction for inter group finance expenses to the external gross finance expense of the worldwide group. The legislation applies if the UK net debt of the group exceeds 75% of the 'worldwide gross debt of the group'. Where the UK net debt does not exceed 75% of the worldwide gross debt of the group, then the debt cap does not apply.

The legislation applies a reduction in the amount of interest which can be deducted where the tested expense amount exceeds the allowable amount. The tested expense amount is the total of the net amount of financing expenses payable by each relevant group company that has net financing expenses. The available amount is the external gross finance expense of the worldwide group of companies.

HMRC have issued a tax information and impact note (TIIN) about amendments to the worldwide debt cap (WWDC) provisions to ensure changes to accounting standards do not create unintended additional corporation tax liabilities. The *Tax Treatment of Financing Costs and Income (Change of Accounting Standards: Investment Entities) Regulations* 2015, which came into force on 2 April 2015, amend the relevant provisions of TIOPA 2010 to increase the measure of a worldwide group's gross finance costs by certain amounts relating to funding from sources external to the worldwide group.

The excess is known as the total disallowed amount. If this is negative for an individual company, then the net financing deduction for the company is nil. Where it is less than £500,000 for an individual company, then it is treated as being nil.

The group is required to notify HMRC of the allocation of the disallowance between relevant group members by submitting an allocation statement to HMRC. This statement must be received by HMRC within 12 months of the end of the period of account. The statement must show the 'tested expense amount', 'available amount' and 'total disallowed amount' and must list companies that are allocated a disallowance, and identify the particular financing expense amount(s) that are to be disallowed for each such company. The statement must confirm that the total of the amounts specified must equal the total disallowed amount. The effect of the statement is that a financing expense amount of a company specified in a statement is not to be brought into account by the company for corporation tax purposes. Where a company has delivered a corporation tax return for a period and because of the revised statement either the amount of profits or any other information in the return changes, then the company is treated as having amended its return.

A revised statement can be submitted to HMRC with subsequent revisions provided this is done within 36 months of the end of the accounting period. The revised statement must indicate the respects in which it differs from the previous and confirm that it supersedes the previous statement.

The statement must be given by a reporting body. The companies to which Part 7 apply may appoint one of their number to exercise functions conferred on the reporting body in relation to the relevant period of account. Such an appointment is of no effect unless it is signed on behalf of each company by the appropriate person. The appropriate person being the proper officer of the company, or such other person as may for the time being have the express, implied or apparent authority of the company to act on its behalf.

Where a disallowance has been made, then an amount of financing income received by one or more UK members of a worldwide group is to be exempted from corporation tax. The total amount of financing income that can be disregarded in this way, is limited by reference to the tested expense amount for a period of account of the worldwide group which is the sum of the net financing deductions of each relevant group company and the available amount.

A statement of allocated exemptions must be made to HMRC within 12 months of the end of the relevant period of account. The format for reporting is similar to that for reporting disallowances, and similar provisions apply to reporting a revised statement of exemptions as that for reporting revised disallowances.

There is a consultation under way, launched on 6 January 2016, entitled *Tax Deductibility of Corporate Interest Expense* (see www.gov. uk/government/consultations/tax-deductibility-of-corporate-interest-expense/tax-deductibility-of-corporate-interest-expense-consultation updated at 26 May 2016). The document notes 'The use of interest expense has been identified as one of the key areas where there is a significant opportunity for BEPS [base erosion and profit shifting] by multinational companies. The OECD report under Action 4 of the BEPS project sets out recommendations for countering this. The Government recognises this risk and so we are reviewing the rules on interest deductibility that apply within the UK in light of the recommendations set out in the OECD report. Consistent adoption and application of rules across all countries would have the benefit of certainty for business as well as ensuring a more level playing field'.

'The government believes that the new rules on interest deductibility as set out in the OECD report are an appropriate response to the BEPS issues identified therein. Due to the importance of this issue, we are publishing this document now to seek views from all stakeholders on how best to respond to the OECD proposals. We are interested in the views of all stakeholders on how to address BEPS issues involving interest expense in an effective and proportionate manner. The results from this consultation will be considered in the development of a future business tax roadmap.'

Legislation: TIOPA 2010, Pt. 7

Tax Reporter: ¶717-570

3174   Derivative contracts

The derivative contracts legislation was introduced by *Finance Act* 2002 and took effect for accounting periods beginning on or after 1 October 2002.

The legislation applies to 'relevant contracts', which are defined as options, futures and contracts for differences, provided that such contracts would be treated as derivative financial instruments for the purposes of Financial Reporting Standard 25 (FRS 25) or for any successor standard thereto (such as the revised versions of IAS 32 *Financial Instruments: Disclosure and Presentation* and IAS 39 *Financial Instruments: Recognition and Measurement*, both issued in December 2003 by the International Accounting Standards Board (IASB) and which apply to listed companies for annual periods beginning on or after 1 January 2005 (or earlier if international accounting standards are adopted by a company before then)). The derivative contracts legislation also applies to certain options, futures or contracts for differences which are not treated as derivative financial instruments for the purposes of FRS, where such derivative contracts are treated as financial assets for the purposes of that standard, and such derivative contracts, or such contracts together with certain associated transactions, are designed to produce a guaranteed interest-type return, or to ensure that the amount payable in respect of the contract does not fall below a guaranteed minimum amount. Finally, the legislation applies to options, futures or contracts for differences which would not otherwise fall within its scope where the underlying subject matter of such derivatives is commodities and also to contracts for differences whose underlying subject matter is intangible fixed assets, weather conditions or creditworthiness (embedded derivatives).

The derivative contracts legislation provides definitions of an option, a future and a contract for differences.

An 'option' is defined as including a warrant. A 'warrant' is in turn defined as an instrument which entitles the holder to subscribe for shares in a company, or for assets representing a loan relationship of a company, whether or not the shares or assets to which the warrant relates exist or are identifiable.

A 'future' is defined as a contract for the sale of property under which delivery is to be made at a future date agreed when the contract is made, and at a price so agreed. The legislation provides that the price will be taken to have been agreed when the contract is made where the price is left to be determined by reference to the price at which a contract is to be entered into on a market or exchange, or could be entered into at a time and place specified in the contract, as well as cases where the price is expressed by reference to a standard lot and quality with provision for a variation in the price to take account of any variation in quantity or quality on delivery.

A 'contract for differences' is defined as a contract the purpose or pretended purpose of which is to make a profit or avoid a loss by reference to fluctuations in the value or price of property described in the contract, or an index or other factor designated in the contract. None of the following will be treated as a contract for differences: a future; an option; a contract of insurance; a capital redemption policy; a contract of indemnity; a guarantee; a warranty; and a loan relationship.

Where the terms of a future or option provide that it is to be settled by a cash payment and do not contain any provision for physical delivery then, except where the underlying subject matter is currency, that contract will be treated as a contract for differences and not as a future or option for the purposes of the derivative contracts legislation.

Debits and credits to be brought into account

Derivatives are taxable and relieved under the following two regimes:

(1) an income regime, where the underlying subject matter is not a chargeable asset; and

(2) a capital gains regime where the underlying subject matter is a chargeable asset which is not held by a bank, financial trader or a CIS.

The capital gains regime does not just apply in relation to disposals, but also to any other gains and losses recognised in the accounts.

The taxation of derivatives is closely aligned with the accounting treatment.

The general rule is that the amounts to be brought into account for tax purposes under the derivative contracts legislation (for both the income regime and the capital gains regime) are the amounts that are recognised in determining the company's profit or loss for the period in question in accordance with generally accepted accounting practice. The legislation also specifically provides that the debits and credits to be brought into account are those which fairly represent, for the accounting period in question:

(a) all profits and losses of the company which (disregarding any charges or expenses) arise to a company from its derivative contracts and related transactions; and

(b) all charges and expenses incurred by the company under or for the purposes of its derivative contracts and related transactions.

Profits and losses are therefore identified separately to charges and expense, which are only allowable if they are incurred directly:

(a) in bringing any of the derivative contracts into existence;

(b) in entering into or giving effect to any of the related transactions (see below);

(c) in making payments under any of those contracts or as a result of any of the transactions (for example, bank charges for the transfer of the funds); or

(d) in taking steps to ensure the receipt of payments under any of those contracts or in accordance with any of those transactions (e.g. legal fees).

Guidance can be found in relation to this in HMRC's Manuals at CFM13566.

In certain circumstances, where a company holds a loan of derivative that is matched with another financial instrument issued by it, GAAP may permit or require the loan or derivative, or amounts arising in respect of it, not to be recognised in determining the company's accounting profits or losses for the period. For example, a company may have made a loan or hold securities from which it receives income in the form of interest, and issued fixed rate preference shares under which matching amounts are paid as dividends. While the interest income and dividend expense match each other economically, following the accounting treatment in such a case gives rise to a tax asymmetry, since interest is normally fully taxable and the dividends are not deductible. Legislation was first introduced in FA 2006 to counter the tax avoidance possibilities from this type of asymmetry, and has been amended in subsequent Finance Acts as new schemes based on derecognition have come to light.

Rather than continue to make additions to the legislation in response to new examples of such avoidance, the Government announced on 6 December 2010 that the legislative approach would be amended to create a general rule that taxable amounts arising on loan relationships and derivative contracts are to be computed as if all profits and losses on derecognised financial instruments were fully recognised for accounting purposes, where the company is party to tax avoidance arrangements. In addition, from the same date a company is denied a tax deduction under the rules on loan relationships and derivative contracts for a loss on derecognition, again where the company is party to tax avoidance arrangements. Legislation introducing these changes was included in *Finance Act* 2011, Sch. 4. Where the new rules apply a company is required to recognise for tax purposes, the full credits arising on the creditor relationship or derivative contract. A further round of consultation on potential changes was launched on 6 June 2013 – see www.gov.uk/government/uploads/system/uploads/attachment_data/file/205432/2013_06_05_Condoc_FINAL_FOR_PUBLICATION.pdf.

Treatment of profits and losses on derivative contracts

Where a company is party to a derivative contract for the purposes of a trade which it carries on and profits arising under the derivative contract are otherwise chargeable to corporation tax as income under the first general rule, the company will be required to bring credits and debits under that derivative contract into account as receipts and expenses of a company's trade.

Where a company is not party to a derivative contract for the purposes of its trade, and profits arising under the contract are chargeable to corporation tax as income, the company must bring such credits and debits into account as non-trading credits and debits under the loan relationship rules.

Legislation: CTA 2009, Pt. 7

Tax Reporter: ¶719-500ff.

Intangible fixed assets

3179   Intangible fixed assets – outline

Finance Act 2002 introduced a regime for the taxation of goodwill and other intangible fixed assets created or acquired after 31 March 2002. This applies only to companies. It follows UK accounting practice as closely as possible in both the scope and calculation methods. The regime should limit the need for adjustments between accounts and tax profits.

The legislation takes the accounting entries ('losses and gains') in relation to intangible fixed assets and allocates corresponding tax debits and tax credits. Some of these can arise throughout the ownership of the intangible asset, whilst others only arise on realisation.

Provision is made in *Finance (No. 2) Act* 2015 to restrict corporation tax relief for the cost of purchased goodwill and 'customer related intangibles' with effect for acquisitions and disposals on or after 8 July 2015. This change follows on rapidly after the announcement that relief would be restricted for certain related party transactions. Companies will no longer be able to claim tax deductions for amortisation or impairment of such assets and debits on the realisation of such assets will no longer be relieved as a trading loss.

Finance Act 2016, s. 52 confirmed how the commencement and valuation rules for intangible fixed assets apply to partnerships that have corporate partners or members. The change will apply in relation to debits and credits accruing on or after 25 November 2015. The following should be read with these changes in mind.

The tax debits and credits are either trade debits and credits, which arise on assets used for the purposes of a trade and are treated as trading receipts and expenditure; or non-trading debits and credits. The non-trading debits and credits are amalgamated for an accounting period. Net credits are charged to corporation tax on income, whereas net debits can be offset against other profits of the company or the group, any excess being carried forward as a non-trading loss.

There is a form of rollover relief where a company realises an intangible fixed asset (the 'old asset') and incurs expenditure on other intangible fixed assets ('other assets').

In order to fall within the regime, an intangible fixed asset must have been created or acquired after 1 April 2002. This means that some intangible assets (e.g. internally generated goodwill) may potentially remain outside the new rules for many years.

An intangible asset takes the meaning it has for accounts purposes, so long as the accounts are drawn up in accordance with generally accepted accounting practice. Intellectual property, (for example patents, trade marks and copyrights) is specifically included by the legislation.

An intangible fixed asset means an intangible asset that is used on a continuing basis in the course of the company's activities, whether or not it is capitalised in the balance sheet. This applies to assets acquired from another party and those created by the company itself. Options to acquire or dispose of intangible fixed assets are to be treated as intangible fixed assets in their own right. The legislation includes goodwill (as defined for accounts purposes) as an intangible fixed asset. It was HMRC's belief (as supported by the Upper Tribunal in the *Greenbank Holidays* case) that goodwill included internally generated goodwill. The law in this regard was clarified in 2009 at which point it was also made clear that goodwill is created in the course of carrying on the business in question.

Assets excluded by the legislation include:

- rights over intangible fixed assets;

- financial assets;

- rights in companies, trusts, etc.;

- intangible fixed assets held for a non-commercial purpose.

Legislation: CTA 2009, Pt. 8, s. 712(1), 715 and 883–885

Case: *Greenbank Holidays Ltd v R & C Commrs* [2011] BTC 1,696

Other Material: HMRC Brief 25/11

Corporation tax

Tax Reporter: ¶722-000ff.

3183   Debits for intangible fixed assets

Accounting losses relating to intangible fixed assets are not immediately deductible for tax purposes. Instead, they give rise to deductions via the notion of a corresponding tax debit. As can be seen from the table below however, in many cases no adjustment to the accounting loss is necessary to arrive at the tax debit.

In order to get an accounting loss, there must be expenditure on intangible fixed assets. This is defined as expenditure (including abortive expenditure):

- for the purpose of acquiring, creating, or establishing title to the asset;

- incurred by way of royalty in respect of the use of the asset; or

- for the purpose of maintaining, preserving or enhancing, or defending title to the asset.

Accounting entries	Tax debit
Expenditure on intangible fixed assets, which is not capitalised but written off to, the profit and loss account incurred.	Company entitled to a tax debit equal to the amount written off, (subject to exclusions for some categories of expenditure not generally deductible for tax purposes, e.g. entertainment, fines and expensive hired cars).
	Royalties would generally fall within this category. For tax purposes these have traditionally been deductible when paid. In future they will follow the accounts treatment, i.e. the accrual basis.
Writing down of an intangible fixed asset capitalised for accounts purposes by way of amortisation or an impairment review.	Company entitled to a tax debit calculated as follows:

$$\text{Accounting loss} \times \frac{\text{Tax value}}{\text{Accounting value}}$$

Accounting entries	**Tax debit**
	Where:

Accounting loss is the amount of the loss (write down) recognised for accounts purposes.

Tax value is the tax written down value of the asset immediately before the amortisation or impairment is recognised.

Accounting value is the value of the asset for accounting purposes immediately before the amortisation or impairment is recognised.

The tax written down value of an asset is the tax cost minus the total amounts of tax debits previously brought into account plus the total amounts of tax credits previously brought into account.

The legislation recognises that in most cases the tax debit will equal the accounting loss. This may not be the case however where reinvestment relief has been claimed for tax purposes.

Example:

Goodwill is acquired for £200,000. For accounts purposes it is written off over ten years on a straight-line basis. For tax purposes the cost is reduced by £50,000 as a result of a reinvestment claim.
The tax debit in year 1 is £20,000 multiplied by £150,000/£200,000 or £15,000.

The tax debit in year 2 is £20,000 multiplied by £135,000/£180,000 or £15,000.

Intangible fixed asset capitalised for accounts purposes but not amortised.	Irrespective of the accounting treatment, a company may elect to write down the cost of the intangible fixed asset at a fixed rate for tax purposes. This will be particularly beneficial where the intangible asset is not amortised in the accounts. The election must be made in writing within two years after the end of the accounting period in which the asset is created or acquired.

The fixed rate tax deduction will be:

- 4% of the cost of the asset for tax purposes (reduced proportionately where the accounting treatment is less than 12 months); or

Accounting entries	Tax debit
	• if less the balance of the tax written down value.
Reversal of accounting gain recognised in a prior period for tax purposes.	A tax debit is available calculated as follows:

$$\text{Accounting loss} \times \frac{\text{Previous credit}}{\text{Accounting gain}}$$

Where:

Accounting loss is the amount of the loss (write down) recognised for accounts purposes.

Previous credit is the amount of the credit previously brought into account for tax purposes. Accounting gain is the amount of the gain that is reversed (in whole or in part).

Legislation: CTA 2009, Pt. 8, Ch. 3

Tax Reporter: ¶723-100

3186　Credits for intangible fixed assets

Accounting receipts and gains of a company relating to intangible fixed assets are again not automatically taxable. Instead they give rise to a series of tax credits.

Accounting entries	Tax credit
Receipts relating to intangible fixed assets recognised in the profit and loss account as they accrue.	Company entitled to a tax debit on an accrual basis in accordance with the accounts.
Revaluations either above original cost or to restore past losses.	The tax credit is restricted to the debits previously deducted by limiting the taxable amount to the lower of: • the increase in value for tax purposes, or • the net aggregate amount of relevant tax debits previously brought into account.

Accounting entries	Tax credit

The increase in value for tax purposes equals:

$$\text{Accounting adjustment} \times \frac{\text{Tax value}}{\text{Accounting value}}$$

Where:

Accounting adjustment is the amount of the increase in the accounting value of the asset.

Tax value is the tax written down value of the asset immediately before revaluation.

Accounting value is the accounting value of the asset immediately before revaluation.

The net aggregate amount of relevant tax debits equals the total amounts of previous debits brought into account for tax purposes less the total amounts of previous debits brought into account for tax purposes.

A tax credit in relation to a revaluation cannot apply where the asset is being written down on a fixed rate basis for tax purposes.

Accounting entries	Tax credit
Negative goodwill acquired on the acquisition of a business and written back to the profit and loss account.	Corresponding credit brought into taxable income.
Reversal of accounting loss recognised in a prior period for tax purposes.	The tax credit is calculated as follows:

$$\text{Accounting gain} \times \frac{\text{Tax debit}}{\text{Accounting loss}}$$

Where:

Accounting gain is the amount of the gain recognised for accounts purposes.

Tax debit is the amount of the debit previously brought into account for tax purposes.

Accounting loss is the amount of the loss that is reversed (in whole or in part).

Legislation: CTA 2009, Pt. 8, Ch. 2

Tax Reporter: ¶723-200

3189   Realisation of intangible fixed assets

Additional debits and credits can arise on the realisation of intangible fixed assets. The proceeds of the realisation are defined as the amount recognised for accounts purposes reduced by any incidental costs of realisation. They are taxed as follows.

Realisation proceeds	Tax treatment
Assets previously written down for tax purposes.	If the proceeds of realisation exceed the tax written down value of the asset, a tax credit arises equal to the excess.
	If the proceeds are less than the tax written down value of the asset, a tax debit arises equal to the shortfall.
Assets shown in the balance sheet but not written down for tax purposes.	If the proceeds of realisation exceed the tax cost of the asset, a tax credit arises equal to the excess.
	If the proceeds are less than the tax cost of the assets, a tax debit arises equal to the shortfall.
	The cost for tax purposes should be the same as the amount capitalised for accounts purposes unless there are circumstances such as reinvestment relief.
Assets never shown in the balance sheet (e.g. if internally generated).	Tax credit is the realisation proceeds.
Abortive expenditure on a realisation.	A corresponding tax debit arises.

Where there is a part-realisation of an asset the tax debits and credits need to be calculated by reference to the percentage reduction in the accounting value of the asset as a result of the realisation. The tax written down value immediately after a part realisation is the previous value reduced in the ratio which the accounting value (i.e. net book value) of the asset in the accounts immediately after the realisation bears to the accounting value immediately before.

Example

Goodwill was acquired for £200,000 on 1 January 2012. For accounts purposes, it is written off over ten years on a straight-line basis. For tax purposes, the cost is reduced by £50,000 as a result of a reinvestment claim. On 1 January 2013, part of the goodwill was disposed of for £150,000. The value of the remaining asset for accounts purposes immediately after the disposal is £60,000.

Debit for year ended 31 December 2012

The accounting amortisation is £20,000 (£200,000/10). The tax debit for the year is £15,000 (£20,000 × £150,000/£200,000)).

Disposal

Immediately prior to the part disposal, the accounts value of the goodwill is £180,000 (£200,000 − £20,000). The tax written down value is £135,000 (£150,000 − £15,000).

The tax written down value of the part of the asset disposed of is calculated as £90,000 (£135,000 × (£180,000 − £60,000)/£180,000)). A tax credit therefore arises on realisation being £60,000 (£150,000 − £90,000).

Immediately after the part disposal, the accounts value of the goodwill is £60,000. The tax written down value is £45,000 (£135,000 × £60,000/£180,000).

Debit for year ended 31 December 2013

The accounting amortisation is £6,000 (£60,000/10). The tax debit for the year is £4,500 (£6,000 × £45,000/£60,000).

Rollover relief

There is provision for a form of rollover relief, modelled very closely on the capital gains tax rules (see 6305). Where a company realises an intangible fixed asset (the 'old asset') and incurs expenditure on other intangible fixed assets ('other assets'), the proceeds from the realisation of the old asset and the tax cost of the other assets are each reduced by the amount available for relief.

The amount available for relief is the amount by which the proceeds of realisation exceed the tax cost of the old asset. However, if the expenditure on replacement assets is less than the proceeds, the amount of available for relief is the difference between the expenditure and the tax cost.

Legislation: CTA 2009, Pt. 8, Ch. 4, Ch. 7

Tax Reporter: ¶723-300 and ¶724-000ff.

3192   Interaction with other schemes

The rules relating to intangible assets interact with a number of other tax treatments.

Computer software

Software acquired with the related hardware often falls to be treated for accounting purposes as part of the cost of that hardware. If this is the case, then the software is excluded from the new rules, except in relation to any royalties which may arise.

Software not acquired with hardware is an intangible asset, and the intangible assets rules override those in respect of capital allowances. This may not be desirable to a company especially if it is entitled to first year allowances. It is therefore possible to make an election to disapply the intangible provisions. The election must be made in writing not more than two years after the end of the accounting period in which the expenditure was incurred. It is irrevocable.

Research and development expenditure

Expenditure on intangible fixed assets can take the form of research and development expenditure. The legislation effectively removes research and development expenditure from the intangible rules except in relation to:

* any receipts recognised as they accrue (e.g. royalties);

* any accounting loss resulting from an adjustment to the value of receipts recognised as they accrue.

Any debits or credits resulting from realisation must be calculated by excluding any research and development expenditure from the cost of the asset.

Transfer of business or trade

Rules exist to ensure continuity of treatment where intangible fixed assets change ownership in the course of a business reorganisation. They are broadly equivalent to those for capital gains tax purposes (see 3415 and 3417).

Transactions between related parties

Where there is a transfer of a chargeable intangible asset between a company and a related party then it is deemed to be transferred at market value, (i.e. the price at which the asset might reasonably be expected to fetch on a sale in the open market). This mirrors the rules for capital gains tax and hence the value is consistent for all parties even though one of the parties may still be under the old rules.

Where a royalty is payable by a company to a related party and for some reason it is not paid within 12 months of the end of the period of account in which it is charged, it does not give rise to a tax debit until such time as it is paid.

Rollover relief may be restricted where related parties are involved in the transaction.

A related party of a company is defined widely and does not necessarily require control. Rather it relies on the concept of a 'major interest' in a company. Also a close company is connected with its participators and the associates of its participators.

Finance Act 2008 introduced anti-avoidance legislation to clarify that, for transactions from 12 March 2008, the effect of the 'related party' rules in the corporate intangible assets regime is unaffected by any administration, liquidation or other insolvency proceedings or equivalent arrangements in which any company or partnership may be involved.

Groups

For commentary on the rules on intangible assets relating to groups of companies, see 3740.

Tax Reporter: ¶722-525, ¶724-600 and ¶725-000ff.

3195   Transfers of income streams

The legislation to prevent the conversion of income into capital where a person sold the right to income but kept the underlying asset generating the income was piecemeal and was the subject of schemes to exploit the inconsistencies and differences between the way the various provisions worked.

Legislation introduced by FA 2009 (and since rewritten as CTA 2010, Pt. 16, Ch. 1) ensures that receipts which would be taxable as income on the transferor continue to be taxable as such following a transfer of the rights to those receipts only. Consequently, the legislation is not concerned with receipts which would not have been taxed as income in the hands of the transferor had the transfer not taken place, nor is it concerned with transfers which involve, or are deemed to involve, the transfer of the underlying asset (subject to exceptions for annual payments and transfers under sale and repurchase agreements).

Corporation tax

Where, on or after 22 April 2009, a company within the charge to corporation tax transfers a right to relevant receipts to another person, but does not also transfer the asset from which the right arises, the charge to corporation tax on income applies to the relevant amount unless an exclusion applies.

The relevant amount is either:

- the amount received for the transfer of the right; or

- the market value of the right at the time of the transfer where no amount is received or the amount received is substantially less than the market value.

Tax is charged in the same way as it would have been had the relevant receipts not been transferred. For example, if the relevant receipts would have been included in calculating the transferor's trading profits, the amount taxable will be so included. If the relevant receipts would not have been wholly taxed as income, the charge to tax is limited to the relevant proportion of the amount received/market value.

Where the taxable amount under these rules does not exceed the consideration received, it is treated as arising when it is recognised in the transferor's profit or loss account or income statement in accordance with GAAP. Where the amount exceeds the consideration received, it is treated as arising at the same time as it would have been recognised, if it did not exceed the consideration received. Where the full amount taxable under these rules would not otherwise be recognised in an accounting period of the transferor, it is to be treated as arising immediately before the time it is reasonable to assume that this will be the case. This is to ensure that the taxable amount is always taxed in full.

If the amount is already taxable as income, or as part of the profits of the transferor, then no charge arises under these rules. Similarly, these rules do not apply if the income is already brought into account by the *Capital Allowances Act* 2001 (e.g. as proceeds on the disposal of an asset qualifying for capital allowances).

Transactions treated as transfers of assets

In the following instances, the underlying asset is treated as transferred and so the rules do not apply:

- the reduction in the transferor's share in the profits or losses of a partnership where either there is a corresponding reduction in the transferor's share in the partnership property, or it is not the main purpose, or one of the main purposes, of the transfer to prevent the relevant receipts from being brought into account for tax purposes as income of any partner;

- the grant or surrender of a lease of land;

- the disposal of an interest in an oil licence;

- the grant or disposal of an interest in intellectual property which constitutes a pre-2002 asset.

The transfer of an asset under a sale and repurchase agreement is not regarded as the transfer of an asset for these purposes and so is within the scope of the rules.

The exception to the general rule

The general rule, that a transfer of a right to relevant receipts will not fall within the rules if the underlying asset is also transferred, is subject to one exception. Where all rights under an agreement for annual payments are transferred, the rules apply even though the underlying asset has been transferred.

Legislation: CTA 2010, Pt. 16, Ch. 1

Tax Reporter: ¶809-000ff.

Particular reliefs and deductions

3200 Use of capital allowances by companies

Capital allowances are given for corporation tax in respect of similar categories of expenditure to those for individuals (although obviously the part private use apportionment does not apply). Further, the methods of giving effect to allowances or taxing balancing charges are substantially the same as for income tax purposes. Commentary on those areas applying with regard to companies only follows. The TAAR in relation to capital allowances has been the subject of litigation and, in the *Lloyds Bank Leasing (No. 1) Ltd* case, it was found that writing down allowances were not available because the obtaining of the allowances was a main object, or one of the main objects of the transactions which the various parties entered into.

Special leasing of plant and machinery

There are special provisions in relation to the special leasing of plant and machinery. The term 'special leasing' of plant and machinery refers to leasing other than in the course of a trade which consists of, or includes, leasing. The general rule is that a charge is treated as income from special leasing, and allowances are given by set off against income from special leasing. Any excess is carried forward to set against future income from special leasing. However, companies may claim to set the excess against current profits, or carry it back. The carry-back period is limited to the length of the current accounting period. This claim must be made within two years of the end of the accounting period in which the excess arose.

Companies with investment business

Companies with investment business may deduct plant and machinery capital allowances from the income of the business. Any excess is added to the company's management expenses. Charges are treated as income of the business.

Annual investment allowance

For many companies, capital allowances are from April 2008 given mainly by way of an annual investment allowance (AIA), allowing full relief for expenditure in the year of up to £200,000 (£500,000 from April 2014 until 31 December 2015 (£250,000 since 1 January 2013)). There have been numerous changes as the threshold was £50,000 before 1 April 2010 and £100,000 after 31 March 2010 and before 1 April 2012 and £25,000 from 1 April 2012 to 31 December 2012. *Finance (No. 2) Act* 2015 set the AIA at £200,000 from 1 January 2016 and it is intended that it remain at that level for the remainder of this parliament. The AIA figure is adjusted pro rata for accounting periods of less than 12 months and there are complex rules dealing with periods that straddle changes in the AIA limits. The AIA is available for 'special rate' items (for example, integral features and long life assets) as well as other expenditure on plant and machinery, but subject to certain exclusions, including cars. Where qualifying expenditure exceeds the maximum AIA figure, the excess may attract writing-down allowances in the same period.

The following restrictions apply for companies:

(1) A company that carries on more than one qualifying activity is only entitled to one AIA in respect of all its qualifying activities in the chargeable period.

(2) A group of companies has to share a single AIA.

(3) A third restriction applies, allowing just one AIA between the various companies, where – in a given financial year – two or more *groups of companies* are controlled by the same person and where they are related to one another.

(4) A single amount of AIA is shared between the various companies, where – in a given financial year – two or more companies are controlled by the same person and where they are related to one another.

(5) There is a restriction where, broadly, qualifying activities are under common control (not necessarily restricted to companies).

Claims for capital allowances

A claim for capital allowances for an accounting period must be included in the company's tax return (see 4305), either as originally delivered, or via an amendment to the return submitted within the normal time-limit. The claim must specify the amount of the allowance. Claims for capital allowances, once made, can only be amended or withdrawn by amendment of the relevant return.

Consequential amendment of return for another accounting period

Where a claim for capital allowances in an accounting period affects the allowances otherwise due for a subsequent period for which a return has been submitted, the company must amend the later period's return within 30 days. If the company fails to do this, HMRC may amend the return (by written notice). An appeal can be made against such a HMRC amendment in the normal way.

Time-limits for capital allowances claims

Subject to HMRC permitting an extension to the time-limit, claims for capital allowances must be made, amended or withdrawn by the *latest* of:

(1) 12 months after the claimant company's filing date for the return for the accounting period covered by the claim;

(2) 30 days after a closure notice is issued on the completion of an enquiry;

(3) 30 days after HMRC issue a notice of amendment to a return following the completion of an enquiry (issued where the company fails to amend the return itself); or

(4) 30 days after the determination of any appeal against a HMRC amendment (as in (3) above).

'Enquiry' in the above does not include a restricted enquiry into an amendment to a return (restricted because the time-limit for making an enquiry into the return itself has expired), where the amendment consists of making, amending or withdrawing a capital allowance claim.

The time-limits above have priority over any other general time-limits for amending returns.

Capital allowance buying

Where there is a change of ownership of a company, long standing legislation restricts or prohibits the carry forward (and carry back) of certain losses and other reliefs. For example, the carry forward and carry back of unutilised trading losses is restricted if there is within a three-year period both a change in ownership of a company and a major change in the nature or conduct of its trade. Similarly, where there is a transfer of a trade between two companies under common ownership, there is a restriction on the ability of the successor to set off trading losses arising before the transfer of the trade (see 3375 below). However, up until 21 July 2009 there were no restrictions on the utilisation of capital allowances on a change in ownership of a company. Many companies were therefore disclaiming capital allowances, or not claiming them in the first place, prior to a change of ownership to avoid the restrictions on losses carried forward. With effect from 21 July 2009 (or 9 December 2009 in respect of the special rules for ships), new legislation restricts the use of capital allowances and the utilisation of losses attributable to capital allowances where there has been, broadly, a change in ownership of a company and there is a deferred tax asset (i.e. broadly, where the tax written down value of the assets exceeds their balance sheet value). The new rules do not just apply where there is a change in ownership of a company but also where there is an increase in the percentage of ownership of a jointly owned company and also where there is a decrease in the profit sharing ratio of a corporate partner in a trading partnership. However, in all cases, the new rules only apply where the main purpose or one of the main purposes of the transaction is to obtain a tax advantage.

The new legislation is consistent with the rules to deter loss buying transactions and will restrict the way in which capital allowances can be utilised following a transfer of entitlement to benefit from those capital allowances. Capital allowances or any loss attributable to a capital allowances claim will only be available to reduce the profits that they would have been able to reduce before the transaction took place.

There are three other conditions that must be met for the legislation to take effect (that is, in addition to the unallowable purpose test). A company must carry on a trade or carry on a trade in partnership with others, that company (or that partnership) must have an excess of capital allowances and there must be a qualifying change in relation to the company. Broadly, a qualifying change is either the sale or partial sale (to create a consortium) of a company, a change in the ownership proportions of a consortium company, a change in the profit sharing ratio of a partnership in which the company is a partner or a transfer of the trade (with the excess of allowances) in circumstances such that the transfers of a trade without a change of ownership provisions (see 3179) apply.

The amount by which the tax written-down value of plant and machinery exceeds the balance-sheet value is the excess of allowances. The legislation operates by allocating an amount of expenditure equal to the excess of allowances in each pool to a new separate pool of the same type (i.e. a new single asset, class or main pool). WDA are calculated on the old and the new pools separately but at the same rate. If, however, in respect of another pool the balance-sheet value of plant and machinery is greater than its tax-written down value, then this difference can be used to reduce the excess of allowances in a pool. To enable the excess of allowances to be calculated, the company's (or the partnership's) accounting period is brought to an end on the day of a qualifying change and a new accounting period begins on the following day.

Capital allowances claimed in respect of expenditure in the new pools may only be used to reduce the profits (or increase the losses) from the trade as it was carried on, and to the extent that it was carried on, before the qualifying change. Any trading activities transferred in to the company or the partnership will be treated as a separate trade for these purposes. Any losses attributable to capital allowances on new pool expenditure may not be surrendered as group relief or set against other profits of the company for the year, unless they could have been used to reduce those profits before the qualifying change.

Example 1

A company C is a member of the X group of companies. It draws up its accounts to 31 December each year. On 31 December 2011 C is sold to the Y group. The X group and the Y group are independent of each other. On 31 December 2011, C's capital allowance pools have the following balances of unrelieved qualifying expenditure: main pool £150,000, short life asset single asset pool £15,000, special rate pool for high emission cars £50,000. The balance sheet value of the relevant assets are: short life asset £10,000, high emission cars £75,000 other plant and machinery (main pool) £50,000. The company has been loss making and is being sold primarily for the purpose of enabling Y group to benefit from the capital allowances. For the accounting period ended 31 December 2012, C incurs a trading loss of £100,000 (before the deduction for capital allowances).

The capital allowance pools in C on 1 January 2012 will be as follows:

- main pool: 'new' pool: £75,000; 'old' pool: £75,000 (assuming that the excess of the balance sheet value over the tax written down value of the high emission cars is set off against the main pool);

- special rate pool for high emission cars: 'old' pool: £50,000;

- short life single asset pool: 'new' pool: £5,000; 'old' pool: £10,000.

Assuming that there are no additions or disposal of qualifying assets in the year ended 31 December 2012, C's entitlement to capital allowances for that year will be:

- main pool: new pool £15,000, old pool £15,000;

- special rate pool: £5,000;

- short life asset pool: new pool £1,000, old pool £2,000.

The trading loss for the year ended 31 December 2012 after capital allowances will therefore be £138,000. £122,000 of the loss is unrestricted and can be set off against C's other income and gains in the year ended 31 December 2012, carried back against profits of earlier accounting periods in the normal way or surrendered as group relief to other members of the Y group. £16,000 of the loss is restricted under the new capital allowance buying provisions and can only be set off against income in the same or earlier accounting periods from qualifying activities (e.g. an ordinary property business, an overseas property business, managing the investments of a company with investment business, etc.) that were carried on by C prior to the change in ownership, or carried forward against future profits of the trade. It is worthy of note that the restricted loss cannot be set off against capital gains in C in the accounting period ended 31 December 2012 or earlier years even if the relevant asset was owned by C prior to the change of ownership because a capital gain will not be a profit from a qualifying activity.

Example 2

Same facts as Example 1 above. Z, a company in the Y group carries on a similar trade to C and after the acquisition of C, the trade of Z is transferred to C so as to amount to an extension of C's trade. In the year ended 31 December 2012, the newly extended trade of C produces a profit, before capital allowances, of £50,000.

Only the capital allowances from the 'old' pools (i.e. £22,000) can be deducted in calculating the taxable trading profits of C. The profits of C after the change in ownership will need to be streamed and the capital allowances due on the 'new' pools will only be available to deduct in arriving at the taxable profits of the stream that relates to the part of the trade that was carried on by C before the change in ownership.

Example 3

Same facts as Example 1 but after acquisition of C, the Y group recapitalises C and the funds are utilised by C in repaying bank borrowings. As a result of the lower interest costs, the trade of C becomes profitable.

In these circumstances, there is no restriction on the use of the capital allowances and the capital allowances in all the pools, totalling £38,000, can be deducted.

Tax credits

Loss-making companies that incur expenditure on certain 'green' technology from 1 April 2008 are able to surrender their losses in return for a cash payment from HMRC, but only if such companies are otherwise unable to use their losses against their own profits or those of a group member. The rules are directly linked to the first-year allowances that are given for expenditure on energy-saving plant and machinery or environmentally beneficial plant and machinery. In this way, companies can gain an immediate cash payment rather than carrying losses forward indefinitely in the hope of obtaining relief when profits start to be realised in the future.

The main features of the relief are as follows:

- relief may be given for expenditure incurred on technology currently qualifying for 100% FYAs under either the 'energy-saving' plant and 'environmentally beneficial' plant provisions;

- the scheme is available to companies (small, medium or large) but not to excluded companies (e.g. charities, scientific organisations, etc.), or to any sole traders, partnerships or other entities; and

- companies may surrender losses, to the extent that they are attributable to qualifying expenditure, so as to receive a percentage (currently, 19% – but subject to a limit of £25,000 or, if higher, the amount of the company's PAYE and NIC liabilities for the period) of the surrendered loss as a tax-free cash payment from HMRC.

A payment in respect of a first-year tax credit is not treated as income of the company for any tax purpose.

Legislation: FA 1998, Sch. 18, Pt. IX; CAA 2001, Pt. 2, Ch. 16A, s. 262A and Sch. A1, para. 23

Case: *Lloyds Bank Leasing (No. 1) Ltd* [2015] TC 04578

Tax Reporter: ¶709-600ff.

Research and development tax credits

3210   Introduction and key concepts

Additional relief for expenditure on qualifying research and development was introduced by *Finance Act* 2000 for small or medium-sized enterprises (SMEs) and by *Finance Act* 2002 for large companies. It is now provided for by CTA 2009, Pt. 13. The relief is generous, particularly for SMEs: a typical SME will save tax of £46 for every £100 of qualifying expenditure incurred on R&D. However, there are a number of conditions to satisfy, many of which have changed in recent years. The changes made in 2012 (increasing the enhanced relief from 100% to 125%, the removal of the £10,000 limit on expenditure and the cap on refunds and reduce the rate of payable credit for SMEs to 11%) were followed by the payable credit being increased to 14.5% from 1 April 2014. Further changes have been made from 1 April 2015. Consequently, the rate of relief applying to SMEs increased from 225% to 230% and the above the line credit for large companies increased from 10% to 11%.

An above the line tax credit for R&D is available from 1 April 2013 to encourage more research and development by large companies. The current deduction system is to be replaced by a payable credit (the ATL credit) for all large companies, including those who have no liability to corporation tax. The ATL credit is introduced, in CTA 2009, Pt. 3, Ch. 6A, alongside the existing additional relief for expenditure on R&D under CTA 2009, Pt. 13 (known as the super-deduction) but will replace the super-deduction from 1 April 2016. The underlying rules for identifying qualifying activity and calculating qualifying expenditure remain unchanged and the new credit will be calculated as a percentage by reference to the amount of qualifying expenditure on R&D. However, changes to the rules on R&D tax credits for large companies are included in *Finance (No. 2) Act* 2015 so that credits are not available to universities and charities in respect of expenditure incurred from 1 August 2015. These measures affect a university's or charity's own independent research and R&D undertaken as sub-contractors.

In calculating the payable element, the credit will be used firstly to reduce the corporation tax liability of the claimant company for the same accounting period, any payable element will then be limited by the PAYE/NIC liabilities of the company's R&D staff and those of Externally Provided Workers from group companies. There are detailed rules providing for the amount that may be carried forward and treated as a credit for the following year.

Meaning of R&D

The term 'research and development' is defined at CTA 2010, s. 1138. The core of this definition is that activities will amount to R&D if 'generally accepted accounting practice' classifies them as such. However, the activities must also fall within guidelines issued by the Secretary of State for Trade and Industry and developed by the DTI and HMRC. The key theme is that the activities must be creative or innovative work in the fields of science or technology and undertaken with a view to the extension of knowledge. R&D is characterised by work that contains an appreciable element of innovation and breaks new ground or aims to resolve scientific or technological uncertainties.

The definition of 'SME'

The definition of a SME is based on Commission Recommendation 2003/361/EC of 6 May 2003. To qualify as a SME for this purpose, an enterprise must stay below the staff headcount limit and satisfy at least one of the turnover and balance sheet tests, as follows:

- staff headcount less than 500; and

- turnover not exceeding €100m or balance sheet total not exceeding €86m.

Where the enterprise is an autonomous enterprise, the staff headcount and financial tests will be met by reference to the accounts of that enterprise only. Where an enterprise is a partner or linked enterprise, it will be necessary to take account of the headcount, turnover and balance sheet totals of other enterprises. Broadly:

- an enterprise is an autonomous enterprise if it is not a partner enterprise or a linked enterprise;

- enterprises are partner enterprises if they are not linked enterprises and if one holds 25% or more of the capital or voting rights of the other (either on its own or jointly with other linked enterprises); and

- enterprises are linked enterprises if one is able to exercise control over the other.

Finance Act 2012 also:

- clarifies the existing definition of when a company is a 'going concern' to confirm that companies in administration or liquidation are excluded from relief; and

- widens the scope of the definition of an 'externally provided worker'.

Legislation: CTA 2009, Pt. 13

Other Material: Commission Recommendation 2003/361/EC (reproduced at HMRC *Corporate Intangibles Research and Development Manual* CIRD 91000); DTI Guidelines (2004) (reproduced at CIRD 81900); June 2011 R&D consultation response document available on the HM Treasury website at www.hm-treasury.gov.uk/d/consult_r_d_tax_credits. pdf

Tax Reporter: ¶715-000ff.

3212   Reliefs available to SMEs

Small and medium-sized enterprises (SMEs) may claim additional relief for qualifying R&D expenditure. The additional relief enables an amount equal to 230% (225% from 1 April 2012 to 31 March 2015, 200% before 1 April 2012 and 175% before 1 April 2011) of the qualifying expenditure for an accounting period to be deducted in computing profits/losses. This is made up of the normal deduction of 100% and the additional deduction of 130% (or 125%, 100% or 75%, see above).

Example 1

Henderson Ltd incurs qualifying expenditure on R&D of £100,000 in its accounting period ended 31 December 2012. Of this amount, £15,000 was incurred before 31 March 2012. Henderson Ltd is entitled to a deduction of £221,250 in respect of this expenditure in calculating its trading income for its accounting period ended 31 December 2012. The deduction is made up of the following amounts:

- with regard to the expenditure incurred before 1 April 2012, £15,000 at 200% equals £30,000; and

- with regard to the expenditure incurred on or after 1 April 2012, £85,000 at 225% equals £191,250.

Qualifying R&D expenditure incurred by a SME during an accounting period which cannot be relieved because it is unrelated to the carrying on of a trade (perhaps because the company is not yet trading or the trade that is carried on is unrelated to the expenditure), but which would have been allowable as a deduction if the company had been carrying on trading activities that were relevant to the expenditure, may be subject to an election. The effect of the election is to treat the unrelieved qualifying R&D expenditure as if it were a trading loss of the accounting period, equal to 230% (or 225%, 200% or 175%, see above) of the expenditure.

Loss-making SMEs also have the option of surrendering part of the loss for a payable tax credit equal to 14.5% (11% prior to 1 April 2014 and 12.5% for expenditure incurred before 1 April 2012) of the amount surrendered. The amount of loss surrendered cannot exceed the R&D relief claimed for the accounting period. In addition, the tax credit cannot exceed the total of the company's PAYE and NIC liabilities for all employees for payment periods ending in the accounting period. This cap was removed by *Finance Act* 2012 for accounting periods ending on or after 1 April 2012.

Example 2

Before taking account of the relief calculated in Example 1, Henderson Ltd has a trading profit of £15,000 for its accounting period ended 31 December 2012. It has no other income and is unable to make a claim to carry the loss back. Henderson Ltd has the option of surrendering part of its trading loss for a payable tax credit. Assuming the maximum surrender is made, and ignoring the PAYE cap, the amount of the payable tax credit is calculated as follows:

---

(1)   with regard to the expenditure incurred before 1 April 2012, the surrenderable amount is £15,000, being the lower of the loss (profit of £15,000 less R&D relief of £30,000 equals £15,000) and the R&D relief (£30,000). This loss can be surrendered for a payable tax credit of £1,875 (£15,000 at 12.5%); and

(2)   with regard to the expenditure incurred on or after 1 April 2012, the surrenderable loss is £191,250 (the full amount of the relief increasing the loss calculated at (1) above) and this amount can be surrendered for a payable tax credit of £21,037.25 (£191 at 11%).

Henderson Ltd's trading income for its accounting period ended 31 December 2012 is £nil (profit of £30,000 less R&D tax relief £221,250 plus losses surrendered £206,250).

Had Henderson Ltd made a trading profit of £45,000, a payable tax credit could have been claimed, calculated as follows:

(1)   with regard to the expenditure incurred before 1 April 2012, the surrenderable amount is £nil as a profit remains after deducting the R&D relief (profit of £45,000 less R&D relief of £30,000 equals profit of £15,000) and therefore no tax credit is due; and

(2)   with regard to the expenditure incurred on or after 1 April 2012, the surrenderable amount is £176,250 being the lower of the loss (profit of £15,000 less R&D relief of £191,250 equals loss of £176,250) and the R&D relief (£191,250). This amount can be surrendered for a payable tax credit of £16,637 (£151,250 at 11%).

Henderson Ltd's trading income for its accounting period ended 31 December 2011 would have been £nil (profit of £45,000 less R&D tax relief £221,250 plus losses surrendered £176,250).

The reliefs available to SMEs are only available where:

- prior to 1 April 2012, the SME's total qualifying expenditure in the accounting period is £10,000 or more (adjusted pro rata for accounting period of less than 12 months);

- the SME is a going concern;

- the expenditure is not subsidised; and

- the total relief claimed by the SME does not exceed the cap imposed to meet State Aid rules (7.5m Euros).

For expenditure incurred in an accounting period ended before 9 December 2009, it was also necessary for any intellectual property created as a result of the R&D to which the expenditure related to be vested in the company.

Where a SME is unable to claim relief under the SME scheme because of the subcontractor rules (see 3216), because it is subsidised or because the cap on R&D relief has been breached, it may claim relief under the large company scheme.

Legislation: F(No. 3)A 2010, s. 13; FA 2011, s. 43; *Finance Act 2011, Section 43 (Appointed Day) Order* 2011 (SI 2011/2280)

Other Material: HMRC guidance on how to calculate the payable tax credit where an accounting period straddles a change in the rates, HMRC *Corporate Intangible Research and Development Manual* CIRD 90000

3214   Large companies

Large companies may claim additional relief for qualifying R&D expenditure where that expenditure equals or exceeds £10,000 (adjusted pro rata for accounting period of less than 12 months). The additional relief enables an amount equal to 130% of the qualifying expenditure for an accounting period to be deducted in computing profits/losses.

Although the reliefs available to SMEs are more generous than that available to large companies, the large companies scheme is subject to fewer restrictions and is easier to understand and apply as a result. The 'above the line' (ATL) tax credit goes further in making the benefit of this incentive explicit and provide greater financial and cash flow support to companies with no corporation tax liability. The new rules are effective for qualifying expenditure incurred on or after 1 April 2013. An explanatory note of the ATL regime is available via the HM Treasury website at www. hm-treasury.gov.uk/finance_bill_2013.htm. It should be noted that several changes were made to the draft legislation published in December 2012. In particular, the scope of the PAYE/NICs cap on the payable credit to companies with no corporation tax liability is increased as this now takes into account the full PAYE/NICs of a company's R&D staff within the claim and the PAYE/NICs of externally provided workers from a group company that relate to its qualifying expenditure.

3216   Qualifying expenditure

In order to be qualifying R&D expenditure, the expenditure must be:

(1) not capital;

(2) attributable to relevant R&D directly undertaken by the company or on its behalf (subject to the subcontracting rules; see below); and

(3) incurred on any of the following:

   (a) staff costs;

   (b) software and consumables;

(c)   externally provided workers;

(d)   subcontracted R&D.

Changes have been made in *Finance Act* 2015 to the relief for consumables. The measure restricts the expenditure in respect of consumable items that qualifies for R&D tax credits where the company sells the products of its R&D activity as part of its normal business. The revised definition of qualifying consumable items makes it clear that the cost of materials incorporated in such products that are then sold will not be eligible for the relief. The intention is that the measure will increase the focus of the tax credit regime on the real costs of carrying out R&D activity. Qualifying expenditure on consumable items are thus limited to the cost of only those items fully used up or expended by the R&D activity itself and do not go on to be sold as part of a commercial product.

The subcontracting rules can best be summarised in tabular form, as follows:

Contractor	Sub-contractor	Who can claim	Under which regime
SME	SME	Contractor (SME)	SME regime
SME	Large company	Contractor (SME)	SME regime
Large Company	SME	Sub-contractor (SME)	Large company regime
Large Company	Large company	Sub-contractor (Large)	Large company regime
Large Company	Qualifying body	Contractor (Large)	Large company regime
Person otherwise than in course of trade	SME	Sub-contractor (SME)	Large company regime
Person otherwise than in course of trade	Large company	Sub-contractor (Large)	Large company regime

A qualifying body is as defined in CTA 2009, s. 1142 and regulations.

Where a SME makes a payment to another person in respect of R&D subcontracted out to that person, only 65% of the payment will qualify for relief unless the SME and subcontractor are connected or a joint election is made for connected persons treatment to apply.

Legislation: *Research and Development Qualifying Bodies (Tax) Order 2009 (SI 2009/1343)*

Cases: *Gripple Ltd v R & C Commrs* [2010] BTC 873

3220   Land remediation relief

Land remediation relief allows a company to claim relief for qualifying expenditure incurred on remedying contaminated land, and to claim an enhanced deduction for that expenditure. The land must have been acquired by the company for the purposes of a trade or UK property or business carried on by it. Land is in a contaminated state if it is in such a condition because of the substances in, on or under the land that harm is being caused or there is the possibility of harm being caused or pollution of controlled waters is being or is likely to be caused. Though for this purpose a nuclear site is not land in a contaminated state.

It was announced as part of Budget 2011 that relief for the remediation of contaminated or derelict land would be abolished after 2012, subject to consultation. This proposal has been dropped.

Relevant land remediation

Relevant land remediation in relation to the land means the doing of any works, carrying out of any operations or the taking of any steps in relation to the land in question, controlled waters affected by the land or any land adjacent or adjoining the land. The purpose of the activities must be to prevent, or minimise, or remedy or mitigate, the effects of any harm, pollution of controlled waters by which the land is in a contaminated state or to restore the land or waters to their former state. This would include any preparatory activities undertaken for the purpose of assessing the condition of the land or waters concerned.

Qualifying expenditure

For this purpose, qualifying expenditure is expenditure on land in a contaminated state which would not have been incurred if the land was not in a contaminated state, the expenditure is on work undertaken by the company itself or on its behalf. The expenditure must be on staffing costs, materials or qualifying expenditure on sub-contracted remediation.

The relief

Providing all the conditions are met, the company can claim that the qualifying capital expenditure on land remediation is to be allowed as a deduction, in calculating the profits of a UK property business or trade for the period in which the expenditure is incurred. The election to claim this relief must be made in writing to HMRC and must be given before the end of the period of two years, beginning immediately after the end of the accounting period to which the election relates. The company can claim an additional relief where expenditure on land remediation has been allowed as a deduction in calculating the profits of the business or trade for the period. The additional amount of the relief is 50% of the expenditure allowed. Where a company has a qualifying land remediation loss for a period, the company is entitled to a land remediation tax credit for the period. The tax credit is 16% of the land remediation loss.

Derelict land

Finance Act 2009 made modifications to the rules on land remediation and in particular brought land in a derelict state within the scope of the legislation. For this purpose, derelict land is not in productive use, and cannot be put into productive use without the removal of buildings or other structures. In addition, the land must have been in a derelict state throughout the period beginning with the earlier of 1 April 1998, and the date on which a major interest in the land was first acquired by the company or a person who was connected with the company. The amended land remediation relief applies to expenditure incurred on or after 1 April 2009.

Legislation: CTA 2009, Pt. 14

Other Material: May 2011 consultation document on the proposed abolition of land remediation relief available on the HM Treasury website at www.hm-treasury.gov.uk/d/consult_removal_36_tax_reliefs.pdf.

Tax Reporter: ¶715-600

Charitable donations

3230   Charitable donations relief

For accounting periods ending on or after 1 April 2010, relief for qualifying charitable donations is provided by CTA 2010, Pt. 6. For earlier periods, relief was available as a charge on income (see 3235).

For commentary on the definition of charity, see 900.

Manner in which relief is given

Where a company makes a qualifying charitable donation, a deduction is allowed against that company's total profits for the accounting period in which the donation is made. However, an exception is made where a donation is paid to a charity of which the company is a 100% subsidiary (see below). The deduction is to be made after any other relief but before group relief. However, the amount of the deduction is limited to the amount which reduces the company's taxable total profits for the period to nil. Where this restriction applies, the excess amount can not be offset against the profits of earlier or later periods. Relief is only available for the excess amount by way of surrender as group relief and by set off against the apportioned profits of a CFC.

Example

A company (company A) which is a 100% subsidiary of another company (company B) makes a qualifying charitable donation of £100,000 during its accounting period ended on 30 April 2011. Company A's total profits for that period, before deducting the charitable donations relief due, are £80,000. The amount of charitable donations relief which can be claimed by company A is limited to £80,000, being the amount which reduces its taxable total profits for that period to nil. Company A is unable to claim relief in respect of the excess amount of £20,000. However, it may be possible to surrender the excess amount as group relief to company B.

Restrictions on relief

The relief is not available in respect of payments which are otherwise deductible (for example, gifts of trading stock by a trading company to charities and other bodies including designated educational establishments and gifts for humanitarian purposes of medical supplies and equipment where they are held as trading stock which, in either case, would be deductible for tax purposes in calculating the profits of the trade).

With effect for donations made on or after 1 April 2011, relief is denied where the donation is a 'tainted charity donation'. The tainted charity donations provisions were introduced by *Finance Act* 2011 to deny relief for donations where, broadly, the donor has entered into arrangements to obtain a financial advantage from the charity and that advantage has not already been taken into account in calculating the relief due. As such, they will only be relevant in a small number of cases.

Qualifying payments

A payment to a charity will be a qualifying payment for charitable donations relief purposes if each of the following conditions are met:

(a) the payment must be a sum of money;

(b) it must not be subject to a condition as to repayment (except where the company is wholly-owned by the charity and both the charitable payment and the repayment are made in order to reduce the company's taxable profits to nil and the repayment is made within 12 months of the end of the accounting period);

(c) the company making the payment must not be a charity;

(d)   the payment must not be disqualified on the basis that there is an associated acquisition (being, broadly, an acquisition of property by the charity from the company making the payment or a person associated with it);

(e)   the payment must not be disqualified on the basis that it is regarded as a distribution. A non-dividend payment made by a company which is wholly owned by a charity is not regarded as a distribution for this purpose; and

(f)   the payment must not be disqualified on the basis that benefits are associated with the payment unless the total value of the benefits associated with the payment are less than £2,500 (£500 for payments made in an accounting period ended before 1 April 2011) and the total value of the benefits associated with the payment is less than the variable limit, which is, where the payment is £100 or less, 25% of the amount of the payment, where the payment is between £101 and £1,000, £25; and where the payment is £1,001 or over, 5% of the amount of the payment.

Qualifying donations to charity

Where a company makes a donation to a charity in the form of a qualifying investment, charitable donations relief will be available where the company is not itself a charity and where it makes a claim. For these purposes, a 'qualifying investment' is defined as:

- shares or securities which are listed on a recognised stock exchange or dealt in on a designated market in the UK;

- units in an authorised unit trust scheme;

- shares in an open-ended investment company;

- an interest in an offshore fund; and

- a qualifying interest in land (being, broadly, a freehold interest in land in the UK and a leasehold interest in UK land which is a term of years absolute). In this situation, relief is clawed back if the donor company becomes within six years entitled to an interest in all or part of the land concerned is party to an arrangement whereby it enjoys some right in relation to all or part of that land.

The amount of relief due in respect of the donation of a qualifying investment is to be determined in accordance with one of the two formulas at CTA 2010, s. 206 – one applying where the disposal is a gift and the second applying where the disposal is at an undervalue. In both cases, if the amount given by the formula is a negative amount, the amount of the relief is nil.

Finance Act 2010 introduced new rules to block tax avoidance schemes that exploit the rules for tax relief on gifts of qualifying investments to charities. The legislation does not affect charities; it operates by restricting tax relief to a donor on gifts of qualifying investments to charities. The avoidance depends on the donor receiving tax relief at their marginal rate of tax on the full market value of the qualifying investments at the date of the gift where the donor acquired the investments at below market value as part of a scheme or arrangement or the market value of the investment is artificially inflated at the date of the gift to charity. The new anti avoidance provision adjusts the amount of relief to the donor to the economic cost of acquisition of the gift to the donor where the qualifying investment gifted to the charity (or anything from which the investment derives) was acquired within four years of the date of disposal and the main purpose, or one of the main purposes, of acquiring the qualifying investment was to dispose of it to a charity and claim the tax relief.

Legislation: CTA 2010, Pt. 6 and 21B; FA 2010, Sch. 6; FA 2011, s. 27, 41 and Sch. 3

Tax Reporter: ¶716-600ff.

3235   Relief for 'charges on income' of company

Since 2005 and prior to the enactment of the *Corporation Tax Act* 2010, relief for charges on income was, in effect, restricted to qualifying donations to charity. Although the legislation applying to charges on income had formerly been of wide application, much of the substance of the relief was removed with the introduction of the loan relationships regime in 1996. Further rationalisation was made in 2002, with the removal of royalties from the charges on income regime, and again in 2005 with the removal of annuities and annual payments. With effect for accounting periods ending on or after 1 April 2010, the legislation relating to relief for charitable donations was rewritten, and renamed as charitable donations relief (see 3870), by CTA 2010. As a result, the concept of 'charges on income' was consigned to history.

As the purpose behind the enactment of CTA 2010 was to change the way in which the law is expressed and arranged, and not the law itself, the commentary in 3870 above on the relief available for charitable donations also applies for accounting periods ended before 1 April 2010.

Tax Reporter: ¶716-680ff.

Share schemes

3245 Corporation tax deduction for employee share acquisitions

For the position where an employee acquires shares in pursuance of an option granted by the employer, see 3250. This section deals with the corporation tax deduction available where an employee acquires shares in the employing company (and certain other companies) by reason of his employment otherwise than in pursuance of an option.

Share awards can take many different forms and there are several different approved share schemes still in existence. Unapproved schemes are also widely used by employers. Share schemes are usually considered to be an effective way of incentivising employees to contribute to the performance of the company as a whole and retaining them for a longer period of time. A corporation tax deduction is normally available to the employing company in respect of the award of shares to employees.

For accounting periods commencing on or after 1 January 2003, for the purpose of calculating the amount of the corporation tax deduction in respect of such awards, the amount charged to the profit and loss account of the company is generally ignored. The deduction is prescribed by statute at the time the employee acquires his shares. These statutory provisions, explained below, were originally contained in FA 2003, Sch. 23 but have now been rewritten as CTA 2009, Pt. 12. For accounting periods commencing prior to this date, there were no prescriptive provisions in relation to corporation tax deductions for share awards to employees. Companies would, generally, have been able to claim deductions in accordance with the amounts charged in their accounts in respect of the share awards.

A corporation tax deduction for an award of shares can now only be obtained where the conditions of CTA 2009, Pt. 12 are met (other than for Share Incentive Plans where relief is given under what is now CTA 2009, Pt. 11). Part 12 is exclusive and implicitly precludes any other deduction in any accounting period (commencing on or after 1 January 2003, deductions in previous years are not disrupted) in relation to the cost of shares, by the employing company or any other company. Transitional rules exist where costs of awarding shares have been deducted in accounting periods commencing prior to 1 January 2003, so that a deduction can be obtained under Pt. 12 in relation to costs to the extent that the market value of the shares at the time of relief under Part 12 exceeds the amounts previously deducted.

Where the conditions of Pt. 12 are met, corporation tax relief is given for the amount equal to the market value of the shares at the time of acquisition by the employee (or other person in relation to the employee's employment), less any consideration provided by anyone for the shares.

Relief can only be obtained by the legal employer of the employee who acquires the shares. There are also conditions to be met in relation to the business to which the award is made, the company whose shares are acquired, and the income tax position of the employee.

The business to which the award is made must be carried on by the employing company and be within the charge to corporation tax.

The company whose shares are acquired does not have to be the same company as the legal employer. For example, it is possible to have three different companies within the same group that play separate roles (e.g. legal employer, parent company (the shares in which are awarded to employees of the legal employer)), and a company carrying on a trade in which the employees are active. In this example, the legal employer (provided it is carrying on a trade of being a service company) would be the company which obtains the Pt. 12 deduction. It would be likely that in this example, there would be recharges in relation to the cost of awarding the shares. Whichever company suffers the ultimate cost would have a corporate tax disallowance for the charge to the profit and loss account.

In order for the employing company to obtain relief, it must be the case that the employee for whose employment the shares are awarded is subject to income tax or would be subject to income tax if the employee were UK resident and ordinarily resident at all material times and the duties by reason of which the share award is made were performed in the UK at all material times.

The shares acquired by reason of the employment must be ordinary shares that are fully paid up and not redeemable, and must be shares in any one of the following categories:

- listed on a recognised stock exchange;
- shares in a company not controlled by any other company;
- shares in a company that is under the control of a listed company.

Furthermore, the shares must be shares in the employing company (i.e. the company which employs the employee in respect of whose employment the award is made), or a company that is the parent company of the employing company at the time the shares are acquired. Alternatively, the shares could be in:

- a company that is a member of a consortium that owns either the employing company or the parent company of the employing company; or

- where the employing company or its parent company is a member of a consortium, then shares in a company that is a member of that consortium or its parent company, or, shares in a company which is a member of the same commercial association of companies as the consortium company.

Legislation: CTA 2009, Pt. 12, Ch. 2

Tax Reporter: ¶716-475ff.

3250 Corporation tax deduction where employee obtains options to acquire shares

Corporation tax relief can be obtained under Part 12 where an employee or another person acquires shares pursuant to an option awarded as a result of employment.

In most circumstances, the relief is straightforward and is obtained at the time the shares are acquired (not the time that the option is granted). The amount of the corporation tax deduction is an amount equal to the market value of the shares less any consideration paid.

Conditions must be satisfied in relation to the company whose shares are acquired, which are broadly the same as where shares are acquired absent an option (see 3425 above), except the conditions must be met at the time of the grant of the option.

The acquisition of the shares must be an event that would give rise to a tax charge for the employee in respect of whose employment the option has been granted (see 326).

Where the event would have been a chargeable event had the employee been resident and ordinarily resident in the UK at all material times and had the duties of the employment by reason of which the shares were awarded been performed in the UK at all material times, then the condition in relation to income tax position of the employee will still be met. Similarly, corporation tax relief is preserved where the employee is exempt from income tax on the exercise of his share options under an approved share option scheme (e.g. an EMI Option scheme).

The amount of relief given in relation to shares acquired pursuant to an option is the difference between the market value of the shares at the time they are awarded and the consideration given in respect of the option or the shares.

Special rules apply if employees acquire qualifying shares which are:

- subject to a risk of being forfeited (forfeitable shares);

- subject to other kinds of restrictions (other restricted shares); or

- convertible into other shares or securities (convertible shares).

From 1 September 2003, these special rules broadly align the timing and amount of deductions for the employer with the timing and amount of charge to tax on the employee as employment income in respect of:

- the acquisition of the shares; and

- subsequent post-acquisition events.

Legislation: CTA 2009, Pt. 12, Ch. 3

Tax Reporter: ¶716-475ff.

3255 Corporation tax deduction for contributions to employee benefit trusts

Prior to 23 November 2002, no specific tax provision applied to contributions to employee benefit trusts (EBTs): contributions were deductible for corporation tax purposes in accordance with normal corporation tax principles. This means that contributions prior to that date were normally deductible on being made (but subject to case law and accounting principles). Company contributions to an employee benefit trust after 23 November 2002 will now usually fall within CTA 2009, s. 1290. Under s. 1290, any act or omission by an employer (e.g. payment of a contribution to the EBT) which results in value being added to an employee benefit trust, will result in a disallowance for corporation tax purposes for the employer company. A deduction can be obtained subsequently where, broadly, remuneration is paid out of the EBT to an employee or, if the trust funds are applied in acquiring shares in the employing company (or certain other companies), under the rules described in 3425 and 3250 when the shares are acquired from the trustees by employees. However, a corporation tax deduction is not obtainable where benefits in kind are provided out of the trust to an employee or anyone else, even where the benefits are taxable on the employee.

The Special Commissioners decided in *Sempra Metals Ltd v R & C Commrs* that the provisions of what was then FA 2003, Sch. 24 (now CTA 2009, s. 1290) applied to disallow a corporation tax deduction for a contribution to a trust where the beneficiaries were family members of the employees and not the employees themselves.

Legislation was introduced in 1989 providing for, in particular, corporation tax relief on contributions to a specific type of employee benefit trust, called a QUEST (Qualifying Employee Share Ownership Trust). QUESTs required, in particular, that all employees and directors were beneficiaries of the trust and that the majority of trustees were employees who were not directors. Contributions by a company into a QUEST prior to 31 December 2002 were deductible for corporation tax purposes. For accounting periods beginning on or after 1 January 2003, contributions to QUESTs are no longer specifically deductible for corporation tax purposes but fall within the general provisions outlined above.

Legislation: CTA 2009, s. 1290

Case: *Sempra Metals Ltd v R & C Commrs* (2008) Sp C 698

Tax Reporter: ¶703-250

Losses

3300 Introduction

The losses incurred by a company can be generally divided into two groups:

(1) trading losses (see 3310); and

(2) non-trading losses, such as capital losses (see 3355), property income losses (formerly Sch. A) (see 3345) and miscellaneous income (formerly Sch. D, Case VI) source losses (see 3350).

Tax Reporter: ¶730-000ff.

Trading losses

3310 Meaning of trading losses for companies

A company's trading losses (formerly Schedule D, Case I losses) in any accounting period are losses arising from the company's trade in that period. They are determined after the deduction of capital allowances given in taxing the trade.

The principal reliefs available for trading losses are current period relief (see 3315), preceding period's relief (see 3320) and future period's relief (see 3330).

Whilst losses on investments would, except in the case of dealing companies, be capital losses, special relief is given for investment companies (see 5265).

Special provisions may limit the amount effectively regarded as a trading loss of a company involved in a partnership or receiving first-year allowances from a leasing contract which it transfers to another person.

Prior to 1 April 2010, charges on income were, in theory, treated as trading losses where those charges were greater than the profits of the same period (see 3235). The relief was, in theory, available for charges on income incurred by the company wholly and exclusively for the purposes of its trade. The difference between the company's profits and the total charges on income were in practice added to the company's trading losses for the accounting period. Relief was available up to the lower of:

- excess charges; or

- payments made wholly and exclusively for the purposes of the trade.

Consequently, for this purpose, non-trade charges were deemed to be used before trade charges.

Although that was the position in theory for accounting periods ending before 1 April 2010, in practice, due to the introduction of the loan relationship rules in 1996 and other changes to legislation in 2005, only donations and gifts to charities fell to be taken as charges on income. The provisions allowing for the carry forward of excess charges on income therefore had no application as it is difficult to imagine circumstances where a donation or gift to a charity (which is not deductible in computing trading profits) would have been incurred wholly and exclusively for the purposes of the company's trade. In recognition of this, the rewritten legislation in CTA 2010 has renamed 'charges on income' 'charitable donations relief' and has removed the provisions allowing for a carry forward of excess charges on income. For accounting periods ended on or after 1 April 2010, excess charitable donations made by a trading company (A) for an accounting period can only be relieved by being surrendered as group relief or set against the income of a controlled foreign company apportioned to A in the same accounting period.

Legislation: CTA 2010, Pt. 4, Ch. 2

Tax Reporter: ¶730-000ff.

3315   Company trading losses: offset against current profits

A company's 'trading losses' (see 3310) may be set off against total profits made in the same accounting period. A company wishing to set off losses in this way must make a claim within two years after the end of the accounting period in which the losses occur.

Example

A company makes a trading loss of £60,000. In the same accounting period, it receives rents of £20,000 and bank interest of £15,000.

	£
Property income	20,000
Non-trading loan relationship credit	15,000
Total profits	35,000
Less: loss under CTA 2010, s. 37(3)(a)	(35,000)
Chargeable profits	Nil

Profits of an accounting period for the purpose of loss relief can include dividends on investments and interest which would fall to be taxed as trading receipts but for the fact that they have been taxed under other provisions. In the case of industrial and provident societies, this is extended by concession to amounts assessable under miscellaneous income (formerly Sch. D, Case IV and V) as well as most interest. A shipping company contended that interest it received on money invested to provide a fund to replace ships in its fleet was trading income eligible for loss relief. It was held that the interest was investment income and not trading income and that loss relief was not available.

There are certain trading losses to which relief does not apply. These are losses from foreign trading (i.e. where the trade is carried on wholly outside the UK) and from trades carried on a non-commercial basis, without a view to realising a gain. A business or part of a business is only conducted on a commercial basis if it is conducted with a view to making a profit, though it suffices that it is conducted so as to afford a reasonable expectation of profit. If a business, or part, begins or ceases to be conducted on a commercial basis, it is treated as conducted throughout the accounting period in the way in which it was being conducted by the end of the period.

If a company makes a loss in the trade of farming or market gardening, it cannot claim relief against its other taxable income and gains when it has incurred a loss in carrying on that trade in each of the five years prior to the start of the accounting period when the loss is made. The company may still carry forward the trading loss against future trading income.

Relief may be denied in respect of certain losses from dealing in commodity futures or qualifying options.

For accounting periods ending before 1 April 2010 where it was not possible to deduct charges on income incurred wholly and exclusively for the purpose of the trade because of insufficient profits or loss claims, it was possible for the charges to be carried forward to set-off against future trading income (see 3310 and 3330).

Legislation: CTA 2010, s. 37, 44, 47

Tax Reporter: ¶730-150

3320   Company trading losses: offset against previous profits

A company's 'trading losses' can, to the extent that they cannot be used against the current period's profits (see 3315), also be carried back against profits arising in the previous 12 months, any necessary apportionment of the results of a previous accounting period being made to effect this. Terminal losses (see 3335) can be carried back for a period of three years and a temporary extension applies for accounting periods ended after 23 November 2008 and before 24 November 2010 (see 3325).

There are certain trading losses to which relief does not apply. These are losses from foreign trading and from trades carried on on a non-commercial basis, without a view to realising a gain (see 3315).

A company must make its claim for relief within two years of the end of the accounting period in which it made the loss, or within such further period as HMRC may allow.

Relief is given against profits of a later accounting period before those of an earlier accounting period.

Example

H Ltd prepares accounts to 30 June each year. For the year to 30 June 2012, H Ltd made a trading profit of £20,000. For the year to 30 June 2013, H Ltd made a trading loss of £12,000. The company also had chargeable gains of £5,000 in the year to 30 June 2012 and £3,000 in the year to 30 June 2013.

On a claim, the trading loss for the year to 30 June 2013 will first be set against the chargeable gains for that year (see 3315), the balance being set against the trading profit for the year to 30 June 2010 as follows:

	Year to 30 June 2012 £	Year to 30 June 2013 £
Trading profit	20,000	–
Less: loss carried back	(9,000)	
	11,000	–
Chargeable gains	5,000	3,000
Less: current year loss		(3,000)
Chargeable profits	16,000	Nil

The trading loss in the year to 30 June 2011 is thus utilised as follows:

	£
Trading loss y/e 30/6/2013	12,000
Set-off against chargeable gains of same period	(3,000)
(CTA 2010, s. 37(3)(a))	
	9,000
Set-off against profits of previous accounting period	(9,000)
Loss carried forward	–

For the purposes of the carry-back of losses, repayment interest is to be calculated by reference to the accounting period in which the loss is incurred rather than the period to which the loss is carried back except where this is wholly within the previous 12 months (see 4370).

Legislation: CTA 2010, s. 37, 44

Tax Reporter: ¶730-200ff.

3330 Company trading losses: offset against future profits

Any trading losses of a company which are not relieved by offset against current profits (see 3315) or previous profits (see 3320) are carried forward to be set off against the first available profits of the same trade for subsequent accounting periods. Relief is given automatically.

The loss can be carried forward indefinitely subject to provisions dealing with reconstructions and changes in company ownership (see 3370 and 3375) or where a government investment in the company is written off. There is a proposal to consider restricting the carry forward to loss relief whilst broadening the scope of the profits that the loss can be set against. In brief, it is suggested that:

- losses arising from 1 April 2017 will be available to be carried forward and set against different types of taxable profits within that company and against the taxable profits of its group members;

- losses arising prior to April 2017 would remain subject to existing restrictions as to the profits they can be offset against;

- the amount of annual profit that will be able to be relieved by carried-forward losses would be limited to 50% from 1 April 2017, subject to an allowance of £5m per group;

- there would be no restrictions on the carry-back of losses and groups would have full discretion as to where the £5m allowance is used within the group;

- the definition of group for the purpose of the allowance (as opposed to that for the purpose of allowing carried forward losses in one company to be used by another) will be based on 'control' or 'association'.

Legislation: CTA 2010, s. 45 and 92

Tax Reporter: ¶730-300

3335   Company terminal trading losses

When a company ceases trading, a trading loss incurred in the 12 months beforehand can be set off against the trading income of the company made in the three preceding years. If the final accounting period is less than 12 months, a proportionate part of the penultimate accounting period's loss can be used to produce a final 12-month loss.

Where a trade is transferred between two companies, there is a cessation of the trade in the hands of the transferring company. Where the companies are in common ownership, for certain aspects, the trade is treated as continuing throughout (see 3370). This treatment is applied to what would otherwise be terminal losses of a transferring company. Thus, losses accruing in the 12 months prior to the transfer of a trade to another company in common ownership will not qualify for the extended, three-year, carry-back.

With effect for cessations occurring on or after 21 May 2009, terminal loss relief is not available where a trade is transferred to a person outside the charge to corporation tax under a scheme or arrangement entered into to secure that relief. This amendment was made to counter a specific scheme notified to HMRC under the DOTAS rules.

As with the calculation of the final 12-month trading loss, if the final accounting period is less than 12 months (and ends before 1 April 2010), a proportionate part of the penultimate accounting period's excess trade charges on income can be used to calculate the amount available to increase the loss.

Legislation: CTA 2010, s. 39, 41

Tax Reporter: ¶730-225

3340   Pre-trading expenditure by company

Expenditure incurred by a company for the purposes of a trade before that trade commences may in some respects be regarded as a loss but is treated for corporation tax as trading expenditure incurred on the day trading starts. The expenditure must not be incurred more than seven years before trading commences and is allowable as a deduction in computing trading profits only if it would have been allowable had trading commenced (essentially as for income tax) at that time.

However, this does not apply to expenditure that would fall under the loan relationships provisions. A company may elect to delay accounting for what would be a non-trading debit until it begins trading. The expenditure will then be treated as a trading debit in the accounting period in which the trade began.

It is HMRC's view that pre-trading expenditure does not include costs incurred by persons other than the eventual trader: for example, where an individual incurs the expenditure but incorporates when trading begins; or where one company in a group incurs the expenditure and a fellow group member then starts to carry on the trade.

There are special rules for preparation of waste disposal sites which apply to corporation tax in essentially the same way as to income tax (see 2053).

Legislation: CTA 2009, s. 61

Tax Reporter: ¶707-410ff.

Non-trading losses

3345   Losses from UK and overseas property businesses

Where a loss is made in a UK property business for an accounting period, that loss can be set against the company's total profits of that period. To the extent that the loss cannot be so set off, it is carried forward for set-off against future total profits, as long as the company continues to carry on the UK property business.

Where a loss is made in an overseas property business (formerly a Sch. D, Case V loss), the loss is a carried forward for offset against future profits of that business.

Relief is given automatically in both cases, there being no need to make a claim.

Where a company carries on a furnished holiday lettings business (see 1255), a loss in respect of that business will be treated as a trading loss. However, and from April 2011, relief for that loss will only be available against future profits from the same business (and not against general profits of the year of the loss and the preceding year as was the case previously).

Where a company with investment business also has a UK property business, and it ceases to carry on that property business, any unrelieved loss is treated as an expense of management of the succeeding accounting period.

As with trading losses (see 3315), loss relief is only available for a UK or overseas property business conducted on a commercial basis or in the exercise of statutory functions.

Legislation: CTA 2010, Pt. 4, Ch. 4

Tax Reporter: ¶730-650 and ¶730-700

3350 Losses from miscellaneous transactions (formerly losses under Sch. D, Case VI)

A company which makes a loss on a miscellaneous transaction can offset that loss against the earliest available miscellaneous income (being income chargeable under CTA 2010, s. 1173 with the exception of offshore income gains), whether in the same or subsequent accounting periods. A transaction is a miscellaneous transaction if, had it given rise to income, that income would have been chargeable to corporation tax as miscellaneous income.

Legislation: CTA 2010, s. 91

Tax Reporter: ¶730-800

3355 Capital losses of companies

Allowable capital losses can only be set against chargeable gains of the same or subsequent accounting periods. Losses must be set against current period gains before future gains. The set-off is mandatory. Losses must be set against gains at the earliest opportunity.

Example

A company makes a chargeable gain of £100,000 and an allowable loss of £175,000 in the year to 31 March 2012. In the year to 31 March 2013, it makes a chargeable gain of £250,000.

The allowable loss of £175,000 is first set against the gain of the same accounting period so as to reduce net gains to nil. The balance of £75,000 is then set against the gain for the year to 31 March 2013, leaving net gains of £175,000 to be included in the company's profits chargeable to corporation tax for that period.

Allowable capital losses cannot be set against trading profits.

Targeted anti-avoidance rules (TAARs) were introduced with effect from 5 December 2005 to prevent the avoidance of tax through the creation and use of capital losses by companies. The legislation is targeted specifically at the following three areas of avoidance:

(1) the contrived creation of capital losses;

(2) the buying of capital gains and losses; and

(3) the conversion of income to capital and using capital losses to create a deduction against income.

From 21 March 2007, new legislation prevents schemes that exploited an exception in existing anti-avoidance rules. Broadly, the new measures are intended to prevent groups of companies obtaining a tax advantage where a company changes ownership (see 3375) and one of the main purposes of the arrangements is for the new owners to gain access to the company's capital losses or gains.

HMRC have provided reassurance that the legislation will not apply where there is a genuine commercial transaction that gives rise to a real commercial loss as a result of a genuine commercial disposal.

Legislation: TCGA 1992, s. 8, 16A and 184A–184I

Tax Reporter: ¶753-150ff.

Particular situations

3370   Change of trader without change in ownership

If a company (C) stops trading and a second company (S) starts to carry on the same trade, and the shareholders who held 75% (or more) of the ordinary share capital of C within one year before the change hold 75% (or more) of the ordinary share capital of S within two years after the change, C and S are treated as one company when calculating the capital allowances and losses of the trade in so far as S is entitled to reliefs to which C would have been entitled.

It is the activity of C, rather than the trade as such, which must be carried on by S.

Loss relief is restricted where the predecessor company is insolvent at the time it ceases to carry on the trade or part of a trade. Where the predecessor company's 'relevant liabilities' exceed its 'relevant assets', the entitlement of the successor company to the predecessor company's losses is restricted to the excess of the losses over the amount by which relevant liabilities exceed relevant assets.

Example

Predecessor company has losses of £50,000, relevant liabilities of £250,000 and relevant assets of £230,000.

(1)   Excess of liabilities over assets = £250,000 − £230,000 = £20,000

(2)   Losses = £50,000

(3)   Excess of losses over the amount by which liabilities
       exceed assets = £50,000 − £20,000 = £30,000

'Relevant liabilities' are those outstanding and vested in the predecessor company immediately prior to cessation of trade and not transferred to the successor. A liability representing the predecessor's share capital, share premium account, reserves or relevant loan stock is not a relevant liability.

'Relevant assets' are all assets which were vested in the predecessor company immediately before its cessation of trade which were not transferred to the successor company.

If S only takes over part of the activities of C, that part is treated as a separate trade and a just apportionment of the income and expenses is made. The need to 'stream' income in order to determine the availability of loss relief is the subject of an appeal against a determination by HMRC (*Leekes Ltd v HMRC*). The taxpayer was successful in the First-tier Tribunal but the decision was reversed in the Upper Tribunal that held that streaming was necessary.

C and S are not treated as a single company when dealing with losses other than trading losses, i.e. allowable capital losses, nor in dealing with surplus franked investment income.

Legislation: CTA 2010, Pt. 22, Ch. 1

Case: *Falmer Jeans Ltd v Rodin (HMIT)* [1990] BTC 193

Tax Reporter: ¶709-820ff.

3375   Change in company ownership

A company cannot carry forward losses arising in a period prior to a change in ownership to set off against the profits of an accounting period after a change of ownership if that change and a major change in the nature or conduct of the company's trade occurred within three years of each other. Nor can a company carry back losses incurred after the change in ownership against profits before the change.

The company cannot carry forward losses if there is a change of ownership at any time after the activities in a trade carried on by a company have become small or negligible but before there is any considerable revival of trade.

When a company is calculating the losses which it cannot carry forward, the capital allowances for accounting periods before the change of ownership are treated as a first charge against the profits of those periods. This results in an increase in the trading losses which cannot be carried forward.

Similar provisions prevent a taxpayer using unrelieved management expenses (and similar reliefs available to companies with investment business), in respect of ownership changes occurring after 28 November 1994, unless in pursuance of a contract entered into before that date.

Rules also apply from 1 April 1998 to prevent a UK property income loss (formerly Sch. A) arising before a change of ownership of a company carrying on a UK property income (formerly Sch. A) business being relieved against profits of an accounting period after the change in ownership.

Major change in nature or conduct of trade

A statement of practice explains the basis on which HMRC interpret the term 'a major change in the nature or conduct of a trade'.

In addition to the qualitative issues included in statute (matters to be considered in determining whether something is a change), HMRC will also have regard, if appropriate, to changes in such other factors as the location of the company's business, the identity of its suppliers, management, or staff, its methods of manufacture, or its pricing or purchasing policies. With respect to the quantitative component (whether a change is a major change), HMRC will not regard as a major change those alterations made to increase efficiency, to keep pace with developing technology in the industry concerned or with developing management techniques. Similarly, a rationalisation of product range by withdrawal of unprofitable items and, possibly, replacement by items related to existing products will not amount to a major change.

The statement also refers to the position where a company carries on a trade (comprising activities A and B) and transfers part of the trade (comprising activity A) to another company under similar control (so as to treat losses as being carried over, etc. see 3370), such that the second company may carry on activity A as a separate trade or as part of a combined trade. The transfer will not, by itself, be regarded as a major change in any separate trade comprising activity A or any separate trade comprising activity B. However, activity A after the transfer (whether amounting to a separate trade or part of a combined trade) will be compared with activity A before the transfer and activity B after the transfer will be compared with activity B before the transfer. Also, where the transfer occurs after the change in ownership, in determining whether there has been a major change in respect of the original trade (activities A and B), HMRC will not contend that the transfer constitutes a major change if, within the relevant period, there is no other change in the original trade or, after the division, in activities A and B.

The statement also includes some examples to assist in showing where HMRC consider the borderline falls:

'Examples where a change would not of itself be regarded as a major change

a. A company manufacturing kitchen fitments in three obsolescent factories moves production to one new factory (increasing efficiency).

b. A company manufacturing kitchen utensils replaces enamel by plastic, or a company manufacturing timepieces replaces mechanical by electronic components (keeping pace with developing technology).

c. A company operating a dealership in one make of car switches to operating a dealership in another make of car satisfying the same market (not a major change in the type of property dealt in).

d. A company manufacturing both filament and fluorescent lamps (of which filament lamps form the greater part of the output) concentrates solely on filament lamps (a rationalisation of product range without a major change in the type of property dealt in).

e. A company whose business consists of making and holding investments in UK quoted shares and securities makes changes to its portfolio of quoted shares and securities (not a change in the nature of investments held).

Examples where a major change would be regarded as occurring

f. A company operating a dealership in saloon cars switches to operating a dealership in tractors (a major change in the type of property dealt in).

g. A company owning a public house switches to operating a discotheque in the same, but converted, premises (a major change in the services or facilities provided).

h. A company fattening pigs for their owners switches to buying pigs for fattening and resale (a major change in the nature of the trade, being a change from providing a service to being a primary producer).

i. A company whose business consists of making and holding investments in UK quoted shares to investing in real property for rent (a change in the nature of investments held).'

Change in ownership

A company has a change of ownership if one person acquires more than half of its ordinary share capital other than as an unsolicited gift or by succession on death.

There is a change of ownership also if two or more persons acquire more than half of the company's ordinary share capital and each acquires at least 5% of that capital or has a holding of at least 5% as a result of the acquisition.

Where a change in ownership would be treated as occurring after 13 March 1989, any actual change in ownership of a company will be taken as an acquisition by the person(s) involved of relevant shares owned by the company so as to bring about possible changes in ownership of companies in which those shares subsist. No deemed acquisition will take place if the change in ownership of the company can be disregarded because the company remains throughout a 75% subsidiary of any company – with comparable entitlements to profits and assets available for distribution to equity holders (see 3695).

Changes have been made to the legislation to ensure that these rules cannot be circumvented by the immediate transfer of the trade following a change of ownership (see FA 2013, s. 32).

Legislation: CTA 2010, Pt. 14;

Case: *Willis (HMIT) v Peeters Picture Frames Ltd* [1983] BTC 325

Other Material: *Statement of Practice* SP 10/91, Loss loop-hole closure rules: www.hmrc.gov.uk/budget2013/ct-loss-loophole-closure-rules.pdf; HMRC helpsheet for advance clearances at http://tinyurl.com/ps5plke

Tax Reporter: ¶731-050

Chargeable gains

3400   Introduction

Capital gains made by a company are not generally chargeable to capital gains tax. Rather, a company pays corporation tax on its chargeable gains; other capital gains are outside the scope of the UK tax net unless they are to be specifically taxed under income provisions.

It is important to make this distinction between companies and other persons because the general rules relating to capital gains will not necessarily apply to companies, although corporation tax does apply 'capital gains tax principles'.

The exception to the above rule is the charge on the disposal of a property that has been within the scope of the ATED (annual tax on enveloped dwellings). Specific rules were enacted in FA 2013 to ensure that gains accruing after 6 April 2013, in respect of such properties is chargeable at the special rate of 28%. It should be noted that losses in respect of ATED properties are to be 'ring-fenced' (see HMRC manual at CG 73602 for further details www.hmrc.gov.uk/manuals/cgmanual/cg73602.htm).

Finance Act 2015, s. 37 and Sch. 7 extended the charge to CGT to certain companies disposing of residential property – see 3407.

Tax Reporter: ¶753-000ff.

Computational issues

3405   Calculation of chargeable gains of companies

Chargeable gains and allowable losses are calculated according to the normal capital gains tax rules (see 5221ff.) except that accounting periods are treated as if they are years of assessment. However, indexation (see 5280ff.) continues to apply for the purposes of corporation tax on chargeable gains. Indexation allowance is not available to create or to augment a loss. The indexation allowance is limited to the amount of the unindexed gain.

The gains of a company to be included in total profits chargeable to corporation tax (see 3400) for an accounting period are calculated by setting off allowable losses suffered in the same and earlier accounting periods. There are special provisions for groups (see 3625.) and the loss offset may be restricted in the case of gains on assets transferred in to a company by a fellow group company to soak up allowable losses attributable to periods before the company joined the group (see 3630).

Example

Company Ltd prepares accounts annually to 30 June. In March 2013 (i.e. in the year to 30 June 2013), it sold a chargeable asset for £500,000. The asset was purchased in July 1998 for £200,000. The company also sold a chargeable asset in January 2013 for £100,000 that it had purchased in January 2005 for £120,000.

The company also made trading profits of £2,000,000 for the year to 30 June 2013.

Company Ltd's total taxable profits for the period are computed as follows.		
Asset 1		£
Disposal proceeds		500,000
Less: acquisition cost		(200,000)
Unindexed gain		300,000
Less: indexation allowance say		
0.526 × £200,000		(105,200)
Chargeable gain		194,800
Asset 2		£
Disposal proceeds		100,000
Less: acquisition cost		(120,000)
Allowable loss		(20,000)
Total taxable profits– y/e 30/6/2013	£	£
Trading profits		2,000,000
Chargeable gain	194,800	
Less: allowable loss	(20,000)	
		147,800
Total taxable profits		2,174,800

Legislation: TCGA 1992, s. 8

Tax Reporter: ¶753-000ff.

3406   Calculation of chargeable gains on ATED properties

Finance Act 2013 contains the details of the charge to capital gains tax (CGT) on both UK and non-UK resident non-natural persons (NNPs) in respect of gains accruing on the disposal of interests in high value residential property that are the subject of the annual tax on enveloped dwellings (ATED). Broadly, for the purposes of this legislation, NNPs will be companies and certain collective investment schemes. Companies that are within the charge to UK corporation tax will thus be liable to this CGT charge in respect of such disposals rather than corporation tax. The charge applies to gains on disposals on or after 6 April 2013 and increases (and decreases) in the value of property before then are outside the new charge but remain subject to the existing corporation tax rules on capital gains. As these rules are closely linked, the legislation should be read alongside the legislation (and guidance material) introducing ATED. The computation is potentially extremely complex as it is necessary to split any gain to that attributable to the property use within the scope of the ATED rules and that which is not as well as determining the extent to which any pre-April 2013 gain is excluded from the charge.

3407 UK residential property owned by non-resident taxpayers

Finance Act 2015 introduced a charge to CGT on UK residential property owned by non-resident taxpayers. The charge takes effect from April 2015. Complex rules dealing with the interaction between this new charge and the ATED rules are included.

3408 Interest on capital not deductible for chargeable gains of companies

For accounting periods ending after 31 March 1996, the rules applicable to the taxation of loan relationships in the hands of companies apply (see 3164). The assumption is that relief will be afforded for such interest under those rules and therefore relief against capital gains will be prevented from applying by the general prohibition against deductions in calculating chargeable gains for expenditure which is allowable in arriving at income. However, it is possible for a company to own a capital asset now in respect of which interest was incurred in accounting periods ended before 31 March 1996 which was capitalised (so as not to have been an allowable deduction against income for corporation tax purposes). In these circumstances, the capitalised interest will be an allowable deduction in calculating the chargeable gain on a disposal of the asset.

Legislation: TCGA 1992, s. 39 and 40

Tax Reporter: ¶760-350

3410 Shareholders liable to pay company's tax on capital gains

Shareholders connected with a UK-resident company may be liable to pay the tax on the capital gains made by that company where they receive a capital distribution; this does not apply where the distribution represents a reduction of capital.

A shareholder is connected with a company if he has control of it alone or together with other persons connected with him.

A person is connected with their spouse and other 'relatives' (or spouses thereof); that person is also connected with relatives of their spouse (or spouses of those relatives). 'Relative' includes brother, sister, ancestor and lineal descendant.

'Control' has the same meaning as applies to close companies (see 4000).

Circumstances in which shareholder liable

A shareholder who qualifies for liability to the tax will be held liable where the distribution is made after a disposal of assets which results in a capital gain by the company or where the distribution amounts to a disposal of assets.

When a shareholder becomes liable

If the corporation tax for the accounting period in which the capital gain is made is not paid by the company within six months from the date it became payable, a shareholder who has received a distribution may be assessed and charged to corporation tax; the assessment must be made within two years of the date when the tax became payable.

Limit on the amount of the liability

The amount of corporation tax charged on a shareholder must not exceed the amount of the capital distribution and a portion of the tax charged on the gain in proportion to the recipient's share of the distribution.

The shareholder so charged is entitled to reclaim the corporation tax paid and any interest on overdue tax from the company.

Capital distributions

Capital distributions are distributions which are not income in the hands of the recipient for income tax purposes (see 5890).

All distributions in a winding-up are capital distributions. The enactment of ESC C16 has been made by inserting new s. 1030A and 1030B into CTA 2010. In consequence certain distributions on the striking off of a company under CA 2006, s. 1000 procedure are also treated as being of a capital nature.

It is to be noted that the dissolution of a company under the *Companies Act* 2006, s. 1000 or 1003 (or corresponding overseas provisions) is not a formal winding up and so a distribution by it of any surplus assets to its shareholders would in strictness be an income distribution for corporation tax purposes. New s. 1030A provides that in specified circumstances a distribution made prior to the dissolution of a company is not an income distribution for the purposes of corporation tax. If the conditions are met, then the distribution is treated as a capital payment to be taken into account in determining the capital gains tax liability of a shareholder in the company. Section 1030B disapplies s 1030A should the company, within two years of a distribution, have not been dissolved or secured, as far as was reasonably practicable, payment of all sums due to it or satisfied all of its debts and liabilities.

Most capital distributions to shareholders and debenture holders are treated as resulting from disposal of an interest in those shares and debentures, and the gains over the cost of acquisition are taxable.

This rule does not apply to the issue of shares and debentures. The shares resulting from a capital distribution are identified with the original holding and no acquisition or disposal is deemed to occur, e.g. when a company makes a bonus issue of shares or debentures to its shareholders or a rights issue in proportion to each holding, or alters rights attached to issued shares or reduces capital.

Legislation: TCGA 1992, s. 189 and 286; CTA 2010, s. 450

Tax Reporter: ¶598-050ff.

Reconstructions and reorganisations

3415   Company reconstruction or amalgamation

Where, under a scheme of reconstruction or amalgamation, one company transfers the whole or part of its business to another company it is treated as a transfer resulting in neither a gain nor a loss to the company making the transfer and the transferee will take over the assets as if it had acquired them on the same date as the person making the transfer.

Both companies must be resident in the UK at the time of the transfer and, from 19 March 1990, the transferee must not be exempt from tax under a double tax treaty on a notional gain in respect of the disposal of the assets in point. From 30 November 1993, any such company would, in any case, be regarded as resident outside the UK, and therefore outside the scope of these provisions (see 3020).

The transferor must receive no consideration for the company's business.

To be treated as a reconstruction, the transaction must be for bona fide commercial purposes so that there is no reconstruction where an arrangement is effected to avoid liability to corporation tax.

Once HMRC decide that the transaction is not bona fide and that the company would be assessed to tax if it were not in liquidation, it may charge tax on the company which receives the assets or its shareholders.

There is machinery for a prospective transferee to apply in writing to the Board for a ruling that HMRC is satisfied with the scheme before the transfer takes place. It must supply all material facts and details to the Board after which the Board has 30 days in which to ask for further information. It then has a further 30 days to give its decision. If the applicant wishes to challenge the finding, it may refer to the special commissioners. Further details of the approach set out by HMRC is set out at www.hmrc. gov.uk/cap/.

Reconstruction involving an issue of shares or securities

Where in a scheme of reconstruction or amalgamation, shareholders of a company receive shares in another company and the old shares are either retained or cancelled, they may in certain circumstances be treated as having exchanged their original holdings for the new holdings so as to obtain a tax deferral: provided the tax avoidance motive test is passed (or advance clearance obtained) as in relation to the relief for certain actual exchanges, that relief applies notwithstanding that there is no general offer or resultant substantial holding (for discussion of the exchange relief, see 3417). Where the new holding comprises debentures or gives right to the issue of debentures which, rarely, would not constitute a debt on a security they are treated as such; hence, unless they are qualifying corporate bonds they do not fall outside the chargeable gains net (see 6183). By virtue of an Extra-statutory Concession, published on 12 May 1995, costs incurred as part of a share exchange, company reconstruction or amalgamation treated as a share reorganisation under these provisions may be treated as an additional payment for the new shares or debentures and consequently treated as allowable expenditure when the shares are disposed of.

What is a reconstruction?

In the *South African Supply and Cold Storage* case Buckley J said at p. 286:

> 'What does 'reconstruction' mean? ... It involves, I think, that substantially the same business shall be carried on and substantially the same persons shall carry it on. But it does not involve that all the assets shall pass to the new company or resuscitated company, or that all the shareholders of the old company shall be shareholders in the new company or resuscitated company. Substantially the business and the persons interested must be the same.'

As a general rule, therefore, a scheme of reconstruction is considered to entail the second company carrying on substantially the same business with the same members as the first. Therefore, the division of a company's undertaking into two or more companies owned by different sets of shareholders would not be a reconstruction. In practice, however, for capital gains purposes, HMRC do not insist upon identity of shareholdings in the old and new companies where a division of companies is carried out for bona fide commercial reasons.

A scheme whereby the shares are reorganised into separate classes under which new companies are formed to take over separate parts of the undertaking allocated to the different classes and each group of shareholders receives shares in a separate company, is treated as a scheme of reconstruction. This is so even though the new companies have no common shareholder provided that there is a segregation of businesses and not just assets. For this purpose, it is enough that there are identifiable parts of a trade or business which can be carried on in their own right. A later chargeable disposal of shares in one or more of the newly created companies does not on its own prevent the division of the original company being recognised as a reconstruction. In the context of demergers, a shareholding in a company which is a 75% subsidiary of the distributing company is treated as constituting an identifiable part of the trade or business of the distributing company. Therefore, the division of a company involving the transfer of shares in a subsidiary to a newly formed company by way of a demerger is also regarded as a scheme of reconstruction.

HMRC have confirmed that, in their view, relief is available for a scheme of reconstruction which involves an arrangement under CA 2006, s. 899 where shares in a company (company A) are cancelled, new shares in company A are issued to a new company (company B) and company B issues its own shares to the former members of company A pro rata to their holdings in company A.

What is an amalgamation?

An amalgamation occurs when two or more businesses merge within one company. The resulting company must be one of the participating companies to which the business of another company is transferred. Alternatively, the company must have been formed specially to accommodate the enterprises.

The shareholders in the new company must be all the shareholders in the participating companies.

Again in the *South African Supply and Cold Storage* case, Buckley J said at p. 287:

> 'The difference between reconstruction and amalgamation is that in the latter is involved the blending of two concerns one with the other, but not merely the continuance of one concern … It is not necessary that you should have a new company. You may have a continuance of one of the two companies upon the terms that the undertakings of both corporations shall substantially be merged in one corporation only.'

It is possible for an amalgamation to take place within a series of arrangements which are not made primarily for purposes of amalgamation.

The position post-16 April 2002

The statute governing schemes of reconstruction and amalgamation was replaced by FA 2002 with effect from 17 April 2002. However, the effect of the legislation remains largely unchanged, except that it now contains practice previously outlined in Statement of Practice SP 5/85.

Legislation: TCGA 1992, s. 136–139 and Sch. 5AA

Cases: *Re South African Supply and Cold Storage Co* [1904] 2 Ch 268; *Crane Fruehauf Ltd v IR Commrs* [1975] 1 All ER 429

Other Material: *Extra-statutory Concession* ESC D52

Tax Reporter: ¶756-900ff.

3417 Exchange of shares or securities

The provisions relating to the reorganisation of share capital which broadly defer chargeable gains by disregarding the disposal and treating the replacement securities as if they were the original shares (see 5900 to 5910) apply where:

(1) company A issues shares or debentures to a person in exchange for shares or debentures of company B if:

    (a) company A holds (or, because of the exchange, will hold) more than 25% of company B's ordinary share capital; or

    (b) company A issues the shares, etc. in exchange for shares as a result of a general offer which is made to shareholders of company B, and is made initially on a condition that, if satisfied, company A would have control of company B; and

(2) the exchange is for bona fide commercial reasons and is not a tax avoidance manoeuvre). This condition is satisfied if advance clearance for the exchange of shares is obtained from HMRC (see below).

The ICAEW have published a guidance note containing the text of an exchange of letters between themselves and HMRC concerning the above clearance procedure – it sets out certain matters concerning the way in which a request should be drafted.

By virtue of an Extra-statutory Concession, published on 12 May 1995, costs incurred as part of a share exchange, company reconstruction or amalgamation treated as a share reorganisation under these provisions may be treated as an additional payment for the new shares or debentures and consequently treated as allowable expenditure when the shares are disposed of.

Where the new holding comprises debentures or gives right to the issue of debentures which, rarely, would not constitute a debt on a security they are treated as such; hence, unless they are qualifying corporate bonds they do not fall outside the chargeable gains net (see 6183).

The position post-16 April 2002

The statute governing exchanges of shares or securities was replaced by FA 2002 with effect from 17 April 2002. However, the effect of the legislation remains largely unchanged, except that it now applies in relation to companies without share capital.

Legislation: TCGA 1992, s. 135 and 137–139

Other Material: ICAEW Guidance Note, TR 657; *Extra-statutory Concession* ESC D52

Tax Reporter: ¶757-400

Disposal of substantial shareholdings

3425   Introduction

Finance Act 2002 introduced an exemption for capital gains and losses on disposals by companies with substantial shareholdings in other companies. The exemption, which is effective from 1 April 2002, essentially applies where:

- an independent trading company or a company which is a member of a trading group disposes of a substantial shareholding in another company which is itself a trading company or the holding company of a trading group; and

- the investing company has held 10% or more of the ordinary shares of the company invested in for a period of at least 12 months in the two years before the share sale.

The rules apply equally whether the shares being disposed of are in a UK or overseas company. Where the exemption applies, no claim is necessary. Any gain on the disposal of the shares is not chargeable to tax and any loss is not available to set against other gains.

The exemption will not apply where there is a major change in the trade of the company in between the acquisition and disposal of its shares.

In addition to the main exemption, other subsidiary exemptions apply (see 3435 below), being:

- the disposal of assets relating to shares; and

- disposals where the main exemption was previously met.

Legislation: TCGA 1992, s. 192A and Sch. 7AC

Tax Reporter: ¶759-800ff.

3430 Conditions for exemption

In order to qualify for the main or subsidiary exemptions detailed conditions must be complied with. Care needs to be exercised to ensure that the favourable treatment will apply.

Following changes made by FA 2011, the exemption may now apply where a divisionalised company transfers one or more of its businesses into a new group company prior to the sale of that company (i.e. where there is a qualifying transfer of trading assets within a group). Broadly, and for share disposals taking place on or after 19 July 2011 (or 1 April 2011 in some cases), it is provided that the company making the disposal (A) is treated as having held the substantial shareholding in the company disposed of (B) at any time in the 12-month period ending on the date of disposal when the asset transferred to B was used by A or another group company (C) for trading purposes. A similar modification has been made to the qualifying period rule applying with regard to the company invested in. Briefly, the company invested in is treated as having been a trading company at any time during the 12 months ending with the date of disposal when the asset transferred to it was used by the transferor or another group company for trading purposes.

Substantial shareholding requirement

The investing company must have held a substantial shareholding in the company invested in throughout a 12-month period beginning not more than two years before the date on which the disposal took place (see above for changes made by FA 2011). More complex rules cover situations involving reconstructions or reorganisations.

For the purposes of this legislation, a company has a substantial shareholding in another company if:

- it holds not less than 10% of the company's ordinary share capital;

- it is beneficially entitled to not less than 10% of the profits available for distribution to equity holders of the company; and

- it would be beneficially entitled on a winding up to not less than 10% of the company available for distribution to shareholders.

It is possible therefore to hold 10% of the shares of a company but for the shareholding not to be a substantial shareholding. This may be the case if there are different classes of share, low profits available for distribution or a low asset value.

A company that is a member of a group is able to include shares (and interests in shares) held by any other member of the group in determining whether a substantial shareholding exists.

The investing company

The investing company must be:

- either a sole trading company or a member of a qualifying group throughout the qualifying period; and

- either a sole trading company or a member of a qualifying group immediately after the time of the disposal.

Broadly, a qualifying group is a trading group. There are careful definitions of what is meant by 'trading'.

The qualifying period begins with the start of the latest 12-month period by which the substantial shareholding requirement is met and ends at the time of disposal.

The company invested in

The company invested in must be both a qualifying company throughout the qualifying period and a qualifying company immediately after the time of the disposal (see above for changes made by FA 2011).

A qualifying company is a:

- trading company;

- the holding company of a trading group; or

- the holding company of a trading sub-group.

Tax Reporter: ¶759-850ff.

3435 Subsidiary exemptions

There are two subsidiary exemptions available.

Assets related to shares

Where a company meets the conditions for the main exemption and it also owns 'assets related to shares' of the company invested in, it may also be possible to dispose of these assets without chargeable gain. Assets related to shares include for example, an option to acquire or dispose of shares or an interest in shares in that company.

Disposals where main exemption previously met

Special rules apply where a disposal of shares or assets related to shares is made at a time when the substantial shareholding requirement is met, but the other requirements are not. If it can be determined that a disposal at any time in the previous two years would have qualified for the exemptions, then generally the disposal can occur without any gain being chargeable to tax or any loss being available to set against other gains. The rules are complex and require careful consideration, but the intention is to bring within the exemption gains which would not otherwise qualify – e.g. gains made while the company invested in is in liquidation. It is also intended to preclude losses being made allowable that would previously have been within the exemption.

Tax Reporter: ¶759-810, ¶760-130 and ¶760-140.

3440   Interaction with other legislation

Negligible value claims

It is possible to backdate negligible value claims (see 5090). The operation of this rule is modified in relation to substantial shareholdings so that a loss which would otherwise fall within the exemption cannot be backdated to before the exemption was introduced.

Degrouping charges

Where a company leaves a group within six years of acquiring an asset from another group company, a gain or loss can arise under the degrouping charge rules (see 3645). If, on a hypothetical disposal of the asset at the time of the degrouping, a chargeable gain would have been prevented from arising as a result of the application of the substantial shareholdings rules, the deemed sale and reacquisition under the degrouping charge rules is treated as taking place immediately before the degrouping.

Share for share exchanges

The substantial shareholdings rules apply in priority to TCGA 1992, s. 127 (share reorganisations not treated as involving a disposal). Where this is the case, the new shares are treated as having been acquired at market value.

Legislation: TCGA 1992, Sch. 7AC, para. 38; TCGA 1992, Sch. 7AC, para. 33; TCGA 1992, Sch. 7AC, para. 4(1)(b)

Tax Reporter: ¶760-150 and ¶760-100

Transactions involving a non-resident company

Transfer of foreign branch to foreign company

3460   Transfer of assets to a non-resident company

If a company decides to transfer the business of a foreign branch to a company not 'resident in the UK' (see 3020) any net chargeable gain made on the transfer can be rolled over for a potentially indefinite period to the extent that shares are received in return. The net chargeable gain is the aggregate of chargeable gains arising from the transfer after the deduction of allowable losses so arising.

This rule only applies if the transferor is a UK-resident company which carries on a trade through a foreign permanent establishment. The transferor must transfer the business and all its assets in the branch to a non-resident company and must hold not less than 25% of the ordinary share capital of the transferee company after the transfer.

Where applicable, the transferor can choose between this deferral and the relief by reference to notional tax in the home territory, if it is within the EU (see 3490).

Time when deferment ends

The deferment of tax will come to an end when the shares are disposed of or the assets transferred are disposed of (see 3465, 3470 and 3475).

When there is a disposal of this kind, the deferred gain is chargeable to corporation tax along with the consideration for the disposal.

Portion of gain chargeable

If shares are received by the transferor as part consideration for the transfer, only a fraction of the gain is taken into account when the deferment comes to an end. The fraction is the proportion which the market value of the shares bears to the total consideration.

If the shares received by the transferor company represent the whole of the consideration for the transfer, the whole of the gain can be deferred.

Example

Company A merges its US branch with S Inc (incorporated in US) in 2011. Total consideration for transfer of assets in US branch (market value):

	£
£1 shares in the merged US company issued to A to value of	40,000
Cash payment	60,000
	100,000

Assume the net gain to A on transfer (ignore indexation) is £30,000. Shares form only part of the consideration.

Therefore, fraction of gain deferrable is

$$\frac{\text{market value of shares}}{\text{market value of total consideration}} = \frac{£40,000}{£100,000} = \frac{4}{10}$$

The gain deferred is £30,000 × $^4/_{10}$ = £12,000.

Legislation: TCGA 1992, s. 140(1)–(3)

Tax Reporter: ¶758-850ff.

3465 Disposal or part disposal of foreign transferee's shares by transferor

If, following relief on the transfer of assets to a non-resident (see 3460), the transferor disposes of all or a part of the shares issued to him, and the disposal takes place on or after 6 January 2010, the whole or the appropriate proportion of the deferred gain is deemed to accrue to the transferor company in addition to any gain or loss that actually accrues on the disposal of the securities. For disposals before that date, the consideration which the transferor company received for the disposal was increased by the appropriate proportion of the deferred gain so far as not previously brought back into account. In both cases, the fraction of the gain brought into account on the part disposal is the proportion of the market value of the shares disposed of to the market value of the shares held immediately before the disposal.

Example

Assume the same facts as contained in the example in 3460.

In 2012, shares issued to A rose in value to £60,000. A decided to sell 15,000 at market value which is £22,500.

Fraction of capital gain brought into account:

$$\frac{\text{market value of shares disposed of}}{\text{market value of total shares prior to disposal}} = \frac{£22,500}{£60,000} = \frac{3}{8}$$

The gain brought back into charge is $^3/_8 \times £12,000 = £4,500$

Legislation: TCGA 1992, s. 140(4)–(8)

Tax Reporter: ¶759-100

3470 Disposal by foreign transferee of assets within six years of transfer

If, following relief on the transfer of assets to a non-resident (see 3460), the transferee disposes of the whole or part of the assets received within six years of the transfer, the transferor is assumed to make a chargeable gain. The fraction of the deferred gain brought into account on a part disposal is the proportion of the capital gain deferred on the part disposed of to the total chargeable gain on the whole of the assets held immediately before the disposal (but see also 3475).

Example

Assume the same facts as contained in the example in 3460.

In 2012 S Inc disposes of the buildings, which it received on the merger, for £60,000.

Market value	2011	Gain on deferral	2012
	£	£	£
Building	40,000	15,000	60,000
Plant and machinery	25,000	4,000	30,000
Goodwill	35,000	11,000	50,000
Total market value	100,000	30,000	140,000

Fraction of deferred gain attributable to company A ($^4/_{10}$; see 3460):

> $$\frac{\text{capital gain deferred on building}}{\text{capital gain deferred on whole}} = \frac{£6,000}{£12,000} = \frac{1}{2}$$
>
> The gain crystallising is $\frac{1}{2} \times £12,000 = £6,000$

Tax Reporter: ¶759-150

3475 Assets disposed of by foreign transferee after sale of shares by transferor

If, following relief on the transfer of assets to a non-resident (see 3460), a transferee disposes of the assets acquired after the shares held by the transferor have been sold, only the part of the deferred chargeable gain not dealt with in the earlier transaction is brought into account (see also 3465 and 3470).

> **Example**
>
> (Applying the rule to the facts in the example in 3465 followed by that in 3470.) Fraction of chargeable gain brought into account on disposal by S Inc:
>
> $$\frac{\text{capital gain deferred on building}}{\text{capital gain deferred on whole}} = \frac{£6,000}{£12,000} = \frac{1}{2}$$
>
> The capital gain brought into account is calculated as follows:
>
> $\frac{1}{2} \times$ (total capital gain − fraction already accounted for)
>
> $= \frac{1}{2} \times (£12,000 − £4,500)$
>
> $= \frac{1}{2} \times £7,500 = £3,750$
>
> In the reverse situation, where the transferee makes the first disposal, the fraction is calculated:
>
> $$\frac{\text{market value of shares disposed of}}{\text{market value of total shares prior to disposal}}$$
>
> $\frac{3}{8} \times (£12,000 − £6,000)$
>
> $\frac{3}{8} \times £6,000 = £2,250$

Tax Reporter: ¶759-150

3480 Transfer of company residence

A company ceasing to be 'UK-resident' (see 3020) or becoming dual-resident may be subject to a charge to tax on chargeable gains (an 'exit charge').

When a company ceases to be resident in the UK, there is a deemed disposal of all chargeable assets, except those which relate to any UK branch and which are retained in the UK, on the date the transfer of residence takes place. Replacement rollover relief is also denied where the emigration falls between the disposal and acquisition (see 6305ff.). There are provisions to ensure that payment of the tax occurs prior to the company becoming non-resident. However, FA 2013 introduces two options for companies to defer payment for UK corporation tax where it arises under provisions taxing unrealised profits and gains when the company ceases to be resident in the United Kingdom or a non-resident company ceases to carry on all or part of its business in the UK. The exit charge payment plans are available to companies incorporated in the European Union or European Economic Area (EU/EEA), including UK companies, which transfer their business and their place of residence for tax purposes to another member state. The deferred tax payments will be subject to interest under the usual rules.

The gain (net of any losses) can be postponed if the company is a '75% subsidiary' (see 3610) of a UK-resident company after migration or becoming a dual resident. The two companies must elect for postponement within two years of migration. If the company disposes of its assets within six years, the UK parent is deemed to incur the relevant part of the postponed gain. Similarly, the postponed gain will crystallise if the 75% relationship is broken or the parent becomes non-UK resident.

Example

S Ltd is a wholly-owned subsidiary of P Ltd, which is UK-resident. When S Ltd ceased to be UK-resident on 15 October 2011, the two companies elected to postpone the gain which was deemed to arise, as shown below.

	Asset A £	Asset B £	Asset C £	Asset D £	Total £
Deemed gains	50,000	30,000	80,000		160,000
Deemed losses				(40,000)	(40,000)
Postponed net gain					120,000

Within six years of ceasing to be resident in the UK, S Ltd disposes of asset A. At that time P Ltd (not S Ltd) is deemed to realise a gain of £37,500, which is calculated as follows:

$$\frac{50,000}{160,000} \times £120,000 = £37,500$$

At a later date, but still within the six-year period, S Ltd disposes of asset B.

At that time P Ltd is deemed to realise a gain of £22,500 being:

$$\frac{30,000}{110,000} \times (£120,000 - £37,500 \text{ already assessed})$$

At a later time, P sells all of its shares in S Ltd and so P Ltd is deemed to realise at that time a gain of £60,000 (being the postponed gain of £120,000 less the previously assessed gains of £37,500 and £22,500).

Losses

If at any time the company, which ceases to be UK-resident or becomes dual resident, has allowable losses which have not been deducted from chargeable gains, but the principal company is assessed in the manner explained above, then the two companies can elect to deduct the loss in whole or part from the gain; the election needs to be made in writing to the inspector within two years of the gain arising.

Legislation: TCGA 1992, s. 185–188; TMA 1970, s. 59FA and Sch. 3ZB

Tax Reporter: ¶592-400

3485   Transfer of UK branch trade to UK company

For disposals made prior to 1 April 2000, a specific provision provided that a company which was not 'resident in the UK' (see 3020) could transfer the business of a UK permanent establishment to a UK company without an immediate capital gains charge.

To qualify for relief, the transferor had to dispose of assets (after 19 March 1990) at a time when the two companies would have been members of the same group for chargeable gains purposes (see 3625) if the transferor were UK-resident; a claim had to be made by the two companies within two years of the end of the accounting period of the transferee company during which the disposal occurred.

The transfer was treated as taking place on a no gain/no loss basis.

The assets must have been within the corporation tax net as regards the transferor.

The relief did not apply where the transferee company was a dual resident investing company or an investment trust or (prior to 30 November 1993) a company which at that time would be exempt from tax under a double tax treaty on a notional gain in respect of the disposal of the assets in point.

For disposals of assets on or after 1 April 2000, an express provision is no longer required due to the removal of the UK residence requirement in the provisions dealing with the transfer of assets between group companies.

3490 Transfer of non-UK branch trade to company in another EU member state

In consequence of the EC mergers directive, the UK has provided for relief where a UK-resident company transfers a branch or agency situated in another EU member state to a company resident outside the UK (but within the EU). Any net gains can be taxed in the UK with relief for notional tax relevant in the state in which the branch or agency is situated. The provisions for taxing the net gains are set out below; the provisions for providing for the appropriate double tax relief are discussed at 1789 and 1792.

Where it is applicable, the taxpayer can choose between this treatment and the deferral for domestication of certain foreign branches (see 3460).

Except as noted below, a claim for this treatment may be made by the transferor in respect of the transfer of the whole of the trade assets (with the possible exception of cash) at least partly for securities.

The transfer of the trade (or part) must meet a tax avoidance motive test. The relief does not apply unless the transfer is effected for bona fide commercial reasons and does not form part of a scheme or arrangements of which the main purpose or one of the main purposes is avoidance of liability to income tax, corporation tax or capital gains tax. Advance clearance can be obtained from the Board. The test and clearance procedure are largely the same as in relation to company reconstructions, etc. (see 3417) and various administrative provisions are imported therefrom.

If a valid claim is made, chargeable gains and allowable losses arising on the transfer are aggregated so as to produce a single net chargeable gain. There are special rules for certain insurance business.

Legislation: TCGA 1992, s. 140(6A), 140C and 140D; EC Directive 90/434

Tax Reporter: ¶759-200

3495 Transfer of UK branch trade between companies in different EU member states

In consequence of the EC mergers directive, the UK has provided for relief where a company resident in one EU member state transfers all or part of its UK trading operations to a company resident in another member state in exchange for securities issued by the transferee company.

In the case of the domestication of a UK branch (i.e. the transfer of a UK branch of a non-resident company to a UK-resident company), a similar relief otherwise exists where the two companies would be part of the same chargeable gains group if the overseas company were incorporated under the Companies Acts and UK-resident – although there is no tax avoidance motive test and the issue of securities as consideration is not a necessary condition (see 3485).

A joint claim can be made by the transferor and transferee in respect of assets 'included in' the transfer of the whole or part of the trade; there must be no other consideration for the transfer other than the issue of securities. The transferee must be exposed to UK tax in respect of the assets.

No claim can be made if the transfer fails a tax avoidance motive test. The relief does not apply unless the transfer is effected for bona fide commercial reasons and does not form part of a scheme or arrangements of which the main purpose or one of the main purposes is avoidance of liability to income tax, corporation tax or capital gains tax. Advance clearance can be obtained from the Board. The test and clearance procedure are largely the same as in relation to company reconstructions, etc. (see 3417) and various administrative provisions are imported therefrom.

If a valid claim is made, the transfers are treated on a no gain/no loss basis; if the occasion is one on which a non-resident ceases to carry on its branch activities, the general rule providing for a deemed market value disposal and reacquisition immediately before the transfer (see 5705) does not apply.

Consequential amendments are made to deny re-basing to 31 March 1982 on the transfer (see 5302), to extend deferral in respect of the replacement of a security by a qualifying corporate bond (see 5865), to extend the restriction of allowable losses by reference to capital allowances to those given to the transferor (see 5226), to extend the dividend stripping rules to losses avoided by such a transfer before ultimate disposal (see 3545) and to deny indexation allowance in respect of linked company shares by reference to the transferor rather than the transferee (see 5280).

Legislation: TCGA 1992, s. 140A and 140B; EC Directive 90/434

Tax Reporter: ¶759-200

'Bed and breakfast' transactions

3510   Company bed and breakfasting shares

A 'bed and breakfast' transaction is a term commonly used where a person has losses on shares which are realised by a sale and immediate repurchase to avoid disposing of them permanently, and to crystallise the capital gains loss.

To control these transactions by companies, there are statutory provisions which govern the order in which shares so dealt with are identified with other shares acquired just before or after the transaction (see 3515). They apply where the company disposing of the shares holds at least 2% of the total of shares in the same class at any time within six months prior to the disposal.

Tax Reporter: ¶556-600

3515   Order of identification of shares for bed and breakfasting

Shares disposed of by a company are identified where possible with shares which it acquires within six months before or after the disposal (or one month for quoted shares) as set out below. The shares are identified with shares acquired before rather than after the disposal and nearer to rather than further from the disposal date. They are also identified with disposals by the company acquiring them rather than with another group member. A disposal of acquired shares already identified with a disposal by another group member must be identified with shares acquired by that other member.

The rules which govern the acquisition or disposal of shares on the same day (see 5826) have priority over rules of identification except where there are more shares disposed of than are acquired.

Tax Reporter: ¶556-600

Value shifting

3525   Value shifting

The value shifting provisions are designed to target arrangements whereby:

- in certain circumstances, value is shifted from one person to another without there being a disposal of an asset (in which case TCGA 1992, s. 29 applies to impose a deemed disposal); or

- the value of an asset has been reduced prior to its disposal and a tax-free benefit is conferred on the person making the disposal or a connected person (in which case TCGA 1992, s. 30 applies to adjust the consideration for the disposal and so to counteract the advantage).

Prior to changes made by FA 2011, TCGA 1992, s. 30 was modified by former TCGA 1992, s. 31–34 where the reduction in value resulted from a transaction within a group of companies. The rule operated where a reduction in value could be attributed to the distribution of profits or to the transfer of an asset at under value (see 3530). Former TCGA 1992, s. 31–34 were repealed by FA 2011 with effect for disposals of shares or securities taking place on or after 19 July 2011.

For disposals of shares or securities taking place on or after 19 July 2011, the targeted anti-avoidance rule (TAAR) at TCGA 1992, s. 31 applies instead of s. 30. The TAAR is invoked where a company (the 'disposing company') disposes of shares in, or securities of, another company and:

(1) arrangements have been made whereby the value of those shares or securities, or of any asset which, at the time of the disposal, was owned by a company in the same group as the disposing company, is materially reduced;

(2) the main purpose, or one of the main purposes of the arrangements is to avoid a liability to corporation tax in respect of chargeable gains for the disposing company or any other person; and

(3) the arrangements do not consist solely of the making of an exempt distribution (being a distribution which falls within CTA 2009, s. 931H or which would do if the company was not small; see 3900).

Where the TAAR applies, the allowable loss or chargeable gain on the disposal is to be calculated as if the consideration were increased by an amount which is just and reasonable having regard to the arrangements and any tax that would have been avoided had the TAAR not applied.

Legislation: TCGA 1992, s. 29, 30 and 31; FA 2011, Sch. 9, para. 2 and 6

Tax Reporter: ¶760-800ff.

3530   Rules applying before 19 July 2011

Dividends from artificial profits

An adjustment may have been made to a chargeable gain or allowable loss on shares if the value of the shares had been reduced by a dividend paid (principally to the chargeable company or a fellow group company) out of artificial profits.

Such profits were:

- profits on certain intra-group disposals of capital assets which were for tax purposes on a no gain/no loss basis;

- profits on an exchange of shares or debentures in any company for shares or debentures in another company in the same group which was not regarded as a disposal for tax purposes;

- revaluation reserves (not generally distributable for UK companies anyway by virtue of Companies Acts restrictions);

- distributions from other companies out of similar profits.

Example

Company X wanted to dispose of its shares in its wholly-owned subsidiary, company Y, when its value was £2,500,000 in circumstances where the substantial shareholding exemption (see 4035) did not apply. The base cost to company X was £100. Company Y had no distributable reserves but owned an asset worth £1,110,000 for which its base cost (and carrying value in the accounts) was £700,000.

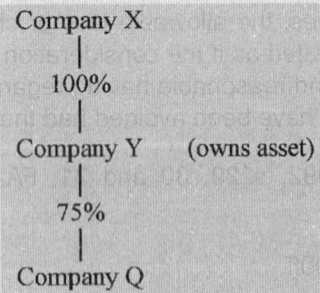

A simple sale of its shares in company Y would have resulted in a chargeable gain accruing to company X of £2,499,900 (ignoring indexation).

Instead, company X decided to reduce its exposure before the sale. Company Y disposed of the asset to its 75% subsidiary, company Q, for its full value. For tax purposes, this transaction took place on a no gain, no loss basis. Company Y then distributed the accounting surplus of £410,000 to company X by way of dividend, reducing the value of company X's holding in company Y by a corresponding amount.

On the sale of its shares in company Y, there accrued to company X a chargeable gain of only £2,089,900 (ignoring indexation). This gain could have been adjusted.

Disposals intra-group at an artificial discount

An adjustment may have been made to a chargeable gain or allowable loss on shares if the value of the shares had been reduced by a transfer of an asset intra-group at a discount below both cost and market value.

The asset transfer must have been no gain/no loss for tax purposes by virtue of the transferor and transferee companies being members of the same group.

Legislation: TCGA 1992, s. 31, 32 and 33(1)–(6) and (8)

Tax Reporter: ¶761-250ff.

3540   Consequences of a depreciatory transaction by a company

If a company sells shares at a loss and tries to claim an allowable loss on the transaction, the claim will be limited by the extent of any depreciatory transactions effected within the period of six years ending with the disposal (for disposals taking place before 19 July 2011, the rules applied to transactions effected on or after 31 March 1982). However, the provisions do not apply to increase a gain. Thus, a transaction reducing a gain from £500,000 to £1, is not depreciatory within these rules so that, other things being equal, the gain will be £1.

If the company making the final disposal is not a member of the group when the shares are disposed of, the loss will not be reduced according to the depreciatory transaction which occurred when that company was not a member of the group.

However, allowance can be made for any other transaction by which the value of the company's assets is increased and the value of assets of any other group member is depreciated.

Where the allowable loss claimed is reduced and shares in any other company which was a party to the depreciatory transaction are (within six years of the depreciatory transaction) disposed of resulting in a chargeable gain, that gain will be reduced by the same amount as the reduction in the earlier loss.

What is a 'depreciatory transaction'?

A 'depreciatory transaction' is where one group member disposes of any assets to another group member for a consideration other than market value, or when the company whose shares are finally disposed of or its 75% subsidiary was a party to the transaction and where the parties to the transaction include two or more companies which were members of the same group when the transaction took place.

Example

Company A purchases shares in company B so that B becomes a 75% subsidiary of A. The purchase price reflects underlying assets held by B. B transfers assets to A at an undervalue.

Shares in B held by A lose their value and A sells those shares at a loss. A then claims a capital loss on the sale.

That loss is one created by a depreciatory transaction.

Legislation: TCGA 1992, s. 176

Tax Reporter: ¶756-650

3545   Dividend stripping

Dividend stripping is the practice of paying dividends out of a company so as to reduce the value of another person's holding in that company pending a disposal of that holding.

A capital loss on such a disposal may be disallowed where one company has a holding in another company which is the whole or part of 10% of all holdings of the same class in that other company. A company's holding of whatever size is treated as a 10% holding if the total of its holding together with those of any 'connected persons' (see 3410) amounts to 10% of all shares in that class.

The capital loss will only be disallowed if certain conditions also exist. The holding company must not be a 'dealing company' in relation to the holding. In other words, it must be a capital asset of that company. There must also have been a distribution in respect of that holding resulting in the net value of the holding being 'materially reduced'.

A company is a dealing company in relation to a holding if a profit on its sale would be taken into account in calculating the company's trading profits. All the company's holdings of the same class in another company are treated as a single holding.

There is no statutory indication of the meaning of 'materially reduced'. Although there are no decided cases on the point, each case will presumably depend on its particular facts and all the circumstances surrounding them.

The disallowance cannot be avoided by transfer of the shares to an affiliate, etc. under no gain/no loss provisions before ultimate disposal.

The primary purpose of this legislation is anti-avoidance. It aims to attack the sort of transaction where a company with a substantial cash surplus and distributable reserves is acquired and a large distribution made prior to resale at a reduced value. HMRC have confirmed that they will not generally treat as a depreciatory transaction a dividend paid out of post-acquisition reserves (commonly called a 'pre-sale' dividend); nor generally will they apply the principle of looking at the overall effect of certain composite transactions (see *Furniss v Dawson* and similar decisions) to the payment of dividends in order to reduce the value of shares before their sale.

Legislation: TCGA 1992, s. 177

Tax Reporter: ¶756-750

Groups of companies

Introduction to groups

3600   Basis of group taxation

In general, the same rules relating to corporation tax apply to groups of companies as to individual companies: each company is taxed separately and there is no consolidated tax treatment. However, there are specific provisions which apply solely to a recognised 'group of companies' (see 3610).

These specific provisions deal mainly with the following:

- transfers of assets (within the chargeable gains regime) between members (see 3630);

- replacement of business assets by group members (see 3660);

- the recovery from other members of the group of unpaid tax on chargeable gains (see 3665);

- the surrender of losses for offset by another member (group relief: see 3690);

- transfers of intangible fixed assets between members (see 3740);

- transfers to shareholders of shares in, or business of, subsidiary members on a demerger (see 3750);

- the surrender of a tax refund, etc. (including, under self assessment, repayments of instalments paid by large companies) within a group (see 3760).

In order to understand these provisions, it is necessary to consider a number of definitions in relation to the meaning of group (see 3610).

Legislation: CTA 2010, Pt. 5

Tax Reporter: ¶735-000ff.

3610 What is 'a group of companies'?

Basically, there is no single definition of a 'group of companies' since the meaning may vary for different purposes.

Provisions relating to groups generally apply by reference to 75% subsidiaries and 51% subsidiaries:

- a company is a **75% subsidiary** of another company if, and so long as, not less than 75% of the ordinary share capital is owned directly or indirectly by that other company (see below); and

- a company is a **51% subsidiary** of another company if, and so long as, more than 50% of its ordinary share capital is owned directly or indirectly by the other company (see below).

These requirements are further refined in relation to each specific relief. Ownership also generally requires certain minimum rights to income, and to assets on a winding-up. Generally, holdings by share dealers are ignored.

In general terms, the two types of company qualify the groups of which they are part for the following reliefs:

75% subsidiary

- group relief for losses etc.;
- surrenders of repayments to another group company; and
- capital gains reliefs.

51% subsidiary

- following the abolition of ACT and the need for group income elections in 1999 and 2001, the concept of 51% subsidiary is now most relevant in the context of capital gains reliefs where, in additional to being a 75% subsidiary, a subsidiary also has to be an effective 51% subsidiary (see 3625).

Certain reliefs are also available for particular forms of shareholding arrangements known as consortia including certain reliefs by reference to 90% subsidiaries. Effect (from 10 December 2014) was given to the measure to simplify the link company requirements for consortium claims by removing all requirements relating to the location of a link company so that group relief may flow regardless of where the link company is based. These provisions were not included in *Finance Act* 2015 but have been included in the *Finance (No. 2) Act* 2015.

Ownership of ordinary share capital

'Ordinary share capital' is all issued share capital of a company except that capital which carries a right to fixed rate dividend but with no other right to a share in the company's profits.

Such capital is owned directly or indirectly where it is held directly by the company itself, through another company or companies or partly directly and partly indirectly through another company.

Example

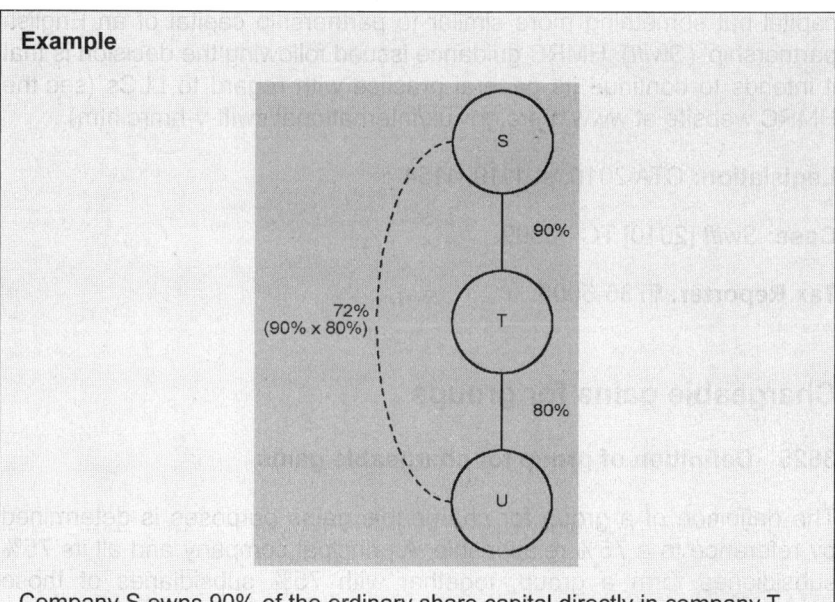

Company S owns 90% of the ordinary share capital directly in company T.

Company T owns 80% of the ordinary share capital directly in company U.

Therefore, S is treated as owning 72% (90% × 80%) of the ordinary shares in U through T.

Thus, T is a 75% subsidiary of S.

U is a 75% subsidiary of T.

U is a 51% subsidiary of S.

HMRC have set out in HMRC Brief 87/09 their views on the meaning of 'ordinary share capital' in the context of overseas companies. The Brief includes specific comments in relation to Delaware Limited Liability Companies (DLLCs) and German GmbH.

In relation to DLLCs, HMRC believe that there is legal authority for such entities to issue 'shares' under the *Delaware Limited Liability Act*, s. 18–702(c). Where 'shares' are issued in this way, HMRC will accept that they may be regarded as 'ordinary share capital' for the purpose of the definition of 'ordinary share capital' in CTA 2010, s. 1154. This means that such an LLC may be a '75% subsidiary'. It follows that it is possible for an LLC to:

- be a member of a capital gains group; and

- be a member of the same group as another company for the purposes of group relief.

This continues to be the case even though the First-tier Tribunal found that a member's interest in a particular Delaware LLC was 'not similar to share capital but something more similar to partnership capital of an English partnership' (*Swift*). HMRC guidance issued following the decision is that it intends to continue its general practice with regard to LLCs (see the HMRC website at www.hmrc.gov.uk/international/swift-v-hmrc.htm).

Legislation: CTA 2010, s. 1119, 1154

Case: *Swift* [2010] TC 00399

Tax Reporter: ¶736-500ff.

Chargeable gains for groups

3625 Definition of group for chargeable gains

The definition of a group for chargeable gains purposes is determined by reference to a 75% relationship. A principal company and all its 75% subsidiaries form a group, together with 75% subsidiaries of those subsidiaries, etc. (for the required ownership, see 3610). Non-UK resident companies can be a member of the group (see further 3640).

However, companies which satisfy the 75% test at any link in the chain are excluded if they are not 'effective 51% subsidiaries' of the principal company.

A company is an effective 51% subsidiary of its parent if:

- the parent is beneficially entitled to more than 50% of any profits available for distribution to equity holders ('income'); and

- the parent would be beneficially entitled to more than 50% of any assets available for distribution to equity holders on a winding-up ('assets').

Example

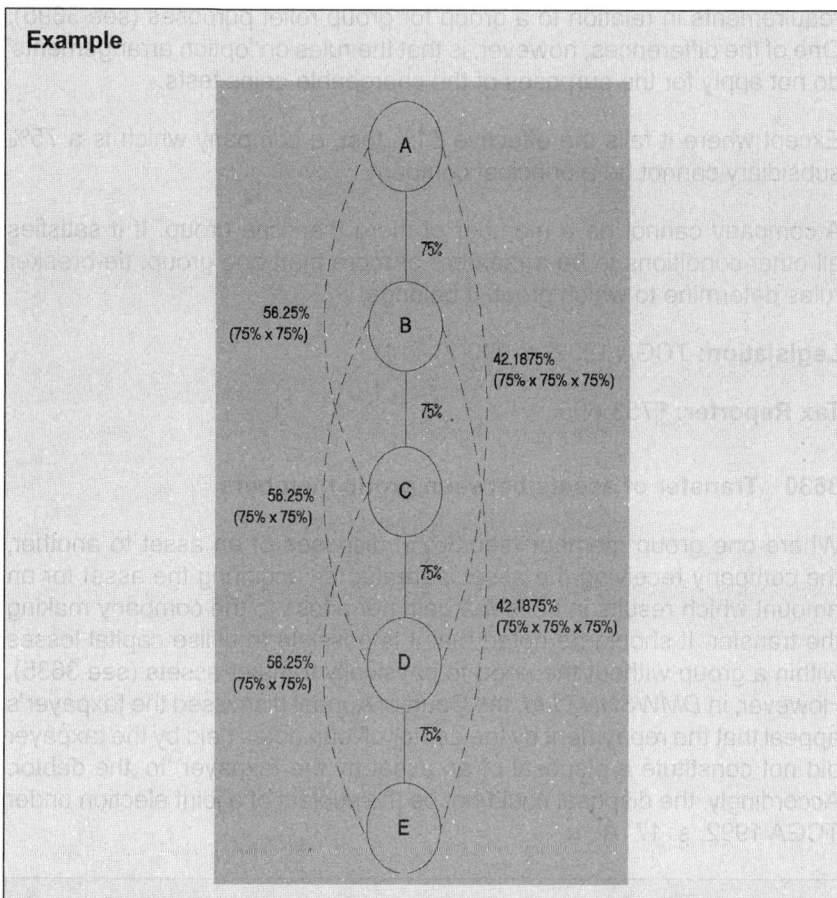

A is the principal company of a chargeable gains tax group comprising A, B and C. B is a 75% subsidiary of A and C is a 75% subsidiary of B, C is also an effective 51% subsidiary of A, A being entitled to 56.25% (75% × 75%) of its income or assets in a winding up. D is not a member of A's chargeable gains group. Although it is a 75% subsidiary of A, it is not an effective 51% subsidiary of A. A is only entitled to 42.1875 (75% × 75% × 75%) of its income or assets in a winding up.

> C, D and E cannot form a separate chargeable gains group because C is a 75% subsidiary and as such cannot be a principal company. Similarly, B, C and D, cannot form separate chargeable gains group; B, being a 75% subsidiary of A, cannot be a principal company. D is however a principal company of a separate chargeable gains group comprising D and E.

The definition of 'equity holder' and the determination of the extent of equity holdings are essentially those used for the purposes of similar requirements in relation to a group for group relief purposes (see 3695). One of the differences, however, is that the rules on 'option arrangements' do not apply for the purposes of the chargeable gains tests.

Except where it fails the effective 51% test, a company which is a 75% subsidiary cannot be a principal company.

A company cannot be a member of more than one group. If it satisfies all other conditions to be a member of more than one group, tie-breaker rules determine to which group it belongs.

Legislation: TCGA 1992, s. 170(2)–(14)

Tax Reporter: ¶753-600

3630 Transfer of assets between group members

Where one group member (see 3625) disposes of an asset to another, the company receiving the asset is treated as acquiring the asset for an amount which results in neither a gain nor a loss to the company making the transfer. It should be noted that it is possible to utilise capital losses within a group without the need to physically transfer assets (see 3635). However, in *DMWSHNZ Ltd*, the Court of Appeal dismissed the taxpayer's appeal that the repayment by the debtor of loan notes held by the taxpayer did not constitute a disposal of an asset by the taxpayer 'to' the debtor. Accordingly, the disposal could not be the subject of a joint election under TCGA 1992, s. 171A.

Example

Blot Ltd and Elder Ltd are members of the same chargeable gains group. In January 2011, Blot acquires from outside the group an asset costing £100,000, which it transfers to Elder in December 2011. At that time, the market value of the asset is £150,000. In July 2012, Elder sells the asset to Mr. Smith for £180,000.

Since Blot and Elder are companies within the same group, the disposal by Blot is regarded as being one giving rise to neither gain nor loss. The calculation of the disposal proceeds is as follows:

	£	£
Deemed consideration (December 2011)		106,000
Less: cost (January 2011)	100,000	
Less: indexation allowance (est.)	6,000	(106,000)
Gain		Nil

When Elder sells the asset it realises a chargeable gain (ignoring incidental costs, etc.) as follows:

	£	£
Sale proceeds (July 2012)		180,000
Less: deemed consideration (December 2011)	106,000	
Less: indexation allowance (est.)	2,438	(108,438)
Gain		71,562

Exceptions

The no gain/no loss transfer rule does not apply to certain excluded disposals. In particular, the rule does not apply to a disposal of a debt owing by one member of a group when another member satisfies the whole or part of that debt. It does not apply on the redemption of redeemable shares in a company or to a disposal by or to an investment trust, or to a disposal to a dual resident investing company. Nor does it apply to disposals to a company which, at that time, would be exempt from tax under a double tax treaty on a notional gain in respect of the disposal of the assets in point.

Anti-avoidance

The ability to transfer an asset tax-free to a fellow group company led to the practice of buying in capital losses, or more precisely buying and bringing into the group a company with unused allowable losses: assets pregnant with gain could be transferred to the loss company before realisation, thereby permitting any chargeable gain to be relieved by the allowable losses.

The set-off of capital losses brought into a group of companies as a result of a company joining the group is restricted to certain permissible gains by the pre-entry losses rules. Significant changes to these rules were made by FA 2011 and, with effect for accounting periods beginning on or after 19 July 2011, the rules apply to losses realised before the company joined the group only. Previously, the rules applied equally to the pre-entry proportion of a loss on an asset held at the time of entry by the loss company, or later transferred to it within the group, without there having been a disposal outside the group since that date (the restriction applied to a time-apportioned amount of the loss or, by election, to an amount calculated by reference to market value on entry to the group).

The changes made to the pre-entry losses rules by FA 2011 reflect that fact that, from 5 December 2005, a more targeted anti-avoidance provision has existed to counteract the effect of arrangements that have as their main purpose, or one of their main purposes, the securing of a tax advantage and involve a change of ownership of a company, the conversion of income into capital or the creation of a deduction against income for an expense that would otherwise be relieved against chargeable gains.

Legislation: TCGA 1992, s. 171, 184A–184I and Sch. 7A; FA 2011, Sch. 11, para. 11

Cases: *Westcott (HMIT) v Woolcombers Ltd* [1987] BTC 493; *DMWSHNZ Ltd (in members'; voluntary liquidation) v R & C Commrs* [2015] BTC 32

Tax Reporter: ¶753-850ff., ¶755-000ff. and ¶755-810ff.

3635   The transfer of gains and losses within a group

Following the enactment of FA 2009, it is possible for chargeable gains and allowable losses to be transferred within a group. For gains and losses made before 21 July 2009, this result could only be achieved by electing for the notional transfer of an asset before its disposal to a third party (see below). However, it was only possible to do this where the asset was to be sold to a third party and so an election could not be made where an asset was destroyed, where a group company was liquidated or on the making of a negligible value claim. Therefore, the rules currently in place provide a simpler and more comprehensive means of transferring gains and losses within a group.

This election can only be made where:

(a) a chargeable gain or an allowable loss accrues on or after 21 July 2009 to a company (Company A) in respect of an asset;

(b) at that time, Company A and another company (Company B) are members of the same group; and

(c) had Company A transferred the asset to Company B immediately before the time of the accrual, the transfer would have taken place on a tax neutral basis under TCGA 1992, s. 171(1).

Following changes made by FA 2011, an election can now be made in respect of a degrouping charge (see 3645).

There is provision to allow gains or losses to be transferred to a non-resident company provided that the company carries on a trade through a permanent establishment.

Where Company A and Company B have made such an election the effect is to treat the gain or loss as accruing to company B. The election can be made for all or part of the gain or loss, but cannot exceed the amount of the gain or loss. Where the election exceeds these amounts, the election is ineffective, a parliamentary reply suggests that there is nothing to prevent a revised election being submitted.

Gains or losses accruing before 21 July 2009

In relation to disposals after 1 April 2000 but before 21 July 2009, it was possible to utilise capital losses in different group companies without an actual physical transfer of the asset involved between group companies on a no gain/no loss basis. Such an election saved the group incurring the compliance costs associated with an actual intra-group transfer.

Where two companies (A and B) were members of a group (see 3625) and one of those companies (A) disposed of an asset to a person who was not a member of a group (C), the two group companies (A and B) could jointly elect for the purposes of corporation tax on chargeable gains that the asset in question was treated as transferred from A to B on a no gain/no loss basis immediately prior to the transfer to C and that B disposed of the asset to C. Furthermore, the actual incidental costs of disposal by A were deemed to be the incidental costs of disposal by B; thus B could get a deduction in computing the chargeable gain on its disposal to C even though B did not actually incur those costs.

The election had to be made on or before the second anniversary of the end of the accounting period of A in which the disposal to C was made.

Legislation: TCGA 1992, s. 171A and 171B

Tax Reporter: ¶753-925 and ¶753-950

3640   Non-UK residents

The ability of companies to transfer assets on a no gain/no loss basis (including across residence barriers) was enhanced significantly from 1 April 2000, with associated anti-avoidance measures applying from 21 March 2000. From that date, membership of a chargeable gains group (see 3625) is not restricted to UK-resident companies. Transfers within the group can be made on a tax neutral basis if the asset remains within the UK tax net. So, for example, a transfer of an asset can be made on a tax neutral basis between a UK resident member of a group and a non-UK resident member of the group if the asset is used by the non-resident member for the purposes of a trade carried on in the UK through a UK permanent establishment.

The change means, that for example, transfer of assets are possible between UK-resident subsidiaries with a non-resident parent on a no gain/no loss basis, where the subsidiaries and parent are members of a chargeable gains group. Previously, the transfer between the subsidiaries would have been treated as if the subsidiary making the disposal had disposed of it at market value, irrespective of the actual consideration.

Also from 1 April 2000, the transfer of assets from one company to another company as part of a scheme of reconstruction or amalgamation will attract tax relief irrespective of where the participating companies are resident, provided the assets remain in the UK tax net.

Prior to 1 April 2000, companies which were not UK-resident could not generally benefit from the no gain/no loss provisions (see 3625). However, relief was available in the case of the transfer of a UK branch or agency to a UK-resident company.

Further forms of relief applied in respect of the transfer by a UK-resident company to a company resident in another EU member state of a non-UK branch (see 3490) and in respect of the transfer between EU member states involving at least one non-resident company of a UK branch (see 3495).

If a company ceases to be resident, it is normally required to notify HMRC and to pay tax on any capital gains which have accrued on assets which it holds (though this does not apply to relevant assets that continue to be employed in a UK trade, and so remain within the charge to UK tax). This requirement has been removed in the case of companies which cease to be UK-resident by virtue of the provisions that treat dual resident companies which are not treated as resident in the UK by virtue of a double taxation agreement as not resident for all tax purposes (see 3020). In certain circumstances, any gains which accrued whilst the company was UK resident can, by election, be treated as deferred ('postponed gains') until the assets are sold (or certain other events occur).

Where an asset ceases to be a chargeable asset as a result of a company ceasing to carry on a trade in the UK through a branch or agency, there is a deemed disposal (except where the cessation is in connection with certain no gain/no loss transfers).

Legislation: TCGA 1992, s. 25 and 171, 185, 187

Tax Reporter: ¶753-600

3645 Consequences when a member leaves a group

Where a company leaves a group within 6 years of having acquired an asset from another group member on a no gain/no loss basis, a gain or loss may arise under the degrouping charge rules. Significant changes to these rules were made by FA 2011 with effect for degrouping charges triggered by a company leaving a group on or after 19 July 2011 (or 1 April 2011 where an early commencement election is made).

Where the degrouping charge rules apply, the gain or loss is calculated as if the company had sold and immediately re-acquired the asset at its market value.

Example 1

Sunspot Ltd has two wholly-owned subsidiaries: Mabel Ltd and Spotlight Ltd. In January 2008, Mabel Ltd acquired a warehouse from Spotlight Ltd when it was worth £200,000. Spotlight Ltd had purchased the warehouse in March 2004 for £100,000. Mabel Ltd was sold by Sunspot Ltd in November 2011.

The gain arising under the degrouping charge rules is computed as follows:

	£
Market value (at January 2008)	200,000
Less: Original cost	(100,000)
Indexation March 2004 to January 2008 (£100,000 × say 10%)	(10,000)
Chargeable gain	90,000

Where the gain/loss arises because the company ceased to be a member of the group in consequence of a disposal of shares on or after 19 July 2011, the gain/loss will be taxable/relievable by reference to the company making the disposal of shares (a gain being added to the consideration, and a loss being added to the allowable expenses, in calculating the chargeable gain or allowable loss on the disposal of the shares). In any other case, the gain/loss will be taxable/relievable by reference to the company which acquired the asset.

Example 2

The facts are as in Example 1. Sunspot Ltd sold its shares in Mabel Ltd for £2,000,000. The indexed base cost of the shares is £300,000. The gain or loss arising under the degrouping charge rules of £90,000 accrues to Sunspot Ltd as follows:

	£
Proceeds received for the shares	2,000,000
Gain arising under degrouping charge rules	90,000
Total consideration	2,090,000
Less: Indexed base cost	(300,000)
Capital gain/loss	1,790,000

Where the degrouping charge is taxable or relievable by reference to the company disposing of the shares, and the substantial shareholdings exemption (see 3425) applies with regard to the gain or loss on those shares, the exemption will also apply with regard to the gain or loss arising under the degrouping charge rules.

If a company would cease to be a member of a group by failing the effective 51% subsidiary test when the principal company joins a new group, the deemed disposal is not triggered until the company also fails to meet the 75% test with any company in the new group; the gain or loss then arises at the time of the original transfer.

The deemed disposal does not apply to:

(1) a company which ceases to be a member of a group on the winding-up or dissolution of itself or in consequence of another group member ceasing to exist;

(2) certain mergers if the company leaves the group for bona fide commercial reasons (see 3750);

(3) any asset acquired by one company from another in the same sub-group if they leave a group at the same time (see below); and

(4) any asset (or property to which a chargeable gain is carried forward from the asset on a replacement of business assets: see 6305ff.), which is held as trading stock by the chargeable company or its associate which is also leaving the company.

Prior to changes made by FA 2011, the exclusion at (3) above applied with regard to 'associated' companies. The associated companies exemption was replaced with the sub-group exemption in order to provide clarity; questions having been raised as to at what point companies had to be associated in order to benefit from the associated companies exemption. The sub-group exemption is designed to reflect HMRC's view of how the associated companies exemption applied, as supported in part by the decision of the Court of Appeal in the Johnston Publishing case. For the sub-group exemption to apply, the transferee must have been a 75% subsidiary and an effective 51% subsidiary of the transferor (or vice versa) at the time of the transfer and must have remained so until immediately after they left the group or both companies must have been 75% subsidiaries and effective 51% subsidiaries of another company and must have remained so until immediately after they left the group.

A degrouping charge can be reallocated to another group member (see 3635 for the position following the changes made by FA 2011). Where the degrouping charge arises as a result of a company leaving a group on or after 19 July 2011, it is possible to make a claim for the charge to be reduced if, in the absence of such a claim, the charge would give rise to double taxation. Prior to changes made by FA 2011, it was possible for the gain or loss to be held over by investing the deemed proceeds in new qualifying assets.

Legislation: TCGA 1992, s. 179 and 179ZA; FA 2011, Sch. 10, para. 9

Case: *Johnston Publishing (North) Ltd v R & C Commrs* [2008] BTC 443

Tax Reporter: ¶754-400ff.

3650 Acquisition or disposal of trading stock within group

If one member of a 'group' (see 3625) acquires an asset as trading stock from another group member for which it was not trading stock, the acquirer is treated as acquiring it other than as trading stock and then immediately appropriating it to trading stock, so that a chargeable gain or allowable loss will result (see 5145).

Example ignoring indexation

Company A is a member of a group of companies.

A has a capital asset acquired in 2007 for £50,000. In 2012, it is worth £75,000.

A transfers the asset in 2012 to B, another group member, who acquires it as trading stock.

The capital asset is treated as sold by A to B for	£50,000
B's deemed appropriation to trading stock is treated as a gain made by B of:	£
Market value	75,000
Deemed acquisition cost	(50,000)
	25,000

B is therefore liable to pay any tax assessed on that gain. If the asset is appropriated by B for use in a UK trade, B is able to make an election to reduce the acquisition cost of the asset by an amount equal to the chargeable gain, and so 'eliminate' such gain.

If a group member disposes of assets from trading stock to be used for some other purpose by the acquirer, the disponor is treated as appropriating that asset for that other purpose immediately before the disposal; this will effectively result in a market value transfer from revenue to capital account (see 636 and 5145).

Legislation: TCGA 1992, s. 173(1) and (2), 161

Cases: *Coates (HMIT) v Arndale Properties Ltd* [1984] BTC 438; *Reed (HMIT) v Nova Securities Ltd* [1985] BTC 121

Tax Reporter: ¶754-200

3660 Replacement of business assets by group members

All trades carried on by members of a 'group' (see 3625) are treated as a single trade for the purpose of applying the rules relating to the replacement of business assets. This allows a gain arising on an asset owned by one member to be rolled over into the cost of an asset acquired by another member. This extends to treating the members of a group as a single person.

However, this rule does not apply where the replacement is made by a dual resident investing company.

Although rollover relief is denied for acquisitions of assets by group companies in a no gain/no loss transaction, rollover relief for disposals of land under compulsory purchase orders is extended to those situations in which the disposal of the land and the acquisition of its replacement are made by different group companies.

The rules applicable to depreciating assets apply to the group members as if the group were one person and as if all trades were the same trade (see 6310).

Legislation: TCGA 1992, s. 175 and 247(5A)

Tax Reporter: ¶756-100ff.

3665 Recovery within group: failure to pay tax on chargeable gains

If a member of a 'group' (see 3625) makes a chargeable gain and fails to pay the tax assessed thereon within six months of it becoming payable, the inspector may recover that tax from the principal company in the group at the time of the gain, or from any company which was a member of the group within the two years before the date when the gain was made and which owned the whole or part of the asset disposed of or an interest in it.

The tax inspector has two years from the date when the tax became payable to make such an assessment. The assessment is in the name of the company which made the gain. The amount of tax charged must not exceed the corporation tax payable on the gain at the rate in force when that gain was made.

A company so charged may recover the tax (and any interest on overdue tax) from the company which made the gain or from the principal company of the group. If the principal company repays the tax, then it may in turn recover the sum from the company which made the gain or from any other group member which owned the asset disposed of whilst it was a member of the group. The amount recoverable from such a company is in proportion to the value of the asset when that company disposed of it.

Similar provisions apply specifically in relation to tax charged when a company leaves a group with an asset transferred to it intra-group (see 3630).

Legislation: TCGA 1992, s. 190

Tax Reporter: ¶760-650

Group relief

3690 Nature of group relief

One advantage of being a member of a group is that it is possible to transfer the benefit of some corporation tax reliefs between members by way of group relief. Similar benefits apply as between consortium members and companies owned by the consortium.

Subject to certain restrictions (see 3715), this may be particularly useful where one company incurs large trading losses which it cannot expect to relieve against its own income in the foreseeable future but another company has profits against which to set off the losses. Commentary on group relief follows and a comprehensive example is provided at 3735.

Extension of group relief to non-UK resident companies

In recent years, principles established in cases heard before the European Court of Justice (ECJ) have lead to the enactment of legislation which has extended group relief to non-UK resident companies. Recent changes include:

(1) from April 2000, permitting groups and consortia to be established through the presence of non-resident companies and extending

group relief to UK branches of overseas companies (*Imperial Chemical Industries plc v Colmner*);

(2) from April 2006, allowing losses in overseas subsidiaries in another EEA country to be offset as group relief (*Marks and Spencer v Halsey*; see below); and

(3) from July 2010, allowing group relief to be claimed through a link company established in the EEA (*Philips Electronics UK Ltd v R & C Commrs*; see 3698).

Although foreign losses can now be relieved in the UK ((2) above), this is only possible where all possibilities of relief have been exhausted, and future relief is unavailable, in the country where the losses were incurred or in any other country. It is widely believed that the way in which these restrictions are enacted go beyond the limitations which the ECJ found to be acceptable in *Marks and Spencer v Halsey*. In 2008, the European Commission sent the UK a formal request to implement properly the judgement of the ECJ. However, the European Court of Justice (ECJ) has rejected a challenge by the European Commission that UK legislation on the tax relief available for losses incurred by foreign-based subsidiaries of UK companies unfairly limited the possibility of claiming cross-border group relief. The court has now dismissed the Commission's claim that the changes made in 2006 were not compatible with EU law.

In *Philips Electronics* (Case C-18/11), the Advocate General's opinion considered that a UK permanent establishment of a Dutch company could surrender its losses to a UK company where those same losses could be utilised in the Netherlands.

Legislation: CTA 2010, Pt. 5

Cases: *Marks and Spencer plc v Halsey (HMIT)* (Case C-446/03) [2006] BTC 318; *Marks and Spencer plc v Halsey (HMIT)* [2006] BTC 346; *Marks and Spencer plc v Halsey (HMIT)* [2007] BTC 204; *Marks and Spencer plc* [2009] TC 00181; *Marks and Spencer plc v R & C Commrs* [2010] BTC 1,550; *Imperial Chemical Industries plc v Colmner* [1999] BTC 440; *Boake Allen Ltd & Ors (including NEC Semi-conductors Ltd) v R & C Commrs* [2007] BTC 414; *Pilkington Bros Ltd v IR Commrs* [1982] BTC 79; *Shepherd (HMIT) v Law Land plc* [1990] BTC 561; *Steele (HMIT) v EVC International NV* [1996] BTC 425; *Scottish and Universal Newspapers Ltd v Fisher (HMIT)* (1996) Sp C 87

Other Material: *Statement of Practice* SP 3/93; *Extra-statutory Concession* ESC C10; Inland Revenue Tax Bulletin, Issue 26, December 1996, p. 372

Tax Reporter: ¶736-300ff.

3695 Application of group relief

One company, the claimant company, may obtain relief against its profits (see 3705) for a trading loss or similar amount (see 3700), incurred by another company, the surrendering company, in the same accounting period. The surrendering company must consent to the arrangement.

This rule applies where either company is a '75% subsidiary' (see 3610) of the other or they are both 75% subsidiaries of a third company. Alternatively, either company must be a member of a consortium and the other must be one of the following:

- a trading company owned by the consortium and which is not a 75% subsidiary of any company;

- a trading company which is a '90% subsidiary' of a holding company owned by the consortium and which is not a 75% subsidiary of a company other than the holding company; or

- a holding company owned by the consortium and which is not a 75% subsidiary of any company.

A company is owned by a consortium if 75% or more of its ordinary share capital is owned by companies, each owning at least 5% of that share capital.

A company is a 'member of a consortium' if it is one of the companies owning at least 5% of the ordinary share capital of the consortium company, above.

A 'trading company' is a company the business of which consists wholly or mainly in the carrying on of a trade or trades. A 'holding company' is a company the business of which consists wholly or mainly in the holding of shares or securities of companies that are its 90% subsidiaries and are trading companies.

A '90% subsidiary' is defined in the same way as a 75% subsidiary (see 3610) – that is, not less than 90% of its ordinary share capital is owned directly or indirectly by the other company. A company will not, however, be a 75% subsidiary or a 90% subsidiary unless:

- it is beneficially entitled to at least 75% or, as the case may be, 90% of the subsidiary's profits distributable to its equity holders (see below); and

- it is beneficially entitled to not less than 75% or, as the case may be, 90% of the subsidiary's assets distributable to its equity-holders (see below) on a winding-up.

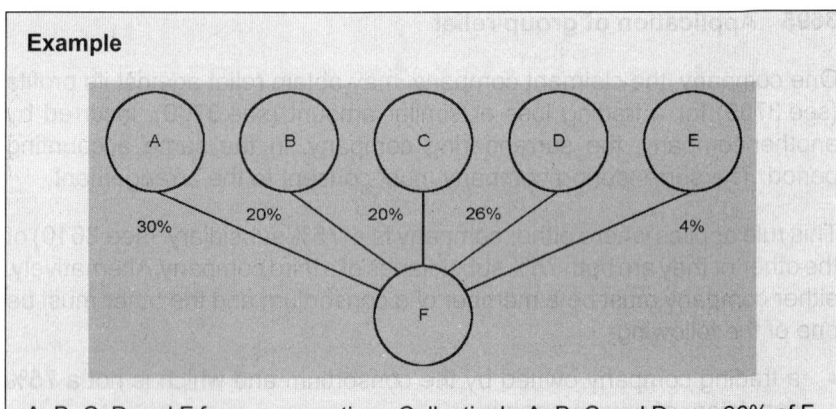

Example

A, B, C, D and F form a consortium. Collectively, A, B, C and D own 96% of F, and each company individually owns more than 5% of F. E is not a consortium member as it owns less than 5% of F.

For the purposes of calculating the amount of group relief that may be surrendered to, or claimed by, a company, a consortium member's share ('ownership proportion') in a company owned by the consortium is the lowest of the following:

- the percentage of the ordinary share capital of the other company beneficially owned by that member;

- the percentage of any profits distributable to equity holders (see below) of the other company to which the member is beneficially entitled;

- the percentage of the other company's assets distributable to its equity holders (see below) on a winding-up to which the member company is beneficially entitled; and

- (for accounting periods beginning on or after 12 July 2010) the proportion of the voting power in the company that is directly possessed by the member company.

This ownership proportion places a limit on the proportion of the losses of the surrendering company that can be claimed by the claimant company (where the surrendering company is the company owned by the consortium), and on the proportion of the profits of the claimant company against which losses can be surrendered (where the claimant company is the company owned by the consortium).

If there are any fluctuations in any of the percentages during the surrendering company's accounting period, the average percentage over the period is used. In determining the average percentage, HMRC apply a weighted average rather than a flat average, to prevent the percentage being manipulated by changes in shares for a short period towards the end of the accounting period.

An arrangement to change the rights in the future may be given effect immediately. Anti-avoidance rules operate to deny group relief in certain situations where 'arrangements' are in place. These are discussed at 3715.

If group relief is given, no further relief may be claimed for the same loss. No relief will be given if, in any accounting period, the share of the claimant, as a member of a consortium, in the surrendering company is nil or if any profit on the sale of the shares in the surrendering company is a trading profit of the claimant.

'Equity holder'

An 'equity holder of a company' is any person who:

- holds 'ordinary shares' in the company; or

- is a 'loan creditor' of the company for a loan which is not a 'normal commercial loan'.

'Ordinary shares' are all a company's shares except restricted preference shares. To qualify as restricted preference shares, shares must, in particular, not carry a right to a dividend other than a restricted right to dividends. This latter phrase means:

(a) the rate of dividend on the shares is no more than a reasonable commercial return on the new consideration given for the shares; and

(b) the dividends are of a fixed amount or at a fixed percentage rate (or a fluctuating rate where the rate fluctuates in accordance with the RPI or other similar general index of prices issued by the Government) of the nominal value of the shares and the company must not be entitled to reduce the amount of, or not pay, the dividends. However, this latter restriction (i.e. that the company must not be entitled to reduce the amount of or not pay the dividend) is removed for accounting periods beginning on or after 1 January 2008 where the company is only entitled to reduce the amount of or not pay the dividends in 'special circumstances', or, having regard to all the circumstances, it is reasonable to assume that the company is only likely to reduce the amount of, or not to pay, any of the dividends in such circumstances. 'Special circumstances' are when the company is in severe financial difficulties or when it is unable to pay all or part of a dividend because of a recommendation by the Financial Services Authority or a similar body.

It should be noted that non-cumulative preference shares are not therefore restricted preference shares (because the dividend is not fixed – depending on the level of reserves the dividend might be at a rate below the quoted coupon rate) and so would be regarded as ordinary shares which could lead to two companies which would otherwise have qualified for group relief ceasing to qualify.

In addition to these conditions on the restricted right to dividends, shares have to meet the following conditions in order to qualify as a restricted preference shares:

(a) the shares were issued for a consideration which includes new consideration (so, for example, shares issued on a bonus issue can not be restricted preference shares);

(b) the shares do not carry the right to conversion into other shares or securities (except into other restricted preference shares or shares or securities of the company's quoted parent company);

(c) the shares do not carry any right to the acquisition of other shares and securities; and

(d) on repayment, the shares do not carry the right to an amount exceeding the new consideration given for the shares (except so far as those rights are reasonably comparable with those generally carried by listed fixed dividend shares).

A 'loan creditor' of a company is a person to whom the company owes a debt for the following:

- money borrowed;

- capital assets acquired;

- any right of the company to receive income created in favour of the company;

- consideration which, at the time the debt was incurred, was to the company substantially less than the amount of the debt (including any premium on the debt); or

- any redeemable loan capital issued by the company.

A 'normal commercial loan' is a loan:

- wholly or partly of new consideration;

- which gives no right to conversion into, or acquisition of, additional shares or securities (except conversion as mentioned below);

- the interest on which is no more than a reasonable commercial return on the new consideration, and is not dependent on either the company's profitability or the value of its assets (except where the rate reduces/increases, when the results of the debtor company's business improve/worsen or the value of its assets increase/decrease and except in respect of non-recourse loans made on terms which restrict the security for the payment of interest or principal to non-dealing land); and

- which does not give a right to more than a reasonable commercial premium on redemption.

Subsidiary companies issuing certain types of convertible shares or securities will not be prevented from being members of groups. A share or loan may as a result be convertible into restricted preference shares or a normal commercial loan which do not themselves carry conversion or additional acquisition rights and would not be regarded as equity. They may also be convertible into shares or securities in the quoted parent company (i.e. one for which the subsidiary is a 75% subsidiary, which is not itself a 75% subsidiary of any company and whose shares are listed, including the USM) or in a 'quoted unconnected company', or into restricted preference shares or a normal commercial loan themselves convertible into such shares or securities.

Legislation: CTA 2010, Pt. 5, Ch. 2 and 6

Cases: *J Sainsbury plc v O'Connor (HMIT)* [1991] BTC 181; *Imperial Chemical Industries plc v Colmer (HMIT)* [1999] BTC 440; *Imperial Chemical Industries plc (ICI) v Colmer (HMIT)* (Case C-264/96) [1998] BTC 304; *Philips Electronics UK Ltd* [2009] TC 00176

Tax Reporter: ¶736-300ff.

3698   Company simultaneously a member of a group and a consortium

Group relief is also available where at the same time a company is in the same group as one or more other companies and is also either a company owned by a consortium or it, or another company in its group, is one of the members of a consortium (see 3695). In this situation it is possible for:

- a loss or other amount of the surrendering company to be claimed partly as group relief and partly as consortium relief; and

- for consortium relief to 'flow through' the consortium member (the 'link company') to and from other companies in the consortium member's group.

The relaxations aim to give such companies greater flexibility in using group and consortium relief.

For accounting periods beginning before 12 July 2010, the link company had to be resident in the UK or carrying on trade in the UK though a UK permanent establishment. This was found to be contrary to the freedom of establishment principle of EU law (*Philips Electronics UK Ltd v R & C Commrs*) and consequently legislation was introduced in F(No. 3)A 2010 to enable relief to be claimed through a link company which is established in the EEA. A company is established in the EEA if it is constituted under the law of the UK or an EEA territory and if it has its registered office, central administration or principal place of business within the EEA. But even then relief is not given if the 'group' relationship between the link company and the claimant or service company is only sustained with the involvement of a company not established in the EEA. The changes apply with effect for accounting periods beginning on or after 12 July 2010. Further changes have been made taking effect from 10 December 2014 by removing all requirements relating to the location of a link company so that group relief may flow regardless of where the link company is based.

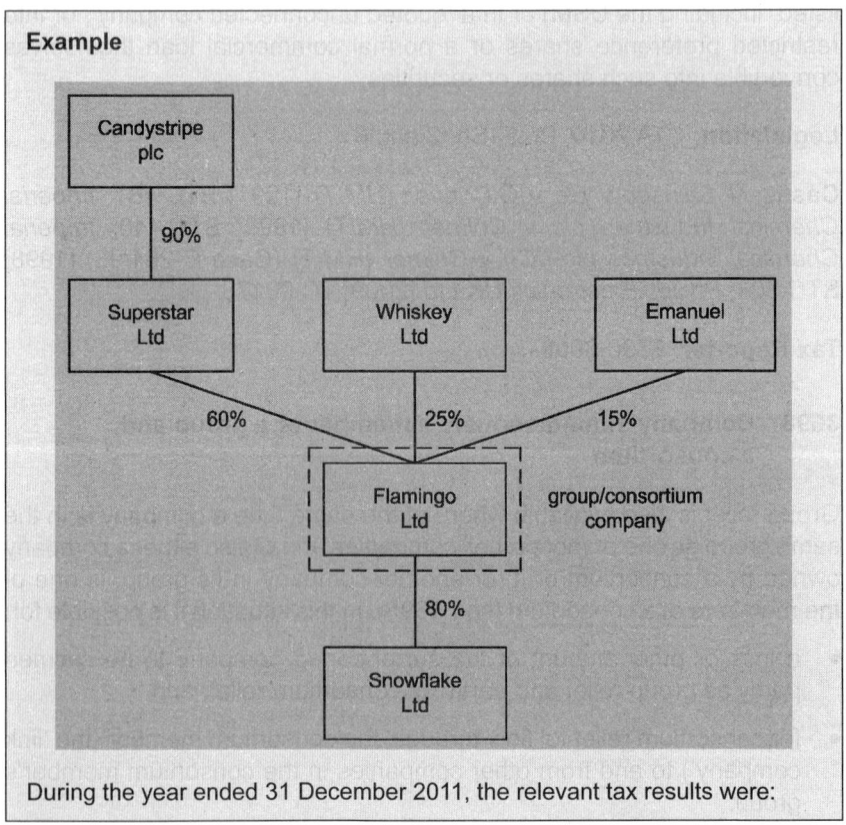

Example

During the year ended 31 December 2011, the relevant tax results were:

		£
Superstar Ltd	Total profits	250,000
Flamingo Ltd	Trading loss	(360,000)
Snowflake Ltd	Total profits	90,000

Flamingo Ltd is a group/consortium company. Superstar Ltd is one of the members of a consortium, and also a member of a group.

Superstar Ltd's claim for consortium relief against its profits would be 60% of Flamingo Ltd's loss after taking into account the potential group relief claim by Snowflake Ltd (whether or not the claim is actually made), i.e. £162,000 (60% × (£360,000 – £90,000)).

As £162,000 is lower than Superstar Ltd's available profits of £250,000, the amount surrendered is £162,000.

Superstar Ltd's final taxable profits would then be:

	£
Profits	250,000
Less: consortium relief	(162,000)
Taxable profits	88,000

If the tax results for the relevant companies for the year ended 31 December 2011 were as follows:

		£
Candystripe plc	Total profits	328,000
Superstar Ltd	Total profits	80,000
Flamingo Ltd	Trading loss	(220,000)
Snowflake Ltd	Trading loss	(10,000)

Then the maximum loss which Flamingo Ltd can surrender to Superstar Ltd is £132,000 (60% × £220,000). This would then be reduced to £80,000, being Superstar Ltd's total profits available to relieve the surrendered loss.

However, the surrender of the full £132,000 can be split between Candystripe plc and Superstar Ltd, in whatever proportion they may decide.

Legislation: CTA 2010, Pt. 5, Ch. 2, Ch. 4

3700 Amounts available for group relief

The losses and other amounts which a company may be able to surrender as group relief are split into two categories:

(1) trading losses, excess capital allowances, and a non-trading deficit on the company's loan relationships (see below for these); and

(2) qualifying charitable donation (previously charges on income, see 3235), UK property business losses (see below), management expenses, and a non-trading loss on intangible fixed assets.

Subject to the detailed provisions in the rest of the group relief rules (see 3690), the above amounts may be set off against the claimant company's total profits for its corresponding accounting period. If the accounting periods of the claimant and the surrendering company do not coincide, apportionment of their respective profits and loss must be made.

Amounts in category (1) above (trading losses, excess capital allowances and non-trading deficits on loan relationships) may be surrendered as group relief even if the surrendering company has other profits in the same accounting period against which they could be set. A deficit on a non-trading loan relationship can only be surrendered as group relief if a claim is made to treat it as eligible for group relief (see 3168).

Amounts in category (2) above (charitable donations, property losses, management expenses and non-trading loss on IFAs) may only be surrendered as group relief to the extent that in aggregate they exceed the surrendering company's 'gross profits' (see below) for the surrender period. Any excess surrendered is taken to consist first of charitable donations, then property losses, management expenses and finally non-trading loss on IFAs (in that order).

The surrendering company's 'gross profits' comprise its profits for the period without deduction either for:

(1) the losses, allowances or other amounts of the accounting period which are potentially available for surrender as group relief (see above); or

(2) any other losses or allowances, etc. of any other accounting period, whether or not within that description.

Excess capital allowances

The excess capital allowances which can be surrendered as group relief are defined as the excess in an accounting period of a company's capital allowances which are to be given by discharge or repayment of tax over the income against which they are primarily available. Allowances carried forward from an earlier period do not affect this calculation. Allowances or losses of any other period cannot be deducted from the income against which the allowances above are primarily available.

Dual resident investing companies

The amounts which may be surrendered are subject to the restriction on group relief which can be surrendered by dual resident investing companies (see 3725).

Companies owned by consortia

The amount of group relief which can be surrendered by a company owned by a consortium is restricted. Such a company is deemed to use up as much as possible of its trading losses by setting them off against its other profits of the same accounting period (see 3315) before it is allowed to surrender any of them as group relief. The restriction applies whether or not the company in fact makes a current period set-off claim. The restriction also applies before any reduction of the amount which can be claimed or surrendered by a company which is both a member of a group and of a consortium (see 3690).

Legislation: CTA 2010, Pt. 5, Ch. 2

Tax Reporter: ¶738-000

3705 Set-off of group relief

Group relief can be set off against the total profits of the claimant before they are reduced by any relief derived from a subsequent accounting period, but after all other reliefs are deducted. The claimant is assumed to set off all trading losses and capital allowances against total profits of the same accounting period, in so far as they exceed income from the same source.

Relief derived from a subsequent accounting period includes relief on trading losses given against profits of a preceding accounting period (see 3320) and relief on capital allowances given against profits of a preceding accounting period. This also applied to 'terminal loss relief' (see 3335) on a loss incurred in an accounting period after the end of the accounting period in which the profits were being calculated.

Where the claimant is a member of a consortium, it can only set off a fraction of the surrendering company's loss equal to the percentage of the ordinary share capital of the surrendering company or its holding company held by it. Where the surrendering company is a member of a consortium, the loss cannot be set off against more than a fraction of the total profits of the claimant.

Differing accounting periods

If the accounting periods of the claimant and the surrendering company do not coincide, apportionment of their respective profits and loss must be made.

Example

Blue Ltd, Green Ltd and Red Ltd are trading companies in the same group for group relief purposes. Blue Ltd and Green Ltd make their accounts up to 31 December each year. For the accounting period ending 31 December 2011, their tax adjusted results are profits of £2,000,000 for Blue Ltd and £600,000 for Green Ltd. Red Ltd makes its annual accounts up to 30 September each year. Its tax adjusted result for the accounting period ending 30 September 2011 is a loss of £2,080,000. Blue Ltd claims the maximum possible group relief for Red Ltd's loss of the overlapping period. Subsequently Green Ltd also makes a maximum claim for group relief from Red Ltd. All necessary consents to surrender are given. All apportionments are on a time basis.

The overlapping period in this case is nine months (from 1 January 2011 to 30 September 2011).

Blue Ltd's claim will be £1,500,000 since this is the lesser of:

- Blue Ltd's otherwise unrelieved profits for the overlapping period, £1,500,000 ($£2,000,000 \times {}^9/_{12}$); and

- Red Ltd's otherwise unutilised loss for the overlapping period, £1,560,000 ($£2,080,000 \times {}^9/_{12}$).

Blue Ltd's chargeable profit for the accounting period ending 31 December 2011 after group relief will be £500,000 (profit £2,000,000 less group relief £1,500,000). Blue Ltd will be unable to make any further group relief claims in respect of this overlap period since all of its apportioned profit has been relieved.

Green Ltd's later claim will be £60,000, since this is the lesser of:

- Green Ltd's otherwise unrelieved profits for the overlapping period, £450,000 ($£600,000 \times {}^9/_{12}$); and

- Red Ltd's otherwise unutilised loss for the overlapping period, £60,000 ($£2,080,000 \times {}^9/_{12} = £1,560,000$ less £1,500,000) (being the relief already given).

Green Ltd could claim further losses (from other group companies) for this overlap period of £390,000 (£450,000 less £60,000 (losses already claimed)).

Red Ltd has obtained full relief for its group relievable losses, £1,560,000, of the period from 1 January 2011 to 30 September 2011 (£1,500,000 to Blue Ltd and £60,000 to Green Ltd). No further surrender of relief can be made in respect of this period. The loss for the period 1 October 2010 to 31 December 2010 cannot be used for any overlapping period beginning after 31 December 2010.

Legislation: CTA 2010, s. 138–142

Tax Reporter: ¶737-750

3710 Group relief claims under CTSA

Under corporation tax self-assessment (CTSA), a claim to group relief for any accounting period must be included in the claimant company's return (either as originally delivered, or via an amendment to the return submitted within the normal time-limit). The claim must specify the amount of relief and the surrendering company (or companies), which must provide a notice of consent to the surrender. However, the Treasury has the power to make regulations dispensing with the requirement for a company to file a copy of the notice of consent from the surrendering company with any group relief claim. The Treasury may also regulate that the dispensation is dependent on the agreement of the group company authorised to amend the returns for group purposes.

It is not necessary to claim all of the relief(s) available for surrender; a lesser amount of relief may be requested. However, if a claim exceeds the 'amount available for surrender', it will be ineffective. It seems that this may mean that the whole claim will be disregarded, not just the excess amount. Claims to group relief, once made, cannot be amended but may be withdrawn (by amendment to the relevant company tax return) and if necessary replaced by another claim.

All claims, surrenders of losses, etc. by companies in a group can be administered by one group company on behalf of all group members.

Amounts available for surrender

To determine the 'amount available for surrender':

(1) on the basis of the company's tax return (see 4305), determine the total amount available for surrender according to 3700; then

(2) deduct all amounts included in extant notices of consent.

In (1) above, any company's amendments to its return which are made during an enquiry into the return are disregarded.

Multiple claims

Where, in the case of multiple claims, some are withdrawn and some are made on the same day, the withdrawals are given effect to first. However, where multiple claims exceed the amount available for surrender, HMRC have the power to determine which claims will be ineffective, so as to bring the total claimed within the limit available.

Reduction in amount available for surrender

Where, after notice(s) of consent have been given, the amount available for surrender is reduced below the amount of relief consented to, the company must withdraw the notice(s) of consent to bring the amount surrendered to an acceptable level. If necessary, new notices can be issued, to ensure the surrender limit is not exceeded. All affected claimant companies, and HMRC, must be notified in writing of any consent withdrawals and reissues in different amounts. Where a surrendering company fails to withdraw consent, HMRC may by notice issue such directions as are necessary to prevent any over-surrender of reliefs. All parties affected by such a direction must receive notification in writing. Claimant companies must amend their self-assessments upon receiving details of any alterations to the amount(s) surrendered. Surrendering companies may appeal against any directions issued by HMRC regarding these matters.

Assessment to recover excessive group relief

If HMRC discover that excessive group relief has been given, they may recover the amount that they consider excessive by assessment, without prejudice to the general power to make discovery assessments.

Legislation enables recovery from other specified beneficiaries of tax arising from an excessive claim to group relief. Where tax relating to the excessive claim remains unpaid six months after the expiry of the final time-limit for a claim for the period, HMRC can have recourse to other claimant companies which have benefited from the same surrender, subject to a maximum of the tax which those other companies have saved.

For accounting periods ending after 1 April 2000, in consequence of the extension of the group relief rules to encompass groups with non-resident members, the tax payable by the non-resident can be recovered from other members of the group in the event of default.

Joint amended returns

The Treasury may make regulations modifying, as they see fit, any of the provisions relating to making and withdrawing claims in order to facilitate arrangements whereby one person may be authorised to act on behalf of two or more companies (in the same group) as far as the amendment of returns to revise group relief claims is concerned.

Consent to surrender

All claims to group relief require the consent of the company surrendering relief. Where there is a consortium claim, each member of the consortium must also consent.

Any such consent(s) must be given in writing at or prior to the time that the corresponding claim is made, to the officer of the Board to whom the surrendering company renders returns. Failure to provide such a consent renders the claim ineffective, because all claims to group relief (and consortium relief) must be accompanied by a copy of the relevant consent(s) to be valid.

However, the Treasury has the power to make regulations dispensing with the requirement for a company to file a copy of the notice of consent from the surrendering company with any group relief claim. The Treasury may also regulate that the dispensation is dependent on the agreement of the group company authorised to amend the returns for group purposes.

Notice of consent by surrendering company

To be effective, a consent notice must include all of the following details:

- the name of the surrendering company and its tax district reference;

- the name of the claimant company and its tax district reference;

- the amount of relief being surrendered; and

- the accounting period of the surrendering company to which the surrender relates.

Once given, a notice of consent may not be amended but it may be withdrawn (by notice to HMRC) and a new notice issued. However, the withdrawal of a consent notice is not permitted without the permission of the claimant company, which must amend its return if such permission is given. An exception to the requirement of obtaining the claimant company's permission is when withdrawal of consent is required because the amount available for surrender is reduced.

Notice of consent requiring amendment of return

Where a notice of consent is given after the delivery of a surrendering company's tax return (see 4305), an amendment to that return must be made, fully reflecting the effect(s) of the surrender of relief(s). Failure to make such an amendment renders the notice of consent ineffective.

Time-limits for group relief claims

Subject to HMRC permitting an extension to the time-limit, claims to group relief must be made (or withdrawn) by the *latest* of:

(1) 12 months after the filing date for the claimant company's tax return for the accounting period covered by the claim;

(2) 30 days after the issue of a closure notice is issued on the completion of an enquiry;

(3) 30 days after HMRC issue a notice of amendment to a return following the completion of an enquiry (issued where the company fails to amend the return itself); or

(4) 30 days after the determination of any appeal against a HMRC amendment (as in (3) above).

'Enquiry' in the above does not include a restricted enquiry into an amendment to a return (restricted because the time-limit for making an enquiry into the return itself has expired), where the amendment consists of a group relief claim or withdrawal of claim.

The above time-limits have priority over any other general time-limits for amending returns.

Legislation: FA 1998, Sch. 18, para. 63–65 and Sch. 18, Pt. VIII; *Corporation Tax (Simplified Arrangements for Group Relief) Regulations* 1999 (SI 1999/2975)

Tax Reporter: ¶739-600

3715 Loss of group relief where arrangements are in existence

A group of companies may make relevant 'arrangements' in relation to the group structure. Relevant arrangements include all kinds of arrangements whether oral or in writing.

If two companies (A and B) satisfy the criteria for being members of the same group in a particular accounting period but, at some time during or after that period:

(1) A could cease to be a member of the same group as B and become a member of the same group as a third company, C;

(2) any person or persons could obtain control of A but not of B; or

(3) C could begin to carry on a trade which is carried on by A, as A's successor, or as the successor of another company which began to carry on the same trade during or after the accounting period,

then, for group relief purposes, A is not treated as a member of the same group as B.

C is a company that is not, apart from any of the arrangements at (1) to (3) above, a member of the same group of companies as A. Group relief is not denied for the whole of the accounting period; the group relationship is only broken for the period from the beginning of the arrangements until their termination, apportionments of results being made as necessary.

Example

Company A is a parent company. Company S is its subsidiary. S purchases capital assets and is entitled to capital allowances which it cannot use. A is not in a position to use them if S surrenders the allowances to it (see 3700).

Therefore, A sells its equity in S to B. Company S is now B's subsidiary. Subject to possible limitation (see 3730), B is then entitled to S's allowances which are surrendered as group relief.

However, if A had retained an option to buy back its equity (at a price taking into account the reliefs which B was given), B and S would not be treated as members of the same group, and the reliefs granted above would not apply.

If a company is the subject of relevant arrangements in an accounting period, and it is a trading company, it loses any right to surrender available reliefs to a member of a consortium if any of the following circumstances exist at some time during or after that period:

(1) the trading company could become a '75% subsidiary' (see 3610) of a third company;

(2) the owner(s) of less than 50% of the ordinary share capital of the trading company has or could obtain control of that company;

(3) a person, other than a holding company of which the trading company is a '90% subsidiary' (see 3610), holds or could hold, or controls or could control alone or with 'connected persons' the exercise of at least 75% of the votes on a poll taken at a general meeting of the trading company, In that or a later accounting period; or

(4) a third company could begin to carry on the trade which, at any time in that accounting period, is carried on by the trading company, either as that company's successor or that of another company which has begun to carry on that trade during the same accounting period.

This rule similarly applies in relation to a holding company of which a trading company is a 90% subsidiary.

Certain arrangements entered into by a joint venture company, and certain mortgage arrangements, in either case entered into in accounting periods beginning on or after 1 March 2012 are, subject to conditions, not to be counted as arrangements for the above purposes.

Definition of 'connected persons'

A 'person' is connected with his/her spouse, any of his/her relatives, i.e. brother, sister, ancestor or lineal descendant, and any such relative of his/her spouse.

A trustee of a 'settlement' is connected with the 'settlor' (see 1071), any person connected with the settlor and any company connected with the settlement. A company is connected with a settlement if:

(1) it is a close company (see 4005) (or only not a close company because it is not resident in the UK) and the participators (see 4010) include the trustees of the settlement; or

(2) it is under the control of a company within (1) above.

A company has control of another company if it can secure, by means of shares or voting power, or by virtue of articles of association or other document, that the company's affairs are conducted in accordance with its wishes.

A 'partner' is connected with any person with whom he is in partnership, his/her relatives and the relative of any partner.

A 'company' is connected with another company if they are both controlled (see above) by the same person, or one person controls it who also controls the other together with connected persons or where the other company is controlled by connected persons alone. Companies are also connected where they are both controlled by the same group of persons or are under the control of different groups but members of one group are connected with members of the other group.

Arrangements

HMRC have published a statement of practice concerning the terms 'arrangements' and 'option arrangements'; it includes the following views:

• if an agreement provides for the creation of specified option rights exercisable at some future time, option arrangements come into existence when the agreement was entered into;

• neither a public offer nor private negotiations for the disposal of shares, etc. will generally give rise to arrangements until an offer is accepted (usually subject to contract or some similar conditional basis) or, where required, shareholder approval is given (or effectively definite) or the parties come to an understanding in the nature of an option (e.g. an offer allowing the purchaser to choose the moment to create a bargain);

- arrangements may exist between parties even though they are not enforceable.

Power of HMRC to request information

If HMRC have reason to believe that any 'relevant arrangements' may exist, they may serve notice in writing on the company requiring it to make a written declaration that those arrangements do or do not exist and/or any other information he may require. The company is given 30 days to supply that information.

Legislation: CTA 2010, s. 154–156

Cases: *Boake Allen Ltd (including NEC Semi-conductors Ltd) v R & C Commrs* [2007] BTC 414; *Marks & Spencer plc v Halsey (HMIT)* (Case C-446/03) [2006] BTC 318; *Pilkington Bros Ltd v IR Commrs* [1982] BTC 79; *Shepherd (HMIT) v Law Land plc* [1990] BTC 561; *Steele (HMIT) v EVC International NV* [1996] BTC 425; *Scottish and Universal Newspapers Ltd v Fisher (HMIT)* (1996) Sp C 87

Other Material: *Statement of Practice* SP 3/93; *Extra-statutory Concession* ESC C10

Tax Reporter: ¶737-350

3720 Group relief: foreign and non-commercial trades

There are certain trading losses to which group relief does not apply. These are losses from foreign trading and from trades carried on on a non-commercial basis, without a view to realising a gain (see 3700). The exclusion in respect of foreign trading does not apply in the special case of surrenders by non-UK resident, EEA companies.

Legislation: CTA 2010, s. 100(2)

Tax Reporter: ¶738-025

3725 Group relief: dual resident companies

Losses made by dual resident companies are frequently available for worldwide tax relief twice. Many countries have provisions permitting the aggregation or consolidation of profits and losses within a group of resident companies. Some countries determine residence by reference to incorporation and some by other means, e.g. place of management, hence the concept of dual resident companies.

Provisions were enacted in 1987 to remove the tax advantage in the UK from the deliberate setting up of dual resident companies financed by borrowing, but not adversely to affect genuine trading companies.

Any loss or other amount is unavailable for set-off by way of group relief if the surrendering company is a dual resident investing company which meets either of these conditions, viz:

- not a trading company; or

- its main function, or one of its main functions, is, broadly, to borrow money, pay interest or charges, or acquire shares (or that such types of activity are carried on to an extent that does not appear to be justified by any trade the company carries on).

Legislation: CTA 2010, s. 109

Tax Reporter: ¶738-300

3730   Group relief where a member joins or leaves a group

If a new company joins or an existing member leaves a group before the end of its accounting period, that period comes to an end and another begins for purposes of group relief. The claimant and surrendering companies must be members of the same group in or during some part of the surrendering company's accounting period and of the corresponding accounting period of the claimant. The part which coincides is the 'overlapping period', and group relief is limited by reference to the part of the surrender period of the surrendering company that coincides with any part of the claim period of the claimant company.

Example

C owns 83% of the ordinary share capital of S when S joins the group on 1 August 2011. S incurs losses of £20,000 for period 1 November 2010 to 31 October 2011. C makes a profit of £60,000 for period 1 May 2011 to 30 April 2012. The overlapping period, being the period which is (1) common to the claim period and the surrender period and (2) throughout which the companies were members of the same group, is 1 August 2011 to 31 October 2011 (3 months).

S's loss apportioned: $3/_{12}$ × £20,000 = £5,000.

Profits of C available: $3/_{12}$ × £60,000 = £15,000.

C has sufficient profits to absorb the loss of £5,000.

It has been held that if the surrendering company leaves the group after the end of the accounting period to which the claim relates, relief will still be available to the claimant company and may be claimed (within the appropriate time-limits) even though the surrendering company is not a member of the group at the time the claim is made.

Only one claim allowed

A group of companies may claim relief only once for the same loss. Where more than one company claims relief for one loss, they may obtain in total only the same relief which would be available to a single company whose corresponding period coincides with that of the surrendering company.

Legislation: CTA 2010, s. 137(7), 138–142

Case: *AW Chapman Ltd v Hennessey (HMIT)* [1982] BTC 44

Tax Reporter: ¶737-650

3735 Comprehensive example of group relief

A comprehensive example of group relief is provided below.

Example

Aster (Holdings) plc has four wholly owned subsidiaries: Lilliput Ltd, Meteor Ltd, Milady Ltd and Pompone Ltd. Milady Ltd was acquired on 1 November 2011.

All companies prepared accounts for the year ended 31 March 2012. A summary of the tax computations, incorporating the group relief claims, is shown below:

	Aster plc	Lilliput Ltd	Meteor Ltd	Milady Ltd	Pompone Ltd
	£	£	£	£	£
Trading profit/(loss)	1,777,100	460,900	217,300	(78,000)	143,300
Trading profit/(loss) b/fwd (max £672,000)		(460,900)			
Trading profit/(loss) c/fwd					
Non-trading income (see below)	425,000	1,400			1,200
Rental income			12,400		(20,700)
Chargeable gain	33,400				4,600
Non-trading loan (interest paid to Aster (Holdings) plc)			(425,000)		
Gift aid donation	(5,000)				
	2,230,500	1,400	(195,300)	(78,000)	128,400
Less: group relief					

	Aster plc	Lilliput Ltd	Meteor Ltd	Milady Ltd	Pompone Ltd
	£	£	£	£	£
Non-trading loan deficit	(126,900)		195,300		(68,400)
Milady Ltd's trading losses	(32,500)			32,500	
PCTCT	2,071,100	1,400	Nil		60,000
Loss c/fwd		(211,100)		(45,500)	
CT payable					
at 26%	538,486				
at 20%		280			12,000

Lilliput Ltd cannot surrender its brought forward losses.

Meteor Ltd can make a claim to surrender £195,300 of its loan relationship deficit by way of group relief. It does not have to apply its loan relationship deficit in reducing its other profits first but may do so. £68,400 is allocated first to Pompone Ltd to bring its profits down to the lower limit for small profits rate purposes – £60,000 (i.e. £300,000 ÷ 5). The balance is surrendered to Aster (Holdings) plc.

As Milady Ltd joined the group on 1 November 2011, it can only surrender $^5/_{12}$ of its loss of £78,000. The remaining £45,500 has been carried forward.

Pompone Ltd's rental business loss of £20,700 cannot be group-relieved as it does not exceed the company's total profits.

3740   Intangible fixed assets

For the purposes of the rules relating to intangible fixed assets (see 3179), a group is defined in a similar way to that used for chargeable gains purposes (see 3625). The single company rules are extended in a number of group situations including:

- transfers of intangible fixed assets within a group;
- rollover relief on reinvestment: application to group members;
- companies ceasing to be members of a group (degrouping);
- payments between group members in respect of reliefs.

Transfers of intangible fixed assets within a group

Where an intangible fixed asset is transferred between two companies which are members of the same group and the asset is a chargeable intangible asset immediately before and after the transfer, then the transfer is treated as being tax neutral. A tax-neutral transfer is not regarded as a realisation by the transferor. The transferee is treated as though it has held the asset for the same length of time as the transferor and has done all the things that the transferor did in relation to the asset.

Rollover relief

The rollover relief for reinvestment into intangible fixed assets is extended where a company is a member of a group. Where a company which is a member of the same group as the company realising the old assets incurs the expenditure on new assets, the reinvestment relief can apply. The relief does not apply if the company incurring the expenditure is a dual resident investing company or if the expenditure on other assets relates to assets acquired from another member of the group by a tax-neutral transfer.

Reinvestment relief is also extended under certain circumstances to reinvestment in shares in a company where the assets of that company include chargeable intangible fixed assets.

Degrouping

The degrouping provisions apply if a company, which has acquired a chargeable intangible asset by way of a tax-neutral transfer, leaves a group within six years (see 3645). If the company leaving the group (or an associated company also leaving the group) still owns the intangible asset at the time, then the provisions have effect. The transferee company is deemed to realise and immediately reacquire the asset immediately after the transfer at its market value at that time. The resulting amendments to the tax debits and credits are brought into the computation in the period in which the company leaves the group.

Under certain circumstances, it may be possible:

- for the deemed realisation under the degrouping rules to be subject to a reinvestment relief claim;
- for a remaining member of a group to elect jointly that the degrouping tax credit be brought to account by them rather than the departing company;
- for the company which elects to take on the degrouping charge to make a claim for reinvestment relief in relation to the deemed realisation.

Payments between group companies in respect of reliefs

Where there are payments between group members for group rollover relief or for the reallocation of a degrouping charge, then the payments shall not be taken into account in computing profits or losses for corporation tax purposes.

Corporation tax

Legislation: CTA 2009, Pt. 8

Tax Reporter: ¶724-500ff.

3750 Company mergers

A 'merger' is an arrangement between several parties, which may include a non-resident company, whereby the merging company acquires one or more interests in the whole or part of the business of the leaving company. The members of the group which that company has left then acquire an interest in the business carried on by either the merging company itself or its '90% subsidiary' (see 3610) before the merger. In either case, the interest acquired must be at least 25% of the ordinary share capital of the relevant company. The remaining interest may include shares and/ or debentures. The interest must not be acquired with an intention to dispose of it.

If a company leaves a group as part of a 'merger' which is not taking place to avoid tax, the charge which arises in respect of assets transferred to that company intra-group (see 3630) is disapplied.

Legislation: TCGA 1992, s. 181

Tax Reporter: ¶754-700

3760 Surrender of tax refund within group

Companies in a group can effectively offset underpayments and overpayments within the group in calculating interest on overdue tax payable by any individual company. Under self-assessment (CTSA), the ability to surrender repayments of tax to other group members is extended to cover payments of corporation tax under self-assessment, i.e. including repayments of instalments paid by large companies.

The offset is treated as having been made for all purposes of the Tax Acts. A consequent adjustment will also be made in any tax-geared penalty arising as a result of failing to deliver a tax return on time.

Membership of a group for this purpose is essentially the same as for group relief, although the two (or more) companies involved must have coterminous accounting periods, and must also be members of the group throughout the period from the start of the relevant accounting period until the date on which the offset election is made (see 3690).

Legislation: CTA 2010, s. 963

Tax Reporter: ¶735-475ff.

3770 Arrangements with respect to payment of corporation tax

Under its 'care and management' powers, the Board may enter into arrangements with a group of companies to allow one member to discharge the corporation tax liabilities of the group (effective from 31 July 1998). The arrangements aim to ease the transition to quarterly payments. 'Group' for these purposes is a company and all of its 51% subsidiaries, any 51% subsidiaries of those subsidiaries and so on. Any such payment will not have to be broken down between the respective group members at the time of payment, but will be allocated to them as their tax liabilities arise under self-assessment.

Such arrangements may include provision for, inter alia:

(a) companies joining or leaving a group;

(b) payment of interest and penalties on corporation tax;

(c) amounts treated as corporation tax (i.e. liabilities under the provisions for loans to participators: see 4040 and controlled foreign companies: see 4150ff.);

(d) ending the arrangements; and

(e) any other necessary or expedient provision.

Arrangements entered into will not impact on the actual liability, or the duty to pay corporation tax of any company covered by the arrangements, or any other tax liabilities. Therefore, if a subsidiary's corporation tax is not paid under a group arrangement, that subsidiary is still liable to pay that tax and any collection, interest, etc. provisions of the legislation will continue to apply.

HMRC have published details of the way payment arrangements operate for groups of companies liable to pay their corporation tax by quarterly instalments. They allow groups of companies that wish to do so to account for corporation tax (including quarterly instalment payments) on a group basis, instead of by individual company. Companies which undertake to pay tax under the arrangements must make such payments by electronic funds transfer. Once in place, the arrangements will generally apply automatically to subsequent accounting periods, but there are procedures which cover changes in the members of the group or if it transpires that the conditions for the arrangements have been breached.

In addition to the points already made above, it should be noted that:

• companies whose tax affairs are in arrears cannot apply;

• generally, the accounting period must be that of all the participating companies, but there will be adaptations for a company or companies joining a group and aligning their accounting period with that of the group;

- not all companies in the group need be UK resident, *but* the company nominated to pay on behalf of the companies covered by the arrangement must be resident;

- not all members of the group need be covered by the group payment arrangements; and

- there may be more than one arrangement for different sub-groups.

For further details and if groups wish to take advantage of these arrangements, companies should register their interest by contacting the group payment team at the HMRC Accounts Office to which their CT payments are normally made.

Legislation: TMA 1970, s. 59F

Tax Reporter: ¶735-450

Distributions

Identifying a distribution

3800 Dividends and other distributions to shareholders

A company does not exist in isolation and the shareholders who invest in it expect to get some financial benefit when the company makes a profit. A company confers some benefit on its shareholders in the form of distributions which it makes from time to time. The distribution will usually take the form of a dividend but there are other types of distribution. Not all distributions are 'distributions' for tax purposes (see 3805 and 3810).

Following the Summer 2015 Budget announcement of wide-ranging changes to the taxation of dividends, the Government consulted on the rules for company distributions in Autumn 2015. In addition, changes have been made on the transaction in securities rules and a targeted anti-avoidance rule (TAAR) introduced to counter arrangements designed to permit profits to be extracted in capital form.

Following the abolition of ACT (advance corporation tax) in 1999, the major tax implication of a payment made by a company being treated as a distribution is that the payment will not be deductible for corporation tax purposes.

The distributions a company makes are subject to special rules when calculating the tax payable on them by the recipient of the distribution.

The tax treatment of a company distribution in the hands of the shareholder may depend on whether it is a 'qualifying distribution', in which case there is an associated tax credit, or a non-qualifying distribution (see 3910). The tax treatment of distributions in the hands of corporate recipients is considered at 3900. For commentary on where a distribution is received by an individual, see 1350.

Special provisions apply to stock dividends (see below).

Information relating to distributions

For dividends or payment of interest which are deemed to be distributions, payment must be accompanied by a statement from the company (and in the case of payments via nominees, by such nominees) showing, in the case of a qualifying distribution, the amount and accompanying tax credit or, in the case of interest which is not a qualifying distribution, the amount gross and net of any tax deducted at source. The penalty is £60 per offence, restricted to £600 per distribution. The recipient of a qualifying distribution may also call for a statement from the payer showing the amount and accompanying tax credit.

Returns relating to distributions

Electronic delivery of returns is possible provided the sender notified the recipient in advance that he intends to use electronic format, the recipient agrees, and the electronic format used is designed to prevent alteration of what is delivered.

Stock dividends

In general terms, a stock dividend is share capital issued by a 'UK-resident' (see 3020) company either instead of a dividend or as a bonus issue to which there is a right under the terms on which the original shares were issued. They are not regarded as distributions for tax purposes.

An individual is charged to higher rate tax in respect of the appropriate amount in cash, which is generally the amount foregone unless the market value is substantially different); HMRC regard 15% as substantial. The charge is modified in relation to personal representatives and discretionary trustees, and a statement of practice has been published which sets out the tax treatment of enhanced stock dividends received by trustees of interest in possession trusts. Company recipients are generally treated as having received capital under general principles and so are not subject to corporation tax in respect of stock dividend. For the chargeable gains position in respect of stock dividends, see 5915.

Legislation: CTA 2010, Pt. 23, Ch. 6; ITTOIA 2005, Pt. 4, Ch. 5; *Income and Corporation Taxes (Electronic Certificates of Deduction of Tax and Tax Credit) Regulations* 2003 (SI 2003/3143)

Case: *IR Commrs v Blott* [1921] 2 AC 171

Other Material: *Statements of Practice* SP A8 and SP 4/94

Tax Reporter: ¶743-000ff.

3805   What is a 'distribution' for tax purposes?

Although any detailed discussion of what is meant by a distribution would require an excursion into the world of company law, it is necessary to have, at least, a basic definition in order to understand their tax treatment. Distributions include those matters set out below.

(1)   Any dividend paid by the company, including a capital dividend.

(2)   Any other distribution out of assets of the company (whether in cash or otherwise) in respect of shares in the company, except any part of the distribution which:

   (a)   represents a repayment of capital (see below); or

   (b)   is equal to any new consideration received by the company for the distribution.

'Shares' include stock and any other interest of a member in the company. Something is done in respect of a share if it is done to a person as the current or former holder of a share, or because of a right granted or offer made with reference to the share. Anything done in respect of shares referring to a shareholding at a particular time is done to the then shareholder or to his personal representatives.

'New consideration' is consideration not provided directly or indirectly out of the assets of the company. It does not include amounts retained by the company by capitalising a distribution. So for example, a bonus issue of securities or redeemable shares will not be treated as issued for new consideration and so will be a distribution. A bonus issue of ordinary (non-redeemable) shares is also not for new consideration but it would not normally be out of assets of the company and so not a distribution. A premium paid when shares are issued and later used to pay up share capital may be treated as new consideration. The making of a loan is generally matched by new consideration of the obligation to repay; if the obligation is released, this can result in a charge to tax if the loan is by a close company to its participators (see 4060).

A distribution is made out of assets of a company if the cost falls on the company.

(3) Any redeemable share capital or any security:

(a) issued by the company in respect of shares in the company; or

(b) issued by the company after 5 April 1972 in respect of securities in the company

otherwise than for new consideration.

(4) Any interest or other distribution out of assets of the company in respect of 'non-commercial' securities of the company (but see also 3810). Securities issued by a company are 'non-commercial' if the consideration given by company for the use of the principal represents more than a reasonable commercial return.

(5) Any interest or other distribution out of assets of the company in respect of 'special securities'.

The following securities issued by a company are 'special securities' for these purposes:

(a) securities issued under (3) but not including those issued before 6 April 1965;

(b) securities convertible directly or indirectly into shares in the company, or securities issued after 5 April 1972 with a right to receive shares in or securities of the company (unless the securities are listed or the terms are reasonably comparable with listed securities);

(c) securities which have variable interest according to the results of the business of the company;

(d) securities connected with shares in the company. 'Connected with' means that because of the terms, conditions or rights attached to the securities, it is necessary or advantageous for a person holding them to hold, dispose of or acquire a proportionate holding of the shares; or

(e) in respect of interest, etc. paid after 14 May 1992, 'equity notes' issued by the company and held by an associated company or a company funded in respect thereof by the issuer or an associated company; equity notes are broadly securities with a term of at least 50 years and companies are associated if they are under 75% common control (normal inter-company indebtedness, bank overdrafts, bank deposits and demand loans are not equity notes).

(6) A transfer of assets between a company and its members if the benefit received by the member exceeds any new consideration given in return. The value of any benefit is decided according to its market value. The company is treated as making a distribution of an amount equal to the difference between the two figures. In HMRC's view, 'assets' for these purposes do not include cash.

(7) An issue of paid up share capital after a repayment of share capital. A distribution is treated as made in respect of bonus shares on the later issue. The amount of the distribution is limited to the difference between the total share capital repaid and any amount treated previously as a distribution. Where the bonus share capital is issued after 5 April 1973, this provision is only applicable if:

(a) the issue is made within ten years of redeemable shares; and

(b) the issue is of redeemable share capital.

but the provision applies in full if:

(a) the company is under the control of five or fewer persons;

(b) the company is unlisted;

(c) where the company is controlled by another company, the controller fulfils these conditions.

Limited meaning of distribution in respect of interest

Finance Act 1982 introduced a limitation to the meaning of distribution in respect of interest payments falling within 3805(5)(a)–(d) above, with effect for payments after 8 March 1982.

The limitation was introduced to stop lenders, principally banks, from converting an interest receipt (taxable) into a non-taxable distribution by the simple expedient of linking part of the interest to the results of the borrower. It excludes such interest from being a distribution if it is paid out of the assets of the borrower to another company within the charge to corporation tax (see 3030) and it is not excessive.

A distribution is also still treated as occurring for corporation tax purposes if the company to which the interest or other distribution is paid is entitled to a tax exemption on that payment other than by virtue of the fact that UK company distributions are not chargeable to corporation tax.

Repayment of share capital

Where a company issues any share capital other than by the receipt of new consideration and any amount so paid is not a distribution, then any subsequent distributions within ten years of issue will not be treated as repayments of share capital, except to the extent that those distributions, together with any previous distributions, exceed the amounts so paid up on such shares after that date which are not qualifying distributions.

All shares of the same class are treated as representing the same share capital; and where shares are issued in respect of other shares, or converted into or exchanged for other shares, they are treated as representing the same share capital.

Where share capital is issued at a premium representing new consideration (see (3) above), the premium is part of the share capital to decide whether any repayment is a distribution. Otherwise, any premium paid on the redemption of share capital is not a repayment of share capital and consequently is a distribution.

Legislation: CTA 2010, Pt. 23, Ch. 2

Other Material: Law Society's *Gazette*, 24 February 1993; TAX 5/93

Tax Reporter: ¶743-300ff.

3810 Non-distributions

In defining a distribution for tax purposes (see 3805), a further complication arises because, besides the specific distributions, etc. made by a company which are not treated as distributions for tax purposes (see 3810), there are also a number of general descriptions of transaction which are not regarded as distributions for tax purposes.

Company transactions which are not distributions for tax purposes include:

- distributions made in respect of share capital on a winding-up (see 4240);
- payments made to a charity under a covenant for annual payments over a period which may exceed three years;
- group relief payments (see 3690);
- share or loan interest paid by a registered industrial and provident society;
- building society interest or dividends;
- dividends or bonuses deductible in calculating the tax chargeable on trading profits made by an industrial or provident society;
- taxable stock dividends (see 3800);
- small distributions on the dissolution of an unincorporated association of a social or recreational nature which has not carried on a trade or investment business;

- certain demergers (see 3830);

- certain purchases by a company of its own shares (see 3850).

If one company transfers assets or liabilities to another company, it will not be treated as a distribution if both companies are resident in the UK and neither is a 51% subsidiary of a foreign company and they are not under common control (see 3610) or if both companies are UK resident and one is a 51% subsidiary of the other or both are 51% subsidiaries of another UK resident company.

A distribution does not occur where fully paid preference shares are repaid and those shares existed on 6 April 1965 or were issued after that date for new consideration not derived from ordinary shares and remain fully paid until the date of repayment.

Legislation: CTA 2010, Pt. 23, Ch. 3

Tax Reporter: ¶743-600 and ¶743-800

Demergers

3830 Demergers which are not distributions

A 'demerger' is a transaction whereby trading activities carried on by a single company or group are divided so that they are carried on by two or more companies not belonging to the same group or by two or more independent groups.

If a company makes a distribution to facilitate a demerger, that distribution is exempt from the usual tax treatment and it is an 'exempt distribution' (see 3810). However, this exemption is hedged by numerous conditions and exclusions which must be considered at some length to acquire a full understanding of its application. There is a corresponding chargeable gains deferral for the shareholders.

Conditions for exemption

A distribution will not qualify for exemption unless it is one of the following.

(1) A distribution consisting of a transfer of shares by a company to all or any of its members of shares in one or more companies which are its 75% subsidiaries. The shares must be irredeemable and constitute the whole or substantially the whole of the distributing company's holding of the ordinary share capital of the subsidiary. The distribution must confer the whole or substantially the whole of the distributing company's voting rights in the subsidiary. The distributing

company must, after the distribution, be either a trading company or the holding company of a trading group. The latter condition does not apply where the transfer relates to two or more 75% subsidiaries of the distributing company and that company is dissolved without any net assets remaining after the distribution which are available for distribution in a winding up.

(2) A distribution consisting of the transfer by the distributing company to one or more other companies of a trade or shares in one or more companies which are 75% subsidiaries of the distributing company. Before this can apply:

(a) if a trade is transferred, the distributing company must either not retain any interest or retain only a minor interest in that trade;

(b) if shares in a subsidiary are transferred, they must constitute the whole or substantially the whole of the distributing company's voting rights in the subsidiary;

(c) the only or main activity of the transferee company after the distribution must be the carrying on of a trade or the holding of shares transferred to it;

(d) shares issued by the transferee company must not be redeemable, must constitute the whole of the issued ordinary share capital and must confer most of the voting rights in that company;

(e) the distributing company must, after the distribution, be either a trading company or the holding company of a trading group. This is not applicable if there are two or more transferee companies, each of which has shares in a separate 75% subsidiary of the distributing company transferred to it and the distributing company is dissolved without any net assets available for distribution in a winding-up after the distribution.

Further conditions require the distributing company, its subsidiaries and the transferee companies to be 'UK-resident' (see 214) at the time of the distribution and a subsidiary whose shares are transferred to be either a trading company or the holding company of a trading group at that time.

For distributions made on or after 11 November 2009, this requirement is replaced with a requirement that the companies must be resident in an EU member state (*Corporation Tax (Implementation of the Mergers Directive) Regulations* 2009 (SI 2009/2797)).

The distribution must be made wholly or mainly for the purpose of benefiting some or all of the trading activities which before the distribution are carried on by a single company or group and after the distribution will be carried on by two or more companies or groups.

Ineligible distribution

A distribution will not be eligible for exemption if it forms part of a scheme or arrangement whose main purpose is:

- to avoid tax;

- to make a chargeable payment or what would be a chargeable payment if any company taking part were unquoted (i.e. not listed) (see 3835);

- for any person or persons other than members of the distributing company to acquire control of that company or another company in the same group; or

- to enable trading to cease or the business to be sold after the distribution.

75% subsidiaries

If a company is a 75% subsidiary of another company, the group to which the distributing company belongs when the distribution occurs must be a trading group. That distribution must be followed by one or more distributions which result in a member of the holding company of the group, to which the distributing company belonged at the time of the distribution, becoming a member of one of the following:

- the transferee company to which a trade was transferred by the distributing company;

- the subsidiary whose shares were transferred by the distributing company; or

- a company of which the company is a 75% subsidiary.

By concession, relief is still available if the company retains, after the distribution, sufficient funds to meet the cost of liquidation and to cover what will usually be the negligible amount of share capital remaining. The concession only applies where the company retains no more than a negligible amount of share capital.

Legislation: TCGA 1992, s. 192; CTA 2010, Pt. 23, Ch. 5

Other Material: *Statement of Practice* SP 13/80

Tax Reporter: ¶743-950ff.

3835 Chargeable payments made after an exempt distribution

Where, after a demerger, a chargeable payment is made less than five years after the exempt distribution is made (see 3830), the amount paid is treated as income chargeable to tax under miscellaneous income or an annual sum payable otherwise than out of profits or gains charged to income tax, except where the payment is a transfer of money's worth. Where appropriate, that amount is also treated as a distribution which is not deductible for corporation tax purposes. It may also be deemed to be a payment which cannot be a repayment of capital.

A 'chargeable payment' embraces the transfer of money's worth including the assumption of a liability and is any of the following:

- a payment which is not made for bona fide commercial reasons; or

- a payment which forms part of a scheme or arrangement whose main purpose is to avoid tax.

Any such payment must also be:

- a payment made by a company concerned in an exempt distribution directly or indirectly to a member of that company or of any other company concerned in the distribution;

- a payment connected with the shares of that company; or

- a payment which is not a distribution or an exempt distribution or made to any other company which belongs to the same group as the company making the payment.

Chargeable payments and unquoted companies

If an unquoted company (i.e. one which is not listed) is concerned with an exempt distribution, a chargeable payment will include any payment made by or to another person under a scheme or arrangement made with the unquoted company. This only applies if the unquoted company is under the control of no more than five persons and not under the sole control of a company which is not itself under the control of fewer than five persons.

Legislation: CTA 2010, s. 1088, 1089 and 1090

Tax Reporter: ¶744-300

Purchase of own shares

3850 Purchase by an unquoted trading company of its shares

The *Companies Act* 2006, Pt. 18 provides a system whereby a limited company can buy back its own shares out of distributable profits or proceeds from a new share issue. A payment made to shareholders in this way would normally constitute a distribution (see 3800 and 3805) but for a corporate vendor would still be taken into account in the capital gains calculation (see 3400 and 5890).

Certain payments by a company on the redemption, repayment or purchase of its own shares are not treated as distributions by the company. The company must be an unquoted company (i.e. one which is neither listed, nor a 51% subsidiary of a listed company) and a trading company or the holding company of a trading group.

There are two sets of circumstances in which the tax treatment following such purchase applies. Either the purchase, redemption or repayment is made wholly or mainly for the purpose of benefiting a trade carried on by the company or by any of its 75% subsidiaries, or the whole of the payment is applied by the recipient in meeting an inheritance tax liability arising on death (see below).

Legal expenses incurred are not likely to be deductible (see 2068).

Payment for benefit of trade

The redemption, repayment or purchase must be made wholly or mainly to benefit the company's trade or that of any of its 75% subsidiaries (see 3610).

It must not form part of a scheme or arrangement set up mainly to allow the share owner to participate in the company's profits without receiving a dividend or to avoid tax.

If the inspector has reason to believe that the payment by the company does form part of a scheme, he may require the company to supply him with a declaration in writing whether or not such a scheme exists. The company must also supply any other information the inspector may reasonably require to decide whether there is a scheme or arrangement and whether the payment is to benefit the trade of the company. The company has at least 60 days to comply with this requirement, or any longer time which the inspector specifies.

Discharge of inheritance tax liability

The whole or substantially the whole of the payment must be used by the person who receives it to discharge a liability for inheritance tax he has incurred on a death within two years after that death. The payment will still be treated as a distribution if the recipient could have settled the tax liability from some other source without undue hardship.

Other conditions

There are further rules (see 3855 and 3885) to be complied with before payments by a company to purchase its own shares can be exempted from treatment as a distribution.

Legislation: CTA 2010, s. 1033

Other Material: ICAEW Technical Release, TR 745; *Statement of Practice* SP 2/82; HMRC helpsheet for advance clearances at *http://tinyurl.com/ ps5plke*

Tax Reporter: ¶744-550ff.

3855 Vendors qualifying for relief on buy-back of shares

In order for a purchase of its own shares by a company not to involve a distribution (see 3850), the person selling the shares or his nominee where applicable must be 'resident' (see 213 and 214) and, in the case of an individual, etc. 'ordinarily resident' (see 216) in the UK in the year of assessment when the payment is made; if that person is a personal representative, his residence is taken as that of the deceased immediately before his death.

The vendor must also have owned the shares for five years prior to and ending with the date of sale.

Where the vendor acquired the shares as a beneficiary under a will, he must have owned the shares for a period of three years ending with the date of purchase; any period when the shares were owned by the deceased is treated as a period of ownership by the vendor.

If the vendor acquired shares of the same class at different times, the shares acquired earlier are taken into account before those acquired later; any previous disposal of shares of the same class is treated as a disposal of the later rather than the earlier acquired shares.

Legislation: CTA 2010, s. 1034–1036

Tax Reporter: ¶744-750 and ¶744-800

3860 Required reduction of vendor's interest in company on buy-back

In relation to the vendor (see 3855) of shares in a company to that company, if the vendor owns shares in the company immediately after the repurchase, etc. is made, his interest (or the interest of his associates: see 3875) as a shareholder must be substantially reduced to qualify for relief from normal distribution treatment (see 3850); for group holdings see (3865).

A vendor's interest will only be treated as substantially reduced if the total nominal value of the shares owned by him immediately after the purchase expressed as a fraction of the issued share capital of the company at that time does not exceed 75% of the same fraction prior to the purchase (see, however, 3870).

Example

The issued share capital of Brown Ltd comprises 1,000 ordinary shares of £1 each. Mr Brown owns 400 of these shares with the remaining 600 being held by unconnected parties.

If Brown Ltd acquires 100 of Mr Brown's shares, Mr Brown will have retained 300 shares and the company's issue share capital will be 900.

Mr Brown's interest will have fallen from 40% to $33\frac{1}{3}$%, which is less than a one-quarter reduction. In order to attain the necessary reduction, Mr Brown must dispose of at least 143 shares to Brown Ltd. This is determined by using the formula below.

$$R = (A \times B) / (4B - 3A)$$

where:

R   is the minimum number of shares needed to achieve a substantial reduction;

A   is the nominal value (before the sale) of the vendor's shares;

B   is the nominal value (before the sale) of the company's issued share capital.

Thus:

$$(400 \times 1,000) / (4,000 - 1,200) = 400,000 / 2,800 = 143 \text{ shares}$$

Legislation: CTA 2010, s. 1037

Tax Reporter: ¶744-850

3865   Required reduction of vendor's interest in group on buy-back

A company making a purchase may be a member of a group immediately before the purchase and then, immediately after the purchase, the vendor may own shares of one or more other group members, or alternatively, after the purchase, the vendor may own shares of the company making the purchase and immediately before he may have owned shares of other group members. In either of these circumstances, the vendor's interest as a shareholder in the group must be substantially reduced (or the interests of its associates: see 3875). For present purposes, a *group* means a company which has one or more 51% subsidiaries, but is not itself a 51% subsidiary of any other company, plus all its subsidiaries; there are certain rules to prevent a company leaving the group artificially.

Ascertainment of vendor's interest

The vendor's interest as a shareholder in a group is ascertained by the following steps.

(1) Express the total nominal value of the shares owned by him in each relevant company as a fraction of the issued share capital of the company.

(2) Add the fractions together.

(3) Divide the result by the total number of relevant companies including any in which he owns no shares.

Example

A group of companies is made up of five members.

Company A has issued share capital of 50,000 £1 shares

Company B has issued share capital of 100,000 £1 shares

Company C has issued share capital of 75,000 £1 shares

Company D has issued share capital of 60,000 £1 shares

Company E has issued share capital of 50,000 £1 shares

$$\text{V owns} \quad 20,000 \text{ shares in A} = \text{fraction } \frac{20,000}{50,000} = \frac{2}{5}$$

$$30,000 \text{ shares in B} = \text{fraction } \frac{30,000}{100,000} = \frac{3}{10}$$

$$6,000 \text{ shares in D} = \text{fraction } \frac{6,000}{60,000} = \frac{1}{10}$$

$$25,000 \text{ shares in E} = \text{fraction } \frac{25,000}{50,000} = \frac{1}{2}$$

Add fractions together:

$$\frac{2}{5} + \frac{3}{10} + \frac{1}{10} + \frac{1}{2} = \frac{13}{10}$$

> *Divide* by total group members:
>
> $\dfrac{13}{10} \div 5 = \dfrac{13}{50} = 26\% =$ vendor's interest in group

The vendor's interest as a shareholder in a group will be substantially reduced only if it does not exceed 75% of the corresponding interest immediately before the purchase. In the last example, this would mean that V's interest after a purchase by a group member must not exceed 75% of 26%, i.e. 19.5% of his interest before purchase.

Legislation: CTA 2010, s. 1039 and 1040

Tax Reporter: ¶744-850

3870 Buy-back where continued economic ownership by vendor

A buy-back of shares will not qualify for non-distribution treatment (see 3850) if the vendor's interest in the group is not substantially reduced (see 3865) and it will not be considered to be so reduced where he would be entitled to a significant share of the profits if every company distributed all its profits available for distribution immediately after the purchase. To be significant that share, when expressed as a fraction of the total distributable profits, must exceed 75% of the corresponding fraction immediately before the purchase. If a person is entitled to receive a fixed amount from the company making the purchase, he is treated as being entitled to that same amount if the company made a distribution immediately after the purchase.

Profits available for distribution

Profits available for distribution are a company's accumulated and realised profits not previously used in a distribution or capitalisation less its accumulated realised losses if they have not already been written off in a reduction or realisation of capital.

The amount of profits available for distribution is assumed for present purposes to be increased by £100 plus, where a person is entitled to a fixed periodic distribution (see 3805), a sum equal to the amount of that distribution.

Legislation: CTA 2010, s. 1038 and 1041

Tax Reporter: ¶744-850

3875   Buy-back where vendor's associates continue to hold shares

If a vendor's 'associate' (see 4025) owns shares of the company immediately after the purchase, their combined interests as shareholders must be substantially reduced to obtain non-distribution treatment on a buy-back (see 3850); the reduction is calculated as for the vendor (see 3860). This may be relaxed in relation to a vendor who agrees to the purchase in order for another vendor to satisfy the condition.

Legislation: CTA 2010, s. 1037(2), 1039(4) and 1043

Tax Reporter: ¶744-850

3880   Buy-back where vendor remains connected with company

A payment to purchase a company's own shares will not be exempt from treatment as a company distribution (see 3850) if it is only made as part of a scheme or arrangement designed to give, or which is likely to give, the vendor or his associate interests in the company which prevent him from satisfying the conditions for exemption or if the vendor remains 'connected with the company'.

Legislation: CTA 2010, s. 1042

Tax Reporter: ¶744-900

3885   HMRC approval in advance of buy-back

It is possible for a company wishing to redeem shares to apply in writing to the Board for its approval of the redemption. The application must give full details of the relevant transactions and the Board has 30 days after receiving the application to request further details. If the company does not provide these within 30 days, the Board need not go any further with the application. Otherwise, the Board has 30 days in which to give its decision whether the payment will be treated as exempt from being a distribution or not. This 30-day period runs from either the date of receipt of the application or the date the company complies with the Board's request for further details, whichever is applicable.

If the company fails to give all relevant details, the Board's decision may be void.

Legislation: CTA 2010, s. 1044 and 1045

Tax Reporter: ¶744-950

3900 Distributions paid on or after 1 July 2009

A number of significant changes were made to the taxation of distributions received by UK companies by FA 2009. The changes were made as a result of the Government's review of the taxation of foreign profits. For most companies, the most important of these changes was the replacement of the exemption for UK distributions, and the credit system for the taxation of foreign dividends, with a broad exemption applying to UK and foreign dividends received by companies. The changes were introduced by CTA 2009, Pt. 9A as inserted by FA 2009, s. 34 and Sch. 14, and apply to distributions received on or after 1 July 2009.

Although Pt. 9A has the effect of removing most distributions from the charge to corporation tax on income, it begins by applying that charge. Distributions are then removed from the charge to corporation tax on income if they are exempt. As originally enacted, Pt. 9A did not apply to distributions of a capital nature but *Finance (No. 3) Act* 2010 amended the legislation (retrospectively with effect from 1 July 2009) so that all company distributions that are distributions for tax purposes now fall within Pt. 9A irrespective of whether they are income or capital distributions. Matters that are specifically regarded for tax purposes as *not* being distributions fall outside the scope of Pt. 9A and will be taxed according to the rules applying to chargeable gains. The most commonly met examples will be distributions in respect of share capital on a winding up and repurchase by a company if its own shares (in the latter case, if certain conditions are met – see 3850).

For capital gains purposes, a capital distribution is defined as a distribution from a company which is not treated as income for income tax purposes or, in the case of a company, not treated as income for corporation tax purposes. It is now specifically provided that a distribution that would be taxable under Pt. 9A were it not exempt, is to be treated as income for corporation tax purposes and therefore not a capital distribution for the purposes of corporation tax on chargeable gain. The definition of capital distribution for the purposes of corporation tax on chargeable gains is therefore now effectively limited to those company distributions that are outside the scope of Pt. 9A, typically because they are not distributions for tax purposes (for example, distributions in respect of share capital in a winding up and some repurchases by a company of its own shares).

The rules for exempting distributions received by small companies are distinct from the rules for medium and large companies. The result in each case is that the great majority of distributions will be exempt from corporation tax.

Distribution received by a small company

For a distribution received by a small company to be exempt, the following conditions must be met:

(a) the payer is a resident of (and only of) the UK or a qualifying territory at the time that the distribution is received;

(b) the distribution is not of a kind mentioned in paragraph (4) or (5) of 3805;

(c) no deduction is allowed to a resident of any territory outside the UK under the law of that territory in respect of the distribution; and

(d) the distribution is not made as part of a tax advantage scheme.

A qualifying territory is a territory with which the UK has a double taxation treaty that includes a non-discrimination provision in a standard form.

A company is defined as a 'small company' in an accounting period if it is in that period a micro or small enterprise, as defined in the Annex to Commission Recommendation 2003/361/EC of 6 May 2003. That is a company with less than 50 employees or has a turnover of balance sheet total not exceeding €10,000,000. But a company is not a 'small company' in an accounting period if it is at any time in that period an open-ended investment company, an authorised unit trust scheme, an insurance company, or a friendly society.

Distributions received by medium and large companies

A distribution received by a company which is not small will be exempt if:

- it is not of a kind mentioned in paragraph (4) or (5) of 3805;

- no deduction is allowed to a resident of any territory outside the UK under the laws of that territory; and

- it falls into an exempt class.

The exempt classes are:

- dividends or other distributions paid by the distributing company to the controlling company;

- distributions paid on non-redeemable ordinary shares;

- dividends from portfolio holdings where there is an interest of less than 10%;

- dividends derived from transactions not designed to reduce tax, or if there is a reduction of tax, the reduction is minimal or not the main purpose of the transaction;

- dividends paid from shares which would be classified as debt under GAAP which means either International Accounting Standard (IAS) 32 or the UK equivalent Financial Reporting Standard (FRS) 25.

The exemptions are subject to a number of anti-avoidance provisions which largely apply where there is a tax avoidance motive.

A company can elect that a distribution which qualifies as exempt be treated as taxable. This would be advantageous where an exemption distribution would lead to a higher rate of withholding tax or where dividends can only be taken into account for the purposes of the CFC acceptable distribution policy exemption (see 4155) if they are subject to tax. The election must be made within two years of the end of the accounting period in which the distribution is received.

Legislation: CTA 2009, Pt. 9A; FA 2009, s. 34, Sch. 14

Tax Reporter: ¶745-300ff.

Qualifying and non-qualifying distributions

3910 Importance of qualifying nature of distribution

Once a company has decided that a transaction which it has made is a distribution for tax purposes (see 3805), it must perform yet another task before it can deal with and account for the payment. It must consider whether that distribution is a qualifying or a non-qualifying distribution. This will determine whether the person receiving the distribution is entitled to an associated tax credit.

A person receiving a non-qualifying distribution or not entitled to a tax credit may be liable to higher rate income tax on the amount or value of the distribution; there is relief for a subsequent repayment of share capital constituting a distribution.

Legislation: CTA 2010, s. 1109

Tax Reporter: ¶747-550

3915 What is a 'qualifying distribution'?

All distributions of a company are 'qualifying distributions' except:

- any bonus security or any bonus redeemable share capital issued by a company after 5 November 1972 in respect of securities of the company to the extent that it is not referable to new consideration;

- a distribution by company A of any bonus share capital or bonus security of company B received directly or indirectly by company A where the bonus security is a non-qualifying distribution of company B.

Legislation: CTA 2010, s. 1136

Tax Reporter: ¶747-150

3920 Treatment of qualifying distributions

From 6 April 1999, where a UK-resident company makes a distribution, and the person receiving the distribution is another UK-resident company or a UK-resident person other than a company, the recipient is entitled to a tax credit. The value of the tax credit is determined in accordance with the fraction in force at the time the distribution was made. Since 6 April 1999, the fraction has been one-ninth.

> **Example**
>
> Sharing Ltd pay a dividend of 90 pence per share in July 2008. In the hands of the recipient, there is an associated tax credit of 10 pence per share (90 pence × $1/_9$).

If a company makes a qualifying distribution (see 3915) to another UK-resident company, the company which receives the distribution is entitled to a tax credit. Following the abolition of ACT with effect from 6 April 1999, the tax credit is fixed at 10% of the dividend plus the tax credit.

A non-resident company may be entitled to an amount (often known as a 'tax credit') under the appropriate 'double tax treaty' (see 1780) calculated as a portion of the tax credit given to UK companies less a withholding of income tax.

An individual is treated as receiving an amount of income equal to the cash dividend and the tax credit (see 1350). That tax credit is only payable in limited circumstances after 5 April 1999.

The distribution plus the tax credit in the hands of a recipient company is called 'franked investment income'.

Franked investment income does not include group income, either:

- before 6 April 1999, where the group or consortium has elected to pay dividends within the group without ACT being paid (see 3665); or

- after 5 April 1999 and the abolition of ACT, where the distributions have been made by members of the same group.

Rectification of excessive

An inspector may make any necessary assessments to rectify an excessive offset or payment of tax credit, including interest thereon.

Legislation: CTA 2010, s. 1109, 1110, 1126

Tax Reporter: ¶747-550

3925 Qualifying distributions in the hands of a dealer

With effect for distributions and manufactured payments made after 1 July 1997, the legislation recognises the principle that where shares in UK companies are held as trading assets, rather than as investments, distributions relating to those shares should be treated as trading income. The rules ensure that *all* UK distributions (and manufactured payments representing such distributions) received by dealers are chargeable to corporation tax. (Prior to 6 April 1999, this was net of their tax credit, which was available to set against franked payments.)

Legislation: CTA 2009, s. 130

Tax Reporter: ¶714-750

Transfer pricing

3950 Introduction

The price charged between associated enterprises on the transfer of property or services is known as a transfer price. Due to the relationship between the parties to the transfer, the transfer price may not be the price that would be charged between independent enterprises. Where this is the case, profits taxable in one jurisdiction may be higher, and profits taxable in another jurisdiction may be lower, than would otherwise have been the case. To ensure that the taxing rights of each jurisdiction are protected, and to avoid double taxation, the OECD member countries have adopted the arm's length principle under which taxable profits are calculated by reference to the price which would have been charged between independent enterprises. It should be noted that the transfer pricing regime is not confined to transactions across borders.

As an OECD member country, the UK has introduced legislation which is based on, and must be construed with, the OECD's guidelines on transfer pricing (TIOPA 2010, Pt. 4). The legislation is built round a basic rule; where associated enterprises are party to a transaction other than on an arm's-length basis, and that transaction has the potential to give rise to a UK tax advantage for one of the parties, the taxable profits and losses of that party are to be calculated as if the transaction had been made on an arm's length basis (see 3952). Exemptions apply (see 3954), most notably for enterprises which are not large, and provision is made for compensating adjustments (subject to anti-avoidance rules) and balancing payments. Although transfer pricing largely concerns companies carrying on business internationally as part of a group, it is not confined to corporate bodies, nor to transactions across national frontiers.

HMRC have published an amended technical note on compensating adjustment rules, following consultation on proposals to counter avoidance. Legislation giving effect to the changes came into force on 25 October 2013 and under the new regime, persons (other than companies) within the charge to income tax will be prevented from claiming a compensating adjustment where the counterparty is a person within the charge to corporation tax.

The legislation is silent on how to determine the arm's length price of a transaction and instead reference must be made to the Guidelines published by the OECD (see 3956). In most cases, the arm's length price will be based on comparable uncontrolled transactions, being transactions undertaken between independent enterprises in similar circumstances to the transaction between associated enterprises. Where this is not possible, perhaps because comparable transactions cannot be identified, it may be appropriate to use one of the other methods recommended by the OECD. Whichever method is used, documentation in support of the transfer price should be prepared and maintained.

HMRC have produced very useful guidance on their approach and this has recently been rewritten to ensure that it has a logical structure and presents a consistent approach. The old guidance (INTM430000) has been withdrawn and replaced by new pages starting at INTM410000. A destination table is at INTM489030.

Legislation: TIOPA 2010, Pt. 4

Other Material: HMRC's *International Manual* INTM410000ff; the 2010 edn of the OECD's *Transfer Pricing Guidelines for Multinational Enterprises and Tax Administrations* (available from the OECD bookshop which can be accessed here www.oecd.org)

Tax Reporter: ¶767-000ff.

3952 The basic rule

The basic transfer-pricing rule is set out in TIOPA 2010, Pt. 4, Ch 1 and can be expressed in the following simple terms: where associated enterprises are party to a transaction other than on an arm's-length basis, and that transaction has the potential to give rise to a UK tax advantage for one of the parties, the taxable profits and losses of that party are to be calculated as if the transaction had been made on an arm's length basis. However, it should be noted that the rule is 'basic' in that it provides the foundation on which the UK's transfer pricing code is built; it is not *basic* in terms of expression or scope. There can be no substitute for looking at the rule in detail and gaining an understanding of the terminology used (key terms are shown in quotation marks below).

The basic transfer-pricing rule applies where all of the following conditions are met:

(1) a provision ('the actual provision') has been made or imposed between any two persons ('the affected persons') by means of a transaction or a 'series of transactions';

(2) at the time the actual provision was made or imposed (or within the six-month period beginning on the date on which the actual provision was made or imposed where the actual provision related to financial arrangements) either:

   (a) one of the affected persons was 'directly or indirectly participating in the management, control or capital' of the other; or

   (b) the same person (or persons) was directly or indirectly participating in the management, control or capital of each of the affected persons;

(3) the actual provision differs from the provision which would have been made had the persons been independent enterprises ('the arm's length provision'); and

(4) the actual provision confers 'a potential advantage' in relation to UK tax on one or both of the affected persons.

Where all of the above conditions are met, the effect of the basic transfer-pricing rule is that 'profits and losses' of the 'advantaged person' or persons are to be calculated for tax purposes as if the arm's length provision had been made or imposed instead of the actual provision. This is subject to a number of exceptions discussed at 3954.

Where an adjustment is made as a result of applying the basic transfer pricing rule, the adjustment may be made by way of discharge or repayment of tax, by the modification of any assessment, or otherwise.

Although the basic transfer pricing rule applies with regard to the profits and losses of the advantaged person only, the 'disadvantaged person' can claim a compensating adjustment where certain conditions are met. Alternatively, a balancing payment could be made or, in certain situations, an election can be made for the disadvantaged person to pay the advantaged person's additional tax liability.

3954   Exemptions from the basic rule

However, the basic transfer-pricing rule does not apply:

- where the exemptions for small or medium-sized enterprises (SMEs) or dormant companies provided by TIOPA 2010, Pt. 4, Ch. 3 apply (see below);

- with regard to exchange gains or losses on loan relationships or derivative contracts;

- with regard to the calculation of a capital allowance or balancing charge (there being capital allowances provisions which import market value for sales to a connected person, etc.);

- with regard to the calculation of any chargeable gain or allowable loss (there being provisions in TCGA 1992 which impose market value in some instances); and

- with regard to transactions and deemed transactions in oil treated as made at market value by any of sections ITTOIA 2005, s. 225F–225J or CTA 2010, s. 281–285.

Dormant companies

The basic rule does not apply where the 'potentially advantaged person', being the affected person expected to benefit from the actual provision, is a company that was dormant throughout the three months ended on 31 March 2004, or throughout the accounting period ended on 31 March 2004 where there was such a period, and has continued to be dormant at all times since. The exemption will not apply where a company which was dormant before 1 April 2004 becomes active after that date only to return to being dormant.

SMEs

The basic rule is also disapplied where the company is a SME. The definition of SME for this purpose is based on Commission Recommendation 2003/361/EC. A company will be a SME for a period if it stays below the headcount limit (250) and has either a turnover of less than €50m or a balance sheet total of less than €43m.

Where the enterprise is an autonomous enterprise, the staff headcount and financial tests will be met by reference to the accounts of that enterprise only. Where an enterprise is a partner or linked enterprise, it will be necessary to take account of the headcount, turnover and balance sheet totals of other enterprises. Broadly:

- an enterprise is an autonomous enterprise if it is not a partner enterprise or a linked enterprise;

- enterprises are partner enterprises if they are not linked enterprises and if one holds 25% or more of the capital or voting rights of the other (either on its own or jointly with other linked enterprises); and

- enterprises are linked enterprises if one is able to exercise control over the other.

The SME exemption does not apply where:

(1) the SME so elects;

(2) the other affected person, or a party to a relevant transaction, is a resident of a non-qualifying territory at the time the actual provision is made or imposed; and

(3) in the case of medium-sized enterprises only, where the medium-sized enterprise receives a transfer pricing notice.

A 'non-qualifying territory' is a territory with which the UK does not have double taxation arrangements which include a non-discrimination provision (see INTM432112 for a list of arrangements which do include a non-discrimination provision).

3955 Disposal of stock other than in trade and of intangible assets

The legislation relating to the transfer of trading stock and intangible assets is being amended to ensure that disposals made other than in the normal course of business are brought into account for tax purposes at full open market value. The amendments are intended to stop corporate groups from using a transfer pricing override to manipulate the value of assets in intergroup transfers. The measure will have effect for transfers of trading stock or intangible fixed assets made on or after 8 July 2015. The proposed revisions will ensure that transactions between related parties can remain subject to further adjustment required under the market value rules in CTA 2009 or ITTOIA 2005 and are intended to ensure that between them, the amended rules will bring into overall charge an amount not less than the market value of what has been transferred.

3956 Determining an arm's length price

The arm's length principle is the transfer pricing standard which the OECD member counties have agreed should be used for tax purposes. The authoritative statement of the arm's length principle can be found in Art. 9 of the OECD Model Tax Convention, where it is provided that:

> '[When] conditions are made or imposed between ... two [associated] enterprises in their commercial or financial relations which differ from those which would be made between independent enterprises, then any profits

which would, but for those conditions, have accrued to one of the enterprises, but, by reason of those condition, have not so accrued, may be included in the profits of that enterprise and taxed accordingly.'

The UK's transfer pricing legislation is based on, and in most cases must be construed with, the arm's length principle as expressed in the OECD model and applied by the OECD's transfer pricing guidelines. In addition, the question of how to determine the arm's length price is largely left to the OECD guidance, which sets out a number of acceptable methods. For accounting periods beginning on or after 1 April 2011, the transfer pricing guidelines are the OECD's Transfer Pricing Guidelines for Multinational Enterprises and Tax Administrations as approved on 22 July 2010 (the 'Guidelines'). For earlier periods, the Guidelines in place before 1 May 1998 applied (the '1998 Guidelines').

The Guidelines recognise five transfer pricing methods, grouped as follows:

(1) **traditional transaction methods**:

(a) **comparable uncontrolled price method**. This method requires a comparison between the controlled transaction and 'a comparable uncontrolled transaction in comparable circumstances';

(b) **resale price method**. This method starts with the price at which the product is sold to an external party (the resale price) and works backwards to arrive at the arm's length price for the original sale between the associated enterprises; and

(c) **cost plus method**. Under this method the arm's length price is the total of the costs incurred by the supplier plus an appropriate mark-up; and

(2) **transactional profit methods**:

(a) **profit split method**. Under this method profits are split between the associated enterprises on the basis of the functions performed by each and in linc with the division that would have been expected by independent enterprises; and

(b) **transactional net margin method**. Under this method the net profit relative to an appropriate base (e.g. cost, sales) that a taxpayer realises from a controlled transaction is compared to the margin enjoyed by the same enterprise in uncontrolled transactions or, where this is not possible, the margin enjoyed by other enterprises in uncontrolled transactions.

Although it is possible to use a method other than one described in the Guidelines, this should only be the case where the method chosen is more appropriate to the facts and circumstances of the case. OECD guidance is that taxpayers using such a method must be prepared to explain why the method was used in preference to an OECD-recognised model.

Preference is given in the Guidelines to the traditional transaction models which are regarded as 'the most direct means of establishing whether conditions in the commercial and financial relations between associated companies are arm's length'. Where a traditional transaction method and a transactional profit method can each be expected to give a reliable result, the traditional transaction method should be used in preference to the transactional profit method. However, it is acknowledged in the Guidelines that there will be cases where it is more appropriate to use a transactional profit method (for example, where the parties engage in highly integrated activities or where they make unique contributions to the transaction).

There has been a softening in the OECD's approach to the use of the transactional profit methods. In the 1998 Guidelines, use of these methods was restricted to 'cases of last resort'. Although preference for the traditional transaction methods remains, it is now accepted that a transactional profit method can provide a better result in some cases and in particular where appropriate comparables are difficult to find.

Close companies

4000 Introduction to close companies

Alongside the sometimes complex provisions which govern the taxation of companies generally, there are further special provisions which relate to the taxation of close companies.

When a company is closely controlled by a few persons, it is possible for them to reduce the tax payable on the profits made. The directors may be content to plough back the company's profits into the business, take some as directors' remuneration and make no distributions; alternatively they may take cash out of the company by way of loan or may receive non-cash benefits. Since 95% of all companies in England are small private companies, the Government takes the view that such artificial influences are unsatisfactory and the purpose of the legislation is to ensure that such persons do not gain a material advantage.

Certain investment-type close companies (close investment-holding companies) are prevented from using the small profits rate (formerly, small companies' rate) of corporation tax.

There are also special rules governing the tax treatment of gains realised by non-resident close companies (see 5720).

Before setting out how the legislation applies, it is important to define certain terms which occur throughout the provisions so that they can be understood.

Legislation: CTA 2010, s. 34

Tax Reporter: ¶776-000

Key terms

4005   What is a 'close company'?

A 'close company' is a company which is 'UK-resident' and not otherwise excluded (see below) which is controlled by five or fewer participators or by participators who are directors or a company over half of whose assets could be distributed on a notional winding-up between five or fewer participators or director participators (for the meaning of 'participator' and 'director', see 4010 and 4015).

Where a non-resident company would be a close company if it were resident in the UK, any UK company which controls it is deemed to be a close company for the purposes of this rule.

Exclusions

If a company has allotted ordinary share capital to the public which carries 35% of its total voting power, it will not be treated as a close company if those shares have been dealt in and listed by a recognised stock exchange (as defined) in the last 12 months. A stock exchange listing alone is not enough. The shares must be dealt in and held by the public. Despite this exception, a company will still be regarded as a close company if its principal members control more than 85% of the voting power. Principal members of a company are the five persons who have individual control of the largest percentage of the voting power. Each person must control at least 5%. The voting power exercisable by their nominees and associates and companies under their control is attributable to them.

A company is not deemed to be close if it fulfils the conditions only because it is controlled by or on behalf of the Crown.

A registered industrial and provident society and a building society are not close companies.

If the controlling shareholders of a company are one or more companies which are not close companies, and that company is only treated as a close company if a non-close company is included as one of its five or fewer controlling participators, it may be treated as a non-close company.

This will occur if the company would not be a close company but for the fact that the participators include loan creditors which are companies other than close companies.

Legislation: CTA 2010, s. 439

Tax Reporter: ¶776-350ff.

4010 What is a 'participator' in a close company?

In relation to a 'close company' (see 4005), a 'participator' is any person who has, or is entitled to acquire, share capital or voting rights in the company, a person entitled to participate in distributions by the company, a person entitled to have income or assets of the company applied for his benefit or a 'loan creditor'.

A 'loan creditor' is a creditor in respect of any debt incurred by the company for money borrowed, or for capital assets purchased by the company, or for a right to receive income in favour of the company, or for consideration which was worth substantially less to the company than the amount of the debt. The definition also includes any person who is not a creditor but who has a beneficial interest in any loan capital or debt regarding which another person is a loan creditor.

A banker is not a loan creditor as regards any loan capital or debt issued or incurred by the company for money lent by him in the ordinary course of his business. A person who is not a creditor in respect of, but has a beneficial interest in, any debt or loan capital, is deemed to be a loan creditor to the extent of that interest.

Legislation: CTA 2010, s. 453 and 454

Tax Reporter: ¶776-050.

4015 What is a 'director' of a close company?

In relation to a 'close company' (see 4005), a 'director' is any person who occupies the position of director whatever his title, and any person on whose instructions or directions the directors are accustomed to act, and the manager of a company if he holds or controls 20% of its ordinary share capital either alone or with his associates.

A person is not a director where the company's articles of association allow the appointment of that person as a special, executive or assistant director on condition that such a person shall not be regarded as a member of the company's board or of any committee and shall only attend board meetings at the invitation of the board, and shall have no power to vote.

A person is not a director merely because the directors act upon his professional advice. He must be in the habit of directing company policy and company affairs and the directors should act frequently on those directions.

Legislation: CTA 2010, s. 452

Tax Reporter: ¶776-250.

4020   What is 'control' of a close company?

The tests to determine control of a company so as to make it a close company refer to a single person; control by more than one person applies by aggregation. Except as noted below, a person controls a company if he directly or indirectly controls the company's policies and has power to appoint and dismiss the directors by ordinary resolution in general meeting.

A person is also in control of a company if he is entitled to acquire more than half of its nominal or issued share capital or voting power. Hence, if a person holds convertible debentures in a company he may have potential control if the majority of voting power were to rest in him if the debentures were turned into ordinary shares.

Example

A holds 100 convertible debentures in company X. Each debenture is convertible into five ordinary shares. A would therefore hold 500 ordinary shares if the debentures were converted.

Total ordinary share capital in X is 1,350 shares:

B holds 200 ordinary shares

C holds 100 ordinary shares

D holds 150 ordinary shares

E holds 150 ordinary shares

F holds 50 ordinary shares

Other persons each with less than 50 shares hold the balance of 700 shares.

Therefore, company X is controlled by five or fewer participators.

A controller includes a person who holds or is entitled to acquire issued share capital with a right to receive more than half the company's income if it were all distributed. Amounts payable to loan creditors are not taken into account.

Any person entitled to more than half the company's net assets distributable amongst participators on a winding-up is also a controller.

In determining control, a person is treated as having the rights and powers of his associates.

Legislation: CTA 2010, s. 450

Tax Reporter: ¶776-300

4025　What is an 'associate' of a participator in a close company?

An 'associate' of a participator is:

- any relative or partner of the participator;
- a trustee of a settlement created by the participator or any relative of his;
- where the participator holds trust shares in the company, the trustee of the relevant settlement and, if the participator is a company, any other company interested in the trust; excluded from aggregation with the participator's shares are the personal shares of other beneficiaries of the trust.

Legislation: CTA 2010, s. 448 and 451

Case: *Willingale (HMIT) v Islington Green Investment Co* (1972) 48 TC 547

Tax Reporter: ¶776-150

4030　What is an 'associated company' for close company purposes?

A company is associated with another at a particular time if, at that time or within the past year, one of the companies is or has been in control of the other or both are or have been under the control of the same persons, or where both together would form a group.

Two or more companies are not necessarily associated merely because they are controlled by the same 'loan creditor' (see 4010), provided that the loan creditor is a non-close company or some other bona fide loan creditor. There must be no other connection between the companies.

Legislation: CTA 2010, s. 449

Tax Reporter: ¶776-200

Loans to participators

4040 Charge on loans to participators by close companies

If a company makes a loan to one of its 'participators' (see 4010) or an 'associate' (see 4025) outside the ordinary course of its business, it is chargeable to tax for the accounting period when the advance was made. This rule applies even though the whole or any part of the loan or advance may have been repaid before the charge is raised. However, in such circumstances, the company remains entitled to the proper measure of relief (see 4050). Changes have been made, with effect from 20 March 2013 by *Finance Act* 2013 to deal with loans to partnerships and trusts, arrangements whereby a benefit is conferred on a participator and the repayment rules are abused. A consultation on potentially far reaching changes to the basis for charging tax on loans to participators concluded that no changes should, at present be made (see www. gov.uk/government/consultations/reform-of-close-company-loans-to-participators-rules). The Chartered Institute of Taxation (CIOT) has written to HMRC voicing its disappointment that the Government has decided, without explanation, not to make any further changes following its review. In particular, they are asking HMRC to advise on the reasons for the decision, whether another review is planned once FA 2013 regime has had time to bed in and for an update on whether HMRC guidance at CTM61642 would be amended to reflect HMRC's interpretation of CTA 2010, s. 464C(6).

However, following the changes to the personal tax on dividend income and the abolition of the tax credit, the rate of tax accountable on loans has, from 6 April 2016, been increased from 25% to 32.5%.

The money-lending exemption is really two tests:

(1) the company must carry on the business of lending money in general and not just to a single participator; and

(2) the loan must be in the ordinary course of that business; HMRC's view is that this would not be the case where the size, terms or conditions of the loan differed from those which normally applied.

The rate of charge is fixed at 25% of loans or advances made on or after that date. A consultation document was been issued setting out alternative options to this charge including an annual, non-refundable, charge   (see www.gov.uk/government/consultations/reform-of-close-company-loans-to-participators-rules).

Close companies must notify HMRC of loans to participators, etc. and must notify both chargeability and liability to tax.

Legislation: CTA 2010, s. 455 and 456

Cases: *Steen v Law (Liquidator of International Vending Machines Pty Ltd)* [1964] AC 287; *Earlspring Properties Ltd v Guest (HMIT)* [1995] BTC 274

Tax Reporter: ¶776-900ff.

4045   What is a 'loan' to a participator?

A close company is treated as making a loan to another person if that person incurs a debt to the company or assigns a debt owed to a third person to the company. The amount of the debt is treated as the loan.

Exception

A debt will not be treated as a loan to a participator if it is incurred for the supply of goods or services by the company in the ordinary course of its business. However, this will not apply where either more than six months' credit is given or if a longer credit period than that normally given to the company's customers is given.

Small loans

If the company makes a small loan to a restricted class of participators, it is not chargeable to corporation tax, but there are some conditions which must be fulfilled. A company may make a loan to a director or an employee of up to £15,000 if that person is a full-time employee of the company or its associate who has no material interest in that company.

A person will have a material interest in a company if he or his associate is the beneficial owner of, or can control directly or indirectly, more than 5% of its ordinary share capital or if more than 5% of the company's assets on a notional winding-up could be distributed to him and/or his 'associate' (see 4025).

Legislation: CTA 2010, s. 455(4), 456 and 457

Case: *Grant v Watton (HMIT)* [1999] BTC 85

Tax Reporter: ¶777-000 and ¶777-150

4050   Payment of tax on loan to participator

The tax payable on loans to participators (see 4040) must be paid within nine months after the day after the end of the accounting period.

If the loan is wholly or partly repaid more than nine months after the end of the accounting period in which it was made, relief for the repayment is not given before nine months after the end of the accounting period in which the repayment occurred. However, if the loan is wholly or partly repaid within nine months after the end of the accounting period in which it was made, relief can take effect as soon as the tax falls due, the company having to make its claim within six years after the end of the financial year in which the loan was repaid.

Relief from a charge is extended to include circumstances where the debt in respect of the loan is released or written off, in addition to where it is repaid. Such an event could lead to a refund of any tax paid on the amount of the loan or advance repaid, released or written off. Interest on the refund of such a charge also applies where a loan debt is released or written off and not just when the loan is repaid. This brings the interest provisions into line with the tax repayment provisions.

Legislation: ICTA 1988, s. 826(4); CTA 2010, s. 455(3) and 458

Tax Reporter: ¶776-950

4055 Loans made indirectly to participator

If a close company makes a loan indirectly to one of its participators, it is treated as a loan subject to a corporation tax charge (see 4040).

Example

A close company lends money to a bank which would not normally be chargeable to corporation tax. The bank then makes a loan to one of the company's participators. The loan made by the close company to the bank is, in these circumstances, treated as a loan made directly to the participator.

Where a transaction which might amount to an indirect loan takes place in the ordinary course of the company's business, the rule now being considered does not apply. This is also the case where the loan is treated as part of the total income of the participator (see 4010).

For the purposes of this rule, a participator includes a company receiving a loan in a fiduciary capacity or as a representative, and a non-resident company.

FA 2013 extended the scope of the charge to s. 455 by providing that the following are also within the charge:

(1) Loans made by a close company to an intermediary (an LLP or other partnership).

(2) Loans made by a close company to a trust, where one or more of the trustees or actual/potential beneficiaries is a participator in the company (or an associate of a participator – for example, because the settlor is a participator).

(3) Certain arrangements where close companies transfer value to participators (or their associates), other than by way of loan.

Legislation: CTA 2010, s. 459

Tax Reporter: ¶777-200

4060 Loans to participator written off by a close company

If a close company releases or writes off the whole or part of a debt created by a loan to a participator which is assessed to tax (see 4040), a tax charge may arise. The amount written off or released is grossed up by reference to the dividend ordinary rate (10% for 2011–12) and included in the participator's total income for the year.

For commentary on the consequences for the close company, see 3164.

Legislation: ITTOIA 2005, s. 416

Case: *Collins v Addies (HMIT)* [1992] BTC 532

Tax Reporter: ¶777-050 and ¶777-100

4065 Loans to participator in close company by controlled company

Where a close company 'controls' another company (see 4020) and that other company makes a loan, that loan is treated as if the close company made it in relation to the charge to tax for loans to participators (see 4040).

If a company is controlled by a close company after it makes a loan, the close company is regarded as making the loan immediately after it acquires control.

If there are two or more close companies which control the company making the loan, they are both treated as making the loan in proportion to their interests in the company which they control.

The above rules do not apply where the company making the loan can show that there was no arrangement connecting the making of the loan and the close company acquiring control, or the close company providing funds for the company making the loan.

A close company is deemed to provide funds for a company if it directly or indirectly makes any payment or transfers any property to or releases or satisfies a liability of the company making the loan.

Legislation: CTA 2010, s. 460

Tax Reporter: ¶777-200

4070   Anti-avoidance

Specific anti-avoidance rules have been introduced to counter abusive arrangements and further consultation is expected on further changes. In broad terms, the following additional circumstances will need to be considered:

- where a loan is made by a close company to an intermediary;

- loans made by a close company to a trust where the trustees hold shares in the company or where the trustees are associates of a participator (for example, because the settlor is a participator);

- certain arrangements where close companies transfer value to participators other than by way of loan;

- where a loan to a participator is repaid within nine months of the end of the company's accounting period, a s. 455 charge does not arise. However, companies have sought to avoid the charge by arranging for the loan to be repaid shortly before the nine months expire and then making a new loan shortly afterwards. A new 30-day rule will be introduced to prevent bed and breakfasting in respect of repayments of more than £5,000.

Close investment holding companies

4080   Introduction to close investment-holding companies

Certain close companies which are of an investment nature, close investment-holding companies (CICs), are prevented from benefiting from the small profits rate of corporation tax or marginal relief. This is of little relevance for accounting periods and parts of accounting periods after 31 March 2015 as the standard and small companies rates of corporation tax are the same.

Legislation: CTA 2010, s. 18

Tax Reporter: ¶777-350ff.

4085 Definition of close investment-holding company

All close companies are close investment-holding companies (CICs) unless they satisfy certain requirements.

A company must satisfy any one requirement, although it may also satisfy more than one. In outline, they relate to the following types of company:

- trading companies;

- commercial property investment companies;

- group-holding or group-finance companies;

- administrative co-ordination companies;

- group-service (trade) companies;

- group-service (property investment) companies.

In more detail, to be excepted from being a CIC, a close company must exist wholly or mainly for one or more of the required purposes. The test must be satisfied for each accounting period in point, and throughout the period.

A company in liquidation is normally a CIC, any trade or business which it continues to carry on during its winding up is likely to be incidental to its main purpose of winding up its affairs although in such case its status would be continued for the first accounting period after commencement of the winding up; if trade ceased before the winding up, protected status is not generally applicable.

Legislation: CTA 2010, s. 34

Tax Reporter: ¶777-450

4110 Extended meaning of distribution for close companies

In addition to the normal payments which are treated as distributions by all companies (see 3805), there are additional payments which are artificially treated as distributions by close companies. Such payments cannot be deducted from the company's profits for corporation tax purposes. They are treated as the income of the recipient and subject to a charge to income tax at the appropriate rate (see Key Data).

The payments that are treated as distributions by a close company are any net expenses incurred by the company to provide its participators with accommodation, entertainment, domestic or other services, or other benefits or facilities of whatever nature. A participator includes an associate of a participator, and a participator in a company which controls the company making the payment.

There are certain exceptions to this rule, such as pensions, annuities, lump sum payments or gratuities paid to the spouses, children or dependants of a person which are payable on or as a result of that person's death or retirement, and certain transfers of assets or liabilities between companies which are UK-resident, and where one of the companies is a 51% subsidiary of the other, or where both companies are 51% subsidiaries of a third UK-resident company.

If there are reciprocal arrangements between unconnected close companies to attempt to circumvent a charge to tax, then any payments or facilities provided will be treated as provided to each participator by the close company in which he is himself a participator.

Legislation: CTA 2010, s. 1064

Tax Reporter: ¶776-650ff.

4120   Transfers of value by close companies

Capital gains implications

If a close company transfers an asset, otherwise than to a group member, for consideration less than its market value, the difference between the market value and the consideration is apportioned between the shareholders and reduces the base cost of their shares in the company.

Where the transferee is a participator, the transfer is instead treated as an income distribution or as a capital distribution. Where the transferee is an employee, that amount will be taxed as employment income.

If the transfer is to an employee benefit trust for the benefit of employees of the transferee company, the apportionment to shareholders is of an amount equal to the difference in the consideration paid by the EBT and either the market value of the asset, or, if lower, the acquisition cost of the asset.

Inheritance tax implications

When a transfer of value is made by a close company, the value transferred is apportioned amongst the company's participators although the actual IHT due is primarily payable by the company itself. IHT is charged as though each individual participator has made a transfer of value of the amount apportioned to him. Such transfers are not potentially exempt transfers and so are immediately chargeable to IHT.

In March 1975, HMRC issued a statement of practice in respect of certain close company transactions. This statement clarified the position concerning dividend payments and transfers of assets from a subsidiary company to a parent or sister company as appropriate. In HMRC's view, a dividend paid by a subsidiary company to its parent is not a transfer of value. Similarly HMRC do not feel that they can justifiably treat a transfer of assets between a wholly-owned subsidiary and its parent or between two wholly-owned subsidiaries as a transfer of value.

The value transferred by a close company will be apportioned amongst its participators according to their respective rights and interests in the company immediately before the transfer and, if one of those participators is itself a close company, that amount will be further sub-apportioned. Rights and interests in a company include rights and interests in the assets of the company available for distribution amongst the participators in the event of a winding up or in any other circumstances.

If a disposal of an asset by a close company (the transferor) to another member of the same 'group' gives rise to a transfer of value, then, provided the effect on the rights of the minority participators is small, no amount will be apportioned to those minority participators unless the transferor company is the principal member of the group. Group has the same definition as that for the purposes of chargeable gains (see 3625). A minority participator is a person who is not, and is not a person connected with, a participator of the principal member of the group or of any of the principal company's participators.

No apportionment will be made in the following instances:

(a) if the value transferred is liable to income tax or corporation tax;

(b) if the value is attributable to property outside the UK and the participator is domiciled outside the UK.

In addition, under normal inheritance tax principles, dispositions which are not intended to confer any gratuitous benefit on any person are not transfers of value and so would fall outside these close company provisions. This is likely to remove from the scope of these provisions most transactions undertaken by close companies in the normal course of their trade or business (but see below in relation to HMRC's views on contributions to employee benefit trusts). Similarly, any disposition that is an allowable deduction in computing the company's corporation tax liability is not a transfer of value.

In practice, potential IHT charges can arise in connection with contributions by close companies to employee benefit trusts. Under normal IHT principles, dispositions made by companies into trusts for the benefit of their employees are not transfers of value but this exemption does not apply if any participators owning 5% or more of the share capital can benefit under the trust. Also, since November 2002, a contribution by a company into an employee benefit trust is not deductible for corporation tax purposes in the year in which it is made, but a deduction is often available later when the trust makes payments out to the employees. In HMRC's view, relief from IHT is only available under (b) above to the extent that a deduction is allowable to the company for the accounting period in which the contribution is made. Also, in HMRC's view, it will often be difficult for close companies to argue that there is no intention to confer any gratuitous benefit when making a contribution to an employee benefit trust because, for example, it is common for the beneficiaries of such trusts to include wives, husbands, children and stepchildren of the employee.

HMRC's views in relation to the IHT implications of contributions by close companies to employee benefit trusts is set out in HMRC Brief 49/09.

Legislation: IHTA 1984, s. 12; TCGA 1992, s. 122, 125 and 239(3); CTA 2010, s. 1000(1) and 1020

Tax Reporter: ¶520-290 and ¶603-700.

Controlled foreign companies

4150   Scope of CFC legislation for accounting periods beginning before 1 January 2013

Provisions were introduced in 1984 to prevent UK companies from avoiding UK tax by diverting income to subsidiaries in tax havens. Significant changes have been made to take effect for CFC accounting periods beginning after 31 December 2012. See at 4180 for further detail. Consideration will also need to be paid to the diverted profits tax introduced in *Finance Act* 2015.

The CFC provisions are changed by *Finance (No. 2) Act* 2015 so as to remove the ability of companies to use UK losses and reliefs against a CFC charge from 8 July 2015. The intention is to improve the effectiveness of the CFC regime in both deterring the diversion of profits and in taxing any profits that are diverted. Anti-avoidance legislation was introduced in *Finance Act* 2015 restricting the ability of companies to use carried-forward losses in relation to profits that arise in connection with certain arrangements. The proposed measure includes commencement provisions which are intended to ensure that profits are allocated appropriately to the periods before and after the commencement date. Changes will also be made to CTA 2010, Pt. 14B to clarify that it also applies to arrangements involving the use of carried-forward losses against profits apportioned under the CFC rules.

The CFC provisions apply to any 'controlled foreign company', i.e. a company which:

(1) is not resident in the UK (see 3020 regarding companies which cease to be UK-resident under the provisions applicable to dual resident companies), but which is controlled by individuals or companies that are UK-resident; and

(2) is subject to a level of tax on income less than three-quarters of what it would have been had it been resident in the UK.

Note that the comparison between the tax which would have been paid in the UK and that which applies in the other country should be made by reference to the amount of tax actually *paid* and not the tax rate applying to the profits of the CFC (see example below).

A number of exemptions apply to prevent an apportionment from being made (see 4155). For example, companies with foreign subsidiaries which are engaged in genuine trading activities in their country of residence will be unlikely to be affected by the CFC regime.

In recent years, much attention has focused on the interaction between the UK's CFC regime and EU law. Following the *Cadbury Schweppes* case, legislation was introduced in *Finance Act* 2007 to make the UK rules compliant with EU law. However, the changes do not appear to have gone far enough as, in May 2011, the European Commission formerly requested that the UK amend its legislation to better take into account the rulings of the EU's Court of Justice on the tax treatment of controlled foreign corporations.

Control and the '40%' test

Control is defined as the ability to secure that a company's affairs are conducted with the wishes of the person exercising the control, whether through share or votes or via the articles of association of other documents. In addition, a '40% test', similar to that applying under the 'transfer pricing regime' is used to determine whether or not a CFC is under the control of two persons, at least one of whom is UK resident. The test is satisfied where each of the two persons, who together control the company, have at least 40% of the interests, rights and powers. The test is of use to HMRC where one of the persons satisfying the 40% test is non-resident. The effect is to extend control by UK residents to include the situation where:

- the company is controlled by two persons who together meet the new definition of control;

- each of them individually satisfies the 40% test; and

- only one of them is UK resident.

The company is deemed to be controlled by the UK resident and is potentially a CFC.

The territory of residence

A company's residence is the territory in which it is liable to tax by reason of domicile, residence or place of management.

If there is more than one such territory, its residence is the place where it is effectively managed. After corporation tax self-assessment, where the normal rules do not produce a single territory of residence, holders of a majority UK assessable interest in the CFC (see 4160) may elect for it to be treated as resident in a specific territory; if no election is made, HMRC may designate, on a just and reasonable basis, the territory of residence.

Excluded countries list

A company which is resident and carrying on business in a country appearing on a list (originally published by the Revenue on 5 October 1993) will be treated as meeting the statutory exclusion conditions, subject to any qualification set out in the list for the country concerned (see 4155).

Responsibility for establishing a charge

Prior to the introduction of self-assessment (CTSA), a charge to tax only arises if HMRC so direct. A direction will not be made unless the UK company, together with connected or associated persons, has at least a 10% 'share' of the CFC's profits.

Under CTSA, this direction requirement is removed, so that the charge applies automatically if the necessary conditions are met. A charge will not apply unless the UK company, together with connected or associated persons, has at least a 25% 'share' of the CFC's profits. The onus is on the UK company to include an apportionment of the profits of a CFC in its annual return. A special supplementary page is provided for this purpose. In the original consultation document announcing the CTSA proposals for CFCs it was stated:

> 'Penalties would not be charged where a company could demonstrate that it had made reasonable efforts to get its self assessment of its CFC liabilities right.'

The charge to tax

The charge is calculated by reference to the profits of the overseas company. The home country currency (that in which the accounts are required) is to be used to compute the profits which are then translated on a closing rate basis.

Regulations dealing with various features specific to CFCs carrying on general insurance business have been published. In particular, the regulations will allow companies using a recognised form of non-annual accounting to benefit from the exemption for CFCs.

The following example illustrates the above points:

Example

Transalp Ltd is a company not resident in the UK but controlled by UK residents. It has income for an accounting period of £500,000 on which it has suffered tax in a third country, other than its country of residence, of £50,000. Assuming a rate of taxation in its own territory of 25% and UK corporation tax of 33%, the comparison is made as follows:

	Own territory		UK equivalent	
	%	£	%	£
Full rate of tax	25	125,000	33	165,000
Relief for foreign tax		(50,000)		(50,000)
Net tax payable		75,000		115,000
Total tax bill		125,000		165,000

Comparison – more than $^3/_4$ (75%) of UK CT?

Tax rate:	$^{25}/_{33}$	= 75.76% not statutory test
Total tax:	$^{125,000}/_{165,000}$	= 75.76% not statutory test
Local/UK tax:	$^{75,000}/_{115,000}$	= 65.22% *statutory test*

Transalp Ltd is subject to a lower level of taxation and is therefore a CFC potentially subject to a charge unless it qualifies for one of the available exceptions (see 4155). In determining whether or not its overall tax burden is more than three-quarters of the total equivalent UK charge, tax in another territory is deducted.

Legislation: ICTA 1988, s. 747–756 and Sch. 25

Cases: *Cadbury Schweppes plc v IR Commrs* [2008] BTC 52; *Vodafone 2 v R & C Commrs* [2009] BTC 273

Tax Reporter: ¶770-000

4155 Companies excluded from CFC provisions for accounting periods beginning before 1 January 2013

No charge is made on some CFCs' income because of a variety of exemptions in the legislation (see below). However, the Treasury has the power to specify, in regulations, jurisdictions where the exemptions will not apply. Thus, all CFCs in that jurisdiction would be within the charge to tax. The aim is to protect the UK against jurisdictions indulging in 'harmful tax practices'.

The exemptions referred to above have been subject to considerable change in recent years. For accounting periods of the CFC beginning on or after 1 January 2011, the exemptions are as follows:

(1) the '**exempt activities**' test. No charge will arise in respect of a CFC for an accounting period throughout which it is engaged in 'exempt activities'. To meet this test, the CFC must have a business establishment in the territory in which it is resident, and its business affairs must be effectively managed there. In addition, its main business must not consist of investment business or dealing in goods for delivery to or from the UK. The purpose of this test is to exclude automatically those CFCs which, because of the nature of their activities, can reasonably be assumed not to be being used to avoid UK tax.

(2) the '**limited UK connection**' tests. No charge will arise if the CFC qualifies for the exemption applying where a trading company has limited connection with the UK or the exemption applying where a company exploiting intellectual property has limited connection with the UK. Each test is built around a number of conditions applying with regard to the CFC's business establishment, activities, level of UK connection and income.

Where an apportionment would be avoided as a result of the application of a limited UK connection exemption, but that exemption is not available as a result of a relevant failure, an application can be made with the effect that, broadly, the limited UK connection exemption applies to profits not connected with the relevant failure.

(3) the '**small chargeable profits**' test. No charge will arise if the CFC's profits for a 12-month period do not exceed £50,000;

(4) the '**small relevant profits**' test: No charge will arise if the CFC's relevant profits for a 12-month period do not exceed £200,000.

A company's relevant profits are, broadly, its accounting profits calculated in accordance with GAAP, excluding any distributions which would be exempt under the broad exemption for distributions provided by CTA 2009, Pt. 9A;

(5) the '**exempt period**' test. No charge will arise if the accounting period of the CFC ends during an exempt period. The exempt periods begins, broadly, when the company falls within the CFC rules and lasts three years unless there is an early termination event in which case the length of the exempt period is reduced. In certain circumstances, the effect of the exempt period can be preserved to an extent after the exempt period has come to an end; and

(6) the '**motive**' test. No charge will arise if the CFC's transactions were carried out for bona fide commercial reasons, and it was not the main purpose of these transactions to achieve a significant reduction of UK tax, nor a main reason for the company's existence to divert profits from the UK. See above regarding HMRC clearance that a company satisfies the motive test.

The exemptions available in earlier periods were as follows:

- for accounting periods beginning before 1 January 2011, the exempt activities, small chargeable profits and motive tests as above;

- for accounting periods beginning before 1 July 2009 (subject to transitional arrangements), the exempt activities, small chargeable profits and motive tests and an additional test, the 'acceptable distribution policy' (ADP) test, applying where the CFC remitted, by way of dividend, a certain proportion of its profits to UK residents; and

- for accounting periods beginning before 6 December 2006, the exempt activities, small chargeable profits, motive and ADP tests and an additional test, the 'public quotation' test, applying where the CFC's shares were listed and dealt in on a recognised stock exchange.

Prior to changes made by *Finance Act* 2009, the exempt activities exemption was available to local holding companies, non-local holding companies and superior holding companies. For CFCs which are not qualifying holding companies, only the local holding company exemption remains after 1 July 2009. For CFCs which are qualifying holding companies, the non-local holding companies and the superior holding companies exemptions remain, subject to additional conditions, but only until 1 July 2012 (note that the transitional period was extended by a year by *Finance Act* 2011). Broadly, a CFC is a qualifying holding company if it was an exempt holding company in relation to the last accounting period to end before 1 July 2009. A company will have been an exempt holding company in respect of that period if it was engaged in exempt activities within the meaning of ICTA 1988, Sch. 25, Part 2 throughout the period and if the special rules which applied to non-local and superior holding companies applied to the company in relation to the period.

'Excluded countries list'

The 'excluded countries list' may be referred to in order to establish whether or not a company located in a particular country can be regarded as prima facie outside the CFC provisions providing it is resident *and* carrying on business in that country. Originally, the list was published as part of a Revenue press release although it has been updated since then. Under CTSA, regulations replace the non-statutory excluded countries list.

The list was first published as an indication that a company satisfied the motive test (see above) although it appears to be based on levels of taxation. It is in two parts:

Part I – companies resident in countries in this part will not be charged under the CFC provisions; and

Part II – companies resident in countries in this part will only be charged under the CFC provisions if they benefit from specified reliefs (which usually provide for a favourable tax rate or exemption from tax altogether).

Legislation: ICTA 1988, s. 748, 748A, 751AB, 751AC and Sch. 25; FA 2011, Sch. 12, para. 14; *Controlled Foreign Companies (Excluded Countries) Regulations* 1998 (SI 1998/3081)

Tax Reporter: ¶771-800ff.

4160 Apportionment of chargeable profits for accounting periods beginning before 1 January 2013

Where a tax charge arises in respect of a CFC, the notional UK tax is apportioned to persons with an interest in the CFC. An interested person is one who:

(1) possesses or is entitled to acquire shares or voting rights in the CFC;

(2) possesses, or is entitled to acquire, a right to receive distributions or any payment to loan creditors by way of premium on redemption;

(3) is entitled to secure that income or assets of the company will be applied directly or indirectly for its benefit (unless the entitlement is contingent upon default of the company under any agreement and the default has not occurred);

(4) has control of the CFC either alone or together with others.

Rights which a person has as a loan creditor do not constitute an interest in the company for the above purposes.

Method of apportionment

Once it has been decided who has an interest in the CFC, the next step is to determine the proportion in which the CFC's chargeable profits are to be allocated to those persons. The profits (and 'creditable tax') are apportioned according to the respective interests of the persons who at any time during the accounting period in question have had an interest.

The self-assessment rules enable a UK company to apportion to itself the appropriate amount of a CFC's chargeable profits and creditable tax. Where all holdings in a CFC are by means of ordinary shares, the apportionment will be made in direct proportion to the percentage of issued ordinary shares. In any other case, apportionment will be made on a just and reasonable basis among the persons who have 'relevant interests' in the CFC at any time in the relevant accounting period. A means of establishing which interests are relevant interests is provided, the aim being to identify the UK-resident company or companies which hold the most direct interest in the CFC. The rules are put into practical effect by a formula to establish the proportion of ordinary shares represented by an indirect holding of ordinary shares, and a formula to compute the relevant interest where this varies during the accounting period.

Legislation: ICTA 1988, s. 749(5)–(7), 749B, 752, 752A–752C and 756(3)

Tax Reporter: ¶770-900ff.

4170   Designer rate regimes for accounting periods beginning before 1 January 2013

Broadly, for accounting periods beginning on or after 6 October 1999, anti-avoidance rules apply to counter the use of so-called 'designer tax regimes'.

The legislation deems a company resident outside the UK, but subject to an effective rate of tax of 75% or more of the UK equivalent tax on those profits, nevertheless to be subject to a lower level of taxation for CFC purposes in the accounting period concerned where the local tax is determined by 'designer rate' provisions. The legislation does not actually define 'designer rate' regimes beyond granting the power to name them in regulations. In practice, the provisions are directed towards territories that effectively permit a company resident there to choose its rate of tax to enable it to circumvent the three-quarters of UK tax rule.

The regimes already named in regulations are those which apply to the following bodies:

- Guernsey – bodies with international tax status;

- Jersey – international business companies;

- Isle of Man – international companies;

- Gibraltar – income tax qualifying companies; and

- Ireland – companies taxed in accordance with the *Irish Taxes Consolidation Act* 1997, s. 448(7).

Legislation: ICTA 1988, s. 750A

Tax Reporter: ¶770-450

4175 Interim improvements

A limited number of changes were made by FA 2011 to provide temporary relief in anticipation of the full reform in FA 2012. In particular:

- increase in the de minimis limit from £50k to £200k;

- codification of the 'year of grace' and an extension to three years;

- new exemptions for:

  - certain intra-group trading transactions with little UK connection;

  - CFC's with a main business of IP exploitation, where IP and CFC have minimal UK connection.

4180 CFC rules for accounting periods commencing after 31 December 2012

Finance Act 2012, s. 180 and Sch. 20 contains the legislation for the reformed CFC regime (Controlled Foreign Companies and Foreign Permanent Establishments) Pt. 1 of Sch. 20 deals with Controlled Foreign Companies and Pt. 2 with Foreign Permanent Establishments. Part 1 inserts new Pt. 9A into TIOPA 2010 and Pt. 2 amends CTA 2009, Pt. 1, Ch. 3A. With a raft of consequential amendments and commencement provisions the legislative changes are extensive. Based on the document *Consultation on Controlled Foreign Companies (CFC) Reform* published in June 2011, the new regime was to operate by:

(1) identifying companies that are CFCs;

(2) exempting companies that pose a low risk to the UK tax base;

(3) imposing a CFC charge where no exemptions are available.

Corporation tax

Finance Act 2013 makes amendments to the new CFC rules introduced in *Finance Act* 2012. These amendments counter two tax planning opportunities and make consequential changes to ensure the rules work as intended, together with minor mechanical amendments again to ensure the CFC rules operate as intended. The amendments, one of which is subject to a transitional rule, will have effect from 1 January 2013 in line with the commencement date for the new CFC rules.

Finance Act 2014 inserts anti-avoidance provisions to counter arrangements exploiting the complete or partial exemption from CFC apportionment for group finance companies. Guidance has been issued by HMRC and is available at www.hmrc.gov.uk/drafts/additional-conditions.pdf.

4185 Fundamental principles of new legislation

At the outset, it should be noted that only artificial diversion of profits from the UK is now being targeted. However, the new 'Gateway' test broadly follows a principle of 'all out unless in'. The regime will thus apply to all overseas subsidiaries of UK Companies and potentially creates enormous compliance issues. Fortunately, the Gateway, Safe Harbour or Entity Level Exemptions will remove most companies from the charge. Helpfully, partial exemption is possible if full exemption is not available and, in addition there are more relaxed regimes for CFCs 'actively managing' IP and group treasury and finance CFCs. The Gateway is better defined than it was in the original Finance Bill draft and is actually called a 'Gateway' in the legislation: the gateway is the entry to the CFC regime and a company will only pass through Gateway, and into the regime, if one or more of five chapters of the legislation apply.

Structure of legislation – key parts

The legislation is extensive comprising 22 Chapters: In summary, the Chapters are:

- Chapter 2: the basic details of the CFC charge, details the Gateway and the steps to be taken for charging the CFC charge
- Chapter 3: the 'Initial Gateway': how to determine which (if any) of Chapters 4 to 8 apply in relation to profits of a CFC
- Chapters 4 to 8: how to determine which profits (if any) of a CFC pass through Gateway.
- Chapter 9: exemptions for profits from qualifying loan relationships
- Chapters 10 to 14: the 'entity level exemptions'
- Chapter 15: how to determine persons whose interests in CFC are relevant to CFC charge

- Chapter 16: how to determine creditable tax of CFCs

- Chapter 17: how to apportion CFCs chargeable profits and creditable tax among persons who have relevant interests in CFC

- Chapter 18: concept of 'control'

- Chapter 19: concepts of 'assumed taxable total profits', 'assumed total profits' and 'the corporation tax assumptions'

- Chapter 20: rules for determining the territory in which CFC is resident

- Chapter 21: provisions about management of CFC charge, including collection of sums charged

- Chapter 22: supplementary provisions and definitions

Chargeable Profits

The *Taxation (International and Other Provisions) Act* 2010 Pt. 9A, Ch. 2 sets out the steps for determining if a CFC charge arises once it has been established that a foreign company is a CFC. There is a CFC charge only if the CFC has 'chargeable profits', none of the CFC exemptions apply and there is a UK 'interest holder' that is not exempt and who together with connected companies, holds at least a 25% interest.

The Gateway

The basic mechanism of the legislation is to use Chapter 3 to determine if any of Chapters 4–8 apply ('Initial Gateway'). A company is only in the CFC regime if one or more of these Chapters apply. If none apply, then none of the CFCs 'assumed total profits' pass through the Initial Gateway. The principal Chapters are Chapters 4, 5 and 6.

Profits attributable to UK activities (Chapter 4)

Chapter 4 applies unless filtered out by any one of conditions A, B, C or D in Chapter 3. The conditions are:

- Condition A: a test of the purpose of the arrangements whereby the CFC holds its assets and bears its risks. The condition is met if the arrangement does not have as its main purpose, or one of its main purposes, the reduction or elimination of a UK or overseas tax liability.

- Condition B: at no time during the accounting period does the CFC have any UK managed assets or bears any UK managed risks.

- Condition C: at all times during accounting period the CFC itself has the capability to ensure that its business would be commercially effective were:

  - the UK managed assets of the CFC; and

  − the UK managed risks borne by the CFC

to stop being UK managed.

- Condition D: the CFC's assumed total profits consist only of one or both of:

  − non-trading finance profits (dealt with by Chapter 5);

  − property business profits (outside scope of CFC charge).

If none of the Chapter 3 conditions A–D are met, it is necessary to apply Chapter 4 and use the OECD guidelines ('Report on the Attribution of Profits to Permanent Establishments' – (the 'AOA') to apportion profits to UK SPFs (significant person functions) and then to consider the exclusions (safe harbours) from Chapter 4. The exclusions and safe harbours from Chapter 4 are broadly in relation to:

- where most of the SPFs are not UK SPFs;

- there is substantial non-tax value;

- independent company arrangement;

- commercial activities – trading safe harbour;

- specific rules for banking and insurance.

The Trading safe harbour exempts all trading profits of the CFC in certain circumstances.

Non-trading finance profits (NTFP) (Chapter 5)

Chapter 3 also filters out certain profits from investment of funds held for:

- trade of CFC: if no profits of that trade pass through Gateway;

- purpose of CFC's UK or overseas property business.

A safe harbour is available so as to exclude from charge if the NTFPs are less than 5% of profits. If the NTFP is not filtered out by Chapter 3, then Chapter 5 applies. Specifically included are profits that arise from:

- funds or other assets invested from the UK;

- a loan to UK resident connected company, where reasonable to assume main reason for loan rather than dividend is tax-related; or

- a finance lease of asset to UK Co or UK PE of non-UK Co connected with CFC, where it is reasonable to assume it was tax-motivated.

If Chapter 5 applies, then it is necessary to take similar steps as for profits attributable to UK activities in Chapter 4 to apportion NTFPs to UK using the 'AOA'.

Trading finance profits (Chapter 6)

This applies if the CFC has trading finance profits and at any time during the accounting period has funds or other assets which derive from UK connected capital contributions. If the CFC is a group treasury Co, notice can be given for it to be treated under NTFPs rules in Chapter 5 (and Chapter 9 (Profits from qualifying loan relationships)). There is an option for the CFC to claim NTFPs profits on QLRs (qualifying loan relationships) within Chapter 9 rather than Chapter 5. QLR profits are:

- profits on loans by CFC to non-UK resident connected Co controlled by same UK resident person(s) who control CFC; and

- consequential profits and losses, such as forex adjustments.

There are exclusions from QLRs where the:

- ultimate debtor is UK resident;

- borrower is a UK PE of the debtor;

- borrower is a UK property business of the CFC;

- ultimate debtor CFC to which Chapter 3–8 or Chapter 12 (low profit exemption) applies and the loan relationship debits are taken into account.

Entity level exemptions

There are, in addition, a number of entity level exemptions, which provide full exemption from the CFC charge. Specifically, the following should be noted:

- exempt period exemption (Chapter 10);

- excluded territories exemption (Chapter 11);

- low profits exemption (Chapter 12);

- low profit margin exemption (Chapter 13);

- tax exemption (Chapter 14).

Detailed guidance is available on the HMRC website – see www.hmrc. gov.uk/drafts/cfc.htm.

Other Material: *Consultation on Controlled Foreign Companies (CFC) Reform* available on the HM Treasury website at www.hm-treasury.gov. uk/d/consult_cfc_detailed_proposals.pdf

Special companies and activities

Companies with investment business

4200 Introduction to companies with investment business

Generally, companies with investment business are taxed in the same way as any other company, with the exception that deductions available in computing the non-trading profits of such companies are subject to greater restrictions than is the case with a trade. Holding companies in a group will often be companies with investment business but need not necessarily be so.

The definition of 'company with investment business' (see 4205) does not preclude such a company from carrying on a trade. Commentary on trading companies generally applies equally to investment companies carrying on a trade.

Legislation: CTA 2009, Pt. 16

Tax Reporter: ¶713-000ff.

4205 Definition of a company with investment business

Finance Act 2004 extended relief for expenses of management to companies with investment business. A company carries on an investment business if its 'business consists wholly or partly of making investments'. Prior to the changes made by *Finance Act* 2004, relief for expenses of management could only be claimed by an investment company, being 'a company whose business consists wholly or mainly in the making of investments and the principal part of whose income is derived therefrom'. Although the term 'company with investment business' is more inclusive than the term 'investment company', extending relief to many companies which previously did not qualify for it, both phrases focus on the making of investments. Consequently, previous decisions in the courts and other interpretations relating to investment companies continue to be of valid application in the context of the definition, and understanding, of what constitutes a company with investment business. They are summarised below.

It is now well established that the making of investments will not also require that the investments be turned over and that making an investment is not of itself trading. It follows that a holding company can be an investment company or have investment business. Also, in principle, a company can carry on a business of investment even though its investments provide no income but whether it actually does so is a matter of fact in each case. It does not necessarily follow that, because a company's formal object was to carry on the business of an investment company, the company in fact carried on that business.

The parent company of a trading group, which also provided head office services to its subsidiaries, was found to be an investment company in *Dawsongroup Ltd v R & C Commrs* (the Upper Tribunal overturning an earlier ruling by the First-tier Tribunal). Although the case is now mainly of historical interest only, in view of the widening in 2004 of the circumstances in which a company can claim a deduction for expenses of management, the Upper Tribunal Judge made some important observations. He ruled that it was incorrect to separate the holding of shares from the exercise of control which that holding enables the holder to do and that, therefore, exercising control by means of holding shares can be part of the investment activity and not necessarily a trading activity.

Residents' associations were found not to constitute investment companies (*Tintern Close Residents Society Ltd v Winter (HMIT)*). The businesses of the companies concerned did not consist wholly or mainly in the making of investments: further, the principal part of the companies' business was not derived from the making of investments. However, the High Court found that a housing society was an investment company. Although the object of the society was to acquire housing for renting with a social, rather than a profit, purpose, it did not follow that the houses were not investments. In fact, the houses were income-producing investments and the business of the society consisted in the making of investments (*Cook (HMIT) v Medway Housing Society Ltd*). It was also found to be irrelevant that the profit realised was to be used in furthering the objects of the society and not to be distributed to members.

Legislation: CTA 2009, s. 1218

Cases: *IR Commrs v Tyre Investment Trust Ltd* (1924) 12 TC 646; *Simpson (HMIT) v The Grange Trust Ltd* (1935) 19 TC 231; *Cook (HMIT) v Medway Housing Society Ltd* [1997] BTC 63; *Dawsongroup Ltd v R & C Commrs* [2010] BTC 1,528; *Tintern Close Residents Society Ltd v Winter (HMIT)* (1995) Sp C 7

Tax Reporter: ¶713-100

4210   Management expenses of an investment company

In computing the profits for an accounting period of a 'company with investment business' (see 4205), certain expenses commonly referred to as management expenses are deductible. Such expenses are deductible if they qualify as 'expenses of management', an expression which is not defined in relation to either investment companies or life assurance companies. Although the specific limitations on what may or may not be included in expenses of management differ for investment companies and life assurance companies the expression 'expenses of management' applies equally for both. Confusingly, qualifying (deductible) management expenses are often referred to as 'management expenses'.

For the means by which relief is obtained, see 4230.

Certain expenses are specifically excluded from inclusion in management expenses and some expenses are made specifically deductible. There is also judicial authority relating to whether certain items are or are not management expenses.

Legislation: CTA 2009, s. 1219

Tax Reporter: ¶713-250

4215 Management expenses: expenses not deductible

The rules governing management expenses remained largely unchanged until 2004 when changes were made to reflect a more modern business climate. Those changes included, amongst other things, an unallowable purpose rule.

Since the 2004 changes, various attempts have been made to circumvent the unallowable purpose rule and/or to create contrived expenses that could be deducted as expenses of management under ICTA 1988, s. 75 (see 4210). HMRC do not consider that these schemes succeed but their use has shown that the 'unallowable purpose' rule is not a sufficient deterrent. *Finance Act* 2007, s. 28, which received Royal Assent on 19 July 2007, therefore introduced a targeted anti-avoidance rule (TAAR) for management expenses. It also amended the existing unallowable purpose rule, so that similar provisions apply to both the purpose for which investments are held and the purpose for which management expenses are incurred. Both new provisions apply to expenses of management paid on or after 20 June 2007, the date the measure was announced.

The new TAAR will apply where the main purpose or one of the main purposes of arrangements is to seek to produce a wholly or partly contrived deduction for management expenses or other tax advantage. It is based upon the principle that relief for expenses of management should only be available where a company has genuinely incurred expenditure in the course of managing its investment business. Where the rule applies, its effect is to disallow relief for expenses of management where companies enter into arrangements where tax avoidance is the main purpose or one of the main purposes of the arrangements. The provisions are unlikely to affect the vast majority of companies, only those which have deliberately and knowingly entered into a scheme to avoid tax.

In addition, the following expenses are not deductible management expenses (i.e. are not 'expenses of management'):

- any amount disbursed which is deductible in computing profits apart from as expenses of management;

- expenses of a capital nature unless falling within any of the categories in 4220 below or are employer contributions to a pension scheme;

- expenses for which there is a statutory prohibition on deduction (e.g. business entertaining and gifts, crime-related payments, remuneration not paid within nine months of the end of the accounting period, contributions to employee benefit trusts, penalties, interest and VAT surcharges, a proportion of the hire costs of cars costing more than £12,000, etc.);

- brokerage and stamp duty on the purchase and sale of investments;

- the costs of raising finance, such as the issue of the debentures;

- payments that are not wholly for the purposes of the company's business, such as excessive directors' fees or administrative expenses paid to a parent company otherwise than pursuant to an agreement;

- exchange losses on payment of interest on capital liability (in relation to exchange losses generally see SP 1/87 with particular reference to para. 31);

- premiums for insurance against war risk;

- certain payments for war injuries to employees;

- certain payments in respect of unapproved retirement benefits schemes (whether by contribution or pension, etc.) unless and until the recipient is charged to income tax on them; certain foreign arrangements are treated as approved;

- rent in excess of commercial amounts paid under lease-back arrangements;

- rent for leased-back assets to the extent of any capital sums received under a lease-back arrangement, although strictly the deduction is not prevented, an equal amount being charged to corporation as miscellaneous income (formerly, under Sch. D, Case VI).

At first, the courts put a narrow interpretation on what constituted expenses of management. In *Capital and National Trust Ltd v Golder*, the Court of Appeal interpreted expenses of management as those involved in taking managerial decisions, but excluding expenses involved in carrying them out. This narrow interpretation was rejected by the House of Lords in *Sun Life Assurance v Davidson*, where the question at issue was whether the life assurance company could include, as expenses of management, sums representing brokerage and stamp duties incurred in connection with purchases and sales of investments made in the course of its business. Although the House found that the brokerage and stamp duties were not expenses of the management of the company's business, being too closely linked with the purchases and sales, it did reject the narrow construction put on 'expenses of management' adopted in *Capital and National Trust Ltd v Golder*. This wider interpretation of 'expenses of management' was also favoured by the Court of Appeal in *Hoechst Finance Ltd v Gumbrell*, where commission payments were considered.

The general principle established by this line of cases is that to be deductible, expenses of management have to be expenses of managing the investment business, rather than the investment themselves. So, expenses that relate to the purchase or sale of a particular investment will not generally be deductible as expenses of management.

Professional advisers' fees in connection with an aborted acquisition were held to be deductible expenses of management in *Atkinson v Camas plc* and professional advisers' fees in connection with an investigation into the affairs of a company in which an investment had previously been made were also held to be deductible expenses of management in *Holdings Ltd v IR Commrs*. Expenses incurred in 2000 (before the statutory prohibition on the deduction for expenses of management of capital nature was introduced) in connection with the delisting of a company's shares from the Stock Exchange were, unsurprisingly, held not to be deductible expenses of managing its investment business in *Dawsongroup Ltd v R & C Commrs*.

Legislation: CTA 2009, s. 1219 and Pt. 16, Ch. 4; CTA 2010, s. 838

Cases: *Bennet v Underground Electric Railways Co of London Ltd* (1923) 8 TC 475; *London County Freehold and Leasehold Properties Ltd v Sweet (HMIT)* (1942) 24 TC 412; *Capital and National Trust Ltd v Golder (HMIT)* (1949) 31 TC 265; *Sun Life Assurance Society v Davidson (HMIT)* (1957) 37 TC 330; *LG Berry Investments Ltd v Attwooll (HMIT)* (1964) 41 TC 547; *Fragmap Developments Ltd v Cooper (HMIT)* (1967) 44 TC 366; *Hoechst Finance Ltd v Gumbrell* [1983] BTC 66; *Atkinson v Camas plc* [2004] BTC 190; *Holdings Ltd v IR Commrs* (1997) Sp C 117; *Dawsongroup Ltd v R & C Commrs* [2010] BTC 1,528

Tax Reporter: ¶713-600

4220 Management expenses: deductible expenses

Expenses of management (i.e. deductible management expenses) include certain expenses by operation of statute; this covers 'commissions' and the following expenses:

- any statutory redundancy payment and corresponding employer's other payments in excess of the recoverable rebate (including payments after discontinuance of trade);

- any payment which is made after discontinuance of trade in addition to a statutory redundancy payment or other employer's payment up to three times the redundancy payment or other employer's payment provided it would be deductible under general principles if made before discontinuance;

- costs of establishing share options and profit sharing schemes;

- contributions to certain profit-sharing schemes;

- contributions to an agent's expenses under a payroll deduction scheme (see 2240);

- outplacement counselling expenses;

- contributions to certain pension schemes;

- the costs of valuing the fixed assets of the company, where such valuation is necessary to comply with CA 2006, s. 461 which requires the reporting of significant changes in the company's fixed assets;

- any expenditure attributable to employing a person whose services are made available on a temporary basis either to a charity;

- any expenditure incurred by an employer in paying or reimbursing 'relevant expenses' in connection with a 'qualifying course of training' undertaken by an employee who holds or held an office or employment under the employer, with a view to 'retraining' the employee;

- certain payments to the Export Credits Guarantee Department.

Expenditure incurred by an investment company on professional fees of accountants and solicitors in investigating the financial and legal affairs of a trading company in which it had a 50% shareholding qualified as allowable 'expenses of management'.

Legislation: CTA 2009, s. 1219 and Pt. 16, Ch. 3

Case: *Holdings Ltd v IR Commrs* (1997) Sp C 117

Tax Reporter: ¶713-450ff.

4225 Capital allowances for investment companies

The management of an investment company is a qualifying activity for the purposes of claiming capital allowances on plant and machinery. Relief is given by deduction from the income of the accounting period.

Any capital allowances that cannot be given against the income of the period are added to the company's management expenses and may be carried forward to subsequent accounting periods.

Legislation: CAA 2001, s. 253

Tax Reporter: ¶713-700

4230 Method of relief for deductions of an investment company

In computing an investment company's profits for an accounting period, expenses of management (i.e. deductible management expenses: see 4210) are first deducted from income from sources not charged to tax (except franked investment income, group income (in relation to distributions made before 6 April 1999) and regional development grants) and next from the company's other income and gains in the period.

If in an accounting period, the expenses of management together with qualifying charitable donations (for accounting period ended before 1 April 2010, charges on income) paid wholly and exclusively for purposes of the business exceed the profits for that period, the excess is carried forward to the next accounting period and treated as expenses of management of that period.

The excess expenses of management may alternatively be surrendered as group relief (see 3690) to be set off against the profits of the claimant company's corresponding accounting period. Expenses of management brought forward from previous years cannot be surrendered. Group relief is available for expenses of management whether or not the claimant company is an investment company.

Detailed provisions apply to changes in ownership of investment companies which seek to prevent exploitation of unrelieved management expenses and other similar reliefs available to investment companies.

Legislation: CTA 2009, s. 1219; CTA 2010, Pt. 14, Ch. 3

Tax Reporter: ¶713-800ff.

4240   Companies in liquidation or receivership

The position of the liquidator of a company in relation to that company differs from that of the receiver or administrator of the assets of the company whose powers are governed by the terms of his appointment.

Liquidation

On commencement of the winding-up of a company, its accounting period comes to an end and a new one starts; thereafter, until the completion of the winding-up, each accounting period spans 12 months except that an accounting period ends if a date is agreed with HMRC as a likely completion date.

Where a company ceases to be in liquidation without actually being wound up, then the fixed 12-month accounting period rule that is normal from the start of liquidation will cease to apply.

A company in liquidation may well be a close investment-holding company (see 4080).

For the financial year in which the winding-up is completed, special provisions may determine which rate of corporation tax is applicable. Interest on overpaid tax will be taxable unless it does not exceed £2,000 (see 4370).

On its liquidation, the company ceases to be the beneficial owner of its assets and accordingly various reliefs applicable to groups may cease to be available (see 3600); however, the capital gains group is preserved.

Receivership or administration

There are a variety of circumstances in which a receiver or administrator may be appointed to realise all or part of a company's assets or to run the company's business. The appointment does not affect the continuation of the company's trade in itself.

The commencement of administration will cause one accounting period to end and another to start, as will the date a company comes out of administration. In a parallel move to put administration on the same footing as liquidation, administrators will be able to calculate tax based on an earlier period's rates and to self-assess the compay's corporation tax liability early.

Legislation: TCGA 1992, s. 170(11); CTA 2009, s. 9–12; CTA 2010, Pt. 13, Ch. 5 and s. 1030

Tax Reporter: ¶802-300ff.

4250 Miscellaneous bodies

Special rules apply to a number of other types of bodies including, but not limited to:

- insurance companies (see Tax Reporter ¶780-000ff.);

- collective investment schemes and investment trusts (see Tax Reporter ¶782-000ff.);

- Real Estate Investment Trusts (REITs; see Tax Reporter ¶788-000ff.);

- shipping companies (tonnage tax; see Tax Reporter ¶790-000ff.);

- oil companies (see Tax Reporter ¶795-000ff.);

- corporate members of Lloyds (see Tax Reporter ¶802-900ff.);

- friendly societies (see Tax Reporter ¶805-200ff.);

- industrial and provident societies (see Tax Reporter ¶805-450ff.); and

- companies carrying on a mutual business (see Tax Reporter ¶806-800ff.).

Administration and compliance

4300 Introduction

In recent years, the move has been towards a harmonised system for the administration of taxes including with regard to HMRC powers, record-keeping obligations and penalties. The new powers extend to corporation tax in most cases and commentary can be found at 11000ff. Commentary on compliance and administration issues of relevance to companies only follows.

4305 Duty to give notice of chargeability

The duty to give notice in relation to a company coming within the charge to corporation tax is dealt with by FA 1998, Sch. 18, para. 2. In relation to such accounting periods, a company chargeable to corporation tax for an accounting period that has not received a notice to deliver a return is required to give notice within 12 months from the end of the accounting period that it was so chargeable. From 1 April 2010, penalties are provided for by FA 2008, Sch. 41 (see 12120). Prior to 1 April 2010, tax-geared penalties applied where the tax due in relation to the accounting period in question remained unpaid 12 months after the end of the accounting period.

Finance Act 2004, s. 55 introduced an additional and more burdensome rule with effect for accounting periods beginning on or after 22 July 2004. After this date, a company is obliged to give notice to HMRC of its coming into charge to corporation tax. A company will come into charge to corporation tax either at the beginning of its first accounting period or at the beginning of any subsequent accounting period that does not immediately follow the end of a previous accounting period, for example when a company begins to trade after a period of dormancy. A company must notify HMRC of its chargeability to corporation tax within three months of the beginning of the relevant accounting period. The notice must be in writing, it must state the date that the accounting period began and it must also include within the notice the information as prescribed by *Corporation Tax (Notice of Coming within Charge – Information) Regulations* 2004 (SI 2004/2502), reg. 2.

Where a company has a reasonable excuse for not fulfilling its obligation to give notice to chargeability within the three months from the beginning of the accounting period, so long as the company gives notice as soon as the excuse has been resolved, then the company will not be regarded as having failed to comply with that obligation.

Prior to 1 April 2010, failure by a company to notify HMRC of its coming into charge to corporation tax could have resulted in penalties being levied against the company. An initial penalty of £300 could have been levied in the event of such a failure and a further £60 per day could have been levied for each day the failure continued after the day on which the initial £300 penalty has been levied. Where a company had notified HMRC of its chargeability to corporation tax but had done so in a way that was fraudulent or negligent thus resulting in incorrect information appearing on the notification, the above penalties of £300 and £60 were increased to £3,000 and £600 respectively.

FA 2008, Sch. 41 (see 12120) has removed with effect from 1 April 2010 the old penalty regime which applied where a company failed to notify its coming into charge to corporation tax under FA 2004, s. 55 but has not extended the new Sch. 41 penalty regime to such a failure. It is assumed that this is an oversight by the parliamentary draftsman.

Legislation: FA 1998, Sch. 18, para. 2; FA 2004, s. 55; FA 2008, Sch. 41; *Corporation Tax (Notice of Coming within Charge – Information) Regulations* 2004 (SI 2004/2502), reg. 2

4310   Company tax return

A notice to make a company tax return must specify a period to which it relates. If a company accounting period ends during, or at the end of, the specified period, a return must be made for that period. Separate returns are required for each such accounting period within the specified period. If no accounting period ends during a specified period, but one begins (e.g. where a company first becomes chargeable to UK corporation tax), a return is required for that part of the specified period immediately before the accounting period began. If a company is outside the scope of UK corporation tax throughout the period, a return for the whole period is required. In any other case, no return is needed.

Return to include a self-assessment

Any company tax return must include a self-assessment of corporation tax due based on the information, etc. in the return, taking into account any reliefs or allowances (and including amounts due on close company loans to participators (see 4040) and on controlled foreign company profits (see 4713ff.) for the return period).

Accounts required in case of Companies Act companies

Where a UK-resident company is required to prepare accounts for *Companies Act* 2006 purposes (or Northern Ireland equivalent Orders), a company tax return may only require such accounts (together with annexed documents and information) as are required to be prepared under the Act (or Order).

In June 2010, HMRC issued guidance on the form of accounts that need to be submitted with the company tax return. This is available on HMRC website at www.hmrc.gov.uk/ct/company-accounts.pdf.

Filing date

The normal filing date, where a company produces annual accounts, is twelve months from the end of the company's accounting period. However, there are special rules to accommodate long periods of account (which include more than one accounting period) and for cases where the notice requiring a return is delayed. Thus, the filing date is the later of:

- twelve months from the end of the period to which the return relates;

- for long periods of account that are less than eighteen months long, twelve months from the end of the period of account;

- for long periods of account over eighteen months, 30 months from the start of the period of account; and

- three months from the date on which the notice requiring a return was served.

Example

A Ltd prepares accounts for the 12 months to 30 September 2011, and receives a notice to make a return for this period. If the notice was issued on 22 October 2011, the filing date would be 30 September 2012.

For the purposes of the three-month rule (above), HMRC assume that a notice which is served by post will be received four working days after it is issued.

Example

A Ltd prepares accounts for the 12 months to 30 September 2011, and receives a notice to make a return for this period. If the notice was issued on Friday 30 July 2012, it would be deemed to be received on Thursday 5 August 2012, and the filing date would be 5 November 2012.

Claims and elections to be included in returns

Generally, all elections and claims for relief or credit that can be made for a specified period must be made in the company tax return. (Time-limits for claims, elections, etc. are unaffected by this provision: see 4375.) This includes making a claim, election, etc. via an amendment to a return (see below). Certain claims can only be made by being included (via amendment, if necessary) in a return. These are claims:

(1) for group relief;

(2) for capital allowances;

(3) to repay income tax because a company is exempt or excluded from liability to income tax; and

(4) to tax credits (unless the company is exempt from corporation tax completely or exempt from corporation tax regarding everything bar trading profits).

In (4), tax credits subject to the payment on account rules for insurance companies carrying on pension business are excluded.

Amendment and correction of returns

A company may amend its tax return at any time within 12 months of the filing date. HMRC can specify the form that an amendment must take and can require any reasonable statement or information in support of the amendment to accompany it.

HMRC can, by notice, correct any 'obvious errors or omissions' in a return. These include errors of principle, arithmetic or otherwise. The normal time-limit for such corrections is nine months from the date the return is submitted; however, if a correction is needed following a company's amendment to a return, the time-limit is nine months from the date the amendment was made.

A company may amend a return that has been corrected by HMRC, within the normal time-limit for amending returns, so as to reject HMRC's correction. If this time-limit has expired, a HMRC correction can be rejected by the issue of a notice, to the officer who made the correction, within three months of date that the correction was made.

Conclusiveness of return

Once an amount in a return can no longer be altered, whether by the company itself or by HMRC, it is regarded as conclusive for the purposes of tax payable for another accounting period of that company, or the tax liability for any accounting period of another company.

See above and the ensuing paragraphs in this chapter for the various ways in which a company's return may be altered.

Time limit for enquiries

For accounting periods ending after 31 March 2008, the enquiry window for most returns delivered by, or on, the filing date will close 12 months from the day on which HMRC receive the return. For example, if a return for an accounting period ended 30 June 2008 is received by HMRC on 26 January 2009, the enquiry window will close on 26 January 2010, i.e. 12 months after delivery.

For accounting periods ending on or before 31 March 2008, the enquiry window for returns filed early closed 12 months from the statutory filing date, which was normally 12 months after the end of the accounting period.

Penalties

For penalties in relation to returns, see 4385.

Legislation: FA 1998, Sch. 18, para. 2–16 and 88; *Corporation Tax (Notice of coming within charge – Information) Regulations* 2004 (SI 2004/2502)

Other Material: www.hmrc.gov.uk/ct/company-accounts.pdf

Tax Reporter: ¶811-600ff.

4315   Compulsory electronic filing of corporation tax returns

Electronic filing is mandatory for corporation tax returns delivered after 31 March 2011 for accounting periods ending after 31 March 2010, subject to exceptions for companies which are in administration or liquidation and to transitional arrangements applying with regard to smaller charities. It should be noted that no exemption is provided for solvent dissolutions where the company seeks informal striking off or enters a Members' Voluntary Liquidation (MVL) although HMRC have published guidance on how the rules will be applied in such cases.

The return must be provided in iXBRL (inline eXtensible Business Reporting Language) format using either the filing product provided by HMRC on its website or commercially available software that meets all the relevant requirements (details of which can be found on HMRC's website; see below). The company's computations and accounts must also be submitted in iXRBL format (a joint filing service with Companies House is available). Other information included as part of the return must be sent as PDF files.

HMRC have published guidance on how it will manage the transition to compulsory online filing and on what counts as a reasonable excuse for failing to file on time. HMRC agreed in June 2012 to retaining the MTLs (minimum tagging list) and not moving to full tagging. The full HMRC statement is available at www.hmrc.gov.uk/ct/ct-online/file-return/xbrl-tagging-120531.pdf. HMRC have added a new document, Company Tax return – taxonomy for new financial reporting standards to their taxonomies guidance. The Financial Reporting Council (FRC) published a new XBRL taxonomy which supports tagging under the new UK GAAP Financial Reporting Standards (FRS) and also under EU-adopted IFRS. HMRC are mandating the use of the new taxonomy as they have updated their systems in December 2014. Accounts prepared under the new accounting standards; submitted as part of a company tax return; and filed with HMRC on or after 1 April 2015 must be tagged with the new taxonomy.

Legislation: *Income and Corporation Tax (Electronic Communications) Regulations* 2003 (SI 2003/282); *Directions under regulations 3 and 10 of the Income and Corporation Taxes (Electronic Communications) Regulations* 2003 (SI 2003/282)

Other   Material: www.hmrc.gov.uk/efiling/ctsoft_dev.htm   (HMRC guidance on how it will manage the transition to electronic filing); www.hmrc.gov.uk/ct/ct-online/flow-diagram.pdf (flow diagram incorporating links to other guidance); www.hmrc.gov.uk/efiling/ctsoft_dev.htm (details of suppliers of software); and www.hmrc.gov.uk/ct/mvl-guidance.pdf (guidance on how the rules apply with regard to solvent dissolutions)

Tax Reporter: ¶811-770

4320 Preservation of company records

The records that must be maintained and retained by a company in support of its company tax return are wide-ranging and extensive. Records (or the information contained within them) of the amounts and nature of receipts and expenses, including all purchases and sales of stock, where relevant, together with supporting documents in the form of receipts, vouchers, contracts, deeds, books and accounts, are included.

For commentary on the rules applying from 1 April 2009, see 12405. Before 1 April 2009, the records that had to be kept must have been preserved for six years from the end of the period for which it may have been required to make a return. If a notice to deliver a return was issued within the six-year period, the records must have been preserved beyond the six-year period until either any enquiry into the return was completed or, in the absence of an enquiry, HMRC no longer had the power to make an enquiry into the return. If a notice to deliver a return was issued after the end of the six-year period, all extant records that would have assisted in the making of the return must have been preserved, again, until either any HMRC enquiry was complete, or, in the absence of an enquiry, HMRC no longer had the power to make an enquiry into the return.

Where a company fails to keep and preserve the records needed to enable it to deliver a correct and complete CTR for the requisite period, or fails to produce documents when required to do so, it may be liable to a penalty (see 4385).

Legislation: FA 2008, s. 115 and Sch. 37; FA 1998, Sch. 18, para. 21 and 22

Tax Reporter: ¶812-100

Payment of corporation tax

4325 Due date for payments

Corporation tax is due on the day following nine months after the end of the accounting period to which it relates.

Example

A company prepares accounts to 30 September each year. In respect of its accounting period ending 30 September 2011, tax is payable by 1 July 2012.

If the 'tax payable' is then exceeded by the total of any 'relevant amounts previously paid' (as stated in the relevant company tax return), the tax will be repaid. The 'tax payable' is the amount computed in accordance with FA 1998, Sch. 18, para. 8.

'Relevant amounts previously paid' are any of the following, so far as relating to the accounting period in question:

- any amount of corporation tax paid by the company and not repaid;

- any corporation tax refund surrendered to the company by another group company;

- any excess of the amounts available for set off against overall tax liability under Step 4 of the calculation in FA 1998, Sch. 18, para. 8 (for example income tax borne by deduction);

- any deductions from payments to sub-contractors treated as corporation tax paid in respect of profits of the company.

The above is subject to the payment of corporation tax by instalments.

Electronic payment of corporation tax is mandatory from 1 April 2011.

Legislation: TMA 1970, s. 59D, 59DA and 59E; *Income and Corporation Tax (Electronic Communications) Regulations* 2003 (SI 2003/282)

Tax Reporter: ¶811-000ff.

4330 Repayment claims

A company which has paid corporation tax for a period and which has, following a change in its circumstances, grounds for believing that the amount paid exceeds its probable tax liability for the period, may claim repayment of the excess. The claim must state the grounds for believing that the amount paid is excessive. Companies will either be able to claim repayment nine months after the end of the accounting period to which the overpayment relates or at the earlier date or dates provided by regulations where the corporation tax was paid by quarterly instalments.

A company which has appealed against an assessment or an amendment to an assessment may apply to the commissioners who will hear the appeal to determine the amount that should be repaid. The application may be combined with an application to postpone payment of tax.

A claim (for repayment of the excess) or application (to the commissioners) can be heard and determined in the same way as an appeal.

A company that wishes to include amounts deducted under the subcontractor's scheme in its provisional repayment must have delivered a company tax return for the period.

The above is subject to the payment of corporation tax by instalments (see 4340).

Legislation: TMA 1970, s. 59D, 59DA and 59E

Tax Reporter: ¶811-600ff.

4335 Recovery of excessive repayments

Where it appears that HMRC has paid, repaid or set-off against other liabilities:

- tax (including income tax and tax credits);
- repayment supplement; or
- interest on overpaid tax,

that appears to be excessive, an assessment may be issued to recover the excess amount(s). Interest may be charged on the excessive repayment, etc. from the date it was paid to the company to the date it was recovered. The normal four-year (six years prior to 1 April 2010) time-limit for making assessments is overridden where a recovery assessment is made either:

(a) before the end of the accounting period after the one in which the excess repayment was made; or

(b) if later, before the expiry of three months after the conclusion of an enquiry into the company's return.

(In order for this extension to apply, there does not have to have been a loss of tax brought about carelessly or deliberately (or, prior to 1 April 2010, fraud or negligence on the part of the company). Where there *has* been a loss of tax brought about carelessly or deliberately, then the further extended six-year (for carelessness) or 20-year (otherwise) time-limit may be invoked by HMRC to recover the excess.)

Legislation: FA 1998, Sch. 18, para. 52, 53

Tax Reporter: ¶812-000

4340 Recovery of overpaid tax

The error or mistake provisions allow a taxpayer to claim repayment of tax overpaid where there is an overpayment of tax as a result of a relevant mistake in a return.

Finance Act 2009 inserted a new para. 51 to FA 1998, Sch. 18, and allows a company to claim repayment of tax overpaid where a person has paid an amount by way of tax but believes that the tax was not due, or a person has been assessed as liable to pay an amount by way of tax, or there has been a determination or direction to that effect, but the person believes that the tax is not due.

The claim will only be possible where there is no other statutory route to recover the overpaid tax when a person first becomes aware, or might reasonably be expected to be aware, that they have overpaid. The person must also have used any appeal rights that were available and the claim will have to be made within time-limits. A claim under para. 52 may not be made more than four years after the end of the relevant accounting period.

Legislation: FA 1988, Sch. 18, para. 51

Tax Reporter: ¶811-900

4345 Large companies: corporation tax payable in instalments

A quarterly instalment payment system applies to 'large' companies under CTSA. For these purposes, 'large' companies are companies with profits in excess of the upper relevant maximum amount for the purposes of small profits rate (including reductions in that amount to reflect associated companies and short accounting periods: see 3100). 'Profits' means chargeable profits shown in an assessment (or determination) plus franked investment income (excluding group income).

The arrangements for filing the tax returns under CTSA of large companies are the same as for other companies (see 4305).

For these purposes, 'corporation tax' includes any amounts due under the legislation applicable to loans to participators, etc. (4040) and controlled foreign companies (4713).

Outline of instalments regime

Large companies (broadly, those with profits of more than £1.5m, or less if the company has other associated companies) have to pay their corporation tax in instalments starting during the accounting period for which the tax is payable, rather than in one lump sum nine months and one day after the end of the accounting period. This connection test is to be referred to as 'related 51% group companies' as a consequence of changes being made in *Finance Act* 2014 to deal with the alignment of the standard and small companies rates from April 2015. For a normal 12-month accounting period, this will result in quarterly instalments starting in month seven during the accounting period (therefore, two of which will be before the end of the accounting period).

The instalment regulations provide a de minimis limit to prevent companies in large groups having to make instalment payments of small liabilities. The limit is currently £10,000.

Where companies become large for the first time, they will be protected from any unanticipated liability to payment in instalments. Instalment payments will not be required if:

- the corporation tax profits for the accounting period do not exceed £10m (reduced where there are associated companies by reference to the number of associated companies at the end of the immediately preceding accounting period or, where there is no such period, at the beginning of the period concerned); and

- the company was not a large company for the previous year (either because it did not exist – or did exist but had no accounting period – or because it was not a large company for an accounting period ending in the preceding 12 months).

Pattern of instalments

A maximum of four instalments will be due six months and thirteen days after the beginning of an accounting period, carrying on, where the length of the period allows, at three-monthly intervals and ending three months and fourteen days (i.e. on the fourteenth day of the fourth month) after the end of the accounting period.

For a 12-month period, this simply translates into instalments being due quarterly on the fourteenth day of:

(1) month 7 after the beginning of the accounting period;

(2) month 10;

(3) month 13; and

(4) month 16 (the final instalment).

These are intended to reflect the dates which used to apply to most companies for the payment of any liability to advance corporation tax, prior to abolition, albeit starting later in the period.

New corporation tax payment dates will be introduced for companies with annual taxable profits of £20m or more with effect for accounting periods beginning on or after 1 April 2019 (this was originally intended to apply from April 2017). For such companies, corporation tax will be paid in quarterly instalments in the third, sixth, ninth and twelfth months of their accounting period and the £20m threshold will apply on a group-wide basis.

Example 1

Gross plc is a large company which has a 12-month accounting period which ends on 31 December. Instalment payments will be due on:

- 14 July and 14 October in the course of the accounting period for which the corporation tax is due; and

- 14 January and 14 April in the following year.

One quarter of Gross plc's corporation tax liability for an accounting period will be payable on each of those dates.

If, in the calendar year 2011, Gross plc changed its accounting reference date to 30 September, it would have a nine-month accounting period ending on 30 September 2011. Its instalment dates for that accounting period would be 14 July 2011 and 14 October 2011 with a final instalment on 14 January 2012. There would only be three instalment dates for the short period. If Gross plc continues to use 30 September as its year-end after 2011, it would revert to a pattern of four instalments for each accounting period thereafter.

Amount of instalments

Instalment payments will be based on a large company's total liability for the accounting period. By the very nature of the system, this will have to be based on estimated figures, at least initially. For these purposes, the 'total liability' is:

(1) corporation tax included in an assessment or a determination, less any subcontractors' tax deducted; and

(2) the aggregate of any liabilities under the provisions for:

    (a) close company loan to participators; and

    (b) controlled foreign companies.

Instalments are intended to be in equal amounts: however, this will not always be the case. Accordingly, the amount of each instalment is calculated according to a formula:

$$\frac{3}{n} \times CTI$$

Where CTI is the amount of the company's total liability for the period and n is the length of the accounting period in months. The amount of tax due on the first instalment date will be the *smaller* of CTI and the amount produced by the above formula. For subsequent instalments, the amount due will be the smaller of the balance of tax left after the previous instalment and the amount produced by the formula. Thus there may not be the maximum number of instalments for the period where all the tax is payable in less than four instalments.

Example 2

From Example 1 above, Gross plc has a corporation tax liability for the nine-month accounting period ended 30 September 2011 of £2.5m. Its instalments are calculated as follows:

CTI = £2,500,000

n = 9 months

		Cumulative total of tax paid

First instalment:

$$\frac{3}{9} \times 2,500,000$$

Lesser of CTI and formula = 833,333.33	due 14 July 2011	833,333.33

Second instalment:

$$\frac{3}{9} \times 2,500,000$$

= 833,333.33   A

Balance of tax after first instalment	1,666,666.67 B	
Lesser of A and B	833,333.33 due 14 October 2011	833,333.33

Third instalment:

$$\frac{3}{9} \times 2,500,000$$

= 833,333.33   C

Balance of tax after first and second instalments	833,333.33 D	
Lesser of C and D	833,333.33 due 14 January 2012	833,333.33

Total tax paid in instalments		2,500,000.00

If, using the same corporation tax liability, Gross plc instead ended its accounting period on 15 May 2011, its instalments would be reduced in number as follows:

CTI = £2,500,000

n = 4.5 months

			Cumulative total of tax paid
First instalment:			
	$\dfrac{3}{4.5} \times 2{,}500{,}000$		
Lesser of CTI and formula	= 1,666,666.67	due 14 July 2011	1,666,666.67
Second instalment:			
	$\dfrac{3}{4.5} \times 2{,}500{,}000$		
	= 1,666,666.67	A	
Balance of tax after first instalment	833,333.33	B	
Lesser of A and B	833,333.33	due 29 August 2011	833,333.33
Total tax paid in instalments			2,500,000.00

Repayments of excessive instalments

Any instalment payments already made will normally be repaid if a company decides on reflection that they ought not to have been paid and the aggregate amount already paid exceeds the aggregate amount which should have been paid using the revised total liability. A claim can be made for repayment of the excess amount. Such a claim must give the amount being reclaimed and the grounds for making the claim. The commissioners may determine the amount which should be repaid where an assessment is under appeal prior to determination of the final liability. An application to the commissioners for such a determination will be treated like an appeal.

Repayments will carry interest (see below). Repayments of excess instalments may also be surrendered within a group.

Miscellaneous requirements

The following matters are also covered by the regulations:

- HMRC's right to request such information, including copies of books, documents and other records, relating to the calculation of instalments as they may 'reasonably require'; and

- the right of inspection of any records so required.

For arrangements for groups of companies, including arrangements whereby one company will be able to make instalment payments on behalf of the group, see 3770.

Legislation: TMA 1970, s. 59D, 59DA, 59E and 87A; ICTA 1988, s. 826A; *Corporation Tax (Instalment Payments) Regulations* 1998 (SI 1998/3175)

Tax Reporter: ¶811-050ff.

4355 Interest on overdue or overpaid tax

Unpaid or underpaid corporation tax carries interest from the due date, nine months after the end of the accounting period. Companies are able to claim relief for the interest where it relates to an accounting period within self-assessment.

From a date yet to be announced, *Finance Act* 2009 introduces a new penalty regime for late payment of corporation tax (see 12210).

HMRC must pay interest to a taxpayer company on certain refunds of tax. The refunds in question relate to the following:

- corporation tax;

- income tax deducted at source from amounts received by the company; and

- tax credits on franked investment income (see 3920).

Interest on corporation tax runs from the later of the date on which the tax is paid or nine months after the accounting period; for income tax and tax credits it runs from nine months after the accounting period in which the company receives the income.

Companies are taxable on interest on overpaid tax.

Legislation: TMA 1970, s. 87 and 87A; ICTA 1988, s. 826 and 826A; FA 1989, s. 178

Tax Reporter: ¶811-350

4360   Time-limits for claims and elections

With effect from 1 April 2010, a claim must be made within four years from the end of the accounting period to which it relates, unless a longer or shorter time-limit is given by a specific provision.

Example

A company makes up its accounts to 31 December. A claim is required in respect of the accounting period ended 31 December 2005. The claim could have been made at any point up to 31 March 2010 as at that date a time-limit of six years applied and so the period during which the claim could be made had not elapsed. The claim cannot be made on or after 1 April 2010 as from that date the time-limit is four years and so the period during which the claim could be made ended on 31 December 2009.

Transitional rules are provided.

For claims made before 1 April 2010, the claim had to be made within six years from the end of the accounting period to which it related, unless a longer or shorter time-limit was given by a specific provision. If a mistake was discovered in any claim or election, a company was able to make a supplementary claim, etc. within the time-limit for making the original claim or election. All claims to reliefs, allowances or repayments had to be for specific quantified amounts.

For commentary on the special CTSA provisions relating to claims for capital allowance, see 3070 and, for group relief, see 3710.

Claims or elections not included in returns

If a claim or election can be made without being included in a return (for example, because the time-limit for making an amendment to the return has expired), the administrative rules of TMA 1970, Sch. 1A apply (see 2684).

Consequential claims

Following the closure of a HMRC enquiry (see 2684) or the issue of an assessment that results in more tax being payable, it is possible to make further claims and elections (or revoke existing claims, etc.) to reduce the tax due to the amount originally returned. Such further claims must be made within 12 months of the end of the accounting period in which the closure notice or assessment is made. Claims that could affect the liability of other parties (e.g. companies in the same group) require their written approval. Where the assessment is made as a result of a loss of tax brought about carelessly or deliberately (or, for periods prior to 1 April 2010, as a result of fraudulent or negligent conduct of the company or its servants, etc.) (see 4410), the scope for making additional claims, etc. is restricted to those that could have been made within the normal time-limit for the accounting period concerned.

Late claims

Late claims for losses, capital allowances or group relief may be accepted, provided the delay was for reasons beyond the company's control. HMRC's approach is set out in SP 5/2001.

Legislation: FA 1998, Sch. 18, para. 54–65; *Finance Act 2008, Schedule 39 (Appointed Day, Transitional Provision and Savings) Order 2009 (SI 2009/403)*

Other Material: SP 5/2001

Tax Reporter: ¶812-150ff.

4365 Determinations and assessments by HMRC

If no return is delivered by a company following the issue of a notice, or if a notice to deliver a return is complied with only partially, HMRC may determine to the best of their information and belief the amount of tax payable by a company.

Determinations to have effect as self-assessments

Such determinations are treated as self-assessments for most practical purposes, including:

- payment of tax due;
- collection and recovery proceedings;
- interest on overdue tax;
- tax related penalties; and
- assessment of unpaid tax on other persons (to enable collection to be effected).

In the absence of adequate information regarding the matter, the period covered by the determination is to be treated as an accounting period of the company.

When return not delivered

A determination made in the absence of any return may be made after the filing date for that return has passed. If, for some reason (e.g. lack of information about the commencement of an accounting period) the filing date cannot be ascertained, the exercise of determination powers may be made after the later of 18 months from the end of the period specified in the notice to deliver the return and three months from the date the notice was served.

Determination of tax payable if notice complied with in part

A determination made because a return for only part of the period specified in the notice has been delivered may be made after the filing date for the outstanding return has passed. If for some reason the filing date cannot be ascertained, the exercise of determination powers may be made after the later of 30 months from the end of the period specified in the notice and three months from the date the notice to deliver a return was served.

Time-limit for determinations

No determination may be made more than three years (five years for determinations made prior to 1 April 2010) after the date that the power to make a determination first arose. If a company can show that a determination should not have been made (e.g. because it has actually delivered a return for the period, or that the period covered by the determination was not an accounting period, etc.) the determination will be treated as having no effect.

Determinations superseded by actual self-assessments

If, after a determination has been made (and within the later of five years of the date that the power to make a determination first became exercisable and 12 months from the date of the determination) a company delivers a return, the self-assessment in the return supersedes the determination. The delivery of a self-assessment in these circumstances does not delay or impede any tax recovery proceedings in relation to the determination. The period of five years was reduced to three years with effect from 1 April 2009.

Legislation: FA 1998, Sch. 18, para. 36–40

Tax Reporter: ¶812-000

4370   Penalties under CTSA

Failure to deliver a return within the time-limit

A company which has had a notice to make a tax return and fails to deliver it by the filing date may become liable to a flat-rate penalty of:

(1)   £100; if it is delivered within three months of the filing date; and

(2)   £200; if it is delivered after three months.

Corporation tax

The penalty under (1) is increased to £500 and under (2) to £1,000 if the returns for the two immediately previous consecutive accounting periods were also late.

It should be noted that penalty is set by statute and no reduction is to be made by reference to the income of the company or to its tax liability (the case of *Somercombe OTS No 39 Ltd*).

Excuse for late delivery of return

No flat-rate penalty is due if a company is required to deliver accounts under the *Companies Act* 2006 (or equivalent Northern Ireland Order) and submits its return within the time allowed for delivering the accounts to the Registrar of Companies.

Tax-geared penalty

Where a company tax return is delivered later than 18 months after the end of the accounting period (i.e. more than six months after the filing date, in the usual case of a company with a regular 12-month accounting period), a further tax-geared penalty will become due (in addition to the flat-rate penalties shown above). The tax-geared penalty is:

(1) 10% of the unpaid tax, if it is delivered within two years of the end of the period for which the return is required (i.e. within 12 months of the filing date in the usual case of a company with a regular 12-month accounting period); or

(2) 20% of the unpaid tax, if it is delivered after the two-year period in (1) above.

New penalty regime for late filing of CT returns

From a date yet to be announced, *Finance Act* 2009 introduced a new flat rate and tax-geared penalty regime for the late filing of corporation tax returns. The new regime is considered at 12210.

Penalties for incorrect returns or accounts

Finance Act 2007 introduced a new regime for penalties in respect of incorrect documents submitted to HMRC for documents in respect of income tax, capital gains tax, corporation tax, PAYE, Class 1 and Class 4 NICs, Construction Industry Scheme and VAT. The new penalty regime applies for returns for periods commencing on or after 1 April 2008 and due on or after 1 April 2009. The new regime is considered at 12002.

Under the old rules, a penalty of up to an amount equal to the tax understated may have been charged if:

- an incorrect company tax return was fraudulently or negligently delivered; or

- a company discovered an 'innocent' error in a submitted return and failed to remedy the error without 'unreasonable delay'.

A penalty of up to an amount equal to the tax understated may have been charged if a company fraudulently or negligently:

- submitted to HMRC incorrect accounts in connection with its tax liability; or

- made any incorrect return, statement or declaration regarding a claim for any allowance, deduction or relief.

Accounts submitted on behalf of a company were regarded as submitted by the company unless it could be shown that they were submitted without its 'consent or connivance'.

Failure to keep and preserve records

Where a company fails to keep and preserve the records needed to enable it to deliver a correct and complete tax return for the requisite period (broadly six years from the end of the period covered by the company tax return), it may be liable to a penalty of up to £3,000. For further commentary, see 12407.

Failure to produce documents

From 1 April 2009, the new information powers in FA 2008, Sch. 36 apply.

Prior to 1 April 2009 where a company failed to produce documents or information required in a formal notice served during an enquiry into a return or amendment to a return, a penalty of £50 could have been charged. Where the failure continued daily, penalties could have been imposed for each day of continued failure:

- £30 per day, if the daily penalty was determined by an officer of the Board under TMA 1970, s. 100; or

- £150 per day if the daily penalty was determined by the commissioners under TMA 1970, s. 100C.

Multiple tax-geared penalties in respect of same accounting period

Where a company incurs more than one tax-geared penalty, the total penalty chargeable by reference to any particular portion of tax shall not exceed the largest of the individual penalties chargeable on that portion.

Where it is necessary to calculate the 'tax understated' for the purposes of a tax-geared penalty, no account is taken of any deferred relief for the repayment of loans made to participators in close companies where the repayment was made more than nine months after the end of the accounting period in which the loan was made (see 4050).

Legislation: FA 1988, Sch. 18, para. 17–19, 23 and 90; FA 1998, Sch. 18, para. 2; FA 2007, s. 97 and Sch. 24; FA 2008, Sch. 36; FA 2009, s. 95, Sch. 47, para. 40A and Sch. 55; *Finance Act 2007, Schedule 24 (Commencement and Transitional Provisions) Order* 2008 (SI 2008/568)

Tax Reporter: ¶812-050

4375   Collection and recovery from companies

Corporation tax is generally collected direct from the taxpayer, although there are certain amounts from which income tax will have been deducted at source (see 1370, 1402, 1652, 1654 and 3125).

HMRC issue payslips and reminders as follows:

- a notice requiring a return to be made contains a payslip;
- about a month before the due date, a payment reminder and a further payslip will be sent;
- where appropriate, a further reminder and payslip will be sent about a month after the due date.

Payment is, of course, due without the need for any action on the part of HMRC.

PAYE procedures apply to companies largely as they apply to individuals.

Collection of tax from UK paying or collecting agents in respect of certain foreign dividends receivable by non-residents is broadly the same as for individuals (see 1654).

Unpaid tax may be recovered by the Crown in the following ways:

- by levying distress upon the lands or goods of the person in default;
- by action to recover the debt through court proceedings;
- by bankruptcy proceedings.

These remedies apply in relation to corporation tax much as they apply in relation to income tax (see 2804ff.).

Legislation: CTA 2010, s. 710 and 713

Tax Reporter: ¶805-100

4380 Deduction of income tax

Where a company has made a payment under deduction of tax, it must account to HMRC for the tax deducted. It does this through a system commonly known as the 'quarterly accounting' system.

Return periods

For this purpose, the company's accounting period is divided into return periods, based on the quarterly dates 31 March, 30 June, 30 September and 31 December. Where the accounting period does not end on one of these dates, there will be two short return periods. For instance, if a company produces accounts for the year to 31 July, its return periods will be:

- 1 August to 30 September;
- 1 October to 31 December;
- 1 January to 31 March;
- 1 April to 30 June; and
- 1 July to 31 July.

A return of relevant payments (i.e. those made under deduction of tax) is due within fourteen days of the end of the return period. The tax is paid at the same time.

Relief for tax suffered at source

Where a company has suffered income tax deducted at source, relief can be obtained through the quarterly accounting system. The tax suffered may be used to reduce the amount of tax owing in respect of relevant payments. It may also be used to obtain repayment of income tax paid in earlier return periods in the same accounting period.

Income tax suffered at source which is not relieved in this way may be set against corporation tax due for the accounting period. If the corporation tax liability is insufficient to cover this, then any remaining income tax is repaid.

Legislation: ITA 2007, Pt. 15, Ch. 15

Tax Reporter: ¶812-400

4385 Senior accounting officers

For financial years beginning on or after 21 July 2009, senior accounting officers of large qualifying companies are required to take reasonable steps to ensure that the company establishes and maintains appropriate tax accounting arrangements and must in particular, take reasonable steps:

(a) to monitor the accounting arrangements of the company; and

(b) to identify any respects in which those arrangements are not appropriate tax accounting arrangements.

The senior accounting officer must give a certificate for each financial year to HMRC stating whether the company had appropriate tax accounting arrangements throughout the financial year, and if it did not, give an explanation of the respects in which the accounting arrangements of the company were not appropriate tax accounting arrangements. This certificate must be given to HMRC no later than the end of the period for filing the companies accounts.

The senior accounting officer is liable to a penalty of £5,000 if he fails to provide a certificate to HMRC or provides a certificate that contains a careless or deliberate inaccuracy. An inaccuracy is careless if the inaccuracy is due to a failure by the senior accounting officer to take reasonable care. An inaccuracy in a certificate that was neither careless nor deliberate when the certificate was given is to be treated as careless if the senior accounting officer discovered the inaccuracy some time later, and did not take reasonable steps to inform HMRC.

Senior accounting officer, in relation to a company that is not a member of a group, means the director or officer who, in the company's reasonable opinion, has overall responsibility for the company's financial accounting arrangements. While senior accounting officer in relation to a company that is a member of a group, means the group director or officer who, in the company's reasonable opinion has overall responsibility for the company's financial accounting arrangements.

Appropriate tax accounting arrangements means accounting arrangements that enable the company's relevant liabilities, as follows, to be calculated accurately in all material respects as regards:

- corporation tax (including any amount assessable or chargeable as if it were corporation tax);

- value added tax;

- amounts for which the company is accountable under PAYE Regulations;

- insurance premium tax;

- stamp duty land tax;

- stamp duty reserve tax;

- petroleum revenue tax;

- customs duties;

- excise duties.

A qualifying company is liable to a penalty of £5,000 if for a financial year, the commissioners are not notified of the name or names of its senior accounting officer or officers.

A company is a qualifying company in relation to a financial year if the qualification test was satisfied in the previous financial year.

The qualification test is that the company or the company and its subsidiaries satisfied either or both of the following requirements:

(1)   relevant turnover more than £200m; and

(2)   relevant balance sheet total, being the aggregate of assets, more than £2bn.

The legislation does not apply to non-resident companies, partnerships, charities, Crown Estates or public bodies.

Provision is made in the legislation for assessing and appealing any penalty levied. HMRC have amended their guidance on these rules and, in HMRC Brief 19/13 (www.hmrc.gov.uk/briefs/company-tax/brief1913.pdf). These updates do not represent changes in policy and will apply from the date of publication (5 August 2013).

Legislation: FA 2009, s. 93 and Sch. 46

Tax Reporter: 813-600ff.

4390   Large business tax compliance

In the Summer Budget 2015, it was announced that additional resources will be committed to large business compliance work to combat tax evasion, avoidance and aggressive tax planning by large businesses. The Government will also consult on new measures to increase compliance and tax transparency in relation to large business tax strategies. These will include the introduction of a 'special measures' regime to tackle businesses that persistently adopt highly aggressive behaviours including around tax planning, a voluntary Code of Practice defining the standards HMRC expect large businesses to meet in their relationship with HMRC and the need for companies to publish a 'tax strategy' document (further detail in the guidance note published by HMRC at www.gov.uk/guidance/large-businesses-publish-your-tax-strategy).

Capital allowances

KEY POINTS

- Capital allowances provide tax relief for certain types of capital expenditure by prescribing a statutory rate of depreciation for tax purposes, in place of that used for accounting purposes. Where none of the forms of capital allowances that are available apply, the capital expenditure remains non-deductible.

- The Annual Investment Allowance gives full tax relief for expenditure incurred by a business on plant and machinery to a maximum of £200,000 p.a. for expenditure incurred on or after 1 January 2016. Previously, the maximum amount was £500,000 until 31 December 2015 (since 1 April 2014) (see 4615).

- First year allowances are only available for a few specified categories of plant and machinery such as that which meets certain energy-saving criteria (see 4620).

- The main rate of writing down allowances for expenditure on plant and machinery is 18% p.a. (20% before April 2012).

- The special rate of writing down allowances for expenditure on plant and machinery is 8% p.a. (10% before April 2012).

- The rates of capital allowances available for cars are based on the level of CO_2 emissions (see 4650).

- There is no statutory definition of plant and machinery. The legislation includes lists of assets that are 'treated as buildings' or constitute excluded 'structures, assets and works', which prescribes items which do not qualify for plant and machinery allowances. Otherwise the definition can only be found by reference to case law (see 4560).

- Special provisions apply to plant and machinery fixtures which in law form part of the land to which they are attached (see 4605).

- Plant and machinery allowances are given through a system of pooling with new expenditure being added and sales proceeds being subtracted and allowances given on the value of the pool at the end of the chargeable period (see 4660).

- In addition to plant and machinery capital allowances are given for certain expenditure on the renovation of business premises, mineral extraction, research and development, know-how, patents and dredging (see 4530).

- The phasing out of industrial and agricultural building allowances (including hotels and commercial buildings in enterprise zones) was completed in 2010–11 and the allowances are no longer available from April 2011 (see 4800).

- Flat conversion allowances were abolished from 1 April 2013 (see 4820).

- Capital allowances are generally available by reference to the time the expenditure is incurred (see 4540).

- The amount of expenditure qualifying for capital allowances is reduced to the extent that it is met by a subsidy from a third party (see 4545).

- A person contributing to expenditure incurred by another may be entitled to allowances (see 4550).

4520   Nature of capital allowances

The initial cost and accounting depreciation of a capital asset purchased by a business are not allowed as deductions in computing taxable profits. However, capital allowances, which are a form of statutory depreciation, may be available.

The law relating to capital allowances is mainly to be found in the *Capital Allowances Act* 2001, although amendments have been made in more or less every subsequent Finance Act not all of which have been incorporated into the 2001 Act.

The general rule is that capital allowances are included as a deduction in the calculation of income for income tax purposes, or the calculation of profits for corporation tax purposes.

In the following commentary, references to dates for financial years have been taken to be those relevant for corporation tax (1 April to 31 March) rather than income tax (6 April to 5 April). In all cases except where otherwise stated, the dates are interchangeable depending on the form of taxation being considered.

Corporation Tax (Northern Ireland) Act 2015

The *Corporation Tax (Northern Ireland) Act* 2015 received Royal Assent on 26 March 2015. It devolves a power to the Northern Ireland Assembly to set a Northern Ireland corporation tax rate for certain trading profits, from a date to be set by Statutory Instrument. The Act includes amendments to facilitate a potential rate differential between the UK main rate regime and the Northern Ireland regime, including amendments to CAA 2001 on how to compute amounts related to capital allowances.

Tax Reporter: ¶235-000ff.

4525   Major changes to capital allowance regime

Important changes to capital allowances have been introduced in recent years. The following notes provide an overview of these changes.

First-year allowances (plant and machinery)

First-year allowances for expenditure on 'green' technology are available at 100%. Companies are eligible to surrender losses arising from such expenditure in return for a cash payment.

Annual investment allowance (plant and machinery)

The Annual Investment Allowance (AIA) applies to expenditure incurred from 1 April 2008. The AIA gives full tax relief for expenditure incurred by a business on plant and machinery in its chargeable accounting period, to a maximum of:

- £200,000 p.a. (1 January 2016 onwards);

- £500,000 p.a. (1 April 2014 to 31 December 2015); and

- £250,000 p.a. (1 January 2013 to 31 March 2014).

The AIA offers full and immediate tax relief, for all sizes of business, for the first £200,000 of expenditure on plant and machinery in the period. The maximum annual allowance is proportionately increased or reduced if the chargeable period is greater or shorter than one year. Special rules apply to accounting periods straddling the dates when changes are made to the maximum amount.

Small pools allowance

From 1 April 2008, a new rule was introduced to ease the administrative burden on businesses with low levels of capital expenditure. General and special rate pools of under £1,000 now attract balancing allowances to reduce them to zero. This removes the need to maintain the pool going forward for an ever-diminishing benefit.

Reduction in rate of writing-down allowances for general pool plant and machinery

The rate of writing-down allowances (WDAs) for plant and machinery in the general pool was reduced from 20% to 18% for chargeable periods beginning from 1 April 2012. A hybrid rate applied for chargeable periods straddling the date of change, including in respect of single-asset pools, such as short-life assets.

Capital allowances

The reduction in the rate of WDAs is for plant and machinery allowances only. Many of the minor allowances continue to have 25% WDAs (business premises renovation conversion allowances, for example, are normally given by way of a full initial allowance).

Reduction in rate of writing-down allowances for special rate pool plant and machinery (long-life assets and integral features)

The rate of WDAs for long-life asset (LLA) expenditure was increased from 6% for chargeable periods beginning on 1 April 2008 at the same time the integral features rules were introduced. Both types of assets attracted WDAs of 10% until 1 April 2012 when the rate was reduced to 8%.

Payable tax credits (plant and machinery)

Loss-making companies that incur expenditure on certain 'green' technology from 1 April 2008 are able to claim a cash payment if they are otherwise unable to use their losses against their own profits or those of a group member. In this way, companies can gain an immediate cash repayment rather than carrying losses forward indefinitely in the hope of obtaining relief when profits start to be realised in the future.

Cars

Capital allowances for cars were reformed for expenditure incurred from 1 or 6 April 2009 (for corporation tax and income tax respectively). The £3,000 annual cap on allowances for cars costing more than £12,000 was removed and a revised system was introduced whereby allowances are linked to the CO_2 emissions of the vehicle (see 4645).

Industrial and agricultural buildings allowances

From April 2008, WDAs on industrial and agricultural buildings were gradually phased out, with final withdrawal completed in April 2011. To prepare the way for final abolition, most balancing adjustments, and the recalculation of WDAs on sale, were effectively withdrawn from 21 March 2007.

Flat conversion allowances

The allowances for capital expenditure incurred on the renovation or conversion of vacant or underused space above shops and other commercial premises to provide flats for rent was withdrawn from 1 April 2013.

Legislation: CAA 2001; FA 2008, Pt. 3, Sch. 26 and 27; FA 2009, s. 24; FA 2011, s. 10 and 11; FA 2013, s. 7 and Sch. 1

Tax Reporter: ¶235-025

4530   Categories of expenditure/asset

The legislation dealing with capital allowances is a core part of the UK's tax system.

The most familiar allowances are those available for capital expenditure on plant and machinery. For many businesses, however, expenditure on plant and machinery will determine only part of their overall capital allowance claims. Depending on the nature of the business, claims may be made under different rules in respect of any of the following:

- plant and machinery;

- renovation of business premises;

- mineral extraction;

- research and development;

- know-how;

- patents; and

- dredging.

The distinction between assets qualifying for these various different types of allowance is not always clear-cut. Occasionally, it is up to the taxpayer to decide which claim to make.

In many cases, the decision results in a timing benefit only. However, the abolition of industrial buildings allowances (IBAs) and agricultural buildings allowances (ABAs) has impacted on many businesses that previously were content to treat all the expenditure as qualifying for IBA/ABA in the knowledge that they would obtain 100% of the tax relief over time, which is no longer the case.

For affected businesses, the question of whether or not an asset is plant and machinery has become more critical. If an asset can be shown to constitute plant or machinery, then a reasonably generous rate of tax allowances may be due. If, on the other hand, the asset is deemed to be part of a building then no tax relief is due at all (though some relief may be available for fixtures in a building). Unfortunately, there are still many borderline cases where the answer is not clear cut, even though the principles that govern the making of this distinction are based on over a hundred years of case law and legislation.

Legislation: CAA 2001

Tax Reporter: ¶235-000

4535 Tax years and basis periods for income tax

Capital allowances are generally given effect for a chargeable period. For corporation tax, this means an accounting period of a company.

For income tax this is the same as the period of account. There can be complications in the opening and closing years or where there is a change in accounting date. Where two basis periods overlap, the period common to both is deemed to fall in the first period only; where there is a 'gap period', the interval is treated as part of the first period of account. Where the accounts are made up to a date more than 12 months after the previous accounts date, the first 12 months is taken as one period with the remainder (up to a further 12 months) forming another period and so on.

Legislation: CAA 2001, s. 6

Other Material: www.gov.uk/guidance/capital-allowances-accounting-periods-which-are-more-or-less-than-a-year

Tax Reporter: ¶235-150

4540 Timing and extent of expenditure incurred

Capital allowances are generally available by reference to the amount of capital expenditure incurred in the chargeable period. Capital expenditure is normally treated as incurred for capital allowance purposes on the date when the obligation to pay it becomes unconditional, whether or not a later date for payment is specified.

There are a number of exceptions to the general rule. Where any payment is due more than four months after the date when the obligation becomes unconditional, such payment is not taken to be incurred until it has to be paid. Where a stage payment is made under a 'milestone' contract and the specified conditions are met the expenditure is treated as incurred before the end of the chargeable period if the obligation to pay becomes unconditional within one month of the end of the period. There is also an anti-avoidance measure which provides that where a date is inserted solely or mainly to accelerate entitlement to a capital allowance, the date is to be disregarded and the allowance will be given instead when payment is due.

VAT can be included within the capital expenditure to the extent that it cannot be recovered as input tax by the taxpayer:

The capital allowances system also takes account of retrospective adjustments made under the VAT Capital Goods Scheme to the amount of VAT recoverable on certain assets.

Legislation: CAA 2001 s. 5 and 235

Tax Reporter: ¶235-125

4545 Subsidies and grants

Expenditure is not generally regarded as having been incurred by any person in so far as it has been or is to be met directly or indirectly by the Crown or by any government or public or local authority, whether in the UK or elsewhere, or by any other person entitled to capital allowances or a trading deduction on that amount. This means that capital allowances may be claimed only on the cost of the asset less any grants or subsidies.

Prior to 1 April 2013, where capital allowances were restricted to the extent that the expenditure was met by a grant which was later repaid, HMRC would treat the repayment as expenditure on which capital allowances could be given, provided the repayment fell to be taxed on the recipient through a balancing adjustment or as a trading receipt. This concession was withdrawn from 1 April 2013.

Legislation: CAA 2001, s. 532–536

Tax Reporter: ¶235-300

4550 Contributions

A person contributing to expenditure incurred by another person may be entitled to allowances if:

- the contribution is a capital sum;
- that expenditure would have been treated as incurred by the recipient; and
- if it had been incurred by the recipient, it would have entitled him to receive capital allowances.

Legislation: CAA 2001, s. 537–543

Tax Reporter: ¶235-350

4555 Capital allowances on a succession

Where a person ceases to carry on a qualifying activity, another person may begin to carry on that activity (typically transferring all the assets on which that person has claimed capital allowances).

In the case of a partnership, where on an admission or retirement, the partners elect that the qualifying activity should be considered to continue, the successor partnership generally steps into the shoes of the predecessor as regards capital allowances.

Otherwise, if there is a transfer of assets on a succession, without a sale, the assets will be treated as having been sold at market value. For plant and machinery only, where the parties are connected persons (using an extended definition for these purposes), an election may be made to treat the transfer as being at tax written down value.

Legislation: CAA 2001, s. 263–268 and 557–560

Tax Reporter: ¶235-450

4557 Capital allowances on sale to connected person

Alternatively, a person may sell off all or any of their assets to a connected person to further their business activities. In these cases, the normal balancing adjustments will apply subject to the amendments set out below.

- For plant and machinery, there are provisions to ensure that the buyer obtains writing-down allowances only on the disposal value the seller brings into account, or if none, the lower of market value or original cost to the seller. Further restrictions may apply if the purpose of the transaction is to obtain a tax advantage.

- For most other types of asset, if the parties are connected (or under common control) or the transaction is structured to obtain a tax advantage, there will be taken to be a market value sale, subject to an election to avoid any balancing charge by treating the sale as being at tax written down value if that is less than market value.

Legislation: CAA 2001, s. 213–218A and 567–570A

Tax Reporter: ¶235-550; ¶235-600

4560   Meaning of 'plant and machinery'

There is no statutory definition of 'plant and machinery'. The legislation includes two lists of assets that cannot by statute be plant and machinery. List A contains assets to be treated as buildings (including walls, floors, ceilings and windows) and List B contains assets to be treated as structures (including tunnels, bridges, canals and reservoirs).

A third list of assets, List C, contains assets that are not within the general exclusion of buildings and structures. They include manufacturing, catering, sanitary and computer equipment. Items falling within List C are typically eligible for capital allowances but whether they do in fact qualify can only be decided by reference to case law.

The classic legal definition of plant can be found in the case of *Yarmouth v France* where it was stated that it 'includes whatever apparatus is used by a businessman for carrying on his business – not his stock-in-trade ... but all goods and chattels, fixed or moveable...which he keeps for permanent employment in his business'.

Some of the assets that have been held by the courts to be plant include:

- books purchased by a practising barrister;
- a dry dock;
- a swimming pool at a caravan park;
- knives and lasts used by a shoe manufacturer together with machinery;
- concrete grain silos;
- warehouse storage platforms;
- decorative window screens; and
- pictures on walls in a hotel.

On the other hand, the courts have held the following assets not to be plant·

- a canopy in a self-service petrol station;
- an inflatable cover for a tennis court;
- a prefabricated gymnasium and laboratory in a school;
- a vessel used as a floating restaurant; and
- permanent quarantine kennels.

The current state of the law on the meaning of 'plant' derives from the decision in the case of *Wimpy International Ltd v Warland*, and

Associated Restaurants Ltd v Warland in the late 1980s. A small number of subsequent cases have been decided using the same basic principles.

In both *Wimpy* and *Associated Restaurants*, the taxpayers improved and modernised their restaurants. They claimed plant and machinery allowances on items such as replacement shop fronts, floor and wall tiles, murals, lighting, water tanks, staircases and raised floors. The Special Commissioners followed the Scottish and Newcastle decision and allowed such things as murals, decorative brickwork and wall panels, but disallowed the rest apart from the water tanks. The companies appealed to the High Court and then the Court of Appeal. The Special Commissioners' decision was upheld apart from one item – the Wimpy light fittings.

In his judgment, Hoffman J said that there were three tests, all of which could be called 'functional', to be considered when deciding whether an item was plant. These tests are the following.

(1) Is the item stock in trade?

(2) Is the item the business premises or part of the business premises (known as 'the premises test')?

(3) Is the item used for carrying on the business (the 'business use test')?

The fact that an item passes the business use test is not enough to make it plant. If the business use is as stock in trade (i.e. if the answer to 1) above is 'yes'), then the item is not plant. Furthermore, it is not sufficient that the asset is used in the business – it must be employed in carrying on the business.

Hoffman J also said that an item used for carrying on the business is not plant if the business use is as the premises (or part of the premises) or place in which the business is conducted – the 'premises test' (i.e. if the answer to 2) above is 'yes') then the item is not plant.

He suggested four general factors to be considered in deciding whether an item is part of the premises:

(1) Does the item appear visually to retain a separate identity?

(2) To what degree of permanence has it been attached to the building?

(3) To what extent is the structure complete without it?

(4) To what extent is it intended to be permanent? Is it likely to be replaced within a short period?

These are questions of fact and degree. They are not absolute hurdles, each of which must be surmounted.

Legislation: CAA 2001, s. 21–23

Cases: *Bradley (HMIT) v London Electricity plc (No. 2)* [1996] BTC 451; *Attwood (HMIT) v Anduff Car Wash Ltd* [1996] BTC 44; *Gray (HMIT) v Seymours Garden Centre (Horticulture)* [1995] BTC 320; *Wimpy International Ltd v Warland (HMIT)* [1989] BTC 58; *IR Commrs v Scottish and Newcastle Breweries Ltd* [1982] BTC 187; *Yarmouth v France* (1887) 19 QBD 647

Tax Reporter: ¶244-500; ¶244-800; ¶245-025

4570   Incidental building alterations

Expenditure on alterations to an existing building incidental to the installation of plant and machinery is treated as if it were on the provision of the plant and machinery. Although the provision has been in place for over 60 years the scope of its application has only recently been considered by the courts. In the case of *JD Wetherspoon v R & C Commrs* it was concluded that it was fairly limited, the alterations having to be truly incidental rather than consequential upon the installation of plant. The purpose of the provision is to allow the cost of alterations to facilitate the installation of plant in an existing building that would not be required if the same plant were to be installed in a new building.

Legislation: CAA 2001, s. 25

Cases: *JD Wetherspoon v R & C Commrs* [2012] UKUT 42 (TCC); [2012] BTC 1,578

Tax Reporter: ¶245-480

4605   Fixtures

To be eligible for plant and machinery allowances an asset must, prima facie, belong to the taxpayer in consequence of his incurring the expenditure in question. Expenditure by tenants on items which become fixtures would not, without further provision, qualify for allowances.

Fixtures are items that are so installed or fixed in a building as to become, in property law, part of that building. In property law, all such items are treated as belonging to the freeholder. In consequence, and in the absence of the provisions in CAA 2001, a tenant installing a central heating system in a warehouse, for example, would not receive any capital allowances, as the item would in law belong to the freeholder.

The legislation overcomes this problem by treating the entitlement to capital allowances as attaching to the interest in land held at the time by the person who incurred the capital expenditure on the plant and machinery.

Capital allowances

Other rules prevent more than one person claiming allowances on the same fixture at the same time, while further rules restrict the amount of allowances that can be claimed by the current owner when there has been a claim by a prior owner.

Finance Act 2012 introduced new rules for purchasers of fixtures. The new rules apply to new expenditure incurred on or after 1 April 2012 for corporation tax purposes and on or after 6 April 2012 for income tax purposes.

The new rules make the availability of capital allowances to a purchaser of fixtures conditional on:

- previous business expenditure on qualifying fixtures being pooled before a subsequent transfer on to another person (the 'pooling requirement'); and

- the seller and purchaser formally agreeing the value of fixtures within two years of a transfer (the 'fixed value requirement'); or, exceptionally

- the past owner providing a written statement of the amount of the disposal value of the fixtures, which he had some time earlier been required to bring into account (for example, when a person permanently ceases a business) within two years of a later sale of the property (the 'disposal value statement requirement').

If these requirements are not met, the qualifying expenditure of the new owner is to be treated as nil.

Neither the pooling requirement nor the fixed value requirement apply to the expenditure of a past owner where the period of ownership was entirely before 1 April 2012 for corporation tax purposes and 6 April 2012 for income tax purposes.

Pooling requirement

The pooling requirement in CAA 2001, s. 187A(4) applies in any case where the new rules apply, i.e. where the past owner was entitled to claim allowances. The requirement will be met even if the allowances claim is reduced to nil. The requirement does not apply to property traders or tax exempt entities such as charities and pensions funds that are not entitled to allowances.

The pooling requirement is that:

- the historic expenditure on fixtures has been allocated to a pool in a chargeable period beginning on or before the day on which the past owner ceases to be treated as the owner of the fixture; or

- a first-year allowance has been claimed on whole or part of the historic expenditure.

The introduction of the pooling requirement was delayed until 1 April 2014 for corporation tax purposes and 6 April 2014 for income tax purposes, meaning that in the two year period between April 2012 and April 2014, only the fixed value requirement (or exceptionally the disposal value statement requirement) applied. The pooling requirement does not apply where the period of ownership of the past owner ended no later than two years from the commencement date, i.e. 31 March 2014 for corporation tax purposes and 5 April 2014 for income tax purposes.

Fixed value requirement

The fixed value requirement in CAA 2001, s. 187A(6) applies where the past owner is or has been required to bring a disposal value into account (as a result of having made a claim) following the sale of the qualifying interest or grant of a lease for a premium (items 1, 5 or 9 in table in CAA 2001, s. 196).

The fixed value requirement is met (except in cases where there is an intermediate owner who was not entitled to claim allowances) by the making of a relevant apportionment of the apportionable sum. The making of such apportionment is achieved by:

- one of the parties making an application to the tribunal to determine the part of the apportionable sum that constitutes the disposal value within two years of the sale or grant; or

- the parties making a joint election under either CAA 2001, s. 198 or 199 within two years of the sale or grant (or before any application to the tribunal is determined or withdrawn, if later).

Where the requirement applies, i.e. where a past owner who owned the fixture on or after 1 (or 6) April 2012 claimed allowances, the use of the election will in practice become mandatory, unless the parties cannot reach agreement and one or both choose to refer the matter to the tribunal.

The legislation also makes provision for cases where there is an intermediate owner who was not entitled to claim allowances (such as charities that are not chargeable to tax) and referred to as the 'purchaser from the past owner (or as the case may be lessee)'. In these cases, the fixed value requirement can be met by the current owner obtaining the following written statements:

- from the purchaser from the past owner that a relevant apportionment has not been and is no longer capable of being met; and

- from the past (taxpaying business) owner of the amount of the disposal value actually brought into account.

Disposal value statement requirement

The disposal value statement requirement applies where the past owner is required to bring a disposal value into account (as a result of having made a claim) where the sale is deemed to be at market value as a result of a cessation of ownership (items 2 or 3 in table in CAA 2001, s. 196 or item 7 in table in CAA 2001, s. 61). It is anticipated that this will apply in a very limited number of other circumstances where a disposal event may have occurred. For example, the cessation of a business followed some years later by the sale of the former business premises.

The current owner must obtain from the past owner a written statement of the disposal value brought into account and made within two years of cessation of ownership.

The new rules apply in addition to existing legislation in place prior to FA 2012 to prevent the double claiming of capital allowances on fixtures when a property changed hands, which legislation continues to apply and provides as follows:

Where plant and machinery allowances have previously been claimed, the maximum allowable amount available to the purchaser will be restricted to the prior claimant's disposal value. The disposal value is required to be equal to the purchaser's apportionment of the purchase price, subject to a maximum of the amount of capital expenditure incurred by the prior claimant. Further complications will arise when there has been an intervening owner who had no interest in capital allowances.

Where the property is the subject of a sale and leaseback transaction, then in the absence of any claim by the seller, the buyer will usually be restricted to the amount paid by the seller for the plant and machinery.

Election to fix apportionment

An election under CAA 2001, s. 198 (or 199) provides the opportunity to choose how the overall value of a purchase and sale agreement should be allocated between different elements. Following the changes made in *Finance Act* 2012, the making of an election has in practice become mandatory unless one or both parties choose to apply to the tribunal for a determination of the disposal value. The amount cannot be more than the expenditure incurred by the seller on the fixtures, nor the price paid for the property, but can be as little as £1. An election can only be made following the sale of the qualifying interest or grant of a lease in cases where a disposal value is required to be brought into account (items 1, 5 or 9 in table in CAA 2001, s. 196, i.e. where the person ceasing to own the qualifying interest has claimed capital allowances).

There is no set format for an election but it should contain the following information:

- the amount fixed by the election;

- the name of each person making the election;

- information sufficient to identify the fixture and the relevant land;

- particulars of the interest acquired by or the lease granted to the purchaser;

- the unique taxpayer reference of each of the persons making the election (or a statement that they do not have such a reference).

The time limit for making the election is two years.

Where the buyer is paying a premium for the grant of a new lease rather than a transfer of an existing interest in land, then a separate election will be required to transfer the entitlement to allowances to the lessee. The only exception to this rule is where the lease is granted by the developer (e.g. an individual unit on a business park), in which case the entitlement to allowances transfers automatically.

Legislation: CAA 2001, s. 172–204

Tax Reporter: ¶242-800ff.

4607 Integral features

A new category of qualifying expenditure on 'integral features' was introduced in April 2008. The following items are integral features:

- an electrical system (including a lighting system);

- a cold water system;

- a space or water heating system, a powered system of ventilation, air cooling or air purification, and any floor or ceiling comprised in such a system;

- a lift, an escalator or a moving walkway; and

- external solar shading.

One of the benefits of these rules is that they allow some taxpayers to benefit from allowances where none were available before. For example, lighting in an office building (in contrast to that in say a retail shop) would not normally qualify for allowances under the old rules but will now do so as an integral feature. A further benefit is that such lighting may also potentially qualify under the enhanced capital allowances scheme (see 4625).

The reason given for the removal of the first four of these items from List C referred to in 4560 was that the rate of tax relief should more closely reflect accounting depreciation. Capital expenditure on integral features is added to the special rate pool and a reduced writing-down allowance of 8% p.a. is available (10% before April 2012).

The legislation also includes a rule that prevents a revenue deduction being obtained where expenditure is incurred that represents more than 50% of the cost of replacing the integral feature.

Legislation: CAA 2001, s. 33A

Tax Reporter: 243-400ff.

4610 Allowances for plant and machinery generally

Allowances are available in respect of expenditure on plant and machinery if a person who is carrying on a qualifying activity incurs qualifying expenditure. If a person carries on more than one qualifying activity, then allowances must be calculated separately for each.

Plant and machinery allowances are given through a system of pooling, whereby most expenditure is merged within a single, ongoing calculation, the value of the pool increasing as new expenditure is incurred but reducing as allowances are given or sale proceeds are received.

Certain types of asset are not pooled as such (though the legislation uses the term 'single asset pool'). A third category of assets can be pooled with one another but have to be kept separate from the main pool of expenditure ('class pools').

For the majority of businesses, capital allowances are from April 2008 given mainly by way of the annual investment allowance, giving full relief for expenditure in the year it is incurred.

First-year allowances are available in some cases, depending on the nature of the expenditure. Where available, such allowances are given at 100% (i.e. full tax relief in the year in which the expenditure is incurred), though there is generally an option to accept a lower rate of allowance.

Where first-year allowances are available, no writing-down allowances are given in the same period. In contrast, the same expenditure may attract both an annual investment allowance and writing-down allowance in the same period.

Balancing allowances or balancing charges may arise where an asset is sold or otherwise disposed of. Balancing charges can never exceed the total allowances that have been given for the asset in question.

Cash basis for small businesses

From the tax year 2013–14 onwards, some small self-employed businesses that opt to use the cash basis to calculate taxable profits can generally claim a deduction for capital expenditure on plant and machinery (other than cars) rather than capital allowances. In the case of cars, the business has the alternative option of using the simplified expenses flat rate for mileage.

Tax Reporter: ¶236-000

4615   Annual Investment Allowances

The Annual Investment Allowance (AIA) first applied to expenditure incurred from 1 April 2008.

In essence, the AIA gives full tax relief (similar in effect to a 100% first-year allowance) for a fixed amount of annual expenditure incurred by a business on plant and machinery.

The amount of the AIA has changed regularly since its introduction:

*   £50,000 p.a. (1 April 2008 to 31 March 2010);

*   £100,000 p.a. (1 April 2010 to 31 March 2012);

*   £25,000 p.a. (1 April 2012 to 31 December 2012);

*   £250,000 p.a. (1 January 2013 to 31 March 2014) (initial temporary increase);

*   £500,000 p.a. (1 April 2014 to 31 December 2015) (increase and extension of temporary increase); and

*   £200,000 p.a. (1 January 2016 onwards).

Finance (No. 2) Act 2015 permanently increased the annual allowance to £200,000, with effect for expenditure incurred on or after 1 January 2016. The annual allowance was due to fall back to £25,000 from 1 January 2016 following the expiry of the temporary increases which were introduced from 1 January 2013.

Expenditure must be incurred by a 'qualifying person', defined to mean an individual, a partnership consisting only of individuals, or a company. Expenditure is said to be 'AIA qualifying expenditure' if it is incurred by such a person and is not subject to any of the general exclusions. The person claiming the allowance must own the plant or machinery at some time during the chargeable period for which the claim is made.

Cars and expenditure on 'green' technology continue to be treated separately, but the AIA is available for expenditure on all other plant and machinery, including long-life assets and 'integral features'. Expenditure in excess of the AIA may attract writing-down allowances in the same accounting period.

The AIA is optional and so does not have to be claimed. A business may also choose the category of assets on which to claim AIA to maximise their tax relief in a year.

Example

A business spends £150,000 on general plant and machinery and £150,000 on integral features in the year ended 31 March 2017. It will wish to treat the whole of the integral features expenditure and £50,000 of the plant and machinery expenditure as AIA qualifying expenditure so that the remaining £100,000 can attract allowances at the main WDA rate of 18% rather than at the lower rate of 8% (if the AIA were allocated first against plant and machinery expenditure).

Where an asset is provided partly for purposes other than those of the qualifying activity carried on by the person, AIAs may be given to the extent that is just and reasonable in relation to the proportion in which the expenditure was incurred for the purposes of the qualifying activity. So if an asset costs £200,000, and is used one-quarter for private purposes, AIAs can be claimed on £150,000. It would seem to follow, from the way that the legislation is worded that when calculating the remaining AIA available, the business can take just the £150,000 claimed into account. So, if the amount of AIA were for example £200,000, AIAs can be claimed on other expenditure of up to £50,000 (rather than nil).

The legislation specifies that a person may not claim an AIA and a first-year allowance in respect of the same expenditure. Now that all remaining first-year allowances are given at 100%, the provision appears to simply remove any possibility of claiming double relief for the same expenditure.

Chargeable periods spanning date of increase or reversion

Where a chargeable period spans the above dates of change, the maximum AIA is calculated by splitting the chargeable period into separate periods falling before and after each of the dates of change. Transitional rules are then applied to determine the maximum AIA available in respect of the total chargeable period and the maximum AIA that may be allocated against qualifying expenditure incurred in each of the separate periods.

Transitional measures: 31 December 2015 reversion to £200,000

Where a business has a chargeable period that spans the date of end of the temporary increase on 31 December 2015, the maximum allowance for that business' transitional chargeable period comprises two parts:

(a) the AIA entitlement, based on the temporary £500,000 annual cap for the portion of the period falling before 1 January 2016; and

(b) the AIA entitlement, based on the £200,000 cap for the portion of the period falling on or after 1 January 2016.

Example

A company with a 12-month chargeable period from 1 April 2015 to 31 March 2016 would calculate its maximum AIA entitlement based on:

(a) the proportion of the period from 1 April 2015 to 31 December 2015, that is $\frac{9}{12} \times £500,000 = £375,000$; and

(b) the proportion of the period from 1 January 2016 to 31 March 2016, that is $\frac{3}{12} \times £200,000 = £50,000$.

The company's maximum AIA for this transitional chargeable period would therefore be the total of (a) + (b) = £375,000 + £50,000 = £425,000, although in relation to (b) (the part period falling on or after 1 January 2016) no more than £50,000 of the company's actual expenditure in that part period would be covered by its transitional AIA entitlement.

Transitional measures: 1 (or 6) April 2014 increase to £500,000

Where a business has a chargeable period of 12 months that spans the operative date of the increase on 1 (or 6) April 2014, the maximum allowance for that business' transitional chargeable period comprises two parts:

(a) its AIA entitlement, based on the £250,000 annual cap for the portion of the period falling before 1 (or 6) April 2014; and

(b) its AIA entitlement, based on the £500,000 cap for the portion of the period falling on or after 1 (or 6) April 2014.

Example

A company with a 12-month chargeable period from 1 January 2014 to 31 December 2014 would calculate its maximum AIA entitlement base on:

(a) the proportion of the period from 1 January 2014 to 31 March 2014, that is, $\frac{3}{12} \times £250,000 = £62,500$; and

(b) the proportion of the period from 1 April 2014 to 31 December 2014, that is, $\frac{9}{12} \times £500,000 = £375,000$.

> The company's maximum AIA for this transitional chargeable period would therefore be the total of (a) + (b) = £62,500 + £375,000 = £437,500, although in relation to (a) (the period falling before 1 (or 6) April 2014, no more than a maximum of £250,000 of the company's actual expenditure in that particular part period would be covered by its transitional AIA entitlement (the maximum claimable before the increase to £500,000).

Earlier transitional measures: 1 January 2013 increase

Where a business has a chargeable period that began before 1 January 2013, that period must be considered separately and a maximum AIA entitlement based on the £25,000 annual cap that applied before 1 January 2013, for the portion of the period falling before that date.

> **Example**
>
> A business with a chargeable period of 18 months from 1 December 2012 to 31 May 2014 would calculate its maximum AIA entitlement based on:
>
> (a) the proportion of the period from 1 December 2012 to 31 December 2012, that is, $^1/_{12} \times$ £25,000 = £2,083;
>
> (b) the proportion of the period from 1 January 2013 to 5 April 2014, that is, $^{15}/_{12} \times$ £250,000 = £312,500; and
>
> (c) the proportion of the period from 6 April 2014 to 31 May 2014, that is, $^2/_{12} \times$ £500,000 = £83,333.
>
> So, the business' maximum AIA for this transitional chargeable period would be the total of (a) + (b) + (c) = £2,083 + £312,500 + £83,333 = £397,916.
>
> However, in relation to (a) (the part period falling before 1 January 2013), the maximum allowance for expenditure actually incurred in this period is the amount that would have been the maximum allowance for the whole of the chargeable period if neither the temporary increase in the AIA to £250,000 nor the temporary increase in the AIA to £500,000 had been made. So, for expenditure incurred in period (a), the maximum allowance would be:
>
> • $^1/_{12} \times$ £25,000 = £2,083;
>
> • $^{15}/_{12} \times$ £25,000 = £31,250; and
>
> • $^2/_{12} \times$ £25,000 = £4,167
>
> Total £37,500
>
> In relation to (b) (the part period falling before 1 (or 6) April 2014), the maximum allowance is again calculated by reference to the amount that would have been the maximum allowance for the whole of the chargeable period but this time ignoring only the later increase from £250,000 to £500,000. Therefore,

in relation to expenditure incurred in period (a) + (b), a maximum allowance would be:

- $\frac{1}{12} \times$ £25,000 = £2,083;

- $\frac{15}{12} \times$ £250,000 = £312,500; and

- $\frac{2}{12} \times$ £250,000 = £41,667

Total £356,250

There are also more detailed transitional rules about entitlement to AIA in relation to group companies, or when businesses under common control are regarded as 'related'. These transitional rules are based on similar time-apportionment principles as applied to the rules in CAA 2001, s. 51K (operation of the annual investment allowance where restrictions apply).

Legislation: CAA 2001, s. 38A, 51A, 52A; FA 2011, s. 11; FA 2013, Sch. 1; *Finance Act* 2014, Sch. 2

Case: *Keyl v R & C Commrs* [2015] BTC 523

Tax Reporter: ¶236-400

4620   First-year allowances

For various reasons, the Government has decided that it is appropriate in particular circumstances to allow tax relief at a faster rate for certain types of expenditure. From April 2008, this is generally by way of the annual investment allowance discussed at 4615. First-year allowances (FYAs) have now largely been withdrawn.

For FYAs to be available, a person must incur 'first-year qualifying expenditure' and must own the asset in question at some time during the chargeable period in which the expenditure is incurred. Any first-year allowance is then made for that chargeable period.

Where an asset is provided partly for purposes other than those of the qualifying activity carried on by the person, FYAs may be given to the extent that is just and reasonable in relation to the proportion in which the expenditure was incurred for the purposes of the qualifying activity.

The legislation identifies several types of first-year qualifying expenditure which are listed in the table below:

Expenditure incurred on	Qualifying period	Rate	Authority (CAA 2001)	Comment
Energy-saving plant or machinery	From 1 April 2001	100%	s. 45A–45C	Loss making companies may claim a payable tax credit from 1 April 2008 until 31 March 2018.
Cars with low CO_2 emissions	From 17 April 2002	100%	s. 45D	Expenditure incurred until 31 March 2018 (as extended from 31 March 2015 for both corporation tax and income tax).
Zero-emission goods vehicles	From 1 April 2010	100%	s. 45DA	Expenditure incurred before 1 April 2018 (corporation tax) or 6 April 2018 (income tax) (as extended from 31 March/5 April 2015).
P&M for gas refuelling station	From 17 April 2002	100%	s. 45E	Expenditure incurred until 31 March 2018 (for both corporation tax and income tax) (as extended from 31 March 2015).
P&M for use in a ring fence trade	From 17 April 2002	100%	s. 45F	Special rules apply to this type of expenditure.
Environmentally beneficial plant and machinery	From 1 April 2003	100%	s. 45H	Loss making companies may claim a payable tax credit from 1 April 2008 until 31 March 2018.
P&M for use in designated assisted areas	From 1 April 2012	100%	s. 45K	Initially for five years but increased to eight years (I.e. until 31 March 2020)

Recent and forthcoming changes

At Budget 2016, the Government announced the following changes:

- extension to April 2021 of 100% first-year allowances for businesses purchasing low emission cars; and

- reduction in the first-year allowance threshold for low emission cars to 50g/km of CO_2 from April 2018 (currently 75g/km).

Other recent changes include:

- extension to 31 March 2018 (corporation tax and income tax) for enhanced capital allowances for gas refuelling equipment and low CO_2 emission cars (previously due to end 31 March 2015);

- reduction in qualifying threshold for low CO_2 emission cars (for these purposes) from 95g/km to 75g/km for expenditure incurred on or after 1 April 2015 (for corporation tax and income tax);

- extension to 31 March 2018 (corporation tax) and 5 April 2018 (income tax) of enhanced capital allowances for zero-emission goods vehicles (previously due to end 31 March 2015 (corporation tax) and 5 April 2015 (income tax)); and

- from 1 April 2015 (corporation tax) and 6 April 2015 (income tax), the ECA for zero-emission goods vehicles is not available, or is withdrawn, if another form of state aid has or will be received (in essence, a choice must be made between claiming the ECA or receiving a grant or other payment that is a state aid).

Legislation: CAA 2001, Pt. 2, Ch. 4, s. 262A and Sch. A1

Tax Reporter: ¶237-000ff.

4625 Enhanced capital allowances

The term 'enhanced capital allowances' (ECAs) is often applied to expenditure under the following headings:

- Energy-saving plant or machinery.

- Low emission cars.

- Environmentally beneficial plant and machinery.

Key features of the scheme are as follows:

- all businesses can claim ECAs, regardless of size, industrial or commercial sector or location;

- only investments in new and unused plant and machinery can qualify;

- eCAs allow the full cost of the investment to be relieved for tax purposes against taxable income of the period of investment;

- qualifying technologies have to meet defined energy-saving criteria published in a list;

- there is an annual review of technologies and criteria;

- there are no territorial restrictions on manufacturers wishing to place their products on the list, or the source of products.

Although the capital allowances legislation does not use the term ECAs, there is some logic in it: all three categories relate to environmentally conscious expenditure and all offer businesses of whatever size the chance to obtain full tax relief in the year in which the expenditure is incurred. Nevertheless, different rules apply and the best approach is to recognise the overlapping concepts but to apply the legislation on a case-by-case basis.

Under the energy-saving rules, for example, manufacturers need to register their products for inclusion on the Energy Technology List published on the government website, www.etl.decc.gov.uk, which contains details of how to go about this. To be included, products must normally meet the scheme's published energy-efficiency criteria, though separate conditions are imposed for certain product types (including lighting).

Care is needed since, as the website states, 'it is the purchaser's responsibility to check with the manufacturer whether their products meet the criteria'. The end-user or his adviser therefore needs to go to the same website and, under 'product search', can choose (for example) to search for lamps. The site lists many thousands of items (and their manufacturers) that qualify under the energy-saving scheme. If the business wants to buy from a particular manufacturer, it can select that name, but often that will not be necessary.

Leasing of assets qualifying for enhanced capital allowances

The question of whether enhanced allowances are available for 'energy-saving' or 'environmentally beneficial' plant and machinery and low emission cars can be complex. As far as these three categories of asset are concerned, the position may be summarised as follows:

- expenditure on plant and machinery for leasing or letting on hire does not generally qualify for FYAs;

- the exclusion does not apply to the schemes for FYAs for 'energy-saving' or 'environmentally beneficial' plant and machinery and, before 1 April 2013, low emission cars for leasing;

- the exclusion applies to the scheme for FYAs for low emission cars for leasing from 1 April 2013;

- the denial of FYAs for 'energy-saving' or 'environmentally beneficial' plant and machinery will still apply unless the plant and machinery is provided for leasing under an excluded lease of 'background' plant and machinery for buildings, within the meaning of CAA 2001, s. 70R.

Legislation: CAA 2001, s. 45DB, 46

Tax Reporter: ¶237-100

4630 Payable enhanced capital allowances

Loss-making companies that incur expenditure on certain 'green' technology from 1 April 2008 to 31 March 2018 are able to claim a cash payment if they are otherwise unable to use their losses against their own profits or those of a group member. The rules are directly linked to the FYAs that are given for expenditure on 'energy-saving' plant and machinery or 'environmentally beneficial' plant and machinery. In this way, companies will gain an immediate cash repayment rather than carrying losses forward indefinitely in the hope of obtaining relief when profits start to be realised in the future.

The main features of the relief are as follows:

- Relief will be given for expenditure incurred on technology currently qualifying for 100% FYAs under either CAA 2001, s. 45A or 45H (respectively covering 'energy-saving' plant and 'environmentally beneficial' plant).

- The scheme will be available to companies (small, medium or large) but not to excluded companies, or to any sole traders, partnerships or other entities.

- Companies will be able to surrender losses, to the extent that they are attributable to qualifying expenditure, so as to receive a percentage of the surrendered loss as a tax-free cash payment from HMRC.

A payment in respect of a first-year tax credit is not treated as income of the company for any tax purpose.

Surrenderable loss

A company is said to have a 'surrenderable loss' in a given chargeable period if, in that period:

- the company is entitled to a FYA under CA 2001, s. 45A or 45H;

Capital allowances

- the expenditure is incurred on or after 1 April 2008;

- it is incurred for the purposes of a qualifying activity of which the profits are chargeable to corporation tax; and

- the company incurs a loss in that qualifying activity.

The amount of the surrenderable loss is the lower of the following figures:

- so much of the loss incurred in carrying on the qualifying activity as is unrelieved; or

- the amount of the FYA claimed in respect of the relevant first-year expenditure in the chargeable period in question.

Calculating the credit

Companies will be able to receive a percentage of the surrenderable loss as a cash repayment. That percentage figure is set at 19% (whatever the size and corporation tax rate of the company), though the Treasury has the power to substitute a higher or lower figure and is applied to the amount of the 'surrenderable loss'.

Example 1

A company makes a profit of £50,000, before deduction of £90,000 of qualifying FYAs. The company thus has a loss of £40,000 which can be surrendered. The company will then receive a cash payment of £7,600 (£40,000 at 19%).

Example 2

A second company makes a loss of £50,000, before deduction of £90,000 of qualifying FYAs (entirely incurred on energy efficient plant and machinery included on the Energy Technology List). The company thus has an overall loss of £140,000 and its surrenderable loss is £90,000. The company can therefore surrender that £90,000 in return for a cash payment of £17,100 (£90,000 at 19%).

A company may claim either the whole or part of the tax credit.

A cap is set on the amount of tax that can be reclaimed under these rules, for each chargeable period, at the higher of:

- the level of the company's PAYE and NIC liabilities for payment periods ending in the chargeable period for which the claim has been made; and

- £250,000.

Availability of the first-year tax credit has been extended to 31 March 2018.

Legislation: CAA 2001, Sch. A1; SI 2013/464

Tax Reporter: ¶242-000; ¶242-040

4640 Energy-saving plant and machinery

FYAs for energy saving plant and machinery were originally introduced by *Finance Act* 2001. The primary legislation allows the Treasury to designate technologies and products qualifying under the scheme by reference to a list published by the Department for Energy and Climate Change (DECC). The scope of the scheme has been widened by the inclusion of new technologies and changes to the criteria each year since its introduction.

Full information about the scheme is published on a website (www.etl. decc.gov.uk) produced by the Carbon Trust in collaboration with DECC and HMRC. Under the scheme, businesses are able to claim 100% first-year allowances on investments in energy-saving plant and machinery. There are currently 16 energy-saving technologies appearing on the Energy Technology List that meet the relevant energy-saving criteria:

- air-to-air energy recovery;
- automatic monitoring and targeting (AMT);
- boiler equipment;
- combined heat and power (CHP);
- compressed air equipment;
- heat pumps for space heating;
- heating ventilation and air conditioning (HVAC) zone controls;
- high speed hand air dryers;
- lighting;
- motors and drives;
- pipe work insulation;
- radiant and warm air heaters;
- refrigeration equipment;
- solar thermal systems;
- uninterruptible power supplies; and
- waste heat to electricity conversion equipment.

The latest version of the list was published on 7 September 2016.

The Energy Technology List is comprised of two lists: the Energy Technology Criteria List (ETCL) and Energy Technology Product List (ETPL). The ETCL presents the energy-saving performance criteria that ECA qualifying equipment must meet, whereas the ETPL is a register of products that have been assessed as being compliant with ETCL criteria. Also published are lists of products removed from the list.

Automatic Monitoring and Targeting (AMT) systems, lighting equipment, pipework insulation and air source split and multisplit heat pumps (including VRF) are not listed on the ETPL. Spending on these types of equipment which meets ETCL criteria can qualify for an ECA. Businesses should seek confirmation from their installer that the equipment complies with ETCL criteria prior to purchase.

Combined Heat and Power (CHP) equipment is also not listed on the ETPL. However, in this instance businesses are required to verify ECA compliance by having their equipment design assessed and a DECC certificate of energy-efficiency issued.

Performance benchmarks, in terms of energy efficiency requirements, have been defined for all product descriptions and manufacturers, suppliers and distributors can provide customers with advice as to whether products qualify. Under the scheme, manufacturers are encouraged to adopt and label their products with lighting fitting efficiency codes.

CHP is the simultaneous generation of heat and power (usually electricity) in a single process. CHP schemes are by their nature bespoke and approval of a given CHP manufacturer or product would not provide sufficient assurance of environmental benefit. With CHP, case by case certification is needed to ensure support is provided for 'good quality' CHP. Certification is achieved using the CHP Quality Assurance Programme (CHPQA). Because a certificate is used, no specific products appear on the Energy Technology Product List. Guidance on claiming Enhanced Capital Allowances for CHP is available on the GOV.UK website.

Allowances for a product on the Energy Technology Product List can be claimed on the price paid for the item and any costs that are directly associated with the provision of the product. Guidance published on the GOV.UK website suggests that these may include:

- transportation and installation costs, including, for example, project management costs and commissioning;

- professional fees directly related to the acquisition and installation of the asset; and

- costs of alterations to an existing building incidental to the installation of the asset.

When a larger item of plant and machinery is acquired that has a qualifying product already installed in it as a component, then the proportion of the cost that relates to the qualifying product will qualify for the ECA scheme. The remainder of the equipment will attract allowances at the normal rate. The Government specifies the amount that can be claimed for a qualifying product incorporated into another piece of equipment; this information can be found on the ECA website.

Feed-in tariffs and the renewable heat incentive

Legislation included in FA 2012 means enhanced capital allowances are no longer available for expenditure on plant and machinery where tariff payments are received under either of the renewable energy schemes. The changes apply from April 2012 with the exception of combined heat and power equipment to which they apply from April 2014. Enhanced capital allowances will still be available on qualifying equipment as long as no tariffs are paid.

Solar panels

Solar panels are treated as special rate expenditure (see 4660) from 1 April 2012 qualifying for writing down allowances at the lower rate of 8%.

Legislation: CAA 2001, s. 45A–45C;   SI 2001/2541;   SI 2002/1818; SI 2003/1744; SI 2004/2093; SI 2005/2424; SI 2006/2233; SI 2007/2165; SI 2008/1916; SI 2009/1863; SI 2010/2286; SI 2011/2221; SI 2012/1832; SI 2013/1763; SI 2014/1868; SI 2015/1508

Tax Reporter: ¶237-400ff.

4645   Environmentally beneficial plant or machinery

Finance Act 2003 introduced environmentally beneficial plant and machinery as a category of expenditure qualifying for 100% FYAs. Specified qualifying plant and machinery are set out in the Water Technology List, the latest version of which (as published June 2016) includes 15 categories of sustainable water use products, namely:

- cleaning in place equipment;

- efficient showers;

- efficient taps;

- efficient toilets;

- efficient washing machines;

- flow controllers;

- greywater recovery and reuse equipment;

- leak monitoring and control equipment;

- meters and monitoring equipment;

- rainwater-harvesting equipment;

- small-scale slurry and sludge de-watering equipment;

- vehicle wash waste reclaim units;

- water efficient industrial cleaning equipment;

- water management equipment for mechanical seals; and

- water reuse systems.

Legislation: CAA 2001, s. 45H–45J; SI 2003/2076; SI 2004/2094; SI 2005/2423; SI 2006/2235; SI 2007/2166; SI 2008/1917; SI 2009/1864; SI 2010/2483; SI 2011/2220; SI 2012/1838; SI 2012/2602; SI 2013/1762; SI 2014/1869 and SI 2015/1509

Tax Reporter: ¶237-600

4648 Enterprise zones

One hundred per cent enhanced capital allowances are available for expenditure incurred by trading companies on plant and machinery primarily for use in designated assisted areas in certain enterprise zones. The enhanced allowances were initially introduced for expenditure incurred in the period of five years beginning with 1 April 2012 but FA 2014 extended the period to eight years from 1 April 2012 (i.e. to 31 March 2020).

Finance Act 2016 makes further amendments to ensure that all zones are able to offer enhanced capital allowances for eight years following the date of designation and establishment of the ECA site.

In July 2016, further areas were designated by SI 2016/751, with effect in relation to expenditure incurred on or after 18 March 2015 and 16 March 2016.

Further guidance on state aid in assisted areas is available on the GOV.UK website per the link below.

Legislation: CAA 2001, s. 45K; SI 2015/2047; SI 2016/751

Other Material: www.gov.uk/government/publications/state-aid-assisted-areas-introduction; www.gov.uk/government/publications/enterprise-zones

Tax Reporter: ¶237-610

4650 Cars

The tax rules granting relief for business expenditure on cars were changed quite radically from April 2009.

The underlying principle had always been that a business should obtain tax relief on the amount by which the value of a car has fallen over the period of ownership. If, for example, a business buys a car for £20,000 and sells it three years later for £7,500, then it will be able to reduce its taxable profits by £12,500 (albeit subject to a likely private use adjustment if the car is not owned by a company). What the tax system does not do, though, is to give tax relief on a timescale that mirrors commercial depreciation; rather, it contains its own fairly complex rules to determine the timing of the tax deductions.

The changes applying from April 2009 relate almost entirely to the timing of that tax relief. In the past, the main factor that determined the speed at which relief could be gained was the cost of the car: more expensive cars were discouraged by slowing down the percentage of relief given in the early years. Now, the rate of relief is determined primarily by the level of engine emissions, the idea being to encourage businesses to buy cars that are more fuel efficient and have a less damaging environmental impact.

Definition of 'car'

The capital allowances definition of 'car' is given at CAA 2001, s. 268A. The term covers any 'mechanically propelled road vehicle' except:

- a motor cycle;

- a vehicle of a construction primarily suited for the conveyance of goods or burden of any description (e.g. a van); or

- a vehicle of a type not commonly used as a private vehicle and unsuitable for such use (e.g. a police car).

The definition is similar (but not identical) to that used for the purposes of determining benefits in kind on company cars. Some of the case law that has helped clarify the definition in that area of the legislation may be applied equally to the capital allowances definition.

Motor cycles

The exclusion of motor cycles was a change introduced from April 2009. This means that motor cycles are now treated for capital allowances purposes like any other asset, rather than being subject to the special rules applying for cars. One effect of this is that the annual investment allowance is now available for motor cycles, whereas this was not previously the case.

Overview of the rules

The key features of the rules introduced from April 2009 are as follows.

- The concept of 'expensive' cars is abolished and the rate of tax relief instead depends on the level of the vehicle's CO_2 emissions.

- Qualifying expenditure is normally allocated to one of the two main pools for plant and machinery. Expenditure on 'main rate cars' (those with emissions of up to 130g/km (160g/km before April 2013)) goes into the main plant and machinery pool, attracting allowances at 18% (20% before April 2012). Cars with higher emissions (over 130g/km or 160g/km before April 2013) attract allowances at just 8% in the 'special rate' pool (10% before April 2012).

- A 'main rate car' is defined as including any car first registered before 1 March 2001; a car with low CO_2 emissions (as defined for *these purposes*: see below); or a car that is electrically propelled.

- A car has low CO_2 emissions (for *these purposes*) if when first registered, it is registered on the basis of a qualifying emissions certificate; and the applicable CO_2 emissions figure in relation to the car does not exceed 130g/km (160g/km before April 2013). At Budget 2016, the Government announced that the CO_2 emission threshold for the main rate of capital allowances for business cars will be further reduced from 130g/km to 110g/km from April 2018.

- Cars with private use are kept in a single-asset pool but the rate at which allowances are given is still determined by reference to the same emission principles.

- For cars bought before April 2009, allowances are normally calculated according to principles applying up to that date, though the transitional provisions are quite complex.

- Car leases that began before 1 April 2009 broadly continue to be subject to the former rules. For new leases of vehicles above the 130g/km (160g/km before April 2013) threshold, a flat-rate disallowance is made, calculated as 15% of 'relevant payments'. New cars with lower emissions suffer no disallowance.

- Certain hire cars (e.g. taxis) that were exempt from the restrictions for expensive cars are from April 2009 subject to the new rules. Conversely, motor cycles were previously classified as cars for capital allowances purposes but are excluded from the definition from April 2009.

- The 100% first-year allowance for cars with very low emissions is currently available until 31 March 2018 but at Budget 2016, the Government announced that the period will be further extended until April 2021 (for both corporation tax and income tax). The applicable CO_2 emissions figure for *these purposes* is 75g//km (or less) for expenditure incurred on or after 1 April 2015 and is due to be reduced to 50g/km (or less) from April 2018 previously, the limits were for expenditure incurred after 1 April 2013 and 110g/km for expenditure incurred before April 2013) (see also 4620 and 4625).

When compared with the system applying before April 2009, the pooling of expenditure on cars may have a short-term advantage as annual writing-down allowances are no longer capped at £3,000. However, there is a significant cash-flow disadvantage in the longer term as there is no balancing allowance on sale of the vehicle.

Example

A company director drives a company car with emissions of 170g/km. The vehicle is bought in year one for £40,000 and sold in year four for £18,000. Under the old rules, the company would obtain tax relief on £3,000 in each of years one to three and £13,000 (by way of a balancing allowance) in year four.

Under the new rules, the company will initially be slightly better off, but will lose out when the car comes to be sold. Allowances will not be calculated separately for the car but will effectively be £3,200, £2,944, £2,708 and (adjusting for the sale proceeds) £1,052. The loss on the car is £22,000 but less than half of that loss has attracted tax relief by the time the car is sold. The balance of the relief will be obtained over an indefinite future period.

Legislation: CAA 2001, s. 54, 104A and 104AA

Tax Reporter: ¶238-500ff.

4654 Short life assets

One effect of having writing-down allowance of 18% p.a. (20% before April 2012) is that capital allowances will not have been given for the full cost of an asset having a short useful life until long after it ceased to be used for the purposes of the trade. An election can be made to allow a business to obtain special treatment for expenditure on such an asset.

The consequence is that qualifying expenditure in respect of a short-life asset is excluded from the main pool and included in a single asset pool of its own.

Writing-down allowances are still given at 18% p.a. (20% before April 2012) but the advantage of the election is that if the asset is disposed of before the '8 year cut-off' (four years before April 2011), then a balancing allowance is given (or charge made) so that capital allowances are given on the actual cost of the asset to the business over the period of ownership. Where the business still owns the asset after the 'cut-off' then the balance of the qualifying expenditure is transferred to the general pool.

Certain classes of asset are excluded including special rate expenditure.

Legislation: CAA 2001, s. 83–89

Tax Reporter: ¶239-000

4656 Long life assets

A long-life asset is defined as plant and machinery that can reasonably be expected to have a useful economic life of at least 25 years. The useful economic life is taken as the period from first use until it is likely to cease to be used as a fixed asset of any business.

Plant and machinery provided for use in a building used wholly or mainly as a dwelling house, showroom, hotel, office or retail shop or similar premises, or for purposes ancillary to such use, cannot be a long-life asset.

There is also a monetary limit which must be exceeded for the legislation to apply. Where the total expenditure on long-life assets does not exceed £100,000 in the chargeable period (which figure is increased or reduced for chargeable periods that are not of 12 months), the long-life asset rules do not apply to expenditure.

Capital expenditure on long life assets is added to the special rate pool and a reduced writing-down allowance of 8% p.a. is available (10% before 1 April 2012). Prior to *Finance Act* 2008, there was a separate long-life asset pool that contained all the expenditure on long-life assets.

Legislation: CAA 2001, s. 90–104

Tax Reporter: ¶239-500ff.

4658 Leasing

The entitlement to capital allowances on plant and machinery has always, with few exceptions, followed the legal ownership. The lessor claimed capital allowances in respect of expenditure on the asset and was taxed on the full rental income. The lessee on the other hand claimed no capital allowances, but deducted the full amount of the rent payable. In the case of a finance lease, the lessor again claimed capital allowances and was taxed on the full finance lease rentals. The lessee again claimed no capital allowances, but was allowed a deduction in the period in which the lease expense was correctly accounted for under Statement of Standard Accounting Practice 21.

The major changes made with effect from 1 April 2006 are intended to align the tax treatment of leased plant and machinery with that obtained using other forms of finance. When the lease is a 'long-funding lease' the lessee now has the right to claim capital allowances.

A long-funding lease is defined in the legislation as a lease of more than five years that is a finance lease or an operating lease that meets certain defined conditions.

When the rules apply and the lease is a finance lease, the lessor can no longer claim capital allowances, but will only be taxed on the finance charge element of the lease rentals. The lessee will claim the capital allowances and will be allowed a deduction for the finance charge.

When the rules apply and the lease is an operating lease the lessor can no longer claim capital allowances but will only be taxed on the full rental income less the amortisation of the decrease in asset value. The lessee will claim the capital allowances and will be allowed a deduction for the full lease rentals less the amortisation of the decrease in asset value.

The majority of typical property leases where plant and machinery fixtures are leased with land are excluded from the scope of the long funding lease rules.

Tax Reporter: ¶240-000ff.

4660 Pooling

Many businesses spend substantial amounts of money on plant and machinery, ranging from computer equipment to cars and sophisticated electrical systems to items which are specific to the business in question. Clearly, it would be impractical to produce separate tax computations to claim relief on every individual item. For this reason, the legislation provides for a 'pooling' system which enables the majority of the expenditure to be dealt with in a single computation.

The general principle is that expenditure has to be pooled for the purpose of calculating a person's entitlement to writing-down allowances and balancing allowances and any liability to balancing charges. If the same person carries on more than one qualifying activity, a separate pool (or set of pools) is required for each activity.

The legislation provides for a main pool but also for 'single-asset pools' and 'class pools'. Certain assets are stated to belong to the single-asset or class pools and all other expenditure is allocated to the main pool.

Single-asset pools

As the name suggests, such pools may contain expenditure relating to only one asset. Items in the following categories must go into a single asset pool (and no other items may do so):

- expensive cars bought before April 2009 (but any cars still held as of the first day of the first chargeable period beginning on or after 1 April 2014 are transferred to the main pool at that time);
- short-life assets;
- ships;
- items used partly for non-trade purposes;
- assets where a partial depreciation subsidy has been received; and
- plant and machinery contribution allowance payments.

Class pools

Class pools are required for special rate expenditure (CAA 2001, s. 104C) and for assets used for overseas leasing (CAA 2001, s. 107).

The 'special rate pool' includes expenditure on:

- thermal insulation;
- integral features;
- long-life assets;
- cars (excluding main rate cars);
- provision of cushion gas; and
- solar panels

and allowances are given at 8% (10% before 1 April 2012).

Entitlement or liability

CAA 2001 uses two key concepts to determine whether a person is entitled to writing-down allowances or a balancing allowance, or is liable to a balancing charge, for a chargeable period. The calculation is made separately for each pool of qualifying expenditure and depends on the 'available qualifying expenditure' (AQE) and 'the total of any disposal receipts to be brought into account' (TDR).

The legislation says, simply enough, that if AQE exceeds TDR then a writing-down allowance or balancing allowance will be due for the period in question. If the reverse is true, then there will be a balancing charge for the period.

The principles apply equally to any single asset pools, any class pools and the main pool.

The allowances given where AQE exceeds TDR will always be writing-down allowances except in the final chargeable period, when it will be a balancing allowance.

Legislation: CAA 2001, s. 55–66

Tax Reporter: ¶238-000; ¶238-050

4800   Industrial building allowances

Industrial Buildings Allowances (IBAs) have been withdrawn with effect from 1 April 2011.

In the March 2007 Budget, the Chancellor announced that IBAs (and ABAs – see 4815) would be phased out over a four-year period. *Finance Act* 2007 contained provisions that prevented the making of any balancing adjustments on disposals of industrial buildings (with the exception of disposals of buildings in enterprise zones) from 21 March 2007. *Finance Act* 2008 then implemented a phased withdrawal of the relief. The effective rate of WDAs was reduced to 3% from April 2008, to 2% from April 2009 and to 1% from April 2010.

The allowances were also given for expenditure on qualifying hotels.

Legislation: CAA 2001, Pt. 3; FA 2007, s. 36; FA 2008, s. 84–87

Tax Reporter: ¶246-750

4805　Enterprise zones

For information about the enhanced capital allowances available in some of the new enterprise zones (see 4648). The old enterprise zone rules formed part of the overall IBA legislation. Unless otherwise specified, qualifying expenditure on an enterprise zone building was treated for IBA purposes in the same way as any other qualifying expenditure.

For enterprise zone expenditure only, balancing adjustments can still be made following the withdrawal of IBAs. It will be possible for a person to incur a balancing charge up to 5 April 2018 in relation to such expenditure. A balancing charge will (from April 2011) arise if:

- an initial allowance or writing-down allowance has been made under the IBA rules;

- an event occurs which would have given rise to a balancing charge under those rules; and

- a balancing event occurs within seven years of the date on which the building was first used.

Similarly, an initial allowance for qualifying enterprise zone expenditure will be withdrawn if:

- an event occurs which would have caused the allowance to be withdrawn if (from April 2011), CAA 2001, s. 307 had not been withdrawn; and

- a balancing event occurs within seven years of the end of the chargeable period for which the allowance was made.

Legislation: CAA 2001, s. 271(1)(b)(iv), 281, 298, 305, 310(1)(a); FA 2008, s. 86

Tax Reporter: ¶251-000

4810　Business Premises Renovation Allowance

Business Premises Renovation Allowance (BPRA) gives 100% tax relief for the costs of renovating or converting certain unused business property in any of 2,000 or so areas of the UK that are designated as disadvantaged. Allowances can be claimed by an individual or company incurring capital expenditure on bringing qualifying business premises back into business use. The allowances are available both to landlords and to businesses occupying their own properties.

The original intention was that the relief would be available for five years from 2005 but, in the event, the five-year period ran from 11 April 2007.

The period was then extended for a further five years from April 2012 and is due to end on 31 March 2017 (corporation tax purposes) and 5 April 2017 (income tax purposes). At Budget 2016, the Government confirmed that the scheme will end on those dates.

Allowances are due only to the person incurring the expenditure. They can be clawed back if there is a sale or other 'balancing event' within seven years from the date on which the premises are first brought back into use (or on which they are first made suitable and available for letting). A subsequent purchaser of the property has no entitlement to allowances.

Entitlement to BPRA depends on three conditions:

- a person must incur qualifying expenditure;

- that expenditure must be on a qualifying building; and

- the person must have the relevant interest in that building.

Qualifying expenditure means capital expenditure on:

- the conversion of a qualifying building into qualifying business premises;

- the renovation of a qualifying building if it is or will be qualifying business premises; or

- repairs to a qualifying building that are incidental to expenditure in these two categories.

For expenditure incurred on or after 1 April 2014 (corporation tax) or 6 April 2014 (income tax), a further condition (Condition B) must be satisfied; that the expenditure is incurred on:

(a) building works;

(b) architectural or design services;

(c) surveying or engineering services;

(d) planning applications, or

(e) statutory fees or statutory permissions.

Expenditure not falling within condition B will qualify to the extent that the expenditure (in total) does not exceed 5% of the qualifying expenditure listed in (a) to (c) of condition B.

A qualifying building means a building (or part of a building) that:

- is situated in a disadvantaged area;

- was unused during the period of one year ending on the date renovation or conversion work begins;

- was last used for business purposes; and

- was not last used as a dwelling.

Finance Act 2014 introduced a number of further amendments to the rules, with effect from 1 April (corporation tax) or 6 April (income tax) 2014:

- relief will not be available if another form of State aid (such as regional aid funding) has or will be received in respect of the same building and on the same single investment project;

- relief will be withdrawn where the works, services or other matters to which the expenditure relates are not completed within 36 months of months of the expenditure being incurred, however, relief will be available subsequently by treating the expenditure as incurred at the time the works, services or other matters are completed or provided;

- clarification of the 'unused for one year' requirement by precluding relief for expenditure incurred where the building has been used at any time during the period of 12 months ending with the day on which the expenditure is incurred; and

- the period in which balancing adjustments must be made if certain events occur is reduced from seven years to five years.

Further guidance on state aid in assisted areas is available on the GOV.UK website per the link below.

Legislation: CAA 2001, Pt. 3A; *Assisted Areas Order* 2007 (SI 2007/107)

Case: *Senex Investments Ltd* [2015] TC 04312

Other Material: www.gov.uk/government/publications/state-aid-assisted-areas-introduction

Tax Reporter: ¶252-500ff.

4815 Agricultural land and buildings

Agricultural Building Allowances (ABAs) have been withdrawn with effect from 1 April 2011.

The withdrawal was phased over four years in the same manner as IBAs.

Legislation: CAA 2001, Pt. 4

Tax Reporter: ¶253-000ff.

4820 Flat conversion allowances

Flat conversion allowances (FCAs) were abolished in respect of expenditure incurred on or after 1 April 2013 for corporation tax purposes and 6 April 2013 for income tax purposes (FA 2012, s. 227 and Sch. 39, para. 36 and 37). The entitlement to claim writing-down allowances on any residual expenditure was also withdrawn from that date.

Previously, both owners and occupiers could claim tax relief on capital expenditure incurred on or after 11 May 2001 on the renovation or conversion of vacant or underused space above shops and other commercial premises to provide flats for rent.

Capital expenditure could qualify for the allowances if it was incurred on, or in connection with:

- converting part of a qualifying building into a qualifying flat;
- renovating an existing flat in a qualifying building if the flat is, or will be a qualifying flat;
- repairs incidental to conversion or renovation of a qualifying flat; and
- the cost of providing access to the flat(s).

A person could claim flat conversion allowances if he or she incurred qualifying expenditure converting or renovating a qualifying property to make one or more qualifying flats for letting. The person must have held a relevant interest in the flats and met various other conditions relating to the age of the property and the rental value.

The rules for flat conversion allowances were similar to those for IBAs but the flat conversion allowance was considerably simpler. In particular:

- 100% initial allowances were generally available;
- there were no balancing charges for events more than seven years after the completion of the flat; and
- entitlement to allowances was not transferable.

Legislation: CAA 2001, Pt. 4A

Tax Reporter: ¶254-000ff.

4825 Mineral extraction allowances

Mineral extraction allowances (MEAs) are available for expenditure incurred on mineral exploration.

Capital allowances

To obtain MEAs, the taxpayer must carry on a 'trade of mineral extraction', i.e. a trade which consists of or includes the working of a 'source of mineral deposits', including exploration and gaining access thereto or restoration within a three-year period thereafter. A 'source of mineral deposits' includes a mine, an oil well and a source of geothermal energy. Pre-trading expenditure is subject to special rules.

With effect in relation to claims made on or after 1 April 2014 (corporation tax) or 6 April 2014 (income tax), *Finance Act* 2014 includes legislation which aligns the treatment of MEAs with the existing principles for plant and machinery allowances and confirms that for the purposes of MEAs a mineral extraction trade consists of activity within the charge to UK tax. *Finance Act* 2014 also amends the legislation to confirm that activity of an exempt foreign permanent establishment (FPE) is treated as a separate mineral extraction trade for the purposes of MEAs and to confirm that notional allowances will be given automatically in calculating the profits or losses of the exempt FPE as if the exempt FPE were within the charge to UK tax (with effect in relation to elections under CTA 2009, s. 18A which start to have effect on or after 1 April 2014).

'Qualifying expenditure' is capital expenditure on:

- mineral exploration and access;

- the acquisition of a mineral asset;

- construction of works which, when the source is worked out, are likely to have little or no remaining value;

- construction of works in connection with a foreign concession, which are likely to have no value to the trader when the commission ends; and

- certain capital contributions to the cost of foreign works for the provision of utilities or facilities for employees and their dependants.

In order to be 'qualifying expenditure', the capital contributions must be incurred for the purposes of the claimant's trade of mineral extraction and the utilities or facilities must be likely to have little or no residual value to the business. With effect from 17 July 2014, expenditure incurred on seeking planning permission will qualify as expenditure on mineral exploration and access whether the planning permission is successful or not. Previously, where planning permission was granted, the expenditure was treated as acquiring a mineral asset and eligible for relief at the lower rate of 10%.

Limitations on qualifying expenditure

Where an allowance is claimed in respect of a mineral asset and that expenditure includes expenditure on the acquisition of an interest in land, so much of the expenditure as represents 'undeveloped market value' of the interest in land does not constitute qualifying expenditure. Similar provisions apply to exclude the 'undeveloped market value' of the interest from disposal receipts.

The allowances available to the trader ('the buyer') are restricted where they are claimed in respect of assets previously owned by another trader, whether or not that trader was entitled to an allowance in respect of their qualifying expenditure. If the previous trader was entitled to an allowance, then the buyer's qualifying expenditure cannot exceed the residue of the previous trader's qualifying expenditure. If the previous trader was not entitled to an allowance or the previous owner did not carry on a mineral extraction trade, then the buyer's qualifying expenditure cannot exceed the amount of the previous trader's qualifying expenditure or the previous owner's overall expenditure.

Where a mineral asset is transferred from one company to another company within the same group, the transferee company's qualifying expenditure is limited to that of the transferor.

Specifically excluded from the definition of qualifying expenditure is the cost of certain land and expenditure ancillary to the mining function, except offices falling within a 10% de minimis limit.

Allowances and charges

For the chargeable period in which the qualifying expenditure is incurred an allowance may be claimed equivalent to the 'appropriate percentage' of the excess of qualifying expenditure over disposal receipts required to be brought into account.

For any subsequent period the allowance which may be claimed is equivalent to the 'appropriate percentage' of the excess of qualifying expenditure over the aggregate of allowances already given in earlier periods together with any disposal receipts required to be brought into account.

The 'appropriate percentage' is 25%, except in relation to expenditure on the acquisition of a mineral asset where the 'appropriate percentage' is 10%. Whatever the appropriate percentage, it is adjusted if the chargeable period is not one year in length.

The disposal value of any asset which ceases to be used for the purposes of the trade must be brought into account as a receipt.

Where disposal receipts and allowances previously given exceed qualifying expenditure (plus certain demolition costs) in any period a balancing charge will arise. Conversely, a balancing allowance equivalent to the whole expenditure outstanding may be applicable in the case of permanent discontinuance, loss, destruction or change of use.

Legislation: CAA 2001, s. 394–436

Tax Reporter: ¶255-500ff.

4830 Dredging allowances

Where a person incurs capital expenditure on dredging for the purposes of any qualifying trade (maintaining or improving the navigation of a harbour, estuary or waterway), a writing-down allowance of 4% of cost p.a. is available.

Legislation: CAA 2001, s. 484–489

Tax Reporter: ¶258-000ff.

4840 Know-how allowances

'Know-how' means any industrial information and techniques likely to assist in the manufacture or processing of goods or materials, or in the working of a mine, oil well or other source of mineral deposits or in the carrying out of any agricultural, forestry or fishing operation.

Know-how allowances are not given for expenditure incurred by companies after 1 April 2002. Such expenditure is now dealt under the intangible assets regime introduced by *Finance Act* 2002.

Other traders may continue to claim the allowances on qualifying expenditure and the rules are generally similar to those for calculating the amount of plant and machinery allowances. However, the rate of writing-down allowances has remained at 25%.

Legislation: CAA 2001, s. 452–463

Tax Reporter: ¶257-000ff.

4841 Patent right allowances

'Patent rights' means the right to do or authorise the doing of anything which would, but for that right, be an infringement of a patent.

Patent allowances are in practice not given for expenditure incurred by companies after 1 April 2002. Such expenditure is now dealt under the intangible assets regime introduced by *Finance Act* 2002.

The rules are generally similar to those for calculating the amount of plant and machinery allowances. However, the rate of writing down allowances has remained at 25%.

Legislation: CAA 2001, s. 464–483

Tax Reporter: ¶257-500ff.

4845 Research and development allowances

Research and development allowances (RDAs) are available for certain capital expenditure on research and development. A separate relief is available for qualifying revenue expenditure on research and development.

Research and development is defined in the legislation as meaning activities that fall to be treated as research and development in accordance with generally accepted accounting practice and includes oil and gas exploration and appraisal.

Expenditure on research and development includes both expenditure incurred on carrying out research and development, and providing facilities for carrying out research and development.

'Qualifying expenditure' for R&D purposes must meet the following conditions:

- a person must incur capital expenditure on research and development;
- the expenditure must be undertaken directly by the person incurring the expenditure, or undertaken on his behalf;
- if he is already carrying on a trade when the expenditure is incurred, then the research and development must relate to that trade; or
- in any other case, he must after incurring the expenditure set up a trade that is connected with the research and development.

A 100% capital allowance is available in the relevant chargeable period:

- for capital expenditure on research and development related to a trade incurred whilst carrying on that trade; or
- for capital expenditure on research and development where the person undertaking the research (or on whose behalf it was undertaken) later commences a trade connected with that research.

Capital allowances

There is a form of balancing adjustment where an asset ceases to belong to the trader by way of an additional trading deduction or receipt representing the difference between the disposal value and, effectively, the expenditure (including certain demolition costs) less the allowance.

Legislation: CAA 2001, Pt. 6

Case: *Gaspet Ltd v Elliss (HMIT)* [1987] BTC 218

Tax Reporter: ¶256-000ff.

Capital gains tax

KEY POINTS

- There are two main rates of capital gains tax for individuals: a standard rate of 10% (from 6 April 2016, previously 18%) and a higher rate of 20% (from 6 April 2016, previously 28%). The higher rate applies to gains in excess of any unused part of the income tax basic rate band (see 5410).

- The standard rate for trustees, personal representatives and ATED related gains is 20% (from 6 April 2016, previously 28%).

- The rate applicable for non-resident CGT disposals (NRCGT gains) is 18% or 28% for individuals and 20% for companies.

- A special rate of 10% applies to gains eligible for entrepreneurs' relief.

- A charge to capital gains tax (CGT) arises where there is a chargeable person, a chargeable disposal of a chargeable asset and a chargeable gain (see 5001).

- A person who is resident (or, for tax years before 2013–14, ordinarily resident) in a tax year is liable to CGT on chargeable gains made in that year (see 5004).

- A person who is not resident will be chargeable to capital gains tax in respect of gains arising on assets used or held for the purposes of a trade carried on in the UK via a branch or agency (see 5715) and from 6 April 2015, on gains accruing on the disposal of UK residential property (see 5717).

- A disposal occurs when an asset is sold, given away or exchanged or when a capital sum is received as a result of the ownership of an asset (see 5060).

- In most cases, the disposal proceeds are the total proceeds received on disposal of the asset (see 5062).

- In certain situations the acquisition of the disposal of an asset is deemed to be at market value (see 5100ff.).

- In computing net gains on which CGT is charged, it is necessary to take account of allowable losses (see 5260ff.).

- For disposals after 5 April 2008 entrepreneurs' relief (which replaced taper relief) may be available (see 5293ff.).

- Indexation allowance, other than for companies, was frozen for periods after 6 April 1998 and is only allowed in respect of disposals on or before 5 April 2008 (see 5268ff.).

- The base costs of assets held at 31 March 1982 and disposed of after 5 April 1988 are rebased to their 31 March 1982 values (see 5320ff.).

- Special rules apply to wasting assets (i.e. assets with a predictable useful life of less than 50 years) (see 5330).

- Disposals between husband and wife, and between civil partners, are on a no gain/no loss basis (see 5500).

- The CGT treatment of trust property depends on the nature of the beneficial interest in the property (see 5550ff.).

- There is no CGT liability on death. The assets of a deceased person are deemed to be acquired by his personal representatives at the market value at the date of death, giving a tax-free uplift on death (see 5680).

- Partnership gains are assessed and charged on the partners separately and for CGT purposes partnership dealings are treated as dealing by the partner and not by the firm (see 5760).

- Special rules apply to identify the cost price for each share for computing capital gains arising on disposals (see 5820ff.).

- An individual has an annual exemption for each tax year and a liability to CGT only arises if net gains exceed this exempt amount (see 6150).

- Various miscellaneous exemptions exist to take certain assets outside the charge to CGT (see 6155ff.).

- Generally, a gain made by an individual on the whole or part of a dwelling-house which is his only or main residence is not liable to CGT. Where the gain is liable to CGT, it will not be wholly liable (see 6220ff.).

- In certain circumstances, it is possible to roll over the gain on the disposal of an asset (see 6302ff.).

- Capital gains tax is normally due by 31 January after the end of the tax year (see 6470).

- Targeted anti-avoidance rules exist to prevent tax avoidance in respect of capital gains tax specifically (see 6410). The general anti-abuse rule also applies to capital gains tax (see 6410A).

Introduction to capital gains tax

5000   History of capital gains tax

Capital gains tax (CGT) was introduced by *Finance Act* 1965. The object of the legislation was to tax gains made by individuals and companies on the disposal of assets, and it supplemented existing legislation introduced in 1962 which charged short-term gains to income tax. The latter charge was abolished in 1971.

The *Taxation of Chargeable Gains Act* 1992 (TCGA 1992) consolidated the chargeable gains provisions. The chargeable gains of companies are liable to corporation tax, not CGT (with the exception of gains on high value residential property), and are dealt with at 3050ff., but reference should also be made to the present division for special reliefs and the general principles which apply equally to companies. The previous consolidating Act was the *Capital Gains Tax Act* 1979 (CGTA 1979) which excluded provisions relating exclusively to companies.

Capital gains tax applies to disposals of assets after 6 April 1965, whenever the assets were acquired.

Tax Reporter: ¶500-000

5001 Scope of CGT

There is a charge to CGT where there is:

- a chargeable person (see 5004);

- a chargeable disposal (including a deemed chargeable disposal) (see 5060ff.) of a chargeable asset (see 5008ff.); and

- a chargeable gain on the disposal (in accordance with the computation provisions and provided that there is no exemption: see 5008ff. and 6140).

Allowable losses follow in a similar manner (see 5260).

Of course, the distinction between a revenue gain (e.g. arising in the course of a trade), which may be liable to income tax, and a capital gain (which may be liable to CGT) must be borne in mind (see 186).

There are a large number of exemptions and reliefs applying to CGT (see 6150ff.).

For the rates of CGT, see 5410ff.

Tax Reporter: ¶500-200

5004 Who is liable to CGT?

Except as noted below, any person who is resident (or, for tax years prior to 2013–14, ordinarily resident) (see 213, 216) in the UK during the tax year is liable to CGT on chargeable gains made in that year. From 2013–14 onwards, if the tax year is a split year (a year in which the individual comes to or leaves the UK), the individual is not chargeable to capital gains tax in respect of any chargeable gains accruing in the overseas part of the year but neither are losses accruing in that part of the year allowable.

A person who is not resident (and prior to 2013–14 not ordinarily resident) will nevertheless be chargeable to capital gains tax in respect of gains arising on assets used or held for the purposes of a trade carried on in the UK via a branch or agency (see 5715) and from 6 April 2015, on gains arising on the disposal of UK residential property (see 5717).

A further exception to the general principle that being non-resident (and prior to 2013–14 not ordinarily resident) will take a person outside the scope of UK capital gains tax concerns temporary non-residents. Individuals who acquire assets whilst resident in the UK and who then leave the UK for a period of less than five complete tax years, during which time the assets are disposed of, remain liable to UK capital gains tax on the disposals – which are brought into charge in the tax year that residence is resumed.

Subject to the above exceptions, persons who are not resident (and prior to 2013–14, not ordinarily resident) are not liable to UK capital gains tax on gains arising on the disposal of UK situs assets. For a discussion of CGT and the foreign element, see 5698ff.

Certain persons, such as charities, approved superannuation funds and foreign diplomats are generally exempt from CGT (see 5800ff.).

Companies are chargeable to corporation tax in respect of their chargeable gains (see 3050), with the exception of:

- ATED related gains (on high value residential property) (see 5150); and

- NRCGT gains (non-resident disposals of UK residential property interests) from 6 April 2015 (see 5717),

which are chargeable to capital gains tax and not corporation tax.

Legislation: TCGA 1992, s. 1(2), (2A), 2(1B), 10 and 10A

Tax Reporter: ¶500-650

5007 What is chargeable to CGT?

Capital gains tax is charged on chargeable gains accruing on *disposals of assets*.

There is no general definition of 'disposal' apart from a statement to the effect that it includes a part disposal. It is thought that the transfer of the legal but not beneficial ownership would not generally constitute a disposal, in view of legislative provisions which treat the acts of bare trustees and nominees as dealings by the beneficial owner, and which treat trustees as a single continuing body of persons. A disposal will normally involve the transfer, assignment or other divesting of beneficial ownership, and will include a gift. Further, certain events are deemed to be disposals, and disposal includes a part disposal (see 5060ff.).

Legislation: *Turner v Follett (HMIT)* (1973) 48 TC 614; TCGA 1992, s. 21(2)

Cases: *Drummond v R & C Commrs* [2008] EWHC (Ch) 1758; [2008] BTC 473

Tax Reporter: ¶514-000

5008 Assets

'Assets' include all kinds of property, whether situated in the UK or not, including:

- stocks and shares;
- options, debts and incorporeal property;
- land and buildings;
- business assets (e.g. goodwill);
- any currency other than sterling; and
- any form of property created by the person disposing of it, or otherwise coming to be owned without being acquired.

Though options are specifically included as assets so that any sale of an option would be potentially chargeable, other special provisions apply to them (see 5980). For debts and CGT, see 6183ff.

A right to receive an unascertained sum sometime in the future upon the occurrence of a contingency is also an asset (a 'chose in action') capable of being valued (see 5235).

Difficulty is sometimes encountered in discerning the extent of any given asset and whether more than one asset exists, in particular in the case of land. Land and the buildings on it may be treated as separate assets so as to enable a negligible value claim or loss on destruction (see 5086 and 5090). HMRC generally argue that goodwill is distinct from any land in respect of which it has been generated. HMRC also generally accept that assets such as milk and potato quotas are separate from the land to which they relate (see 6306).

Legislation: TCGA 1992, s. 21(1), 144

Cases: *Marren (HMIT) v Ingles* (1980) 54 TC 76; *Mertrux Ltd v R & C Commrs* [2012] UKUT 274 (TCC)

Tax Reporter: ¶508-000

5009   Exempt assets

The disposal of some assets does not give rise to a charge to CGT (or to an allowable loss). Such exempt assets include:

- private cars;
- personal effects and goods worth £6,000 or less when disposed of;
- UK Government or 'gilt-edged' securities (e.g. savings certificates, premium bonds and loan stock issued by the Treasury);
- gains made within tax-free investment savings accounts, such as individual savings account (including junior ISAs and child trust fund accounts) and PEPs;
- gains in respect of certain enterprise investment scheme shares (e.g. EIS, SEIS, SITR);
- foreign currency for personal use;
- life assurance policies and deferred annuity contracts, unless purchased from a third party;
- the disposal of an only or main residence;
- betting, lottery or pools winnings; and
- personal injury compensation.

For further details of exemptions and reliefs, see 6140ff.

Tax Reporter: ¶508-400

5010   Gains chargeable to tax

Capital gains tax is charged in respect of the total amount of chargeable gains in point for any tax year, all 'gains' being 'chargeable gains' in the absence of express exemptions, etc. The appropriate total is the aggregate of those amounts which arise in the tax year after deducting the following:

- any allowable losses accruing in that tax year; and
- allowable losses of any previous year which have been brought forward.

For the computation of gains and losses, see 5220ff.

Legislation: TCGA 1992, s. 1(3), 2(2), 15(2)

Tax Reporter: ¶500-700

5013   Location of assets

Most of the provisions in the capital gains tax legislation do not include any restrictions related to the location of an asset and, therefore, the charge to capital gains tax is not normally dependent on where in the world an asset is situated. The charge is not restricted to gains on assets situated in the United Kingdom nor are reliefs dependent on assets being situated in the UK and accordingly, when dealing with such provisions, it is not necessary to decide precisely where the asset is situated.

However, in some circumstances, it is necessary to determine the location of the asset. These circumstances include:

- non-UK residents with a UK branch or agency, see 5715;

- non-UK residents disposing of UK residential property (from 6 April 2015), see 5717;

- temporary non-residents, see 5004;

- non-UK resident companies with a UK permanent establishment, see 5715;

- remittance basis of taxation, see 5710;

- deemed disposals by non-residents, see 5715; and

- the restriction of roll-over relief for non-residents, see 6305.

For these purposes, it is necessary to decide whether or not an asset is situated in the UK (see 5698).

For example, shares and securities, and intellectual property rights (patents, trade marks, etc.), are situated in the country where they are registered. Also, a debt which is owed by a bank and is not in sterling and is represented by a sum standing to the credit of an account in the bank of a non-UK domiciled individual is only treated as situated in the UK where that individual is resident in the UK. The branch of the bank at which the account is maintained must also be situated in the UK.

For capital gains tax purposes, the UK includes the territorial sea of the UK. The UK does not include the Isle of Man or the Channel Islands.

Legislation: TCGA 1992, s. 10(1), 10A, 10B, 12, 25, 275, 276, Sch. 4ZZA

Tax Reporter: ¶591-000ff.

Disposals

Introduction to disposals

5060   Importance of 'disposal'

Capital gains tax (CGT) is charged on chargeable gains accruing on the disposal of assets.

A disposal occurs when an asset is sold, given away or exchanged or when a capital sum is received as a result of the ownership of an asset.

A 'disposal' includes a part disposal, a part disposal occurring where an interest or right in or over the asset is created by the disposal (e.g. the creation of a lease) and where any part of the asset remains undisposed of. For the computation, see 5229.

Deemed disposals

In some cases, there may be a deemed disposal (e.g. when a person becomes absolutely entitled to trust property: see 5575); in others there may be an acquisition but no disposal (e.g. property passing to personal representatives: see 5680), or a disposal but no acquisition (as with sums derived from assets: see 5080).

Value shifting

Previously, certain specific transactions involving the reduction in value of an asset and a related tax-free benefit (value shifting) were treated as disposals, whether or not there was any consideration. The rules were aimed at specific tax avoidance schemes involving:

- share transactions by controlling shareholder;
- sale and leaseback, where there was a subsequent adjustment of the rights in favour of the lessor;
- the extinction, etc. of rights subject to which an asset was held; and
- share transactions.

These rules were changed in *Finance Act* 2011, removing the focus on specific types of transactions and, instead, replacing them with a wide motive-based test. Broadly, now, the rules will apply if there are arrangements in place which materially reduce the value of shares or securities, or an asset underlying shares or securities, with the main purpose of creating a tax advantage.

Where the rules apply, HMRC will require the consideration for the disposal to be adjusted so that a 'just and reasonable' amount is brought into account when calculating the capital gain on the disposal.

There is no time limit during which the previous arrangements must have taken place for the value shifting rules to be applied. A company will need to look back when considering whether the rules will apply to a particular transaction. The wider motive test also means that transactions which would previously have been outside the scope of the rules will need to consider them.

There are some specific exceptions, where the rules will not apply, particularly where the 'arrangements' are solely the making of an exempt distribution, so that a pre-sale dividend will not trigger the value shifting rules. In addition, the test does not need to be considered where the substantial shareholdings exemption applies.

The transfer, etc. of an asset by way of the giving of a mortgage or charge is not a disposal of the asset for value shifting purposes, and a person dealing with the asset so as to enforce the charge does so as nominee for the person who is the owner of the asset subject to the charge.

Legislation: TCGA 1992, s. 1(1), 15(1), 21(2), 26(1), (2), 29(4), (5), 30, 31

Tax Reporter: ¶514-000, ¶514-050 and ¶519-400

5062 Disposal proceeds

In most cases, the disposal proceeds are the total proceeds received when the asset is disposed of. This may include cash that is payable at the time of the disposal or at a future date, the value of any asset received in exchange for the asset that is disposed of or the value of the right to receive future payments (see also 5235 for treatment of deferred consideration).

In some cases, the market value is used in the computation in place of the actual disposal proceeds. This will be the case when the disposal is made to a connected person or by way of a bargain not at arm's length. For further details, see 5100ff.

Case: *Cooling* [2015] TC 04416

Tax Reporter: ¶518-400ff.

5065   Exit charges where asset leaves UK tax net

There are various deemed disposals of assets when they leave the UK tax net by virtue of a person ceasing to be UK-resident, a person becoming exempt under a tax treaty, an asset of a non-resident becoming situated outside the UK, or a UK branch ceasing to trade in the UK (see 5715).

Tax Reporter: ¶592-300

5068   Date of disposal: acquisition under contract and hire-purchase transactions

Where an asset is disposed of and acquired under a contract, the time at which the disposal is made is the time the contract is made. However, if the contract is conditional (e.g. conditional on the exercise of an option), the time at which the disposal is made is the time when the condition is satisfied.

A hire-purchase transaction is treated as a disposal at the beginning of the hire period. This treatment extends to any transaction whereby the use and enjoyment of an asset is passed but transfer of title and consideration is deferred.

Legislation: TCGA 1992, s. 27, 28

Cases: *Lyon (HMIT) v Pettigrew* [1985] BTC 168; *Underwood v R & C Commrs* [2009] BTC 26

Tax Reporter: ¶515-400ff.

Loss of assets and sums derived from assets

5080   Capital sums derived from assets

In general, there is a disposal of assets where any capital sum (i.e. money or money's worth) is derived from assets. This is irrespective of whether an asset is acquired by the person making the payment. In particular, there is, prima facie, a disposal (at the time of receipt) where such a capital sum is received:

- in compensation for damage or injury to assets or when an asset is lost, destroyed or dissipated, or in compensation for any depreciation or risk of depreciation (e.g. compensation for infringement of copyright);

- under an insurance policy against risk of damage or injury to, or the loss or depreciation of, an asset;

- in return for the forfeiture or surrender of rights, or for refraining from exercising rights (e.g. compensation for not enforcing a restrictive covenant);

- for the use or exploitation of an asset,

though relief is available where the ultimate benefit is minimal (see 5083). There are exemptions in respect of trees for the occupier of the woodlands on which they stand.

Cash received by depositors when a building society is taken over is not chargeable to CGT. However, members of a society (such as share account holders and other investors or borrowers with membership rights) who receive a cash bonus on the conversion of their account are liable to CGT in respect of that bonus.

The extinction of an asset is treated as a disposal for the purpose of creating an allowable loss. However, where a person exercises or abandons an option he holds, there is only a disposal for CGT purposes if there is consideration for the abandonment.

Where there is a statutory right to compensation for loss of or damage to an asset, the compensation will frequently not be liable to CGT.

Certain compensation receipts (made under the *Foreign Compensation Act* 1950) in respect of property which has been confiscated or destroyed are exempt. The exemption was originally given by concession (ESC D50) and enacted by TCGA 1992, s. 268B, with effect for capital sums received on or after 1 April 2010 (for corporation tax) or 6 April 2010 (for capital gains tax). The rules are aimed at situations where special legislative provision is made for compensation for losses arising in exceptional circumstances which involved the destruction or confiscation of property, and applies to compensation received after 18 December 1994, and to any case where compensation was received before then but where the liability of such compensation had not been finally determined by that date.

By concession (ESC D33), damages for any wrong or injury suffered by an individual in a personal or professional capacity are exempt from CGT. The concession was amended from 27 January 2014 so that only the first £500,000 of such compensation will be automatically exempt. A claim in writing is required for amounts above £500,000 to also be exempt. A consultation was published on 31 July 2014 seeking views on increasing the limit to £1,000,000 and making the limit an absolute limit so that amounts above the limit are liable to CGT. The consultation closed on 15 September 2014 and the response was published on 5 November 2015. The response indicates that the Government will discuss the issues in more detail with those respondents to ensure that the concerns they raised are fully understood. The response is available at www.gov.uk/government/uploads/system/uploads/attachment_data/ file/473989/Legislating_Extra_Statutory_Concession_D33_summary_ of_responses.pdf.

Legislation: TCGA 1992, s. 22, 144, 250, 268B

Cases: *Davis (HMIT) v Powell* (1976) 51 TC 492; *O'Brien (HMIT) v Benson's Hosiery (Holdings) Ltd* (1979) 53 TC 241; *Davenport (HMIT) v Chilver* [1983] BTC 223; *Drummond (HMIT) v Brown* [1984] BTC 142; *Zim Properties Ltd v Procter (HMIT)* [1985] BTC 42; *Golding (HMIT) v Kaufman* [1985] BTC 92; *Powlson (HMIT) v Welbeck Securities Ltd* [1987] BTC 316; *Kirby (HMIT) v Thorn EMI plc* [1987] BTC 462; *Davis v Henderson* (1995) Sp C 46; *Pritchard v Purves* (1995) Sp C 47; *Foster and Horan v IR Commrs* (1997) Sp C 113; *Williamson Tea Holdings Ltd* [2010] TC 00589

Other Material: ESC D33

Tax Reporter: ¶514-350ff.

5083 Compensation and insurance money: minimal benefit

Generally, there is deemed to be no disposal if a capital sum is derived from an asset in the situation where:

- the sum is wholly applied in restoring the asset; or

- the sum is largely applied in restoring the asset (HMRC consider that at least 95% of the sum should be so applied); or

- the sum is small (not more than 5%) compared with the value of the asset,

provided that a claim is made by the recipient of the money for the disposal to be ignored and for his allowable expenditure to be reduced by an equivalent amount.

Example 1

Sue owns an antique violin which she bought for £10,000. The violin is accidentally dropped and it costs £700 to repair it. Sue recovers £700 under her insurance policy. Ordinarily, Sue would be treated as making a disposal when she receives the money, but she makes an election for the disposal to be ignored. Sue's acquisition cost is reduced by £700 (£10,000 − £700 = £9,300). However, the £700 spent on the restoration is in itself allowable expenditure and so Sue's revised allowable expenditure is £9,300 + £700 = £10,000.

However, the relief does not strictly apply to an asset which is a wasting asset (see 5330) or one that is lost or destroyed (see 5086). Insurance proceeds used to restore damage to property held on a short lease are disregarded.

If the allowable expenditure is insufficient to absorb the whole of the reduction, the disposal cannot be ignored but rather than the usual proportion (see 5229), the whole of the allowable expenditure is deductible from the consideration for the part disposal.

Where the capital sum received is only partly used to restore an asset and the rest is not a relatively small amount the recipient may make a claim that the amount spent in restoration should not be treated as consideration for the disposal but instead should be deducted from allowable expenditure. However, a part disposal does take place. (For details of the part disposal calculation, see 5229.)

Example 2

John buys an asset for £20,000. It is later damaged and the cost of restoration is £5,000. However, John receives £7,000 under an insurance policy. The market value of the asset after restoration is £30,000. The part disposal is calculated as follows:

	£
Consideration received for part disposal	2,000.00
Less: allowable expenditure on part disposal	
$(£20,000 + £5,000) \times \dfrac{£2,000}{£2,000 + £30,000}$	(1,562.50)
	437.50

On an eventual disposal of the asset, the deductible expenditure carried forward from the part disposal is calculated as follows:

	£	£
Acquisition cost		20,000.00
Expenditure in restoring asset		5,000.00
		25,000.00
Less:		
(1) allowable expenditure on part disposal	1,562.50	
(2) amount not treated as consideration for part disposal		
	5,000.00	
		6,562.50)
Deductible expenditure		18,437.50

Legislation: TCGA 1992, s. 23(1)–(3), (6)–(8)

Tax Reporter: ¶514-800; ¶514-850

5086   Assets lost or destroyed

In general, on the entire loss, destruction, dissipation or extinction of an asset there is a deemed disposal irrespective of whether compensation is received. However, if the owner receives compensation which he applies in acquiring a replacement asset within one year of receipt (or longer, if HMRC allow), the charge to CGT is deferred if the relevant claim is made.

If only part of the proceeds is used to replace the asset, full deferral is not possible but the taxpayer may claim to deduct part of the replacement expenditure in the computation in respect of the old asset rather than on disposal of the replacement; the part deductible is determined so as to leave chargeable the gain which is not reinvested, the gain being the last part of the proceeds to be so reinvested.

Where a building is destroyed or irreparably damaged and a capital sum received by way of compensation is wholly or partly applied in constructing or otherwise acquiring a replacement building elsewhere, both the original and replacement buildings may be treated as distinct assets separate from the land on which they stand, for the purposes of a claim to defer the charge to CGT.

If the asset is tangible moveable property, see 6155.

Legislation: TCGA 1992, s. 23(4)–(6), 24(1)

Tax Reporter: ¶514-900; ¶515-100

5090   Assets becoming of negligible value

The owner of an asset which has become of 'negligible value' (which HMRC view as an amount considerably less than 5% of the value, effectively 'worth next to nothing') may make a claim to treat the asset as if it had been sold and immediately reacquired at that negligible value at the time of the claim or at an earlier time specified in the claim. This allows the owner to establish an allowable loss.

The earlier time specified in the claim must be:

(1)   no more than two years before the beginning of the tax year in which the claim is made; or

(2)   (for corporation tax purposes) on or after the first day of the earliest accounting period ending not more than two years before the time of the claim.

However, for the purposes of the restriction on indexation losses (see 5280), indexation relief is calculated as if the sale and reacquisition took place at the time of the claim.

Land and buildings

A building may be treated as a separate asset from the land on which it stands so as to enable a negligible value claim by reference to the value of the building alone or so that its destruction, etc. will be regarded as a chargeable event; however, where the taxpayer chooses to treat them as separate assets so as to give rise to a deemed disposal of the building, the separate asset which comprises the land must also be treated as disposed of (and reacquired) for its market value at that time.

A list of shares formerly quoted on the London Stock Exchange, which have been declared of negligible value is available at www.gov.uk/ negligible-value-agreements-to-30-june-2014. The list was last updated on 24 June 2016.

Legislation: TCGA 1992, s. 24(2), (3)

Cases: *A Director v HMIT* (1998) Sp C 161; *Lewis* [2016] TC 05029

Other Material: HMRC's *Capital Gains Manual* CG13118ff.

Tax Reporter: ¶515-150

Market value

5100 Disposals deemed to be at market value

In general, any acquisition or disposal of an asset is deemed to be for market value if the transaction:

- is not at arm's length, e.g. a gift, a transfer into a settlement by the settlor, a distribution from a company in respect of shares in the company, or a transaction between connected persons (see 5130);

- is wholly or partly for a consideration that cannot be valued;

- is in connection with the loss of an office or employment or diminution of emoluments; or

- is in recognition of past, present or future services.

However, the market rule does not apply to the acquisition of an asset if there is no corresponding disposal and no consideration in money or money's worth (or the consideration is less than the market value).

Re-basing to 31 March 1982 involves a deemed disposal and reacquisition at market value on that date (see 5320).

Legislation: TCGA 1992, s. 17, 149A

Tax Reporter: ¶514-150; ¶518-850; ¶519-200

5103 What is 'market value'?

The 'market value' of an asset is generally the amount it might reasonably fetch on the open market. Regard is not taken for any reduction in the market value due to the whole of an asset being placed on the market at the same time, e.g. disposal of a large shareholding might lead to a reduced valuation for each share, but this is not taken into account. However, there is a concession for valuing shares at 31 March 1982 where they formed part of a larger holding of a spouse or fellow group company on that date (see 5320).

Where the market value of an asset forming part of a deceased's estate has been ascertained for determining the amount chargeable to inheritance tax, this value may be accepted for CGT purposes at the date of death.

Special provisions apply to the determination of market value for certain disposals between connected persons (see 5136).

The person having custody or possession of any property must permit an authorised Revenue officer to inspect that property in order to ascertain its value.

Legislation: TMA 1970, s. 111; TCGA 1992, s. 272(1), (2), 274 and Sch. 11, para. 8

Case: *Bullivant Holdings Ltd v IR Commrs* [1998] BTC 234

Tax Reporter: ¶518-850

5105 Quoted shares and securities

The market value of shares or securities quoted in the Stock Exchange Daily Official List is, in general, either:

- the lower of the two prices shown in the quotations for the shares or securities in the Stock Exchange Daily Official List for the relevant date plus one-quarter of the difference between the two prices ('quarter-up value'); or

- half way between the highest and the lowest prices at which bargains were recorded on that date ('mid-market price').

If the London trading floor is closed on the relevant date, the market value is calculated according to the latest previous date or the earliest subsequent date on which it is open. The figure taken is that which gives the lower value.

For valuing quoted shares and securities on 6 April 1965, a slightly different formula is used.

Legislation: TCGA 1992, s. 272(3), (4), (6) and Sch. 11, para. 3, 6, 7

Tax Reporter: ¶528-500

5110 Unquoted shares and securities

For unquoted shares or securities disposed of, the market value at any time is the price they would fetch in the open market where the prospective purchaser has all the information that a prudent purchaser might reasonably require were he proposing to purchase the asset from a willing vendor by private treaty and at arm's length.

Securities which are dealt in on the Alternative Investment Market (AIM) are not listed in the Stock Exchange Daily Official List and so fall to be treated with other unquoted securities for this purpose. However, in practice, initial evidence of their value will be suggested by bargains done at or near the date in point, though other factors may be more important.

HMRC Shares and Assets Valuation (SAV) is a specialist area within HMRC that undertakes the valuation of a wide range of assets for tax purposes, including valuations of unquoted shares for CGT purposes (e.g. at 31 March 1982). When the open market value of assets is relevant to a person's tax affairs, the individual's Tax Office may instruct SAV to consider the value of the asset in question. Alternatively, in some circumstances, it may be possible to ask SAV to consider the value once the transaction has occurred but before the tax return is filed using the Post Transaction Valuation Check (PTVC) service.

Legislation: TCGA 1992, s. 273

Cases: *Marks* [2011] TC 01086; *Foulser* [2015] TC 04413

Tax Reporter: ¶528-800; ¶529-000

5115 Unit holders in unit trusts

Where the managers of a unit trust regularly publish buying and selling prices, the market value of a unit holder's rights in the unit trust is the buying price on the relevant date or, if none were published on that date, the price published on the latest date before that relevant date.

Legislation: TCGA 1992, s. 272(5)

Tax Reporter: ¶528-600

Disposals between connected persons

5130   Disposals between connected persons generally

Transactions between 'connected persons' (see 5142) are treated as made other than by way of bargain at arm's length and are, therefore, deemed to be for a consideration equal to market value (see 5100ff.).

If a loss is incurred when a disposal is made between connected persons, the disponor may not treat it as an allowable loss; the only exception to this rule is where a chargeable gain is made on a later disposal between the same connected persons while they are still connected.

Further, where the disponor grants an option to a connected person, a loss made by the acquirer when he disposes of the option is only an allowable loss if the disposal is on an arm's length basis to a person who is not connected with him.

For married couples, see 5460ff. For same-sex couples, see 225.

Gifts in settlement

Transactions by trustees are generally subject to the same provisions as other transactions though, by virtue of the limited number of persons with whom they are connected, their application is restricted to transactions with the settlor or persons connected with the settlor (see 5142).

HMRC no longer consider the transfer of unused losses to beneficiaries to be prevented where they are connected with the trust (see 5575).

Disposals made as gifts in settlement are not subject to the rule regarding losses on a disposal to a connected person if the gift and the income from it is wholly or primarily applicable for educational, cultural or recreational purposes. The persons who benefit from it must be restricted to members of an association of persons for whose benefit the gift was made and all or most of whom are not connected.

Schemes which rely on the availability of gifts relief on the disposal of assets to the trustees of trusts which are settlements in which the settlor has an interest are subject to anti-avoidance provisions (see 5550ff. for further details).

Legislation: FA 2004, s. 116 and Sch. 21; TCGA 1992, s. 18(1)–(5)

Case: *Kellogg Brown & Root Holdings Ltd v R & C Commrs* (2008) Sp C 693

Tax Reporter: ¶518-900; ¶524-700; ¶519-050

5133 Additional charge on series of transactions

Separate disposals by a person within six years of each other to another person or persons connected with him (see 5142) are each treated as made for a consideration equal to a proportion of the aggregate market value of the assets disposed of, had they been the subject of a single transaction.

Not only may there be a greater CGT liability on a second or later transaction, by virtue of these provisions, but liability in respect of earlier transactions in a series may be increased.

Although the legislation is clearly aimed at the 'fragmentation' of majority shareholdings in companies, or of 'sets' of antiques, in theory it may also catch what at first sight appear to be totally unrelated transactions, since the only requirement for the provisions to apply is that the aggregate value if disposed of together is greater than the sum of the individual values.

There are detailed provisions for determining the original market value and the aggregate market value for this purpose.

Legislation: TCGA 1992, s. 19, 20

Tax Reporter: ¶519-250

5136 Disposals subject to right or restriction

Basically, if there is a disposal between connected persons (see 5142) and the person making the disposal, or a person connected with him, has any right or restriction over the asset, then the market value of that asset is calculated as the market value of the asset without the right or restriction, less the lower of the following:

- the market value of the right or restriction; and

- the amount by which the value of the asset would increase were the right or restriction extinguished.

Example

Andy gives as a wedding present to his daughter a plot of land which has planning permission for a house. The gift is subject to a restriction in favour of Andy that no building may be built on the land. His daughter accepted the gift knowing about the restriction.

The land is valued as follows:

	£
Land with planning permission	50,000
Land with restriction	(10,000)
Increase in value on extinction of restriction	40,000
Market value of restriction	£12,000

On making the gift, Andy is treated as making a disposal of £50,000 less the lower of:

(1) £12,000 (market value of the restriction);

(2) £40,000 (increase in value on extinction of restriction),

i.e. A is treated as making a disposal for £38,000.

Legislation: TCGA 1992, s. 18(6)

Tax Reporter: ¶503-800

5142 'Connected persons' for CGT

Individuals

A person is connected with an individual if he is:

(1) the individual's spouse or civil partner;

(2) the individual's relative;

(3) the spouse or civil partner of a relative of the individual;

(4) a relative of the individual's spouse;

(5) the spouse or civil partner of a relative of the individual's spouse or civil partner.

'Relative' means brother, sister, ancestor or lineal descendant.

Example

The following is H's family tree:

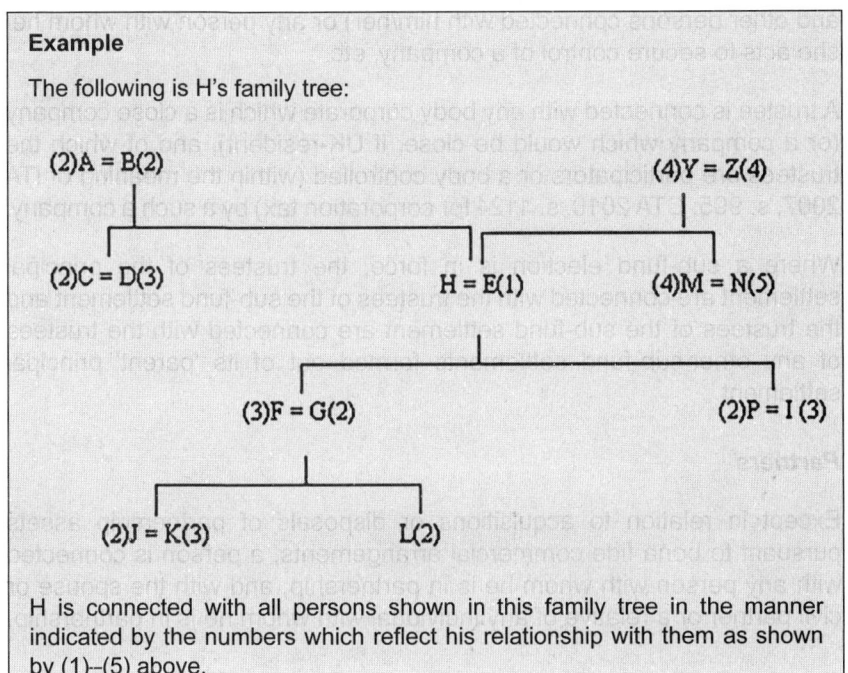

H is connected with all persons shown in this family tree in the manner indicated by the numbers which reflect his relationship with them as shown by (1)–(5) above.

Trustees

The settlor of a settlement and any trustee of the settlement are connected (TCGA 1992, s. 286(1), (3)). The terms 'settlement' and 'settlor' were originally imported from what is now ITTOIA 2005, s. 620. Thus a settlement is 'any disposition, trust, covenant, agreement, arrangement or transfer of assets' involving an element of bounty.

For periods prior to 6 April 2006, a settlor was 'any person by whom the settlement was made'. However, *Finance Act* 2006 replaced that imported definition with a general definition applicable for most capital gains purposes. In essence, it still refers to a person who 'makes' a settlement, but expands to deem other actions to be making a settlement also.

Also with effect from 6 April 2006, a specific definition of 'trustee' is now provided for 'connected persons' purposes. Where there would otherwise be no trustee, any person in whom the settled property is vested or who is charged with the management of that property is to be treated as a trustee.

A trustee is also connected with any other person who is connected with the settlor, e.g. a fellow trustee in relation to the same trust, members of the settlor's family (see previous subheading), a person with whom the settlor is in partnership, a company controlled by the settlor (or by him/her and other persons connected with him/her) or any person with whom he/she acts to secure control of a company, etc.

A trustee is connected with any body corporate which is a close company (or a company which would be close, if UK-resident), and of which the trustees are participators or a body controlled (within the meaning of ITA 2007, s. 995; CTA 2010, s. 1124 for corporation tax) by a such a company.

Where a sub-fund election is in force, the trustees of the principal settlement are connected with the trustees of the sub-fund settlement and the trustees of the sub-fund settlement are connected with the trustees of any other sub-fund settlements formed out of its 'parent' principal settlement.

Partners

Except in relation to acquisitions or disposals of partnership assets pursuant to bona fide commercial arrangements, a person is connected with any person with whom he is in partnership, and with the spouse or civil partner or a relative of any individual with whom he is in partnership.

Companies

A company is connected with another company:

- if the same person has control of both, or a person has control of one and persons connected with him, or he and persons connected with him, have control of the other; or

- if a group of two or more persons has control of each company, and the groups either consist of the same persons or could be regarded as consisting of the same persons by treating (in one or more cases) a member of either group as replaced by a person with whom he is connected.

A company is connected with another person, if that person has control of it or if that person and persons connected with him together have control of it.

Any two or more persons acting together to secure or exercise control of a company are to be treated in relation to that company as connected with one another and with any person acting on the directions of any of them to secure or exercise control of the company.

'Company' includes unincorporated associations but excludes partnerships.

> **Example**
>
> (1) Alan has voting control of A Ltd. Alan's brother, Bertie, has voting control of B Ltd. A Ltd and B Ltd are connected. A Ltd is connected with Alan and B Ltd is connected with Bertie.
>
> (2) Z Ltd possesses 51% of the issued share capital in X Ltd and owns 49% of Y Ltd's issued share capital and has an option to purchase a further 2%. X Ltd, Y Ltd and Z Ltd are connected.

Legislation: TCGA 1992, s. 286, 288(1)

Case: *Foulser v MacDougall (HMIT)* [2007] BTC 95

Tax Reporter: ¶503-800

5145 Appropriations to and from trading stock

If an asset is not initially acquired as trading stock but is subsequently transferred or appropriated to a trade as trading stock there is a deemed disposal for CGT purposes at the asset's market value (see 5100ff.). The trade is then treated as if the asset was purchased for that value. An election can be made for income tax purposes to bring the asset into trading stock at its market value appropriately reduced (or increased) by the chargeable gain (or allowable loss). The otherwise chargeable gain is thus eliminated by the adjustment to the cost of the trading stock.

The election must be made within 12 months of the 31 January immediately following the end of the tax year during which the period of account in which the appropriation takes place ends.

If the trader appropriates an asset from his trading stock, his acquisition cost for CGT purposes is the amount he brings into his trading accounts for tax purposes.

Legislation: TCGA 1992, s. 161

Tax Reporter: ¶515-300

5150 Disposals of high-value residential property by non-natural persons: ATED related gains

Finance Act 2013 introduced a new charge to capital gains tax for companies (both UK resident and non-UK resident) and other non-natural persons disposing of high-value residential properties. The charge for companies will be capital gains tax and not corporation tax; an exception to the usual rule that companies are subject to corporation tax on gains. The charge has been introduced to reduce the use of 'wrappers' for residential property, where the 'wrapper' would be sold, rather than the property itself.

'High-value' has the same meaning as for the Annual Tax for Enveloped Dwellings (see 9246), that is residential property worth over £500,000 for disposals in the tax year 2016–17 (previously, £1m for 2015–16 and £2m for 2013–14 and 2014–15) and is intended to remain aligned with that tax.

'Residential property' is an interest in land which is a single dwelling, so that this charge will not apply to a block of flats where each flat is worth less than £500,000 but the aggregate may be worth more.

A 'non-natural' person is a legal person other than an individual, trustees of a settlement, or personal representatives (whether holding in their own right, or as members of a partnership or a collective investment scheme).

Gains and losses attributable to periods before the property becomes liable to ATED are excluded from the charge to CGT on ATED related gains. This is achieved by 'rebasing' to 5 April in the relevant year (2013, 2015 or 2016). Alternatively, a taxpayer can elect for rebasing not to apply and the gain or loss is calculated by reference to the whole period of ownership. In most cases, it will not be beneficial to make the election unless the value of the property has fallen since the relevant date.

The rate of CGT charged on disposals of high value residential property is 28%.

A tapering relief is applied to ensure that the chargeable gain cannot be more than $5/3$ of the difference between the consideration received for the disposal and the threshold value at which property is considered 'high value'. This is intended to compensate for the fact that the vendor could have sold the property for less than the threshold value without paying capital gains tax.

Example

A Ltd sells a single dwelling for £600,000 at a gain of £450,000. Assuming that the entire gain arises after 6 April 2016, the chargeable gain is the lower of:

- £450,000; and

- $5/3$ of the difference between the consideration for disposal (£600,000) and the threshold amount (£500,000) = £166,667.

In this case, the chargeable gain would be limited to £166,667.

ATED related gains and losses for a tax year are aggregated with any net gain chargeable to capital gains tax. To the extent that ATED related losses exceed gains, the excess if carried forward but can only be set against ATED related gains in later years; excess ATED related losses may not be carried back.

> ATED related gains and losses are effectively ring-fenced in that only ATED related losses can be set off against ATED related chargeable gains and they cannot be set off against chargeable gains of any other description.

Legislation: TCGA 1992, s. 2B–2F and Sch. 4ZZA

Tax Reporter: ¶808-000ff.

5160 Exemption from capital gains tax for disposals by businesses using the cash basis for tax accounting

From 2013–14, very small unincorporated businesses are able to elect to prepare accounts on a 'cash basis' rather than using GAAP accounting standards (see 589).

For businesses using the cash basis, a disposal of certain business assets is effectively outside the scope of capital gains and will not lead to a chargeable gain or an allowable loss. A number of conditions must all be met for this to apply, so that there is no chargeable or allowable loss where:

(a) the asset is tangible movable property and a wasting asset; and

(b) at any time during the period of ownership of the person making the disposal, the asset has been used for the purposes of a business carried on by that person; and

(c) a cash basis election has been made in relation to the business at the time of the disposal; and

(d) any expenditure on the asset or interest has been brought into account the profits of the business on the cash basis, or any expenditure would have been so brought into account if a cash basis election had effect in relation to the business at the time the expenditure was paid.

Where the asset was used partly for the business and partly for other purposes, or has only been used for the purposes of the business for part of the ownership period, then:

(a) the consideration for the disposal, and any expenditure attributable to the asset or interest is apportioned by reference to the extent to which that expenditure was, or would have been, brought into account as required in condition (d) above; and

(b) the computation of the gain is made separately in relation to the apportioned parts of the expenditure and consideration; and

(c) the exemption from capital gains tax applies to any gain accruing by reference to the computation in relation to the part of the consideration apportioned to use for the purposes of the business.

If a business leaves the cash basis and then disposes of a business asset acquired whilst in the cash basis, the capital gains tax rules will apply to that disposal as if the expenditure on the asset had qualified for capital allowances, with some modifications. In particular:

(a) TCGA 1992, s. 39 (exclusion of expenditure by reference to tax on income) will not apply in relation to the relevant expenditure; and

(b) the provisions of TCGA 1992, s. 41 (restriction of losses by reference to capital allowances and renewals allowances) have effect as if:

(i) the cash basis election had not had effect at the time the relevant expenditure was incurred; and

(ii) the reference in s. 41(7) to qualifying expenditure included a reference to expenditure which, if that election had not had effect at that time, would have been qualifying expenditure; and

(c) the provisions of TCGA 1992, s. 45 (exemption for certain wasting assets) and s. 47 (wasting assets qualifying for capital allowances) have effect as if the cash basis election had not had effect at the time the relevant expenditure was incurred.

Legislation: TCGA 1992, s. 47A, 47B

Tax Reporter: ¶500-000ff.

Computation of gains and losses

Introduction to computation of gains and losses

5220   History of computational changes in gains and losses

The rules for computing chargeable gains have changed radically since the introduction of CGT in 1965. General principles on the deduction of allowable expenditure and the treatment of losses apply throughout the lifetime of CGT. Indexation allowance was introduced in 1982, amended in 1985 and potentially restricted with effect from November 1993. The basic rule after April 1988 is that only post-1982 gains and losses are taken into account.

Tax Reporter: ¶500-000ff.

5221   Basic computation

Basically, CGT is computed by deducting 'allowable expenditure' from the 'disposal proceeds'. Expenditure which is allowable is generally limited by statute (see 5223) and there are specific disallowances (see 5226). Special rules apply to part disposals, contingent liabilities and deferred consideration (see 5229, 5232 and 5235).

In its simplest form, the following pro forma can be used to compute the gain.

	£	£
Disposal proceeds		x
Less: allowable expenditure		
Acquisition costs (A)	x	
Incidental costs of acquisition (B)	x	
Enhancement expenditure (C)	x	
Total allowable expenditure		x
Incidental disposal costs		(x)
Gain before indexation		x
Less: indexation allowance on A, B and C[(1)]		(x)
Chargeable gain (allowance loss)[(2)]		x

[(1)] Indexation allowance was only available for individuals, trustees and personal representatives for periods to 5 April 1998 (see 5280ff.). Indexation allowance continues to be available for companies.

[(2)] Taper relief, which reduced the amount of the chargeable gain, was available for individuals, trustees and personal representatives where the asset was held after 5 April 1998 and a gain arose on or before 5 April 2008 (see 5268). Taper relief was abolished with effect from 5 April 2008 and replaced with entrepreneurs' relief (see 5293).

It has been held that, on general principles, there can be no allowance for inflation in the computation of chargeable gains and allowable losses. Hence, except to the extent to which indexation allowance for disposals on or before 5 April 2008 provided some degree of relief against the loss in purchasing power of the amounts spent on an asset, no account is taken of inflation.

In certain cases, exemptions and reliefs may be available to further reduce the gain. These are dealt with at 6150ff..

For specific provisions applying to shares and securities, see 5820ff..

Legislation: TCGA 1992, Part II

Cases: *Secretan v Hart* [1969] 1 WLR 1159; *Drummond v R & C Commrs* (2007) Sp C 617; *Bentley v Pike (HMIT)* (1981) 53 TC 590; *Stanton (HMIT) v Drayton Commercial Investment Co Ltd* [1982] BTC 269; *Fielder (HMIT) v Vedlynn Ltd* [1992] BTC 347; *Capcount Trading v Evans (HMIT)* [1993] BTC 3

Tax Reporter: ¶518-000; ¶518-050

5223   Allowable capital gains expenditure

In the calculation (see 5221), the following amounts are specifically deductible in calculating the amount of a chargeable gain (for limited exceptions, see 5226).

Acquisition cost

The acquisition cost is the cost of acquiring the asset. This will normally be the purchase price, though in some circumstances, for example if the asset was a gift, the acquisition cost is taken to be the market value at the date of acquisition (see 5100ff. for further examples of where the market value may be used instead).

Where the asset is one which the owner has created himself, the acquisition cost is the capital expenditure incurred wholly and exclusively in creating the asset (if any). Such assets may include, for example, a copyright or patent or the goodwill in a business.

Where the asset is inherited or the owner acquires it as a result of becoming absolutely entitled to settled property, the acquisition cost is the market value at the date of death, or the date on which the owner become absolutely entitled to the property, was appropriate, rather than the market value on the date on which the property was actually acquired.

As far as shares are concerned, the acquisition cost is generally the amount paid for the shares. However, special rules apply where shares of the same class in the same company have been acquired on different occasions. The special rules applying to shares and securities are dealt with at 5820ff..

Incidental costs of acquisition

Also allowable are any incidental costs of acquisition. These are costs incurred wholly and exclusively on the acquisition of the asset and include such costs as the fees, commission, etc. paid for the professional services of a surveyor, valuer, auctioneer, accountant, agent or legal adviser as well as the costs of transfer or conveyance (including stamp duty or stamp duty land tax). However, the incidental expenses of valuation allowed extend only to the initial valuation made in order to comply with the requirements for making a return and not to expenditure incurred for pursuing a dispute with HMRC.

Enhancement expenditure

Enhancement expenditure is expenditure incurred wholly and exclusively in enhancing the value of the asset, and reflected in the asset at the time of sale (but which is more than simply expenditure on maintenance). This does not include the estimated cost of the taxpayer's own labour.

Incidental disposal costs

Incidental costs of disposal, as for incidental costs of acquisition, are allowable. These include the fees, commission, etc. paid for the professional services of a surveyor, valuer, auctioneer, accountant, agent or legal adviser as well as the costs of transfer or conveyance. Also included are the costs of advertising for a buyer and the costs of valuation, e.g. to ascertain market value, for the purposes of computing CGT liability. They do not, in HMRC's view, include the costs of negotiating the value with them.

Other allowable expenditure

Also allowable as a deduction in computing the chargeable gain is expenditure wholly and exclusively incurred by the taxpayer in establishing, preserving or defending his title to, or to a right over, the asset. The costs of personal representatives in establishing title to an asset are also deductible. A HMRC statement of practice sets out a scale of allowable expenditure regarding expenses incurred by personal representatives (see 5695).

As far as legatees and beneficiaries are concerned, a person who disposes of an asset to which he became absolutely entitled as a legatee or as against the trustees of settled property is entitled to deduct, as allowable expenditure, any expenses incurred by him and the personal representatives or trustees in transferring the asset to him (see 5690).

Where value added tax (VAT) suffered on the purchase of an asset is unavailable for set-off in the purchaser's VAT account, the cost for CGT purposes is inclusive of the VAT borne.

Example 1

Anthony buys a George III bureau for £7,000. It is restored at a cost of £3,000. Anthony sells the bureau at auction for £18,000. He pays 10% commission to the auctioneer. The chargeable gain is calculated as follows (ignoring indexation):

	£	£
Sale price		18,000
Less: cost of acquisition	7,000	
enhancement of value	3,000	
disposal costs: commission	1,800	
Total allowable expenditure		(11,800)
Chargeable gain		6,200

Example 2

Barry buys a small hotel for £200,000. The legal fees on acquisition were £1,200. A tennis court was added at a cost of £10,000. However, Barry subsequently does away with the tennis court and builds in its place a swimming pool at a cost of £30,000. Barry sells the hotel for £350,000. Agents commission and legal fees on sale are £3,500. The chargeable gain is calculated as follows (ignoring indexation, etc.):

	£	£
Sale price		350,000
Less: cost of acquisition	200,000	
legal fees on acquisition	1,200	
enhancement: swimming pool	30,000	
disposal costs: commission, etc.	3,500	
Total allowable expenditure		(234,700)
Chargeable gain		115,300

No relief is available for the cost of the tennis court because the expenditure is not 'reflected in the state of the asset at the time of disposal'.

Wasting assets

The acquisition cost is written off over the life of certain wasting assets, so that allowable expenditure is reduced (see 5330ff.).

Rebasing

Where the disponor did not hold the asset on 31 March 1982 but is treated for rebasing purposes as if he did so, he is also treated as having incurred any enhancement expenditure which arose between that date and the time that he actually acquired it.

Legislation: TCGA 1992, s. 38(1), (2), (4), 43, 52(1)

Cases: *IR Commrs v Richards' Exors* (1971) 46 TC 626; *Oram (HMIT) v Johnson* (1980) 53 TC 319; *Chaney v Watkis (HMIT)* [1986] BTC 44; *Couch (HMIT) v Caton's Administrators* [1997] BTC 360; *Drummond v R & C Commrs* [2009] BTC 312; *Flutter* [2015] TC 04443; *R & C Commrs v Blackwell* [2015] BTC 526; *Mulloy* [2016] TC 05019

Other material: VAT statement of practice D7; SP 2/04 (replaces SP 8/94 from 6 April 2004)

Tax Reporter: ¶519-550ff.

5226 Expenditure statutorily disallowed in computing gains

The following items of expenditure are not generally deductible when computing the CGT liability:

- interest payments, except in relation to the financing of certain building work by companies;

- expenditure allowable in computing the profits, etc. of a trade, profession or vocation for income tax purposes;

- expenditure to the extent that it is covered directly or indirectly by the Crown or any Government, public or local authority, in the UK or elsewhere, by way of a grant, reimbursement, etc. If the recipient of the grant has to repay it either directly or through a reduction in the amount of a later grant otherwise receivable, HMRC permit the consideration received for the asset in question to be reduced by the amount repaid;

- insurance premiums;

- where there is a loss on a disposal, any capital allowance or renewals allowance made in respect of that asset to the disponor or, in certain cases previous transferors.

Legislation: TCGA 1992, s. 38(3), 39, 41, 50, 52(5), 205

Other Material: ESC D53, *Section 50 Taxation of Chargeable Gains Act 1992: grants repaid*

Tax Reporter: ¶519-850; ¶519-900; ¶519-950

5229 Computation on part disposal

A part disposal occurs when some part of the asset remains undisposed of where a person disposes of an interest or right in or over an asset (see 5060).

Where a part disposal occurs the cost of the asset allowable as a deduction is apportioned between the part of the asset disposed of and the part remaining, according to the value of each part immediately after the disposal. The effect of the apportionment is to reduce the allowable expenditure on a later disposal of the remaining part of the asset. The following fraction is applied to allowable expenditure for the purpose of the apportionment:

$$\frac{A}{A + B}$$

A   is the consideration received for the part disposed of; and

B   is the market value of the property which remains undisposed of.

Example

Adam purchases a plot of land for £100,000. He splits it up into two equal plots. He then sells one plot to Bradley for £70,000.

Adam is treated as making a chargeable gain which is calculated as follows:

	£
Market value of part disposed of	70,000
Market value of part retained	70,000

Allowable expenditure on this disposal:

$$\frac{A}{A+B} \times \text{purchase price}$$

$$\frac{£70,000}{£140,000} \times 100,000 = £50,000$$

Chargeable gain: £70,000 − £50,000 = £20,000. (Incidental expenses and indexation, etc. have been disregarded for the purposes of this example.)

The allowable expenditure on a calculation of the gain or loss made when the land remaining is disposed of will also be £50,000.

Where the facts of a particular case show that any expenditure related wholly to the part disposed of, or to the remaining part, it will be treated as relating to that part alone and no apportionment takes place.

In the case of part disposals of land, HMRC allow an alternative basis of valuation for the part retained, i.e. the part disposed of is treated as a separate asset, and any fair and reasonable method of apportioning the allowable expenditure relating to both the part disposed of and the part retained is accepted (e.g. a reasonable valuation of the part disposed at the date of acquisition).

Example

Alastair buys 600 acres of farmland for £100,000 on 6 October 1991. He sells 150 acres for £50,000 on 4 May 2010. If Alastair elects for the alternative basis, he will not have to obtain a valuation of the part retained as at 4 May 2010. Instead, HMRC will accept an apportionment based on the value on 6 October 1991. Thus, the CGT payable is calculated on the price received on the sale less the valuation made of the part disposed:

$$£50,000 - £25,000 \text{ (i.e. } \frac{150}{600} \times £100,000) = £25,000$$

(Incidental costs of acquisition and disposal, indexation, taper relief, etc. have been ignored.)

The carry forward of the part retained will be £100,000 − £25,000 = £75,000.

For certain small part disposals of a holding of land the transferor may make a claim for the transfer not to be treated as a disposal and the base cost of the total holding is reduced by the consideration received for the disposal. These rules apply where the amount or value of the consideration does not exceed the lower of one-fifth of the market value of the holding as it subsisted immediately before the transfer and £20,000, or if the land was compulsorily acquired or could have been so acquired by the transferee.

Example

Rupert buys Blackacre, a 100 acre farm, for £10,000. He sells five acres for £750 and makes a s. 242 claim. The remaining 95 acres will have a base value of (£10,000 − £750) = £9,250.

If the allowable expenditure is insufficient to absorb the whole of the reduction, the disposal cannot be ignored but, rather than the usual proportion, the whole of the allowable expenditure is deductible from the consideration for the part disposal. Similar rules apply to compensation for assets not lost or destroyed (see 5083), capital distributions (see 5890) and premiums on conversion of securities (see 5913).

Apportionment on a part disposal takes place before applying any rule which has the effect of producing neither a gain nor a loss on a disposal, for instance a disposal between a husband and a wife (see 5500) and replacement rollover relief (see 6305ff.).

Capital gains tax

A reasonable rather than strict valuation is acceptable where a first or subsequent interim distribution is made during the course of the liquidation of an unquoted company. Shares and securities are dealt with at 5820ff.

There is also a simplified tax scheme for individuals investing regular sums in monthly savings schemes of authorised unit trusts and approved investment trusts.

Legislation: TCGA 1992, s. 23(6)–(8), 42, 242, 243, 244

Other Material: SP D1, *Part Disposals of Land*

Tax Reporter: ¶510-450; ¶520-050

5232 Contingent liabilities

Contingent liabilities are not generally taken into account in initially determining CGT liability. If a contingent liability, such as a payment under a warranty has become enforceable, subsequent adjustments are made on a claim by discharge or repayment of tax.

Legislation: TCGA 1992, s. 49

Tax Reporter: ¶518-720

Case: *Morrison v R & C Commrs* [2015] BTC 1

5235 Deferred consideration (ascertainable and unascertainable)

No allowance is made for delay in receipt of deferred consideration (e.g. a purchase price paid by instalments) in computing CGT liability; however, a distinction needs to be drawn between consideration of a known amount (ascertainable) and consideration which cannot be quantified until the happening of some later event or contingency (unascertainable).

If the amount of that deferred consideration can be ascertained at the time of the disposal, it is to be brought into account in calculating the chargeable gain/allowable loss at its full amount without any discount to recognise delay in payment or the risk of non-payment.

However, if the amount of that consideration cannot be ascertained at the date of disposal, the right to receive that unascertainable consideration is itself an asset (a 'chose in action') which is acquired on the disposal of the original asset at its market value at that time. The subsequent receipt of the proceeds, once ascertained by the happening of the contingency, is a capital sum derived from the chose in action and therefore a disposal (see 5080). It is therefore possible for a chargeable gain or allowable loss (see 5265 for loss relief) to arise on the chose in action based on the differences between the value of the right to receive the unascertainable consideration at the date of the original disposal and the actual consideration subsequently received.

The fact that the deferred consideration is subject to a maximum amount or a ceiling is irrelevant in deciding whether the deferred consideration is ascertainable or not. Also, deferred consideration which is ascertainable but contingent is treated in the same way as all other ascertainable amounts.

Where there is deferred consideration, the computation is based on the total amount of the consideration but, if there would otherwise be hardship, payment may be made by instalments.

Any part of the deferred consideration which is subsequently shown to be irrecoverable is taken account of by later adjustments.

Legislation: TCGA 1992, s. 48, 280

Cases: *Marren (HMIT) v Ingles* (1980) 54 TC 76; *Goodbrand (HMIT) v Loffland Bros North Sea Inc* [1998] BTC 297; *Garner (HMIT) v Pounds Shipowners and Shipbreakers Ltd* [2000] BTC 190

Tax Reporter: ¶508-100; ¶518-650

Capital gains losses

5260 Relevance of losses for CGT

Capital gains tax is charged on capital gains less 'allowable losses'. There are rules for establishing the amount of allowable losses (see 5263) and for determining the manner in which they are relieved (see 5265).

Tax Reporter: ¶523-900

5263 Establishing allowable losses

The following general rules apply to the calculation of losses for the purposes of tax on chargeable gains.

- *Computation:* losses arising on a disposal are computed in the same way as gains though, when formerly available indexation allowance and taper relief could not generally be used to create or increase a loss (see 5280). Losses must be set off against gains arising in the same tax year and only the excess of losses over gains may be carried forward.

- *Losses which are not allowable*: where if a gain arose on a disposal it would not be a chargeable gain, a loss arising on such a disposal cannot be an allowable loss.

- *Non-residents*: a loss accruing to a person in a tax year during which he is not resident (nor, for tax years prior to 2013–14, ordinarily resident) in the UK is not an allowable loss. Exceptions are that:

  – a non-resident trading through a branch or agency in the UK who is liable to CGT is entitled to relief for losses on those assets which, had there been a gain on disposal, would have given rise to a chargeable gain; and

  – an NRCGT loss accrued by a person on chargeable non-resident disposals of UK residential property interests when non-UK resident will also be general allowable losses for use against chargeable gains when UK resident (see also 5265).

- *Non-domiciles*: losses accruing to an individual who is not domiciled in the UK on the disposal of foreign assets are not allowable losses unless an election is made under TCGA 1992, s. 16ZA, even if a gain arising in similar circumstances would have been a chargeable gain. If there is an election, then foreign losses are allowable, subject to special rules. The making of an election is linked to the individual's claiming the remittance basis of taxation (see 5710 and 5712).

- *Anti-avoidance*: a capital loss accruing to any person (individual, trustee or company) will not be an allowable loss where it accrues as a result of or in connection with 'arrangements' and the main purposes, or one of the main purposes, of such arrangements is to secure a tax advantage (introduced with effect for disposals on or after 6 December 2006).

A mechanism is provided for making a claim to a loss in a schedule to the tax return. This means that it is not necessary to wait until there are capital gains to offset before agreeing the amount of a loss. Losses claimed under these provisions take priority over losses brought forward from earlier tax years/accounting periods.

Legislation: TCGA 1992, s. 2, 16, 16ZA–16ZD, 16A

Case: *Carey* [2015] TC 04634

Tax Reporter: ¶523-950; ¶523-975

5265   Relief for capital losses

The following rules relate to the use of 'allowable losses' (see 5260) for CGT purposes.

- *Losses and gains in the same year*: allowable losses must first be relieved against chargeable gains arising in the same tax year (see 5010) even if this has the effect of reducing total gains below the annual exemption.

- *Carry-back*: allowable losses cannot be carried back and relieved against gains of earlier years, except in certain circumstances:

  - on death (see 5685);

  - where the loss accrues on expiry or termination of a mineral lease or agreement;

  - where a right to unascertainable consideration (see 5235) was received as the whole or part of the consideration on the disposal of an asset, it may be possible to elect (under TCGA 1992, s. 279A) for a loss accruing on or after 10 April 2003 on the disposal of the right to be carried back and treated as if it occurred in a tax year of a disposal of the original asset.

- *Carry-forward*: allowable losses can be carried forward indefinitely, but they must be set off against gains at the earliest opportunity (see 5010). Losses brought forward are deducted after losses accruing in the year of assessment and need only be used to reduce gains to the level of the 'annual exempt amount' (see 6150) for that year, and surplus losses may continue to be carried forward. Losses brought forward from 1996–97 and later years (i.e. post self-assessment) must be used before losses brought forward from earlier years.

- *Deduction in most beneficial way*: with the introduction of up to three rates of capital gains tax with effect from 23 June 2010, it is specifically provided that allowable losses may be set against gains in the most beneficial way to the taxpayer. Thus, they should be set primarily against those gains bearing the highest rate of capital gains tax.

- *Loss relief*: relief for losses can be given once only. No additional relief is available where relief has already been given under the Income Tax Acts.

- *Transactions between connected persons*: losses arising to a person on disposals between connected persons may not be relieved against chargeable gains except those arising to him on some other disposal to that same connected person (see 5130ff.).

- *Set-off against income*: capital losses cannot generally be set off against income.

- *Anti-avoidance*: A general anti-avoidance rule applies from 6 April 2006 (see 5263).

- *Finance Act* 2007 introduced a measure to stop groups of companies engaged in buying and selling companies, securing a tax advantage through gaining access to their capital losses and gains.

- *ATED related losses* (the excess over ATED related chargeable gains) are ring-fenced and are carried forward and available for set off in future tax years, but only against ATED related chargeable gains in later years. Excess ATED related allowable losses cannot be carried back and set off against chargeable gains in any tax year before the one in which they accrued.

- *NRCGT losses* are also ring-fenced and can only be used against gains from other UK residential property in the same year or a subsequent year. NRCGT losses may not be carried back but may also be used against general chargeable gains if the person subsequently becomes UK resident.

Example 1

In 2016–17, Jake has chargeable gains of £15,000 and allowable losses for the year of £12,000. As the losses and gains arise in the same year, the allowable losses must be set in full against the gains, reducing the net chargeable gains to £3,000. As this is below the annual exemption, no CGT is payable. There are no losses to carry forward.

Example 2

Nigel has chargeable gains of £6,000 and allowable losses of £9,500 in 2016–17. The allowable losses are set against the gains so as to fully extinguish them, leaving allowable losses of £3,500 (£9,500 – £6,000) to be carried forward.

Example 3

In 2016–17, Emily realises chargeable gains of £14,000. She has losses brought forward of £10,000. The annual exemption is £11,100.

The losses brought forward are set against the gain so as to reduce it to the level of the annual exemption. Thus, £2,900 of the brought forward loss is used in 2016–17, leaving allowable losses of £7,100 (£10,000 – £2,900) to be carried forward.

Where a company may set off trading losses against any of its profits liable to corporation tax, these include chargeable gains.

Legislation: TCGA 1992, s. 2(2), (3), 3(5), 4B(2), 14D–14E, 184A, 202, 279A–279D; FA 1995, s. 113(2); FA 2003, s. 162

Tax Reporter: ¶510-770; ¶524-050; ¶524-250

Taper relief (to 5 April 2008)

5268 Introduction

Taper relief applied from 6 April 1998 to 5 April 2008 in respect of disposals by individuals, trustees and personal representatives. It did not apply to companies, which generally continued to be subject to the indexation regime (see 5280).

Taper relief was also not available to set against chargeable gains which were treated as accruing to beneficiaries of an offshore trust under the anti-avoidance provisions in TCGA 1992, Sch. 4C, para. 11.

Any deferred gain brought into charge by TCGA 1992, s. 284A(3) was not eligible for taper relief.

Indexation relief was withdrawn for disposals after 5 April 1998 and replaced by taper relief which reduced the amount of the chargeable gain the longer the asset was held after 5 April 1998, with a greater reduction for business assets. However, the gain could not be reduced to nil; the maximum reduction, which applied after a qualifying holding period of four years (or ten years for non-business assets), was 75% for business assets but only 40% in other cases. Taper relief was based on the size of the gain and the length of time an asset had been held. The relief ignored the amount of the initial investment.

For assets acquired prior to 1 April 1998, indexation, from acquisition (or March 1982, if later) to April 1998, was given in arriving at the chargeable gain, which was then reduced by taper relief. In assessing the chargeable gain eligible for taper relief on a disposal after 5 April 1998, the cost taken was the indexed cost up to 1 April 1998.

In order to be eligible for taper relief, the asset either had to be a business asset owned for at least one complete year after 5 April 1998, or a non-business asset owned for at least three complete years after 5 April 1998. (This was subject to certain special provisions for assets owned prior to 17 March 1998.)

Legislation (all prior to repeal or amendment by FA 2008): FA 1998, Sch. 21, para. 8; TCGA 1992, s. 2A, 3(5)–(5C) and Sch. A1

Other Material: CGT 1, *Capital gains tax: an introduction* – obsolete, with the abolition of taper relief in 2008, but still available at webarchive. nationalarchives.gov.uk/20140109143644/http://www.hmrc.gov.uk/ leaflets/obsolete-cgtfs1.pdf

Tax Reporter: ¶521-050

5269 Losses: calculation of the relief

For disposals prior to 6 April 2008, taper relief was applied after deducting allowable losses. The annual exemption was set against the net tapered gains (see 6150, 6152). Losses brought forward from an earlier year, or carried back from the year in which a person died (see 5685), need only be used to the extent to which it was necessary to reduce the untapered net gains to the level of the annual exemption (see 6150).

Legislation (all prior to repeal or amendment by FA 2008): FA 1998, Sch. 21, para. 8; TCGA 1992, s. 2A, 3(5)–(5C) and Sch. A1

Other Material: CGT 1, *Capital gains tax: an introduction* – obsolete, with the abolition of taper relief in 2008, but still available at webarchive. nationalarchives.gov.uk/20140109143644/http://www.hmrc.gov.uk/ leaflets/obsolete-cgtfs1.pdf

Tax Reporter: ¶521-200

5270 Qualifying holding period

For disposals prior to 6 April 2008, the qualifying holding period was the time from 6 April 1998, or the date of acquisition of the asset if later, to the date the asset was disposed of.

The qualifying holding period of an asset was generally calculated on the basis of ownership of the asset after 5 April 1998 on the basis that before April 1998 indexation relief was available to reduce the chargeable gains.

Bonus year

However, in the case of non-business assets owned (for whatever period) before 17 March 1998, one year was automatically added to the qualifying holding period. Thus, if a non-business asset was owned before that date, the disposal had to occur after 5 April 2000 before any taper relief would apply.

As far as business assets were concerned, the position was slightly more complicated. If the business asset was acquired before 17 March 1998 and the disposal took place before 6 April 2000, the bonus year was available and the number of complete years that the asset was held after 6 April 1998 was increased by one.

However, in consequence of the introduction of a more generous taper for business assets disposed of after 6 April 2000, the bonus year did not apply if the business asset was disposed of after that date, irrespective of whether the asset was acquired before 17 March 1998.

> **Example 1**
>
> Matthew acquired a non-business asset on 22 May 1996. He disposed of it on 24 April 2007. For taper relief purposes, Matthew held the asset for nine complete years from April 1998 to the date of its disposal. However, as the asset was held on 17 March 1998, Matthew qualified for the bonus year. Thus, the taper relief was calculated as if the asset had been held for ten years after April 1998 (nine years actual holding plus the bonus year). Indexation relief was available for the period from acquisition in May 1995 to April 1998.

> **Example 2**
>
> Jackie acquired a non-business asset on 30 June 1998. She disposed of it on 27 August 2007. At the time of disposal, she had held the asset for nine complete years. As the asset was acquired after 17 March 1998, the bonus year was unavailable. Thus taper relief was based on the actual holding period of nine years.

Where the asset was acquired after 16 March 1998, the bonus year was not in point. Taper relief was based on the actual number of years for which the asset had been held at the date of its disposal.

For these purposes, a year is any continuous period of 12 months. A year did not have to coincide with a tax year (though it will do so for assets acquired before 6 April 1998 because of the deemed starting date). Fractions of years were ignored. If an asset was disposed of and the anniversary of its acquisition, HMRC accept that it had been held for a complete number of years.

Legislation (all prior to repeal or amendment by FA 2008): FA 1998, Sch. 21, para. 8; TCGA 1992, s. 2A, 3(5)–(5C) and Sch. A1

Other Material: CGT 1, *Capital gains tax: an introduction* – obsolete, with the abolition of taper relief in 2008, but still available at webarchive. nationalarchives.gov.uk/20140109143644/http://www.hmrc.gov.uk/ leaflets/obsolete-cgtfs1.pdf

Tax Reporter: ¶521-150

5271 Percentage of gain chargeable

For disposals before 6 April 2008, taper relief operated in accordance with the tables at 84, which set out the reduction in the percentage of gain chargeable for business and non-business assets.

The period over which taper relief reduced the gain for business assets was decreased from four years to two years in respect of disposals after

5 April 2002. However, the bonus year (see 5270) applying to assets held before 17 March 1998 was not in point where the disposal is after 6 April 2000.

Percentage of gain chargeable on non-business assets

The chargeable gain from a non-business asset reduced by 5% p.a. after a 'qualifying holding period' of at least three years. If the asset had a qualifying holding period of ten years or more, only 60% of the gain was chargeable.

Example 1

Penny acquired a non-business asset on 26 January 1998. She disposed of it on 3 May 2007. The gain (after indexation allowance) was £12,000.

At the date of disposal she had held the asset for nine complete years since 6 April 1998. As the asset was acquired before 17 March 1998, she qualified for the bonus year. The taper relief was thus based on a holding period of ten years and thus 60% of the gain (£7,200, i.e. £12,000 × 60%) was chargeable.

Percentage of gain chargeable on business assets

For disposals after 5 April 2002 but before 6 April 2008, the chargeable gain reduced by 50% after the first year, and by 25% after the second year, so that after a two year qualifying holding period only 25% of the gain was chargeable.

Example 2

Louise acquired a business asset on 5 May 2000 and sold it on 10 June 2002, realising a gain of £12,000. It was a business asset throughout her period of ownership.

Because it had been held for more than two whole years at the time of disposal, only 25% of the gain was chargeable to tax (£3,000, i.e. £12,000 × 25%).

For disposals between 6 April 2000 and 5 April 2002, the chargeable gain reduced by 12.5% p.a. for the first two years of the qualifying holding period then by 25% p.a. for the next two years, so that after four years only 25% of the gain was chargeable. The bonus year did not apply if the disposal of the business asset was after 6 April 2000, even if it was acquired before 17 March 1998.

Example 3

Greg acquired a business asset on 24 July 1998. He sold it on 15 September 2001. At the time of disposal, he had held the asset for three

---

> complete years. Taper relief, based on a qualifying holding period of three years, reduced the gain so that only 50% of it was chargeable.

Legislation (all prior to repeal or amendment by FA 2008): FA 1998, Sch. 21, para. 8; TCGA 1992, s. 2A, 3(5)–(5C) and Sch. A1

Other Material: CGT 1, *Capital gains tax: an introduction* – obsolete, with the abolition of taper relief in 2008, but still available at webarchive. nationalarchives.gov.uk/20140109143644/http://www.hmrc.gov.uk/leaflets/obsolete-cgtfs1.pdf

Tax Reporter: ¶521-100

5272 Conditions for shares to qualify as business assets (pre- 6 April 2008 disposals)

The following shares were treated as business assets if they were within the widened definition of a 'qualifying company'. Broadly, a 'qualifying company' was a trading company or the holding company of a trading group and one or more of the following conditions applied:

- the company was unlisted;

- the individual was an officer or employee of the company, or of a company having a relevant connection with it; or

- the individual was able to exercise not less than 5% of the voting rights.

Business assets taper relief was available on the shares held by an officer or employee in a non-trading company, being the employing company or a company connected with the employing company, provided the officer or employee did not have a material interest in the company or a company controlling the company. The officer or employee had a material interest if he or she held, or was entitled to hold, more than 10% of: the voting rights, any shareholding, profit distribution rights, or asset distribution rights. It should be noted that the holdings, or entitlements, of persons connected with the officer or employee (e.g. a husband or wife, relatives, and certain trusts and companies) were taken into account for determining whether a material interest exists.

As far as trustees of a settlement are concerned, the company was a qualifying company if it was a trading company or a holding company of a trading group and the company was unlisted, either:

(i) an eligible beneficiary was an officer or employee of the company, or of a company having a relevant connection with it; or

(ii) the trustees were able to exercise at least 5% of the voting rights.

Business assets taper relief was also available on shares in a non-trading company, as applied to an officer or employee, for trustees where an eligible beneficiary was likewise an officer or employee. The trustees could not have a material interest, i.e. one which was determined in a similar way as that for officers or employees.

Where the disposal was made by the individual's personal representative, the company was a qualifying company provided that it was a trading company or a member of a trading group and the company was unlisted and/or the personal representatives were able to exercise at least 5% of the voting rights in the company.

Legislation (all prior to repeal or amendment by FA 2008): TCGA 1992, s. 2A, 3(5)–(5C) and Sch. A1; FA 1998, Sch. 21, para. 8; FA 2000, s. 67; FA 2001, s. 78 and Sch. 26

Other Material: CGT 1, *Capital gains tax: an introduction* – obsolete, with the abolition of taper relief in 2008, but still available at http://webarchive. nationalarchives.gov.uk/20140109143644/http://www.hmrc.gov.uk/ leaflets/obsolete-cgtfs1.pdf

Tax Reporter: ¶521-400; ¶522-150

5273 Conditions for other assets to qualify as business assets (pre-6 April 2008 disposals)

Individuals

An asset disposed of by an individual must have satisfied one of the following conditions to qualify as a business asset (other than shares).

(1) It must have been used for the purposes of a trade carried on by the individual or by a partnership of which he is a member. Alternatively, the asset owned by the individual could have been used for the purposes of a trade carried on by a trading company or holding company of a trading group provided one of the following conditions was met:

    (a) the company was unlisted;

    (b) the individual worked either part- or full-time for the company; or

    (c) the individual held 5% or more of the voting shares.

(2) An asset qualified as a business asset if it was owned by the individual and used for the purposes of a trade carried on by a subsidiary company of a trading group where the holding company was a qualifying company.

(3)   An asset qualified as a business asset if it was used for the purposes of an office or employment held by the individual with a person carrying on a trade.

Note that FA 2003 relaxed the condition that the individual worked for the company. For periods of ownership from 6 April 2004, assets used for the purposes of the trade carried on by an individual, trustees of settlements, personal representatives or certain partnerships qualified as business assets irrespective of whether the owner of the asset was involved in carrying on the trade concerned.

Trustees and personal representatives (pre-6 April 2008 disposals)

An asset owned by trustees qualified as a business asset if it was used for the purposes of:

- a trade carried on by the trustees, by an eligible beneficiary (see above) or by a partnership in which either the beneficiary was a member or the trustees were a member;

- a trade carried on by a trading company or member of a trading group where the group holding company or the trading company was unlisted or the trustees had 5% or more of the voting rights or the beneficiary was an officer or employee of the company in which the asset was used; or

- an office or employment held by an eligible beneficiary with a person carrying on a trade.

Broadly similar rules applied to assets used for the purposes of a trade carried on by personal representatives.

Note that FA 2003 relaxed the condition that trustees of settlements and personal representatives were involved in the company. For periods of ownership from 6 April 2004, assets used for the purposes of trades carried on by trustees of settlements or personal representatives qualified as business assets irrespective of whether the owner of the asset was involved in carrying on the trade concerned.

Legatees (pre-6 April 2008 disposals)

An asset may have qualified if acquired by a person as legatee (see 5690) who then disposed of it and it did not qualify as a business asset in the legatee's hands but did qualify as such in the personal representatives' hands.

Apportionment for non-business use (pre-6 April 2008 disposals)

Apportionments were made where assets had been business assets for only some of the relevant period of ownership, or were (in the case of assets apart from shares) used only partly for business purposes.

Legislation (all prior to repeal or amendment by FA 2008): TCGA 1992, s. 2A, 3(5)–(5C) and Sch. A1; FA 1998, Sch. 21, para. 8; FA 2003, s. 160

Case: *Allen* [2016] TC 05100

Other Material: CGT 1, *Capital gains tax: an introduction* – obsolete, with the abolition of taper relief in 2008, but still available at http://webarchive.nationalarchives.gov.uk/20140109143644/http://www.hmrc.gov.uk/leaflets/obsolete-cgtfs1.pdf

Tax Reporter: ¶521-450

5274   Taper relief: special cases (pre-6 April 2008 disposals)

Options

Where an asset was acquired by exercising an option, the taper period ran from the time of exercise. Whether the gain arising qualified for business or non-business taper depends on the underlying asset.

Assets derived from other assets

Where assets had been merged or divided, the taper period could run from the earliest time when an interest was acquired in the original asset.

Assets transferred between spouses

Where an asset had been transferred between spouses who live together (see 5500), the taper relief on a subsequent disposal was based on the combined period of ownership of the spouses. Whether an asset was a business asset at any time in that period was determined by the use made of it by the spouse holding it at that time.

Held-over gains, rolled over gains and other deferred gains

For other no gain/no loss transfers and for gifts holdover relief, the taper operated by reference to the holding period of the new holder. Where gains had been relieved under a provision which reduced the cost of a replacement asset (e.g. rollover relief for business assets), the taper operated by reference to the holding period of the new asset. Where a relief deferred the gain on a disposal until a later occasion, such as on the relief on reinvestment in a venture capital trust, the taper operated by reference to the holding period of the asset on which the deferred gain arose.

Anti-avoidance provisions

Anti-avoidance provisions aimed to prevent persons claiming taper relief on an artificially extended qualifying holding period. Thus, for example, the taper period stopped running at any time that the holder of an asset was not exposed to changes in the value of the asset.

Settled property originating from more than one settlor

Where settled property originated from more than one settlor, the property was treated as comprised in different settlements.

Legislation: TCGA 1992, s. 2A, 3(5)–(5C) and Sch. A1; FA 1998, Sch. 21, para. 8

Other Material: CGT 1, *Capital gains tax: an introduction* – obsolete, with the abolition of taper relief in 2008, but still available at webarchive. nationalarchives.gov.uk/20140109143644/http://www.hmrc.gov.uk/leaflets/obsolete-cgtfs1.pdf

Tax Reporter: ¶522-700

Indexation allowance (to 5 April 2008)

5280 Introduction

Finance Act 2008 contained provisions for the withdrawal of indexation allowance in respect of disposals by individuals and trustees occurring on or after 6 April 2008. It remains available in respect of disposals by companies within the charge to corporation tax on chargeable gains. The commentary in the following paragraphs is therefore only applicable for periods up to 5 April 2008 in respect of CGT.

Since the introduction of CGT, the effect of inflation often meant that increases in the value of assets were much greater than otherwise might have been and that CGT was taxing gains due to inflation rather than real gains.

A measure of relief was introduced in 1982 by a complex system of indexing items of 'allowable expenditure' (see 5223). This is done by effectively adjusting allowable expenditure for increases in the Retail Prices Index (RPI), though the adjustment is a single item to be set against the gain;

as before 6 April 1985, for disposals after 29 November 1993 this cannot generally create or increase a loss (see also 5283).

For individuals or trusts made before 30 November 1993, indexation effectively lost under the above rules in respect of disposals before 6 April 1995 gives rise to an 'indexation loss' which, in certain circumstances, can be relieved. Such indexation losses for 1993–94 reduce net gains otherwise brought into charge – 'relevant gains' – for that year, any excess being carried forward and added to indexation losses in 1994–95 for relief in that year; the maximum relief is generally £10,000. There are special rules for appropriations to/from trading stock and where the taxpayer also seeks income relief for a disposal of shares in a qualifying trading company.

Before the general restriction of indexation allowance from 30 November 1993 where it would create or increase a loss (see above), the allowance was removed or restricted to prevent losses in respect of the following:

- transfers of debts or redeemable preference shares between associated companies or companies within a group involving 'linked company financing' – aimed at preventing the artificial arrangement of a debt on a security between related companies which could be repaid in full but with an allowable loss equal to the indexation allowance;

- shares in a building society or registered industrial and provident society – aimed at preventing the former practice of closing share accounts in order to crystallise an allowable loss equal to the indexation allowance;

- deposit-based unit trust and offshore funds where at least 90% of the market value of the investment property consists of non-chargeable assets and/or shares in building societies;

- certain oil-industry assets.

Replacement of indexation allowance by taper relief

For disposals after 5 April 1998 and before 6 April 2008 by individuals, trustees and personal representatives, indexation allowance was replaced by a taper which reduced the amount of the chargeable gain the longer the asset was held after that date, with a greater reduction for business assets (see 5268).

Indexation allowance is only given in the months after April 1998 for companies within the charge to corporation tax. Indexation allowance was frozen for periods after April 1998 in respect of assets held by all other persons where the asset was disposed of before 6 April 2008. Thus for individuals, trustees and personal representatives who disposed, before 6 April 2008, of assets acquired before 1 April 1998, indexation allowance was computed only up to April 1998. The withdrawal of the allowance was meant to be compensated for by the introduction of taper relief.

Following the withdrawal of taper relief with effect from 6 April 2008, the frozen indexation allowance has also been withdrawn. Instead, capital gains are taxed at a lower rate of tax than income. Entrepreneurs' relief is available for business assets only (5293).

Legislation: TCGA 1992, s. 53(1)–(2A), (4)

Other Material: CGT 1, *Capital gains tax: an introduction* – obsolete, with the abolition of taper relief in 2008, but still available at webarchive. nationalarchives.gov.uk/20140109143644/http://www.hmrc.gov.uk/leaflets/obsolete-cgtfs1.pdf

Tax Reporter: ¶523-250

5283 Description of indexation allowance

For the availability of indexation allowance on disposals after 5 April 1998, see 5268.

The indexation allowance applied to items of allowable expenditure, thereby adjusting for changes in the Retail Prices Index between acquisition (or 31 March 1982, if later) and disposal.

Where allowable expenditure is written down over the life of an asset (see 5330ff.), the written-down value is the value to which the indexation allowance applies.

Other Material: CGT 1, *Capital gains tax: an introduction* – obsolete, with the abolition of taper relief in 2008, but still available at webarchive. nationalarchives.gov.uk/20140109143644/http://www.hmrc.gov.uk/leaflets/obsolete-cgtfs1.pdf

Tax Reporter: ¶523-300

5284 Substitution of March 1982 values

Where an asset was held on 31 March 1982, a gain may, since 1988, be re-based to that date (see 5320ff.); the manner in which this is effected brings about a deemed disposal and reacquisition at that date so that, in such cases, indexation allowance automatically becomes based on the 1982 value. Before re-basing was introduced, where a taxpayer held the asset on that date (or it existed on that date and had been the subject of only no gain/no loss transfers since then) he could nonetheless claim to have the indexation allowance based on the asset's market value (see 5103) at that date rather than on expenditure incurred before that date – this uplift continues to be relevant where re-basing does not apply, though no claim is required. If the disposal takes place after 29 November 1993, indexation allowance cannot create or increase a loss (see 5280); however, an exception is made where the disponor is treated as having held the asset on 31 March 1982 for indexation purposes following one or more no gain/no loss transfers – i.e. indexation allowance to the date of any transfer to him before 29 November 1993 can create or increase his loss. In practice, where re-basing is competent even though the disponor did not hold the asset on 31 March 1982, indexation applies to all enhancement expenditure incurred after that date, whether by the disponor or another person (see 5286).

The Shares Valuation Division may begin negotiations in respect of the value of unquoted shares before a referral from HMRC, usually for indexation allowance and re-basing purposes (see 5103).

Legislation (prior to introduction of TCGA 1992, s. 52A): TCGA 1992, s. 53(3), 55

Other Material: CGT 1, *Capital gains tax: an introduction* – obsolete, with the abolition of taper relief in 2008, but still available at webarchive. nationalarchives.gov.uk/20140109143644/http://www.hmrc.gov.uk/leaflets/obsolete-cgtfs1.pdf

Tax Reporter: ¶523-450

5286 Computation of indexation allowance

For the availability of indexation allowance on disposals after 5 April 1998, see 5268.

Although there were special rules for most shares (see 5826), the indexation allowance was generally calculated as follows.

Step 1

Identify each item of allowable expenditure.

Step 2

Calculate the indexed rise in that expenditure.

This is done by applying the following formula (expressed as a decimal and rounded to the nearest third decimal place) to each item of allowable expenditure:

$$\frac{RD - RI}{RI}$$

RD is the RPI for the month of disposal; and

RI   is the RPI for the later of (a) March 1982, (b) the month of the expenditure (see Key data for monthly RPI figures).

The resultant figure is the indexed rise for that item of expenditure.

Step 3

Add together the indexed rise for each item of expenditure. The final total is the indexation allowance, subject to possible restriction where it would create or increase a loss (see 5280).

Expenditure on the enhancement, etc. of an asset was generally assumed to have been incurred when the expenditure became due and payable; where the disponor was treated as if he held the asset on 31 March 1982, this applied equally to enhancement or title expenditure which he was deemed to have incurred (see 5223). There were special provisions for certain call options.

Example

Toby bought a house in January 1987 which was not his sole or main residence (so not exempt from charge).

Step 1

He had the following items of allowable expenditure:

	£
(1) purchase price	50,000
(2) legal fees	400
(3) survey fees	150
(4) cost of extending central heating in October 1988	1,500

He sold the house in January 1997 for £92,000 incurring incidental costs of £500.

The RPI is   100.0 for January 1987

109.5 for October 1988

154.4 for January 1997

Step 2

Calculate indexation allowance for purchase price and incidental costs of acquisition:

$$£50,550 \times \frac{(154.4 - 100)}{100}$$

i.e. £50,550 × 0.544 = £27,499.

Calculate indexation allowance for enhancement expenditure:

$$£1,500 \times \frac{(154.4 - 109.5)}{109.5}$$

i.e. £1,500 × 0.410 = £615

Step 3

Add indexation allowances together:

£27,499 + £615 = £28,114 total indexation allowance.

Toby's chargeable gain was therefore:

	£	£
Sale price		92,000
Less: purchase price	50,000	
legal fees	400	
survey fees	150	
central heating	1,500	
disposal costs	500	
		(52,550)
Unindexed gain		39,450
Less: indexation allowance		(28,114)
Chargeable gain		11,336

Where one asset was derived from another asset (perhaps rather than being acquired), expenditure on the original asset was apportioned between the two assets or, if the original asset ceased to exist, was attributed to the new asset (see 5223); by concession, HMRC would allow indexation allowance on the costs of acquisition of a lease to be calculated by reference to the date it was acquired, even though it ceased to exist on the acquisition of a superior interest in the property, such as the freehold reversion.

A gain realised on the disposal of assets acquired before the introduction of CGT in 1965, and to which the indexation allowance provisions applied, was computed by applying the time-apportionment rules after deduction of indexation allowance. This continued to be relevant where re-basing is excluded.

Legislation (prior to introduction of TCGA 1992, s. 52A): TCGA 1992, s. 54, 114, 145

Case: *Smith (HMIT) v Schofield* [1993] BTC 147

Other Material: ESC D42; CGT 1, *Capital gains tax: an introduction –* obsolete, with the abolition of taper relief in 2008, but still available at webarchive.nationalarchives.gov.uk/20140109143644/http://www.hmrc.gov.uk/leaflets/obsolete-cgtfs1.pdf

Tax Reporter: ¶523-350

5289   Indexation allowance on part disposals

For the availability of indexation allowance on disposals after 5 April 1998, see 5268.

On a part disposal of an asset, allowable expenditure was apportioned between the part disposed of and the part retained (see 5229). This apportionment was to be made before the calculation of the indexation allowance; thus, the expenditure apportioned to the part retained was not taken into account in determining the indexation allowance.

In certain circumstances, the whole (or part) of the allowable expenditure could be taken into account in calculating the gain on the part disposed of with a corresponding reduction in the allowable expenditure on the part retained; in such cases as set out below, indexation allowance was calculated in respect of the subsequent disposal (of the part originally retained) on the amount without reduction and was then reduced by the amount of a notional indexed adjustment based on:

- the allowance already given against a receipt of compensation or insurance money (see 5083);

- the allowance already given against a capital distribution (see 5890);

- the allowance already given against a premium on conversion of securities (see 5913);

- the allowance already given against a gain from a small part disposal (see 5229).

Legislation (prior to introduction of TCGA 1992, s. 52A): TCGA 1992, s. 56(1), 57

Tax Reporter: ¶523-550

5292 Indexation allowance: disposals on a 'no gain/no loss' basis

For the availability of indexation allowance on disposals after 5 April 1998, see 5268.

There were special rules for calculating indexation allowance in respect of disposals to which certain types of tax deferral apply, so that the transferor was treated as making neither a gain nor a loss on his disposal (e.g. the relief for the replacement of business assets, see 6305). Basically, the indexation allowance was calculated and was set off against a deemed gain of an equal amount so that there was no gain/no loss after indexation; any remaining gain was effectively rolled over to the transferee.

Example

Harry made a gift of a non-business asset to his wife, Janet. Harry's acquisition cost was £13,000. At the date of disposal there was an accrued gain of £5,000 and, say, an indexation allowance of £3,000.

The disposal was regarded as being on a no gain/no loss basis, but only after the indexation allowance had been taken into account. Thus Janet was treated as having acquired the asset for £13,000 + £3,000 = £16,000.

Notwithstanding the above, where a person was deemed to have held an asset at 31 March 1982 following a no gain/no loss transfer of it to him, the acquisition cost could be reduced by an amount equivalent to the rolled-up indexation allowance to the date of transfer to accommodate the fact that indexation allowance was computed on market value at 31 March 1982 (see 5283).

Disposals after 29 November 1993

Where a disposal took place after 29 November 1993, following a no gain/no loss transfer before that date, the indexation allowance to the date of transfer would be deducted from the base cost under the rule outlined in 5283. However, where a loss arose, with the result that some or all of the indexation allowance was wasted, indexation allowance up to the date of the no gain/no loss transfer could be preserved.

Legislation (prior to introduction of TCGA 1992, s. 52A): TCGA 1992, s. 55(6)–(8), 56(2)

Tax Reporter: ¶523-500

Entrepreneurs' relief

5293 Introduction

Entrepreneurs' relief was a hastily produced solution to a problem created by the Government's decision, announced in the 2007 Pre-Budget Report, to 'simplify' capital gains tax by abolishing taper relief and setting a single rate of tax at 18% (see 5410 for current rates). The problem was that under the taper relief regime, most business owners were expecting to pay an effective rate of only 10% on the disposal of their businesses. In order to placate the criticism which resulted, this new relief was proposed. It is largely based on the old retirement relief which was last available in 2002–03 and its effect is to preserve the effective 10% rate for businesses which applied under taper relief.

The relief is to be given upon a claim being made in respect of 'qualifying business disposals', of which there are three:

(1) a material disposal by an individual;

(2) a disposal by an individual which is associated with a material disposal; and

(3) a disposal by a trustee.

In contrast to both retirement relief, upon which it is based, and taper relief, which it replaced, entrepreneurs' relief must be claimed. That claim must be made by the first anniversary of 31 January following the year of the qualifying business disposal. In practice, however, the self-assessment return will include the facility to make a claim when returning the chargeable gains for the year.

'Relevant gains' arising on qualifying business disposals are to be aggregated with any 'relevant losses' arising on such disposals. The resulting net gains arising on disposals occurring on or after 23 June 2010 are charged to capital gains tax at a rate of 10%. Where the net gains arose on disposals before that date, the resulting gains were to be reduced by $^4/_9$ ths. Thus only $^5/_9$ of the net relevant gains were chargeable gains and were charged at the 18% capital gains tax rate then applicable, giving an effective rate of 10% on the full amount of the gains.

Although the effective tax rate remained the same, the method of calculation changed for disposals made on or after 23 June 2010, so that the capital gains tax rate for gains subject to entrepreneurs' relief will be unaffected by any change in the standard rate of capital gains tax. (See 5410 for current rates of CGT.)

If the result of the aggregation is a net loss, then obviously no relief is in point. To the extent that the relevant loss has not been set off against relevant gains of that year, it is allowed against any chargeable gains in the same or subsequent years. The rule requiring aggregation means that relevant losses arising in a year are to be set against relevant gains of that year in priority to any other losses of that or any previous year.

The relief is limited to the prevailing lifetime threshold of gains at the time of disposal, from which the amount of any net relevant gains on previous disposals is deducted. The threshold is as follows:

- £1m for disposals occurring in the period 6 April 2008 to 5 April 2010;

- £2m for disposals occurring in the period 6 April 2010 to 22 June 2010;

- £5m for disposals occurring in the period 23 June 2010 to 5 April 2011; and

- £10m for disposals occurring on or after 6 April 2011.

Relevant gains and losses

Where the disposal is of company shares or securities, the relevant gain or loss is that accruing on those shares, etc. as computed under normal capital gains rules and assuming, in the case of a loss, that a claim has been made. In other cases, the relevant gains or losses are those which arise on 'relevant business assets' similarly computed and, again in the case of losses, assuming that a claim has been made.

Earlier relevant qualifying business disposals

In the case of an individual, these are his previous qualifying disposals plus any previous qualifying disposals by the trustees of a settlement in respect of which he was the qualifying beneficiary. Similarly, in the case of trustees, these are their previous disposals which have qualified for relief plus any disposals made by the qualifying beneficiary in his own right.

Legislation: TCGA 1992, s. 169M and 169N

Tax Reporter: ¶572-500; ¶572-550

5294   Restriction to relevant business assets

Where the qualifying business disposal is one comprising the disposal of the whole or part of a business, the 'relevant gains or losses' to be taken into account in computing relief are those which arise on 'relevant business assets'. These are defined as specifically including goodwill (but see below regarding disposals to a related company from 3 December 2014), and:

- in the case of the disposal of a business (or part of a business) carried on by the individual or by a partnership of which he was a member, the assets used for the purposes of that business;

- in the case of a trustees' disposal assets used for the purposes of a business carried on by a qualifying beneficiary either as a sole trader or in partnership with others;

- in the case of an associated disposal assets used for the purposes of a business carried on by the partnership or company concerned; and

- in all cases, excluding shares, securities and other assets held as investments.

Because the relief is given for the disposal of a business rather than individual assets, the intention behind this restriction is to deny relief to those assets forming part of the business which are held as investments or are otherwise not used for business purposes. To apply the restriction to associated disposals seems unnecessary as such a disposal can only occur if the asset is in use for the purposes of the business concerned.

There is no corresponding restriction where the business asset comprises of a holding of company shares; in such a case, relief is either due on the whole gain or it is not.

Goodwill transferred to a related party

From 3 December 2014, goodwill is not included as a 'relevant business asset' on which relief is available in certain circumstances. The restriction was introduced in order to counter a previously well used means of extracting funds from the business at the lower rate of CGT rather than normal rates of income tax and National Insurance.

As originally introduced, the restriction applied on satisfaction of three conditions:

(1) that a person (P) disposes of goodwill as part of a qualifying business disposal directly or indirectly to a close company (C);

(2) that P is a related party in relation to C at the time of the disposal; and

(3) that P is not a 'retiring partner' (in other words, the relief is not restricted if P retires from the business).

Finance Act 2016, however, changes the conditions so that the concepts of 'related' party and 'retiring partner' are removed, with effect retrospectively in relation to disposals of goodwill to a related company on or after 3 December 2014.

Capital gains tax

As amended by *Finance Act* 2016, the restriction applies where:

(1) the disposal is made directly or indirectly to a close company; and

(2) immediately after the disposal, the person making the disposal and any 'relevant connected person' together own more than 5% of the ordinary share capital or hold more than 5% of the voting rights of the company or any company that is a member of its group.

Additionally, even if condition 2 is satisfied, entrepreneurs' relief may still be claimed if the following conditions are satisfied:

(1) The person making the disposal and any relevant connected person dispose of all of their shares to another company (A) before the end of the 'relevant period'.

(2) If A is a close company, the person making the disposal and any relevant connected person together own less than 5% of its share capital and hold less than 5% of its voting rights immediately before the end of the relevant period.

The relevant period means the period of 28 days beginning with the date of the qualifying business disposal, or such longer period as HMRC may by notice allow

(TCGA 1992, s. 169LA(1A)–(1C), as inserted by FA 2016, s. 85).

A 'relevant connected person' is either a company or trustees connected with the person making the disposal (TCGA 1992, s. 169LA(8), as amended).

Anti-avoidance

Goodwill is also not treated as a 'relevant business asset' where the person disposing of goodwill is party to 'relevant avoidance arrangements' (s. 169LA(6)).

Legislation: TCGA 1992, s. 169L, 169LA

Tax Reporter: ¶572-600

5295 Personal company

Where a material disposal or a trustees disposal is one of company shares or securities, the company concerned must be the individual's (or, in the case of a trustees' disposal, the qualifying beneficiary's) 'personal company'.

In addition, in the case of an associated disposal, where the asset was being used in a business carried on by a company, that company also has to be the individual's personal company.

The term 'personal company' is defined as a company in which the individual (or qualifying beneficiary, as the case may be) not only holds at least 5% of the 'ordinary share capital' (nominal value) but also is able to exercise at least 5% of the voting power by virtue of that shareholding. Where the person concerned has a joint holding with another, only his proportionate share of that joint holding is taken into account for these purposes. In the case of a trustee's disposal of shares, those shares are ignored in determining whether the company concerned is the qualifying beneficiary's personal company; the beneficiary does not hold the shares, nor does he exercise voting power, those are the functions of the trustees. Therefore a trustee's disposal of shares can never qualify for relief unless the qualifying beneficiary already has beneficial ownership of at least 5% of the company's ordinary share capital (nominal value) and voting power.

Ordinary share capital is defined by ITA 2007, s. 989 as:

> '"**ordinary share capital**", in relation to a company, means all the company's issued share capital (however described), other than capital the holders of which have a right to a dividend at a fixed rate but have no other right to share in the company's profits.'

The meaning of 'ordinary share capital' in the context of determining whether the requisite 5% shareholding is held has recently been considered in two cases: *Castledine* and *McQuillan*. In *Castledine*, deferred shares were held by the FTT to form part of the ordinary share capital of the company which resulted in the appellant's percentage holding falling below the 5% limit (denying enterpreneurs' relief). By contrast in *McQuillan*, the FTT held that a right to no dividend was a right to a dividend at a fixed rate (albeit a nil rate) for purposes of the definition of ordinary shares and consequently, redeemable shares in that case did not form part of the ordinary share capital and did not serve to dilute the appellant's shareholding below the requisite 5%.

Legislation: TCGA 1992, s. 169S

Cases: *Prowting 1968 Trustee One Ltd v Amos-Yeo* [2015] BTC 33; *Castledine* [2016] TC 04930; *McQuillan* [2016] TC 05074

Tax Reporter: ¶572-650

5296   Trading company or holding company of a trading group

The definitions of 'trading company' and 'trading group' adopted are the same as those applying for the holdover relief on gifts of business assets and which were also applicable for the now-abolished taper relief.

Trading company

A trading company is one 'carrying on trading activities whose activities do not include, to a substantial extent, activities other than trading activities'. It therefore follows that a company is either a trading company or it is not; there are no half measures. Where a company carries on non-trading activities, it may still qualify as trading provided those activities are not 'substantial'. HMRC's view on how this term was to be interpreted for taper relief purposes was provided in the *Capital Gains Manual* at CG64090. In essence, HMRC's view is that substantial means 20% or more, measured in terms of income, asset value, costs and management time incurred or the company's recent history, whichever is appropriate.

Trading activities, apart from those undertaken for the trade currently being carried on, are defined as including those for the purposes of acquiring or setting up a proposed new trade, provided that where a new trade is acquired, the company starts to carry on that trade as soon as reasonably practical. Also included are activities undertaken with a view to acquiring a 'significant interest' in the ordinary share capital of another company which is itself a trading company or the holding company of a trading group and is not already a member of the same group of companies as the company concerned. Again, that acquisition must be made as soon as reasonably practical. A significant interest for these purposes means either more than 50% or a qualifying interest in a joint venture company but without making the two companies members of the same group.

Holding company of a trading group

A holding company is a company that has one or more 51% subsidiaries. A 51% subsidiary is a company in which the holding company holds more than 50% of the ordinary share capital.

A group of companies comprises the holding company and all its 51% subsidiaries.

A trading group of companies is one where at least one of its members carries on trading activities and, if the activities of all of the group members are taken together, they do not include, to any substantial extent, any non-trading activities.

In a group context, the definition of trading activities is identical to that in respect of singleton companies, but modified to refer to activities carried on by a member of the group. The activities of all the members of the group are to be treated as one business and therefore intra-group activities are disregarded. Thus, where one group member holds all the properties within a group and lets them out to other group members, those non-trading activities will fall to be disregarded in considering whether the group as a whole was a trading group.

Entrepreneurs' relief: trading company, etc.

From 18 March 2015, the meaning of 'trading company' and 'trading group' as those terms apply for the purposes of entrepreneurs' relief were amended by FA 2015 so as to remove an unintended facility under the entrepreneurs' relief rules whereby relief could be claimed by an individual who, whilst holding 5% of a company's shares, did not have a similar stake in the trade which gave the shares their value.

However, *Finance Act* 2016 introduces a new definition of 'trading company' and 'trading group', with effect retrospectively from 18 March 2015 and replaces the definitions inserted by FA 2015.

As originally introduced by FA 2015, the definition of 'trading company' and 'trading group' for entrepreneurs' relief purposes followed TCGA 1992, s. 165 (and TCGA 1992, s. 165A) subject to modifications:

(1) activities of joint venture companies in which a company holds shares are no longer be treated as carried on by the shareholder company;

(2) in determining whether a company which is a member of a partnership is a trading company, activities carried on by the company as a member of the partnership are treated as non-trading activities; and

(3) in determining whether a group of companies is a trading group in a case where one or more companies is a member of a partnership, activities carried on by such a company as a member of the partnership are treated as non-trading activities (TCGA 1992, s. 169S(4A)).

As amended by *Finance Act* 2016, the definitions are set out in a new Sch. 7ZA (as introduced by new s. 169SA). Under Sch. 7ZA, the definition of 'trading company' and 'trading group' are as provided by TCGA 1992, s. 165 subject to modifications in Sch. 7ZA, Pt. 2, with Pt. 2 introducing rules for deciding when a proportion of the activities of a joint venture company (JVC) may be treated as carried on by a company which holds its shares. In summary, for entrepreneurs' relief purposes, a JVC's activities will only be attributed to a company which holds its shares if the individual claiming entrepreneurs' relief (referred to as P) passes two tests:

(1) the shareholding test: in summary, P must own at least 5% of JVC's ordinary shares, either directly or indirectly through investing companies (Sch. 7ZA, para. 5–8); and

(2) the voting rights test: in summary, P must hold at least 5% of the voting rights in JVC, either directly or indirectly through one or more investing companies (Sch. 7ZA, para. 9–12).

Schedule 7ZA, Pt. 3 outlines how the activities of a company in its capacity as a member of a partnership are to be treated for the purposes of determining a claimant's eligibility for entrepreneurs. In summary, the activities of a company as a member of a partnership are treated as non-trading activities unless the claimant (referred to as P) passes two tests in relation to the partnership:

(1) the profits and assets test: in summary, P passes this test if he or she has an interest (held directly or indirectly through one or more direct interest companies) of at least 5% in the partnership throughout the 'relevant period' (normally the year ending with P's disposal of shares) (Sch. 7ZA, para. 15–20); and

(2) the voting rights test: in summary, the sum of the 'direct voting rights percentage' and the 'indirect voting rights percentage' held by the claimant P throughout a specified relevant period must be at least 5% (Sch. 7ZA, para. 21–23).

The activities of a corporate partner in that capacity are also treated as not being trading activities if the company has not been a member of the partnership for the 'relevant period' specified in para. 25 (normally the year ending with P's disposal of shares).

Legislation: TCGA 1992, s. 165A, 169SA and Sch. 7ZA

Tax Reporter: ¶572-700; ¶572-750

5297   Material disposals by individuals

A 'material disposal' is one of business assets which have been owned for a minimum of one year and falls into one of four categories:

(1) the whole or part of a business;

(2) assets used in a business at the time it was discontinued;

(3) shares in or securities of a 'personal company' (see below and 5295); or

(4) for disposals on or after 6 April 2013, relevant Enterprise Management Incentive shares (see below and 5297A).

For such a disposal to qualify as a material disposal, the business, shares or option must have been owned by the individual throughout the period of one year ending with the disposal.

Relief is not confined to sole traders. In the case of a partnership business, it is treated as owned by each individual who is a member of the partnership at that particular time and the disposal by an individual of his interest in partnership assets is treated as the disposal of the whole or part of the business carried on by the partnership.

In addition, it is provided that a sole trader who takes another person into partnership, thus disposing of an interest in the assets of his business, is to be treated as disposing of a part of his business.

A business or part of a business

A business is something more than a mere collection of assets. For the purposes of entrepreneurs' relief, it is defined as a trade, profession or vocation which is conducted on a commercial basis with a view to profit (TCGA 1992, s. 169S(1)). Thus relief is not due where an individual or partnership sells one or more of its business assets whilst continuing with its business as before.

The requirement that there must be a disposal of a business or part of a business was also a feature of retirement relief and resulted in a string of cases before the court relating to farming, where the point at issue was whether a disposal of part of the farmland was the disposal of part of the farming business. The principles established by these cases will be relevant for entrepreneurs' relief.

Disposal of assets after business discontinued

To cater for situations where an outright sale of a business is not possible, relief is also available where business is discontinued and there are subsequent disposals of the individual assets which were used in that business at the time of its cessation.

The conditions to be satisfied are:

- the business must have been owned by the individual throughout the period of one year ending with the cessation of the business; and

- the date of the disposal must be within three years of that cessation.

A disposal of assets used in a partnership business which has been discontinued also qualifies as a material disposal subject to the same conditions.

Disposal of shares in a personal company or EMI shares

A disposal of shares or securities in a company is a material disposal where:

- throughout a qualifying period of one year ending with the disposal:
  - the company is the individual's 'personal company';
  - that company is a trading company or the holding company of a trading group (see 5296); and
  - the individual is an officer or employee of the company or of one or more companies in the same trading group; or
- for a disposal on or after 6 April 2013 (subject to the transitional provisions in FA 2013, Sch. 24, para. 6) the assets disposed of are 'relevant EMI shares'; and:
  - the EMI option was granted at least one year before the disposal and throughout the period of one year ending with the disposal (rather than the EMI option having to be exercised at least one year before disposal, recognising that many option holders will only exercise the option immediately before the sale of the shares);
  - the company is a trading company or the holding company of a trading group; and
  - the individual is an officer or employee of the company or of one or more companies in the same trading group.

Where the company ceases trading or ceases to be the holding company of a trading group before the disposal occurs, the conditions outlined above have only to be satisfied for an alternative qualifying period of one year ending with that event, provided that event occurs no more than three years before the disposal, and:

(1) if the event is the company ceasing to trade, it is not thereafter a member of a trading group and does not become a member of such a group; or

(2) if the event is the company ceasing to be a member of a trading group, it ceases to be a trading company and does not become one.

If a company falls within (1) above because it remains a member of a trading group despite having ceased to trade, then relief should still be available under TCGA 1992, s. 169I(6) if the company is the holding company of the group. HMRC take the view that the conditions in that subsection can be satisfied if throughout part of the qualifying period of one year ending with the disposal, the company was a trading company and throughout the remainder of the period was the holding company of a trading group (*Capital Gains Manual* CG 63975).

However, this will not apply where an individual holds shares in a trading subsidiary which is a member (but not the holding company) of a trading group. If, before the share disposal, that company ceases to trade but remains a member of that group, the conditions in TCGA 1992, s. 169I(6) will not be satisfied throughout the qualifying period ending with that disposal. The relaxation provided for in s. 169I(7) will not apply as the company has remained a member of the group following the cessation of trade.

There is no requirement that the individual, in his capacity as an officer or employee, must actually work for the company for any minimum number of hours per week. However, whilst it is possible to be a non-executive director, it is difficult to see how an individual could be an employee and yet perform no duties.

Legislation: TCGA 1992, s. 169I

Cases: *Carver* [2015] TC 04362; *Patel* [2016] TC 04871

Tax Reporter: ¶572-800ff.

5297A   Relevant EMI shares

'Relevant Enterprise Management Incentive (EMI) shares' are shares acquired by an individual which are either:

(1)   shares acquired on or after 6 April 2013 as a result of the exercise of a qualifying EMI option, or qualifying replacement option (see 335) where the option is exercised on or before the tenth anniversary of the date of grant, or if it is a replacement option, the date of the grant of the original option, provided that such exercise was not more than 90 days (40 days prior to 17 July 2013) after a disqualifying event. Where the options were exercised within 90 days (40 days prior to 17 July 2013) of a disqualifying event, the date of disposal for the purposes of testing whether the option was granted at least 12 months earlier is the date of the disqualifying event; or

(2)   shares acquired as replacements for qualifying EMI shares as a result of a reorganisation of share capital (see 5920) which is a qualifying reorganisation for EMI purposes, where the new company in which shares are acquired as a result of the exchange meets the independence requirement and the trading activities requirement.

On a qualifying reorganisation, or a qualifying replacement of EMI options, the 12-month period during which the EMI option must be held is calculated from the date of grant of the original option.

The legislation provides for entrepreneurs' relief to be available for disposals of relevant EMI shares made on or after 6 April 2013, where the shares were acquired on or after 6 April 2013. Relief will also be available for EMI shares acquired during the 2012–13 tax year, provided that the option was held for at least a year, where no disposals of shares of that class were made in the 2012–13 tax year. If disposals of shares of that class were made, the shares acquired in 2012–13, the individual may elect for the shares acquired in 2012–13 to be regarded as relevant EMI shares within the scope of entrepreneur's relief on election by the individual. Note that this election had to be made by 31 January 2014, and cannot be revoked after that date.

Legislation: TCGA 1992, s. 169I(7A)–(7R); FA 2013, Sch. 24, para. 6

Tax Reporter: ¶572-950

5298 Associated disposals

Where an asset used in the business of a partnership or trading company is owned personally by a partner or director, relief is available for a disposal of these assets where they are associated with a material disposal.

For disposals on or after 18 March 2015, amendments were introduced by FA 2015 to prevent individuals claiming relief on the disposal of private assets used in a business without permanently reducing their participation in the business by a meaningful amount.

However, *Finance Act* 2016 retrospectively changes the conditions which must be met in order for an individual to claim entrepreneurs' relief on an associated disposal, with effect from 18 March 2015.

Disposals on or after 18 March 2015

As originally amended by FA 2015, a disposal qualifies as an associated disposal if:

(1) condition A1, A2 or A3 is met; and

(2) conditions B and C are met.

Condition A1: the disposal is of all or part of the individual's interest in a partnership, that interest is at least a 5% interest in the partnership's assets and there must be no 'partnership purchase arrangements' in force at the date of that disposal.

Condition A2: the disposal (which must not be a capital distribution treated as a disposal under TCGA 1992, s. 122 unless it is made in the course of winding up or dissolution) is of ordinary shares in a company that constitute at least 5% of the company's ordinary share capital, carrying at least 5% of the voting rights and there must be no 'share purchase arrangements' in existence at the date of disposal.

Condition A3: the disposal is of securities that represent at least 5% of the value of the company's securities and there must be no 'share purchase arrangements' in existence at the date of disposal.

Conditions B and C are the same as applied for disposals prior to 18 March 2015 with the addition that the disposal is not treated as made as part of a withdrawal from the business for the purposes of condition B if there exist at the date of disposal any partnership purchase arrangements or arrangements under which the individual (or any connected person) may acquire further shares or securities (TCGA 1992, s. 169K(3A)–(3C)).

Finance Act 2016 introduces a new alternative condition 'Condition A1A' which relaxes the requirement in condition A1 that the interest disposed of must be at least a 5% interest in the partnership's assets. The new condition applies if the 'material disposal of business assets' associated with the disposal of personal assets is a disposal of the whole of the claimant's interest in a partnership. Where this is the case, the material disposal may be of less than a 5% interest in the assets of the partnership, providing the claimant has owned 5% or more for three years in the eight years preceding the disposal. The new condition also requires that, consistent with the original condition, no partnership purchase arrangements exist at the date of disposal.

Finance Act 2016 further introduces a new fourth condition, 'Condition D' which must also be satisfied for the disposal to qualify as an associated disposal.

Condition D is that the associated disposal must be of an asset that the individual has owned for at least three years ending with the date of the disposal (new TCGA 1992, s. 169K(4A)), with effect in relation to disposals of assets which are acquired on or after 13 June 2016. Previously, there was no requirement for any minimum ownership period (although Condition C imposes a minimum period for which the asset must have been used in the business).

Disposals prior to 18 March 2015

There were three conditions to be satisfied for a disposal to qualify as an associated disposal:

(1) The individual must make a material disposal of either his interest in a partnership, or of shares/securities in a company (condition A).

(2) He makes the associated disposal as part of a withdrawal from participation in the business carried on by the partnership or by the company (or a fellow member of a trading group) (condition B).

(3) The asset which is the subject of the associated disposal has been in use for the purposes of that business throughout the one-year period ending with the material disposal, or, if earlier, the date on which the business was terminated (condition C).

The legislation, like that for retirement relief, does not actually specify that both the material and associated disposals should take place at the same time, or indeed, in any particular order. They must, however, share the same objective: that of enabling the individual to withdraw from the business concerned.

Under retirement relief, HMRC took the view that a withdrawal from the business required only that the individual should reduce his interest in the partnership or holding in the company. It did not mean that he should withdraw from working in the business concerned. This view is also taken for entrepreneurs' relief (see *Capital Gains Manual* CG 63995).

Relief for associated disposals is restricted where:

- the assets concerned have been used for the purposes of the business during only part of the individual's period of ownership;

- only a part of the asset has been so used;

- the individual was a partner, officer or employee for only part of the period in which the assets were used for business purposes; or

- during any part of the period when the asset was in use for the purposes of the business, that use by the partnership or company was dependent upon the payment of rent (or any other form of consideration for its use: TCGA 1992, s. 169S(5)).

Where these conditions are satisfied, the relief is to be restricted to an amount which is 'just and reasonable'. In other words, only the just and reasonable part of the gain is to be reduced by the relief and the balance remains taxable in full.

In arriving at the relievable amount of the gain, consideration is to be given to the periods of time concerned in the situations in the first two bullet points, the proportion of the asset used in situations in the third and, in the final situation, the extent to which the rent paid was less than a commercial rent.

Similar restrictions were previously applicable for both retirement and taper relief. However, whilst retirement relief was restricted where rent was paid for the use of the asset, taper relief was not. The decision to reintroduce a restriction where rent is paid introduces a degree of retrospective taxation because it applies where rent has been charged at any time in the period of business use. This period, of course, will probably stretch back beyond April 2008 when rent may have been charged, because under the taper relief regime it was perfectly acceptable.

The expanded definition of rent to include other forms of consideration will also catch situations where an enhanced partnership profit share is received in recognition of the use of the asset or where the partnership pays the interest on a loan taken out by a partner to purchase the asset concerned.

Legislation: TCGA 1992, s. 169K, 169P

Tax Reporter: ¶573-000; ¶573-050

5299   Disposals by trustees

Trustees are not entitled to an 'allowance' of entrepreneurs' relief in the same way as individuals. Any relief given to trustees is treated as having been given to the 'qualifying beneficiary' and serves to reduce his entitlement for future disposals.

Where there are two qualifying disposals made on the same day, one by the trustees and the other by an individual who is also a qualifying beneficiary of that trust, the trustees' disposal is to be treated as having occurred after the one made by the individual.

The effect of these provisions is to restrict an individual's relief threshold by the relief granted to trustees of a settlement of which he is a qualifying beneficiary.

A qualifying beneficiary is one who has an 'interest in possession' in that part of the settled property which includes the assets, shares or securities which are the subject of the disposal.

Legislation: TCGA 1992, s. 169J, 169N

Tax Reporter: ¶573-100; ¶573-200

5299A   Entrepreneurs' relief where held-over gains become chargeable

From 3 December 2014, entrepreneurs' relief may be claimed in respect of gains on qualifying business disposals that are deferred under the enterprise investment scheme (see 5923) or investments in social enterprise (see 5297). Previously, gains deferred under either scheme could not also be the subject of a claim for entrepreneurs' relief.

Entrepreneurs' relief will be available where:

(1) a gain representing all or part of a gain which has previously been deferred (or 'held-over') under the enterprise investment scheme or investment in social enterprise accrues under either TCGA 1992, Sch. 5B, para. 4 (EIS) or Sch. 8B, para. 5 (SITR) ('the first eventual gain');

(2) the disposal which originally gave rise to the first eventual gain (before any deferrals) must be a 'relevant business disposal' (defined by TCGA 1992, s. 169U(9) as effectively a disposal that would qualify for entrepreneurs' relief) (so gains which are deferred more than once by being serially reinvested must be traced back to the original 'underlying disposal');

(3) the claim to entrepreneurs' relief in respect of the first eventual gain is made on or before 31 January in the year immediately following the tax year in which the first eventual gain accrues by the same person who made the disposal which originally gave rise to the first eventual gain; and

(4) the first eventual gain is the first gain treated as accruing in respect of a particular deferred gain (i.e. where part of a deferred gain has previously accrued without a claim to entrepreneurs' relief being made in respect of it, it is not possible to claim entrepreneurs' relief under these new provisions when another part of the same gain subsequently accrues)

(TCGA 1992, s. 169U).

Where the above conditions are all met, the first eventual gain is treated as a gain on which entrepreneurs' relief is due, subject to the 'lifetime limit' applicable to the total amount of relief given. However, the gain is not to be treated as a chargeable gain except for entrepreneurs' relief purposes. In other words, to the extent that entrepreneurs relief is given in respect of it, the first eventual gain is not treated as a gain for other purposes of TCGA 1992 (TCGA 1992, s. 169V(2)). This avoids taxing the same gain twice.

Where the first eventual gain does not represent the whole of the deferred gain, the rest of the deferred gain (which it is finally treated as accruing) is also treated as an amount on which entrepreneurs' relief is due without the need for further claims to entrepreneurs' relief on the later accrual(s). As before, the gains which are subject to entrepreneurs' relief are not treated as gains for other purposes of TCGA 1992 (TCGA 1992, s. 169V(3)).

Relief may only be claimed in respect of gains which have as their source a qualifying business disposal on or after 3 December 2014 (FA 2015, s. 44(2)).

Legislation: TCGA 1992, Pt. 5, Ch. 4; FA 2015, s. 44(2)

Tax Reporter: ¶573-500

Investors' relief

5310 Introduction

From 6 April 2016, *Finance Act* 2016 introduces a new relief which applies a 10% rate of CGT to gains accruing on the disposal of (and disposals of interests in) qualifying shares in an unlisted trading company held by individuals. Qualifying shares must have been newly issued to the individual on or after 17 March 2016, and have been held for a period of at least three years starting from 6 April 2016. Gains which qualify for the relief are subject to a lifetime limit of £10m.

Relief can be claimed in respect of any number of gains accruing in tax year 2019–20 or later years, but the total gains eligible for investors' relief may not exceed £10m.

Relief must be claimed on or before the first anniversary of 31 January following the tax year in which the disposal is made. Where the claim is in respect of a disposal by trustees of a settlement, the claim must be made jointly by the trustees of the settlement and the eligible beneficiary (TCGA 1992, s. 169VM).

Legislation: TCGA 1992, s. 169VA–169V and Pt. 5, Ch. 5

Tax Reporter: ¶573-600; ¶573-635

5311 Qualifying shares

There are three types of share which may be contained in a holding of shares immediately before a disposal of all or part of that holding:

(a) qualifying shares;

(b) potentially qualifying shares;

(c) excluded shares.

Qualifying shares

A share is a 'qualifying share' at any time if it meets the following conditions:

(a) it was subscribed for by the person making the disposal ('the investor');

(b) the investor has held the share continuously from issue until immediately before the disposal ('the share-holding period');

(c) the share was issued on or after 17 March 2016;

(d) at the date the share was issued, none of the shares or securities of the company were listed on a recognised stock exchange;

(e) the share was an ordinary share within the meaning given in ITA 2007, s. 989 both when it was issued and immediately before the disposal;

(f) the company that issued the share was a trading company or holding company of a trading group when the share was issued and has remained so throughout the share-holding period;

(g) at no time in the share-holding period was the investor or a person connected with the investor a relevant employee in respect of that company; and

(h) the period beginning with the date the share was issued (or 6 April 2016 if later) and ending with the date of disposal is at least three years (TCGA 1992, s. 169VB(2), (6), (7)).

Potentially qualifying shares

These are shares that meet tests at (a)–(g) above but do not pass the test at paragraph (h) because they have not been held for three years ending with the date of the disposal. They may become eligible for relief in future.

The necessary three-year holding period is extended where the shares in question were issued before 6 April 2016, so that no claim may be made in respect of a disposal made before 6 April 2019.

Excluded shares

These are shares which are neither qualifying shares nor potentially qualifying shares and can never qualify for the investors' relief (e.g. if they were purchased before commencement of the relief).

Value received

Shares are disqualified where value is received by the investor (TCGA 1992, s. 169VB(5)).

Legislation: TCGA 1992, s. 169VB

Tax Reporter: ¶573-630

5312 The relief

Investors' relief applies where a 'qualifying person' disposes of a holding or part of a holding of shares in a company, some or all of which are 'qualifying shares' and a chargeable gain accrues. If a claim for relief is made, the rate of tax in respect of the 'relevant gain' is 10% (TCGA 1992, s. 169VC(1), (2)), subject to an overall cap of £10m (TCGA 1992, s. 169VC(4)).

If, immediately before the disposal, all of the shares in the holding are 'qualifying shares', the 'relevant gain' is the chargeable gain arising on the disposal. If not, the 'relevant gain' is the 'appropriate part' of the chargeable gain (TCGA 1992, s. 169VC(3)). A 'holding' of shares means a holding that is treated by TCGA 1992, s. 104(1) as a single asset. The chargeable gain on the disposal (or the appropriate part of that gain) is the chargeable gain after deduction of allowable losses that fall to be made (TCGA 1992, s. 169VC(5)).

Qualifying person

A 'qualifying person' is an individual or the trustees of a settlement.

Joint holdings

Relief is available in respect of interests in a relevant holding as well as a disposal of a relevant holding of itself.

A disposal of a relevant holding is a disposal a number of shares of the same class acquired in the same capacity jointly by two or more persons including a qualifying person or solely by the qualifying person.

An interest in a relevant holding means any interest of the qualifying person in any of the shares in the relevant holding which are regarded by virtue of TCGA 1992, s. 104, as a single asset (and references to an interest includes a part of an interest).

Cap on relief

Relief is limited to an aggregate of £10m gains in respect of any individual which is calculated as to include any gains by the trustees of a settlement in respect of which the individual was an eligible beneficiary as well as relief claimed in respect of disposals by the individual himself. Accordingly, the trustees of a settlement must take into account an individual's past claims history and any prior settlement gains in respect of which relief has been claimed pertaining to that particular eligible beneficiary in order to determine the availability of relief and the amount of the £10m limit remaining available where part of this has been previously used.

Legislation: TCGA 1992, s. 169VC, 169VK, 169VL

Tax Reporter: ¶573-625

5313 Disposal where holding consists partly of qualifying shares

When an individual disposes of shares from a holding but not all the shares in the holding are qualifying shares, only the 'appropriate part' of the gain which accrues on the disposal is relieved under s. 169VC.

The 'appropriate part' of the gain is found by multiplying the chargeable gain on the disposal by the appropriate fraction, given by Q/T, where:

Q   is all the qualifying shares in the holding at the time immediately before the disposal concerned, or if less, such number of those qualifying shares as equals the number of shares disposed of in that disposal; and

T   is the total number of shares disposed of.

For the purposes of determining the appropriate part of the total gain, qualifying shares in a holding are treated as being disposed of in priority to other types of share.

Legislation: TCGA 1992, s. 169VD

Tax Reporter: ¶573-680

5314 Determining shares in a holding

Special rules apply for determining the composition of a holding of shares from which there has been an earlier disposal. In order to determine the number of qualifying shares, potentially qualifying shares and excluded shares in the holding, it is necessary to determine the number of each type disposed of on earlier occasions. There are two special rules which apply depending upon whether there has been a previous claim for investors' relief or not (TCGA 1992, s. 169VE).

Previous claim for investors' relief

In summary, shares which were qualifying shares at the time of the earlier disposal are treated as having been disposed of first; then shares which were excluded shares at that time, and then shares which were potentially qualifying shares. The objective is to preserve the maximum potential investors' relief to be claimed on future disposals (TCGA 1992, s. 169VF).

No previous claim for investors' relief

In summary, shares which were excluded shares at the time of the earlier disposal are treated as having been disposed of first; then shares which were potentially qualifying shares at that time, and then shares which were potentially shares. The objective is to preserve the maximum potential investors' relief to be claimed on future disposals (TCGA 1992, s. 169VG).

Legislation: TCGA 1992, s. 169VE–169VG

Tax Reporter: ¶573-685

5315 Disposals by trustees: further conditions for and restriction of relief

Where a disposal is made by the trustees of a settlement, investors relief will not apply to the disposal unless there is at least one individual who is an eligible beneficiary in respect of the disposal (TCGA 1992, s. 169VH(1)).

An individual is an 'eligible beneficiary' if:

(i)   at the time immediately before the disposal, the individual has under the settlement an interest in possession in settled property that includes or consists of the holding of qualifying shares;

(ii) the individual has had that interest in possession through the three years ending with the date of the disposal;

(iii) the individual has not been a relevant employee at any time during the three years ending with the date of the disposal; and

(iv) the individual has elected (by telling the trustees by whatever means) to be treated as an eligible beneficiary in respect of the disposal (and has not withdrawn that election prior to the claim being made)

(TCGA 1992, s. 169VH).

Reduction of relief in certain cases

Relief may be restricted where, immediately before the disposal, two or more persons have an interest in possession in the settled property. In such cases, relief is restricted to the portion of the gain that relates to the eligible beneficiary (or eligible beneficiaries if more than one) calculated on an X/Y basis where:

X   is the interest in possession held by the eligible beneficiary (or beneficiaries if more than one) in the income from the holding; and

Y   is all interests in possession in the income of the holding under the settlement.

Legislation: TCGA 1992, s. 169VH–169VI

5316 Reorganisations

Special rules apply where, before a disposal, there has been a reorganisation of a company's share capital within TCGA 1992, s. 126 and no new consideration was given for the new holding of shares in order to determine how many shares held after the reorganisation are qualifying, potentially qualifying or excluded shares for investors' relief purposes when they come to be disposed of. The treatment depends on whether the reorganisation falls within TCGA 1992, s. 126, being a reorganisation or reduction of a company's share capital or within TCGA 1992, s. 135–136 (takeovers and reconstructions).

Reorganisation within s. 126 and no consideration given

Where, before a disposal, there has been a reorganisation of a company's share capital within TCGA 1992, s. 126 and no new consideration was given for the new holding of shares, the new holding of shares after the reorganisation is treated as having the same proportions of the three types of share as the original holding before the reorganisation.

Where shares in the original holding had been subscribed for and held continuously by the claimant, the corresponding shares in the new holding are treated as having been likewise subscribed for and held for the same period

(TCGA 1992, s. 169VN and 169VO).

Reorganisation within s. 126 and consideration given

Where, before a disposal, an individual holds qualifying shares and there has been a reorganisation within TCGA 1992, s. 126, but consideration was given by the individual for new shares, shares received for consideration given as part of the reorganisation are treated for investors' relief purposes as having been issued when they actually were issued, and not when the original shares from which they were derived were issued. Shares for which consideration was not given are collectively subject to the rules in s. 169VN and 169VO (above)

(TCGA 1992, s. 169VP).

Exchanges and reconstructions within s. 135 or 136

Where there has been either an exchange within TCGA 1992, s. 135 or reconstruction within s. 136, the rules in s. 169VN and 169VP are applied as if the two companies involved in the exchange or reconstruction were the same company and as if the transaction were a reorganisation (TCGA 1992, s. 169VQ and 169VR). However, in order to determine whether a share is a qualifying share or a potentially qualifying share, the conditions in s. 169VB(2) (see 5311) are modified as follows:

> 'The conditions in new s. 169VB(2)(f) requiring the company that issued the share to be and remain either a trading company or the holding company of a trading group and in new s. 169VB(2)(g) that the investor or connected person must not be an officer or employee of the company must be met in relation to the original share for the period from issue until the date of the reorganisation and in relation to the share that represented the original share for the period from the reorganisation to the date of disposal (new TCGA 1992, s. 169VS).'

Election to disapply s. 127

TCGA 1992, s. 169VT allows a claimant to elect to disapply the normal tax treatment of a reorganisation of share capital or a share exchange. Where an election is made, for investors' relief purposes, there is deemed to be disposal of the original shares and a gain eligible for relief is treated as accruing. This means that investors' relief is not lost where shares which would produce a relievable gain on a normal sale are exchanged for (or converted into) shares or securities which are not eligible for relief. The election is only effective if the original shares qualified for the relief at the time the reorganisation or exchange of shares occurred.

An election must be made on or before the first anniversary of 31 January following the tax year in which the reorganisation or exchange takes place (TCGA 1992, s. 169VT(4)).

Legislation: TCGA 1992, s. 169VN–169VT

Tax Reporter: ¶573-700; ¶573-710; ¶573-720

5317 Definitions

'Subscribed for'

A person subscribes for shares if they are issued to that person for consideration consisting wholly of cash. Both the subscription and the issue must be for genuine commercial reasons and not for the avoidance of tax. 'Tax' in this context is not limited to capital gains tax. Where shares are transferred between spouses or civil partners, the transferee is treated as having subscribed for and acquired the shares at the same time as the transferor did so.

'Trading company' and 'holding company of a trading group'

'Trading company' and 'holding company of a trading group' take the meanings given by TCGA 1992, s. 165A. Furthermore, a company is not regarded as ceasing to trade because it has gone into liquidation or receivership for genuine commercial reasons.

Relevant employee

A relevant employee is an officer or employee of the issuing company or a connected company but an unpaid director is not regarded as a relevant employee by reason of the directorship alone provided he (nor any connected person) has not previously been connected with the issuing company nor involved in carrying on the issuing company's business (or the business of any connected company).

Where a person becomes a relevant employee part way through the relevant period but not within the first 180 days, provided there was no reasonable prospect (more likely than not) at the beginning of the period that the individual would become an employee during the relevant period and provided the individual is not a director at any time during the relevant period, the individual is treated as not being a relevant employee for the relevant period.

Unpaid director

An unpaid director will qualify as such notwithstanding receiving certain payments including:

(i)   a payment or reimbursement of travelling or other expenses, incurred wholly, exclusively and necessarily in the performance of the duties as director;

(ii) a reasonable commercial rate of interest on money lent to the issuing company or a related person;

(iii) any dividend not exceeding a normal return on the investment to which it relates;

(iv) payment for goods not in excess of market value;

(v) payment for rent not in excess of a reasonable and commercial rate,

(vi) any necessary and reasonable remuneration for qualifying services provided to the issuing company or a related person in the course of a UK trade or profession and taxed accordingly.

Related persons means a connected company of which the person is a director or any person connected with the issuing company or any connected company of which the person is a director.

Further general definitions are provided by TCGA 1992, s. 169VY.

Legislation: TCGA 1992, s. 169VU–169VY

Tax Reporter: ¶573-605; ¶573-610

5318   Disqualification of shares

Sch. 7ZB overrides the definitions of qualifying shares or potentially qualifying shares at s. 169VB (see 5311). Where the specified conditions are met, shares which would otherwise be qualifying shares or potentially qualifying shares at a given time are instead treated as excluded shares. This will be the case when, broadly, the shareholder has received value in some form from the company which issues the shares he has subscribed for. The value may be received at any time in the period starting one year before and (usually) ending three years after the shares are issued to him. The purpose of these rules is to ensure that the cash subscribed for the shares serves genuinely to increase the funds available to the company and does not represent a recycling of the company's existing resources.

All receipts of value from the company during the specified 'period of restriction' are aggregated, and if the total is not an amount of insignificant value (does not exceed £1,000 in aggregate), then the shares subscribed for are treated as excluded shares.

The circumstances in which an investor 'receives value' from a company for the purposes of Sch. 7ZB are based on the definitions which apply for the purposes of the enterprise investment scheme (see 5923).

A receipt of value from a company will not result in the recipient's shares being treated as excluded shares provided further conditions are met, which are, broadly, that the recipient restores an equal amount of value to the company, or otherwise effectively reverses the receipt. The share subscription itself cannot represent this 'replacement value' given to the company.

Legislation: TCGA 1992, Sch. 7ZB

Tax Reporter: ¶573-750ff.

Rebasing to 31 March 1982

5320   Base value for disposals after 5 April 1988

For a post-5 April 1988 disposal of an asset held on 31 March 1982, the base value against which the chargeable gain is computed is the value on 31 March 1982 (for exceptions, see 5322). This is achieved by assuming that the asset was sold and immediately reacquired by the disponor on 31 March 1982 at market value. When it was available, the indexation allowance was calculated on the basis of the March 1982 base value (see 5283).

Capital gains tax

Prior to *Finance Act* 2008, where rebasing was not deemed to have occurred, the taxpayer could elect for rebasing to apply, to override the exceptions to rebasing. The simplification of capital gains tax in FA 2008 made rebasing to 31 March 1982 mandatory for individuals and trustees (but not for companies) for disposals on or after 6 April 2008 and so this election is no longer applicable.

Example

Tim bought a chargeable asset in 1975 for £10,000. He sells it in January 1997 for £25,000.

Value of asset on 31 March 1982 was £11,000.

	£
Disposal consideration	25,000
Allowable expenditure	(11,000)
Unindexed gain	14,000
Indexation allowance (£11,000 × 0.891)	(9,801)
Chargeable gain	4,199

Where an asset is acquired after 31 March 1982, the base value is the cost of acquisition and indexation allowance was also based on acquisition cost, subject to certain exceptions (see 5292); however, relief may have been available in specific cases. There was no rebasing in certain circumstances.

For market value, see 5103ff.

For the interaction of the MV82 rebasing, provisions with the no gain/no loss transfer provisions for assets subject to inter-spouse transfers prior to onward disposal, see 5500.

Where shares formed part of a larger holding of a spouse or fellow group company on 31 March 1982 (but have been transferred to the taxpayer on a no gain/no loss basis), they may be valued by reference to the size of the larger holding if the taxpayer so claims; for disposals after 15 March 1993, a claim must be made within two years of the end of the tax year and, for disposals made before that date, a claim must be made before the liability in point is finally determined. This may raise the base value of shares, particularly where a majority holding has been split to utilise reliefs, e.g. to use the annual exemptions of both husband and wife (see 6150).

The Shares and Assets Valuation would agree to certain approaches to value unquoted shares before a referral from HMRC, largely for indexation allowance and rebasing purposes (see 5103). For rebasing and shares generally, see 5826.

Legislation: TCGA 1992, s. 35(1), (2), 55(6) and Sch. 3, para. 1A

Other Material: Former ESC D44, *Rebasing and indexation: shares derived from larger holdings held at 31 March 1982*

Tax Reporter: ¶520-350

5322 Exceptions to rebasing

A simplified rebasing scheme could be applied by election (see below) but, otherwise, prior to 6 April 2008 there was no rebasing to 1982 values in the following cases:

- where 1982 rebasing would produce a gain but a smaller gain would be produced without rebasing, the pre-1988 rules continued to apply. This exception ensured that the taxpayer was not worse off under the rebasing rules;

- where 1982 rebasing would produce a loss but a smaller loss would be produced without rebasing, the pre-1988 rules continued to apply. This ensured that the taxpayer was not unjustifiably better off under the rebasing rules;

- where 1982 rebasing turned what would be a gain without rebasing into a loss or what would be a loss without rebasing into gain. In either case the disposal must be treated as producing neither loss nor gain, i.e. the chargeable gain/loss is nil;

- if neither a gain nor a loss would occur without rebasing either on the facts of the case or under the special rules for pre-1965 assets, those pre-1988 rules continued to apply; and

- where neither a gain nor a loss would accrue by virtue of certain specified provisions, rebasing did not override the existing no gain/no loss transfers.

Prior to 6 April 2008 (and still for companies), a 'kink-test' comparison after time apportionment was required where there was no deemed disposal on 31 March 1982. The prior acquisition of the asset remained critical subject to special rules for assets held on 6 April 1965 – referred to above, as a whole, as the pre-1988 rules.

Legislation (prior to amendment by FA 2008): TCGA 1992, s. 35(3), (4), (10) and Sch. 3, para. 6

Tax Reporter: ¶520-550

5323   Election for 1982 valuation on all assets

Prior to FA 2008, and still for companies, it was necessary for the necessity for the retention by taxpayers of to retain pre-1982 records and the complexity of tax computations were made on more complex by the alternative bases available. However, taxpayers could elect that their capital gains and losses on all assets held as at 31 March 1982 be calculated by reference to March 1982 values. Such an election would displace the operation of the exceptions to 1982 rebasing. From 6 April 2008, rebasing has been mandatory and this election is no longer applicable for individuals and trustees.

Special provisions determine the nature of the election for groups. Plant and machinery generally and certain mining or oil-related assets are excluded from the election.

An election made by a person in one capacity did not cover disposals made by him in another capacity. In this respect, HMRC have indicated that:

- a partner could make an election in respect of a disposal of his interest in partnership assets but it was not necessary for all partners to make elections; if an individual was a member of more than one partnership, a separate election was required for each; a separate election was required for assets held privately;

- where assets were otherwise held jointly, each individual's share or holding would be covered by an election made by him in his capacity as an individual;

- an election by a sole trader applied to business and private assets;

- an election by the single body formed by all the trustees of a settlement applied only to that one settlement.

Time-limit

Once made, an election was irrevocable and it had to be made by notice in writing to HMRC before 6 April 1990 or within two years after the end of the tax year within which the first relevant disposal was made or such later time as HMRC may have allowed. Simply submitting a computation which was based only on the 31 March 1982 value did not, in HMRC's view, in itself constitute a claim. For tax years after 1995–96, the time-limit was 12 months from the 31 January next following the tax year in which the disposal took place; that is, approximately 22 months from the end of the tax year.

A Revenue statement of practice clarified the operation of the time-limit for the rebasing election. The statement treated certain disposals which would not produce chargeable gains as not being 'relevant disposals' and accordingly such disposals could be left out of account in timing any election. Disposals included were of private cars; chattels below the value of the chattel exemption; chattels which were wasting assets; government non-marketable securities; gilt-edged securities and qualifying corporate bonds; rights to compensation for an injury or wrong suffered by an individual in his person, profession or vocation; shares held as part of a personal equity plan, etc; life assurance policies, etc. unless purchased from a third party; foreign currency for personal expenditure; most debts held by the original creditor; BES shares in respect of which relief had been given and not withdrawn; gifts of works of art, etc; decorations for valour, etc; betting winnings and rights to certain superannuation allowances, annuities, etc.

In determining the time-limit for an election, HMRC would also omit those disposals which in practice did not give rise to a chargeable gain or allowable loss, the main examples being building society withdrawals, dwelling-houses where the whole gain qualified for private residence relief, most no gain/no loss provisions. Discretion would also be exercised so as to ignore disposals where no election for the simplified re-basing scheme was possible. The statement also gave guidance for persons who became resident in the UK after 6 April 1988, for disposals of non-UK assets by individuals resident but not domiciled in the UK and for disposals by a UK resident during a period of non-residence.

Legislation: TCGA 1992, s. 35(5)–(8) and Sch. 3, para. 7, 8

Other Material: SP 4/92

Tax Reporter: ¶520-400

Wasting assets

5330 Importance of 'wasting assets'

A 'wasting asset' is an asset with a predictable useful life of no more than 50 years as ascertainable at the time of acquisition. Thus, a lease granted for a term of no more than 50 years is a wasting asset (see further 5333). The following general rules apply:

- plant and machinery are in all cases wasting assets, even where the asset is considered to have a useful life of more than 50 years. HMRC have confirmed that they regard such items as antique clocks, vintage cars and sailing vessels propelled by engines as 'machinery' (see HMRC's *Capital Gains Manual* CG76900ff., which also gives a fuller list of specific items considered to be machinery);

- a life interest in settled property is a wasting asset where the life expectancy of the life tenant is 50 years or less (as ascertained from actuarial tables);

- freehold land is never a wasting asset, regardless of its nature (e.g. eroding cliff-side property).

The nature of wasting assets requires special rules of computation for CGT purposes. Since the owner will have had the use and enjoyment of the wasting asset, the basic rule is that the acquisition expenditure must be written off, save for a residual or scrap value. Any comparison of the price at which the asset is sold with the original purchase price is not a comparison of like with like, and any 'gains' or 'losses' arising would be an unsound basis for taxation.

The legislation deals with wasting assets in various ways.

- Wasting assets which are 'tangible moveable property' (chattels) are generally exempt from CGT unless they are used for a trade, profession or vocation as mentioned below. This prevents claims for allowable losses on, e.g. household furniture.

- Wasting assets which have been used throughout the disponor's period of ownership for the purposes of a trade, profession or vocation and in respect of which the disponor was entitled to claim capital allowances are liable to CGT to the extent so used; there is no writing-off of expenditure. However, where a tangible moveable asset is not exempt as a wasting asset because capital allowances have been claimed against it, on disposal it will be exempt from CGT if it is sold for less than £6,000, irrespective of its trade use (see 6155).

- Quoted options to subscribe for shares, traded options, commodity and financial futures involving certain approved financial institutions, etc. or a dealer on a recognised futures exchange and most options to acquire assets for trade purposes: there is no writing-off of expenditure (see 5980 and 5985).

- Short leases of land: allowable expenditure is written off at a specified rate (see 5333).

- Other wasting assets: allowable expenditure is written off evenly over the life of the asset (see 5336).

Legislation: TCGA 1992, s. 44(1), (3), 44, 45, 47, 262

Other Material: RI88

Case: *Lord Howard of Henderskelfe (Deceased) v R & C Commrs* [2013] BTC 1,750

Tax Reporter: ¶508-700

5333 Short leases of land

Notwithstanding the general rules as to the meaning of wasting assets (which would apply by reference to the term of a lease: see 5330), leases with unexpired 'duration' of 50 years or less are, in general, wasting assets. A lease is widely defined and specific provisions determine the duration of a lease. The possibility of a claim for extending a lease by 50 years under the *Leasehold Reform Act* 1967 did not prevent a lease with 16 years to run from having a duration not exceeding 50 years, the High Court has held.

The allowable expenditure for CGT purposes is treated as wasting away over the length of the lease in accordance with calculations based on a formula which amounts to the following table:

Years	%	Years	%
Years	*%*	25	81.100
50 (or more)	100	24	79.622
49	99.657	23	78.055
48	99.289	22	76.399
47	98.902	21	74.635
46	98.490	20	72.770
45	98.059	19	70.791
44	97.595	18	68.697
43	97.107	17	66,470
42	96.593	16	64.116
41	96.041	15	61.617
40	95.457	14	58.971
39	94.842	13	56.167
38	94.189	12	53.191
37	93.197	11	50.038
36	92.761	10	46.695
35	91.981	9	43.154
34	91.156	8	39.399
33	90.280	7	35.414
32	89.345	6	31.195
31	88.371	5	26.722
30	87.330	4	21.983
29	86.226	3	16.959
28	85.053	2	11.629
27	83.816	1	5.983
26	82.496	0	0

Capital gains tax

The allowable expenditure can be calculated according to the formula:

$$\frac{X}{Y} \times Z$$

X   is the percentage (taken from the table) for the number of years remaining when the lease is disposed of;

Y   is the percentage for the number of years remaining when the lease was acquired; and

Z   is the cost at acquisition.

The resulting figure is subtracted from the consideration received on disposal to give the chargeable gain.

Example

Charlie acquired a 12-year lease for a sum the capital element of which (i.e. excluding any amount chargeable to income tax under the property income rules in ITTOIA 2005) was £10,000. Seven years later he assigned the lease to David for a premium the capital element of which was £7,000.

Chargeable gain

	£
Price at disposal	7,000.00
Less: allowable amount:	
$\dfrac{26.722}{53.191} \times £10,000$	(5,023.78)
Chargeable gain	1,976.22

Enhancement expenditure, if any, is discounted by applying the same formula:

$$\frac{X}{Y} \times Z$$

but now Y is the percentage for the number of years remaining when the enhancement expenditure is incurred and Z is the enhancement cost.

If the duration of the lease is not an exact number of years the percentage derived from the table is calculated using the lower of the nearest two exact year percentages plus one twelfth the difference between the two percentages for each odd month. In this context an incomplete month is counted if it comprises 14 days or more.

Special rules apply to subleases granted out of short leases.

Premiums for leases

A person who requires a premium under a lease of land is treated as making a part disposal, i.e. the premium is chargeable to CGT.

Any part of a premium for a lease which is liable to a charge to income tax as income from a property business (see 1260ff.) is deducted from the amount liable to CGT.

A number of amendments have been made to the tax treatment of certain sums treated as additional lease premiums. The sums in question are amounts received in lieu of rent or as consideration for the surrender of a lease, and amounts received as consideration for the variation or waiver of any of the terms of the lease.

A premium deemed to be received for the surrender of a lease is treated as a disposal by the landlord of his interest in the lease.

A premium deemed to be received in lieu of rent or as consideration for the variation or waiver of any of the terms of the lease is treated as a further part-disposal of the asset out of which the lease was granted, taking place on the date the premium is due.

Relief is allowed where the lessee of property on a lease which has 50 years or less to run receives insurance payments which are applied in discharging an obligation to restore any damage to the property (see 5083).

Legislation: TCGA 1992, s. 240, Sch. 8, para. 1, 3–6, 8, 10

Tax Reporter: ¶509-600ff.

5336 Wasting assets other than leases of land

Subject to special rules for tangible moveable property, assets used for a trade, short leases of land and various options or futures (see 5330), allowable expenditure attributable to wasting assets is written off evenly over the useful life of the asset so as to leave the residual or scrap value. The 'residual or scrap value' is the predictable value (as ascertainable at the time of acquisition) which the asset will have at the end of its predictable useful life, having regard to the purpose for which the asset was acquired.

The expenditure which is disallowed is calculated by using the following formulae:

Capital gains tax

(1) *Expenditure on cost of acquisition:*

$$(A - S) \times \frac{O}{L} = \text{expenditure disallowed.}$$

(2) *Expenditure on enhancing the value of the asset:*

$$E \times \frac{T}{L - (O - T)} = \text{expenditure disallowed.}$$

A   is the cost of acquisition.

E   is expenditure on enhancing the value of the asset.

L   is the predictable life of the asset as at the time of acquisition.

O   is the period of ownership.

S   is the residual or scrap value.

T   is the period during which E is reflected in the asset value.

Example

Peter buys a wasting asset with a predictable life of 20 years. The cost of acquisition is £10,500. Peter spends £5,000 on the asset after three years of ownership. He sells the asset after five years of ownership for £9,000. The scrap value of the asset is £500.

The calculation to ascertain CGT liability is as follows:

(1) $(£10,500 - £500) \times \dfrac{5}{20} = £2,500$

The acquisition cost (£10,500) is reduced by £2,500 to give allowable expenditure of £8,000.

(2) $£5,000 \times \dfrac{2}{20 - (5 - 2)} = £588.24$

The cost of enhancement (£5,000) is reduced by £588.24 to give allowable expenditure of £4,411.76.

The two resultant figures for allowable expenditure (£8,000 and £4,411.76) are added together, giving a total of £12,411.76. Thus, there is an allowable loss of £12,411.76 − £9,000 = £3,411.76.

Leases of property other than leases of land are subject to broadly similar provisions to those relating to leases of land (see 5333).

Legislation: TCGA 1992, s. 44(2), (3), 46 and Sch. 8, para. 9

Tax Reporter: ¶508-850

Assets held on 6 April 1965

5380   Introduction to assets held on 6 April 1965

For disposals after 5 April 1988, chargeable gains or allowable losses are computed as if the asset in point had been disposed of and reacquired on 31 March 1982 at its market value at that time; however, prior to the mandatory re-basing for individuals and trustees introduced in FA 2008, such re-basing did not apply in certain cases where the former provisions would have dictated a result of a different nature. Hence, special rules applicable to assets held at 6 April 1965 continued to be relevant to disposals prior to 6 April 2008 even after the introduction of re-basing to 31 March 1982. The rules will continue to have some limited relevance, to those companies with assets acquired over 50 years ago.

Capital gains tax and corporation tax on chargeable gains were introduced in 1965. It was not intended that the charge should be retrospective and rules were provided with the broad objective of restricting any chargeable gain or allowable loss to that which had accrued after 6 April 1965.

It was considered administratively impossible and undesirable to require that all assets held on 6 April 1965 should be valued at that time. The rule for most assets was therefore that any gain or loss should be time-apportioned to determine the amount attributable to the post-6 April 1965 period which should be within the scope of the chargeable gains regime. However, an election was provided for taxpayers to choose instead to value an asset at its value on 6 April 1965. Special rules applied to quoted securities, where a market value at 6 April 1965 was readily available, and to land reflecting development value on that date, where such valuation was likely to have been available and where time apportionment would be wholly inappropriate.

The rules applied also to an asset held by a taxpayer's spouse at 6 April 1965 but later transferred on a no gain/no loss basis.

Legislation: TCGA 1992, s. 35(9) and Sch. 2

Other Material: ESC D34; SP 5/89

Tax Reporter: ¶520-750; ¶520-800

5383   Quoted securities held on 6 April 1965

For quoted shares or securities held at 6 April 1965, where there was a market value readily available, the asset was deemed to have been acquired on 6 April 1965 for its market value at that time, unless a smaller gain or loss would result from the use of actual costs; there was also the possibility of pooling shares or securities of the same class at their value at that date, so that gains or losses were calculated on the basis of the pool value irrespective of the actual cost position.

Legislation: TCGA 1992, Sch. 2, para. 1, 2(1), (2), 4–7

Tax Reporter: ¶520-800

5386 Land with development value at 6 April 1965

On a disposal or part disposal of land held at 6 April 1965, it was generally treated as if it had been acquired at its market value at 6 April 1965. A similar exercise took place each time there is a part disposal, so that additional considerations which had arisen could be taken into account in the valuation process; each earlier part disposal as then recalculated on the basis of the revised assumptions. This deemed acquisition did not apply where a smaller gain or loss would arise if the actual costs were used nor if a gain would be turned into a loss or vice versa, in which case there was deemed to be no gain/no loss.

Land to which rules apply

These rules apply only to land situated in the UK.

Land which was acquired by gift prior to 6 April 1965 fell within these provisions in the same way as land acquired for consideration.

The disposal consideration must have exceeded the current use value at the time of the disposal or some material development of the land must have been carried out since the disponor acquired it.

Legislation: TCGA 1992, Sch. 2, para. 9–15

Cases: *Mashiter (HMIT) v Pearmain* [1985] BTC 105; *Morgan (HMIT) v Gibson* [1989] BTC 272

Tax Reporter: ¶520-800

5389 Time apportionment: pre-1965 gains or losses

For assets other than quoted shares or securities (including units in a unit trust scheme) and land reflecting development value, unless the taxpayer elected to apply the market value at 6 April 1965, the gain or loss was deemed to accrue on a straight-line basis over the period of ownership and only that part which was apportioned to the period after 6 April 1965 was a chargeable gain or allowable loss.

The taxpayer could elect (subject to certain conditions) to have the 6 April 1965 value substituted as the base value. Under self-assessment, the election had to be made within 12 months from 31 January following the tax year in which the disposal was made or, for corporation tax purposes, within two years from the end of the accounting period in which the disposal is made.

Legislation: TCGA 1992, Sch. 2, para. 16, 17

Case: *Smith (HMIT) v Schofield* [1993] BTC 147

Other Material: ESC D10

Tax Reporter: ¶520-800

Rates of capital gains tax

5410   Rates of capital gains tax

Finance Act 2016 reduces the main rates of capital gains tax to 10% and 20% from 6 April 2016 (previously 18% and 28% respectively). The new main rates do not apply to 'upper rate gains' which consist of:

- residential property gains;

- NRCGT gains; or

- gains accruing under TCGA 1992, s. 103KA(2) or (3) (carried interest).

The rates of 18% and 28% continue to apply to gains within the above categories.

The rate of capital gains tax is determined by aggregating the individual's taxable income and chargeable gains. To the extent that gains fall within the individual's basic rate band, the lower rates (of 10% or 18%) apply. To the extent that gains exceed the individual's basic rate band, the higher rates (of 20% and 28%) apply on the excess.

The rates applicable to trustees and personal representatives from 6 April 2016 are 28% on upper rate gains and otherwise 20% (previously, the rate applicable was 28% regardless of the category of gain).

Gains eligible for entrepreneurs' or investors' relief (as introduced from 6 April 2016) are charged at 10% (see 5293 and 5310).

ATED related gains are chargeable at 28% (see 5150).

Pre-6 April 2016

From 23 June 2010, there were two rates of capital gains tax applicable to individuals: a basic rate of 18% and a higher rate of 28%, determined by aggregating the individual's taxable income and chargeable gains. Trustees and personal representatives were charged at a rate of 28%.

The rate of tax on non-resident disposals (from 6 April 2015) was 18% or 28% for individuals and 20% for companies (see 5717).

From 23 June 2010, a special 10% flat rate applied to gains eligible for entrepreneurs' relief (see 5293).

Pre-23 June 2010

Between 6 April 2008 to 22 June 2010, capital gains tax was charged at a single flat rate of 18%, regardless of the person chargeable, the nature of the asset involved or the length of ownership of that asset.

Prior to 6 April 2008, individuals were charged to capital gains tax at their marginal income tax rate, so that gains within the basic rate band were charged at the basic rate and any excess was charged at the higher rate.

An effective rate of tax of 10%, known as entrepreneurs' relief was introduced for eligible gains from 6 April 2008 to replace taper relief. Between 6 April 2008 and 22 June 2010, such gains were charged at the 18% rate after being reduced by 4/9 to produce an effective 10% rate.

Individuals

The rate of capital gains tax payable by individuals is determined as follows:

- if any of the gains are on qualifying business disposals which attract entrepreneurs' relief (see 5293) or investors' relief, those gains will always be taxed at 10% (TCGA 1992, s. 169N(3));

- where, for the tax year in which the gains arise, an individual is liable to pay income tax at the higher rate or dividend upper rate, chargeable gains (other than those eligible for entrepreneurs' relief) are taxed at 28% on upper rate gains and 20% otherwise (TCGA 1992, s. 4(4));

- where part of the individual's income tax basic rate band is unused, special rules apply to determine the rate of CGT applicable:

  - where an individual has gains subject to entrepreneurs' relief or investors' relief (known as 'special rate gains', those gains are included in the total of chargeable gains for the purposes of determining the rate applicable in respect of other gains and are treated as being the lowest part of that total (TCGA 1992, s. 4(6) and (6A)). The effect of this is the unused amount of an individual's income tax basic rate band is reduced by the amount of any gains that are taxed at the special CGT rates and limits or eliminates access to the lower rates of CGT (10% or 18%) where those reliefs are due, pushing other gains into the 20% and 28% rates;

- when part of the individual's income tax basic rate band is unused and the individual has gains from residential property or carried interest (upper rate gains), the rules allow him or her to choose which chargeable gains are subject to the appropriate lower rate of CGT, up to the unused amount. For these purposes, again, the unused amount is reduced by the amount of any gains that are taxed at the special CGT rate under entrepreneurs' relief or investors' relief. Gains which are not charged at a lower rate are charged at the higher rate appropriate to their nature. This means that any unused basic rate band can be used in the most beneficial way to reduce CGT charged (TCGA 1992, s. 4BA).

For these purposes, an individual's taxable income is the figure calculated at Stage 3 of the prescribed method of calculating income tax liabilities and the unused part of his basic rate band is the excess of the basic rate limit over that taxable income.

The income calculated at Stage 3 is to be modified for these purposes by being:

(1) reduced by any deficiency relief due in respect of life insurance contracts;

(2) reduced by any reduction in residuary income as a result of inheritance tax being charged on accrued income; and

(3) reduced by the amount of any gains on life policies in excess of the annual equivalent of those gains.

(The reliefs at (1) and (2) above are normally given by means of a tax reduction at Step 6 of the income tax calculation, whilst the gains on life policies are included in total income in full but subject to top-slicing relief being given as a tax reduction at Step 6.)

Where 'top-slicing relief' has been given in respect of a gain on a life policy and the calculation of the individual's income tax liability on the gain does not involve higher rate income tax, then he is to be treated as not having paid tax at that rate when it comes to determining the rate of capital gains tax applicable.

Trustees and personal representatives

Chargeable gains arising on disposals on or after 6 April 2016 are charged at 20% other than 'upper rate gains' (residential property gains, NRCGT gains and carried interest gains) which are charged at 28% and gains eligible for entrepreneurs' relief, when the rate is 10%. Prior to 6 April 2016 (from 23 June 2010), the rate was 28% on all gains other than gains eligible for entrepreneurs' relief which were charged at 10%.

Losses and annual exemption

Because it is possible for a number of rates of capital gains tax to be chargeable for the same year, the question arises as to how to allocate allowable losses and the annual exemption. It is specifically provided that losses and the annual exemption may be used in the way most beneficial to the taxpayer. Thus, they should be set primarily against the gains bearing the highest rate of tax.

This provision does not, however, override any other provision which restricts the set-off of losses, such as losses arising on a connected persons transaction which can only be set against gains arising on a transaction with the same person.

Legislation: TCGA 1992, s. 4, 4A, 4B, 4BA

Tax Reporter: ¶500-220

5415   CGT rates and annual exemption for trusts

Chargeable gains arising on disposals on or after 6 April 2016 are charged at 20% other than 'upper rate gains' (residential property gains, NRCGT gains and carried interest gains) which are charged at 28% and gains eligible for entrepreneurs' relief, when the rate is 10%. Prior to 6 April 2016 (from 23 June 2010), the rate was 28% on all gains other than gains eligible for entrepreneurs' relief which were charged at 10%.

For the period 6 April 2008 to 22 June 2010, capital gains tax was charged at a single flat rate of 18%, regardless of the person chargeable, the nature of the asset involved or the length of ownership of that asset.

For the years up to and including 2007–08, the rate of capital gains tax for trustees was the 'trust rate', which was a flat 40% for 2007–08.

The annual exemption for trusts continues and is in most cases one-half of that applying to individuals (but see 5595 concerning trusts for the disabled). However, where there is more than one settlement by the same settlor, that half is divided amongst them, but subject to a de minimis figure of 10% of the full exempt amount for each trust.

For a table of rates and thresholds, see Key Data.

Legislation: TCGA 1992, s. 4 and Sch. 1, para. 2

Tax Reporter: ¶500-250; ¶535-125

5417 Capital gains tax and income tax separate taxes

CGT and income tax remain separate and distinct. Income tax reliefs and allowances cannot generally be set against chargeable gains. Personal allowances against income tax which are unused in any year are lost (see 1840); they cannot be used to reduce liability to CGT. Neither can capital losses (generally) or the annual CGT exemption (see 6150) be set against taxable income.

Tax Reporter: ¶500-000ff.

Spouses and civil partners: capital gains tax

5460 Independent taxation for CGT

Spouses are taxed separately on their chargeable gains. The effect on CGT is that a wife's gains are not attributed to her husband, each spouse is entitled to a separate annual exemption (see 6150) and one spouse's unrelieved losses cannot be deducted from the other's gains. Disposals between husband and wife are on a no gain/no loss basis (see 5500).

The *Civil Partnership Act* 2004 took effect from 5 December 2005. Broadly, the Act allows registered same-sex couples the same legal rights and protections as married couples (see 230 for further commentary on this).

Same sex marriages were legalised by the *Marriage (Same Sex Couples) Act* 2013, which received Royal Assent on 17 July 2013.

In the remainder of this chapter, references to a spouse also apply equally to civil partners.

Case: *Jolaoso* [2011] TC 00921

Tax Reporter: ¶504-000

5490 'Living together' for CGT

A married woman is treated as living with her husband unless:

- they are separated under a court order or deed of separation; or
- they are in fact separated in such circumstances that the separation is likely to be permanent.

Legislation: TCGA 1992, s. 288(3)

Case: *Holmes v Mitchell (HMIT)* [1991] BTC 28

Tax Reporter: ¶504-050

5500 Transfers between spouses and civil partners

Transfers of assets between husband and wife, or civil partners, 'living together' (see 5490) have always generally been on a no gain/no loss basis, the gain on the whole period of ownership being brought into charge when the asset is eventually disposed of.

Example

Hugh and Winnie are husband and wife living together. Hugh buys a painting for £15,000 and then two years later gives the painting to Winnie when it is worth £18,000. Winnie sells it ten years after that for £22,000. Winnie is treated as having acquired the painting for £15,000. The gain attributable to Winnie is therefore £7,000. No chargeable gain arises on Hugh's disposal to Winnie.

In the case of recipients of inter-spouse transfers made after 31 March 1982 (or of transfers from civil partners after 5 December 2005), they would not be entitled to rebasing as they did not hold the asset on 31 March 1982. Prior to April 2008, TCGA 1992, Sch. 3, para. 1(1) deemed the recipient of an asset which was the subject of a no gain/no loss disposal (including inter-spouse and civil partner transfers) to have held the asset on 31 March 1982 where it was so held by the transferring spouse or civil partner. With effect from 6 April 2008, TCGA 1992, Sch. 3 is only relevant for corporation tax purposes and para. 1(1) has been amended to refer to intra-group transfers only. However, the position of spouses and civil partners was maintained by the insertion of a new provision which applies where:

(1) the person making the disposal (on or after 6 April 2008) had acquired the asset concerned after 31 March 1982 and before 6 April 2008;

(2) the transaction by which the asset was acquired was one which the legislation treated as a no gain/no loss disposal. If there was more than one disposal of the asset since 31 March 1982, all must have been so treated;

(3) the person making the disposal must not have held the asset at 31 March 1982 (this is to cover cases where the asset had previously been owned by the person making the disposal)

(TCGA 1992, s. 35A(1)).

In such cases, the consideration deemed to have been given for the acquisition of the asset in the no gain/no loss transaction is to be determined on the basis that rebasing applied to that transaction and that an unindexed gain accrued which was equal to the indexation allowance due to the transferor (TCGA 1992, s. 35A(2)). The effect is therefore to treat the acquisition cost of the asset as being the sum of the value of the asset at 31 March 1982 plus indexation allowance from that date to the date of the no gain/no loss transaction (or to April 1998 if earlier).

The question then is what happens where, say, a spouse acquired an asset before 31 March 1982, but the transfer takes place after 6 April 2008? TCGA 1992, s. 35A cannot apply, as condition (1) is not satisfied (i.e. the person making the disposal must have acquired the asset before 6 April 2008). However, s. 35(1) and (2) apply to the first spouse as he or she held the asset in 1982 and is the one making the disposal after 6 April 2008. The *Taxation of Chargeable Gains Act* 1992, s. 58 applies to treat a transfer by the first spouse as a no gain/no loss disposal, so that his or her disposal value is equal to the March 1982 value and it is this value which is the second spouse's acquisition value in relation to the final disposal. Therefore, rebasing still applies to the recipient spouse, although it is not that obvious.

Where a shareholding is split between the couple after 31 March 1982, the market value on that date of the part holdings can be determined by reference to the larger holding.

For application of inter-spouse transfer rules on transfers of employee shareholder shares and interaction with the lifetime CGT exemption limit, see 5929A.

Legislation: TCGA 1992, s. 35, 35A, 58

Tax Reporter: ¶504-050; ¶520-300

5502 Jointly held assets

For CGT purposes, the assets of each spouse are treated separately, with separate relief and exemptions (see 5460). HMRC have clarified that the CGT treatment of assets held jointly by husband and wife may be summarised as follows:

- gains are apportioned in accordance with beneficial interests at the time of the disposal;

- where the split of beneficial interests between them is clear, because, for example, they have a legal agreement between them, or where there is an agreement that one is merely a nominee and has no beneficial interest, gains should be apportioned on that basis;

- where the split of beneficial interests is unclear, HMRC will normally accept that the couple hold the asset in equal shares;

- for income tax purposes, despite the usual presumption that the couple are equally entitled to the income, where assets and the rights to income from them are held in the same unequal shares, the couple can declare this to HMRC and be charged to income tax (and CGT) according to that split. It is presumed that where a couple make a declaration for income tax purposes, the same split applies for CGT.

Case: *Koshal* [2013] TC 02806

Other Material: HMRC Press Release dated 21 November 1990

Tax Reporter: ¶504-100

5505   Sole or main residence for married couple

A husband and wife or civil partners 'living together' (see 5490) can have only one sole or main residence for the purpose of the principal private residence exemption (see 6233).

Tax Reporter: ¶546-000

Trusts and settlements for capital gains tax

Types of trust for CGT

5550   General CGT considerations for settlements

Settlements are used for a number of different purposes; for example, to:

- put assets into the hands of trustees who are better able to administer the assets than the intended beneficiaries;
- separate the ownership of income and capital so that for the present income is employed for one person but the capital is held long-term for another;
- avoid the ownership of a particular asset having to be determined at a given time; and
- take advantage of tax planning opportunities.

Settlements do not exist wholly for tax planning purposes; it is the flexibility that can be achieved through the use of a settlement that most often makes them attractive. Successive governments have therefore accepted that the settlement vehicle should continue to exist but have repeatedly attempted to restrict the tax planning opportunities that it may offer.

The terms 'settlement' and 'trust' are often used interchangeably. However, in this division, the term 'settlement' is used to refer to the overall arrangement whereby property is held by a body of persons (the 'trustees') 'on trust' for the benefit of others (the 'beneficiaries').

A 'trust' is the obligation which binds the trustees to hold property and apply it or the income derived from it for the benefit of the beneficiaries. A trust is generally created by a person, known as the settlor, who transfers funds to the trustees directing the way in which the property transferred is to be held and administered. The trustees have a fiduciary duty to deal with the trust property according to the terms of the trust.

Tax Reporter: ¶576-000; ¶350-000ff.

Handout: Capital gains tax and UK trusts

5552   Absolute and beneficial entitlement

The concept of absolute entitlement against the trustee(s) is important in connection with the taxation of chargeable gains and settlements. Determining whether property is settled may hinge on whether a beneficiary is absolutely entitled as against the trustee and the occasion of a person becoming absolutely entitled as against the trustee may trigger a charge to tax (see 5575).

For capital gains tax, a person is absolutely entitled as against the trustee where he has an exclusive right to direct how a trust asset should be dealt with, subject only to the satisfaction of any outstanding charge, lien or other right of the trustees to resort to the asset for payment of any outgoings.

A person may be absolutely entitled even though not beneficially entitled to property as against the trustees. Where trustees exercise a power as a result of which assets are held on new trusts, the new trustees may be absolutely entitled as against the former trustees.

Trustees of any settlement are a separate and continuing body (see 5565). Where trustees advance property so that assets are held on new trusts, even though the trustees of both settlements may actually be the same persons, this may occasion a deemed disposal within TCGA 1992, s. 71 (see 5575). This is an area that has caused difficulty and there is a series of cases that have considered the question of whether an appointment of assets on new trusts gives rise to a capital gains tax charge.

Legislation: TCGA 1992, s. 60(2)

Capital gains tax

Cases: *Hoare Trustees; Gardner; Hart v Briscoe* (1977) 52 TC 53; *Roome v Edwards (HMIT)* (1981) 54 TC 359; *Bond (HMIT) v Pickford* [1983] BTC 313; *Swires v Renton* [1991] BTC 362

Other Material: SP 7/84, *Exercise of a Power of Appointment or Advancement over Settled Property* (supersedes SP 9/81)

Tax Reporter: ¶351-075; ¶351-560

5555   Nominees and bare trustees for CGT

Assets held for another by a nominee or bare trustee are treated as if they are vested in the person for whom the assets are held: the beneficiary. The acts of the nominee or trustee in relation to those assets are treated as the acts of the beneficiary. For CGT purposes, therefore, a bare trust is treated as being transparent and any capital gains or losses of the bare trust are treated as those of the person who is entitled to the underlying assets of the trust.

A 'bare trustee' is a person who holds property for someone who is (or would be but for being an infant or mentally handicapped) absolutely entitled as against the trustee, i.e. he has exclusive right, subject to any outstanding charge, lien, etc. for the payment of taxes and the like, to direct the trustee how to deal with the asset. The same applies where two or more persons are, or would be, jointly entitled (see Examples 2 and 3 below). For the trustee to be a bare trustee, the beneficiary must have a vested and indefeasible interest.

Example 1

Trustees hold property in trust for such of the settlor's children as should attain 18 years or marry under that age. During the time that the children are unmarried infants, the trustees dispose of investments comprised in the trust fund and a gain accrues. The trustees are not bare trustees because it cannot be said that if the beneficiaries were not infants at the time of the sale they would be absolutely entitled to call for the money and be able to give a good receipt. The interests of the infants are contingent on their reaching 18 years. The gains, therefore, accrue to the trustees and not to the beneficiaries. (This example is based on *Tomlinson (HMIT) v Glyns Exor & Trustee Co* (1969) 45 TC 600.)

Example 2

Jack and Julie are trustees for sale of certain land for their own benefit as tenants in common. The land is sold and a gain accrues. Jack and Julie do not have interests in a settlement but are bare trustees – a chargeable gain, therefore, accrues to each of them. The situation would be the same if Jack and Julie were joint tenants.

Example 3

Trustees are directed to hold a trust fund for Anita for life with remainder to Beatrice absolutely. Although Anita and Beatrice may join together to direct the trustees how to deal with the property, they are not 'jointly' entitled, i.e. they have successive rather than concurrent interests. The trustees are not bare trustees and so the property is settled property.

Funds in court are treated as bare trusts.

Legislation: TCGA 1992, s. 60, 61

Cases: *Kidson (HMIT) v MacDonald* (1973) 49 TC 503; *Jenkins (HMIT) v Brown; Warrington (HMIT) v Sterland* [1989] BTC 281

Tax Reporter: ¶351-375; ¶357-075; ¶357-100

5562 Settlor

Finance Act 2006 introduced a definition of 'settlor' for all capital gains tax purposes, based on the wider definition in the settlements anti-avoidance legislation in ITTOIA 2005.

With effect from 6 April 2006, a 'settlor' is the person who 'makes' the settlement, or is treated as so doing (TCGA 1992, s. 68A(1)(a)). Three examples are given of persons who are deemed to have made a settlement. These are persons:

- who made or entered into the settlement, either directly or indirectly (TCGA 1992, s. 68A(2)(a));

- who have provided property, directly or indirectly, for the purposes of the settlement, or have undertaken to do so (s. 68A(3)); and

- as a result of whose death, the settled property, or property derived from the settled property, included property which they were competent to dispose (s. 68A(2)(b), (5)).

If A enters into a settlement where there are reciprocal arrangements with B, B is treated as the settlor for these purposes.

The legislation now identifies the settlor where there is a transfer of property between settlements made for no consideration or less than full consideration. Where property is disposed of from settlement 1 and acquired by settlement 2 (even if in a different form), the settlor(s) of settlement 1 will be treated as the settlor(s) of settlement 2 unless the transfer occurs because of a will variation.

The legislation also now identifies the settlor in relation to will and intestacy variations occurring on or after 6 April 2006 regardless of the deceased's date of death where there is a variation in accordance with TCGA 1992, s. 62(6) and property which was not settled property under the will becomes settled. In this case, a person mentioned in the group below is treated as having made the settlement and providing the property for it:

- a person who immediately before the variation was entitled to the property, or to property from which it derives, absolutely as legatee (as defined);

- a person who would have become entitled to the property, or to property from which it derives, absolutely as legatee but for the variation;

- a person who immediately before the variation would have been entitled to the property, or to property from which it derives, absolutely as legatee but for being an infant or other person under a disability; and

- a person who would, but for the variation, have become entitled to the property, or to property from which it derives, absolutely as legatee if he had not been an infant or other person under a disability.

If property would have been comprised in a settlement as a result of the deceased's will but the effect of the variation is that it becomes comprised in another settlement, the deceased will be treated as the settlor. He or she will also be the settlor if an existing settlement of which the deceased was settlor becomes comprised in another settlement. In both cases, the deceased is treated as having made the settlement immediately before his or her death unless the settlement arose on the person's death.

Legislation: TCGA 1992, s. 68A–68D

Tax Reporter: ¶351-000

5565   Trustees of a settlement

The trustees of a settlement are treated as a single and continuing body of persons, distinct from the persons who may from time to time be the trustees; thus, a change in the trustees of a settlement will not in itself give rise to a charge to CGT, whilst gains arising to the trust are dealt with separately from gains arising to trustees as individuals. See 5630ff. for non-resident trusts.

The liability of trustees to UK tax is determined by residence status. If the trustees are resident (and, for tax years prior to 2013–14, ordinarily resident) in the UK, they are subject to capital gains tax on the disposal and deemed disposal of assets in the UK and abroad. For the residence of trustees and non-resident trusts, see 5630ff.

Where part of the settlement property is vested in one trustee and part in another, they are together treated as constituting a single body of trustees.

Trustees of a settlement and any settlor in relation to that settlement are connected persons and so any disposal or acquisition between trustee and settlor is at market value (see 5100ff.).

For the annual exemption for trustees, see 5415 and 5595.

Legislation: TCGA 1992, s. 65(2), 69(1), (3)

Tax Reporter: ¶351-625; ¶357-050; ¶358-000; ¶358-125

Charges to CGT on settlement events

5570 Transfers into CGT settlement

A transfer of property into a 'settlement', whether revocable or irrevocable, is a chargeable disposal at market value by the disponor to the trustees, irrespective of whether the disponor retains an interest in the property or the disponor is a trustee of the settlement. The whole of that property is deemed to be disposed of at market value notwithstanding that the disponor has some interest as a beneficiary under the settlement. This provision, therefore, relates to what otherwise would be considered a part disposal.

A limited hold-over relief in respect of assets transferred into settlements is available where:

- the disposal is also a chargeable transfer for inheritance tax purposes (see 6287); or
- where the asset transferred is a business asset in respect of which hold-over relief applies (see 6325).

Legislation: TCGA 1992, s. 70

Case: *Bond (HMIT) v Pickford* [1983] BTC 313

Tax Reporter: ¶357-150; ¶357-175

5575 Assets leaving CGT settlements

Trustees are liable to capital gains tax in the normal way wherever a chargeable gain accrues in respect of disposals and deemed disposals by them. Chargeable gains are generally computed according to the computational rules. Trustees' expenses may be relievable as allowable expenses and they may set their annual exemption against any resulting gain.

Where an allowable loss accrues in respect of a disposal or deemed disposal by trustees, it may generally be set off against chargeable gains in the same tax year or carried forward to be set against future gains. However, there are restrictions and it is important for trustees to watch that they do not dispose of assets resulting in the creation of capital losses which cannot be utilised. In particular, where a loss arises on the disposal of an asset to a connected person, relief for the loss is restricted so that the loss may only be set against gains accruing on a disposal to the same connected person (trustees being connected with the settlor, any person connected with the settlor and with any corporate body deemed connected with the settlement (see 5142)).

Where a person becomes absolutely entitled (see 5552) to any settled property as against the trustee (or would be so entitled had he not been an infant or mentally handicapped) all the assets forming part of the settled property to which the person becomes entitled are deemed to have been disposed of and immediately reacquired by the trustee as a bare trustee (see 5555) for a consideration equal to market value.

See 5585 for the position where a person becomes absolutely entitled on the death of a person with an interest in possession or annuitant.

See 5929B for relief from the deemed disposal charge under s. 71 where trustees of a settlement ('the acquiring settlement') become absolutely entitled to settled property as against the trustees of the settled property ('the transferring trustees') and the settled property consists of shares which qualify for relief for disposals to employee-ownership trusts.

Allowable losses where beneficiary absolutely entitled

Where a person becomes absolutely entitled to an asset standing at a loss, the loss which is deemed to arise on the disposal by the trustees, to the extent that it cannot be deducted from gains accruing to the trustees on or before the deemed disposal, is treated as belonging to the beneficiary. Where the trustees have a loss on the occasion of absolute entitlement, that loss is set against available gains, those arising on the same occasion or earlier in the tax year, in priority to any other loss, but solely for the purpose of determining the amount of loss treated as belonging to the beneficiary. Any such loss that is treated as belonging to the beneficiary can only be set against chargeable gains accruing on the same asset, or any asset deriving from it and is set against the gain in priority to any other rules about the order of losses.

On the deemed disposal of various assets under TCGA 1992, s. 71(1), chargeable gains may accrue on some, and losses may arise on the remainder of the assets to which the beneficiary becomes absolutely entitled. Where claims to hold-over relief are made in respect of some or all of the assets on which chargeable gains accrue, relief should first be given under TCGA 1992, s. 165 and the losses set-off only against such of the gains (if any) as remain chargeable after the grant of hold-over relief.

Legislation: TCGA 1992, s. 71

Tax Reporter: ¶358-650; ¶358-700

5580 Termination of life interests for CGT (otherwise than on death)

Where a life interest terminates a distinction is made between:

- property which continues to be settled; and
- property which ceases to be settled.

Where there is a termination of a life interest otherwise than on death and the property ceases to be settled (another person becomes absolutely entitled to the property), the trustee is deemed to have disposed of the property and reacquired it, with an associated chargeable gain or capital loss (see 5575).

Where there is a termination of a life interest otherwise than on death and the property remains settled, there is no deemed disposal for the purposes of TCGA 1992, s. 71(1) as no one has become absolutely entitled as against the trustee.

Life interest

Interests in possession can be either life interests or other interests; a beneficiary with an interest in possession which will come to an end when he or she reaches a specified age is not a life interest.

'Life interest' includes a right to income of, or the use or occupation of, settled property for the life of another. However, a right which is contingent on the exercise of a discretion of the trustee or some other person is not a life interest. A right to an annuity payable out of settled property is only a life interest if part of the settled property is appropriated by the trustees as a fund out of which the annuity is payable.

A life interest 'in possession' is one which is not a reversionary interest, i.e. it is not expectant on the termination of a prior interest. However, the House of Lords has held (in a capital transfer tax case) that an 'interest in possession' exists where there is an immediate entitlement to income. A power of accumulation prevents there being an interest in possession.

Legislation: TCGA 1992, s. 71

Case: *Pearson v IR Commrs* [1981] AC 753

Tax Reporter: ¶358-835; ¶358-840

5585 Termination of life interests for CGT (on death)

Where a life interest terminates on death, again, a distinction is made between:

- property which continues to be settled; and
- property which ceases to be settled.

The following provisions apply equally on the death of an annuitant.

Property remains settled property

Where the life interest is terminated by the death of the person entitled to it (or where the life tenant dies but the interest does not terminate) and the property continues to be settled property, the capital gains tax treatment depends upon whether or not the interest in possession is one to which the person became entitled on or after 22 March 2006.

Where the life interest terminated by death is a post-22 March 2006 interest, there is no effect for CGT (no deemed disposal and reacquisition of the settled property and no CGT charge (so no death uplift)) unless the interest falls within one of the types specified by TCGA 1992, s. 72(1A) (see (2) below).

Where, on the death of the person entitled to an interest in possession:

(1) that person became entitled to that interest before 22 March 2006; or

(2) the entitlement arose on or after 22 March 2006; and

    (a) the person died under the age of 18 and the property in which the interest subsisted was comprised in either an age '18–25' trust (see 7004) or a 'bereaved minors' trust' (see 7003) for the purposes of inheritance tax; or

    (b) the assets in which the interest subsisted formed part of the deceased's estate for inheritance tax purposes as a result of:

        (i) an 'immediate post death interest' (see 6907);

        (ii) a 'disabled person's interest' (see 7011); and

        (iii) a 'transitional serial interest' (see 6908),

then TCGA 1992, s. 72(1) deems the whole or a corresponding part of each of the assets forming part of the settled property (and not ceasing to be settled property) to be disposed of by the trustees and immediately re-acquired at market value, but no chargeable gain arises (the 'tax-free uplift on death').

From 5 December 2013, the s. 72 capital gains tax uplift provisions are extended to include trusts for the benefit of a disabled persons where the beneficiary has no entitlement to the income of the trust (thus, affording such trusts the same treatment as where the beneficiary does have an interest in possession).

A life interest which is a right to part of the income of settled property is treated as a life interest in a corresponding part of the settled property; a life interest in the income of part of the settled property (where there is no right of recourse to the remainder of the settled property) is treated as a life interest in a separate settlement consisting of the property in which the interest exists.

Property ceases to be settled property

Where the death of a life tenant leads to the termination of a life interest and the property ceases to be settled property by virtue of a beneficiary becoming absolutely entitled as against the trustee, again, the capital gains tax treatment depends upon whether or not the interest in possession is one to which the person became entitled on or after 22 March 2006.

Where the life interest terminated by death is a post-22 March 2006 interest, TCGA 1992, s. 71 applies and there is a deemed market value disposal unless the interest falls within one of the types specified by TCGA 1992, s. 73(2A) (see (2) below).

Where:

(1)   the deceased acquired his interest before 22 March 2006; or

(2)   that interest was acquired on or after that date; and

   (a)   the person died under the age of 18 and the property in which his interest subsisted was comprised in either an 'age 18–25' trust (see 7004) or a 'bereaved minors' trust' (see 7003); or

   (b)   the assets in which the interest subsisted formed part of his estate for inheritance tax purposes as a result of:

      (i)   an 'immediate post death interest' (see 6907);

      (ii)   a 'disabled person's interest' (see 7011); and

      (iii)   a 'transitional serial interest' (see 6908),

the *Taxation of Chargeable Gains Act* 1992, s. 71 still applies and trustees are deemed to dispose of and immediately re-acquire the settled property at market value but TCGA 1992, s. 73(1) provides that no chargeable gain accrues on the disposal. The consequence is that the beneficiary who becomes absolutely entitled to the asset has a base cost that is equivalent to market value on the date of the deemed disposal and reacquisition (the 'tax-free uplift').

Example

Under the terms of a settlement, property is settled on Andrew for life, with remainder to Brian. On Andrew's death, Brian will become absolutely entitled against the trustees. Thus, if on Andrew's death, the market value of the trust fund is £20,000, the trustees are deemed to have disposed of those assets for £20,000 and to have reacquired them (as bare trustees) at the same value. (In this example, there would be no charge to CGT though Brian's base value for CGT purposes will have been uplifted).

The *Taxation of Chargeable Gains Act* 1992, s. 73 also modifies the s. 71 deemed disposal charge where:

- the property reverts to the settlor, in which case the trustee's s. 71 disposal is deemed to be on a 'no gain/no loss' basis;

- the deceased life tenant's interest extended to only part of the settled property to which s. 71 applies, in which case the chargeable gain is reduced to the extent that the interest forms part of the whole property (though the reduction may be smaller where a clawback of the same proportion of any held over gain is necessary following hold-over relief, as below).

Hold-over relief on termination of life interest

Where hold-over relief for gifts (see 6287 and 6325ff.) was given on the transfer into settlement and the interest in possession arose either before 22 March 2006 or is one to which the special rules in TCGA 1992, s. 72(1A) or TCGA 1992, s. 73(2A) applies (the effect of which is a CGT free uplift on death), TCGA 1992, s. 74(2) disapplies the no gain rules in s. 72(1)(b) and s. 73(1)(a) but restricts the amount of the gain arising as a result of the deemed disposal and re-acquisition rules to the amount of the held over gain.

Example

Settled property is held in trust for Adam for life, with his life interest commencing in 2000, then Betty for life, then Christopher absolutely. The settled fund has a CGT base value of £20,000. On Adam's death, the assets in the fund are deemed to have been sold and reacquired by the trustees at the then market value (say, £30,000). There is no liability to CGT at this point and £30,000 will be the new base value for CGT purposes.

Legislation: TCGA 1992, s. 72, 73, 74

Tax Reporter: ¶358-850 to ¶358-975

5590   Disposals of interests in settlements for CGT

In general, no chargeable gain arises to a beneficiary where he disposes of an interest under a settlement (e.g. a life interest, an annuity, a reversionary interest), provided that he or someone before him did not acquire his interest for consideration in money or money's worth, other than consideration consisting of another interest under the settlement.

Originally, the exemption was disapplied where, *at the time of the disposal of the interest*, the trustees were neither resident nor ordinarily resident in the UK (TCGA 1992, s. 85(1)). It was therefore possible to get the benefit of the exemption in respect of an interest in a non-resident settlement by ensuring the trustees became UK resident before a beneficiary disposed of his interest. This resulted in tax avoidance by trustees of an offshore trust which had realised substantial gains. The offshore trustees could pay the cash out to the UK-resident and domiciled beneficiary but this would trigger a CGT charge. Instead, the trustees would bring the trust into the UK by resigning in favour of the resident trustees who would appoint the funds to the beneficiary contingently on his surviving for a short period. The beneficiary would then sell his interest under the trust to a third party for cash. (The third party might be exempt from tax and therefore the cash in the trust could later be appointed to that party by the trustees tax free.) No CGT was charged on the sale by the beneficiary because the settlement was resident in the UK at the time of the disposal (so s. 85(1) did not override s. 76(1)) and the beneficiary was able to get the value of the gains out of the settlement tax free.

To counter such arrangements, further legislation was introduced which provides that the exemption does not apply where the interest is under a settlement where the trustees have at *any time* been non-resident (or, for tax years prior to 2013–14, neither resident nor ordinarily resident) in the UK or if, despite being resident, they were regarded as 'dual resident' (see 5645). In addition, the exemption does not apply if the interest is in a settlement which is, or includes, property which is derived, directly or indirectly, from such a non-resident or dual resident settlement (TCGA 1992, s. 76(1A), (1B)). For special provisions where the trustees become non-resident at some time after the person obtains the interest, see 5640.

Where an interest in a settlement in which the settlor has an interest is disposed of for a consideration, the assets to which the interest relates are deemed, for CGT purposes, to have been disposed of and reacquired by the trustees at their market value. Any resulting gains are chargeable on the settlor under normal provisions. Holdover relief (see 6144) is unavailable in respect of gains arising on the disposal.

The rule also applies to any property that formed part of a settlement in which the settlor had an interest at any time in the two previous tax years, or at any time in the period beginning when the contract for sale of the interest is entered into and ending when the transaction is completed.

From 6 April 2006, the definition of a settlor-interested trust is extended to include accumulation and maintenance trusts set up by parents. The legislation provides that a settlor has an interest in a settlement where property is or may be comprised in a settlement, or may become payable for the benefit of the settlor's dependent child, or the child derives any benefit from it whatsoever either directly or indirectly.

Legislation: TCGA 1992, s. 76, 76A, 77, 85(1), Sch. 4A

Tax Reporter: ¶357-450; ¶357-475; ¶357-500; ¶357-525; ¶359-050; ¶359-475

5592 Transfers of value

Anti-avoidance measures counter the use of loans taken out by trustees to enable gains to be extracted without a CGT liability, or with reduced CGT liability.

Broadly, if trustees transfer or lend property to another person, for example another trust, at a time when the trust's borrowed funds have not been used for regular trust purposes, the assets remaining in the trust are deemed to have been sold for their market value. Any resulting gain is chargeable on either any UK-resident settlor or any UK-resident beneficiaries who are to receive any capital payments. Where the trustees make a transfer of value on or after 6 April 2008 any gains previously unattributed may also be attributed to beneficiaries, including UK-resident non-domiciled beneficiaries.

Finance Act 2003 introduced measures to ensure that schemes designed to avoid a charge on UK beneficiaries receiving payments from trustees of offshore settlements who realise gains (see 5635) are subject to the anti-avoidance legislation contained in FA 2000. The rules bring the stranded gains into a pool so that they can be attributed to, and charged to CGT on, any beneficiary who receives capital payments from relevant trustees.

There is also a rule that requires payments to beneficiaries who are not domiciled and resident in the UK to be ignored in computing the amounts that may be charged on beneficiaries.

Legislation: FA 2003, s. 163; TCGA 1992, s. 76B, 85A, Sch. 4B, Sch. 4C

Tax Reporter: ¶360-350ff.

5595 Trusts for the disabled and CGT

Annual exemption

The trustees of settlements for certain disabled persons may, unlike the trustees of other settlements (see 5415), be entitled to the full annual exemption.

For 2013–14 and subsequent years, the full annual exemption is available to trustees if, during a year of assessment, the whole or part of the trust fund is held on trust for a 'disabled person' such that, during the person's lifetime:

- if any of the property is applied for the benefit of a beneficiary, it is applied for the disabled person's benefit; and

- either the disabled person is entitled to all of the income (if there is any) arising from any of the property or if any such income is applied for the benefit of a beneficiary, it is applied for the disabled person's benefit.

Previously, the full annual exemption was available where the settled property was held on trusts which provided that during the lifetime of a mentally disabled person or a person in receipt of an attendance allowance:

- at least half of the property applied was applied for his benefit; and

- he was entitled to at least half of the income arising out of the property, or that no income arising from the property may be applied for the benefit of any other person.

Where there is more than one 'qualifying settlement' (a disabled settlement, other than a non-resident or charitable settlement, created on or after 10 March 1981) comprised in a group, the full annual exemption is divided by the number of such settlements but with a minimum amount due to each settlement of one-tenth of the full amount.

Trusts with vulnerable beneficiaries

There is a specific tax regime for certain trusts with vulnerable beneficiaries. Under the provisions, certain trusts and beneficiaries can elect into the regime and, where a claim for special tax treatment is made for a tax year, no more tax will be payable in respect of the relevant income and gains of the trust for that year than would be paid had the income and gains accrued directly to the beneficiary.

For CGT purposes, the special capital gains tax treatment will apply in relation to chargeable gains arising to the trustees of a settlement if the following conditions are met in relation to the tax year in question:

- chargeable gains ('qualifying trusts gains') arise in the tax year to the trustees on the disposal of settled property held on qualifying trusts for the benefit of a vulnerable person;

- the trustees would be chargeable to capital gains tax in respect of those gains were it not for the application of the new rules in FA 2005, Ch. 4;

- the trustees are resident (or, for tax years prior to 2013–14, ordinarily resident) in the UK during any part of the tax year; and

- the trustees make a claim for special tax treatment for the tax year.

Under the special regime, the trustees' liability to CGT for the tax year will be reduced by an amount determined by using a formula set out in the legislation. Broadly, the amount is equal to the difference between two quantities. The first quantity is the capital gains tax liability that the trustees would have in respect of the qualifying trusts gains were it not for the regime contained in FA 2005. The second quantity is the amount of extra tax to which the vulnerable person would be liable to under the new rules, subject to making certain assumptions, in relation to the qualifying trusts gains.

Legislation: TCGA 1992, Sch. 1, para. 1(1); FA 2005, s. 23–45 and Sch. 1

Tax Reporter: ¶355-000ff; ¶358-275

5600 Persons chargeable in respect of trustees' liability to CGT

Capital gains tax in respect of gains accruing to trustees may be charged on and in the name of one or more trustees; but where an assessment is not made on all the trustees the persons assessed cannot include a person who is not resident (or, for tax years prior to 2013–14, ordinarily resident) in the UK (see 213 and 216).

A CGT assessment may be made on any one or more of the 'relevant trustees'. Trustees in the tax year in which the chargeable gains accrued, and any subsequent trustees are 'relevant trustees'.

If CGT assessed on any trustee is not paid within six months from the time it becomes payable and the asset (or the proceeds) in respect of which the gain accrued is transferred by the trustees to a person who is absolutely entitled, that person may instead be assessed (in the name of the trustees) at any time within two years from the time the tax became payable.

If the trustees of a UK-resident trust become not resident (nor, for tax years prior to 2013–14, ordinarily resident) in the UK, they may be subject to an exit charge; if the tax is not paid within six months from the time it becomes payable, HMRC may in some cases have resort to a past trustee for payment (see 5640). There can be no assessment on a person who ceased to be a trustee before the migration of the trust, and who can show that, at the time of cessation, there was no proposal for the trust to migrate.

Legislation: TCGA 1992, s. 65, s. 82

Tax Reporter: ¶358-000; ¶359-400

5620 Sub-funds

From 6 April 2006, sub-funds are recognised for both capital gains and income tax purposes. The new provisions enable trustees to elect for a specified part of settled property (a sub-fund) to be treated as a separate settlement subject to various conditions being satisfied. One consequence of such an election is that the trustees of the principal settlement will also be a trustee of the sub-fund.

The election must be made by the first anniversary of the 31 January filing date for the tax year when it takes effect. The creation of a sub-fund will result in a capital gains tax disposal, so they are most likely to be of benefit when a new trust is created.

Legislation: TCGA 1992, Sch. 4ZA

Tax Reporter: ¶358-750ff.

Non-resident and dual resident trusts

5630 Residence of trusts

From 6 April 2007, common rules determine the residence of trustees and trusts. Trustees will together be treated as if they were a single person and the deemed person will be treated as resident (and, for tax years prior to 2013–14, ordinarily resident) in the UK when all of the trustees are resident; or at least one trustee is resident and at least one is not and the settlor is resident or domiciled (or, prior to 2013–14, ordinarily resident) in the UK when the settlement was created.

Under the common rules, a non-resident trust must have all non-resident trustees if it has a UK resident or domiciled settlor. If the settlor is non-resident and non-domiciled, there can be a majority of UK trustees provided that one of them is non-resident.

Where the relevant residence condition(s) are not satisfied, no tax can be charged even if the assets concerned are located in the UK unless, for disposals on or after 6 April 2015, the asset is a UK residential property interest (see 5717), in which case the trustees are chargeable to capital gains tax in respect of any chargeable NRCGT gain (see 5717) accruing in the tax year (TCGA 1992, s. 14D(1)).

However, because offshore trusts are not otherwise chargeable to capital gains tax, a number of anti-avoidance provisions have been introduced under which:

- gains are attributed to UK resident beneficiaries (see 5635);
- gains are attributed to UK domiciled settlors (see 5637);
- a charge arises on exporting a UK resident settlement (see 5640 and 5645).

Legislation: TCGA 1992, s. 69 and Pt. 3, Ch. 2

Tax Reporter: ¶358-025; ¶359-200ff.; ¶591-450

5632 Settlements with foreign element: special returns

HMRC have extensive powers to obtain information in relation to non-resident or dual-resident settlements and the settlor, the trustees and persons who transfer property to the trustees must submit certain information to HMRC if the trust is, or becomes, non-resident; there are exclusions from the requirements to provide information where it has already been supplied as a result of some other provision.

Legislation: TCGA 1992, Sch. 5A

Tax Reporter: ¶359-525; ¶359-825

5635 Gains of offshore trusts apportioned to beneficiaries

In relation to any settlement where the trustees are not resident (or, for tax years prior to 2013–14, ordinarily resident) in the UK gains (after deduction of losses) accruing to trustees are, within certain limits, attributed to beneficiaries who receive capital payments from the trustees, etc. See 5645 for extension of charge in respect of dual resident settlements.

Capital payment

A capital payment is a transaction not at arm's length representing:

- any payment on which the beneficiary is not liable to pay income tax; or

- any payment received other than as income by a beneficiary who is resident (or, for tax years prior to 2013–14, ordinarily resident) outside the UK,

where 'payment' includes the transfer of an asset and any other benefit conferred on the beneficiary and also applies to any occasion on which a person becomes absolutely entitled to settled property. In order to put demand loans to offshore trustees on to a commercial footing, it may have been necessary for the trust to pay a sum in lieu of interest in respect of periods to 5 April 1992 (see SP 5/92); HMRC have expressed the view that such payment would be a capital payment to the recipient for the purposes of potential apportionment.

Interest-free loans, repayable on demand, made by offshore trusts to UK-resident beneficiaries constitute a capital payment so long as the loan remains outstanding.

The charge (from 2008–09)

The basic operation of s. 87 is as follows:

(1) Calculate any chargeable gains accruing to the trustees (the amount on which the trustees would be chargeable to capital gains tax but for their non-resident status), (this is called the 'section 2(2) amount' because it is the amount on which the trustees would have been chargeable under TCGA 1992, s. 2(2));

(2) If there are any gains attributable to the settlor under s. 86 (see 5637), these are deducted in calculating the section 2(2) amount;

(3) Capital payments made by the trustees to the beneficiaries are then matched with the section 2(2) amount for the year, or any earlier tax year;

(4) The amount matched is treated as a chargeable gain accruing to the beneficiary.

Where, for tax years 2015–16 and subsequent years, the trustees make a non-resident CGT disposal (see 5717), then to the extent that an NRCGT chargeable gain or allowable loss accrues, it is not treated as forming part of the s. 2(2) amount (TCGA 1992, s. 87(5A)). Consequently, it cannot be attributed to the beneficiaries as it is in fact assessable on the trustees.

The beneficiary will be charged to capital gains tax only if they are resident in the UK. If the beneficiary is not UK domiciled and is a remittance basis user (see 5710), the remittance basis will apply to their gains (and the gains are treated as foreign chargeable gains, assessed on amounts remitted to the UK).

With effect from 2013–14, where the tax year is a split year for the beneficiary for residence purposes (see 224), the beneficiary will be subject to tax on the matched amount that would otherwise have been chargeable, apportioned to the UK part of the split year on a time basis.

In HMRC's view, gains which would otherwise be charged on UK charities under these provisions may attract the exemption discussed at 5800.

Where a beneficiary had deemed gains under these provisions in 2010–11, such gains were treated as arising before 23 June 2010 and taxable at 18% if the deemed gain arises from being matched a capital payment made before that date. Deemed gains arising from being matched with capital payments on or after 23 June 2010 were treated as arising after that date and so taxable at 28%.

The matching rules

Payments are matched first with section 2(2) amounts of the same year. If there are unmatched payments, these are matched against section 2(2) amounts of earlier years taking the latest year first. If there are still unmatched payments, these are carried forward and matched against section 2(2) amounts of later years.

With one exception, capital payments are matched whether the beneficiary will be charged on the s. 87 gain or not. So, if the trustees make capital payments to non-resident beneficiaries, this will reduce the section 2(2) amount but no UK tax will be paid. The exception is that capital payments made on or after 6 April 2008 are ignored if they are made to a non-resident close company.

Example 1

The non-resident trust's section 2(2) amounts are as follows:

	£
2010–11	20,000
2011–12	–
2012–13	15,000
2013–14	40,000
2014–15	–
2015–16	–
2016–17	80,000

Capital payments to two UK resident beneficiaries of £30,000 and £70,000 respectively were made in June 2016:

- the section 2(2) amount for 2016–17 is £80,000. As this is less than the capital payments of £100,000, the section 2(2) amount is matched with the relevant proportion of each capital payment:

Payment		Gain matched (proportion of gain)	
2016–17	£30,000	2016–17	£24,000
			((£30,000/£100,000) × £80,000)
2016–17	£70,000	2016–17	£56,000
			((£70,000/£100,000) × £80,000)

- the section 2(2) amount for 2016–17 is reduced to nil (the full gain of £80,000 has been matched), however, there remains £20,000 (£100,000 − £80,000) of unmatched capital payments which are then allocated against the next most recent years (unmatched) section 2(2) amounts (i.e. 2013–14):

Payment		Gain matched (remainder of capital payment)	
2016–17	£30,000	2013–14	£6,000
			(£30,000 − £24,000)
2016–17	£70,000	2013–14	£14,000
			(£70,000 − £56,000)

- as the capital payments are now nil, the process stops.

The recipients of the capital payments of £30,000 and £70,000 will be assessed on gains of these amounts in 2016–17.

The section 2(2) amounts for all relevant years are now as follows:

	£
2010–11	20,000
2011–12	–
2012–13	15,000
2013–14	20,000
	(£40,000 − £6,000 − £14,000)
2014–15	–
2015–16	–
2016–17	–

Supplementary charge

A supplementary charge is also made in relation to capital payments, where there is a delay between the non-resident trustees realising a gain and the distribution of that gain to beneficiaries. Broadly, the effect of the provisions is to increase the CGT payable by beneficiaries by 10% for each complete tax year for which the trust gains are not distributed to beneficiaries, though the period for which this additional charge may be levied is limited to six years. The supplementary charge can therefore never exceed 60% of the tax charged on the gain, nor can it increase the total tax payable to an amount in excess of the capital payment. For the purpose of calculating the supplementary charge, HMRC take the gains assessable to be the lowest slice of the beneficiary's total capital gains for the year, thus benefiting from the annual exemption.

The chargeable period in respect of which the charge is levied begins on the later of:

- 1 December in the tax year immediately after the year in which the trustees' gain arose; and

- 1 December falling six years before 1 December in the tax year following that in which the capital payment is made,

and ends on 30 November in the tax year following that in which the capital payment is made (TCGA 1992, s. 91(4), (5)).

Example 2

In example 1, as £20,000 of the capital payments made in 2016–17 were matched with gains arising in 2013–14, the chargeable period runs from 1 December 2014 to 30 November 2017 so the tax charged on gains of £6,000 and £14,000 respectively will be increased by 30%.

Years up to 2007–08

Finance Act 2008 introduced a new method of matching from 2008–09. For years up to and including 2007–08, trustees' gains and capital payments were considered on a cumulative basis, irrespective of the years in which they arose. In effect, this required the maintenance of a 'pool' of trust gains of a number of years which would be diminished as capital payments were matched (and the equivalent amount of gain charged on the beneficiary) and enlarged as the trustees realised more gains. For the tax year 2008–09, it was, therefore, necessary to establish a starting point at 5 April 2008 by allocating the amount of trustees' gains for the year 2007–08 and each preceding year and also identify the total of those gains which had been attributed to beneficiaries as a result of the receipt of capital payments. This established what is termed the 'section 2(2) amount' for 2007–08 and earlier years (in other words, the amount of the trustees' gains which had not yet been attributed to the beneficiaries – known in common parlance as the 'stock-piled gains').

Finance Act 2008 changes also removed the exemption from the charge for non-domiciled beneficiaries. Prior to April 2008, the charge on capital payments received from a non-resident settlement did not apply to non-domiciled beneficiaries and a form of 'rebasing election'is available to trustees so that where a disposal occurs in 2008–09 or later years, that element of the gain which relates to the period of ownership prior to 6 April 2008 is excluded from the charge (FA 2008, Sch. 7, para. 126).

Inter-settlement transfers of property

Where property is transferred from one settlement to another, otherwise than for money or money's worth, and the transferor settlement is non-resident, the section 2(2) amounts of the transferee settlement for the year of transfer or earlier years is increased by the section 2(2) amounts of the transferor settlement for those years which have not been matched with capital payments.

Where the transferee settlement is, and has always been, UK resident, then the section 2(2) amounts are still transferred as above but the transferee settlement is treated as if it were a migrant settlement (see 5640) and TCGA 1992, s. 89(2)–(4) applies as if the year of transfer were the last year of non-residence prior to a period of residence for those purposes (TCGA 1992, s. 90(6)).

The transferred section 2(2) amount is reduced proportionately where only part of the settled property is transferred with the amounts being calculated based on market value of the part transferred as a proportion of market value of the whole prior to the transfer.

Where the transfer is for a consideration which is less than the market value of the property transferred, (transfers at full consideration are ignored), the transferred section 2(2) amounts are reduced to the extent that consideration has been received for the transfer.

Where the transfer between settlements is a 'transfer of value', it is ignored for these purposes and does not have the effect of increasing the transferee settlement's trust gains, however, special anti-avoidance rules within TCGA 1992, Sch. 4B and 4C apply to attribute gains to beneficiaries following 'transfers of value' (see 5592) which were designed to counter avoidance arrangements known as 'flip-flop' schemes.

Similar provisions applied to increase the trust gains of the transferee settlement for the year of transfer prior to 6 April 2008.

Legislation: TCGA 1992, s. 2(4), (5), 87–87C, 90–97

Cases: *Marshall (HMIT) v Kerr* [1994] BTC 258; *De Rothschild v Lawrenson (HMIT)* [1995] BTC 279; *Billingham (HMIT) v Cooper* [2000]

BTC 28; *Herman v R & C Commrs* (2007) Sp C 609; *Futter v Futter* [2010] BTC 455; *Bowring v R & C Commrs* [2015] BTC 530

Other Material: ESC D40; SP 5/92

Tax Reporter: ¶359-850ff.; ¶199-387; ¶593-150

5637 Gains of offshore trusts attributed to the settlor

Where a number of conditions are fulfilled, a charge to tax is levied on the settlor of a non-resident trust in respect of the gains arising to the non-resident trustees which are attributed to the settlor and treated as the highest part of his total chargeable gains for the year. The effect is therefore to bring into charge the otherwise non-taxable gain and to provide that the annual exemption and any personal losses are set first against personal gains and only any excess set against the 'attributed gains'.

The charge does not apply where the only members of the settlor's family who can benefit from the trust are children under 18, unborn children, or future spouses of the settlor or his children.

The conditions for the charge to apply are as follows:

- the settlement is a 'qualifying settlement' in the year (TCGA 1992, Sch. 5, para. 9);

- the trustees are not resident (nor, for tax years prior to 2013–14, ordinarily resident) in the UK, or are dual resident and deemed to be resident outside the UK at some time during the tax year;

- the settlor (or one of the settlors if there were more than one in relation to the settlement) is domiciled in the UK at some time during the tax year and resident (or, for tax years prior to 2013–14, ordinarily resident) for that year;

- at some time during the year the settlor (or members of his family or certain companies controlled by them) has 'an interest in the settlement';

- that property originating from the settlor is disposed of by the trustees in respect of which a charge to capital gains tax would arise if the trustees were resident and ordinarily resident in the UK throughout the tax year and if no double taxation arrangements applied.

There are a number of exceptions to the charge including where the settlor, etc. dies in the year.

HMRC have confirmed that a settlor with a life interest in all the assets of a trust will not be regarded as adding funds to the trust if he fails to exercise a right to reimbursement out of trust income.

The settlor is entitled to recover any tax payable under these provisions from the trustees of the settlement, and for this purpose the inspector of taxes is obliged to provide a certificate showing the gains assessed and the tax paid.

Amounts subject to the charge

The charge is in respect of disposals of settled property originating from the settlor on which the trustees would be chargeable to CGT if they were resident (or, for tax years prior to 2013–14, ordinarily resident) in the UK throughout the tax year, and if no double taxation arrangements applied, but subject to the following:

- any annual exemption which would be due to the trustees is ignored;

- a deduction may be made for the trustees' losses of the tax year or losses brought forward in so far as they relate to property originating from the settlor (for the meaning of 'originating', see TCGA 1992, Sch. 5, para. 8); for this purpose, the provisions which disallow losses of non-residents (see TCGA 1992, s. 16(3)) are ignored and losses in respect of disposals before 19 March 1991 are not to be taken into account; and

- if the trustees are participators in a non-resident company in respect of shares which originate from the settlor, any gains or losses of that company which would have been treated as accruing to the trustees under TCGA 1992, s. 13 had they been UK-resident and ordinarily resident may be taken into account.

Where the trustees make a disposal of property on or after 6 April 2015 which is a non-resident CGT disposal (see 5717), any gain or loss will only be taken into account in ascertaining the amount on which the trustees would have been chargeable if UK resident if it is not an NRCGT gain or loss (TCGA 1992, s. 86(4ZA)). Thus, NRCGT gains or losses are not attributed to the settlor (the logic clearly being that they are in fact assessable on the trustees (see 5717) therefore there is no need to attribute them to the settlor).

Special rules apply where the trustees are dual-resident and part of the settled property is represented by 'protected assets' (see 5645).

Property put into the trust by a company may be treated as originating from the settlor if he controls it (with or without his associates, as in relation to close companies: see 4005ff.). Extra-statutory Concession D40 excludes a beneficiary of the trust from being automatically treated as a participator in determining control of a company.

A statement details the practice HMRC will follow in applying the rules in various different circumstances; in particular, it includes transactions entered at arm's length, close companies, transactions with wholly-owned companies, loans made to settlements, loans made by trustees, failure to exercise rights to reimbursement, administrative expenses, life tenants, indemnities and guarantees, variations and ultra vires payments.

Interaction with other charges

Any amount which would otherwise be charged on beneficiaries (see 5635) for a particular tax year is reduced by any amount chargeable on the settlor under these rules for the same tax year.

Where an amount is chargeable on the settlor under anti-avoidance rate rules, and an amount is also chargeable on him under these procedures for the same tax year, any tax recoverable by the settlor from the trustees under the provisions of the rate rules is to be calculated on the basis that gains under these procedures form the next highest part thereof.

Avoidance of double charge

A double charge to CGT is prevented on gains arising to the trustees of an offshore settlement as a result of the CGT charges imposed on non-residents. Non-resident settlors who return to the UK after a period of temporary residence abroad (less than five years) suffer CGT in the year of return in respect of gains realised by offshore trusts during their period of temporary non-residence (see 5004). However, UK-resident beneficiaries may have already paid tax on some of those gains if capital payments have been made to them while the settlor was abroad.

In these circumstances, the gains which would fall to be charged on the settlor on his return to the UK will be reduced by the amount of the gains which have been charged on UK-resident beneficiaries of the settlement during that period (see 5635).

Legislation: TCGA 1992, s. 2(4), (5), (7), 86, 86A, Sch. 5; FA 1998, s. 131, 132, Sch. 22, 23

Case: *Coombes v R & C Commrs* [2008] BTC 884

Other Material: ESC D40; SP 5/92

Tax Reporter: ¶359-550ff.; ¶593-100

5640 Migrant settlements

Exporting a settlement (the 'exit' charge)

At the time ('the relevant time') when trustees of a UK-resident trust become not resident (nor, for tax years prior to 2013–14, ordinarily resident) in the UK, they are deemed for CGT purposes to have disposed of and reacquired, at market value at that time, 'the defined assets', i.e. all of the assets which constituted the property settled in the trust immediately before the relevant time other than:

- assets situated in the UK and used in or for the purposes of a trade which, immediately after the relevant time, the trustees carry on in the UK through a branch or agency, or

- assets which would not be regarded as liable to CGT, if they were disposed of immediately before the relevant time, by virtue of double taxation arrangements, thereby crystallising capital gains and losses in relation to those defined assets.

A former trustee may be required to pay the tax in some circumstances if it is unpaid.

The charge is limited where the change in residence status is caused by the death of a trustee and the former status is resumed within six months.

Rollover relief on replacement of business assets (see 6305) is unavailable where the old assets are disposed of before the relevant time but the new assets are not acquired until after that time unless the new assets, at the time they are acquired, are situated in the UK and used in or for the purposes of a trade carried on by the trustees in the UK through a branch or agency, or used or held for the purposes of the branch or agency (TCGA 1992, s. 80(6), (7)).

Deemed disposal of UK residential property interest

Where the trustees of a settlement cease to be UK resident and a disposal (and immediate reacquisition) by the trustees of all the settled property is deemed to be made (by TCGA 1992, s. 80(2)) immediately before they become non-resident, special rules are applied by TCGA 1992, s. 80A if the deemed disposal takes place on or after 6 April 2015 and the settled property includes a UK residential property interest (see 5717). These rules recognise the fact that, unlike other assets that are the subject of a deemed disposal by the trustees, UK residential property interests are not removed from the scope of CGT when the trustees cease to be UK resident (see 5717). They provide that, if the settled property includes a UK residential property interest that would have given rise to an NRCGT gain or loss if the disposal had been a non-resident CGT disposal (see 5717), the trustees may elect under s. 80A(2) for the following to apply:

- no gain or loss accrues on the disposal; and

- on a subsequent disposal of all or part of the interest in land, all or a corresponding part of the gain or loss that would have arisen by virtue of s. 80(2) is deemed to accrue to the trustees (in addition to any gain or loss that actually accrues) and is treated as an NRCGT gain or loss.

Note: an election under s. 80A(2) does not set aside the deemed disposal and reacquisition rules; it simply provides that no gain or loss accrues, and therefore the base cost of the asset is uplifted to market value. When the gain or loss is deemed to accrue on a subsequent disposal (and treated as an NRCGT gain or loss), it is computed on the basis of a deemed disposal immediately before the trustees ceased to be UK resident, therefore the special computational rules for disposals of UK residential property interests (see 5717) are not applicable.

Emigration (Re-emigration)

If resident trustees are replaced by non-resident trustees, with the result that a non-resident period follows one or more periods of residence, any capital payment made to a beneficiary while the trustees were resident in the UK is ignored for the purposes of the apportionment to beneficiaries of non-resident trust gains (see 5635) if the payment was not made in anticipation of a disposal by the non-resident trustees.

Where there is a subsequent period of non-residence and gains brought forward from the previous non-resident period have still not been exhausted, they will be taken into account in the first year of the subsequent non-resident period (see 5630 for residence).

Immigration

In the opposite situation, where non-resident trustees are replaced by resident trustees, any s. 2(2) gains of the non-resident trustees which have not been attributed to a beneficiary (see 5635) continue to be allocated and treated as chargeable gains made by the beneficiaries who later receive capital payments from the resident trustees.

Inter-settlement transfers of property

If property is transferred to the trustees out of another non-resident trust, otherwise than for money or money's worth, the unallocated section 2(2) trust gains of the transferor trust are effectively transferred as well in such a way as to be available for apportionment to its beneficiaries, whether or not the transferee trust would otherwise be subject to these apportionment provisions (i.e. even if the transferee trust is resident).

Disposal of interest following migration

Where trustees migrate so that the above exit charge provisions apply, and after the relevant time a person disposes of an interest in the settlement which was created for or acquired by him before that time, any chargeable gain on the disposal of the interest is to be calculated on the basis that the person disposing of it acquired it immediately before the migration of the trustees (any gain up to the date of migration would be exempt). This deemed disposal and reacquisition is required to mitigate the double taxation which would otherwise occur; the trustees would have been treated as having disposed of all the settlement assets immediately before migration at market value (the exit charge – see above) and the gain charged on the beneficiary on the subsequent disposal of his interest (see also 5590) would, because of his nil-base cost, have included the same gains. The effect of this provision is that the beneficiary's deemed disposal is treated as taking place whilst the trustees are still UK resident and thus the TCGA 1992, s. 76(1) (see 5590) exemption applies. His chargeable gain on the disposal of the interest will therefore be limited to the excess of the consideration he receives over the market value of the settlement assets just before the migration of the settlement.

These provisions do not apply if:

- before the interest disposed of was created for or acquired by the person disposing of it, the trustees had become dual resident giving rise to a charge to tax (see 5645);

- between the creation or acquisition of the interest and the trustees ceasing to be UK resident, they become dual resident (in such a case, any chargeable gain on the disposal of the interest is computed on the basis that it had been the subject of a disposal and reacquisition at its market value at the time when the trustees became dual-resident – or at the time they first became dual resident if that happened more than once (TCGA 1992, s. 85(5)–(9)) (see 5645);

- the settlement has 'relevant offshore gains' at the time when the trustees became non-resident (the 'material time') (TCGA 1992, s. 85(10)). A settlement has 'relevant offshore gains' at any time where there are gains arising on actual trustees' disposals or deemed disposals in connection with a 'transfer of value' which have not yet been matched with capital payments and attributed to beneficiaries and, if the tax year was to end at that time, those gains would be treated as accruing to the beneficiaries in the following tax year (TCGA 1992, s. 85(11)) (see 5635).

Legislation: TCGA 1992, s. 80–82, 85, 89, 90

Case: *Davies (Inspector of Taxes) v Hicks* [2005] BTC 331

Tax Reporter: ¶359-300; ¶360-350ff.

5645 Dual resident trusts

On a trust becoming dual resident, there is a deemed disposal and reacquisition, by the trustees, at market value at that time, of all their relevant assets. 'Relevant assets' means all those assets which are settled property and which are covered by the double taxation relief arrangements. This provision operates at the time, 'the time concerned' that trustees of a settlement become dual resident (that is, even though they remain UK-resident for UK tax purposes generally, they become also resident in some other territory under the laws of that territory), and by virtue of double taxation relief arrangements they are consequently not liable to UK tax on gains.

Where dual resident trustees acquire 'new assets' which would normally qualify for rollover relief on replacement of business assets (see 6305), relief will not be allowed if those new assets are covered by double taxation relief arrangements (so that any gains on disposal by the trustees would not attract UK tax) at the time of acquisition.

Special rules apply in respect of the s. 86 charge on the settlor (see 5637) where the trustees are dual-resident and part of the settled property is represented by 'protected assets'. These are assets which fall within a description specified by the double taxation agreement concerned and on which, if they were to be the subject of a disposal at a time when that agreement regarded the trustees as resident outside the UK, any gain would not be liable to UK tax (TCGA 1992, Sch. 5, para. 1(8), (9)). The charge on the settlor may be reduced or eliminated entirely. It is necessary to calculate gains chargeable on the settlor according to the rules described at 5637 and compare that with the amount of the gain if only protected assets are taken into account. If the latter produces a smaller gain, that figure is the chargeable amount and if it produces no gain, then there is no charge on the settlor (TCGA 1992, Sch. 5, para. 1(4)).

The charge on beneficiaries as applies to non-resident trusts (see 5635) is extended to apply to dual-resident settlements; for this purpose the s. 2(2) gains are the smaller of the total net gains on which the trustees would be chargeable if the double tax treaty did not apply and the net gains on assets 'protected' under the treaty on which they would be so chargeable if the treaty did not apply.

Legislation: TCGA 1992, s. 83, 84, 86, 88 and Sch. 5

Tax Reporter: ¶359-250; ¶359-425; ¶359-450; ¶359-575; ¶360-050

Capital gains of estates in administration

5680   Death and the assets of the deceased

Assets of a deceased person are deemed to be acquired by his 'personal representatives' (see 5685) at the market value (see 5103) of the assets at the date of death; however, the assets are not deemed to be disposed of and, therefore, there is no CGT liability on death.

> **Example**
>
> Horace dies on 10 April 2016. His estate includes 10,000 XYZ Ltd shares which H purchased on 2 March 2005 for £20,000. The probate value of the shares is £25,500. The personal representatives sell the shares on 5 July 2016 and realise £30,000 from the sale. They are deemed to have acquired the shares for £25,500 and, therefore, are treated as having made a gain of £4,500 in 2016–17.

Assets of the deceased include a share in property to which he was beneficially entitled as joint tenant, e.g. a husband and wife owning a house as joint tenants are treated as having a half share each.

A notional market value gain held over where qualifying corporate bonds (QCBs) are issued in exchange for shares or securities which are not QCBs (see 5865) is in effect wiped out by the subsequent death of the holder.

Legislation: TCGA 1992, s. 62(1), (10)

Tax Reporter: ¶367-000

5685   Liability to CGT of personal representatives

Personal representatives are treated as a single and continuing body and not as individuals. Thus, any change in the personal representatives does not give rise to a gain or loss.

Personal representatives are treated as having the deceased's 'residence' (see 224) ('ordinary residence' prior to 6 April 2013) and 'domicile' (see 227) at the date of death. Thus, if the deceased were resident (and, for tax years prior to 2013–14, ordinarily resident) abroad, his personal representatives would be regarded as so resident (and, for tax years prior to 2013–14, ordinarily resident) even though some or all of them may in fact be resident, etc. in the UK. However, as personal representatives are not regarded as individuals, advantage cannot be taken of the provisions regarding the non-remittance of foreign gains by a non-domiciled individual who was resident (or, prior to 6 April 2013, ordinarily resident) at the date of death (see 5710, 1600ff.).

> **Example**
>
> Edward dies resident and domiciled in the Isle of Man in 2016. His estate has been left to his children who are all resident, and domiciled in England. The personal representatives dispose of many of the estate assets at a substantial gain. This gain will not be subject to capital gains tax because the personal representatives are treated as being resident and domiciled in the Isle of Man.

Capital gains tax in respect of gains accruing to personal representatives may be charged on and in the name of one or more of them and not on anyone else; but where an assessment is not made on all of them, the persons assessed cannot include a person who is not resident (or, for tax years prior to 2013–14, ordinarily resident) in the UK (see 224).

A CGT assessment may be made on any one or more of the 'relevant personal representatives'. Personal representatives in the tax year in which the chargeable gains accrued, and any subsequent personal representatives are 'relevant personal representatives'.

Personal representatives are liable for any CGT charged upon the deceased and still unpaid. Any allowable losses sustained by the deceased in the tax year of his death may be carried back and set against the gains of the three preceding tax years. The order in which losses are set off against gains is as follows:

- against gains made in the tax year of death;

- against gains made in a later year before gains made in an earlier year.

> **Example**
>
> Derek dies having made a chargeable gain of £10,000 in the year of death (2016–17). He also made an allowable loss of £19,000 in that year. £10,000 of the loss is set off against the 2016–17 gain. The remaining £9,000 of allowable losses may, similarly, be set against any unrelieved gains for 2015–16, 2014–15 and 2013–14 in that order (but so as not to reduce those gains below the annual exemption: see further 5697).

Losses sustained by personal representatives cannot be passed on to beneficiaries and can only be relieved against chargeable gains accruing to the personal representatives in the same or subsequent tax years.

Disposals of assets by personal representatives are only liable to CGT if the asset is not acquired by a legatee (see 5690). A notional market value gain held over where qualifying corporate bonds (QCBs) are issued to the personal representatives in exchange for shares or securities which are not QCBs (see 5865) crystallises on disposal of the QCBs or, if they transfer them to legatees, when the legatees dispose of them.

Legislation: TCGA 1992, s. 62(2)–(4), 65

Tax Reporter: ¶367-100ff.; ¶367-500ff.

5690   Legatees and CGT

On a person acquiring an asset as a legatee, no chargeable gain accrues to the personal representatives and the legatee is treated as if the personal representative's acquisition of the asset had been his acquisition of it, i.e. the legatee's base cost for CGT purposes is the market value of the asset at the deceased's death.

Example

Bert dies on 21 January 2016. Alice is the residuary legatee. Bert's residuary estate consists of 10,000 quoted shares in ABC Ltd with a value of £20,000 at 21 January 2016. The shares are transferred to Alice on 24 February 2017 when the administration of the estate is completed. The shares are then worth £30,000. However, no gain accrues to the executors and Alice is regarded as having acquired the shares for £20,000 on 21 January 2016.

Where the legatee disposes of an asset held by him on 31 March 1982, the base value will be the 1982 value (see 5320ff.).

Example

Will dies in February 1980 and Frank is legatee of property worth £20,000 at that time. The March 1982 value is £25,000. If Frank disposes of the property in January 2016, his base value will be £25,000.

'Legatee' includes any person taking under a testamentary disposition or on an intestacy or partial intestacy. Whether he takes beneficially or as trustee, a person taking under a donatio mortis causa (a gift made in contemplation of death, i.e. before death but conditional upon it) is treated as a legatee and such gifts are specifically exempted from CGT.

A residuary legatee, of course, has no vested interest in the estate. Only when the personal representatives have ascertained the residue can the residuary legatee's interest be vested. Generally, at that stage, if the personal representatives have not distributed the estate, they are deemed to have absented themselves as trustees: as was said in one case, it 'is for the executors ... to determine what particular assets should be realised to enable them to satisfy prior purposes and vested rights antecedent to those of the residuary beneficiary', and thus any gains arising during the administration accrue to the personal representatives and not to the residuary legatee.

A legatee is entitled to deduct the cost of transferring assets to him from any gains made by him on a subsequent disposal of those assets.

A notional market value gain held over where qualifying corporate bonds (QCBs) are issued to the personal representatives in exchange for shares or securities which are not QCBs (see 5865) crystallises, if they transfer them to legatees, when the legatees dispose of them.

The provisions above apply equally in Scotland and Northern Ireland, subject to the fact that: in Scotland, on the death of a liferenter, the person (if any) who, on the death of the liferenter, becomes entitled to possession of the property as fiar shall be deemed to have acquired all the assets forming part of the property at the date of the deceased's death for a consideration equal to their market value at that date; and in Northern Ireland, a person who acquires property in fee simple absolute or fee tail in possession as a consequence of the deceased's death shall be deemed to have acquired all the assets forming part of the property at the date of the deceased's death for a consideration equal to their market value at that date.

Where an estate is administered under foreign law, the legatee's date of acquisition is governed by that foreign law.

Legislation: TCGA 1992, s. 62(4), (5), 63, 63A, 64

Cases: *Cochrane's Exors v IR Commrs* (1974) 49 TC 299; *Bentley v Pike (HMIT)* (1981) 53 TC 590; *Passant v Jackson (HMIT)* [1986] BTC 101

Tax Reporter: ¶365-500; ¶367-000; ¶367-275; ¶367-700ff.

5692 Instruments of variation

Whether or not administration is complete, the beneficiaries may effect an 'instrument of variation' (or deed of variation or of family arrangement) redirecting the deceased's property without tax penalty; provided certain conditions are met, any variation or disclaimer by a beneficiary does not constitute a disposal by him and the variation is treated as if made by the deceased or a disclaimed benefit is treated as it had never been conferred. The variation must be made within two years of the person's death. There is no requirement to notify HMRC (for variations made after 1 August 2002), provided there is a statement in the instrument effecting the variation that it is intended to be effective for CGT purposes. There can be no consideration in money or money's worth other than a reciprocal variation.

The deeming provisions of TCGA 1992, s. 62 were considered by the House of Lords in *Marshall (HMIT) v Kerr* [1994] BTC 258 who held that the rules deeming a variation to have been effected by the deceased did not apply for the purpose of determining the identity of the settlor of a trust created by a deed of variation. The settlor of the trust was the beneficiary who had effected the deed of variation, not the deceased, and the deeming provisions applied only for the purposes of providing that the disposition arising as a result of variation itself was not a disposal chargeable to capital gains tax and to enable the substituted legatee to acquire the asset for capital gains tax purposes at the market value at the date of death (i.e. at the same value as the original legatee would have acquired the asset).

Legislation: TCGA 1992, s. 62

Case: *Marshall (HMIT) v Kerr* [1994] BTC 258

Tax Reporter: ¶367-825ff.

5695 Personal representatives: allowable capital gains expenditure

A gain arising on a disposal by personal representatives is liable to CGT (unless the person acquiring the asset does so as legatee: see 5690). In computing their chargeable gains, the personal representatives may set off the costs of obtaining probate, etc. relating to that asset (i.e. expenditure incurred in 'establishing, preserving or defending' title to the asset concerned: see 5223). Thus, in one case, the personal representatives succeeded in a claim to set off against gains made on the disposal of stocks and shares a proportion of solicitor's fees incurred in obtaining probate.

As it is often difficult to establish the appropriate proportion relating to a particular asset, HMRC have issued a scale of expenses which are allowable as being the costs of establishing title. The scale is contained in a statement of practice and is set out below:

Gross value of estate		Allowable expenditure
A	Not exceeding £50,000	1.8% of the probate value of the assets sold by the personal representatives.
B	Over £50,000 but not exceeding £90,000	A fixed amount of £900, to be divided between all the assets in the estate in proportion to the probate values and allowed in those proportions on assets sold by the personal representative.

C	Over £90,000 but not exceeding £400,000	1% of the probate value of the assets sold.
D	Over £400,000 but not exceeding £500,000	A fixed amount of £4,000 to be divided as at B above.
E	Over £500,000 but not exceeding £1,000,000	0.8% of the probate value of the assets sold.
F	Over £1,000,000 but not exceeding £5,000,000	A fixed amount of £8,000, to be divided as at B above.
G	Over £5,000,000	0.16% of the probate value of the assets sold, subject to a maximum of £10,000.

HMRC generally accept computations based on the above scale or on actual expenditure incurred.

Where it can be ascertained, actual expenditure can be claimed even where it exceeds the scale rates.

For allowable expenditure generally, see 5223.

Case: *IR Commrs v Richards' Exors* (1971) 46 TC 626

Other Material: SP 2/04, *Allowable expenditure: expenses incurred by personal representatives and corporate trustees* (replaces SP 8/94 from 6 April 2004)

Tax Reporter: ¶367-575

5697 Personal representatives: rate of tax and annual exemption

The personal representatives of a deceased person (and the trustees of all other types of trust as well) are liable to capital gains tax at 20% in respect of non-'upper rate gains' and at 28% on 'upper rate gains' (see 5410) for disposals on or after 6 April 2016.

Between 23 June 2010 and 5 April 2016, the rate was 28% regardless of the type of gain. Earlier rates were 18% between 6 April 2008 and 22 June 2010, and 40% between 6 April 2004 and 5 April 2008. This rate is applied to the chargeable gains of personal representatives irrespective of the status of either the deceased person or the beneficiaries of the estate.

Tax is only due in respect of certain disposals, where the assets have risen in value from the probate value at which the personal representatives acquired them to the date of disposal and after losses and any annual exemption have been taken into account.

For a table of rates and thresholds, see Key Data.

Legislation: TCGA 1992, s. 3(7), 4

Tax Reporter: ¶367-600

Capital gains tax: the foreign element

5698   Introduction

The UK's power to tax capital gains depends primarily on the residence status of the person making the gain and, in certain cases, the location of the asset concerned.

The territorial limits of the UK are therefore important for determining where taxpayers are resident and whether assets are located here. The UK consists of Great Britain (that is, England, Wales and Scotland) and Northern Ireland. It does not include the Channel Islands or the Isle of Man. The sea within a bay is brought 'onshore' if it lies on the landward side of a line not exceeding 24 miles in length which joins the low-water lines of the natural entrance points of the bay. The UK is further extended to 12 nautical miles from the coastline.

Dwellers on boats within UK coastal waters are thus within the scope of UK taxation.

Certain offshore oil and gas assets are also within the scope of the charge to tax, by virtue of being treated as either sited in the UK or used for the purposes of a trade carried on in the UK through a branch or agency.

Situs and territorial scope

The location of an asset is of relevance where:

- an individual making the disposal is not domiciled in the UK; in such a case, chargeable gains on assets sited abroad may, in certain circumstances, be taxable only to the extent that they are remitted to the UK (see 5710);

- a person who is not resident (nor, prior to 2013–14, ordinarily resident) in the UK is carrying on a trade here, via a branch or agency. Chargeable gains only arise on the disposal of assets situated in the UK which were in use, or are intended for use, for the purposes of that trade, or where the asset becomes situated outside the UK, or the trade is discontinued without an actual disposal of the assets (see 5715).

For disposals on or after 6 April 2013, chargeable gains may also arise in respect of high-value UK residential property owned by a non-resident 'non-natural' person. Only the gain accruing since 6 April 2013 is chargeable (see 5725).

Similarly, for disposals on or after 6 April 2015, the charge to capital gains tax was further extended to gains accruing to a non-resident person (including individuals, trustees and personal representatives and certain (close) companies) on the disposal of UK residential property. Only to the gain accruing since 6 April 2015 is chargeable (see 5717).

Legislation: TCGA 1992, s. 276(1); *Territorial Sea Act* 1987, s. 1

Case: *Davies (HMIT) v Hicks* [2005] BTC 331

Other Material: SP D23, *Non-resident company: section 13 TCGA 1992 (section 15 CGTA 1979)*

Tax Reporter: ¶591-000

5700 Foreign assets: delayed remittances

If, in the case of any resident (or, prior to 2013–14, ordinarily resident) taxpayer, a chargeable gain cannot be remitted to the UK (where the assets are sited abroad), the taxpayer can defer the assessment of the gain, if:

(1) a claim is made within four years from the end of the tax year or accounting period. Prior to 1 April 2010, the time limit for a claim was the fifth anniversary of 31 January next following the end of the relevant tax year for those chargeable to capital gains tax and in the case of a company, six years from the end of the accounting period in which the gain accrued;

(2) the gain was unable to be remitted to the UK because of the laws of the country where the asset was situated, or because of the executive action of its government, or because it was impossible to obtain foreign currency; and

(3) the inability to remit the gain was not due to any want of reasonable endeavours on his or her part (TCGA 1992, s. 279(3)(c)); it is understood that HMRC have in the past interpreted 'reasonable endeavours' strictly.

The gain is deferred until the year of assessment in which the conditions set out in (2) above cease to be satisfied.

In the case of an individual who has died, his personal representatives may make any claim which the individual could have made.

Where any of the amount due is received by the taxpayer through a form of insurance cover arranged with the Export Credit Guarantee Department (ECGD), the amount cannot be treated at any time as unremitted.

Legislation: TCGA 1992, s. 279

Tax Reporter: ¶591-150

5701 Residence and ordinary residence – individuals

Subject to a few limited exceptions, an individual's capital gains for a tax year are subject to UK capital gains tax if the residence condition is met, i.e. he is resident in the UK for the year in question (prior to 2013–14 an individual's was liable to capital gains tax if he was resident in the UK for any part of the tax year or ordinarily resident for that year. In order to be outside the scope of the tax, the person had to be *both* not resident and not ordinarily resident).

From 2013–14, a new Statutory Residence Test has been enacted to determine the residence status of an individual (see 224).

For 2013–14 onwards, an individual who is subject to the split year treatment (see 224) will not be chargeable to capital gains tax in respect of any chargeable gains accruing in the overseas part of the year, however, this rule does not apply where gains are charged on a non-resident trading in the UK (see 5715) and is subject to the rules for temporary non-residents (see 5004).

Prior to 2013–14, the absence of a statutory test led HMRC to publish their working interpretation of the law in HMRC booklet *HMRC6: Residence, Domicile and the Remittance Basis* (which replaced booklet IR20 Residents and Non-Residents: Liability to Tax in the UK from 6 April 2009). This was applied to CGT as it was to income tax.

Legislation: *Finance Act* 2013, Sch. 45

Tax Reporter: ¶591-400

5702 Partnerships

The residence of a partnership is not of importance: a partnership's capital gains are assessed separately on the partners, so any individual or corporate partner's liability to tax on the partnership's gains depends on that partner's residence status.

Legislation: TCGA 1992, s. 59(a)

Tax Reporter: ¶591-500

5703   Companies

A UK-resident company is liable to tax in respect of its worldwide gains, while a non-resident company is only liable in respect of the gains of a permanent establishment in the UK. A company is resident in the UK if it is:

(1)   incorporated in the UK; or

(2)   'centrally managed and controlled' in the UK.

Consequently, there are exit charges where a company becomes non-resident, ceases to be chargeable to tax in respect of branch assets or becomes dual resident so as to shelter any gains under a double tax treaty.

Legislation: CTA 2009, s. 14

Tax Reporter: ¶591-550

5710   Foreign assets: non-domiciliaries and the remittance basis

The relevance of domicile (see 227) in the context of capital gains tax is in connection with gains arising on disposals of assets situated outside the UK. For the remittance basis to be applicable for capital gains tax, the individual must be non-domiciled.

For years up to and including 2007–08, gains on such assets were only within the charge to tax to the extent that they were remitted to the UK. Corresponding overseas losses were not available for relief against gains on either overseas or UK assets, presumably on the basis that, whilst it is possible to remit funds which represent a gain, it is not, by definition, possible to remit funds which represent a loss. With the changes introduced by *Finance Act* 2008, the universal right of UK resident but non-domiciled individuals to be taxed on the remittance basis was withdrawn. Instead, the automatic right to the basis is restricted to two categories of non-domiciliaries:

- individuals whose unremitted foreign income or gains for the year are less than £2,000;

- individuals who:
  - (i)   have no UK source income or gains (other than taxed investment income) exceeding £100 for the tax year concerned;
  - (ii)   do not remit in that year any relevant income or gains (foreign income or gains to which the remittance basis applies whensoever arising); and

(iii) have been UK resident for not more than six of the immediately preceding nine tax years or are under the age of 18 throughout the tax year concerned (FA 2008, Sch. 7, para. 85),

and the remainder are given the opportunity to make a claim for the remittance basis to apply. (Individuals falling within the automatic entitlement categories may also give notice to disapply the remittance basis for the year).

Those who make a claim for the remittance basis to apply for a particular year lose their entitlement to the annual exemption for that year regardless of whether there are remitted foreign gains in that year or not.

Where the remittance basis applies for capital gains tax for a tax year and an amount of 'foreign chargeable gains' has been remitted to the UK in that year, the individual is deemed to have realised chargeable gains equal to the amount of the remittance. Foreign chargeable gains, in this context, are gains on the disposal of assets which are situated outside the UK. However, foreign gains arising to a remittance basis user in the overseas part of a split year of residence and remitted in the UK part of the year are not charged to tax.

A charge for using the remittance basis of taxation applies if the claimant is aged 18 or over at any time in the tax year and satisfies either the seven-year residence test or the 12-year residence test. From 2015–16 onwards, the charge is imposed at one of three rates:

- £90,000 for those who have been resident in at least 17 out of the 20 immediately preceding tax year (the '17-year test');

- £60,000 for those who have been resident in at least 12 of the 14 immediately preceding tax years (the '12-year test'); and

- £30,000 for those who have been resident in at least seven of the nine immediately preceding tax years (the 'seven-year test') and who do not satisfy the 12-year test.

Domicile reform

At Summer Budget 2015, the Government announced that it will legislate so that, from 6 April 2017, anybody who has been resident in the UK for more than 15 of the past 20 tax years will be deemed to be domiciled in the UK for all tax purposes. This will mean that from their 16th tax year of residence, long-term residents will no longer be able to access the remittance basis and will be subject to tax on an arising basis on their worldwide gains. Additionally, the £90,000 remittance basis charge payable by those who have been resident for 17 out of 20 years will be redundant as such persons will be taxable on an arising basis after

15 years. The £30,000 and £60,000 remittance basis charges remain unchanged.

Also from April 2017, individuals who are born in the UK to parents who are domiciled here will no longer be able to claim non-domicile status whilst they are resident in the UK even if they can show they have acquired a foreign domicile of choice. The new rules will mean that the former UK doms returning to the UK after having settled overseas will be taxed as UK domiciled for tax purposes on their return irrespective of their intentions or domicile status under general law.

All non-dom reforms are to be legislated in Finance Bill 2017 (Budget 2016).

A consultation on domicile reform, including the need to retain a de minimis exemption beyond 15 years where total unremitted foreign income and gains are less than £2,000 p.a. (ITA 2007, s. 809D(2)) ran from 30 September 2015 to 11 November 2015 and is available at www.gov. uk/government/consultations/reforms-to-the-taxation-of-non-domiciles.

A technical briefing note was also published on 8 July 2015 and is available at www.gov.uk/government/publications/technical-briefing-on-foreign-domiciled-persons-changes-announced-at-summer-budget-2015.

Legislation: TCGA 1992, s. 3(1A), 12; ITA 2007, Ch. A1

Tax Reporter: ¶199-620ff.; ¶591-750

5712 Foreign losses: non-domiciliaries and the remittance basis

Losses on non-UK assets arising before 6 April 2008 to remittance basis users were not allowable losses. For tax year 2008–09 onwards, an individual may elect that such 'foreign losses' which arise in the year of election or subsequent years are allowable, subject to certain special rules (see below), against chargeable gains (TCGA 1992, s. 16ZA).

The election is irrevocable and has effect in the year it is made and all subsequent years. The election must be made by an individual for the first tax year in which the individual claims the remittance basis and is not domiciled in the UK. This is known as the relevant tax year. The procedure and time limit for making an election are governed by the rules for claims to relief, etc. in the *Taxes Management Act* (i.e. the election must be made within four years after the end of the 'relevant year'). A failure to make such an election will mean that foreign losses for the relevant year *and all subsequent years* in which the individual is non-UK domiciled will not be allowable losses (TCGA 1992, s. 16ZA(3)). Note that TCGA 1992, s. 16ZA does not itself provide for foreign losses to be allowable – that is achieved by TCGA 1992, s. 16. The effect of s. 16ZA is to prevent foreign losses being allowable, unless an election is made.

The special rules for giving relief in respect of foreign losses have two main effects:

- They prevent any loss (not just a foreign loss) of a later year being allowed against a foreign chargeable gain which arose in an earlier year but which is not remitted (and so not taxed) until the year of the loss or later (TCGA 1992, s. 16ZB). This is analogous to the 'no carry back' rule where the remittance basis is not in point (see 5265).

- They limit the amount of losses available for relief against chargeable gains in a year by imposing a strict order in which they are matched with gains of various classes, including unremitted foreign chargeable gains (TCGA 1992, s. 16ZC).

Correct operation of these rules is likely to demand careful record-keeping by the taxpayer.

Legislation: TCGA 1992, s. 16ZA–16ZD

Tax Reporter: ¶591-750

5715 Non-residents trading in the UK

Gains on trading assets

Persons other than companies
The general rule is that if a person is not resident (and, for tax years prior to 2013–14, not ordinarily resident) in the UK but is carrying on a trade, profession or vocation in the UK through a UK branch or agency, then that person is liable to tax on gains arising from the disposal of those assets situated in the UK which are used for the purposes of the trade, etc. or used/held for the purposes of the branch or agency (TCGA 1992, s. 10(1), (5)). The term 'branch or agency' is defined in TCGA 1992, s. 10(6). A branch or agency means any factorship, agency, receivership, branch or management. However, general agents and brokers are not included as a branch or agency for this purpose of capital gains tax.

Companies
In the case of a company, one looks at a permanent establishment, hence this approach follows more closely the approach taken by double taxation agreements.

Under TCGA 1992, s. 10B(1), the profits chargeable to corporation of a company, which is not resident in the UK but which is carrying on a trade in the UK through a UK permanent establishment, include the chargeable gains accruing to the company on the disposal of:

(1) assets situated in the UK and used in, or for the purposes of, the trade at or before the time the gain accrued;

(2) assets situated in the UK and used, or held, for the purposes of the UK permanent establishment at or before the time the gain accrued; or

(3) assets situated in the UK and acquired for use by, or for the purposes of, the UK permanent establishment.

It is important, though, for the chargeable gains to be included in the profits chargeable to corporation tax; that the disposal, giving rise to the chargeable gains, is made when the company is carrying on a trade in the UK through the permanent establishment concerned.

Under TCGA 1992, s. 10B(3), the company's chargeable gains would not be included in its profits chargeable to corporation tax where it is exempt from corporation tax on the profits of the permanent establishment because of the use of double taxation relief rules.

In order to counter avoidance of the charge on non-residents carrying on a trade in the UK, i.e. by ceasing to trade in the UK, TCGA 1992, s. 25 provides that when a non-resident trader ceases to trade in the UK, there is a deemed disposal and reacquisition of the branch or permanent establishment asset (at market value) immediately before that occasion.

Legislation: TCGA 1992, s. 10, 10B, 25

Case: *Puddu v Doleman (HMIT)* (1995) Sp C 38

Tax Reporter: ¶592-500; ¶592-550

5717 Non-residents disposing of UK residential property: NRCGT disposals

From 6 April 2015, the charge to capital gains tax was extended to non-residents disposing of an interest in UK residential property in order to bring the UK into line with many other countries that charge CGT on the basis of the location of the property.

The charge applies to disposals of UK residential property; defined as property suitable for use as a dwelling with communal residential property being excluded from the charge.

The charge applies to non-resident persons that own UK residential property, in particular:

- non-UK resident individuals;

- non-UK resident trusts;

- personal representatives of a deceased person who was non-UK resident; and

- non-UK resident companies controlled by five or fewer persons, except where the company itself, or at least one of the controlling persons is a 'qualifying institutional investor'.

The rate for companies is 20%, however, the charge will remain at 28% on disposals of property subject to ATED (see 5725) and where part of the gain could be subject to both ATED-related CGT and the new CGT charge the ATED-related CGT charge will take precedence.

The rates for non-resident individuals are 18% or 28% depending on whether the gain falls within the individuals' basic rate income band or above it (see 5410) and non-resident individuals will have access to the annual exempt amount of taxable gains, in line with UK residents.

The charge only applies to the amount of gain relation to periods post 6 April 2015 with the default method of calculating the post April 2015 gain or loss being to establish the market value of the property at 5 April 2015 and calculate the gain or loss in the normal way (allowing deductions for enhancement expenditure and incidental costs).

Alternatively, an election may be made for straight-line time apportionment or for the retrospective basis of computation whereby the gain is calculated on the basis of the whole period of ownership (which will be relevant for establishing losses).

Example 1: default (rebasing) calculation		
	£	£
Disposal proceeds		1,250,000
Incidental disposal costs		(30,000)
Net disposal proceeds		1,220,000
Market value at 5 April 2015	1,000,000	
Enhancement costs	0	
Total cost	1,000,000	(1,000,000)
Gain over period from 5 April 2015 market value		220,000
[Further apportionment is made for mixed use]		

Example 2: straight-line time apportionment

Total ownership 65 months, period from 5 April 2015 to disposal
(6 June 2016) was 14 months, proportion of ownership relates to period
from 5 April 2015 to disposal (14/65).

	£	£
Disposal proceeds		1,250,000
Incidental disposal costs		(30,000)
Net disposal proceeds		1,220,000
Acquisition cost	750,000	
Incidental costs of acquisition	40,000	
Enhancement costs	0	
Total acquisition cost	790,000	790,000
Gain over period of ownership		430,000
Time apportioned gain post-5 April 2015 (× 14/65)		92,615

[Further apportionment is made for mixed use]

Example 3: retrospective basis over whole period of ownership

[Apportion for periods of non-residential use]

	£	£
Disposal proceeds		1,250,000
Incidental disposal costs		(30,000)
Net disposal proceeds		1,220,000
Acquisition cost	750,000	
Incidental costs of acquisition	40,000	
Enhancement costs	0	
Total acquisition cost	790,000	790,000
Gain over period of ownership		430,000

[Further apportionment is made for mixed use]

Legislation: TCGA 1992, s. 1(2A), 4(3B), 14B–14H, Sch. 4ZZB

Tax Reporter: ¶510-750ff.

5720   Non-resident close companies: attribution of gains to UK-resident participators

Special rules apply where chargeable gains accrue to a company which:

(1) is not resident in the UK; and

(2) would be a close company if it were resident in the UK.

In such a case, chargeable gains accruing to the company may be apportioned to participators in proportion to their interest as a participator in the company.

The attribution of gains to UK resident participators does not apply to Annual Tax on Enveloped Dwellings (ATED) related gains chargeable to capital gains tax under TCGA 1992, s. 2B (see 5725).

Unlike gains, losses arising on a disposal by a non-resident close company are not apportioned to the UK-resident shareholders. Where the non-resident company realises a loss which would be an allowable loss if the company were UK resident, that loss can be set against gains arising in the same accounting period and only the net gain is apportioned to the shareholders.

These rules were challenged by the European Commission on the basis that they were incompatible with the European Treaty freedoms as no apportionment was made to participators of gains accruing to a UK-resident close company (EC Press Release IP/11/158). Following consultation, *Finance Act* 2013, s. 62 modified the provisions to also exclude from charge the following, with effect from 6 April 2012:

- gains on assets used for the purposes of economically significant activities (i.e. the provision of goods or services on a commercial basis with appropriate substance) carried on wholly or mainly outside the UK;

- gains where neither the acquisition or disposal of the relevant asset was a part of arrangements put in place with the intention of avoiding tax.

The charge was already disapplied in respect of gains accruing on the disposal of an asset used solely for the purposes of a trade, or part of a trade, carried on wholly outside the UK, and gains in respect of which a company is chargeable to tax by virtue of TCGA 1992, s. 10B (Non-resident company with UK-permanent establishment) (see 5715).

Legislation: TCGA 1992, s. 13, 13A

Tax Reporter: ¶592-900

5725 Non-resident non-natural persons disposing of high-value UK residential property: ATED related gains

Finance Act 2013 introduced a capital gains tax charge on non-natural persons disposing of high value residential property in the UK. Tax is charged at 28% on a chargeable gain arising on a disposal by a non-natural person on or after 6 April 2013, although the chargeable gain is limited to that accruing since 6 April 2013.

A 'non-natural person' is broadly anyone within the scope of the Annual Tax on Enveloped Dwellings other than an individual, a trustee, or a personal representative and includes companies (both resident and not resident), partnerships with a corporate partner (both UK and non-UK resident) and collective investment schemes. The charge is on the non-natural person disposing of the property and not, for example, the shareholders of a company owning residential property. 'High value' property is that worth more than the specified threshold amount, unless the disposal is a part disposal or the disposal of a joint interest, in which case the threshold amount is reduced so that only the relevant part of the interest is subject to capital gains tax. See 5150 for further details of the charge.

Legislation: TCGA 1992, s. 2B–2E, Pt. 2, Ch. 5, Sch. 4ZZA

Tax Reporter: ¶808-000ff.

5730 Double taxation relief on gains

Many countries tax their residents (e.g. the UK) and/or their citizens (e.g. the US) on their worldwide income and gains. Most countries also tax, to some extent, income and gains arising within their jurisdictions. There is, accordingly, ample scope for double taxation. The UK is party to a large number of double tax treaties and is also a member of the Organisation for Economic Co-operation and Development (OECD). Most of the modern treaties to which the UK is party are based on OECD models, which aim to ensure that a resident of a territory which is party to a double tax treaty is only taxed in one state; persons who are resident in both territories are usually treated, *for the purposes of applying the provisions of the treaty*, as resident in the territory with which they are most closely related under a 'tie-breaker' clause.

There is considerable scope for income and gains to be taxed twice. Double taxation is generally seen as a clog on trade and international investment, and most countries give their taxpayers some form of relief for overseas taxes suffered.

Foreign tax can be relieved in three ways:

(1) as a deduction from the amount on which tax is charged;

(2) by offset against domestic tax; or

(3) by exempting certain items of income or gains from taxation (tax sparing).

The UK gives relief for foreign tax by way of credit against domestic tax, either unilaterally (where no treaty relief is available) or under an agreement with the other country. If the foreign tax is less than the corresponding UK tax, then relief is restricted to the foreign tax suffered; if the foreign tax exceeds the UK tax, then relief is restricted to the UK tax payable.

The legislation governing unilateral and bilateral relief for foreign income taxes is found in the *Taxation (International and Other Provisions) Act* 2010 ('TIOPA 2010').

A HMRC statement of practice deals with double taxation relief and CGT. The statement provides clarification, particularly in respect of situations where charges to foreign and UK tax on the same gain do not arise at the same time. It gives the following useful examples:

> 'HMRC's view is that the following sets of circumstances fall within the terms of the standard credit article and may therefore give rise to a credit for overseas tax against CGT or UK corporation tax on chargeable gains.
>
> (i) The overseas tax charges capital gains as income.
> (ii) Overseas tax is payable on a disposal falling within TCGA 1992, s. 171 (transfers within a group of companies treated as taking place on a no gain/no loss basis (see 3630)) and a liability to UK tax arises on a subsequent disposal.
> (iii) An overseas trade carried on through a branch or agency is domesticated (i.e. transferred to a local subsidiary) and relief is given under TCGA 1992, s. 140 (see 3490 and 3495). There is a subsequent disposal of the securities (or the subsidiary disposes of the assets within six years) giving rise to a liability to UK tax and overseas tax is charged in whole or in part by reference to the gain accruing at the date of domestication.
> (iv) Overseas tax is payable by reference to increases in the value of assets although there has been no disposal. There is a subsequent disposal of the assets on which a liability to UK tax arises.'

Where gains of non-resident companies are apportioned to UK resident (or, for tax years prior to 2013–14, ordinarily resident) shareholders, double tax relief extends in such cases to overseas tax paid by the company.

Foreign tax for which no credit relief is available can be deducted in computing the income or gain.

Capital gains tax

Legislation: TIOPA 2010, Pt. 2

Other Material: SP 6/88, *Double taxation relief: chargeable gains*

Tax Reporter: ¶593-300

Partnership gains

5760 Introduction to partnership gains

Tax in respect of chargeable gains accruing on the disposal of chargeable assets is assessed and charged on the partners separately and partnership dealings are treated as dealings by the partners and not by the firm.

The practical application of CGT to partnership transactions is detailed in an important HMRC statement of practice (SP D12). The latest version of SP D12 was published on 14 September 2015. The following paragraphs outline the main points of that practice statement. However, the acquisition or disposal of an asset is deemed to be for a consideration equal to market value where the transaction is not made at arm's length (see 5100ff.) and a transaction is not at arm's length if it is made between connected persons (see 5130ff.), for which purpose a person is, inter alia, connected with:

- any person with whom he is in partnership (i.e. existing partners);

- the spouse or relative of any individual with whom he is in partnership.

Excepted from this definition of 'connected persons' is any acquisition or disposal of assets made pursuant to a bona fide commercial arrangement. In cases where the exception applies, market value is not substituted for actual consideration. However, strictly speaking, the exception does not apply where parties to the transaction are connected persons for reasons other than partnership, e.g. father and son.

Legislation: TCGA 1992, s. 286(4)

Other Material: SP D12, *Partnerships*

Tax Reporter: ¶503-200; ¶503-800; ¶290-060

5765 Partnership assets

Chargeable gains accruing on the disposal of partnership assets are assessed separately on individual partners. Each partner is regarded as owning a share of the partnership assets. The size of that share is usually determined by the partnership agreement specifying the respective shares in asset surpluses. Where the agreement does not so specify, each partner's share will depend on the treatment of asset surpluses in the accounts. Where any surplus is not allocated among the partners, regard is had to the ordinary profit-sharing ratio.

Example

Annie, Bella and Chloe are partners. The profit-sharing ratios are 2:2:1 respectively. The partnership agreement does not deal with the division of surpluses arising from the disposal of assets. The partnership sells certain assets making a gain of £25,000. This surplus is not allocated among the partners but put into a common reserve. The gain apportioned to Annie and Bella is £10,000 each. £5,000 is apportioned to Chloe.

Expenditure on acquiring an asset is allocated similarly at the time of the acquisition.

Other Material: SP D12, *Partnerships*

Tax Reporter: 290-080

5770 Partnership assets received in kind

A partner receiving a partnership asset in kind is not regarded as disposing of his share in it. The asset is taken by the partner at its market value reduced by any gain attributed to his share. This will be his acquisition cost which he carries forward. Any gains attributed to the other partners are subject to CGT. The same principles apply where a loss results from the disposal.

Example

Alex, Brandon and Callum are partners, each having a one-third fractional share in asset surpluses. Alex and Brandon plan to retire soon and Callum agrees to take a heavier burden in the partnership business. The partnership premises, with a current market value of £50,000, are transferred to Callum. The premises were purchased for £44,000. At the time of distribution, a chargeable gain of £2,000 arises to each of Alex and Brandon. Callum is not regarded as making a chargeable gain. Instead, his base value for CGT purposes is reduced from £50,000 to £48,000 (i.e. by the gain attributed to him).

If, instead of a gain, there had been an overall loss of, say, £6,000, C's share (£2,000) would have been added to the current market value to give a carry-forward value of £52,000.

Other Material: SP D12, *Partnerships*

Tax Reporter: ¶290-090

5775 Changes in partnership-sharing ratios and CGT

A change in partnership-sharing ratios (including changes to sharing ratios made when a partner joins or leaves the firm), in general, gives rise to loss a potential charge to capital gains tax, subject to possible rollover relief.

A partner increasing their share of the profits is treated as having made an acquisition of a corresponding share of each asset owned by the partnership. A partner reducing their share is deemed to have disposed of a corresponding share of each of those assets. The cost of the part disposed of is calculated on a fractional basis.

Example

Alice, Brenda, Christine and David are partners in a firm. Share ratios in asset surpluses are 3:1:1:1. The firm takes Emily on as a new partner. Emily is given a one-sixth share and Alice's share is reduced similarly. The current balance sheet value of the principal asset is £90,000, since the asset has not been revalued in the accounts since acquisition.

Alice is treated as disposing of a one-sixth share in the asset for consideration equivalent to base cost of £15,000 (a no gain/no loss disposal). £15,000 also becomes Emily's acquisition cost and the base cost of Alice's remaining interest is reduced to £30,000.

There are certain qualifications to this position, and these are dealt with at 5780 and 5785.

Other Material: SP D12, *Partnerships*; SP 1/89, *Partnerships: further extension of statement of practice D12*

Tax Reporter: ¶290-100

5780 Partnership accounting adjustments and CGT

In the case of partnership accounting adjustments, upward revaluations alone are not occasions of charge and, therefore, do not give rise to chargeable gains. However, if there is a subsequent reduction in a partner's sharing ratio, he is regarded as disposing of a fractional share of the partnership asset (i.e. the fractional difference between his old and new share). The deemed consideration is that fraction of the current book value. The partner with the increased share has a similarly increased acquisition cost to carry forward. The same principles apply to a downward revaluation.

Example

Alan, Brian, Charles and Daniel are partners in a firm. Each is entitled to a quarter share in capital profits from the disposal of Blackacre. Blackacre was acquired for £100,000 in January 1994 and is revalued in the partnership accounts from £100,000 to £240,000 in September 2004. Following the revaluation, the share ratios are altered in January 2015 when Alan becomes entitled to a half share and Brian, Charles and Daniel have their shares reduced to one-sixth each.

There is no chargeable gain at the time of revaluation; but a gain arises to each of Brian, Charles and Daniel on the alteration of ratios. Each is treated as having disposed of a one-twelfth share (i.e. $1/4 - 1/6$) for a consideration of £20,000 (£240,000 × $1/12$). Alan is regarded as acquiring a quarter share in Blackacre for a consideration of £60,000. Alan's acquisition cost carried forward is £85,000 (i.e. £60,000 + £25,000 attributable to his original one-quarter share). Brian, Charles and Daniel have each made a gain of £11,667.

	£
Proceeds	20,000
Cost (£100,000 × $1/12$)	(8,333)
Gain	11,667

Tax Reporter: ¶290-140

5785 Payments by partners outside accounts for CGT

Payments made outside the partnership accounts upon the change of partnership sharing ratios are included as part of the consideration for the disposal of a partner's share. For example, such payments may be for goodwill not included in the balance sheet, in which case the partner receiving the consideration will have no acquisition cost to set off against his CGT liability (unless he himself made a payment for the share he is now disposing of). However, if the payment is clearly payment for a share In assets which are included in the balance sheet, the partner receiving it will be able to deduct the amount of the acquisition cost relative to that share.

Other Material: SP D12, *Partnerships*

Tax Reporter: ¶290-160

5790 Transfers between partners not at arm's length

Changes in partnership sharing ratios do not in themselves normally give rise to chargeable gains or allowable losses (see 5775) unless payments are made outside the accounts (see 5785). However, there is a charge to tax when the transactions are not between persons at arm's length. Market value is substituted for any deemed or actual consideration for the disposal (see 5100ff.).

The transaction is not at arm's length if the parties are 'connected' (see 5130). Often transactions between existing partners will be bona fide commercial transactions and the market value rule will not apply. But market value is substituted where the partners are connected other than by partnership (e.g. father and son).

Market value is not substituted if nothing would have been paid if the parties had been at arm's length or if the sum paid would have been paid if the parties had been at arm's length.

Other Material: SP D12, *Partnerships*

Tax Reporter: ¶290-100

Gains of special taxpayers

5800 Charities, local authorities, health service bodies, public institutions

Gains accruing to charities are exempt from taxes on chargeable gains if they are applicable and applied for charitable purposes only; in this regard, the exemption may be restricted to the extent that the charity incurs non-qualifying expenditure, as in relation to income tax. Gains accruing to trustees under a will have been held not to be exempt from CGT, although charities were among the residuary beneficiaries. However, donations from one charity to another (giving rise to capital gains) may be exempt from CGT although the recipient charity merely adds the donations to its general funds and does not distribute them.

If property ceases to be held for charitable purposes (including where the charity ceases to be a charity), there is a deemed market value disposal which is not exempt; further, if that property was acquired on a disposal of other assets held on charitable trusts the previous exemption for that disposal is lost.

There is no charge to CGT where a charity or any of a list of specified public benefit bodies becomes absolutely entitled to settled property as against the trustees (see 6189).

Local authorities, local authority associations and health service bodies are also exempt from tax on capital gains.

There are also exemptions for the Crown, the Treasury, etc. various museums and other public institutions, for consular officials, and for the issue departments of the central banks of India and Pakistan.

Legislation: TCGA 1992, s. 256(1), 271(1)(a), (f), (5)–(8)

Case: *IR Commrs v Helen Slater Charitable Trust Ltd* (1981) 55 TC 230

Other Material: Former ESC D47, *Temporary loss of charitable status due to reverter of school and other sites*

Tax Reporter: ¶589-100; ¶815-440

5803 Scientific research associations

Scientific research associations within the definition in CTA 2010, s. 469 are exempt from CGT, although a claim must be made for exemption.

Legislation: TCGA 1992, s. 271(6)(b)

Tax Reporter: ¶589-650

5810 Lloyd's underwriters

Annual deemed gains or losses on assets forming part of a Lloyd's underwriter's premiums trust fund or special reserve fund are subject to income tax as part of the proceeds of a trade of insurance, as are any gains/losses arising from actual disposals of those assets.

Other fund assets are subject to CGT in the usual manner, the member being treated as absolutely entitled to the assets.

Individual members of Lloyd's who participate in syndicates through a Members' Agent Pooling Arrangement (MAPA), can to treat their share of the various syndicate capacities held through the MAPA as if it were a single direct holding of syndicate capacity, so reducing the number of CGT computations needed when the MAPA manager buys and sells syndicate capacity or when other members join or leave the MAPA. Further, all syndicate capacity, whether held directly or through a MAPA, is eligible for CGT rollover relief on acquisitions or disposals.

Legislation: FA 1993, s. 176(1), Sch. 20A; FA 1999, s. 82, 83

Tax Reporter: ¶588-300; ¶588-550

5813   Pension funds

Gains accruing to a person on the disposal of investments held in registered pension schemes, personal pension schemes and most other types of superannuation fund are exempt.

The relief also covers capital gains arising from options and futures contracts dealt in by occupational or personal pensions schemes, etc.

Legislation: TCGA 1992, s. 271

Tax Reporter: ¶535-300

5816   International organisations and officers

There are exemptions for various designated international organisations and for foreign diplomats, consular officials, etc. The exemption does not extend to gains on private immovable property situated in the UK, unless held for the relevant country on behalf of the diplomatic mission.

Legislation: TCGA 1992, s. 11, 265, 271

Tax Reporter: ¶589-400; ¶591-160; ¶592-150

5817   Carried interest

Managers of investment funds are rewarded in a variety of ways. Management fees are charged to tax as income, and legislation in FA 2015 ensured that fee income could not be disguised as a form of capital receipt (ITA 2007, Pt. 13, Ch. 5E).

Managers also receive performance-based rewards, sometimes known as 'carried interest'. This is based on the performance of the funds that they manage and can take the form of a share in the fund's total return. Legislation in *Finance (No. 2) Act* 2015 ensures that where carried interest is taxable as a chargeable gain, the full amount will be taxable without reduction through arrangements such as 'base cost shift' (TCGA 1992, Pt. 3, Ch. 5).

Finance Act 2016 makes further changes and introduces a new test to determine whether performance based rewards (or 'carried interest') paid to asset managers should be taxed as income or as chargeable gains. The new legislative test replaces the case law tests based around the 'badges of trade'. ITA 2007, Pt. 13, Ch. 5F (as inserted by FA 2016, s. 37 provides for the circumstances in which carried interest is treated as 'income-based carried interest'. Where the carried interest falls outside Ch. 5F, it will be within the scope of the charge to capital gains tax.

Carried interest arises from an individual's participation in an investment vehicle, typically a partnership. Sums allocated to an individual in satisfaction of carried interest are treated, for tax purposes, as though the individual and not the partnership had carried out the transactions which gave rise to the sums in question. Where a chargeable asset held by a partnership is disposed of, a chargeable gain accrues to the individual and is calculated in accordance with the chargeable gains legislation. HMRC have published Statement of Practice D12 (SP D12) which sets out an agreed interpretation of how the chargeable gains legislation operates in these circumstances. The application of SP D12, together with tax planning techniques, could result in fund managers being charged to capital gains tax on amounts significantly lower than their actual economic returns.

When carried interest arises on or after 8 July 2015, the gain will normally be equal to the sum received. Deductions will be allowed only for actual acquisition costs paid in the form of money (and not as money's worth) and for amounts previously taxed as earnings.

Where an individual performs investment management services for a collective investment scheme through an arrangement involving one or more partnerships, then any sums received in respect of carried interest under that arrangement will constitute a chargeable gain and be subject to capital gains tax. This will cover the entire sum received by an individual, regardless of the items notionally applied to satisfy the carried interest at the level of the partnership or other entity in the fund structure. Only specified sums will be allowable as a deduction against the sum received when calculating the chargeable gain to ensure that individuals are charged to tax on their true economic profit. In particular, a deduction will only be allowed for consideration actually given by the individual (if any) in return for the carried interest rather than for the amount that would be allowed under SP D12. Provision will be made to ensure that credit is given for employment income tax charges where relevant.

Legislation: TCGA 1992, Pt. 3, Ch. 5

Other material: HMRC guidance 'Investment Managers: Capital Gains Tax treatment of carried interest (July 2015)' (www.gov.uk/government/ publications/investment-managers-capital-gains-tax-treatment-of-carried-interest-july-2015/investment-managers-capital-gains-tax-treatment-of-carried-interest-july-2015)

Gains in respect of shares and securities

5818 Nature of CGT treatment of shares and securities

Incorporeal property is specifically included as an asset for the purposes of chargeable gains (see 5008). Two of the most important types of incorporeal property are shares and securities.

'Shares' are defined to include stock, but otherwise there is no statutory definition for capital gains tax purposes. According to HMRC's *Capital Gains Manual*, the word 'share' must be given its ordinary meaning, which is 'a definite portion of a company's share capital'. The term 'securities' sometimes encompasses shares, although the most widely adopted treatment defines them separately to distinguish between the owners of the company and investors in the company, although the distinction is usually blurred.

There are special rules for identifying shares and securities involving, in some cases, the pooling of those of the same class in the same company (see 5820ff.).

There are a number of exemptions and reliefs which specifically apply to the disposal and/or the acquisition of shares or securities (though others may do so). In particular, as well as various provisions of notable importance to companies (see 3400ff.), special rules apply to:

- government securities and qualifying corporate bonds (see 5860);
- reorganisations of share capital (see 5900);
- shares in special schemes, plans or arrangements (see 5923ff.);
- transfer of a business to a company in exchange for shares (see 6302);
- disposals of shares to qualifying employee share ownership trusts (see 5929B);
- gains which are reinvested in shares of qualifying unlisted trading companies, etc. (see 5923ff.).

The House of Lords has held that, in order to determine the date on which shares are issued, the crucial date is the date of registration and not the date of allotment. The question arose in relation to the now-abolished Business Expansion Scheme but it appears to have wider implications.

The charge to CGT is postponed in certain circumstances where a person sells company shares or debentures wholly or partly for the right to receive an uncertain amount of another company's shares or debentures at a later date. Such rights are known as 'earn-out rights' and they are sometimes used where a company is sold for amounts which depend on the future profitability of the company's business. This postponement of the tax charge can be overridden by an election by the vendor of the shares.

Legislation: TCGA 1992, s. 138A

Cases: *National Westminster Bank plc v IR Commrs; Barclays Bank plc v IR Commrs* [1994] BTC 236

Tax Reporter: ¶555-000; ¶561-550; ¶561-600

Share identification

5820 Need for share identification rules

Where shares of the same class in the same company have been acquired at different times and at different prices, some form of identification rules are needed to establish which of those shares have been sold, where a sale takes place which is of less than the full amount of the total holding.

For all in-date years, there are three sets of identification rules applicable to:

(1) disposals from 6 April 2008 onwards by individuals and trustees;

(2) disposals in the years up to 5 April 2008 by individuals and trustees;

(3) disposals by companies.

Tax Reporter: ¶556-500

5826 Identification rules for individuals and trustees: 2008–09 onwards (and years to 2007–08 inclusive)

Disposals on or after 6 April 2008 are to be identified with acquisitions in the following order:

(1) same-day acquisitions;

(2) acquisitions within the following 30 days on the basis of earlier acquisitions in that period, rather than later ones (a FIFO basis); and

(3) securities within the expanded 's. 104 holding' (see below), which specifically does not include acquisitions under (1) and (2) above.

Where the number of securities which comprise the disposal exceed those identified under the above rules, that excess is identified with subsequent acquisitions beyond the 30-day period referred to above.

Capital gains tax

Same day transactions

Before a disposal is identified with any previous acquisition or pool, it is matched, as far as possible, with acquisitions on the same day which are made in the same capacity. For this purpose, all acquisitions on the same day are treated as if they were made by a single transaction and all disposals on that day are similarly treated as made by a single transaction.

A 'bear' transaction is one whereby the taxpayer disposes of shares or securities which he intends to acquire but does not hold at the time of the disposal. In such a case, unless the taxpayer is a company and the disposal is identified with acquisitions according to other 'prescribed period' anti-avoidance provisions, the disposal is matched with the first shares or securities of that type subsequently acquired by the taxpayer in the same capacity. If there remains a balance of unmatched shares or securities, they are identified with the next subsequent acquisition, and so on.

HMRC have confirmed (*Tax Bulletin 52*) that this same-day rule, which treats a disposal as being identified with an acquisition on the same day, does not serve to frustrate a 'negligible value' claim. Concern had been expressed that the interaction the same-day rule and such a claim, which deems there to be a disposal and an immediate re-acquisition, would mean that, on the deemed disposal, neither a gain nor a loss would arise because the securities disposed would be treated as being those deemed to have been re-acquired. It also follows that where a deemed disposal and re-acquisition would give rise to a gain, that gain cannot be avoided by relying on the same-day rule.

Alternative treatment of shares acquired on the same day

Because of the general identification rule, employees who acquired shares under an approved share option scheme at a low base cost and, on the same day, acquired other shares of the same class at a higher value, would find that the acquisition costs would be averaged.

Where an individual:

- has acquired two or more holdings shares on or after 6 April 2002 as a result of transactions on the same day and in the same capacity, referred to as the 'relevant shares';

- those shares are all of the same class; and

- some of those shares were acquired under an Enterprise Management Initiative or an approved share option scheme, without incurring a charge to income tax,

he may elect an alternative identification rule to apply on any subsequent disposal of any of the relevant shares.

The time limit for the election is the first anniversary of 31 January next following the end of the tax year in which the first disposal of any of the relevant shares is made; in other words, 22 months after the tax year concerned. Once made, the election will apply to that disposal and all subsequent disposals of the relevant shares.

Under the alternative identification rule, the approved scheme shares and the remaining shares are treated as acquired in separate single transactions. Subsequent disposals are then identified with the remaining shares in priority to the approved scheme shares. As the remaining shares can be expected to have a higher base cost for future disposal purposes than the approved scheme shares, the effect would be to produce a lower chargeable gain on the earlier disposals than would be the case otherwise. Clearly, for this election to be relevant, there needs to be only a part disposal of the relevant shares.

Where the shares in question attracted EIS income tax relief or capital gains deferral relief, the alternative identification rule is adapted to ensure that the existing identification rules for EIS shares are not displaced. The EIS rules provide for shares acquired on the same day to be put into different categories, but if any of the categories contains approved-scheme shares and remainder shares, the remaining shares are treated as disposed of before the approved-scheme shares. Thus, for EIS purposes, the alternative identification rule works within the existing categories for same-day acquisitions.

Where EIS shares are transferred between husband and wife, the person to whom the shares are transferred is treated as having acquired the shares on the date on which they were issued, ensuring consistency with existing EIS rules.

Acquisitions within 30 days of disposal – individuals and trustees only

Under the capital gains rules as originally enacted, it was possible to realise a gain or loss for tax purposes, while effectively continuing to hold the asset after completion of the transaction. A 'bed and breakfast' transaction was a term commonly used where a person wishing to crystallise an allowable loss (to set against other chargeable gains in the period) or a chargeable gain (to utilise the annual exempt amount or other exemptions or reliefs) usually in respect of shares, without disposing of them permanently, sold the shares (e.g. at the close of business one day) and reacquired them (e.g. at the opening of business on the following day).

Under current legislation, where a person disposes of shares and then acquires shares of the same class in the same company within 30 days following that disposal, the shares disposed of are matched with the subsequent acquisitions in priority to any acquisition of such shares before the date of the disposal. Where there is more than one acquisition in that 30-day period, the earliest acquisition is matched first.

In *Tax Bulletin 52*, HMRC confirmed that an acquisition on the same day as the disposal was not 'within the period of 30 days after the disposal' and therefore the 30-day rule would not frustrate a 'negligible value claim'. They also opined that the 30-day rule could not be used to nullify gains arising on a deemed disposal and re-acquisition as, for example, on a settlement becoming non-resident.

However, that opinion was not upheld in the High Court. As a result of the decision in *Davies (HMIT) v Hicks* [2005] BTC 331 and disclosures under the avoidance scheme disclosure regime, an amendment was introduced by *Finance Act* 2006. The matching is disapplied in respect of disposals on or after 22 March 2006 when the subsequent acquisition is at a time when the taxpayer is:

- not resident (nor, for tax years prior to 2013–14, ordinarily resident) in the UK; or

- resident (or, for tax years prior to 2013–14,ordinarily resident) but treated as 'treaty non-resident'.

A person is treaty non-resident at any time when he is treated as resident in another territory under the terms of a double taxation agreement between the UK and that territory.

The 's. 104 holding' from 6 April 2008 – individuals and trustees only

Under the rules applying for years to 2007–08, two separate pools could be in existence: the '1982 holding' (comprising shares acquired in the period 6 April 1965 and 5 April 1982) and the 's. 104 holding' (comprising shares acquired in the period 6 April 1982 and 5 April 1998). The changes introduced by *Finance Act* 2008 removed the provision which prevented securities acquired prior to 6 April 1982 from forming part of the s. 104 holding (TCGA 1992, s. 104(2)(a) prior to its omission by *Finance Act* 2008). The effect was therefore to expand the s. 104 holding to include all acquisitions of securities of the same class held in the same capacity.

The s. 104 holding from 6 April 2008 therefore now includes:

- any securities remaining in the existing s. 104 holding at 6 April 2008 (see 5828);

- any securities remaining in the 1982 holding at that date (see 5828);

- any securities acquired in the period 6 April 1998 to 5 April 2008 which had not already been identified with disposals in years prior to 2008–09; and

- any securities acquired prior to 6 April 1965 which also had not been previously identified with disposals.

Identification rules for individuals and trustees in the years to 2007–08 inclusive

Disposals on or before 5 April 2008 were identified with acquisitions in the following order:

(1) same-day acquisitions (TCGA 1992, s. 105 – see above);

(2) acquisitions within the following 30 days on the basis of earlier acquisitions in that period, rather than later ones (a FIFO basis) (TCGA 1992, s. 106A(5) – see above);

(3) previous acquisitions after 5 April 1998, identifying the most recent acquisitions first (a LIFO basis) (TCGA 1992, s. 106A(6));

(4) any shares acquired in the period 6 April 1982 to 5 April 1998; these were collectively termed 'the s. 104 holding' (see 5828) and it was regarded as a single asset or 'pool';

(5) any shares acquired in the period 6 April 1965 to 5 April 1982; these were termed 'the 1982 holding' (see 5828) which was also regarded as a single asset; and

(6) any shares acquired before 6 April 1965 (TCGA 1992, s. 106A(7), (8), see 5828).

Where the number of shares which comprise the disposal exceed the acquisitions identified under the above rules, that excess was identified with acquisitions occurring after the disposal (TCGA 1992, s. 105(2)).

Legislation: TCGA 1992, s. 104, 105, 105A, 105B, 106A

Tax Reporter: ¶556-525; ¶556-550; ¶556-650; ¶556-700; ¶556-825

5828   Identification rules for disposals by companies

The order of identification is:

- with any acquisition on the same day (TCGA 1992, s. 105(1), see 5826);

- with acquisitions within the previous ten days (TCGA 1992, s. 107(3), see below);

- with acquisitions since 6 April 1985, 'the s. 104 holding' (TCGA 1992, s. 107(8)), previously termed 'the new holding' (see below);

- with acquisitions in the period 6 April 1965 to 5 April 1982, the '1982 holding' (TCGA 1992, s. 107(9) – see below); and

- lastly, with those held on 6 April 1965, in respect of which no election has been made to include them in the pre-1982 pool; these will be identified on a last-in, first-out (LIFO) basis (TCGA 1992, s. 107(9) – see below).

These rules for separately categorising securities do not affect the determination of their market value, which is ascertained on the basis of, inter alia, aggregate holdings (TCGA 1992, s. 104(5)).

Acquisitions within ten days of disposal – companies only

Before a disposal is identified with any shares or securities, it is matched with acquisitions made on the same day and then with acquisitions in the previous ten days made in the same capacity, if both disposal and acquisition would otherwise fall within the 'new holding' or 's. 104 holding' provisions, being of the same class.

Where there is more than one such acquisition in the ten-day period, the disposal is matched with them on a first-in, first-out (FIFO) basis. If the shares or securities acquired in the matched acquisition exceed those similarly disposed of, any excess is subject to the normal 'new holding/s. 104 holding' rules, mentioned above. If the shares or securities disposed of exceed those acquired in any matched acquisition (i.e. one or more matched acquisitions), any excess is identified with other securities in the normal manner.

Even where, within the ten-day period, the acquisition and disposal straddle a month-end, the benefit of indexation allowance is withdrawn – such an acquisition is taken for indexation purposes to consist of 'relevant securities', so that no indexation allowance is available where a disposal of securities takes place within ten days of their acquisition.

If the taxpayer is a company and the company has a sufficiently large holding of the issued shares or securities of that class, this rule may be overridden by provisions matching the disposal with acquisitions made within a 'prescribed period' before or after the disposal.

The 's. 104 holding' for companies (and for individuals and trustees for years to 5 April 2008 only)

Shares or securities of the same class acquired by a person in the same capacity after the end of 1981–82 were pooled together, as a 's. 104 holding', except where a sub-fund election was in force.

Pooling is an arrangement for treating a person's holding of shares of the same class as a single asset which grows as further shares are acquired and diminishes when there is a disposal of part of the holding. Under this arrangement, when there is a disposal of only some of the shares in the holding, it is treated as a disposal of part of an asset and the acquisition cost of those shares for chargeable gains purposes is not their actual cost but a proportionate part of the cost of all shares in the holding.

Because pooling did not originally apply between the end of 1981–82 and the end of 1984–85, the pool was first created with those shares or securities, if any, which were acquired before 6 April 1982 and were still held at 6 April 1985 (or 1 April for companies) with indexation allowance calculated to that date; the pool was then indexed from that date to any following event which increased or decreased the size of the pool – an 'operative event' – and between successive events of that type.

The value of shares depended upon the extent of the holding; for the purposes of determining the value of any holding at 31 March 1982, HMRC permitted all the shares or securities held to be considered together irrespective of whether they were to be pooled together or whether they were acquired subsequently on a no gain/no loss basis.

If a holding of shares treated as a single asset by way of the 's. 104 holding' pool was transferred in a no gain/no loss transaction after 29 November 1993, the recipient was treated as having acquired the shares for their original cost, and only this amount was added to the recipient's unindexed pool of expenditure. However, the indexed rise in the cost of the shares at the date of the transfer was added to the recipient's indexed pool of expenditure; this was an amount of indexation allowance in the hands of the transferee, which was therefore subject to the same use restrictions as other indexation allowance. The indexation allowance available on the disposal of any of the shares was the difference between the relevant proportions of the unindexed and indexed pools of expenditure. However, this allowance could only reduce a chargeable gain to £nil.

Certain shares and securities did not fall to be pooled as part of the s. 104 holding:

- securities within the accrued income scheme;
- qualifying corporate bonds; and
- material interests in non-qualifying offshore funds.

For these securities, the special identification rules applied.

There were also special identification rules for certain shares or securities held by insurance companies or underwriters and a simplified regime was applied, in practice, for individuals investing regular sums in monthly savings schemes of authorised unit trusts and approved investment trusts.

The '1982 holding' for companies (also for individuals and trustees for years to 5 April 2008 only)

Shares or securities of the same class acquired by a person in the same capacity between 6 April 1965 and the end of 1981–82 were pooled together, as part of a '1982 holding', except when a sub-fund election was in effect.

The '1982 holding' pool treated a person's appropriate pre-1982 holding of shares or securities of the same class as a single asset which diminished when the disposal was only part of the holding; however, it could not grow by the addition of further shares or securities, though the value of the pool could be enhanced if there was a bonus or rights issue or other reconstruction involving the shares or securities.

Being a pool of shares or securities held at 31 March 1982, the 1982 holding was eligible for rebasing to the value at that date, in accordance with the usual rules (see 5320). The value of shares depended upon the extent of the holding; for the purposes of determining the value at 31 March 1982, HMRC permitted all the shares or securities held to be considered together irrespective of whether they were to be pooled together or whether they were acquired subsequently on a no gain/no loss basis.

Quoted shares and securities acquired before 6 April 1965 for companies (also for individuals and trustees for years to 5 April 2008 only)

Quoted shares or securities were treated as individual assets which were acquired on 6 April 1965, the date capital gains tax came into force, at their market value on that date. However, they were included in the 1982 holding if an election was made before 6 April 1985 (or 1 April 1985 for companies) requiring them to be pooled at their value at 6 April 1965.

If no such election was made, the taxpayer had a further chance to elect for them to be included in the 1982 holding; alternatively, he had another chance to elect for them to be pooled only with other similar shares held at 6 April 1965. Being held at 31 March 1982, all such shares or securities were eligible for rebasing to the value at that date in accordance with the usual rules (see 5320).

See also 5383 for computation of gains/losses.

Legislation: TCGA 1992, s. 105, 107, 109, 110, 110A, 113 and Sch. 2

Tax Reporter: ¶556-600; ¶556-750; ¶556-850; ¶557-500

5830   Special rules for relevant securities

There are various securities ('relevant securities') which are excluded from the general pooling and identification provisions (see 5826 and 5828), namely:

- securities falling within the accrued income scheme;
- qualifying corporate bonds;
- material interests in non-reporting offshore funds,

though the special rules do not apply to either quoted shares/securities unless an election was made for them to be pooled at their market value on 6 April 1965 or to unquoted shares/securities held at that date.

The general rule is that, notwithstanding any identification specified in transfer documents, as regards securities of the same class and disposals made in the same capacity, earlier disposals are to be considered before later ones. It should not be forgotten that, with an unconditional contract, a disposal takes place at the time of the contract and not the transfer or delivery date.

Legislation: TCGA 1992, s. 108, 119

Tax Reporter: ¶558-100

Government securities and qualifying corporate bonds

5860   Non-marketable government securities

Savings certificates and non-marketable securities (i.e. non-transferable securities or securities transferable only with the appropriate official consent) are not chargeable assets and are exempt from CGT.

Legislation: TCGA 1992, s. 121

Tax Reporter: ¶508-420

5865　Gilt-edged securities and qualifying corporate bonds

Where gilt-edged securities or qualifying corporate bonds (or options on them) are disposed of, the gain on disposal is exempt from CGT. The closing out of an option by a person entering into a reciprocal option is a disposal for this purpose. In consequence, losses accruing on disposals are not generally allowable, though a limited relief for loans may be available.

'Gilt-edged securities' are, for this purpose, those government securities set out in a prescribed list and any additional securities which may be specified subsequently by statutory instrument.

Qualifying corporate bonds

A 'qualifying corporate bond' (QCB) is, broadly:

- for corporation tax purposes in relation to accounting periods ending after 31 March 1996, any asset representing a 'loan relationship' of a company; or

- a security which represents a normal commercial loan and which is expressed in sterling with no provision for conversion into or redemption in another currency.

For corporation tax purposes in relation to accounting periods ending after 31 March 1996, foreign currency loan relationships, unit trusts and offshore funds held in exempt circumstances are not QCBs.

Before 14 March 1989, there was a requirement that the securities must since their issue have been quoted on a UK stock exchange or dealt in on the Unlisted Securities Market (for the date of issue, see 5818).

Because of the exemption for QCBs, special provisions apply to reorganisations, conversions and reconstructions which would otherwise be treated as not involving a disposal or acquisition in such a way that the new holding is broadly treated as if it were the original shares (see 5900), if either the original shares or the new holding but not both include QCBs. The usual rules do not apply to the extent that QCBs are involved:

- if the QCBs represent the old asset, there is a disposal and acquisition at market value, as adjusted for the acquisition by other consideration passing;

- if the QCBs represent the new asset, a notional market value gain or loss is postponed until subsequent disposal of the new asset, unless other consideration also passes; if there is an exempt gift of the bonds to charity (see 6189), the deferred gain does not crystallise either on the donor or on the charity on a subsequent disposal.

The notional market value gain is in effect wiped out by the subsequent death of the holder; if the shares or securities are held by personal representatives at the time of the reorganisation, the gain crystallises if the personal representatives dispose of the QCBs or, if they transfer them to legatees (see 5690), when the legatees dispose of them. If the consideration received on a share exchange is only partly in the form of QCBs, the shares inherit a just and reasonable proportion of the base cost while the remainder is used to calculate the notional market value gain deferred until disposal of the QCBs.

Legislation: TCGA 1992, s. 115–117B, 132 and Sch. 9

Cases: *Weston v Garnett (HMIT)* [2005] BTC 113, [2005] BTC 342; *Klincke* [2009] TC 00122; *R & C Commrs v Hancock* [2016] BTC 503; *R & C Commrs v Trigg (a partner of Tonnant LLP)* [2016] BTC 505

Tax Reporter: ¶559-000ff.

5890   Capital distributions

A capital distribution received from a company in respect of any shares in that company is treated as consideration for the disposal of an interest in the shares (unless the distribution is 'small'). A capital distribution is, generally, any distribution not subject to income tax in the hands of the recipient, but it also includes consideration for disposal of a member's right in respect of a provisional allotment of shares or debentures. Ordinarily, a distribution by a company by way of dividends of gains arising on the sale of capital assets is liable to income tax; however, a repayment of share capital on a dissolution or winding-up of the company will be a capital distribution. (See also 5905.)

If a capital distribution is small and less than the allowable expenditure in relation to the value of the shares in respect of which the distribution is made, then, except as noted below, the distribution is not treated as a disposal but is deducted from allowable expenditure. However, in practice, HMRC have confirmed that a taxpayer can insist that a small capital distribution be treated as a part disposal and can ask HMRC not to make a direction ignoring the disposal.

HMRC interpret 'small' as meaning less than 5% of the value of the holding, but accept that a receipt with a value of £3,000 of less will be small whether or not it is less than 5%.

If the allowable expenditure is less than the amount distributed, there is a part disposal but rather than the usual apportionment (see 5229), the taxpayer can elect to have the whole of the allowable expenditure deducted on the part disposal.

Where a company purchases its own shares from a corporate shareholder in circumstances that amount to a distribution, the amount of the distribution is nonetheless included in the consideration for chargeable gains purposes. HMRC's view is that the distribution does not suffer a charge to tax as income within the terms of TCGA 1992, s. 37(1). In the case of a corporate shareholder, it is not therefore excluded from the capital gains computation so as to escape tax altogether. Where a company purchases its own shares from an individual shareholder, provided the conditions set out in the legislation from CTA 2010, s. 1033–1043 are satisfied (see 3850), the consideration received by the shareholder as a result of a company purchasing its own shares is not a distribution (so falls to be treated as a capital distribution and as disposal for capital gains tax purposes). Where a company purchases its own shares and the aforementioned conditions are not satisfied, the consideration received by a shareholder falls to be a distribution that is subject to income tax.

Legislation: TCGA 1992, s. 122, 123

Case: *O'Rourke (HMIT) v Binks* [1992] BTC 460

Other Material: Revenue Interpretation 157; SP 4/89, *Company purchase of own shares: capital gains treatment of distribution received by corporate shareholder*; SP 2/82, *Company's purchase of own shares: ICTA 1988*

Tax Reporter: ¶562-000ff.; ¶562-150

Reorganisation of share capital

5900   Importance of a 'reorganisation'

A 'reorganisation of share capital' is not exhaustively defined but specifically includes the case where persons are allotted shares in, or debentures of, a company in respect of and in proportion to their holdings of shares in that company or where there is more than one class of shares and rights attaching to a class of shares are altered – thus, a reorganisation of share capital occurs when there is a bonus issue, or a rights issue, of shares.

Except in certain cases involving qualifying corporate bonds (see 5865), a reorganisation is not treated as involving any disposal of shares held before the reorganisation ('the original shares') or any acquisition of new shares or debentures ('the new holding') which represent the original shares; the new holding is treated as having been acquired at the same cost and at the same time as the original shares and CGT will only apply on a disposal of the new holding.

If there is consideration received by the taxpayer other than the new holding, there is a part disposal of the original shares effectively before (or at the same time as) the equation of the old and new holdings; the apportionment of the cost of acquisition of the original shares is carried out not on the usual part disposal basis (see 5229) but by reference to market value on the date of disposal.

If there is additional consideration given by the taxpayer, it is treated as if it had been given for the original shares so that it forms part of the acquisition cost of the new holding treated as incurred as the original cost had been. Indexation allowance (see 5280) has complicated matters where consideration is given for any part of the new holding since, for that purpose, the actual date of the additional consideration is used to index that amount.

The CGT treatment of the reorganisation of share capital also applies to the conversion of securities (see 5913) and certain company takeovers and reconstructions (see 5920). If an open offer is made to shareholders, then HMRC will treat any subscription for shares which is equal to or less than the shareholder's minimum entitlement as a share reorganisation. Any shares subscribed for in excess of the minimum entitlement will be treated as a separate acquisition.

For the treatment of collective investment schemes, see 5917.

For the interaction between the reorganisation provisions and the employee shareholder shares exemption, see 5929A.

Legislation: TCGA 1992, s. 126–129, 131

Case: *Dunstan (HMIT) v Young, Austen & Young Ltd* [1989] BTC 77

Tax Reporter: ¶560-000ff.

5905   Bonus and rights issues

Bonus issues

Bonus issues are free distributions of shares (e.g. two new shares for each share already held), treated as a reorganisation (see 5900).

Example

In 2000, Richard purchased 300 ordinary shares in S Ltd at £3 per share, total cost £900 (ignoring expenses for the purposes of the example). In 2006, Richard received a bonus issue of 300 shares.

He then held 600 shares at £1.50 per share. They are all treated as purchased in 2000.

Rights issues

Rights issues are treated in the same way as bonus issues except that any consideration given for the new holding (or any part of it) is added to the original acquisition cost and treated, for most purposes, as if incurred when the original expenditure was incurred. However, for the purposes of the indexation allowance for companies, the additional consideration for the new holding is treated as a separate item of allowable expenditure incurred when it was due and payable (see 5900).

Example 1

A Ltd owns 10,000 ordinary shares in H Ltd, which it bought in 2001 for £20,000 (including expenses). H Ltd makes a one for five rights issue in 2016 at £1 per share.

A Ltd's total acquisition cost for 12,000 shares is: £20,000 + £2,000 = £22,000.

Example 2

The facts are the same as in Example 1.

A Ltd sells the shares at a gain in, say, 2016. Its allowable expenditure will include not only the acquisition costs (£22,000) but also indexation calculated separately on:

- the original cost of £20,000;
- the additional cost of £2,000.

A disposal of rights to acquire shares is treated as if the consideration for the disposal were a capital distribution by the company (see 5890).

Example 3

The facts are the same as in Example 1, but A Ltd sells its rights for 150p per share (i.e. £3,000) when each share is worth 250p. A Ltd's gain is calculated as follows:

	£
Consideration for rights	3,000.00
Less: apportioned acquisition cost (below)	(2,142.86)
Gain	857.14

The acquisition cost attributable to the rights shares is calculated as with part disposals:

$$\text{Acquisition cost of shares} \times \frac{\text{Consideration for sale of rights}}{\text{Market value of original shares} + \text{Consideration for sale of rights}}$$

$$£20,000 \times \frac{£3,000}{£25,000 + £3,000} = £2,142.86$$

If the consideration for the rights had been less than 5% of the market value of the original shares, there would (if A Ltd had made a claim) have been no disposal at this stage. Instead, the acquisition cost of A Ltd's original shares would have been reduced by the amount of the consideration (see 5890).

Tax Reporter: ¶560-100; ¶560-700

5910 Composite new holdings

A reorganisation of share capital may result in the new holding consisting of more than one class of securities (e.g. shares and debentures). The apportionment of the acquisition cost between the different classes of securities must be made upon a part disposal of the new holding.

The rules of apportionment differ depending on whether the new holding includes any quoted securities.

Unquoted securities

Where none of the securities in the new holding are quoted, the apportionment is made by reference to their market value at the date of the disposal.

Legislation: TCGA 1992, s. 129, 130

Tax Reporter: ¶560-100

5913 Conversion of securities

The CGT treatment of the reorganisation of share capital (see 5900 to 5910) also applies to the conversion of securities, e.g. a conversion of loan stock of a company into shares in the company; 'security' means loan stock or similar security (whether secured or unsecured) of any government, or of any public or local authority, or any company. It also includes alternative finance arrangements such as alternative investment bonds.

If a sum of money or premium is received on the conversion, there is a part disposal of the original securities (see 5900) but if it is small (see 5890 for discussion of what counts as 'small') in relation to the value of the securities in respect of which the premium is given, then, except as noted below, the receipt of the premium is not treated as a disposal but the amount is deducted from allowable expenditure. If the allowable expenditure is less than the premium, there is a part disposal but rather than the usual apportionment (see 5229) the taxpayer can elect to have the whole of the allowable expenditure deducted on the part disposal; it is likely that the considerations as to whether the premium must be small for this purpose apply in the same way as for capital distributions (see 5890).

Where gilt-edged securities are received in recompense for the compulsory acquisition of shares, this is not treated as a conversion because of the exemption for gilts (see 5865); instead, a notional market value gain or loss is calculated but postponed until subsequent disposal of the gilts. For the effect on re-basing, see 5323.

Any gain on a non-QCB security, whilst it is chargeable to CGT, will remain chargeable. Where the terms of such a security change, converting it to a QCB, any deferred capital gains from reorganisations and reconstructions are postponed until the disposal of the QCB.

Legislation: TCGA 1992, s. 132–134

Cases: *R & C Commrs v Hancock* [2016] BTC 503

Tax Reporter: ¶560-800

5915   Stock dividends

A stock dividend is an issue of shares in lieu of a cash dividend are treated as free-standing acquisitions, rather than reorganisations of share capital, with an acquisition cost of the cash equivalent of the shares issued.

Legislation: TCGA 1992, s. 142

Tax Reporter: ¶560-550

5917   Collective investment schemes

Authorised unit trust schemes are collective investment schemes under which the property in question is held on trust for the participants (*Financial Services and Markets Act* 2000); they are treated as UK resident companies in which the participants' rights are shares but, to the limited extent that they are not exempt, are subject to CGT rather than corporation tax on chargeable gains.

Gains accruing to an authorised unit trust, an investment trust, a court investment fund, a venture capital trust or a unit trust wholly for exempt unit-holders, are exempt. Exemption is not withheld from a unit trust because of any temporary holding necessary under ordinary arrangements of the trust for the issue and redemption of units.

Finance Act 2004 introduced provisions, essentially clarificatory, amending the legislation relating to authorised unit trusts (AUTs) to bring its treatment of 'umbrella schemes' strictly into line with HMRC's established interpretation of the current rules. The amendments take effect for chargeable periods beginning on or after 1 April 2004. The legislation treats a unit trust scheme as though it were a company and the units held by investors as though they were shares in that company. An 'umbrella scheme' is an AUT whose investments are split into a number of separate sub-funds, usually having different investment strategies. The holders of units in the scheme have rights over individual sub-funds, and are entitled to switch their entitlements between different sub-funds. The new provisions make explicit provision for each sub-fund of an umbrella scheme to be treated as though it were an AUT, and for the scheme itself not to be a unit trust scheme for such purposes.

Transfer of company's assets to investment trust

Where a company becomes an investment trust so as to benefit from the above exemption, there is a crystallisation by virtue of a deemed disposal and reacquisition at market value of assets transferred on a tax-free reconstruction. The chargeable gain or allowable loss crystallises at the end of the accounting period before the one in which the company becomes an investment trust, rather than at the time of the transfer of all or part of its business.

Legislation: TCGA 1992, s. 99–101C

Other Material: Former ESC D17, *Unit trusts for exempt holder: section 100(2) TCGA 1992*

Tax Reporter: ¶782-050

5920 Company takeovers and reconstructions

The acquisition of a company (or at least 25% of the ordinary share capital thereof) in exchange for shares or a reconstruction involving the issue of shares may, in some cases, be treated as a tax-free reorganisation. This can have an unfortunate side-effect; if the consideration for the whole transaction consists of a future allocation of shares contingent on some event, such as attainment of specified profit levels, rather than an immediate issue of shares-for-shares. On a strict interpretation of the reorganisation relief rules, no relief would be due in relation to the value of the new shares issued on the happening of the contingency, because the initial disposal would be in exchange for the right to the future, contingent issue, not for actual shares in the company. A concession prevents this loss of relief.

Where consideration received on a share exchange is partly in the form of qualifying corporate bonds (QCBs), the shares inherit a just and reasonable proportion of the base cost while the remainder is used to calculate the notional market value gain deferred until disposal of the QCBs (see 5865).

Tax Reporter: ¶561-000ff.

Investment schemes

5923 EIS

The enterprise investment scheme (EIS) has three features:

- income tax relief on qualifying investments in eligible companies (see 1930);
- capital gains tax exemption on disposals of qualifying investments, provided the income tax relief is not withdrawn; and
- capital gains tax deferral on the disposal of any asset where sales proceeds are re-invested in qualifying EIS investments.

EIS deferral relief is a holdover relief, not a rollover relief. In other words, the gain is simply held in suspense until the happening of a chargeable event. The consideration for the disposal of the original asset and for the acquisition of the relevant shares is not reduced as a consequence of relief. When the relevant shares are sold, the gain on those shares will be calculated on normal rules and will be chargeable in addition to any deferred gain which is deemed to accrue.

The deferred gain is the chargeable gain which would, in the absence of a claim, arise on the original disposal. It is therefore the gain after any of the following reliefs:

- business asset rollover relief;
- incorporation relief; and
- business asset gift relief.

Where a claim for relief is made, an amount of qualifying expenditure is set against the gain concerned. A corresponding part of the gain is then treated as not having accrued on the date it would otherwise have accrued, but as accruing on the occurrence of a chargeable event in relation to the eligible shares. That part of the gain is deferred until the chargeable event occurs.

The amount of the deferred gain is determined by the claimant specifying the amount of the qualifying expenditure to be set against the gain, the only limitations being:

- the available qualifying expenditure is that part of the total expenditure on the relevant shares remaining after previous claims; and

- the claim cannot exceed the amount of the gain remaining after previous claims under these provisions and claims for the relief that used to be available for investment in venture capital trusts.

For entrepreneurs' relief on deferred gains, see 5299A.

Legislation: TCGA 1992, s. 150A, 150C and Sch. 5B

Cases: *Blackburn v R & C Commrs* [2009] BTC 39; *Daniels v R & C Commrs* (2005) Sp C 489; *East Allenheads Estate Ltd* [2015] TC 04513; *Ames* [2015] TC 04523; *Stolkin v R & C Commrs* [2016] BTC 19

Tax Reporter: ¶565-400; ¶565-550; ¶568-000

5925   Venture capital trusts

If an individual disposes of shares in a venture capital trust (VCT) (see also 1950ff.), the gain will be exempt from CGT if the original acquisition cost of the shares did not exceed the permitted maximum (currently £200,000) in any one tax year.

A disposal is a qualifying disposal for these purposes if it is made by an individual aged 18 or over, and is made of shares which were acquired for bona fide commercial purposes (i.e. not as part of a tax avoidance scheme). The shares disposed of must not have exceeded the permitted maximum in the tax year in which they were acquired, with the definition of permitted maximum, and the rules for identifying those shares which exceed the permitted maximum being imported from ITA 2007, Pt. 6, Ch. 2 (see 1954) for this purpose.

Identification of shares disposed of

In addition to the rules imported from ITA 2007, Pt. 6, Ch. 2 (see above) regarding identification of shares disposed of, a further provision ensures that shares acquired when the company was not an approved VCT are assumed to be disposed of before shares acquired when the company was an approved VCT. Once this provision has been applied, any shares acquired on different days are deemed to be disposed of on a FIFO basis, and shares acquired on the same day are deemed to be disposed of with those shares (if any) which exceed the permitted maximum being disposed of first.

Withdrawal of approval

Where approval of a VCT is withdrawn, then an individual holding shares in the VCT is deemed to have disposed of those shares and immediately reacquired them for their market value. The disposal is deemed to take place whilst the VCT is still approved, so that no chargeable gain or allowable loss arises, but the reacquisition, for the purposes of the share pooling rules (see 5826), is deemed to take place immediately after the company ceases to be a VCT.

Supplementary provisions

Where shares which enjoy different tax reliefs (specified in TCGA 1992, s. 151B(3)) are involved in a reorganisation under TCGA 1992, s. 126, then the shares are treated as being different holdings according to the different tax reliefs they enjoy. If a reorganisation such as a rights issue affects an existing holding, and results in the individual holding shares in a VCT (as defined in TCGA 1992, s. 151B(3)(a)–(c)), then the reorganisation provisions contained in TCGA 1992, s. 127–130 will not apply to the existing holding.

On a reconstruction, the rules contained in TCGA 1992, s. 135, 136 are disapplied where a VCT acquires another company which is not a VCT, or is acquired by such a company.

Legislation: TCGA 1992, s. 151A, 151B(6), (7)

Tax Reporter: ¶565-300

5926 Seed enterprise investment scheme (SEIS)

The seed enterprise investment scheme was introduced from 6 April 2012 as an investment scheme designed to help start-up companies obtain initial investment. Initially introduced for a five-year period only (and due to end on 5 April 2017), the scheme and associated capital gains tax reinvestment relief were made permanent by *Finance Act* 2014. The scheme complements the EIS and venture capital reliefs described above but is designed to precede both schemes and a company which has already raised finance under either the EIS or VCT scheme is precluded from raising finance under the SEIS scheme. The rules have been designed to mirror those of EIS as it is anticipated that companies may want to go on to use the EIS or VCT scheme after an initial investment under SIES.

SEIS provides:

- income tax relief on investment in new shares (with a maximum qualifying investment of £100,000);

- capital gains tax exemption on sale of qualifying seed enterprise investment shares, provided that income tax relief has not been withdrawn;

- capital gains tax exemption on the disposal of assets where the gains are reinvested in qualifying SEIS shares.

The disposal relief provides an exemption from capital gains tax in respect of a gain arising on the disposal shares where an investor has received income tax relief (which has not subsequently been withdrawn) on the cost of the shares, and the shares are disposed of after they have been held for at least three years. However, if no claim to income tax relief is made, then any subsequent disposal of the shares will not qualify for exemption from capital gains tax.

The reinvestment exemption is available in respect of a gain arising on the disposal of any asset with so much of the gain as is matched with the relevant percentage of qualifying SEIS expenditure being exempt from capital gains tax (subject to the £100,000 investment limit). The relief was originally introduced in respect of gains accruing in 2012–13 and matched with investment in 2012–13 then extended in relation to gains accruing in 2013–14 and matched with investment in 2013–14 but with a limit on the amount that was treated as not being a chargeable gain of 50% of the qualifying SEIS expenditure. The relief was made permanent by *Finance Act* 2014 for 2014–15 and subsequent years at the 50% rate.

The asset does not have to be disposed of first; the investment in SEIS shares can take place before the disposal of the asset, providing that both the disposal and investment take place in the same year. However, investors who make use of the 'carry-back' facility for the purposes of SEIS income tax relief should note that to the extent that shares are treated as issued in the previous tax year for the purposes of income tax relief, those shares will also be treated as issued in the previous tax year for the purposes of reinvestment relief. Accordingly, as gains must be matched with investment in the same tax year, if an investor is issued with SEIS shares in 2013–14 and wants to claim SEIS income tax relief as if all or some had been issued in 2012–13, then the shares treated as issued in 2012–13 are treated as issued in 2012–13 for the purposes of reinvestment relief and reinvestment relief cannot be claimed on gains made in 2013–14 in respect of those shares.

Legislation: TCGA 1992, s. 150G and Sch. 5BB

Tax Reporter: ¶568-500ff.

5927   Social investment tax relief

The social investment tax relief (SITR) is a scheme designed to support social enterprises seeking external finance by offering a range of tax reliefs to individual investors who invest in new shares or new qualifying debt investments in those social enterprises. The rules are similar to those applying to other investment schemes, but relief is not available on any investment in respect of which the investor has obtained relief under EIS, SEIS or CITR. SITR applies for investments made on or after 6 April 2014 and before 6 April 2019 and provides:

- income tax relief on investments in new shares or new qualifying debt investments (with a maximum annual investment of £1,000,000) (see 1958);

- capital gains tax exemption on the disposal of qualifying investments shares that have been held for at least three years, provided that income tax relief has not been withdrawn; and

- capital gains tax deferral on the disposal of assets where the gains are reinvested in qualifying shares or debt instruments which also qualify for income tax relief.

The disposal relief provides an exemption from capital gains tax in respect of the disposal of an investment where the investor has received income tax relief (which has not subsequently been withdrawn) on the cost of the investment, and the investment is disposed of after it has been held for at least three years. However, if no claim to income tax relief is made, then any subsequent disposal of the investment will not qualify for exemption from capital gains tax.

The deferral relief enables the payment of tax on a capital gain to be deferred where the gain is reinvested in shares or debt investments which also qualify for SITR income tax relief. It is not, however, necessary for the investor to have made a claim for SITR income tax relief. The gain can arise from the disposal of any kind of asset, but must arise in the period from 6 April 2014 to 5 April 2019. The SITR qualifying investment must be made in the period one year before or three years after the gain arose. There is no minimum period for which the investment must be held; the deferred capital gain is brought back into charge whenever the investment is disposed of or the social enterprise ceases to meet the requirements of the scheme, but if an amount equal to the gain is once more invested in shares or debt investments which also qualify for SITR income tax relief then the gain may be held-over again.

For entrepreneurs' relief on deferred gains, see 5299A.

Legislation: TCGA 1992, s. 255A–255E and Sch. 8B

Tax Reporter: ¶569-300ff.

Employee share schemes

5928 Share option scheme shares

There are certain provisions which apply to options generally (see 5980).

Except as noted below, where an income tax charge is made in respect of shares (or an option to acquire shares) under an employee share scheme, this is taken into account in computing chargeable gains so as not to charge the amount to tax more than once; the relevant amount is added to what would otherwise be the allowable acquisition cost.

The release of an employee share option by the option holder in return for a replacement option does not give rise to a capital gain for the option holder or the grantor of the new option on the occasion of a takeover of the employing company.

Legislation: TCGA 1992, s. 120, 238

Tax Reporter: ¶565-000; ¶565-050

5929 Enterprise management incentives

The enterprise management incentives scheme is designed to help small potentially high risk companies to recruit and retain high calibre individuals. Provided that the scheme has been operated correctly and the value of the company increases, individuals will face a capital gains tax liability at the time that they sell their shares. Where the option has been granted at full market value, this will represent the difference between proceeds and cost. Where the grant took place at a discount, the gain chargeable to CGT will, essentially, be calculated on the difference between (a) the sale proceeds and (b) the cost plus the amount on which income tax has already been paid or is payable on acquisition of the shares, upon option exercise. In the vast majority of cases, this amount charged to income tax will be calculated by reference to the market value of the shares at the date that the option was granted (see ITEPA 2003, s. 531).

Where options are granted under the scheme, on the sale of the shares, taper relief was, until 5 April 2008 (see 5268ff.) normally available from the date on which the options were granted, rather than from the date of exercise.

Holders of share options under an enterprise management incentive scheme are able to benefit from entrepreneurs' relief in certain circumstances (see 5297A).

Legislation: TCGA 1992, s. 169I, 238A and Sch. 7D, Pt. 4

Tax Reporter: ¶466-720

5929A   Employee shareholder shares

A limited relief by way of exemption is available for gains arising on or after 1 September 2013 on the disposal of 'employee shareholder shares'. These are shares which an employee acquires under an employee shareholder agreement (see 360). Note that an employee with a material interest (or with a connected individual who has a material interest) in the company either at the time the employee shareholder shares are acquired or at any time within the year before such acquisition cannot benefit from this relief.

Finance Act 2016 introduces a lifetime limit of £100,000 on the CGT exempt gains that a person can make on the disposal of shares acquired under employee shareholder agreements entered into after 16 March 2016 (TCGA 1992, s. 236B(1A)–(1C)). Any gains which accrue on disposals of employee shareholder shares that were issued in respect of employee shareholder agreements made on or before 16 March 2016 will not count towards the limit. Taxpayers will need to keep a record of CGT exempt gains which count towards the limit. When employee shareholder shares issued as consideration for entering into employee shareholder agreements after 16 March 2016 are disposed of, gains made in excess of the lifetime limit will be charged to CGT.

Subject to the lifetime disposal limit, gains on employee shareholder shares are fully exempt from capital gains tax if the total value of qualifying shares owned by the employee shareholder in that company immediately after acquisition is less than or equal to £50,000. If the total shares acquired are worth more than £50,000 immediately after an acquisition of such shares, only a proportion of the shares in the latest acquisition round can be treated as qualifying. The amount is determined by a formula:

$$\frac{(50,000 - B)}{T}$$

where–
  B = total value of employee shareholder shares previously acquired; and
  T = total value of employee shareholder shares acquired in the latest tranche.

Qualifying shares are employee shareholder shares of either the employer company or an associated company of the employer company, acquired by the employee in consideration for an employee shareholder agreement. Companies are 'associated' if one has control of the other, or both are under the control of the same person.

The share identification rules (see 5820 onwards) do not apply to employee shareholder shares. An owner of such shares who also owns non-exempt shares can choose whether to treat shares disposed of as being a disposal of exempt shares or of non-exempt shares.

Reorganisations of share capital

The *Taxation of Chargeable Gains Act* 1992, s. 127 (the share-for-share exchange rules) do not apply to exempt employee shareholder shares, so that on an exchange of shares, the new shares do not inherit the base cost of the exempt employee shareholder shares, or the exemption (per HMRC guidance published 3 September 2013). However, *Finance Act* 2016 makes amendments to this rule, with effect in relation to disposals made after 16 March 2016. Where an exempt employee shareholder (EES) share is disposed of on a reorganisation, it is to be treated as disposed of for consideration (the 'relevant amount') calculated as follows:

(i) where a notional gain would arise if the EES share were disposed of for consideration equal to market value and that gain would be chargeable under TCGA 1992, s. 236B(1A), i.e. because the gain exceeds the £100,000 exemption limit), the consideration is deemed to be for an amount that gives rise to neither a gain nor a loss;

(ii) where a notional gain would arise if the EES share were disposed of for consideration equal to market value but only part of that gain would be chargeable under TCGA 1992, s. 236B(1A), i.e. because part of the gain falls within the £100,000 exemption limit), the consideration is deemed to be for an amount not exceeding market value that secures no gain nor loss arises;

(iii) where a notional gain would arise if the EES share were disposed of for consideration equal to market value and no part of the gain is chargeable under TCGA 1992, s. 236B(1A), i.e. because it all falls within the £100,000 exemption limit), the consideration is deemed to be market value at the time of the disposal;

(iv) where no notional gain arises if the EES share were disposed of for consideration equal to market value, the consideration is deemed to be for an amount which gives rise to neither a gain nor a loss.

Inter-spouse transfers

Transfers between spouses and civil partners take place on a no gain/ no loss basis under TCGA 1992, s. 58 (see 5500). *Finance Act* 2016 amends s. 58 to deal with inter-spouse transfers in consequence of the introduction of the introduction of the lifetime limit. Broadly, where employee shareholder shares are transferred between spouses or civil partners and a CGT exempt gain would otherwise accrue (ignoring inter-spouse transfer rules), the disposal is treated as taking place for consideration which will result in that exempt gain. The effect is to limit the exemption to the gain that arises during the period that the employee shareholder holds the shares and to transfer the benefit of that exemption from the transferor to the transferee by increasing the transferee's allowable cost of the shares.

Accordingly, where the whole of the transferor's lifetime allowance has already been used up before the disposal, the inter-spouse transfer rules under s. 58 apply and the transfer will be treated as if the shares were acquired from the transferor on a no-gain, no-loss basis. Where the transferor's gain would be less than the balance remaining of his or her lifetime allowance, s. 58 does not apply and the disposal is treated under normal rules as being for consideration of an amount equal to the market value of the shares transferred. Where, if s. 58 did not apply, the transferor's gain would be more than the balance remaining of his or her lifetime allowance, then s. 58 applies subject to the modifications given in new subsection (5). In that situation, the disposal is treated as being for consideration which gives rise to a gain of an amount equal to the balance of the lifetime allowance.

Example 1: No lifetime limit remaining

Mrs A owns £75,000 worth of shares which cost £20,000 (and stand at a gain of £55,000). She has none of her £100,000 lifetime CGT exemption remaining. She transfers the shares to Mr A. Mrs A has neither a gain nor a loss. The deemed cost to Mr A for any future disposal is £20,000.

Example 2: Sufficient lifetime limit remaining to cover gain

Mrs B owns shares worth £75,000 which cost £5,000 (and stand at a gain of £70,000). She has previously used up £90,000 of her lifetime CGT exemption remaining. She transfers the shares to Mr B and has an exempt gain of £70,000 and £20,000 lifetime CGT exemption carried forward. The deemed cost to Mr B for any future disposal is the market value of £75,000.

Example 3: Insufficient lifetime limit remaining to cover gain

Ms C owns shares worth £75,000 which cost £5,000 (and stand at a gain of £70,000). She has only £20,000 of her lifetime CGT exemption remaining. She transfers the shares to her civil partner, Ms D. The consideration treated as received by Ms is fixed at £25,000, giving her an exempt gain of £20,000 and no lifetime CGT exemption carried forward. The deemed acquisition cost for Ms D for any future disposal is £25,000.

Disguised fees and carried interest

Finance Act 2016 also inserts subs. (2A) into TCGA 1992, s. 236B to ensure that a gain on disposal of shares is not exempt under the employee shareholder rules where the proceeds of the disposal constitute either a disguised investment management fee under ITA 2007, Pt. 13, Ch. 5E, or carried interest under ITA 2007, s. 809EZC. The new rules apply to relevant disposals of shares made on or after 6 April 2016.

Legislation: TCGA 1992, s. 58, 236B–236G

Tax Reporter: ¶565-050

5929B Employee ownership trusts

From 6 April 2014, disposals of shares to a trust with specified characteristics which benefits all employees of a company (or group) may be wholly relieved from capital gains tax if certain criteria are met. These are that:

- the trading requirement: the company whose shares are disposed of must be a trading company, or the parent company of a trading group;

- the all-employee benefit requirement: the trust which acquires the shares must operate for the benefit of all employees;

- the controlling interest requirement: the trust must have a controlling interest in the company at the end of the tax year, which it did not have at the start of that year;

- the limited participation requirement: certain participators must be excluded from being beneficiaries of the trust; and

- neither the claimant (nor anyone connected with him) has previously received relief on the same company's (or any group company's) shares.

The relief operates by disapplying TCGA 1992, s. 17(1); (market value disposals) and treats the disposal (and acquisition by the trustees) as for such consideration as to secure that neither a gain nor a loss accrues on the disposal. The relief is available on disposals which take place in a single tax year; disposals may be made by more than one person and can be of any number of shares. Where a disqualifying event (broadly, the relief requirements cease to be met) occurs in the following tax year, any relief given is withdrawn and where a disqualifying event occurs in any later tax year, this triggers a deemed disposal and reacquisition at market value by the trustees.

The relief may also be claimed against the deemed disposal charge arising under TCGA 1992, s. 71(1) (see 5575) by reason of the trustees of a settlement ('the acquiring settlement') becoming absolutely entitled to settled property as against the trustee of that settled property ('the transferring trustee'). Where the relief requirements are met and the transferring trustee makes a claim for relief (under TCGA 1992, s. 236Q), TCGA 1992, s. 17(1) (market value disposals) is disapplied and the TCGA 1992, s. 71(1) deemed disposals is treated as being made for such consideration as to secure that neither a gain nor a loss accures on the disposal. Relief is again withdrawn where a disqualifying event occurs in the following tax year.

Legislation: TCGA 1992, s. 236H–236U

Tax Reporter: ¶361-400ff.

Other share provisions

5930   Shares in close companies

A close company may be broadly described as one that is under the control of a small number of persons who can direct its affairs.

A chargeable gain of a company which is not a close company by virtue only of the fact that it is not resident in the UK may be apportioned to UK-resident shareholders (see 5698). The apportionment is based on the shareholder's interest as a participator in the company. Where a member has paid tax on an apportioned gain and within two years of the date the gain accrued to the company, the company distributes an amount in respect of that gain, the participator may offset the tax already paid against the tax liability on the distribution received. As a result, the existing provision allowing tax paid on an apportionment to be set against the CGT liability arising on the disposal of the shares causing the apportionment is revised.

See 5720 for details of attribution of capital gains of non-resident companies to UK-resident shareholders.

Legislation: TCGA 1992, s. 13, 124, 125; SI 2009/730

Tax Reporter: ¶592-900

5940   Distributions in a winding up

From April 2016, *Finance Act* 2016 introduces a targeted anti-avoidance rule which provides that certain distributions in a winding up are treated as distributions subject to income tax rather than capital gains tax if certain conditions are met (see 1352).

5950   Value shifting and shares

Provisions treat and tax as a disposal any transaction whereby control of a company is exercised so that value passes out of shares or rights owned by one person into other shares or rights in the same company.

The provisions also apply where value is shifted so as to set up an otherwise allowable loss.

Where value of an asset is materially reduced and matched by a tax-free benefit, the chargeable gain or allowable loss on disposal of the asset may be adjusted so far as just and reasonable. The charge is discussed elsewhere in greater detail to the extent that it specifically relates to companies (see 3525), although in so far as it does so the adjustment is expanded so as to relate also to relevant assets (see 5060).

Legislation: TCGA 1992, s. 29(1)–(3), 30

Tax Reporter: ¶524-600; ¶760-800ff.

Gains on futures, options and other derivatives

5980   CGT treatment of options

Though options are specifically included as assets (see 5008) so that any sale of an option would be potentially chargeable, the grant of an option is initially treated as a separate disposal (of the option even though the grantor may have divested himself of part of the equitable interest in the underlying asset) unless and until the option is exercised, when it is merged with the resulting sale or acquisition for both parties. Consequently, a charge may arise on the grant of an option even if the option is never exercised. Notwithstanding the merger of the transactions, where a company acquires an option binding the grantor to sell – a 'call option' – and subsequently exercises the option, indexation allowance applies to the amount paid for the option and the amount paid for the underlying asset from the dates those amounts are actually given.

On exercise, if the sole effect is monetary – a 'cash-settled option' – as well as a deemed disposal of an asset by the person receiving the payment, there is a deemed disposal of an asset by the payee and the payment is treated as if it were an incidental cost of that disposal, so that he obtains CGT relief for the payment.

Traded options are not subject to the write-down in allowable expenditure (see 5336) associated with other wasting assets. Where a taxpayer closes out a traded option by acquiring a matching option, the costs of obtaining the match are allowable in computing the gain on the disposal which arises when he granted the first option.

There are certain other rules relevant to option arrangements:

- replacement rollover relief may be available by reference to the underlying nature of the asset which is the subject of the option (see 6308);

- the amount chargeable on a company when it grants an option to an employee under a share scheme is limited to the sum paid by the individual;

- unlike other wasting assets (see 5336), there is no write-down in allowable expenditure on a quoted option to subscribe for shares; similarly there is no write down in respect of an option to acquire assets for use in a trade, except on transfer of an option over quoted shares;

- a quoted option to subscribe for shares which is dealt in within three months of a reorganisation, etc. is equated with the original shares in the same way as would be the underlying shares.

Legislation: TCGA 1992, s. 144, 144A, 146–148

Case: *Strange v Openshaw (HMIT)* [1983] BTC 209

Tax Reporter: ¶563-000ff.

5985 CGT treatment of commodity and financial futures

Transactions in commodity and financial futures and traded options on recognised exchanges are treated as capital in nature unless they are regarded as profits or losses of a trade. HMRC have given guidance on those transactions in futures and options which would be treated as trading transactions and those which would be treated as capital transactions giving rise to capital gains or losses.

Where a futures contract is not closed out so that a person makes a payment in settlement, as well as a deemed disposal of an asset by the person receiving the payment, there is a deemed disposal of an asset by the payee and the payment is treated as if it were an incidental cost of that disposal (so that he obtains CGT relief for the payment) but, unlike other wasting assets (see 5336), there is no write-down in allowable expenditure.

Legislation: TCGA 1992, s. 143

Other Material: SP 14/91, *Tax treatment of transactions in financial futures and options*

Tax Reporter: ¶508-500

5990 CGT treatment of derivatives other than options or futures

Apart from options and futures (see 5980 and 5985), there are few specific provisions dealing with derivatives, so that general principles apply.

Profits and losses on qualifying contracts are to be recognised for tax purposes as they accrue and taxed or relieved as income receipts or deductions. However, these rules apply in relation to various amounts of an income nature or treated as of an income nature; there are no specific rules to deal with any balance of gains within the chargeable gains net.

Case: *Whittles (HMIT) v Uniholdings Ltd (No. 3)* [1996] BTC 399

Tax Reporter: ¶720-200

Exemptions and reliefs

Types of exemption and relief from tax on capital gains

6140 Circumstances in which there is no charge to tax on gains

There are a number of circumstances in which general rules would result in a charge to tax in respect of a capital gain but there is a fiscal desire to reduce, postpone or eliminate the liability. Although there is no hard and fast rule, the term 'exemption' is generally given to rules taking a matter outside the charge to tax while the term 'relief' is generally given to something which postpones or reduces the charge to tax.

An exemption might work by treating a person or an asset as exempt from tax (see 5004 and 5009) or by deeming a gain not to be a 'chargeable gain' (see 5010).

A relief might treat a gain as being a chargeable gain only to an extent specified or in so far as it exceeds a certain level. Alternatively, it might deem a disposal to be at such amount as produces neither a gain nor a loss. Certain rules adopt a form of relief specific to taxes on chargeable gains (whether corporation tax or CGT): 'rollover reliefs' or 'holdover reliefs' provide a temporary (if sometimes lengthy) deferral (see 6144).

Tax Reporter: ¶535-000ff. and ¶540-000ff.

6144 Concept of rollover and holdover reliefs

The general scheme of rollover and holdover reliefs is to give a measure of relief from CGT on business assets in a variety of circumstances where its charge might otherwise be unfairly onerous. This is done by deferring the CGT payable until some subsequent disposal or event: a rollover defers tax until a subsequent disposal while a holdover generally has some time limitation (though the legislation often refers to gains being 'held-over' in either case). Some rollovers are given by deeming a disposal to take place at no gain/no loss for both transferor and transferee: this rolls over the gain to the transferee; some rollovers are given by reducing the disposal consideration so that there is no gain/no loss in the hands of the transferor, with the acquisition cost of a replacement asset being reduced by a corresponding amount – the transferee's acquisition cost is not amended; further rollovers deem there to have been no disposal and equate the replacement asset with the original asset.

Example

H Ltd enters into a transaction with J Ltd, disposing of an asset, for consideration of £40,000. H Ltd later acquires a replacement asset for £40,000. A rollover relief is available on H Ltd's indexed gain of £10,000. Depending upon the nature of the deferral in point, the disposal by H Ltd may be ignored and the replacement asset treated as if it had been the original asset. Alternatively, H Ltd may be treated as having made neither a gain nor a loss and the base value for capital gains purposes either of the replacement asset or of the original asset in the hands of J Ltd may be reduced by the amount of the indexed gain (i.e. £10,000); if, in either case, the asset is later sold for, say, £50,000, the gain would be calculated as follows:

	£	£
Sale proceeds		50,000
Acquisition cost	40,000	
Less: rollover relief	(10,000)	
Base cost as reduced	30,000	
Indexation allowance at, say, 38%		
38% × £30,000	11,400	
Indexed base cost		(41,400)
Indexed gain		8,600

(Note: indexation continues to apply as this is a disposal by a company.)

Tax Reporter: ¶570-200

6147   Incorporation using relief for gifts of business assets

Conditions to be met

As far as its application to business incorporation is concerned, the general scheme of TCGA 1992, s. 165 is uncomplicated. The first and overriding condition is that the relief applies to disposals 'otherwise than by way of bargains at arm's length'. Consequently, it applies both to outright gifts and sales which occur at a value less than market value. There are then three other types of condition for a claim to be made, which are:

(1)   the transfer must be made by an individual;

(2)   the transfer must be made to a person who is resident (and, for tax years prior to 2013–14, ordinarily resident) in the UK (unless the asset is chargeable to NRCGT in the hands of the transferee (see 5717 and 6325)); and

(3)   the assets transferred must be used in a trade, profession of vocation carried on by the transferor.

In the first condition, the term individual includes partners (other than corporate partners). In some circumstances, it also applies to trustees.

Except where there are restrictions because an asset has not always been used for trade purposes, if no payment is received for the disposal, the full amount of the gain may be held over that otherwise would have been chargeable. So, there is no chargeable gain at the time of the disposal, but the amount of the held over gain is deducted from the transferee company's base cost. The held over gain is therefore brought into the capital gains computation automatically on any subsequent disposal of the assets by the company.

Example

B, who is 45, has carried on a business trading in architectural reclamations for ten years. He wishes to transfer his business to a newly incorporated company, B Ltd. He has business assets, as follows:

	£
Freehold premises	470,000
Goodwill	200,000
Stocks	150,000
Debtors	90,000
Cash	25,000

B purchased the premises, when he set up the business, for £85,000. B is making a gift of his business assets to B Ltd.

	£	£
Disposal consideration – premises (market value)	470,000	
Less: cost	85,000	
Gain	385,000	
Disposal consideration – goodwill (market value)	200,000	
Less: cost	0	
Gain	200,000	
Total gains on transfer to company		585,000

Because B received no payment from B Ltd, he is entitled to claim holdover relief for the full amount of the gains. When B Ltd sells the assets, its allowable expenditure is the amount it is deemed to have given for the assets (market value at the date of transfer) less the amount of the held over gain.

If the transferor does receive payment, but it does not exceed his or her allowable expenditure for capital gains tax purposes, the treatment for hold over relief is the same as though he or she received no payment at all. If, however, the transferor receives a payment that exceeds that allowable expenditure, there is a restriction on the amount of the gain that may be held over. The amount of the gain which may be held over is reduced by the amount by which the payment received exceeds the allowable expenditure.

Emigration of the donee

One of the conditions that must be satisfied for holdover relief to apply is that the donee must be UK resident. Should the transferee company become non-UK resident while still holding the assets gifted to it, the legislation, under the general rules, imposes a deemed disposal of all assets except any assets situated in the UK and used for the purposes of a UK permanent establishment or that remain chargeable under NRCGT rules. The deemed disposal takes effect immediately before the company moves its tax residence to the UK.

Making the choice: incorporation relief (see 6302) or gift of business assets relief

Which of the two methods is preferable depends entirely on the circumstances of the case but, on balance, the gifts of business assets route is probably used more widely. Its relative popularity is due principally to the perceived defect in s. 162 that all assets (other than cash) have to be transferred to the company. This can involve considerable amounts of stamp duty and tax being payable where the business assets include a substantial property.

However, the stamp duty land tax problem is at least a 'one-off' at the time of the transfer. A much more significant problem arises, using

s. 162, where the business is of a type that requires large premises that appreciate in value. In so far as it is commercially possible, it is good tax planning to keep such assets outside a company, to avoid the owner being exposed to a potential double capital gains charge (once when the company sells the premises) and again, indirectly, when the owner sells his or her shares in the company. Using the gifts of business assets rules selectively enables the business owner to keep such assets outside the company.

Additionally, the amendments by *Finance Act* 2015 that deny entrepreneurs' relief in respect of certain gains arising on goodwill will also reduce the appeal of incorporation using gift relief (see 5294).

Legislation: TCGA 1992, s. 165

Tax Reporter: ¶574-400ff.

Annual exemption and miscellaneous exempt assets

6150 Annual exemption

An individual is not liable to CGT if his taxable amount (i.e. net gains) for any tax year does not exceed 'the exempt amount' for the year (unless that individual has claimed the benefit of the remittance basis of taxation for any tax year from 2008–09 onwards). The exempt amount is linked to the Retail Prices Index (RPI), unless Parliament determines otherwise the 'exempt amount' is £11,100 for 2016–17 and 2015–16. For a table of figures for earlier years, see Key Data.

Allowable losses carried forward or back which are available to be set off against chargeable gains need only be used to reduce the gains for the tax year to the exempt amount for that year. This leaves more losses to be carried forward to subsequent years.

Husband and wife, and civil partners, are each entitled to a separate annual exemption (see 5460). For the annual exempt amount for trustees and personal representatives, see 5415, 5595 and 5697.

The annual exemption may be set against both gains chargeable to CGT by virtue of TCGA 1992, s. 2 and also NRCGT gains chargeable to CGT by virtue of s. 14D (see 5717) (TCGA 1992, s. 3(5)).

Legislation: TCGA 1992, s. 3

Tax Reporter: ¶535-100

6152 Annual exemption and taper relief

The annual exemption is set against net gains (tapered for disposals made before 6 April 2008; see 5268). Losses brought forward from an earlier year, or carried back from the year in which a person dies, need only be used to the extent to which it is necessary to reduce the net gains to the level of the annual exemption.

Tax Reporter: ¶535-100

6155 Chattels sold for £6,000 or less

An asset which is tangible moveable property (e.g. a painting, carpet, piece of furniture or jewellery) may, subject to limited exclusions, be disposed of without liability to CGT so long as the consideration for the disposal is not more than £6,000.

If the consideration is greater than £6,000, the chargeable gain is either five-thirds of the difference between £6,000 and the value of the consideration, or the actual gain, whichever is the lesser amount.

Losses

Relief for losses is available in full except that if the consideration for the disposal is less than £6,000, the consideration is deemed to be £6,000 and allowable losses are restricted in this way.

> **Example**
>
> Freddy sells a painting for £5,900. Allowable expenditure is £6,500. Ordinarily, his allowable loss would be £600 but this is restricted to £500 (£6,500 − £6,000).

> **Example**
>
> If Freddy had sold the painting for £9,000, with allowable expenditure of £2,000, the chargeable gain would have been the lesser of:
>
> (a) $5/3 \times (£9,000 − £6,000) = £5,000$, and
>
> (b) the actual gain $(£9,000 − £2,000) = £7,000$
>
> So Freddy's chargeable gain would have been £5,000, before considering the annual exemption.

Sets of articles

There are provisions to prevent avoidance of CGT by breaking up a set of articles (e.g. a set of antique chairs, an issue of postage stamps, a canteen of cutlery or a set of books) and selling the individual items by separate transactions, in order to take advantage of the relief for chattels.

Where:

- two or more assets which have formed part of a set of articles owned by the same person are disposed of by two or more transactions, which may take place at the same or different times; and

- the disposals are to the same person, or to persons acting together 'in concert', or to persons who are 'connected persons': see 5142,

then the transactions are treated as a single disposal of one asset.

Example

Janice buys a matched pair of antique duelling pistols for £5,400. She sells one to Emma in March 2007. In May 2015, Janice sells the other to Emma. On both occasions Emma pays Janice £3,500. Janice is treated as having made one disposal for £7,000 and hence not within the chattel exemption, although five-thirds of the difference between £6,000 and the value of the consideration may be substituted, if less than the actual gain.

In many cases, these special provisions will be subject also to the general anti-avoidance computational rules relating to series of transactions (see 5133). Thus, in the above example, the gain on each occasion would most likely be calculated on one-half the market value of *two pistols* – probably a much greater sum than £7,000.

Part disposals

If a person disposes of a right or interest in a chattel, for the purposes of the chattels' exemption, the consideration for the part disposed of is, in the first instance, regarded as being the aggregate of:

- the actual consideration received for the part disposed of; and

- the market value of the part retained.

If this total exceeds £6,000 then the *limit* of consideration liable to CGT is calculated by applying the following formula:

$$((A + B) - £6,000) \times \frac{A}{A + B} \times \frac{5}{3}$$

A   is the consideration received for the part disposal; and
B   is the market value of the part retained by the disponor.

Capital gains tax

In the case of a loss, where the aggregate of:

(1) consideration for the part disposed; and

(2) market value of the part retained,

is less than £6,000, then any loss is restricted by deeming the consideration to be the amount arrived at by applying the following formula:

$$A + \frac{(£6,000 - (A + B)) \times A}{A + B}$$

A   is the consideration received for the part disposal; and

B   is the market value of the part retained by the disponor.

Example

Julia buys an article for £6,800. She sells an interest in it for £2,400. The value of the share retained is £2,600. Julia is deemed to have received an amount calculated as follows:

$$£2,400 + \frac{(£6,000 - (£2,400 + £2,600)) \times £2,400}{£2,400 + £2,600} = £2,880$$

The loss is therefore limited to:

	£
Deemed disposal proceeds	2,880
Cost: $\dfrac{2,400}{£2,400 + £2,600} \times £6,800 =$	(3,264)
Allowable loss	(384)

Special rules apply to small part disposals of land (see 5229).

Currency disposals and dealings in commodities

The chattel exemption does not apply to the disposal of currency (note: currency in sterling is not a chargeable asset) or to a disposal of commodities on a terminal market.

Legislation: TCGA 1992, s. 262

Tax Reporter: ¶509-050; ¶509-100

6162   Winnings and damages

Winnings from betting, including pool betting, or lotteries or games with prizes, are not chargeable gains and, therefore, not liable to CGT. No chargeable gain or allowable loss can accrue on the disposal of rights to such winnings.

There is also no chargeable gain on the receipt of damages or compensation for personal injury, or a wrong suffered personally or in the person's profession or vocation. The exemption is limited to damages for these purposes only; compensation received for damage to property (real or intangible, including the loss of contractual rights derived from assets) is capable of being a chargeable gain (see 5080ff.).

Legislation: TCGA 1992, s. 51(1)

Tax Reporter: ¶535-700

6169   Mortgages and charges for capital gains

The conveyance or transfer by way of security of an asset (or an interest in it or right over it) does not involve any acquisition or disposal for CGT purposes; if the person entitled to the benefit of the charge enforces the security he is treated as doing so as nominee for the person entitled to the asset (subject to the security) (see 5060).

Tax Reporter: ¶511-500

6170   Gains from life assurance and other insurance policies

The rights of an insurer under an insurance policy (other than a life assurance policy) do not constitute a chargeable asset; however, the rights of the insured do constitute a chargeable asset to the extent that those rights relate to assets on the disposal of which a gain may accrue (see 5080ff.).

Example

Duncan takes out a policy of insurance on a house against fire damage. The property suffers severe fire damage and the insurance company agrees to pay £75,000 under the policy. Duncan assigns his rights to receive the money to Claire. The money is paid to Claire. Duncan is regarded as having made a part-disposal of a chargeable asset (see 5229).

There is normally no chargeable gain (and, therefore, no liability to CGT) where a person disposes of an interest in, or rights under, a life assurance policy or a deferred annuity contract; however, there may be a liability to CGT where the disponor is not the original beneficial owner and he acquired the rights or interest for a consideration in money or money's worth. Rights under a policy or contract are regarded as disposed of if the policy is held to maturity (or in the case of a deferred annuity payment of the first instalment) or surrendered.

The transfer of investments direct to the policyholder is a disposal which is, in the case of a non-life policy, automatically at market value.

Sums received for loss or depreciation of assets are derived from the assets (see 5080).

For annuities other than deferred annuities and for amounts paid out of superannuation funds or schemes, see 6186.

Legislation: TCGA 1992, s. 204, 210

Tax Reporter: ¶514-750

6175 Passenger vehicles are not chargeable assets

Motor cars and other road vehicles are not chargeable assets if the vehicle is constructed or adapted for the carriage of passengers and is of a type commonly used as a private vehicle. This provision is largely designed to prevent claims for losses on motor cars.

Other motor vehicles which do not meet the dual tests of being both passenger vehicles and commonly used as private vehicles may still be exempt as 'wasting assets' which are also chattels, provided the assets do not qualify for capital allowances. HMRC accept that the following vehicles may qualify for exemption as wasting assets:

- taxi cabs;
- racing cars and single seat sports cars;
- commercial vehicles (vans lorries, etc.);
- motor cycles and scooters; and
- railway locomotives, tramway and traction engines.

Legislation: TCGA 1992, s. 263

Tax Reporter: ¶535-350

6178 Gains exempt if decorations for valour

No chargeable gain arises on the disposal of a decoration awarded for gallantry unless it was acquired for money or money's worth.

Legislation: TCGA 1992, s. 268

Tax Reporter: ¶535-400

6180 Gains on foreign currency for personal expenditure

No chargeable gain (or allowable loss) arises on the disposal of currency acquired by an individual for the personal expenditure outside the UK of himself or his family or dependents. This includes expenditure on providing or maintaining a residence outside the UK.

For foreign currency bank accounts, see 6183.

Legislation: TCGA 1992, s. 269

Tax Reporter: ¶535-450

6183 Debts and tax on capital gains

The basic rule is that a person who is owed money 'disposes' of an asset (the debt) whenever repayment or satisfaction of the debt is made, or when he assigns, etc. the debt to a third party. However, no chargeable gain or allowable loss accrues to the disponor (or his personal representative or legatee: see 5690) if the disponor was the original creditor.

> **Example**
>
> Edward makes an unsecured loan of £8,000 to his sister and later accepts £6,000 in full satisfaction. As Edward is the original creditor, no allowable loss arises.

The above rule does not apply to foreign currency bank accounts which do not represent amounts for personal expenditure (see also 6180) or to a 'debt on a security'. There is no definition of a 'debt on a security' only of 'security' which for this purpose which means any loan stock or similar security of any government or any public or local authority or of any company, whether secured or unsecured. The courts have held that the fact that a debt is evidenced by some form of certificate, note, or similar document is insufficient of itself to make a loan a 'debt on a security'. The essential feature of such an asset has been held to be its genuine transferability and marketability. The case of *W T Ramsay Ltd v IR Commrs* contains a useful summary of the position, which was relied on in a special commissioners decision. In another decision, the fact that an intra-group loan, evidenced by a promissory note, had no fixed term and was repayable on demand led to the conclusion that it lacked the permanence to be truly marketable and was thus not a debt on a security.

Capital gains tax

There are various events which are treated as disposals of debts and which determine the extent of the gain or loss. These do not apply to debts which are debts on a security (Revenue correspondence with the Law Society's Revenue Law Committee). In other words, if there has been an intra-group transfer of a debt on a security (which is not a QCB), a loss realised on a disposal by a group transferee is capable of being an allowable loss.

In the case of debts which are settled property, a person becoming absolutely entitled as against the trustee is treated as the original creditor.

Legislation: TCGA 1992, s. 132(3)(b), 251(1)–(5), 252

Cases: *WT Ramsay Ltd v IR Commrs* [1982] AC 300; *Tarmac Roadstone Holdings Ltd v Williams (HMIT)* (1996) Sp C 95; *Taylor Clark International Ltd v Lewis (HMIT)* [1998] BTC 466; *Cann v Woods (HMIT)* (1999) Sp C 183

Tax Reporter: ¶510-900; ¶511-500; ¶535-470

6184 Loans for trade purposes

Relief for losses is available in respect of certain loans to traders. Relief is available for 'a qualifying loan', i.e. a loan in the case of which:

- the money lent is used by the borrower wholly for the purposes of a trade, profession or vocation (or for setting up such a trade, etc.) carried on by him (but which does not include the lending of money);

- the borrower is 'resident in the UK' (see 224); and

- the debt is not a debt on a security (a loss on which may be allowable under general rules: see 6183).

The lender may make a claim for an allowable loss where any part of the loan becomes irrecoverable and relief is otherwise unavailable. A special commissioner has held that loans made by a taxpayer to a company which he controlled became irrecoverable when he sold its subsidiary, which he had for some years been supporting by making loans to keep it trading. The taxpayer could not have been expected to continue to support the company indefinitely. By the time of the sale, the company was insolvent. Unless the taxpayer provided further money, it would have had to cease trading.

The loss arises when the claim is made, though the claim may specify an earlier time, which must be:

(1) no more than two years before the beginning of the tax year in which the claim is made; or

(2) (for corporation tax purposes) on or after the first day of the earliest accounting period ending not more than two years before the time of the claim.

Relief is also available to a person who has given a guarantee in respect of a qualifying loan which has become irrecoverable from the borrower, under similar conditions. In neither case must the borrower and lender be spouses, or companies in the same 'group' (see 3625). It has been held that a payment made by a guarantor could only be relieved to the extent that it was not recoverable from co-guarantors. The time-limit for claims is four years after the end of the year of assessment in which the payment was made or, for corporation tax purposes, within four years after the end of the accounting period in which the payment was made.

Where loss relief has been granted under these provisions, there will be a clawback if there is a subsequent recovery of principal or interest by the lender or guarantor, who will be treated as making a chargeable gain, equal to the amount recovered, at the time of recovery.

Legislation: TCGA 1992, s. 253

Case: *Leisureking Ltd v Cushing (HMIT)* [1993] BTC 22

Tax Reporter: ¶511-150ff.

6186 Gains on disposal of annuities, annual payments

No chargeable gain arises on the disposal of a right to:

- any allowance, annuity or capital sum paid under a superannuation scheme established solely or mainly for persons (and their dependents) employed in a trade, profession, undertaking or employment;

- unsecured annual payments due under a covenant.

For deferred annuities under life contracts, see 6170.

Legislation: TCGA 1992, s. 237

Tax Reporter: ¶535-300

6189 Gifts exempt from tax on capital gains

Gifts to charities, etc.

Gifts or disposals where the consideration does not exceed the acquisition cost and other allowable expenditure of the person making the disposal are exempt from CGT if the disposal is to a charity or for national purposes, i.e. to one of the bodies or institutions set out in IHTA 1984, Sch. 3 (see 7198) (e.g. the National Gallery, the British Museum, museums or galleries maintained by local authorities or universities, health service bodies, etc.). The exemption in relation to a gift to a charity does not apply if the disposal is one of shares previously held in a venture capital trust.

Gifts of national heritage property

Gifts of property (including works of art, scientific collections, etc. of national, scientific, historic or artistic interest) are exempt from CGT if also exempt from inheritance tax (see 7346ff.).

Gifts to housing associations

Where there is a disposal of an estate or interest in land in the UK otherwise than by arm's length bargain to a registered housing association, the transferor and the association may make a claim, of which the effect is to displace the normal rule where the consideration is deemed to be market value where the transaction is not at arm's length (see 5100). If the disposal is by way of gift or for a consideration not exceeding allowable deductions, the disposal is treated as a no loss/no gain disposal and the association's base cost is treated as being the same as the transferor's base cost, i.e. the transferor's gain is held over.

There are also certain exemptions in respect of the transfer of assets between the Housing Corporation, Housing for Wales or Scottish Homes and housing associations or between housing associations (including those in Northern Ireland).

Legislation: TCGA 1992, s. 218–220, 257–259

Tax Reporter: ¶535-600ff

6197 Capital gains: employee trusts

Disposals by close companies or individuals to trustees of employee trusts which are not liable to inheritance tax are exempt from CGT. For the meaning of 'employee trust', see 7159.

A Revenue concession (now enacted, for disposals on or after 6 April 2009) removes a CGT charge on the trustees of employee trusts where the employee is liable to income tax on the full market value of assets transferred to the trustees; it effectively displaces the normal market value rule (see 5100).

Legislation: TCGA 1992, s. 239, 239ZA (formerly ESC D35)

Tax Reporter: ¶361-200

Private residence relief

6220   Relief from CGT for private residences

The general rule is that a gain made on the disposal by an individual of the whole or part of a dwelling-house (or an interest in a dwelling-house) which is his only or main residence is not liable to CGT, or if liable not wholly liable (see 6244).

A 'dwelling-house' has been held to include a caravan raised up on bricks. However, a mobile caravan not connected to an electricity or a water supply has been held not to be included.

A 'dwelling-house' will not be a 'residence' in the context of this relief if the claimant cannot show that the occupation of the property has some degree of actual permanence and continuity, or some expectation of such continuity and as such is not merely a temporary accommodation.

Legislation: TCGA 1992, s. 222(1)(a), 223(1)

Cases: *Makins v Elson (HMIT)* (1976) 51 TC 437; *Moore v Thompson (HMIT)* [1986] BTC 172; *Goodwin v Curtis (HMIT)* [1998] BTC 176; *Dutton-Forshaw* [2015] TC 04644; *Harrison* [2015] TC 04693; *Kothari* [2016] TC 04915

Tax Reporter: ¶540-000ff.

6222   Garden or grounds

The garden or grounds of the dwelling-house up to half a hectare, inclusive of the site of the house – or such larger area as is required for the reasonable enjoyment of the house as a residence – may also be sold without liability to CGT if sold with the dwelling-house or at a time when the house is the main residence of the person making the disposal. This has been held not to apply to the sale of the garden of a house after the house itself had been sold. HMRC have confirmed that where a dwelling-house and garden are sold together, but after the taxpayer has ceased to occupy the property, they do not seek to charge the sale of the garden to CGT.

In one case, a special commissioner decided that a taxpayer was entitled to private residence relief on the sale of two building plots which comprised a field which she had, until the time of disposal, enjoyed with her residence. It did not matter that the field did not adjoin the residence. In the light of this decision, HMRC have set out their interpretation of the garden or grounds provisions. The relevant extract is reproduced below:

'HMRC do not accept that land is garden or grounds merely if it is in the same ownership as the residence and is used as a garden. However, land which can be shown objectively, on the facts, to be naturally and traditionally the garden of the residence, so that it would normally be offered to a prospective purchaser as part of the residence, will be accepted. An example of this is where, as in some villages, it is common for a garden to be across the street from the residence. The separation itself would not be regarded as a reason for denying relief.

It must be stressed that these cases will be rare and if land is separated from the residence by other land which is not in the same ownership as the residence, it will usually not be part of the garden or grounds. For example, land bought some distance from the residence due to an inadequate garden at the residence and which is cultivated and regarded as part of the garden will not qualify for relief.'

In *Fountain* [2015] TC 04596, Mr and Mrs Fountain divided an area of land behind their home into five building plots. Two of the plots were sold together with a field and one plot was gifted to their son. Mr and Mrs Fountain built a new home on one of the plots and moved into this. The former residence was sold together with a field and then the final plot (Plot 2) was also sold. The First-tier Tribunal ruled that Plot 2 did not qualify for private residence relief because although it formed part of the grounds of Mr and Mrs Fountain's original home, the question to be considered following *Varty v Lyne*, was whether, at the time it was sold, it formed part of the garden or grounds of the new residence? The FTT concluded that relief was not available because at the time of sale the plot had been levelled, was uncultivated and physically separated from the taxpayers'; residence and fenced off from other plots.

Legislation: TCGA 1992, s. 222(1)(b), (2)–(4)

Cases: *Varty (HMIT) v Lynes* (1976) 51 TC 419; *Wakeling v Pearce* (1995) Sp C 32; *Fountain* [2015] TC 04596

Other Material: *Tax Bulletin* Issue 18

Tax Reporter: ¶545-600

6224 More than one building

It is clear from the authorities that where there is more than one building in the same grounds, CGT private residence relief (see 6220) may extend to more than one of them. Buildings which form part of the dwelling-house are clearly eligible for relief (these may include garages and fuel stores); buildings which are ancillary to the garden or grounds (such as greenhouses, gazebos and sheds) only qualify for relief if they fall within the permitted area; other buildings do not qualify for relief.

A 'dwelling-house' can comprise several dwellings not physically joined: e.g. a separate garage, a studio, or a self-contained staff flat.

The following two conditions if satisfied are indicative that the buildings constitute a single dwelling-house:

- the occupation of the building in dispute must increase the taxpayer's enjoyment of the main house; and

- the disputed building must be very closely adjacent to the main house. In determining that, the scale of the buildings as a group must be considered.

The proximity test

However, whilst proximity or otherwise of the building is an important factor, it is insufficient in itself to conclude that two buildings constitute separate dwellings. It is important that all of the facts are considered.

The courts have also applied the test of whether a subsidiary dwelling-house was appurtenant to and within the curtilage of the main house (the 'proximity test'). This approach also avoided the difficulty that a second dwelling-house, used for the enjoyment of the main house, might otherwise qualify for relief even if it were outside the 'permitted area' of garden and grounds.

HMRC have indicated that they would draw a distinction between the curtilage of a main house and the curtilage of an estate as a whole, and that the fact that a whole estate may be contained within a single boundary does not mean that buildings on the estate should be regarded as being within the curtilage of the main house.

Cases: *Batey (HMIT) v Wakefield* (1981) 55 TC 550; *Markey (HMIT) v Sanders* [1987] BTC 176; *Williams (HMIT) v Merrylees* [1987] BTC 393; *Lewis (HMIT) v Lady Rook* [1992] BTC 102; *Honour (HMIT) v Norris* [1992] BTC 153

Tax Reporter: ¶545-300ff.

6226   Joint owner occupiers

Joint owner occupiers who are not husband and wife, or civil partners, may benefit from full CGT private residence relief (see 6220) if they have unrestricted access to the whole property, even though some areas are not actually used by both. Where such owners do not have access to the whole property, they may be able to exchange their interests so as to acquire sole ownership without tax penalty, providing relief similar to compulsory purchase (see 6300 [AF1]).

Capital gains tax

Legislation: TCGA 1992, s. 248A

Tax Reporter: ¶546-050

6228 Purchase for gain

Private residence relief (see 6220) is unavailable where the residence was acquired in whole or in part to make a gain on its disposal, even if the taxpayer lives in the house for a time before he sells it.

Legislation: TCGA 1992, s. 224(3)

Tax Reporter: ¶546-700

6230 More than one residence

When a taxpayer has more than one residence, he may elect by notice in writing to treat one or other residence as his main residence for CGT purposes. The election has to be made within two years of the time that the taxpayer first has an interest in two or more residences. An election may be varied subsequently, but not so as to take effect earlier than two years before the notice of variation.

This time limit may be extended where a taxpayer was unaware of the need to nominate a main residence but where his interest in each of them (or each of them except one) has no more than a negligible capital value, e.g. a short-term rented flat.

A non-UK resident person (subject to a charge to capital gains tax on a disposal of UK residential property from 6 April 2015) may also determine which of two or more residences their main residence is for any period at the time of disposal and any such determination may vary any notice already given in respect of another property (provided the individual has not already disposed of the other property) (TCGA 1992, s. 222A).

Legislation: TCGA 1992, s. 222(5), 222A

Case: *Griffin (HMIT) v Craig-Harvey* [1994] BTC 3

Other Material: ESC D21, *Private residence exemption: late claims in dual residence cases*

Tax Reporter: ¶545-950

6233 Private residence relief and spouses

In the case of a married couple, or civil partners, 'living together' (see 5490), there can be only one sole or main residence for the purposes of the CGT private residence exemption (see 6220) and, where an election is made as to which house this applies to (see 6230), such election must generally be made jointly.

If the conditions in relation to absence are satisfied by an individual so that the absence is treated as a period of residence (see 6247), they are treated as satisfied also in relation to that individual's spouse provided they are living together.

HMRC's *Capital Gains Manual* refers to the various possibilities as regards elections by a newly-married couple, which depend upon the two individuals' previous ownership of property.

A spouse, or civil partner, who inherits a dwelling-house from the other spouse, or civil partner, also inherits the latter's period of ownership for private residence relief purposes. (This is not overridden by the rule that a legatee acquires an inherited asset for CGT purposes on the date of death: see 5690.) The result of this is that periods of ownership, before the death of the first spouse or civil partner, to die, also fall to be taken into account in determining qualifying 'periods of residence' (see 6244).

Legislation: TCGA 1992, s. 222(6), (7)(a), 223(3)

Other Material: HMRC *Capital Gains Manual*

Tax Reporter: ¶546-000

6235 Private residence relief: trustees and personal representatives

The CGT private residence exemption (see 6220) applies to trustees where, during the period of ownership of the trustee, the house has been the only or main residence of a person entitled to occupy it under the terms of a settlement ('B').

The criteria for the relief to be available as set out in TCGA 1992, s. 222–224 in relation to the occupation of the dwelling house, residence in a territory, or meeting the day count test must be satisfied by B.

Example

A dwelling-house is vested in trustees on trust for sale and to pay the income of property, until sale, to Frank, with a power to let Frank into occupation pending a sale. Frank is let into occupation until sale. The house is treated as Frank's principal private residence and is not liable to CGT.

A 'person entitled' may include a discretionary beneficiary.

This relief is extended to personal representatives where the dwelling house disposed of has been the only or main residence, both before and immediately after the deceased's death, of individual(s) who under the will or on intestacy are entitled to 75% or more of the net proceeds of disposal (either absolutely or via an interest in possession) ('the qualifying individual(s)'). Again, the criteria set out in TCGA 1992, s. 222–224 in relation to the occupation of the dwelling house, residence in a territory, or meeting the day count test must be satisfied by the qualifying individual(s).

In making an election to determine which residence is the main residence of a person (see 6230), such notice of election must be given jointly by the trustees or personal representatives and the person entitled to occupy the house.

Private residence relief is denied where the residence was acquired under a hold-over election on certain disposals to trusts under TGCA 1992, s. 260 (TCGA 1992, s. 226A and 226B). Relief is denied where the subsequent disposal of the residence takes place on or after 10 December 2003. Transitional relief is available where the hold-over disposal was before 10 December 2003 whereby any gain is time apportioned and only the gain proportionate to ownership prior to 10 December 2003 is eligible for private residence relief. There is an exception for maintenance funds for historic buildings (TCGA 1992, s. 226B).

Legislation: TCGA 1992, s. 225, 225A; FA 2004, s. 117–226B

Case: *Sansom v Peay (HMIT)* (1976) 52 TC 1

Tax Reporter: ¶546-750; ¶546-900; ¶546-975

6238   Private residence relief and dependent relatives

Relief in respect of a residence occupied rent-free by a dependent relative was available for disposals up to 5 April 1988, subject to transitional provisions which preserve the relief where the relative was occupying the property on 5 April 1988, until such time as he ceases to reside there.

A 'dependent relative' is:

- any relative of a taxpayer or of his or her spouse who is incapacitated by old age or infirmity from maintaining him or herself; or

- the mother of a husband or wife who is either widowed or living apart from her husband, or is a single woman because of the dissolution or annulment of marriage.

By concession, the conditions that the occupation be 'rent-free' were satisfied even where the dependent relative paid all or part of the owner's council tax and the cost of repairs to the home attributable to normal wear and tear; further, the relief was not lost where the relative made other payments in respect of the property, provided no net income was receivable by the individual taking one year with another. If the dependent relative paid the mortgage, the dwelling ceased to qualify.

Legislation: TCGA 1992, s. 226(6), (7)

Other Material: ESC D20, *Private residence exemption: residence occupied by dependent relative*

Tax Reporter: ¶546-800

6241   Job-related accommodation and private residence relief

For private residence relief (see 6220), a house is treated as occupied by an individual as his residence where during his ownership of the house, he resides in other accommodation which is 'job-related' and he intends in due course to occupy the house as his only or main residence.

The relief extends to self-employed people under a contractual requirement to live in accommodation provided as part of the terms of their trade, profession or vocation but who are buying a home of their own.

Legislation: TCGA 1992, s. 222(8), (9)

Tax Reporter: ¶546-100

6244   Extent of exemption under private residence relief

To obtain complete exemption from CGT under the private residence provisions (see 6220), the house must have been the individual's only or main residence throughout the period of ownership, except for the whole or any part of the last 18 months of ownership.

The final period exemption was reduced from 36 months to 18 months with effect for disposals made on or after 6 April 2014 with an exception for individuals who are disabled or in a care home and with no other property who continue to be entitled to a 36-month final period exemption.

'Period of ownership' is determined by reference to the first interest obtained in the property and may include that of a spouse but does not include any period before 31 March 1982 (TCGA 1992, s. 223(7)(a)).

In determining the amount of relief attributable to NRCGT gains on disposals on or after 6 April 2015, 'period of ownership' excludes periods prior to 6 April 2015 unless an election has been made for the NRCGT gain to be calculated using the retrospective basis of computation (see 5717) (TCGA 1992, s. 223(7)(b) and (7A)).

By concession, where there is a short delay in taking up residence, the period before taking up residence will be treated as a period of occupation for the purposes of the relief in the following circumstances:

- where an individual acquires land on which a house is built which is then used as the only or main residence; or

- where an existing property is purchased but before using it as the only or main residence, the individual arranges for alterations or redecorations or completes the necessary steps for disposing of the previous residence.

The concession applies to a period of up to one year unless there are good reasons outside the individual's control in which case the period may be extended up to a maximum of two years.

Where the house has not been the only or main residence throughout the period of ownership (exclusive of the last 18 or 36 months), only a fraction of the gain is not liable to CGT. That fraction is:

$$\frac{A + B}{C}$$

A   is the period after 31 March 1982 during which the house was the individual's only or main residence (but not including the last 18 or 36 months (as applicable) of the period of ownership);

B   is the last 18 or 36 months of ownership (plus up to 24 months initial period); and

C   is the total period of ownership after 31 March 1982.

Example

Jack buys a house on 1 June 2005 for use as his only residence. He lives in the house for seven years and six months (90 months) before moving out and immediately occupying a nearby flat which he also owns. He elects for the flat to be his only or main residence from 1 December 2012 (date of initial occupancy). Jack does not return to live in the house and it remains empty until he sells it on 31 May 2016, making a gain of £82,500. The chargeable gain covering Jack's 11 years (132 months) of ownership is calculated as follows:

	£
Indexed gain	82,500

Private residence exemption

Using $\dfrac{A + B}{C}$ formula above

A = 90 months	
B = 18 months	
C = 132 months (11 × 12)	
$\dfrac{90 + 18}{132}$ × £82,500 =	(67,500)
Chargeable gain	15,000

The gain is also apportioned where part of the dwelling-house is used exclusively for the purposes of a trade, business, profession or vocation and the consideration may be apportioned where otherwise necessary. HMRC no longer apply the rule-of-thumb that one-third of a farmhouse is used for business purposes – each case must be considered on its particular circumstances.

Relief may be adjusted where there is a change in the extent to which a property is used as an individual's residence, etc. There are also provisions relating to periods of absence which may be treated as periods in which the property was used as the individual's only or main residence (see 6247).

Legislation: TCGA 1992, s. 222(7), (10), 223(1), (2), (5)–(7), 224(1), (2), 225E

Other Material: ESC D49, *Private residence relief: short delay by owner-occupier in taking up residence*

Tax Reporter: ¶546-450; ¶546-650

6245 Private residence relief: non-qualifying tax years

For disposals on or after 6 April 2015, a residence will be treated as not being occupied as a residence for a tax year (the 'deeming' rule) when it is located in a territory in which neither the person making the disposal nor their spouse or civil partner is tax resident and they (either the person making the disposal or their spouse) are not present in it for at least 90 midnights during the year (the '90-day' rule). Where the property is owned for part of a year, the 90-day rule is reduced by a proportionate amount. Where more than one residence is owned in the same territory during the year, the 90-day rule applies across the properties (TCGA 1992, s. 222B–222C).

Except where the disposal is an NRCGT disposal (see 5717), this restriction only applies for tax years 2015–16 onwards (TCGA 1992, s. 222B(2)).

This day count test does not prevent absence reliefs (see 6241 and 6247) applying in respect of a non-qualifying year (TCGA 1992, s. 222B(11)).

Legislation: TCGA 1992, s. 222B

Tax Reporter: ¶545-925

6247 Private residence relief: periods of absence

Although the extent of exemption in respect of a private residence (see 6220 and 6245) is determined by reference to that part of the period of ownership in which it is used as the only or main residence (see 6244), in some cases a period of absence from the dwelling house is, nevertheless, treated as a period during which the house was occupied by the individual as a residence. These comprise:

(1) any periods of absence for any reason totalling up to three years;

(2) employment wholly abroad; and

(3) employment (or self-employment) elsewhere up to four years (including where an employer reasonably requires the individual live elsewhere).

There is a requirement that the property must have been occupied as the individual's residence before the period of absence (condition A) and after the period of absence (condition B), however, the requirement that the individual must resume occupation of the house as his principal residence in order for a period of absence to be treated as one of residence (condition B), is waived in respect of periods of absence falling within (2) or (3) above, where the individual is prevented from resuming residence in the house because of the situation of his or her work, or because of a condition imposed by his employer requiring him to live elsewhere for the effective performance of his duties. The requirement is also waived (in respect of absences within (2) or (3)) where the individual is prevented from resuming residence because of the workplace or employment conditions of a spouse or civil partner.

In determining whether condition A is satisfied in respect of NRCGT disposals (on or after 6 April 2015 (see 5717) and whose period of ownership is treated as beginning on that date (see 6244), periods prior to 6 April 2015 are ignored unless the person elects and specifies the date as to when, prior to 6 April 2015, the property was the person's only or main residence for the purpose of meeting condition A. Where such an election is made, relief is calculated as if the period of ownership included the period beginning with the day specified in the election and ending with 5 April 2015 (the bridge period) and any period of absence within that period count towards the maximum periods or maximum aggregate periods as specified above (TCGA 1992, s. 223A).

If the conditions are satisfied by an individual, they are treated as satisfied also in relation to that individual's spouse provided they are living together (see 6233). An individual may have a qualifying period of absence under more than one head and these may be added together.

Legislation: TCGA 1992, s. 223(3), (3A), (3B), 233A

Tax Reporter: ¶546-200ff.

6250   Lettings relief: private residence relief

Individuals can let all or part of their homes to residential tenants without losing all of the principal private residence exemption (see 6220). The dwelling-house house (or part of it) must have been the individual's only or main residence for some part, at least, of his ownership period.

Where a gain accrues on disposing of a dwelling-house which (or part of which) has been let as residential accommodation, then any gain which would have been chargeable because of the letting is exempt to the extent that it does not exceed the lesser of:

- £40,000; or

- such an amount as is exempt from CGT because of the private residence exemption (see 6220).

Example 1

Peter buys a house in 2006. He lets one of the three floors of the house. The remaining two-thirds of the house form his only residence. He sells the house in May 2016. He makes a gain of £10,500. Disregarding the lettings relief, £7,000 (i.e. £10,500 × $2/_3$) of this gain would be exempt from CGT under the private residence exemption following apportionment of the gain.

However, because of the letting relief, the amount of the gain attributable to the letting (£10,500 × $1/_3$ = £3,500) is also wholly exempt because it does not exceed the exempt gain of £7,000 or the absolute ceiling of £40,000.

Thus all of the gain is exempt.

Example 2

Polly bought a house on 1 June 2005 as her only or main residence. She lived there for 12 months after which she moved into a bungalow that she had inherited. She let the house as residential accommodation for the next 24 months, following which she re-occupied it as her only or main residence. She remained there for eight years (96 months) until 31 May 2016 when she

---

sold the house, realising a gain of £82,500. The chargeable gain, taking into account private residence relief and lettings relief, is calculated as follows:

	£
Indexed gain	82,500

(a)   Private residence relief

Using $\dfrac{A + B}{C}$ (see 6244)

A = 12 + 78 [96–18]

B = 18

C = 132

$\dfrac{90 + 18}{132} \times £82,500$ (67,500)

Gain after private residence relief, but

before lettings relief   15,000

(b)   Lettings relief

Gain attributable to period of letting

$£82,500 \times \dfrac{24}{132} = £15,000$

Letting relief is the lower of:

• £15,000; and

• £40,000   (15,000)

Chargeable gain   Nil

A lodger living as a member of a person's family does not affect that person's private residence relief and the lettings relief provisions are, therefore, not relevant to such a situation.

Legislation: TCGA 1992, s. 223(4)

Other Material: SP 14/80, *Relief for owner occupiers*

Tax Reporter: ¶546-850

6255   Use of relocation business to sell private residence

Where work is being relocated and the employer sets up arm's length arrangements under which an employee, office holder or person sharing with them, moves home because of the relocation and sells his or her home to his employer or to a relocation business with a right to share in any later profit made on a subsequent sale, the right will generally be exempt to the same extent as the home itself is (see 6220ff.). Thus if, for example, the home was used partly for business purposes, or was not the main home throughout the employee's period of ownership, only a corresponding proportion of any gain relating to the right to later profits will also be exempt.

This relief does not apply when the right is held by the employee for more than three years.

Legislation: TCGA 1992, s. 225C

Tax Reporter: ¶547-000

General gifts relief

6285 Former general gift relief

There was a general CGT holdover relief for gifts made before 14 March 1989. The principles of the relief may still be important in so far as they affect the transferee where holdover was claimed before that date (see 6289).

The relief applied to a transfer with an element of gift if:

- it was between individuals resident or ordinarily resident in the UK (see 224) and made after 5 April 1980 where both transferor and transferee claimed relief within six years from the end of the relevant tax year;

- it was made after 5 April 1981 by an individual to trustees of a settlement resident in the UK, where the transferor made a claim; or

- it was a distribution out of a trust made after 5 April 1982, where both transferor and transferee made a claim.

Computation of relief

Where the conditions for general gift relief were satisfied, relief was provided by reducing to nil the amount of the chargeable gain accruing to the transferor and reducing the transferee's deemed consideration (i.e. his allowable expenditure on a subsequent disposal) by the same amount (referred to as the held over gain; see 6144).

Legislation: Former FA 1980, s. 79

Tax Reporter: ¶548-950

6287 General gifts outside potentially exempt transfer regime

Where inheritance tax (IHT) is charged on a lifetime transfer, there remains the spectre of double taxation so provision has been made for continuing the general holdover relief for gifts (see 6285) in such circumstances where the recipient of the gift is an individual or the trustees of a settlement. The relief continues as for gifts before 14 March 1989 in respect of IHT chargeable transfers but not potentially exempt transfers (see 6610). Holdover relief also continues for certain transfers which are exempt from IHT anyway (i.e. such transfers do not attract IHT or immediate CGT liability). Transfers included are those to political parties, for public benefit, transfers to maintenance funds for historic buildings and of property designated by the Treasury as conditionally exempt.

As for gifts before 14 March 1989 (see 6285), the holdover relief does not apply where the transferee is not resident (nor, for tax years prior to 2013–14, ordinarily resident); nor does it apply where, though resident (or, for tax years prior to 2013–14, ordinarily resident) in the UK, the transferee would not be liable to CGT on any subsequent disposal by him because of double taxation treaty relief.

However, where the disposal in relation to which a claim could be made under s. 260 is a disposal of a UK residential property interest to a non-resident and a gain arises that would be a chargeable NRCGT gain (5717), holdover relief will still be available despite the non-resident status of the recipient. This is because the asset remains within the scope of capital gains tax (TCGA 1992, s. 261ZA).

Where the general holdover relief applies to gifts after 13 March 1989, the rollover relief for gifts of business assets (see 6325) is not available as well. However, the general holdover relief takes priority over the rollover relief for gifts of business assets.

If a disposal to which the general gift relief applied before 14 March 1989 was a chargeable transfer for inheritance or capital transfer tax purposes, the transferee, on an ultimate disposal by him, was entitled to deduct from any chargeable gain accruing to him, the lesser of:

- the amount of inheritance or capital transfer tax on the original transfer (whether paid by the transferor or transferee);

- the chargeable gain on the transferee's disposal.

This rule is equally applicable under the post 13 March 1989 regime. Where the original transfer was potentially exempt but subsequently proves to be chargeable, necessary adjustments must be made.

Further, the exemption is unavailable in respect of a disposal to a dual resident trust eligible for a treaty exemption, i.e. if:

- the trustees to whom the disposal was made were treated as UK-resident even though the general administration of the trust is ordinarily carried on outside the UK (see 5630); or

- the trustees would be exempt from tax in respect of any gains on the asset under a double tax treaty.

There are circumstances in which HMRC will not need to agree at the time of the gift the market value of assets for which relief is claimed, applicable as in relation to gifts of business assets (see 6325).

Legislation: TCGA 1992, s. 165(3)(d), (10), 169, 260, 261, 261ZA

Tax Reporter: ¶548-700

6289 Emigration of transferee following general gift relief

In general, where a gift was made to a UK resident (or, for tax years prior to 2013–14, ordinarily resident) person (see 224) and holdover relief has applied (see 6285 or 6287), then a chargeable gain equal to the held over gain is deemed to accrue to the transferee if he becomes non-resident (and is not for tax years prior to 2013–14, ordinarily resident) in the UK within six years of the gift.

However, where a gain on a deemed disposal would otherwise be deemed to accrue under s. 168 at the time the transferee ceases to be UK resident, it will instead accrue at the time the asset is subsequently disposed of if the gain at that time would be a chargeable NRCGT gain (TCGA 1992, s. 168A).

Additionally, if the reason that the transferee becomes non-resident is that he works in an employment or office all the duties of which are performed outside the UK and he again becomes resident (or, for tax years prior to 2013–14, ordinarily resident) in the UK within three years, during which time he has not disposed of the asset, the held-over gain does not crystallise.

Legislation: TCGA 1992, s. 67, 168, 168A

Tax Reporter: ¶548-700

6300 Relief on compulsory purchase

A disposal of land to an authority having compulsory purchase powers may give rise to a CGT liability. The timing of any disposal not made under contract is determined by reference to the agreement of compensation or the date of seizure, etc. Rollover relief may be claimed by the landowner where, in general:

- the landowner took no steps (e.g. by advertising) to dispose of the land or make known his willingness to dispose of it; and

- the consideration for the disposal is applied in acquiring other land which is not the sole or main residence of the landowner or will not be such a residence within six years of acquisition.

The landowner's gain is rolled over to the new land purchased by him.

Where the new land is a depreciating asset, the gain is held over until the earlier of:

- the date of disposal of the land acquired; or

- ten years from the date of acquisition of the land.

HMRC accept that rollover relief is available where a tenant exercises the following rights to acquire an interest in the tenanted property from the landlord:

- the right to acquire the freehold reversion or an extension of the lease under the *Leasehold Reform Housing and Urban Development Act* 1993, or

- the right to buy or acquire the freehold or an extension of the lease under the *Housing Acts* 1985–96.

This effectively brings leasehold tenants within the scope of the meaning of a person or body of persons with compulsory purchase powers.

Provisional claims may be made, enabling rollover relief to be given before the reinvestment is made.

Legislation: TCGA 1992, s. 243, 245–248

Case: *Ahad* [2010] TC 00291

Other Material: SP 13/93 (revised June 2005); HMRC *Capital Gains Manual* 61940

Tax Reporter: ¶547-050

Transfer of business to a company

6302 Conditions for relief on transfer of business to a company

For rollover relief on the transfer of business assets to a company, etc. the following conditions must be satisfied:

- the transferor of the business must be a sole trader or a partnership;

- the transfer must be to a body corporate or unincorporated association;

- the transfer must be of the business as a going concern together with all assets of the business (though cash may be excluded); and

- the transfer must be wholly or partly in exchange for shares issued by the transferee to the transferor (if liabilities are taken over this is not regarded as consideration).

Legislation: TCGA 1992, s. 162(1), (5)

Other Material: ESC D32, *Transfer of a business to a company*

Tax Reporter: ¶574-100

6303   Amount of relief on transfer of business to a company

If the conditions for rollover relief on transfer of a business to a company are satisfied (see 6302), the gain arising on the disposal to the company can be deferred or 'rolled over' (see 6144) until the eventual disposal of the shares.

Where the consideration for the transfer is wholly in the form of shares, there is no CGT liability at the time of the transfer. Instead, the cost price, or base value of the shares for CGT purposes, is reduced by the amount of the gain on the transfer.

If there is also cash (or other consideration) for the transfer, the gain is apportioned by applying the fraction:

$$\frac{A}{B}$$

A   is the cost of the shares; and

B   is the total consideration received by the transferor.

Example

Joel is a sole trader. He transfers his business to X Ltd in exchange for 10,000 ordinary shares in X Ltd and £9,000 cash. The value of the shares when allotted to Joel is £40,000. Details of Joel's business assets are as follows:

Assets	Base cost	Market value on transfer	Gain
	£	£	£
Freehold property	10,000	30,000	20,000
Goodwill	–	5,000	5,000

Capital gains tax

Assets	Base cost	Market value on transfer	Gain
	£	£	£
Trading stock	2,000	7,000	–
Plant and machinery	5,000	3,000	–
Debtors	–	5,000	–
	17,000	50,000	25,000
Liabilities			
Trade creditors	–	1,000)	–
	17,000	49,000	25,000

The rolled-over gain for Joel on the transfer is:

$$\frac{£40,000}{£49,000} \times £25,000 = £20,408$$

The assessable gain is, therefore, £4,592 (being £25,000 – £20,408). The balance of the gain (£20,408) is rolled over. On a later sale of the 10,000 shares in X Ltd, Joel's base value for those shares will be reduced by £20,408. Thus, if he later sells the shares for £50,000, Joel will be liable to CGT on a gain of £30,408 (ignoring any available annual exemption or other reliefs), which is calculated as follows:

	£	£
Sale proceeds of shares		50,000
Market value on acquisition shares	40,000	
Less: rolled over gain	(20,408)	
		(19,592)
Gain		(30,408)

Example

Suppose that B has a balance sheet as follows:

	£
Business assets – chargeable to CGT (e.g. land/buildings)	200,000
Business assets – non chargeable (e.g. trade debtors, cash)	50,000
	250,000
Less: trade creditors	20,000
	230,000
Capital and reserves	230,000

Of the non-chargeable assets, £15,000 is cash. The balance sheet amounts are stated at cost. The chargeable assets, purchased several years earlier, have a current market value of £500,000. The non-chargeable assets' value is as stated in the balance sheet. No individual asset is standing at a loss. The company, B Ltd, to which B is transferring his business is issuing B with ordinary shares. B Ltd is not taking over the liabilities, nor having the business' cash transferred to its account.

The calculation of the relief then proceeds as follows:

Calculate the gain on the chargeable assets.

	£
Market value of chargeable assets	500,000
Less: cost	200,000
Gain	300,000

Calculate the value of the shares.

The value of the shares issued as consideration by B Ltd is the net value of assets transferred. This is:

	£
Chargeable business assets	500,000
Non chargeable business assets (NB cash not transferred)	35,000
Total value	535,000

Since the value transferred to the company exceeds the gains on the chargeable business assets, the whole gain may be rolled over, and so none is immediately taxable. The cost of B's shares in B Ltd is then reduced by the gain:

	£
Consideration for shares	535,000
Less: rolled over gain, s. 162 relief	300,000
Revised acquisition cost carried forward	235,000

Claiming the relief

There is no need to make a claim for relief on incorporation, because, provided the conditions are satisfied, it applies automatically.

It is possible to elect to disapply incorporation relief. The election must be made by the second anniversary of 31 January following the tax year of the incorporation. So if the incorporation took place in 2016–17, the election must be made by 31 January 2020. However, if all the shares acquired on incorporation are disposed of by the end of the tax year following incorporation, the election must be made by 31 January following that later tax year. So if the incorporation took place in 2016–17, and the shares were all sold by 5 April 2018, the election would have to be made by 31 January 2019.

Legislation: TCGA 1992, s. 36, 162(2)–(5), 162A and Sch. 4, para. 2, 9

Case: *Colley v Clements (HMIT)* (2005) Sp C 483

Tax Reporter: ¶574-200

Replacement of business assets

6305   Replacement rollover relief in outline

Rollover relief applies in certain instances where consideration received for the disposal of business assets is applied in acquiring new assets for the purposes of a business (see further 6306 to 6309). The relief is strictly limited to the specific categories of asset set out in the legislation (see 6306).

This form of rollover relief only applies if the new assets are also chargeable, i.e. if the taxpayer is not resident (or, for tax years prior to 2013–14, ordinarily resident) (see 224) immediately after acquisition or is so resident but not then chargeable because of double taxation treaty relief, the relief is unavailable. The same disqualification applies to dual resident companies which are deemed to be non-resident for tax purposes. A further disqualification applies in relation to old assets disposed of before that event and new assets acquired after that event where a company ceases to be UK-resident or becomes dual-resident.

Relief is not denied in respect of an NRCGT gain where the new assets are chargeable to NRCGT.

For the concept of relief by way of rollover, see 6144.

Legislation: TCGA 1992, s. 152(1), 153A, 159, 159A, 185(3)

Tax Reporter: ¶570-100

6306   Assets to which replacement rollover relief applies

'Replacement rollover relief' (see 6305) applies only to the following classes of assets used only for the purposes of a trade.

- Buildings and land occupied for the purposes of the trade, provided the trade is not one of dealing in or developing land nor one of providing services for the occupier of land in which the trader has an interest or estate.

- Fixed plant or machinery which does not form part of a building. Movable plant or machinery is ineligible for rollover relief for business assets.

- Ships, aircraft and hovercraft.

- Satellites, space stations and spacecraft (including launch vehicles).

- Goodwill.

- Milk quotas and potato quotas.

- Ewe and suckler cow premium quotas.

- Fish quota.

- Entitlements under the EU's single farm payments scheme.

- Entitlements under the EU's new basic payment scheme of income support for farmers (from 20 December 2013).

Both assets disposed of and assets acquired must be within one of these classes, but not necessarily the same class.

Payments under the single farm payments scheme (currently the EU's main agricultural subsidy scheme for farmers under common agricultural policy) ceased from 2014 and have been replaced by payments under the EU's new basic payment scheme (BPS) from 1 January 2015. Payment entitlements under the BPS are included within the list of classes of assets eligible for roll-over relief with effect in relation to disposals of old assets and acquisitions of new assets from 20 December 2013 (the date the relevant EU regulation came into force).

Legislation: TCGA 1992, s. 155, 156; *Finance Act 1993, Section 86(2), (Fish Quota) Order* 1999 (SI 1999/564)

Cases: *Williams v Evans (HMIT)* [1982] BTC 155; *Cottle v Coldicott* (1995) Sp C 40

Tax Reporter: ¶571-000

6307   Businesses to which replacement rollover relief applies

'Replacement rollover relief' (see 6305) is available for the disposal of assets used by any of the following:

- trades, professions or vocations, including certain commercial letting of furnished holiday accommodation (see 1255) and partners (often extending to assets used by the partnership;

- offices and employments (often extending to assets used by the employer rent-free and without any formal tenancy, etc.);

- public authorities;

- commercial woodlands;

- a trade association which has activities directed to the protection or promotion of the interests of its members who carry on a trade;

- professional associations which are non-profit making;

- non-profit making unincorporated associations and other bodies chargeable to corporation tax, i.e. trade unions, sports clubs, etc. (including claims for assets held by a company owned by such association).

As a result of a 1999 change, the relief now applies for UK oil licence gains.

Legislation: TCGA 1992, s. 158, 193, 241(4), (5); former TCGA 1992, s. 193; FA 1999, s. 103

Other Material: SP 5/86, *Relief for replacement of business assets: employees and office holders*

Tax Reporter: ¶570-450

6308 Conditions for replacement rollover relief to apply

In addition to the restriction of relief to certain businesses (see 6307) and to certain classes of assets (see 6306), certain other conditions must be met before the relief can be obtained, as set out below. If the disponor is an individual, the trade in point may be carried on by him or by his 'personal company'. HMRC's view is that the asset must be used by the same personal or family company and not, for example, by a subsidiary of the personal or family company.

(1) Except as noted below, the asset disposed of must have been used solely for the purposes of the business throughout the period of ownership (disregarding any period before 31 March 1982).

Apportionment takes place where the asset is not used for the business throughout the disponor's ownership or where the asset is not used only for the purposes of the trade; the part which has not been used for the trade is treated as being a separate asset. The gain on disposal is apportioned between the two notional assets on a 'just and reasonable basis' and only the gain attributable to the notional asset used in the trade is eligible for rollover.

(2) The consideration for the disposal of the assets must be used to acquire new business assets within the specified classes; such consideration is determined after other reliefs and may be a just and reasonable portion of the proceeds of a larger disposal. The new

asset may be used in any business carried on by the person acquiring the asset, i.e. it need not be used in the same business for which the old asset was used. All trades carried on by companies within a group are treated as a single trade (see 3695), though the disponor and acquiring company need not be members at the same time and the property holding company in a group is generally regarded as trading for this purpose. Special conditions apply where assets are only partly replaced.

Concessionary relief is also given where the proceeds of sale are used to enhance the value of other assets, to acquire a further interest in an asset already in use for the person's trade or, in purely commercial transactions where the same assets are repurchased. In HMRC's view, relief is applicable only to actual rather than deemed disposals. In principle, there is no reason why relief should not be available where the consideration for the acquisition is satisfied by the issue of shares.

(3) The new assets must be acquired (or an unconditional contract for their acquisition entered into) within a four-year period beginning 12 months before the disposal of the old assets and ending three years after the disposal; HMRC (but not the tax tribunal, etc.) have a discretion to allow an extension, which they will use, inter alia where the intention to acquire assets is frustrated by matters outside the taxpayer's control and where following compulsory purchase land is leased back to the trader until the authority is ready to build on it – relief may be given provisionally in the interim period where an unconditional contract has been entered into. In preparation for self-assessment, provisions were enacted to allow provisional claims to be made where there is an intention to reinvest (see below).

(4) The new assets must be acquired for use in the business and not wholly or partly for the purpose of realising a gain on the disposal of the new assets.

(5) The new asset(s) must be taken into use 'on' the acquisition. In one case, the taxpayer company's claim to rollover relief failed because there was a delay of eight months between completion of the sale and occupation of the premises. A delay to enable capital expenditure to be used to enhance the property before use is often permitted, provided it is not let before use.

(6) Where part of a newly acquired asset is sold shortly after the purchase, it is not possible to claim rollover relief in respect of any gain arising by identifying the part sold as the 'old' asset and the original acquisition (within the prior 12 months) as the 'new' asset.

(7) The person carrying on the business must make a claim for the relief. Under self assessment, provisional claims for rollover relief can be made where there is an intention to reinvest the proceeds in acquiring

new assets and the taxpayer makes a declaration to that effect. Such declarations enable provisional relief to be given until the earliest of:

- the date the declaration is withdrawn;
- the date it is superseded by a valid rollover relief claim;
- in the case of CGT, the third anniversary of 31 January following the tax year in which the disposal took place or, for corporation tax purposes, the fourth anniversary of the end of the accounting period in which the disposal took place.

Relief may be available in relation to the grant of an option over land if it would be due on the disposal of the underlying land.

Legislation: TCGA 1992, s. 23(6)–(8), s. 152, 153, 153A, 157, 175(2B)

Cases: *Tod (HMIT) v Mudd* [1987] BTC 57; *Campbell Connelly & Co Ltd v Barnett (HMIT)* [1994] BTC 12; *Watton (HMIT) v Tippett* [1997] BTC 338; *Steibelt (HMIT) v Paling* [1999] BTC 184

Other Material: ESC D16, *Relief for replacement of business assets: repurchase of the same asset*; ESC D22, *Relief for the replacement of business assets: expenditure on improvements to existing assets*; ESC D24, *Relief for the replacement of business assets: assets not immediately brought into trading use*; ESC D25, *Relief for the replacement of business assets: acquisition of an interest in an asset already used for the purposes of the trade*; SP D6, *Replacement of business assets: time limit*; 1991/26, Technical Information Release, October 1991; Technical Release TAX 15/92

Tax Reporter: ¶570-400ff.; ¶570-700ff.

6309 Effect of claim for replacement rollover relief

If all the conditions for 'replacement rollover relief' are satisfied (see 6308), then the disposal of the old assets is deemed to be on a 'no gain/no loss' basis and the consideration for the new assets is reduced by the amount of the gain.

> **Example**
>
> In 1996, Z & Co purchased (for £70,000) a 99-year lease of offices for the purposes of its business of management consultants. The partnership occupied the premises until 2001 when it assigned the unexpired term of its lease for £100,000. In 2000, the partnership acquired new office premises in anticipation of the sale of its old offices. The new premises were acquired for £180,000. The new premises are sold in 2016 for £200,000 and the partnership dissolved. The disposal of the old assets is deemed to be made at neither a gain nor a loss. Thus Z & Co pay no CGT on the first disposal

> but, ignoring incidental expenditure, on the disposal of the new premises the
> partnership gain is £50,000 (i.e. £200,000 − (£180,000 − £30,000)).
>
> *Note*: The tax treatment of the other party to these transactions is unaffected
> by any claim made by Z & Co.

Order of reliefs

In HMRC's view, claims to rollover relief take priority over the relief for the
transfer of a business to a company rules (see 6302).

Legislation: TCGA 1992, s. 152(1), (2)

Other Material: Inland Revenue Manual *Capital Gains*, vol. VI, CG61560

Tax Reporter: ¶570-200

6310 Replacement by depreciating assets

Where, in a claim for 'replacement rollover relief' (see 6308), the new
asset acquired is a 'depreciating asset' or will become a depreciating
asset within ten years (so basically, an asset with a predictable life of
not more than 60 years from the date of acquisition (50 years plus ten
years)) the gain on the disposal of the old asset is not so much rolled
over as held over. HMRC consider that whether new constructions (or
the addition of fixtures) on leasehold land are depreciating assets is
determined by reference to the duration of the lease at that time.

In this case, instead of being deducted from the cost of the new assets
(see 6309), the gain is deferred until the earliest of the following events:

- the claimant disposes of the new asset;
- he ceases to use the asset for the purposes of his business otherwise
  than on death; or
- the expiry of ten years from the date of acquisition of the new asset.

If the claimant later acquires another asset ('asset No. 3') which is not
a depreciating asset and the acquisition is made before any of these
events occurs, the postponed gain from the old asset may be rolled over
to asset No. 3.

> **Example**
>
> X Ltd buys factory premises (freehold) for its business. The purchase price
> is £100,000. Two years later, X Ltd sells the factory for £150,000 and buys
> a second factory (35-year lease unexpired) for £170,000. A claim is made for

> relief. The gain (£50,000) on the disposal of the first factory is postponed until one of the events above takes place.
>
> Five years later, X buys a third factory (freehold) for £180,000 and sells the second factory. X Ltd may make a claim to roll over the postponed gain (on the sale of the first factory) to the third factory, i.e. the acquisition cost of the third factory will be £180,000 − £50,000 = £130,000.

Special provisions exist where only part of the postponed gain is carried forward.

ESC D45

On 20 July 2015, HRMC published the response to a consultation issued on 2 October 2014 regarding the withdrawal of extra-statutory concessions including ESC D45. ESC D45 ensures that a capital gains tax (CGT) charge does not arise where roll-over relief has been claimed and the claimant later dies by making clear that the general exemption that death is not an occasion of charge applies in all cases. HMRC's view is that the concession is not needed as the existing legislation already gives this result. Accordingly, HMRC will formally withdraw the ESC from April 2016 and guidance will be clarified to make the position certain. The consultation response is available at www.gov.uk/government/consultations/withdrawal-of-extra-statutory-concessions#history.

Legislation: TCGA 1992, s. 154(6)

Other Material: ESC D45, *Rollover into depreciating assets*; Consultation outcome: Withdrawal of extra-statutory concessions: www.gov.uk/government/consultations/withdrawal-of-extra-statutory-concessions#history

Tax Reporter: ¶571-500ff.

6314 Employee share ownership plans

Capital gains tax rollover relief is available to enable shares to be transferred to the trustees of the plan trust of an approved employee share ownership plans in a tax efficient manner. The relief operates so as to deem the consideration in respect of the disposal to be at such an amount as gives rise to neither a gain or a loss. Partial relief is available where not all the consideration is reinvested, provided that the amount not reinvested is less than the gain.

Conditions

For the relief to be available, the following conditions must be satisfied:

- at the time of the disposal the employee share ownership plan must be a Schedule 2 SIP under ITEPA 2003, Sch. 2;

- the shares disposed of to the plan (the 'relevant shares') must meet the requirements of ITEPA 2003, Sch. 2, Pt. 4 except that they must not be listed on a recognised stock exchange (the listing requirement is treated as omitted);

- during the entitlement period, the trustees must hold for the beneficiaries of the plan trust at least 10% of the ordinary share capital of the company and carry rights to at least 10% of the profits available for distribution to the shareholders and the assets of the company available for distribution to its shareholder in the event of a winding up. Shares held within the plan on behalf of an individual are treated as being held by the trustees for the purposes of the calculation until such time as they cease to be subject to the plan. The entitlement period is 12 months from the date of the disposal; and

- during the prescribed period, there must be no unauthorised arrangement that would enable the claimant or a person connected with him to acquire from the trustees, directly or indirectly, shares (or an interest in or right deriving from them). The proscribed period is the period from the date of the disposal to the date of acquisition, or, if later, the date on which the trustees satisfy the 10% holding requirement.

Example 1

Pauline disposes of 1,000 shares in an unlisted company to the trustees of a Schedule 2 employee share ownership plan. The shares are eligible shares. The consideration is £2.25 per share. Pauline makes a chargeable gain of £1,480. Three months later she invests all the proceeds in chargeable assets. She satisfies the conditions for rollover relief, and within the time-limit makes a claim for relief.

The effect of such a claim is to treat the consideration received from the disposal as being £770 (the actual consideration of £2,250 less the gain of £1,480), being the sum that gives rise to neither a gain nor a loss. The gain is rolled over into the replacement assets.

Example 2

Justin disposes of 1,000 shares to the trustees of a Sch. 2 employee share ownership plan for £3.50 per share. The shares are eligible shares in an unlisted company. He realises a gain of £680. Two months later, he reinvests £3,000 in chargeable assets. He makes a claim for partial relief.

> The sum not reinvested was £500 and this was less than the gain of £680. As a result of the claim, the gain crystallising on the disposal is reduced to £500 (the amount not reinvested), a reduction of £180. The consideration for the replacement assets is deemed to be £2,820 (i.e. the actual consideration of £3,000 less the balance of the gain of £180). Consequently, £180 of the gain is rolled over.

Legislation: TCGA 1992, Sch. 7C

Tax Reporter: ¶361-250ff.

Gifts of business assets

6325   Gifts of business assets by individuals

Relief is provided for certain gifts of business assets. The relief is by way of 'holdover' (see 6144) of the gain otherwise chargeable, i.e. CGT liability is postponed until the transferee subsequently makes a chargeable disposal and his base cost is taken to be the transferor's base cost.

For the relief to apply, there must be a disposal of business assets otherwise than at arm's length bargain and the relief must be claimed within four years of the end of the relevant tax year by both transferor and transferee; where the transferees are trustees of a settlement, the claim for relief should be made by the transferor alone.

The relief applies to the following business assets:

- an asset, or an interest in an asset used for the purposes of a trade, profession or vocation carried on by the transferor, his personal company or a member of a trading group of which his personal company is the holding company, or

- shares or securities of a trading company or of the holding company of a trading group, where either the trading company or holding company is the transferor's personal company (or previously family company), or those shares or securities are not quoted on a recognised stock exchange.

The relief in the first category above expressly includes assets used by a trading group held by the personal company.

Personal company

This is a company in which the individual can exercise 5% or more of the voting power (TCGA 1992, s. 165(8)(a)). (N.B. This differs from the definition of 'personal company' for entrepreneurs' relief, which requires a minimum 5% ordinary shareholding in addition to voting power.) The company may qualify as 'personal' even though its shares may be listed on a recognised stock exchange. However, in such a case, it will only be assets owned by the individual and used by the company for its trade which will be qualifying business assets; the shares in that company will not qualify.

Restrictions

Gains subject to possible holdover on a gift chargeable to inheritance tax (see 6287) have always been excepted from business asset holdover relief; the following exceptions also apply.

- The relief does not apply to disposals of qualifying corporate bonds where a gain crystallises following a company reorganisation involving old assets which were not such bonds (see 5865) – this prevents a further holdover relief for gifts of business assets on the subsequent disposal of the new securities.

- The relief does not apply where the transferee is not resident (nor, for tax years prior to 2013–14, ordinarily resident) in the UK unless the asset is chargeable to NRCGT in the hands of the transferee (in which case the full amount of the held-over gain accrues as a chargeable NRCGT gain for the transferee on their subsequent disposal).

- The relief does not apply where the transferee is resident (or, for tax years prior to 2013–14, ordinarily resident) in the UK but is regarded as a resident outside the UK under any double taxation treaty and under that treaty would not be liable to tax on a gain; if the transferee is a dual-resident company, it is regarded as non-resident and so excluded, even if the treaty does not provide for effective chargeable gains exemption.

- The relief does not apply where the gift of business assets is to a foreign-controlled company (i.e. a company controlled by a person connected with the transferor who is not resident nor, for tax years prior to 2013–14, ordinarily resident in the UK).

Valuations

An HMRC statement of practice explains the circumstances in which they will not need to agree at the time of the gift the market value of assets for which relief is claimed. A valuation may be necessary at some point before disposal as a result of the interaction of the holdover reliefs with other CGT reliefs.

The practice aims to reduce the compliance burden for taxpayers. Valuation negotiations, including those of unquoted shares and land – which can often be both expensive and complex – will be saved. The time it takes to settle holdover relief claims will be reduced as a result. However, the new arrangements are voluntary: HMRC will still agree valuations and calculate the held over gain in any case where the taxpayer wishes it.

The transferor and transferee must both make a request that the valuation be avoided and must provide:

- full details of the asset transferred;
- its date of acquisition;
- its allowable expenditure;
- a statement that they have satisfied themselves that the value of the asset at the date of the transfer was in excess of the allowable expenditure plus indexation to that date.

HMRC stipulate that once a claim made on this basis has been accepted it may not be subsequently withdrawn.

Extension to agricultural property

The relief also extends to agricultural property which is disposed of, even though it does not satisfy the trade use condition; such property is defined by reference to property eligible for inheritance tax agricultural property relief. The relief is given by reference to the nature of the asset, though the inheritance tax relief ultimately depends upon the value of the asset (which excludes hope or development value: see 7292ff.); the relief is, in principle, available on the whole of the gain not just that part which reflects the agricultural value of the property.

Reduction of relief

The relief is reduced where the asset is not used for the purposes of a trade, profession or vocation throughout the transferor's ownership; there are also rules for apportioning the gain where the asset is a building or structure only part of which was used for the trade, profession or vocation. Holdover relief is available only in respect of that part of the gain referable to the business user.

Where the chargeable assets of the company whose shares are being disposed of include assets which are not business assets, the amount of the held over gain allowed is the same proportion as the company's business assets at market value bear to the company's total chargeable assets at market value on the date of disposal. The reduction is only made where the transferor has or has had a significant interest in the company; that is the transferor held at least 25% of the voting rights in the company or the company is his personal company, in each case at some time within the 12 months preceding the disposal.

If a disposal is, or eventually proves to be, also a chargeable transfer, and a claim for business asset rollover relief is made, the transferee can deduct in computing the chargeable gain accruing to him on a subsequent disposal the lesser of:

- the inheritance tax due on the original transfer; or

- the chargeable gain computed apart from this relief.

Legislation: TMA 1970, s. 42; TCGA 1992, s. 165, 166(1), (2), 167, 167A, 169, Sch. 7, para. 1, para. 4–8

Other Material: SP 8/92

Tax Reporter: ¶574-400ff.

6326   Gifts of business assets by trustees

Holdover relief for gifts of business assets can be claimed by trustees, similar in nature to that applicable to individuals (see 6325). Assets included are those used for the purposes of a trade, profession or vocation carried on by the trustees making the disposal or a beneficiary having an interest in possession immediately before the disposal. Alternatively, shares or securities of a trading company are included if they are not quoted or the trustees have at least 25% of the voting rights in the company at the time of the disposal. A further category includes agricultural property.

Legislation: TCGA 1992, Sch. 7, para. 2, 3

Tax Reporter: ¶574-700

Administration of capital gains tax

6400   Care and management of taxes on capital gains

Most of the provisions dealing with the administration of direct UK taxes are to be found in the *Taxes Management Act* 1970 which, so far as it relates to chargeable gains, is construed as one with the *Taxation of Chargeable Gains Act* 1992. The 'care and management' of taxes on capital gains are entrusted to the Board of HM Revenue and Customs.

Regulations have been made to supplement the *Taxes Management Act* 1970, many of whose provisions apply not only to CGT but to income tax and corporation tax as well.

Legislation: *Commissioners for Revenue and Customs Act* 2005; TMA 1970, s. 119(4)

Tax Reporter: ¶180-000ff.

6410 Targeted anti-avoidance rules (TAARs)

There is a targeted anti-avoidance rule (TAAR) to counter schemes to create and use artificial capital losses to avoid tax. The measure is designed to ensure that allowable capital losses are restricted to those arising from genuine commercial transactions. The rule applies in relation to capital losses arising on disposals on or after 6 December 2006.

Where a person has entered into arrangements, and a main purpose of those arrangements is to gain a tax advantage by creating an artificial capital loss, any resulting loss will not be an allowable loss for the purposes of CGT, income tax or corporation tax.

Legislation: TCGA 1992, s. 16A

Tax Reporter: ¶523-975

6410A General anti-abuse rule

A general anti-abuse rule (GAAR), targeting artificial and abusive tax avoidance schemes was implemented in FA 2013, Pt. 5, enabling HMRC to counteract tax advantages arising from arrangements that are considered abusive. It applies to a wide range of taxes, including capital gains tax and has effect for arrangements entered into on or after 17 July 2013.

Arrangements will be considered 'abusive' if they cannot be reasonably regarded as a reasonable course of action in relation to the relevant tax provisions, considering the circumstances in each case. An independent panel will consider individual cases referred to it, and will provide opinions on those cases. These opinions are not binding on HMRC or the taxpayer, so that the normal rights of appeal to the tax tribunal will continue to operate. However, in such tribunal proceedings relating to the GAAR, the burden of proof will be on HMRC to show that there were tax arrangements which were abusive and that their proposed counteraction is just and reasonable.

The GAAR is not expected to result in the repeal of any of the targeted anti-avoidance rules, whether in capital gains tax or elsewhere, but is instead intended as an additional means of dealing with tax avoidance.

Legislation: FA 2013, Pt. 5

Tax Reporter: ¶187-850ff.

Returns of capital gains

6425   Returns in respect of charge to tax on gains

Various persons may be required to supply information to HMRC to enable tax to be properly collected in respect of capital gains. Since chargeable gains form part of the profits of a company which are subject to corporation tax, the returns applicable to corporation tax are relevant to companies (see 4300ff.). A person chargeable to CGT must notify HMRC of that fact and returns in respect of CGT may be required from the taxpayer or a third party (see 6427 and 6429).

Tax Reporter: ¶180-450

6427   Notice of liability to CGT

Under self-assessment, the CGT notice of liability requirements are combined with those relating to income tax (see 2200ff.). The time-limit for notification, if the taxpayer has not already been requested to make a tax return, has become six months from the end of the relevant tax year. Delay is allowed for if the taxpayer has reasonable grounds; the delay may continue so long as the reasonable excuse exists, and when it ceases to apply the taxpayer still has a 'reasonable time' within which to comply.

Legislation: TMA 1970, s. 7(1)

Tax Reporter: ¶180-425

6428   CGT returns by individuals and partnerships

Under self-assessment, the taxpayer may choose to make a self-assessment of his gains; alternatively, HM Revenue and Customs (HMRC) will make an assessment on his behalf – without penalty – if he submits his return before 31 October following the end of the tax year or, if later, within two months of the issue of the notice requiring him to make a return for that year. The filing deadline for the combined income tax and CGT return is the later of 31 January following the tax year and three months after the issue of a notice requesting submission of a return.

If in a tax year:

- the 'taxable amount' does not exceed the 'exempt amount'; and

- the aggregate consideration on disposals on which chargeable gains accrued does not exceed twice the exempt amount, then (unless HMRC otherwise require) a statement that the two conditions are fulfilled is sufficient for compliance with the requirement to make a return of gains.

Valuations

Individuals and trustees liable to CGT may submit draft valuations to their tax office, before they complete their self-assessment returns. Applications should be made on CG34 as soon as possible after the date of the disposal, to allow adequate time for consideration and it should be noted that CG34 currently states that such consideration by HMRC may take at least two months. However, submission of the relevant return should not be delayed if agreement on the valuation has not been reached by the filing date.

Where a self-assessment enquiry (see 12700ff.) is held open pending agreement of a CGT valuation, HMRC will not take advantage of the open enquiry to raise new issues, unless new facts come to light.

Effect of delay

Delay in sending in a return of capital gains may expose a taxpayer to interest on overdue tax and, under self-assessment, a surcharge. There are also penalties (see 12000ff.).

Partnerships

Although a partnership in English law is not a separate legal person and is not itself liable to CGT, the partner required to make a return in respect of the income of the partnership (see 2243) is to include in that return the notional gains of the partnership for tax purposes. This is to include details in respect of disposals of partnership property and particulars of acquisitions of partnership property, subject to the exclusions listed below. The filing deadline may differ for the partnership return (see 2243).

Legislation: TMA 1970, s. 7–8

Other Material: SP 1/99

Tax Reporter: ¶180-000ff.

6428A   Non-resident CGT (NRCGT) returns

Non-residents (i.e. persons not resident nor, for tax years prior to 2013–14, ordinarily resident: see 224) are not normally within the charge to CGT. For the position of non-residents trading within the UK through a branch or agency, see 1672.

A person who makes a non-resident disposal of UK residential property (NRCGT disposal) (see 5717) must notify HMRC of the disposal in an NRCGT return. The return must be made within 30 days of, normally, the time when the property is conveyed.

Finance Act 2016 inserts TMA 1970, s. 12ZBA under which a person who is not required to submit an NRCGT return (under TMA 1970, s. 12ZB(1)) may submit an elective NRCGT return. TMA 1970, s. 12BZA prescribes two circumstances an elective NRCGT return may be submitted. The first is a no gain/no loss disposal under TCGA 1992 and the second is where an arm's length lease is granted to a person unconnected with the grantor for no premium (and so no chargeable gain arises on the disposal).

Where two or more NRCGT disposals are made on the same day, only one return must be made.

The NRCGT return must include 'an advance self-assessment' of the amount that is notionally chargeable for the tax year, or additional amount if a previous NRCGT return for the year has been made, subject to certain exceptions, e.g. if the person is required to make a self-assessment return for the tax year in which the disposal is made or the previous year; or has made an ATED return for the preceding period.

NRCGT returns are treated as self-assessment returns and may be amended within 12 months of the 31 January following the tax year in which the disposal was made. Rules regarding amendments by HMRC, enquiry by HMRC into returns, HMRC assessments including discovery assessments, procedures for claims, etc. mirror those for self-assessment returns.

Individuals who are within self-assessment must also report NRCGT disposals on their self-assesment returns (in addition to filing an NRCGT return).

Legislation: TMA 1970, s. 12ZA–12ZN

Case: *Morris v R & C Commrs* [2007] BTC 448

Tax Reporter: ¶180-000ff.

6429 Information about chargeable gains

Finance Act 2008, Sch. 36 contains a harmonised set of information and inspection powers that can be used to check a person's tax position for income tax, capital gains tax, corporation tax and VAT, with effect from 1 April 2009. See 11900ff. Previously, powers were fragmented according to the particular tax concerned.

Legislation: FA 2008, Sch. 36

Tax Reporter: ¶186-550ff.; ¶180-450

Assessments, determinations and claims for CGT

6437   Claims in respect of CGT

Claims in respect of reliefs from CGT are generally to be made in the same way and subject to the same time-limit rules as for income tax (see 2324).

Tax Reporter: ¶191-585ff.

6440   Scope of assessments to CGT and determinations

The assessable amount for CGT is the taxable amount of chargeable gains less allowable losses and net of the exempt annual amount (see 6150). Under self-assessment, where a taxpayer fails to submit his return on time HMRC may determine income and gains (see 2324ff.).

Apart from discovery assessments (see 2330), HMRC have powers to make estimated assessments or determinations by reference to the taxpayer's return (or his failure to make a return) or to adjust a taxpayer's self-assessment, depending upon whether the tax year is a self-assessment year. The rules apply in much the same way as for income tax (see 2324ff.).

Capital gains tax assessments may be made on various persons chargeable in a representative capacity, as they can for income tax; this might apply to, for example, personal representatives, guardians and receivers, while there is statutory protection for certain trustees, agents and receivers.

Legislation: TMA 1970, s. 71–77

Tax Reporter: ¶184-275ff.

6442   CGT assessments in respect of partnerships

Even though an individual partner makes a return of partnership gains (see 6428), the tax on chargeable gains is to be charged (and assessable) on the partners separately.

Legislation: TCGA 1992, s. 59

Tax Reporter: ¶290-040

6446 Arrears of CGT due to official error

In some circumstances, arrears of CGT are wholly or partly waived by concession if they have arisen through failure by HMRC to make proper and timely use of information supplied by the taxpayer (see 2362).

Other Material: ESC A19, *Giving up tax where there are Revenue delays in using information*

Tax Reporter: ¶193-660

Appeals in respect of capital gains

6450 Scope of appeals in respect of capital gains

An appeal may be brought against a determination of the amount of any tax (or an assessment to tax) or against a decision on a claim by notice of appeal in writing, given within 30 days of the date of the notice of assessment or decision. Except as noted below, the rules are the same as for income tax.

However, because one taxpayer's disposal value is another taxpayer's acquisition value, specific provisions are applicable for capital gains tax purposes where market value or any kind of apportionment of consideration is an issue. Therefore, regulations were made, by statutory instrument, to ensure, where a market value or apportionment of value affects more than one person, that each person has a say in deciding the value or apportionment. The regulations also try to ensure that the same value or apportionment is used in all CGT computations affected by the amounts concerned.

Where the market value of an asset on a particular date, or an apportionment, may affect the liability to capital gains tax for any period of two or more persons, and it is not a material question in an appeal already brought by any of them, then any of them may apply to the tribunal to determine the market value or the manner in which the apportionment should be made (SI 1967/149, reg. 9(1)).

Land

Where an appeal against an assessment to tax (whether to CGT or corporation tax) on chargeable gains involves a question as to the value of any land or of a lease of land that question must be determined by a special tribunal. If the land is in England or Wales, the question is to be determined on a reference to the Upper Tribunal; if in Northern Ireland by the Lands Tribunal for Northern Ireland; if in Scotland by the Lands Tribunal for Scotland.

Legislation: TMA 1970, s. 46D; SI 1967/149

Other Material: HMRC: *Litigations and settlement strategy*

Tax Reporter: ¶190-390ff.

Collection of CGT

6470   Collection of CGT generally

The rules applicable to the payment of capital gains tax and the charging of interest and surcharges are the same as those applicable to income tax (see 2350ff.).

If the taxpayer cannot make payment, they should contact HMRC's Business Payment Support Service before the payment deadline, to see whether it is possible to be given time to pay.

If the taxpayer does not make payment, HMRC have a number of methods of recovery open to them including collection through PAYE, taking control of goods, magistrates court proceedings, county court proceedings and insolvency proceedings.

Date of payment

Capital gains tax for any tax year is due (in accordance with a person's self-assessment or HMRC's calculation thereof on his behalf) on 31 January which is ten months after the end of the tax year or, if later (provided he notified HMRC of his chargeability within six months of the end of the year), three months from the issue of the notice requiring him to make a return of his income or gains. There are penalties for late payments, and interest runs on overpayments and underpayments from the due dates (see 2368 and 6484). Additional tax payable as a result of an amendment to the self-assessment figure becomes due as above or, if later, 30 days from the notice of the amendment. Further tax payable if HMRC make a 'discovery assessment' (see 2330) is due 30 days from the notice of assessment.

Autumn Statement 2015 announced that from April 2019, a payment on account of any CGT due on the disposal of residential property will be required to be made within 30 days of the completion of the disposal. This will not affect gains on properties which are not liable for CGT due to Private Residence Relief. The Government will publish draft legislation for consultation in 2016 (Finance Bill 2017).

NRCGT liabilities

Payment on account of capital gains tax to be made for a tax year when an NRCGT return contains an advance self-assessment for the year (see 6428A). The amount payable is the difference between the amount notionally chargeable in relation to the return and the payments (if any) made towards that amount. Payment is due on the filing date for the return (i.e. within 30 days of completion).

Individuals within self-assessment are not required to make payment until the normal due date for the tax year as set out above (but have the option to make payment on filing the NRCGT return).

Payment by instalments of CGT on gifts

Tax can be paid in ten equal annual instalments where there is a disposal by way of gift or a deemed disposal on a beneficiary becoming absolutely entitled against the trustees of a settlement, or a deemed disposal on the termination of a life interest on death. The disposal must also be one to which the relief for gifts of business assets or the relief accorded for gifts on which inheritance tax is chargeable in various circumstances does not apply, or would not apply were a claim made. The first instalment is due on the day on which, had the tax been payable normally, it would have been payable; however, tax payable by instalments carries interest from the normal due date so that each instalment is increased to reflect the interest element. A taxpayer wishing to pay off outstanding instalments not yet due may do so at any time, though interest is payable up to the date of settlement.

Legislation: TMA 1970, s. 59AA, 59B; TCGA 1992, s. 281

Tax Reporter: ¶182-750; ¶183-000; ¶183-025

6474   Recovery of CGT from person not primarily liable

A number of provisions enable CGT to be collected from someone other than the person primarily liable for the tax (see below).

Settlements

If CGT assessed on the trustees of a settlement is not paid within six months of its becoming payable and before or after the six-month period, the asset on which the gain arose or the proceeds of sale from it is transferred to someone, who is absolutely entitled to it as against the trustees, the recipient can be assessed to the tax, or a proportion of it, within two years of the tax becoming payable (see 5600).

Gifts

If a gain accrues on the disposal of an asset by way of gift or otherwise by way of a bargain at arm's length and the tax assessed on the donor is not paid within 12 months of its becoming payable, the donee may be assessed and charged within two years of the tax becoming payable in the name of the donor. The amount in respect of which the assessment is made is not to exceed the lesser of (a) the chargeable gain accruing on the disposal and (b) the amount of CGT unpaid grossed-up at the marginal rate; the donee is given a right of recovery against the donor.

Non-residents trading through a branch or agency

Where non-residents carry on a trade in the UK through a branch or agency, HM Revenue and Customs will, broadly, treat that branch or agency as the non-resident's 'UK representative', and look to it for the performance of various tax obligations (see further 1672).

Company reconstructions and amalgamations

Where neither of the rollover reliefs on share exchanges and company reconstructions apply by virtue of failing the tax avoidance motive test (see 3415 and 3417) and tax is payable but is not paid within six months of when it is payable, any person who has acquired the original taxpayer's holding on a no gain/no loss transfer between spouse or within groups may be assessed to the tax within two years of its becoming payable.

Legislation: TCGA 1992, s. 137(4), 282

Tax Reporter: ¶188-345ff.

Interest on overdue and overpaid CGT

6480   Interest on overdue CGT

For interest on overdue CGT, surcharges, etc., see 2368.

Tax Reporter: ¶182-925

6484   Interest on overpaid CGT ('repayment supplement')

Where there has been an overpayment of CGT and repayment is made, in some circumstances, it is to be made with a tax-free supplement.

Under self-assessment any repayment by HMRC of CGT, penalties, surcharges, etc. are to be increased by a repayment supplement, equal to interest at a rate fixed by the Treasury, between the date of payment of the tax, etc. and the date of repayment.

For rates of interest and interest factor tables, see Key Data.

Legislation: ICTA 1988, s. 824(8); TCGA 1992, s. 283

Tax Reporter: ¶182-975

6490   General penalties in relation to CGT

For failures in relation to compliance requirements, see 12000ff.

Tax Reporter: ¶180-000ff.

Inheritance tax

KEY POINTS

- Inheritance tax is a tax on the transfer of value by individuals, including executors and trustees (see 6525).

- Transfers of value may be chargeable transfers, exempt transfers or potentially exempt transfers (see 6525 and 6610ff.).

- As regards lifetime transfers, the value is determined by the reduction in the transferor's estate (see 6526).

- Property is generally valued for IHT purposes at the price that it would fetch in the open market (see 6570ff.).

- On death, there is a deemed transfer of value (see 6526).

- Higher rates of inheritance tax apply to transfers on death than apply to lifetime transfers (see 6526).

- Additional tax may be due on lifetime transfer if death occurs within seven years. Death within seven years of making a PET will bring the PET into charge (see 6800ff.).

- Taper relief may apply to reduce the tax charge where additional tax is due on a lifetime transfer because the donor dies within seven years of making the transfer (see 6801).

- Reduced 36% rate of IHT where more than 10% of a taxable estate (as defined) is donated to charity. Estate to be divided into three components and each component can be separately entitled to the reduced rate.

- Reduced 36% rate can be extended to GWR assets by election to merge separate components.

- As far as settled property is concerned, inheritance tax distinguishes between trusts where someone is beneficially entitled to an interest in possession (see 6526ff.), discretionary trusts and trusts with no qualifying interest in possession (see 6940ff.) and special trusts, such as employee trusts or protective trusts (see 6998).

- Most trusts are subject to an inheritance tax charge on each ten-year anniversary (see 6943ff.).

- An exit charge applies where property leaves most trusts (see 6962 and 6964).

- Anti-avoidance provisions exist regarding pre-owned assets (see 6725).

> • Various exemptions and reliefs apply to remove or reduce any charge to inheritance tax (see 7150ff.).
>
> • Various administrative requirements apply in relation to inheritance tax, including the delivery of accounts and the payment of the tax (see 7500ff.).
>
> • Inheritance tax on trusts is brought within the disclosure of tax avoidance schemes but application of DOTAS to a wider range of planning arrangements has been temporarily withdrawn but with detailed proposals later in 2016 (see 6976).

Inheritance tax in the UK

6505   Estate duty, capital transfer tax and inheritance tax

In 1974, capital transfer tax (CTT) replaced estate duty, an eighty-year old duty which had been levied on all property passing on death. Capital transfer tax was a tax on both inter vivos gifts and upon the estate of a deceased. In its short life CTT was much amended. From 25 July 1986, CTT was renamed inheritance tax (IHT) and its operation was substantially modified so as to exclude many, though not all, charges on inter vivos transfers. Inheritance tax was in some ways a return to the old concept of estate duty, but the central idea of CTT, that a lifetime transfer of value was to be measured by the loss to the donor's estate, was retained (see 6525).

Legislation: *Inheritance Tax Act* 1984

Other Material: *HMRC Inheritance Tax: Customer Guide* available on the HMRC website at www.hmrc.gov.uk/cto/customerguide/page1.htm

Tax Reporter: ¶600-100

6507   Consolidation of IHT legislation

The provisions of the *Finance Acts* 1975–1984 concerning CTT were consolidated in the *Capital Transfer Tax Act* 1984. The consolidation Act is effective from 1 January 1985. Since the passing of *Finance Act* 1986, the *Capital Transfer Tax Act* 1984 is cited as the *Inheritance Tax Act* 1984. Furthermore, after 25 July 1986 all references to capital transfer tax are construed as references to IHT where they appear:

• in any other enactment passed before or in the same session as *Finance Act* 1986; or

• in any document executed, made, served or issued on or before the passing of the 1986 Act or at any time after its passing.

Legislation: *Inheritance Tax Act* 1984

Tax Reporter: ¶600-500

6520   Interaction between IHT and other capital taxes

If there is a disposal by way of a *sale* at arm's length between unconnected persons, there may be a liability to CGT but not to IHT – there is a presumption of a transaction at proper value.

If there is a disposal by way of a *gift*, there may be a liability to both IHT and CGT, but CGT hold-over relief may be available depending upon the type of asset where there is an immediate charge to IHT or if the gift is a PET of business or agricultural assets.

If there is a disposal *on death*, there may be liability to IHT but not to CGT.

Tax Reporter: ¶617-400

An outline of IHT

6525   Persons and property chargeable to IHT

Inheritance tax is charged on individuals, including executors and trustees, but it does not apply to transfers of value by companies (other than close companies: see 6555).

All property is liable to be charged to IHT. However, there is no charge where an individual domiciled outside the UK transfers property 'situated outside the United Kingdom' although the proposals to extend 'deemed domicile' *for all taxes* from 6 April 2017 once an individual has been resident for 15 out of 20 years may bring more value into the UK tax charge (see 6550).

Transfer of value

Inheritance tax is charged on the value transferred by chargeable transfers. A transfer of value is determined by reference to a 'disposition' (see 6660) which results in a reduction in the value of the transferor's total property, i.e. his 'lifetime estate' (see 6630) (see further 6612). However, there is also a deemed transfer of value of the whole of a person's 'estate on death' (see 6780ff.). For these purposes, transfers of value are of three kinds, namely, chargeable transfers, exempt transfers and potentially exempt transfers. There are also certain special charges in respect of settlements.

Chargeable transfer

A 'chargeable transfer' is any transfer of value other than an exempt transfer (see 7192ff.) or a potentially exempt transfer (see 6611).

Legislation: IHTA 1984, s. 1, 2, 3(1), 3A

Other Material: *HMRC Inheritance Tax: Customer Guide* available on the HMRC website at www.hmrc.gov.uk/cto/customerguide/page1.htm

Tax Reporter: ¶601-250

6526   Scope of IHT charges

The deemed transfer of value made on death (see 6525) is liable to be charged to IHT. The tax also applies to potentially exempt lifetime transfers which are made less than seven years before the death of the transferor and to transfers inter vivos which do not qualify as 'potentially exempt transfers' (see 6611). The tax also applies to settled property.

Certain dispositions are not charged to IHT (see 6528).

Lifetime transfers

Inheritance tax is a cumulative tax (see 6527), charged on the value transferred by a chargeable transfer made inter vivos. It is charged by reference to the amount by which the transferor's estate has been reduced. It should be noted that the transferor's estate will be reduced by the IHT payable on the gift as well as by the gift itself (unless, of course, the transferee agrees to pay the tax). No other tax is taken into account when calculating the loss to the transferor's estate. Obviously, if there is a 'disposition' (see 6660) for market value, there will be no diminution in the value of the transferor's estate.

There are now three rates of inheritance tax: 0%, 40%, and a lower 36% rate which applies, on death on or after 6 April 2012, if more than 10% of a taxable estate, as defined, is given to charity the lower rate of 36% can apply (see 6806) (with tax on certain lifetime transfers chargeable at half rates – 20%). Relevant property (discretionary) trusts are charged at 30% of the lifetime rate which is why we talk of a 6% rate applying here. The range of transfers made inter vivos which qualify as chargeable transfers is limited so as to exclude exempt transfers (see 7192ff.). 'Potentially exempt transfers' (PETs: see 6611) are treated as exempt transfers unless and until the transferor dies within seven years of making the transfer. Thus, IHT is now largely a tax on transfers on or within a short time before death.

Death

When someone dies there is a deemed transfer of all the property to which he was beneficially entitled immediately before his death. The transfer on death is cumulated with previous chargeable lifetime transfers within the last seven years (see 6527). The higher rate of IHT applies to transfers on death.

Death may also bring about a tax charge or increased tax charge on transfers within seven years before death. If death occurs within seven years after making a chargeable transfer, additional tax may have to be paid by the transferee (see 6610). A potentially exempt transfer will also become chargeable if made within seven years of death and tax may become payable by the transferee as a result (see 6611).

Settled property

(1)   Interest in possession

An interest in possession in settled property, generally from arrangements made before 22 March 2006, exists where the person having the interest has the immediate entitlement to any income produced by that property as the income arises. However, a discretion or power that can be exercised after the income arises which has the effect of withholding the income from that person, negates the existence of an interest in possession. A 'qualifying interest in possession' is an interest in possession to which an individual (or in certain circumstances a company) is beneficially entitled.

Example

Andrew transfers property to Brian and Claire (as trustees) on trust for Duncan for life with remainder to Emma for life and then Florence absolutely. Duncan has an interest in possession since he is entitled to the income from the property for his life. Emma does not have an interest in possession but will do so when Duncan dies.

For interests in possession, see 6903ff.

(2)   No interest in possession

Under discretionary settlements there is no interest in possession since there is no interest until that discretion is exercised.

Example

Alan leaves property on trust to Bella and Charlie (as trustees) to appoint to such of his five children as they in their absolute discretion see fit. None of Alan's children at this stage has an interest in possession. As soon as

---

> Bella and Charlie appoint the property or part to one or all of Alan's children, an interest in possession will arise on the value appointed.

The principal charge to IHT here occurs where, immediately before a ten-year anniversary, all or part of any property comprised in a settlement is 'relevant property' (see 6940). The ten-year anniversary occurs every ten years after the commencement of the settlement. However, no anniversary before 1 April 1983 was a chargeable event.

The charge at other times occurs when property ceases to be relevant property or where trustees dispose of property and thereby reduce the value of relevant property in the settlement.

Finance Act 2006 made radical changes to the taxation of settled property. From 22 March 2006, only lifetime gifts to an individual, into a disabled trust (see 7011), into a bereaved minor's trust (see 7003) on the coming to an end of an immediate post-death interest (see 6907) and on the creation of a transitional serial interest (see 6908) qualify for 'potential exemption'. Lifetime interest in possession trusts created on or after 22 March 2006, other than those mentioned above, are taxed under the 'relevant property regime' (see 6880ff.). Trusts created on or after 22 March 2006 can no longer qualify as accumulation and maintenance trusts (see 7002).

Legislation: FA 2006, s. 157; IHTA 1984, s. 59(1)

Case: *Pearson v IR Commrs* [1981] AC 753

Other Material: *HMRC Inheritance Tax: Customer Guide*

Tax Reporter: ¶600-700

6527 Cumulation

The position before 1981 used to be that all chargeable transfers made by a person during his lifetime would be cumulated. This meant that the rate of IHT payable on later transfers would be worked out by looking at the total of all previous chargeable transfers. The combination of a limitless cumulation period and graduated rates of tax ensured a penal rate on later transfers. However, a ten-year maximum period on cumulations was introduced in 1981, and in respect of transfers after 17 March 1986, the cumulation period was further reduced to the current seven years.

The deemed transfer on death is also cumulated with previous lifetime transfers within the last seven years.

For the effect on the calculation of tax, see 6614 and 6800.

Legislation: IHTA 1984, s. 7(1)

Other Material: *HMRC Inheritance Tax: Customer Guide*

Tax Reporter: ¶604-150

6528   Dispositions not charged to IHT

No liability to IHT will arise if the disposition is deemed not to be a transfer of value (see 7150ff.) or if the transfer is exempt (see 7192ff.) or potentially exempt (see 6611), or if the disposition is one of excluded property (see 7397). The legislation defines the circumstances in which the exceptions occur.

Reliefs are given in various ways:

- relief for transfers of business and agricultural property is given by reducing the value transferred (see 7253 and 7292);

- relief for woodlands is given by leaving property out of account (see 7320);

- relief for successive transfers is given by quick succession relief which reduces the IHT chargeable on the second chargeable transfer.

Legislation: IHTA 1984, s. 3A, 10–42

Other Material: *HMRC Inheritance Tax: Customer Guide*

Tax Reporter: ¶601-250

6530   Crystallisation of IHT liability

For events that occur on or after 6 April 2014, the date on which any tax due, and the date on which returns must be made to HMRC, is aligned so that both forms and tax are now due six months after the end of the month in which the relevant event occurred.

For events that occurred before 6 April 2014, the transferor or trustees if settled property is involved had, within 12 months of the lifetime transfer, to deliver an account of the transfer to HMRC, or within three months of the beginning of the day on which the person who is to make the return became liable for the IHT if that date was later. However, the tax was due six months after the end of the month in which a chargeable transfer is made, except for transfers made between 5 April and 1 October in any year otherwise than on death, when the tax becomes due at the end of April in the next year.

Where the IHT charge occurs on death, an account of the deceased person's estate must be delivered to HMRC otherwise a grant of representation cannot be obtained. Delivery of the account must be within 12 months of the end of the month in which the transferor's death took place or within three months of the date when the personal representatives first act or have reason to believe that an account is required. Personal representatives must pay all the tax for which they are liable on delivery of their account. The 12-month time-limit after death also applies to tax on a potentially exempt transfer which becomes chargeable because of the donor's death within seven years.

Legislation: IHTA 1984, s. 216

Other Material: *HMRC Inheritance Tax: Customer Guide*

Tax Reporter: ¶180-725

6540 Domicile for IHT

The question of 'domicile' is important if the assets to be transferred are located outside the UK (see 6550). A person's domicile for tax purposes may be determined by general law (a domicile of origin/dependency or a domicile of choice: see 219) or it could be a fiscal domicile by operation of law – deemed or elected domicile (as for IHT, see below).

Domicile has an extended meaning for IHT purposes. A person who is not domiciled under the general law of the UK will be treated as domiciled in the UK for IHT purposes only at the relevant time:

- if he was domiciled in the UK within the three years immediately preceding the relevant time; or

- if he was resident in the UK in not less than 17 of the 20 tax years ending with the tax year in which the relevant time falls (though any dwelling-house available for use in the UK has always been ignored: see 213).

But see the post 5 April 2013 rules for non-UK domiciled spouses, to elect to be UK domiciled (6541) below where an individual with an elected domicile retains, that domicile for four complete tax years from the date of departure. Note the election is automatically disapplied after four tax years of absence, so if the couple go abroad and become non-resident for more than four tax years, the need to renew the election must be considered on their return.

Note the Summer 2015 Budget proposal to extend UK domicile from 6 April 2017, initially to be included in *Finance Act* 2016 but now to be included in Finance Bill 2017 (following consultation), to apply *for all tax purposes* (not just for deemed IHT domicile) to long-term residents in the

UK where they have been resident in the UK for 15 out of the previous 20 years which will replace the current 17 out of 20 year rule.

Exceptionally, the question of domicile for IHT is determined by reference to the UK, while for the purposes of the general law one is domiciled in one of the three jurisdictions within the UK (England and Wales, Scotland, or Northern Ireland).

Example

Bob is an American citizen who has been living and working in Britain for the past 18 tax years, during which time he has made frequent visits to the USA and reiterated his desire to return there permanently. Bob makes a gift of £100,000 to his daughter.

Under general law, Bob is domiciled in Florida. For the purposes of UK IHT, Bob is treated as domiciled in the UK under the 17 out of 20 tax year rule. Accordingly, if Bob dies within seven years, the gift will be liable to tax regardless of where the property gifted is located although if this was the only gift Bob made the practical impact is that the gift will be within Bob's nil-rate band so the effect will be to increase the tax on the death estate.

HMRC have issued revised guidance which states that it will consider making an enquiry where domicile could be an issue, or making a determination of IHT in such cases, only where there is a significant risk of loss of UK tax.

The significance of the risk will be assessed by HMRC using a wide range of factors which will include:

- a review of the information available to HMRC about the individual on HMRC databases; and

- whether there is a significant amount of tax (all taxes and duties, not just IHT) at risk.

HMRC do not state the amount of tax they would consider to be significant but a comparison to other circumstances might suggest a relatively modest amount.

Finance Act 2013, s. 178 increases the lifetime exemption available on transfers to non-domiciled spouses/civil partners up to the current nil-rate band of £325,000 with the intention that, for the future, any increase in the nil-rate band will apply here as well (see 7192).

In addition, an individual not UK domiciled under general law (or through the deeming provisions) will be able to elect to be UK domiciled if married or in a civil partnership with a UK domiciled partner. The election can only be made once the marriage/civil partnership is in place (see 6541).

Where an election to be made, it would continue to have effect for four complete tax years after leaving the UK. Presumably, this change is more likely to apply to EU citizens of modest means where the current rules for inter spouse/civil partner transfers and the (old) £55,000 non-domiciled spouse limit caused hardship or where the surviving partner is much younger and is likely to survive at least four years.

Legislation: IHTA 1984, s. 267; FA 2013, s. 178

Case: *Allen (Executors of Johnson dec'd) v R & C Commrs* (2005) Sp C 481

Other Material: HMRC Brief 34/10; *HMRC Inheritance Tax: Customer Guide*

Tax Reporter: ¶684-400

6541 Electing to be UK domiciled for IHT

Before 6 April 2013, an individual's domicile status (when affecting their IHT liability) was determined as a matter of law. An individual was either UK domiciled or non-UK domiciled but where an individual had been resident in the United Kingdom for 17 tax years out of 20 tax years they became deemed domiciled so that they then became liable to IHT on worldwide assets. Anyone who is non-UK domiciled only pays UK IHT on UK situs assets.

Finance Act 2013, s. 177 introduced provisions which allow an individual (or their executors) by the introduction of (new) IHTA 1984, s. 267ZA to elect to be UK domiciled. Under (new) IHTA 1984, s. 267ZA(1) an individual can elect to be treated as UK domiciled from a specified date, which cannot be earlier than 6 April 2013, where either Condition A (new) IHTA 1984, s. 267ZA(3) or Condition B (new) IHTA 1984, s. 267ZA(4) are satisfied.

Condition A is that the individual is not domiciled in the United Kingdom at the date of the election and the individual's spouse or civil partner is UK domiciled.

Condition B requires that the electing individual not be UK domiciled at the date of death of their spouse or civil partner (provided that date is on or after 6 April 2013) and that spouse or civil partner was UK domiciled at the time of their death.

Executors can only elect if Condition B applies – it would seem that the circumstances where a death election is made may be exceptional. Perhaps a *commorientes* situation where the UK domiciled spouse/civil partner is the older partner. A death election must be made within two years of the death of the UK domiciled spouse/civil partner, or such additional time as HMRC may allow.

The election does not exclude the current exemption from IHT of Government Securities free of tax whilst in foreign ownership and other savings specified in IHTA 1984, s. 6(2), (3) or 48(4).

The election is also to be ignored (new) IHTA 1984, s. 267ZA(6) in determining or applying any qualifying double tax relief arrangements under IHTA 1984, s. 158(6).

The election can only apply to events on or after 6 April 2013 but the following factors are relevant to the making of a valid election:

- The election must be made by notice in writing (*HMRC do not produce a form*).

- The election can specify the date from which it is to apply but that date cannot be more than seven years back and cannot apply earlier than 6 April 2013 or the date of marriage if later. If no date is mentioned in the election, then a lifetime election takes effect from the date it is signed.

- If a death election is made, that election is deemed to have taken place immediately before the death of the UK domiciled spouse or civil partner but the death cannot be more than two years before the date of the election.

- An election can only be made, to cover a relevant period, where the individual was either married or in a civil partnership with the relevant spouse throughout the period.

Example

Orlando (who is Italian domiciled) is married to Judith (UK domiciled) and he has only been in the United Kingdom for five years at 30 June 2013 (so is not deemed domiciled). If he elects to be UK domiciled he can only elect to be so domiciled from 6 April 2013.

Example

Antonia (who is Spanish domiciled) has been living in the UK since May 2009 and married Paul (UK domiciled) on 1 July 2013. She can only elect to be UK domiciled, under these rules, from 1 July 2013, the date of marriage.

Any election, lifetime or death, cannot be revoked but will cease to have effect once the individual who made the election ceases to be resident in the United Kingdom for a period of four successive tax years beginning any time after the date the election was made.

Example

Gaston (who is French domiciled) elected to be UK domiciled on 5 January 2014 just before the death of his wife. This was so that he could inherit his UK domiciled spouse's assets free of UK IHT. However, it was always his intention to return to France and it would follow that if, for example, he left the United Kingdom in January 2016 that after 6 April 2020 he will then have been non-resident (it is assumed) for four successive tax years and the election would then lapse. It will also follow that Gaston will be at risk of UK IHT on worldwide assets for a four-year period but in making the election he would have to balance the IHT avoided on his wife's death against the IHT that would apply on his worldwide assets, his state of health and how likely it is that he would die within four years.

Note the Summer 2015 Budget proposal to extend UK domicile from 6 April 2017, initially proposed to be included in *Finance Act* 2016, to apply *for all tax purposes* (not just for deemed IHT domicile) to long-term residents in the UK where they have been resident in the UK for 15 out of the previous 20 years which will replace the current 17 out of 20 year rule has been delayed until Finance Bill 2017.

Legislation: FA 2013, s. 177

Tax Reporter: ¶644-900

6550   Location of assets for IHT

Property situated outside the UK is 'excluded property' (i.e. not within the charge to IHT: see 7397) if, and only if, the person beneficially entitled to it is an individual domiciled (see 6540) outside the UK: in other words, for persons domiciled abroad, IHT generally applies only to their UK assets. (If an individual is domiciled in the UK, then any assets can be charged to tax regardless of their location.) It may therefore be important to know in what country certain property is located. Where there are no special rules governing the location of assets, the question is determined by the general law.

The potential charge to inheritance tax from holdings by foreign investors in UK-authorised funds was removed for transfers on or after 16 October 2002. The rules apply to the holding of non-UK domiciled investors or their trusts in authorised unit trusts and open-ended investment companies. IHT relief is also extended to losses on the sale of listed shares in open-ended investment companies.

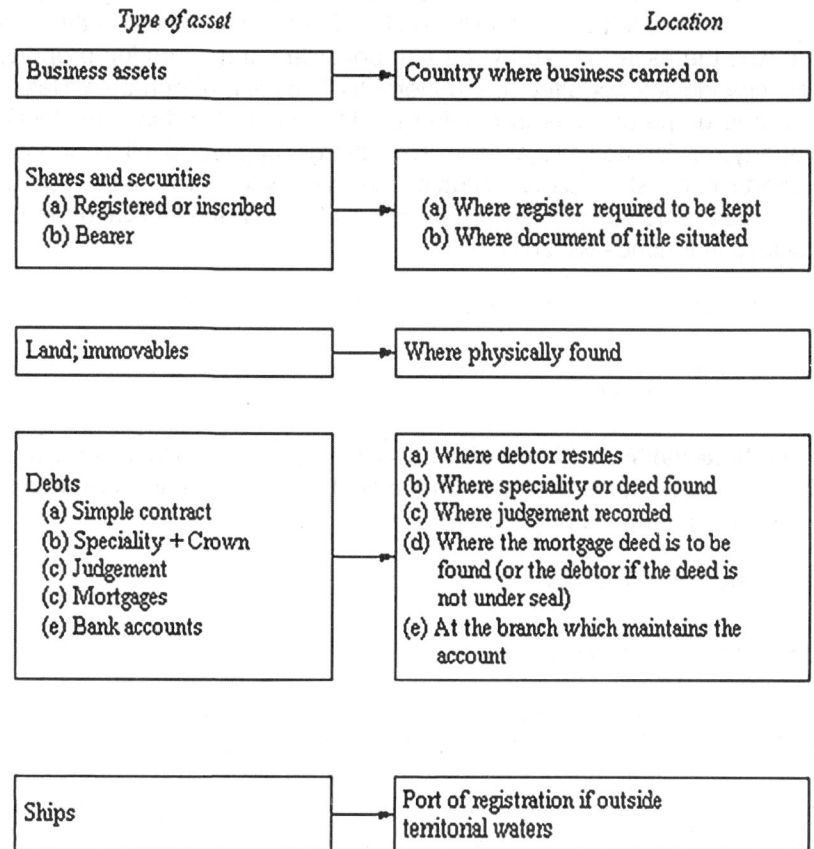

Type of asset	Location
Business assets	Country where business carried on
Shares and securities (a) Registered or inscribed (b) Bearer	(a) Where register required to be kept (b) Where document of title situated
Land; immovables	Where physically found
Debts (a) Simple contract (b) Speciality + Crown (c) Judgement (c) Mortgages (e) Bank accounts	(a) Where debtor resides (b) Where speciality or deed found (c) Where judgement recorded (d) Where the mortgage deed is to be found (or the debtor if the deed is not under seal) (e) At the branch which maintains the account
Ships	Port of registration if outside territorial waters

The Privy Council has held that the location of a non-negotiable promissory note is determined like that of most other debts (see above) and is accordingly located wherever it can be enforced (i.e. normally the country where the debtor resides). However, negotiable instruments are situated wherever there is an available market for their negotiation.

Where foreign works of art are normally kept outside the UK, they could be outside the scope of IHT as discussed above; if the owner dies while they are in the UK for exhibition, cleaning or restoration, any liability will be waived. Chattels are normally located where they are physically situated.

The Summer 2015 (post-election) Budget included an announcement to ensure that from 6 April 2017 all UK residential property owned by non-domiciles, regardless of their residence status for tax purposes, through any offshore structure, whether trust or closely controlled company will be brought within the charge to UK inheritance tax. It was mainstream tax planning to avoid the London property being UK situs assets; a London property would be owned, for example by a Jersey company with the shares then owned by a non-UK trust so it was any interest in the trust that was the asset owned by the non-domicile not the London property. This change will not affect the general IHT position of non-domiciles or excluded property trusts in relation to UK assets other than residential property, or for non-UK assets. The charge applies to all residential property not just property occupied by the owner as a home, so an investment portfolio of flats would be included with the legislation being included in Finance Bill 2017.

Legislation: IHTA 1984, s. 3(2), 48, 82; FA 2003, s. 185

Case: *Kwok Chi Leung Karl (Exor of Lamson Kwok) v Commr of Estate Duty* [1988] BTC 8,073

Other Material: ESC F7, *Foreign owned works of art*; HMRC *Inheritance Tax: Customer Guide* available on the HMRC website at www.hmrc.gov. uk/cto/customerguide/page1.htm

Tax Reporter: ¶602-150

6555   Close companies and IHT

Inheritance tax is chargeable only on individuals, except in relation to dealings in settled property. This means that companies are not liable to IHT when they make transfers of value. However, there are special provisions in the legislation which deal with close companies. A transfer of value by a close company is apportioned to the company's participators (a wider definition than simply shareholders) though the IHT is primarily payable by the company itself. Such transfers are immediately chargeable; they are not PETs (see 6611).

Further, since (by virtue of the rules mentioned above) an interest in possession to which a close company is entitled is attributed to its participators, when a participator disposes of any part of his shareholding, in addition to any charge in respect of the actual shares, a charge can also arise in respect of the settled property (see 6909).

Neither a dividend paid by a subsidiary to its parent nor a transfer of assets between a wholly-owned subsidiary and its parent (nor between two wholly-owned subsidiaries) is a transfer of value.

Apportionment

The value transferred by a close company will be apportioned amongst its participators according to their respective rights and interests immediately before the transfer and, if one of those participators is a close company, that amount will be further sub-apportioned to the participators in that company.

No apportionment will be made for any value attributable to any payment or transfer of assets to any person who brings it into account for the purposes of their income tax or corporation tax computations (including UK company dividends and other distributions not chargeable to income tax or corporation tax). Nor will any apportionment be made for an amount attributable to an individual domiciled outside the UK which is attributable to any property outside the UK.

Alteration of share or loan capital

An alteration or extinguishment of a close company's 'unquoted' (see 6571) share or loan capital, or any 'rights' over that capital, resulting in value being transferred between shareholders, is treated as a 'disposition' (see 6660) made by the participators. 'Rights' here include rights in the assets of the company available for distribution among the participators in a winding up. Such alterations are not PETs (see 6611).

Liability for IHT

The company is primarily liable for IHT. However, if tax remains unpaid, the persons to whom any amounts in excess of 5% have been apportioned and any individual whose estate has been increased by the transfer are liable for any unpaid tax.

An individual will only be liable for an amount of tax corresponding to the value apportioned to them or, in the case of an increase in their estate, will be liable only for the amount of the increase.

Legislation: IHTA 1984, s. 94–102, 202; CTA 2009, s. 1285

Tax Reporter: ¶603-700

Valuation rules for IHT

6570 Valuation generally for IHT

The value of any property for IHT purposes is the price which the property might reasonably be expected to fetch if sold on the open market at that time. However, the price must not be assumed to be reduced merely because all the property is on the market at one time.

It must be assumed that there is both a willing buyer and a willing seller and that the asset is sold in the most advantageous way, e.g. well advertised, put into its most saleable form, etc. to maximise value.

There are a number of specific reliefs applicable on death (see 6810); subject to those, there are some specific rules which should be considered (see 6571 to 6573).

Legislation: IHTA 1984, s. 160

Other Material: Revenue Interpretation, *Inheritance tax: valuation of assets at the date of death*

Tax Reporter: ¶637-300

6571 Valuation of quoted shares

Stocks and shares which are 'quoted' (i.e. listed on a recognised stock exchange) are valued at the lower of:

- the 'quarter up' value; and
- the mid-market value.

The quarter value is found by taking the lower of the selling price and buying price at close on the day of death, plus one-quarter of the difference between the two.

The mid-market value is the halfway price between the lowest and highest marked bargains for the day.

If the Stock Exchange is closed on the day in point, then the last previous quotation or the next quotation after that day may be taken. If the investment is quoted cum dividend, this means that the buyer will get the benefit of the next dividend and the price will, therefore, include that accrued net income. However, if the investment is quoted ex dividend, the dividend less any income tax must be brought into account since the price will not reflect the accrued net income.

Example

John died on 18 July 2015. His net free personalty included:

	Investments	Quotation
(a)	5,000 10p ordinary shares in A plc	50–58p
(b)	2,000 £1 ordinary shares in B plc (dividend due on 19 August is 20p per share)	60–66 ex div.

	Valuation	£
(a)	5,000 10p ordinary shares in A plc at 52	2,600
(b)	2,000 ordinary shares in B plc at 61¹/₂ ex div.	1,230
(c)	Dividend of 20p per share on (b)	400

Note that the valuation basis of shares for capital gains tax, corporation tax and income tax purposes has been changed by SI 2015/616 (*Market Value of Shares, Securities and Strips Regulations* 2015) but the above rules still apply for IHT purposes.

Legislation: IHTA 1984, s. 160; *Market Value of Shares, Securities and Strips Regulations* 2015 (SI 2015/616)

Other Material: Revenue interpretation, 'Inheritance tax: valuation of assets at the date of death'

Tax Reporter: ¶638-300

6572   Valuation of unquoted shares

If stocks and shares are not 'quoted' on a stock exchange, etc. (see 6571), their market value must be estimated. The following matters will be considered, although they will not all necessarily carry equal weight:

- the size of the hypothetical sale;
- dividend record;
- profit cover for dividends;
- earnings yield and price/earnings ratio;
- general economic climate;
- value of assets per share;
- how fashionable is the business being valued;
- comparisons with similar quoted companies;
- restrictions on transfer; and
- management.

Further, in arriving at a hypothetical open market value, evidence of open market sales of the same or similar property are particularly relevant and admissible, even if not conclusive. Similarly, the Court of Session has held that agreements between taxpayers and HMRC as to value are also relevant. The court said that the best evidence of open market value would be evidence of sales of the same or similar property, though if conditions had changed the evidence might have to be qualified by taking account of other evidence.

It could not be said to follow from the fact that the value was to be ascertained on a hypothetical basis that any evidence of actual transactions should be ruled out. The same approach applied to agreements with HMRC, though the evidence might not carry much weight. In reality, modest shareholdings in private companies do not change hands so the valuation process is entirely artificial.

Legislation: IHTA 1984, s. 168

Other Material: Revenue interpretation, 'Inheritance tax: valuation of assets at the date of death'

Tax Reporter: ¶638-450

6573   Valuation of land

The valuation of land is negotiated between the representatives of the transferor and HMRC. HMRC usually refer the matter to the District Valuer. In arriving at a value, recent sales of similar property in the area will be relevant although not conclusive. Also, if the property is subsequently sold, the actual sale price will not automatically upset the value placed on the property by HMRC or the District Valuer. However, if land is sold less than three years after death for less than its valuation at death, the sale price may be substituted provided that it was the best reasonably obtainable in an arm's length transaction between unconnected persons; sales to connected persons (even if the sale were at an auction) do not allow a value reduction (see 6810).

Where the transferor and HMRC cannot agree, a value will be placed on the land. The taxpayer can appeal against the valuation. Appeals may be made direct to the Upper Tribunal for England and Wales, the Lands Tribunal for Scotland or the Lands Tribunal for Northern Ireland, depending on where the land is situated.

Leased or tenanted property

A property that is subject to a lease is often worth much less than if sold on the open market with vacant possession. The method of valuation will depend on the length of the unexpired lease. Where the lease is to expire in the reasonably foreseeable future, its value will be its vacant possession value reduced by an appropriate percentage. However, if the lease is a long one which is not due to come to an end in the foreseeable future, the value is generally determined by reference to the value of income (after deduction of reasonable outgoings) received from it.

Farm cottages

Farm cottages which are valued as part of an agricultural property and are occupied by persons employed solely for agricultural purposes are valued without regard to their value on the open market if they were not so occupied.

Legislation: IHTA 1984, s. 160, 169, 170

Cases: *Alexander v IR Commrs* [1991] BTC 8,024; *IR Commrs v Gray* [1994] BTC 8,034; *Walton (as surviving executor of Walton) v IR Commrs* [1996] BTC 8,015

Other Material: Revenue interpretation, 'Inheritance tax: valuation of assets at the date of death'

Tax Reporter: ¶637-800

6575 Related property

Where the value of any property comprised in the estate would be less than the appropriate portion of the aggregate value of that and any related property, IHT is charged on the appropriate portion of the aggregate value.

Property is related to the property comprised in a person's estate if:

(1) it is comprised in the estate of the spouse or civil partner; or

(2) it is or has been within the preceding five years:

    (a) the property of a charity, or held on trust for charitable purposes only; or

    (b) the property of a body mentioned in IHTA 1984, s. 24, 24A, or 25 (see 7195ff.);

    and became so on a transfer of value which was made by him or his spouse or civil partner after 15 April 1976 and was exempt to the extent that the value transferred was attributable to the property.

With the exception of shares, the appropriate portion is the proportion that the property transferred bears to the sum of all items of related property if valued individually. This portion is then applied to the aggregate value.

Example

Jack owns one of a pair of Ming vases. His wife owns the other. Valued individually, the vases are worth £7,000 each. However, valued as a pair, they are worth £20,000.

> On Jack's death, his vase is valued at £10,000. The appropriate portion is 50%, and 50% of the aggregate value is £10,000. If the vases were instead owned by Jack and his sister then each vase would only be worth the standalone value of £7,000 because in that instance they are not related property.

As far as shares are concerned, the appropriate portion is determined by reference to the numbers of shares held, rather than to their value.

Example

Hugo and Wendy, husband and wife, each own 49% of the shares of their family company, HW Ltd. Each holding is 'related' to the other, therefore on a transfer of value each holding would be valued, not as a 49% holding, but as one-half ('the appropriate portion') of the value of a 98% holding ('the aggregate').

Where related property is sold within three years of death, and the sale price is less than the value determined on death in accordance with the related property provisions, the value at death may be recalculated ignoring any related property (see 6815).

Legislation: IHTA 1984, s. 161

Other Material: *HMRC Inheritance Tax: Customer Guide* available on the HMRC website at www.hmrc.gov.uk/cto/customerguide/page1.htm; HMRC Brief 71/07: IHT and the valuation of property owned jointly by spouses or civil partners

Tax Reporter: ¶637-450

Lifetime transfers

6610   IHT and lifetime transfers: IHT and PETs

Inheritance tax is charged on the value transferred by chargeable transfers of value made *inter vivos* after 26 March 1974 (see 6525). For these purposes, there are three kinds of transfer of value:

- chargeable transfers;
- exempt transfers; and
- potentially exempt transfers.

A 'chargeable transfer' is any transfer of value other than an exempt transfer or a potentially exempt transfer (see 6525).

An 'exempt transfer' is any transfer described as such in the IHT legislation (see 7192ff.).

A 'potentially exempt transfer' (PET) is described at 6611 below; a PET made seven years or more before the death of the transferor is an exempt transfer but if the transferor dies within seven years of making the PET the transfer then becomes a chargeable transfer. Until it becomes clear that a PET is chargeable, the transfer is assumed to be exempt. The personal representatives may well be liable for the additional tax but there is limited relief where they have proceeded on the understanding that there were no appropriate transfers (see 7533).

Legislation: IHTA 1984, s. 2, 3A

Other Material: *HMRC Inheritance Tax: Customer Guide* available on the HMRC website at www.hmrc.gov.uk/cto/customerguide/page1.htm

Tax Reporter: ¶607-000

6611   'Potentially exempt transfer'

A 'potentially exempt transfer' (PET) is a transfer of value:

*   which is made by an individual after 17 March 1986;

*   which is a gift to another individual, or (prior to 22 March 2006 into an accumulation and maintenance settlement) a disabled person's trust; and

*   which would otherwise be a chargeable transfer.

Further, if the transfer is a gift to another individual then it must be one whereby the property concerned becomes comprised in the estate of the transferee or whereby the estate of the transferee is increased even though the property in question does not become comprised in that estate. In the case of a gift subject to reservation of benefit by the donor, there is a PET at the time any reservation is released (see 6785). A PET may also take place where certain debts or encumbrances are discharged (see 6782).

There was considerable criticism that the definition of a PET did not include a transfer into settlement where there was an interest in possession or any disposition of the settled property by the tenant for life. Since the tenant for life of settled property, generally in respect of pre-22 March 2006 arrangements, is treated as though he were absolute owner for IHT purposes, it was felt to be a startling anomaly that transfers by him or to him were not potentially exempt. That anomaly was corrected and potential exemption was extended to such transfers in

1987. The definition of a PET included any transfer after 16 March 1987 to 21 March 2006:

- which is attributable to property in which an individual became entitled to an interest in possession; or

- which increased the value of property in which an individual was entitled to an interest in possession.

Further, transfers by the tenant for life and the termination of his interest will be potentially exempt provided they satisfy the conditions for potential exemption generally, i.e. the transferee must be an individual, or (prior to 22 March 2006 an accumulation and maintenance trust) a trust for the disabled.

Until 22 March 2006, gifts to either interest in possession or accumulation and maintenance trusts were regarded as PETs (see above). From that date, this exemption no longer applies. In addition, the ten-year and exit charges, which previously only applied to discretionary trusts, now also apply to all trusts other than those which are specifically exempt.

For a further discussion of the rules and anti-avoidance provisions preventing property being transferred free of tax into discretionary trusts by means of short interests in possession, see 6909ff..

Deemed transfers of value, such as transfers on death, are not PETs.

Legislation: IHTA 1984, s. 3A; *Finance Act* 2006, s. 156 and Sch. 20

Other Material: *HMRC Inheritance Tax: Customer Guide* available on the HMRC website at www.hmrc.gov.uk/cto/customerguide/page1.htm

Tax Reporter: ¶607-100

6612 Value transferred by lifetime transfer

A transfer of value is any disposition made by the transferor as a result of which the value of his estate immediately after the disposition is less than it would be but for the disposition. The amount by which it is less is the value transferred by the transfer (the loss to the estate rule) – if the transferor pays any IHT due that is also a reduction in the estate and a grossing up process is necessary (see 6620). The reduction in the donor's estate may not match the increase in the donee's estate.

Example

Albert transfers a 2% shareholding in TPMC Ltd into a discretionary trust. Immediately before the transfer, he had a 51% holding. There are 10,000 issued shares in the company. Values per share are as follows:

% holding	£ per share
51	12
49	7
2	2

The diminution in value of his estate is calculated as follows:

	£
Before	
5,100 shares at £12	61,200
After	
4,900 shares at £7	(34,300)
Diminution in value	26,900

If Albert pays any IHT due in consequence of the disposition, the above amount must be grossed up to give the aggregate diminution in value of his estate and hence the value transferred by the transfer of value (before business property relief if applicable; see 7253ff.).

No account is taken of the value of excluded property which ceases to form part of a person's estate as a result of a disposition (see 7394). Apportionment is made where the value has to be determined by reference to the value of other property. For detailed valuation rules, see 6570ff.

Usually, a chargeable disposition will involve the transfer of property to a donee, but any destruction, abandonment or omission which results in a loss to the estate of the transferor are all chargeable unless there is no gratuitous intent (see 7153).

Certain dispositions are treated as not involving transfers of value (see 7150ff.).

Legislation: IHTA 1984, s. 3(1); *Inheritance Tax (Indexation) Order* 2003 (SI 2003/841)

Other Material: *HMRC Inheritance Tax: Customer Guide* available on the HMRC website at www.hmrc.gov.uk/cto/customerguide/page1.htm

Tax Reporter:¶ 607-300

6614 IHT rates on lifetime transfers

Originally, there were two separate tables detailing the different rates of IHT applicable to transfers on or within three years of death and other transfers. Since 1986, there has only been one set of rates.

Inheritance tax

For tables of past and current IHT rates, see *Hardman's Tax Rates and Tables* at 6-000.

Legislation: IHTA 1984, s. 7, 8 and Sch. 1

Other Material: *HMRC Inheritance Tax: Customer Guide* available on the HMRC website at www.hmrc.gov.uk/cto/customerguide/page1.htm

Tax Reporter: ¶604-500

6616   Seven-year rule

As originally formulated IHT, when known as capital transfer tax, was a lifetime cumulative tax, i.e. all inter vivos transfers were accumulated and aggregated with property passing on death. Tax was charged at the time of each transfer and the higher the cumulative total, the greater the tax rate. A ten-year cumulative period was introduced in 1981, and for transfers after 17 March 1986 the cumulation period is reduced to seven years.

To ascertain the amount of tax payable on a chargeable transfer, it is necessary to take into account the donor's chargeable transfers in the previous seven years (so at this stage PETs are ignored).

The steps in the calculation are:

Step 1

Work out the value of the current transfer (i.e. work out the loss to the transferor as the result of the transfer, deduct reliefs and exemptions).

Step 2

Ascertain the transferor's total of chargeable transfers in the seven years before the current transfer.

Step 3

Add the values in Step 1 and Step 2 to create an 'aggregate chargeable transfer'.

Step 4

Deduct the tax threshold (the amount up to which tax is payable at 0% ascertained at the date of the current transfer) from the aggregate chargeable transfer. If the aggregate chargeable transfer is below the tax threshold, there is no lifetime tax to pay.

Step 5

Work out the tax at half rate (i.e. 20%) on the value ascertained in Step 4 (i.e. the excess over the tax threshold).

Step 6

If the value in Step 2 (the previous lifetime transfers) exceeds the tax threshold, repeat Steps 4 and 5 with the value in Step 2. Deduct this notional tax from the tax on the aggregate chargeable transfer to calculate the tax on the current transfer.

Example

George made the following chargeable lifetime transfers (after all reliefs and exemptions) into separate discretionary trusts:

5 December 2008	£200,000
11 May 2015	£180,000
12 January 2016	£160,000
14 March 2016	£50,000

The lifetime tax payable on the transfers is calculated as follows (assuming the tax is payable by the transferee, i.e. the trustees):

Tax on transfer 5/12/07

Steps 1–3	£
Transfers in 7 years prior to this transfer	Nil
Add: value of this transfer	200,000
Aggregate chargeable transfer	200,000

Step 4
Below tax threshold (£300,000) @ 5/12/08

Tax on transfer 11/5/15

Steps 1–3	£
Transfers in 7 years prior to this transfer	200,000
Add: value of this transfer	180,000
Aggregate chargeable transfer	380,000

Step 4
Deduct tax threshold @ 11/5/15

£(380,000 − 325,000) =	£55,000

Step 5
Work out tax

£55,000 × 20% =	£11,000

Step 6

Transfers in the seven years before this transfer are below the tax threshold so no adjustment for tax on this value needs to be made.

Tax on transfer 12/1/16

Steps 1–3	**£**
Transfers in 7 years prior to this transfer	180,000
Add: value of this transfer	160,000
Aggregate chargeable transfer	340,000

Step 4

Deduct tax threshold @ 12/1/16

£(340,000 − 325,000) =	£15,000

Step 5

Work out tax

£15,000 × 20% =	£3,000

Step 6

Transfers in the 7 years before this transfer are below the tax threshold so no adjustment for tax on this value needs to be made.

Tax on transfer 14/3/16

Steps 1–3	**£**
Transfers in 7 years prior to this transfer	340,000
Add: value of this transfer	50,000
Aggregate chargeable transfer	390,000

Step 4

Deduct tax threshold @ 14/3/16

£(390,000 − 325,000) =	£65,000

Step 5

Work out tax

£65,000 × 20% =	£13,000

Step 6

Notional tax on previous transfers

£(340,000 − 325,000) =	£15,000

Work out tax

£15,000 × 20% =	£3,000
Tax on current transfer £(13,000 − 3,000) =	£10,000

You will see that the tax on the current transfer is £50,000 × 20% = £10,000 as all of the transfer is chargeable above the tax threshold.

For chargeable transfers followed by death within seven years where PETs then get taken into account to determine the revised tax charges, see 6803.

For PETs followed by death within seven years, see 6802.

Legislation: IHTA 1984, s. 7

Other Material: *HMRC Inheritance Tax: Customer Guide* available on the HMRC website at www.hmrc.gov.uk/cto/customerguide/page1.htm

Tax Reporter: ¶611-100

6620   Reduction in value of estate: grossing-up

Inheritance tax is charged on the value transferred by a chargeable transfer. The value transferred is measured by reference to the diminution in the value of the transferor's estate. Where the transferor pays the IHT on the transfer, the diminution in the value of his estate will be twofold: the property or sum gifted and the tax paid. In order to find the IHT payable by a transferor in such circumstances the value of the gift must be grossed up at the appropriate rate and that rate should then be applied to the gross sum so found.

The calculation is performed as follows:

Step 1

Work out the value of the current transfer (i.e. work out the loss to the transferor as the result of the transfer, deduct reliefs and exemptions).

Step 2

Ascertain the transferor's total of chargeable transfers in the seven years before the current transfer (so at this stage, PETs are ignored). If this value exceeds the tax threshold (the amount up to which tax is payable at 0% ascertained at the date of the current transfer), deduct the tax threshold from it and then work out notional tax at half rate (i.e. 20%) on this value (i.e. the excess over the tax threshold). Deduct the notional tax from the total of transfers to give the net value of transfers brought forward. If the value is below the tax threshold, the net and the gross values of the b/f transfers are the same.

Step 3

Add the values in Step 1 and Step 2 to create an 'aggregate net chargeable transfer'.

Step 4

Deduct the tax threshold from the aggregate net chargeable transfer. If the aggregate net chargeable transfer is below the tax threshold, there is no lifetime tax to pay.

Step 5

Work out the tax on the value in Step 4 using the grossing up rate. This is found by dividing the lifetime rate by (100 minus the lifetime rate). Thus, where the lifetime rate is 20%, the grossed up rate is 1/4 (20/80) or 25%.

Step 6

Deduct any notional tax calculated in Step 2 from the tax on the aggregate net chargeable transfer to calculate the tax on the current transfer.

Step 7

Add the tax found after Step 6 to the current transfer to give the gross chargeable transfer to be carried forward in the cumulation.

Example

On 31 May 2015, Harry transferred £420,000 into a discretionary trust for the benefit of his children. Harry agreed to pay the lifetime tax due. Harry had made one chargeable transfer in the previous seven years, with a value of £150,000. For the purposes of this example, the annual exemption is ignored.

The tax payable on the transfer in May 2015 is calculated as follows:

Step 1

Value of current transfer is £420,000.

Step 2

Transfers in seven years prior to this transfer are £150,000 which is below tax threshold so gross and net value is £150,000.

Step 3	£
Net transfers in seven years prior to this transfer	150,000
Add: value of this transfer	420,000
Aggregate net chargeable transfer	570,000

Step 4

Deduct tax threshold @ 31/5/15	£245,000
£(570,000 − 325,000) =	

Step 5

Work out tax

£245,000 × 1/4 = £61,250

Step 6

Transfers in the 7 years before this transfer are below the tax threshold so no adjustment for tax on this value needs to be made.

Step 7

Chargeable transfer to carry forward in cumulation is:

£(420,000 + 61,250) = £481,250

Example

Assume in the above example that Harry had previously made a chargeable transfer of value of £350,000, instead of £150,000.

The tax payable on the transfer in May 2015 is calculated as follows:

Step 1

Value of current transfer is £420,000.

Step 2

Notional tax on previous transfers

£(350,000 − 325,000) =	£25,000
Work out tax	
£25,000 × 20% =	£5,000
Net value of transfers b/f £(350,000 − 5,000)	£345,000

Step 3 £

Net transfers in seven years prior to this transfer	345,000
Add: value of this transfer	420,000
Aggregate net chargeable transfer	765,000

Step 4

Deduct tax threshold @ 31/5/15

£(765,000 − 325,000) = £440,000

Step 5

Work out tax

£440,000 × 1/4 = £110,000

Step 6

Tax on current transfer £(110,000 − 5,000) = £105,000

Step 7

Chargeable transfer to carry forward in
cumulation is:

£(420,000 + 105,000) =   £525,000

Once again, the tax on the current transfer is £420,000 × 25% = £105,000 as
all of the transfer is chargeable above the tax threshold.

If George had not agreed to pay the tax, then the tax would simply have
been 20% of the chargeable amount; multiplying the chargeable amount by
$1/4$ allows for grossing up.

Grossing-up does not apply where the transferee agrees to pay the tax.

Other Material: *HMRC Inheritance Tax: Customer Guide* available on the
HMRC website at www.hmrc.gov.uk/cto/customerguide/page1.htm

Tax Reporter: ¶602-450

6630 Meaning of lifetime 'estate'

A person's estate is the total of all the property to which he is beneficially
entitled. 'Property' includes rights and interests of any description. A
person who has a general power which enables him, or would if he was
of full age, to dispose of any property other than settled property, or to
charge money on any property other than settled property, will be treated
as beneficially entitled to the property or money. 'General power' means
a power or authority enabling the person by whom it is exercisable to
appoint or dispose of property as he thinks fit. Therefore, property would
include:

- houses, cars, land, caravans, any real property;
- shares, debentures, mortgages, insurance policies;
- options, rights, easements;
- businesses, woodlands, agricultural property;
- money whether in banks, building societies, or found at home;
- furniture, paintings, sculptures;
- beneficial interests in settled property.

Legislation: IHTA 1984, s. 5, 272

Tax Reporter: ¶624-000

6660 Meaning of 'disposition'

A transfer of value is any 'disposition' made by a person ('the transferor') as a result of which the value of his estate immediately after the disposition is less than it would be but for the disposition (see 6525). The word 'disposition' is not defined in the legislation, though it is stated that a disposition includes a disposition effected by 'associated operations' (see 6670). However, the word clearly has a very wide meaning.

Loans

There is an element of disposition where a person is allowed the use of money on soft terms (a low rate of interest, although in the current climate that will mean a very low rate indeed, or a long repayment period) or is allowed the use of property for less than full 'rent'; hence, exemptions apply as if it was an outright gift. The waiver of a loan would also appear to be a disposition, though HMRC only accept that a loan made between individuals has been waived by the lender (so that the lender's estate is reduced for IHT purposes by the amount of the loan released) if the waiver is effected by deed.

Dispositions by omission

It is also provided in the legislation that where the value of a person's estate is diminished and that of another person's estate (or of settled property in which no interest in possession subsists) is increased by the omission to exercise a right, he will be treated as having made a disposition at the latest time when he could have exercised that right, unless he shows that the omission was not deliberate.

Example

Anthony owes Ben £150,000 for some capital equipment that he purchased. Anthony decides not to pay Ben and Ben decides not to take any action against Anthony. Ben has made a disposition in respect of the £150,000 debt that he has failed to claim from Anthony.

Non-resident trusts

If a settlor fails to exercise a right to recover CGT from a trustee of a non-resident trust where trust gains are treated as his (see 5637), this may fall to be regarded as a transfer of value.

Survivorship clauses

Dispositions made subject to a survivorship clause (whether on survival or death) are treated as effected when the potential entitlement arises. Dispositions which do not involve the transfer of property until a date more than 12 months thereafter do not give rise to a transfer until the later event.

Legislation: IHTA 1984, s. 3(3), 29, 92, 262

Case: *Duke of Northumberland v A-G* [1905] AC 406

Tax Reporter: ¶607-900

6670 Associated operations

A 'transaction' includes a series of transactions and any associated operations. The statutory definition of 'associated operations' is any two or more operations of any kind being:

- operations affecting the same or related property or income arising from that property; or

- any two operations which are directly or indirectly related to each other,

whether those operations are effected by the same person or different persons, and whether or not they are simultaneous; and 'operation' includes an omission.

Example 1

William, who has already made previous chargeable transfers in excess of his NRB and is thus liable to IHT at the lifetime rate of 20%, transfers property to his wife Betty who has made no previous chargeable transfers. This is an exempt transfer and, therefore, no tax is payable. However, before transferring the property, William obtains Betty's agreement to transfer it on to certain discretionary trusts. When Betty transfers the property HMRC will treat William as the transferor since these are associated operations and William will be liable for any IHT.

It could be argued that if there is a binding obligation on Betty (wife) to pass on the property to Charlie, then Betty at no time becomes the owner. If, however, William transfers to Betty property of which she becomes the owner where she has the option of either keeping the property or transferring it to Charlie or any other person, then it is argued this will not be viewed as an associated operation but good tax planning.

If Betty receives some benefit from the property whilst she is the owner, such as the income generated by the property, that might, depending upon the period of her ownership, suggest associated operations were not an issue. The longer the period is between the two transactions, in the indicated William and Betty arrangements, the less likely it is that associated operations will be an issue. Equally, if there is a difference between the asset received by Betty and the asset passed to Charlie, then again it is less likely that associated operations will be an issue.

> **Example 2**
>
> Michael owns a set of four paintings worth £200,000, but individually only worth £25,000 each. He gives two of the paintings to Lynne in 2012. In 2015, he gives Lynne the other two in the set. Michael will be treated as having made a transfer of value of £200,000 by associated operations.

Where there are associated operations, the transfer of value is treated as taking place at the time of the last of the operations. If the earlier operation is also a transfer of value, it will reduce the value transferred by all the operations unless the earlier transfer is exempted as a transfer between spouses.

The House of Lords has held that to be chargeable, the associated operation must form part of, and contribute to, a scheme which confers a gratuitous benefit.

Grant of a lease

Leases granted for full consideration in money or money's worth are not associated with any operation effected more than three years after the grant, and no operation effected after 26 March 1974 will be taken to be associated with an operation effected before that date.

Legislation: IHTA 1984, s. 268

Case: *Macpherson v IR Commrs* [1988] BTC 8,065

Other Material: *HMRC Inheritance Tax: Customer Guide* available on the HMRC website at www.hmrc.gov.uk/cto/customerguide/page1.htm

Tax Reporter: ¶608-150

6675 Operation of the Ramsay principle

From the line of cases beginning with *W T Ramsay Ltd v IR Commrs* [1982] AC 300, it has been established that if a transaction or a series of transactions contains a step which has no commercial purpose apart from the avoidance or mitigation of tax, and at the time the step was taken the whole process was pre-ordained so as to produce a given result, the courts have power to ignore the inserted step and treat the series of transactions as one composite transaction for tax purposes.

On the face of it, this principle bears a resemblance to the associated operations rule for IHT discussed at 6670. Most of the cases through which the *Ramsay* principle evolved were concerned with CGT, but it is clear that its scope is much wider. The first case in which the applicability of the rule to IHT was considered, albeit obiter only, concerned an (unsuccessful) attempt to pass down property free of tax by means of two deeds executed on two consecutive days. The judge said that had he been asked to decide on the issue, he would have read the two deeds together on the basis that the parties never intended the situation brought about by the first deed to last more than one day.

On inter-spouse transfers, HMRC have said in a letter dated 20 September 1985 to the ICAEW that 'the circumstances of such transfers always need to be carefully examined to ensure, among other things, that the transaction has substance as well as form. For example, an understanding between the spouses on the ultimate destination of the assets would be important in this connection.'

In one case, HMRC chose to attack a scheme to avoid CTT on the basis of the *Ramsay* principle rather than the associated operations rule. Following the death of the tenth Earl Fitzwilliam, the executors considered various proposals for mitigating CTT on the distribution of his large estate. The scheme finally adopted involved use of the surviving spouse exemption (the transitional relief retained after estate duty), the relief for distributions within two years of death out of a discretionary trust set up by will, the relief for mutual transfers, and the provisions then in force relating to the termination of an interest in possession and reverter to settlor. The taxpayers argued that by deft manipulation of these provisions they had achieved the appointment of some £3.8m out of the estate to one of the beneficiaries without incurring any liability to tax. HMRC issued notices of determination on the basis that the steps taken to mitigate tax constituted a single composite transaction within the *Ramsay* principle. The House of Lords held that, on the evidence, the steps taken were not pre-ordained from the beginning, and did not fulfil the conditions previously laid down by the House: there was no person whose guiding could procure that the scheme as planned would be carried out nor could it be said that there had been no practical or real likelihood that the scheme would not be completed.

Case: *Countess Fitzwilliam v IR Commrs* [1993] BTC 8,003

Tax Reporter: ¶608-650

6690 Voidable transfers

Where a chargeable transfer has been set aside as voidable through law, any IHT paid or payable will be repaid or not payable as the case may be. The transfer is treated as if it had never taken place for IHT purposes. The chargeable transfer may be set aside as voidable or otherwise defeasible by virtue of an enactment or rule of law.

From 1 April 2011, a claim must be made not more than four years after the claimant knew or ought reasonably to have known, that the relevant transfer has been set aside.

Legislation: IHTA 1984, s. 150; *Finance Act 2009, Schedule 51 (Time Limits For Assessments, Claims, Etc.) (Appointed Days and Transitional Provisions) Order* 2010 (SI 2010/867)

Tax Reporter: ¶615-000

6710   Annuity purchased in conjunction with a life policy

Where a life insurance policy is issued, made, varied or substituted after 26 March 1974 and an annuity on the life of the insured is purchased and the benefit of the policy is vested in someone other than the person who purchased the annuity, then a transfer of value will be treated as having been made, unless it can be shown that the making of the insurance and the purchase of the annuity were not associated operations (see 6670). The person who purchased the annuity will be treated as having made the transfer of value by a disposition at the time the benefit of the policy became vested.

The value transferred is the lesser of:

(1)   the total of:

  (a)   the price of the annuity; and

  (b)   the premium paid or consideration given under the policy on or before the transfer; or

(2)   the greatest value capable of being conferred at any time by the policy calculated as if that time were the date of the transfer.

Example

John, who expects to die very shortly, buys an annuity for £1,500,000 which will give him £150,000 for the rest of his life, and concurrently John's daughter Molly assures her father's life for £1,450,000. The first premium payable is £150,000, and the annuity payments are set against this and subsequent premiums. If John then died Molly would receive £1,450,000. However, John is treated as having made a transfer of value to Molly when the benefit of the policy is vested in her. The value transferred is the lesser of:

(1)   the price of the annuity (£1,500,000) plus any premium paid on or before the transfer (say £150,000) which together make it £1,650,000; and

(2)   the greatest value capable of being conferred at any time by the policy as if that time were the date of the transfer (£1,450,000).

Therefore, the value transferred is treated as being £1,450,000.

Legislation: IHTA 1984, s. 263

Other Material: SP E4

Tax Reporter: ¶630-600

6720 Timing and order of transfers

It is important to establish clearly the precise date of any lifetime transfers since reliefs (small gifts and annual exemptions) and any additional IHT charge on death may be affected. The most important rules are as follows.

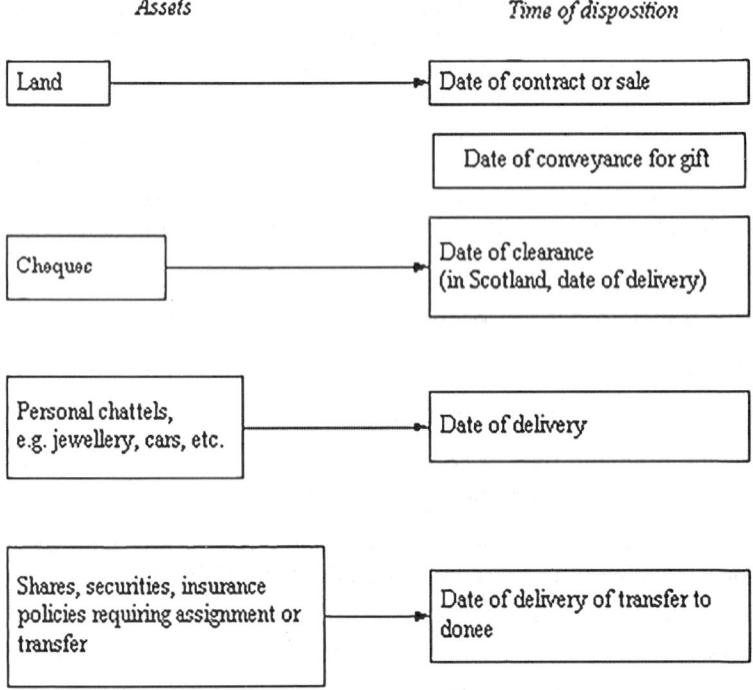

Where the value transferred by more than one chargeable transfer made by the same person on the same day depends on the order in which the transfers are made, they will be treated as made in the order which results in the lowest value chargeable. The rate at which tax is charged on such transfers is the effective rate at which tax would have been charged if those transfers had been a single chargeable transfer of the same total value.

> **Example**
>
> Tim transfers £290,000 each to discretionary trusts A and B on the same day, 8 September 2010. The total IHT payable is £51,000 (no annual exemptions available) and each trust will bear half the charge (subject to grossing up if Tim pays the tax). Had the transfers been on different days, the earlier transfer would not have incurred a tax charge and the later a charge to £51,000.

If a transferor makes two transfers on the same day, the earlier one not required to be grossed up and the later one requiring grossing up (as above), then the total IHT is calculated by treating the later transfer (the one requiring grossing up) as having been made first.

Equally try to use the £3,000 annual exemption by arranging immediately chargeable transfers before PETs.

Legislation: IHTA 1984, s. 266

Tax Reporter: ¶614-850

Pre-owned assets

6725 Overview

For 2005–06 onwards, an income tax charge arises on benefits received by the former owners of property, referred to as pre-owned assets. Broadly, the charge applies to individuals (the chargeable person) who continue to receive benefits from certain types of property they once owned after 17 March 1986 but have since disposed of.

The property within the scope of the charge can be grouped into three headings:

- land;
- chattels; and
- intangible property.

If the chargeable person has either disposed of any property within these headings by way of gift or, in some circumstances, sale, or contributed towards the purchase of the property in question and they continue to receive some benefit from the property they are potentially liable to the charge. The benefit may be occupation of the land, use of the chattel or the ability to receive income or capital from a settlement holding intangible property.

Certain transactions are excluded from the charge (see below). There are also provisions exempting the relevant property from the charge where the property is subject to a charge to inheritance tax or where specific protection from inheritance tax is given by legislation.

The conditions required for the charge to apply are virtually identical where the property in question is land or chattels but they differ slightly in respect of intangible property. However, be aware that although HMRC publish detailed notes concerning their view as to how the rules are to apply that these are often updated without indication of the date of change. If providing advice on an issue always download the section of the manual and date it so it is linked to the advice.

6730   Land and chattels

The charge applies where the chargeable person occupies any land or uses or possesses any chattels, either alone or with other persons, and either the 'disposal condition' or the 'contribution condition' is met.

Broadly, the disposal condition will apply if the chargeable person, at any time after 17 March 1986, owned relevant land or chattels, or other property whose disposal proceeds were directly or indirectly applied by another person towards the acquisition of the relevant land or chattels, and then disposed of all or part of their interest in the relevant land or chattels (or other property).

The contribution condition will apply if the chargeable person, at any time after 17 March 1986, provided any of the consideration given by another person for the acquisition of an interest in the relevant land or chattel, or for the acquisition of any other property, the proceeds of the disposal of which were directly or indirectly applied by another person towards an acquisition of an interest in the relevant land or chattel. As with the disposal condition, if the provision of the consideration qualifies as an excluded transaction, this condition will not apply.

Intangible property

The charge applies where the chargeable person settles intangible property or adds intangible property to a settlement after 17 March 1986 on terms that any income arising from the settled property would be treated under ITTOIA 2005, s. 624 (income arising under a settlement where the settlor retains an interest) as income of the chargeable person as settlor and any such income would be so treated even if s. 624(2) did not include any reference to the spouse of the settlor.

Excluded transactions

There are a number of situations where a charge to tax will not arise. Certain transactions are excluded from the charge and there are also exemptions from the charge where certain conditions are met. The concept of excluded transactions has no application to intangible property. They only serve to exclude from the income tax charge certain transactions relating to land and chattels.

For the purposes of the disposal conditions relating to land and chattels, the disposal of any property is an excluded transaction in relation to the chargeable person if:

- it was a disposal of their whole interest in the property, except for any right expressly reserved by them over the property, either by a transaction made at arm's length with a person not connected with them, or by a transaction such as might be expected to be made at arm's length between persons not connected with each other;

- the property was transferred to their spouse or civil partner, or former spouse or civil partner where the transfer has been ordered by a court;

- the disposal was by way of gift (or in accordance with a court order for the benefit of a former spouse or civil partner) by virtue of which the property became settled property in which his spouse or civil partner or former spouse or civil partner is beneficially entitled to an interest in possession. The spouse or civil partner must take an interest in possession from the outset. It is not an excluded transaction, however, if the interest in possession of the spouse or civil partner or former spouse or civil partner has come to an end other than on their death unless the spouse or civil partner or former spouse or civil partner has become absolutely entitled to the property in which case it would be accepted that the benefit of the exclusion is not lost;

- the disposal was a disposition falling within IHTA 1984, s. 11 (disposition for maintenance of family);

- the disposal is an outright gift to an individual and is wholly exempted from inheritance tax by either IHTA 1984, s. 19 (£3,000 annual exemption); or s. 20 (£250 small gifts exemption).

For the purposes of the contribution conditions relating to land and chattels, the provision by the chargeable person of consideration for another's acquisition of any property is an excluded transaction in relation to the chargeable person if:

- on its acquisition the property became settled property in which their spouse or civil partner or former spouse or civil partner is beneficially entitled to an interest in possession. The spouse or civil partner must take an interest in possession from the outset. It is not an excluded transaction, however, if the interest in possession of the spouse or civil partner or former spouse or civil partner has come to an end otherwise than on their death unless the spouse or civil partner or former spouse or civil partner has become absolutely entitled to the property; or the other person was their spouse or civil partner, or former spouse or civil partner where the transfer has been ordered by a court;

- the provision of the consideration constituted an outright gift of cash by the chargeable person to the other person and was made at least seven years before the earliest date on which the chargeable person occupied the land or had possession or use of the chattel;

- the provision of the consideration is a disposition falling within IHTA 1984, s. 11 (maintenance of family);

- the provision of the consideration is an outright gift to an individual and is for the purposes of IHTA 1984 a transfer of value that is wholly exempt by virtue of s. 19 (£3,000 annual exemption) or s. 20 (£250 small gifts exemption).

Gifts with reservation

The charging provisions also do not apply to a person at a time when, for IHT purposes, the relevant property or property deriving its value from relevant property falls within the Gifts with Reservation provisions set out in FA 1986 (FA 2004, Sch. 15, para. 11(3)), see 6785.

De minimis

An exemption from charge applies where in relation to any person in a year of assessment, the aggregate of the amounts specified below in respect of that year do not exceed £5,000.

The tax charge

The approach to valuing property for the purpose of the pre-owned assets rules is generally the same as for IHT purposes (IHTA 1984, s. 160). In other words, it is the price that the property might reasonably be expected to fetch if sold in the open market at that time, without any scope for a reduction on the ground that the whole property is to be placed on the market at one and the same time.

The valuation date for property subject to the charge is 6 April in the relevant year of assessment or, if later, the first day of the taxable period.

When valuing relevant land or a chattel, it is not necessary to make an annual revaluation of the property. The property should rather be valued on a five-year cycle. Before the first five-year anniversary, the valuation of the property will be that set at the first valuation date. Thereafter, the valuation at the latest five-year anniversary will apply.

6740   Land

The chargeable amount in relation to the relevant land is the appropriate rental value, less the amount of any payments which the chargeable person is legally obliged to make during the period to the owner of the relevant land in respect of their occupation.

The appropriate rental value is:

$$R \times \frac{DV}{V}$$

R   is the rental value of the relevant land for the taxable period;

DV   is:

- where the chargeable person owned an interest in the relevant land, the value as at the valuation date of the interest in the relevant land that was disposed of by the chargeable person or, where the disposal was a non-exempt sale, the 'appropriate portion' of that value;

- where the chargeable person owned an interest in other property, the proceeds of which were used to acquire an interest in relevant land, such part of the value of the relevant land at the valuation date as can reasonably be attributed to the property originally disposed of by the chargeable person or, where the original disposal was a non-exempt sale, to the appropriate portion of that property;

- if the contribution condition applies, such part of the value of the relevant land at the valuation date as can reasonably be attributed to the consideration provided by the chargeable person;

V   is the value of the relevant land at the valuation date.

The 'rental value' of the land for the taxable period is the rent which would have been payable for the period if the property had been let to the chargeable person at an annual rent equal to the annual value. The annual value is the rent that might reasonably be expected to be obtained on a letting from year to year if the tenant undertook to pay all taxes, rates and charges usually paid by a tenant, and the landlord undertook to bear the costs of the repairs and insurance and the other expenses, if any, necessary for maintaining the property in a state to command that rent.

FA 2004, Sch. 15, para. 4(4) introduces the concept of a 'non-exempt sale' for a disposal which is a sale of the chargeable person's whole interest in the property for cash, but which is not an excluded transaction as defined in para. 10. The 'appropriate proportion', which is relevant for ascertaining the appropriate rental value is calculated as follows:

$$M - \frac{P}{MV}$$

MV   is the value of the interest in land at the time of the sale; and

P   is the amount paid.

6750   Chattels

The chargeable amount in relation to any chattel is the appropriate amount, less the amount of any payments that the chargeable person is legally obliged to make during the period to the owner of the chattel for the possession or use of the chattel by the chargeable person.

The appropriate amount is:

$$N \times \frac{DV}{V}$$

N   is the amount of the interest that would be payable for the taxable period if interest were payable at the prescribed rate on an amount equal to the value of the chattel at the valuation date. The prescribed rate is the official rate of interest at the valuation date; with effect from 6 April 2015, the rate is 3% (remaining unchanged from 6 April 2016 and 3.25% for 2013–14).

6755   Intangible property

The chargeable amount in relation to the relevant property is:

$$N - T$$

N   is the amount of the interest that would be payable for the taxable period if interest were payable at the prescribed rate on an amount equal to the value of the relevant property at the valuation date. The prescribed rate is the official rate of interest at the valuation date (as above);

T is the amount of any income tax or CGT payable by the chargeable person in respect of the taxable period by virtue of any of the following provisions: ITTOIA 2005, s. 624 or TCGA 1992, s. 86; so far as the tax is attributable to the relevant property.

IHT election

The provisions of the pre-owned assets legislation are optional. The reason for this is that the provisions are simply a device to prevent the avoidance of IHT by exploiting possible gaps in the gifts with reservation legislation. The legislation has therefore provided taxpayers the opportunity to opt back into the IHT rules. Such an option has to be made by the taxpayer in the form of an election.

There is a time-limit for making an election, which is the same as the self-assessment deadline for making a return for the tax year in which an individual is first liable for the pre-owned assets charge. From 21 March 2007, HMRC may accept late elections for IHT treatment that would otherwise be too late.

HMRC state that they will accept late elections where an event occurs which is 'beyond the chargeable person's control'. In general, HMRC will accept a late election if the chargeable person can show that an event beyond their control prevented them from sending the election by the relevant filing date. If the chargeable person was able to manage the rest of their private or business affairs during the period in question, HMRC are unlikely to accept that they were genuinely prevented from delivering the election on time. Examples of such circumstances include an unforeseen event disrupting the normal postal service; loss of records, etc. through fire, flood or theft; serious illness; or the death of a close relative or partner.

In addition, there may be cases where, given the overall circumstances, HMRC will accept a late election even where the chargeable person cannot show that the reasons for the late election were beyond their control. Essentially, this will be where the chargeable person can show that they were unaware – and could not reasonably have been aware – that they were liable to an income tax charge under Sch. 15, and elected within a reasonable time of becoming so aware.

Legislation: FA 2007, s. 66; FA 2004, Sch. 15; *Income Tax (Benefits Received by Former Owner of Property) (Election for Inheritance Tax Treatment) Regulations* 2007 (SI 2007/3000); *Charge to Income Tax by Reference to Enjoyment of Property Previously Owned Regulations* 2005 (SI 2005/724)

Other Material: IHT500: *Election for inheritance tax to apply to asset previously owned*; HMRC website www.hmrc.gov.uk/poa/poa_guidance. htm

Tax Reporter: ¶614-800

Transfers on death

6770   Charge to IHT on death

Where an individual dies, IHT is charged on their estate as if they had made a transfer of value of the whole of their estate immediately before their death (see 6525). This is a deemed transfer of value. The usual effect is that on death, one of the first jobs of the executor is to value the deceased's assets.

Legislation: IHTA 1984, s. 4(1)

Other Material: *HMRC Inheritance Tax: Customer Guide* available on the HMRC website at www.hmrc.gov.uk/cto/customerguide/page1.htm

Tax Reporter: ¶624-000

Meaning of 'estate' on death

6780   Types of property included in death estate

A person's estate is the aggregate of all the property to which they are beneficially entitled, except that the estate of a person immediately before their death does not include 'excluded property' (see 7397). Included in the estate of the deceased would be:

- *real property* (land and interests in land), including any property over which they had a general power of appointment (unless that property over which they had a general power of appointment was settled property);

- *chattels* – cars, jewellery, furniture, boats, etc.;

- *insurance policies* where the deceased was entitled to be paid a sum of money;

- *a business or interest in a business*;

- *guaranteed annuities* if the deceased was receiving payments under an annuity and died before the end of the annuity period, the right to receive the remainder of the payments is an asset of the estate;

- *shares and securities,* either quoted or unquoted;

- *debts due* to the deceased (unless recovery is not reasonably practicable and has not been made so by the actions of the deceased);

- *settled property* in which the deceased had an interest in possession (or would have had if the administration of an estate had been completed). The estate of a deceased person does not include an interest in settled property where the person became beneficially entitled to the interest in possession on or after 22 March 2006, and the interest in possession is not an immediate post-death interest, a disabled person's interest, and not a transitional interest;

- *the undivided share of a tenant in common*;

- *the undivided and severable share of a joint tenant*;

- *cash* in banks or building societies or in the deceased's possession;

- *property subject to a reservation in favour of the deceased* (see 6785).

Survivorship clauses

Dispositions made subject to a survivorship clause (whether on survival or death) are treated as effected when the potential entitlement arises.

For details of types of property specifically excluded from the estate at death, see 6790.

Legislation: IHTA 1984, s. 5(1), (1A), 91, 92, 152, 166

Cases: *Singh Anand v IR Commrs* (1996) Sp C 107; *Marquess of Linlithgow v R & C Commrs* [2010] BTC 487

Tax Reporter: ¶624-250

6782   Deductions from the estate on death

Liabilities may generally be offset only to the extent that reimbursement cannot reasonably be expected.

Allowance is made for reasonable funeral expenses, including the cost of mourning and a tombstone or gravestone.

Where property is situated outside the UK, an allowance may be made against the value of the property to be included in the estate for expenses incurred in administering or realising the property, where they are attributable to the situation of the property. This is subject to an upper limit of 5% of the gross value of all foreign property in the estate.

FA 2013, s. 176 and Sch. 34 introduce restrictions for, generally, debt incurred on or after 6 April 2013 whereby it must first be deducted from the asset whose purchase it funded irrespective of the asset on which it is secured. The position for UK domiciled individuals, for debt incurred before 6 April 2013 is that it is deducted from the asset on which it is secured.

Where, however, non-UK domiciled individuals have secured debt on UK situs assets (i.e. assets subject to UK IHT), to reduce the UK taxable value, but the debt was then used to purchase excluded assets then the debt cannot be deducted from the UK taxable value irrespective of when the debt was incurred for IHT events on or after 17 July 2013 (Royal Assent for *Finance Act* 2013).

Finance Act 2014 introduced rules to cover a loophole that arose in the FA 2013 rules. If the debt, secured on UK situs assets was used to fund a UK based foreign currency bank account, the bank account was not excluded property but was equally not subject to UK IHT at an IHT event. With effect from Royal Assent of *Finance Act* 2014 (17 July 2014), the related debt in the indicated circumstances will not be deductible against assets subject to UK IHT.

Legislation: FA 1986, s. 103; IHTA 1984, s. 162, 172, 173

Other Material: SP7/87, *Inheritance tax: reasonable deduction for funeral expenses*; *HMRC Inheritance Tax: Customer Guide* available on the HMRC website at www.hmrc.gov.uk/cto/customerguide/page1.htm

Tax Reporter: ¶625-450

6785   Gifts with reservation: introduction

Where an individual dies and immediately before their death, there is any property which in relation to them is property subject to a reservation, that property is treated for IHT purposes as property to which the individual was beneficially entitled before his death and valued at the higher of value at death or when first given away where the reservation still exists at death.

Where, after 17 March 1986, an individual disposes of property by way of gift, except for certain specified exempt transfers (see 6787), and either:

(1)   possession and enjoyment of the property is not bona fide assumed by the donee at or before the beginning of the 'relevant period' (see also substitutions and accretions at 6788); or

(2)   at any time in the relevant period the property is not enjoyed to the entire exclusion, or virtually to the entire exclusion, of the donor and of any benefit to him by contract or otherwise (see 6786),

the property concerned is referred to as 'property subject to a reservation'. For settled gifts, see 6789.

The 'relevant period' is a period ending with the individual's death and commencing seven years before or on the date of the gift, if it is later.

The *Dexter Lyon* case confirmed, in relation to a settlement, that the ability to potentially receive benefit was enough to cause reservation of benefit; it was not necessary to actually receive a benefit (although, in that case, the Special Commissioners also decided that the actual benefit received was not de minimis).

It is possible that the gifts-with-reservation rules result in a double charge. For example, a gift to discretionary trusts where the settlor is an object of the discretion would not be potentially exempt and would therefore be chargeable. The property would also fall into charge on the settlor's death under the gifts-with-reservation rules. Regulations eliminate such double charges (see 6830).

Where property ceases to be property within (1) or (2) above, the transferor is treated as making a 'potentially exempt transfer' (see 6610) at the date of such cessation.

Agricultural property and business property

Business and agricultural property reliefs (see 7253 and 7292) are preserved in respect of property which is included in the transferor's estate because it was the subject of a gift with reservation. Special provision is necessary because ownership (and occupation, in the case of agricultural property) will usually have been assumed by the transferee, thus rendering it impossible for the transferor to meet the qualifying conditions in respect of the transfer immediately before death. Accordingly, in determining whether the property qualifies for relief, the transferee's occupation and ownership (taken in combination, where necessary, with the transferor's) is counted.

Legislation: FA 1999, s. 104; FA 1986, s. 102 and Sch. 20, para. 8

Cases: *Exors of Harry Dexter Lyon dec'd v R & C Commrs* (2007) Sp C 616

Other Material: *HMRC Inheritance Tax: Customer Guide* available on the HMRC website at www.hmrc.gov.uk/cto/customerguide/page1.htm

Tax Reporter: ¶625-350

6786 Gifts with reservation: property not enjoyed to exclusion of donor

In determining whether any property falls to be regarded as disposed of by a gift with reservation as being property not enjoyed to the entire exclusion, or virtually the entire exclusion, of the donor and of any benefit to them by contract or otherwise (see 6785), the following points should be noted.

'Virtually' is not defined, though HMRC have expressed the view that property is enjoyed to 'virtually' the entire exclusion of a donor where the benefit to them is small.

A benefit received by the donor by virtue of 'associated operations' (see 6670) is treated as a benefit to them by contract or otherwise and there are specific rules for certain land, chattels and life policies. In particular, in the case of property which is an interest in land or a chattel, retention or assumption by the donor of actual occupation or actual enjoyment or actual possession of the property shall be disregarded if it is for 'full consideration in money or money's worth'. Further, in the case of an interest in land any occupation by the donor of the land or part is disregarded if:

- it results from an unforeseen change in the donor's circumstances not designed to exploit the provision;

- it occurs when the donor has become unable to maintain themself through old age or infirmity;

- it represents reasonable provision for the donor by the donee; and

- the donee is a relative of the donor or their spouse.

To determine whether the donor is entirely excluded from benefit, it is necessary to identify the subject-matter of the gift. There is a difference between giving away property and then retaining some interest (which would constitute reservation of a benefit) and carving out a lesser interest from that which is owned and giving away that lesser interest (no reservation of a benefit).

Some of the old estate duty cases give illustrations of this distinction. In one such case, the deceased gave away grazing land to his son and then later entered into partnership with his son, the grazing land being brought in as partnership property. It was held that the deceased was not excluded from benefit in respect of the land and it was dutiable on his death. However, in another case, the deceased agreed with his children that his business as grazier should be carried on by them as partners but with himself as manager. Ten years later he gave part of the grazing land to each child, subject to the partnership agreement. It was held that the subject-matter of each gift was the appropriate portion of the land subject to the partnership rights. In those circumstances, there was no reservation of benefit and the land was not dutiable on the death of the deceased.

Applied to settled property, the reservation-of-benefit rules are not triggered if the donor retains a reversionary interest or if the reversion comes back to him by operation of law. The donor is treated as making a partial gift in those circumstances.

However, if the donor is an object of a discretionary trust, he is treated as not entirely excluded from benefit and the whole of the settled fund will be included in his estate on death. It is HMRC's view that if the donor can become eligible to benefit under a discretionary trust, in any circumstance, because of a power contained in the settlement, he will be treated as reserving a benefit, even if he never actually benefits. If the donor is only a trustee of a settled property, that, of itself, will not trigger the reservation-of-benefit/exclusion-from-property rules. The result is the same where there is entitlement to reasonable remuneration for acting as trustee. Where, however, the settlor can use his position as trustee to obtain a personal benefit, e.g. where trust shares give him majority voting rights in a company in which he owns shares beneficially, the result may be otherwise.

The original rules introduced in 1986 were intended to prevent the avoidance of the IHT charge on death through a lifetime gift aimed at reducing the value of the donor's estate for the purposes of the tax, without the donor having to give up enjoyment of the asset concerned. In *IR Commrs v Eversden*, the Court of Appeal held that the rules do not work when gifts made by a married person are routed through a trust for their spouse. Further to this, where gifts to a spouse are made on or after 20 June 2003:

- the property becomes settled property by virtue of the gift;

- the trusts of the settlement give an interest in possession to the donor's spouse, so that the gift is exempt from IHT by reason of the exemption for transfers between spouses and the rule which treats an interest in possession as equivalent to outright ownership;

- between the date of the gift and the donor's death the interest in possession comes to an end; and

- when that interest in possession comes to an end, the beneficiary does not become beneficially entitled to the settled property, or another interest in possession in it.

Gifts from 2005–06 onwards

Over recent years various schemes have been marketed which use artificial structures to avoid the existing rules about gifts made with reservation (see above). Broadly, such schemes enabled people to remove assets from their taxable estate but continue to enjoy all the benefits of ownership. *Finance Act* 2004 introduced measures to block this sort of avoidance by implementing an income tax charge on this type of transaction from 2005–06 onwards (see 6725). The charge will not apply to the extent that:

- the property in question ceased to be owned before 18 March 1986;
- property formerly owned by a taxpayer is currently owned by their spouse or civil partner;
- the asset in question still counts as part of the taxpayer's estate for inheritance tax (IHT) purposes under the existing 'gift with reservation' (GWR) rules;
- the property was sold by the taxpayer at an arm's length price, paid in cash: this will not be restricted to sales between unconnected parties;
- the taxpayer was formerly the owner of an asset only by virtue of a will or intestacy which has subsequently been varied by agreement between the beneficiaries; or
- any enjoyment of the property is no more than incidental, including cases where an out-and-out gift to a family member comes to benefit the donor following a change in their circumstances.

There is a de minimis threshold of £5,000 per year.

Gifts of interests in land made after 8 March 1999

For gifts of interests in land made on or after 9 March 1999, the gift is treated as being a gift with reservation if there is some interest, right or arrangement which enables or entitles the donor to occupy the land concerned to a material degree without paying full consideration.

The change does not apply to a gift where:

- the right or interest concerned is negligible so that the donor is virtually entirely excluded from any enjoyment of the land;
- the donor may occupy the land or enjoy some right in relation to it only when the interest that he/she has given away comes to an end;
- the gift is made more than seven years after the right or interest concerned is granted or acquired;

- the gift is itself covered by the main exemptions from IHT, including transfers between spouses; or

- the donor is effectively forced to reoccupy the land concerned due to some unforeseen downturn in his/her financial circumstances.

The gift of an undivided share in land, which the donor occupies jointly with the other owner ('donee') will not be a gift with reservation, providing the donor receives no material benefit at the donee's expense in connection with the gift. This puts on a statutory footing the *Hansard* statement on joint occupation issued by the minister in 1986.

Legislation: FA 2004, s. 84 and Sch. 15; FA 2003, s. 185; FA 1999, s. 104; FA 1986, s. 102A–102C and Sch. 20, para. 6, 7

Cases: *IR Commrs v Eversden (Executors of Greenstock dec'd)* [2003] BTC 8,037; *Chick v Commr of Stamp Duties* [1958] AC 435; *Commr for Stamp Duties of New South Wales v Perpetual Trustee Co Ltd* [1943] AC 425; *Munro v Commr of Stamp Duties* [1934] AC 61

Other Material: *HMRC Inheritance Tax: Customer Guide* available on the HMRC website at www.hmrc.gov.uk/cto/customerguide/page1.htm

Tax Reporter: ¶625-350

6787   Gifts with reservation: exclusion of specified exempt transfers

The gifts-with-reservation rules (see 6785) do not apply if, or to the extent that, the gift is an exempt transfer of any of the following kinds:

- transfers between spouses or civil partners (see 7192);

- small gifts (see 7223);

- gifts in consideration of marriage or civil partnership (see 7229);

- gifts to charities (see 7195);

- gifts to political parties (see 7195);

- gifts to housing associations (see 7196);

- gifts for national purposes (see 7198);

- maintenance funds for historic buildings (see 7040);

- employee trusts (see 7005).

Legislation: FA 1986, s. 102(5)

Tax Reporter: ¶614-350

6788 Gifts with reservation: substitutions and accretions

If at any time before 'the material date' the donee ceases to have the possession and enjoyment of gifted property subject to a reservation or any part of it, the gifts-with-reservation rules (see 6785) apply instead to any property received by the donee in substitution for such property as he ceases to possess and enjoy, in addition to any gifted property retained by him.

The relevant rules prevent the avoidance of the gifts-with-reservation rules where the donee replaces property and allows the donor some benefit from the property substituted.

The 'material date' means the date of the donor's death, or any earlier date on which the property ceases to be subject to a reservation.

These rules do not apply to property which becomes settled by virtue of the original gift, or to sums of money in sterling or any other currency.

If the donee disposes of the gifted property for less than full consideration or for no consideration he is treated as continuing to have possession and enjoyment of it, unless the property has been returned to the donor.

Where the donee acquires a further interest in property in which he already has an interest resulting from a gift with reservation, the merger of the two interests will not prevent the transaction from being one whereby the donee voluntarily divests himself of property. He is therefore treated as continuing to have enjoyment and possession of the property subject to a reservation.

Bonus and rights issues

Where shares or debentures are comprised in a gift, and the donee receives a bonus issue or a rights issue in respect of those shares or debentures, the additional shares or debentures are treated as comprised in the original gift.

Donee predeceasing the material date

If the donee dies before the 'material date' (see above), the acts of the donee's personal representatives are deemed to be his acts and, consequently, his trustees are treated as continuing to have the possession and enjoyment of the property. He is treated as having voluntarily divested himself of the gifted property in favour of his legatees.

Legislation: FA 1986, Sch. 20, para. 1–4

Tax Reporter: ¶614-600

6789 Gifts with reservation: settled gifts

The rules relating to accretions and substitutions (see 6788) do not apply where the property subject to a reservation becomes settled as a result of the gift by the donor. However, the other rules relating to gifts with reservation (see 6785) still apply as regards exclusion of benefit in relation to reversions to settlor and the settlor becoming an object of the trust, see 6786. Further, those rules apply to any property comprised in the settlement which consists of property originally settled by the donor or represents or is derived from such property.

If the settlor dies without having released his interest in the settled property, the property subject to a reservation and comprised in the original gift will be included in his estate on death for IHT purposes (see 6780).

If, however, the settlement terminates before the material date, i.e. before the release of the settlor's interest or his death, special tracing rules apply to determine which of the settled property is to be treated as comprised in the original gift. Where such a settlement terminates, in whole or in part, then the following are treated as comprised in the original gift:

- any property which, had the settlor died immediately before the termination, would have been treated as comprised in the gift, except any such property to which the settlor becomes absolutely and beneficially entitled; and

- any consideration given by the settlor for any property to which he becomes absolutely and beneficially entitled.

Legislation: FA 1986, Sch. 20, para. 5

Tax Reporter: ¶614-750

6790 Exclusions from estates of deceased

Certain types of property are excluded when calculating the value of a person's estate on death. These are:

- 'excluded property' (see 7397);

- an interest in or under a registered pension scheme, a qualifying non-UK pension scheme or a section 615(3) scheme or by way of remuneration for acting as trustee, if it ends on that person's death;

- overseas pensions from certain former colonies that become payable on death (also excluded are returned contributions);

- reversion to settlor on death of an interest in possession in settled property, unless the settlor purchased that reversion;

- interest in possession passing to settlor's spouse or civil partner, on death of deceased, unless the spouse or civil partner was not domiciled in the UK at the time of death or the settlor or his spouse had purchased the reversion. A 'spouse' includes a widow or widower if the settlor dies less than two years before the deceased; and

- certain payments received under schemes which provide compensation for wrongs suffered during the Second World War era are left out of account in determining the chargeable value of the estate for the purposes of IHT on death (such amounts are deemed to remain in the recipient's estate). Thus the gift of any funds so received would be regarded as a PET and drop out after seven years but the value received would then also be exempt from IHT.

Foreign bank accounts of persons who were not domiciled in the UK and who were not resident or ordinarily resident there immediately before death, are left out of account in determining the value of the person's estate immediately before death but see 6782 for the interaction of debt deduction and foreign bank accounts.

Legislation: IHTA 1984, s. 54, 90, 151, 153, 157

Other Material: ESC F20 *Late compensation for World War II claim schemes*

Tax Reporter: ¶625-850

6800   IHT rates on death

Except as noted below, IHT is charged on a death at the full rates laid down in the Table in IHTA 1984, Sch. 1 (see *Hardman's Tax Rates and Tables* at 6-050) as if the deceased had made a transfer of value immediately before death and the value transferred had been equal to the value of the estate at that time; unless Parliament specifically provides otherwise, the threshold(s) included in the Table are indexed. There is therefore in general no grossing-up on death and for 2015–16 and 2016–17 a single rate of 40% applies where the value of the estate together with other gross cumulative transfers exceeds £325,000. The steps in the calculation are:

Step 1

Work out the value of the chargeable estate (after reliefs and exemptions).

Step 2

Ascertain the transferor's total of chargeable transfers in the seven years before death.

Step 3

Add the values in Step 1 and Step 2 to create an 'aggregate chargeable transfer'.

Step 4

Deduct the tax threshold (the amount up to which tax is payable at 0% ascertained at the date of death) from the aggregate chargeable transfer. If the aggregate chargeable transfer is below the tax threshold there is no tax to pay on the death estate.

Step 5

Work out the tax at full rate (i.e. 40%) on the value ascertained in Step 4 (i.e. the excess over the tax threshold).

Step 6

If the value in Step 2 (the lifetime transfers) exceeds the tax threshold, repeat Steps 4 and 5 with the value in Step 2. Deduct this notional tax from the tax on the aggregate chargeable transfer to calculate the tax on the estate.

Example

Yvonne died on 8 April 2015 leaving an estate of £330,000 which is chargeable to IHT, having made transfers amounting to £126,000, net of all exemptions within the previous seven years.

The tax on the estate is calculated as follows:

Steps 1–3	£
Transfers in 7 years prior to death	126,000
Add: value of estate	330,000
Aggregate chargeable transfer	456,000

Step 4	
Deduct tax threshold @ 8/4/15	
£(456,000 − 325,000) =	£131,000

Step 5	
Work out tax	
£131,000 × 40% =	£52,400

Step 6

Transfers in the seven years before death are below the tax threshold so no adjustment for tax on this value needs to be made. It would only be if the transfers in the seven years before death exceeded the tax threshold (NRB) that tapering of the tax would need to be considered (see 6801).

Legislation: IHTA 1984, s. 7–9 and Sch. 1

Other Material: *HMRC Inheritance Tax: Customer Guide* available on the HMRC website at www.hmrc.gov.uk/cto/customerguide/page1.htm

Tax Reporter: ¶604-500

6801 Taper relief

Where tax, or additional tax, becomes due because the donor dies within seven years of making a lifetime gift, relief is available if more than three years have elapsed between the date of the gift and the date of the death. The amount of the charge is tapered as follows:

More than	But less than	Percentage of full rate
3 years	4 years	80
4 years	5 years	60
5 years	6 years	40
6 years	7 years	20

It should be noted that it is the rate of tax, rather than the value transferred, that is tapered.

For examples of the application of taper relief, see 6802.

Legislation: IHTA 1984, s. 7(4)

Other Material: *HMRC Inheritance Tax: Customer Guide* available on the HMRC website at www.hmrc.gov.uk/cto/customerguide/page1.htm

Tax Reporter: ¶611-400

6802 PET becomes chargeable

No tax is due on a potentially exempt transfer (PET) at the time that it is made. If the donor survives seven years, the transfer becomes exempt, but if the donor dies within seven years of the date of the PET, then the transfer is brought into charge.

The steps in the calculation are:

Step 1

Work out the value of the PET (i.e. work out the loss to the transferor as the result of the transfer, deduct any reliefs and exemptions).

Step 2

Ascertain the transferor's total of chargeable transfers in the seven years before the PET. Remember that this will include both lifetime chargeable transfers and PETs – but only those made within the seven years before death.

Step 3

Add the values in Step 1 and Step 2 to create an 'aggregate chargeable transfer'.

Step 4

Deduct the tax threshold (the amount up to which tax is payable at 0% ascertained at the date of the death (but not any transferrable nil-rate band which can only be set against the death estate) from the aggregate chargeable transfer. If the aggregate chargeable transfer is below the tax threshold, there is no tax to pay on the PET.

Step 5

Work out the tax at full rate (i.e. 40%) on the value ascertained in Step 4 (i.e. the excess over the tax threshold).

Step 6

If the value in Step 2 (the previous lifetime transfers) exceeds the tax threshold, repeat Steps 4 and 5 with the value in Step 2. Deduct this notional tax from the tax on the aggregate chargeable transfer to calculate the death tax on the PET.

Step 7

Check whether taper relief is available. If so, take the appropriate percentage of the death tax to arrive at the tax payable as a result of the PET coming into charge.

Example

Reginald died on 22 May 2015. He had given his daughter Eleanor a gift of £150,000 in September 2009 and his son Brian a gift of £160,000 in March 2005. He had also made a chargeable lifetime transfer of £200,000 in June 2009. For the purposes of this example, the annual exemption is ignored.

As a result of Reginald's death, IHT is payable on the gift to Eleanor. The gift to Brian is exempt as it is a PET made more than seven years before death.

The tax on the gift to Eleanor is:	
Step 1–3	£
Transfers in seven years prior to PET	200,000
Add: value of PET	150,000
Aggregate chargeable transfer	350,000
Step 4	
Deduct tax threshold @ 22/5/15	
£(350,000 − 325,000) =	£25,000
Step 5	
Work out tax	
£25,000 × 40% =	£10,000
Step 6	
Transfers in the seven years before this transfer are below the tax threshold so no adjustment for tax on this value needs to be made.	
Step 7	
Death occurred between four and five years after gift and taper relief applies, so that 60% of the death tax is payable.	
Tax payable is £10,000 × 60% =	£6,000

Legislation: IHTA 1984, s. 7, 131–140, Sch. 2, para. 1A

Other Material: *HMRC Inheritance Tax: Customer Guide* available on the HMRC website at www.hmrc.gov.uk/cto/customerguide/page1.htm

Tax Reporter: ¶612-850

6803 Death within seven years of a chargeable lifetime transfer

Where a donor dies within seven years of making a chargeable lifetime transfer, tax must be recalculated using the full rates applicable at death. If this amount, after any taper relief, exceeds the tax payable at the time of the transfer, additional tax is payable.

The steps in the calculation are:

Step 1

Write down the value of the chargeable lifetime transfer (already ascertained in lifetime).

Step 2

Calculate the transferor's total of chargeable transfers in the seven years before the lifetime transfer. Remember that this will include both lifetime chargeable transfers and also PETs made within seven years before death.

Step 3

Add the values in Step 1 and Step 2 to create an 'aggregate chargeable transfer'.

Step 4

Deduct the tax threshold (the amount up to which tax is payable at 0% ascertained at the date of the death (but not any transferrable nil-rate band which can only be set against the death estate) from the aggregate chargeable transfer. If the aggregate chargeable transfer is below the tax threshold there is no death tax to pay (see also Step 8).

Step 5

Work out the tax at full rate (i.e. 40%) on the value ascertained in Step 4 (i.e. the excess over the tax threshold).

Step 6

If the value in Step 2 (the previous lifetime transfers) exceeds the tax threshold, repeat Steps 4 and 5 with the value in Step 2. Deduct this notional tax from the tax on the aggregate chargeable transfer to calculate the death tax on the current transfer.

Step 7

Check whether taper relief is available. If so, take the appropriate percentage of the death tax to arrive at the adjusted death tax on the lifetime transfer.

Step 8

Deduct any lifetime tax already paid, to give the additional tax on the transfer as the result of death. If the lifetime tax is equal to or exceeds the adjusted death tax, there is no further tax to pay (but no repayment of lifetime tax).

Example

Peter died on 2 June 2015. He made a gift into a discretionary trust on 2 April 2010 of £330,000 on which the trustees paid the lifetime tax of £1,000. He also made a gift to his sister of £110,000 in December 2009 and a previous gift to the trust in January 2003 of £38,000. For the purposes of this example, the annual exemption is ignored.

The death tax payable on the transfer to the trust in April 2010 is:

Steps 1–3	£
Transfers in seven years prior to this transfer	148,000
Add: value of the current transfer	330,000
Aggregate chargeable transfer	478,000

Step 4

Deduct tax threshold @ 2/6/15

£(478,000 – 325,000) =	£153,000

Step 5

Work out tax

£153,000 × 40% =	£61,200

Step 6

Transfers in the seven years before this transfer are below the tax threshold so no adjustment for tax on this value needs to be made.

Step 7

Death occurred between five and six years after gift and taper relief applies, so that the adjusted death tax is 40% of the death tax.

Adjusted death tax is £61,200 × 40% =	£24,480

Step 8

Additional tax payable on death is:

£24,480 – 1,000	£23,480

Legislation: IHTA 1984, s. 7 and Sch. 2, para. 2

Other Material: *HMRC Inheritance Tax: Customer Guide* available on the HMRC website at www.hmrc.gov.uk/cto/customerguide/page1.htm

Tax Reporter: ¶624-100

6804   Transfers within seven years before death

Relief is available where a PET becomes chargeable or additional IHT becomes payable in respect of a transfer other than a PET, because of the death of the transferor within seven years, and either:

- there has in the intervening period been a fall in value of the gifted property in the transferee's hands; or

- the transferee has previously sold the property outright to an unconnected purchaser at arm's length for a price which is lower than its value at the date of the original transfer.

In these circumstances, unless the property is tangible moveable property which is a wasting asset, the transferee can elect within four years of the transferor's death, to calculate any additional tax payable on the lower value or sale price. The market value for this purpose may be enhanced or reduced by reference to the difference brought about by any change in circumstances between the time of the transfer and the death/sale.

Legislation: IHTA 1984, s. 131–140

Tax Reporter: ¶611-100

6805   Instruments of variation and disclaimers

If, within two years of death, a disposition is varied or disclaimed, the disclaimer or variation is treated as if made by the deceased and will not be a transfer of value by the beneficiary. It is possible to vary an inheritance under a will, the distribution of an estate on intestacy or the passing of an interest in property held as joint tenants by survivorship and to disclaim a gift. Tax will then be charged as though the deceased had left the estate as so varied, not as had originally passed on death. Accordingly, if tax has already been paid on the death estate, and less tax is due following the variation or disclaimer, the difference may be reclaimed from HMRC. It is not possible to vary a life interest, which terminates on the death of the life tenant after their death,

To qualify for this treatment, the variation or disclaimer must take place within two years after the death and must be made in writing by the original beneficiary or beneficiaries. In the case of a variation (not a disclaimer) for variations made after 31 July 2002, there is no need to notify HMRC, within six months of the variation, for variations made after 31 July 2002, there is no longer any need to notify HMRC unless extra IHT results. Although execution of certain documents by deed is vital, it is not necessary for alterations of dispositions taking effect on death but, as a prudent precaution, a deed is normally used.

If one of the beneficiaries dies before a variation is made, HMRC take the view that the legal personal representatives of the deceased beneficiary may enter into a variation and sign an election.

When a variation results in more IHT being payable, the personal representatives must join in the notice to HMRC.

A second variation which alters the dispositions made by an earlier variation does not fall within the relief even if both are effected within the two-year period.

Instruments of variations are likely to be the favoured method of altering a will because it is then possible to direct the unwanted inheritance in a particular direction. By contrast, a disclaimer is a blunt instrument in that all it achieves is the disclaimed inheritance falling back into the estate to become part of the residue which is then redistributed on the basis of who receives the residue (which might result in some value passing back to the disclaimer).

Variations and disclaimers do not affect the IHT due where a gift with reservation is brought into charge under the provisions discussed at 6785.

Rectification

The High Court has rectified deeds of variation to correct errors which, if left uncorrected, would have nullified the tax saving which the documents were intended to achieve.

However, rectification is likely to be refused where there is no adequate evidence of what the parties intended.

However, a recent case (*Chadda*) suggests that the quality of evidence required is different depending upon whether the intention is either inherently probable or inherently improbable – '*something inherently improbable requires strong evidence, it follows that something less improbable requires less evidence*'.

Applications to the court for family provision and 'legitim'

Where as a result of an application under the *Inheritance (Provision for Family and Dependants) Act* 1975 an order is made making reasonable financial provision for the applicant out of the deceased person's estate, IHT is payable on the estate as though the estate had been distributed ab initio subject to the provisions of the order. Thus, if the order has the effect of depriving a person of property received, either by gift or by bequest, on which tax may have been payable, the tax charge can be adjusted in consequence of the order.

From 1 April 2011, a claim must be made not more than four years after the date on which the order is made.

In Scotland the surviving spouse and descendants of the deceased are entitled to claim a fixed share of the estate, called legal rights; the child's share is known as legitim. These rights may be renounced in favour of the provisions in the deceased's will. Where the estate is insufficient to meet claims for legitim on the basis of an intended disposition to the spouse, the executors or judicial factor of the testator may choose whether IHT should be charged on the basis that any disposition to the spouse is fully paid out or reduced by any legitim not renounced.

Distributions within two years of death out of discretionary trust set up by will

A similar relief is available where a distribution is made within two years of death out of a discretionary trust set up by the will of the deceased (see 7023).

Where capital is appointed under a will, for deaths on or after 10 December 2014, then IHTA 1984, s. 144 is amended, where property was left in trust, and subsequently appointed to the surviving spouse or civil partner of the deceased, such that the appointment will be treated as having been made by the will notwithstanding that the appointment was within the first three months after death (for appointments in the first three months, previously, a tax charge could have arisen as a result of the *Frankland* trap). This change was included within *Finance (No. 2) Act* 2015, s. 14 and applies to cases where the testator's death occurs on or after 10 December 2014.

Legislation: IHTA 1984, s. 142, 146, 147, 218A

Cases: *Racal Group Services Ltd v Ashmore* [1995] BTC 406; *Matthews v Martin* [1991] BTC 8,048; *Seymour v Seymour* [1989] BTC 8,043; *Lake v Lake* [1989] BTC 8,046; *Russell v IR Commrs* [1988] BTC 8,041; *Re Slocock's Will Trusts* [1979] 1 All ER 358; *Chadda* [2014] TC 04154; *Frankland v IR Commrs* [1997] BTC 8,045

Other Material: Revenue interpretation, IRInt. 1003 'Inheritance tax: Variation of inheritance following a death', Revenue interpretation, IRInt. 1006 'Post Death Variation of inheritance by survivorship'

Tax Reporter: ¶632-000

6806   Reduced rate of IHT as a consequence of charitable donations

To encourage charitable giving a potential reduction in the IHT death rate from 40% to 36% was introduced for deaths on or after 6 April 2012. The reduction is achieved where 10% or more of an individual's taxable estate passes to charity. The concept is simple but, as always, issues arise within the detail. Initial reaction suggested that the relief was initially used by those who were already making significant charitable donations so the new regime was not changing, as had been hoped, taxpayer behaviour. However, there is now some indication that some are now being encouraged to increase their charitable activity.

Under these rules, an individual's estate has to be divided into potentially three components (ignoring deemed elements such as GWR or failed PETs):

- the survivorship component;
- the settled property component; and
- the general component.

The survivorship component is the aggregate of all property within an individual's estate that, immediately before their death, was joint (or common property) that passes either by survivorship (in England, Wales and Northern Ireland) or under a special destination (Scotland). If the property is situated outside of the United Kingdom and the passing is under a law that corresponds to survivorship or special destination then it is comprised within the survivorship component.

Settled property is property in which an interest in possession exists in the estate of the deceased where the deceased was beneficially entitled immediately before death (typically pre-22 March 2006 IIP trusts but also, potentially trusts for vulnerable persons).

The general component is everything else but specifically excludes property deemed to be in an individual's estate under the gift with reservation rules.

It is possible to make a charitable donation in respect of a single component of the estate, and obtain 36% IHT on that component or on the estate as a whole. Donated amounts are those within IHTA 1984, s. 23(1).

Where the net estate consists of all three components any available nil rate band, including transferable nil rate band from a former spouse or civil partner, is apportioned proportionally between the three components or if an estate also consists of GWR assets then any available nil rate band is divided between the four elements. Available nil rate band being the nil rate band (including transferable nil rate band) less any failed PETs.

The charitable donation is described in the legislation (IHTA 1984, Sch. 1A, para. 2(5)) as 10% of the baseline amount where the baseline amount is the taxable proportion of the estate calculated in accordance with the following steps:

Step 1 Determine the part of the value transferred by the chargeable transfer that is attributable to property in that component (net of APR or BPR or charitable donations and other deductions).

Step 2   Deduct from the amount determined under step 1 on the appropriate proportion of the nil rate band.

'The appropriate proportion' is a proportion equal to the proportion that the amount determined under step 1 bears to the value transferred by the chargeable transfer as a whole.

'The available nil rate band' is the amount (if any) by which:

(a)   the nil rate band maximum (increased, where applicable, in accordance with s. 8A) exceeds

(b)   the sum of the values transferred by previous chargeable transfers made by the deceased in the period of seven years ending with the date of the relevant transfer.

Step 3   Add to the amount determined under step 2 an amount equal to so much of the value transferred by the relevant transfer (the charitable gift) as (in total) is attributable to property that:

(a)   forms part of that component; and

(b)   is property in relation to which s. 23(1) applies.

The result is the baseline amount for that component from which the 10% (minimum) charitable legacy is then calculated, described, in the legislation, as 'the appropriate proportion'.

The charitable donation is defined in the legislation as 'the appropriate proportion' (Sch. 1A, para. 5). If an appropriate proportion charitable legacy is restricted to a single component, then IHT is reduced to 36% on that single component with other components subject to 40%.

In determining the taxable value of the estate, and hence the calculation of the baseline amount, full relief is taken for available nil rate bands (including transferable nil rate band from a former spouse or civil partner) and any available APR or BPR (or other deductions). The APR or BPR will relate to a specific asset within a particular component so in the relevant calculations that component gets the benefit of the APR or BPR.

The charitable donation does not have to be paid out of every single component. The executors can choose the component from which the payment is to be made and if that exceeds 10% of the baseline amount in the total estate they can merge separate components, by election within two years of death, and obtain the 36% IHT rate across all three components.

An election to merge (Sch. 1A, para. 7) must be signed by the appropriate persons for each separate component (Sch. 1A, para. 7(6)) where these are:

- in respect of the survivorship component the appropriate person(s) is the person who acquires the property on death;

- in respect of settled property it is the trustees of the settled property;

- in respect of the general component all the personal representatives of the deceased must join in the election. In the event that there are no personal representatives, those liable for the inheritance tax on the general component are the appropriate persons; and

- in respect of any GWR assets elected to merge with one or more of the above indicated components the appropriate persons to sign the election are the legal owners of the asset or assets.

The election can be withdrawn within two years, one month of the deceased's death (Sch. 1A, para. 9(2)) with the election to withdraw being made by the same relevant persons indicated above.

In exceptional circumstances, an officer of Revenue and Customs can agree to extend either the time limit for making an election or the time limit for withdrawing the election.

Equally an election can be made to exclude a component of the estate from the 36% IHT rate, assuming that sufficient aggregate charitable donations have been made, to treat the charitable donation as though it were less than 10% of the baseline amount. HMRC suggest this might be where the cost of asset valuation exceeds the 4% tax saving.

If the appropriate amount is being made out of the general component

The mechanics, and options, indicated above can be illustrated by the following example:

Example

Peter is widowed, has an estate with a value of £1,500,000 which comprises assets that pass by survivorship of £400,000, settled property, where Peter had an interest in possession, with a value of £600,000 and a general component (everything else) with a value of £500,000. In addition, there are deemed assets, because Peter retained a benefit from assets given previously with a value of £300,000. Within the general component, there are assets that qualify for 100% BPR with a value of £200,000.

Peter's executors have transferable nil rate band from his wife of £325,000 and, from Peter, £275,000, net of lifetime gifts made in the seven years before death. His will included a charitable gift of £20,000 from general component.

The position is as the following example:

	Survivorship	Settled	General	GWR	Total
Assets	400,000	600,000	500,000	300,000	1,800,000
Less: BPR			200,000		200,000
	400,000	600,000	300,000	300,000	1,600,000
Less: Legacy			20,000		20,000
	400,000	600,000	280,000	300,000	1,580,000
Less: NRB	151,898	227,848	106,330	113,924	600,000
Taxable elements	248,102	372,152	173,670	186,076	980,000
Add: Legacy			20,000		
Baseline amounts	248,102	372,152	193,670		

Thus, the £20,000 from general component satisfies the 10% test so £173,670 is taxed at 36% with the remainder of the estate taxed at 40%.

However, whenever additional charitable legacy is made, to top up the charitable legacy to 10% (even within a single component), the NRB allocation will alter. Suppose, in the above example, the executors decided to make a further charitable donation of £25,000 but from the survivorship component which based upon the above calculation suggests, it is within the 10% parameter. The revised position, without merger election would be as follows.

	Survivorship	Settled	General	GWR	Total
Assets	400,000	600,000	500,000	300,000	1,800,000
Less: BPR			200,000		200,000
	400,000	600,000	300,000	300,000	1,600,000
Less: Legacy	25,000		20,000		45,000
	375,000	600,000	280,000	300,000	1,555,000
Less: NRB	144,695	231,511	108,039	115,755	600,000
Taxable elements	230,305	368,489	171,961	184,245	955,000
Add: Legacy	25,000		20,000		
Baseline amounts	255,305	368,489	191,961	184,245	

The 10% baseline limit for survivorship component is £25,531 so a legacy of £25,000 does not result in a reduction to 36%. Care is required in the calculations and account needs to be taken of the NRB reallocation.

If the executors decided to make a global charitable donation of £82,000, ignoring the GWR component, and make an election to merge all three components then the position might be as follows (because the reduction in the taxable estate then increases the NRB allocated to the GWR element).

	All components	GWR	Total
Assets	1,500,000	300,000	1,800,000
Less: BPR	200,000		200,000
	1,300,000	300,000	1,600,000
Less: Legacy	82,000		82,000
	1,218,000	300,000	1,518,000
Less: NRB	481,423	118,577	600,000
Taxable elements	736,577	181,423	918,000
Add: Legacy	82,000		
Baseline amounts	818,577	181,423	

Thus, 10% baseline amount is £81,858 so £82,000 satisfies the parameter and the 36% rate applies to the non GWR components.

If the executors decided to make a charitable donation of £100,000 and include the GWR asset within the election, then 36% would extend to the GWR asset (£1,600,000 - £600,000 - £100,000 = £900,000 + £100,000 = £1,000,000 so 10% baseline amount = £100,000).

If there were failed PETs in the seven years before death, they would be deducted from any available NRB and only any remaining balance of NRB then allocated proportionately between the relevant components.

Where the legacy is created by a variation of the will be aware that only one bite at the cherry is generally permitted so the legacy needs to be precisely calculated if the aim is to be as close to 10% as possible.

Failed PETs and applicable tax rate

If the failed PETs exceed the available NRB, then any failed PET excess is taxed at 40% subject to rate taper for gifts made between three and seven years before death. Taxable failed PETs cannot benefit from the 36% rate.

Interaction with spouse/civil partner exemption

It is the net taxable estate that determines the calculation of the baseline amount and hence the calculation of the appropriate proportion. It therefore follows that if an individual, on death, transfers assets to a surviving spouse or civil partner, then that value is excluded from calculation of the baseline amount.

Example

Helen, who is married to Fred, has an estate of £1,200,000, consisting solely of general component and at her death left £550,000 to Fred, a charitable legacy of £13,000 and the residue to her daughter Susan. Without taking any action the position is as follows:

Total estate			1,200,000
Less:	Spouse / CP exemption	550,000	
	NRB	325,000	
	(Assume full)		875,000
Potentially taxable estate			325,000
Less: Charitable legacy			13,000
Taxable estate			312,000
Add: Charitable legacy			13,000
Baseline amount			325,000

Because the £13,000 charitable legacy is less than 10% of the baseline amount the estate is subject to 40% IHT. Without action Helen's executors have an IHT liability of £124,800.

IHT (312,000 @ 40%)	124,800
Charity legacy	13,000
Spouse	550,000
Susan	512,200
Total estate	1,200,000

If the charitable legacy is increased to £32,500 (10% of the baseline amount) then the position is as below:

Total estate			1,200,000
Less:	Spouse / CP exemption	550,000	
	NRB	325,000	
	(Assume full)		875,000
Potentially taxable estate			325,000
Less: Charitable legacy			32,500
Taxable estate			292,500
Add: Charitable legacy			32,500
Baseline amount			325,000

So, with a 10% legacy, the position is as follows:

IHT (325,000 – 32,500 @ 36%)	105,300
Charity legacy	32,500
Spouse	550,000
Susan	512,200
Total estate	1,200,000

Thus, the charity receives £19,500 extra but it does not cost the residuary beneficiary anything. The executors pay £32,500 to charity at a nil cost to the residuary beneficiary because in the above example, the initial legacy was 4% of the taxable value of the estate. So increasing the charitable legacy to 10% of the baseline amount means that a charitable legacy can be made at no cost to the residuary beneficiary. If the charitable legacy is more than 4%, but less than 10% of the baseline amount, then the amount receivable by the residual beneficiary will actually increase.

Impact upon 'free of tax legacies'

The issues are complex and if it is not immediately apparent that the charitable legacy satisfies the 10% baseline test then two sets of calculations need to be undertaken, initially at 40% and then at 36% once it is clear the legacy satisfies the 10% baseline threshold. The following example from the HMRC manual on the reduced IHT rate illustrates the position. Reference should be made to the manual in practice as the computations are complex.

Example

Stephen died on 11 September 2015 leaving an estate valued at £1,000,000 after deduction of liabilities, consisting solely of general component. The will left pecuniary legacies of £245,000 free of tax to his children and 10% of the residue to the RSPCA. To qualify for the reduced rate of tax, the amount passing to charity might be thought to be at least £67,500 (£1,000,000 – £325,000 = £675,000 × 10%).

Ignoring grossing up, the residue of the estate is £1,000,000 – £245,000 = £755,000. The donated amount would be £75,500 and so, initially, the estate appears to qualify for the reduced rate. But because there are legacies that are left free of tax, they must be grossed up to reflect the fact that in reality, the residue and so the share passing to charity will be reduced by the tax paid by the executors. If the estate is grossed up at 40%, the calculations are as follows:

Initial residue (1,000,000 – 245,000)	755,000
Less; initial exempt residue	75,500
Initial chargeable residue	679,500
Initial chargeable estate (245,000 + 679,500)	924,500

Tax on initial estate (924,500 – 325,000 @ 40%)		239,800
Gross up gifts at estate rate		
(245,000 × (924,500 / (924,500 – 239,800)		330,805
Final residue (1,000,000 – 330,805)		669,195
Donated amount (1,000,000 – 330,805 @ 10%)		66,919

Grossing up the pecuniary legacies at full rate has increased their value for tax to £330,805. This must be fed into the calculation to determine the baseline amount as follows:

Estate on death	1,000,000	
Legacy to charity (donated amount)	66,919	
Chargeable transfer	933,081	(step 1)
Less; NRB	325,000	
	608,081	(step 2)
Add back legacy	66,919	
Baseline amount	675,000	(step 3)

The donated amount (£66,919) is less than 10% of the baseline (£67,500) so the estate does not qualify for the reduced rate when the legacy is grossed up at the full rate.

If the estate is grossed up at 36%, however, the calculations are as follows:

Initial chargeable estate (245,000 + 679,500)		924,500
Tax on initial estate (924,500 – 325,000 @ 36%)		215,820
Gross up gifts at estate rate		
(245,000 × (924,500 / (924,500 – 215,820)		319,611
Final residue (1,000,000 – 319,611)		680,389
Donated amount (1,000,000 – 319,611 @ 10%)		68,039

Here, the value of the legacies is grossed up to £319,611. The value of the residue is not reduced by quite so much as when the legacies are grossed up at 40%, so the donated amount is slightly higher.

The baseline calculation is as follows:

Estate on death	1,000,000	
Legacy to charity (donated amount)	68,039	
Chargeable transfer	931,961	(step 1)
Less: NRB	325,000	
	606,961	(step 2)
Add back legacy	68,039	
Baseline amount	675,000	(step 3)

The donated amount (£68,039) is now greater than 10% of the baseline (£67,500) so the estate qualifies for the reduced rate. The grossed up value of the legacies and the chargeable estate must be calculated using the 36% rate grossing calculator.

Other matters

The full 40% rate must also apply to charges under IHTA 1984, s. 128, where woodlands relief no longer applies, and under IHTA 1984, s. 78 in relation to conditionally exempt occasions involving settled property.

HMRC are awake to the possibility that dishonest executors will vary an estate, to indicate a charitable donation of an appropriate amount but then fail to pay the donation over to the charity. The reduced 36% rate is only available where the executors can show that the charity has been notified that the disposition of the estate has been varied in their favour. This is achieved by amending IHTA 1984, s. 142 to insert IHTA 1984, s. 142(3A).

In a husband and wife, or civil partnership situation, where the couple are minded to make a charitable donation but on the first death the whole of the estate will pass to the survivor it will make financial sense for the charitable donations to be made on the second death. This is because if the gift to charity is on the first death no relief for the charitable donation, and hence no rate reduction, will be obtained. This is because the transfer to the surviving spouse/civil partner remains exempt.

Most commercial precedent drafters include a specimen clause in their precedent database. The Society of Trust and Estate Practitioners (STEP) have published on their website a specimen and HMRC have also issued a precedent with some commentators suggesting that if a non HMRC precedent is used there may be a review that might not otherwise arise.

Testators will have to consider whether they wish to make the charitable gift by way of legacy or by instrument of variation after the death. Perhaps an instrument of variation has more flexibility, but less certainty for the charity. Some practitioners express concern that if the charitable donation is achieved within the will that consequent interest from the charity may impact upon the efficient administration of the estate. Perhaps the better view, particularly if the gifts are to be more than the 10% minimum, is to leave the charities out of the will and to deal with the matter by appointment, under the terms of a letter of wishes, or under a discretionary trust or by way of a deed of variation.

It is important to remember that the requirement is for the charitable donation to be at least 10% of the baseline amount which in most cases is unlikely to be 10% of the gross estate. It therefore follows that an individual with a substantial estate, but one which is eligible for BPR/APR on a significant proportion of that estate, can make a charitable donation which only represents a modest proportion of the gross estate and reduce the tax rate to 36%. It still has to satisfy the 10% of the baseline amount test but, in these circumstances, perhaps it is a more palatable donation to make.

Consider the following example:

Example

Jason has an estate of £5,000,000, all of which is general component, comprising APR/BPR eligible assets with a value of £3,500,000 and other assets with a value of £1,500,000. There is a full transferable NRB from his wife's estate available and Jason also has a full NRB available. The current position is:

Gross estate	5,000,000
Less: APR /BPR (100%)	3,500,000
	1,500,000
Less: NRB (325,000 × 2)	650,000
Taxable estate	850,000
Tax at 40%	340,000

A charitable legacy of £85,000, equivalent to only 1.7% of the gross estate achieves a reduction in the tax rate to 36%.

Taxable estate	850,000
Less: Charitable legacy	85,000
	765,000
Add: Charitable legacy	85,000
Baseline amount	850,000
10%	85,000

Taxable estate is £765,000 so tax at 36% is £275,400

So the net cost is £20,400 (£340,000 − £275,400 = £64,600 tax reduction − £85,000), no more than 0.41% of the gross estate; an amount that might be regarded as loose change in such an estate.

What is not clear, and may not be clear for some time, is whether this allowance will change testator's plans. Experience suggests that most testators leave significantly less than 10% to charity and the modest cost of increasing charitable legacies is unlikely to change that. Those who already leave substantial sums to charity do not need persuasion, and the reduced tax rate, so what is the true relevance of this complicated regime which may benefit very few estates each year?

Legislation: IHTA 1984, Sch. 1A

Tax Reporter: ¶629-520

6810   Value transferred on death and subsequent disposals

There is a deemed transfer of value immediately before death of the whole of the deceased's estate (see 6770). The value of any property for IHT purposes is generally the price it might reasonably be expected to fetch if sold in the open market at that time (see 6570), though there are certain reliefs and liabilities to be taken into account on death (see below).

If the deceased was a sole trader or a member of a partnership, the business assets (including goodwill) must be valued and any liabilities deducted – the valuation will be on the basis that the business is a going concern unless more could be realised by discontinuing the business and selling the separate assets. Chattels, including cars, furniture, jewellery, collections, boats, etc. will generally be accepted at the executor's valuation, but professional valuations should be carried out for such things as antiques, etc. Debts owed to the deceased will form part of his estate at face value unless they are impracticable to recover. Life policies are valued as the amount assured, plus any bonus or share of profit.

Legislation: IHTA 1984, s. 5

Tax Reporter: ¶602-400

6815   Reliefs in relation to disposals shortly after death

Shares

If 'qualifying investments' are sold within 12 months of death at a lower value than at death or, in certain cases, it is otherwise recognised that they lose their value within that time frame, then from 1 April 2011, relief must be claimed, within four years from the end of the 12-month period.

'Qualifying investments' comprise 'quoted' (see 6571) investments, holdings in authorised unit trusts and shares in a common investment fund. The relief is calculated by adding together the price received from the sale of all qualifying investments within the 12-month period and subtracting this figure from the value as at the date of death. If shares or securities are bought within the period from the date of death and two months after the last sale within the 12 months after death, the relief may be wholly or partly lost.

Example

Personal representatives of Arnold sell shares quoted at £4,000 on his death for £3,000. Therefore, the value of shares on death will be reduced by £1,000. They purchase further shares for £2,000. Part of the relief of £1,000 will be lost, calculated as follows:

$$\frac{2,000}{3,000} \times £1,000 = £666.66$$

Thus, the value of shares on death will be treated as £3,333.34.

If a person other than a trustee or personal representative purchases further shares then they must be of the same description as those sold.

The relief also applies to loss in value recognised within the 12-month period by cancellation of the investments (a notional sale for £1 immediately before cancellation) or by suspension of 'listing' (a notional sale at market value at the 12-month date).

Land

If 'land' is sold within three years of death for less than its valuation at death, the sale price may be substituted, provided that the sale price was the best reasonably obtainable in an arm's length transaction between unconnected persons. Again, sales at a loss and sales at a profit in the three year period are netted off and the relief is restricted for purchases made within four months of the last sale in the three year period. From 1 April 2011, a claim must be made within four years from the above period. This relief does not apply if the sale is between connected persons even if the sale is by public auction.

Sales in the fourth year after death at a loss are deemed to be made in the three year period so the time limit for claim is unchanged. Sales at a profit in the fourth year are ignored and fourth year sales do not affect the restriction for purchases.

'Land' is defined as including buildings and interests in land. Therefore, a lease would be within the definition.

Related property

Where related property is sold within three years of death by the person in whom the property became vested on death or by the deceased's personal representatives, and the sale price is less than the value determined and the value is less than that determined in accordance with the related property provisions (see 6575), the value on death may be redetermined by ignoring the related property provisions and instead using the value that would have applied had the property in question been valued on its own.

Example

Mavis owns half an antique tea set. Her husband owns the other half. Individually, each half of the tea set is valued at £4,000. However, the complete set has a value of £20,000. Mavis dies. Under the related property provisions (see 6575), her property is valued as a 50% share of the whole set, i.e. 50% of £20,000 = £10,000.

However, six months after her death, Mavis's daughter, who was left her mother's half of the tea set on her death, sells it for £6,000. As the actual sale price is less than the value determined in accordance with the related property provisions of £10,000, the value at death is redetermined, ignoring the related property provisions. Taking the half-tea set alone, the value at death is revised to £4,000.

Legislation: IHTA 1984, s. 178–198; *Finance Act 2009, Sch. 51 (Time Limits For Assessments, Claims, Etc.) (Appointed Days and Transitional Provisions) Order* 2010 (SI 2010/867)

Tax Reporter: ¶627-900

6818   Treatment of liabilities

Any liabilities due at death together with the interest thereon are deductible provided they were incurred for full consideration in money or money's worth.

However, no deduction is allowed in respect of the liabilities of the deceased to the extent that the creditor has received gifts from the deceased. If and to the extent that it is shown that the loan was not made to the deceased out of property derived from him or out of consideration provided by someone who had in his resources property derived from the deceased, the disallowance will not operate (see 6782).

In valuing the deceased's estate no account is taken of liabilities arising in connection with a policy of life assurance made after 30 June 1986 unless the sums assured form part of the deceased's estate immediately before death.

Reasonable funeral expenses are deductible, but executorship and administration costs are not (although SP2/04 allows a modest deduction for executorship and administration costs against capital gains made by executors although, alternatively, actual costs can be used if they give a greater deduction subject to the usual self-assessment tests of being able to justify whatever deduction is claimed). If the property is located outside the UK, there is a special relief for the additional cost of administration arising through the location of the property, but the allowance cannot exceed 5% of the gross value of all foreign property in the estate.

Also, see 6819 below as some debts may not be deductible on death if they are not repaid, unless there is a commercial reason for the debt to be left unpaid. Alternatively, for debt incurred on or after 6 April 2013 the debt may not be deducted from the asset on which it is secured, but instead must be deducted from the asset whose purchase was effected. Where debt is secured on private assets but used to purchase APR or BPR, etc. relievable assets then the application of this rule will increase the taxable value of the estate.

Legislation: FA 2013, s. 176 and Sch. 36; IHTA 1984, s. 5(3)–(5)

Tax Reporter: ¶617-400

6819   Interaction of liabilities and other reliefs

Finance Act 2013, s. 176 and Sch. 36 introduce provisions, applying from 6 April 2013, that restrict the ability to deduct liabilities over and above the existing restrictions.

Special rules apply where a loan was secured on UK situs assets but where the proceeds of the loan are used to purchase excluded property. This rule applies at the date of the IHT event (provided it is on or after 17 July 2013) so even if the finance arrangement was effected many years ago the debt is deducted from the asset whose purchase was arranged. The consequence is to increase the taxable value of the UK estate.

Where a loan has been taken out to acquire excluded property, that is assets situated outside the UK owned by a non-domiciled individual, then that debt will only be UK deductible where either the excluded property has been disposed of and the proceeds of sale are no longer excluded property (provided the proceeds have not then been used to acquire, maintain or enhance further excluded property) or used to repay a liability that would not have been deductible. The liability may be deducted only if disposal is at full value and the proceeds form part of the UK estate so that they are then chargeable to IHT (new) IHTA 1984, s. 162A.

If a loan has been used to acquire assets which have become excluded property and the loan exceeds the asset value, at the date of IHT event, then only the excess can be deducted provided, and this is a catch-all, the debt was not incurred as a result of arrangements that were intended to result in a tax advantage of any sort. Tax advantage is defined in (new) IHTA 1984, s. 162A(8).

Where the liability has been incurred, on or after 6 April 2013, to acquire property that is otherwise relievable because, for example, APR or BPR or Woodlands Relief can be deducted, then the debt, even if it is not secured on the relievable property, has first to be deducted from the value of that relievable property before determining what remaining value is then eligible for APR or BPR, etc. This is designed to stop a range of tax planning schemes but including arrangements which many thought unobjectionable.

Prior to the introduction of (new) IHTA 1984, s. 162B the preferred planning in relation to assets eligible for APR or BPR (or equivalent reliefs) was to secure the debt, if possible, on an asset not eligible for APR or BPR so the taxable value of the relievable asset became £nil (value less APR or BPR, etc.) but the debt was still deductible against the general estate. That preferred result still applies provided the debt was taken out, and in place, before 6 April 2013.

Example

Susanna wished to expand her farming business and in May 2009 purchased farmland with a value of £750,000 with the aid of a bank loan of £500,000. Susanna lives in a mansion house that is not believed to qualify for APR. She arranged for the debt to be secured on the mansion house.

At the date of an IHT event, assumed on or after 6 April 2013, her position will be as follows: Land Value £750,000 less APR £750,000 = £nil chargeable value (once the farmland qualifies for APR) with the £500,000 loan then deductible from the value of Susanna's other assets (including the mansion house).

If the same debt arrangement took place on or after 6 April 2013, then the position will be as follows: Land Value £750,000 less bank loan £500,000 = chargeable value of £250,000 from which APR of £250,000 would then be deducted to leave a taxable value of £nil but no further deduction for the loan. The second example further illustrates the issues.

Example

Henry, the controlling shareholder in Henry Trading Ltd wishes to purchase in October 2012, personally, an additional factory at a cost of £2m with the aid of a bank loan of £1.5m. The position at an IHT event on or after 6 April 2013, because the loan was in place before 6 April 2013, will be as follows: Factory Value − £2m less BPR at 50% of £1m = chargeable value of £1m (once the asset qualified for BPR) and then a separate deduction for the debt of £1.5m assuming it could be secured on private (that is non APR or BPR relievable) assets.

If the same debt arrangement takes place on or after 6 April 2013, then the position will be as follows: Factory Value − £2m less loan of £1.5m = chargeable value £500,000 less BPR (at 50%) to give a chargeable value of £250,000.

In both examples, the effect of the debt being deducted from the financed asset (before BPR, etc. is considered) is to increase overall taxable value of the estate at the date of an IHT event.

However, the provisions go further. Under (new) IHTA 1984, s. 162C which states that where a loan has been used for the acquisition of a mixture of excluded property, relievable property and other property, then in reviewing the deductibility of the debt (if any), any loan repayments are deemed to be first applied in reducing any loan used to acquire, effectively, private chargeable assets, in preference to any other part of the loan.

Example

Christine took out a loan of £1,000,000 in July 2013 of which £750,000 was used to acquire BPR relievable assets and £250,000 was used to acquire a seaside cottage. In December 2015 at an IHT event, the debt has been reduced to £850,000. The full repayment is treated as reducing the debt on the (non-relievable) seaside cottage so the consequence is to increase the taxable value within the estate but the remaining £750,000 is still matched against the relievable assets.

In addition, if the debt is not repaid after the IHT event, then there can be further restrictions on the ability to deduct the debt at all under (new) IHTA 1994, s. 175A where the effect is as follows:

A deduction for a liability will only be allowed to the extent that it is repaid to the creditor, unless it can be shown that there is a commercial reason for not repaying the liability and it is not left unpaid as part of arrangements to obtain a tax advantage.

What does 'commercial reason' mean? Presumably, it should include circumstances where property was jointly owned with other individuals where as a result of the death of one joint owner any funding arrangements continue with the inheritor of the deceased's share taking over responsibility for their share of the debt? Would taking on a 'family debt' count as a commercial reason? HMRC manual from IHTM28010 onwards refers to 'commercial terms' which points towards loans having the characteristics of borrowing from a third party. So the loan should have the following characteristics: repayment over time – by monthly or quarterly instalments; interest calculation basis specified; an agreed time frame for loan repayment; security and do the parties think it is arms length? Consider the following HMRC examples:

Example 1

Kevin's estate is valued at £750,000, £700,000 of which is attributable to his home. A mortgage of £100,000 is secured against the house. The executors borrow £100,000 to repay the mortgage and secure the new loan on the

---

house, so that the beneficiary receives the property charged with the new debt. You may accept that the liability has been discharged out of the estate. There is no need to raise any enquiries into the source of funds lent to the executors, including whether or not the beneficiary is the creditor for the new loan. Provided the mortgage has actually been repaid from funds charged against the estate, the deduction may be allowed as this has the same effect as the liability being discharged out of the estate had there been sufficient liquid assets.

Example 2

David's estate includes a house valued at £800,000. There is a commercial mortgage of £200,000 from a family trust charged against the property. David leaves his house to his son, Roger. The trustees are content that the house can be transferred to Roger provided that Roger takes over the mortgage and continues to make the repayments. Although the liability has not been repaid, the arrangements are commercial and there is no tax advantage arising from Roger taking over the mortgage, so the liability may be allowed as a deduction against the estate.

However, the ease in which 'repayment' of the debt is evidenced in the majority of cases (as in the above examples) would suggest that HMRC have particular avoidance arrangements in mind, such as loans under employee benefit trusts (which are typically not collected on death).

Certainly, if the loan arrangements contain characteristics that a commercial lender would never countenance such as deferral of interest, no interim capital repayments or repayment only required after a family event such as the death of a parent, then the loan is unlikely to be on commercial terms.

There are many possible circumstances which cause concern. Suppose the debt is waived by the creditor to avoid hardship. Does that count as being left unpaid as part of an arrangement to obtain a tax advantage? HMRC guidance as to their view of 'commercial reason' is not terribly clear. If we have to wait several years for tax cases to determine what 'commercial reason' means, then that is surely an unsatisfactory arrangement.

The restriction may apply to a nil-rate band debt scheme involving a loan arrangement. Suppose the loan is waived instead of being repaid after the second death. To get a deduction, the debt has to be repaid, perhaps challenging if the only trust asset is a property or an interest in a property which cannot be sold. Will it be possible to create a debt that can be classified as 'money's worth' under (new) s. 175A(1)(a)?

It seems equally possible that the new rules affect equity release schemes, perhaps not where the borrowed money has been spent (the usual expectation) but if invested in assets that attract BPR (a more unusual expectation).

Certainly, if the loan proceeds were gifted, the residual debt would not be deductible.

Trustees as well as individuals will also be subject to the rules with the exception that the unpaid liabilities rule will not apply to the calculation of the value of the estate for the purposes of the ten-year anniversary charge. That is presumably on the basis that the date of the ten-year anniversary charge is an entirely artificial event and therefore requiring repayment of the loan at the date of a ten-yearly charge could cause hardship.

When transferring property to a trust subject to a debt (assuming it has been acquired for a commercial purpose), care will need to be taken that the commercial reason is not thereby negated.

The rules apply, equally, to property owned by a non-UK domiciled individual which would be excluded property and therefore not subject to IHT under UK rules. If debt were secured on UK situs assets (historically, a mainstream planning device), but the assets funded by the loan were situated outside the UK, then where the IHT event is on or after Royal Assent to FA 2013 (17 July 2013) that debt cannot be deducted from the taxable value of the UK situs assets irrespective of when the debt was taken out.

What is clear is that this is a belt and braces approach to prevent a deduction for debt unless it can clearly been shown to be for a commercial reason. What is objectionable is that this is retrospective in that the new rules impact upon what was previously regarded as acceptable planning.

However, the relative ease with which 'repayment' can be demonstrated in straightforward cases may suggest that HMRC have particular schemes in mind such as employee benefits trusts (where it is understood that in many cases any outstanding loan is automatically waived on death so perhaps ought never to have been deducted because it was never a genuine debt) so perhaps conventional estates may not have many concerns.

Legislation: FA 2013, s. 176 and Sch. 36

Tax Reporter: ¶626-250

6820 Quick succession relief

Where the value of a person's estate was increased by a chargeable transfer made not more than five years before his death, the IHT chargeable on death is reduced by a percentage of the tax charged on so much of the value transferred by the first transfer as is attributable to the above increase. The relief applies only where there has been a transfer to the deceased within five years before his death and where the second occasion of charge is his death. The percentages are:

- 100% if the first transfer is made within one year of death;
- 80% if the first transfer is made within two years of death;
- 60% if the first transfer is made within three years of death;
- 40% if the first transfer is made within four years of death;
- 20% if the first transfer is made within five years of death.

Relief is calculated using the formula:

$$\text{tax on gift} \times \frac{\text{increase in second transferor's estate}}{\text{value transferred}} \times \text{percentage}$$

If there is more than one later transfer, the reduction is only available in respect of the earliest of them. However, if the reduction is less than the whole of the IHT charged, a reduction may be made in respect of the later transfers (in chronological order) until reductions representing the whole of that tax have been made.

Any 'excluded property' (see 7397) consisting of a reversionary interest to which the transferor became entitled on the occasion of, or before, the chargeable transfer, will be disregarded in determining the increase in his estate from a chargeable transfer.

Relief is thus given by way of credit against the IHT bill attributable to the later transfer.

Example

Richard dies and as part of his will he makes a chargeable transfer of £140,000 to Anne. It is assumed that tax of £10,000 was payable on the gift.

Eighteen months later, Anne dies. In calculating the tax payable on her estate, quick succession relief is available in respect of the bequest by Richard as follows:

$$£10,000 \times \frac{(£140,000 - £10,000)}{£140,000} \times 80\% = £7,428$$

Legislation: IHTA 1984, s. 141

Tax Reporter: ¶627-400

6830   Avoidance of double charge

Regulations eliminate a double charge to IHT by setting off the value transferred by one transfer against the value transferred by another or by setting the tax paid on one transfer against the tax paid on another or by both. The regulations deal with situations where, as a result of the provisions relating to PETs and gifts with reservations (see 6610 and 6785ff.), the same property forms or is treated as forming part of one person's estate more than once for IHT purposes.

The regulations apply so as to charge whichever of the transfers produces the higher amount of tax. The transfer which produces the lower amount of tax is then ignored.

Legislation: FA 1986, s. 104; *Inheritance Tax (Double Charges Relief) Regulations* 1987 (SI 1987/1130)

Tax Reporter: ¶614-300

Inheritance tax and settled property

Scope of IHT charges on settled property

6880   Types of settled property for IHT

Finance Act 2006 introduced changes to the inheritance tax (IHT) treatment of trusts that were the most far-reaching reforms of capital taxation for some 20 years. The announcement of the changes in March 2006 led to widespread criticism from the professions and the financial press. The professions were particularly concerned that a consultation process on trusts had been ongoing for two years with no mention of the proposed reform to IHT. Whilst a number of amendments were made at Committee stage, the changes mean that the majority of trusts will now be subject to the 'relevant property' rules In IHTA 1984, Pt. III that were previously restricted to discretionary trusts.

Interest in possession trusts created before 22 March 2006 will continue to be taxed under the old rules as long as the interest of the life tenant benefiting at that date continues. If an interest in possession comes to an end during the life tenant's lifetime, the trust will then fall within the 'relevant property' regime subject to transitional rules for trusts created before 22 March 2006. Under the transitional rules, where the trust is replaced by a further interest in possession trust, the new interest in possession trust will be taxed under the old rules.

Accumulation and maintenance trusts created before 22 March 2006 continued to be taxed under the old regime until 6 April 2008. From 6 April 2008, accumulation and maintenance trusts created before 22 March 2006 continued to be taxed under the old rules if the beneficiaries have the right to capital on or before the age of 18. Where the beneficiary in an existing accumulation and maintenance trust will take the trust assets absolutely no later than age 25, the trust will be taxed under the provisions for the new age 18 to 25 trusts. New trusts created on or after 22 March 2006 can no longer qualify as accumulation and maintenance trusts.

From 18 March 1986 to 21 March 2006, lifetime gifts into accumulation and maintenance trusts and disabled trusts qualified as potentially exempt transfers. Gifts into interest in possession trusts qualified as PETs from 17 March 1987 to 21 March 2006. If the settlor survived seven years from the date of the gift, no tax was payable.

Transfers into 'relevant property' give rise to an immediate tax charge, where the value of the gift to the trust and any chargeable transfers made by the settlor in the seven years prior to the creation of the trust exceed the level of the nil rate band, at half the rates set out in IHTA 1984, Sch. 1 (see *Hardman's Tax Rates and Tables* at 6-000). If the settlor then dies within seven years, extra tax might be payable if the amount chargeable (at full rates 6-050) at the time of death, after taper relief, exceeded the amount paid when the transfer was made.

From 22 March 2006, only lifetime gifts to another individual, into a disabled trust (7011), into a bereaved minor's trust (7003) on the coming to an end of an immediate post-death interest (6907) and the creation of a transitional serial interest (6908) will qualify as PETs. If the settlor survives seven years from the date of the gift, no tax will be payable.

Lifetime gifts to other trusts are chargeable transfers and will give rise to an immediate tax charge where the value of the gift to the trust and any other chargeable transfers made by the settlor in the seven years prior to the creation of the trust exceed the level of the nil rate band, and will be charged at half rates (20%) set out in IHTA 1984, Sch. 1. If the settlor then dies within seven years, extra tax might be payable if the amount chargeable (at full rates – 40%) at the time of death, after taper relief, exceeds the amount paid when the transfer was made.

Example

In May 2013, Robin created a 'relevant property', the assets of which amounted to £150,000, under which the income was payable to his daughter, Jenny, for life, with the remainder to Jenny's daughter, Emma. Chargeable transfers in the previous seven years amounted to £100,000. He has used his annual exemptions.

As the value of the gift to the trust and the chargeable transfers (gifts that might eventually become exempt PETs are ignored) made in the previous seven years (ignoring annual exemptions) is below the nil rate band of £325,000, no tax is payable on the transfer to the trust.

Example

If Robin had made chargeable transfers of £200,000 in the previous seven years, an immediate tax charge would arise on the gift to the trust.

£350,000 – £325,000 = £25,000 @ 20% = £5,000 (if the tax is paid by the trust fund, otherwise grossing up applies)

If, in the second example above, Robin had created the trust in February 2006 (before the rules changed), the gift to the trust would have qualified as a PET. If he had then survived seven years from the date of the gift, no tax would have been payable by Robin.

Legislation: FA 2006, s. 156 and Sch. 20; IHTA 1984, s. 43–93

Other Material: *HMRC Inheritance Tax: Customer Guide* available on the HMRC website at www.hmrc.gov.uk/cto/customerguide/page1.htm

Tax Reporter: ¶362-000

6883 Creation of a settlement

The first occasion when tax becomes payable earlier than transfers between individuals is when property is settled. If the trust is created on or after 22 March 2006 and is not a trust for the disabled (7011), a transitional serial interest (6908), or bereaved minor's trust (7003) on the coming to an end of an immediate post-death interest (6907), the transfer is not a potentially exempt transfer. Tax is chargeable – at half rates (6-000) – when the transfer is made where the transfer to the trust and any chargeable transfers made by the settlor in the seven years prior to the creation of the trust exceed the level of the nil rate band. If the settlor dies within seven years after making the transfer, extra tax may be payable to bring the total up to the full rates applicable at the time of the death.

Where a settlement terminates so the capital leaves the trust due to the impossibility of achieving its purposes, a charge to tax may arise.

Example

Charles creates a settlement for the benefit of his children, and transfers £100,000 into the settlement. Tax is payable on the creation of the settlement. Charles dies without having any children. The purposes of the settlement have failed and so the settlement terminates. A charge to tax will also arise on the termination.

Tax Reporter: ¶362-025

6884 Variation of an existing settlement

It may be desirable for the trustees of an existing settlement to vary its purposes, either under a power given to them in the terms of the trust, or by application to the court under the *Variation of Trusts Act* 1958, s. 1 (or the *Trusts (Scotland) Act* 1961, s. 1). Such a variation could give rise to a charge to inheritance tax, depending on the effect which it has on the nature of the beneficiaries' interests. For example, if the variation involves property being made over to a beneficiary absolutely, a charge may arise. Likewise, the creation or termination of an interest in possession may have tax consequences.

Example

Trustees hold £500,000 in a settlement in which no interest in possession subsists. The trust is varied in such a way that a beneficiary becomes entitled to receive one-fifth of the income arising. Inheritance tax will be payable by the trustees on £100,000. If the tax is paid out of the £100,000, no grossing-up is required; if it is paid out of other trust funds, grossing-up is required.

Tax Reporter: ¶362-050

6885 Distributions and appointments by trustees

Generally, any capital distribution to a beneficiary out of the trust fund is an event likely to give rise to a charge to tax. The same is true where an interest in possession is created in property in which no such interest previously subsisted.

The charge is not avoided by making dispositions to beneficiaries by indirect means, e.g. by an omission by the trustees to exercise a right, or by causing settled property to become 'excluded property'. Certain distributions/dispositions made by trustees are not chargeable to IHT. These include:

(1) costs and expenses of administration of the settlement;

(2) payments of income to beneficiaries;

(3) a grant of a tenancy of agricultural land for full consideration;

(4) a commercial bad bargain which reduces the value of the settled fund but where there was no gratuitous intent;

(5) gifts to charities, political parties and gifts for national purposes (provided certain conditions are fulfilled).

Tax Reporter: ¶362-075

6886   Depreciatory transactions

Where the trustees of a settlement enter into an agreement with a beneficiary, potential beneficiary or a person connected with either, and because of the agreement the value of the settlement is reduced, then there is a charge to tax on that reduction. A commercial arrangement between the trustees and a beneficiary, where there is no gratuitous intent, is not a depreciatory transaction and will not give rise to a charge.

Examples of depreciatory transactions are the granting of a lease at less than the market rent, the granting of a loan of money at less than market rates (whether in terms of interest rates or repayment terms), and a sale at an undervalue.

Tax Reporter: ¶362-100

6887   Ten-yearly charge on 'relevant property' settlements

For trusts created before 22 March 2006, the ten-yearly or 'principal charge' only applied to discretionary trusts (i.e. settled property in which no interest in possession subsisted). Following the changes in the *Finance Act* 2006, all new trusts created on or after 22 March 2006 during the lifetime of the settlor will be subject to the 'relevant property' regime, the only exceptions being trusts for the disabled (7011) and where new interest in possession trusts were created out of existing ones (transitional serial interests 6908) before 6 October 2008.

The principal charge arises on the tenth anniversary of the commencement of the settlement, and subsequent anniversaries at ten-yearly intervals. The rate of tax is 30% of the appropriate lifetime rate (half rate – 20%) so a maximum of 6%.

Example

Alastair leaves property to Basil and Charles (as trustees) for those of his children (Wendy, Xavier, Yvonne and Zak) as Basil and Charles, in their absolute discretion, see fit. There is an interest in possession in the property for the first three years. Ten years after the discretionary trust has been set up, a charge to IHT arises on the value of 'relevant property' (see 6940) in the trust. The rate of tax will be reduced by twelve-fortieths in arriving at the amount chargeable to tax (representing the three years' interest in possession outside the discretionary trust regime) so the ten-yearly charge will be $^{28}/_{40}$ of a full ten-year charge.

Changes to the basis upon which periodic charges in relevant property trusts are calculated from 6 April 2014 apply following ongoing consultation with HMRC over their desire to 'simplify' the basis upon which periodic charges are calculated. However, *Finance Act* 2014 confirms two changes which will apply from 6 April 2014.

(1) The date on which any tax due, and the date on which returns must be made to HMRC, will be aligned so that both forms and tax will be due six months after the end of the month in which the relevant event occurred.

(2) Income which the trustees hold, which has never been formally accumulated often because the trust deed does not require accumulation will, for purposes of calculating the periodic charge, be deemed, for this purpose only, to have been accumulated after five years.

HMRC had concerns that some trustees were leaving income unaccumulated far beyond periods which might be considered appropriate under the terms of the trust deed or where, for example, income which had not been formally accumulated had, in effect, been accumulated because the funds had been used to purchase long term investments rather than left as cash.

This has been a long running issue although given that HMRC could have litigated to achieve certainty, it might, perhaps, not be an unreasonable conclusion to think that the advice HMRC had was that if the policy of particular trustees was in accordance with the trust deed that any argument that income had been accumulated by passage of time might not have been successful. The unaccumulated five years' income would be taxed at the normal periodic charge rate for that particular trust. This can be contrasted with the position where assets are added to a settlement part way through a ten-year period where a reduced periodic charge applies in the first ten-year charge after the assets are added (as the Alastair example above).

Example

The Farrow Discretionary Trust was due a ten-year periodic charge on 30 September 2015 and at that date, the assets of the trust are quoted shares with a value of £1,700,000, farmland with a value of £2,000,000 (agricultural value £1,800,000) and unaccumulated income at 30 September 2015 of £150,000. The net of tax income for the five years to 30 September 2015 (ignoring income distributions) was £90,000 so £60,000 relates to the period before 30 September 2010. There were no intermediate distributions and a full NRB is available.

Quoted shares		1,700,000
Farmland	2,000,000	
BPR	(1,800,000)	200,000
Unaccumulated income		60,000

	1,960,000
Less: Nil-rate band	(325,000)
	1,635,000
Tax at 20% lifetime rate	327,000
Tax rate	$^{327,000}/_{1,960,000}$ = 16.68%
Effective rate	30% × 16.68% = 5%
Periodic charge = 1,960,000 × 5% = £98,000 of which £3,000 is attributable to the unaccumulated income	

These rules apply to any charge due from 6 April 2014. If, for example, a periodic charge was due on 30 September 2015, the trustees would have to look back and see whether there was any income that had not been accumulated in the period before 30 September 2010; any periodic charge that arises on unaccumulated income to be deducted from income account in accordance with the usual procedures.

HMRC offer detailed guidance on this issue at IHTM42166 but in the absence of contrary information that income received can be treated as distributed on a 'first-in, first-out' basis. Thus, the trustees would take the balance on income account and divide it into two parts – net of tax income received in the five years before a periodic charge (ignoring all income distributions in the most recent five-year period) and the balance. Unless the trust minutes state, for example, that an income distribution made in 2015–16 was specifically made out of the income for that year that the normal presumption would be that income distributions, whenever made, were allocated to income receipts on a first-in, first-out basis; against the oldest income first.

Most trusts will make their accounts up to 5 April (to match the tax year) but only exceptionally will a trust be established on 5 April. Thus, suppose a ten-year charge is due 30 September 2016. It will be necessary to apportion the accounts for the two years to 5 April 2017 and 5 April 2011 to establish the net of tax income for the last five years. It is understood that HMRC will accept any reasonable apportionment so long as it is consistently applied.

The consultation document 'Inheritance Tax: A fairer way of calculating Trust charges', issued on 6 June 2014, and subject to much critical response from professional organisations was withdrawn on 3 December 2014 and replaced by further changes. Since the underlying objective of previous consultation was to attack 'Pilot Trusts', the current proposals, which will apply to charges on or after 18 November 2015 (the date of Royal Assent to *Finance (No. 2) Act* 2015), have the degree of simplicity.

The proposals state that where property is added on or after 10 December 2014 to two or more settlements on the same day, and after the commencement of those settlements, the value of the added property, together with the value of the property settled at the date of commencement (that is not already in a related settlement), is brought into account in calculating the rate of tax for the purpose of ten-year charges, for exit charges before the first ten-year anniversary and for exit charges between anniversaries (as well as for the charges on 18–25 trusts).

However, there is a de minimis exemption such that the same day addition of amounts of less than £5,000 in aggregate, but only if made during the settlor's lifetime, will not be regarded as same day additions. This may cover the situation where the settlor may pay the administration fees of the trust or add capital to meet an IHT charge where the trusts are illiquid. *Finance (No. 2) Act* 2015, Sch. 1 contains anti-fragmentation provisions to prevent the same-day rules being avoided by adding amounts in excess of £5,000 in multiples of £5,000.

In some circumstances, there can be a same-day addition where there is an increase in the value of the property contained within the settlement even though there was no increase in the amount of the property.

There is a transitional period for the proposed regime not to apply (so that each pilot trust would be treated independently as was previously the position) where a settlor dies on or before 5 April 2017 (a March Budget 2015 change – the transitional period had previously been announced as ending 5 April 2016), where the transfer of value is on or after 10 December 2014. However, to take advantage of the transitional arrangements, the will that applies in respect of the death on or before 5 April 2017 has to be a 'protected testamentary disposition' as defined. This means that the transfers into trust under the will are in substance the same as they would have been immediately before 10 December 2014.

> **Example**
>
> George created seven pilot trusts on seven successive days in July 2010 with initial capital of £50 in each trust. On his death on 31 May 2016, £250,000 was added to each settlement. For the purposes of calculating future relevant charges, any liability on each separate trust is calculated by reference to the individual trust's assets plus related settlements with an aggregate value of £1,250,250 (5 × £250,050).

Can a codicil to a will executed on or after 10 December 2014 taint a pre-10 December 2014 will? HMRC initially suggested that if the codicil altered, in any way, the disposition of the estate, then the will was no longer a 'protected testamentary disposition'. But most advisers consider that the requirement to be 'in substance, the same' only covers those parts of the will that refer to the use and indication of value relating to pilot trusts. It is understood that HMRC now accept that a codicil or new will does not automatically prevent a 'protected testamentary disposition' but it would be important to keep the pre-10 December 2014 will as evidence. Equally it seems certain that altering the terms of the pilot trust dispositions through an instrument of variation will cause the transitional protection to be lost because that is not a testamentary disposition. Thus, for example, if in the George example the capital into each trust was altered post death to £300,000, it cannot be said that the will is 'in substance, the same'.

By contrast if the will stated, for example, that the value into each pilot trust was one-seventh of the residue (and the expected value was £250,000 per trust), the inclusion in a codicil (or new will) of a new legacy that left each trust still receiving one-seventh of the residue but reduced each share to £200,000 would still be regarded 'in substance, the same' because the share remains one-seventh. Presumably this is on the basis that until the testator dies no one knows what (in our example) one-seventh might amount to.

Where the settlor survives beyond 5 April 2017, then the will is no longer a 'protected testamentary disposition' so changes are, in any event, then likely to be required and best advice must be to revisit the will where the potential testator survives beyond April 2017.

Pilot trusts that were in place, with full capital, before 10 December 2014 are equally not caught by these changes and will continue as independent settlements each with their own nil rate band.

Tax Reporter: ¶362-175

6889   Meaning of settlement and settlor, etc.

The meaning of a settlement for inheritance tax purposes is in IHTA 1984, s. 43(2), which states that 'settlement' means any disposition or dispositions of property whether effected by instrument, by parol or by operation of law, or partly in one way and partly in another, whereby the property is for the time being:

(1) held in trust for persons in succession or for any person subject to a contingency;

(2) held by trustees on trust to accumulate the whole or part of any income of the property or with power to make payments out of that income at the discretion of the trustees or some other person with or without power to accumulate surplus income;

(3) charged or burdened (otherwise than for full consideration in money or money's worth paid for his own use or benefit to the person making the disposition) with the payment of any annuity or other periodical payment payable for a life or any other limited or terminable period; or

(4) would be so held or charged or burdened if the disposition or dispositions were regulated by the law of any part of the UK; or whereby, under the law of any other country, the administration of the property is for the time being governed by provisions equivalent in effect to those which would apply if the property were so held, charged or burdened.

One settlement or more than one

It is important to identify in any disposition or dispositions whether one settlement or more than one settlement has been created. For example, every discretionary trust created before 27 March 1974 has its own inheritance tax rate scale. Also, when interests are appointed out of settled property, it is important to know how many settlements exist in order to determine the possibility of certain property qualifying for relief or becoming excluded.

Leases for life

A lease of property which is for life or lives, or for a period ascertainable only by reference to a death, or which is terminated on, or at a date ascertainable only by reference to a death, is treated as a settlement, and the property as settled property. Where a lease not granted as a lease at a rack rent is at any time to become a lease at an increased rent, it is treated as terminable at that time.

The exception is where the lease was granted for full consideration in money or money's worth; hence commercial transactions are not treated as giving rise to a settlement. A statutory tenancy is not a settlement.

Settlor

As a matter of general law, more than one person can be the settlor of the same settlement. The legislation defines 'settlor' in relation to a settlement to include any person by whom the settlement was made directly or indirectly, and in particular to include any person who has provided funds directly or indirectly for the purpose of or in connection with the settlement, or has made with any other person a reciprocal arrangement for that other person to make the settlement. Thus, if a life tenant provides funds to allow the trust to cover an expense, the life tenant becomes a settlor of the contributed amount. That would be so even if the relevant funds never passed through the trustee's bank account; the effect of paying a trust liability means the trustees do not have to pay so effectively the value of the trust fund is maintained.

The legislation continues the definition in relation to multiple settlors, and states that where more than one person is a settlor in relation to a settlement and the circumstances so require, the settled property provisions of the Act shall apply in relation to it as if the settled property were comprised in separate settlements.

An example of a situation where the circumstances so require is where the trustees are resident abroad and tax must be recovered from the settlor. Thus, if A puts £20,000 into a settlement and B puts £40,000 into the same settlement, and the trustees are non-resident, the liability for tax due will be split between A and B in the ratio in which each put money into the trust. The trust itself will be held to be two trusts: A's trust and B's trust; and the tax will be due from each separately, not from both jointly.

It is important to identify the settlor or settlors because their identity and circumstances govern the rate of the ten-year charge for the discretionary trust regime; also, if the settlor is non-resident, then the settled property or part of it could be excluded property.

Trustee

From 6 April 2006, trustees of a settlement are treated as if they were a single person, distinct from the persons who are trustees of the settlement from time to time. Changes in the persona of the trustees have no effect on the trust as such, since the trustees are treated as a separate legal entity.

A bare trustee is not a trustee for inheritance tax purposes, because the property which he holds does not fall within the definition of settled property in IHTA 1984, s. 43(2) (see above). A 'bare' trustee means any person holding property to which another person is absolutely entitled (or would be so entitled if he were not an infant or under some other legal incapacity). Thus, for example, where a person entitled to an interest in possession in settled property becomes absolutely entitled to it, the property ceases at that moment to be settled property for tax purposes, and the person holding the legal title ceases to be a trustee.

Beneficiary

The term 'beneficiary' has no special meaning for inheritance tax. It includes an annuitant, a lessee for life and (in Scotland) a proper liferenter. It includes anyone with either a present or a future right of enjoyment of settled property, including anyone with a contingent interest so long as the contingency is capable of being fulfilled.

The term also includes a person to whom the trustees have given a right of occupation of a dwelling-house comprised in the settled property, provided the rent paid is not a full market rent.

Legislation: TCGA 1992, s. 69(1); IHTA 1984, s. 43(2), (3), 44(1), (2)

Cases: *Re Buttle's Will Trusts* [1977] 3 All ER 1039; *Re Ogle's Settled Estates* [1927] 1 Ch 22; *Vine v Raleigh* [1896] 1 Ch 37

Tax Reporter: ¶351-025

6892   Disclosure of ownership of assets by trusts

There were proposals from the European Commission for a public register of trusts open to public scrutiny that would have included disclosure of the trust assets, disclosure of the trust deed and other documents including the letter of wishes but as at February 2016 that possibility is not currently being pursued although there remain some in Europe who would wish that it were so. Company information is in the public domain, with new legislation to increase company disclosure as to beneficial ownership in respect of persons with significant control (PSC) registers where every company must have in place an appropriate register by 30 June 2016 and update it on an annual basis but, where a trust owns a company, PSC disclosure will only extend to the name of the trust not the underlying beneficiaries.

Guidance was published by the Department for Business, Innovation and Skills on 15 February 2016 and should be required reading for all who are involved in managing trusts. The guidance contains the following:

> 'If an individual has significant influence or control over the activities of a trust or firm, which would be a PSC of the company if it were an individual, then you should enter that person's details on the PSC register. If a registrable relevant legal entity (RLE) controls the trust or firm then its details must be entered on the PSC register. If a legal entity which is not an RLE controls the trust or firm, then you should continue to explore the ownership chain until you have identified an individual or registrable RLE with majority ownership of that legal entity, or are confident none exists. [...] If someone other than the trustees, such as the settlor or beneficiary of the trust, or partners has the right to exercise significant influence or control over the trust or firm, then they would also be shown on the register [...].'

Interest in possession in settled property

6903   Definition of 'interest in possession'

There is no statutory definition of 'interest in possession' in the legislation and, therefore, the ordinary rules of property law must be applied. References to an interest in possession include those equivalent rights in Scotland. A reversionary interest is defined accordingly.

An interest in possession exists when the person having the interest has the immediate entitlement to any income produced by that property as the income arises. The Court of Session has held that an interest in possession was enjoyed where the settlor had an entitlement to income subject to the trustees' powers to appropriate income to meet capital depreciation or for any other reason they might deem necessary. It was held that on the true construction of the trust deed the trustees' powers were administrative only; they did not amount to a power to accumulate and did not prevent an interest in possession existing. Thus, an interest in reversion will not qualify as an interest in possession, whereas a life interest in property will so qualify.

Example

Anna leaves property to Bertie and Caroline upon trust for David for life with remainder to Edward. David has an interest in possession. Edward will acquire an interest in possession when David dies.

In HMRC's view, a discretion or power, in whatever form, which can be exercised after income arises so as to withhold it from that person, negates the existence of an interest in possession. For this purpose, a power to accumulate income is regarded as a power to withhold it, unless any accumulations must be held solely for the person having the interest or his personal representatives. On the other hand, the existence of a mere power of revocation or appointment, the exercise of which would determine the interest wholly or in part (but which so long as it remains unexercised, does not affect the beneficiary's immediate entitlement to income) does not, in HMRC's view, prevent the interest from being an interest in possession. This broadly coincides with the House of Lords later decision in *Pearson v IR Commrs* [1981] AC 753.

Where there is no interest in possession in a dwelling-house, if the trustees permit a beneficiary to occupy it on a non-exclusive basis, this does not usually create an interest in possession. However, an interest in possession may be created indirectly by a direction not to sell the dwelling house. In one case, a testatrix (a tenant in common in the house) left her share of the house to her daughter. However, the executors of her will were directed not to enforce the sale of the house during the lifetime of the testatrix's spouse (the other tenant in common). On the death of the spouse, it was held that he had an interest in possession in the testatrix's share of the house. In another case concerning a trust for sale of a house, the settlor directed that the sale should be postponed for so long as any of the children desired to live there. One son lived in the house, the other did not. On the death of the son who lived in the house, it was held that both sons had an interest in possession and so only half of the value of the house was chargeable on the death.

Legislation: IHTA 1984, s. 46, 47

Cases: *Woodhall (as Personal Representatives of Woodhall dec'd) v IR Commrs* (2000) Sp C 261; *IR Commrs v Lloyd's Private Banking Ltd* [1998] BTC 8,020; *Pearson v IR Commrs* [1981] AC 753

Other Material: SP 10/79 *Power for trustees to allow a beneficiary to occupy a dwelling-house*; HMRC *Inheritance Tax: Customer Guide* available on the HMRC website at www.hmrc.gov.uk/cto/customerguide/page1.htm

Tax Reporter: ¶351-400

6906   Extent of interest in possession

A person beneficially entitled to an 'interest in possession' (see 6903) in settled property prior to 22 March 2006 is treated as beneficially entitled to the underlying property in which the interest subsists, i.e. he is treated as owning it absolutely.

Example

Percy has a pre-March 2006 life interest in Whiteacre, the property passing to his two sons in equal shares on his death. Percy is treated as being beneficially entitled to the whole of Whiteacre. On Percy's death, the value of Whiteacre would be included in the value of his estate for IHT purposes.

Interest in part

If the person entitled to the interest in possession is entitled only to part of the income of the property, he is treated as being beneficially entitled to a proportionate share of that property.

Example

Jack is beneficially entitled to three-quarters of the income from Blackacre for the rest of his life in a pre-March 2006 trust. He is treated as being beneficially entitled to three-quarters of Blackacre.

If the beneficiary is entitled to a specific amount of income in a period, his interest is taken to subsist in such part of the property as produces that amount in that period.

A charge arising on the cessation of an annuity charged on property may be relieved by reference to the extent to which the value of the property in point reflects anticipated rent increases.

Where the person entitled to the interest is not entitled to any income of the property, but is entitled, jointly or in common with one or more other persons, to the use and enjoyment of the property, his interest is taken to subsist in such part of the property as corresponds to the proportion which the annual value of his interest bears to the aggregate of the annual values of his interest and that or those of the other or others.

From 22 March 2006, newly created interest in possession settlements are taxed under the relevant property regime, unless the interest is an immediate post-death interest (6907), transitional serial interest (6908) or a disabled person's interest (7011), so such interests are no longer deemed part of the life tenant's estate.

Lease for life

Where a lease of property for life is treated as a settlement (see 6883), the lessee's interest in the property is taken to subsist in the whole of the property less such part of it as corresponds to the proportion which the value of the lessor's interest bears to the value of the property.

An IPDI can include anyone who will become age 18 within two years of the death of the testator by reason of IHTA 1984, s. 144.

Legislation: IHTA 1984, s. 49(1), 50

Other Material: ESC F11, *Property chargeable on the ceasing of an annuity*; *HMRC Inheritance Tax: Customer Guide* available on the HMRC website at www.hmrc.gov.uk/cto/customerguide/page1.htm

Tax Reporter: ¶350-925

6907   Immediate post-death interest

An immediate post-death interest arises where a life tenant is beneficially entitled on or after 22 March 2006, to an interest in possession in settled property and a number of conditions are satisfied, namely:

(1) the settlement was effected by will or on intestacy;

(2) the life tenant became beneficially entitled to an interest in possession on the death of the testator or intestate;

(3) the trust must not currently be for bereaved minors and the interest is not that of a disabled person;

(4) condition (3) must have been satisfied at all times since the life tenant became entitled to the interest in possession.

Where a trust qualifies as an immediate post-death interest, it will be taxed under the pre-22 March 2006 rules for interest in possession trusts (see 6909).

Legislation: IHTA 1984, s. 49A

Tax Reporter: ¶362-550

6908 Transitional Serial interest

Under now expired transitional provisions an interest in possession could qualify as a transitional serial interest and benefit from the tax treatment that applied to pre-22 March 2006 interests where:

(1) the settlement began before 22 March 2006 and immediately before that date, the property was subject to an interest in possession ('the prior interest');

(2) the prior interest came to an end on or after 22 March 2006 and before 6 October 2008;

(3) the 'current interest' became entitled to an interest in possession at the time that the prior interest ended;

(4) the trust was not for a disabled person nor a bereaved minor.

On the death of spouse or partner on or after 6 October 2008

Alternatively, where a person, 'E' in the legislation, is beneficially entitled to an interest in possession in settled property ('the successor interest'), that interest is a transitional interest where:

(1) the settlement must have commenced before 22 March 2006 and the property comprised in the settlement was property to which a person other than 'E' was beneficially entitled to an interest in possession ('the previous interest');

(2) the previous interest came to an end on or after 6 October 2008 on the death of the other person ('F');

(3) immediately before F died, F was the spouse or civil partner of E;

(4) E became beneficially entitled to the successor interest on F's death;

(5) this was not a settlement for a bereaved minor or a disabled person.

Legislation: IHTA 1984, s. 49C, s. 49D

Tax Reporter: ¶362-575

6909   Charge to IHT on settled property where interest in possession

Consistent with the general rule that a tenant for life of a pre-22 March 2006 interest in possession is treated as though he were the beneficial owner of the settled property (see 6906), transactions involving the life interest are not actual transfers of value. However, subject to limited exceptions:

(1) where a pre-22 March 2006 interest in possession comes to an end, otherwise than on the life-tenant's death, there is a deemed transfer of value equal to the value of the property in which the interest subsisted; this applies also for the purposes of certain exemptions if the transferor notifies the trustees of the availability thereof: or

(2) where the life tenant of a pre-22 March 2006 settlement disposes of his interest, the disposal is not an actual transfer of value, but is treated as the coming to an end of his interest, as above: there is a deemed transfer of value equal to the value of the property in which the interest subsisted, less any consideration received for the disposal.

It may therefore be seen that the usual method of valuing a disposition by reference to the fall in value of the transferor's estate (see 6612) is not applied in the case of deemed transfers of value by a life-tenant. Instead, the deemed transfer of value is measured by reference to the value of property in which the interest subsisted. Moreover, the value is measured in isolation, without reference to any similar property.

Example

Rupert owns 4,000 shares in S Ltd, an investment company, and is also the life-tenant of a settled fund which holds 2,000 shares. There are 10,000 issued shares. Values per share are agreed as follows:

% holding	£ per share
20	5
40	8
60	13

Clearly, if Rupert died, the value of the shares in both his free estate and in the settled fund of which he is a life-tenant would be valued at £13 per share as part of a 60% holding (see 6906).

However, if Rupert assigns the whole of his life-interest, the value transferred will be measured as follows 2,000 shares × £5 = £10,000 (i.e. the value of the 20% holding).

Where the interest is one to which the person became beneficially entitled on or after 22 March 2006, an actual or potential charge to tax will only arise in relation to the coming to an end of the interest only if the interest is an immediate post-death interest (see 6907) or a transitional serial interest (see 6908) and is not an interest in a bereaved minor's trust (see 7003).

Prior to 22 March 2006, the rules governing PETs applied – whether or not that person was an individual – so that, provided the other conditions are satisfied, transfers or deemed transfers to or by a tenant for life were potentially exempt (see 6611).

Example

On 1 August 2005, Arnold settled £100,000 on trust for Billy for life, remainder to Cuthbert absolutely. Billy gave his interest to Diana on 1 December 2005. Both the August 2005 and December 2005, transactions are potentially exempt and there will be no IHT charge provided Arnold did not die before August 2012 and Billy before December 2012.

If Arnold had settled the property on trust on or after 22 March 2006, there would potentially be an immediate charge to tax unless the interest is a transitional serial interest or a disabled person's interest depending upon the settled value.

An interest in possession to which a close company is entitled is attributed to its participators (see 6555); this applies for all IHT purposes, so that a charge can arise when a participator disposes of any part of his shareholding.

Where a close company became beneficially entitled on or after 22 March 2006 to an interest in possession, that interest will also include an immediate post-death interest or a transitional serial interest.

Trustees' annuities

An interest by way of annuity, etc. as commercial remuneration for a trustee's services is not subject to the charge.

Legislation: IHTA 1984, s. 51, 52, 57, 90

Other Material: *HMRC Inheritance Tax: Customer Guide* available on the HMRC website at www.hmrc.gov.uk/cto/customerguide/page1.htm

Tax Reporter: ¶362-675, ¶362-875

6912 Exceptions to deemed transfer of value rules

The deemed transfers of value mentioned at 6909 (*in respect of pre-22 March 2006 trusts*) do not arise in various circumstances.

If the person whose interest has come to an end becomes beneficially entitled to the property or to another interest in possession in the property – unless the new interest is less valuable than the previous interest.

Example 1

Arthur transferred Whiteacre to Bertram and Christine (as trustees) upon trust for Daniel until he attains the age of 25 years and thereafter to Daniel absolutely. When Daniel attains the age of 25 years, his interest in possession in Whiteacre will end, but he will become absolutely entitled to the property so no IHT charge will arise.

Example 2

Arthur transferred Whiteacre and Blackacre to Bertram and Christine upon trust for Daniel until he attains the age of 25 years and, thereafter, Whiteacre is to be transferred to Daniel absolutely and Blackacre to Emily absolutely. Daniel will be treated as having made a transfer of value equal to the value of Blackacre and will be charged to IHT accordingly.

---

(2) If the settled property in question is 'excluded property' (see 7397).

(3) If the interest comes to an end by being disposed of by the person beneficially entitled to it for a consideration in money or money's worth which is equal to or greater than the value of the interest disposed of. If the consideration for the interest is less than the value, there is a deemed transfer on the difference. The value of any reversionary interest in the property, or of any interest in other property comprised in the same settlement, is left out of account.

(4) Where the settlor becomes beneficially entitled to the property in which the interest in possession previously subsisted, provided that the settlor or his spouse had not acquired a reversionary interest in the property for a consideration in money or money's worth.

(5) Where the interest in possession comes to an end and the settlor's spouse becomes beneficially entitled to the settled property in which the interest in possession previously subsisted, provided:

(a) the settlor's spouse is then domiciled in the UK; and

(b) neither the settlor nor the settlor's spouse had acquired a reversionary interest in the property for a consideration in money or money's worth.

Legislation: IHTA 1984, s. 52(2), 53, 54

Other Material: *HMRC Inheritance Tax: Customer Guide* available on the HMRC website at www.hmrc.gov.uk/cto/customerguide/page1.htm

Tax Reporter: ¶362-725

6918 Transactions reducing the value of settled property

Where the value of settled property is reduced before the interest in possession comes to an end by a transaction between the trustees and a person connected with:

- the person beneficially entitled to an interest in the property; or

- a person beneficially entitled to any other interest in that property or to any interest in any other property comprised in the settlement; or

- a person for whose benefit any of the settled property may be applied,

then a corresponding part of the interest is treated as having come to an end. However, this is not so when, had the trustees been beneficially entitled to the property, the transaction would not have been a transfer of value.

Example

Mark transfers property worth £400,000 to James and Caroline (as trustees) upon trust for Thomas until he reaches the age of 25, and thereafter to Thomas absolutely. Shortly before Thomas reaches 25, James and Caroline sell him half of the settled property (worth £200,000) for one-quarter of its value (£50,000). Thus, the value of the settled property has been reduced by £150,000 which is three-eighths of the current value. Thomas's interest in three-eighths of the settled property is treated, for the purposes of the charge on termination of an interest in possession (see 6909), as having come to an end.

The House of Lords has held that an arrangement whereby certain paintings were taken out of the possession of the settlement for a specified period was a chargeable depreciatory transaction.

Where the interest is one to which the person became beneficially entitled on or after 22 March 2006, the above only apply where the interest is an immediate post-death interest (see 6907), a disabled person's interest (see 7011), or a transitional serial interest (see 6908).

Legislation: IHTA 1984, s. 52(3)

Case: *Macpherson v IR Commrs* [1988] BTC 8,065

Other Material: *HMRC Inheritance Tax: Customer Guide* available on the HMRC website at www.hmrc.gov.uk/cto/customerguide/page1.htm

Tax Reporter: ¶362-940

Settlements with no qualifying interest in possession

6940 Types of settlement without qualifying interest in possession

There are special charges to IHT in respect of settlements with no qualifying interest in possession, other than 'privileged trusts' (see 6998). They are designed to ensure that there is an approximation to a full charge to tax in respect of property held in such long-term trusts, once in every 30 years but spread over that time.

Relevant property

More specifically, the special rules apply in respect of relevant property. 'Relevant property' means settled property in which there is no qualifying interest in possession, other than certain types of property, e.g. property held for charitable purposes only. Property in a premiums trust fund or ancillary trust fund of a Lloyd's Name is not relevant property.

'Qualifying interest in possession' means an interest in possession to which an individual is beneficially entitled; it also applies to companies if their business consists wholly or mainly in the acquisition of interests in settled property, and the company has acquired the interest from an individual beneficially entitled to it for a full consideration in money or money's worth.

Property becoming settled on a death

For present purposes, will trusts, etc. are treated as if the property became comprised therein at the time of death.

Undistributed income

For periods until 5 April 2014, undistributed income was taxed within a periodic charge or exit charge only if it was formally accumulated and then only from the date of accumulation. The date of accumulation will depend upon the terms of the trust and the actions of the trustees. Make sure, if it is relevant, that decisions not to accumulate are regularly minuted by the trustees. If income that is supposedly not accumulated is invested in long-term funds that may indicate that de facto accumulation has occurred, notwithstanding what the documentation suggests.

Finance Act 2014 brings, from 6 April 2014, unaccumulated income that has remained unaccumulated for more than five years before the periodic charge event into charge. This income is subject to the full rate of tax rather than the proportionate charge that might otherwise apply if the income had been formally accumulated between ten-year charge dates.

HMRC have published IHTM42166 guidance that, normally, income will be assumed to have been distributed on a first-in, first-out basis (resulting in older income being distributed first). Trustees may need to amend their annual accounts (and minutes) to make it clear that any particular income distribution is not made out of current income, to avoid any claim that, for example, the distributions made in the year to 5 April 2016 relate to income arising in that year resulting in income more than five years old remaining undistributed and thus subject to periodic charges – see 6887.

Legislation: FA 1994, s. 248; IHTA 1984, s. 58, 59, 83, 84

Other Material: SP 8/86, *Inheritance tax: treatment of income of discretionary trusts*; *HMRC Inheritance Tax: Customer Guide* available on the HMRC website at www.hmrc.gov.uk/cto/customerguide/page1. htm; IHTM42166

Tax Reporter: ¶362-200

6943 The charge to IHT on settlements without a qualifying interest in possession

The principal charge to IHT on settlements without a qualifying interest in possession (known as relevant property trusts) occurs immediately before a ten-year anniversary on the value of 'relevant property' (see 6940) in the settlement at that time. A 'ten-year anniversary' means the tenth anniversary of the date on which the settlement commenced and subsequent anniversaries at ten-yearly intervals; no date falling before 1 April 1983 was a ten-year anniversary. The 'commencement of a settlement' is taken to be where property first becomes comprised in that settlement.

The other times at which tax will be charged are where property ceases to be relevant property, e.g. where someone obtains an interest in possession in that property, and where trustees make a disposition reducing the value of settled property which is not of the types mentioned below. Inheritance tax is charged on the reduction in value of the settled property or, if the tax is paid out of the relevant property, it will be charged on an amount which, after deducting tax, is equal to the amount by which the relevant property has been reduced.

From 22 March 2006, any new trust set up during lifetime or on death is subject to the relevant property regime unless it is:

- an immediate post-death interest (see 6907);
- a transitional serial interest (see 6908);
- an age 18–25 trust (see 7004); or
- a trust set up for a disabled person (see 7011).

Certain other trusts are excluded from the definition of 'relevant property', namely charitable trusts, maintenance funds for historic buildings, employee trusts and protective trusts.

No charge is incurred:

- where the event is within the first quarter after commencement of the trust or ten year anniversary (but in that instance CGT holdover will not be available);
- on payments of costs or expenses (payment includes transfer of assets other than money);
- where no gratuitous benefit was intended;
- on property which becomes 'excluded property' (see 7397) by leaving the UK; or
- on property which becomes excluded property because it is invested in certain types of securities and the settlor (or in some cases a previous or subsequent settlor) was not domiciled in the UK at the time.

Legislation: IHTA 1984, s. 60, 61, 63–65, 82(2), (3)

Other Material: *HMRC Inheritance Tax: Customer Guide* available on the HMRC website at www.hmrc.gov.uk/cto/customerguide/page1.htm

Tax Reporter: ¶362-200

6946   IHT on ten-year charge

Each period of ten years (see 6943) is divided into 40 quarters so that property is only charged to IHT for the period that the property is within the relevant property regime but see below for the position in relation to unaccumulated income deemed subject to periodic charge if not formally accumulated within five years of receipt. Inheritance tax will be charged on the value of the property at the time of the charge, reduced by one-fortieth for each quarter that the property is outside the relevant property regime (a quarter being any period of three months).

Example

Alan transfers £500,000 into a relevant property trust in May 2005. In May 2015, the settlement fund is valued at £800,000. There have been no dispositions or distributions by the trustees in the ten-year period and no unaccumulated income of more than five years – see 6887.

Alan had made no transfers of value before setting up the settlement.

	£
Value of relevant property	800,000
Tax on transfer of £800,000 (800,000 – 325,000 @ 20%)	95,000
Effective rate $\dfrac{95{,}000}{800{,}000} \times 100\%$	11.88%
Rate applicable is 30% × 11.885% =	3.56%
Tax payable £800,000 × 3.56% =	£28,480

The rules set out at 6950–6960 apply to settlements with a commencement date after 26 March 1974. Different rules apply in the case of settlements created before 27 March 1974.

Legislation: IHTA 1984, s. 63, 85

Other Material: *HMRC Inheritance Tax: Customer Guide* available on the HMRC website at www.hmrc.gov.uk/cto/customerguide/page1.htm

Tax Reporter: ¶362-300

6950   Rate of ten-yearly charge

Inheritance tax is charged at 30% of the half rate applicable to chargeable lifetime transfers (see 6614) which is determined by assuming that a chargeable transfer has been made on the following basis:

- that the value assumed to have been transferred is equal to the total, at the time of the charge, of all 'relevant property' (see 6940), non-relevant property which was not relevant property at the commencement of the trust and remained non-relevant property (but only for charges arising before Royal Assent to *Finance (No. 2) Act* 2015 (18 November 2015) as a result of changes announced in the 3 December 2014 Autumn Statement), and the value immediately after a 'related settlement' commenced of the property then comprised in it;

- that it is assumed to have been made immediately before the ten-year charge by an assumed transferor whose cumulative total value of previous chargeable transfers is assumed to be equal to the total of any chargeable transfers made by the settlor of the trust in the seven years before the settlement commenced and the value of any distributions made out of the trust in the ten years before the charge.

'Related settlements' are those where the settlor is the same in each case and they commenced on the same day, unless all the property held in one or both settlements is charitable property. This rule remains unchanged after the 3 December 2014 Autumn Statement but note that the relevant legislation was included within *Finance (No. 2) Act* 2015.

Added property

Where property is added to the settlement, if the total value of the settlor's chargeable transfers in the seven years preceding the addition is higher, that latter value will be substituted in the calculation of the rate of IHT for the total of his chargeable transfers in the seven years before the settlement commenced.

Legislation: IHTA 1984, s. 62, 66, 67

Tax Reporter: ¶362-325

6954   First ten-year charge

As regards settlements made on or after 27 March 1974, the following procedure is followed to calculate the first ten-year charge, where there have been no additions to the trust (see further below).

The steps in the calculation are:

Step 1

Work out the value of a hypothetical transfer which is the aggregate of:

(a) the value of the relevant property in the settlement immediately before (i.e. day before) the anniversary date (including unaccumulated income received more than five years before the charge date);

(b) the value of any other property in the same settlement that is not relevant property (for example, property in which there is an interest in possession) at its value immediately after becoming comprised in the settlement (where a charge arises on or after 18 November 2015 (date of Royal Assent to *Finance (No. 2) Act* 2015) this step is ignored); and

(c) the value of any property comprised in all related settlements (i.e. made by the same settlor on the same day as this settlement, other than a non-temporary charitable settlement) at its value immediately after becoming comprised in the related settlement.

Step 2

Calculate the 'special cumulation' which is an imaginary cumulation total found by aggregating:

(a) the settlor's total of chargeable transfers in the seven years before the commencement of the settlement; and

(b) the amounts on which exit charges have been imposed in the last ten years.

Step 3

Add the values in Step 1 and Step 2 to create an 'aggregate chargeable transfer'.

Step 4

Deduct the tax threshold (the amount up to which tax is payable at 0% ascertained at the anniversary date) from the aggregate chargeable transfer. If the aggregate chargeable transfer is below the tax threshold, there is no tax to pay.

Step 5

Work out the tax at half rate (i.e. 20%) on the value ascertained in Step 4 (i.e. the excess over the tax threshold).

Step 6

If the value in Step 2 (the special cumulation) exceeds the tax threshold, repeat Steps 4 and 5 with the value in Step 2. Deduct this notional tax from the tax on the aggregate chargeable transfer to calculate the tax on the hypothetical transfer.

Step 7

Calculate the effective rate by dividing the tax on the hypothetical transfer by that transfer and multiplying by 100.

Step 8

Calculate the actual rate of tax by taking 30% of the effective rate found in Step 7.

Step 9

Multiply the actual rate by the current value of relevant property in the trust (step 1(a)) to obtain the tax payable by the trustees.

Position before Royal Assent to Finance (No. 2) Act *2015* (*18 November 2015*)

Example

Charles, who had made a chargeable transfer of £30,000 in 1997, creates a settlement on 8 May 2005, transferring property worth £300,000. Half of the fund is held on discretionary trusts, the other half being subject to an interest in possession for Charles' son. No tax was payable on the creation of the settlement as the value of the property held on discretionary trust was below the threshold and the creation of the interest in possession qualified as a PET. No exit charges occurred in the first ten years of the trust's life.

On 7 May 2015, the value of the whole trust fund is £800,000. The ten-year charge is calculated as follows:

Step 1

Hypothetical transfer	£
(a) current value of relevant property (1/2 × £800,000)	400,000
(b) value of other property in settlement immediately after commencement (non-relevant property) – historical value (1/2 × £300,000)	150,000
(c) value of property in related settlement immediately after commencement	n/a (in this case)
Hypothetical transfer	550,000

Step 2

Special cumulation	£
(a) settlor's total of chargeable transfers in seven years before the commencement of the settlement	30,000
(b) the amounts on which exit charges have been imposed in the last ten years	n/a
Special cumulation	30,000

Step 3

	£
Special cumulation	30,000
Add: value of this transfer	550,000
Aggregate chargeable transfer	580,000

Step 4

Deduct tax threshold @ 8/5/15 £(580,000 – 325,000) =	£255,000

Step 5

Work out tax on aggregate chargeable transfer

£255,000 × 20% = £51,000

Step 6

The special cumulation is below the tax threshold so no adjustment for tax on this value needs to be made.

Step 7

Effective rate

$$\frac{51,000 \times 100}{550,000} = 9.27273\%$$

Step 8

Actual rate

9.27273% × 30% = 2.78182%

Step 9

Tax payable by trustees

2.78182% × £400,000 = £11,127

Where property has been added to the settlement which is relevant property at the anniversary date, an adjustment needs to be made to the actual rate of tax on such property. This is to ensure that the added property is only taxed for the period when it was in the settlement (this reduction does not apply to the value of unaccumulated income received more than five years before the charge date which is subject to the full ten-year rate).

Position on or after Royal Assent to Finance (No. 2) Act 2015 (18 November 2015)

With effect from Royal Assent to *Finance (No. 2) Act* 2015, non-relevant property (within the relevant property trust) will be ignored when calculating any relevant tax charges but the related settlement rules remain (because otherwise the anti-pilot trust changes would not work). Thus, the following example (with identical facts to the previous example) would ignore the 50% held on interest in possession trusts for any charge arising on or after Royal Assent to *Finance (No. 2) Act* 2015.

Example

David who had made a chargeable transfer of £30,000 in 2000, creates a settlement on 8 October 2006, transferring property worth £300,000. Half of the fund is held on discretionary trusts, the other half being subject to an interest in possession for David's son. No tax was payable on the creation

---

of the settlement as the value of the property held on discretionary trust was below the threshold and the creation of the interest in possession qualified as a PET. No exit charges occurred in the first ten years of the trust's life.

On 7 October 2016, the value of the whole trust fund is £800,000. The ten-year charge is calculated as follows:

Step 1

Hypothetical transfer	£
(a) current value of relevant property (1/2 × £800,000)	400,000
(b) value of other property in settlement immediately after commencement (non-relevant property) (historically 1/2 × £300,000) but zero as post 17 November 2015	n/a
(c) value of property in related settlement immediately after commencement	n/a (in this case)
Hypothetical transfer	400,000

Step 2

Special cumulation	£
(a) settlor's total of chargeable transfers in seven years before the commencement of the settlement	30,000
(b) the amounts on which exit charges have been imposed in the last ten years	n/a
Special cumulation	30,000

Step 3

	£
Special cumulation	30,000
Add: value of this transfer	400,000
Aggregate chargeable transfer	430,000

Step 4

Deduct tax threshold @ 7/10/16	
£(430,000 – 325,000) =	£105,000

Step 5

Work out tax on aggregate chargeable transfer	
£105,000 × 20% =	£21,000

Step 6

The special cumulation is below the tax threshold so no adjustment for tax on this value needs to be made.

Step 7

Effective rate

$$\frac{21,000 \times 100}{400,000} = 5.25\%$$

Step 8

Actual rate

$5.25\% \times 30\% = 1.575\%$

Step 9

Tax payable by trustees

$1.575\% \times £400,000 =$ | £6,300

Notea: in calculating an exit charge post 18 November 2015 where the rate had been calculated on the pre-18 November basis item, recalculate the rate on the post 18 November basis (the same principle as would apply if the NRB charged) and use that to calculate the exit charge.

Legislation: IHTA 1984, s. 64, 66

Other Material: *HMRC Inheritance Tax: Customer Guide* available on the HMRC website at www.hmrc.gov.uk/cto/customerguide/page1.htm

Tax Reporter: ¶363-350

6960   Second and subsequent ten-year charge

As regards settlements made on or after 27 March 1974, the rules for computing the tax on the second and subsequent anniversaries are the same as for the first one. However, it should be remembered that only those existing charges within the ten years before each anniversary are taken into account.

Example

The facts are the same as in the example in 6954 above. In February 2016, the trustees appoint £50,000 (gross) to Donald out of the discretionary part of the fund. In 2017, the interest in possession comes to an end and that half of the fund is made over to Eric (the beneficiary with the interest in possession) absolutely. Assume on 7 May 2023, the remaining relevant property fund is worth £900,000.

The ten-year charge in 2023 will be calculated as follows (assuming the threshold for 2015–16 applies).

Step 1

Hypothetical transfer	£
(a) current value of relevant property	900,000
(b) value of property in related settlement immediately after commencement	n/a (in this case)
Hypothetical transfer	900,000

Step 2

Special cumulation	£
(a) settlor's total of chargeable transfers in seven years before the commencement of the settlement	30,000
(b) the amounts on which exit charges have been imposed in the last ten years	50,000
Special cumulation	80,000

Step 3

	£
Special cumulation	80,000
Add: value of hypothetical transfer	900,000
Aggregate chargeable transfer	980,000

Step 4

Deduct assumed tax threshold @ 8/5/23

£(980,000 − 325,000) =	£655,000

Step 5

Work out tax on aggregate chargeable transfer

£655,000 × 20% =	£131,000

Step 6

The special cumulation is below the tax threshold so no adjustment for tax on this value needs to be made.

Step 7

Effective rate

$$\frac{131,000}{900,000} \times 100 = 14.5555\%$$

Step 8

Actual rate

14.5555% × 30% = 4.36666%

Step 9

Tax payable by trustees on relevant property

4.36666% × £900,000 = £39,300

This example confirms that non-relevant property is ignored in calculating any charges on or after 18 November 2015 (Royal Assent to *Finance (No. 2) Act* 2015) but the related settlement rules still apply – the relevant legislation is included in *Finance (No. 2) Act* 2015.

Legislation: IHTA 1984, s. 64, 66

Other Material: *HMRC Inheritance Tax: Customer Guide* available on the HMRC website at www.hmrc.gov.uk/cto/customerguide/page1.htm

Tax Reporter: ¶363-375

6962　Exit charge before the first ten-year anniversary

The rate of tax charged on an exit charge prior to the first ten-year anniversary (on or after 18 November 2015 (Royal Assent to *Finance (No. 2) Act* 2015) is determined in accordance with the following procedure.

The steps in the calculation are:

Step 1

Work out the value of a hypothetical transfer which is the aggregate of:

(a) the value of the settled property in the settlement at its value immediately after becoming comprised in the settlement (but relevant property only);

(b) the value of any property comprised in a related settlement (i.e. made by the same settlor on the same day as this settlement, other than a non-temporary charitable settlement) at its value immediately after becoming comprised in the related settlement; and

(c) the value of any property added to the settlement after commencement at its value immediately after becoming comprised in the settlement.

Step 2

Ascertain the value of the settlor's total of chargeable transfers in the seven years before the commencement of the settlement.

Step 3

Add the values in Steps 1 and 2 to create an 'aggregate chargeable transfer'.

Step 4

Deduct the tax threshold (the amount up to which tax is payable at 0% ascertained at the exit charge date) from the aggregate chargeable transfer. If the aggregate chargeable transfer is below the tax threshold, there is no tax to pay.

Step 5

Work out the tax at half rate (i.e. 20%) on the value ascertained in step 4 (i.e. the excess over the tax threshold).

Step 6

If the value in step 2 (the amount of the settlor's transfers in the seven years before commencement) exceeds the tax threshold, repeat steps 4 and 5 with the value in step 2. Deduct this notional tax from the tax on the aggregate chargeable transfer to calculate the tax on the hypothetical transfer.

Step 7

Calculate the effective rate by dividing the tax on the hypothetical transfer by that transfer and multiplying by 100.

Step 8

Calculate the actual rate of tax by taking 30% of the effective rate found in step 7 and then multiply the result by the 'appropriate fraction'. If there have been no additions to the settlement, the 'appropriate fraction' is as many fortieths as there are complete successive quarters beginning with the day that the settlement commenced and ending with the day before the event causing the exit charge. For these purposes, 'quarter' means a period of three months.

Step 9

If the trustees pay the tax out of relevant property, a grossing up rate needs to be calculated by dividing the actual rate by (100 minus the actual rate). Otherwise, the actual rate is used. In both cases, charge is on the loss in value of relevant property as a result of the exit charge.

Example

On 1 February 2008, Paul, who had made a chargeable transfer of £82,000 on 1 May 2002, transferred £400,000 to a new discretionary trust. IHT of £46,000 was paid by the trustees.

On 1 November 2016 (35 complete quarters since commencement), the trustees make a capital payment to Sharon of £220,000. Sharon pays the tax due, which is calculated as follows:

Step 1

Hypothetical transfer	£
(a) the value of the settled property in the settlement at its value immediately after becoming comprised in the settlement (whether or not relevant property) £(400,000 – 46,000)	354,000
(b) the value of any property comprised in a related settlement at its value immediately after becoming comprised in the related settlement	n/a
(c) the value of any property added to the settlement after commencement at its value immediately after becoming comprised in the settlement	n/a
Hypothetical transfer	354,000

Step 2

Amount of settlor's total of chargeable transfers in seven years before the commencement of the settlement	82,000

Step 3

	£
Transfers b/f	82,000
Add: value of hypothetical transfer	354,000
Aggregate chargeable transfer	436,000

Step 4

Deduct tax threshold @ 1/11/16	
£(436,000 – 325,000) =	£111,000

Step 5

Work out tax on aggregate chargeable transfer	
£111,000 × 20% =	£22,200

Step 6

The amount of the settlor's total of transfers is below the tax threshold so no adjustment for tax on this value needs to be made.

Step 7

Effective rate

$$\frac{22,200}{354,000} \times 100 = 6.27119\%$$

> **Step 8**
>
> Actual rate
>
> 6.27119% × 30% × 35/40 = 1.646188%
>
> **Step 9**
>
> Tax payable by Sharon
>
> 1.646188% × £220,000 = £3,622

Legislation: IHTA 1984, s. 68

Other Material: *HMRC Inheritance Tax: Customer Guide* available on the HMRC website at www.hmrc.gov.uk/cto/customerguide/page1.htm

Tax Reporter: ¶363-800

6964   Exit charge between ten-year anniversaries

After the first ten-year anniversary has passed, the exit charge rate is based on the rate of the most recent ten-year charge; a rate known as the 'anniversary rate'. The exit charge rate is calculated by multiplying the anniversary rate by the appropriate fraction, i.e. as many fortieths as there are complete successive quarters in the period beginning with the most recent anniversary and ending with the date before the event causing the exit charge.

Changes in rates of tax

Where rates change, the exit charge is recalculated as if the new rate has applied at the time of the previous ten-year anniversary. This means recalculating a notional rate for the ten year charge.

Property added since last anniversary

The rate of the exit charge is reduced in respect of property that has entered the settlement, or has become relevant property since the most recent anniversary. The appropriate fraction relating to that property is calculated by omitting any quarter expiring before the day on which the property became (or last became) relevant property. If that day falls in the same quarter as the day before the event causing the exit charge the quarter will be counted, whether or not complete (this reduction does not apply to the value of unaccumulated income received more than five years before the charge date which is subject to the full ten-year rate).

As the added property was not in the settlement at the last anniversary, it is given a hypothetical value at that date, so that the exit charge reflects the addition. This is done by recalculating the ten year charge as if the fund included the added property at the anniversary date. The added value is brought in at its value when it entered the settlement (or the date on which it became relevant property, if later).

The added property must be brought into account, even where the exit charge is on property comprised in the original fund and regardless of whether or not the added property is still in the settlement.

Legislation: IHTA 1984, s. 68, 69 and Sch. 2, para. 3

Other Material: *HMRC Inheritance Tax: Customer Guide* available on the HMRC website at www.hmrc.gov.uk/cto/customerguide/page1.htm

Tax Reporter: ¶363-825

6966   Death of settlor

Where the settlor dies shortly after settling property on a discretionary trust, there are two main consequences:

(1) If the death is within seven years after the transfer into the trust, extra tax is payable in respect of that transfer. Liability for the extra tax falls on the trustees and on any person who has benefit out of the fund. However, it has no effect on the rate of tax chargeable on the ten-year and exit charges.

(2) If, within seven years before death and before the creation of the settlement, the settlor made any potentially exempt transfers (see 6611) which become chargeable, this will affect the special cumulation and is thus likely to affect the rate of tax chargeable on the ten-year and exit charges.

Legislation: IHTA 1984, s. 7, 64–69

Other Material: *HMRC Inheritance Tax: Customer Guide* available on the HMRC website at www.hmrc.gov.uk/cto/customerguide/page1.htm

Disclosure of inheritance tax avoidance schemes

6976   Disclosure of tax avoidance schemes

In July 2015, HMRC published draft changes to the DOTAS regime to include IHT planning within mainstream guidance but the proposals were the subject of much critical comment from all professional organisations on the basis the proposed draft rules were too overreaching and would have brought within the net transactions which many thought were standard and uncontroversial arrangements. This was partly because of the proposal that a transaction would, for the future, be within the DOTAS regime if a main purpose was to obtain an IHT advantage, if it was 'contrived, or unlikely to have been made if there was no tax advantage'. Although transactions organised through a will were excluded, many other arrangements were not and the original proposals could have caught anodyne tax planning such as lifetime gifts to members of an individual's family!

So far as other taxes are concerned, the *Tax Avoidance Schemes (Prescribed Descriptions of Arrangements) (Amendment) Regulations* 2016 (SI 2016/99) come into effect from 23 February 2016 and it should be noted that the previous exemption for arrangements that could be 'grandfathered' and remain outside the new regime is no longer included in the amended regulations. HMRC have agreed to currently exclude IHT from the amended regulations but will come back with revised proposals later in 2016; therefore, the description of the current DOTAS rules in (6980) and (6981) below, so far as they relate to IHT are very much at the end of their application.

In the June 2010 Budget, the Government announced its intention to bring IHT on trusts within the disclosure of tax avoidance schemes (DOTAS) regime. (For details of the DOTAS regime, see 230).

Following the consultation, from 6 April 2011, arrangements must be notified to HMRC if:

(1) as a result of any element of the arrangements, property becomes relevant property (see 6940); and

(2) a main benefit of the arrangements is that an advantage is obtained in relation to a relevant property entry charge.

The Regulations prescribe the information which is to be notified in relation to inheritance tax arrangements and the time limits within which that information is to be provided so that, where:

(1) a person is party to notifiable arrangements prescribed by the Regulations; and

(2) that person is required to make a return to HMRC under IHTA 1984, s. 216 in respect of a transaction forming part of the notifiable arrangements,

the prescribed information shall be notified to HMRC in the return.

Where a person who is party to notifiable arrangements is not required to make a return under the regulations, information should be provided separately and 'in such form and manner as they may specify' within a period of 12 months of the end of the month in which the first transaction forming part of the arrangements is entered into.

Inheritance tax

In order for an inheritance tax scheme to be disclosable, the arrangements must result in property becoming relevant property which does not include, for example, property held on charitable trusts, a qualifying interest in possession or a disabled person's interest.

It is important to note that it does not matter whether or not property becomes relevant property straight away or whether it remains relevant property; a scheme will require disclosure if, at any point in the arrangements or proposed arrangements, property becomes relevant property.

The claiming of a relief or increased relief is included within the definition of 'advantage'. This means that where the relevant property entry charge is relieved then disclosure may be required. However, where there are no wider arrangements other than a single step claim to relief or exemption or use of the inheritance tax nil rate band then arrangements would not be disclosable.

There were further consultations to extend DOTAS further into the inheritance tax regime – see 'Strengthening the Tax Avoidance Disclosure Regimes' (31 July 2014) which seem to suggest that DOTAS disclosure will be required where an otherwise unobjectionable relief or arrangement is not used in a straightforward way. Thus, for example, para. 2.47 of the consultation document confirms that buying AIM shares in order to become entitled to BPR and then transferring them into trust once BPR is established is acceptable but if the potential settlor borrowed funds to purchase the investments (and secured that debt on a non-relievable asset) and then gave the shares into trust so that the debt remains deductible against the non-relievable asset would be an objectionable use of the relief. On the basis, presumably (see 6819) that, post 5 April 2013, if the AIM shares were retained, the debt would have been deducted from the share value before any entitlement to BPR was calculated.

Legislation: *Tax Avoidance Schemes (Prescribed Descriptions of Arrangements) (Amendment) Regulations* 2016 (SI 2016/99)

6980 Grandfathering

One of the stated aims of the extension of the disclosure rules to inheritance tax is to restrict disclosure to those schemes which are new or innovative. This is achieved by exempting from disclosure those schemes which are the same or 'substantially the same' as arrangements made available before 6 April 2011.

The regulations provide for the exemption from disclosure of arrangements which are the same or substantially the same as arrangements:

* which were first made available before 6 April 2011;

- in relation to which the date of any transaction forming part of the arrangements falls before 6 April 2011; and

- in relation to which a promoter first made a firm approach to another person before 6 April 2011.

What constitutes a change in a scheme or arrangement so that it is no longer substantially the same is a matter which needs to be considered on each occasion.

Schemes not within the current regulations

HMRC guidance provides an extensive list of schemes not within the regulations. Included in the list are:

- The purchase of business assets with a view to transferring the assets into a relevant property trust within two years, or the purchase of agricultural assets with a view to transferring the assets into a relevant property trust after two or seven years.

- The establishment of pilot settlements with a nominal sum (regardless of the number of settlements and whether they are created on successive days) would not require disclosure where there is no advantage obtained in relation to the relevant proposed entry charge. An advantage in respect of the ten-year anniversary and exit charges is not disclosable under the regulations but note that 3 December 2014 Autumn Statement effectively denies the tax advantages that otherwise may have arisen in respect of pilot settlements by requiring all pilot trusts, where capital is added to the separate trusts on the same day, to be aggregated for the purposes of calculating periodic and other charges (notwithstanding the original pilot trusts were nearly always created on separate days).

- Discounted gift trusts where the residual trust is a bare trust would not require disclosure as there is no property becoming relevant property. Where property becomes relevant property then disclosure will not be required where the grandfathering provisions apply.

- Property which is transferred in excluded property trusts, disabled trusts, employee benefit trusts and a qualifying interest in possession trust does not become relevant property and is therefore not disclosable unless, as a further element of the arrangements, property does become relevant property and an advantage is obtained in respect of the relevant entry charge. This will be subject to the grandfathering rules applying.

- A transfer into a relevant property trust made under the terms of a person's will or paid into a relevant property trust on a person's death will not require disclosure.

- The transfer of pension scheme death benefits into a relevant property trust where the scheme member retains the retirement benefit will not in itself require disclosure. However, where the transfer is part of arrangements which enable an advantage to be obtained in respect of the relevant entry charge then disclosure may be required.

- Where property is transferred into a relevant property trust and the settlor retains a reversionary interest then the transfer will not require disclosure as long as it can be shown that the grandfathering rule applies.

Legislation: FA 2004, s. 306ff.; *Inheritance Tax Avoidance Schemes (Prescribed Descriptions of Arrangements) Regulations* 2011 (SI 2011/170); *Tax Avoidance Schemes (Information) (Amendment) Regulations* 2011 (SI 2011/171); *Tax Avoidance Schemes (Information) Regulations* 2004 (SI 2004/1864)

Other Material: HMRC guidance at www.hmrc.gov.uk/aiu/

Tax Reporter: ¶192-410

6981 Examples of arrangements not exempted from disclosure

Examples of arrangements which would not be excluded from disclosure include arrangements where property becomes relevant property and an advantage is obtained in respect of the relevant property entry charge:

- where the claim that there is no transfer of value relies on a series of transactions where, in the absence of all other intervening steps, there would have been a transfer of value and a relevant property entry charge;

- where reliefs and exemptions are used in such a way that the arrangements are not covered by the grandfathering rule; and

- where an individual makes a potentially exempt transfer to another person and the arrangements are such that the subject matter of the transfer becomes relevant property then, unless the arrangements are covered by the grandfathering rule, disclosure will be required.

Other Material: HMRC guidance at www.hmrc.gov.uk/aiu/

Privileged trusts and special transfers

6998   Property leaving temporary charitable trusts

Where settled property is held temporarily for charitable purposes only, it will be charged to IHT:

- where it ceases to be held for charitable purposes, unless it is applied for charitable purposes; and

- in any other case, where the trustees make a disposition (otherwise than for charitable purposes) as a result of which the value of the settled property is reduced.

Payments of costs or expenses, or which are the income of any person, are excluded from the charge, as are payments which are dispositions not intended to confer gratuitous benefits.

Inheritance tax is charged on the reduction in value of the property comprised in the settlement. There will be grossing up where the tax is paid out of the settled property. The rate at which tax is charged is the total of the following percentages:

- 0.25% for each of the first 40 complete successive quarters in the relevant period;

- 0.20% for each of the next 40;

- 0.15% for each of the next 40;

- 0.10% for each of the next 40; and

- 0.05% for each of the next 40.

The relevant period is the length of time the property has been held on charitable trust (or from 13 March 1975 until the chargeable event, if shorter). Where the property was 'relevant property' (see 6940) immediately before 10 December 1981, and became settled on charitable trusts after that date but before 9 March 1982, the relevant period will commence when the property last became relevant property before 10 December 1981.

Where the amount charged to tax is attributable to 'excluded property' (see 7397), no quarter throughout which that property was excluded property is taken into account in determining the rate of tax to be applied. It is not known whether any such settlements actually exist or whether the charge is just to plug a perceived loophole.

Example

Betty makes a settlement on 1 January 1974 under which the property was held for charitable purposes until 20 June 2010. The property in the settlement was valued at £200,000 on 20 June 2010. There were 141 quarters between 13 March 1975 and 20 June 2010.

Tax payable is at 0.25% for each of the first 40 complete successive quarters, at 0.20% for the next 40 quarters, at 0.15% for the next 40 and 0.10% for the remaining five-quarters. Therefore:

	£
0.25% × 40 × £200,000	20,000
0.20% × 40 × £200,000	16,000
0.15% × 40 × £200,000	12,000
0.10% × 21 × £200,000	4,200
Total tax payable	52,200

Legislation: IHTA 1984, s. 70

Other Material: *HMRC Inheritance Tax: Customer Guide* available on the HMRC website at www.hmrc.gov.uk/cto/customerguide/page1.htm

Tax Reporter: ¶364-500

7002 Accumulation and maintenance trusts

Following changes to the inheritance tax treatment of trusts in *Finance Act* 2006, new trusts created on or after 22 March 2006 cannot qualify as accumulation and maintenance trusts and hence cannot qualify as a PET; they have to be relevant property trusts. New concepts of 'a trust for a bereaved minor' (see 7003) and 'an age 18-to-25 trust' (see 7004) were introduced but these are defined differently from the old accumulation and maintenance trust.

Accumulation and maintenance trusts already in existence before 22 March 2006 continued to be exempt from the 'relevant property' regime and were treated under the old rules detailed below until 6 April 2008 unless, before that date, the interest in possession vests or the trust was restructured so as to accelerate a life interest.

From 6 April 2008, existing accumulation and maintenance trusts must conform to the new rules that require beneficiaries to take the trust assets absolutely on or before the age of 18 to continue to be taxed under the old regime in IHTA 1984, s. 71. Existing accumulation and maintenance trusts where the beneficiary will take the trust assets absolutely no later than 25 are taxed under the new age 18-to-25 trust rules from 6 April 2008.

To qualify as an accumulation and maintenance settlement prior to 22 March 2006, the settlement must have had one or more persons who became beneficially entitled to the settled property, or to an interest in possession in it, on attaining a specified age not exceeding 25. Prior to that person or persons becoming so entitled, no interest in possession must subsist in the property, and the income arising must be accumulated so far as not applied for the maintenance, education or benefit of a beneficiary.

From approximately 1975 but before 22 March 2006, a gift by an individual into an accumulation and maintenance trust was a potentially exempt transfer. After 21 March 2006, a gift by an individual into an accumulation and maintenance trust is no longer treated as a PET.

After 16 March 1987 but before 22 March 2006, a PET also occurred where an individual disposed of or terminated his beneficial interest in possession in settled property by gift and the property was then is settled on accumulation and maintenance trusts. Where an individual had an interest in possession in settled property which was in existence at 22 March 2006 and it terminated before 6 April 2008 with the property settled on accumulation and maintenance trusts then the new interest will come within the old taxing regime.

To qualify as an accumulation and maintenance trust before 22 March 2006, certain statutory requirements had to be met.

Legislation: IHTA 1984, s. 71

Case: *Trustees of the Neil Roy Crawford Settlement v R & C Commrs* (2005) Sp C 473

Other Material: ESC F8, *Accumulation and maintenance settlements*; *HMRC Inheritance Tax: Customer Guide* available on the HMRC website at www.hmrc.gov.uk/cto/customerguide/page1.htm

Tax Reporter: ¶677-700

7003 Trusts for bereaved minors

New trusts from 22 March 2006 will not qualify as an accumulation and maintenance trust (see 7002) but trusts for a bereaved minor created under a will or intestacy will not come within the relevant property regime.

A 'trust for a bereaved minor' applies to settled property (including property settled before 22 March 2006) held on trust for the benefit of a person under the age of 18, at least one of whose parents has died, where the trust is created in one of the following circumstances:

(1) under the will of a deceased parent of the bereaved minor;

(2) under a 'statutory trust' arising on an intestacy; and

(3) under the Criminal Injuries Compensation Scheme.

Where the trust arises under the intestacy rules, the terms of the trust are statutory and therefore invariable, and the trust will automatically qualify.

Where the trust arises under the will of a deceased parent of the minor, or under the Criminal Injuries Compensation Scheme, the trust will need to satisfy some further conditions.

A bereaved minor can be given an interest in possession in the trust (i.e. be entitled to all the income) and the trust will still qualify; unlike the old rules for accumulation and maintenance trusts where one of the conditions was that no interest in possession subsisted in the trust fund.

It should be noted that only will trusts arising on the death of a bereaved minor's parent (or step-parent or guardian) will qualify. Thus, trusts created under the will of a deceased grandparent in favour of a grandchild whose parents predeceased the grandparent will not qualify.

Where a trust qualifies as a trust for a bereaved minor it will be exempt from the relevant property regime, i.e. it will be exempt from the ten-yearly charge, and will be exempt from the exit charge on trust assets. The assets of the trust will also not be treated as part of the bereaved minor's estate (whether or not the bereaved minor has an interest in possession in it).

There will be no charge to tax where settled property ceases to be property to which s. 71A applies as a result of:

- a bereaved minor acquiring an absolute interest in the trust assets on or before the age of 18;

- the death of a beneficiary before attaining the specified age of 18; or

- being paid or applied for the advancement or benefit of the bereaved minor.

Where settled property on a bereaved minor's trust ceases to satisfy the necessary conditions set out in s. 71A (detailed above), then there will be a charge under the rates given at s. 70(6) (the temporary charitable trust exit rates – see 6998).

An example of where the charge may apply is where a bereaved minor dies before the age of 18 but the trust continues after his/her death.

A charge does not arise where settled property held on trust ceases to be so because the bereaved minor becomes absolutely entitled on or before the age of 18 or dies before the age of 18 or the property is applied or advanced to the bereaved minor before the age of 18.

If the trustees make a disposition which reduces the value of the settled property, a charge to tax arises. Tax will be calculated at half rates on the same basis as the mainstream exit charge for relevant property.

Legislation: IHTA 1984, s. 71A–71C

Tax Reporter: ¶677-850

7004   Age 18 to 25 trusts

An age 18 to 25 trust is a trust for the benefit of a person under the age of 25, at least one of whose parents has died, where the trust is established:

- under the will of a deceased parent of the minor; or
- under the Criminal Injuries Compensation Scheme, and which satisfies certain conditions.

Existing accumulation and maintenance trusts which satisfy the conditions for age 18 to 25 trusts (above) by 6 April 2008 will be taxed as an 18 to 25 trust.

Where settled property ceases to satisfy the conditions above, or the trustees make a disposition which reduces the value of the settled property, tax will be charged under IHTA 1984, s. 71E.

The charge will not arise where:

- a beneficiary at or under age 18 becomes beneficially entitled to, or to an interest in possession in, settled property on or before attaining the specified age of 25;
- the beneficiary dies before attaining the age of 18;
- settled property becomes property held under trust for a bereaved minor while the beneficiary is living and under 18;
- settled property is paid or applied for the advancement or benefit of the beneficiary before attaining 18 but while the beneficiary is still living or on attaining 18;
- on the payment of costs or expenses attributable to the property; or
- where any payment is (or will be) income of any person for the purposes of income tax or would be if he were UK resident.

Where tax is calculated, the amount of tax is calculated by:

Chargeable amount × Relevant fraction × Settlement rate

The chargeable amount is the reduction in the value of the trust fund as a result of the transfer grossed-up where the settlement pays the tax.

The relevant fraction is 30% of x/40 where x is the number of complete quarters from the time when the beneficiary attained 18 or, if later, on the day when the property became subject to the 18 to 25 trust to the day before the occasion of charge.

The settlement rate is the effective rate but, as with exit charges part way through the first ten-year period the rate is calculated by reference to the initial value of the fund at commencement. Thus, in the example below, the rate is calculated by reference to the initial value (£500,000) and that rate is then applied to the fund value at age 25. It does not matter, in the case of 18–25 trusts, if the entry into trust was more than ten years before the potential exit charge. So in the example below if C was aged three when the trust was established the initial rate would still be calculated in exactly the same way as indicated below.

The initial value will be either the actual value of assets entering the trust or the value of assets less any IHT on them depending upon whether the will indicates that the relevant IHT liability is to come out of the trust fund or out of residue.

Example

B died on 20 June 2008 leaving all his assets valued at £500,000 (net of any IHT) in trust for C (his son) who was aged under 18 at his father's death. C is 25 on 20 May 2016 and on that date the trustees appoint the capital and any accumulated income to C. The capital and remainder of accumulated income at 20 May 2016 is £550,000. B made no previous chargeable transfers in the seven years prior to his death.

Assumed tax on chargeable transfer at 20 May 2016	£
Value of relevant property on 20 May 2008	500,000
Less: nil rate band	325,000
	175,000
IHT at half rates (£175,000 at 20%)	£35,000

Effective rate

$$\frac{35,000}{500,000} = 7\%$$

Exit charge on C becoming 25 is:

3/10 × 7% = 2.1% × 28/40 × £550,000	£8,085

Where the '18-25' trust commences after the child, or children, are aged 18 then the 28/40 fraction is proportionately reduced to the number of complete quarters between age at commencement and age 25.

Note that where, instead of an immediate trust interest for children, there is an intermediate life interest for a spouse or civil partner that the holder of the intermediate interest is deemed to be the settlor of any subsequent 18–25 trust and it is their nil rate band that is then used to calculate the subsequent exit charge but the trust still derives from the parent who established the trust.

Legislation: IHTA 1984, s. 71D–71E

Tax Reporter: ¶677-950

7005   Property becoming subject to employee trusts

Tax will not be charged in respect of shares or securities of a company which cease to be held in discretionary trust, etc. ('relevant property': see 6940) on becoming held on trusts for the benefit of employees, etc. provided that the following conditions are satisfied:

(1) The persons for whose benefit the trusts permit the settled property to be applied include all or most of the persons employed by, or holding office with, the company.

(2) Where the shares or securities cease to be relevant property, or not more than one year thereafter:

  (a) the trustees hold more than one-half of the ordinary shares of the company and have powers of voting on all questions affecting the company as a whole which, if exercised, would yield a majority of the votes capable of being exercised; and

  (b) there are no provisions in any agreement or instrument affecting the company's constitution or management or its shares or securities whereby the condition as to employee benefit above can cease to be satisfied without the consent of the trustees.

(3) The trusts do not permit any of the settled property to be applied for the benefit of a participator in the company or in any close company that has made a disposition whereby property became comprised in the same settlement, or any person who has been such a participator at any time after, or ten years before, the transfer of value or to be applied for the benefit of any person connected with him.

Employee trusts also benefit from CGT exemptions in respect of transfers to the trustees (see 6197).

Property moving between employee trusts continues to be regarded as held in the original trust (see 7008).

Legislation: IHTA 1984, s. 28, 75

Tax Reporter: ¶678-850

7008 Property leaving employee trusts and newspaper trusts

Where property leaves a trust set up for the benefit of employees or newspaper publishing companies, or a payment is made to a 'qualifying person' or to a person who is connected with (see 7153) a qualifying person, or where the trustees make a disposition which reduces the value of settled property, an IHT charge will arise. The charge also applies to property leaving an employee share ownership plan.

Tax will be charged in the way described in 6998.

A 'qualifying person' is:

- one who has directly or indirectly provided any of the settled property otherwise than by additions not exceeding £1,000 in value in any one year;

- a participator, where the employment is by a close company, and is either beneficially entitled to not less than 5% of its issued share capital or to at least 5% of the assets on a winding up; or

- one who has acquired an interest in the settled property for a consideration in money or money's worth.

Employee trusts also benefit from CGT exemptions in respect of transfers to the trustees (see 6197).

Property moving between employee trusts or newspaper trusts continues to be regarded as held in the original trust.

Legislation: IHTA 1984, s. 72, 86, 87

Other Material: *HMRC Inheritance Tax: Customer Guide* available on the HMRC website at www.hmrc.gov.uk/cto/customerguide/page1.htm

Tax Reporter: ¶679-050

7011 Protective trusts and trusts for the disabled

Except as noted below, where property is held on protective trusts or trusts for the disabled, the principal beneficiary is treated as having an interest in possession in the settled property (potential charges in connection with such interests are set out at 6909).

Gifts into trusts for the disabled (though not protective trusts) are PETs, in respect of which no tax is chargeable if the donor survives for seven years after making the gift.

From 22 March 2006, the changes made to the IHT treatment of interest in possession trusts have required amendments to existing legislation to ensure that disabled person's trusts still continue to benefit from special treatment.

Legislation: IHTA 1984, s. 73, 74, 88, 89

Cases: *Pitt v Holt* Ch D [2010] BTC 235

Other Material: *HMRC Inheritance Tax: Customer Guide* available on the HMRC website at www.hmrc.gov.uk/cto/customerguide/page1.htm

Tax Reporter: ¶678-650

7014 Property becoming held for charitable purposes or by exempt bodies

Inheritance tax will not be charged on property which ceases to be 'relevant property' (see 6940), or ceases to be property to which the provisions for temporary charitable trusts (see 6998), accumulation and maintenance trusts (see 7002), employee or newspaper trusts (see 7008) or pre-1978 protective trusts or historic buildings funds (see 7371) applies, on becoming:

- property held for charitable purposes only without limit of time;

- the property of a political party qualifying for exemption (see 7195);

- the property of a body mentioned in 7198 (national purposes, etc.); and

- the property of a body not established or conducted for profit.

Legislation: IHTA 1984, s. 76

Other Material: *HMRC Inheritance Tax: Customer Guide* available on the HMRC website at www.hmrc.gov.uk/cto/customerguide/page1.htm

Tax Reporter: ¶645-300

7017 Initial interest of settlor, spouse or civil partner

If a settlor or his spouse, or civil partner, is beneficially entitled to an interest in possession in property immediately after it becomes comprised in the settlement, the property will be treated as not being comprised in the settlement on that occasion. However, where any of the same property becomes held on trusts under which neither of the spouses or partners is beneficially entitled to an interest in possession, that property will be treated as becoming comprised in a separate settlement.

A 'spouse of a settlor' includes a widow or widower of a settlor.

Legislation: IHTA 1984, s. 80

Other Material: *HMRC Inheritance Tax: Customer Guide* available on the HMRC website at www.hmrc.gov.uk/cto/customerguide/page1.htm

7020 Property moving between settlements

Where property ceases to be comprised in one settlement and becomes comprised in another, it will be treated as remaining comprised in the first settlement unless any person has become beneficially entitled to that property and not merely to an interest in possession in it.

Legislation: IHTA 1984, s. 48(6), 81

Other Material: *HMRC Inheritance Tax: Customer Guide* available on the HMRC website at www.hmrc.gov.uk/cto/customerguide/page1.htm

7023 Distributions within two years of death

Where property comprised in a person's estate immediately before his death is settled by his will and a chargeable event occurs within the period of three months to two years after his death, IHT will not be charged if no interest in possession has subsisted in the property. This is a relieving provision which disapplies the exit charge which would otherwise apply: for deaths occurring before 10 December 2014, it could not apply during the first three months after the death as there would be no exit charge in any case during this time.

In addition, the distribution was treated as if it was made under the will and is thus effectively 'back-dated' to the date of the testator's death. This 'two-year discretionary trust' can be a favoured tax planning device which may be employed to use up the nil-rate band available to the testator, while the residue of the estate is left to (e.g.) the testator's spouse. Alternatively, the will may create a discretionary trust over the whole estate, so that it can be distributed after the testator's death in the manner then considered to be the most tax-efficient.

Where capital is appointed, under a will, for deaths on or after 10 December 2014, then IHTA 1984, s. 144 has been amended by *Finance (No. 2) Act* 2015, s. 14, reversing the *Frankland* decision, where property was initially left in trust, and subsequently appointed to either the surviving spouse or civil partner of the deceased, then the appointment will be treated as having been made by the will not withstanding that the appointment was within the first three months after death (under the previous position, a charge to tax could have arisen as the spouse/civil partner exemption would not but for this change have been available).

Distributions out of a trust for a charity or other exempt body (see 7014), an employee trust (see 7005) or a national heritage maintenance fund (see 7371ff.) made within two years of the deceased's death are already exempt from any charge. Such distributions will be treated as taking place at the date of death so reducing the deceased's chargeable estate.

Legislation: IHTA 1984, s. 144; *Finance (No. 2) Act* 2015, s. 14

Case: *Frankland v IR Commrs* [1997] BTC 8045

Other Material: *HMRC Inheritance Tax: Customer Guide* available on the HMRC website at www.hmrc.gov.uk/cto/customerguide/page1.htm

Tax Reporter: ¶676-900

7040   Property becoming comprised in maintenance funds

The transfer into trust of various historic buildings or works of art, etc. is either exempt from IHT or conditionally exempt from IHT (see 7346ff. and 7371ff.). There are special modifications to the trust regime to cater for these arrangements where other trusts are involved.

Maintenance funds

Where property leaves a discretionary trust to become comprised in a maintenance fund, the normal exit charge (see 6940ff.) does not apply except to the extent that the amount charged exceeds its value thereafter or the trustees are acquiring it for money or money's worth. Similarly no such exit charge arises if the property temporarily becomes subject to no settlement at all before being transferred by an individual as part of an exempt transfer (within 30 days or two years following death).

Where, within two years after the death of a person with an interest in possession, property becomes comprised in a maintenance fund, it is treated as if it had been settled by the deceased so that no intervening charges arise.

Where, however, the interest is one to which the person became beneficially entitled on or after 22 March 2006, the above only applies where immediately before the person's death, the interest was:

(a) an immediate post-death interest (6907);

(b) a disabled person's interest (7011); or

(c) a transitional serial interest (6908).

Trusts for works of art

Where property which is designated property has been within a discretionary settlement for six years, the provisions for conditionally exempt transfers of such property are modified so as to exclude the property from the normal exit charge (see 6940ff.) on leaving the trust. The usual loss of exemption where a condition is breached, etc. (see 7351) can thereafter apply by reference to the settlor.

Exemption from ten-yearly charge

Further, the ten-yearly charge on discretionary trusts (see 6940) does not apply to that property unless and until any conditions attaching to such property are broken; however, if such event occurs, a charge then arises on the value of the property at that time and the rate at which IHT is charged is the total of the relevant percentages set out at 6998.

Claims

In relation to transfers of property made, or other events occurring, after 16 March 1998, claims must be made within two years from the date of the transfer or other event in question, or such longer period as HMRC may allow. Previously, there was no time-limit.

The Autumn Statement of 3 December 2014 included provisions to amend the current requirement that a claim must be made and the property designated as heritage property before the approaching ten-year anniversary, and replaces it with provisions that allow trustees to make a claim for exemption within two years of the ten-yearly charge arising. This change will apply for those occasions on which tax would fall to be charged on or after Royal Assent to *Finance (No. 2) Act* 2015 (18 November 2015). Thus, the claim may be made within two years of the ten-yearly charge arising or at such later date as HMRC allow. This now means that trustees of relevant heritage property will then be subject to the same requirements as trustees and individuals subject to other IHT charges.

Legislation: IHTA 1984, s. 57A, 57A(1A), 77–79A and Sch. 4, para. 16

Other Material: *HMRC Inheritance Tax: Customer Guide* available on the HMRC website at www.hmrc.gov.uk/cto/customerguide/page1.htm

Tax Reporter: ¶651-900

7055   Property leaving maintenance funds

Where property ceases to be held in a maintenance fund (and does not become part of another such fund) or where works of art, etc. leave a trust (and cease to be designated property), an IHT charge may arise. Further, a disposition by trustees reducing the value of property in a maintenance fund may also give rise to a charge to tax.

Maintenance funds

Where property ceases to be 'relevant property' (see 6940) comprised in a 'maintenance fund' (see 7040) or where trustees make a disposition reducing the value of property in the fund, IHT will be charged on the reduction in value of the settled property. However, tax will not be charged where the property is transferred into another maintenance fund by an individual within 30 days provided that individual did not acquire his interest for a consideration in money or money's worth. If the property which ceases to be comprised in the fund becomes property to which the settlor or his spouse is beneficially entitled or to which the settlor's widow or his spouse is beneficially entitled (if the settlor died within the preceding two years), there will be no charge to tax unless:

- the person acquired his or her beneficial interest for a consideration in money or money's worth;

- the property was held on discretionary trusts, etc. before it became property comprised in the maintenance fund and tax was not chargeable when it ceased to be such 'relevant property' (see 6940);

- the property was previously comprised in a maintenance fund and no tax was charged on becoming comprised in the present maintenance fund; or

- the person who becomes beneficially entitled to the property is domiciled in the UK at the time when he becomes so entitled.

Where property ceases to be part of a discretionary trust, etc. ('relevant property': see 6940) and no IHT is charged on it becoming comprised in a maintenance fund, then the tax to be charged when it leaves the maintenance fund will be the total of the relevant percentages as shown at 6998.

Where the above provision does not apply (i.e. the property was not previously part of a discretionary trust, etc. or tax was charged when it left such trust), the rate at which tax is charged will be the higher of:

- the total of similar percentages to those shown above (where the relevant period begins with the day the property became comprised in the maintenance fund);

- the effective rate at which tax would be charged if the amount were the value transferred by a chargeable transfer (or if the settlor is dead if the amount were treated as the highest part of the value transferred on his death).

There are certain modifications where the property was previously subject to an interest in possession.

Trusts for works of art

The normal exit charge on discretionary trust property (see 6940ff.) will apply unless designated property has been within a discretionary settlement for six years before it ceases to be so held, as in relation to transfers into the trust from another settlement (see 7040); equally, if the property ceases to be designated on leaving the trust (if the appropriate conditions are breached), a charge may arise (see 7351).

Legislation: IHTA 1984, Sch. 4, para. 8–15A

Other Material: IR 67: National Heritage booklet *Capital Taxation and the National Heritage*, *HMRC Inheritance Tax: Customer Guide* available on the HMRC website at www.hmrc.gov.uk/cto/customerguide/page1.htm

Tax Reporter: ¶651-900

Exemptions and reliefs from inheritance tax

Dispositions which are not transfers of value

7150   Introduction to dispositions which are not transfers of value

A transfer of value is any disposition made by a person (the transferor) as a result of which the value of his estate immediately after the disposition is less than it would be but for the disposition and the amount by which it is less is the value transferred by the transfer (see 6525). It is stated in statute that, notwithstanding the above definition, a disposition is not a transfer of value in several specific cases. If a disposition is not a transfer of value, no IHT is chargeable on the transfer.

Legislation: IHTA 1984, s. 1, 2

Tax Reporter: ¶609-350

7153 No gratuitous intent

A disposition is not a transfer of value (see 7150) if it is shown that it was not intended to confer any gratuitous benefit on any person and that it was made in an arm's length transaction between persons not 'connected with' each other, or that it was such as might have been expected to have been made in an arm's length transaction between persons not connected with each other. Thus, if there is no element of gift or giving away, there can be no transfer of value.

Reversionary interests, unquoted securities

The above rule is inapplicable where a person with an interest in possession acquires the reversion expectant on the interest; and it only applies to a sale of 'unquoted' (see 6572) shares or debentures if it is shown that the sale was at a price freely negotiated at the time of the sale, or at such a price as might be expected to have been freely negotiated at the time of the sale.

Example

Agatha transferred property to Beryl and Constance before 22 March 2006 upon trust for Delia for life with remainder to Evelyn. The interest in remainder is valued at £50,000. Delia purchases Evelyn's reversion for £50,000. She is treated as having made a transfer of value of £50,000 since, for IHT purposes, she is treated as being already beneficially entitled to all the property so that the payment of £50,000 is treated as a gift for no consideration.

Connected persons

The following are connected persons.

Individuals

A person is connected with an individual if that person is the individual's husband or wife or civil partner, or a relative of the individual or of the individual's husband or wife or civil partner. For IHT purposes, a relative includes an uncle, aunt, nephew and niece.

Trustees

A person in his capacity as trustee of a settlement is connected with any individual who in relation to the settlement is a settlor, with any person who is connected with such an individual and with a body corporate which is deemed connected with the settlement.

Partners

A person is connected with any person with whom he is in partnership, and with the husband or wife or civil partner or a relation of any individual with whom he is in partnership. This does not apply to the acquisition or disposal of partnership assets pursuant to genuine commercial arrangements.

Companies

A person is connected with a company if that person has control of it or if that person and persons connected with him together have control of it. Any two or more persons acting together to secure or exercise control of a company will be treated in relation to that company as connected with one another and with any person acting on the direction of any of them to secure or exercise control of the company.

A company is connected with another company if:

- the same person has control of both, or a person has control of one and persons connected with him, or he and persons connected with him, have control of the other; or

- an (irreducible) group of two or more persons has control of each company and the groups either consist of the same persons or could be regarded as consisting of the same persons by treating (in one or more cases) a member of either group as replaced by a person with whom he is connected (see the similar rules for CGT at 5142).

'Control' is defined by reference to power over the majority of votes when taken together with related property and powers of trustees in relation to property to which the person in question has a qualifying interest in possession.

Legislation: IHTA 1984, s. 10, 55(2), 269, 270

Case: *IR Commrs v Spencer-Nairn* [1991] BTC 8,003

Tax Reporter: ¶609-350

7156 Dispositions for maintenance of family

Dispositions for the maintenance of family are not transfers of value (see 7150) in certain circumstances.

Between spouses and civil partners, or to children

A disposition is not a transfer of value if it is made by one party to a marriage or civil partnership in favour of the other party for his or her maintenance. A disposition is not a transfer of value if made by one party to a marriage or civil partnership in favour of a child of either party for his or her maintenance, education or training, up to the age of 18 or until the time that the child ceases to undergo full-time education or training if later than 18. This will apply even if the disposition is in favour of a child who is not in the care of a parent of his or hers, but if the disposition is not to be a transfer of value after the child attains 18 years, the child must have been in the care of the person making the disposition for substantial periods before the child attains 18 years of age.

The provisions will apply to an illegitimate child if the disposition is made by the parent of that child.

A 'child' here includes a stepchild and an adopted child and 'marriage' includes a former marriage in relation to a disposition made on the occasion of the dissolution or annulment of a marriage and in relation to a disposition varying a disposition so made. A 'year' means any period of 12 months ending with 5 April.

Dispositions to dependent relatives

A disposition is not a transfer of value if made in favour of a dependent relative of the person making the disposition and is a reasonable provision for his or her care or maintenance. A 'dependent relative' means a relation of a person or a relation of his or her spouse or civil partner, and one who is incapacitated by old age from maintaining himself, or the mother of that person or of his spouse or civil partner, if the mother is living apart from her husband or widowed, or is a single woman in consequence of dissolution or annulment of marriage. (The official view is that the exclusion does not apply to transfers on death.)

In practice, relief is permitted if an unmarried mother is not incapacitated but relies on the child making the disposition.

Legislation: IHTA 1984, s. 11; *Civil Partnership Act* 2005

Other Material: ESC F12, *Disposition for maintenance of a dependent relative*; *HMRC Inheritance Tax: Customer Guide* available on the HMRC website at www.hmrc.gov.uk/cto/customerguide/page1.htm

Tax Reporter: ¶610-200

7159   Dispositions on trust for benefit of employees

Where a close company contributes to an employee trust, described at 7005 or an employee share ownership plan, there is not a transfer of value (see 7150) if the persons for whose benefit the trusts permit the property to be applied include all or most of the employees and office holders of the company and of subsidiary companies if their employees or office holders are also to benefit. Where a subsidiary is to be included, the employees and office holders of the two companies are taken as a single class, so that if the holding company's employees comprised only a minority of the total they could all be excluded.

This will not apply if the trusts allow any benefit to go to any of the following persons (apart from any benefit which would be income of the recipient for the purposes of income tax):

- a participator of the company making the disposition;

- a participator of any close company making a disposition of property into the same settlement;

- anyone who has been a participator in such a company as in the above categories at any time after, or ten years before, the disposition made by that company; or

- any person connected with a person in one of those three categories (see 7153).

'Close company' and 'participator' are explained at 6555. A participator for the above purposes will not include any participator entitled to less than 5% of assets on a winding up of the company.

HMRC have published a Brief which sets out their current view on the IHT position in relation to contributions to an employee benefit trust. The Brief also includes material on various matters not previously addressed including ongoing IHT liabilities of the trust and any sub-trusts it created and the taxation of income arising in offshore employee benefit trusts. HMRC state that existing cases will be taken forward on the basis of the views set out in the Brief.

Where a close company makes a transfer of value to an employee benefit trust an IHT charge arises unless, broadly, the disposition:

- is not a transfer of value under IHTA 1984, s. 10 (dispositions not intended to confer gratuitous benefit), s. 12 (dispositions allowable for the purposes of calculating that person's corporation tax) or s. 13 (dispositions by close companies for the benefit of employees);

- is eligible for relief.

Where there is a transfer of value, it is apportioned between the individual participators according to their respective rights and interest in the company immediately before the contribution to the employee benefit trust is made. There is an immediate charge of 20% on the value transferred (the contribution) in excess of the participator's unused nil rate band. The liability for the charge to IHT that arises under s. 94 is the company or, if the tax remains unpaid, the participator.

Where a disposition is not prevented from being a transfer of value, a charge arises and the transfer of value is apportioned between the individual participators according to their respective rights and interest in the company immediately before the contribution to the employee benefit trust giving rise to the transfer of value.

Ten-year charges and exit charges in respect of any sub-trusts

The HMRC Brief describes how charges to IHT can arise in any employee benefit trust; even where the original disposition into the trust was not made by a close company or individual.

The charge arises where a payment is made from the employee benefit trust into a sub-trust that is not itself a qualifying employee benefit trust. The charge is a flat-rate charge and is dependent on the length of time the property was held subject to the terms of the employee benefit trust. Business property relief will not apply to the flat-rate exit charge in these circumstances.

In addition, where there is a non-commercial loan to a participator then an exit charge may arise.

In general, sub-trusts are not employee benefit trusts and are, therefore, relevant property trusts for IHT purposes. For the purposes of the ten-year anniversary charge, the anniversary is calculated from the date on which the property became settled, that is, the date the employee benefit trust commenced. However, property can only be treated as relevant property when it leaves the qualifying employee benefit trust.

Where the trustees of a sub-trust decide to bring the sub-trust to an end an exit charge will arise.

Payment of ongoing inheritance tax liabilities

Where a transfer is made during the life of the settlor and the trustees are not resident in the UK, then the settlor is liable for the ongoing trust IHT liabilities. The settlor of an employee benefit trust will usually be the company, whether or not it is a close company. In addition where a participator has benefited then they are liable for the ongoing trust IHT.

Spotlight 5

In *Spotlight 5: Using trusts and similar entities to reward employees – PAYE (Pay As You Earn) and National Insurance contributions (NICs), Corporation tax and Inheritance tax*, HMRC state that they are aware that:

> '... companies have been seeking to reward their employees without operating PAYE/NICs by making payments through trusts and other intermediaries that favour the employees or their families. The arrangements usually seek to secure a Corporation Tax deduction, as if the amounts were earnings at the time they were allocated, and also defer PAYE/NICs altogether.'

HMRC's view in these circumstances is that:

> 'an Inheritance Tax charge may arise on the participators of a close company. Unless the participators are excluded beneficiaries and have not had funds applied for their benefit, such as the receipt of a loan, a charge to Inheritance Tax arises on participators of close companies at the time the funds are paid to the trustee by the close company. Relief is only available to the extent that a deduction is allowable to the company for the year in which the contribution is made. Later payments of earnings out of the trust that may trigger a deduction to the company would not qualify for relief.'

Participators affected in this way may need to self-assess a liability to inheritance tax.

Legislation: IHTA 1984, s. 13; s. 72(2)(d) s. 94; s. 201(1)(d); s. 202

Other Material: SP E11, HMRC Brief 18/11, *Spotlight 5: Using trusts and similar entities to reward employees – PAYE (Pay As You Earn) and National Insurance contributions (NICs), Corporation tax and Inheritance tax*

Tax Reporter: ¶610-750

7162   Waiver of remuneration

The waiver or repayment of remuneration will not be a transfer of value (see 7150) if it would have been assessable to income tax under the charge on employment income provisions (see 250) but for the waiver or repayment.

If the amount of remuneration would have been allowed as a deduction in computing profits or gains or losses of the person by whom it is payable or paid, it will not be a transfer of value merely because the waiver or repayment means that it is not then allowed as a deduction or is otherwise brought into charge in computing profits or gains or losses.

Legislation: IHTA 1984, s. 14

Tax Reporter: ¶610-850

7165 Waiver of dividends

A person who waives any dividend on shares of a company within 12 months before any right to the dividend has accrued is not treated as having made a transfer of value (see 7150) merely because of the waiver. Accordingly, best practice would be to have a separate waiver on each occasion a dividend is proposed executed before payment is due.

Legislation: IHTA 1984, s. 15

Tax Reporter: ¶610-900

7168 Dispositions conferring retirement benefits

A disposition made by any person is not a transfer of value (see 7150) if it is a contribution under a registered pension scheme, a qualifying non-UK pension scheme or ICTA 1988, s. 615(3) in respect of an employee of the person making the disposition.

Where the condition is satisfied only to a limited extent, the payment is treated as two separate dispositions: one of which is not a transfer of value, and the other that is.

From 6 April 2011, where a person who is a member of a registered pension scheme, a qualifying non-UK pension scheme or a s. 615(3) scheme omits to exercise pension rights under the pension scheme, there is no transfer of value under IHTA 1984, s. 3(3).

Legislation: IHTA 1984, s. 12(2)–(5), FA 2011, s. 65 and Sch. 16

Tax Reporter: ¶610-800

7172 Dispositions allowable for income tax

A disposition made by any person will not be a transfer of value (see 7150) if it is allowable as a deduction in computing that person's profits or gains for income tax or corporation tax (see 2150ff.).

Legislation: IHTA 1984, s. 12(1), (5)

Tax Reporter: ¶610-600.

7174   Grant of tenancies of agricultural property

Where it is not specifically provided otherwise, the grant of an agricultural tenancy would result in a transfer of value because of the ensuing reduction in the value of the freehold. Accordingly, it is provided that the grant of a tenancy of agricultural property in the UK, the Channel Islands or the Isle of Man for use for agricultural purposes is not a transfer of value by the grantor (see 7150) if he makes it for full consideration in money or money's worth.

Legislation: IHTA 1984, s. 16

Tax Reporter: ¶610-950

7176   Changes in distribution of deceased's estate

Certain changes in the distribution of a deceased's estate are not transfers of value (see 7150):

- a variation or disclaimer made within two years of death (see 6805);

- the renunciation (in Scotland) to a claim to legitim within a specified period (see 6805);

- a transfer within two years of death in accordance with a testator's express wish (but not under the terms of his will) (see 7023); or

- an election by a surviving spouse to have his or her life interest redeemed where the deceased died intestate (the survivor thereafter being regarded as entitled to the capital value).

Note that a review of instruments of variation was announced in the March 2015 Budget to establish if they are being used for tax avoidance purposes with a government response expected as part of the 2015 Autumn Statement.

Legislation: IHTA 1984, s. 17, 145

Other Material: *HMRC Inheritance Tax: Customer Guide* available on the HMRC website at www.hmrc.gov.uk/cto/customerguide/page1.htm

Tax Reporter: ¶611-000

Transfers exempt during life and on death

7192   Transfers between spouses and civil partners

Generally, direct transfers between spouses and civil partners are exempt without limit, both during lifetime and on death even where the couple is not living together (but if not living together the CGT exemption may not apply). Where the transferor is domiciled in the UK, but their spouse or civil partner is not, the exempt amount was restricted to a lifetime total of £55,000 until 5 April 2013. However, FA 2013, s. 178 increased the foreign domiciled spouse exemption to an amount equivalent to the current nil-rate band of £325,000 but this remains a lifetime allowance. This change will apply to deaths on or after 6 April 2013 (with an indication that for the future the relief will match any future increases in the standard nil-rate band).

The increase only applies to transfers of value made on or after 6 April 2013. So, for a period, if domiciled/non-domiciled partners had previously tried to manage their IHT liability by lifetime gifts then before 5 April 2013, there was only the £55,000 limit with any excess deducted from the standard nil-rate band (or any transferrable nil-rate band but on death only) as a PET whereas gifts made on or after 6 April 2013 will be exempt provided they do not exceed £325,000.

Example 1

Tony (UK domiciled) is in a civil partnership with Alfredo (who is Spanish domiciled) and in November 2012 he made a gift of £100,000 to Alfredo. He subsequently made a further gift of £150,000 to Alfredo on 1 August 2013. In respect of the first gift, the excess of £45,000 above £55,000 used up part of the available nil-rate band of Tony but the second gift will be covered by the inter-spouse/civil partner limit of £325,000 (£120,000 remains – £325,000 – £55,000 – £150,000).

Unlike the normal nil-rate band, the limit on transfers to a non-domiciled spouse/civil partner is not refreshed after seven years and where the £55,000 has already been used the transferor will then only have, post-5 April 2013, £270,000 available. In the above example, the post 5 April 2013 increase to £325,000 cannot make the £45,000 PET in November 2012 an exempt gift because the transfer was before the law changed but if Tony survives beyond November 2019 (and the £45,000 was the only gift that reduces the nil-rate band) then the standard nil-rate band would be refreshed.

It follows that once any 'transitional' arrangements have worked their way through that a UK domiciled spouse/civil partner could potentially transfer a total of up to £975,000 (at current nil-rate band) to a non-domiciled spouse/civil partner without any IHT liability arising. That being the aggregate of non-domiciled spouse/civil partner exemption of £325,000, the conventional nil rate band of £325,000 and a full transferrable nil-rate band available on the death of a previous spouse/civil partner.

Example 2

Andrew gave his wife, Beth, £500,000 in September 2012. They are both domiciled in the UK. There will be no IHT charge on this transfer of value.

Example 3

Christopher gave his wife, Jennifer, £500,000 in September 2012. Christopher is domiciled in the UK and Jennifer is domiciled in the USA. There will be a potential charge to tax on £445,000 since only £55,000 was exempt in the event of death within seven years (but any available nil-rate band may reduce the taxable amount).

If Christopher made a further gift to Jennifer in July 2014 of £400,000, the increased non-domiciled spouse exemption would then apply to leave £130,000 potentially subject to tax (£400,000 − (£325,000 − £55,000) = £130,000). Additionally, if Jennifer elected to be UK domiciled under the post-5 April 2013 changes and that election was backdated to 6 April 2013, then the whole of the July 2014 gift would be covered by the spouse/civil partner exemption. However, advice should always be obtained before electing to make sure there is no adverse impact on the original domicile.

The spouse/civil partner non-domicile exemption is a lifetime allowance. It is not refreshed once seven years from the gift have passed.

The exemption will not be given:

- if the gift or bequest is not immediately in favour of the other spouse or civil partner, unless the property is given to a spouse only if he survives the other spouse or civil partner for a specified period;

- if the testamentary or other disposition depends on a condition which is not satisfied 12 months after the transfer; or

- if the property is given in consideration of the transfer of a reversionary interest, if that interest does not form part of the estate of the person acquiring it.

Example 4

Frank leaves property to his wife, Mavis, for life. This will be an exempt transfer since Mavis takes an immediate life interest.

Example 5

Jeremy leaves property to his brother Simon for life with remainder to his wife, Charlotte. The transfer to Simon would not be exempt since Charlotte (his wife) does not get an immediate interest in the property.

Note however that with effect from 6 April 2017, new rules will be introduced, initially in *Finance Act* 2016 but now proposed to be included in Finance Bill 2017 (after consultation) to make individuals who have been UK resident for 15 out of the previous 20 years to be deemed to be UK domiciled *for all tax purposes*. Currently, deemed domicile only applies for IHT purposes with income tax on worldwide income and gains being avoided provided the relevant individual pays an appropriate annual fee.

Legislation: IHTA 1984, s. 18, 56; FA 2013, s. 178

Other Material: *HMRC Inheritance Tax: Customer Guide* available on the HMRC website at www.hmrc.gov.uk/cto/customerguide/page1.htm

Tax Reporter: ¶644-800

7193 Transfer of unused nil-rate band between spouses and civil partners

Finance Act 2008 introduced legislation that allows a claim to be made to transfer any unused IHT nil-rate band on a person's death (no matter what the date of their death) to the estate of their surviving spouse or civil partner who dies on or after 9 October 2007. This applies where the IHT nil-rate band of the first deceased spouse or civil partner was not fully used in calculating the IHT liability of their estate. When the surviving spouse or civil partner dies, the unused amount may be added to their own nil-rate band.

The amount that can be transferred is based on the proportion of the nil-rate band that was unused when the first spouse or civil partner died, and applied in the same proportion to the nil rate band in force at the time of the second death. Historically, transfers between spouses were not always exempt from estate duty. The spouse transfer position historically was as follows: for deaths prior to 21 March 1972, there was no tax free transfer between spouses – spouse transfers used up the nil rate band. Between 21 March 1972 and 12 November 1974, there was a tax free transfer permitted between spouses of up to £15,000 (the then nil rate band) so spouse transfers in excess of £15,000 used up the nil rate band and post 12 November 1974 the monetary limit on transfers between spouses was removed.

Example 1

If on the first death none of the original nil-rate band was used because the entire estate was left to a surviving spouse, then if the nil-rate band when the surviving spouse dies is £325,000 that would be increased 100% to £650,000.

Example 2

If on the first death the chargeable estate is £150,000 and the nil-rate band was £300,000, then 50% of the original nil-rate band would be unused and is available for transfer. If the nil-rate band when the surviving spouse dies is £325,000, then the amount available for transfer would be 50% of £325,000

> or £162,500, giving the surviving spouse's estate a nil rate band of £325,000 + £162,500 = £487,500 in total.

The legislation does not require the first spouse to die domiciled (whether by law or election) or deemed domiciled in the UK.

Note the Summer 2015 Budget proposal to extend UK domicile from 6 April 2017, in (originally) Finance Bill 2016 but now to be included in Finance Bill 2017, to apply *for all tax purposes* (not just for deemed IHT domicile) to long-term residents in the UK where they have been resident in the UK for 15 out of the previous 20 years which will replace the current 17 out of 20 year rule.

Example 3

Anna and Adam had been domiciled for many years in Spain. However, on Adam's death Anna returned to the UK, resuming her domicile of origin. She died in 2008. Adam's unused nil-rate band is available for transfer.

The size of the estate of the first person to die is irrelevant. The question is only what percentage of the nil-rate band did that person use up by making a chargeable transfer on death or by chargeable lifetime transfers that cumulated with his estate on death. So, if, for example, the first spouse's or civil partner's estate was worth only £100,000 and the entire estate was left to the surviving spouse or civil partner, 100% of the nil-rate band is still available for transfer when the surviving spouse or civil partner dies.

Example 4

Mr X died in 2000, having made no lifetime gifts, and leaving everything to his wife, Mrs X. Mrs X died at the beginning of 2016 and shortly before her death in 2015 gave £650,000 to her son which qualified as a potentially exempt transfer (PET). As Mrs X died within seven years of making the gift, it is a failed PET which becomes chargeable on her death. Her remaining estate is worth £500,000.

There will be no IHT to pay on the lifetime gift as two nil-rate bands of £325,000 are allocated against it. The £500,000 left in her estate at death is fully chargeable at 40%.

Example 5

If following the above example, Mrs X instead settled property worth £600,000 on her daughter instead of making an outright gift, this would have been an immediately chargeable transfer. Her nil-rate band of £325,000 would have been allocated against the £600,000 gift to the settlement which would have left tax a tax charge of £275,000 @ 20% = £55,000.

On her death within seven years of making the settlement, additional IHT is potentially payable. However, Mr X's unused nil-rate band is then available to allocate against it and no additional IHT is charged. It should also be noted that there is no refund of the tax charged when the settlement was created.

Example 6

Eric died on 5 April 1973 and left his entire estate valued at £25,000 to his wife Julia. On Julia's death on or after 9 October 2007, her executors will have one-third of Eric's (then) nil-rate band available. The transfer on 5 April 1973 firstly used up the spouse exemption of £15,000 and then £10,000 of the nil-rate band of £15,000.

The amount of additional nil-rate band that can be accumulated by any one surviving spouse or civil partner is limited to the value of the nil-rate band in force at the time of their death. This may be relevant where a person dies having survived more than one spouse or civil partner, and therefore more than one unused nil-rate band could otherwise be transferred to them. This may also be relevant where a person dies having been married to, or the registered civil partner of, someone who had themselves survived one or more spouses or civil partners (see www.hmrc.gov.uk/inheritancetax/intro/transfer-threshold.htm). Divorced couples cannot claim the nil-rate band when an ex-spouse dies. Where the first spouse died before 21 March 1972 (when a restricted spouse exemption was initially introduced) strong evidence will be required to confirm any transferable NRB because before that date the NRB was low and transfers to spouses could have used all or part of any NRB. Before 15 April 1969, the nil rate band was £5,000 which was not much more than the price of a relatively modest property.

Where the new rules have effect, personal representatives will not have to claim for unused nil-rate band to be transferred at the time of the first death. Any claims for transfer of unused nil-rate band amounts will be made by the personal representatives of the estate of the second spouse or civil partner to die. The personal representatives will need to fill in a claim form that will show how much of the nil-rate band is available for transfer. They will also need to provide certain documents to support their claim including:

- the death certificate for the first person to die;
- the marriage certificate or civil partnership certificate for the couple;
- if the spouse or civil partner left a Will, a copy of it;
- a copy of the grant of probate or confirmation; and
- if there is a Deed of Variation, a copy of it.

The personal representatives should send the claim form and the supporting documents to HMRC when they send in the form IHT400 on the death of the surviving spouse or civil partner. The claim must be made within 24 months from the end of the month in which the surviving spouse or civil partner dies. For further information on the making of a claim, see www.hmrc.gov.uk/inheritancetax/intro/transfer-threshold.htm.

The transfer of the unused nil-rate band would appear to negate in some case the need for nil-rate band-planning debt or charge type trusts. However, these may still be good planning for some couples who:

- are not married;
- have more complex situations such as second marriages and stepchildren;
- have assets expected to grow faster than the likely increase in the nil-rate band (currently frozen until 5 April 2021); or
- have assets that are eligible for business property relief (see 7253) or agricultural property relief (see 7292) so that the relief is claimed before it is lost.

For those who have died in the last two years, the nil-rate band trust can be dismantled by an appointment by the trustees in favour of the spouse if it is thought no longer necessary under IHTA 1984, s. 144. However, if someone died more than two years ago, leaving assets into a nil-rate band trust, nothing can be done to take advantage of the new relief.

Note that HMRC will impose a significant penalty if a claim for excess transferable nil-rate band is made (see 7620).

Any transferrable nil-rate band can only be set against the death estate. It cannot be set against PETs or other lifetime transfers that become taxable on death.

The Summer 2015 Budget announced the long awaited increase in nil-rate band to help those who wish to pass on to their children their home tax free. The introduction of a residential nil-rate band (RNRB) is included in *Finance (No. 2) Act* 2015, s. 9 and *Finance Act* 2016, Sch. 15 covers the consequences of downsizing or ceasing to own any residential property on or after 8 July 2015.

This RNRB will initially amount to £100,000 in 2017–18, increase to £125,000 in 2018–19, to £150,000 in 2019–20 and reach £175,000 in 2020–21; thereafter, the amount will be increased by any increase in consumer price index; conveniently reaching £1m (two nil-rate bands plus two RNRB) around the time of the next general election. The RNRB will apply to the main residence (or the proceeds of sale/value of a main residence if funds equivalent to the disposed property's value passes to direct descendents) of a deceased that was occupied by them at some time and if not fully used on the first death any balance can be transferred to the surviving spouse/civil partner.

But note that one part, potentially, of the RNRB already in force is the possible future availability of transferable RNRB from events on or after 8 July 2015. Although the relief cannot be available until after 6 April 2017, a husband or wife (or civil partner) who pre-deceases their partner, on or after 8 July 2015, where the survivor dies on or after 6 April 2017, can generate transferable RNRB. HMRC published on 18 September 2015 a technical note, revised on 7 October 2015, indicating possible circumstances of transferability.

Thus, example 1 is as below.

Example 1

A widow (whose husband died after 7 July 2015) sells a home worth £400,000 in August 2020 and moves to a home worth £210,000. At the time of the sale, the available RNRB is £350,000 as, had she died at that time, her executors would be able to make a claim to transfer all the unused RNRB from her late husband. By downsizing, she has potentially lost the chance to use £140,000 or 40% of the available RNRB which could have applied had the more valuable home not been sold.

When the widow later dies in October 2020, the (new) home is worth £225,000 and is left to her children together with £500,000 of other assets. The estate can (potentially) use an RNRB of £225,000. However, the widow was also eligible for an RNRB of £350,000 had she not downsized. The estate can therefore claim an additional RNRB of 40% of the available RNRB (40% × £350,000) or £140,000. This would give RNRB of £365,000 (£225,000 + £140,000). As this is more than the maximum available RNRB (£350,000), the additional RNRB is restricted to £125,000 to ensure that the total amount used does not exceed the maximum available (£225,000 + £125,000 = £350,000).

In addition, any standard nil-rate band together with any transferable nil-rate band from her late husband's estate can be applied to the remaining assets in the estate.

In example 1, the maximum transferable RNRB is £350,000 but apparently the taxpayer has £365,000 made up of £225,000 (being the value on death of the deceased's current house) plus the difference between the available transferable RNRB and the downsized value (£140,000), but transferable RNRB can never exceed twice the allowance so £365,000 is abated. In this instance, it is the 'potentially transferable' RNRB that is abated.

Example 2 (below) is straightforward and there is only RNRB (not transferable RNRB) available as a result of the transactions undertaken. This might, in some circumstances, be a favourable option if the effect of transferring all the assets of the first deceased to the surviving spouse/ civil partner would then cause RNRB to be abated if the estate at second death then exceeds £2m.

Example 2

A husband sells a home worth £300,000 in July 2020 and moves to a home worth £140,000. At the time, the available RNRB is £175,000. He has potentially lost the chance to use £35,000 or 20% of the available RNRB which could have applied had the more valuable home not been sold.

When he dies in December 2020, the (new) home is worth £175,000 and is left to his son with the remainder of the estate passing to his wife. The estate can use the RNRB of £175,000 to the full and since the RNRB was fully used on death, there is none to transfer to the widow. However, none of the existing nil-rate band has been used, so it can be transferred and will be available on the widow's death along with her own RNRB.

Example 3 confirms that RNRB is not available to set against failed PETs even where that failed PET is the gift of the deceased's former home. RNRB is only available on death transfers but a pre-deceased spouse can still generate entitlement to transferable RNRB.

Example 3

A widower gives away his home worth £400,000 to his children in May 2020 and moves into rented 'later living' accommodation. At the time of the gift, the available RNRB (including transferable RNRB) is £350,000. He has potentially lost the chance to use £350,000 or 100% of the available RNRB which could have applied had he not given away his home.

When he dies in February 2021, within seven years of the gift, his estate is worth £600,000 and is split between his four children. As there is no qualifying residence in his estate, it cannot use RNRB directly. But the estate is eligible for additional RNRB up to a maximum of 100% of the available RNRB at his death or £350,000.

The position for the gift of the house is considered first. RNRB only applies to the assets in the estate, so it is not available in respect of the gift of the house. However, the estate can claim the full transferable nil-rate band (TNRB) of £650,000 so there is no tax to pay on the gift of £400,000. The balance of £250,000 TNRB remains available to be set against the estate.

RNRB is applied first against the estate of £600,000, leaving a remainder of £250,000. The balance of TNRB from his late wife's estate is applied to this amount so no tax is payable as a result of the death.

Example 3 might be represented as follows, following the HMRC guidance.

Value of estate		600,000
Failed PET	400,000	
Less: Available NRB	650,000	
Surplus NRB	250,000*	
Available RNRB		350,000
Potentially taxable		250,000
Less: Surplus NRB		250,000*
Taxable estate		Nil

It would seem, in this case, that the requirement to 'has otherwise ceased to own' their only residence is relevant here and, as assets at least equivalent to the value of the former home have been subsequently inherited by the children, RNRB and transferable RNRB are available in full (even though the relevant asset has also been given to the children). Suppose instead only 50% of the estate (£300,000 in this example) passed to children at death, and the balance (say) to non-family members, then RNRB would be restricted to £300,000 resulting in tax payable.

RNRB is only available in full where the estate has a value of less than £2m. Where the death estate exceeds £2m, RNRB will be clawed back at the rate of £1 for every £2 an estate is above £2m. Consider, as speculated above, that in some circumstances transfers on the first death (contrary to the perceived wisdom following TNRB) may provide an advantage if the survivor's estate can be kept below £2m so that claw back is avoided.

One objective of the change (apart from implementing an election pledge) is to try to reduce the number of estates that pay IHT, on the basis the freezing of the NRB has brought more estates into charge. It is understood the current number of taxable estates has increased over time but the piecemeal way in which the relief is being introduced might suggest that fiscal drag as a consequence of further house price inflation will ensure the government's tax take remains unchanged.

The view of some practitioners is that this arrangement is unnecessarily complex and potentially unworkable so it is likely that, as time passes, more information and clarification will become available to these arrangements.

Legislation: IHTA 1984, s. 8A–8C; FA 2008, s. 10 and Sch. 4; F(No. 2)A 2015, s. 9; FA 2016, s. 93 and Sch. 15

Website: www.hmrc.gov.uk/inheritancetax/intro/transfer-threshold.htm

7195   Gifts to charities and political parties

Transfers of property to charities and political parties are generally exempt from IHT.

A political party is one which before the gift is made had two members elected to the House of Commons or one member was elected and candidates, being members of that party, received at least 150,000 votes.

If the value of the property to the charity is less than the loss in value of the donor's estate, the exemption is not restricted.

Exceptions

The exemptions relating to charities and political parties will not apply to any property if:

- the disposition is not immediately in favour of the charity or political party;
- the disposition depends on a condition which is not satisfied 12 months after the transfer;
- the property is given on consideration of a reversionary interest if that interest does not form part of the estate of the person acquiring it;
- the disposition is defeasible;
- the property given is an interest in other property and that interest is less than the donor's full interest, or given only for a limited period;
- the property is an interest in possession in settled property and the settlement does not come to an end in relation to that settled property on the making of the transfer;
- the property is land or buildings and the donor has obtained the right of occupation for himself or others with whom he is connected at a rent less than market rent;
- the property is not land or buildings and the donor has created or reserved an interest; unless that interest is for full consideration in money or money's worth, or the interest does not substantially affect the enjoyment of the property by the person or body to whom it is given; or
- the property or any part of it may be applied for purposes other than charitable, political, or national purposes.

These exceptions mean that the donor must part with his whole interest in the property transferred and must not affect the enjoyment of those to whom it is given.

Legislation: IHTA 1984, s. 23, 24, 56

Other Material: *HMRC Inheritance Tax: Customer Guide* available on the HMRC website at www.hmrc.gov.uk/cto/customerguide/page1.htm

Tax Reporter: ¶645-250

7196 Gifts to housing associations

Gifts of land to registered housing associations are exempt. A 'registered housing association' is a non-profit making body established for the provision or encouragement of housing.

To be within the exemption, the gift must be immediate and not conditional, defeasible or limited, etc. (as in relation to gifts to charities: see 7195).

Legislation: IHTA 1984, s. 24A, 56

Other Material: *HMRC Inheritance Tax: Customer Guide* available on the HMRC website at www.hmrc.gov.uk/cto/customerguide/page1.htm

Tax Reporter: ¶645-900

7198 Gifts for national purposes

Gifts for national purposes

Gifts for national purposes made to the following institutions are completely exempt from IHT:

- the National Gallery;
- the British Museum;
- the National Museums of Scotland;
- the National Museum of Wales;
- the Ulster Museum;
- any other similar national institution which exists wholly or mainly for the purpose of preserving for the public benefit a collection of scientific, historic or artistic interest and which is approved by HMRC;
- any museum or art gallery in the UK which exists wholly or mainly for that purpose and is maintained by a local authority or university in the UK;
- any library the main function of which is to serve the needs of teaching and research at a university in the UK;
- the Historic Buildings and Monuments Commission for England;

- the National Trust for Places of Historic Interest or Natural Beauty;
- the National Trust for Scotland for Places of Historic Interest or Natural Beauty;
- the National Art Collections Fund;
- the Trustees of the National Heritage Memorial Fund;
- the National Endowment for Science, Technology and the Arts;
- the Friends of the National Libraries;
- the Historic Churches Preservation Trust;
- Commission for Rural Communities;
- Natural England;
- Scottish Natural Heritage;
- the Countryside Council for Wales;
- any local authority;
- any government department (including the National Debt Commissioners);
- any university or university college in the UK; and
- a 'health service body' (see 4635).

Legislation: IHTA 1984, s. 25, 26A, Sch. 3

Other Material: *HMRC Inheritance Tax: Customer Guide* available on the HMRC website at www.hmrc.gov.uk/cto/customerguide/page1.htm

Tax Reporter: ¶646-050

Transfers exempt only during lifetime

7210   Potentially exempt transfers as exempt transfers

Any PET made seven or more years before the death of the transferor is an exempt transfer. Any other PET is chargeable. During the period between the date of the PET and either seven years from that date or, if it is earlier, the date of the transferor's death the PET is assumed to be an exempt transfer (see 6611).

The nature of a PET is discussed at 6611.

Legislation: IHTA 1984, s. 3A

Other Material: *HMRC Inheritance Tax: Customer Guide* available on the HMRC website at www.hmrc.gov.uk/cto/customerguide/page1.htm

Tax Reporter: ¶643-200

7220 Annual exemption

Transfers of value made by a transferor in any one year are exempt up to the value of £3,000. If the value transferred in any one year falls short of £3,000, the shortfall may be added to the £3,000 in the next following year. If the value transferred exceeds £3,000, the excess will be attributed to a later, rather than an earlier, transfer and, if the transfers are made in the same day, the excess will be attributed to them in proportion to the values transferred by them. A 'year' means any period of 12 months ending with 5 April.

Example 1

Margaret gives Lucy £2,800 in year 1 and £3,100 in year 2. The shortfall of £200 in year 1 may be carried forward to be used in year 2. There will be no chargeable (or potentially exempt) transfer in year 2, since £3,200 is then available as an exemption, but the £100 left over from year one, because the current year's £3,000 is used first, cannot be carried forward any further. Since the gift in year 2 is over £3,000, there is no shortfall available for any gifts that may be made in year 3 that are over £3,000.

Example 2

Duncan gives Paul £2,000 in year 1 and £2,500 in year 2 and £3,750 in year 3. The gifts in years 1 and 2 are covered by the exemption since they are under £3,000, but the gift in year 3 will be treated as a chargeable (or potentially exempt) transfer of £250 since only £500 was available as a carry forward from year 2.

The legislation states that, in a tax year where there are both PETs and chargeable transfers, when allocating the annual exemption the PETs are left out of account in the first instance. However, HMRC hold the view that this is inconsistent with other parts of the legislation and that the annual exemption should instead always be allocated in chronological order, regardless of whether the transfer remaining after the exemption is a chargeable transfer or a PET. This is the more logical view since the question of whether a transfer is a PET or a chargeable lifetime transfer is determined after exemptions been taken into account. In practice the point is unlikely to be often encountered.

Legislation: IHTA 1984, s. 19

Other Material: *HMRC Inheritance Tax: Customer Guide* available on the HMRC website at www.hmrc.gov.uk/cto/customerguide/page1.htm

Tax Reporter: ¶643-200

7223 Small gifts

Transfers of value made by a transferor in any one year by outright gifts to any one person are exempt if the values transferred by them do not exceed £250 but the £3,000 exemption and the £250 small gifts relief cannot be aggregated to exempt a gift of £3,250.

Legislation: IHTA 1984, s. 20

Other Material: *HMRC Inheritance Tax: Customer Guide* available on the HMRC website at www.hmrc.gov.uk/cto/customerguide/page1.htm

Tax Reporter: ¶643-700

7226 Normal expenditure out of income

If the transfer of value is part of the 'normal expenditure' of the transferor and it came out of their income so that it left them with sufficient income to maintain their usual standard of living, then the transfer will be exempt from IHT. Potentially, there is no monetary limit to the amount that might be regarded as 'normal expenditure out of income' provided the donor can maintain their required standard of living out of the retained income. The general view is that such gifts must be of cash (see below regarding the purchase of chattels which are then immediately gifted).

Payment, whether directly or indirectly, of an insurance premium on the life of the transferor is not regarded as part of normal expenditure if an annuity has been purchased on their life at any time, unless it can be shown that the purchase of the insurance and annuity were not associated operations (see 6670).

The term 'normal expenditure' connotes expenditure which accords with a settled pattern adopted by the transferor. While that pattern need not be immutable, it must have been intended to remain in place for more than a nominal period. 'Normal' refers to the type, not amount, of expenditure. The amount of the expenditure need not be fixed, nor need the individual recipients be the same (e.g. family members, needy friends). There is no fixed minimum period during which the expenditure has to be incurred. The expenditure need not be reasonable or such that another person would have incurred in similar circumstances. Nor does it matter that the object is to prevent accumulation of income in the transferor's hands, ultimately liable to IHT on his death.

Gifts made to relatives during the last few years of the donor's life were held by a special commissioner not to be 'normal expenditure' because they showed no regular pattern and no prior commitment.

When beginning what is intended to be a series of gifts it makes sense for the donor to include within any letter making the gift a phrase such as 'it is my intention to continue to make gifts out of income for as long as I am able'. If nothing else it sets the tone.

Gifts out of income will generally need to be of cash rather than possessions unless there is clear evidence that a specific possession was purchased with the immediate intention of it being a gift and was so gifted.

Establishing that the normal expenditure out of income applies can be difficult to establish in the absence of detailed lifetime evidence. If the taxable value of the estate can be covered by an aggregate of nil-rate band (including transferrable nil-rate band) plus other reliefs such as APR and BPR, then do not waste time pursuing the claim. The other reliefs are easier to establish.

Legislation: IHTA 1984, s. 21

Cases: *Nadin v IR Commrs* (1997) Sp C 112; *Bennett v IR Commrs* [1995] BTC 8,003

Other Material: *HMRC Inheritance Tax: Customer Guide* available on the HMRC website at www.hmrc.gov.uk/cto/customerguide/page1.htm

Tax Reporter: ¶643-950

7229   Gifts in consideration of marriage

Gifts made in consideration of marriage (or civil partnership) are exempt to a certain extent, depending on the relationship of the transferor to the transferee. The limits are:

- £5,000 in the case of gifts by a parent of either party to the marriage;

- £2,500 in the case of gifts by more remote ancestors (e.g. grandparents) of either party to the marriage;

- £2,500 in the case of gifts by one party to the marriage to the other; and

- £1,000 in any other case (e.g. aunts, siblings).

Both outright gifts and marriage settlements are included in the exemption, but if persons other than those being married, their issue, and the wife or husband of any issue are entitled to benefit, the marriage settlement would not normally qualify for exemption. The gifts must become fully effective on the marriage.

Example

Henry gives marriage gifts of £20,000 to his son and £5,000 to his son's fiancée in June 2015. He dies in December 2015. He has made no chargeable transfers for the year of the marriage. £4,000 of the gift to his son will be exempt and £1,000 to his bride (before considering any annual exemption). The actual calculation is as follows:

	£	£
Transfer	20,000	5,000
Less: exemption apportioned		
in ratio of £20,000 to £5,000 (IHTA 1984, s. 22(1))	(4,000)	(1,000)
	16,000	4,000
Less: £3,000 annual exemption apportioned		
in ratio of £16,000 to £4,000	(2,400)	(600)
	13,600	3,400

Henry has therefore made two PETs: one of £13,600 to his son, and one of £3,400 to his son's fiancée. (The annual exemption for 2015–16 has been allocated in accordance with HMRC's view (see 7220).) Both PETs became chargeable as a result of Henry's death in December 2015.

Legislation: IHTA 1984, s. 22

Other Material: *HMRC Inheritance Tax: Customer Guide* available on the HMRC website at www.hmrc.gov.uk/cto/customerguide/page1.htm

Tax Reporter: ¶644-450

Transfers exempt only on death

7250   Death on active service

Inheritance tax will not be charged if it is certified by the Defence Council or the Secretary of State that the deceased died from a wound inflicted, or an accident occurring when on active service against the enemy, or when on other service of a warlike nature. This will also apply if a disease was contracted at some previous time, the death being due to, or hastened by, the aggravation of the disease while on active service or on other service of a warlike nature.

The deceased must have been a member of any of the armed forces of the Crown (including women's services) or, by concession, a member of the Royal Ulster Constabulary. The exemption can only be claimed after death because the cause of death may not be as a result of a wound inflicted, or an accident occurring when on active service against the enemy, or when on other service of a warlike nature.

The exemption can only be claimed post death because the circumstances of the individual's death may not be a consequence of their service.

This exemption for armed service personnel is extended, in respect of deaths on or after 19 March 2014 to Emergency Service Personnel and Humanitarian Aid Workers by *Finance Act* 2015, s. 75 which inserts new sections, IHTA 1984, s. 153A (emergency services) and 155A (constables and service personnel).

The relevant individual has to be an 'emergency responder' and includes anybody employed in connection with the provision of fire services, rescue services, medical, ambulance or paramedic services, police services, anybody employed for the purposes of providing or engaged in providing the transportation of organs, blood, medical equipment and medical personnel or anyone employed by a government or international organisation, or charity in connection with the provision of humanitarian assistance.

In respect of constables and services personnel, there is a further exemption, again applying from 19 March 2014, if such individuals die from an injury incurred when subject to violence as a consequence of their status as a constable or service person. In this instance, when so targeted, it does not matter whether the constable or service personnel was acting in the course of their duty. The exemption will include PETs but not any additional charge that will arise on chargeable lifetime transfers. According to HMRC, 'people making immediately chargeable transfers are doing so at a time when they are alive and fully aware of what they are doing and the consequences. The exemption is given because the tax liability arises as a result of an unplanned for event: no one plans to die when responding to an emergency'.

HMRC Trusts and Estates Newsletter (December 2014) includes an indication that they will take a pragmatic view as to who comes within the 'emergency services personnel' definition but emergency circumstances does not include death whilst undertaking training presumably on the basis health and safety should determine that there was no risk.

Legislation: IHTA 1984, s. 154; FA 2015, s. 75

Other Material: ESC F5, *Death of members of the Royal Ulster Constabulary (now withdrawn)*

Tax Reporter: ¶646-950

7251 Wartime compensation

Legislation is being introduced in *Finance Act* 2016, s. 95 (inserting IHTA 1984, s. 153ZA and Sch. 5A) to make it clear that the part of a person's estate represented by qualifying compensation received by victims of persecution during the Second World War is exempt from IHT for deaths that occur on or after 1 January 2015. The exemption previously operated by concession principally to Far East Prisoners of War but is now extended to a range of schemes from European funds.

Example

Eric received qualifying compensation of £15,000 and at his death, a full nil-rate band is available. It follows that a total of £340,000 would not be subject to IHT on Eric's death.

The compensation is deemed to be subsumed into the assets at death. Accordingly, if Eric had made a £15,000 gift when the compensation was received six years before death, that gift would now be a failed PET but the original receipt would be exempt.

7252 Partial exemption where further transfer by exempt beneficiary

Where a transfer made on the death of any person is an exempt transfer to a spouse, civil partner, charity, political party, housing association, public body, maintenance fund or employee trust, and the exempt beneficiary, in whole or partial settlement of any claim against the deceased's estate, makes a disposition of property not derived from the transfer on death, the exemption on death is lost to the extent of the value transferred by the exempt beneficiary, i.e. there is a partial exemption.

Note that any order made by the court in recognition of a claim against the deceased's estate under the *Inheritance (Provision for Family and Dependants) Act* 1975 is treated as a disposition effected by the deceased (see 6805). That means that any transfer to give such an order effect is not taxable again but it does not necessarily enjoy exemption. The present provision seems to be an anti-avoidance measure aimed at the following situation.

Example

Thomas agrees with charity X (or any other exempt beneficiary) that he will leave charity X a bequest of £500,000 provided charity X transfers £200,000 of its own property to his daughter (or any other non-exempt beneficiary who may have a claim against the deceased's estate). The effect is that £200,000 passes to a non-exempt beneficiary free of tax. The exemption to the charity

---

is abated to the extent of the charity's transfer, i.e. only £300,000 would enjoy exemption from IHT.

The 1984 Act already contains an 'associated operations' rule (see 6670) so it is arguable that the arrangement above would not have avoided IHT anyway. The provision enables HMRC more easily to charge such an arrangement.

Legislation: IHTA 1984, s. 29A

Other Material: *HMRC Inheritance Tax: Customer Guide* available on the HMRC website at www.hmrc.gov.uk/cto/customerguide/page1.htm

Tax Reporter: ¶646-950

Relief for business property

7253   Introduction to business property relief

Where the value transferred in a transfer of value includes relevant business property, the value transferred may, in certain circumstances, be treated as reduced by:

(1) 100% (50% for transfers or as a result of death before 10 March 1992) if the property consists of a business or interest in a business, or securities of an 'unquoted' company (see 6571) which, together with other securities owned by the transferor and any unquoted shares so owned, gave the transferor control of the company immediately before the transfer (before 6 April 1996, shares giving the transferor control of the company immediately before the transfer were also in this category);

(2) 100% for any unquoted shares in a company (before 6 April 1996, 100% relief is only available where the transferor held shares yielding more than 25% of exercisable votes and had maintained such a holding during the preceding two years; where the transfer was made or death occurred before 10 March 1992, only 50% relief was available in such circumstances);

(3) 50% (30% for transfers or as a result of death before 10 March 1992) if the property consisted of any land or building, machinery or plant which immediately before the transfer was used wholly or mainly for the purposes of a business carried on by a company which the transferor controlled, or by a partnership of which he was then a partner, or by the transferor, and was settled property in which he was then beneficially entitled to an interest in possession; and

(4)   50% for a controlling shareholding in a quoted company.

BPR is available so long as the company is trading and the shares are not quoted on a recognised Stock Exchange. HMRC, from time to time, produce lists of institutions they regard as a recognised Stock Exchange. Such lists are not fixed. HMRC can recognise, at any time, particular organisations as a recognised Stock Exchange. That may have the effect of causing BPR to be lost where, for example, shares were traded through an institution which was not previously a recognised Stock Exchange but which subsequently becomes a recognised Stock Exchange. It is important to continually review the position. The issue will be that any decision to categorise a particular institution as a 'recognised Stock Exchange' is likely to be retrospective so BPR will have been lost before the change has been announced by HMRC.

There is a minimum period of ownership for relief to apply (see 7259) and additional conditions for transfers within seven years before death (see 7260). Certain property is excepted from relief (see 7265). If the property is subject to a contract for its ultimate sale at the time of the transfer, relief may be denied in certain circumstances; HMRC's view is that 'buy and sell agreements' whereby, on death, a person's interest must be acquired by his fellow partners or director shareholders, are sufficient to deny relief.

Where business property is disposed of by way of a gift with reservation, the availability of relief where the reservation is released, or when the donor dies, is determined by treating the shares or securities as having been owned by the donor since the disposal by way of gift, but otherwise determining entitlement to business property relief by reference to the donee (see 6785).

The Court of Appeal has held that settled property (settled land) used for the purposes of the life tenant's business qualified for relief under (1) above. HMRC accept that the higher rate relief is available provided the settled property is transferred along with the business; if the settled property is transferred alone, the lower rate applies.

Where there is a gift of cash which on the construction of a will can only be satisfied by resort to an asset which qualifies for business relief, the gift itself qualifies for business relief.

The owner of the assets must do enough work to be classified as a trader, otherwise the assets may be classified as investments rather than a trade (see 7255 below) resulting in no relief being due.

Legislation: IHTA 1984, s. 103–105, 109A, 113; *Inheritance Tax (Market Makers) Regulations* 1992 (SI 1992/3181) (as amended by SI 2001/3629)

Cases: *McCall (Personal representatives of McClean deceased) v R & C Commrs* [2009] BTC 8,059; *Executors of Piercy (deceased) v R & C Commrs* (2008) Sp C 687; *Trustees of Nelson Dance Family Settlement v R & C Commrs* (2008) Sp C 682; *Russell v IR Commrs* [1988] BTC 8,041; *Fetherstonhaugh v IR Commrs* [1984] BTC 8,046; *Atkinson (Executors of the will of William Mashiter Atkinson (Dec'd))* [2010] TC 00420

Other Material: SP 12/80, *Business relief from inheritance tax: buy and sell agreements*; *HMRC Inheritance Tax: Customer Guide* available on the HMRC website at www.hmrc.gov.uk/cto/customerguide/page1.htm

Tax Reporter: ¶664-000

7255 Excluded businesses

If the business concerned consists wholly or mainly of securities, stocks, shares, land, buildings, making investments, or holding investments, then relief will be denied unless the business is that of a market maker on The Stock Exchange (or a discount house) and is carried on in the UK, or unless that business is to act as a holding company for a company or companies whose business is not one of the above. Market makers on the London International Financial Futures and Options Exchange (LIFFE) are also excluded from the above restrictions.

By contrast, *ICAEW Tax Guide 1/14* sets out HMRC's views in relation to trading companies owned through an LLP (Limited Liability Partnership) responding to questions posed by ICAEW (and others), indicates that where the trade of the LLP consists of the holding of shares in unquoted trading companies, BPR will not be available notwithstanding that if the same structure existed but with a limited liability company (or even a standard partnership) as the holding entity, then in that instance BPR would be available. Relief might still be available to an LLP if the LLP can demonstrate that the shareholdings are an integral part of its commercial activity; for example controlling a company to secure supplies of raw material and to deny such supplies to competitors.

In one case the High Court denied relief where the business of a caravan park was predominantly receiving rents (the caravans were the year-round homes of those paying rent) and was therefore mainly the making or holding of investments, although other caravan parks offering holiday accommodation (where those paying the rent were resident for only a week or two), where the overall commercial arrangements are similar to a holiday camp, may qualify.

The relief is also unavailable where the property is shares or securities of a company that is being wound up, unless the business of the company is to be continued after reconstruction or amalgamation, which must take place no later than one year after the transfer of value.

Recently, the availability of BPR on furnished holiday lettings has been reviewed but ultimately not in favour of the taxpayer. In *Pawson*, the Upper Tribunal found in favour of HMRC on the basis it was not possible to differentiate the profit the Pawson family made from a profit made exploiting property which would have been an investment. Furnished holiday letting continues to work its unsuccessful way through the courts; the 2015 case of *Green* simply confirming that exceptional evidence of trading will be required to overturn *Pawson*. The same conclusion was made in *McCall* where insufficient work was undertaken by the landowner to make the 'farming' a trade even though in that case the amount of work required was modest. Whilst IHTM25278 allows for the possibility of BPR on holiday lettings, there has to be more than just making accommodation available and allowing the tenant to entertain themselves. The HMRC manual refers to being 'substantially involved with the holidaymakers in terms of their activities on and from the premises' so directly linking the accommodation with other activities may be the path to relief. A package, i.e. accommodation plus horse riding or working on a farm sold together or a group of cottages where there is also a social centre, so in that instance the arrangements look more like a holiday camp or hotel, is more likely to fall the BPR side of the line whereas just accommodation with a note to the tenant that there is horse riding available in the locality or as in *Pawson* a single cottage fall on the investment side

The availability of BPR is not a right that can be obtained by placing an appropriate label on a business activity. Remember many activities are businesses but not every business is a trade. Both *Pawson* and *McCall* suggest there is a minimum of additional effort required by a business owner to cross the threshold. If the courts decide not enough extra work has been undertaken then perhaps we should not be surprised if the relief is denied. There have recently been a number of cases before the courts where businesses that essentially owned and exploited property have tried to establish a BPR entitlement. Even where the 'additional services' that were supplied or organised were apparently substantial the taxpayers in *Zetland* and *Best* failed to persuade the courts that those 'additional services' were sufficiently different to the 'ordinary services' that it is expected all landowners might supply. The conservative view might be that any businesses exploiting property will find it extremely difficult to establish an entitlement to BPR because the minimum additional effort is actually quite substantial.

Legislation: IHTA 1984, s. 103–105, 109A, 113; *Inheritance Tax (Market Makers) Regulations* 1992 (SI 1992/3181) (as amended by SI 2001/3629)

Cases: *Weston (Exor of the Will of Weston dec'd) v IR Commrs* [2000] BTC 8,041; *Brander (as personal representative of Balfour)* [2009] TC 00069; *R & C Commrs v Lockyer (personal representatives of Pawson dec'd)*[2013] BTC 1,605; *McCall (personal representatives of McClean, dec'd) v R & C Commrs* [2009] BTC 8,059; *Trustees of David Zetland Settlement* [2013] TC 02690; *Best (Executor of the Estate of Buller dec'd)* [2014] TC 03217; *Green* [2015] TC 04519

Other Material: *HMRC Inheritance Tax: Customer Guide* available on the HMRC website at www.hmrc.gov.uk/cto/customerguide/page1.htm; *ICAEW Tax Guide 1/14*; IHTM25278

Tax Reporter: ¶664-950

7259   Minimum period of ownership for business property relief

To obtain 'business property relief' (see 7253), the property must have either been owned by the transferor for the two years immediately before the transfer, or must have replaced other property which was owned for two out of the five years immediately before the transfer. The value on which relief can be claimed is the lowest value during the five years. The property in either case must be one of the types set out at 7253 that qualify for business relief. If the transferor became entitled to any property on the death of another person, they are deemed to have owned it from that death and, if the deceased was their spouse or civil partner, then they are deemed to have owned it for any periods that the spouse or civil partner owned it.

Relief also will be granted, even though the property has not been owned for two years, if there have been two transfers of value, at least one being made as a transfer on death, and all or part of the earlier transfer qualified for relief; the property that qualified for relief must have become, on that earlier transfer, the property of the person making the later transfer or their spouse or civil partner. If only part of the earlier transfer was eligible for relief, then only a like part of the later transfer will be eligible for relief, and if the property is replacement property, the relief is not to exceed what it would have been had the property not been replaced.

HMRC take the view that where agricultural property is replaced by business property (or vice versa) shortly before the owner's death (see also 7297) the period of ownership of the original property will normally be relevant for applying the minimum ownership condition to the replacement property.

Legislation: IHTA 1984, s. 106–109

Other Material: Revenue interpretation, 'IHT: Business and Agricultural Property Relief', IRInt. 1002 *Tax Bulletin*, December 1994, p. 182; *HMRC*

Inheritance Tax: Customer Guide available on the HMRC website at www. hmrc.gov.uk/cto/customerguide/page1.htm

Tax Reporter: ¶665-500

7260 Transfers within seven years before death and business property relief

Where because of the transferor's death within seven years a PET becomes chargeable or extra tax becomes payable in respect of a chargeable transfer (see 6800), additional conditions have to be met before business property relief (see 7253) is available. They are:

(1) the original transferee must retain ownership of the property originally transferred throughout the period from the original chargeable transfer to the death of the transferor; and

(2) the original property must still fulfil the conditions and requirements of 'relevant business property' at the time of the transferor's death, except that it is not necessary for the transferee to have owned the property for two years if the original transfer was less than two years before the death.

The second condition above does not apply for shares which were 'quoted' (see 6571) at the time of the gift nor for shares which gave the donor control at the time of the gift and were unquoted throughout the period until death (this prevented relief from being lost if, for example, control passed from unquoted shares by virtue of a rights issue which is not taken up or the flotation of the company).

Business property relief is ignored in determining whether there has been a PET or a chargeable lifetime transfer. This is to avoid the argument that a net transfer valued below £3,000 as a result of BPR, for example, could be an exempt transfer under the annual exemption provision.

Where the transferee dies before the transferor, the conditions set out above are treated as satisfied to the extent that they were satisfied at the transferee's death and the IHT payable on the transferor's death is to be reduced accordingly.

Replacement property

The relief is available where the original property is replaced by other qualifying property during the period in question provided that:

• the whole consideration received for any original property disposed of was applied in the acquisition of the replacement property;

- not more than 36 months elapsed between the conclusion of the contract for the disposal of the property sold and the conclusion of the contract for the acquisition of the new property (HMRC may permit a longer period);

- both the disposal and the acquisition were at arm's length;

- the transferee owned either the original property or the replacement property throughout the period from the date of the gift to the transferor's death;

- the replacement property qualifies as 'relevant business property' immediately before the transferor's death.

Legislation: IHTA 1984, s. 113A, 113B

Other Material: *HMRC Inheritance Tax: Customer Guide* available on the HMRC website at www.hmrc.gov.uk/cto/customerguide/page1.htm

Tax Reporter: ¶665-700

7262 Valuation of business property eligible for relief

Business property relief (see 7253) is related to the value of the business transferred; the value of a business, or an interest in a business, is the value of the assets including goodwill, less any liabilities incurred for the purposes of the business. If a company is a member of a group and another company in the group deals in stocks or shares, etc. this company will be ignored when calculating the value of shares in the other companies of the group, unless that company is a discount house or a market maker or is a holding company.

Where a debt has been secured on an eligible asset then the net value is then subject to BPR at the appropriate rate. However, it was previously possible to secure the debt on an assets that did not qualify for either APR or BPR so that 100% APR or BPR on the purchased asset would then reduce the taxable value to nil and the debt could then be set against otherwise taxable assets.

Legislation was introduced in FA 2013, effective from 6 April 2013 (in most instances) to require any debt that was used to purchase an asset, on or after that date, that was otherwise eligible for either APR or BPR (or other exemptions) to first be deducted from the asset whose purchase was funded whether or not it is secured on that asset and APR or BPR then deducted on the net value (see 6819).

Legislation: FA 2013, s. 176 and Sch. 36; IHTA 1984, s. 110, 111

Other Material: *HMRC Inheritance Tax: Customer Guide* available on the HMRC website at www.hmrc.gov.uk/cto/customerguide/page1.htm

Tax Reporter: ¶664-150

7265   Assets excepted from business property relief

Excepted assets are left out of account in the valuation of property which qualifies for relief (see 7262) so the value of excepted assets is potentially taxable. An asset is excepted if it is not used wholly or mainly for the business for the two years immediately before the transfer, or 'required at the time of the transfer for future use for those purposes'. Cash held in a company's bank account at the date of the death of the holder of 50% of the shares was excluded from relief in circumstances where the cash was not used for seven years (*Barclays Bank Trust Co Ltd*) and no credible evidence of intention to be used was available. A special commissioner held that at the time of the death, the money could not be said to be 'required … for future use' if it was not in fact used for such a long period. If, however, there was a realistic prospect of accumulated cash being used for an immediate business purpose, then relief should not be restricted (*Brown's Executors*). Here evidence of intent will be crucial. In *Brown* at the date of the IHT event there was no business, simply cash from a previous business sale but efforts had been made by the deceased to find a new business which the Commissioner thought had been thwarted by the untimely illness and death of the taxpayer.

The key requirement is 'immediate intention'. That does not mean the money must be spent tomorrow, but that there is a definable project for which the cash is required. A company accumulating cash over a number of years to finance a factory extension (perhaps because the company does not want to or cannot borrow) is still an immediate intention. By contrast HMRC in 2014 indicated, via *ICAEW Tax Guide 1/14*, that retaining cash to ride out a future recession or a possible downturn in business is not an 'immediate intention' presumably because the future events may never happen.

If a company is a member of a group, use of an asset by another company in the group will be treated as use for the business concerned, provided that immediately before the transfer and during use, the company is a member of the group and provided the company is not dealing in shares, securities, etc. However, this will not apply to any land or building, machinery or plant used immediately before the transfer, wholly or mainly for a business carried on by a company of which the transferor had control or a partnership of which he was a partner, unless it was so used for two years before the transfer or it replaced another asset so used and the other asset was so used for at least two out of the five years before the transfer. If the two-year ownership requirement is waived because of successive qualifying transfers (see 7259) and the asset is so used between the earlier and later transfer, the condition will be treated as satisfied.

Where only part of any land or buildings is used exclusively for business use, the value of the part so used will be such proportion of the whole as may be just.

Legislation: IHTA 1984, s. 112

Cases: *Barclays Bank Trust Co Ltd v IR Commrs* (1998) Sp C 158; *Brown's Executors v IR Commrs* (1996) Sp C 83

Other Material: *HMRC Inheritance Tax: Customer Guide* available on the HMRC website at www.hmrc.gov.uk/cto/customerguide/page1.htm

Tax Reporter: ¶665-150

7268 Interaction between business property relief and other reliefs

If 'agricultural relief' (see 7292ff.) or 'relief on the disposal of trees or underwood' (see 7320ff.) has already been obtained, then business property relief (see 7253) cannot also be claimed. If any value is included in the value of a person's estate immediately before his death, the value so included will not be reduced by these provisions.

Legislation: IHTA 1984, s. 114

Other Material: *HMRC Inheritance Tax: Customer Guide* available on the HMRC website at www.hmrc.gov.uk/cto/customerguide/page1.htm; *ICAEW Tax Guide 1/14*

Tax Reporter: ¶666-200

Relief for agricultural property

7292 Introduction to agricultural property relief

The value of agricultural property in the UK or a qualifying EEA member state which is transferred will be reduced by 100% (50% for transfers or deaths before 10 March 1992) provided certain conditions are satisfied; there must be a right to vacant possession, or vacant possession must be obtainable within 12 months, otherwise the relief will be limited to 50% (30%). The condition as to vacant possession being obtained or obtainable within 12 months is regarded as satisfied where the transferor's interest in the property either:

- carries a right to vacant possession within 24 months of the transfer; or

- is, notwithstanding the terms of the tenancy, valued at an amount broadly equivalent to the vacant possession value of the property.

Example

Robert has owned and occupied a farm comprising agricultural land and buildings occupied for farming for ten years. He transfers the farm to his son in June 2011. There is a right to vacant possession of the farm. Since Robert is transferring agricultural property and has occupied it for at least two years before the transfer (see 7297) and since there is a right to vacant possession, the value of the property transferred will be reduced by 100%, thereby effectively exempting it from IHT.

Where agricultural property is disposed of by way of gift with reservation, the availability of relief where the reservation is released, or when the donor dies, is determined by reference to the donee (see 6785).

If the property is subject to a contract for its ultimate sale at the time of the transfer, relief may be denied in certain circumstances.

Relief is given to those shareholders who control farming companies (see 7295).

The 100% rate of relief is also available if the interest of the transferor in the property immediately before the transfer does not carry the rights referred to above where the property is let on a tenancy beginning after 31 August 1995 (or, in Scotland, a tenancy acquired after that date by right of succession). In HMRC's view, the 1995 amendments to the agricultural property relief regime applied to all tenancies commencing after 31 August 1995, provided other necessary conditions were satisfied, irrespective of whether the tenancy in question fell within the provisions of the *Agricultural Tenancies Act* 1995.

The availability of agricultural property relief at 100% has been extended to circumstances where farmland subject to an agricultural tenancy is acquired as a result of the death of the previous tenant. This applies where the tenant's death or, in a case involving retirement, the landowner's death occurs after 31 August 1995.

Agricultural property relief has been extended to include land assets taken out of farming and dedicated under a habitat scheme (see 7310).

Legislation: IHTA 1984, s. 115(1), (5), 116, 124; FA 2009, s. 122

Other Material: ESC F17, *Relief for agricultural property*; Revenue interpretation, *Relief for tenanted agricultural land*; *HMRC Inheritance*

Tax: Customer Guide available on the HMRC website at www.hmrc.gov.
uk/cto/customerguide/page1.htm

Tax Reporter: ¶658-000

7295   Agricultural property and its value for relief

Agricultural property relief (see 7292) applies to agricultural property,
which means agricultural land or pasture, including woodland and
buildings occupied for farming. The value of such agricultural property is
determined by treating the property as agricultural property for all time. A
stud farm operation constitutes agriculture. Land used for short rotation
coppice is also treated as agricultural land.

The Court of Appeal has held that the phrase 'agricultural land or
pasture' means bare land or pasture and does not include buildings on
the land. The inclusion of a reference to certain types of buildings later
in the provision was intended to expand the availability of the relief to
the categories of buildings mentioned rather than merely to clarify the
meaning of the basic phrase 'agricultural land or pasture'.

Where there is a transfer of agricultural property which includes a cottage
occupied by a retired farm employee or their widow(er), the requirement
as to occupation for agricultural purposes is regarded as satisfied if
the occupier is a statutorily protected tenant or the occupation is under
a lease granted to the farm employee as part of the employee's contract
of employment by the landlord for agricultural purposes.

Shares or securities giving the transferor control of a company can
constitute agricultural property. Any development premium on farmland
cannot qualify for APR. It can only qualify for BPR so the additional relief
is only available to working farmers. Although investors in farmland can
qualify for APR on the agricultural value of their land, if the tenant occupies
the land for the purposes of agriculture, if there is any development
premium no additional relief is due to them.

APR only applies to the agricultural value of the property. For any value
above agricultural value, a working farmer has to rely on BPR for relief
on any additional value. In *McCall*, the courts decided the landowner was
not undertaking enough work to be a working farmer so BPR was lost.
However, this case turned on its special facts and most working farmers
should not be affected. The excess above agricultural value can arise in
a number of ways: development premium, gravel deposits, etc. It therefore
follows that anyone who owns land as an investor is not eligible for BPR
on any excess above agricultural value because they are not a trader.
Equally in respect of farmhouses and value in excess of agricultural value
cannot qualify for relief at all (see 7296).

Legislation: FA 1995, s. 154; IHTA 1984, s. 115(2)–(4), 122

Cases: *Starke (Exors of Brown dec'd) v IR Commrs* [1995] BTC 8,028; *McCall (personal representatives of McClean, dec'd) v R & C Commrs* [2009] BTC 8,059

Other Material: ESC F16, *Relief for agricultural property and farm cottages*; *HMRC Inheritance Tax: Customer Guide* available on the HMRC website at www.hmrc.gov.uk/cto/customerguide/page1.htm

Tax Reporter: ¶658-250

7296 Agricultural property applicable to farmhouses

For many small farming businesses, the value of the farmhouse is a significant asset within the farming enterprise. APR is only available on the agricultural value of a farmhouse which, typically, might be 70% of open market value. It therefore follows that any excess does not qualify for any relief. It is important, generally, for the farmland and the farmhouse to be under both the same control and direction. In *Higginson*, the farmland was let to a neighbouring farmer by the former farmer (who resided in the farmhouse) so APR was not available on the agricultural value of the farmhouse. By contrast in *Antrobus*, the land was farmed by the owner/occupant of the farmhouse. Accordingly, APR was due on the appropriate proportion of farmhouse value. Even arranging for a land agent to direct farming on your behalf can be fatal to the availability of the relief on the basis the farming is not then directly under the same control and direction.

It is however important for the person who occupies the land (and occupies the farmhouse) to be the person who directs the farming activities. In *Arnander*, the taxpayer had delegated all decisions to an agent, who in turn delegated farming activities to a contractor; the consequence was that the land owner no longer occupied the 'farmhouse' for the purposes of agriculture so relief was no longer available.

A current concern is the availability of APR on a farmhouse where the farmer has to go into residential accommodation and is therefore no longer in physical occupation of the farmhouse, perhaps for respite care, but then returns home for increasingly shorter periods. Does there come a time where the periods in care become so extended that the care home then becomes the individual's home? Is there a definable period in care that results in the relief being potentially lost? As always, it will depend upon the specific facts of each case but can guidance be indicated from the change to the final period of exemption for CGT main residence relief, from 6 April 2014, that reduces the final exempt period to 18 months in most cases but retains the 36-month exemption where an individual is in a residential home for more than three months? Partnerships may be more flexible in that the partnership may be able to arrange for the property to be occupied by another partner but the position for sole traders seem potentially uncertain. Certainly, occupation by a real person rather than 'the partnership' is more likely to allow the relief; see the case explanations below.

The first case involving farmhouses, *Harrold*, failed because, as a question of fact, the property had never been occupied as a farmhouse once renovation was complete. In *Atkinson*, successful at First-tier Tribunal but lost at Upper Tier Tribunal, the farmhouse was not occupied by the farmer (apart from personal effects held for storage) and as such could not be said to be 'occupied for the purposes of agriculture'. Accordingly no APR was then due on the agricultural value. Within a partnership it may be possible to arrange for another partner (or farm worker) to occupy the farmhouse vacated by an older partner to preserve the relief but sole traders would appear to have more difficulty in preserving the relief.

In *JR & C Commrs v Hanson (as Trustee of the William Hanson 1957 Settlement)* [2013] BTC 1,900, the issue of whether ownership of land was important in determining the availability of Agricultural Property Relief was considered. The taxpayer owned a property which was accepted as being an eligible farmhouse except that the amount of land owned by the farmhouse owner was considered insufficient to support a claim for APR on the value of the farmhouse. However in addition to the owned land there was further land rented by the taxpayer from other family interests.

The case turned upon the correct interpretation of IHTA 1984, s. 115(2) which is set out below.

> 'In this Chapter "agricultural property" means (1) agricultural land or pasture and includes (2) woodland and any building used in connection with the intensive rearing of livestock or fish if the woodland or building is occupied with agricultural land or pasture and the occupation is ancillary to that of the agricultural land or pasture; and also includes (3) such cottages, farm buildings and farmhouses, together with the land occupied with them, as are of a character appropriate to the property.'

The judgment splits s. 115(2) into three limbs as indicated, and the issue was the relationship between limb (1) and limb (3). HMRC said there must be common ownership of all property within limb (1) to which the qualification within limb (3) then applied. The judgment refers to *Rosser v IR Commrs* (2003) Sp C 368 but in that case there was a farmhouse, a barn but only three acres owned and occupied by the owner where the farmhouse was not of a character appropriate to the exploited land and therefore no APR was due.

The judgment includes discussion as to what is a farmhouse. It was common ground between HMRC and the taxpayer that the relevant property was a farmhouse. The *Hanson* judgment includes the following phrase:

> 'For a house to be a "farmhouse" there had to be some functional connection between the house and the farm. If that connection ceases to exist, we consider that the house ceases to be a farmhouse. Thus, suppose that the farmer sells the house to a third party who has nothing at all to do with farming and who moves into the house as his family home. The house might well remain of a character appropriate to the farm so that if the farm and the house were again to fall into common ownership with the new owner both farming the land and residing in the house, operating the farming business from it, the house might once again become a farmhouse.'

That view seems to point towards commonality of occupation although, in the example, commonality of ownership could also exist. The judgment also refers to the situation where a tenant farmer occupied property for many years but then acquires the freehold but dies within two years of acquiring the freehold. In that situation, the previous occupation is taken into account in determining whether APR can be due on the freehold now owned by the taxpayer. In that instance, relief is not precluded by IHTA 1984, s. 117(a).

Hanson seems a common sense conclusion. There will be many farmers who own some land and rent other land. That is often the natural farming unit. As such the owner/occupier of the whole farm would on any natural construction of the word 'farmer' consider themselves to be so.

Is it possible APR can be available on the full value of the farmhouse? The starting point, above, is that APR is only available on the agricultural value of the property so, for 100% relief to be available, agricultural value and open market value would have to be the same. Many advisors adopt 70% of open market value as a standard discount but this is a lazy approach which derives from a particular decided case. The correct approach is to assess open market value and agricultural value and that then determines whether any discount is applicable. It is understood that factors which are taken into account in, effectively, bringing open market value down to agricultural value include; the remoteness of the farmhouse, its state of repair (a modernised farmhouse is more attractive to non-farming purchasers) and the overall demand for properties in the particular locality. Thus, farmhouses within easy reach of metropolitan centres, London, Belfast and Edinburgh should attract a premium above agricultural value so a discount will apply. Conversely, where the farm is more remote, and less likely to be used as a 'weekend cottage', within the remote parts of the Scottish Highlands and mid Wales, then it is possible that agricultural value and open market value will be similar.

Legislation: IHTA 1984, s. 115, 117

Cases: *Higginson's executors' v IR Commrs* (2002) Sp C 337; *Lloyds TSB (personal representative of Antrobus deceased) v IR Commrs* (2002) Sp C 336; *R & C Commrs v Atkinson (Executors of Atkinson dec'd)* [2011] BTC 1,917; *Harrold's Executors v IR Commrs* (1996) Sp C 71; *R & C Commrs v Hanson (as Trustee of the William Hanson 1957 Settlement)* [2013] BTC 1,900; *Rosser v IR Commrs* (2003) Sp C 368; *Arnander (Executors of McKenna dec'd) v R & C Commrs* (2006) Sp C 565

7297 Minimum period of occupation or ownership for agricultural property relief

Except as noted below, to obtain agricultural property relief (see 7292), the agricultural property must have been occupied by the transferor (or by a company he controls or by a Scottish partnership of which he is a partner) for two years immediately before the transfer, or owned by him for seven years and, during that time, must have been occupied by someone for the purposes of agriculture (which does not include the grazing of horses used for leisure purposes).

If the transferor became entitled to any property on the death of another person, he will be deemed to have owned it from that death and, if the deceased is his spouse, then he will be deemed to have owned it for any periods that the spouse owned it; this also extends to occupation by the other person but there are additional provisions determining the rate of relief in such cases.

Relief also will be granted, even though the property has not been owned for two years, if there have been two transfers of value, at least one being made as a transfer on death, and all or part of the earlier transfer qualified for relief; the property that qualified for relief must have become, on that earlier transfer, the property of the person making the later transfer or their spouse. If only part of the earlier transfer was eligible for relief, then only a like part of the later transfer will be eligible for relief, and if the property is replacement property, the relief is not to exceed what it would have been had the property not been replaced.

If the agricultural property replaced other agricultural property, relief may similarly be available, but together they must have been occupied for two out of five years or been owned for seven out of the ten years before the transfer. Changes resulting from the formation, alteration or dissolution of a partnership will be disregarded.

See also 7259 regarding HMRC's view where agricultural property is replaced by business property (or vice versa) shortly before the owner's death.

Legislation: IHTA 1984, s. 117–121

Case: *Wheatly's Executors v IR Commrs* (1998) Sp C 149

Other Material: *HMRC Inheritance Tax: Customer Guide* available on the HMRC website at www.hmrc.gov.uk/cto/customerguide/page1.htm

Tax Reporter: ¶658-500

7305 Transfers within seven years before death and agricultural property relief

Where a PET becomes chargeable or extra tax becomes payable in respect of a chargeable transfer other than a PET, by reason of the transferor's death within seven years (see 6800), and agricultural property relief (see 7292) is claimed, the following additional conditions must be met:

- the original transferee must retain ownership of the original property throughout the period from the original chargeable transfer to the death of the transferor ('the relevant period');
- the original property must still be agricultural property when the transferor dies and must have been occupied for the purposes of agriculture by the transferee or another, throughout the relevant period; and
- where relief is claimed in respect of a controlling interest in a farming company, the property owned by the company must have been so owned by the company and occupied for the purposes of agriculture, whether by the company or another, throughout the relevant period.

Agricultural property relief is ignored in determining whether there has been a PET or a chargeable lifetime transfer. See further 7260.

Where the transferee has died within the period between the original transfer and the transferor's death, the conditions set out above will be treated as satisfied, and the tax or additional tax payable on the transferor's death reduced accordingly, to the extent that the conditions were so satisfied at the death of the transferee.

Agricultural relief remains available where, during the relevant period, the original property is replaced by other agricultural property, a farming business is incorporated or there is a reorganisation or reconstruction of shares.

Replacement property

If the original property has been replaced by other property, then the following further conditions must be met before the relief is available:

- the whole consideration received for any original property disposed of must be applied in acquiring the replacement property;

- not more than 36 months must elapse between the conclusion of a contract for the disposal and the conclusion of a contract for the acquisition (HMRC may permit a longer period);

- both transactions must be at arm's length;

- either the original property or the replacement property must have been owned by the transferee throughout the relevant period;

- the replacement property must be 'agricultural property' immediately before the transferor's death; and

- throughout the respective periods of ownership, the properties must have been occupied by the transferee or someone else for the purposes of agriculture.

Legislation: IHTA 1984, s. 124A, 124B

Other Material: *HMRC Inheritance Tax: Customer Guide* available on the HMRC website at www.hmrc.gov.uk/cto/customerguide/page1.htm

Tax Reporter: ¶658-850

7310   Land in habitat schemes

Agricultural property relief (see 7292ff.) has been extended to include land in habitat schemes. All land in such schemes is treated as agricultural land, the management of such land to be agriculture and buildings used in carrying out that management to be farm buildings thus qualifying for relief. Land is treated as being in a habitat scheme for the purposes of relief if an application for aid under one of the enactments listed below has been made and is still in force.

The relevant statutory regulations (as long as the relevant undertaking has been given), which cover the habitat schemes that require land to be taken out of farming for 20 years and therefore come under the extended relief, are the:

- *Habitat (Former Set-Aside Land) Regulations* 1994 (SI 1994/1292);

- *Habitat (Salt-Marsh) Regulations* 1994 (SI 1994/1293);

- *Habitats (Scotland) Regulations* 1994 (SI 1994/2710); and

- *Habitat Improvement Regulations (Northern Ireland)* 1995 (SI 1995/134).

The above has effect in relation to any transfer of value made after 25 November 1996 and in relation to transfers on which IHT becomes chargeable due to events occurring after that date. This covers situations where a gift made before 26 November 1996 becomes chargeable to tax on or after that date due to the donor's death occurring within seven years of making that gift.

Legislation: IHTA 1984, s. 124C

Other Material: *HMRC Inheritance Tax: Customer Guide* available on the HMRC website at www.hmrc.gov.uk/cto/customerguide/page1.htm

Tax Reporter: ¶658-200

7311   Business assets of a farmer

Because APR only applies to land, and interests in land, it follows that a working farmer has to claim BPR on other assets, such as live and dead stock and plant and machinery, used in the farming business as well as any 'development premium' on the land value (provided the underlying land is used for agricultural purposes).

Relief for woodlands

7320   Introduction to relief for woodlands

The IHT which would normally be charged on death in relation to growing trees and underwood can be deferred until sale (see 7323), unless the land is the subject of agricultural relief (see 7292ff.).

Legislation: IHTA 1984, s. 25

Other Material: *HMRC Inheritance Tax: Customer Guide* available on the HMRC website at www.hmrc.gov.uk/cto/customerguide/page1.htm

Tax Reporter: ¶653-150

7323   Deferral of IHT on woodlands until subsequent disposal

If the deceased was beneficially entitled to the land throughout the five years preceding his death, or became beneficially entitled to it for other than a consideration in money or money's worth (e.g. inherited it), and provided there are trees or underwood growing on the land, then the value of those trees or underwood may be left out of account in determining the value transferred on death. An election so to do must be made within two years of the death. It should be noted that IHT will be charged on a subsequent disposal of the trees and underwood (unless the disposal is to a spouse) and the person entitled to the proceeds of sale will be liable to pay the tax (see 7326). *Finance Act* 2009 extended the relief to woodland located in a qualifying EEA member state.

Legislation: IHTA 1984, s. 125; FA 2009, s. 122

Other Material: *HMRC Inheritance Tax: Customer Guide* available on the HMRC website at www.hmrc.gov.uk/cto/customerguide/page1.htm

Tax Reporter: ¶653-650

7326 Value and rate of IHT on disposal after woodlands deferral

If the value of trees has been left out of account on death (see 7323), and they have been subsequently disposed of, IHT will be charged on the net proceeds of the sale if it is a sale for full consideration in money or money's worth or, in any other case, on the net value of the trees or underwood at the time of the disposal. Tax is charged as if the trees or underwood had never been left out of account and had formed the highest part of the value of the deceased's estate on death.

If the property had not been left out of account, and if it would have been taken into account for the purposes of business relief, the amount on which tax is charged will be reduced by 50%. This is an anomaly since the rate of business property relief has been increased to 100%. In most cases, it will be advantageous simply to claim business property relief (if available at 100%) rather than woodlands relief.

The expenses of disposal and replanting within three years of the disposal will be allowed as a deduction in arriving at the net proceeds of sale or the net value of the trees.

Example

Barry died in December 1997 leaving an estate of £650,000, including growing timber worth £85,000 which he had owned since 1966. He left it all to his son Thomas who elected to postpone payment of tax. Thomas died in May 2012 leaving an estate of £1,250,000 to his son Max. The growing timber is now worth £130,000. Max sells the timber in December 2013 for £165,000 net. No tax is chargeable on the value of the timber at Barry's death because the election was made to postpone payment of tax. If an election was also made on Thomas's death, no tax will be payable until the sale by Max. Assuming that Thomas made no chargeable lifetime transfers the tax payable will be on £1,250,000 less £130,000, i.e. on £1,120,000. The tax payable on the disposal of the timber by Max will be on the net sale price which is £165,000. The rate at which it will start is the point on the death scale where Thomas's estate finished, £165,000 will therefore be charged at 40%. Therefore, total tax to be borne by Max is £66,000. Even though Thomas had not owned the timber for five years, the election to postpone could be made since the timber had been inherited.

Legislation: IHTA 1984, s. 126–130

Other Material: *HMRC Inheritance Tax: Customer Guide* available on the HMRC website at www.hmrc.gov.uk/cto/customerguide/page1.htm

Tax Reporter: ¶653-300

Relief for works of art and historic buildings

7346 Introduction to relief for works of art and historic buildings

HMRC may designate certain types of property conditionally exempt from IHT. The property in point relates to artistic works and land or buildings of significant interest (see 7349).

An IHT charge may arise on the breach of any of the required undertakings or on death or disposal (see 7349 and 7351).

There are similar provisions to disapply various discretionary trust charges where designated property is held in such a trust, with corresponding adjustments to the charge on breach of conditions (see 7040 and 7055).

Legislation: IHTA 1984, s. 30, 31

Tax Reporter: ¶650-300

7349 Designated property and undertakings for conditional exemption

HMRC may designate any of the following property to be conditionally exempt (see 7346):

- any 'relevant object' which, or any collection or group of relevant objects which, taken as a whole, appears to HMRC to be pre-eminent for its national, scientific, historic or artistic interest; a 'relevant object' means a picture, print, book, manuscript, work of art or scientific object, or other things not yielding income; and in determining whether an object, etc. is 'pre-eminent', regard is had to any significant association of the object, etc. with a particular place; before 31 July 1998, this first category comprised pictures, prints, books, manuscripts, works of art, scientific collections or other things not yielding income which appeared to HMRC to be of national, scientific, historic or artistic interest;

- any land which in HMRC's opinion is of outstanding scenic or historic or scientific interest;

- any building for the preservation of which special steps should in the opinion of the Board be taken by reason of its outstanding historic or architectural interest (or any land which adjoins it which in HMRC's opinion is essential for the protection of the character and amenities of the building or any object which in HMRC's opinion is historically associated with it).

A claim for the property to be so designated must be made. The provisions will only apply to a transfer of value on death, unless the transferor and/ or his spouse have been beneficially entitled to the property for six years before the transfer, or unless the transferor acquired the property on a death which was the occasion of a transfer of value, which was itself conditionally exempt or left out of account. Conditional exemption may be obtained for designated property held in settlements for six years on the occasion of a ten-year charge or exit charge.

The rules relating to potentially exempt gifts are to be applied to national heritage property before the conditional exemption rules. If a PET becomes chargeable because of the donor's death within seven years (see 6800), it will then be possible to make a claim for conditional exemption. The claim may not extend to any property which has been sold by the donee during the period between the transfer and the donor's death. Further, in determining whether property is appropriate for designation, the circumstances prevailing at the time of death, rather than at the time of transfer, will be taken into account.

Undertakings

A person who HMRC consider to be appropriate, will be required to give an undertaking that the property will not leave the UK without HMRC's approval and that reasonable steps will be taken for the property's preservation and for securing reasonable public access. Before 31 July 1998, public access could be limited to those with a prior appointment. Owners may also now be required to publicise the terms of their undertakings and to disclose any other information relevant to public access: while this gives scope for agreeing terms for publishing certain types of confidential information, it operates subject to a claim to the Treasury not to grant access to such objects as manuscripts on grounds of confidentiality.

In the case of land and buildings, the undertaking will be for the maintenance of the land and preservation of its character or for the maintenance, repair and preservation of the property, as appropriate.

Claims

In relation to transfers made, and other events occurring, after 16 March 1998, claims must be made within two years from the date of the transfer of value giving rise to the claim or, in the case of a PET, two years from the date of death which rendered the PET chargeable, or such longer period as HMRC may allow. Previously, there was no time-limit.

A claim for exemption may be made on 700A. That form provides that an owner who does not live in a house which is or will be open to the public will be able to choose between:

- lending his objects for display in a house which is regularly open to the public;

- lending his objects to public collections on a long-term basis; or

- asking HMRC to arrange for details of the objects to be put on a register maintained by the National Art Library. That register will be available to museums, galleries and members of the public. Owners will be required, on request, to lend the objects for special exhibitions for up to six months in any two-year period and to make arrangements for members of the public to view the objects.

Legislation: IHTA 1984, s. 30(3BA), 35A

Tax Reporter: ¶650-350.

7351 Amount of IHT charged where conditional exemption lifted

In relation to conditional exemption for works of art, historic buildings, etc. (see 7346), breach of an 'undertaking' (see 7349) is treated as a chargeable event, as are the death of the person beneficially entitled to the property and disposal of the property. If the property is sold or given to any of the bodies listed at 7195, or given to HMRC in satisfaction of the tax due, it will not be treated as a chargeable event.

A death or disposal other than by sale will also not be a chargeable event if similar undertakings are given. Undertakings given after 30 July 1998 must comply with the changed requirements outlined at 7349.

The persons liable for the IHT due are:

- in the case of death, the person entitled to the proceeds of sale if sold immediately after death; and

- in the case of a disposal, the person for whose benefit the property is disposed of.

Inheritance tax is charged on an amount equal to the value of the property at the time of the chargeable event. Death rates will apply if the relevant transferor (see below) is dead, as if the amount had been added to the value transferred on his death and had formed the highest part of that value.

The relevant transferor is usually the last person who made a conditionally exempt transfer. However, HMRC may select any person within the last 30 years before the event if there have been two or more such transfers within that period.

Example

Hugo has a very large estate, including valuable books, which are designated conditionally exempt on his death by HMRC. He leaves the books to Sophie and they are conditionally exempt from tax. Five years later, Sophie gives the books to Annabel who gives fresh undertakings so that the conditional exemption is continued. Two years later, Annabel sells the books so that tax becomes chargeable. Since the transfer by Hugo occurred within the 30-year period, HMRC can calculate the tax on the sale by Annabel by reference to Hugo's death. If so, the amount will be added to the value transferred on Hugo's death and tax will be charged as if that amount had formed the highest part of the value transferred on Hugo's death. This in effect prevents the use of Annabel as a middle man to escape tax at the high rates which are chargeable on Hugo's death.

The cumulative total of the last transferor will have to be altered if he is still alive. He will be treated as if he had made a gift of non-exempt property valued at the date of the chargeable event. If the transferor is dead his estate on death will be increased by the amount on which tax was charged on the chargeable event.

Legislation: IHTA 1984, s. 32–35 and Sch. 1

Tax Reporter: ¶650-850

Maintenance funds for historic buildings

7371 Maintenance of historic buildings

There will be no IHT liability where property is put into a settlement in order to repair, maintain or preserve historic buildings if HMRC give the necessary direction (see 7374). A direction may have effect at the time of the transfer or it may be given after that time. In the latter case, in relation to transfers of value made after 16 March 1998, a claim for the direction must be made within two years from the date of the transfer, or such longer period as HMRC may allow.

There may be a charge to tax where property ceases to be subject to maintenance funds or where the trustees make a disposition reducing the fund's value (see 7055).

Legislation: FA 1998, s. 144; IHTA 1984, s. 27, Sch. 4

Tax Reporter: ¶651–900

7374   Requirements for HMRC direction as to maintenance fund exemption

HMRC will give a direction for exemption in respect of donations to maintenance funds for historic buildings, etc. (see 7371) if the settlement meets certain requirements and the property being put into the settlement is of a character and amount appropriate for the purposes of the settlement. The trustees must be resident, must include a professional adviser, and they must be approved by HMRC.

The requirements to be met are that:

- none of the property can, for six years, be used other than for the maintenance, repair or preservation of qualifying property (designated property for which undertakings have been given), or for defraying the expenses of the trustees or for the maintenance, repairs or preservation of property in the settlement;

- none of the property can devolve, otherwise than on any body (see 7195) or charity, on ceasing to be comprised in the settlement; and

- none of the property can be applied at the end of the period except as mentioned above.

The first two requirements do not apply to property which was previously comprised in another settlement and became comprised in the current settlement in circumstances such that no IHT was charged (i.e. property which was exempt under another settlement and which within 30 days becomes comprised in the present settlement).

HMRC will give a direction that a fund qualifies, when a claim is made, if they are satisfied:

(1) that the property is of a character and amount appropriate for the purposes of those trusts and that the property can for six years from the date it became held on the trusts be applied only:

(a) for the maintenance, repair or preservation of, or making provision for public access to, property which is for the time being qualifying property for the maintenance, repair or preservation of property held on the trusts or for such improvement of property so held as is reasonable having regard to the purposes of the trusts, or for defraying the expenses of the trustees in relation to the property so held;

(b) as respects income not so applied and not accumulated for the benefit of a body set up for national purposes or the public benefit (see 7198) or of a preservation charity; and

(c) that none of the property can on ceasing to be held on the trusts at any time within that period, devolve otherwise than on such body or charity and that income arising from such property can only be applied as mentioned above; and

(2) that the trustees are approved by HMRC, include a trust corporation, solicitor, or accountant and are resident in the UK.

There are special provisions regarding property previously comprised in another settlement (see 7040 and 7055).

HMRC may withdraw the direction by notice in writing to the trustees if the facts cease to warrant the continuance of the direction. Where a direction is in force the trustees must furnish such accounts and information relating to the property as HMRC may reasonably require.

Property is qualifying property for these purposes if it is land or a building of appropriate interest and has been designated as such.

Legislation: IHTA 1984, Sch. 4, para. 2(1)

Tax Reporter: ¶652-000

Excluded property

7394 Introduction to excluded property

No account is to be taken of the value of 'excluded property' (see 7397) which ceases to form part of a person's estate as a result of a disposition. A person's estate is the aggregate of all the property to which he is beneficially entitled, except that the estate of a person immediately before his death does not include excluded property.

However, an 'excluded' asset is not always completely irrelevant for IHT purposes. Thus:

- an excluded asset in a person's estate may still affect the valuation of another asset in the estate (e.g. an 'excluded' holding of shares in an unquoted company (see 6572) may affect the value of a similar holding in the estate which is not 'excluded'); or

- the value of an 'excluded' asset at the time the asset becomes comprised in a settlement may be relevant in determining the rate of any tax charge arising in respect of the settlement under the IHT rules concerning trusts without interests in possession (see 6950 to 6960).

Finance Act 2013, s. 176 and Sch. 36 introduced new rules that affect the basis of valuation for excluded property where debt has been taken out which is then secured on UK situs property but which is then used to purchase excluded property. Traditional planning, by non-UK domiciled individuals, to reduce the UK taxable estate, was to take out a loan secured on UK property but used to purchase excluded property where the consequence, before the FA 2013 change, was to reduce the taxable value of the UK estate. FA 2013, s. 176 and Sch. 36 contain provisions that apply, in respect of an IHT event on or after 17 July 2013 (the date of Royal Assent for FA 2013). In these circumstances, the debt is deducted, not from the asset on which it is secured, but from the value of the asset whose purchase was effected. Thus, the taxable value of UK situs property is preserved. The rule applies whenever the loan was taken, so a loan taken out before the date of Royal Assent will still be disregarded at an IHT event on or after 17 July 2013 in the envisaged circumstances. Many will have undertaken what was regarded as mainstream planning now to find their planning has been negated. There are complex provisions for tracing debt from one asset to another to prevent debt being recycled back to the UK situs assets.

Finance Act 2014 included further provisions to counter an unintended loophole in the new debt regime. A UK debt secured on UK property which then was deposited in a UK situs foreign currency bank account was deductible from the UK asset. Although the foreign currency bank account was not excluded property it equally was not subject to UK IHT. This change will apply to all IHT events on or after the date of Royal Assent for *Finance Act* 2014 (17 July 2014).

Legislation: FA 2013, s. 176 and Sch. 36; IHTA 1984, s. 3(2), 5(1)

Tax Reporter: ¶602-150.

7397 Meaning of 'excluded property'

'Excluded property' (see 7394) is determined in accordance with the following rules.

Property 'situated outside the UK' (see 6550) is excluded property (i.e. not within the charge to IHT) if the person beneficially entitled to it is an individual domiciled (see 6540) outside the UK: in other words, for persons domiciled abroad, IHT generally applies only to their UK assets. Further, certain government securities (savings certificates, premium bonds, National Savings Bank deposits, etc.) are also excluded property if the individual is domiciled in the Channel Islands or the Isle of Man.

For transfers of value before 3 December 2014, only decorations awarded for valour or gallant conduct were treated as excluded property if it could be shown that they have never been transferred for consideration in money or money's worth. The rule is strict. If A and B were left the residue of an estate, which included an award, then an agreement whereby A took the award but B a greater share of the residue may be treated as consideration in money or money's worth.

For transfers of value made, or treated as made, on or after 3 December 2014, this exemption is extended to include awards for service in the armed forces and awards made by the state in recognition of achievements in public life, such as an MBE. The exemption is further extended to equivalent orders, decorations or awards made by other countries and territories but the relief still only applies provided the awards have never been transferred for consideration in money or money's worth as before.

Settled property

Slightly different rules apply to property held in a settlement. Property (but not a reversionary interest) comprised in a settlement and situated outside the UK when a chargeable event occurs is excluded property if the 'settlor' (see 6883) was 'domiciled' (see 6540) outside the UK at the time the settlement was made; for this purpose, property becomes comprised in a settlement when it, or other property which it represents, is introduced by the settlor. If the settlor or his or her spouse or civil partner was originally entitled to an interest in possession in the property, it is deemed to be comprised in a separate settlement when that interest ceases (see 7017) so that the settlor must, in addition, have been UK-domiciled when the original settlement was made. Similarly, if property moves between settlements without vesting in someone in between, it is deemed to continue to be held in the original settlement (see 7020), so that the settlor must, in addition, have been UK-domiciled when the second settlement was made.

Addition of assets to existing settlements

In the light of the definition of 'settlement' (see 6883), HMRC's view is that assets added to a settlor's own settlement made at an earlier time when the settlor was domiciled abroad are not 'excluded', wherever they may be situated, if the settlor has a UK domicile at the time of making the addition (see further 6883).

Reversionary interests

A reversionary interest is excluded property unless:

- it has at any time been acquired (whether by the person entitled to it or by a person previously entitled to it) for a consideration in money or money's worth;

- it is one to which either the settlor or his spouse or civil partner is or has been beneficially entitled; or

- it is the interest expectant on the determination of a lease treated as a settlement (e.g. a lease for life: see 6883).

Visiting forces

Certain property of overseas forces visiting the UK is excluded property.

The Summer 2015 (post-election) Budget Statement included an announcement to ensure that from 6 April 2017 all UK residential property (including residential property let out on a commercial basis) owned by non-domiciles, regardless of their residence status for tax purposes, through any offshore structure, whether trust or closely controlled company will be brought within the charge to UK inheritance tax. It was mainstream tax planning to avoid the London property being UK situs assets; a London property would be owned, for example by a Jersey company with the shares owned by a non-UK trust so it was any interest in the trust that was the asset owned by the non-domicile not the London property. This change will not affect the general IHT position of non-domiciles or excluded property trusts in relation to UK assets other than residential property, or for non-UK assets but the charge is extended to residential property held as an investment, for example, residential flats for students. The legislation will be introduced in Finance Bill 2017.

Legislation: IHTA 1984, s. 6, 48, 82, 155; FA 2015, s. 74

Other Material: SP E9, *Excluded property*

Tax Reporter: ¶602-200

7410 Allocation of exemptions where transfer partly chargeable

A transfer of value (particularly a bequest under a will) may be chargeable or exempt; it may also be partly chargeable and partly exempt, e.g. where an exemption limit is exceeded. At the same time, a bequest may be stated to be free of tax or it may 'bear its own tax', i.e. the tax falls on the person who becomes entitled to the property given, etc. In combination, this variety of possibilities raises two separate problems:

- how to ascertain the value for tax of respective gifts and thus calculate the total tax payable on the transfer; and

- how the burden of tax, once calculated, is to be distributed among the donees or beneficiaries.

Specific rules apply where there is an exemption on transfer between spouses or civil partners or other transfers exempt during life and on death (see 7192ff.) or where there is a conditional exemption for the preservation of certain works of art and historical buildings, etc. (see 7346ff.).

Burden of tax

The 'burden of tax' is a term used to show the way in which the allocation of exemptions so as to produce the tax payable affects the distribution of the transfer after tax. This is clearly different from the 'incidence of tax' (see 7539) which refers to funds out of which the tax must be borne.

Notwithstanding the terms of any disposition, no tax is to fall on an exempt specific gift and no tax attributable to the residue is to fall on an exempt share of residue. This provision was considered in a case where a will which gave residue as to half to non-exempt individuals and half to exempt charities was construed, for IHT purposes, as giving the half-share of residue to the exempt beneficiaries after payment of debts, funeral and testamentary expenses, but before payment of IHT. Tax was to be borne by the non-exempt beneficiaries so that, in effect, the net amount which the non-exempt beneficiaries collectively received was less than the amount received collectively by the charities.

Attribution of value to gifts

Gifts are treated as reduced (or 'abated') for IHT purposes to the extent necessary to reduce their value to that of the assets available to meet them. Where gifts take effect out of different funds, the abatement is applied separately to each fund.

If there is a monetary limit on such exemption as is mentioned above, gifts bearing their own tax are covered by the exemption before other gifts; subject to that, the excess over the limit is apportioned rateably according to the amount of each gift.

The value attributed to residuary gifts is determined after value is attributed to specific gifts.

If specific gifts bear their own tax, it makes no difference whether the residue is partly exempt since no tax on the specific gifts will fall on the residue and tax on the chargeable part of the residue cannot fall on any exempt part of it; the value transferred is attributed to any specific gifts according to their actual values, the balance to residue.

If there are specific gifts not bearing their own tax and other chargeable gifts, a specific method is applied involving the attribution of a hypothetical gross value to the tax-free gifts. This value is used to calculate the taxable estate and hence the effective gross value of the gifts.

If part of the value transferred is property eligible for business property relief (see 7253ff.) or agricultural property relief (see 7292), all specific gifts and any non-specific gifts out of the property in point are first reduced to reflect that relief.

Legislation: IHTA 1984, s. 36–42

Case: *Re Benham's Will Trusts* [1996] BTC 8,008

Tax Reporter: ¶602-250

7450   Double tax relief for IHT

Where property suffers a charge to IHT and also to another similar tax in another territory, relief may be given in the UK either in accordance with a treaty between the UK and the other territory or unilaterally.

Treaties made by Order in Council are given effect for IHT purposes.

Unilateral relief is provided where there is no treaty in force. Where the property is situated in the overseas territory and not in the UK, the credit against IHT is equal to the whole of the foreign tax. Otherwise, a proportionate credit is given:

$$\frac{A + B}{A} \times C$$

A   is the amount of IHT;

B   is the overseas tax (or aggregate overseas tax); and

C   is the aggregate of all amounts included in A or B, except the largest.

Legislation: IHTA 1984, s. 158, 159

Tax Reporter: ¶687-000

Administration, liability and incidence

Administration of inheritance tax

7500   Scheme of administration of IHT

The management of IHT is carried out by HM Revenue and Customs (HMRC). HMRC are subject to the authority of the Treasury which is responsible for the imposition and collection of taxation. HMRC report to the Chancellor of the Exchequer. In practice, IHT is administered by

HMRC (Inheritance Tax). The scheme of administration and collection is laid down in IHTA 1984, Pt. VIII. In any correspondence between the transferor and HMRC, the transferor's official reference should always be quoted unless it is not known, in which case the name, date of birth, and if dead the date of death, of the transferor should be given.

Tax Reporter: ¶693-000

7503   Need to deliver IHT accounts

An account (or in Scotland an inventory or additional inventory) must be delivered to HMRC by:

- the transferor for a lifetime transfer chargeable when made (see 6610ff.);

- the trustees for chargeable transfers relating to settled property (see 6880ff.);

- the personal representatives for the estate of a deceased person (see 6770ff.); and

- by the transferee for lifetime transfers chargeable only by reason of the transferor's death within seven years and gifts with reservation (see 6610 and 6785ff.),

specifying to the best of his or her knowledge and belief the value of all appropriate property. Personal representatives must include details of any chargeable transfers made by the deceased within seven years before death.

The form of account (or supporting papers) and exceptions, etc. are determined by HMRC.

Form IHT 400 is used for all estates (other than excepted estates). It comprises a 'core account' with a number of supplementary pages that only need to be completed if relevant to the estate. In certain circumstances (basically where the charity or spouse or civil partner exemption applies and the chargeable estate is below the tax threshold) a reduced account can be filed. In all cases, IHT 421 (form C1 in Scotland) must be filled in, as this shows details of the estate relevant for the issue of a grant of representation (see below).

Providing additional information with the account may result in more focused questions or no question on that asset or deduction: for example, if a large debt owed to the deceased's son or other relative is to be deducted, where a deduction is claimed for a guarantee debt or if it is claimed that some person had an equitable interest in property held by the deceased as sole legal owner.

A person who delivers such an account and later discovers a material defect in it must, within six months of his discovery, deliver a corrective account.

Other than in the largest estates (and a small number of other exceptions), an IHT account will be required only where there is tax to pay. In other cases, contact with the Probate Service will cover both tax and probate formalities (in Scotland a Sheriff Court covers confirmation formalities).

The liability of trustees to deliver an account extends to foreign trustees of a settlement made outside the UK by a person domiciled in the UK, for the purpose of calculating the tax liability arising on the settlor's death.

Grants of representation

In order to obtain a grant of representation, the personal representatives must deliver the account and pay any tax due to HMRC. HMRC then fill in its part of the Form IHT 421 (or form C1 in Scotland) and return it to the personal representatives. They then submit it with the other papers necessary to obtain the grant of representation from the probate registry (Sheriff Court in Scotland). If the personal representatives are unable to ascertain the exact value of any particular property, they must deliver a provisional first account and state it to be provisional and give an undertaking to deliver a further account as soon as its value is ascertained.

If no grant of representation has been obtained within 12 months of the deceased's death, any beneficiary, or any person for whom any of the property is applied, must deliver an account to HMRC of all property in which he has an interest, or which is applicable for his benefit, and the value of that property. This will not apply if HMRC are satisfied that an account will be delivered by the personal representatives in due course.

Excepted estates

Some estates are excepted from the requirement to make an IHT account. The principal criterion for exception is that for deaths on or after 1 September 2006 the gross value of the estate plus the chargeable value of any transfers in the seven years prior to death, does not exceed the nil rate band (see Key Data for current thresholds), or £1m and the net chargeable estate after deduction of the spouse or civil partner and, or, charity exemption only is less than the nil rate band. There are also additional limitations on the following property:

(i)   the limit for the value of foreign property is £100,000;

(ii) the limit for the value of 'specified transfers' is £150,000;

(iii) the limit for the value of settled property is £150,000; and

(iv) the limit for the value of a non-domiciled individual's UK estate is £150,000.

The following amendments have been made to the excepted estates regulations.

An estate benefiting from unused nil rate band (see 7193) will only benefit from the transferred IHT threshold for the purposes of the excepted estates regulations where all of the first deceased's nil-rate band was used.

Estates up to £1m in value qualify as an excepted estate where there is no IHT to pay because the assets passing under the estate are exempt from IHT by virtue of passing either to a surviving spouse or civil partner, or to charity. An amendment to the regulations provides that the total value transferred on that person's death by a spouse, civil partner or charity transfer must be greater than nil. This amendment is intended to prevent the personal representatives of some estates where these exemptions do not apply nevertheless submitting an excepted estate return.

Where, in any tax year in the seven years prior to death, a person has transferred more than £3,000 that would ordinarily be considered exempt as part of normal expenditure out of income (7226), the amount must be notionally included in the value of a person's estate for the purpose of determining whether the personal representatives are excused from the requirement to deliver an inheritance tax account, even though the transfer itself may still qualify for the exemption. This is part of HMRC's risk management of the system.

Excepted terminations and chargeable events

Regulations, which apply for terminations or chargeable events arising under relevant property trusts (see 6940) made on or after 6 April 2007, have been made that mean the trustees do not need to deliver an IHT 100 in respect of those occasions of charge.

Legislation: IHTA 1984, s. 216, 217, 256, 257, 261; *Inheritance Tax (Delivery of Accounts) (Excepted Estates) Regulations* 2004 (SI 2004/2543), (as amended by SI 2005/3230, SI 2006/2141 and SI 2011/214); *Inheritance Tax (Delivery of Accounts) (Excepted Transfers and Excepted Terminations) Regulations* 2008 (SI 2008/605); *Inheritance Tax (Delivery of Accounts) (Excepted Transfers and Excepted Terminations) Regulations* 2008 (Excepted Settlements)

Other Material: SP 2/93, *Inheritance tax: the use of substitute forms*; *HMRC Inheritance Tax: Customer Guide* available on the HMRC website at www.hmrc.gov.uk/cto/customerguide/page1.htm

Tax Reporter: ¶693-800

7506 Time for delivering IHT accounts

An IHT account (see 7503) must be delivered:

- in the case of transfers on death, or PETs which become chargeable, within 12 months after the end of the month in which the death occurred or, if later, three months from the date on which the personal representatives first acted as such;

- in the case of beneficiaries or any person for whom any of the property is applied, within three months of first realising that he must deliver an account; and

- in any other case, within 12 months of the transfer or, if later, three months from the date on which he becomes liable for tax.

There is no requirement to notify HMRC nor to deliver an account on the making of a PET. However, a PET may turn out to be chargeable so records should be kept. Also, the rate at which such a PET is chargeable depends on chargeable transfers made within the seven years before. Therefore, records back to 14 years before the deceased's death may be required by HMRC.

If a transfer is reported late and the tax on a later transfer has been miscalculated as a result, any additional tax may be collected with the tax on the earlier transfer.

See also 7503 above for *Finance Act* 2004 changes.

Legislation: IHTA 1984, s. 216(6), 264

Other Material: *HMRC Inheritance Tax: Customer Guide* available on the HMRC website at www.hmrc.gov.uk/cto/customerguide/page1.htm

Tax Reporter: ¶693-800

7508 Power to require information

HMRC can call for IHT-relevant information, in not less than 30 days, from *any* person, whether or not he or she is liable to pay any IHT or deliver an IHT account. However, a barrister or solicitor cannot be required to give information without his client's consent, except that a solicitor may be obliged to disclose his client's name and address.

Additional powers

HMRC also have additional powers to call, in not less than 30 days, for documents, accounts or particulars from a more limited class of persons. The request can only be made for the purpose of inquiring into an account (see 7503), determining whether such an account is incorrect or incomplete or making a determination (see 7512).

The class of persons involved are those who have delivered or are liable to deliver an account (see 7503). Professional privilege in the conduct of any appeal is protected. There is a right of appeal.

Inspection powers for the purposes of valuation

From 1 April 2010, an HMRC officer or person accompanying the HMRC officer in assistance can enter and inspect premises and any other property on those premises in connection with checking a person's position with regard to inheritance tax. The valuation, measurement or determination of the premises or property must be 'reasonably required' by HMRC.

Legislation: IHTA 1984, s. 219, 219A, 219B; FA 2008, Sch. 36, para. 12A, 12B; FA 2009, s. 96 and Sch. 48, para. 5

Other Material: *HMRC Inheritance Tax: Customer Guide* available on the HMRC website at www.hmrc.gov.uk/cto/customerguide/page1.htm

Tax Reporter: ¶694-300; ¶694-450

7509 Information as to settlements for IHT

If a person, other than a barrister, is concerned with the making of a settlement in the course of a trade or profession carried on by him, he must, within three months of the making of the settlement, make a return to HMRC stating names and addresses of the settlor and trustees if he knows, or has reason to believe, that the settlor was domiciled in the UK and the trustees are not or will not be resident in the UK.

Note however that with effect from 6 April 2017, new rules will be introduced, initially in *Finance Act* 2016 but now to be included in Finance Bill 2017 (after consultation), to make individuals who have been UK resident for 15 out of the previous 20 years to be deemed to be UK domiciled for all tax purposes. Currently, deemed domicile only applies for IHT purposes with income tax on worldwide income being avoided provided the relevant individual pays an appropriate annual fee.

Legislation: IHTA 1984, s. 218

Other Material: *HMRC Inheritance Tax: Customer Guide* available on the HMRC website at www.hmrc.gov.uk/cto/customerguide/page1.htm

Tax Reporter: ¶694-300

7512 Determination of relevant IHT matters by HMRC

In relation to any transfer, HMRC may determine relevant IHT matters which are:

- the date of the transfer;
- the value transferred and the value of any property to which the value transferred is wholly or partly attributable;
- the transferor;
- the tax chargeable and the persons liable;
- the amount of any payment made in excess of the tax for which a person is liable and the rate at which tax or any repayment of tax overpaid carries interest; and
- any other matter which appears to be relevant to HMRC.

Legislation: IHTA 1984, s. 221

Tax Reporter: ¶693-100

Liability and incidence of inheritance tax

7530 Importance of liability and incidence for IHT

Usually, more than one person is liable for the payment of tax and payment can be recovered from any one of them. Liability depends upon the nature of the transfer (see 7533), though there are certain rules to protect those persons who become liable for payment because of their access to the property but upon whom the burden should not fall.

In the absence of any instructions in the will, IHTA 1984, s. 211 treats all IHT due as a testamentary expense payable out of the residue provided the property that generates the liability is UK property vesting in the personal representatives.

It therefore follows that IHT on the items set out below is not a testamentary expense. In all of these instances, provided the will does not specify, for example, that all IHT should be paid out of residue then any IHT (or any foreign equivalent, particularly on foreign property) will be payable by the person or persons in possession of the asset:

- foreign property;
- property that was comprised in a settlement immediately before death where the deceased had an interest in possession (essentially pre-22 March 2006 settlements);

- IHT payable on failed PETs;

- property that passes by survivorship or nomination (e.g. sums passing under a pension scheme);

- gifts 'donatio mortis causa';

- property that is deemed to be part of the estate, typically a gift with reservation; and

- works of art and similar assets, where IHT becomes payable as a result of a sale or the breach of an undertaking which previously deferred IHT.

The incidence of tax effectively refers to the person ultimately required to bear the burden of the tax (see 7539).

Legislation: IHTA 1984, s. 199

Tax Reporter: ¶694-800

7533   Persons liable for IHT

Subject to certain exceptions from liability and certain limitations on the extent of a person's liability for IHT (see 7536), the following rules apply. Generally, if more than one person is liable, each of them is liable for the whole amount.

1   Lifetime transfers

The person primarily liable is the transferor, unless it is agreed that the transferee will pay, in which case there will be no grossing up. The transferor's spouse or civil partner may also be liable if, after the transfer of value, all remaining assets are transferred to the spouse or civil partner. Then the spouse or civil partner would be liable for IHT to the extent of the value of the transfer to them. If payment of tax remains outstanding after the due date, the following persons are also liable:

- the transferee and any person the value of whose estate is increased by the transfer;

- any person who takes the property or a beneficial interest in possession in the property at any time after the transfer; and

- in the case of property transferred into a settlement any person for whose benefit any of the property or its income is applied.

2   Transfers within seven years before death

Where a PET becomes chargeable, or where additional tax becomes payable in respect of a chargeable transfer other than a PET, because of the transferor's death within seven years (see 6800), usually HMRC will look to the transferee to pay the tax due. However, the personal representatives of the transferor are also liable for the tax subject to the limitation on the extent of their liability discussed in 7536.

HMRC has given a limited assurance that where a lifetime transfer made by a deceased person in the seven years before death does not come to light until after a certificate of discharge has been obtained and the estate distributed, a personal representative who has made full and proper enquiries will not usually be pursued for IHT on the transfer.

3 Transfers on death

The persons liable for the tax are:

- the personal representatives in respect of any property which they have collected, or would have collected but for their neglect or default (subject to special rules for Scotland);
- the trustees of settled property which passes on death;
- any person in whom property becomes vested on death;
- where the property was comprised in a settlement, the beneficiaries.

Where a person is entitled to part only of the income of property as a result of death, he will be treated as entitled to an interest in the whole of the property. All IHT on the property passing on death can, therefore, be recovered from any of the beneficiaries.

Legislation: IHTA 1984, s. 199, 200, 203, 205, 209

Other Material: *HMRC Inheritance Tax: Customer Guide* available on the HMRC website at www.hmrc.gov.uk/cto/customerguide/page1.htm

Tax Reporter: ¶694-900.

7536 Exceptions from and limitations of IHT liability

Where the transferor or trustees of a settlement leave tax unpaid, then the other persons potentially liable in relation to that transfer (see 7533) become liable. Where the value transferred is partly attributable to the tax payable on it (i.e. the reduction in value of the person's estate is the value transferred plus the tax payable on it), then those other persons will be liable to no greater extent than they would have been had the value transferred been reduced by the tax remaining unpaid. Liability may also be restricted according to the nature of the person's interest therein as mentioned below.

> **Example**
>
> Ruby transfers £50,000 to Jacob. The tax for which Ruby is liable is £5,000 (assumed figure). Therefore Ruby's estate has been reduced by £55,000. If Ruby only pays £4,000 tax then Jacob's liability will be limited to the excess over £4,000 of tax which would have been payable on value transferred of £54,000 (value transferred £55,000 less tax unpaid £1,000).

1 Purchasers

A purchaser of property, and a person deriving title from him, will only be liable for IHT if the property is subject to a HMRC charge.

2 Personal representatives

Personal representatives are only liable for assets that they received or might have received but for their own neglect or default. Where the tax is attributable to property which was comprised in a settlement immediately before death and consists of land in the UK, a personal representative's liability is limited to so much of that property as is at any time available in his hands for the payment of tax, or might have been available but for his neglect or default.

Personal representatives are liable for any tax payable on the transferor's death within seven years of a PET and for any additional tax payable in respect of a chargeable transfer, other than a PET, within seven years of death only to the extent that there is no recourse against donees, trustees, beneficiaries or nominees or to the extent that tax remains unpaid 12 months after the end of the month of death.

Personal representatives are liable for the tax due on property which is included in the deceased's estate because it was property which the deceased had transferred subject to a reservation (see 6785), to the extent that the tax remains unpaid 12 months after the end of the month of death.

Personal representatives may be liable in respect of pension rights, etc.

3 Trustees

Trustees are only liable to the extent of property that they received or disposed of, or that they have become liable to account for to the persons beneficially entitled thereto, and any other property available in their hands for the payment of tax or property that might have been so available but for their neglect or default. Trustees of pension schemes are not liable in respect of pensions, annuity or death benefits.

4   Life tenants and beneficiaries with an interest in property

A beneficiary is only liable to the extent of any property in which he has a beneficial interest.

5   Beneficiaries with no interest in settled property

Beneficiaries of settled property are only liable to the extent of the amount of the property or income which is applied for their benefit.

6   Designated property

Where a transfer is of designated property, such as a work of art, the person that is liable is determined according to the nature of the event which breaches the conditions (see 7346ff.); generally, it is the trustee, the person that would be entitled to receive the proceeds of sale or the person for whose benefit the property is disposed of.

Legislation: IHTA 1984, s. 204, 207, 210

Other Material: *HMRC Inheritance Tax: Customer Guide* available on the HMRC website at www.hmrc.gov.uk/cto/customerguide/page1.htm

Tax Reporter: ¶695-400

7539   Incidence of IHT

The person liable to pay any IHT due is not always the person out of whose property it should be borne (see 7530). The person liable may apply to HMRC for a certificate showing the tax he has paid so as to be able to claim a refund from the ultimate payee, etc.

On a death, where a will contains no indications to the contrary, the tax attributable to non-settled property in the UK which vests in the executors will be treated as a testamentary expense, coming out of the estate as a whole.

If a person could have paid the tax by instalments (see 7596) and is entitled to recover that tax from another person, then that other person is entitled to refund the tax also by instalments.

Where a person, other than a transferor or the spouse of a transferor, is liable for IHT attributable to the value of any property he can raise the amount of tax by selling, mortgaging or creating a terminable charge on that property whether or not that property is vested in him; where a person has a limited interest in any property, and pays IHT on that property, he will be entitled to a charge on that property.

Inheritance tax on settled property may be paid out of any property comprised in the settlement and held on the same trusts.

An application may be made by the person paying the tax (if that person is not ultimately liable) for a certificate specifying the tax paid and the debts and encumbrances allowed in valuing the property. The certificate is conclusive between the person ultimately liable and the person who paid. Inheritance tax will be repaid to the person producing the certificate.

Inheritance tax here includes interest on the tax and costs properly incurred in respect of the tax.

Legislation: IHTA 1984, s. 211–214

Other Material: *HMRC Inheritance Tax: Customer Guide* available on the HMRC website at www.hmrc.gov.uk/cto/customerguide/page1.htm

Tax Reporter: ¶695-450

Payment and recovery of inheritance tax

7590 Introduction to payment and recovery of IHT

There are various rules for determining the time for payment of IHT (see 7593), though in certain circumstances, payment may be made by instalments (see 7596) or by way of the transfer of property to the Crown (see 7605).

HMRC have certain powers to recover unpaid tax (see 7611) with specific preference over other creditors in respect of the transferred property (see 7608). Interest may also be charged; conversely interest may be due to the taxpayer in respect of overpaid tax (see 7599).

Legislation: IHTA 1984, s. 226–244

Other Material: *HMRC Inheritance Tax: Customer Guide* available on the HMRC website at www.hmrc.gov.uk/cto/customerguide/page1.htm

Tax Reporter: ¶695-600

7593 Time for payment of IHT

Unless it can be paid in instalments (see 7596), IHT is due in accordance with the following rules that are being amended by *Finance Act* 2014.

For transfers involving trusts on or after 6 April 2014, the time limit for submitting the return and paying tax are aligned to six months after the end of the month of the chargeable transfer. For transfers before 6 April 2014, if the chargeable transfer was made between 5 April and 1 October in any year otherwise than on death, tax will be due at the end of April in the next year, where the transfer was made after 1 October the six month rule applied.

Personal representatives must pay the tax on delivering the account. If additional tax is due because the transferor dies within three years of making a lifetime chargeable transfer, tax will be due within six months of death.

The tax due on a PET which becomes chargeable because of the transferor's death within seven years should be paid six months after the end of the month in which death occurs.

Where foreign assets need to be transferred to the UK to meet the liabilities of the deceased, tax may be deferred for so long as they are unremittable.

From 5 November 2007, the provisions for paying IHT by cheque are now a bank approved payslip carrying an IHT reference must be sent with a cheque to the cashiers who are the Banking Team in Cumbernauld. To coincide with the move to Cumbernauld, HMRC IHT will no longer be issuing receipts as a matter of course. You can apply for an IHT reference and payslip online at www.hmrc.gov.uk/inheritancetax/online.htm.

Legislation: IHTA 1984, s. 226

Other Material: ESC F6, *Blocked foreign assets*, IHT and Trusts Newsletter December 2007

Tax Reporter: ¶695-600

7596 Payment of IHT by instalments

Notwithstanding the general rules for payment of IHT (see 7593), tax may be paid in instalments if the tax payable on the value transferred by a chargeable transfer is attributable to the value of the following:

(1) land;

(2) shares or securities of a company which gave the deceased control of that company before death;

(3) 'unquoted' (see 6572) shares or securities if the tax on those shares amounts to at least 20% of his liability on those chargeable transfers that may be paid by instalments, or if the payment of tax in one sum will, in HMRC's opinion, cause undue hardship;

(4) unquoted shares if those shares exceed £20,000 in value and either –

   (a) the nominal value of the shares is at least 10% of the nominal value of all the shares in the company at the time of death; or

   (b) the shares are ordinary shares and their nominal value is not less than 10% of the nominal value of all ordinary shares of the company at the time of death;

(5) a business or an interest in a business (otherwise than a business not carried on for gain) and the value here is the net value and is of the business as a whole and not individual assets; or

(6) timber.

The tax so attributable may be paid in ten equal yearly instalments, if the person paying the tax so elects by notice in writing to HMRC. The first instalment is due at the time the tax would have become due if it had not been for the election to pay by instalments (or six months after the transfer in the case of death or in relation to woodlands). Even if an election to pay by instalments has been made, all the tax may be paid in one sum with interest due to the date of payment if so desired.

If any of the property is sold, all or a proportionate part of the tax will become payable immediately unless the six-month period (see 7593) has not expired.

For both potentially exempt and chargeable transfers which are brought into charge or extra tax is payable because of the death of the transferor within seven years, the option is available only if the same property is owned by the transferee throughout the period or if business or agricultural property has been replaced. For the option to apply to unquoted shares (see above), they must have remained unquoted throughout the period.

Legislation: IHTA 1984, s. 227–229

Other Material: *HMRC Inheritance Tax: Customer Guide* available on the HMRC website at www.hmrc.gov.uk/cto/customerguide/page1.htm

Tax Reporter: ¶695-650

7599   Interest on overdue/overpaid IHT

1   On overdue tax

If payment of IHT is overdue, it carries interest from the due date.

2 On repayment of tax

Any repayment of an amount paid in excess of a liability for tax, or for interest on tax, will carry interest from the date on which the payment was made until the order for repayment is issued.

From 29 September 2009, interest charged on late payments of inheritance tax will be the Bank of England base rate plus 2.5% (currently 3%). From the same date, the interest rate on overpayments is the Bank of England rate minus one, subject to a minimum rate of 0.5% on repayments. For rates of interest, see *Hardman's Tax Rates and Tables* 6-850.

3 On payment by instalments

Where the tax payable on the value transferred by a chargeable transfer is payable by instalments, then interest on the unpaid portion of the tax will be added to each instalment and paid accordingly. This does not apply to dealers in land, buildings or securities, etc. unless the business is that of a market maker on The Stock Exchange (or a discount house) and is carried on in the UK, or unless that business is to act as a holding company for a company or companies whose business is not one of dealing. Market makers on the merged London International Financial Futures and Options Exchange (LIFFE) also fall within the exclusion from the above restriction.

4 Interest-free instalments

Where the tax is attributable to the value of any shares, securities, business or interest in a business, or to the value treated as reduced in agricultural relief (see 7292) or to timber, it will, for the purposes of any interest to be added to each instalment, be treated as carrying interest from the date at which the instalment is payable.

This means that if each instalment is paid as it becomes due it will not carry interest. This will not apply to shares or securities of a company whose business consists wholly or mainly of dealing in securities, etc. land or buildings, or making or holding investments, unless its business is that of a holding company of one or more companies whose business is not dealing in securities, etc. or unless it is a market maker or discount house and its business is carried on in the UK.

Legislation: IHTA 1984, s. 233–236; *Taxes (Interest Rate) Regulations* 1989 (SI 1989/1297); *Inheritance Tax (Market Makers) Regulations* 1992 (SI 1992/3181) (as amended by SI 2001/3629)

Cases: *Richardson v R & C Commrs* (2009) Sp C 730

Other Material: *HMRC Inheritance Tax: Customer Guide* available on the HMRC website at www.hmrc.gov.uk/cto/customerguide/page1.htm

Tax Reporter: ¶695-900

7605   Acceptance of property in satisfaction of tax

HMRC may accept certain types of property in satisfaction of tax. These include:

(1) land;

(2) objects which are, or have been, kept in a building if the building:

    (a) has been accepted in payment or part payment of tax or estate duty;

    (b) belongs to Her Majesty in right of the Crown or of the Duchy of Lancaster, or belongs to the Duchy of Cornwall, or belongs to a government department, or is held for the purposes of a government department;

    (c) is one of which the Secretary of State is guardian under the *Ancient Monuments and Archaeological Areas Act* 1979; or

    (d) belongs to any body specified at 7195;

    (in all such cases it must appear desirable to the Secretary of State that the objects should remain associated with the building);

(3) works of art, etc. (works by living artists have been accepted).

HMRC may waive interest charges where property is accepted in satisfaction of tax at a valuation date earlier than that on which the property is actually accepted.

The basis for negotiations is set out in a statement of practice.

Property otherwise used to pay tax

A person with the power to sell property to raise money to pay tax or interest may, instead, agree that the property be accepted in lieu of tax, as described above.

Where an administration action is pending as regards property to which a disposition relates, the court may provide that it should be used in payment of outstanding tax thereon.

Legislation: IHTA 1984, s. 230–232, 233(1A)

Other Material: SP 6/87, *Acceptance of property in lieu of inheritance tax, capital transfer tax and estate duty*, Capital Taxation and the National

Heritage guidance (replacing R 67: National Heritage booklet: 'Capital Taxation and the National Heritage') published 2011

Tax Reporter: ¶696-050

7608 HMRC charge for unpaid IHT

Where IHT or interest remains unpaid, a protective charge will be imposed for the amount unpaid on any property to which the tax is attributable, or on any property comprised in a settlement. However, the charge will be subject to any encumbrance which is allowable as a deduction when valuing the property for tax.

Where the chargeable transfer is made on death, any personal or movable property of the deceased will be exempt from the charge. However, for deaths occurring after 8 March 1999, the charge can include leasehold interests. Any outstanding tax, charged after that date, in respect of assets previously benefiting from relief for heritage assets has also been brought within the charge.

Heritable property in Scotland is not subject to the charge.

A disposition of property subject to a HMRC charge will take effect subject to that charge. However, if the charge was not registered or protected by a notice in the case of land, or the purchaser had no notice in the case of movables, or a certificate of discharge had been given in the case of any property, then that property will no longer be subject to the charge, but any property representing it will be subject to the charge. Where property is disposed of and it does not cease to be subject to the charge, it will cease to be subject to the charge within six years from the later of the date when the tax becomes due or the date on which a full and proper account of the property was first delivered to HMRC.

Where property has been transferred by a PET which proves to be a chargeable transfer and is sold to a purchaser before the transferor's death, it is not subject to the charge, but any property representing it (e.g. the sale proceeds, or anything bought with them) is subject to the charge. Further, the charge applies to property which has been disposed of before the transferor's death otherwise than to a purchaser.

Legislation: FA 1999, s. 107; IHTA 1984, s. 237, 238

Tax Reporter: ¶695-950

7611 Recovery of unpaid IHT

As announced in the Pre-Budget Report 2009, HMRC will now normally require payment of tax even though a case may be under further appeal.

This has effect in relation to all decisions made by the Tribunals or Courts on or after 1 April 2010. Thus, on an appeal to the Upper Tribunal, the tax in dispute must be paid. If the appellant is successful, the amount will be repaid.

HMRC have stated, however, that they will not enforce payment in cases where an agreement not to do so had been made with the appellant before 9 December 2009. Also, HMRC will not enforce payment in cases where to do so would be likely to drive the taxpayer into liquidation or bankruptcy.

Where there is a judgment in favour of a taxpayer, HMRC must repay overpaid tax, even if that judgment is subject to appeal.

Where HMRC accept the payment of tax in full satisfaction, no proceedings can be brought for the recovery of any additional tax after the expiration of six years beginning with the later of the following dates, namely:

- the date on which the payment (or in the case of tax paid by instalments the last payment) was made and accepted; and

- the date on which the tax or the last instalment became due.

On the expiration of this period, any liability for the additional tax and any charge for that tax will be extinguished. However, if there is fraud, wilful default or neglect the date will start from the discovery of that fraud, wilful default or neglect by HMRC. Tax miscalculated as a result of the failure to report an earlier transfer on a timely basis can be recovered as if it related to the earlier transfer (see 7506).

In Scotland, tax and interest on tax may, without prejudice to any other remedy, and if the amount of the tax and interest does not exceed the sum for the time being specified in the *Sheriff Courts (Scotland) Act* 1971, s. 35(1)(a), be sued for and recovered in the sheriff court.

An authorised officer of the Board may address the court in any sheriff court proceedings for the recovery of tax or interest on tax.

In proceedings for recovery, a certificate by an officer of the Board that the tax or interest is due, or that, to the best of his knowledge and belief, it has not been paid, is sufficient evidence that the sum is due or unpaid as appropriate.

Where too little tax has been paid, the amount underpaid will be payable with interest even if the amount paid was stated in a notice of determination, but subject to the six-year limitation rule set out above.

Where too much tax has been paid, HMRC must repay the excess, again subject to the six-year limitation rule set out above.

Time-limit for fraud

In any case of fraud, wilful default or neglect by a person liable for the tax or the person who is the settlor in relation to a settlement, the time-limit for bringing proceedings for recovery of additional tax is six years from the date when the fraud, etc. comes to HMRC's knowledge.

Finance Act 2009 introduced legislation to align the time limits for changing the amount of tax due by assessment to four years. Time limits for taxpayers' claims are also aligned at four years. The new time limits for making IHT assessments and claims came into force on 1 April 2011.

With effect from 1 April 2011, proceedings in a case involving loss of tax where the loss of tax has been careless may be brought within six years from the later of:

(1) the date on which the payment (or in the case of tax paid by instalments, the last payment) was made and accepted; and

(2) the date on which the tax or the last instalment became due.

Where the loss of tax has been brought about deliberately, proceedings may be brought within 20 years from the later of the dates in (1) and (2) above.

Transitional provisions provide that, where:

(1) the chargeable transfer took place before 31 March 2011; and

(2) a loss of tax is brought about deliberately,

the period within which proceedings may be brought is the earliest of six years beginning when the deliberate conduct comes to HMRC's knowledge, or 20 years from (1) or (2) above.

A new subsection applies to any case where too little tax has been paid, provided that case does not involve a loss of tax brought about deliberately. Where this subsection applies:

(1) no proceedings are to be brought for the recovery of tax after the end of the period of 20 years beginning with the date on which the chargeable transfer was made; and

(2) at the end of that period any liability for the tax and any Inland Revenue Charge for that tax is extinguished.

From 1 April 2011, if tax has been overpaid the Board will repay the excess tax paid (with interest, if appropriate) if the claim for repayment is made within four years of the date of the last payment of tax.

With effect from 1 April 2011, a new section applies where:

(1) information is provided to HMRC;

(2) the person who provided the information, or the person on whose behalf the information was provided, discovers some time later that the information was inaccurate; and

(3) that person fails to take reasonable steps to inform HMRC.

Any loss of tax brought about by the inaccuracy is to be treated as having been brought about carelessly by that person.

Legislation: IHTA 1984, s. 240–244, FA 2009, s. 99 and Sch. 51, para. 11, the *Finance Act 2009, Sch. 51 (Time Limits for Assessments, Claims, etc.) (Appointed Days and Transitional Provisions) Order* 2010 (SI 2010/867)

Tax Reporter: ¶696-400 and ¶696-600

7617 Certificates of discharge

A person liable for tax may apply for a certificate of discharge (IHT 30) which will be granted if the tax has been paid, or HMRC are satisfied that it will be paid. Such a certificate need not be issued unless the transfer is on death. Where a PET becomes chargeable because of the donor's death within seven years, a certificate need not be issued until two years after the death. The certificate will discharge the property from any HMRC charge or all persons from any further claim for the tax, unless there is fraud or failure to disclose material facts.

Legislation: IHTA 1984, s. 239

Other Material: www.hmrc.gov.uk/cto/forms5.htm

Tax Reporter: ¶696-450

Penalties

7620 Incorrect returns of inheritance tax

FA 2008 extended the penalty provisions in FA 2007 which created a single penalty regime to incorrect returns of inheritance tax and all other taxes. The legislation covers errors for periods commencing on or after 1 April 2009 where documents are filed on or after 1 April 2010. Penalties are based on taxpayer behaviour. So there are four categories of taxpayer behaviour: mistake, careless behaviour, deliberate understatement and deliberate understatement with concealment. There is no penalty where a taxpayer makes a genuine mistake, but persuading HMRC where the borderline between a genuine mistake and careless behaviour is may be a difficult boundary to define as may the borderline in the other categories set out below. There will be a maximum penalty of:

- 30% for careless behaviour (defined as failure to take reasonable care);
- 70% for a deliberate understatement; and
- 100% for a deliberate understatement with concealment.

In considering the penalty position with regard to careless, deliberate or deliberate and concealed, HMRC will consider whether the disclosure of an inaccuracy was prompted or unprompted. An unprompted disclosure means that the person has no reason to believe that HMRC IHT have discovered or are about to discover the failure to pay the required contributions. Prompted disclosure is likely to apply in all other cases.

The table below sets out the maximum reductions that can apply to each level of penalty for a prompted or unprompted disclosure. The reduction can never reduce the penalty below a statutory minimum so once the error becomes deliberate there will always be a charge.

Type of behaviour	Statutory maximum penalty	Statutory minimum penalty with unprompted disclosure	Statutory minimum penalty with prompted disclosure
Careless	30%	0%	15%
Deliberate but not concealed	70%	20%	35%
Deliberate and concealed	100%	30%	50%

The current regime also contains a provision that allows a tax-geared penalty to be charged where an inaccuracy in the liable person's document was attributable to another person. This is particularly relevant to IHT, where the personal representatives will inevitably be relying on other people to provide them with information about the deceased's estate.

Where it can be shown that the other person deliberately withheld information or supplied false information to the liable person, with the intention that the IHT account or return would contain an inaccuracy, a penalty may be charged on that other person. But that will not necessarily mean that the personal representatives themselves may not also be chargeable to a penalty. If the withheld or false information gave rise to inconsistencies in the information they had received about the estate and they did not question those inconsistencies, the liable person might still be charged a penalty for failing to take reasonable care as well.

The penalties can also apply if HMRC misinterpret the information provided and under assess or repay too much tax if the taxpayer does not immediately seek to correct any HMRC error.

It is understood that where an incorrect claim for transferable nil-rate band from one spouse to another is made that HMRC will impose a significant penalty on the estate which is likely to be at a level in excess of the penalties indicated in 7625. Remember that before 21 March 1972, there was no tax free transfers between spouses so any transfers used up, what in modern terms, was a modest nil-rate band so firm evidence will be required to support any claim where the first death was before that date. Even in periods where there were tax free transfers between spouses the extent of any nil-rate band must be adequately established to confirm the claim and, as a minimum, provide evidence to support the claim made and defend any penalty impositions. The case of *Hutchings* [2015] TC 04221 is the first case involving FA 2007, Sch. 24, para. 1A, where a penalty was imposed on a beneficiary for failing to disclose details of a gift to executors, resulting in tax being underpaid. The court had to decide if Hutchings had caused the inaccuracy in the documents supplied to HMRC by the executors. Hutchings received a lifetime gift of a Swiss Bank account, amounting to approximately £443,000, from his father only seven months before father's death but did not disclose this to the executors when they asked for details of lifetime gifts. In consequence, the executors claimed a full nil rate band causing an underpayment of IHT. In addition, Hutchings should have paid IHT on the failed PET because the gift exceeded the available nil rate band. Hutchings was assessed to a tax-geared penalty because disclosure was only made when the taxpayer knew that HMRC had information as to the bank account.

Legislation: FA 2008, Sch. 40; FA 2007, Sch. 24

Case: *Hutchings* [2015] TC 04221

Other Material: IHT and Trusts Newsletter April 2009

Tax Reporter: ¶696-700

7625   Failure to deliver an account

Failure to deliver an account attracts a penalty of £100, plus a further penalty not exceeding £60 per day after the day on which the failure is declared by a court or by the tribunal until the account is delivered. Where six months have elapsed since the date when the account ought to have been delivered, and the taxpayer still has not delivered the account at the end of that six-month period, but proceedings in which the failure could be declared have not been commenced (so that the daily penalty cannot be charged), a further penalty of £100 may be imposed. If, however, the tax due is less than any penalties due (i.e. the two penalties of £100), these penalties are limited to the amount of the tax. For other possible mitigations, see below.

Inheritance tax

Where 12 months have passed since the account ought to have been delivered, the taxpayer will be liable to a penalty of an amount not exceeding £3,000.

Finance Act 2009 has introduced a new penalty regime from a date to be appointed. The new regime will treat late filing and late payment (see below) separately. Failure to deliver an account will attract a penalty of £100. Where a penalty has been assessed as payable, and failure continues after three months beginning with the penalty date, a penalty of £10 for each day is charged whilst the failure continues during the period of 90 days beginning with the date specified in the penalty notice given by HMRC. If the failure to pay the penalty continues after the end of the period of six months beginning with the penalty date, then there is a further penalty of 5% of any liability to tax which would have been shown in the return in question or £300, whichever is the greater.

Where the failure to pay the penalty continues after the end of the period of 12 months beginning with the penalty date, there will be a further penalty. That penalty will depend on whether the original inaccuracy was deliberate but not concealed, in which case the penalty will be the greater of 70% of any liability to tax which would have been shown in the return in question, and £300. Where the original inaccuracy was deliberate and concealed then the further penalty will be the greater of 100% of any liability to tax which would have been shown in the return in question and £300. In all other cases, there is a further penalty of the greater of 5% of any liability to tax which would have been shown in the return in question and £300.

A revised penalty regime for the late payment of IHT was introduced by *Finance Act* 2009 from a date to be appointed. A taxpayer is liable to pay a penalty of 5% of the unpaid tax. If this is still unpaid at the end of five months beginning with the penalty date then the taxpayer is liable to a penalty of 5% of that amount. Further, if any of that tax is still unpaid after the end of 11 months beginning with the penalty date, a further 5% is payable.

HMRC IHT may reduce a penalty in special circumstances. However, the inability to pay or the existence of an overpayment will not be classed as special circumstances.

Legislation: IHTA 1984, s. 216, 217, 245; FA 2009, Sch. 55, 56

Tax Reporter: ¶696-700

7630 Failure to make a return disclosing an overseas trust

Failure to provide information as to the making of an overseas trust attracts a penalty not exceeding £300, plus a further penalty not exceeding £60 per day after the day on which the failure is declared by a court or by the tribunal until the return is made.

Legislation: IHTA 1984, s. 218, 245A(1)

Tax Reporter: ¶696-700

7635 Failure to provide information or produce documents

Failure to comply with a notice to provide information attracts a penalty not exceeding £300, plus a further penalty not exceeding £60 per day after the day on which the failure is declared by a court or by the tribunal until the return is made.

Failure to comply with a notice to produce documents (or make originals available for inspection) attracts a penalty not exceeding £50, plus a further penalty not exceeding £30 per day after the day on which the failure is declared by a court or the tribunal until the return is made.

Legislation: IHTA 1984, s. 219, 219A, 245A(2) and (3)

Tax Reporter: ¶696-700

7640 Mitigating provisions

There are certain mitigating provisions which apply to penalties which may be imposed under s. 245 or s. 245A. First, the daily penalty of up to £60 or £30 per day (as the case may be) is not due if the account is delivered before commencement of proceedings in which the failure could be declared. Second, a person who has a reasonable excuse for the failure in question is not liable for a penalty unless the failure continues after the excuse has ceased.

Legislation: IHTA 1984, s. 245(6), (7), 245A(4), (5)

Tax Reporter: ¶696-700

7645 Provision of incorrect information

Any person not liable for tax on the value transferred by a chargeable transfer who fraudulently or negligently furnishes or produces to the Board any incorrect account, information or document in connection with the transfer shall be liable to a penalty not exceeding £3,000.

Further, any person who assists in or induces the delivery, furnishing or production of any account, information or document which he knows is incorrect is liable to a penalty not exceeding £3,000.

If after any information or document has been furnished or produced by any person without fraud or negligence it comes to his notice that it was incorrect in any material respect, then it is treated as negligently furnished or produced unless the error is remedied without unreasonable delay.

Hutchings is the first case involving FA 2007, Sch. 24, para. 1A, where a beneficiary has been subject to penalty for failing to disclose details of a gift they had received to executors, resulting in tax being underpaid. In this case, the issue for the court was whether the actions or inactions of Hutchings had caused the inaccuracy in the documents supplied to HMRC by the executors that gave rise to the underpayment of tax. Hutchings received a lifetime gift of a Swiss bank account from his father of approximately £443,000 some seven months before the father's death but did not disclose this to the executors when they asked for details of lifetime gifts. The consequence was that a full nil rate band was claimed by the executors resulting in an underpayment of IHT on the estate. In addition, Hutchings should also have paid some IHT on the failed PET (which would otherwise have received the benefit of the NRB) because the gift exceeded the available nil rate band. Hutchings was assessed to a tax-geared penalty of £87,533.80. While the case report suggests attempts to deflect blame it indicates that disclosure was only made when the taxpayer knew that HMRC had received information about the bank account by way of an anonymous tip off.

See also the case of *Tager (Personal Representatives of the Estate of Tager (deceased)) v R & C Commrs* for additional confirmation that substantial penalties can be imposed if inaccurate information is supplied to HMRC.

Legislation: IHTA 1984, s. 247(3), (4); FA 2007, Sch. 24, para. 1A

Case: *Cairns (personal representative of Webb, deceased)* (2009) TC 00008; *Hutchings* [2015] TC 04221; *R & C Commrs v Tager (Personal Representatives of the Estate of Tager (deceased))* [2015] BTC 509

Tax Reporter: ¶696-750

7650 Criminal proceedings

It is open to the Board to initiate criminal proceedings instead of, or in addition to, proceedings under the revenue legislation. There have been prosecutions for fraud, although these are unusual and would generally occur in respect of large-scale evasion or persistent non-cooperation. In such cases it is, of course, possible that an offender would be sentenced to imprisonment.

Tax Reporter: ¶696-850

VAT

- Value added tax (VAT) is an indirect tax, charged on taxable supplies of goods and services made in the course of business in the UK, on imports of goods into the UK from outside the EC, and on the acquisition of goods from elsewhere in the EC. VAT is also due on some imports of services.

- The tax is borne by the final consumer and exempt and partially exempt traders within the supply chain.

- Traders must keep records of input and output tax and complete periodic VAT returns (see 8430ff.).

- VAT is primarily a tax on supplies (see 7758ff.).

- VAT is only due if the supply is made by a taxable person in the course of furtherance of his business (see 7792ff.).

- A supply may be a supply of goods or a supply of services (see 7804ff.).

- UK VAT is charge on supplies that are deemed to occur in the UK (see 7816ff.).

- The time of supply (or tax point) is important in that it determines the period for which the supplier must account for tax and therefore the date by which it must be paid over to HMRC (see 7830ff.).

- Importation of goods from outside the EC constitutes a chargeable event and triggers liability to both customs duties and import VAT (see 7880ff.).

- Special rules apply to acquisitions of goods from elsewhere in the EC (see 7972).

- Traders are obliged to account for VAT on taxable supplies and they can recover VAT on supplies made to them according to the normal VAT recovery rules (see 8034ff.).

- A business making both taxable and exempt supplies can, in principle, only recover input tax that relates to the making of the taxable supplies (see 8110ff.).

- Supplies may be taxable or exempt (see 8210ff.).

- Taxable supplies may be taxable at the standard rate, the reduced rate or the zero rate (see 8210 and 8216).

- Exempt supplies fall in to one of 15 groups (see 8228ff.).

- Businesses making taxable supplies in the UK above the registration limit are normally obliged to register with HM Revenue and Customs (HMRC) (see 8250ff.).

- A number of special VAT schemes exist, including retail schemes, flat-rate scheme for farmers, the tour operators' margin scheme, second-hand goods schemes and special schemes for small businesses (see 8365 and 8410).

- VAT returns must be submitted to HMRC by the end of the month following the period to which it relates and any tax due paid by the same date (see 8430ff.).

- A penalty regime provides sanction against offences such as late submission of returns and payments (see 8480ff.).

Outline of value added tax

7700   Application of VAT

Value added tax (VAT) was introduced in the UK on 1 April 1973 shortly after the UK joined what was then the European Economic Community (EEC), now the European Community (EC) or European Union (EU). VAT is the common value added tax of the EC.

Value added tax is charged on taxable supplies of goods and services made in the UK, where these are made in the course of business (see 7798ff.). It is also charged on imports of goods into the UK from outside the EC, on the acquisition of goods from elsewhere in the EC and on many imports of services (see 7880ff. and 7972ff.).

Businesses which make taxable supplies above the registration limit are obliged to register with HM Revenue and Customs (HMRC), the government department which controls the tax (see 8250ff.). Registered businesses are often referred to as 'traders' by HMRC, and more recently as 'customers', although the term 'trader' includes businesses that would not generally be regarded as trades (e.g. a practising solicitor is normally regarded as being engaged in a profession rather than a trade, but in VAT terms would be called a trader).

Other Material: Notice 700, *The VAT guide*

Indirect Tax Reporter: ¶1-100

7706   VAT records and returns

Each registered trader is obliged to keep a record of the supplies which he makes in the course of any business carried on by him, and of the tax due on them. He must also keep a record of tax incurred on supplies to him, and on his imports and acquisitions.

He must then complete a periodical VAT return, and submit this to HMRC with a remittance for any tax due for the period. Returns are normally due quarterly, although some traders complete monthly or annual returns.

The trader must enter on his VAT return the totals of supplies made by him and of supplies (and imports and acquisitions) which he has obtained for the purposes of his business. He must also enter on it the total tax due on the supplies and acquisitions which he has made, and the amount suffered on supplies to him and on imports and acquisitions. He may set the tax incurred by him against the tax due on his own supplies. The tax which he is due to pay to HMRC is the difference between the two. If the tax due on his own supplies is less than the tax which he has suffered, he receives a repayment from HMRC.

Primary legislation requires records to be kept which enable a trader to make accurate returns.

Further details of accounting requirements are given at 8430ff.

Legislation: *Value Added Tax Regulations* 1995 (SI 1995/2518), Pt. V

Other Material: Notice 700, *The VAT guide*; Notice 700/21, *Keeping records and accounts* (April 2016 edn)

Indirect Tax Reporter: ¶4-620

7712   Exemption and partial exemption

Certain supplies are exempt from VAT, so no tax is charged on them. A trader who makes only exempt supplies cannot register for VAT, and so cannot obtain credit for input tax suffered on his business expenses. A trader who makes only taxable supplies can reclaim all of his input tax (except that suffered on certain purchases of motor cars, etc.).

Special rules are needed in the case of a trader who makes both taxable supplies and exempt supplies (referred to as a partially exempt trader), in order to secure a fair and reasonable attribution of input tax.

In principle, a partially exempt trader can reclaim in full any input tax suffered in relation to the making of taxable supplies, and cannot reclaim any input tax suffered in relation to the making of his exempt supplies. Input tax suffered on supplies used both for the purposes of his taxable supplies and for the purposes of his exempt supplies must be apportioned between the two activities, and only the part relating to the taxable supplies made can be reclaimed.

The initial input tax deduction for certain expenditure on land and buildings and on computer equipment must be reviewed by reference to the use of the assets over a review period of five or ten years (see 8182). This is the Capital Goods Scheme.

The detailed application of these general rules, and the different ways of apportioning input tax between the types of activity, is a complex area (see 8034ff.).

Other Material: Notice 706, *Partial Exemption (June 2011 edn)*

Indirect Tax Reporter: ¶3-130

7718   Review of the system for control and enforcement of VAT

Value added tax is administered by HM Revenue & Customs (HMRC). They have a headquarters in London, a VAT Central Unit in Southend, and local VAT offices throughout the UK. Large businesses will have dedicated officers and groups of officers to monitor their activities.

Traders making taxable supplies who are above the registration threshold, must normally register for VAT by submitting a form to one of the registration units. When this is processed the trader's details are entered on the register of taxable traders, and the VAT Central Unit at Southend will periodically issue VAT returns to the trader. Registration is mostly done online, through the HMRC website, although HMRC will accept paper applications forms.

The VAT returns, with the related tax, must be submitted to HMRC by the end of the month following the accounting period concerned and normally online from 2012; however, following appeals against the requirement to file online, the First-tier Tribunal (in the case of *L H Bishop Electric Company Ltd* [2013] TC 02910) ruled that the failure of the VAT Regulations 1995 to take account of a person's ability to comply on account of:

* age;
* disability;
* computer illiteracy (linked to age); or
* remoteness of location;

was a breach of the European Convention on Human Rights (ECHR). HMRC have consulted on this and is currently considering the responses.

The trader is responsible for completing his own VAT returns correctly (see 8454). Failure to submit returns (or any related payments) on time can expose the trader to a penalty (see 8480ff.).

Periodic checks are made on traders by officers from the local VAT office or from one of the large business groups (LBGs). These officers visit the trader's premises to inspect the VAT records to satisfy themselves that VAT is being accounted for correctly. Such visits are referred to as assurance visits (formerly, and still colloquially, control visits). The intervals between visits vary considerably, depending upon the size and type of business and the trader's own record of compliance (or non-compliance) with the VAT accounting requirements. Very large businesses are likely to have frequent control visits, and they will have their own 'customer relationship manager', while smaller businesses may be visited only at intervals of several years. Visits can also be triggered by changes of pattern becoming apparent from the VAT returns submitted by the trader.

If a visit reveals that the trader has underdeclared his VAT liabilities, an assessment will normally be issued to collect the tax. The trader may also become liable to pay interest and penalties in respect of the underdeclaration. Where underdeclarations arise because of dishonesty on the part of the trader, rather than because of errors, penalties may be due either under the civil law or under criminal law. In the latter case, a dishonest trader may also be imprisoned.

Legislation: VATA 1994, Pt. IV; FA 2007, Sch. 24

Other Material: Notice 989, *Visits by Customs and Excise officers*

Indirect Tax Reporter: ¶3-500

Chargeable events – VAT on supplies by the business

7740   Liability to VAT: general

As VAT is in principle a tax on supplies, this generally means that a person has to account for VAT when he makes supplies. There are other occasions when VAT becomes due (see 7880ff. and 7972ff.).

Legislation: VATA 1994, s. 1

7746   When VAT is chargeable

UK VAT is intended to be charged on the consumption of goods or of services within the UK, but is generally levied on the supplier of those goods or services rather than directly on the consumer. Because the tax is generally accounted for by suppliers, rather than the consumers who are ultimately intended to bear it, there are several occasions of charge. This is to prevent consumers from avoiding the tax by, for instance, obtaining taxable supplies from overseas suppliers.

The principal charge is on supplies of goods or of services made within the UK (including certain imports of services). The charge on imports of goods into the UK from outside the EC is covered at 7880ff. and the charge on acquisitions of goods from elsewhere in the EC is dealt with at 7972ff.

Some businesses may become liable to account for VAT on supplies which they are deemed to make to themselves (see 7766).

Legislation: VATA 1994, Pt. I

Case: *Hutchison 3G UK Ltd v C & E Commrs* (Case C-369/04) [2010] BVC 55

Other Material: Notice 700, *The VAT guide*

Indirect Tax Reporter: ¶1-100

7752   VAT on UK supplies

The main charge to VAT in the UK is on supplies made in the UK. As far as the law is concerned, this charging of VAT arises from a single section in the VAT Act and all of the other complexities of VAT flow from this one sentence. This particular provision is so important that it is well worth looking at the words used in the law. The charging provision concerned is VATA 1994, s. 4(1), and it reads as follows:

> 'VAT shall be charged on any supply of goods or services made in the United Kingdom, where it is a taxable supply made by a taxable person in the course or furtherance of any business carried on by him.'

Close examination of this provision reveals that there are five aspects to consider:

(1)   There must be a supply, either of goods or of services (see 7758ff. and 7804ff.).

(2)   The supply must be made in the UK rather than elsewhere.

(3)   The supply must be a taxable supply.

(4)   The supply must be made by a taxable person, rather than by some other kind of person (see 7792ff.).

(5)   The supply must be made in the course or furtherance of a business carried on by the taxable person who makes the supply.

Supplies are divided into taxable supplies and exempt supplies. Some 'supplies' are outside the scope of VAT (see 7786).

Taxable supplies are either:

- zero-rated (in VATA 1994, Sch. 8) supply (see 8222);

- reduced rate of 5% (in VATA 1994, Sch. 7A) (see 8210); or

- standard-rated (done by exception in the legislation, so there is no list of what is standard-rated).

Zero-rated supplies include:

- basic foodstuffs, but not luxuries (Group 1);

- construction and sale (or lease more than 21 years) of new dwellings (including accommodation with care extras (see HMRC Brief 47/11) and conversion of commercial to residential accommodation followed by a sale (or a lease of more than 21 years) (Group 5); and

- children's clothing (Group 16).

Reduced rate supplies include:

- work on certain residential properties (that have been empty for two years or more) (Group 7); and

- domestic fuel and power (Group 1).

Exempt supplies (see 8228) are those in Sch. 9 to VATA 1994 that are specifically exempted from the charge to VAT (but carry no general right of recovery (see 8110)) and include:

- property (Group 1);

- insurance (Group 2); and

- financial services (Group 5).

Legislation: VATA 1994, s. 4(1)

Other Material: Notice 700, *The VAT guide*

Indirect Tax Reporter: ¶10-000

Supply

7758   The meaning of supply

Primarily, VAT is a tax on supplies (see 7752).

The UK law does not give a precise definition of the term 'supply' but states that it includes all forms of supply. Things done for no consideration are not supplies, unless there is specific provision within the law to class them as supplies. Anything done for consideration constitutes a supply.

It is apparent from this that:

- anything which is done for a consideration is a supply for VAT purposes; and

- anything which is not done for a consideration is not a supply unless the law specifically states that it is a supply.

In fact, the law does specify that a transfer of the property in goods, or of their possession, constitutes a supply. It follows that, where goods are provided, a supply arises whether or not there is consideration; only services can be provided for no consideration without a supply arising.

There are other occasions when a supply is deemed to arise, e.g. deregistration and certain self-supplies (see 7762 and 7766).

Legislation: VATA 1994, s. 5(2)(a), (b), Sch. 4, para. 1

Other Material: Notice 700, *The VAT guide*

Indirect Tax Reporter: ¶10-000

7760 Consideration for VAT purposes

The term 'consideration' has long been used in UK law, particularly with reference to contract law. However, the UK law on VAT derives from EC law, and particularly the VAT Directive 2006/112 (this is the recast sixth directive on VAT). The UK courts are, therefore, obliged to construe the UK legislation so as to give effect to the directive.

Although 'consideration' is not defined in the VAT directive, a definition was given in Directive 67/228 (the second VAT directive) as follows:

> 'The expression 'consideration' means everything received in return for the supply of goods or the provision of services, including incidental expenses (packing, transport, insurance etc.) that is to say not only the cash amounts charged, but also, for example, the value of the goods received in exchange or, in the case of goods or services supplied by order of a public authority, the amount of the compensation received.'

In *Apple and Pear Development Council v C & E Commrs* (Case 102/86) (1988) 3 BVC 274, the House of Lords considered that the intended scope of VAT was set by the then sixth directive but that there was no clear authority in European law on the meaning of consideration, and reference was made to the European Court of Justice for guidance on this point. The House of Lords noted the definition of consideration given in the second directive, and presumed that the term had the same meaning when used in the sixth directive. The Advocate General also made reference to the second directive in analysing the meaning of consideration for VAT purposes. The European Court considered that there must be a direct link between the supply made and the consideration received if there is to be consideration in the VAT sense. It has also been held that consideration for VAT purposes must be capable of being expressed in money (*Staatssecretaris van Financiën v Coöperatieve Aardappelenbewaarplaats GA* [1981] ECR 445).

A good rule of thumb is to regard 'consideration' as meaning anything (not only money) provided in exchange for something else, where the one is conditional on the other.

Example

John is a window cleaner. He cleans Emma's windows for £5. He cleans George's windows on condition that George (who is a carpenter) repairs his ladder. He cleans Linda's windows free of charge, because Linda is unwell and John wants to help out. Linda is grateful for John's help and gives him a new sponge.

Clearly John cleaned Emma's windows for consideration, the fee of £5.

He cleaned George's windows for consideration too, the consideration being George's work on John's ladder. By the same token, George mended John's ladder for consideration in the form of John cleaning George's windows. Thus, there are two supplies for consideration in this instance, one by John and one by George.

John did not receive any consideration for cleaning Linda's windows. Although Linda gave him a sponge (and presumably regarded it as a quid pro quo for the cleaning of the windows), she was under no obligation to do this. The cleaning of the windows in this case was done freely, as was the giving of the sponge. Since John was providing services, rather than goods, and there was no consideration, his action did not amount to a supply for VAT purposes.

It should be noted that in practice, where something is done freely but a quid pro quo is received, it may often be difficult to prove that the one is not consideration for the other.

It is also interesting to note that in the above example, while John has not made a supply to Linda, Linda has made a supply to John in giving him the sponge, since the transfer of the property in goods (in this case, the sponge) is a supply. In practice it is likely that no VAT will be due, either because her supply is not made in the course of a business or because it falls into the exclusion for small business gifts. Both of these aspects are covered later in this section.

While the 'anything in exchange' concept gives a good rule of thumb, it cannot be regarded as a complete expression of the law. The exact meaning of consideration is not entirely clear, and continues to be a matter of debate. In one case it was held that the act of arranging promotional parties constituted additional consideration for the supply of cosmetic cream at a reduced price (*Naturally Yours Cosmetics Limited v C & E Commrs* (1988) 3 BVC 428). In another, the handing in of a voucher in exchange for goods was held not to form part of the consideration for the supply of those goods. The voucher was no more than evidence of entitlement to a discount (*Boots Co plc v C & E Commrs* (1990) 5 BVC 21).

The European Court of Justice has held that the payment of a grant by the EC to compensate a farmer who undertook to discontinue milk production did not amount to consideration for a supply, on the ground that VAT was intended to be a tax on consumption and, in these circumstances, there was no consumption by the EC, which was merely acting in the common interest (*Mohr v Finanzamt Bad Segeberg* (Case C-215/94) [1996] BVC 293). Similar treatment will apply to most government grants.

The main thing which the business manager who is not a VAT specialist needs to bear in mind is the potentially wide meaning of 'consideration'. It is often assumed that any VAT liability will be picked up by the ordinary accounting systems of the business. This may often be the case; however, it can be seen that transactions which might not ordinarily enter the accounting systems (as no invoice would be generated) can readily give rise to VAT liability. Managers need to be aware of 'hidden' consideration, and preferably to take account of it when projects are being planned.

Particular care needs to be taken where commercial terminology is used which conceals the true nature of what is happening. This applies particularly where marketing activities are carried on which involve offers of 'gifts' or 'prizes' which are not really free, but have to be earned in some way. Frequently, there is consideration for the provision of the 'gift' or 'prize', and this can affect the VAT position.

The 'anything in exchange' concept referred to above will provide a useful way of spotting potential supplies. As indicated, it should not be relied upon to produce an infallible answer in all cases. The best plan is to use it to spot transactions which might give problems, and to seek expert advice on borderline cases.

Another point worthy of note is that, while the receipt of money will often indicate that consideration is being received for a supply made, there are a number of occasions when money may be received without being consideration, and without there being a supply. A number of these are considered at 7776.

Legislation: The VAT Directive 2006/112; EC Directive 67/228 (the second directive); EC Directive 77/388 (the sixth directive)

Cases: *Staatssecretaris van Financiën v Coöperatieve Aardappelenbewaarplaats GA* [1981] ECR 445; *Naturally Yours Cosmetics Ltd v C & E Commrs* (1988) 3 BVC 428; *Apple and Pear Development Council v C & E Commrs* (Case 102/86) (1988) 3 BVC 274; *Mohr v Finanzamt Bad Segeberg* (Case C-215/94) [1996] BVC 293

Other Material: Notice 700, *The VAT guide*

Indirect Tax Reporter: ¶10-985

7762 Deemed supplies

The law specifically states that some transactions are to be treated as supplies for VAT purposes, whether or not there is consideration present. These are:

- the transfer or disposal of goods which are business assets (done under the directions of the person carrying on that business) so that they are no longer assets of the business. They may be excepted from this as small business gifts or gifts of industrial samples (see below). This includes, in the case of a sole trader business, the transfer of the goods to the sole proprietor in his personal capacity. However, there is no deemed supply unless the trader has been entitled to some input tax credit in respect of the goods;

- fuel for private use is also regarded as a deemed supply and if a trader recovers all of the input tax on fuel (both business and non-business element) then there is a deemed supply for the private element and output tax is due under the fuel scale charge tables. These are amended on 1 May each year (VATA 1994, s. 56 and 57) (note also the advisory fuel rates for employers which have been amended from 1 March 2014);

- the use for non-business purposes of goods which are business assets and in respect of which input tax has previously been recovered. In the case of a sole trader business, this includes use for the personal purposes of the sole proprietor; and

- when a person ceases to be registered for VAT, any goods remaining on hand are deemed to be supplied at that point unless it can be shown that tax has not been reclaimed on their purchase, or that the total tax involved is below £1,000.

It should be noted that, in applying these rules, land is specifically treated as being goods. This becomes especially important when the option for taxation has been exercised (see 8230).

The gift or private use of goods only gives rise to a supply if some part of the VAT on the goods concerned (or component parts) was deductible by the supplier (or some predecessor in the case of goods obtained under a transfer of a going concern).

Exceptions to deemed supply on gift of goods

(1)   Small gifts

Although there is normally a supply of goods where business assets are transferred so as no longer to form part of the assets of the business, this does not apply if a gift is made in the course of the business and the cost of the goods to the business does not exceed £50. If the gift forms part of a series of gifts to the same person, there is no supply unless the cumulative cost of the gifts in a 12-month period exceeds £50.

Where gift goods have been obtained under a transfer of a going concern, the cost for this purpose is the cost to the transferor (or, in the case of a series of such transfers, the first transferor), not the price attributed to them under the transfer.

It should be noted that this relief only applies to genuine gifts. As indicated earlier, there are many occasions where items are described as gifts but, in fact, they are provided in return for consideration.

(2)   Gifts of samples

A gift of a single sample is not treated as a supply. Up to 19 July 2011, repeated samples would be a supply. However, following the EMI case at the ECJ, from 19 July 2011, repeated samples will not be within the deemed supply rules.

Legislation: VATA 1994, Sch. 4, para. 5(2), (3); *Value Added Tax (Refund of Tax) Order* 2006 (SI 2006/1793); EC VAT Directive 2006/112

Other Material: Notice 700/7 (incorporates the old Notice 700/35 – from May 2012), *Business gifts and samples*

Indirect Tax Reporter: ¶10-988

7764   Supplies by a receiver

There is another occasion when a person can be treated as making a supply, without actually making a supply. If a receiver is appointed over assets of a business, then any supplies of goods made by the receiver are treated as if they had been made by the person carrying on the business. In this case, the receiver is liable to account directly to HMRC for the tax due, although the VAT continues to be shown on the trader's return.

This is in contrast to the position where a receiver is appointed over the whole of a company's assets. In this case, the company is regarded as having become incapacitated, and it is for the receiver to make returns and payments of tax currently due on behalf of the company.

Legislation: VATA 1994, Sch. 4, para. 7; *Value Added Tax Regulations* 1995 (SI 1995/2518), reg. 9, 27, 30

Other Material: Notice 700, *The VAT guide*

7766 Self-supplies

In some circumstances, a business can be treated as making supplies to itself. This arises in certain cases specified in statutory instruments, in certain cases relating to land, and in other instances covered below. In these cases, the business must account for tax on the self-supply, but can then treat it as input tax as if the supply had been obtained from another trader. This might seem self-defeating, in that the tax would simply appear on both sides of the VAT return and cancel out, but the effect would be felt by partially exempt businesses that can't recover all the input tax charged to it.

(1) Self-supply of motor car

VAT suffered on the purchase of a motor car cannot be recovered if the car is to be put to any non-business use (such as private mileage, including home to work travel by an employee). Input tax on car purchase is recoverable if the car is to be used wholly for business purposes. However, if VAT is recovered on this basis and the car is subsequently put to non-business use, a self-supply arises.

(2) 'Self-supply' of residential or charitable building (a change of use charge)

A charge to VAT occurs when zero-rating under VATA 1994, Sch. 8, Grp. 5 has been obtained on the purchase or construction of a building for relevant residential or charitable use and, within ten years, the building is put to a non-qualifying use. These provisions are in VATA 1994, Sch. 10, para. 36.

(3) Self-supply of construction services

A self-supply arises if certain works of construction are carried out by a business without using outside contractors. If the value of the works is £100,000 or more, and they would have been positive-rated if bought in, a self-supply arises.

(4) Self-supply on acquisition of business by group

A self-supply arises where a business is transferred, as a going concern, to a VAT group of companies. This is intended to counter certain planning techniques which were previously available. The relevant provisions are in VATA 1994, s. 44.

If the group is partially exempt either during the prescribed accounting period (i.e. VAT return period) in which the supply takes place, or in the 'longer period' (see 8110ff.) which includes it, then a self-supply takes place. However, there is no self-supply if it can be shown that all of the assets transferred were acquired by the transferor more than three years before the transfer.

Legislation: VATA 1994, Sch. 10, para. 36; *Value Added Tax (Self-supply of Construction Services) Order* 1989 (SI 1989/472); *Value Added Tax (Cars) Order* 1992 (SI 1992/3122), art. 5

Indirect Tax Reporter: ¶12-795

7768   Reverse charge supplies

In some instances where a supply is made, it is treated as if it had been made by the customer rather than by the person who made the supply (the 'reverse charge'). This is relevant where the supply is made across an international boundary (see 7820).

The effect is that the customer (if registrable for VAT somewhere in the EC and this includes the UK) must account for output tax on the supply and can treat the same amount as potentially recoverable input tax. The input tax may, or may not, be deductible in full depending on the use to which the supplies are put (i.e. the normal VAT rules apply).

The reverse charge has become particularly important since 1 January 2010 under the new VAT package (see 7820).

Reverse charge supplies also count when considering whether the taxable turnover of the person carrying on the business exceeds the VAT turnover limits, making registration necessary (see 7792ff.).

See also 8492 in respect of the introduction of reverse charge accounting in relation to the supply of certain goods of a kind used in missing trader intra-Community fraud (MTIC).

Further to EU Directive 2013/43/EU introducing the Reverse Charge Mechanism, HMRC have confirmed that the UK will continue to apply the reverse charge for mobile telephones, computer chips and emissions allowances in their current forms. The Reverse Charge Mechanism allows these measures to run until the end of 2018.

Legislation: VATA 1994, s. 8, s. 7A and Sch. 4A

Other material: HMRC Brief 36/13

Indirect Tax Reporter: ¶13-350

7770 Imports and acquisitions

Value added tax arises, not only on supplies, but also on the importation of goods from outside the EC, and on their acquisition from elsewhere in the EC. These chargeable events are covered at 7880ff. and 7972ff.

Indirect Tax Reporter: ¶13-470

Non-supplies (outside the scope supplies)

7776 Receipt of money which is not consideration

When something is done for consideration, there is a supply for VAT purposes (see 7758). It is therefore normal to conclude that, whenever a business receives money, it is likely to be consideration for something so it is likely that there is a supply. However, it is possible to receive money without that money being consideration for anything. Examples of this include:

- receipt of dividends;
- supplies in a warehouse (other than the last supply of certain goods before removal from the warehouse);
- compensation payments (in most cases, except certain payments which are expressed as compensation but are, in reality, consideration for permission to continue the actions giving rise to compensation;
- disbursements, where these represent the recovery of amounts expended which were the liability of the person from whom they are claimed. Recovery of one's own expenses in making supplies represents consideration for those supplies;
- internal payments (i.e. payments flowing within the same legal entity);
- capital introduced into a business (corporate or non-corporate);
- loan repayments;
- gifts of money – provided that they are genuine gifts;

- grants, provided that these amount to no more than deficit funding and do not involve the body making the grant receiving any benefit;

- payments within a group of companies for group relief, provided that the payment is not expressed as encompassing anything other than the group relief (*C & E Commrs v Tilling Management Services Ltd* (1978) 1 BVC 185); and

- payments under a contract of indemnity (such as the payment of a claim by an insurance company).

Legislation: VATA 1994, s. 18

Case: *C & E Commrs v Tilling Management Services Ltd* (1978) 1 BVC 185

Indirect Tax Reporter: ¶10-988

7778 Sale of a business as a going concern

If a business is sold as a going concern, and certain conditions are met, the transaction is treated as not being a supply (although a 'self-supply' charge may arise for a purchaser which is a member of a VAT group).

This non-supply treatment applies where:

- a business, or part of a business, is transferred as a going concern;

- the transfer is part of a business and that part is capable of separate operation;

- the assets transferred are to be used by the transferee in carrying on the same kind of business as that carried on by the transferor; and

- if the transferor is a taxable person, the transferee is also a taxable person (or becomes one as a result of the transfer).

However, extra care is needed if the assets transferred include 'VATed' land or buildings (the supply of which is standard-rated, either because the supplier has waived exemption or because they consist of new freehold non-residential buildings). In this case, the supply of the land and buildings remains standard-rated unless the transferee opts to tax (OTT) the land or buildings, and notifies this to HMRC, before the occurrence of the first tax point in respect of the transfer. It is also necessary that the transferee warrants that the OTT will not be disapplied because of the anti-avoidance provisions in VATA 1994, Sch. 10, para. 12.

HMRC published HMRC Brief 30/12 following their defeat in the tribunal in the *Robinson Family Limited* case. This affects leases carved out of freeholds and whether they qualify as a TOGC or not.

HMRC Brief 27/14 has now been published. This Brief explains a number of changes relating to the transfer of a business as a going concern (TOGC) and explains a number of changes relating to the transfer of a business as a going concern (TOGC):

- a change in HMRC's policy on whether the surrender of a property lease can be a VAT-free TOGC;

- to clarify the scope of certain aspects of the policy change announced in HMRC Brief 30/12;

- to explain a change in policy concerning TOGCs of new residential and relevant charitable developments.

HMRC's policy has been that where a member of a VAT group acquires a business, and thereafter the only supplies are made to other members of that VAT group, the acquisition cannot be treated as the transfer of a business as a going concern for the purposes of the *VAT (Special Provisions) Order* 1995 (SI 1995/1268) (TOGC), art. 5. This is because with all subsequent supplies treated as made to and by the same person, the transferor's business ceases at the point of transfer. Consequently, the supply of the assets of the business by the transferor to the transferee is subject to VAT.

In the case of *Intelligent Managed Services Ltd v R & C Commrs* [2015] BVC 524, IMSL had been developing a banking platform. It sold this part of its business to Virgin Money Management Services Limited (VMMSL). VMMSL continued to develop the software and then supplied software services to Virgin Money Bank Limited (VMBL). VMBL used these services to supply retail banking to its customers. VMMSL and VMBL were at the time members of the Virgin Money Group VAT group (VMG). HMRC considered that the supply of the assets of IMSL's business to VMMSL was subject to VAT because that business ceased at the point of transfer.

The Upper Tribunal disagreed with this conclusion, saying that the transfer of IMSL's banking support services business to VMMSL was the transfer of a business as a going concern (TOGC).

The Upper Tribunal considered that while VAT grouping treats the representative member as carrying on the business of each member of that group, it does not change the nature of the businesses carried on by the individual members whose activities remain separate as a matter of fact. Looked at objectively, VMMSL had not intended to liquidate the transferred assets but rather to carry on the same kind of business as IMSL as part of its own banking support services. Consequently, in its judgment, there is nothing in the VAT group rules that could prevent the transfer of IMSL's business to VMMSL from being a TOGC.

HMRC now accept that if a business is transferred to a company in a VAT group and both:

- that company intends to continue to use the transferred assets to operate the same kind of business in providing services to other group members;

- those other group members use the services to make supplies outside of the group,

then the transfer is a TOGC at the first stage.

Other Material: Notice 700/9, *Transfer of a business as a going concern* (January 2013 edn); HMRC Brief 11/16

Indirect Tax Reporter: ¶54-150

7780 Supplies made outside the UK

United Kingdom VAT is charged only on supplies made within the UK. It is perfectly possible for a business which is established in the UK to make a supply which, although taxed in the UK for other purposes, is regarded as made outside the UK for VAT purposes and so does not attract UK VAT.

The rules for determining whether a supply is made in the UK are quite technical, and are covered at 7816ff.

Indirect Tax Reporter: ¶10-000

7782 Repossessed goods

Certain disposals of goods repossessed by insurance and finance companies, etc. are treated as not being supplies, if their supply by the previous owner would not have attracted VAT, or attracted it on some amount less than the total proceeds.

The transactions affected are:

- the disposal of goods falling within a second-hand goods scheme, or of a used motor car, by a person who repossessed them under a finance agreement, or an insurer who acquired them as part of the settlement of an insurance claim;

- the disposal of a boat by a mortgagee who has taken possession of it under a marine mortgage; and

- the disposal of an aircraft by a mortgagee who has taken possession of it under an aircraft mortgage.

In each case, the relief is denied if the goods have previously been relieved of VAT, as being exported, and have been reimported, or to goods which have been imported into the UK free of VAT. Also, the goods must be resold in the same condition as that in which the person making the disposal acquired them.

Legislation: *Value Added Tax (Cars) Order* 1992 (SI 1992/3122), art. 4

Indirect Tax Reporter: ¶18-660

7784   Gift of motor car

The gift of a motor car is treated as not being a supply if the tax on its acquisition or importation was non-deductible.

Legislation: *Value Added Tax (Special Provisions) Order* 1995 (SI 1995/1268), art. 4(1); *Value Added Tax (Cars) Order* 1992 (SI 1992/3122), art. 4(1)(c)

Indirect Tax Reporter: ¶13-855

Taxable persons and businesses

7792   Taxable persons and businesses for VAT generally

Tax will be due on a supply only if it is made by a taxable person in the course or furtherance of a business carried on by him.

A 'taxable person' is defined as one who is (or is required to be) registered for VAT (VATA 1994, s. 3(1)). The rules governing registration are covered at 8250ff.

Legislation: VATA 1994, s. 3(1), 4(1)

Other Material: Notice 700, *The VAT guide*

Indirect Tax Reporter: ¶43-025

7794   Taxable VAT unit is a 'person'

Although VAT applies to supplies made in the course of a business, the taxable unit is not the business as such but the person who carries it on. This concept is important in the context of the VAT registration limits which apply in the UK. In considering these, all of the taxable supplies made by a particular person must be aggregated, even though they may be made in the course of different businesses. Once a person becomes liable to register for VAT, the tax will apply to all of his business activities.

However, it does not necessarily apply to a business activity carried on by a different person with which he is involved. Thus, the fact that a sole trader is registered for VAT does not automatically affect the position of a partnership in which he is a partner.

The term 'person' is not defined in UK VAT law, but is taken to include any body having separate legal personality (such as a company, an LLP, a trust, a trade union, etc.). A conventional partnership is also regarded as a person for VAT although it does not have separate legal personality (except in Scotland). An unincorporated association (such as a club) is also regarded as a person in practice. The treatment of different types of person is covered at 8316.

7796   Sideline activities and VAT

The taxable person is the accounting unit for VAT purposes (see 7794), so it is necessary when looking at a new business carried on by a person to have regard to other activities which may be regarded as businesses. This is relevant in determining whether registration limits have been reached, and in determining whether VAT has to be accounted for in respect of those other activities.

It also has implications when there are other business activities which give rise to exempt supplies. This can result in unfavourable consequences, of which the businessman needs to be warned, if the exempt supplies cause him to be treated as partially exempt for VAT purposes. In this instance, he will be prevented from recovering part of the VAT input tax arising on his expenses. Unless proper steps are taken, the input tax lost can exceed that relating strictly to the exempt activity. If the main business giving rise to VAT registration includes some exempt supplies, but not enough to lead to partial exemption, an exempt sideline activity can tip the balance and cause significant loss of input tax recovery.

There can also be favourable implications, which may not be immediately obvious. If there is an exempt sideline activity, but the scale of it is too small for the partial exemption rules to apply, then the businessman may find himself with an unexpected bonus. In this case, he will be able to reclaim tax on expenses relating to the exempt sideline business, which he could not have done before.

Example

An individual sets up a new business, and his accountant advises him that he is obliged to register for VAT. The annual taxable turnover of the business is likely to be in the region of £110,000 p.a.

The accountant notices from his client's tax return that he owns three houses, which are rented out and produce gross rentals totalling £8,500 p.a.

> The property-letting activity is a business for VAT purposes. It seems likely that the input tax relating to the exempt activity will be sufficiently low compared with the scale of the new business that the businessman can recover the tax on expenses incurred in relation to the property business. This would include VAT on estate agents' fees for managing the properties as well as on repairs, refurbishment expenses, etc.

Note that the VAT position could alter significantly in a year in which input tax relating to the exempt activity exceeded the partial exemption de minimis limits (see 8110ff.).

This interaction of different activities for VAT purposes affects partnerships and companies just as much as individuals. In these cases, it is usually more obvious that there may be an interaction, since the accounts of a company or partnership are more likely to include all business activities.

7798 VAT only on business activities

Value added tax affects supplies only when they are made in the course or furtherance of a business. So when a VAT registered parent sells a child's old bicycle, no VAT is due since the transaction is a personal one, not done in the course of a business.

(1) Whether a business carried on

It is easy to assume that the term 'business' for VAT is synonymous with the term 'trade' used in income tax law. Indeed, the term 'business' does include a trade, profession or vocation. But the VAT term goes far wider than this, and covers many activities which would be regarded for income tax purposes as generating investment income. For instance, the letting of property is regarded as a business for VAT purposes.

Specific activities treated as business

The following activities are regarded as done in the course of a business by definition:

- the carrying on of a trade, profession or vocation;

- the admission of persons to premises for consideration; and

- the provision by a club or association of benefits to its members for consideration (including subscriptions).

General meaning of business

The list of activities treated as business activities which is given in the *Value Added Tax Act* 1994 (in s. 94) is not complete. The statute merely states that the term includes these activities. Each case has to be looked at on the basis of its facts, to see whether the activities carried on should be regarded as business activities within the ordinary meaning of that term. Furthermore, because VAT stems from European law, it is necessary to bear in mind the terms of the EC VAT Directive 2006/112 when construing the UK law. The directive does not use the term business, but refers to a taxable person as one who 'independently' carries on certain 'economic activities'. The economic activities concerned are those of (Directive 2006/112, art. 9):

> 'producers, traders and persons supplying services including mining and agricultural activities and activities of the professions. The exploitation of tangible or intangible property for the purpose of obtaining income therefrom on a continuing basis shall also be considered an economic activity.'

(2) Whether supply is made in the course or furtherance of business

Once it is established that a business is being carried on it is necessary, in order to establish whether a particular supply may be liable to VAT, to establish whether it is done in the course or furtherance of the business.

The legislation provides that a number of things which might not be seen as done in the course of a business or in its furtherance, such as closing it down, are brought within the meaning of the term by statute. Things which will be seen as done in the course or furtherance of a business are as follows:

- the supply of a business asset or a supply made for business purposes – this is not a specific statutory addition, but a general inference from the legislation and cases;

- things done in connection with closing a business down, such as selling the remaining business assets;

- transferring a business as a going concern; and

- supplies made as the holder of an office by a person carrying on a trade, profession or vocation if he accepted that office in the course of his trade, profession or vocation. An example of this would be a lawyer who accepts office as a director of a company in the course of carrying on his profession.

Legislation: VATA 1994, s. 94

Other Material: Notice 700, *The VAT guide*

Indirect Tax Reporter: ¶18-090

Goods and services

7804 Whether supply is of goods or services

VAT is charged on supplies of goods and supplies of services. There are many detailed rules covering such matters as whether a supply is regarded as made in the UK or elsewhere, the time when the supply is regarded as taking place (and so when the tax on it falls due), and even the amount taxable and the rate of tax applicable, which vary depending on whether the supply is of goods or of services. It is therefore important to distinguish between the two.

The legislation specifies a number of supplies which are to be treated either as supplies of goods or as supplies of services such as electricity (which is deemed to be a supply of goods). Any supply which is not a supply of goods and is done for a consideration, is deemed to be a supply of services.

Legislation: VATA 1994, s. 5(2)(b), Sch. 4

Other Material: Notice 700, *The VAT guide*

Indirect Tax Reporter: ¶10-455

7806 Composite (or compound) and multiple supplies

Before a supply can be classified as being of goods or of services, its real nature must be established. Often this is straightforward. For instance, if a person sells a van for a sum of money, there is clearly a supply of the van. However, if the van which is sold contains a load of carrots, and these pass to the purchaser as well, there may well be two supplies, one of the van and the other of the carrots. So, sometimes what appears to be a single transaction can be made of more than one supply.

There are two possibilities:

- a multiple supply – where the different elements each have their own identity and each has its own VAT treatment; and

- a compound (or composite) supply – where the different elements have one VAT treatment overall and this follows the VAT treatment of the main element, so the other elements lose their VAT identity.

> **Example**
>
> The sale of a calculator with an instruction manual might be looked at as two supplies, one of the calculator (standard-rated) and the other of the manual (zero-rated). In all probability, though, it would be regarded as a single supply of a calculator, the manual being seen as merely incidental to the supply.

> However, consider the position if the manual went beyond the operation of that particular calculator, and covered, for instance, mathematical techniques and number games. If the manual were sufficiently valuable in comparison with the calculator, and was of utility in its own right, the transaction might be regarded as a multiple supply. This would be even more likely if the manual were also available separately to people who did not wish to buy a calculator.

As can be seen, this is an area where great care needs to be exercised. The managers of the business need to be wary of transactions which might be seen in different ways, and take advice on them. It should be noted that HMRC are very much aware of the differences of treatment which can arise depending on how such supplies are viewed.

A line of cases suggests a general principle that, where a transaction includes a number of components, some of which are liable to VAT and some of which are not, it should be seen as involving a number of separate supplies and dissected accordingly if it is practical and realistic to do so. For example, a day excursion with a five-course lunch or dinner on the Orient Express was held to be two separate supplies of transport (zero-rated) and catering (standard-rated). This approach is based on the notion that the exemptions and zero-ratings are a fundamental part of the tax, and that the courts should give effect to the intentions of the legislators. It appears that a major factor in deciding, in borderline cases, whether it is practical and realistic to split the transaction is if the parties have found it possible to apportion the consideration, either in their agreement or when invoicing. Indeed, the Court of Appeal indicated that, while HMRC could seek to split into its components that which the contracting parties had sought to treat as a single supply, they could not join together elements that the parties had themselves split in the contractual arrangements.

Further general guidance was given by the seminal decision of the European Court of Justice in the *Card Protection Plan* case (although the court left it to the national court to apply these principles to the specific facts of the case before it) on the following lines:

(1) Where the transaction involves a bundle of features, regard must be had to all of the circumstances in which the supply takes place.

(2) Every supply of a service must normally be regarded as distinct and independent, but a supply which comprises a single service from an economic point of view should not be artificially split, as this would be distortive.

(3) There is a single supply if one or more elements are to be regarded as constituting the principal service, while other elements are merely ancillary and so share the same tax treatment as the principal

service. A service is ancillary to the principal service if it does not constitute, for customers, an aim in itself, but provides a means of better enjoying the principal service supplied.

(4)   The fact that a single price is charged suggests that there is a single service, but is not decisive. If the circumstances suggested that customers intended to purchase two or more separate services liable at different rates, then the consideration must be apportioned. The simplest method of calculation or assessment should be used for this.

There have been many cases concerned with the fundamental question of what it is that is being supplied. This is ultimately an area for subjective judgment, and cannot readily be codified. It is important to consider the possible different views which might be taken of a particular transaction and, where different tax results might otherwise arise, to take all possible steps to document the true nature of the transaction (e.g. by means of formal contracts).

Example

A business sells a package which is made up of a book, a DVD and a customer support helpline. The sale price of the package is £250. The book and the DVD can be purchased separately for £120 each. Customers can subscribe to the helpline alone for £75 p.a. They can also subscribe to the helpline and take either the book or DVD for £150 p.a.

The helpline and the DVD are standard-rated for VAT, but the supply of the book is zero-rated.

The price of £250 therefore needs to be apportioned. The VAT at 20% is found by applying the fraction 1/6 to the amount relating to the standard-rated supply.

$$£250 \times \frac{75 + 120}{75 + 120 + 120} \times \frac{1}{6} = £25.79$$

Cases: *Sea Containers Services Ltd v C & E Commrs* [2000] BVC 60; *C & E Commrs v Lloyds TSB Group Ltd* [1998] BVC 173; *C & E Commrs v Wellington Private Hospital Ltd* [1997] BVC 251; *Bophuthatswana National Commercial Corporation Ltd v C & E Commrs* [1993] BVC 194; *C & E Commrs v Bushby* (1978) 1 BVC 158; *Card Protection Plan Ltd v C & E Commrs* (Case C-349/96) [1999] BVC 155

Other Material: VAT Information Sheet 02/01 – *Single or multiple supplies – how to decide*

Indirect Tax Reporter: ¶10-000

7808 Supplies of goods

The following are specified as being supplies of goods:

- the transfer of the whole property in goods;

- the transfer of possession of goods under an agreement for the sale of the goods, or under an agreement which expressly contemplates that the property in the goods will also pass at some ascertainable future date;

- the supply of power, heat, refrigeration or ventilation;

- the granting, assignment or surrender of a 'major interest' in land. A 'major interest in land' is the freehold or a leasehold interest having a term certain greater than 21 years; and

- the transfer or disposal of goods which are business assets so that they no longer form part of the business assets is treated as a supply of goods, even if no consideration passes. In view of the first two items above, this last provision seems redundant in the context of distinguishing between supplies of goods and of services. It is presumably included to put it beyond doubt that a gift of goods constitutes a supply, rather than to indicate the classification of the supply.

Legislation: VATA 1994, s. 96(1), Sch. 4, para. 1(1), 3, 4, 5

Other Material: Notice 700, *The VAT guide*

Indirect Tax Reporter: ¶10-455

7810 Supplies of services

The following are specified as being supplies of services:

- the transfer of an undivided share of the property in goods, or a transfer of the possession of goods except under a contract for their sale, etc. An example of the former would be the sale of a half-share in goods; and

- the use of goods which are business assets, under the directions of the person carrying on the business, for a private or non-business purpose, whether or not there is any consideration.

Anything else which is a supply, but is not specifically stated to be a supply of goods, will be a supply of services.

There is a deemed supply of services where input tax is reclaimed on the obtaining of services and these are subsequently put to non-business use for no consideration.

However, this deemed supply does not apply:

- if any part of the tax charged on the original supply of the services was disallowed as not being input tax (i.e. was apportioned as not being used for business purposes);

- to services of car hire where 50% of the input tax has been excluded from credit; or

- to services used for the provision of catering or accommodation for employees falling within VATA 1994, Sch. 6, para. 10 (see 7860).

Legislation: VATA 1994, s. 5(2)(b), Sch. 4, para. 1, 5(4), Sch. 6, para. 10; *Value Added Tax (Supply of Services) Order* 1993 (SI 1993/1507), art. 6A

Indirect Tax Reporter: ¶10-455

Place of supply

7816 Determining where supplies are made

VAT in the UK is charged on supplies which are deemed to occur in the UK, but not on supplies made outside of the UK. It is important, therefore, to be able to tell where supplies are made.

The determination of the place of supply is done separately for each supply made. This is in contrast with other taxes where the determination of tax jurisdiction is generally carried out for the person concerned, rather than for individual transactions. The rules for determining the place of supply fall into two quite distinct sets: one for supplies of goods and the other for supplies of services.

Indirect Tax Reporter: ¶13-350

7818 The place of supply of goods

The UK law on the place of supply of goods is contained in VATA 1994, s. 7, while the equivalent EC provisions are in VAT Directive, art. 31 onwards.

(1) Place of supply of goods: basic rule

The rules governing the place of supply of goods are markedly different from the rules for liability to other taxes, in that they entirely ignore the locations of the parties to the transactions.

The basic rule is that goods are treated as supplied at the place where they are when their dispatch or transport to the customer begins, or the place where they are when the supply takes place if they are not to be dispatched or transported. Effectively, therefore, they are supplied at the place where they are when allocated to the supply in question. The location of the person making the supply does not have any effect on the place of supply of the goods, nor does the place where the goods are at the time when title in them passes. The place of supply is the place where they are when they first become identified with the particular supply.

Example

Terry sells a lathe and a computer to Ben. The lathe is in the US and the computer is in Huddersfield. Both are shipped to Ben's premises in Australia.

The lathe is treated as supplied outside of the UK, since it was outside of the UK when allocated to the supply.

The computer, on the other hand, was in the UK when allocated to the supply, and so is treated as supplied in the UK (this does not necessarily mean that standard-rated VAT will be charged on the supply – in all probability it will be zero-rated as an export of goods).

Terry also sells Ben a printer to go with the computer. Terry is awaiting a consignment of printers from Japan, and when they arrive he will forward one of these to Ben in fulfilment of the contract.

The supply of the printer is treated as made in the UK.

---

(2) Place of supply of installed goods

There is a special rule if the goods are to be installed or assembled by the supplier, or by some other person acting on his behalf (e.g. a sub-contractor). In this case the goods are treated as supplied at the place where installation or assembly takes place.

As a simplification measure, when installed goods are supplied by a supplier registered for VAT in another member state but not in the UK and they are installed in the UK, instead of the supplier being required to register for VAT in the UK, to deal with the installation, his supply is ignored and the customer is treated as making an acquisition in the UK, provided that appropriate formalities are followed.

(3) Supplies on intra-EC journeys

Where goods are supplied during passenger transport within the EC, the supply is treated as made in the Member State of departure.

(4) Distance selling

The broad aim of the distance selling provisions is to prevent consumers in different member states from using the internet, mail order, etc. to obtain goods at lower rates of VAT (they are perfectly at liberty to achieve this end by travelling, and buying in person). They apply where a business in one member state takes orders from an unregistered customer in another member state, and delivers goods to that customer in that other Member State.

To prevent market distortion, a person selling significant quantities of goods (over €100,000 or €35,000 – depending on the member state) to unregistered persons in a particular member state must register there, and charge that state's VAT on these sales. These supplies are deemed to take place in the destination state.

These rules do not apply to the supply of a new means of transport, nor do they apply where there is a deemed supply on a movement of the trader's own goods from one EC location to another, without any actual supply.

(5) Supplies by importers

Where goods are imported into the UK from outside the EC, the supply of the goods by the importer, and any subsequent supplies, are treated as made in the UK.

UK businesses supplying customers elsewhere in the EC should note that other Member States are bound by the same VAT directive as the UK. Thus, the place of allocation of goods, the question of installation, and the mechanics selected for importation into the other state must all be considered to determine whether the UK business has an obligation to register for VAT in the other Member State.

(6) Intra-EC supplies of goods

The position for a supply of goods by a trader registered in one Member State to a trader registered in another is straightforward:

- the supplier must obtain the customer's VAT registration number and show it on the tax invoice (provided that he holds satisfactory evidence of departure from the UK he can then zero rate the supply: see 8220); and

- the customer is liable to pay VAT in his own state on his 'acquisition' of the goods. This VAT is also input tax in his hands (see 7972ff.).

If the customer cannot produce a valid VAT registration number the supplier must charge his own VAT on the supply. However, if his sales to unregistered persons in the member state concerned exceed the relevant threshold, the supplier must register for VAT in that country and his supplies to such unregistered customers are deemed to take place there (see the distance selling arrangements above).

Legislation: VATA 1994, s. 7 and Sch. 2

7820 The place of supply of services

The rules that determine where a supply of services is made are very important where services cross country boundaries. The status of the customer is essential.

The rules for electronic services to B2C customers have also changed from 1 January 2015 – see below.

The basic rules from 1 January 2010 are as follows:

If the customer is a business customer, the service is therefore a B2B (business to business) service and the place of supply is where the customer belongs. The service will therefore be outside the scope of UK VAT. If the customer is in the EC, then that customer will have to bring the VAT to account using the reverse charge mechanism (see below).

If the customer is NOT a business customer, so the supply is B2C (business to customer), then the new rules provide that the place where the service is supplied is the place where the supplier belongs (this is, in effect, a default). There is, however, an override where the B2C customer is outside the EC (see below).

Legislation was introduced in *Finance Act* 2014 to tax intra-EU B2C supplies of telecommunications, broadcasting and e-services in the member state in which the consumer is located.

The changes took effect from 1 January 2015 and implement already agreed EU legislation into UK legislation, ensuring that these services are taxed fairly in the member state of consumption.

The main commercial area that will be affected by this is the supply of electronic services to consumers.

This means services downloaded from the internet with minimal human contact.

Examples would include the downloading of apps, music, games, software, etc.

To alleviate the need for businesses affected by these changes to register for VAT in other member states, a Mini One Stop Shop (MOSS) has been introduced from 1 January 2015.

HMRC have published updated guidance on registration and use of the MOSS with further simplifications (April 2016). This is available on GOV.UK: www.gov.uk/register-and-use-the-vat-mini-one-stop-shop.

This is an IT system that will give businesses the option of registering in just the UK and accounting for VAT due in other member states using a single return. This is an extension of VATA 1994, Sch. 3B, rules.

Even though a trader may be below the UK registration threshold, sales of electronic services to B2C customers in other member states will require the UK trader to account for domestic VAT in the member state where the sale has taken place.

This will require a UK VAT registration (to be able to get into the online HMRC system), but will have nil returns in the UK.

(1) The place where customers and suppliers belong

It is necessary to be able to tell where the customer or supplier belongs in respect of B2B and B2C services. The UK rules follow the EC VAT Directive and are as follows:

For a B2B supply, a business customer belongs in a country if the person has a business establishment or some other fixed establishment there and if there is more than one such country, the country most directly concerned with the supply.

If the supply is a B2C customer, then that person belongs in a country where that person's usual place of residence is.

Legislation: VATA 1994, s. 7A and 9; EC Directive 2006/112, art. 43 onwards

Other Material: Notice 741A (from 1 January 2010), *Place of supply of services*

Indirect Tax Reporter: ¶13-470

7824 Place of supply of services – special rules

The 2010 VAT package, like the pre-existing legislation, has special rules in some circumstances.

There are some general exceptions, and these include:

- services connected with land are treated as supplied where the land is located;

- passenger transport, which is treated as taking place where the transport takes place (this could be in more than one Member State);

- where electronic services (such as website provision and software downloads) take place where the non-business customer belongs. There is, however, a simplified registration facility to save multiple registrations in the EC;

- intellectual services supplied to non-business customers outside the EC (such as accountancy services) – these are supplied where the customer belongs, so no VAT needs to be charged by the EC supplier and the service is outside the scope of their local EC VAT;

- intermediary services (i.e. agents) which are deemed to be supplied in the country in which the underlying principal's service takes place; and

- cultural, educational and entertainment services – treated as taking place where the event takes place.

There are also some exceptions that apply only to B2C services:

The effective use and enjoyment rules

There is a further layer of rules – 'the effective use and enjoyment rules' that modify the rules above. These rules, and the services subject to them, are covered in the EC VAT Directive (art. 43 onwards) and have been adopted by the UK law.

In summary, they say that where the services listed below are supplied to a customer that is in the UK and the services are effectively used and enjoyed outside the EC, then they will not be charged to VAT in the UK.

The reverse also applies if the service is made by a UK supplier to a customer outside the EC and the customer effectively uses them in the UK, then they will be subject to UK VAT.

The services include:

(1)   the hiring of goods;

(2)   telecoms and broadcasting services; and

(3)   electronically supplied services to business customers (i.e. B2B).

Legislation: VATA 1994, Sch. 4A

The reverse charge

Given that the B2B rules make the place of supply generally where the customer belongs, the mechanism by which the VAT is brought to account is the reverse charge and this only happens where the customer is in the EC. If the customer is outside the EC, then there is no VAT to bring to account. There may, however, be local tax implications.

In both cases, the supply is outside the scope of the supplier's member state.

The reverse charge will also be imposed on UK traders that receive supplies of services (other than exempt supplies) from either another EC member state or from a place outside the EC (see VATA 1994, s. 8).

The reverse charge mechanism is similar to the acquisition process for goods. The customer charges himself local VAT and puts this to output tax in his VAT return and then tries to recover as much as possible of this self-charged VAT under the normal VAT recovery rules.

The result of this (like the acquisition process) is that it is neutral whether the customer buys in his own Member State or in another Member State or a third country. The system is therefore anti-market distortion.

The EC Sales List

The EC Sales List is a method of auditing the reverse charge and acquisition process and to allow the tax authorities of the Member States to check that it is being done.

From 1 January 2010, the EC Sales List applies to services as well as goods. Prior to 1 January 2010, it applied to goods only.

Legislation: VATA 1994, s. 7A, 8, Sch. 4A; VAT Directive 2006/112, art 43 onwards

Other Material: Notice 741A, *Place of supply of services*

Indirect Tax Reporter: ¶13-470

Time of supply

7830   Importance of time of supply

The time when a supply is deemed to occur for VAT purposes is important for a number of reasons. First and foremost, it determines the period for which the supplier must account for the tax, and so the date by which it must be paid over to HMRC. It also determines the period for which a VAT-registered customer can reclaim the tax.

When there are changes in the rate of tax, or in the classification of supplies which are exempt or zero-rated, the precise time of supply can be of crucial importance in determining the rate which attaches to supplies made around the time of the change.

The time of supply is also important in ascertaining the calculations of turnover for registration purposes, and partial exemption calculations.

There are slightly different rules for goods and for services, and special rules for a number of specified supplies.

In principle, the time of supply (or 'tax point') is the earlier of:

- the date when the supply is 'really' made, referred to by HMRC as the basic tax point (see 7832);

- the date when a tax invoice is issued in respect of the supply (see 7834); and

- the date when payment is received for the supply (see 7836).

There are a number of refinements to be borne in mind in applying this basic rule and there are also special rules for certain kinds of supply (see 7838).

Other Material: Notice 700, *The VAT guide*

Indirect Tax Reporter: ¶11-700

7832   Time of supply: the basic tax point

Identification of the 'basic tax point' (or the time when the supply actually takes place) is based on different rules depending on whether the supply is of goods or of services. This is yet another area where the VAT law distinguishes between goods and services, and treats them differently.

Example

Alfred dispatches goods to Bert on 15 September. This is the basic tax point. Bert paid for the goods on 25 August, and this is the actual tax point.

If Alfred issued an invoice on 20 September, this further tax point would override the basic tax point, but not the earlier actual tax point.

In this example, the goods are deemed to have been supplied on 25 August.

---

(1)   Basic tax point: goods

In the case of goods which are to be delivered to the customer, or collected by the customer, the basic tax point is the date when delivery commences. If the supply does not involve movement of the goods (e.g. a supply of land, or of goods which are erected on the customer's premises), the basic tax point is the date when the goods are made available to the customer. In the case of supplies of land, the basic tax point is normally the date of completion rather than the date when contracts are exchanged (although the date of exchange of contracts can be important in Transfers of Going Concerns (TOGCs)).

It is possible for goods to be delivered to a potential customer without a supply yet having taken place. This would happen, for instance, if they were sent on approval or on sale or return terms. If goods are delivered on such terms, so that it is uncertain whether there will in fact be a supply of them, the basic tax point does not arise until the supply becomes certain (e.g. by the customer adopting the goods, or the expiry of an agreed period within which they may be returned). However, the basic tax point will in any case arise if the customer holds the goods for 12 months without returning them, even if he still has the right to return them.

(2) Basic tax point: services

The basic tax point for a supply of services arises when the services are performed. HMRC generally take this to be the date when the performance of the service is completed.

Legislation: VATA 1994, s. 6(2)(a), (b), (c), (3)

Other Material: Notice 700, *The VAT guide*

Indirect Tax Reporter: ¶11-750

7834   Time of supply: issue of a tax invoice

The tax invoice is the formal document which a VAT-registered trader must issue to another VAT-registered trader or to a customer in another Member State (and may issue to anyone) in respect of a taxable supply other than a zero-rated supply (in the case of a customer elsewhere in the EC the issuing of the invoice is compulsory for a zero-rated supply also). It provides the evidence which enables another taxable trader to reclaim tax on the supply. For obvious reasons, HMRC does not wish to refund tax in respect of such an invoice unless the supplier has become liable to pay the tax to them, and so the issue of a tax invoice creates a time of supply, even if it occurs before the supply is actually made.

(1) Pro-forma invoices

Often payment is requested by issuing a document similar in appearance to a tax invoice, but which does not have the characteristics of one (e.g. a pro-forma invoice). In such cases, great care should be exercised to ensure that the document cannot be treated as a tax invoice.

No VAT registration number should be quoted, and ideally no separate amount should be shown in respect of VAT. The document should be clearly marked to the effect that it is not a tax invoice. If such documents are to be used with any frequency, or for large amounts, it would be wise to agree the exact form of them with HMRC.

(2) The 14-day rule

If a tax invoice is issued within 14 days after the basic tax point, then the basic tax point can be ignored in fixing the time of supply and the date when the invoice is issued is used instead. This can simplify VAT accounting in practice, as it is often easier to set up systems which operate by reference to the date of the invoice than it is to use the basic tax point.

There is no obligation to use the 14-day rule, and accounting can be done by reference to the basic tax point if this is more convenient. However, a trader who does not wish to use the 14-day rule must notify HMRC of this in writing. This notification will then effectively cancel the 14-day rule for all supplies made by that trader. It is possible to use the 14-day rule for some supplies, but not for others, but in practice this should be agreed with HMRC.

If required, the 14-day rule can be extended. Many businesses with monthly invoicing runs find it convenient to use a 31-day rule. If a longer period than 14 days is required, the trader must ask HMRC to make a direction to that effect. Often, a longer period is used without the issuing of a formal direction. This is unwise, because it will expose the trader to possible penalties and interest for incorrect returns and late payments of tax (8480ff.).

It should also be noted that the 14-day rule only overrides the basic tax point. The issue of an invoice cannot override an earlier tax point triggered by the receipt of payment for a supply (see below).

(3) On-account invoicing

If a tax invoice is issued for only a part of the total price of the supply, this will trigger the tax point only for that part of the supply. The tax point for the remainder of the supply, and the date when the tax on it becomes accountable to HMRC, will be determined separately.

Legislation: VATA 1994, s. 6(5)

Other Material: Notice 700, *The VAT guide*

Indirect Tax Reporter: ¶11-765

7836 Time of supply: date payment received

The date when a payment is received by the supplier triggers the tax point to the extent of the payment, if the tax point has not already arisen by reference to the basic tax point or the issue of a tax invoice.

If a deposit is received from the customer, the precise terms on which it is held need to be considered to decide whether it amounts to payment. Usually a deposit will amount to advance payment for a supply, in which case it gives rise to a tax point. However, a deposit which is merely security for, say, the return of goods which are let on hire, is not payment for a supply (even if forfeited) and so does not give rise to a tax point.

Most advance payments in respect of a supply will bring about a tax point, even if the money is refundable should the supply not proceed.

If a deposit is received for a supply, and represents payment for the supply, then it will be necessary to account for VAT on the amount of the deposit. If the supply is then cancelled by the customer, and the terms are such that the deposit is forfeited, it no longer represents consideration for a supply of any sort. The tax already accounted for can be claimed back on the next VAT return. However, care is needed if the deposit might be seen as consideration for some supply other than the one originally contemplated. In *C & E Commrs v Bass plc* [1993] BVC 34 the court held that a 'no show' fee, chargeable when a hotel customer failed to turn up having made a booking under a guaranteed reservation scheme, amounted to consideration for a supply of holding the room available for use.

Overpayments by customers, retained by the supplier and set against subsequent bills, were held not to give rise to a tax point until applied against those later bills.

Case: *C & E Commrs v Bass plc* [1993] BVC 34

Indirect Tax Reporter: ¶11-900

7838 Special time of supply rules

There are a number of instances in which the normal time of supply rules are overridden and special rules are used instead. These generally operate by ignoring the basic tax point, and using the earlier of the date when an invoice is issued and the date when payment is received as the tax point

The main occasions when the special rules apply are:

- deemed supply when goods or services are put to non-business use;
- deemed supply on import of services;
- compulsory purchase of land, or supply of it when amount of consideration undetermined;
- supply under a major interest lease;
- supply of power, heat, etc.;
- supply involving retention payments;
- continuous supplies of services;
- royalty payments, etc.;
- certain supplies in the construction industry;
- deemed supply on transfer of a going concern to partially exempt group; and
- self-supplies.

Change in rate of tax: consequences

If there is a change in tax rate, or in the liability status of a supply, and the basic tax point falls under one set of rules while the tax point finally determined falls under the other set of rules, the supplier may elect to treat the supply as taking place at the basic tax point. This applies only for determining the rate of tax for the supply. The ordinary tax point is used for all other purposes, such as determining when the tax is payable to HMRC.

If, as a result, it transpires that a tax invoice already issued now bears an excessive amount of tax, the supplier must issue a credit note to reduce the tax within 45 days after the change.

The option to elect for the most favourable tax point does not apply in the case of self-supplies of cars, or in the case of goods sold by a receiver.

The ability to select the most favourable tax point, and therefore rate of VAT, applies to users of the cash accounting scheme as well as to other traders. The cash accounting scheme only affects the date when tax is paid to, or reclaimed from, HMRC, not the underlying tax point.

Legislation: VATA 1994, s. 88, 88(6); *Value Added Tax Regulations* 1995 (SI 1995/2518), reg. 81–93

Other Material: Notice 700, *The VAT Guide*

Indirect Tax Reporter: ¶11-700, ¶12-305, and ¶12-500

Value of supply

7844   Introduction to value of supply

The value of a supply, as determined for VAT purposes, is the amount on which VAT is charged. Clearly, it is important to understand the rules for determining the value of a supply (or the 'taxable amount', as it is called in the EC legislation), since this directly affects the amount of tax chargeable.

As is the case with the law governing the time of supply, there are some basic rules which cover most transactions, and then a set of special rules which apply in specified circumstances.

Legislation: VATA 1994, s. 19(1)

Other Material: Notice 700, *The VAT guide*

Indirect Tax Reporter: ¶14-200

7846   Consideration in money

If a supply is made for consideration, and the consideration is wholly in money, the value of the supply (or taxable amount) is taken to be the amount which, with the addition of the tax chargeable, is equal to the consideration. In other words, if a supply is made for money, the price charged includes the VAT due.

So:

VALUE PLUS VAT = CONSIDERATION

From the supplier's point of view, it is therefore desirable to express the price as being a VAT exclusive amount, with VAT to be added as appropriate.

Example

Alfred sells standard-rated goods to Bert for £3,000.

If the contract price is stated as being VAT-inclusive, the VAT is £500 (1/6 × £3,000).

The value if the supply is therefore £2,500.00.

If the contract price is stated as being excluding VAT, the taxable value of the supply is £3,000 and the VAT is £600.00 (£3,000 × 20%).

Legislation: VATA 1994, s. 19(2)

Indirect Tax Reporter: ¶14-200

7848   Change in value of supply

Although not specifically implemented in the UK legislation, the EC VAT Directive, art. 90, provides for the value of supply (or taxable amount) to be changed in certain circumstances. Its terms are as follows:

> 'In the case of cancellation, refusal or total or partial non-payment, or where the price is reduced after the supply takes place, the taxable amount shall be reduced accordingly under conditions which shall be determined by the Member States.
>
> However, in the case of total or partial non-payment, Member States may derogate from this rule.'

This provision has direct effect in the UK (except in the case of non-payment, where Member States may derogate) and, since the UK government has not taken advantage of its right to impose conditions, it has unconditional effect.

Legislation: EC VAT Directive 2006/211, art. 90

Indirect Tax Reporter: ¶14-200

7850   More than one supply: effect on value of supply

If a consideration in money relates to several items, then it must be split between those so that each supply is treated as made for a monetary consideration equal to the amount of the total consideration which is properly attributable to it.

Legislation: VATA 1994, s. 19(4)

Indirect Tax Reporter: ¶14-200

7852   Change in rate of tax: effect on value of supply

If there is a change in the rate of tax attaching to a supply (including a change in classification of the supply as between standard-rated, zero-rated or exempt), then the consideration due under a pre-existing contract for the supply is automatically adjusted to take account of the change, unless the contract provides to the contrary. The value of the supply remains the same, but the total consideration alters.

Example

Beryl contracts to sell goods to Claire for £5,875 inclusive of VAT. Before the tax point arises, the standard rate of VAT changes from 17.5% to 20%.

The value of the supply, or taxable amount, is £5,000 (£5,875 × $^{40}/_{47}$). This amount, with the addition of tax at 17.5%, comes to £5,875.

On the change in rate, the taxable amount remains the same. The tax chargeable becomes £1,000 (£5,000 × 20%), so the consideration under the contract is increased to £6,000.

Legislation: VATA 1994, s. 89, 89(2)

Indirect Tax Reporter: ¶14-200

7854 Non-monetary consideration

If a supply is made for a consideration which is not in money, or is not wholly in money, then under UK law the value of the supply is taken as being the amount of money which, with the addition of the VAT due, is equal to the value of the consideration.

The incidence of VAT on non-monetary consideration gives rise to an important planning point when framing contracts which is frequently overlooked. As indicated at 7846, it is important (from the supplier's point of view) to state that amounts of monetary consideration mentioned in the agreement do not include any VAT which may be due, and that VAT is to be added as appropriate. However, this is not sufficient if there is also non-monetary consideration. Unless there is specific provision in the contract requiring the customer to pay over any VAT arising on supplies made wholly or partly for non-monetary consideration, the supplier will be left to bear the VAT (although the customer may still be able to recover it as input tax).

Legislation: VATA 1994, s. 19(3)

Indirect Tax Reporter: ¶11-295

7856 Discounts

HMRC have changed the VAT treatment of Prompt Payment Discounts (PPDs). Historically, PPDs have mainly been offered business to business (B2B) and recipients have generally been entitled to recover any VAT charged. PPDs are increasingly being offered to final consumers (B2C) who cannot recover the VAT charged. HMRC have identified several instances of suppliers of B2C services offering PPDs in the telecommunication and broadcasting sectors. Under the existing interpretation, this results in a tax loss where PPDs are not taken up.

This measure has effect for supplies of telecommunication and broadcasting services where there is no obligation to provide a VAT invoice, on and after 1 May 2014. For all other supplies, the measure has effect for supplies made on and after 1 April 2015.

Under the new PPD system, the supplier has to record the full net value of the supply and the full VAT due on the invoice and then says that a reduced payment (with a reduced VAT liability) applies if the customer takes up the PPD within the prescribed time limit.

If the PPD is NOT taken up, then the supplier either has to issue a credit note or to make a bad debt relief claim. It is thought that this cumbersome process may change.

The customer can only claim back the input tax that is actually paid over to the supplier.

Legislation: The Principal VAT Directive (Directive 2006/112), art. 79; VATA 1994, Sch. 6, para. 4 (as amended)

Other material: HMRC Brief 49/14

Indirect Tax Reporter: ¶14-400

7858 Consideration in foreign currency

If a supply is made for a consideration expressed in a foreign currency, certain values must be converted into sterling by reference to the market rate at the time of supply, unless the trader opts to use an exchange rate published by HMRC.

Legislation: VATA 1994, Sch. 6, para. 11

Case: *Willis Pension Trustees Ltd* [2006] BVC 2,045

Indirect Tax Reporter: ¶14-750

7860 Special value of supply rules

There are a number of modifications to the basic rules as to the value of supply:

- HMRC can direct that certain supplies between connected persons be treated as taking place at market value;
- HMRC can direct that certain 'party plan' type supplies be treated as taking place at retail value;
- the sale of a token, stamp or voucher which carries a right to obtain goods or services is treated as taking place at a value limited to any excess of the consideration payable over the face value of the token;

- where there is a deemed supply on a self-supply of a motor car (see 7766), or where goods which are business assets cease to be such, or when a person ceases to be registered for VAT, the value of the supply is deemed to be equivalent to the current value of the goods, taking into account the age and condition of the goods concerned. If this cannot be ascertained, then the value is taken to be equal to that of similar goods or, failing that, the current cost of production of such goods;

- a deemed supply arises when goods which are business assets are put to non-business use for no consideration. The VAT value of such a deemed supply is the full cost to the trader of making the goods available;

- there is a reduction in value for certain supplies of long stay hotel accommodation;

- in the case of the supply to employees of food or beverages (supplied in the course of catering) or of accommodation in a hotel, inn, boarding house, or similar establishment, the value of the supply is restricted to the amount of any money consideration;

- where goods are sold under a second-hand goods scheme (see 8392ff.), the consideration for which they are sold is regarded as limited to any excess of the actual consideration over the cost of the goods to the supplier;

- if a business provides car fuel to an employee, partner, proprietor or director for use for non-business purposes (including home-to-work travelling) free or for less than cost, the supply is treated as being made for a consideration calculated by reference to the cylinder capacity of the vehicle. The value is to be found in a table contained in VATA 1994, s. 57, as amended from time to time.

Legislation: VATA 1994, s. 56, 57 and Sch. 6, para. 1, 2, 6, 7, 9, 10

Chargeable events – VAT on imports from outside the EC

7880 Introduction – imports

The general rule is that the importation of goods from outside the EC is a chargeable event, and VAT is due on the goods, regardless of whether the person importing the goods does so in the course of a business. Only imports from 'third countries' (i.e. non-EC countries) are covered by this charge – 'imports' from elsewhere in the EC are covered by the 'acquisition' rules reviewed at 7972ff. The tax is chargeable as if it were a duty of customs, and is payable at the same time as any customs duty arising.

There are a number of reliefs, and suspensions of liability, available, including some which also apply for customs duty purposes and some which are peculiar to VAT. It is important to appreciate that a customs duty relief will not automatically mean that a VAT relief will follow (for example on outward processing relief (OPR), which is essentially a customs duty relief and not a VAT relief).

As a general rule, VAT on importation is payable when the goods enter the country (or during the month following, under duty deferment arrangements), although in some limited circumstances involving low value goods a registered trader may account for the tax via his VAT return.

This section provides a general outline of the system for applying VAT to imports of goods from countries outside the EC, and of the main reliefs and suspensions available.

In most instances, the mechanics of these rules will be handled for traders by freight forwarders, etc. The important points for traders to bear in mind are to ensure that the right person is named as importer, that the place of supply provisions are properly recognised for any supply by the importer, and that appropriate evidence is held for recovery of input tax. The rules have been modified in part following the adoption of the Union Customs Code (UCC) in May 2016.

Legislation: VATA 1994, s. 1

Other Material: HMRC Notice 702, *Imports* (April 2016 edn)

Indirect Tax Reporter: ¶63-710

7886 The charge to VAT on imports – general

The basic charging provision for VAT on importation is VATA 1994, s. 1.

Tax is due when goods are imported into the EC from a place outside the EC. This is deemed to arise where:

- the goods are removed from a place outside the EC and enter the territory of the EC;

- they either enter the UK directly or enter it via another member state; and

- the circumstances are such that it is on entry into the UK that any liability to customs duty arises (or would arise if the goods were dutiable).

Usually, the charge will arise in the ordinary way, on a direct importation into the UK, at the time when the goods are entered. However, if on arrival in the UK, the goods are entered for some customs duty suspension regime (e.g. warehousing, etc.) the liability arises when they are removed into free circulation.

If goods first arrive in some other member state and are entered into a customs duty suspension arrangement, and are in the UK when removed from this and entered for home use, the VAT charge on importation arises in the UK.

(1)   Import by a business

Most imports are carried out by businesses. Any VAT due on importation will also rank as input tax in the hands of the importer, so is usually recoverable from HMRC via the importer's VAT returns (subject to the usual VAT recovery rules – see 8034ff. and 8110ff.).

(2)   Import by a private individual, etc.

Import VAT is due on importation regardless of the status of the importer. If the importation is by a private individual, or some other entity not carrying on a business, import VAT is due in the ordinary way. In this case there is, of course, no question of recovering a similar amount as input tax. Thus, a non-taxable person who buys goods from outside the EC, and imports them, is put in the same VAT position as a person who buys from a taxable business.

(3)   Zero-rated goods

If the imported goods fall into a zero-rated category, there is no VAT liability on the importation of them, unless the zero-rating provisions in VATA 1994, Sch. 8 provide to the contrary (VATA 1994, s. 30(3)).

Goods excluded from this relief on importation include:

- building materials, etc. (VATA 1994, Sch. 8, Grp. 5, Note 24);

- gold (VATA 1994, Sch. 8, Grp. 10, Note 2); and

- certain drugs and other aids for handicapped persons, unless imported by a handicapped person for his own domestic or personal use, or by a charity for making available to handicapped persons for their own domestic or personal use (VATA 1994, Sch. 8, Grp. 12, Note 1).

(4)   Exempt goods

There is no equivalent provision excluding from the charge on importation goods which would be exempt from VAT if supplied in the UK. This is presumably because, to the extent that the UK exemptions apply to goods, they only apply when the goods are supplied in particular circumstances or by particular persons. The supplier will in each case have suffered irrecoverable input tax on the acquisition or manufacture of the goods, and will normally pass this on in the price of the goods. Relieving from import VAT non-EC goods which do not bear such an underlying VAT burden would create a distortion of competition in favour of non-EC suppliers.

Legislation: VATA 1994, s. 1(4), 30(3), Sch. 8; *Premier Foods (Holding) Ltd v R & C Commrs* [2008] BVC 667

Other Material: Notice 702, *Imports (April 2014 edn)*

Indirect Tax Reporter: ¶63-710

7892   Procedure on importation – general

Goods entering the UK may only be landed at a Customs control area, such as a customs port or airport (CEMA 1979, Pt. III). A person and a vehicle arriving at such an area is obliged to report to HMRC. The importer of goods must enter them, by presenting C88 (the Single Administrative Document, or SAD).

The SAD gives details of the goods being imported, their value for customs and VAT purposes, the name of the importer, etc. Unless the goods are entered for a special regime, such as warehousing (see below), VAT (and any duty) payable on the importation is due at the time of importation (but see 7904), and the goods will not normally be released until payment has been made.

The SAD is normally submitted electronically by direct trader input, or by their agent to CHIEF, the main HMRC computer that deals with imports and exports if goods. In some circumstances, HMRC will complete the SAD for the trader.

For alternative entry procedures, see 7898.

Legislation: CEMA 1979, Pt. III; EC Regulation 2913/92, art. 40ff.

Other Material: Notice 702, *Imports (April 2014 edn)*

Indirect Tax Reporter: ¶63-710

7898   Alternative entry procedures

There are alternatives to the basic entry procedure (7892), the main ones being:

- CFSP – Customs Freight Simplified Procedures – this allows a person to use faster frontier procedures which can result in local clearance at the trader's premises or a less detailed frontier document with the detailed being supplied later;

- postal imports – in this case, where the value of the goods is less than £2,000 and appropriate procedures are followed, the VAT-registered importer can account for the VAT on importation via his VAT return. However, for Datapost packets the Post Office will collect the VAT at the time of delivery. For consignments whose value exceeds £2,000, a declaration must be made and returned to HMRC with payment of the VAT on importation.

Details of the various entry procedures are contained in vol. 3 of the Customs Tariff.

Other Material: CFSP PN 760 (August 2010 edn); PN 144, Trade imports by post.

Indirect Tax Reporter: ¶63-760

7904   Payment of VAT by deferment

Value added tax on importation is, in principle, due for payment at the time of importation.

It is also possible to enter into a deferment arrangement whereby VAT on importation is collected by HMRC, by direct debit, on the fifteenth day of the month following importation. This involves providing HMRC with suitable security to cover deferrable charges (VAT, customs duty, etc.) each month and obtaining their approval. The amount of the guarantee can be topped up occasionally to cover unusually high levels of imports. Approved traders may be able to lower their guarantee through the Simplified Import VAT Accounting (SIVA).

These traders will be given a Deferment Approval Number (a DAN), which is a bit like a credit card and all importations will be put against this number.

Legislation: SI 1973/1223 the Customs Duties (Deferred Payment) Regulations

Indirect Tax Reporter: ¶63-780

7910   Identity of importer

The 'importer' of goods from the time of importation to the time when they are delivered out of charge is defined as including:

'any owner or other person for the time being possessed of or beneficially interested in the goods.'

There is therefore an element of choice as to the identity of the importer in relation to any particular transaction.

In practice, the importer is generally taken as being the person named as such on the Single Administrative Document (SAD). Care needs to be taken in selecting the importer, to ensure that it is someone capable of recovering the tax concerned as input tax (i.e. someone involved in the supply chain, not a mere carrier, etc.), and to avoid any unintended side effects in relation to the place of supply (see 7916).

Legislation: CEMA 1979, s. 1(1)

Other Material: Notice 702, *Imports*

Indirect Tax Reporter: ¶63-760

7916   Interaction with place of supply rules

A supply of the imported goods by the importer of them into the UK is treated as made in the UK, even if delivery in respect of the supply commenced outside the UK.

7922   Value on importation

The value of imported goods for VAT purposes is generally the same as the value for customs duty purposes plus (if not already included) taxes, duties, etc. arising prior to or because of the importation, and all commission, packing, insurance, transport, etc. costs up to the place of importation. If a further destination of the goods within the EC is known at the time of importation, the value for VAT purposes includes the further transport, etc. costs in so far as they result from the transfer of the goods to that further destination. If the value is based on the price at which they are supplied, this is generally reduced to take account of any prompt payment discount.

The value for customs duty purposes is generally based on the price at which the transaction is taking place. Where this is inappropriate there are other possible bases, such as the transaction value of identical or similar goods, or a computed value based on cost (see Regulation 2913/92 on the valuation of goods for customs duties purposes).

Legislation: FA 2006, s. 18; FA 1996, s. 27; VATA 1994, s. 21(2), (3)

Indirect Tax Reporter: ¶14-250

7928   Reliefs – general

There are three main kinds of relief from VAT on the importation of goods from outside the EC:

(1) Suspension of the charge – the charge is not removed, but is suspended while the goods are in some kind of suspension regime (such as warehousing). The liability crystallises, and VAT becomes payable, as and when the goods are removed from the suspension regime for free circulation in the UK.

(2) Temporary admission relief (TA) – this is a customs duty relief under which certain goods brought temporarily to the UK escape the liability to VAT on importation altogether, provided that all appropriate conditions are met and the goods are subsequently re-exported. If the goods remain in the UK beyond the permitted period, a UK VAT liability then arises. Security for the customs duty and the import VAT is normally required.

(3) Absolute reliefs – in some cases there is no liability to VAT on the importation.

The reliefs available are mentioned in 7934ff. Detailed coverage of these reliefs is beyond the scope of this work.

Other Material: Notice 702/8: *Fiscal warehousing;* Public Notice 232 *Customs Warehousing*; Temporary Admission – Public Notices: 200, 306 and 308

Indirect Tax Reporter: ¶63-800

7934   Reliefs – suspension

VAT on importation of goods from outside the EC into the UK is suspended in the following main cases:

- importation into a free zone – in this instance, the import VAT is due only when the goods are removed from the free zone for home use or when they are consumed within the freezone;.

- importation into a customs warehouse, excise warehouse or a fiscal warehouse – in these cases, importation VAT becomes payable, if at all, when the goods are removed from the warehouse for home use;

- inward processing relief (IPR); and

- transit and transhipment.

The low value consignment relief (LVCR) for goods imported from the Channel Islands for goods under £15, has been repealed from 1 April 2012. This move attacks big businesses such as Spec Savers and

HMV that deliberately set up in the Channel Islands to be able to send low value goods to the UK and not have to charge VAT on them.

Legislation: VATA 1994, s. 17–18F; Regulation 2913/92, art. 98 onwards

Other Material: Notice 334: *Free Zones;* Notice 232 *Customs Warehousing*

7940 Reliefs – temporary admission (TA) relief

Relief from both customs duties and import VAT is available for various goods temporarily imported into the UK, including:

- certain personal effects temporarily imported;
- commercial vehicles and aircraft;
- goods for removal to another Member State;
- containers and pallets; and
- various goods specified in the legislation.

TA is primarily a customs duty relief, but the VAT follows the duty treatment.

In each of the above cases, there are a number of conditions to be met – security may be required, and VAT becomes due if the goods remain in the UK beyond a specified period or the conditions for relief are otherwise breached. TI is essentially a customs duty relief, but the import VAT follows the duty treatment. On importation, security may well be required for the customs duty and the import VAT and will be released when the goods are subsequently re-exported.

7946 Reliefs – absolute reliefs

There are a number of absolute reliefs from VAT on importation from outside the EC, including the following:

- reimportation by a person who is not a taxable person and who previously exported the goods, without having been altered, where they have previously borne VAT (which has not been repaid) within the EC and various detailed conditions are met;
- a similar relief for taxable persons (again conditional on any VAT suffered previously not having been reclaimed);
- a further similar relief for reimported motor cars;
- goods specified in the *Value Added Tax (Imported Goods) Relief Order* 1984 (SI 1984/746);

- certain personal property imported by persons entering the UK to take up permanent residence;

- certain goods, such as labels, imported free of charge for incorporation in UK manufactured goods which are to be exported from the EC;

- certain trade samples, imported legacies, awards for distinction, etc.; and

- goods for diplomats.

In each case detailed conditions must be met, and appropriate documentation completed, in order to qualify for relief. In addition, no VAT is payable on imported goods falling within travellers' duty free allowances.

Legislation: VATA 1994, s. 21(4)–(7); *Value Added Tax (Imported Goods) Relief Order* 1984 (SI 1984/746); EC Regulation 684/2009; *VAT (Personal Reliefs for Special Visitors) Order* 1992, SI 1992/3156; *C&E Duties (Goods Permanently Imported) Order* 1992 (SI 1992/3193)

7952 Removal from warehouse, etc.

Import VAT on UK goods placed in a warehouse is due on their removal for home use. Any sales which have taken place in the warehouse are ignored.

However, if the goods are processed in the warehouse so as to lose their character, or mixed with UK-produced goods so that they are no longer identifiable, the position is different. In this case, import VAT is no longer due on their removal from the warehouse. However, if they are supplied while in the warehouse, VAT is due on the last such supply to take place, and is payable by the person removing the goods for home use.

Legislation: VATA 1994, s. 18

Other Material: Notice 200 (March 2012 edn) – *Temporary Admission*; Notice 232 *Customs Warehousing* (June 2014 edn)

Indirect Tax Reporter: ¶63-875

Chargeable events – VAT on acquisitions from elsewhere in the EC

7972 Introduction to VAT on acquisitions

There are particular rules on the acquisition of goods from elsewhere in the EC. There are also special registration requirements for unregistered businesses and other entities acquiring goods in the UK from elsewhere in the EC.

The general rule for goods supplied within the EC is that they are taxed in the Member State to which they are dispatched:

- the supplier in the Member State of dispatch can zero-rate his supply, but only if he is supplying to a VAT-registered customer and quotes the customer's VAT registration number on his invoice (see 7818);

- the customer is liable to account for VAT in the Member State of arrival on his 'acquisition' of the goods;

- to enable the authorities to verify that acquisition tax is properly accounted for, the supplier must submit periodic EC sales listings to which the authorities in the Member State of arrival have access (see 8460);

- a supplier dispatching significant quantities of goods to unregistered persons in another Member State may become liable to register for VAT there, and account for that Member State's VAT on these supplies (see 7818). In such a case, he is relieved of the liability to account for output tax in his own Member State; and

- some unregistered entities acquiring significant quantities of goods from suppliers in other Member States may become liable to register for VAT in respect of these acquisitions. They are then liable to account for their own country's VAT on the acquisitions and their suppliers can zero-rate their supplies in the Member State of dispatch.

Indirect Tax Reporter: ¶64-220

7978   Acquisition – normal procedure

The most common case involving acquisitions from elsewhere in the EC (see 7972) is where a UK business purchases goods from a supplier elsewhere in the EC, who ships the goods to the UK customer. The liability to pay acquisition VAT arises when:

- there is an acquisition of goods in the UK (see 7984 and 8002);

- the acquisition does not involve the supplier in making a UK supply (i.e. it is not caught by the UK's distance selling rules or by the rules for supplies of installed goods – see 7818);

- the person making the acquisition does so in the course of a business;

- the person making the acquisition is a taxable person (i.e. someone who is already registered for VAT, or is liable to be registered, whether under the ordinary VAT system or under the rules for registration of persons making significant UK acquisitions); and

- the acquisition is not exempt or zero-rated.

Legislation: VATA 1994, s. 10

Case: *JP Commodities v R & C Commrs* [2008] BVC 683

Indirect Tax Reporter: ¶64-210

7984   Meaning of acquisition

The term 'acquisition of goods' is defined in the EC VAT Directive 2006/112, art. 20 and, in the UK, in VATA 1994, s. 11. An acquisition arises where goods are removed from one Member State to another and:

- the movement involves a supply by the person dispatching the goods; or

- the person is moving his own goods from one Member State to another.

A taxable person moving his own goods from one Member State to another is deemed to make a supply in the Member State of dispatch and an acquisition in the Member State of arrival.

Legislation: VATA 1994, s. 11; EC VAT Directive 2006/112, art. 20

Indirect Tax Reporter: ¶64-240

7990   Exceptions from normal procedure on acquisition

The basic definition of an acquisition would cover any movement of goods within the EC (see 7984). However, where there would be relief from VAT on import from outside the EC under the *Value Added Tax (Imported Goods) Relief Order* 1984 (SI 1984/746) (see 7946) there is a parallel relief from VAT on acquisition from another Member State.

Similarly, no liability arises where the goods are transferred by a private individual, subject to the exceptions covered below.

(1)   New means of transport

A new means of transport delivered from one Member State to another bears VAT in the Member State in which it is registered, even if the person to whom it is delivered is not a taxable person. Where the customer is a taxable person, the normal rules apply. Where the customer is not a taxable person, he is liable to account for VAT in the state of registration of the means of transport (*Value Added Tax Regulations* 1995 (SI 1995/2518), reg. 148). The person making the acquisition must notify HMRC within seven days of their arrival, and pay the tax due within 30 days of receiving a demand for it.

The supplier of the goods must hold appropriate evidence that tax has been accounted for in the other Member State (where the acquirer is not a taxable person) in order to zero-rate the supply.

A UK supplier of a new means of transport for acquisition in another Member State may need to charge UK VAT in the first instance, pending receipt of evidence that acquisition tax has been accounted for in the other Member State. HMRC can refund the tax at a later date, on receipt of a claim accompanied by suitable evidence.

A 'new means of transport' is, broadly, a new ship, aircraft or land vehicle. Excluded from the definition are ships of 7.5 metres and less, aircraft less than 1,550 kilograms in take-off weight, and land vehicles of less than 48 cc (or electric vehicles using less than 7.2 kilowatts). A means of transport is new until at least three months have elapsed from its entry into service (six months for a land vehicle) or it has had a specified amount of use (VATA 1994, s. 95).

(2) Excise goods

As a general rule, when goods liable to excise duty (such as tobacco products, alcohol, etc.) are delivered by a supplier in another Member State to a UK customer, this will involve a taxable supply in the UK under the distance selling rules (see 7818). This is because no turnover limit applies for the distance selling of excise goods (VATA 1994, Sch. 2, para. 1(3)).

Where the seller is not making the supply by way of business (or is otherwise not registrable in the UK) the customer (including a private individual) is obliged to notify the acquisition and account for VAT on it (*Value Added Tax Regulations* 1995 (SI 1995/2518), reg. 36).

It follows that the only way in which excise goods can enter the UK from elsewhere in the EC without payment of UK VAT (and duty) is if a private individual collects them personally from elsewhere in the EC and brings them back for his own private use. These excise rules require that VAT and excise duty is paid in the Member State in which they were purchased (say in a supermarket).

Legislation: VATA 1994, s. 40, s. 95; Sch. 2, para. 1(3), s. 36A; *Value Added Tax Regulations* 1995 (SI 1995/2518), reg. 36, 148; EC Directive 2008/118, art. 32; HMDP 2010

Indirect Tax Reporter: ¶64-360

7996 Registration in respect of acquisitions

A person in business in the UK, and certain other persons, can become liable to register for VAT in the UK if acquisitions from other Member States exceed a certain threshold (measured from 1 January in the year concerned).

This liability to register affects all businesses, and also any body corporate, club, association, organisation or other unincorporated body carrying on non-business activities.

The liability to register in respect of acquisitions is covered in more detail at 8280ff.

Legislation: VATA 1994, s. 10(3), Sch. 3

Indirect Tax Reporter: ¶64-300

8002 Place of acquisition

If the goods are removed to the UK (the normal case), then the acquisition takes place in the UK.

The other instance where an acquisition might be deemed to take place in the UK arises where a person accepts an intra-EC delivery of goods in another member state, but quotes his UK VAT registration number to enable his supplier to zero-rate the supply (referred to in the legislation as 'making use of a VAT number'). In this instance, an acquisition is deemed to take place in the UK unless the acquirer can show that he has actually paid acquisition tax in the member state of delivery. This facilitates the policing of the system, since the supplier will have included the UK registration number on his EC sales listing (8460).

Legislation: VATA 1994, s. 13

8008 Time of acquisition

An acquisition is deemed to take place on the earlier of the date when the supplier issues an invoice and the 15th day of the month following the date when the goods are removed. The date of payment for the supply is ignored.

Legislation: VATA 1994, s. 12

Indirect Tax Reporter: ¶64-320

8014 Value of acquisition

The value of an acquisition is the value of the transaction under which it takes place. This will normally be the value of the consideration, whether monetary or non-monetary.

There are special provisions to cover special cases (gifts, connected persons, etc.) on similar lines to those relating to supplies of goods.

Legislation: VATA 1994, s. 20 and Sch. 7

Indirect Tax Reporter: ¶64-340

8016 Call-off stocks, consignment stocks and sale or return goods

If a trader ships goods to another member state and holds them as stock under his control, this gives rise to a deemed supply. This is consignment stock. The subsequent supply of the goods to a customer in that other state is a supply made there. The normal EC movement rules apply. The trader will need to have a VAT number in the member state where the goods will be stored and then the trader can zero-rate his supply as a dispatch into the other member state.

However, if goods are shipped to another member state and held under the control of a specific customer there, who can then 'call off' the goods for use as and when required, this is still regarded as a zero-rated supply to the customer (if VAT registered) and an acquisition by the customer in the other member state, both arising at the time of the movement of the goods.

There is no distinction between the two for VAT purposes; both are treated as dispatches and acquisitions. However, there are major contractual and commercial differences. In call-off stock, the title does not pass until the customer calls the stock off.

Goods sent to an overseas customer on sale or return are treated in the same way as consignment stocks.

The same treatment applies to goods shipped to the UK by a supplier in another member state.

Care should be taken in dealings with other member states, as not all of them accept these treatments.

Other Material: Notice 725 – *The Single Market* (February 2011 edn)

Inputs and input tax recovery – general

8034   Overview of input tax recovery

Traders are obliged to account for VAT on taxable supplies which they make. They can also recover VAT charged to them on supplies which they obtain, and on imports of goods from outside the EC and acquisitions of goods from within the EC.

A number of further complexities arise for businesses which make both taxable supplies and exempt supplies (even occasional exempt supplies), see 8110ff.

HMRC have produced a series of toolkits to help taxpayers and agents alike to meet their compliance obligations and to avoid common errors. One of these is on input tax recovery and it can be accessed on the HMRC website. It has been updated in July 2016.

Indirect Tax Reporter: ¶19-000

8040   Definition of input tax

The only tax which may be recovered by a taxable trader is that which falls within the definition of input tax. 'Input tax' is defined as follows:

'... 'input tax', in relation to a taxable person, means the following tax, that is to say–

(a)   VAT on the supply to him of any goods or services;

(b)   VAT on the acquisition by him from another Member State of any goods; and

(c)   VAT paid or payable by him on the importation of any goods from a place outside the Member States,

being (in each case) goods or services used or to be used for the purpose of any business carried on or to be carried on by him.'

It follows from this definition that a number of conditions must be met before a person can treat VAT as input tax. Even where these conditions are met, so that the tax ranks as input tax, some or all of it may still be non-deductible, and this aspect will be considered later. However, there is no possibility of tax being deductible unless it meets the basic criteria set out above.

(1)   Taxable person requirement

A UK 'taxable person' is a person who is registered for VAT in the UK, or is required to be registered (VATA 1994, s. 3(1)). Value added tax in the UK is also deductible by a non-UK taxable person if, broadly, that input tax would have been recoverable if that trader was established in the UK (see 8080). Similarly, a UK taxable person can recover certain VAT suffered in other member states (see 8082).

(2)   Supply, acquisition or importation

It is implicit in the definition of input tax that a supply, acquisition or importation must actually take place for any 'tax' which is sought to be reclaimed to be input tax.

Transactions which do not amount to supplies are covered at 7776ff.

(3)   Supply to or acquisition/importation by taxable person

Where an input tax refund is sought in respect of a supply, it is essential that the supply is made to the taxable person rather than to some other person. This does not necessarily mean that the supply must be paid for by the taxable person, or that all supplies for which a person pays rank as supplies made to that person.

The *Redrow* case concerned a business promotion scheme operated by a housebuilder. The builder would engage estate agents to sell the existing houses of potential customers. Provided the customers then bought new houses from Redrow, it would pay the estate agents' fees. The estate agents contracted separately with the customers for payment of the fees, in the event that the customers did not buy from Redrow. The court held that the estate agents supplied services to Redrow, so that the VAT on their fees was input tax in Redrow's hands.

The outcome of the *Redrow* case depended upon the contractual relationship between Redrow and the estate agents. It should be contrasted with the position where, for instance, a tenant is obliged to pay a landlord's professional costs in connection with a lease variation. In this instance, the tenant has no contractual relationship with the landlord's professional advisers, and the supplies by those advisers are made to the landlord, and not to the tenant. The right to input tax recovery (if any) rests with the landlord and not with the tenant.

This issue has been further under the spotlight with employers trying to recover input tax in respect of pension fund management (see HMRC Brief 8/15 and HMRC Brief 17/15).

In order to recover input tax on an importation of goods from outside the EC, or an acquisition from within the EC, the importation or acquisition must have been made by the claimant.

(4) Legal services relating to insurance claims

When claims are made against people who have insured against such claims, and the claims are resisted, lawyers are often engaged to handle the matter. It is accepted by HMRC that the supply by the lawyer, in this instance, is made to the policyholder rather than to the insurance company, even though the insurance company instructs the lawyer on behalf of the policyholder and the insurance company is ultimately responsible for the lawyer's fees.

(5) Supplies obtained by employees

As a rule, when supplies are ordered by employees of a taxable person for that person's business, it will be clear that the supplies are obtained on behalf of the employer and so no difficulty should arise over the deduction of related input tax. For instance, if a buyer for XYZ Ltd orders 200,000 printed circuit boards from a supplier, no one will be in any doubt that the contract is really between XYZ Ltd and the supplier, and the transaction will proceed accordingly.

There are occasions when employees may obtain supplies in their own right and recharge them to the employer. The most common of these are dealt with on a concessionary basis.

If an employee on a business trip obtains accommodation and meals for business reasons and the business bears the full cost, the tax can be treated as input tax even if the supply was made, in the first instance, to the employee. This will not enable tax to be recovered for business entertaining as such tax is specifically treated as non-deductible, but it does prevent tax on ordinary subsistence expenses from being disallowed on a technicality.

A special provision applies where employees buy petrol for business journeys, and the business reimburses the actual expenditure. In addition, tax can be reclaimed on a reasonable petrol element of mileage allowances paid to employees in respect of business mileage.

(6) Importation by taxable person

Value added tax on the importation of goods from outside the EC ranks as input tax in the hands of the taxable person concerned if it is paid or payable by the taxable person.

Value added tax on importation is payable as if it were a duty of customs (VATA 1994, s. 1(4)). It is therefore payable by the importer. The term 'importer' is defined, in CEMA 1979, s. 1(1), as follows:

"importer', in relation to any goods at any time between their importation and the time when they are delivered out of charge, includes any owner or other person for the time being possessed of or beneficially interested in the goods and, in relation to goods imported by means of a pipe-line, includes the owner of the pipe-line.'

It follows that, in relation to any particular importation, a number of different persons may each be entitled to act as importer. As some of these (such as the carrier of the goods) will usually not be in a position to reclaim the VAT, it is important to ensure that care is taken in deciding who is to act as importer for VAT purposes.

HMRC will regard as the importer for VAT purposes the person named on the import entry documentation as such. Since this documentation must be completed and passed to HMRC before the goods can enter the UK, the decision needs to be taken in advance.

(7) Tax properly chargeable

The tax which can be treated as input tax is the tax properly due on the supply, acquisition or importation concerned. While this seems straightforward, it gives rise to problems in practice.

It is not uncommon for VAT to be charged on transactions where it is not due, usually because of difficulties in understanding the law and a desire by the supplier to 'play safe' in cases where the customer can recover any tax due. In such instances, the tax cannot be treated as input tax in the hands of the customer, as it is not properly chargeable on the transaction.

(8) Domestic accommodation for directors

Tax on supplies, etc. used in providing domestic accommodation for directors is deemed not to be input tax, and so cannot be reclaimed. This rule applies where:

- supplies, acquisitions or imports are to be used by a company in connection with the provision of accommodation by the company; and

- the accommodation is used or to be used for the domestic purposes of a director of the company, or of a person connected with a director.

A 'director' includes an owner/manager who is not formally a director and, in the case of a company managed by its members rather than by a board of directors, a member of the company; a person connected with a director is a director's spouse, and a relative or the spouse of a relative of the director or the director's spouse.

This exclusion from the definition of input tax appears to apply even if the company receives consideration for the provision of accommodation, although its validity in that case appears questionable.

(9) Business use

Tax on supplies obtained by (or importations or acquisitions by) a taxable person cannot rank as input tax unless the goods or services concerned are used, or to be used, for the purposes of a business carried on or to be carried on by that person.

The concept of 'business' is considered at 7798.

It should be noted that the supplies concerned do not have to be put to business use immediately, provided that they are intended for business use and business use ultimately occurs.

Tax on supplies to be used for the purposes of a business not yet operating ranks as input tax. Thus, a taxable person with an existing business ought to have little difficulty in recovering tax on preparatory expenses of a new business not yet commenced, but to be operated by the same person. This view is supported by both UK and EC case law. More difficulty may be encountered where no supplies are yet being made, and HMRC will need to be satisfied that there is a genuine business activity before allowing registration.

It has also been established that input tax recovered in respect of preparatory activities may be retained by the trader, even if the activity proves abortive and no taxable supplies are actually made.

Recovery of VAT that is not input tax

There are some circumstances in which an entity cannot recover input tax because it is not a 'business' as discussed above.

Examples include government departments, local authorities and self-build house builders.

However, the VAT legislation allows for some limited recovery of VAT that is not input tax; local authorities can recover VAT under VATA 1994, s. 33 (see VAT Notice 749), government departments can recover VAT under VATA 1994, s. 41.

The house builders' scheme in VATA 1994, s. 35 and s. 33ff. provides for refunds of VAT in certain cases. HMRC have published revised claim forms and guidance on recovery of VAT under the scheme (April 2015).

In Budget 2015, the Chancellor announced that the list would be extended by adding s. 33C and s. 33C to the *VAT Act* 1994 to allow for medical courier charities (e.g. blood bikes) to recover VAT incurred for their non-business activities (from 1 April 2015).

The same right will also be extended to charities providing palliative care for their non-business activities, also from 1 April 2015.

Legislation: VATA 1994, s. 1(4), 3(1), 24(1), (3), (7), 33, 33C, 33D, 35, 41; CEMA 1979, s. 1(1); *Value Added Tax (Input Tax) (Reimbursement by Employers of Employees' Business Use of Road Fuel) Regulations* 2005 (SI 2005/3290)

Cases: *C & E Commrs v Redrow Group plc* (1999) BVC 96; *Rompelman v Minister van Financiën* (Case 268/83) (1985) 2 BVC 200,157; *Belgium v Ghent Coal Terminal NV*(Case C-37/95) [1998] BVC 139

Other Material: Notice 701/36; Notice 700, *The VAT guide*; VAT Notice 1001 *Refunds of VAT for certain charities* (September 2015); Form VAT 431NB and VAT 431C (April 2015); VAT Notice 749 (August 2015); HMRC Brief 8/15 and HMRC Brief 17/15

Indirect Tax Reporter: ¶19-000

8046   Apportionment of tax

If tax arises on a supply, acquisition or importation used partly for business purposes and partly for other purposes, the taxpayer now has a choice: either to adopt an up-front apportionment (VATA 1994, s. 24(5)) or recover all the input tax up-front and pay the private element back each VAT quarter using the Lennartz principle over the tax life of the asset (120 months for land and buildings and 60 months for other assets).

Legislation: VATA 1994, s. 24(5); *Value Added Tax Regulations* 1995 (SI 1995/2518), Pt. 15A

Cases: *Finanzamt Uelzen v Armbrecht* (Case C-291/92) [1996] BVC 50; *Lennartz v Finanzamt München III* (Case C-97/90) [1993] BVC 202

Indirect Tax Reporter: ¶19-040

Input tax which cannot be deducted

8058   Supplies on which tax is non-deductible

Although the general rule is that input tax is, in principle, deductible by a taxable person when making his VAT returns, there are a number of occasions when the tax cannot be deducted. In particular, there are a number of categories of supply (or importation) the tax on which is specifically treated as non-deductible:

(1) Purchase of a motor car for use in the business, unless:

    (a) the person to whom it is supplied intends to use it primarily:

        (i)   to let with a driver, as passenger transport (e.g. as a taxi);

        (ii) to provide as 'self-drive hire'; or

        (iii) to provide driving instruction;

    (b) the purchaser is a motor manufacturer or dealer for whom the vehicle is to be stock in trade; or

    (c) it is a 'qualifying car', namely where the purchaser has no intention of making it available for any form of private use (a hard test to fulfil, meaning that VAT should not be recovered without proper consideration of the rules).

(2) Leasing or contract hire of a motor car, to the tune of 50% of the input tax incurred. The VAT may be recovered in full if the car falls into the categories identified at (a) to (c) of item (1) above and on any separately identified element of the leasing or contract hire charges relating to maintenance.

    The rules do not apply to vans, or dual-cab pick-ups and HMRC have published a guide on vans and combi-vans and whether they qualify for input tax recovery.

(3) Business entertainment. This means, broadly, input tax on supplies used in the gratuitous provision of hospitality of any kind, including expenses relating to staff acting as hosts, but does not include input tax relating to staff entertainment. Following the *Danfoss* and *AstraZeneca* cases in 2010, HMRC now accept that the block does not apply to overseas entertainment (see HMRC Brief 44/10). Note that this is a fairly limited provision, although the new public notice on entertainment (PN 700/65 – February 2012 edn) allows for modest entertaining at restaurants, but not golf days. Where there is a private benefit for overseas entertainment, this will need a balancing output tax charge to nullify the benefit of recovery.

(4) Certain fittings acquired by the builder of a new dwelling. These are goods to be incorporated in the building by a person intending to grant a major interest in it other than materials, builder's hardware, sanitary ware, or other items of a kind normally installed by builders as fixtures. Items specifically excluded from recovery are:

    (a) finished or prefabricated furniture, other than furniture designed to be fitted in kitchens (this prevents the builder from deducting input tax in respect of fitted wardrobes, etc.; note, however, that many built-in wardrobes making use of alcoves, etc. inherent in the design of the building are not regarded as 'furniture' so no blocking of input tax arises);

(b) materials for the construction of fitted furniture, other than kitchen furniture;

(c) domestic electrical or gas appliances, other than those designed to provide space heating and/or water heating, or such items as ventilation equipment and air-cooling equipment which is now commonly installed in buildings as a requirement of building regulations. The blocking applies, from 1 March 1995, to goods installed in buildings for relevant residential or charitable use as well as to dwellings.

(5) Goods acquired under a second-hand goods scheme.

(6) Certain imports of goods partly owned by another.

Input tax made non-deductible in this way is colloquially referred to as having been 'blocked'.

Legislation: *Value Added Tax (Input Tax) Order* 1992 (SI 1992/3222), art. 5–7

Cases: *McLean Homes Midland Ltd v C & E Commrs* [1993] BVC 99; *Midlands Co-operative Society Ltd v R & C Commrs* [2007] EWHC 1432 (Ch); [2007] BVC 653

Other Material: *Business Brief* 16/04, 9 June 2004, 'VAT – definition of a motorcar'; *Business Brief* 06/04, 27 February 2004, 'VAT avoidance: demonstrator cars'; *Danfoss & AstraZeneca* cases in the ECJ (Case – 371/07); PN 700/65 (February 2012 edn)

Website: www.gov.uk/government/publications/hm-revenue-and-customs-car-derived-vans-and-combi-vans

Indirect Tax Reporter: ¶29-500

8060   Use to which supplies are put

Even where the basic rules relating to input tax are met (see 8040 and 8058), the trader may be prevented from deducting some or all of the input tax arising on supplies to him and importations or acquisitions of goods by him.

The right to deduct input tax is restricted so that, broadly, only tax on supplies and importations used in making taxable supplies may be deducted. Input tax on supplies used in making exempt supplies is, in principle, non-deductible (see 8110ff.).

Indirect Tax Reporter: ¶19-000

8061   Input tax and holding companies

There has been a long history of problems with holding companies deducting input tax. The latest case to address this issue is BAA case and is covered in the HMRC Brief 35/14.

This brief confirms that HMRC have reviewed its policy following the decision of the Court of Appeal in the case of *British Airport Authority (BAA)* ([2013] England and Wales Court of Appeal Civ 112). The decision confirms that VAT is only recoverable where there is a direct and immediate link to taxable supplies. BAA was refused permission to appeal to the Supreme Court. For the purpose of this brief, 'taxable supplies' includes supplies not charged to UK VAT, but which carry a right to input tax recovery.

Legislation: VATA 1994, s. 26(2); *Value Added Tax Regulations* 1995 (SI 1995/2518)

8062   Evidence for deduction of input tax

Before a trader may deduct tax as input tax, he must hold evidence in support of the claim. Furthermore, the evidence must take a specified form which varies depending upon the manner in which the input tax arose. For instance, if the input tax arises on a supply, the evidence required is a valid tax invoice addressed to the claimant.

HMRC have power to accept other evidence for the deduction of tax. This power has been exercised as follows:

- an invoice made out to an employee is acceptable evidence in the case of subsistence expenses and petrol; and

- a tax invoice is not required for expenditure below £25 on telephone calls from public or private telephones, purchases through coin operated machines, car park charges, or privately operated road tolls.

HMRC can be asked to accept alternative evidence in particular cases, and they must act reasonably in the exercise of their discretion.

Case: *Chavda (t/a Hare Wines)* [1993] BVC 1,515

Other Material: Notice 700, *The VAT guide*

Indirect Tax Reporter: ¶63-790

8063   Repayment of input tax on non-payment

Where input tax has been claimed on a supply received by a taxable person and he has not made payment for that supply by the time six months have elapsed from the due date for payment of the supply (or the date of supply itself, if later), the input tax must be repaid to HMRC on the person's VAT return.

Legislation: VATA 1994, s. 26A

Indirect Tax Reporter: ¶19-010

Pre-registration and pre-incorporation supplies/post deregistration supplies

8068   Relief available pre-registration and post-deregistration

Relief is available for certain input tax incurred prior to registration (or, in the case of a limited company, prior to incorporation) and after deregistration. This tax would not, in principle, be deductible as the trader will not have been a registered taxable person at the time when the tax arose. Consequently, there are special provisions to give effect to the relief.

In each case, there are a number of conditions to be met and, even if these are met, the relief remains at the discretion of HMRC (see 8070, 8072 and 8074).

Legislation: *Value Added Tax Regulations* 1995 (SI 1995/2518), reg. 111

Indirect Tax Reporter: ¶43-050

8070   Pre-registration supplies

Relief is available for certain input tax incurred prior to registration (see 8068). The tax which can be reclaimed is:

- tax on supplies of goods obtained within four years before registration, if the goods are still on hand at the date of registration, either in their original state or incorporated into other goods; and

- tax on supplies of services obtained within six months before the registration date and not disposed of before registration.

In order to reclaim the tax, the trader must hold ordinary evidence for deduction of input tax. In addition, the trader must make a list of all the services in respect of which a claim is made, showing their description, date of purchase and (if appropriate) the date of their disposal. A service would be disposed of if it consisted of work done on goods which were then sold.

Where a claim includes input tax relating to supplies of goods obtained before registration, the trader must compile a stock account showing quantities purchased, quantities used in making other goods, date of purchase and date of disposal (either of original goods or of goods made from them).

Indirect Tax Reporter: ¶43-000

8072 Pre-incorporation supplies

A company can reclaim input tax on supplies obtained on its behalf prior to its incorporation (see 8068). The tax covered is the same as that for pre-registration supplies, and the same time-limits apply (see 8070).

In order to qualify for this relief, certain extra conditions need to be met. The supplies must have been obtained for the benefit of the company or in connection with its incorporation. The person who obtained the supply must have become a member, officer or employee of the company, and must not have been a taxable person at the time of the supply or importation. The company must have reimbursed the person who acquired the supplies, or given an undertaking to do so. The goods or services must have been obtained for the purposes of a business to be carried on by the company, and must not have been used (even temporarily) for any other purpose.

The evidence required is as for pre-registration inputs (i.e. normal input tax evidence plus a list of services and/or a stock account).

Indirect Tax Reporter: ¶43-050

8074 Deregistration: relief in respect of services

HMRC also have power to refund tax incurred after deregistration has taken place where this relates to services (but not goods) obtained for the purposes of the business which the person carried on while registered (see 8068). Relief for such input tax is at the complete discretion of HMRC.

Typically, relief is given in respect of services such as those of accountants and lawyers involved in closing the business down, or disposing of it. Normal evidence for input tax deduction must be held.

If possible, the claim should be made by including the tax as input tax on the trader's final VAT return. If this is not possible (e.g. because the work is not done, or a tax invoice is not received, until later), the trader should make a separate claim on form VAT 427. This must be done within four years of the supply.

Legislation: *Value Added Tax Regulations* 1995 (SI 1995/2518), reg. 111

Other Material: Notice 700/11

Miscellaneous input tax matters

8080 Repayments to non-UK traders – 8th EC Council Directive 2008/9 EC and 13th Directive claims

There are provisions permitting repayments of input tax to traders established elsewhere in the EC and to traders established outside the EC.

A claim can be made if the claimant:

- is not registered, liable or eligible to be registered in the UK;

- has no UK business establishment; and

- does not make supplies in the UK, other than certain supplies connected with international freight transport or supplies of services treated as made in the UK merely because that is where the recipient belongs.

No input tax will be repaid under these provisions if the claimant intends to use the inputs in making a UK supply, or to export them from the UK (in either of these cases UK VAT registration is the proper mechanism to obtain a refund). Input tax will only be repaid if it would have been repaid to a similar trader registered for VAT in the UK.

From 1 January 2010, a claim must be made to HMRC via the website. Details of the procedures are given in Notice 723A (March 2016 edn).

Anti-avoidance provisions – MTIC fraud

To prevent goods being sold VAT-free in the UK, a registration requirement applies to businesses that are not registered for VAT and are selling goods in the UK and, either:

- they are overseas businesses (with no business establishment in the UK); or

- they obtained the goods via a VAT-free transfer of a business as a going concern (or a chain of such transfers) from an overseas business.

The provisions were introduced in FA 2000 to counter a scheme known as Missing Trader Inter Community (MTIC) (aka carousel fraud) whereby overseas business claim back VAT brought in the UK and later sell them on in the UK VAT-free.

Legislation: *Value Added Tax Regulations* 1995 (SI 1995/2518), Pt. XX, XXI

Other Material: Notice 723A, *Refunds of VAT in the European Community for EC and non-EC businesses* (October 2011 edn)

Indirect Tax Reporter: ¶55-420

8082   Repayment of input tax to UK traders by other member states

There are equivalent provisions in other member states to the UK provisions discussed at 8080, whereby UK traders can obtain input tax refunds from those states.

Other Material: Notice 723A (October 2011 edn)

8084   Tax repayments to DIY builders

There are special rules enabling recovery of VAT on goods (but not on services) by persons building certain buildings (dwellings or buildings for relevant residential or charitable use), or on goods or services by persons converting certain non-residential buildings for residential use, otherwise than in the course of a business.

Legislation: VATA 1994, s. 35; *Value Added Tax Regulations* 1995 (SI 1995/2518), Pt. XXIII

Indirect Tax Reporter: ¶37-000

8090   Manner of claim for input tax deduction

As a general rule, deduction of input tax is claimed by including the tax on the periodic VAT return form for the period in which the claimed tax arises. In some cases of difficulty, and if authorised by HMRC, an estimated claim may be made and then rectified on a subsequent return. Input tax deduction cannot be claimed more than four years after the due date for submission of the return for the period in which the input tax arose.

In the case of pre-registration or pre-incorporation input tax, the tax should be included on the trader's first VAT return. For tax on supplies of services obtained after deregistration, the tax should be included on the final VAT return if possible, or otherwise claimed separately using VAT 427.

In no case may input tax be reclaimed unless the necessary evidence is held to support the refund. If the evidence is not to hand at the time when the relevant return has to be submitted, it should be notified separately to HMRC (either by letter or using VAT 652). In practice, it will often be included as input tax on a later return, and HMRC have indicated that it will not normally see this as giving rise to a penalty. Such late input tax claims have been implicitly approved of in a number of tribunal decisions.

Legislation: *Value Added Tax Regulations* 1995 (SI 1995/2518), reg. 29(1A), (3)

Other Material: Form VAT 427, 652

Inputs and input tax recovery – partial exemption

8110   Introduction – partial exemption

A trader that makes both taxable and exempt supplies must analyse its input tax, recovering only that which relates to the making of taxable supplies. Input tax related to making exempt supplies is, in principle, non-deductible.

While this is a simple enough idea, its practical implementation is a notoriously complex area.

Partial exemption is widespread. Most traders make exempt supplies at one time or another, and some such supplies can be substantial in relation to the size of the business. Typical exempt supplies which can give rise to partial exemption problems include sale of business premises or land, sale and leaseback of business premises or land, sub-letting of business premises, and issues of shares.

HMRC have produced a series of toolkits to help taxpayers and agents alike to avoid the more common errors in VAT and HMRC have produced a toolkit on partial exemption. It has been updated in July 2016.

Other Material: Notice 706, *Partial exemption*; HMRC toolkit: Partial Exemption (July 2016)

Indirect Tax Reporter: ¶19-400

8116 Partial exemption legislation

The UK legislation on partial exemption is rooted in VATA 1994, s. 26, which establishes the basic principle that the input tax which is recoverable by a trader is that which relates to the making of taxable supplies. It also provides power for HMRC to make regulations setting out detailed rules to give effect to this principle. These detailed rules are contained in the *Value Added Tax Regulations* 1995 (SI 1995/2518), Pt. XIV and XV. The equivalent EC legislation is in the EC VAT Directive 2006/112, art. 167 onwards.

Legislation: VATA 1994, s. 26; *Value Added Tax Regulations* 1995 (SI 1995/2518), Pt. XIV, XV; EC VAT Directive 2006/112, art. 167 onwards

Case: *DCM (Optical Holdings) Ltd v R & C Commrs* [2007] BVC 733

Other Material: Notice 706, *Partial exemption*

Indirect Tax Reporter: ¶19-420

8122 Overview of the partial exemption rules

The general principle is that the input tax for which a trader may obtain credit is that which is attributable to the making of:

- taxable supplies;

- supplies treated as made outside the UK which would be taxable if made inside the UK (this heading includes certain supplies made in warehouse) (these are referred to as 'foreign supplies'); or

- other supplies made outside the UK and certain exempt supplies designated by the Treasury (these are referred to as 'specified supplies').

Specified supplies for the third category above include certain insurance and financial transactions, and the making of arrangements therefor, supplied to persons outside the EC or in connection with the export of goods from the EC, if these supplies are exempt or would be if made in the UK.

Any other input tax is, in principle, non-deductible.

The regulations provide that this basic rule is to be implemented by analysing input tax according to the use to which the related supplies or importations are put. Tax on supplies used solely in making taxable supplies is deductible, while that on supplies used solely in making exempt supplies or for a separable business activity which does not involve the making of supplies is, in principle, non-deductible.

Some supplies obtained will inevitably not fall into one category or the other, being used in support of the business activities generally. The tax on such supplies is referred to colloquially as overhead input tax, or the 'pot', or as 'residual input tax'. This is input tax which cannot be directly attributed either to the making of taxable supplies or the making of exempt supplies. The relative use of supplies used in making both taxable and exempt supplies must be ascertained, and the pot must then be allocated between making taxable supplies and making exempt supplies in the proportion arrived at.

In principle, the input tax attributed to the making of taxable supplies, either directly or indirectly, is deductible while that attributed to making exempt supplies (referred to as exempt input tax) is non-deductible. However, if the exempt input tax falls below the de minimis limit, it too may be deducted.

Example

To summarise the points above, each trader is obliged to analyse input tax as far as possible according to the use to which the related supplies are put, then to reallocate the pot between taxable and exempt input tax as follows:

	Total input tax	Taxable input tax	Exempt input tax	The pot
Primary attribution	X	X	X	X
Secondary attribution of the pot, according to relative taxable and exempt use	–	X	X	(X)
Final attribution	X	X	X	X

If the exempt input tax so calculated is sufficiently small, the whole of the input tax for the period can be recovered. Otherwise, only the taxable input tax can be recovered and the exempt input tax is non-deductible.

This calculation must provisionally be done for each VAT return period, although from 1 April 2009, for each VAT quarter in a partial exemption year, for extra simplicity a trader using the standard method may use the final figure from the previous year (see 8145). At the end of the trader's VAT year, the calculation must be reworked for the year as a whole to calculate the amount of input tax finally deductible. This is done to remove any seasonal distortion. Any under or overpayment arising from the calculations for the return periods is adjusted on the first return of the next period. However, from 1 April 2009, this annual adjustment may be done at the year-end, thus achieving certainty earlier (see 8145).

Legislation: VATA 1994, s. 26; *Value Added Tax (Input Tax) (Specified Supplies) Order* 1999 SI 1999/3121

Other Material: Notice 706, *Partial exemption*

8126   Ignoring partial exemption: de minimis limit

If a trader incurs exempt input tax, that input tax is non-deductible in principle. However, if the exempt input tax falls below the de minimis limit, then the trader's input tax for the period concerned is treated as being wholly attributable to the making of taxable supplies, and therefore deductible.

The exempt input tax falls below the de minimis limit if it does not exceed:

- £625 per month (£7,500 p.a.); and

- 50% of total input tax.

Exempt input tax for this purpose is the aggregate of:

- input tax directly attributed to exempt supplies; and

- the portion of the pot attributed to exempt supplies (*Value Added Tax Regulations* 1995 (SI 1995/2518), reg. 99(1)(a)).

Changes in 2010 make the *de minimis* rules slightly easier to operate (see VAT information sheet 04/10).

Legislation: *Value Added Tax Regulations* 1995 (SI 1995/2518), reg. 99(1)(a), 106

Other Material: Notice 706, *Partial exemption*

Indirect Tax Reporter: ¶19-430

8127   Final attribution of input tax for a tax year or longer period

A trader is normally required to make a provisional attribution of input tax for each prescribed accounting period (or VAT return period) and then review this for a 'longer period'. A business which regularly incurs exempt input tax will almost always have a longer period which is the same as its VAT tax year.

The tax year is a period of 12 months ending on 31 March, 30 April or 31 May, depending upon the business's VAT accounting period. For a business making monthly returns, the tax year will normally end on 31 March.

A trader's first tax year is the first 'full' tax year (the part year from the date of registration to the normal tax year end being known as the 'registration period'). HMRC have power to approve or direct a different first tax year.

A different tax year is sometimes used in order to have a tax year which corresponds with the business's financial year. In the normal course of events, a trader's longer period is the same as the tax year. However, a different longer period may be used by mutual consent of the trader and HMRC.

There are special rules for businesses incurring exempt input tax for the first time, for new businesses, and for businesses ceasing to be registered for VAT.

A different longer period from those set out above can be used if this is approved by HMRC. However, they do not have the power to direct that a different longer period be used against the trader's will.

Legislation: *Value Added Tax Regulations* 1995 (SI 1995/2518), reg. 99(1)(d), (7), 107

Other Material: Notice 706, *Partial exemption*

Indirect Tax Reporter: ¶19-520

8128   Concept of attribution rules

On the face of it, there is little conceptual difficulty in identifying supplies used only in making taxable supplies, or in making exempt supplies (although there may be considerable administrative difficulty). On closer examination, however, there are a number of areas which can give rise to difficulty, such as:

- the treatment of tax on supplies which, while not contributing directly to the making of supplies, are done in the course of the general business activity of making supplies rather than some separate and distinct non-supply activity – this is treated as part of the 'pot' of residual input tax; and

- the treatment of tax on supplies obtained in connection with an exempt supply, where that exempt supply is itself undertaken in support of the general business activity rather than for its own sake.

Importance of intention

A point worth noting is that the attribution of input tax is based on intended future use of the inputs concerned and not simply on the status of the first supply made. It was held in these cases that where inputs were used in making an exempt supply, but there was an intention to make a subsequent taxable supply, the input tax must be apportioned. It was not to be attributed wholly to the first exempt supply.

Case: *C & E Commrs v Briararch Ltd; C & E Commrs v Curtis Henderson Ltd* [1992] BVC 118

Indirect Tax Reporter: ¶19-405

Attribution of the partial exemption pot (overhead input tax)

8144　The standard partial exemption method

Once the primary attribution of input tax has been made, there will almost certainly remain input tax which has not been allocated specifically to the taxable input tax or exempt input tax categories, but is assigned to the pot as relating to both types of supply. It is then necessary to make a secondary analysis to allocate the pot between the making of taxable and exempt supplies.

The method by which this apportionment is normally carried out is 'the standard method' – is set out in the *Value Added Tax Regulations* 1995 (SI 1995/2518), reg. 101(2). The proportion of the pot attributed to taxable supplies, and hence regarded as deductible, is the proportion which taxable turnover bears to total turnover. This is calculated as a percentage, and may be rounded up to the next whole number if the overhead input tax does not exceed £400,000 per month on average. Otherwise, it should be rounded up to two decimal places (reg. 101(5)).

The sum of the input tax directly attributed to exempt supplies, and the exempt proportion of the pot, is referred to as 'exempt input tax'.

Exclusions from turnover under standard method

Certain potentially distortive amounts of turnover are to be excluded from the formula for the apportionment of the pot under the standard method. These are amounts resulting from:

- supplies of capital goods used for business purposes;

- non-taxable amounts relating to the supply of goods on which input tax deduction was blocked (e.g. sale of a business car);

- self-supplies; and

- certain financial and property supplies which are incidental to the trader's business, such as land sales (if they are incidental to the trader's business rather than main business activities).

Following the important House of Lords decision in *C & E v Liverpool Institute for Performing Arts* [2001] BVC 333, certain supplies made outside the UK must also be excluded from the computation (see *Business Brief* 12/2001).

VAT deductions relating to foreign branches

Changes have been announced for partially exempt businesses in respect of deductible VAT in foreign branches of UK businesses. The measure (from August 2015) will result in an amendment to the *VAT Regulations* 1995 (SI 1995/2518) and will mean that supplies made by foreign branches can no longer be taken into account when calculating how much VAT incurred on overhead costs can be deducted by partly exempt businesses in the UK.

It also implements a 2013 decision of the Court of Justice of the European Union (ECJ) (*Credit Lyonnais*).

Up to now, UK law has allowed UK partly exempt businesses to recover VAT on overhead costs used to support foreign branches by reference to supplies made by those branches. This does carry the risk that a business could artificially increase the amount of input tax it is entitled to deduct by over-allocating overhead costs to its non-EU foreign branches.

In *Credit Lyonnais*, the ECJ found that the Principal VAT Directive (PVD) could not be interpreted so as to allow a company to take into account the turnover of its EU or non-EU foreign branches when calculating how much input tax it can deduct in the member state where it has its principal establishment.

Implementing this decision in the UK means that UK businesses will not be able to take into account supplies made by foreign branches when carrying out their partial exemption calculations.

The measure will apply to both the standard method (under reg. 101) and special methods under reg. 102.

8145　The 2009 changes to the standard method

The changes to the partial exemption rules from 1 April 2009, need to considered.

For all accounting periods commencing on or after 1 April 2009, the standard method is changed in respect of the following:

(1) in-year provisional recovery rate;

(2) early annual adjustment;

(3) use-based option for newly partially exempt businesses; and

(4) widening the scope of the standard method.

The first three of these changes are optional. The fourth is mandatory.

In-year provisional recovery rate

Prior to 1 April 2009, all businesses using the standard method were required to make a provisional claim of input tax each quarter, based on sales, and then to do the annual adjustment after the end of each year to firm up the claim.

Businesses now have the option of using last year's recovery rate as a provisional basis for all quarters and then to adjust as normal after the year end. They are not obliged to do this, but this is now the default position (see Notice 706 for details). They can do each quarter as normal on the sales basis if they wish.

Early annual adjustment

The pre-April 2009 position is that all businesses using the standard method, were required to perform an annual adjustment under the *Value Added Tax Regulations* 1995 (SI 1995/2518), reg. 107, and to firm up on their provisional claims made in-year. This was done in the first VAT return after the year end.

The new rules allow businesses that wish to, to bring forward the annual adjustment and to do it in the last quarter of the year (reg. 107(1)(g)).

Use-based option for new partially exempt businesses

This measure allows newly partly exempt businesses to adopt a use-based recovery of input tax in their first year, to avoid unfair recovery.

Widening the scope of the standard method

Prior to 1 April 2009, the standard method only dealt with the recovery of input tax relating to supplies made in the UK. Businesses that made supplies outside the UK had to recover input tax on a use basis under the *Value Added Tax Regulations* 1995 (SI 1995/2518), reg. 103.

The 2009 measure widens the scope of the standard method, so that it now deals with input tax on all supplies made by the business.

Such businesses will still need to perform the annual adjustment.

Standard method override

In order to ensure that taxpayers do not take advantage of the partial exemption rules, it is necessary to substitute a use-based attribution (i.e. based on the use of purchases) if this gives 'substantially' different results from the standard method. 'Substantially' means:

- more than £50,000; or

- more than 50% of the residual input tax (but not less than £25,000).

The effect of this is that no override calculation is necessary if residual input tax is less than £50,000 per year (although this is reduced to £25,000 for group undertakings other than VAT groups).

The need to carry out two calculations inevitably complicates matters for partially exempt businesses that fall above this threshold.

Legislation: *Value Added Tax Regulations* 1995 (SI 1995/2518), reg. 101(2), (3), (4), (5); 106A, 107A to 107E

Other Material: Notice 706, *Partial exemption*

Indirect Tax Reporter: ¶19-400

8146   Use of special partial exemption methods

HMRC may approve or direct the use of a partial exemption method other than the standard method. As a general rule, direct attribution will still be required where possible, and the variation of method will relate to the way in which the pot is apportioned. However, different methods may also be approved for the apportionment of the whole of the input tax.

If a non-standard method is required, written approval should always be obtained.

HMRC have published a new framework to help housing associations agree partial exemption special methods with HMRC.

This Framework has been prepared in conjunction with the National Housing Federation, the Scottish Federation of Housing Associations and Community Housing Cymru, and with the knowledge of the Northern Ireland Federation of Housing Associations. The Framework will be of positive assistance to both housing associations and HMRC officers in agreeing fair PE methods. It will help housing associations and HMRC officers to decide whether the standard method works well (as it often will do) or whether a partial exemption special method (PESM) is needed.

The Framework gives guidance on what is likely to work if a PESM is required. It sets out the range of activities carried out by Housing Associations (HAs). It discusses the challenges they may pose in designing a fair and reasonable PESM and describes ways that those challenges can be overcome. It suggests calculations that are likely to lead to a fair apportionment of input tax. It also goes through when the calculation may need to be split into the operational sectors of the HA in order to arrive at a fair answer.

HMRC have also published a framework document for NHS trusts to help the trusts gain agreement for special methods with HMRC.

Neither of these framework agreements are meant to supersede Public Notice 706, but are meant to augment it.

HMRC have recently lost the Lok'nStore (LnS) case in the Upper Tribunal. LnS provides taxable self-storage facilities in purpose built stores. It also provided exempt insurance for stored goods to all customers who did not otherwise have adequate cover. The issue in this case was the amount of input VAT that could be recovered on general overhead costs, such as those incurred on the construction, maintenance and operation of its stores.

LnS proposed a special method which involved a floor space allocation, resulting in a 99.98% recovery rate for VAT on overheads. HMRC rejected this on the grounds that it did not provide for a better reflection of how the costs were used than the standard method. The UT upheld the taxpayer and said that it was fair (HMRC Brief 34/14).

Legislation: *Value Added Tax Regulations* 1995 (SI 1995/2518), reg. 102(1)

Cases: *R & C Commrs v Lok'Store Group plc* [2014] BVC 523

Other Material: Notice 706, *Partial exemption; Framework for Housing Associations Partial Exemption Special Methods November 2013; Framework for NHS Trusts – October 2013*

Indirect Tax Reporter: ¶19-480

8148 Imposition of a partial exemption method

HMRC have the power to impose a partial exemption method. If HMRC seek to use this power, the trader has a right of appeal to a VAT tribunal.

A method cannot be imposed retrospectively if the trader has been using a method which complies with the law.

Legislation: VATA 1994, s. 83(e); *Value Added Tax Regulations* 1995 (SI 1995/2518), reg. 102(2), (4)

Other Material: Notice 706, *Partial exemption*

Indirect Tax Reporter: ¶19-405

8150 Agreement of partial exemption method

The precise method used by a business to determine the extent to which input tax is recoverable is crucial, and so it is very important to make sure that entitlement to use a particular method is documented. If a special method is to be used, its terms must be considered carefully and documented.

Taxpayers who apply for a special method under reg. 102 will be required to make a formal declaration to the effect that, to the best of their knowledge and belief, the method requested is fair and reasonable. If it transpires that this was not the case, HMRC will be entitled to recoup any VAT that has been incorrectly claimed.

Legislation: *Value Added Tax Regulations* 1995 (SI 1995/2518), reg. 102(9)

Other Material: Notice 706, *Partial exemption*

Indirect Tax Reporter: ¶19-495

8154 The special method override

In parallel with the standard method, the legislation provides for a special method override, such that if the partial exemption method does not fairly and reasonably represent the extent to which goods and services are used in making taxable supplies, then HMRC can impose a notice on the taxpayer, such that he will be required to adjust the attribution and account for the difference.

Legislation: *Value Added Tax Regulations* 1995 (SI 1995/2158), reg. 102A and 102B

Other Material: Notice 706, *Partial exemption*

Indirect Tax Reporter: ¶19-430

Partial exemption: change of use

8158 Special partial exemption provisions for changes of use

There are special provisions to cover the position where input tax is attributed to an intended taxable supply but, in the event, the supply or importation on which the tax arose is actually used in respect of an exempt supply. There are similar provisions to deal with input tax attributed to an intended exempt supply if the supply, etc. is then used in respect of a taxable supply.

These rules are colloquially known as the claw-back and pay-back provisions.

Legislation: *Value Added Tax Regulations* 1995 (SI 1995/2518), reg. 108, 109

Other Material: Notice 706, *Partial exemption*

Indirect Tax Reporter: ¶19-550

Partial exemption: non-supply activities and self-supplies

8174 Partial exemption: non-supply activities

It is possible to incur input tax in respect of activities that are outside the scope of VAT. How are these dealt with for partial exemption purposes? Examples include: sales of assets that are sold as a going concern and the issue (as opposed to the supply) of shares.

In a leading EC judgment, it was held that these inputs can be attributed to the pot, if they cannot be put elsewhere (the *Kretztechnic* case). Where they are directly linked to taxable supplies then they will be attributed there (*Abbey National* case).

Case: *Kretztechnic* and *Abbey National* cases

Other Material: Notice 706, *Partial exemption* (June 2011 edn)

Indirect Tax Reporter: ¶19-600

8176 Self-supplies

It should be borne in mind that input tax arising on self-supplies must be brought into the partial exemption calculations (although the self-supplies themselves are excluded from turnover under the standard method: see 8144).

Input tax on a self-supply cannot be attributed to the self-supply itself.

Legislation: *Value Added Tax Regulations* 1995 (SI 1995/2518), reg. 104

Indirect Tax Reporter: ¶19-670

Capital goods scheme

8182   Nature of the capital goods scheme

The original purpose of the capital goods scheme was to prevent partially exempt traders from making full recovery of input tax on major acquisitions of computers and buildings by putting them wholly to taxable use in the period of acquisition, then switching them to exempt use. Although such planning would now be caught by the partial exemption override rules, the scheme has remained in place.

The scheme allows an initial deduction (or disallowance) to be made in the ordinary way on acquisition, but to review this in later periods and make adjustments to the initial deduction in the light of subsequent taxable use of the asset.

The details of the scheme are set out in the *Value Added Tax Regulations* 1995 (SI 1995/2518), reg. 112–116, and the views of HMRC are set out in Public Notice 706/2.

Adjustments under the capital goods scheme may give rise to the need for adjustments to the accounts, and to capital allowances computations.

Although the capital goods scheme affects partially exempt traders, this does not mean that fully taxable businesses can ignore it. A person who is fully taxable when the input tax arises but becomes partially exempt during the adjustment period must also apply the scheme. A particular danger is that a fully taxable trader may buy a new building, and then sell it within the adjustment period by way of exempt supply. The remaining intervals will be attributed to exempt use, with significant loss of input tax.

Legislation: *Value Added Tax Regulations* 1995 (SI 1995/2518), reg. 112–116

Other Material: Notice 706/2, *Capital goods scheme* (October 2011 edn)

Indirect Tax Reporter: ¶19-800

8184   Input tax affected by capital goods scheme

The capital goods scheme applies to input tax arising on the supply or importation of:

- computer equipment costing £50,000 or more. The £50,000 limit is applied to each item of equipment separately. A system consisting of a number of items each costing less than £50,000 is not affected, even though the total system cost may exceed £50,000;

- land, buildings, parts of buildings, and certain extensions or alterations, costing £250,000 or more. The scheme potentially applies to both freehold and leasehold acquisitions, and to self-supplies. The extensions and alterations affected are those which increase the floor area of the building by 10% or more; and

- civil engineering works costing more than £250,000 and to building refurbishments or fitting out with a capital cost over £250,000 (regardless of any change in floor area).

Legislation: *Value Added Tax Regulations* 1995   (SI 1995/2518), reg. 113(a), (b–f), (g), (h)

Other Material: Notice 706/2, *Capital goods scheme* (October 2011 edn)

Indirect Tax Reporter: ¶19-810

8186   Capital goods scheme: period and manner of adjustment

For the purposes of the capital goods scheme (see 8182), the adjustment period is five years (strictly intervals) for computer equipment (and for leases with less than ten years to run), and ten years for other property.

The initial deduction is made in the ordinary way, but must then be reviewed in each of the remaining years (four for computer equipment or an interest in land having less than ten years to run when acquired, nine for other land) of the adjustment period.

In each year (strictly interval) the taxable use to which the item is put is calculated (using the current year partial exemption recovery percentage) and compared to the original year 1 recovery. If the taxable use has gone up in the year in question, then a bit more input tax may be claimed. If the taxable use has gone down, then a bit of input tax must be repaid.

This adjustment is made on the second VAT return after the end of the period to which it relates (*Value Added Tax Regulations* 1995 (SI 1995/2518), reg. 115(6)).

> **Example**
>
> Kelly Ltd acquired a new building in 2010 for £1m plus £175,000 VAT. In the year of acquisition, its partial exemption method enables it to recover 60% of the VAT on the building. In the next year, the recovery percentage increases to 70% and in the following year it drops to 55%.
>
> In the first year, Kelly Ltd recovers £105,000 of the VAT on the building.
>
> In the next year, it must review the position. The taxable use of the asset has gone up by 10%, so there is an adjustment in respect of $^1/_{10}$ of the total input tax (£17,500). The current amount recoverable is £12,250, compared with £10,500 originally recovered, so an extra £1,750 can be reclaimed.
>
> In the following year, the taxable use to which the item has been put has dropped to 55% from the reference year (year 1) of 60%
>
> So the adjustment is 5% of $^1/_{10}$ of the total input tax. This comes to £875 and because the taxable use has gone down Kelly Ltd must repay £875.

Legislation: *Value Added Tax Regulations* 1995 (SI 1995/2518), reg. 114(3), 115(1), (2), (6)

Other Material: Notice 706/2, *Capital goods scheme* (October 2011 edn)

Indirect Tax Reporter: ¶19-830

8188   Disposals within the adjustment period

If an asset to which the capital goods scheme applies is disposed of within the adjustment period (see 8186), use for the remaining complete intervals of the adjustment period is deemed to be taxable or exempt according to the status of the supply made on disposal of the asset. Computer equipment will always be taxable, so the taxable use for the remaining complete years will be 100%. This may result in repayments of input tax. Land may either be taxable or exempt, depending on circumstances, so a sale within the adjustment period could either be exempt (which could well result in input tax being repaid to HMRC) or taxable which could result in further input tax reclaims. The appropriate adjustment is made at the same time as the adjustment for the period of disposal.

Capping – basic rule

There is special provision that any additional input tax recoverable on disposal must not exceed the output tax due on the disposal (*Value Added Tax Regulations* 1995 (SI 1995/2518), reg. 115(3) proviso). This is intended to prevent recovery where, for instance, a computer system which has fallen rapidly in value is sold for a nominal sum. Without such a provision, the owner might be able to recover the whole of the input tax for the remainder of the adjustment period, even if the bulk of the value of the asset had been exhausted in making, say, exempt supplies.

Capping – special disposal rule

These capping provisions are more stringent where the taxpayer seeks to obtain a tax advantage. The total recovery of input tax over the period of ownership must be compared with the output tax on disposal and (save as the Commissioners otherwise allow) an adjustment must be made to ensure that the *total* recovery does not exceed the output tax. Applied strictly this would result in a restriction on input tax recovery, even in the case of a fully taxable business, in all cases where the asset had diminished in value between purchase and disposal (very likely in the case of computer equipment).

However, HMRC have said that they will not normally require this special disposal rule to be applied in the following circumstances:

(a) sales of computer equipment;

(b) where an owner disposes of an asset at a loss due to market conditions (such as a general downturn in property prices);

(c) where the value of the asset has depreciated;

(d) where the value of the asset is reduced for other legitimate reasons (such as accepting a lower price to effect a quick sale);

(e) where the amount of output tax on disposal is less than the input tax claimed only due to a reduction in the VAT rate;

(f) where the asset is used only for taxable purposes throughout the adjustment period (including the final disposal).

They also say that, where capping does apply, they will not necessarily require it to be fully applied, but only to the extent needed to cancel any 'unjustified tax advantage'.

If an asset is supplied as part of a transfer of a going concern, the new owner takes over the obligation to make adjustments under the capital goods scheme (*Value Added Tax Regulations* 1995 (SI 1995/2518), reg. 114(7)).

If an asset is lost, stolen, or destroyed (or a short lease expires) no further adjustments are made (*Value Added Tax Regulations* 1995 (SI 1995/2518), reg. 115(4)).

Legislation: *Value Added Tax Regulations* 1995 (SI 1995/2518), reg. 114(7), 115(3), (3A), (4)

Other Material: Business Brief 30/97, 19 December 1997; Notice 706/2, *Capital goods scheme* (October 2011 edn)

Indirect Tax Reporter: ¶19-884

Rates of VAT

8210 Standard rate and other rates of VAT

The legislation does not provide a list of standard-rated supplies. Instead, it works by exception. The legislation lists zero-rated supplies (in Sch. 8, VATA 1994), reduced rate supplies (in Sch. 7A, VATA 1994) and exempt supplies (in Sch. 9, VATA 1994). Thus, any supplies not within these schedules but within the scope of VAT MUST be standard-rated (an example is goodwill).

Following the introduction of the 5p charge for plastic bags by retailers, HMRC have highlighted that such a charge is the consideration for a standard-rated supply (see HMRC Brief 14/15).

The standard rate

The standard rate is currently 20% (from 4 January 2011).

The reduced rate

In the UK there is also a reduced or lower rate of 5% which applies to VAT on certain supplies and may be seen in VATA 1994, Sch. 7A.

It should be borne in mind that the Chancellor uses the 5% rate for socially desirable matters – it is not open to him to use the 0% rate as the member states have agreed that no more zero-rates will be applied. The reduced rate includes:

- domestic and charity fuel and power supplies;
- installation of central heating systems and home security goods provided under grants to pensioners and grant-funded heating measures for the less well off;
- supply of children's car seats;
- cost of renovating dwellings that have been empty for at least two years (three years prior to 1 January 2008);
- cost of converting a residential property into a different number of dwellings (e.g. converting a house into flats);

- cost of converting a non-residential property into one or more dwellings, and converting a dwelling into a care home (or for other qualifying relevant residential use), or into a house for multiple occupation (e.g. bed-sit accommodation);

- converting a non-residential property into a care home (or other 'relevant residential' purpose);

- converting a non-residential property into a multiple occupancy dwelling, such as bed-sit accommodation;

- converting a building used for a 'relevant residential' purpose into a multiple occupancy dwelling;

- renovating or altering a care home that has not been lived in for three years or more;

- renovating or altering a multiple occupancy dwelling that has not been lived in for three years or more;

- constructing, renovating or converting a building into a garage as part of the renovation of a property that qualifies for the reduced rate;

- the installation of factory-insulated hot water tanks, micro-combined heat and power systems, and heating systems that use renewable energy, to the extent that the costs of installation are funded by government grants and equivalent local authority schemes;

- the installation of ground source heat pumps;

- air-source heat pumps and micro-combined heat and power units;

- contraceptive products, including 'morning after' contraception (contraceptives which currently qualify for zero-rating are not affected by this provision); and

- mobility aids for the elderly and smoking cessation products. In the case of smoking cessation products, the reduced rate initially applied only for a limited period from 1 July 2007 to 30 June 2008, but this has subsequently been extended.

In Budget 2012, the Chancellor announced that the zero-rate would no longer be available to static caravans that did not meet strict environmental criteria on insulation and would be standard-rated instead. Following a climbdown, he announced that these static caravans will be at the reduced rate of 5% from 6 April 2013 (now in VATA 1994, Sch. 7A, Grp. 12).

The UK has been on the receiving end of EU infraction proceedings and the ECJ has held that the UK has interpreted the provisions of the PVD too widely in VATA 1994, Sch. 7A in respect of Energy Savings Materials (ESMs).

The zero rate

The other main rate of VAT in the UK is the zero rate. Supplies which are zero-rated attract VAT at the rate of 0%. The distinction between zero-rated supplies and exempt supplies is that the makers of zero-rated supplies can (indeed, must) register for VAT if they exceed the VAT registration limit and can recover tax on their expenses (although there is a limited exemption from registration in Sch. 1 to VATA 1994 for these traders – see 8264). As with exempt supplies, the legislation provides a list of supplies qualifying for zero-rating and there is also a general zero-rating which applies to exports of goods from the EC and to certain deliveries of goods to other EC member states (see 8216ff.).

It is possible for a supply to fall within the list of exempt supplies, and also within the list of zero-rated supplies. In this case the zero-rating takes priority, so the supply is treated as zero-rated.

Legislation: VATA 1994, s. 30(1), 31, Sch. 7A, Sch. 1, para. 14

Other Material: Notice 708/6; HMRC Brief 14/15 (August 2015)

Indirect Tax Reporter: ¶3-130

Zero-rated supplies

8216　Meaning of zero-rating

If a supply falls into a zero-rated category, then it is treated as a taxable supply, but the VAT due is calculated at a rate of 0%. Thus, the supplier does not have to account for any effective VAT on the supply. However, since it is a taxable supply, the supplier can register for VAT (indeed must, if taxable turnover exceeds the registration limits and the trader doesn't ask to be released under the VATA, Schedule 1 rules) and so can recover input tax incurred on supplies obtained for the business.

The effect of this is that zero-rated supplies reach the consumer free of VAT, except to the extent that the supplier's costs include items on which the deduction of input tax is specifically blocked. This is in contrast with exempt supplies, where there is always a hidden VAT cost, being the irrecoverable VAT element of underlying costs.

Legislation: VATA 1994, s. 30, Sch. 8

Indirect Tax Reporter: ¶20-000

8220   Zero-rating of exports and dispatches

There is a general zero-rating whereby, if a person supplies goods by way of export from the EC (or by delivery to a taxable person elsewhere in the EC who makes an acquisition of the goods), that supply is zero-rated. However, the form of words used in granting the zero-rating is such that it is not sufficient merely to export the goods in order to qualify for zero-rating. The zero-rating only applies if HMRC 'is satisfied' that the supplier has exported the goods, in other words, the supplier must be able to prove that the goods have been exported.

Supplies of goods can also be zero-rated if the goods are shipped for use as stores on a ship or aircraft with a non-UK destination, provided that certain conditions are fulfilled.

It should be noted that the zero-rating for exports applies only to supplies of goods. There is no general zero-rating for 'exports' of services, although some international supplies of services are relieved from UK VAT by being treated as made outside the UK (see 7816ff.). A supply of services consisting of work on another person's goods to produce goods which are then delivered outside the UK is zero-rated if a supply of the goods themselves would be zero-rated.

HMRC have published a HMRC Brief about VAT: Changes to rules for zero-rating supplies of goods for indirect export outside the European Union.

They are also reviewing the way in which the retail export scheme operates (see HMRC Brief 17/14).

Legislation: VATA 1994, s. 30(2A), (8), Grp. 7, Sch. 8

Evidence of export

HMRC are generally only prepared to be satisfied that the goods have been exported if the supplier retains evidence of this in a form specified by them. Evidence which might be sufficient to satisfy a court that the goods have been exported is insufficient to ensure zero-rating, if it does not take the form specified by HMRC.

The type of evidence required by HMRC varies according to the manner in which the goods are exported. Details of the necessary proof of export are set out in Notice 703.

A common feature of the various proofs of export required is that they are generally obtainable only at the time when the export takes place. For instance, if the export is a postal export of goods requiring a customs declaration, the evidence required is a certificate of posting. The Post Office is not likely to issue such a certificate at some later date.

Any trader who exports goods will therefore be well advised to make a careful study of Notice 703, as it relates to the particular form of export, and ensure that arrangements are in hand to ensure that proper evidence of export is obtained, and retained. Evidence of export must be obtained within three months of the date of the supply to justify the zero-rating.

For dispatches to other EC countries, zero-rating is only available if the customer is a taxable person. This must be evidenced by stating the customer's VAT registration number on the tax invoice.

- The exporter keeps a separate record of the transaction including evidence (such as the order) that the supply is made to an overseas trader.

- The goods are exported within three months of the time of supply.

- Valid proof of export (see above) is obtained within three months of the export.

- The goods are not used in the UK between leaving the exporter's premises and exportation taking place.

In March 2013, HMRC announced that it would review operation of the retail export scheme (tax-free shopping) to make it simpler and to protect UK tax revenue.

It also said that it would consult on changes to the zero-rating of exports for businesses who are VAT registered in the UK but who have no business presence in the UK.

Legislation: VATA 1994, s. 30(2A), (8), (10)

Other Material: Notice 703, *Exports and the removal of goods from the UK* (October 2013 edn)

Indirect Tax Reporter: ¶20-125

8221 EC Sales Lists and Intrastat reporting

In addition to reporting movements of goods to outside the UK on the VAT return, there are two extra layers of reporting:

- The EC Sales Lists (ECSLs or ESLs); and

- The Intrastat Supplementary Declarations (SDs or SSDs).

These are two entirely different systems.

The ECSL is an audit and control mechanism, designed to make sure that the recipient of a good in a member state that has received the good as a zero-rated dispatch, actually performs the two-stage acquisition process.

For fully taxable businesses, this process is tax neutral, but for partially exempt businesses, the taxpayer will have to pay over some VAT at his local VAT rate in his own Member State under the normal acquisition process.

The Intrastat reporting system is statistical only and only records actual movements of goods within the EU. There are two separate legs to the Intrastat system – arrivals (of goods into a member state) and despatches (of goods out of a member state).

The Intrastat thresholds are updated periodically with changes usually taking effect from 1 January. They are £250,000 for despatches and £1,500,000 for arrivals from 1 January 2015 (SI 1992/2790, reg. 3, as last amended by SI 2014/3135).

Legislation: SI 1992/2790, reg. 3

Other material: Notice 60, *Intrastat reporting* (January 2016)

8222   Zero-rating groups in VATA 1994, Sch. 8

There is a statutory list of items to be zero-rated; it consists of a series of 'groups' each of which contains a number of 'items' specifying supplies which are to be zero-rated. The groups are structured so as to contain items which are linked in some general way. For instance, the group headed 'Books, etc.' provides zero-rating for supplies of books and also for supplies of newspapers: essentially, the zero-ratings for supplies of published material are contained in this group.

Although each zero-rating group has a heading, these headings are of no legal force. The headings are there merely to assist in identifying which groups may provide zero-rating for a particular supply. In order to determine whether a zero-rating does, in fact, exist it is necessary to study the items within the groups, to see whether the supply fits precisely into one or other of the descriptions.

Furthermore, there are notes to each group which amplify or modify the meanings of the zero-ratings contained in the items, and these must be studied as well to see whether zero-rating is available.

The zero-rating groups, and a brief description of the supplies zero-rated by them, are set out below.

Group 1 – food (Notice 701/14)

Group 1 zero-rates many supplies of food for human consumption, animal food, seeds for food plants, and live animals used for food purposes. Certain supplies are excluded, particularly supplies in the course of catering (including supplies of hot take-away food) and confectionery.

Budget 2012 has introduced a measure to change the rules on the sale of hot food, such that from 1 October 2012, food that is kept above ambient temperature will be standard-rated regardless of whether the food is consumed hot or cold. This will affect shops that currently sell hot food straight out of the oven but is zero-rated on the grounds that it is merely cooling down. This represents a climbdown by the Chancellor since the original Budget statement.

This will affect shops such as Greggs and supermarkets that sell food straight out of the oven such as rotisserie chickens. This will not affect sales of bread, which can still be sold straight out of the oven and retain its zero-rating.

The consumption of takeaway food in food courts in shopping malls will also be standard-rated from the same date because the concept of 'premises' will be extended to cover adjacent seating.

The second Budget measure to affect the zero-rate in food is the treatment of 'sports drinks'.

The basic shape of the VAT legislation is that 'beverages' are normally standard-rated, but some sports drinks have been able to take the zero-rate because they have such a high food content. This anomaly has been removed from 1 October 2012 and all such sports drinks will are now standard-rated.

There has also been a recent case about confectionery products such as snowballs, where the FTT has agreed that they can be zero-rated as a cake, but has also emphasised that each case will turn on its facts (see HMRC Brief 36/14).

Group 2 – sewerage services and water (Notice 701/16)

Group 2 zero-rates supplies relating to the bulk treatment of sewage, emptying cess pools, etc. and most supplies of water for non-industrial purposes.

Group 3 – books, etc. (Notice 701/10 (June 2015 edn))

Most books, booklets, leaflets, pamphlets, newspapers and periodicals, printed music, maps, etc. are zero-rated, as are ancillary objects such as covers included in the price. The zero-rating does not extend to stationery.

Group 4 – talking books for the blind and handicapped and wireless sets for the blind (Notice 701/1)

Group 4 zero-rating covers supplies (including hire) of certain goods to the Royal National Institute for the Blind, the National Listening Library and similar charities. It also covers supplies (including hire) to any charity of certain equipment which is to be lent, free of charge, to blind persons.

Group 5 – construction of buildings, etc. (Notice 708 – June 2016 edn)

Group 5 zero-rating relates only to dwellings and certain buildings for communal residential use, non-business use by charities, or use by a charity as a village hall or similarly in providing social and recreational facilities.

Zero-rating is provided for:

- supplies in the course of constructing the building;
- the sale of the freehold or long lease of the building by the person constructing it (or, in some instances, the person who created it by converting a non-residential building); and
- the sale of renovated houses that have been empty for ten years or more.

In addition, services in the course of construction of a civil engineering work necessary for the development of a permanent park for residential caravans are zero-rated. However, the sale of such a caravan park does not qualify for zero-rating.

Mains electrical wiring and lighting systems are part of the fabric of the building when determining whether the work qualifies for zero-rating. In the course of a new development, HMRC accept that soft landscaping qualifies for zero-rating. Following the decision in *Rialto Homes plc* [2000] BVC 2,161, HMRC now accept that soft landscaping can extend to planting other than turf, the zero-rating applying to both the labour element and the cost of the plants.

A number of conditions must be met to secure zero-rating.

Group 6 – protected buildings (Notice 708)

A further zero-rating is available for certain protected buildings, if they are 'protected buildings' (these include listed dwellings), relieving from tax substantial reconstruction works prior to the grant of a major interest. From 1 October 2012, the zero-rate no longer applies to 'approved alterations'. The buildings to which the reliefs apply are qualifying buildings which are:

- buildings which are listed buildings under the *Planning (Listed Buildings and Conservation Areas) Act* 1990, or its Scottish or Northern Irish equivalents; or

- scheduled monuments within the meaning in the *Ancient Monuments and Archaeological Areas Act* 1979 or the *Historic Monuments (Northern Ireland) Act* 1971.

HMRC *Business Brief* 11/05 provide a definition of garages within Group 6. *Finance Act* 2012 has introduced a measure to remove the zero-rating for this work, so that from 1 October 2012, all work on protected buildings will be standard-rated. This will affect mostly listed dwellings, but will also affect churches and cathedrals.

Other material: Revised Notice 708 (April 2014), updated to incorporate changes to approved alterations and substantial reconstructions

Group 7 – international services (Notice 741A)

Most supplies of services across national boundaries are dealt with under the 'International services' heading.

There are however two zero-ratings for work carried out on goods for export from the EC, and for the making of arrangements for such a supply, for an export of goods from the EC, or for a supply of services made outside the EC.

Group 8 – transport (Notice 744A, 744B and 744C)

Group 8 provides zero-rating for supplies of ships and aircraft, for the public transport of passengers, for the international transport of goods and passengers, and for international freight handling and storage facilities.

The zero-ratings fall into five main categories:

(1) supplies of ships and of aircraft, including repair, maintenance, hire, etc.;

(2) supplies of lifeboats and certain ancillary equipment to charities;

(3) supplies of passenger transport and public transport services;

(4) supplies of freight transport and related supplies; and

(5) certain supplies by tour operators outside the EC.

Zero-rating applies to passenger transport in vehicles, ships and aircraft which are designed or adapted to carry not less than ten passengers (including the driver).

Also, zero-rating applies to passenger transport in vehicles which are designed or constructed to carry more than ten passengers, but which carry less than ten passengers solely because they are equipped with facilities for persons in wheelchairs.

Group 9 – caravans and houseboats (Notice 701/20 – January 2014 edn)

Group 9 provides zero-rating, broadly, for supplies of caravans and houseboats likely to be used as private residences, putting these on the same basis for VAT as private houses. There is a reduced rate of 5% on large caravans that do not meet the strict environmental criteria from 6 April 2013 (broadly holiday rather than permanent caravans) (see VAT *Information Sheet* 11–12).

Group 10 – gold (Notice 701/21)

Group 10 is of little general interest, and zero-rates supplies of gold held in the UK between Central Banks and members of the London Gold Market.

Group 11 – bank notes

Group 11 is of interest mainly to the Bank of England and the Scottish banks, and zero-rates the issue of bank notes by banks.

Group 12 – drugs, medicines, aids for the handicapped, etc. (Notice 701/7)

The zero-ratings provided by Group 12 are tightly defined, and highly specialised.

The group zero-rates a number of supplies of goods and services for use by people who are handicapped. The supply must be made to the handicapped person or to a charity which makes it available to the handicapped person.

The supplies which can qualify for zero-rating are tightly defined, but include items such as specialised equipment, modifications to buildings, adapted vehicles, etc.

Details are set out in Notice 701/7, which should be studied in detail by anyone making (or receiving) supplies which might be covered.

It should be noted that, to the extent that zero-rating is given for supplies of goods designed or adapted for use by handicapped persons, the tribunals have tended to take a narrow view and deny zero-rating where items have been of particular use to handicapped persons but also of use to the population generally (see, for instance, *Portland College* [1993] BVC 827).

The group also zero-rates the supply of drugs and medicines on prescription.

HMRC have published HMRC Brief 21/14, which covers zero-rating of the dispensing of drugs prescribed by physiotherapists and podiatrists.

Group 13 – imports, exports, etc.

Group 13 provides certain peripheral zero-ratings in relation to international trade.

Group 14 – tax-free shops

Now repealed.

Group 15 – charities, etc. (Notice 701/1)

Group 15 zero-rates a number of supplies to or by charities and related bodies. However, it should be noted that it does not provide any general zero-rating for matters relating to charities. In the main, charities are subject to exactly the same VAT rules as other entities.

The zero-ratings cover some supplies by charities and some supplies to charities. In all cases there are a number of conditions to be met.

The zero rate is available for the sale of donated goods that are offered to sale only to disabled people or people receiving means-tested benefits. From the same date, the zero rate is extended to all supplies of charity advertising in all media.

Group 16 – clothing and footwear (Notice 701/23)

Group 16 zero-rates supplies of children's clothing, of protective boots and helmets for industrial use, and of pedal cycle helmets and motor cycle helmets.

Group 19 – women's sanitary products

As part of the Prime Minister's renegotiation of the UK's relationship with the EU, he managed to secure agreement that women's sanitary products would no longer be subject to the reduced rate of VAT of 5%, but would become eligible for the zero-rate.

Accordingly, the legislation in VATA 1994, Sch. 7A, Grp. 4 has been withdrawn and is now inserted as Sch. 18, Grp. 19 (the zero-rate schedule).

This change is expected to come into force by a statutory instrument expected to be in 2017, but Brexit may affect this.

Legislation: VATA 1994, s. 96(9), (10) and Sch. 8

Cases: *C & E Commrs v Link Housing Association Ltd* [1992] BVC 113; *Portland College* [1993] BVC 827; *Rialto Homes plc* [2000] BVC 2,161; *Procter & Gamble (UK) Ltd v R & C Commrs* [2008] BVC 736

Indirect Tax Reporter: ¶20-200ff.

Exempt supplies

8228   Nature of VAT exempt supplies

The exemption schedule (Sch. 9) operates on similar lines to the zero-rating schedule (see 8222). If a supply falls within one of the categories listed in the groups (but not in their headings, which are merely to help in identification of potential exemptions), then the supply is exempted.

If a supply falls within an exemption category and also within a zero-rating category, then it is treated as zero-rated rather than exempt, since a supply falling within a zero-rated category is treated as zero-rated whether or not tax would otherwise be chargeable on it.

If a supply is exempt from VAT, no VAT is chargeable on it. However, the supplier is not entitled to deduct input tax incurred in connection with an exempt supply (subject to the partial exemption rules – see 8110ff.), so this input tax forms part of the costs of the business.

A person whose only supplies are exempt is not entitled to register for VAT.

Legislation: VATA 1994, s. 26, 30(1) and Sch. 9

Indirect Tax Reporter: ¶26-990

8230   Sch. 9 – the exemptions

The groups contained in the statutory list of exempt supplies (see 8228) and a brief description of the supplies exempted by them, are set out below.

Group 1 – land (Notice 742 (June 2013 edn), Notice 742A (April 2014 edn))

Group 1 exemption covers the grant or assignment of:

- any interest in land;
- any right over land; or
- any licence to occupy land.

As a matter of principle, a right to call for or be granted such an interest, right or licence is itself an interest in land, and so capable of falling within the exemption. However, in Scotland such a personal right is not considered to be a right over land, and the legislation therefore makes specific provision bringing such a right within the exemption.

Some supplies falling within these categories, such as holiday lettings, supplies of sporting rights, etc. are excluded from the exemption.

Finance Act 2012 introduced a measure to remove the exemption for self-storage and for chair rentals in hairdressing salons. These are standard-rated from 1 October 2012.

HMRC Brief 23/13 is a revised VAT Information Sheet which provides an updated guidance on the VAT treatment of the provision of storage facilities.

HMRC have published a new guidance document on caravan pitches and whether they can take the exemption in Group 1:

'You should review the VAT liability of your supplies if you currently treat caravan pitch fees as exempt in any of the following circumstances:

- the pitches are provided for less than a year;
- the pitches are subject to an occupation restriction (such as a planning term stating 'no caravan shall be lived in during February') which prevents them from being lived on at all times throughout the period for which the pitches are provided;
- the pitches are on a holiday/leisure site.

With effect from 1 March 2012, the criteria for treating your pitch fees as exempt will be stricter to ensure that only residential pitches qualify for exemption. Please see the new guidance below for details.'

Budget 2012 also introduces a new measure to restrict the zero-rating of caravans to all year round occupation only. This will remove holiday caravans with all year round restrictions from the zero-rate.

It is possible to opt to tax exempt supplies. The effect of this is to make taxable those supplies which would otherwise be exempt. The election is irrevocable (except for a statutory six-month cooling off period and with the consent of HMRC, after 20 years have passed) so, once made, all future supplies of the land concerned by the elector are standard-rated. The operation and scope of the election to waive exemption are complex. From 1 August 2009, it is possible to revoke the first options to tax made on the introduction of the 'option to tax' legislation.

Supplies in respect of land also extend to:

* surrenders;
* reverse surrenders;
* premiums;
* reverse premiums;
* assignments; and
* reverse assignments.

Group 2 – insurance (Notice 701/36)

The Group 2 exemption covers the provision of insurance or reinsurance. This is generally, but not always by recognised insurance companies, it can also include provision such as credit card protection and funeral plans. It also includes the provision of various intermediary services.

Most intermediary services provided by insurance brokers or insurance agents are covered, but not market research, promotional activities, etc., valuation or inspection services, or supplies of loss adjusters, etc. (except where handling a claim with full written authority to conclude it).

Group 3 – postal services

Group 3 exemption covers supplies of the conveyance of postal packets by the Post Office, and the supply by the Post Office of services in connection with the conveyance of postal packets (other than the hire of goods).

Group 4 – betting, gaming and lotteries (Notices 701/13, 701/26, 701/27, 701/28)

Group 4 exemption applies to supplies of:

- the provision of facilities for placing bets;
- the provision of facilities for playing games of chance; and
- the granting of a right to take part in a lottery.

However, excluded from the exemption are admission charges and gaming machines (fruit machines).

The VAT aspects of gambling are inextricably bound up with excise duty and it is not possible to understand the full picture without both.

Group 5 – finance (Notice 701/49)

Group 5 provides exemption for a wide range of financial transactions, including loans, dealings in money, the sale of stocks and shares (but not the issue of shares – which is outside the scope of VAT), management of special investment funds, etc.

The exemption applies to supplies made in the UK. As a general rule the place of supply will be outside the UK if there is a non-EC customer or an EC customer receiving the supply in a business capacity (see 7824). Where the customer is based outside the EC, related input tax will be recoverable for a supply which would be exempt under this head if made in the UK (*Value Added Tax (Input Tax) (Specified Supplies) Order* 1999 (SI 1999/3121); see 8060).

Group 6 – education (Notice 701/30)

Group 6 provides exemption, in broad terms, for the provision of education or vocational training by private schools (but not state schools), universities, and other 'eligible bodies'. Supplies of research by an eligible body to another eligible body are no longer exempted and have become standard-rated from 1 August 2013.

Supplies of examination services are exempt if the supply is either by or to an eligible body, and also if supplied to a person receiving exempt education or training.

All persons teaching English as a foreign language are regarded as being eligible bodies in respect of these supplies, but this does not necessarily mean that they are eligible bodies in respect of other supplies of education.

Group 6 also exempts certain ancillary supplies, and also the provision of facilities by youth clubs to their members.

HMRC have announced that the exemption for business supplies of research between eligible bodies will be withdrawn on 1 August 2013. The consultation ran until March 2013 and HMRC is expected to draw up secondary legislation in the summer of 2013. The consultation may be seen on HMRC's website.

Group 7 – health and welfare (Notice 701/57)

Group 7 provides exemption for a number of supplies connected with the provision of health and welfare services, and related goods. The views of HMRC on its application are set out in Notice 701/57. It covers supplies by doctors and other qualified health workers, the provision of care in hospitals and other approved institutions, and various related services. See also HMRC Brief 06/07: *Changes to medical services exemption from 1 May 2007.*

Group 8 – burial and cremation (Notice 701/32)

Group 8 exempts supplies of the disposal of the remains of the human dead, and the making of arrangements for and in connection with such disposal.

Group 9 – trade unions and professional bodies

Exemption is provided for supplies made in return for subscriptions by:

- trade unions;
- professional associations;
- learned societies and the like;
- certain trade associations;
- bodies which are made up of the exempt bodies above and which have the same objectives.

In each case, the body seeking exemption must be non-profit making.

The exemption also covers supplies received for payment of membership subscriptions to non-profit making organisations with aims of a political, religious, patriotic, philosophical, philanthropic or civic nature.

Group 10 – sport, sports competitions and physical education (Notice 701/45)

Group 10 exemption applies to the right to enter a sporting competition where all entry fees are returned as prizes, and also the right to enter a sporting competition promoted by a non-profit making body established for the purposes of sport or physical recreation. However, the latter exemption does not apply if the competition involves the free use of facilities for the use of which the body normally makes a charge.

Exemption also applies to supplies of sporting and physical education services to individuals by non-profit making bodies (such as many sports clubs). If the non-profit making body operates a membership scheme exemption only applies to supplies made to members.

At the time of writing, changes are awaited setting out detailed conditions for the recognition of a body as being non-profit making.

A non-profit making body is one that cannot distribute any profits it makes and is not subject to commercial influence.

HMRC have issued HMRC Brief 25/14. Bridport and West Dorset Golf Club is a non-profit making members' golf club. Under EU law, supplies by non-profit making bodies of services closely linked and essential to sport and to persons taking part in sport are exempt from VAT. In UK law, where the body operates a membership scheme, any supplies to individuals who are not members are excluded from the exemption on the basis that the fees received represent 'additional income' for the purposes of EU law.

The *Bridport* appeal concerned green fees paid by visitors (non-members) – Bridport had made a claim for repayment of VAT on green fees arguing that the exclusion of supplies made to non-members was not permissible under EU law.

The European Court of Justice (ECJ) found that where a supply is made by a non-profit making body, it is immaterial whether it is provided to a member of the body or a visitor. It took the view that a member state has no power to exclude certain groups of recipients of services from the benefit of the exemption – 'additional income' could not be construed in such a way that it would lead to such a restriction in the scope of the exemption. The ECJ also rejected the argument that the exclusion of supplies to non-members was permissible on the basis that it had the effect of reducing distortion of competition between members clubs and commercial organisations.

As a result of the ECJ judgment, HMRC accept that supplies of sporting services to both members and non-members of non-profit making sports clubs qualify to be treated as exempt from VAT. This is provided that the services are closely linked and essential to sport and are made to persons taking part in sport. HMRC will legislate by 1 January 2015 to reflect this.

Group 11 – works of art, etc. (Notice 701/12)

Group 11 applies to the disposal of certain works of art, etc. exempted from capital taxes when disposed of by private treaty sale, or by way of acceptance in lieu of tax, under the douceur arrangements.

Group 12 – fund-raising events by charities and other qualifying bodies (Notice 701/1)

Group 12 exempts the supply of goods or services in connection with up to 15 fund-raising events (such as a fete, performance, etc.) by:

- a charity, if the event is organised for charitable purposes by one or more charities; or

- a trade union or professional body within Group 9, or certain bodies with objects of a 'public' nature (VATA 1994, s. 94(3)), if the event is organised solely for the benefit of the body concerned.

In the case of a charity, relief is also available for supplies by a wholly owned subsidiary which covenants the whole of its profits to the charity.

Group 13 – Cultural services (Notice 701/47)

Group 13 provides exemption for supplies by public bodies and eligible bodies of admission to museums, galleries, art exhibitions and zoos, and theatrical, musical, etc. performances of a cultural nature.

Public bodies are local authorities, government departments, and other bodies listed as such by the Office of Public Service. Eligible bodies are non-profit making bodies managed on a voluntary basis by persons with no financial interest in their activities

The exemption for supplies by public bodies only applies where it is not likely to cause distortions of competition with taxable persons.

Group 14 – Supplies of goods where input tax cannot be recovered

Group 14 provides exemption for goods where input tax cannot be recovered. The exemption prevents the double taxation on the supply of goods where no tax is deductible on the purchase, acquisition, importation or production of the goods because they are used for making exempt transactions or because the tax is blocked by a specific exclusion.

An example would be the sale of an input tax blocked car.

Legislation: VATA 1994, Sch. 9

Indirect Tax Reporter: ¶27-000ff.

Registration and deregistration

8250   Importance of registration

Businesses making UK supplies

Persons carrying on businesses of making taxable supplies in the UK (often referred to as traders) are generally obliged to register with HMRC However, not everyone who makes taxable supplies by way of business is forced to register. If the value of taxable supplies is below certain registration limits, set out at 8256, then the trader is not obliged to register for VAT.

A trader who wishes to register, but is not obliged to register, can voluntarily apply for registration. If HMRC (or, on appeal, a VAT tribunal) is satisfied that the trader is carrying on a business and either makes taxable supplies already or intends to do so in the future, then the trader is entitled to registration. Similarly, registration can also be obtained by a person with a UK business establishment who makes (or intends to make) supplies overseas which would be taxable if made in the UK.

Intra-EC acquisitions of goods and distance selling

There are special rules requiring registration of UK businesses and other organisations making acquisitions of goods from elsewhere in the EC, and of EC businesses making distance sales of goods to UK customers who are not taxable persons (see 8280 and 8294).

Disposals of assets for which a VAT repayment is claimed

To prevent avoidance of VAT by overseas businesses, overseas businesses will need to register for VAT in the UK where they are not currently registered, but are making supplies in the UK and, either:

- they are overseas businesses with no business establishment in the UK; or
- they obtained goods via a VAT-free transfer of a business as a going concern (or a chain of such transfers) from an overseas business.

Legislation: VATA 1994, Sch. 1, 2, 3, 3A

Other Material: Notice 700/1, *Should I be registered for VAT?* (June 2016 edn)

Indirect Tax Reporter: ¶5-050

Registration – UK supplies

8256   Taxable turnover limits

The rules for determining whether a trader's business is sufficiently large to make registration mandatory are based upon the trader's taxable turnover. This refers to the amount of the trader's taxable supplies (including zero-rated supplies) in a given period (£83,000 from 1 April 2016). Consequently, it is not a measure of the size of the trader's business in terms of the profits which can be derived from it, but a measure of the value of supplies which are made to others.

It is always the person who is registered and not the business (see *Christodoulou* [2013] TC 02819).

Turnover for VAT includes all taxable supplies made in the course of a business, except that supplies of goods which are capital assets of the business may be ignored in determining whether the turnover limits have been reached. However, capital supplies of land which are taxable at the standard rate may not be ignored (VATA 1994, Sch. 1, para. 1(8)).

These turnover limits are based on the actual value of taxable supplies made, whether standard-rated or zero-rated. It is not permissible to reduce the turnover for any notional figure of VAT included in it. In allocating supplies to particular periods, the ordinary VAT time of supply rules apply. However, a person who is not registered for VAT cannot issue an invoice which meets the technical definition of a tax invoice, so the date of invoicing does not affect the time of supply. In general, a supply is treated as made at the earlier of the date when the supply is actually made and the date when the payment is received for it.

When services are acquired from overseas by a person carrying on a business in the UK, they are treated as supplies made both by and to the importer (VATA 1994, s. 8). Thus, they add to the importer's taxable turnover. These supplies count when checking whether the registration limits have been exceeded. This is the reverse charge mechanism.

The rules for determining whether a person is liable to register for VAT in respect of UK supplies made are covered in VATA 1994, Sch. 1. Broadly speaking, a person is liable to register for VAT if he makes taxable supplies and his taxable turnover has exceeded the historic turnover limit, or there are reasonable grounds for believing that it will exceed the future turnover limit.

Legislation in *Finance Act* 2012 removes the threshold for non-UK established businesses making taxable supplies in the UK from 1 December 2012. Schedule 1A has been created as a result. HMRC have published an updated version of PN 701/1 *Should I be registered for VAT?* (October 2015 edn). Notice 700/1 and 700/11 Supplement October 2015.

Annual turnover limit: historic

The historic turnover limit must be considered at the end of each calendar month, and is based on taxable turnover for the 12 months then ending. If the trader's turnover for the 12 months has exceeded the annual turnover limit, then registration is generally required; however, the trader need not be registered if he can satisfy HMRC that his turnover for the forthcoming 12 months will not exceed the deregistration annual turnover limit (see 8274). There are tables of registration and deregistration limits in the Key Data section.

Where a trader has become liable to register for VAT because of the historic turnover limit, he must notify HMRC of this within 30 days from the end of the calendar month for which the relevant turnover limit was exceeded. HMRC will then register him with effect from the end of the month following that in which the turnover limit was exceeded. However, registration can take effect from an earlier date if HMRC and the trader jointly agree to this (VATA 1994, Sch. 1, para. 5).

Example

On 30 June, John calculates that his taxable supplies for the previous 12 months have exceeded the registration threshold. John is liable to be registered for VAT from 30 June and must notify HMRC by 30 July. During July, John makes sales of £15,000. HMRC will register John from 1 August, unless an earlier date is agreed. John is not required to charge VAT on his supplies in July.

Turnover limit: future

The future turnover limit applies where there are reasonable grounds for supposing that the trader's taxable turnover within the next 30 days will exceed the current turnover limit (£83,000 from 1 April 2016). There is a table of limits in the Key Data section.

A person who becomes liable to register for VAT because of anticipated turnover for a future period of 30 days, must notify HMRC of this by, at latest, the end of the 30-day period. HMRC will then register him from the start of the 30 days or, if agreed by HMRC and by the trader, from some earlier date.

In practice, this may often mean that almost immediate notification is necessary. It is likely that a very small period of grace will be allowed before penalties are imposed for late registration, but this should not be reckoned as being any more than is necessary to allow for ordinary postal delay (i.e. one or two days). If notification is made by post, this should be followed up by telephone to ensure that the notification has arrived. Ideally the form should be sent by recorded delivery and HMRC should be told of its dispatch by telephone.

Example

On 12 May, James expects his taxable supplies in the next 30 days to exceed the current registration threshold. He is therefore liable to register for VAT from 12 May and must notify HMRC by 11 June. The effective date of registration will be 12 May.

Legislation: VATA 1994, s. 8 and Sch. 1, para. 1, 5, 6, Sch. 5

Case: *Christodolou* [2013] TC 02819

Other Material: Notice 700/1, *Should I be registered for VAT?*; HMRC Brief 31/12 – Removal of the VAT registration threshold for non-established businesses.

Indirect Tax Reporter: ¶43-025

8258 Registration procedure

When a person becomes liable to register for VAT, he must notify HMRC. In doing this, he is obliged to use the VAT registration form VAT 1. This may be downloaded from the HMRC website and completed online by himself or his agent. In addition, if the trader is a partnership, VAT 2 must be completed. This gives details of all of the partners.

Legislation: *Value Added Tax Regulations* 1995 (SI 1995/2518), reg. 5(1)

Other Material: Form VAT 2; Notice 700/1, *Should I be registered for VAT?*

Indirect Tax Reporter: ¶43-000

8260 Voluntary registration: supplies

A trader who already makes taxable supplies, but is not obliged to register for VAT by reason of either the historic or future turnover limits, can still seek registration if he wishes to do so. Provided that the trader can satisfy HMRC that taxable supplies are being made in the course of business, they are obliged to make the registration.

The application for registration by a trader seeking voluntary registration should be made on VAT 1, as for a trader who is obliged to register (see 8258).

Example

Nicky intends to open a corporate flower supply business. She estimates that her turnover in the first year will be £50,000, which is below the VAT registration threshold. However, she will suffer input tax on her direct costs and expenses. She intends to charge her customers an additional £5,000 to compensate for the VAT she will have to incur.

If Nicky registers for VAT, she will charge output tax of £10,000 (£50,000 × 20%). If her customers are VAT registered, they will be able to reclaim this VAT, so the overall cost to the customers is £50,000. This enables Nicky to be more competitive than if she went ahead and charged the £55,000 she planned.

Nicky can also recover nearly all of her input tax, so she will be no worse off because of the VAT registration.

Other Material: Form VAT 1; Notice 700/1, *Should I be registered for VAT?*

Indirect Tax Reporter: ¶43-000

8262 Intending trader registration

A person who does not yet make taxable supplies, but intends to do so, can also apply to be registered for VAT. Such a person will typically have started business already but still be at the stage of developing products or markets, so that taxable supplies have yet to be made.

If HMRC (or a VAT tribunal) are satisfied that taxable supplies are intended to be made, they must allow such a registration. If the business fails before taxable supplies are made, the intending trader remains entitled to retain input tax recovered in anticipation of making taxable supplies.

Cases: *Merseyside Cablevision Ltd* (1987) 3 BVC 596; *Rompelman v Minister van Financiën* (Case 268/83) (1985) 2 BVC 200,157

Other Material: Notice 700/1, *Should I be registered for VAT?*

Indirect Tax Reporter: ¶43-000

8264 Exemption from registration

A trader who makes mostly zero-rated supplies can, if he wishes, apply to be exempted from registration even though his taxable turnover exceeds the registration limits. This allows a trader who would only be reclaiming tax from HMRC, not paying tax into it, to escape from the administrative requirements of VAT registration. The cost to him is the input tax which he would otherwise be able to reclaim.

Legislation: VATA 1994, Sch. 1, para. 14(1)

Other Material: Notice 700/1, *Should I be registered for VAT?*

Indirect Tax Reporter: ¶43-000

8266 Registration by reference to overseas supplies

A trader established in the UK can be registered for VAT without making any UK taxable supplies. This applies if the trader:

- makes supplies outside of the UK which would be taxable if made within the UK; or

- makes supplies in a bonded warehouse which would otherwise be taxable (since these supplies are deemed to take place outside the UK, and so fall within the category above).

Such a trader can apply to HMRC to be registered for VAT (but is not obliged to register).

A business will also need to register if it is not already registered for UK VAT and they are selling goods in the UK and either:

- it is an overseas business with no business establishment in the UK; or

- it obtained the goods via a VAT-free transfer of a business as a going concern (or a chain of such transfers) from such an overseas business.

The purpose of this requirement is to prevent the avoidance schemes whereby overseas businesses claim back VAT on assets bought in the UK and later sell them in the UK VAT-free.

Legislation: VATA 1994, Sch. 1, para. 10, Sch. 3A

Indirect Tax Reporter: ¶43-045

8268 Registration by reference to previous owner's turnover

There is a special rule for determining taxable turnover for the purposes of the registration limits where a business has been taken over as a going concern. In determining whether the new owner is liable to be registered for VAT, he is deemed to have made the taxable supplies of that business before the transfer as well as after it. Thus, he has to count the previous owner's turnover as well as his own in checking whether he has reached the turnover limits.

This rule applies only if the person who previously carried on the business was himself a taxable person.

Legislation: VATA 1994, s. 49(1)(a)

Other Material: Notice 700/1, *Should I be registered for VAT?*

Indirect Tax Reporter: ¶43-000

8270 Effective date of late registration

A person who becomes liable to register for VAT may not realise this until some time later (in some cases, years later). Where this happens, the liability to be registered will still have existed from the proper time. Furthermore, the trader will (unknowingly) have been a taxable person throughout, since a taxable person is defined as one who makes taxable supplies and either is or is required to be registered.

In order to reflect this position, the registration of such a person will be made with retrospective effect to the proper registration date. He will be required to account for any output tax which has become due from that effective registration date. By the same token, he can reclaim input tax arising from then, provided that he holds the necessary evidence for reclaim.

Apart from the tax itself, a person registering late may be liable to a penalty for late registration. It should also be noted that there is no relief from the tax liability merely because customers would have been able to reclaim any tax charged to them.

Legislation: VATA 1994, s. 3(1), 67; *Value Added Tax Regulations* 1995 (1995/2518), reg. 25(1)(b)

Other Material: Notice 700/1, *Should I be registered for VAT?*

Indirect Tax Reporter: ¶43-149

8272 HMRC may require security

Although it is not strictly a registration matter, it is worth noting that HMRC have the power to require security from a taxable person. Making taxable supplies without providing the security required under this provision is a criminal offence punishable by a fine at level 5 on the standard scale contained in the *Criminal Justice Act* 1982.

Legislation: VATA 1994, s. 72(11), Sch. 11, para. 4(2)

Indirect Tax Reporter: ¶3-750

8274 Deregistration: supplies

A person who ceases to make taxable supplies is no longer a taxable person, and must notify HMRC that supplies are no longer being made within 30 days.

A trader who carries on making taxable supplies can also apply to be de-registered on the basis of reduced turnover. If HMRC is satisfied that turnover for the next 12 months will be below the deregistration limit (see Key Data), the trader ceases to be liable to be registered and so can be removed from the register. However, this does not apply if the reason for the drop in turnover is that the trader is about to cease trading, or intends to suspend the making of supplies for a period of 30 days or more.

A deemed supply of goods on hand arises on deregistration (see 7762). There are special arrangements permitting a refund of input tax on services (but not goods) arising after deregistration (8074).

Legislation: VATA 1994, Sch. 1, para. 3, 4(2), 11, 12

Other Material: Notice 700/11

Indirect Tax Reporter: ¶510

Registration – acquisitions of goods from other EC countries

8280 EC acquisitions and registration

There is a possible liability to register by a person who acquires goods from EC suppliers not registered for VAT in the UK. The effect of registration is to bring these acquisitions into the UK VAT net, instead of that of the other EC countries concerned, and prevents substantial 'VAT rate shopping' between Member States.

This provision applies not only to (exempt) businesses, but also to clubs, associations, bodies corporate and unincorporated associations acquiring goods for non-business activities.

This provision does not apply to businesses that are otherwise registered for VAT in the UK; they will account for VAT on acquisitions in the normal way (see 7972).

If the value (net of VAT) of intra-EC acquisitions by a person since 1 January of a calendar year exceeds the acquisitions limit (see 8284) that person becomes liable to register for VAT.

The effects of registration are:

- the overseas supplier can zero-rate its supplies, quoting the organisation's (new) UK VAT registration number on its invoice; and

- the UK organisation becomes liable to account for UK VAT on its acquisitions from elsewhere in the EC.

Other Material: Notice 700/1

Indirect Tax Reporter: ¶45-100

8282 Persons affected by acquisitions registration requirement

Obviously, businesses which are already registered for VAT, or already liable to be registered in respect of supplies made, can ignore the provisions requiring registration by reference to the level of EC acquisitions (see 8280). They are already obliged to account for VAT on acquisitions of goods from elsewhere in the EC.

The liability to register in respect of acquisitions is therefore of importance to persons not already registered, or liable to be registered, for UK VAT. The liability to register arises under VATA 1994, s. 10 and Sch. 3, and applies to:

- any person carrying on a business; and

- a body corporate, club, association, organisation or unincorporated body carrying on a non-business activity.

Where such a person acquires goods from a taxable person in another Member State, and the place of acquisition is the UK, the transaction counts for acquisition tax purposes.

Legislation: VATA 1994, s. 10, Sch. 3

Other Material: Notice 700/1

Indirect Tax Reporter: ¶45-100

8284 Acquisitions limit for VAT registration

A person may be affected by VAT registration rules dependent upon the level of acquisitions from elsewhere in the EC (see 8282). The level of such acquisitions is generally changed by statutory instrument and might require him to be registered if:

- at the end of any month, the value of acquisitions from the previous 1 January to the month end exceeds the annual turnover limit (see Key Data); or

- at any time, there are reasonable grounds for believing that the value of acquisitions in the following 30 days will exceed the annual turnover limit (see Key Data).

The value of acquisitions for this purpose is reckoned exclusive of any overseas VAT charged. Acquisitions of new means of transport, and of excise goods, are ignored as there are alternative provisions rendering these liable to UK VAT (see 7990).

A person who becomes liable to register because of past acquisitions has 30 days from the end of the month in which the limit was exceeded in which to notify HMRC, and the Commissioners must register him from the end of the month following that in which the limit was exceeded (or a mutually agreed earlier date).

A person who becomes liable to register because of anticipated acquisitions must notify HMRC of this before the end of the 30-day period concerned, and they must register him from the beginning of that period (or a mutually agreed earlier date).

Where a taxable person becomes liable to register in respect of zero-rated acquisitions, he may apply for exemption from registration.

Legislation: VATA 1994, Sch. 3, para. 8

Other Material: Notice 700/1

Indirect Tax Reporter: ¶45-100

8286 Voluntary registration: acquisitions

It is also possible to register voluntarily in respect of EC acquisitions (see 8280), or intended acquisitions, regardless of the amounts involved. This may be advantageous either because the rates of VAT are higher in the supplier countries, or as a matter of administrative convenience where it is expected that the registration thresholds will in any case be exceeded before long.

HMRC may impose conditions on such a voluntary registration.

Legislation: VATA 1994, Sch. 3, para. 4

Other Material: Notice 700/1, *Should I be registered for VAT?*

8288   EC acquisitions: ceasing registration

As a general rule, a person who voluntarily becomes registered in respect of acquisitions (see 8280) must remain registered for at least two years. Where a registration is cancelled, it will normally be from 1 January on, or following, the effective registration date.

However, if the person was never, in fact, registrable, or was in breach of a condition for voluntary registration, deregistration may take place from some earlier date.

Legislation: VATA 1994, Sch. 3, para. 7(3)

Other Material: Notice 700/1

Indirect Tax Reporter: ¶45-100

Registration – distance selling to the UK

8294   Distance selling and required registration generally

A trader established elsewhere in the EC can become liable to register for VAT in the UK in respect of sales of goods to UK customers who are not registered for VAT (see 7818). The place where such supplies are deemed to be made is then the UK, and the overseas supplier must account for VAT accordingly. The distance selling regime also works to make UK traders liable in other Member States if they breach the relevant distance selling threshold in that member state (member states choose either €100,000 or €35,000).

The distance selling registration provisions apply to a person who makes 'relevant supplies', being supplies of goods which involve the removal of the goods to the UK from another Member State, and their acquisition in the UK by a person who is not a taxable person.

Legislation: VATA 1994, Sch. 2, para. 10

Other Material: Notice 700/1

Indirect Tax Reporter: ¶63-240

8296   Distance selling registration limit

A person who makes relevant supplies (see 8294) of excise goods – goods liable to a duty of excise, such as tobacco products, alcoholic beverage, petrol, etc. – becomes liable to register as soon as such supplies are made; there is no turnover limit. A person who is not otherwise liable to register for VAT becomes liable to register on a day when the total value of his other relevant supplies to the UK since the previous 1 January exceed the distance selling threshold (£70,000). There is a table of limits in the Key Data section.

The value of relevant supplies for this purpose is reckoned exclusive of any overseas VAT charged.

Notification must be made to HMRC within 30 days from the time when the liability to register arose, and they must register him with effect from the day when the liability arose (or from a mutually agreed earlier date).

The same notification and registration rules apply as for registration when the turnover limit is exceeded.

Legislation: VATA 1994, Sch. 2, para. 1(1), (3), 3

Other Material: Notice 700/1

Indirect Tax Reporter: ¶63-240

8298   Voluntary registration: distance selling

A person belonging in another member state who has elected to treat his UK distance sales (see 8294) as taking place outside that state becomes liable to register in the UK when he makes such a supply.

The same notification and registration rules apply as for the other categories of distance selling registration (see 8296).

A person intending to make an election to treat his UK distance sales as made outside his own member state, or who has made such an election, and intending to make distance sales to the UK, may request registration as a distance seller, and HMRC may impose conditions on such a registration (VATA 1994, Sch. 2, para. 4). However, if the person also qualifies for voluntary registration as a UK intending trader or as a person making supplies outside the UK and having a business establishment in the UK, he will be registered under those rules rather than the distance selling rules.

A person who has registered on the basis of an intended election, or intended distance sales to the UK, must notify HMRC within 30 days of the intended election or sales taking place.

Legislation: VATA 1994, Sch. 2, para. 1(2), 4(3), 5(2)

Other Material: Notice 700/1

8300 Distance selling: ceasing registration

A person registered under the distance selling rules (see 8294) ceases to be registrable if a position arises where he is neither obliged, nor able, to register under any of the UK VAT provisions, taking each separately. He must notify HMRC of this within 30 days of ceasing to be registrable (VATA 1994, Sch. 2, para. 5(1)).

A person who ceases to be liable to be registered may have his registration cancelled, provided he is not liable to be registered under other provisions (VATA 1994, Sch. 2, para. 6(1), 7(1)). Also, HMRC may cancel the registration of a person who has registered voluntarily, and who has failed to make the intended election or supplies, or has breached any conditions imposed (VATA 1994, Sch. 2, para. 6, 7).

Legislation: VATA 1994, Sch. 2, para. 5(1), 5(4), 6, 7

Other Material: Notice 700/1

Indirect Tax Reporter: ¶43-030

8306 Registration of UK suppliers in other member states

A UK trader making distance sales to other member states, but not compulsorily registered there, can make elections similar to those mentioned in 8298; distance sales to the other member states concerned are then treated as made in those member states and not in the UK.

Such an election must be notified to HMRC within 30 days before the date on which the first supply under it is to be made, and the trader must within 30 days of making that first supply provide documentary evidence of having notified the other member state of the election. If the election is subsequently withdrawn, the trader must notify HMRC of this within 30 days before the first supply intended following such withdrawal. However, the withdrawal cannot take effect before 1 January which is, or follows, the second anniversary of making the first supply under the election.

A trader voluntarily electing to treat distance sales to another member state as being made in that state is, therefore, bound by that election for a period of two to three years.

Legislation: VATA 1994, s. 7(5); *Value Added Tax Regulations* 1995 (SI 1995/2518), reg. 98

Other Material: Notice 700/1

Indirect Tax Reporter: ¶43-030

Other matters relating to registration

8312   Tax representatives

A person who is liable to be registered for VAT in the UK, but who has no UK business establishment, may be required by HMRC to appoint a UK VAT representative. Such a VAT representative is responsible for his principal's compliance with UK VAT requirements, and is jointly and severally liable for any tax and penalties due.

A person who fails to appoint a VAT representative when so directed may be required to provide such security as HMRC thinks fit.

However, a non-established person in a member state of the EC or in countries that have a suitable mutual assistance arrangement with HMRC cannot be forced to appoint a UK VAT representative.

Legislation: VATA 1994, s. 48

Indirect Tax Reporter: ¶63000

8314   Changes in circumstances

A person who is registered for VAT is obliged to notify HMRC of such changes as changes of name, constitution or ownership of the business, and any other changes which may necessitate the variation of the register or cancellation of the registration. Notification must be made within 30 days after the change.

Legislation: *Value Added Tax Regulations* 1995 (SI 1995/2518), reg. 5(2)

8316   Scope of registration and person registered

When a person is registered for VAT the registration covers all of that person's business activities and, in the case of a partnership, covers activities of other partnerships having the same partners. This is because it is the partners themselves who are registered for VAT rather than the partnership as such.

Although a change in partners does not trigger a new registration, merely an amendment to the register, a change from a partnership to a sole trader, or vice versa, does involve a new registration and all of the formalities of deregistration and notification of liability to register must be observed.

Joint owners of property, even though not in partnership, can be registered jointly on similar lines to a partnership.

In the case of a group of companies for which group treatment has been obtained, the registration of the representative member of the group covers the activities of all of the companies within the group. In effect, the companies are treated as if they were a single taxable person. There are complex provisions covering the formation, variation and dissolution of VAT groups, and preventing their use for tax avoidance purposes.

Under the current rules, two or more bodies corporate are eligible to be treated as members of a VAT group if each is established or has a fixed establishment in the UK and they are under common 'control'. The present definition of control is taken from UK company law and is wide in scope. The group registration rules were amended from 1 August 2004 in order to counter VAT avoidance. The existing eligibility rules for VAT grouping were retained but two additional tests now apply where:

(1) a jointly owned company, or a wholly owned subsidiary run by a third party, makes or intends to make positive-rated supplies to a member of the VAT group which it wants to join (other than supplies which are incidental or ancillary to its business activities); and

(2) the VAT group would be unable to recover VAT on such supplies in full.

Limited partnerships will be subjected to these additional tests too. These partnerships can join a VAT group because for VAT purposes they are identified with the general partner of the partnership.

The two additional tests in these limited circumstances will be based on economic benefits and on consolidation in group accounts. The first test will not allow grouping where the majority of the economic benefits from the entity in question go to a third party. The second test will be that under generally accepted accounting practice, the entity's accounts are consolidated in the group accounts for the person controlling the VAT group (or would be so consolidated if that person prepared group accounts). Both of these tests will have to be satisfied.

Example

P Ltd makes taxable supplies to the New Group, which cannot recover all the VAT charged by P Ltd. P Ltd is jointly owned by O Ltd and Q Ltd, a third party. Q Ltd has the right to more than 50% of the dividends from P Ltd. P Ltd is not consolidated into the group accounts.

P Ltd is not eligible to join the New Group's VAT registration.

In the case of a company organised in divisions, it is possible to arrange for each division to be entered in the register so that separate returns can be submitted but there is still, in principle, a single registration covering all of the divisions.

Example

A garage has the following departments:

* car sales;

* servicing; and

* petrol sales.

Each department has its own accounting records, and the supplies are taxable.

The garage would satisfy the requirements for divisional registration.

A club, association, etc. is registered in its own name. Responsibility for meeting VAT obligations rests with its president, chairman, treasurer, etc. or, if none, its committee or, if none, with every member.

Legislation: VATA 1994, s. 43–46(1) and Sch. 9A; *Value Added Tax Regulations* 1995 (SI 1995/2518), reg. 8

Indirect Tax Reporter: ¶43-000

8318   Splitting a business to avoid registration – anti-avoidance

There is a special provision to counter attempts to avoid registration by splitting a business activity among several legal entities, each with turnover below the VAT registration threshold. This entitles HMRC to make a direction treating the persons named in it as being one person for VAT purposes, and so liable to be registered with effect from the date of direction. Further persons can, if necessary, be added to the direction and such additions to an existing direction can have retrospective effect.

HMRC is entitled to make a direction under this provision if they are satisfied that:

- each person named therein makes taxable supplies;

- the activities in the course of which the supplies are made form part of a business described in the direction, the remaining activities of that business being carried on by the other persons named in the direction; and

- when the whole of the activities of the business are considered together the person carrying it on is liable to be registered for VAT.

Example

Terry and June run a bar and restaurant. Terry runs the bar, whilst June serves all the meals in the restaurant. They maintain separate records of their takings, which are as follows: Bar (£72,000), Restaurant (£14,000) – Total (£86,000).

Terry and June share a business bank account. No rent is paid to either party for use of equipment or premises.

HMRC are likely to consider this situation to be an artificial separation of activities.

Legislation: VATA 1994, Sch. 1, para. 1A, 2

Indirect Tax Reporter: ¶43-710

8320 Transfer of registration number

Where a business is transferred as a going concern (TOGC) and the transferor ceases to be registered for VAT, it is possible for the registration number to be transferred to the transferee by mutual consent of the parties. In such a case, the transferee takes over any VAT liabilities of the transferor. It is generally considered to be good practice to drop the old VAT registration number on a TOGC.

Legislation: *Value Added Tax Regulations* 1995 (SI 1995/2518), reg. 6

Indirect Tax Reporter: ¶43-775

8322 Supplies contracted before registration

It should be noted that, once registered, a trader is liable to account for VAT on all supplies whose tax point arises on or after the effective date of the registration. This has been thought to mean that liability can arise in respect of supplies contracted for (and even performed) before registration. It is therefore important, if registration is a possibility, to ensure that contracts and terms of trading provide for the addition of VAT if applicable. However, in the case of *BJ Rice & Associates v C & E*

Commrs [1996] BVC 211 the Court of Appeal held that VAT was not due on a supply made before registration and having a payment tax point after registration.

Cases: *BJ Rice & Associates v C & E Commrs* [1996] BVC 211; *Madisons* (1987) 3 BVC 638

Other Material: Notice 700/41, *Late registration penalty (February 2011 edn) (for late registrations up to April 2010)*

Indirect Tax Reporter: ¶43-150

8324   Penalties for late registration

From 1 April 2010, FA 2008, Sch. 41 applies to late registration and the penalty which applies is 30% of the potential lost revenue. This rises for a deliberate, but not concealed act to 70% and it can rise to 100% for a deliberate and concealed act.

There are reductions for disclosure.

Legislation: FA 2008, Sch. 41

Other Material: CC/FS 11 *Compliance checks*, HMRC website

Indirect Tax Reporter: ¶43-000

Special VAT schemes

Agents and VAT

8350   Areas of difficulty for agents

Two areas of difficulty arise in respect of agents, or persons describing themselves as such. The first is that of determining whether there is in fact an agent/principal relationship. If there is, the further difficulty arises in applying the special rules for agents.

A person who is an agent is one empowered to act on behalf of his principal in some matter. The concept does not extend, say, to a motor distributor who describes himself as an agent for a manufacturer, but in fact buys and sells as principal. The importance of the legal arrangements between the parties, and of recording these, is emphasised by the case of *C & E Commrs v Music and Video Exchange Ltd* [1992] BVC 30.

The basic rule is that the supplies arranged by an agent for his principal are supplies to or by the principal, and do not affect the agent's VAT position in any way. The agent is making a separate supply of agency services to the principal, for a fee or commission, and this will normally be taxable at the standard rate (although it may sometimes be exempt or zero-rated or outside the scope of UK VAT if it is made across national boundaries – see 7824).

Other Material: *C & E Commrs v Music and Video Exchange Ltd* [1992] BVC 30

8352   Agent acting in own name

In some cases, an agent may appear to act in his own name, so that the parties with whom he deals are not aware that they are really dealing with the principal. Supplies of goods through such an agency arrangement are treated as supplied both to and by the agent. HMRC have the power to extend this treatment to supplies of services through an agent acting in his own name. This enables a selling agent to issue tax invoices to third parties, and receive equivalent tax invoices from the principal, so that the agent takes part in the underlying supply chain. Similarly, a buying agent can obtain tax invoices from the third parties, reclaiming the VAT as input tax, while passing on similar invoices (and accounting for output tax).

Such an agent must still account for VAT in the ordinary way on his agency fee or commission.

Legislation: VATA 1994, s. 47(2A), (3)

Indirect Tax Reporter: ¶54-100

8354   Agent for non-resident importer

If goods are imported into the UK from outside the EC (or acquired from another Member State) by a taxable person, and supplied by him as agent for a person who is not a taxable person, he is treated as having imported (or acquired) the goods, and supplied them, as principal. Consequently, he is liable to account for any tax due on the supply, and can also recover the VAT on the importation (or acquisition).

In applying this provision, if the principal is non-resident and has his principal place of business outside the UK, he can be treated as not being a taxable person in respect of the transaction (even though he is really a taxable person) if he is not registrable by reference to some other activity.

Legislation: VATA 1994, s. 47(1), (2)

Indirect Tax Reporter: ¶54-050

8360 Bad debt relief

A special relief is available to a supplier who is not on cash accounting and who makes a taxable supply (and so becomes liable to pay the tax on it) but does not receive payment from his customer. Relief is available when:

- at least six months have elapsed from the due date for payment of the supply (or the date of supply itself, if later);
- the supplier has formally written the debt off for VAT purposes; and
- the supplier holds the necessary records.

When these conditions are met, the supplier can recover from HMRC, the VAT originally accounted for on the supply, by including an equivalent amount in the input tax box of the VAT return. If payments are subsequently received in respect of the debt, the VAT element must be repaid to HMRC.

The claim must be made within three years and six months of the due date for payment of the supply (or the actual date of supply if later).

VAT: refunds for bad debts account

A claimant under these provisions is required to maintain a record, known as the 'refunds for bad debts account' containing details of supplies in respect of which bad debt relief is claimed. There is no requirement that this forms part of the claimant's ordinary accounting system, so it can be maintained as a separate schedule in the VAT working papers.

The information to be recorded in respect of each claim made is:

(1) for each taxable supply on which the claim is based:

    (a) the amount of tax chargeable;

    (b) the period in which the tax was accounted for and paid to HMRC;

    (c) the date and number of the related tax invoice, or other information showing the time, nature and purchaser of the supply; and

    (d) any payment received for the supply;

(2) the outstanding amount to which the claim relates;

(3) the amount of the claim; and

(4) the period in which the claim is made.

All relevant records must be preserved for a period of four years from the date of the claim (*Value Added Tax Regulations* 1995 (SI 1995/2518), reg. 169).

Effect of claim on customer

If the customer does not pay the invoice, then he must automatically repay input tax to HMRC where payment has not been made within six months of the supply (or the date on which payment is due, if this is later). This is done by adjusting the input tax claim for the period in which the end of the six months falls.

Amount of relief

The amount of bad debt relief available is generally the VAT fraction of the outstanding debt. In the case of supplies under the second-hand goods scheme or the tour operators margin scheme, the relief due is the VAT fraction of the margin for the supply or the VAT fraction of the outstanding debt, whichever is less.

Legislation: VATA 1994, s. 26A, 36; *Value Added Tax Regulations* 1995 (SI 1995/2518), reg. 165 onwards; *Value Added Tax Regulations* 1999 (SI 1999/3029)

Indirect Tax Reporter: ¶18-900

8365 Flat-rate scheme for small businesses

Some small businesses may be eligible for the flat-rate scheme (FRS), which can confer administrative and cash-flow savings on the taxpayer.

Conditions for FRS authorisation

The conditions for a person being eligible to be authorised to use the FRS include:

(1) there are reasonable grounds for believing that the VAT-exclusive annual taxable (being zero and positive-rated) turnover will not exceed £150,000. A supply is disregarded if it is a capital asset of the business or a reverse charge on a supply from abroad.

Future turnover may reasonably be forecast from past results and projections which supported applications for loans. The calculation of future turnover should be in writing and retained in case HMRC query the matter using hindsight;

(2) the person is not a tour operator;

(3) the person is not required to adjust input tax under the capital goods scheme;

(4) the person does not intend to use a margin scheme;

(5) in the previous year, the person has not operated the FRS and has a satisfactory compliance record; and

(6) in the previous 24 months, the person has not been part of a group, or 'associated' with another person unless HMRC are satisfied that authorisation poses no risk to the revenue. The FRS is to help those who run a stand-alone business, i.e. the business is not part of a larger undertaking.

Repayment traders

Persons who usually receive VAT repayments from HMRC cannot use the FRS because the FRS calculates VAT due to HMRC and is unsuitable for regular repayment traders.

Calculation of VAT due to HMRC

FRS users avoid accounting internally for VAT on all their purchases and sales. They calculate the VAT due to HMRC by applying the appropriate flat-rate percentage for their trade category to the VAT-inclusive turnover, including all reduced-rated, zero-rated and exempt supplies. These trade categories are available on the HMRC website and are in the *Value Added Tax Regulations* 1995 (SI 1995/2518), reg. 55K.

There have been a number of HMRC challenge to the flat rates chosen by some taxpayers, especially in respect of the default 'services not described elsewhere' rate of 12.5% and seeking to place mechanical engineers into the: 'architect, civil and structural engineer or surveyor' type of business (14.5%). The tribunal has found for the taxpayer in a number of these cases and apparently HMRC are now taking more care in these challenges.

Persons using the FRS can choose:

(1) whether to account for VAT on a quarterly basis; and

(2) whether to combine the FRS with the annual accounting scheme.

The record of turnover is based on:

(1) cash receipts (i.e. similarly to the cash accounting scheme);

(2) daily gross takings (i.e. similar to a retail scheme); or

(3) invoices issued.

Users of the FRS:

(1) still issue VAT invoices where the customer is VAT-registered, showing VAT at the normal rate for the supply (i.e. not at a flat rate).

Such customers treat these as normal VAT invoices and so they are unaffected by whether they deal with an FRS user; and

(2) still retain all sales and purchase invoices for six years.

Input tax and FRS users

Generally, no claim for input tax or for VAT on imports or acquisitions is due because the flat-rate percentage takes account of normal background input tax. However, subject to the usual conditions, an FRS user can claim input tax outside the FRS in respect of:

(1) capital expenditure on goods with a value exceeding £2,000 including VAT; and

(2) goods-on-hand at registration.

However, where capital purchases are dealt with outside the FRS, output tax on their disposal (or deemed disposal for assets held at deregistration) is also dealt with outside the FRS.

An FRS user is treated as fully taxable and need not consider partial exemption calculations: the flat-rate calculation takes irrecoverable VAT into account.

Record keeping

The FRS should simplify VAT accounting, because there is no need to identify VAT and value separately in the sales and purchase records. However, FRS users must keep a record of the flat-rate calculation showing:

(1) the flat-rate turnover for the period;

(2) the flat-rate percentage used; and

(3) the VAT calculated as due.

Leaving the FRS

Generally, a person ceases to be authorised to use the FRS if:

(1) at any anniversary of his start date, his income in the one year then ending totals more than £225,000, unless HMRC are satisfied that the total value of his taxable supplies in the one year then beginning will not exceed £150,000;

(2) there are reasonable grounds to believe that the total value of his income in the 30 days, then beginning will exceed £225,000;

(3) he becomes a tour operator;

(4) he intends to acquire, construct or otherwise obtain a capital item which requires an adjustment under the capital goods scheme;

(5) he opts to use a margin scheme;

(6) he becomes part of a group, or becomes associated with another person;

(7) he notifies HMRC in writing that he wishes voluntarily to withdraw from the FRS. A person cannot rejoin the FRS for at least one year, so persons cannot decide whether to use the FRS on a return-by-return basis; or

(8) HMRC terminate his authorisation to protect the revenue or because a false statement was made in relation to the application for authorisation.

Legislation: VATA 1994, s. 26B; *Value Added Tax Regulations* 1995 (SI 1995/2518), reg. 55A onwards

Other Material: Notice 733, *Flat-rate scheme for small businesses (May 2016 edn)*(May 2016 edn)

Indirect Tax Reporter: ¶55-350

8366 Farmers' flat-rate scheme

A flat-rate scheme is available for farmers. This is based on the provisions of the EC VAT Directive 2006/211.

A farmer who chooses to use the scheme ceases to be registered for VAT in respect of his farming activities, and so ceases to be able to recover input tax. However, he is able to charge a 'flat-rate addition' (FRA) at a special rate of 4% on supplies to taxable persons (and not to unregistered persons). These customers can recover the FRA as input tax, but the flat-rate scheme farmer is allowed to retain the money instead of paying it over to HMRC.

Legislation: VATA 1994, s. 54; *VAT (Flat-rate Scheme for Farmers) (Designated Activities) Order* 1992 (SI 1992/3220); *VAT (Flat-rate Scheme for Farmers) (Percentage Addition) Order* 1992 (SI 1992/3221); *Value Added Tax Regulations* 1995 (SI 1995/2518), reg. 202–211; EC VAT Directive 2006/211, art. 295ff.

Other Material: Notice 700/46, *Agricultural flat-rate scheme*

Indirect Tax Reporter: ¶53-500

8374 Monthly payments on account by large traders

There are provisions under which certain businesses have to make monthly payments on account of their VAT liability during a prescribed accounting period, any underpayment or overpayment being settled when the return for the period is submitted.

Broadly speaking, this requirement affects businesses whose net VAT payments exceed £2m p.a. A first payment on account is required by the end of the month following the first month of a period, a second one a month later, the balance being cleared by submission of the return at the end of the month following the period end. The amount of each interim payment on account is one twenty-fourth of the estimated annual liability.

There is provision for escaping this requirement where, in a subsequent 12-month period, the net VAT liability falls below £1.6m.

Legislation: VATA 1994, s. 28; *Value Added Tax (Payments on Account) Order* 1993 (SI 1993/2001)

Other Material: Notice 700/60, *Payments on account*

Indirect Tax Reporter: ¶55-410

8380 Local authorities, government departments and similar entities

Local authorities are liable to be registered in respect of taxable business activities, whatever their level of turnover. Business activities of local authorities are taxed in the ordinary way, and input tax blocked in respect of exempt business activities.

As far as non-business activities of local authorities, and certain similar entities, are concerned no output tax is chargeable, but the local authority, etc. is entitled to reclaim input tax (VATA 1994, s. 33(1)).

The bodies to which this relief applies include such entities as local authorities, water authorities, port health authorities, police authorities, the BBC, etc. and any body specified in a suitable Treasury order. Local authorities include the council of a city, district, London borough, parish or group of parishes, etc.

Government departments are treated slightly differently. They too will be bound by the normal VAT rules and may have to charge VAT on their non-statutory activities (their statutory activities are outside the scope of VAT). VAT charged to them may be recoverable under a special Treasury scheme under VATA 1994, s. 41.

Certain museums and galleries, which do not charge members of the public for admission, can claim a refund of input tax.

The input tax must be in respect of those supplies made to an applicable body that are attributable to the provision by that body of free rights of admission to a relevant museum or gallery. The Treasury may, by order, list applicable bodies and relevant museums and galleries for this purpose. Furthermore, HMRC will apportion the input tax where the bought-in supplies are attributable to both free admissions and other supplies.

Legislation: VATA 1994, s. 33(1), 33A(3), 41, 42

Indirect Tax Reporter: ¶51-000

8386 Retail schemes

In principle, VAT is due on each supply made, and should be computed separately for each supply. In order to save retailers from having to keep a detailed record of each sale made, retail schemes are available to them. Under these, a record is kept of daily gross takings (which includes credit sales). The output tax due is then calculated by estimating the proportion of takings which represent standard-rated sales and applying the VAT fraction to arrive at the VAT element contained therein.

Retailers with a turnover exceeding £10m p.a. cannot use a retail scheme without the specific agreement of HMRC, and other retailers may be refused the use of the scheme where it is practicable to account for VAT according to the normal rules.

Other Material: Notice 727, *Retail schemes* (May 2012); Notice 727/2, *Bespoke retail schemes*; Notice 727/3, *Retail schemes: How to work the point of sale schemes*; Notice 727/4 (January 2013 edn), *Retail schemes: How to work the apportionment schemes*; Notice 727/5, *Retail schemes: How to work the direct calculation schemes*

Indirect Tax Reporter: ¶45-000

8392 Second-hand goods schemes

Value added tax is intended ultimately to be collected at the retail stage of the supply chain. When a taxable supply is made by a trader to a final consumer, tax is accountable on the supply but cannot be recovered by the consumer. This works well for goods and services which are fully consumed by the consumer, but difficulties arise in the case of certain more durable goods which may pass back into the business system.

Under the basic VAT rules, if goods which have borne tax are sold by the consumer back into the business sector, then supplied again to another consumer, tax will arise on this new transfer into the non-business sector. As a result, the same article will be subjected to VAT twice.

In order to provide some measure of relief from this double taxation, the Treasury has power to make orders reducing the tax due on such transactions. This is the margin scheme.

The margin scheme is available for most supplies of second-hand goods, and can also be applied by an agent selling any goods in his own name.

The basic idea of the second-hand goods schemes is to restrict the amount of tax due on goods sold under them to tax on the trader's margin, rather than on the entire amount charged on reselling the goods. The trader must calculate the difference between the price at which he buys the goods and that at which he sells them, and account for tax out of the gross profit.

Where goods have been obtained under a transfer of a going concern their cost for margin scheme purposes is the cost to the transferor (or, if there have been two or more going concern transfers, the original transferor).

As a general rule the margin calculation must be made for each item separately. However, a global scheme can be used for goods costing £500 or less.

Other material: Notice 718/1, *The VAT margin scheme on secondhand cars* (January 2016 edn)

8398   Self-billing

It is sometimes desirable that a customer generates the tax invoice for a supply. This is appropriate where the customer controls or wishes to control events

These arrangements are particularly useful where it is the supplier who calculates the amount of the consideration for the supply, under a pre-agreed formula (such as royalties due under a publishing contract, where it is the publisher who has the information on sales made, and advises the author of the amount of the royalties due).

Where a trader (usually the customer) wishes to use self-billing, he must comply with the rules set out in a notice and obtain written approval of this from HMRC. In order to obtain this, he must ensure that all of the suppliers concerned agree to the arrangement, and that they undertake not to issue tax invoices themselves for the transactions covered by it. The normal requirements for the contents of tax invoices apply, so the customer must satisfy himself that he has all relevant information.

The normal procedure is then that the customer generates the tax invoices, retains a copy for himself to act as evidence for his claim for input tax, and provides a copy to his supplier to enable him to account for output tax.

There is a special provision whereby, if a customer using a self-billing arrangement generates a self-billing invoice which understates the tax due, HMRC may elect to recover this from the customer rather than from the supplier.

Legislation: VATA 1994, s. 29; *Value Added Tax Regulations* 1995 (SI 1995/2518), reg. 13(3)

Other Material: Notice 700/62, *Self Billing*

Indirect Tax Reporter: ¶56-200

8404   Tour operators

A special tour operators' margin scheme (TOMS) applies to businesses who make supplies which include 'designated travel services'. These are known as 'tour operators'.

A supply of designated travel services is a supply of goods or services which the tour operator obtains, and resupplies without material alteration or further processing.

The broad basis of the scheme is that the tour operator cannot recover input tax on designated travel services, but the tax on his onward supplies to travellers is due only on his margin. The margin is calculated for the tour operator's supplies as a whole, the calculation being based on his financial accounts.

Legislation: VATA 1994, s. 53; *Value Added Tax (Tour Operators) Order* 1987 (SI 1987/1806)

Case: *R & C Commrs v Dunwood Travel Ltd* [2007] BVC 406

Other Material: Notice 709/5, *Tour operator's margin scheme (November 2009 edn)*

Indirect Tax Reporter: ¶54-450

8410   Special schemes for small businesses

In addition to the Flat Rate Scheme and the Flat Rate Farmers' Scheme, two other special schemes are available to businesses with relatively low turnover. These are the cash accounting scheme and the annual accounting scheme.

Cash accounting

The cash accounting scheme is intended to permit small businesses to account for VAT by reference to payments made and received, rather than the time when supplies are made and received. It is available to businesses with annual taxable turnover up to £1.35m. Once in the scheme, businesses can continue to use the scheme until their annual taxable turnover exceeds £1.6m. It is not necessary for businesses to have been trading before applying to join the cash accounting scheme. It is possible for businesses to be in both schemes at the same time, provided they satisfy both schemes' conditions.

Details of the scheme are contained in Notice 731, and the relevant legislation is in the *Value Added Tax Regulations* 1995 (SI 1995/2518), Pt. VIII.

Businesses that operate the cash accounting scheme do not have to claim bad debt relief for output tax paid on sale proceeds not received (see 8360). Conversely, such businesses cannot deduct input tax on purchases from their output tax in their VAT returns until payment has been made for those purchases.

Annual accounting

The annual accounting scheme is available only to businesses which regularly pay tax to HMRC and not to repayment traders. Its use is optional, so businesses which prefer to account for tax quarterly (or monthly) can continue to do this.

The turnover figure below which a business is eligible to use the annual accounting scheme is £1,350,000. The turnover figure above which a business must leave the Scheme is £1,600,000.

Businesses opting for annual accounting make VAT returns only once a year. However, they are obliged to make payments on account (POAs) of the ultimate liability.

The POAs are set at either:

- a 'quarterly sum', payable on the last day of months four, seven and ten of the year; or

- a 'monthly sum' in nine equal instalments, starting on the last day of month four.

At the end of the year, the trader makes a return for the whole year and this is due (with any final balancing payment) two months after the end of the year.

Legislation: *Value Added Tax Regulations* 1995 (SI 1995/2518), Pt. VII, VIII

Other Material: Notice 731, *Cash accounting*; Notice 732, *Annual accounting (April 2014 edn)*

Indirect Tax Reporter: ¶55-300 and ¶55-450

VAT payment and accounting requirements

8430   VAT payment dates

The VAT return must be submitted by the end of the month following the period to which it relates, and any tax shown on it as due to HMRC must be paid to them by the same date.

Taxpayers are now required to submit returns online and pay online. This procedure gives them an extra seven days to fulfil their compliance requirements.

In response to appeals against the requirement to file online, the First-tier Tribunal (in the case of *L.H. Bishop Electrical Co Ltd. A F Sheldon t/a Aztec Distributors*) ruled that UK VAT law failed to take account of a person's ability to comply on account of:

- age;
- disability;
- computer illiteracy (linked to age);
- remoteness of location

and, as such, was a breach of the European Convention on Human Rights (ECHR).

The judge also held that HMRC could not rely on the fact that telephone filing had been made available to certain businesses to cure the aforementioned human rights breach as it had not been legislated for or properly publicised.

Changes to legislation

Following a formal consultation exercise, *VAT Regulations* 1995 (SI 1995/2518), reg. 25A has been amended to:

- enable HMRC to make a Commissioners' direction approving telephone filing as an alternative method of electronic filing for use by businesses that satisfy HMRC that it is not reasonably practicable for them to use the current method of online filing; and

- provide an additional exemption from electronic filing for businesses that satisfy HMRC that it is not reasonably practicable for them to use an online channel with the result that such businesses will be able to file on paper.

Changes to legislation took effect from 1 July 2014.

(HMRC have published HMRC Brief 29/14 that gives guidance on traders who are unable to file electronically).

Failure to pay on time any VAT shown as due on a return can give rise to a liability to a surcharge (see 8516).

Taxpayers with problems paying should contact HMRC as soon as possible. Assistance under the Business Payment Support Service may be available.

HMRC have published VAT Notice 700/45 (October 2011) How to correct VAT errors and make adjustments or claims.

Legislation: VATA 1994, s. 59; *Value Added Tax Regulations* 1995 (SI 1995/2518), reg. 25, 40

8436   Importance of VAT records

Because VAT is ultimately collected at the level of individual supplies, it is important that records should exist of all transactions. This becomes even more important given the provisions for refund of tax, so that one trader may be seeking repayment from HMRC of tax which should have been paid to them by another trader. Not surprisingly, HMRC are anxious to be able to verify that the tax has in fact been paid.

In order to meet this need, HMRC have a general power to require traders to keep such records as they may require. Their general requirements are set out in the *Value Added Tax Regulations* 1995 (SI 1995/2518), Pt. V.

From the trader's point of view, proper records are important in order to prevent HMRC from making assessments for tax which they might reasonably deduce to be due, but which is not in fact due when the full information is examined. The trader also needs to hold evidence when reliefs from tax are sought. Examples include the refund of input tax, and claiming zero-rating for a supply.

Legislation: VATA 1994, Sch. 11, para. 6(1); *Value Added Tax Regulations* 1995 (SI 1995/2518), Pt. V

Other Material: Notice 700, *The VAT guide*; Notice 700/21, *Keeping records and accounts* (July 2015 edn)

Indirect Tax Reporter: ¶58-800

8442 General VAT accounting requirements

The general requirements as to record keeping for VAT are set out in the *Value Added Tax Regulations* 1995 (SI 1995/2518), reg. 31. Each taxable person has an obligation to keep and preserve his business and accounting records, copies of all tax invoices issued by him, tax invoices received by him, documentation relating to his imports and exports, and to his intra-EC acquisitions and dispatches of goods, credit notes, debit notes or other documents received which evidence changes in the consideration for supplies made or received, copies of such documents which he issues, and a value added tax account containing information specified in the regulations.

Such records must be preserved for a period of six years, unless HMRC allows a shorter period.

Legislation: *Value Added Tax Regulations* 1995 (SI 1995/2518), reg. 31

Other Material: Notice 700/21, *Keeping records and accounts*

Indirect Tax Reporter: ¶58-800

8448 Special VAT record-keeping requirements

Apart from the records needed by traders generally, it should be borne in mind that traders operating special schemes are usually subject to special record-keeping requirements (for special schemes and general records, see 8350ff. and 8442). These may be specified by HMRC in Notices, which have the force of law for this purpose. For instance, a car dealer who wishes to use the second-hand goods scheme for second-hand cars has no legal entitlement to do this unless records are kept in accordance with the scheme rules, providing acquisition and disposal details for each car dealt with under the scheme.

Other areas where special record-keeping requirements arise include retail schemes, retail export schemes, reclaim of pre-registration input tax, bad debt relief claims, and the cash accounting scheme.

Legislation: *Value Added Tax Regulations* 1995 (SI 1995/2518), reg. 31(2)

Other Material: Notice 700/21, *Keeping records and accounts*

Indirect Tax Reporter: ¶58-800

8454   VAT returns

Each trader must make a periodical VAT return to HMRC, showing amounts of output tax to be accounted for and of deductible input tax. The return also gives statistical information on the value of supplies made and received and intra-EC imports and exports of goods. The requirements of HMRC as to the way in which the amounts for supplies made and received are to be arrived at are set out in *Filling in your VAT return –* Notice 700/12.

The VAT return period differs between traders. Generally, returns are submitted quarterly, the quarter end to be used being notified to the trader by HMRC. Traders who regularly receive repayments of VAT (i.e. those who normally make zero-rated supplies) usually make a return each month, rather than each quarter. In some cases, notably when a business starts or finishes, it may be necessary to submit a return for a non-standard period.

The VAT return must be submitted by the end of the month following the period to which it relates, and any tax shown on it as due to HMRC must be paid to them by the same date. Failure to pay on time any VAT shown as due on a return can give rise to a liability to a surcharge (8516).

Large traders (with VAT liabilities of more than £2m annually), are required to make payments on account (POAs).

HMRC have recently published an updated version of the VAT Notice 700/60 Payments on Account

HMRC have been encouraging traders to file online and offer encouragement for this. Online filers must also pay online, but they have an extra seven days in which to pay. As a disincentive to paper filers, from April 2010, the return must be accompanied by cleared funds rather than by a cheque by the due date.

Correction of errors

There is specific provision that, if an error is made in a return, it is to be corrected in such manner and at such time as HMRC may require.

The general requirements for the correction of errors are set out in Notice 700/45 (July 2010 edn). In addition, there are special provisions allowing current period adjustment of earlier errors discovered. For accounting periods beginning after 1 July 2008, traders will only be required to disclose errors where they exceed the greater of £10,000; or 1% of quarterly turnover up to a limit of £50,000. Under this limit, a taxpayer may self-correct the error. There are also special provisions for reclaiming tax incorrectly paid over to HMRC. Errors cannot be corrected if they are over four years old (from 1 April 2009).

Other Material: Notice 700/12, *Filling in your VAT return*; Notice 700/45, *How to correct errors you find on your VAT return*

Indirect Tax Reporter: ¶55-200

8460   Additional returns for intra-EC trade

Apart from the VAT return itself (see 8454), further returns must be made by traders engaged in intra-EC movements of goods and services. The returns are:

- Quarterly or monthly 'EC sales listings' (ESLs) required of all traders (this may be annually for very small traders); and

- Monthly 'Supplementary Statistical Declarations' (SSDs), more commonly known as Intrastat returns, are required of all but the smallest traders.

EC sales list

The EC Sales list (ESL) must be produced for each calendar quarter or month, as appropriate, and must be submitted to HMRC within 14 days of the reporting period for paper returns and 21 days for electronic submission.

The ESL is submitted on form VAT 101, and consists of a list of all customers elsewhere in the EC to whom supplies of goods (and from 1 January 2010, services as well) have been made in the period, their VAT registration numbers (including country prefixes) and the value of supplies of goods to them during the period. It is also possible to submit the information by way of plain paper reports or by electronic transmission.

The transactions which figure on the ESL are, broadly, supplies of goods delivered to other member states for acquisition by taxable persons and services subject to the reverse charge (generally, supplies made to business customers). In general, the values and timing of supplies for ESL purposes are as for VAT return purposes. The value includes freight, etc. costs charged by the supplier to the customer. There are some transactions with special treatment for ESL purposes.

From 1 January 2010, businesses have to submit ESLs for taxable supplies of services made to business customers in other EU countries where the customer is required to account for VAT under the reverse charge procedure.

Monthly ESLs are required for supplies over £70,000 in the current or four previous quarters.

Annual ESLs are allowed (a trader must contact HMRC for approval), if the trader's total annual turnover does not exceed £145,000, the annual value of supplies to other member states is not more than £11,000 and the trader does not supply new means of transport.

Intrastat Statistical Declarations (Intrastat)

The Intrastat Statistical Declaration (SD), or Intrastat, is a monthly return detailing all movements of goods between the UK and other member states. It covers transfers between branches of the same business as well as purchases and sales of goods, and provides the information needed for the trade statistics. The obligation to submit SDs arises under the *Statistics of Trade (Customs and Excise) Regulations* 1992 (SI 1992/2790).

The obligation to submit SDs arises separately for imports and exports and depends on the value of the movements.

Intrastat – changes from 1 January 2015

VAT-registered businesses that are required to submit declarations of arrivals (EU imports) trade received from other EU member states and/or provide Delivery Terms information on an Intrastat declaration.

Changes to Intrastat thresholds from 1 January 2015

- the exemption threshold for arrivals is increased from £1,200,000 to £1,500,000;

- the Delivery Terms threshold is increased from £16m to £24m (where more details are needed); and

- the exemption threshold for dispatches (EU exports) remains unchanged at £250,000.

(See PN 60 – September 2015 edn.)

The SD must give details of each shipment, including such matters as the detailed trade classification of the goods, quantities, shipping costs, countries of departure and arrival, etc.

Changes to submitting Intrastat declarations from 1 April 2012

HMRC have withdrawn paper Intrastat forms. All Intrastat declarations must be submitted in an electronic format.

Change to monthly deadline

HMRC have brought forward the monthly deadline for submitting Intrastat declarations from the last day to the 21st day of the month.

For example, HMRC must receive your September Intrastat declaration by 21 October.

Movements of goods excluded from SDs

The following movements of goods should not be included on the SD:

- goods dispatched to another EC country for a period of less than two years, if they would qualify for temporary importation relief if arriving from outside the EC (e.g. exhibition goods);

- goods transferred temporarily for hire, lease or loan, or for use in carrying out a service in another member state;

- industrial or commercial samples sent to actual or potential customers free of charge;

- goods sent to another Member State for examination, analysis or testing followed by return or destruction, or the return of such goods after testing, etc.; and

- dispatches of goods (other than excise goods or new means of transport) to unregistered customers.

Electronic submission of returns

Because of the large amounts of detailed information required in these statistical returns, arrangements are available whereby they can be submitted electronically. Possible means of submission include magnetic media, such as disks and tapes, and direct transmission of information to HMRC's computer.

Register of temporary movements of goods

The movement of a business's own goods from one Member State to another generally gives rise to a deemed supply in the state of departure and an acquisition in the state of arrival. However, certain temporary movements of goods are excepted from this procedure.

In order that such temporary movements can be controlled, it is a requirement that the taxable person keeps a register of them, giving dates of removal and return, details of the goods, and of processing of them, etc.

Legislation: *Statistics of Trade (HMRC and Excise) (Amendment) (No. 2) Regulations* 2008 (SI 2008/2487)

Other Material: Notice 60, *The intrastat general guide* (January 2014); HMRC Brief 69/09

Indirect Tax Reporter: ¶64-600

VAT enforcement – the penalty regime

8480   Nature of VAT penalties

A revised civil penalty regime for errors has been introduced across all the major taxes, including VAT, for return periods starting on or after 1 April 2008 that are filed on or after 1 April 2009. See 8520 for further details.

Legislation: FA 2007, Sch. 24

8486   Late notification of liability to register for VAT

See 8324.

8492   Criminal fraud: VAT

Criminal fraud arises, broadly, where a person knowingly takes steps to evade tax, or to enable another person to do so.

The penalties for criminal fraud apply, not only to the concealment of liability to account for tax, but also to such matters as the overstatement of claims for the repayment of input tax.

A criminal fraud penalty can only arise as a result of criminal proceedings, in which case the level of penalty depends whether the conviction secured is a summary conviction (i.e. before magistrates) or a conviction on indictment (i.e. before a jury). In either case, the penalty consists of a fine and/or imprisonment.

On conviction on indictment the maximum term of imprisonment is seven years, while the level of fines is unlimited; summary conviction also carries a possible prison term or a fine.

The following measures apply in an effort to combat missing trader fraud:

- HMRC officers have specific powers to enter premises, to inspect and mark goods with a date stamp and to record details of the goods by any means, including the electronic scanning of barcodes; and

- HMRC may also give directions to businesses to require them to keep specified records relating to certain goods that they have traded (such as unique reference numbers for mobile phones). Failure to comply with such a direction will give rise to specified penalties.

The Missing Trader Intra-Community (MTIC) reverse charge accounting requirement was introduced from 1 June 2007. The main features of the scheme are:

- it applies to mobile telephones and integrated circuit devices, such as microprocessors and control processing units, wholesale gas and electricity and emission allowances;

- mobile phones supplied with an airtime contract are outside the scope of the reverse charge but 'pay as you go' ('prepay') phones are within the scope of the reverse charge;

- a 'de minimis' limit of £5,000 applies to the total value of goods subject to the reverse charge supplied together and detailed on a single invoice;

- businesses on the Payments on Account (POA) scheme affected by reverse charge accounting will be entitled to base their eligibility to POA and payments due thereunder on their notional liability excluding the reverse charge VAT;

- suppliers of goods subject to reverse charge accounting are required to submit web-based Reverse Charge Sales Lists giving information on their sales, in addition to their normal VAT returns; and

- suppliers of goods subject to reverse charge accounting will be required to include a specific annotation on their invoices.

Legislation: VATA 1994, s. 55A; *Value Added Tax (Section 55A) (Specified Goods and Excepted Supplies) Order* 2007 (SI 2007/1417)

Other Material: HMRC Notice 735 *VAT Domestic reverse charge on specified goods and services*

Website: www.ec.europa.eu/taxation_customs/taxation/tax_cooperation/reports/index_en.htm

Indirect Tax Reporter: ¶60-715

8498   Civil fraud: VAT

Civil fraud arises where a person takes steps, or omits to take steps, in order to evade tax. This is now dealt with under the new penalty regime (see 8520).

8500 Disclosure

Businesses with supplies of £600,000 or more are required to disclose the use of specific avoidance schemes that are included in HMRC's published list. This must be done within 30 days of the date when the first return affected by the scheme becomes due after 'listing'. Failure to disclose will incur a penalty of 15% of the tax avoided. Businesses with supplies exceeding £10m a year are required to disclose the use of schemes that have certain hallmarks of avoidance. This must be done within 30 days of the date when the first return affected by the scheme becomes due. There is a voluntary facility for those who devise and market VAT avoidance schemes (promoters) to register schemes that have the hallmarks of avoidance with HMRC. A business using a scheme registered by a promoter will not have to make a separate disclosure of its use. Failure to disclose will incur a flat rate penalty of £5,000.

Legislation: *The Value Added Tax (Disclosure of Avoidance Schemes) Regulations* 2004 (SI 2004/1929); *The VAT (Disclosure of Avoidance Schemes) (Designations) Order* 2004 (SI 2004/1933)

Indirect Tax Reporter: ¶60-850

8504 Unauthorised issue of VAT invoices

Up to April 2010, where a person who is not registered for VAT, or otherwise authorised to issue tax invoices (e.g. a receiver selling business assets owned by a taxable person can validly issue a tax invoice), issues an invoice which purports to include VAT, he is liable to a penalty of the greater of £50, or 15% of the purported tax, whether or not the amount of 'tax' is shown separately.

The penalty will not be due if it can be shown that there is a reasonable excuse (see 8556), and the amount of the penalty may be mitigated by HMRC or, on appeal, by the VAT tribunal.

Legislation: VATA 1994, s. 67

From 1 April 2010, the provisions of s. 67 cease to apply and the provisions of FA 2008, Sch. 41 apply. Penalties of 30, 70 and even 100% may apply depending on the taxpayer's behaviour.

Legislation: FA 2008, Sch. 41

Indirect Tax Reporter: ¶18-043

8510 Breaches of VAT regulations: records and payments

There are penalties for breaches of VAT Regulations of any kind in VATA 1994, s. 69.

The amount of penalty varies with the type and frequency of the breach concerned. The basic penalty is at a rate of £5 per day while the breach continues. This is increased to £10 per day if there has been an earlier breach of the same regulation within the previous two years, and £15 per day if there has been more than one such earlier breach.

In some cases, this basic daily penalty is increased to a daily percentage of the tax involved, if this is greater. The percentage rises in line with the number of previous breaches, in exactly the same way as the basic daily penalty. The possible percentages are $1/6$%, $1/3$% and $1/2$%. The equivalent annual rates are approximately 61%, 122% and 183%.

The offence of failing to preserve records for the required period gives rise to a fixed penalty of £500.

An assessment for a daily penalty is subject to a maximum of 100 times the daily amount.

No penalty can be imposed under this provision, other than for failure to keep records or failure to notify end of liability or entitlement to be registered, unless HMRC has given the trader written warning concerning compliance with the requirement concerned within two years preceding the assessment.

An offence which has given rise to a criminal conviction, or a penalty for civil fraud or serious misdeclaration, cannot also be treated as a breach of regulations.

The following table shows the types of regulatory breach and the penalties which attach to them.

Breach	Penalty
Failure to notify cessation of taxable supplies	Fixed daily rate
Failure to make records	Fixed daily rate
Failure to retain records for six years	£500
Failure to furnish information and documents	Fixed daily rate
Failure to make a VAT return by the due date	Greater of fixed daily rate and tax-geared percentage rate
Failure to pay the tax due on a VAT return by the due date	Greater of fixed daily rate and tax-geared percentage rate
Any other breach of regulations	Fixed daily rate

The amount of tax on which the tax-geared percentages are to be based is the tax shown as due on the return for the period concerned. If no return has been made, it is the amount assessed as due for the period by HMRC.

The levels of penalties can be altered by statutory instrument, to take account of inflation.

A statutory defence is provided whereby no penalty is due if the trader can satisfy HMRC (or a VAT tribunal) that there is a reasonable excuse for the breach (see 8556). No mitigation is available for these penalties.

Legislation: VATA 1994, s. 69, 76(2)

Indirect Tax Reporter: ¶850

8516   Default surcharge

The default surcharge penalises traders who submit their VAT returns late, or submit the returns on time but defer payment of the related tax. The amount of the surcharge can range from a minimum of £30 to a maximum of 15% of the tax due for the period depending on the frequency of late submission. The mechanics for fixing liability to surcharge, and its amount, are complex and are set out below.

If a return (or the payment due with it) is late in arriving with HMRC, the trader concerned is 'in default'. This does not, of itself, give rise to liability for default surcharge.

A surcharge liability notice is issued following a single default. This will specify a surcharge liability period beginning with the date the notice is issued and ending one year after the end of the period for which the trader is in default. Further defaults for return periods ending within the surcharge liability period may then attract a penalty.

A second default then attracts a surcharge liability of 2% of the tax, a third and fourth are liable at 5% and 10% respectively, while a fifth or later default is liable at 15%. On a second or subsequent default within a surcharge period, the period is extended.

However, late returns do not attract a penalty in themselves, unless some or all of the tax due is paid late. Nil or repayment returns attract no penalty. Such a late return will still enable HMRC to extend the surcharge liability period, but will not attract a penalty itself, nor lead to an escalation in the rate of penalty for a subsequent default. The default surcharge system also applies to payments on account by larger traders (see 8374).

A trader who is late submitting a return is not liable to a default surcharge (and the late submission does not count in terms of a notice, etc.) if one of two defences can be substantiated to HMRC, or to a VAT tribunal:

- the trader can show that the return (or payment) was sent at such a time, and in such a manner, that it was reasonable to expect that HMRC would receive it by the due date; or

- there is a reasonable excuse for the late submission or payment (see 8556).

No mitigation is available for default surcharge.

Legislation: VATA 1994, s. 59, 59A

Other Material: Notice 700/50, *Default surcharge* – new version (December 2011)

Indirect Tax Reporter: ¶60-450

8520 The penalty regime for errors from 1 April 2009

HMRC introduced a new penalty regime for errors, which applies across all the major taxes including VAT. Penalties are linked to the behaviour that gives rise to the error. People who take reasonable care when completing their returns will not be penalised. If they do not take reasonable care, errors will be penalised, and the penalties will be higher if the error is deliberate. Disclosing errors to HMRC early will substantially reduce any penalty due.

'Reasonable care' varies according to the person, the particular circumstances and their abilities. Every person is expected to make and keep sufficient records for them to provide a complete and accurate return. A person with simple, straightforward tax affairs needs only keep a simple system of records, which are regularly and carefully updated. A person with larger and more complex financial tax affairs will need to put in place more sophisticated systems and maintain them equally carefully. HMRC believe it is reasonable to expect a person who encounters a transaction or other event with which he is not familiar, to take care to check the correct tax treatment, or to seek suitable advice. HMRC expect people to take their tax seriously.

The new penalties apply to errors on VAT returns and also (among others) to corporation tax and income tax.

The penalties apply to returns or other documents for return periods starting on or after 1 April 2008 that are due to be filed on or after 1 April 2009.

The penalty charged will be a percentage of the extra tax due. The rate depends on the behaviour that gave rise to the error. The less serious the behaviour, the smaller the penalty will be. The charges are as follows:

- Reasonable care: no penalty;
- Careless: minimum penalty 0% up to maximum of 30%;
- Deliberate: minimum penalty 20% up to maximum 70%; and
- Deliberate and concealed: minimum penalty 30% up to maximum 100%.

Finance Act 2008 extended the new penalties for incorrect returns across most taxes, levies and duties, for incorrect returns for periods commencing from 1 April 2009 where the return is due to be filed from 1 April 2010.

Legislation: FA 2007, Sch. 24

Other Material: Notice 700/45 *How to correct VAT errors* (July 2015 edn)

8522 Repayment supplement

A repayment supplement is added to certain late repayments of VAT shown as repayable on a VAT return. Any overpayment may often be offset against any underpayment by the taxpayer of tax, penalty, interest or surcharge.

In order to qualify for such a supplement, the return or, as regards local authority, etc. refunds, claim must have reached HMRC by the proper due date for its submission.

Repayment supplement is then due if HMRC fail to issue the written instruction directing the making of the repayment within 30 days of the later of:

- the end of the period concerned; and
- the date when HMRC received the return.

In determining whether the instruction is issued within the 30-day period, certain periods are ignored. These periods are those taken in making reasonable enquiries about the return, or correcting errors in the return, and periods in which the trader has failed to submit other returns, or pay the tax due on them or on assessments issued by HMRC, or comply with the conditions concerned with the production of documents or the giving of security.

If the return overstates the amount of the repayment due by more than the greater of 5% and £250, no supplement is payable.

The supplement is the greater of 5% of the repayment due or £50. There is a table of rates in the Key Data section.

Legislation: VATA 1994, s. 79

Indirect Tax Reporter: ¶60-650

8528 The misdeclaration penalty

This has now been replaced by the new errors penalty regime (see 8520 above) from 1 April 2009.

8544 Interest on underpaid VAT

The legislation provides for charging 'default interest' on assessable VAT paid late.

These provisions do not apply to tax properly shown on a VAT return, but paid over late, such late payments being covered by the default surcharge provisions (see 8516ff.) or dealt with as a breach of regulations (see 8510).

They apply, broadly, to tax which is recovered by way of assessment, or which could have been so assessed but is collected via a return instead.

Interest will arise in cases where:

(1) an assessment is made to recover extra tax for a period for which a return has already been made, or an assessment in lieu of a return issued;

(2) such an assessment could be made, but the tax is recovered on a later return instead;

(3) a person has failed to notify liability to register, or made late notification, and an assessment covering a period longer than three months is made to recover the tax;

(4) such an assessment could be made, but the tax is recovered by means of a 'long' first return period;

(5) a person exempted from registration has failed to notify a change in circumstances which makes him registrable, and the tax is recovered by way of a 'long period' assessment or return; or

(6) an invoice purporting to include VAT has been issued by a person not authorised to issue tax invoices.

In practice, default interest will only be due from a person who has registered late if he fails to pay the tax by the due date for the long first return period. Even then, it only runs from the due date, not from the dates when the tax would have been payable if he had registered at the proper time.

As a general rule, default interest runs from the due date for the submission of the VAT return for the period concerned until the date when the person pays the tax. However, if the assessment is to recover tax which has been incorrectly repaid by HMRC, interest runs from seven days after the date when HMRC issued a written instruction authorising the repayment. In the case of the issue of an invoice by an unauthorised person, interest runs from the date of the invoice.

The rate of interest is fixed by Treasury order, and is intended to reflect commercial rates of interest (there is a table of rates in the Key Data section). Default interest does not rank as an allowable expense for income tax and corporation tax purposes (see, 3027).

Default interest is capped, so that it only runs for the last three years of the period. However, if the trader then fails to pay the assessment on time, interest will continue to run.

In practice, HMRC does not assess for default interest in cases where there has been no commercial loss to them, as when a trader has failed to charge output tax but, if tax had been charged, it would have been recoverable in the hands of the customer.

Also, interest is not charged in respect of net errors below £10,000, which could be adjusted on a subsequent return.

The practice of not charging default interest on net errors of £10,000 or less separately notified to HMRC ceased with effect from 1 September 2008. The decision in *Wilkinson v IR Commrs* deemed this practice to be unlawful. All error notifications (previously known as voluntary disclosures) requiring an assessment may be subject to a default interest charge, irrespective of the amount involved. However, as before, de minimis net errors can continue to be corrected on a VAT return and will not attract interest.

Legislation: VATA 1994, s. 74

Cases: *C & E Commrs v Peninsular and Oriental Steam Navigation Co* [1994] BVC 57; *C & E Commrs v Peninsular and Oriental Steam Navigation Co* [1992] BVC 170

Other Material: HMRC Brief 38/08; Notice 700/43, *Default interest (May 2010 edn)*

Indirect Tax Reporter: ¶60-680

8550   Incorrect certificates

Certain zero-ratings (particularly in connection with property) depend upon the supplier obtaining a certificate of use from the customer. If an incorrect certificate is issued, HMRC may assess the customer for a penalty of 100% of the tax 'saved' by the issue of the certificate.

The usual statutory defence of reasonable excuse applies for this penalty (see 8556), but there is no provision for mitigation.

Legislation: VATA 1994, s. 62

Indirect Tax Reporter: ¶60-200

8556   Reasonable excuse: VAT

There are some VAT penalties which are remitted if the taxpayer has reasonable excuse. These are reduced in number as the penalty regime in VATA 1994 has been replaced by the pan-tax penalty regime – see 8520.

The term 'reasonable excuse' has not been defined in the legislation. However, the legislation does specify that the following are not to give rise to a reasonable excuse:

- an insufficiency of funds to pay any tax due; and

- the fact of reliance on another to perform any task, or dilatoriness or inaccuracy on the part of the person relied upon.

Legislation: VATA 1994, s. 71(1)

Indirect Tax Reporter: ¶60-037

8562   Mitigation of VAT penalties

The mitigation of VAT penalties in the VATA 1994, has largely been replaced by the pan-tax regimes in FA 2007, FA 2008 and FA 2009.

- Penalty for late registration and unauthorised issue of invoice (see 8504 and 8510).

Mitigation can be up to 100%, and is exercisable by HMRC or, on appeal, the tribunal; the tribunal has power to reduce the mitigation allowed by HMRC as well as to increase it.

No account is to be taken of the following in considering mitigation (VATA 1994, s. 70(4)):

- insufficiency of funds to pay either tax or a penalty;

- the fact that there has been no significant loss of tax;
- the fact that the trader (or his representative) has acted in good faith.

Legislation: VATA 1994, s. 70, 70(4)

Indirect Tax Reporter: ¶59-730

8574 Failure to submit EC sales list

Failure to submit an EC sales list (ESL) by the due date can give rise to a civil penalty at a daily rate.

If an ESL is not submitted by the due date, HMRC may issue a notice. If the ESL is not submitted within a further 14 days, then a penalty will be due. Penalties can also be levied (regardless of whether the first late ESL attracts a penalty) for any further late ESLs until 12 months have elapsed without an ESL being submitted late.

The penalty is at a rate of £5 per day for the first default, £10 per day for the second, and £15 per day for any subsequent default.

Legislation: VATA 1994, s. 66

Indirect Tax Reporter: ¶64-920

8586 Assessment of penalties

HMRC have the power under VATA 1994, s. 76 to assess amounts due by way of default surcharge or default interest (see 8516 and 8544).

Legislation: VATA 1994, s. 76

VAT assessments, appeals and disputes

8606 VAT assessment powers

In the ordinary course of events, the amount of VAT due is established by reference to returns submitted by the taxable person. Where this procedure breaks down, liability to tax is established by means of an assessment issued by HMRC.

HMRC have the power to assess tax due where:

- a person has failed to submit returns, or it appears that the returns are incomplete or incorrect;
- an incorrect credit or refund of input tax has been made for a period;

- a person has acquired, imported or been supplied with goods and is unable to account for those goods;

- a non-taxable person has acquired goods subject to excise duty, or a new means of transport, from another Member State and has failed to account for the VAT due on the acquisition.

They also have power to assess amounts due by way of penalties and interest.

The making of an assessment, and its due notification to the person concerned, establishes (subject to any appeal) the person's liability to pay the amount assessed.

Legislation: VATA 1994, s. 73(1), (2), (7), 75, 76

Indirect Tax Reporter: ¶58-520

8612 Time-limits and notification of VAT assessment

Except in cases involving fraud or dishonesty, there is an overall time-limit for the making of an assessment of four years from the end of the prescribed accounting period to which it relates (VATA 1994, s. 77(1)). In cases of fraud this time-limit is extended to 20 years (VATA 1994, s. 77(4)). In the case of a deceased trader, there is a further overriding time-limit of four years from the date of death (VATA 1994, s. 77(5)).

Apart from these overriding time-limits, an assessment must be made by the later of:

- two years from the end of the prescribed accounting period concerned; and

- one year after evidence of facts, sufficient in the opinion of HMRC to justify the making of the assessment, comes to their knowledge (VATA 1994, s. 73(6)).

If further information subsequently becomes available, HMRC can issue a further assessment. Even if no further information comes to light, HMRC can still make a supplementary assessment provided that this is done within the relevant time-limit (VATA 1994, s. 73(6)).

If an assessment is made after the time-limit for making it has expired, it is invalid. If a global assessment is made (i.e. a single assessment covering a number of periods, rather than breaking the tax down between the different prescribed accounting periods), and it is out of time as regards one of the prescribed accounting periods included in it, then the whole assessment falls. Provided that a breakdown is given, the mere fact that assessments for a number of periods are listed in a single notification does not in itself mean that a global assessment has been made.

However, the High Court has held that HMRC was entitled to delay making a 'best judgment' assessment until they had not only material justifying the making of an assessment but also material on which to calculate the amount of the liability.

In order for an assessment to be valid, it must not only be made on time, but also be correctly notified. There is no specifically prescribed form for notification, but the courts have held that the person assessed is entitled to be notified, in reasonably clear terms, of the identity of the person assessed, the amount of the assessment, the reasons for it, and the period or periods to which it relates (see, for example, *House t/a P & J Autos v C & E Commrs*). If the notification is deficient in any of these respects, it may be possible to overturn the assessment.

As stated above, under current law, HMRC can only issue an assessment to recover VAT from a taxpayer within one year of the full facts coming to their attention. This has caused problems where the facts have remained constant but a change in the interpretation of the VAT law has led to a different outcome.

Legislation: VATA 1994, s. 73(6), 77(1), (4), (5)

Cases: *BUPA Purchasing Ltd v R & C Commrs* [2007] BVC 603; *House (t/a P & J Autos) v C & E Commrs* [1996] BVC 116

Indirect Tax Reporter: ¶58-205

8618 Matters which may invalidate a VAT assessment

When HMRC exercises its power to assess, the Commissioners must do so to the best of their judgment. This means that they must consider fairly the material before them, taking account of all matters which are relevant and ignoring matters which are not. They do not have to make exhaustive enquiries provided that they have some material on which they can form a judgment, but will generally be acting unreasonably if they ignore information provided to them by the trader.

Frequently, it is necessary to carry out some degree of estimation in order to arrive at the amount of an assessment, if exact figures are not readily available. In such cases, it is permissible to use observations made for a sample period to estimate the amount of tax due for a longer period.

The main grounds on which an assessment may be invalid, and on which an appeal may therefore be successful, may be summarised as follows:

- the assessment is wrongly based in law (for example, it is based on the notion that a supply is a standard-rated one and it is, in fact, zero-rated);

- the assessment has been made out of time (see 8612);

- the notification of the assessment is procedurally incorrect (see 8612);

- the assessment has not been made to the best of HMRC's judgment; or

- although the assessment is procedurally and legally correct, and has been made to the best of HMRC's judgment, the appellant is able to bring evidence which convinces the tribunal not only that the amount of it is wrong but also what amount is to be preferred.

Legislation: VATA 1994, s. 73

Indirect Tax Reporter: ¶58-300

8620   Reviews and appeals

The whole process of reviews and appeals has changed as a result of the *Tribunals, Courts and Enforcement Act* 2007 (TCEA 2007) and the statutory instruments that give effect to the detail. The whole system changed on 1 April 2009.

The TCEA replaces the old tribunal structure with a new lower tax tribunal, called a First-tier Tribunal that hears basic VAT appeals and an Upper Tribunal that hears appeals from the lower tribunal and, in the first instance, more complex cases.

The appellate structure in the UK has also been modified, such that an appeal from the First-tier Tribunal will normally be heard in the Upper Tribunal, so in effect, this replaces the High Court. Appeals beyond this are as before: to the Court of Appeal and the Supreme Court (which replaces the House of Lords Appellate Committee).

When there is a dispute between a taxpayer and HMRC, the new process is as follows:

The taxpayer is notified of the decision (this could be, say, an assessment) and at that point HMRC must offer the taxpayer a review of the decision under VATA 1994, s. 83A.

If the taxpayer accepts the offer of a review within the statutory 30 days, then HMRC are bound to review the decision under s. 83C and notify the results of the review to the taxpayer.

The taxpayer may choose not to request a review and instead go straight to an appeal under s. 83G. This must be done within 30 days of the disputed decision. It is not possible to request a review and go to an appeal at the same time (s. 83C).

The review must be conducted and the results notified to the taxpayer within 45 days of the relevant date (normally the date of acceptance of the offer of the review).

The review will either confirm, vary or cancel the decision. The taxpayer can still appeal the review decision within 30 days of the conclusions of the review.

Legislation: VATA 1994, s. 82 onwards; *Tribunal Procedures (First-tier Tribunal) (Tax Chambers) Rules* 2009, SI 2009/273; *Tribunal Procedure (Upper Tribunal) Rules* 2008, SI 2008/2698

8624 Appealable matters: VAT

The matters on which an appeal lies to a VAT tribunal are listed in VATA 1994, s. 83, being decisions of HMRC with respect to various things such as an assessment, the registration of a person, the tax chargeable on a supply, the amount of input tax which may be credited, etc. This is a complete list, and anything which does not appear in it is not appealable to the tribunal (although there may be an alternative remedy by way of judicial review).

Legislation: TCEA 2007; VATA 1994, s. 83 onwards

Cases: *R & C Commrs v Church of Scientology Religious College Inc* [2007] EWHC 1329 (Ch); [2007] BVC 743

Indirect Tax Reporter: ¶61-400

8630 Time-limit for VAT appeal and local review

As a general rule, notice of appeal against an assessment or other decision must be lodged with the Tribunal Centre within 30 days of the disputed decision or the conclusions of a review (see 8620).

Legislation: VATA 1994, s. 83G

Indirect Tax Reporter: ¶61-410

8636 VAT appeal procedures

The procedures governing appeals to the VAT tribunals are set out in the *Tribunal Procedure (First-tier Tribunal) (Tax Chamber) Rules* 2009 (SI 2009/273) and the *Tribunal Procedure (Upper Tribunal) Rules* 2008 (SI 2008/2698).

A tribunal may, in particular, require the taxpayer:

- to deliver to them such particulars as they may require for the purpose of determining the appeal; and

- to make various documents available for inspection.

Any party to an appeal may adduce lawful evidence and may call witnesses. A tribunal has the power to summon any person (other than the appellant) to appear before them and give evidence. Witnesses may be examined on oath.

Professional advisers (e.g. barristers, solicitors or accountants) may appear on behalf of any party to the appeal.

A tribunal has the power to award costs, although in the new system these are uncommon.

Legislation: *Tribunal Procedure (First-tier Tribunal) (Tax Chamber) Rules* 2009 (SI 2009/273) and the *Tribunal Procedure (Upper Tribunal) Rules* 2008 (SI 2008/2698)

Indirect Tax Reporter: ¶61-140

SDLT

9000 Background

Stamp duty land tax (SDLT) was introduced in the Chancellor's 2003 Budget and resulted in the new legislation contained in FA 2003, Pt. 4 and 5. The new tax was introduced with effect from 1 December 2003 and replaced the old stamp duty regime on UK land and buildings. Subsequent Finance Acts have made further changes to the new regime to clarify points of uncertainty, to counter avoidance and extend some reliefs.

Stamp duty (SD) in effect only comes into play for sales of unlisted companies. However, if you buy stocks and shares for £1,000 or less, you do not normally have to pay any stamp duty. You also do not have to tell HMRC about the transaction.

All you need to do is:

- make sure the first exemption certificate on the back of the stock transfer form has been completed (you do not need to complete this certificate if you do not pay anything for the shares);

- send the stock transfer form and the share certificate to the registrar of the company you have bought shares in – whether you gave anything for the shares or not.

The address of the registrar is on the share certificate. The registrar will then issue you with your own share certificate.

Sales of shares in listed companies are covered by the stamp duty reserve tax (SDRT) regime.

Legislation: FA 1986, Pt. 4; FA 1999, Sch. 13; FA 2003, Pt. 4, Sch. 3–20

9010   Outline of the SDLT regime

SDLT is a self-assessed tax rather than a duty collected by the payment for stamps (and it is no longer a tax on documents – FA 2003, s. 42(2)). Consequently, since 1 December 2003, taxpayers no longer need to submit documents to HM Revenue & Customs (HMRC) for stamping. Instead, they must (in most circumstances) notify liability to tax using a land transaction return.

SDLT returns are now normally submitted online, although paper SDLT return are acceptable and must be submitted, within 30 days of completion, to HMRC's central processing centre: HMRC Stamp Taxes, Comben House, Farriers Way, Netherton, Merseyside, L30 4RN.

Details of the online filing process can be found on HMRC's website (now largely migrated to the GOV.UK website).

Payment can be made by a number of methods, including: online or telephone banking, CHAPS, Bacs, or sending a cheque though the post. Tax is due 30 days after the 'effective date', which is normally the date of completion, or the date 'substantial performance' occurs, if before completion.

The taxpayer then obtains a stamp duty land tax certificate (an SDLT5), which is either downloaded (for online submission) or sent (for paper submission), which they, or their agent, should submit to the Land Registry in order to register ownership of land or to record a deed, as appropriate.

Under the 'process now, check later' system, HMRC have a period of nine months from filing in which to open an enquiry for all transactions (see below).

SDLT is charged on land transactions. It is chargeable:

- whether or not there is an instrument effecting the transaction;

- if there is such an instrument, whether or not it is executed in the UK; and

- whether or not any party to the transaction is present, or resident, in the UK.

It applies to transactions effected on or after 1 December 2003.

A 'land transaction' means any acquisition of a 'chargeable interest' (FA 2003, s. 43). A chargeable interest is widely defined in FA 2003, s. 48 as an estate, interest, right or power in or over UK-situated land, or the benefit of an obligation, restriction or condition affecting the value of such estate interest right or power, other than certain exempt interests. A charge to SDLT is imposed however the acquisition is effected, whether by act of the parties, by order of a court or other authority, by or under any statutory provision or by operation of law. In particular:

- the creation of a chargeable interest is:

  - an acquisition by the person becoming entitled to the interest created; and

  - a disposal by the person whose interest or right is subject to the interest created;

- the surrender or release of a chargeable interest is:

  - an acquisition of that interest by any person whose interest or right is benefited or enlarged by the transaction; and

  - a disposal by the person ceasing to be entitled to that interest;

- the variation of a chargeable interest is:

  - an acquisition of a chargeable interest by the person benefiting from the variation; and

  - a disposal of a chargeable interest by the person whose interest is subject to or limited by the variation.

The variation of a lease is only an acquisition and disposal of a chargeable interest where it takes effect or is treated, for the purposes of the SDLT legislation as the granting of a new lease or where the variation is to reduce the amount of the rent.

There are a number of exempt interests, which are primarily set out in FA 2003, s. 48 and Sch. 3. The main exemptions are:

- mortgages and similar security interests;
- licences to use or occupy land;
- tenancies at will;
- transactions for no chargeable consideration;
- grants of certain leases by social landlords;
- transactions in connection with divorce or the dissolution of a civil partnership made in pursuance of an order of the court;
- assents and appropriations by personal representatives; and
- variation of testamentary dispositions within two years of death.

The rates of SDLT are given in FA 2003, s. 55 (see 9070).

Legislation: FA 2003, Pt. 4, s. 43–48, 55, 76–78, Sch. 10, s. 42, 43(1), 48, Sch. 3, Sch. 19, para. 2; FA 2010, s. 6 and 7

9020   Contract and conveyance

Where a land transaction is to be completed by conveyance, the general rule is that the contract and the transaction effected on completion are treated as parts of a 'single land transaction'. Under those circumstances, the 'effective date' of the transaction is the date of completion. However, if the contract is substantially performed without having been completed, the contract is treated as if it were itself the transaction provided for in the contract. In this case, the effective date of the transaction is when the contract is substantially performed.

A contract is 'substantially performed' when:

- the purchaser, or a person connected with the purchaser, takes possession of the whole, or substantially the whole, of the subject matter of the contract; or
- a substantial amount of the consideration is paid or provided.

For this purpose, possession includes receipt of rents and profits or the right to receive them. It is immaterial whether possession is taken under the contract or under a licence or lease of a temporary character.

If none of the consideration is rent, a substantial amount of the consideration is paid or provided where the whole or substantially the whole of the consideration is paid or provided.

If the only consideration is rent, a substantial amount of the consideration is paid or provided when the first payment of rent is made.

If the consideration includes both rent and other consideration, a substantial amount of the consideration is paid or provided when:

- the whole or substantially the whole of the consideration other than rent is paid or provided; or

- the first payment of rent is made.

In a case of substantial performance, if the contract is subsequently completed by a conveyance both the contract and the transaction effected on completion are notifiable transactions. Tax is chargeable on the conveyance to the extent (if any) that the amount of tax chargeable on it is greater than the amount of tax chargeable on the contract. If the contract is (to any extent) afterwards rescinded or annulled, or is for any other reason not carried into effect, the tax paid on substantial performance is repayable accordingly. Repayment must be claimed by amendment of the relevant land transaction return.

Legislation: FA 2003, s. 44

9030   Pre-completion transactions (formerly sub-sales)

Finance Act 2013 introduced a new regime for transfers of rights – now referred to as pre-completion transactions. This replaces the older lexicon of 'sub-sales and transfers of rights'. It was introduced in 2013 and was retrospective to 21 March 2012.

A sub-sale is where someone (B) enters into a contract to buy land from the seller (A), and then enters into a contract with a third person (C) for the sale of the land, with completion of both contracts taking place at the same time. Sub-sales are common and take place for a variety of reasons. Sometimes, the initial buyer (B) is a property investor and wants to make a profit on a property. In other cases, the end buyer (C) wants to avoid (A) knowing that he is the real buyer and so uses (B) to hide his identity.

In FA 2013, HRMC changed the legislation, because sub-sales were also increasingly used for tax avoidance. Avoidance schemes often relied on the A–B transaction being disregarded for tax under the 'transfer of rights' rules and a claim that no charge arises on C either because C pays no consideration for the transfer or claims the benefit of a relief or exemption. The new SDLT rules are designed to close this loop hole.

The new regime inserted a new FA 2003, Sch. 2A.

The new rules broadly follow the old rules and allow SDLT relief for B in the A-B-C chain referred to above, such that in simple terms, only C (referred to as the transferee) pays SDLT on the chain transaction. However, there are two important points to note:

(1) B (now referred to as the transferor) must now claim the relief on an SDLT return (before it was disregarded); and

(2) there is complex anti-avoidance legislation to protect the measures being used by tax planners.

The new regime applies to:

- assignments of rights, where C (the transferee), acquires rights under the original contract; and

- free-standing transfers, where C does not acquire rights under the original contract.

The new rules also apply to novations, following the 2013 *Allchin* case in the First-tier Tribunal (FTT), where a precise planning scheme, a novation, which crucially depended on the timings of payments under a novated contract, was struck down by the FTT.

In *APVCO 19 Ltd*, the courts rejected an application for judicial review on the new legislation. See Spotlight 25 (August 2015).

Legislation: FA 2003, s. 45, 45A, Sch. 2 (as amended by FA 2013)

Cases: *Allchin* [2013] TC 02613; *R (on the application of APVCO 19 Ltd) v R & C Commrs* [2015] BTC 26

Other material: See *Spotlight 25: SDLT avoidance in sub-sale relief* (August 2015)

9040 Options and pre-emption rights

The acquisition of an option binding the grantor to enter into a land transaction is treated as a land transaction distinct from any land transaction resulting from the exercise of the option, though they may be 'linked transactions' within FA 2003, s. 108.

Similarly, the acquisition of a right of pre-emption preventing the grantor from entering into, or restricting the right of the grantor to enter into, a land transaction, is also treated as a land transaction distinct from any land transaction resulting from the exercise of the right.

An option binding the grantor to enter into a land transaction includes an option requiring the grantor either to enter into a land transaction or to discharge his obligations under the option in some other way (e.g. by the payment of cash).

The effective date of the transaction in the case of the acquisition of such an option or right is when the option or right is acquired, as opposed to when it becomes exercisable.

Where an option is exercised, the grant and exercise of the option may be regarded as a single transaction in accordance with the 'linked transactions' rules (FA 2003, s. 108). This affects the rate of SDLT that is chargeable on the exercise, because the consideration for the grant of the option and the consideration payable on exercise have to be aggregated (FA 2003, s. 55(4)). In practice, the tax on the grant is calculated without having regard to the amount payable on exercise. The tax payable on exercise is then the difference between tax on the combined consideration and the tax paid on the grant.

Some option agreements provide that on exercise, the option sum is returned to the original grantee, or knocked off the exercise price. This may be helpful if the combined sums take the transaction over into the next SDLT rate band.

Example

Pat pays Reg £1,000 for an option to purchase Reg's land for £299,000.

No SDLT is payable in respect of the grant of the option because of the £1,000 is covered by the 0% band. If Pat exercises the option, however, the total consideration considered is £300,000 on which SDLT at 3% is payable. This gives rise to a liability of £9,000.

Had some SDLT been payable when the option was granted, a corresponding deduction would be made to the liability when the option was exercised.

Legislation: FA 2003, s. 46

Exchanges

9050   General

Where a land transaction is entered into by a purchaser (alone or jointly) wholly or partly in consideration of another land transaction being entered into by him (alone or jointly) as vendor, each transaction is treated as distinct and separate from the other.

These transactions with an effective date after 19 July 2007 are not 'linked transactions' within s. 108. A transaction is treated as being entered into wholly or partly in consideration of another land transaction where an obligation to give consideration for a land transaction that a person enters into as purchaser is met wholly or partly by way of that person entering into another transaction as vendor. The SDLT liability on each transaction is the appropriate percentage of the market value of the property.

Example 1

George and Jim agree to exchange their homes. George's home is worth £400,000; Jim's is worth £600,000. George agrees to pay Jim £200,000 additional consideration.

George will be liable to pay SDLT of 4% of £600,000 (i.e. £24,000).

Jim will be liable to pay SDLT of 3% of £400,000 (i.e. £12,000).

The £200,000 of cash is ignored.

The rules on exchanges were modified in March 2011, to attack planning schemes. These rules are unlikely to affect innocuous exchanges and the rules largely continue as before.

Example 2 (from HMRC's Stamp Tax Bulletin 02/2011)

A grandmother gives her £1m home to her grandson, in exchange for his £300,000 flat. The grandson must pay SDLT on £1m (the market value of the interest acquired – this is greater than the consideration he gave). The grandmother must pay SDLT on the greater of the market value of the interest acquired (£300,000) and the chargeable consideration given. The consideration she gave was £1m but this must be apportioned on a just and reasonable basis between the chargeable consideration given for the flat and the element of gift to her grandson. A just and reasonable apportionment results in the chargeable consideration given being £300,000 and a gift of £700,000. So the grandmother pays SDLT on £300,000. There is unlikely to be any element of gift in any transaction which has a commercial flavour.

Example 3 (from HMRC's Stamp Tax Bulletin 02/2011)

Ahmed and Katrina decide to exchange their homes. Ahmed's is valued at £375,000, but Katrina's is valued at £400,000, so Ahmed gives Katrina £25,000 in cash as well. Ahmed pays tax on chargeable consideration of £400,000 since this is both the value of the interest he acquires and the amount of consideration he gives to acquire it. It is just and reasonable for Katrina to apportion the £400,000 market value of her house (i.e. the value of what she gave) under paragraph 4 as to £375,000 for the property and £25,000 for the cash received. The chargeable consideration is £375,000 for Katrina's acquisition – this is equal to both the value of the interest she acquired and the amount of apportioned consideration she gave to acquire it.

Where one of the transactions consists of the grant of a lease, the rent payable under the lease is included in the chargeable consideration for the acquisition.

Legislation: FA 2003, s. 47, Sch. 4, para. 5 (as amended by FA 2011)

Other Material: Stamp Tax Bulletin 02/2011

9060   Reliefs for certain acquisitions of residential property

There are a number of reliefs available in respect of certain acquisitions (generally by property traders) of residential property. They apply only in respect of areas of land that do not exceed the 'permitted area'.

The definition of 'permitted area' follows that in the capital gains tax main residence relief – i.e. any property with an area of 0.5 ha or less will qualify. Larger properties will also qualify if 'required for the reasonable enjoyment of the dwelling as a dwelling having regard to its size and character'.

A property trader is a business that buys and sells dwellings. It can be a company, LLP or partnership whose members are all companies or LLPs.

Acquisition by house-building company from individual acquiring new dwelling

This is a relief which relieves a double charge to SDLT when a private individual buys a house from a housebuilder and as part of that purchase, sells his house to the housebuilder. The first leg (the sale of the old house to the housebuilder) is exempt from the charge and SDLT is only charged when the housebuilder on-sells the property.

Where a dwelling ('the old dwelling') is acquired by a house-building company, or a company connected with it, from an individual (whether alone or with other individuals), the acquisition is exempt from SDLT if the following conditions are met:

- the individual (whether alone or with other individuals) must acquire a new dwelling from the house-building company;

- the individual:

  – must have occupied the old dwelling as his only or main residence at some time in the period of two years ending with the date of its acquisition by the house-building company; and

  – must intend to occupy the new dwelling as his only or main residence;

- each acquisition must be entered into in consideration of the other; and

- the area of land acquired by the house-building company must not exceed the 'permitted area' (see above).

If the area of land acquired by the house-building company exceeds the permitted area, the chargeable consideration for the acquisition is taken to be the amount calculated by deducting the market value of the permitted area from the market value of the old dwelling.

A 'house-building company' is a company that carries on the business of constructing or adapting buildings or parts of buildings for use as dwellings.

Acquisition by a 'property trader' from individual acquiring new dwelling

Where a dwelling ('the old dwelling') is acquired by a property trader from an individual (whether alone or with other individuals), the acquisition is exempt from charge if the following conditions are met:

- the acquisition must be made in the course of a business that consists of or includes acquiring dwellings from individuals who acquire new dwellings from house-building companies;
- the individual (whether alone or with other individuals) must acquire a new dwelling from a house-building company;
- the individual:
  - must have occupied the old dwelling as his only or main residence at some time in the period of two years ending with the date of its acquisition; and
  - must intend to occupy the new dwelling as his only or main residence;
- the property trader must not intend:
  - to spend more than the 'permitted amount' on refurbishment of the old dwelling;
  - to grant a lease or licence of the old dwelling for more than six months; or
  - to permit any of its principals or employees (or any person connected with any of its principals or employees) to occupy the old dwelling; and
- the area of land acquired by the property trader does not exceed the permitted area.

The 'permitted amount' for refurbishment is the greater of £10,000 or 5% of the consideration for the acquisition of the dwelling, subject to a maximum of £20,000.

> **Example**
>
> Steve is a property trader who purchases three residential properties for £120,000, £300,000 and £800,000 respectively.
>
> Five per cent of the consideration for the acquisition of each dwelling amounts to £6,000, £15,000 and £40,000.
>
> In respect of the first property, the maximum that may be spent on refurbishment is £10,000; on the second, £15,000; on the third, £20,000.

If the area of land acquired by the property trader exceeds the permitted area, the chargeable consideration for the acquisition is taken to be the amount calculated by deducting the market value of the permitted area from the market value of the old dwelling.

Acquisition by a property trader from personal representatives

Where a dwelling is acquired by a property trader from the personal representatives of a deceased individual, the acquisition is exempt from charge if the following conditions are met:

- the acquisition must be made in the course of a business that consists of or includes acquiring dwellings from personal representatives of deceased individuals;

- the deceased individual must have occupied the dwelling as his only or main residence at some time in the period of two years ending with the date of his death;

- the property trader must not intend:

  - to spend more than the permitted amount on refurbishment of the dwelling;

  - to grant a lease or licence of the dwelling; or

  - to permit any of its principals or employees (or any person connected with any of its principals or employees) to occupy the dwelling; and

- the area of land acquired must not exceed the permitted area.

The 'permitted amount' is as defined above.

If the area of land acquired exceeds the permitted area, the chargeable consideration for the acquisition is taken to be the amount calculated by deducting the market value of the permitted area from the market value of the dwelling.

Relief is not permitted if the deceased did not occupy the property as a main residence within the two years before the date of death. Thus, the estate of an individual who leaves the home to live in a nursing home will not be entitled to this relief if the individual lives for a further two years.

Acquisition by a property trader from individual where chain of transactions breaks down

Where a dwelling ('the old dwelling') is acquired by a property trader from an individual (whether alone or with other individuals), the acquisition is exempt from charge if:

- the individual has made arrangements to sell a dwelling ('the old dwelling') and acquire another dwelling ('the second dwelling');
- the arrangements to sell the old dwelling fail;
- the acquisition of the old dwelling is made for the purpose of enabling the individual's acquisition of the second dwelling to proceed;
- the acquisition is made in the course of a business that consists of or includes acquiring dwellings from individuals in those circumstances;
- the individual:
  - occupied the old dwelling as his only or main residence at some time in the period of two years ending with the date of its acquisition; and
  - intends to occupy the second dwelling as his only or main residence;
- the property trader does not intend:
  - to spend more than the permitted amount on refurbishment of the old dwelling;
  - to grant a lease or licence of the old dwelling for more than six months; or
  - to permit any of its principals or employees (or any person connected with any of its principals or employees) to occupy the old dwelling; and
- the area of land acquired does not exceed the permitted area.

The 'permitted amount' is as defined above.

If the area of land acquired exceeds the permitted area, the chargeable consideration for the acquisition is taken to be the amount calculated by deducting the market value of the permitted area from the market value of the old dwelling.

Acquisition by an employer in cases of relocation

Where a dwelling is acquired from an individual (whether alone or with other individuals) by his employer, the acquisition is exempt from charge if:

- the individual occupied the dwelling as his only or main residence at some time in the period of two years ending with the date of the acquisition;

- the acquisition is made in connection with a change of residence by the individual resulting from relocation of employment;

- the consideration does not exceed the market value of the dwelling; and

- the area of land acquired does not exceed the permitted area.

If the area of land acquired exceeds the permitted area, the chargeable consideration for the acquisition is taken to be the amount calculated by deducting the market value of the permitted area from the market value of the dwelling.

This is a slightly more complicated provision. The 'relocation of employment' must be to facilitate becoming an employee of the employer (and employer includes a prospective employer), due to an alteration of the duties of the employee with his employer or because of an alteration of the place where the duties are normally performed. A change of residence is only a relocation of employment if the change is made wholly or mainly to allow the individual to have his residence within a reasonable daily travelling distance and his former residence was not within a reasonable daily travelling distance of the new place of employment.

This relief is not available if it is not the vendor whose employment gives rise to the relocation. Thus, if A and B live together in A's house and they are required to move because of B's job, the relief will not be available in respect of a purchase of the property by B's employer from A.

Acquisition by a property trader in cases of relocation

Where a dwelling is acquired by a property trader from an individual (whether alone or with other individuals), the acquisition is exempt from charge if:

- the acquisition is made in the course of a business that consists of or includes acquiring dwellings from individuals in connection with a change of residence resulting from relocation of employment;

- the individual occupied the dwelling as his only or main residence at some time in the period of two years ending with the date of its acquisition;

- the acquisition is made in connection with a change of residence by the individual resulting from relocation of employment;

- the consideration does not exceed the market value of the dwelling;

- the property trader does not intend:
  (a) to spend more than the permitted amount on refurbishment of the dwelling;
  (b) to grant a lease or licence of the dwelling for a period of more than six months; or
  (c) to permit any of its principals or employees (or any person connected with any of its principals or employees) to occupy the dwelling; and

- the area of land acquired does not exceed the permitted area.

The 'permitted amount' is as defined above.

If the area of land acquired exceeds the permitted area, the chargeable consideration for the acquisition is taken to be the amount calculated by deducting the market value of the permitted area from the market value of the old dwelling.

Withdrawal of relief

Finance Act 2003, para. 11, Sch. 6A provides that the foregoing reliefs are withdrawn in certain circumstances:

Where relief has been given to a property trader, relief will be withdrawn if the property trader:

- spends more than the permitted amount on refurbishment of the old dwelling;

- grants a lease or licence of the old dwelling for a period of more than six months; or

- permits any of its principals or employees (or any person connected with any of its principals or employees) to occupy the old dwelling.

There is no such withdrawal of relief in cases where the acquisition is from a house-building company or the vendor's employer in cases of relocation.

Leases or licences of up to six months, however, are permitted where the relief is in respect of an acquisition:

- from an individual acquiring a new dwelling;

- from an individual whose chain has broken down; or

- from an individual whose employment is relocated.

The lease or licence must be to the individual from whom the dwelling is acquired.

Leases or licences of the dwelling are not permitted in any circumstances if the acquisition by the property trader was from an individual's personal representatives.

Legislation: FA 2003, Sch. 6A, para. 1, 2, 3, 4, 5, 6, 8, 11

9070   Rates of SDLT and chargeable consideration

The rate of charge for land transactions depends on the amount paid for the transaction (this includes 'any payment or consideration' for linked transactions), whether paid in money or money's worth, by the purchaser or a person connected with him.

Where a single bargain includes more than one interest in land, or an interest in land and another interest or asset, the amount paid should be apportioned between the interests. Anything paid for goodwill that cannot be sold separately from the land is part of chargeable consideration.

VAT is included in chargeable consideration only where it is paid as part of the transaction, or where a landlord has elected on or before the grant of a new lease to charge VAT on the rents under that lease (FA 2003, Sch. 4, para. 2).

Arrangements for certain transactions may provide for consideration to be paid in one or more instalments after the effective date of the transaction. Where:

- there is uncertainty about whether anything more will be paid, and/or about the amount of additional consideration due; and

- at least one instalment might be more than six months after the effective date.

It is possible to apply to HMRC to defer payment of tax until the amount to be paid is determined.

The rates of charge (dependent on the chargeable consideration) are set out in FA 2003, s. 55.

They are, for *residential property* (purchased by individuals) up to 3 December 2014:

- relevant consideration of not more than £125,000, rate of 0%;

- relevant consideration above £125,000 and not more than £250,000, 1%;

- relevant consideration above £250,000 and not more than £500,000, 3%;

- relevant consideration above £500,000 and not more than £1m, 4%;

- relevant consideration of more than £1m and not more than £2m, 2% (from 6 April 2011);

- relevant consideration of more than £2m, 7% (from 22 March 2012).

It is important to appreciate that this is the slab system that has been in place for SDLT since its inception in 2003.

From 4 December 2014, the slab system has been replaced by the new progressive system:

Residential land or property SDLT rates and thresholds from 3 December 2014

Purchase price of property	Rate of SDLT
Up to £125,000	Zero
Over £125,000 to £250,000	2%
Over £250,000 to £925,000	5%
Over £925,000 to £1.5m	10%
Over £1.5m	12%

From 4 December 2014, each new SDLT rate will only be payable on the portion of the property value which falls within each band (rather than tax being due at one rate on the entire value).

So for a property purchased for £400,000, under the old system, the purchaser would have paid 3% on the whole of the price, so £12,000.

Under the new system, the purchaser pays 0% on the first £125,000, 2% on the next £125,000 and 5% on the last £150,000. So £10,000 in all.

The higher 15% of SDLT for the acquisition of residential property transactions by certain 'non-natural persons' (NNPs) (broadly companies, collective investment schemes and partnerships with a member who is a company or a collective investment scheme) where the chargeable consideration exceeded £2m applied from 21 March 2012, subject to transitional provisions for pre-existing contracts (see also 9246 for the annual charge (ATED) on these properties).

Legislation introduced in *Finance Act* 2014 reduced this threshold to £500,000. The new threshold applies to land transactions where the effective date is on or after 20 March 2014.

In the Autumn Statement 2015, the Chancellor announced that as part of a five-point housing plan, purchasers of domestic property as a second home or a buy-to-let, are subject to a 3% surcharge from 1 April 2016 as follows:

Band	Existing residential SDLT rates	New rates from 1 April 2016
£0 to £125,000	0%	3%
Over £125,000 to £250,000	2%	5%
Over £250,000 to £925,000	5%	8%
Over £925,000 to £1.5m	10%	13%
Over £1.5m	12%	15%

Transactions under £40,000 do not require an SDLT return to be filed with HMRC and are not subject to the higher rates.

HMRC example

An additional residential property is purchased for £200,000. SDLT is calculated as follows:

- 3% on the first £125,000 = £3,750;

- 5% on the remaining £75,000 (the portion between £125,000 and £200,000) = £3,750;

- the total SDLT due is therefore: £3,750 + £3,750 = £7,500.

It should be noted that the central test is: at the end of the day of the transaction, how many residential properties are owned? If a single residential property has been replaced by another residential property, then the surcharge will NOT apply (regardless of what purpose the second property is put to).

But it is not quite that simple.

If the first residential property which is a main residence is not sold when the second property (which is going to replace the main residence) is purchased, then the central test is met: there are two properties at the end of the day of the transaction and the higher rate will apply.

However, if the first residential property is sold within 36 months (announced in Budget 2016 and replacing the earlier announced 18-month limit), then a repayment of the excess SDLT is allowed.

> If a person owns both a main residence and a second home and sells the main residence and purchases a new one, the new higher rates will NOT apply. Although that person has two properties at the end of the day of the transaction, he or she has replaced the main residence.

Spouses/civil partners

The Government will treat married couples and civil partners living together as one unit.

Married couples and civil partners who own one property at the end of the day of a transaction will not pay the higher rates of SDLT. However, if either of them owns more than one residential property, they may pay the higher rates when purchasing another property.

> **HMRC example**
>
> Mr and Mrs M are married. Mr M owns a home (which he purchases on his own before he was married) where the couple live as their main residence. Mrs M then buys a property to be rented out. At the end of the day of the transaction, they own more than one residential property and are not replacing their main residence, so the higher rates will apply.

HMRC have published a guidance note on the application of the higher rates in March 2016.

Corporate landlords

The Government consulted on whether to relax the rules for the higher rate on 15 or more purchases by corporate landlords, but in Budget 2016, the Chancellor announced that this would not be available.

However, the Government has also made it clear that the new rates will apply when a corporate body buys its first residential property, as an anti-avoidance measure, to stop an individual buying a second property through a company.

HMRC have published guidance on the higher rates of SDLT and this can be found at www.gov.uk/guidance/stamp-duty-land-tax-buying-an-additional-residential-property.

SDLT on mixed/commercial land and buildings

In *Finance Act* 2016, the Chancellor made announcements in respect of the structure of the charge to SDLT for mixed/commercial land and buildings.

From 1 April 2016, the slab system has been repealed and a progressive system has been introduced for these purchases. The rates are as follows:

Value of the purchase	SDLT rate
Up to £150,000	0%
£150,001 to £250,000	2%
The remaining amount	5%

Legislation: FA 2003, s. 55 and Sch. 4, para. 2; FA 2010, s. 7 and Sch. 4A; FA 2016, s. 127 and 128

9090   Relief from charge

There are a number of reliefs in the SDLT regime where certain transactions are exempt from the charge to SDLT. Technically, these are different from the exemptions given in FA 2003, Sch. 3. The difference is that the exemptions within Sch. 3 do not require an SDLT return to HMRC. The other reliefs do require an SDLT return to HMRC, even though no SDLT is payable.

The Sch. 3 exemptions are:

- no chargeable consideration – a true gift;

- transactions in connection with divorce or dissolution of a civil partnership;

- transfers under a will; and

- will variations within two years of death.

For further information, please see 9190.

It is essential to differentiate between a true gift (no strings attached) where no SDLT return is due and a gift with strings where an SDLT return will be due.

Examples of gifts with strings would include a person bringing a future spouse onto the house deeds and the incoming spouse takes over half the mortgage. As debt and the assumption of debt is chargeable consideration (FA 2003, Sch. 4, para. 8), then SDLT may be due if the debt assumed is over the nil-rate band for SDLT. A return will be due even if there is no SDLT payable, as the Sch. 3 exemption only covers true gifts.

Reliefs that have been carried forward from the old stamp duty regime include:

- acquisitions by a charity;

- transfers between group companies;

- transfers arising from company reconstructions;

- certain purchases by registered social landlords;

- acquisitions of land in disadvantaged areas; and

- Crown exemption.

New reliefs for FA 2003 include:

- acquisitions of dwellings by a house-building companies in part-exchange for the sale of a new home;

- acquisition of dwellings by relocation companies;

- acquisitions by local authorities or other public bodies under compulsory purchase orders;

- acquisitions by local authorities or other public bodies under the terms of planning arrangements; and

- first-time buyers' relief on properties with low-value relevant consideration.

Reliefs

9100   Relief for first time buyers for residential property

This was a relief which effectively replaced the 0% rate for certain properties. It provided a relief for first-time buyers where the value of the property was between £125,000 and £250,000. The relief was given in FA 2010 which amends FA 2003 by the insertion of s. 57AA. It was available from 25 March 2010 to 24 March 2012.

9110   Sale and leaseback

A 'sale and leaseback' arrangement means an arrangement under which:

- A transfers to B a major interest in land (the 'sale'); and

- out of that interest B grants a lease to A (the 'leaseback').

The relief for sale and leaseback is available on the leaseback element of a sale and leaseback, but not on the sale element. The leaseback element of a sale and leaseback arrangement is exempt from SDLT if:

- the consideration for the sale does not consist of or include anything other than the payment of money or the assumption, satisfaction or release of a debt; and

- the leaseback is of the same premises that were the subject of the sale.

Where the leaseback element of a sale and leaseback arrangement qualifies for relief under this rule (whether or not relief is claimed), the chargeable consideration for the sale is taken to be not less than the market value of the interest transferred (calculated as if it were not part of a sale and leaseback arrangement), though increasingly HMRC stamp taxes are accepting the argument that the obligation to lease back should be taken into account.

Under FA 2003, Sch. 17A, para. 11, the first assignment of a lease following a sale and leaseback is taxed as if it were the grant of a new lease.

Legislation: FA 2003, s. 57A

9115   Lease and leaseback

Stamp duty land tax treatment of shared ownership properties in lease and leaseback arrangements.

Finance Act 2015 extends the scope of SDLT multiple dwellings relief so that purchases from housing associations of superior leasehold interests in property subject to shared ownership leases can attract relief, where the transaction is part of a 'lease and leaseback' arrangement.

This will reduce the SDLT cost to investors participating in funding arrangements of this kind and HMRC hope that this will encourage private investment in shared ownership properties as the SDLT burden on investors is reduced, enabling more housing association properties to be built without reliance on grant, and may bring forward development plans.

HMRC say that this will help achieve the Government's objective of increasing the provision of low-cost home ownership.

Legislation: FA 2015, s. 69

9120   Disadvantaged areas

Following legislation at FA 2012, Sch. 39, s. 227, Disadvantaged Areas Relief (DAR) has been abolished for transactions with an effective date on or after 6 April 2013.

The relief applied to purchases of residential property in qualifying areas where the purchase price did not exceed £150,000. The following is a description of the measure.

Meaning of 'disadvantaged area'

A 'disadvantaged area' means an area designated as a disadvantaged area by the *Stamp Duty (Disadvantaged Areas) Regulations* 2001 (SI 2001/3747), which are derived from FA 2003, Sch. 6, para. 1. A comprehensive list is available on HMRC's Stamp Taxes website, which is at www.hmrc.gov.uk/so/index.htm.

Legislation: FA 2003, Sch. 6, para. 1 and 2; FA 2003, Sch. 6, para. 5; FA 2003, Sch. 6, para. 6; FA 2003, Sch. 6, para. 9; FA 2003, Sch. 6

Other Material: *Statement of Practice* SP 1/03 (which has some useful flowcharts); *Statement of Practice* SP 1/04

9130 Compulsory purchase facilitating development

A compulsory purchase facilitating development is exempt from charge to SDLT.

'Compulsory purchase facilitating development', in relation to England and Wales or Scotland, means the acquisition by a person of a chargeable interest in respect of which that person has made a compulsory purchase order for the purpose of facilitating development by another person. It does not matter how the acquisition is effected, so the provision applies where the acquisition is effected by agreement.

In relation to Northern Ireland, it means the acquisition by a person of a chargeable interest by means of a vesting order made for the purpose of facilitating development by a person other than the person who acquires the interest. A 'vesting order' means an order made under any statutory provision to authorise the acquisition of land otherwise than by agreement.

'Development' means the carrying out of building, engineering, mining or other operations in, on, over or under land, or the making of any material change in the use of any buildings or other land (*Town and Country Planning Act* 1990, s. 55; *Town and Country Planning (Scotland) Act* 1997, s. 26; *Planning (Northern Ireland) Order* 1991, art. 11).

The following operations or uses of land are deemed not to involve development of the land:

* the carrying out, for the maintenance, improvement or other alteration of any building, of works which:

- – affect only the interior of the building;
- – do not materially affect the external appearance of the building; and
- – are not works for making good war damage or works begun after 5 December 1968 for the alteration of a building by providing additional space in it underground;

- the carrying out, on land within the boundaries of a road by a local highway authority, of any works required for the maintenance or improvement of the road;

- the carrying out, by a local authority or statutory undertakers, of any works for the purpose of inspecting, repairing or renewing any sewers, mains, pipes, cables or other apparatus, including the breaking open of any street or other land for that purpose;

- the use of any buildings or other land within the curtilage of a dwelling house for any purpose incidental to the enjoyment of the dwelling house as such;

- the use of any land for the purposes of agriculture or forestry (including afforestation) and the use for any of those purposes of any building occupied together with land so used; and

- in the case of buildings or other land which are used for a purpose of any class specified by regulations, the use of the buildings or other land or, subject to the provisions of the order, of any part of the buildings or the other land, for any other purpose of the same class.

The use as two or more separate dwelling-houses of any building previously used as a single dwelling-house involves a material change in the use of the building and of each part of it which is so used.

The deposit of refuse or waste materials on land involves a material change in its use, notwithstanding that the land is comprised in a site already used for that purpose, if:

- the superficial area of the deposit is extended; or

- the height of the deposit is extended and exceeds the level of the land adjoining the site.

Legislation: FA 2003, s. 60

9140   Compliance with planning obligations

A land transaction that is entered into in order to comply with a planning obligation or a modification of a planning obligation is exempt from SDLT if:

- the planning obligation or modification is enforceable against the vendor;

- the purchaser is a 'public authority'; and

- the transaction takes place within the period of five years beginning with the date on which the planning obligation was entered into or modified.

Legislation: FA 2003, s. 61

9150 Alternative finance (Islamic finance)

A number of reliefs are available to facilitate the use of Sharia compliant finance products. These are discussed below. They are generally only available where one of the parties is a 'financial institution', which includes:

- a bank;

- a building society;

- a wholly owned subsidiary of a bank;

- a person licensed under Consumer Credit legislation.

Finance Act 2015 expands the definition of a financial institution for the purposes of the stamp duty land tax (SDLT) alternative property finance reliefs to enable users of home purchase plans to benefit from the reliefs.

Home purchase plans are a way of financing a home purchase that does not involve the payment of interest and are regulated in a similar way to conventional mortgages.

Land sold to a financial institution and leased to a person

Relief from SDLT is granted for certain transactions carried out in pursuance of alternative financing arrangements, originally designed as Sharia compliant 'mortgages'. The steps envisaged are:

- the purchase by a financial institution of a major interest in the property concerned (the 'first transaction');

- the grant to a person out of that interest of a lease (if the interest acquired is freehold or in Scotland, that of the owner) or a sub-lease (if the interest acquired is leasehold) (the 'second transaction'); and

- the agreement between the institution and the person that gives the person a right to require the institution or its successor in title to transfer the major interest to that person (either in a single transaction or in a series of transactions).

This relief is also available if the interest purchased is an undivided share of a major interest in the property concerned. In such a case, the major interest must be held on trust for the institution and the person as beneficial tenants in common.

The first transaction is also exempt from SDLT if the vendor is the person concerned (e.g. in the case of a 'remortgage') or another financial institution by whom the interest was acquired under similar arrangements between it and the person.

The second transaction is exempt from SDLT if the provisions relating to the first transaction are complied with (including the payment of any tax chargeable).

Any transfer in accordance with the agreement is exempt from SDLT and (except in Scotland) is not a notifiable transaction if:

- the provisions relating to the first and second transactions are complied with; and
- at all times between the second and the further transactions:
  - the interest purchased under the first transaction is held by a financial institution; and
  - the lease or sub-lease granted under the second transaction is held by the person.

The agreement relating to the transfer of the interest to the person is not treated as substantially performed unless and until the whole of the interest purchased by the institution under the first transaction has been transferred. It is not treated as a distinct land transaction by virtue of the rules relating to options and rights of pre-emption.

Land sold to a financial institution and resold to a person

A similar relief is available where a financial institution purchases a major interest in land ('the first transaction'), and sells that interest to a person ('the second transaction'), and where the person grants the institution a legal mortgage over that interest. The effect is to relieve the second transaction from SDLT.

The first transaction is also exempt from SDLT if the vendor is:

- the person concerned; or
- another financial institution by whom the interest was acquired under other similar arrangements.

The second transaction is exempt from SDLT if the financial institution complies with the provisions relating to the first transaction (including the payment of any tax chargeable on a chargeable consideration that is at least the market value of the interest (or, in the case of the grant of a lease at a rent, the rent).

It should be noted that FA 2008 enacted FA 2003, s. 73AB, which stipulates that s. 71A, 72 and 72A do not apply to alternative finance arrangements if those arrangements, or any connected arrangements, include those for a person to acquire control of the relevant financial institution. The changes have effect in relation to alternative finance arrangements entered into on or after 12 March 2008.

Legislation: FA 2003, s. 71A–72A, 72A–73, 73A, 73B

9160 Charities relief

A land transaction is exempt from SDLT if the purchaser is a charity and the following conditions are met.

The first condition is that the purchaser must intend to hold the subject matter of the transaction for qualifying charitable purposes, that is:

- for use in furtherance of the charitable purposes of the purchaser or of another charity; or

- as an investment from which the profits are applied to the charitable purposes of the purchaser.

The second condition is that the transaction must not have been entered into for the purpose of avoiding SDLT (whether by the purchaser or any other person).

Where the first condition is not met because the whole of the property is not held for qualifying purposes, if the purchaser intends to hold the greater part of the subject-matter for qualifying charitable purposes and the second condition is met, then that transaction will also be exempt from charge.

A 'charity' means a body or trust established for charitable purposes only.

HMRC are now considering claims for overpaid SDLT following the *Pollen Estate and King's College London* cases.

In June 2013, the Court of Appeal released its judgment in respect of *Pollen Estate Trustee Co Ltd v R & C Commrs*.

Essentially, the court held that, when a charity purchases property jointly with another person who is not a charity ('non-charity purchaser'), relief from SDLT under *Finance Act* 2003, Sch. 8, para. 1 is available on the charity's share of the property. Relief is subject to a test based on the extent to which the charity's share is used for charitable purposes.

In light of that judgment, HMRC are now inviting claims for any overpaid SDLT from charities that purchased a property jointly with a non-charity purchaser, satisfied the relevant conditions, but did not claim the relief. Relief is limited to circumstances where the charity used the greater part of its share of the property for a charitable purpose.

Finance Act 2003, s. 68 provides that claims for charities relief must be made in a land transaction return or in an amendment to a return. Under FA 2003, Sch. 10, para. 6, an amendment can be made no later than 12 months after the filing date for the return. The filing date for a land transaction return is 30 days after the effective date of the transaction (this is normally the completion date). Claims made after the expiry of the 12 month amendment period will be time-barred.

Withdrawal of relief

Relief is withdrawn if a disqualifying event occurs:

- before the end of the period of three years beginning with the effective date of the transaction; or
- in pursuance of, or in connection with, arrangements made before the end of that period.

However, relief is not withdrawn unless at the time of the disqualifying event the purchaser holds a chargeable interest:

- that was acquired by the purchaser under the relevant transaction; or
- that is derived from an interest so acquired.

An appropriate proportion of the relief is withdrawn where the purchaser continues to hold only part of the interest purchased for which relief was obtained.

The amount chargeable on withdrawal of relief is the amount that would have been chargeable in respect of the relevant transaction but for charities relief or, as the case may be, an appropriate proportion of the tax that would have been so chargeable.

For these purposes, a 'disqualifying event' is either:

- the purchaser ceasing to be established for charitable purposes only; or
- the subject-matter of the transaction, or any interest or right derived from it, being used or held by the purchaser otherwise than for qualifying charitable purposes.

Where the transaction is exempt because the greater part only of the property will be used for qualifying charitable purposes, there are two additional disqualifying events, namely: a transfer by the purchaser of a major interest in whole or part of the subject matter not made in furtherance of its charitable purposes and a grant by the purchaser of a low-rental lease of whole or part of the property not in furtherance of the purchaser's charitable purposes.

Legislation: FA 2003, Sch. 8, para. 1, 2

Case: *Pollen Estate Trustee Co Ltd v R & C Commrs* [2013] BTC 606

9170   New zero-carbon homes

Finance Act 2007 introduced legislation that permits relief to be given on the first acquisition of a 'zero carbon home'.

The rules do not operate beyond 30 September 2012.

Legislation: FA 2003, s. 58B, 58C; The *Stamp Duty Land Tax (Zero-Carbon Homes Relief) Regulations* 2007 (SI 2007/3437)

9180   Certain acquisitions by RSLs

Registered social landlords ('RSLs') have been entitled to an exemption from charge on certain acquisitions since the introduction of SDLT

A land transaction where the purchaser is an RSL is exempt where:

* the landlord is controlled by its tenants;
* the vendor is a qualifying body; or
* the transaction is funded with the assistance of a public subsidy.

An RSL is controlled by its tenants if the majority of its board members are tenants occupying properties owned or managed by it. Qualifying bodies are:

* RSLs;
* housing action trusts established under the *Housing Act* 1988, Pt. 3;
* a principal council within the meaning of the *Local Government Act* 1972;
* the common council of the City of London;
* the Scottish Ministers;
* a council constituted under the *Local Government etc. (Scotland) Act* 1994, s. 2;

- Scottish Homes;
- the Department of Social Development for Northern Ireland; and
- the Northern Ireland Housing Executive.

A public subsidy is any grant or other financial assistance made or given by way of distribution pursuant to the *National Lottery etc. Act* 1993, s. 25, or under the *Housing Act* 1996, s. 18, the *Housing Grants, Construction and Regeneration Act* 1996, s. 126, the *Housing (Scotland) Act*, or the *Housing (Northern Ireland) Order*, art. 33 or 33A.

Legislation: FA 2003, s. 71

9190 Exempt transactions

The following transactions are exempt, and no return is required in respect of them.

No chargeable consideration

A land transaction is exempt from charge if there is no chargeable consideration for the transaction (e.g. a gift or transfer on death).

All no-strings gifts are exempt from stamp duty land tax.

Grant of certain leases by registered social landlords

The grant of a lease of a dwelling is exempt from charge if the lease:

(a) is granted by a registered social landlord to one or more individuals; and

(b) is for an indefinite term or is terminable by notice of a month or less.

This exemption applies to arrangements between a registered social landlord and a housing authority under which the landlord provides, for individuals nominated by the authority in pursuance of its statutory housing functions, temporary rented accommodation which the landlord itself has obtained for a term of five years or less.

A 'housing authority' means:

- in relation to England and Wales:
    - a principal council within the meaning of the *Local Government Act* 1972; or
    - the Common Council of the City of London,

- in relation to Scotland, a council constituted under s. 2 of the *Local Government etc. (Scotland) Act* 1994, c. 39; and

- in relation to Northern Ireland:

  - the Department for Social Development in Northern Ireland; or

  - the Northern Ireland Housing Executive.

Transactions in connection with divorce, dissolution of civil partners etc.

A transaction between one party to a marriage and the other is exempt from charge if it is effected:

- in pursuance of an order of a court made on granting a decree of divorce, nullity of marriage or judicial separation;

- in pursuance of an order of a court made in connection with the dissolution or annulment of the marriage, or the parties' judicial separation, at any time after the granting of such a decree;

- in pursuance of:

  (a) an order of a court made at any time under the *Matrimonial Causes Act* 1973, s. 22A, 23A or 24A; or

  (b) an incidental order of a court made under the *Family Law (Scotland) Act* 1985, s. 8(2) by virtue of s. 14(1) of that Act; or

- at any time in pursuance of an agreement of the parties made in contemplation or otherwise in connection with the dissolution or annulment of the marriage, their judicial separation or the making of a separation order in respect of them.

A transaction between one party to a civil partnership and the other is exempt from charge if it is effected:

- in pursuance of an order of a court made on granting in respect of the parties an order or decree for the dissolution or annulment of the civil partnership or their judicial separation;

- in pursuance of an order of a court made in connection with the dissolution or annulment of the civil partnership, or the parties' judicial separation, at any time after the granting of such an order or decree for dissolution, annulment or judicial separation;

- in pursuance of:

  (a) an order of a court made at any time under any provision of the *Civil Partnership Act* 2004, Sch. 5 that corresponds to the *Matrimonial Causes Act* 1973, s. 22A, 23A or 24A; or

  (b) an order of a court made at any time under any provision of the *Civil Partnership Act* 2004, Sch. 5 that corresponds to the *Matrimonial Causes Act* 1973, s. 22A, 23A or 24A,

- at any time in pursuance of an agreement of the parties made in contemplation of or otherwise in connection with the dissolution or annulment of the civil partnership, their judicial separation or the making of a separation order in respect of them.

Variation of testamentary dispositions, etc.

A transaction following a person's death that varies a disposition (whether effected by will, under the law relating to intestacy or otherwise) of property of which the deceased was competent to dispose is exempt from charge if the following conditions are met:

(a) the transaction must be carried out within the period of two years after a person's death; and

(b) no consideration in money or money's worth other than the making of a variation of another such disposition must be given for it.

This exemption applies whether or not the administration of the estate is complete or the property has been distributed in accordance with the original dispositions.

This provision is drawn in terms similar to the provisions of IHTA 1984, s. 142 and facilitates the variation of a will after the death of the deceased in a tax-effective way.

A common technique is for wills to be varied by giving a surviving spouse or civil partner the residue of the estate but to allow an amount equal to the nil-rate band to be transferred to a discretionary trust. In many cases, the only substantial asset in the deceased's estate is the couple's residence. HMRC have stated that some methods of effecting such arrangements (where the surviving spouse/civil partner effectively gives consideration for the interest in the land) will not attract relief from SDLT. Care therefore needs to be taken when drafting such arrangements to ensure that an SDLT liability is averted.

Assents and appropriations by personal representatives

The acquisition of property by a person in or towards satisfaction of his entitlement under or in relation to the will of a deceased person, or on the intestacy of a deceased person, is exempt from charge unless the person acquiring the property gives any consideration for it, other than the assumption of secured debt.

Finance Act 2003, Sch. 3 contains two paragraph 3As: one deals with assents and appropriations by personal representatives, the other with transactions in connection with the dissolution of a civil partnership, inserted by FA 2004 and the *Tax and Civil Partnership Regulations* 2005 respectively.

Legislation: FA 2003, Sch. 3, para. 1, 2, 3–3A, 4

Company reorganisations, reconstructions, acquisitions, etc.

9200   Intra-group transfers

Group relief

There are a number of tax reliefs that are available for companies in 75% relationships. These include group relief for corporation tax and chargeable gains. SDLT has similar provisions.

A transaction is exempt from SDLT if the vendor and purchaser are companies that are members of the same group as at the effective date of the transaction.

For this purposes 'company' means a body corporate, so unincorporated associations are not covered. Companies are members of the same group if one is the 75% subsidiary of the other or both are 75% subsidiaries of a third company.

A company ('company A') is the 75% subsidiary of another company ('company B') if company B:

- is beneficial owner of at least 75% of the ordinary share capital of company A;

- is beneficially entitled to at least 75% of any profits available for distribution to equity holders of company A; and

- would be beneficially entitled to at least 75% of any assets of company A available for distribution to its equity holders on a winding-up.

Restrictions on availability of group relief: 'arrangements'

Group relief is not available if, at the effective date of the transaction, there are 'arrangements' in existence by virtue of which, at that or some later time, a person has or could obtain, or any persons together have or could obtain, control of the purchaser but not of the vendor. This does not apply to arrangements entered into with a view to an acquisition of shares by a company in relation to which stamp duty acquisition relief will apply and as a result of which the purchaser will be a member of the same group as the acquiring company.

Group relief is not available if the transaction is effected in pursuance of, or in connection with, arrangements under which:

- the consideration, or any part of the consideration, for the transaction is to be provided or received (directly or indirectly) by a person other than a group company; or

- the vendor and the purchaser are to cease to be members of the same group by reason of the purchaser ceasing to be a 75% plus subsidiary of the vendor or a third company.

Nor is group relief available if the transaction:

- is not effected for bona fide commercial reasons; or

- forms part of arrangements of which the main purpose, or one of the main purposes, is the avoidance of liability to tax.

'Tax' here means stamp duty, income tax, corporation tax, capital gains tax or SDLT.

Thus no SDLT relief will be available if the arrangements are part of a scheme to save (say) corporation tax.

A 'group company' means a company that at the effective date of the transaction is a member of the same group as the vendor or the purchaser.

'Arrangements' includes any scheme, agreement or understanding, whether or not legally enforceable.

'Control' has the meaning given by CTA 2010, s. 450.

Withdrawal of group relief on degrouping event

Group relief is withdrawn if the purchaser ceases to be a member of the same group as the vendor:

- before the end of the period of three years beginning with the effective date of the transaction; or

- in pursuance of, or in connection with, arrangements made before the end of that period.

However, it is withdrawn only if at the time of the degrouping event ('the relevant time'), the purchaser or a relevant associated company holds a chargeable interest:

- that was acquired by the purchaser under the intra-group transaction; or

- that is derived from a chargeable interest so acquired,

and that has not subsequently been acquired at market value under a chargeable transaction for which group relief was available but was not claimed. There is a proportionate withdrawal if part only of the asset is held at the date of the degrouping event.

The amount chargeable is the tax that would have been chargeable in respect of the relevant transaction if the chargeable consideration had been an amount equal to the market value of the subject matter of the transaction, or an appropriate proportion of that tax. If the acquisition was the grant of a lease at a rent, then the amount chargeable is based upon that rent.

'Arrangements' includes any scheme, agreement or understanding, whether or not legally enforceable.

'Relevant associated company', in relation to the purchaser, means a company that:

- is a member of the same group as the purchaser immediately before the purchaser ceases to be a member of the same group as the vendor; and

- ceases to be a member of the same group as the vendor in consequence of the purchaser so ceasing.

Cases in which group relief not withdrawn

Group relief is not withdrawn in some cases, for example, where the purchaser ceases to be a member of the same group as the vendor by reason of the winding up of the vendor or another company that is above the vendor in the group structure.

The degrouping rules do not apply when the vendor company leaves the group.

Cases involving successive transactions

Group relief can also be withdrawn if:

- there is a change in the control of the purchaser that occurs:
  - before the end of the period of three years beginning with the effective date of the relevant transaction; or
  - in pursuance of, or in connection with, arrangements made before the end of that period;
- apart from this rule, group relief in relation to the relevant transaction would not be withdrawn; and

- any previous transaction falls within the following:

  - the previous transaction is exempt from charge by virtue of:
    (i)   group relief (see above);
    (ii) reconstruction relief (see below); or
    (iii) acquisition relief (see below);

  - the effective date of the previous transaction is less than three years before the date of the change in the control of the purchaser;

  - the chargeable interest acquired under the relevant transaction by the purchaser in relation to that transaction is the same as, comprises, forms part of, or is derived from, the chargeable interest acquired under the previous transaction by the purchaser in relation to the previous transaction; and

  - since the previous transaction, the chargeable interest acquired under that transaction has not been acquired by any person under a transaction that is not exempt from charge by virtue of:
    (i)   group relief (see above);
    (ii) reconstruction relief (see below); or
    (iii) acquisition relief (see below).

Where these conditions are satisfied, the group relief withdrawal rules apply in relation to the relevant transaction as if the vendor in relation to the earliest such 'previous transaction' were the vendor in relation to the relevant transaction.

For these purposes, there is a change in the control of a company if:

- any person who controls the company (alone or with others) ceases to do so;

- a person obtains control of the company (alone or with others); or

- the company is wound up.

'Control' is read in accordance with CTA 2010, s. 450. This treatment does not apply where there is a change in the control of the purchaser because a loan creditor, within the meaning of s. 417 obtains, or ceases to have, control of it and the other persons who controlled the purchaser before that change continue to do so. 'Arrangements' includes any scheme, agreement or understanding, whether or not legally enforceable.

Recovery of group relief from another group company or controlling director

Where tax is chargeable as a result of the withdrawal of group relief, the amount of tax has been finally determined, and the whole or part of that amount is unpaid six months after the date on which it became payable, the unpaid tax can be recovered from the following persons:

- the vendor;

- any company that at any relevant time was a member of the same group as the purchaser and was above it in the group structure; and

- any person who at any relevant time was a controlling director of the purchaser or a company having control of the purchaser.

Legislation: FA 2003, Sch. 7, para. 1, 2, 3, 4, 4A, 4ZA, 5–6

Other Material: *Tax Bulletin*, Issue 70 (April 2004)

9210 Reconstruction relief

A land transaction entered into for the purposes of, or in connection with, the transfer of an undertaking or part of an undertaking in a reconstruction is exempt from SDLT.

The envisaged circumstances are that a company ('the acquiring company') acquires the whole or part of the undertaking of another company ('the target company') in pursuance of a scheme for the reconstruction of the target company, and the conditions set out below are met.

The first condition

This is that the consideration for the acquisition consists wholly or partly of the issue of non-redeemable shares in the acquiring company to all the shareholders of the target company. Where the consideration for the acquisition consists only partly of the issue of non-redeemable shares, the rest of the consideration must consist wholly of the assumption or discharge by the acquiring company of liabilities of the target company.

The second condition

This is that after the acquisition has been made:

- each shareholder of each of the companies is a shareholder of the other; and

- the proportion of shares of one of the companies held by any shareholder is the same, or as nearly as may be the same, as the proportion of shares of the other company held by that shareholder.

Thus, the relief is not available in the context of company partitions, but acquisition relief may be available.

The third condition

This is that the acquisition is effected for bona fide commercial reasons and does not form part of a scheme or arrangement of which the main purpose, or one of the main purposes, is the avoidance of liability to stamp duty, income tax, corporation tax, capital gains tax or SDLT.

Legislation: FA 2003, Sch. 7, para. 7

9220 Acquisition relief

A land transaction entered into for the purposes of or in connection with the transfer of the undertaking or part is charged to SDLT at the rate of 0.5%. The envisaged circumstances are that a company ('the acquiring company') acquires the whole or part of the undertaking of another company ('the target company'), and the conditions set out below are met.

The first condition

This is that the consideration for the acquisition consists wholly or partly of the issue of non-redeemable shares in the acquiring company to the target company, or all or any of the target company's shareholders.

Where the consideration for the acquisition consists partly of the issue of non-redeemable shares, the rest of the consideration must consist wholly of:

- cash not exceeding 10% of the nominal value of the non-redeemable shares so issued;
- the assumption or discharge by the acquiring company of liabilities of the target company; or
- both of those things.

The second condition

This is that the acquiring company is not associated with another company that is a party to arrangements with the target company relating to shares of the acquiring company issued in connection with the transfer of the undertaking or part.

Companies are associated if one has control of the other or both are controlled by the same person or persons.

'Arrangements' includes any scheme, agreement or understanding, whether or not legally enforceable.

CTA 2010, s. 450 definition of control applies.

The third condition

This is that the undertaking or part acquired by the acquiring company has as its main activity the carrying on of a trade (as defined for CTA 2010 in s. 1119) that does not consist wholly or mainly of dealing in chargeable interests.

The fourth condition

This is that the acquisition is effected for bona fide commercial reasons and does not form part of arrangements of which the main purpose, or one of the main purposes, is the avoidance of liability to tax. Tax is defined to be any of stamp duty, income tax, corporation tax, capital gains tax or SDLT.

'Arrangements' includes any scheme, agreement or understanding, whether or not legally enforceable.

Legislation: FA 2003, Sch. 7, para. 8

9230 Withdrawal of reconstruction or acquisition relief

Relief is withdrawn if control of the acquiring company changes:

- before the end of the period of three years beginning with the effective date of the transaction; or
- in pursuance of, or in connection with, arrangements made before the end of that period.

However, it is withdrawn only if at the time control of the acquiring company changes ('the relevant time'), it or a relevant associated company holds a chargeable interest:

- that was acquired by the acquiring company under the relevant transaction; or
- that is derived from an interest so acquired,

and that has not subsequently been acquired at market value under a chargeable transaction in relation to which reconstruction or acquisition relief was available but was not claimed.

The amount chargeable is the tax that would have been chargeable in respect of the relevant transaction if the chargeable consideration had been an amount equal to the market value of the subject matter of the transaction or an appropriate proportion of that tax. If the acquisition was the grant of a lease at a rent, then the amount chargeable is based upon that rent.

'Relevant associated company', in relation to the acquiring company, means a company:

- that is controlled by the acquiring company immediately before the control of that company changes; and

- of which control changes in consequence of the change of control of that company.

'Arrangements' includes any scheme, agreement or understanding, whether or not legally enforceable.

'Control' is construed in accordance with CTA 2010, s. 450.

Control of a company changes if the company becomes controlled:

- by a different person;

- by a different number of persons; or

- by two or more persons at least one of whom is not the person, or one of the persons, by whom the company was previously controlled.

Cases in which reconstruction or acquisition relief not withdrawn

Reconstruction or acquisition relief is not withdrawn in the following cases.

The first case: divorce

This is where control of the acquiring company changes as a result of a share transaction that is effected in connection with divorce, etc.

The second case: variation of testamentary disposition

This is where control of the acquiring company changes as a result of a share transaction that is effected in pursuance of the variation of a testamentary disposition.

The third case: exempt intra-group transfer

This is where control of the acquiring company changes as a result of an exempt intra-group transfer, i.e. a transfer of shares which is effected by an instrument exempt from stamp duty under FA 1930, s. 42 or *Finance Act (Northern Ireland)* 1954, s. 11, in relation to transfers between associated bodies corporate.

The fourth case: acquisition relief

This is where control of the acquiring company changes as a result of a transfer of shares to another company in relation to which share acquisition relief applies.

The fifth case: control by loan creditor

This is where:

- control of the acquiring company changes as a result of a loan creditor becoming, or ceasing to be, treated as having control of the company; and

- the other persons who were previously treated as controlling the company continue to be so treated.

'Loan creditor' is defined in CTA 2010, s. 453.

Withdrawal of reconstruction or acquisition relief on subsequent non-exempt transfer

In the third case referred to above, reconstruction or acquisition relief in relation to the relevant transaction; or an appropriate proportion of it, is withdrawn if a company holding shares in the acquiring company to which the exempt intra-group transfer related, or that are derived from shares to which that transfer related, ceases to be a member of the same group as the target company:

- before the end of the period of three years beginning with the effective date of the relevant transaction; or

- in pursuance of or in connection with arrangements made before the end of that period.

However, relief is withdrawn only if the acquiring company or a relevant associated company, at that time ('the relevant time'), holds a chargeable interest:

- that was transferred to the acquiring company by the relevant transaction; or

- that is derived from an interest that was so transferred, and that has not subsequently been transferred at market value by a chargeable transaction in relation to which reconstruction or acquisition relief was available but was not claimed.

In the fourth case referred to above, reconstruction or acquisition relief in relation to the relevant transaction, or an appropriate proportion of it, is withdrawn if control of the other company mentioned in that provision changes:

- before the end of the period of three years beginning with the effective date of the relevant transaction; or

- in pursuance of or in connection with arrangements made before the end of that period,

at a time when that company holds any shares transferred to it by the exempt transfer, or any shares derived from shares so transferred.

However, relief is withdrawn only if the acquiring company or a relevant associated company, at that time ('the relevant time'), holds a chargeable interest:

- that was transferred to the acquiring company by the relevant transaction; or

- that is derived from an interest that was so transferred,

and that has not subsequently been transferred at market value by a chargeable transaction in relation to which reconstruction or acquisition relief was available but was not claimed.

The amount chargeable is the tax that would have been chargeable in respect of the relevant transaction if the chargeable consideration had been an amount equal to the market value of the subject matter of the transaction, or an appropriate proportion of that tax.

Recovery of reconstruction or acquisition relief from another group company or controlling director

Where tax is chargeable as a result of the withdrawal of reconstruction or acquisition relief, the amount of tax has been finally determined, and the whole or part of that amount is unpaid six months after the date on which it became payable, the unpaid tax can be recovered from the following persons:

- any company that at any relevant time was a member of the same group as the acquiring company and was above it in the group structure; and

- any person who at any relevant time was a controlling director of the acquiring company or a company having control of the acquiring company.

Legislation: *Finance Act (Northern Ireland)* 1954, s. 11; FA 2003, Sch. 7, para. 9, 10, 11, 12

9240   Incorporation of an LLP

Incorporation of limited liability partnerships

This exemption effectively allows an existing partnership to transfer property to an LLP upon the existing partnership incorporating without an SDLT charge arising. Where a transaction involves the transfer of a chargeable interest by a person to an LLP in connection with the incorporation of that LLP it will be exempt from charge if:

- the effective date of the transaction is not more than one year after the date of incorporation of the LLP;

- at the relevant time of the transfer, the transferor was a partner of a partnership, the partners of which all are, or are all to be members of the LLP; and

- the proportion of the interest transferred to which the partners of the original partnership are entitled immediately after the transfer are the same as they were at the relevant time, or where there are differences, they have not arisen as part of a scheme or arrangement the main or one of the purposes of which was the avoidance of liability to any duty or tax.

The 'relevant time' is in a case where the transferor acquired the interest after the incorporation of the LLP, immediately after it was acquired, or in any other case immediately before the incorporation of the LLP.

Legislation: FA 2003, s. 65

9245   Leases

SDLT applies to leases as well as purchases of property. The basic shape of the legislation is that the 'purchaser' (lessee) will pay SDLT, but the method of calculation is different. If a person buys a leasehold property, say a flat, the SDLT is paid on the purchase price in the normal way (because it is a capital sum). The fact that the incoming purchaser will have to pay the ground rent is not relevant. This is merely an undertaking by the purchaser and the ground rent generally does not enter the SDLT calculation.

If, however, the lease is the *grant* of a new lease, then the special SDLT rules come into play. There are two sorts of consideration for the grant of a lease:

- Where the consideration is a premium, then this lump of cash is treated as a sale and purchase in the normal way and the s. 55 rates apply.

- If the consideration is rent, then the special rules in Schedules 5 and 17A apply.

The lessee is required to calculate the Net Present Value (NPV) of the rental stream over the life of the lease and then apply an SDLT rate to that NPV.

If the property is residential, then the following rates apply:

- £0 to £125,000 (0%);
- over £125,000 (1%).

If the property is non-residential (or mixed), then the rate bands are as follows:

- £0 to £150,000 (0%);
- over £150,000 (1%).

If the rental stream increases after the end of the fifth year, then the increase is ignored and the calculation uses the highest rent in the first five years to all the years that follow.

This is clearly advantageous to lessees, but to prevent abuse up to 2013, there has been an override rule that kicked in when the rental increase is 'abnormal' (in essence a doubling or more of a rent after the five-year threshold).

The lessee must review the lease every five years after the end of the fifth year and if the rent has doubled or more, then the abnormal increase will be treated as an extra lease and the lessee will have to pay SDLT on the excess and submit another SDLT return.

From Royal Assent of FA 2013, the abnormal increase rules have been abolished. The abolition of the rules on abnormal rent increases will apply to any increases on or after that date.

HMRC say that this is a simplification of the tax. Lessees will no longer be required to complete the complex calculations to determine whether their rent increase is 'abnormal'.

Finance Act 2013 also simplifies the SDLT reporting system when leases are extended after the end of the original end-date or an agreement for a lease is substantially performed before the actual lease is granted.

In Budget 2016, SDLT on leases were changed with the introduction of an additional higher rate (of 2%) to the extent that the net present value (NPV) of the rents receivable under the lease exceeds £5m.

Legislation: FA 2003, Sch. 5 and 17A

Returns

9250 SDLT returns

SDLT returns are either submitted online or, if the taxpayer wishes, by paper submission.

HMRC have updated their list of commercial software providers for online submission of SDLT returns in June 2016 and this may be found at www.gov.uk/government/publications/stamp-duty-commercial-software-suppliers/stamp-duty-land-tax-commercial-software-suppliers.

9255 SDLT paper returns

The guide for completing paper stamp duty land tax (SDLT) 1 returns (PDF 118K) has been revised (September 2013).

HMRC have published a new guide on completing paper SDLT1 forms (April 2014). Information regarding the switch off of SDLT in Scotland has been added to these Guidance Notes.

Completing the main land transaction return (SDLT1)

For most straightforward cases, such as simple residential conveyances, only the SDLT1 is needed. A taxpayer or agent (normally a solicitor) sends the completed SDLT1 to HMRC, together with payment of any SDLT that's due on the transaction. No other paperwork is needed.

For more complicated transactions, additional forms may need to be completed (see below).

Note that each SDLT1 form has its own Unique Transaction Reference Number printed on it, so you can only use it for that particular transaction. Photocopies of the SDLT return for different transactions cannot be used

Transactions that require additional forms

In some cases, extra SDLT forms may need to be completed as well as the SDLT return.

The additional forms are:

- SDLT2 – where there are either more than two purchasers or more than two sellers;
- SDLT3 – where either more than one property is purchased or where only one property is purchased but you can't fit all the address details into the space provided on the SDLT1 form;

- SDLT 4 – where there's a complex lease, multiple grants of lease or a complex commercial transaction;

- ordering the additional forms.

You can order forms SDLT2, SDLT3 and SDLT4:

- online, by completing and submitting the online order form;

- by post, using the online order form;

- by telephoning the HMRC orderline.

Ordering SDLT forms online is quick and efficient. There's no telephone waiting time and the forms are prepacked ready for sending out.

Completing the paper SDLT return

From 1 October 2014, if you file a return on paper (form SDLT1, 3 and 4), you must enter a valid local authority code. Returns which do not include a valid code will be rejected.

9256   Exempt transactions that do not require an SDLT return

Some land and property transactions are exempt from stamp duty land tax (SDLT) regardless of their value and therefore don't need to be notified to HM Revenue & Customs (HMRC) on an SDLT return.

These include:

- transactions where there is no chargeable consideration;

- property left in a will; and

- transfers of property in a divorce or when a civil partnership is dissolved.

A land transaction is notifiable (and thus needs an SDLT return) if it is:

- an acquisition of a major interest in land that does not fall within one or more of the exceptions in s. 77A;

- an acquisition of a chargeable interest other than a major interest in land where there is chargeable consideration in respect of which tax is chargeable at a rate of 1% or higher or would be so chargeable but for a relief;

- a land transaction that a person is treated as entering into by virtue of s. 44A(3); or

- a notional land transaction under s. 75A (anti-avoidance procedures).

The s. 77A exceptions referred to above are as follows:

- an acquisition which is exempt from charge under Sch. 3;

- an acquisition (other than the grant, assignment or surrender of a lease) where the chargeable consideration for that acquisition, together with the chargeable consideration for any linked transactions, is less than £40,000;

- the grant of a lease for a term of seven years or more where:
  - any chargeable consideration other than rent is less than £40,000; and
  - the relevant rent is less than £1,000;

- the assignment or surrender of a lease where:
  - the lease was originally granted for a term of seven years or more; and
  - the chargeable consideration for the assignment or surrender is less than £40,000;

- the grant of a lease for a term of less than seven years where the chargeable consideration does not exceed the zero-rate threshold (as defined);

- the assignment or surrender of a lease where:
  - the lease was originally granted for a term of less than seven years; and
  - the chargeable consideration for the assignment or surrender does not exceed the zero-rate threshold (as defined).

Legislation: FA 2003, s. 77, 77A

9260 Land transaction errors

Where there is an error in a land transaction return, FA 2003 and FA 2009 provide for the repayment of overpaid tax. Where a person believes that he has paid tax under an assessment that was excessive by reason of some mistake in a land transaction return, he may make a claim for relief against any excessive charge. Such a claim must be made not more than six years after the effective date of the transaction, or, from 1 April 2011, not more than four years after the effective date of the transaction in question. Where it is still possible to amend the land transaction it should be amended, rather than claiming a repayment. FA 2010 legislated for future changes to these provisions.

Legislation: FA 2003, Sch. 10, para. 34; FA 2009, s. 99

9270 Penalties

Late filing penalties and interest

For SDLT returns that are not filed by the 30-day filing date, automatic fixed penalties apply. The amount of the penalty depends on how late the return is filed.

If the return is filed:

- within three months after the filing date, the penalty is £100;

- more than three months after the filing date, the penalty is £200.

Returns that are filed after 12 months from the filing date, you'll have to pay a tax-based penalty as well as the fixed penalty. The tax-based penalty can be up to the full amount of the tax due on the return.

The late filing penalties will not apply where a taxpayer has a reasonable excuse.

Late paid tax will also attract interest charges from the filing date to the date the tax is paid at the official rate of interest.

Late payment interest charges are not appealable.

Errors on SDLT returns

If SDLT returns are submitted with errors on, then the error regime in FA 2007, Sch. 24 operates. This is a pan-tax regime that also covers SDLT.

The penalty is levied on incorrect claims on returns (understatements of tax and overstatements of claims). The penalty can range from 0% of the error to 100% of the error, depending on the taxpayer's behaviour.

The standard amount of the penalty payable is 30% of the error for careless action; for deliberate but not concealed action, 70% of the error and for deliberate and concealed action, 100% of the penalty.

These standard amounts may be reduced for disclosure.

Legislation: FA 2003, Sch. 10, para. 3; FA 2007, Sch. 24; FA 2009, Sch. 55

Record keeping

9280   Introduction

A purchaser who is required to submit an SDLT return is required to keep and preserve records for six years from the effective date of the transaction.

Legislation: FA 2003, Sch. 10, para. 9

9290   Enquiries

HMRC have nine months from the due date (or actual filing date, or date of amendment, if later) to start an enquiry into a return or amended return. After that, if new information comes to light under-reported tax can still be recovered. Persons knowingly concerned in fraud relating to tax will be liable to prosecution under a provision similar to that for income tax.

The details in respect of enquiries are in FA 2003, Sch. 10.

Legislation: FA 2003, Sch. 10, para. 12

Other indirect taxes

KEY POINTS

- Customs duty is a tax levied on goods imported into the European Community from outside. 'Free circulation' goods may move around EC countries without a liability to further Customs charges (see 9500).

- These goods are also subject to import VAT. The customs duty is never recoverable, whilst the import VAT is potentially recoverable under the normal VAT recovery rules.

- There are a number of significant customs duties reliefs including inward processing relief (IPR) and end use relief.

- There is also customs control on the export of goods, although there is rarely any duty to be paid. HMRC have introduced a new edition of export procedures (PN 275 (July 2013 edn)).

- Excise duties are generally charged on the production (or importation), rather than the sale, of a wide range of goods and services including alcohol (see 9710), betting and gaming (see 9660 and 9690), tobacco (see 9720) and mineral oils (see 9730).

- Air passenger duty (APD) was introduced in November 1994. The amount due is dependent on the final destination and class of travel of the chargeable passenger. Until 31 March 2015, there were four destination bands (A, B, C and D). From 1 April 2015, there are only two bands. There are three rates of APD for each destination band depending on the class of travel: reduced, standard and higher. Flights from Northern Ireland are treated differently from the rest of the UK. Air passenger duty may be replaced with a new aviation duty but this is not imminent. New rates of APD apply from 1 April 2016 (see 9760).

- Insurance premium tax (IPT) is charged on all risks in the UK, except those falling within certain specified exemptions (see 9800).

- Landfill tax is charged on 'taxable disposals' of waste made at landfill sites (see 9950).

- Climate change levy (CCL) is levied on supplies of electricity, gas and coal to industry, commerce, agriculture and the public sector for their business use of light, heat and power. CCL is not levied on supplies of taxable commodities for domestic or charity use. CCL is the vehicle through which proper pricing of carbon (the carbon price floor) takes place from 2013 (see 10020).

- Aggregates levy is charged per tonne of taxable aggregate that is subject to commercial exploitation (see 10040).

> • The Government has introduced a road user levy for heavy goods vehicles, 12 tonnes or more, aimed at ensuring these vehicles make a contribution to the wear and tear of the UK road network. This levy was introduced by the *HGV Road User Levy Act* 2013 and began on 1 April 2014 (see 10250).

Customs duties

9500   Introduction to customs duties

Customs duties are levied on goods imported into the European Community (EC) from third countries, i.e. those outside the EC. The EC is a customs union, which means that the countries in full membership have no customs duty barriers between them, but have a common customs duty tariff against goods from outside the EC. This is to protect EC traders against foreign competition as well as being a producer of tax revenue.

If goods are in 'free circulation', they are free to circulate within the EC without any liability to pay further customs charges when they move from one member state to the other. The term 'free circulation' means that either:

- the goods originate in the EC; or
- if imported from outside the EC, that all customs duties and similar charges have been paid and have not been refunded.

These goods are referred to as 'community goods' in the EC legislation.

The EC's common external tariff ensures that goods imported from non-EC countries are subject to the same customs duties wherever they arrive in the EC. The goods will also be subject to import VAT, but the rate of VAT will vary depending upon which member state the goods arrive in.under Customs Control (PCC);

The main legal provisions from 1 May 2016 for the customs union are in the Union Customs Code (UCC) (Regulation (EU) 952/2013). The detail is contained in two further regulations: the Delegated Regulation (Regulation 2015/2446) and the Implementing Regulation (Regulation 2015/2447).

Somewhat confusingly, HMRC refer to these as the Delegated Act (DA) and the Implementing Act (IA) (see Notice 3001) respectively.

The main changes from 1 May 2016 are:

- all communications between customs authorities and economic operators must be electronic – paper declarations are being phased out;

- mandatory guarantees for most special procedures (see below) and TS – this only applies to new authorisations;

- the ability to make some movements under temporary storage (TS) rather than national transit or electronic transit system (ETS) – formerly new computerised transit system (NCTS);

- the removal of inward processing (IP) drawback, type D Custom Warehouses (CW) and Processing under Customs Control (PCC);

- the removal of the 'earlier sales provisions' in customs duties valuation.

Some procedures and reliefs ceased or changed on 30 April 2016. These are:

- the €10 waiver of customs duty for free circulation customs declarations – where customs duty is payable no de minimis exemption will apply – this does not affect any community system of duty reliefs (CSDR) duty reliefs;

- goods being declared to onward supply relief (OSR) (customs procedure code 42 series) – can only be entered using a full customs declaration or the simplified declaration procedure (SDP);

- processing under customs control (PCC) authorisation holders will be given an inward processing (IP) authorisation number which must be used for new importations after 30 April 2016.

Type D customs warehousing authorisation holders will be given a new authorisation number with a prefix of C (for type D authorisation), or E (for a type E warehouse with type D rules of assessment) – these must be used for entries to customs warehouses after 1 May 2016, the normal debt rules of assessment will apply. At the heart of the UCC are the customs special procedures (formerly known as Customs Procedures with Economic Impact (CPEI)), which are:

- storage, comprising of Customs Warehousing (CW) and Free Zones;

- specific use comprising of Temporary Admission (TA) and End-Use (EnU);

- processing, comprising Inward and Outward Processing;

- transit, comprising external and internal transit.

These are discussed below.

Legislation: UCC, (Regulation 952/2013), art. 210; Guidance: Notice 3001 (July 2016 edn)

Other indirect taxes

The customs territory of the EU

The member states and territories of the customs territory of the European Community are listed below:

(1) The Republic of Austria;

(2) The Kingdom of Belgium;

(3) The Kingdom of Denmark;

(4) The Republic of Finland;

(5) The French Republic;

(6) The Federal Republic of Germany;

(7) The Hellenic Republic (Greece);

(8) The Republic of Ireland;

(9) The Italian Republic;

(10) The Grand Duchy of Luxembourg;

(11) The Kingdom of the Netherlands in Europe;

(12) The Republic of Portugal;

(13) The Kingdom of Sweden;

(14) The Kingdom of Spain;

(15) The United Kingdom of Great Britain and Northern Ireland;

(16) Cyprus;

(17) Czech Republic;

(18) Estonia;

(19) Hungary;

(20) Latvia;

(21) Lithuania;

(22) Malta;

(23) Poland;

(24) Slovakia;

(25) Slovenia;

(26) Romania;

(27) Bulgaria; and

(28) Croatia.

Included are:

(1) The Isle of Man;

(2) The Austrian territories of Jungholz and Mittelberg, and the territories of the Principality of Monaco;

(3) The Portuguese Islands of Azores and Madeira;

(4) The following special territories of the EC, although included in the Customs territory, are excluded from the fiscal territory (i.e. the VAT territory) of the Community:

  (a) Canary Islands (Spain);

  (b) Channel Islands;

  (c) French Overseas Departments of Guadeloupe, French Guiana, Martinique, and Reunion;

  (d) Mount Athos – also known as Agion Poros (Greece).

Excluded from the customs territory are:

(1) The Faroe Islands and Greenland;

(2) The French overseas territories;

(3) The Islands of Heligoland and the territory of Büsingen;

(4) The Italian communes of Livigno and Campione d'Italia;

(5) The territory of the Republic of San Marino and the national waters of Lake Lugano which are between the bank and the political frontier of the area between the Ponte Tresa and Porto Ceresio;

(6) The North African enclaves of Ceuta and Melilla;

(7) The Principality of Andorra.

There is a customs union between the Republic of San Marino and the EC.

There is a customs union between the Principality of Andorra and the EC for certain goods.

There is a customs union covering most goods between the EC and Turkey.

The Channel Islands

Although the Channel Islands (the islands of Jersey, Guernsey, Alderney, Sark and their respective dependencies) are included in the customs territory of the EC, they are excluded from the fiscal (VAT) territory of the Community.

Other indirect taxes

Under the VAT Directive (Directive 2006/112), all goods from the Channel Islands must be declared to Customs. For goods imported from the Channel Islands which are subject to customs charges, including excise duty and/or import VAT with a value in excess of £600, a full 'single administrative document' (SAD) declaration is required (see 9510). For goods which are not subject to customs charges and are not restricted nor prohibited, no import SAD is required and commercial documents may be used to constitute the declaration. For consignments below a value of £600 subject to customs charges, a simplified import declaration can be made.

For goods exported from the UK to the Channel Islands a non-statistical export declaration is required. However, for consignments from certain South Coast ports a combined 'consignment note and customs declaration' (CNCD) can be used.

When Community goods move direct between the Channel Islands and the UK (in either direction), no Community transit (CT) or status documents are needed, provided that the movement is cleared at the frontier.

The Isle of Man

As a general rule, goods moving between the Isle of Man and the UK, including any goods previously imported from non-EC countries on which the proper duty and tax have been paid, are considered not to be imported into, or exported from, either the Isle of Man or the UK, as the case may be. Such goods are not subject to customs control other than controls applicable to similar goods moving on the British mainland, e.g. for warehouse goods. There are restrictions on the movement of explosives.

Controls in intra-EC trade

There are no controls on the vast majority of EC goods moving within the Community. However, as non-EC goods can be in transit in the Community without payment of duty and Common Agricultural Policy (CAP) charges due on them, some controls remain on these goods moving within the Community – although these controls are now mainly documentary (see 'Community transit' below).

Prohibitions and restrictions

Despite the free movement of goods in free circulation within the Community, the member states can impose restrictions or prohibitions for certain reasons such as health, public morality and security, etc. In addition, there are provisions under art. 115 of the Treaty of Rome and the Treaty of Paris to restrict the importation via another member state of certain non-EC goods in special circumstances, even if those goods are in free circulation.

Anti-dumping duty

Anti-dumping duty (ADD) is an additional duty on imports providing protection against the dumping of goods in the EC at prices substantially lower than the normal value. In most cases, the normal value is the price which the foreign producer charges for comparable sales in his own country. Each anti-dumping duty covers specified goods originating in, or exported from, named countries or exporters. ADD is chargeable in addition to, and is independent of, any other duty to which the imported goods are liable. Whether ADD applies to particular goods at a particular time will be shown in the tariff. The indicator ADD and the country code will be shown on column 3 of the schedule in volume 2, against the commodity code of the goods in question. Where necessary, more detailed information is given as footnotes, or notes at the end of the relevant chapter in the tariff. The principal law relating to ADD is contained in Council Regulation 384/96.

In the UK, the overall responsibility for policy matters surrounding ADD rests with the Department for Business, Innovation and Skills. HMRC are responsible for the collection of the duty.

An investigation into an alleged dumping can be triggered by any business or representative body in the EC, which must present proof that the dumping of certain goods has, or will, cause real economic hardship or injury in the Community. The commission will then investigate the case, at which point a provisional ADD may be imposed for a period of up to nine months. At the end of the investigation, the provisional ADD may be made definitive or may lapse or be cancelled. Provisional ADD must be secured by either a cash deposit or guarantee. Deposits will be refunded without the need for prior application if the provisional ADD is cancelled, lapses or is not replaced in full by a definitive duty.

Anti-dumping duties imposed pursuant to the above regulation may be extended to imports of like products from third-world countries, or parts of products, when circumvention of the measure in force is taking place. A Commission Regulation will instruct EC customs authorities to make these imports subject to registration, or to request security by guarantee. Products will not be subject to registration where they are accompanied by a customs certificate declaring that the importation of the goods does not constitute circumvention.

Where an importer can show that the products imported were not dumped, or that the margin of dumping was less than that on which anti-dumping measures were based, the anti-dumping duties already collected may be partially or fully repaid.

Where goods are exported from a country against which an ADD measure applies and exemption from ADD is claimed on the grounds that the goods did not originate in that country, a 'certificate of origin' will need to be presented when the goods are declared.

Transit

Under the new UCC, there are two main versions of transit:

External transit

Under the external transit procedure, non-Union goods may be moved from one point to another within the customs territory of the Union without being subject to import duty (art. 226, UCC).

Internal transit

Under the internal transit procedure, Union goods may be moved from one point to another within the customs territory of the Union, and pass through a country or territory outside that customs territory, without any change in their customs status (art. 227, UCC).

Legislation: UCC, art. 226ff.

9510 Import procedures

From 1 May 2016, the *Union Customs Code (UCC) Council Regulation (EU) 952/2013* enters into force. One of the major changes is that all communications, unless there are specific exemptions in place, between customs and businesses (known as economic operators) will have to be made electronically.

Most commercial importers and exporters (economic operators) already clear goods electronically, including using the Direct Trader Input (DTI) of customs declarations into the official declaration processing system (Customs Handling of Import and Export Freight add (CHIEF).

The UK currently has a small number of economic operators who continue to use the manual customs declaration procedure (Customs Input Entry (CIE)). In these situations, an economic operator can submit a paper declaration using form C88 to HMRC for keying and electronic processing by HMRC staff.

Except in specific circumstances, this will no longer be a lawful method following the introduction of the UCC.

All goods exported from, or imported into, the EC from outside the member states must be declared to the customs authorities ('customs'). In the UK, the customs authority is HM Revenue and Customs (HMRC). Goods moving to or through other member states and EFTA countries are controlled under the Community transit (CT) procedure (see 9500). Where necessary, declarations for all three purposes are made in all EC and EFTA countries using a standard form called the single administrative document (SAD). In the UK, this is known as a C-88.

Declarations may be made by any person who is able to present the goods in question, or to have them presented, with all the documents that are required to be produced.

Any person may appoint a representative to perform the formalities laid down by customs, and this can be by way of direct or indirect representation. Direct representatives act in the name of, and on behalf of, another person. Indirect representatives act in their own name, but on behalf of another person. A representative must:

- state that he is acting on behalf of the person he is representing;
- specify whether the representation is direct or indirect; and
- be empowered to act as a representative.

If the representative does not do any of the above properly, he will be deemed to be acting in his own name and on his own behalf.

Representation is important both for the principals and their agents such as freight forwarders. For direct representation, only the principal is liable for duties. In indirect representation, both the principal and the agent are liable.

Whoever signs a declaration attests to the accuracy of the information being given, the authenticity of the documents attached and compliance with all the obligations relating to the goods in question under the procedure concerned.

There are special rules for merchandise in baggage and there is an updated notice (Public Notice 6 (January 2016 edn)).

Import control system (ICS)

The ICS is an EC wide electronic communications system that enables EC customs authorities to talk to each other and to carriers. It is an anti-terrorist system and is part of the safety and security amendments to the EC customs legislation implemented following the 9/11 attacks.

The ICS has been adopted by the UK from 1 January 2011. Most goods now arriving into the EC must be **pre-notified** by an Entry Summary Declaration (ENS) which is submitted to the office of first entry (OoFE) in the EC.

The ENS must be lodged by the carrier of the goods, who must have an EORI number. The information is analysed for risk and if the consignment is low risk then a Movement Reference Number (MRN) is issued to the carrier.

If the consignment is considered high risk, then positive actions may be taken against the consignment. These include passing information to the airport, diverting the goods, or even instructing them not to be loaded at all into container ships at the port of departure in a third country outside the EC.

Presentation

When the goods are imported they must be 'presented' to customs by the person who brought them into the EC, or the person who has responsibility for their onward carriage, such as freight haulage companies and shipping and aircraft lines, etc. The implementation of the ICS does not affect this requirement (see the europa website).

Goods may be presented by using an approved computerised trade inventory system linked to HMRC's system or by lodging a form (C1600A) at a designated HMRC office. All goods must be presented within three hours of their arrival at the place of unloading. If the HMRC office is closed, presentation must be made within an hour of its reopening.

Imported goods may be put into temporary storage (TS) for a maximum of 90 days subject to a mandatory guarantee.

Import declaration (aka the SAD or C88)

An import declaration in electronic form is only required for the following categories of goods on arrival into the EC. That are:

- goods arriving direct from a non-EC country;

- goods arriving from a non-EC country via another EC country which have not already been cleared into free circulation; and

- goods from the following special territories of the EC, namely the Channel Islands, French Overseas Department (for example, Martinique), the Canary Islands, Mount Athos and the Vatican City.

When the goods are imported into the EC, it is the responsibility of the importer or his authorised agent to declare them to customs. In most cases, a SAD is used for this purpose. In the UK, the import declaration is then usually entered on to HMRC's entry processing computer which in the UK is known as 'CHIEF'. The input of data to CHIEF by traders direct is known as 'direct trader input' (DTI).

In signing an import declaration, the signatory accepts full legal responsibility for all the information it contains, including that which was provided in the country of export. Any inaccuracies must be corrected, and these corrections must be drawn to HMRC's attention when the declaration is presented. If necessary, a fresh import declaration should be completed.

Customs clearance

Customs clearance is normally carried out at the port or airport of importation, but clearance facilities for goods transported in secure vehicles or containers are, with some exceptions, provided at specified inland premises.

All imported goods are liable to be examined by customs and this is normally carried out at the place where they are declared for importation.

Customs duties, and other charges that are due, must be paid, deferred or secured before the goods are cleared by customs. The deferred payment of customs duties and other charges is subject to the provision of adequate security and to other conditions of the 'duty deferment scheme'.

When the precise amount of duty, etc. cannot be assessed at the time, the declaration is presented, clearance can usually be allowed on payment of a deposit, or provision of security to cover the element of duty in dispute. This may be equal to the full duty amount or the difference between the two potential duty amounts. For non-VAT-registered traders, the amount of VAT consequently in dispute must be secured. For VAT-registered traders, VAT is normally paid outright based on the value, which includes the highest potential duty regardless of whether this is secured by cash or cash less security.

Legislation: EC Regulation 952/2013 (UCC), art 127ff.; Notice 199 (April 2016 edn)

9520   Valuation for customs duty

The majority of goods imported into the EC are subject to an ad valorem, rather than a specific duty. While the *rate* of customs duty payable is determined by the tariff heading under which the goods are classified and, consequently, by the commodity code given, the actual amount on which duty is payable is determined by the value placed on goods as importation.

The General Agreement on Tariffs and Trade (GATT) agreed a valuation code which was adopted by the EC in 1980. The GATT lays down six methods under which imported goods must be valued for duty purposes.

With one exception, the methods must be used in strict hierarchical order, i.e. if Method 1 is not applicable, Method 2 must be considered and so on. The exception is that Method 4 does not have to be tried before Method 5. They can be swapped.

Valuation for customs duty purposes is a complex area, and even when using the most usual method, Method 1, detailed negotiation with HMRC may be required to reach an appropriate value. The six methods are as follows:

(1) The transaction value (i.e. sale) method (Method 1);

(2) The sale value of identical goods method (Method 2);

(3) The sale value of similar goods method (Method 3);

(4) The deductive method (Method 4);

(5) The computed value method (Method 5); and

(6) The 'fall-back' method (Method 6).

Nearly all goods arriving into the EC are sold into the EC, so Method 1 is by far the most common method. Under Method 1, the value of the goods will need to be adjusted in accordance with the rules in the Customs Code, for example adding in the insurance and freight costs up to the place of introduction into the community.

The other valuation methods are only used when Method 1 can not be used, i.e. when there is no sale. So goods imported under a lease or goods given free, for example, cannot use Method 1.

Under the new UCC, from 1 May 2016, the old 'earlier sales' provisions are no longer available. Only the latest sale value will be permitted.

The rules in respect of royalty payments and licence fees have also been changed, such that most royalty payments and licence fees are now included automatically.

Legislation: EC Regulation 952/2013 (UCC), art. 70 and 74; Implementing Regulation 2447/2015, art. 127ff.);

Other Material: Notice 252 (April 2016 edn); PN 702, *Imports* (April 2016 edn)

9530   Tariff classification procedure

The integrated tariff

Customs duty is charged according to the Community code shown in the tariff. Both the UK tariff and the combined nomenclature of the EC (the CN) are based on the internationally agreed system of classification known as the 'Harmonised System'. This nomenclature provides a systematic classification procedure for all goods in international trade, designed to ensure, with the aid of the 'general rules for the interpretation of the nomenclature' and notes to the sections, chapters and subheadings, that any product or article falls to be classified in one place and one place only.

As a result, it should be possible to accurately (if laboriously) identify the amount of duty payable.

The tariff consists of three volumes:

(1)   general information;

(2)   the schedule, which gives the description, commodity code and full rates of duty, preferential duty rates, tariff quotas and ceilings, duty suspensions and anti dumping duties;

(3)   detailed directions for completing the SAD and related documentation and import procedures and requirements.

Classification

In order to determine the proper classification within the tariff for any goods imported into the EC, the appropriate heading for those goods (i.e. the appropriate four-digit heading printed in bold capitals in the schedule) must first be established. It may be helpful to refer to the list of section and chapter titles immediately before the schedule in Volume 2 of the tariff which, in many cases, will immediately indicate the chapter or chapters in which the appropriate tariff heading will be found. However, these titles are only provided for reference purposes. They have no legal force and it is essential that reference is made to any relevant section or chapter notes since these may define the scope of the relevant heading.

Access to the tariff is available through GOV.UK.

Other Material: The principal legal basis for the Volume 2 information is the Combined Nomenclature Regulation 2658/97; Public Notice 600, *Classifying your imports and exports* (July 2016 edn)

9540   EC preferences

The EC has a number of preferential trade arrangements with certain individual countries or groups of countries outside the EC. These provide for particular goods originating in the countries concerned to be imported and entered to free circulation at nil or reduced rates of customs duty. Details of these rates are shown in column 6 of the Schedule in Volume 2 of the tariff.

Other indirect taxes

The different countries and groups of countries are referred to at the head of column 6 or in the footnotes to the schedule. An alphabetical list of countries and specific information concerning country codes and preference types is in Part 7 of Volume 1 of the tariff.

To be admissible to a preference, imported goods must:

(1) be of a description shown in the schedule as being eligible for the preference;

(2) qualify as 'originating' in the preference country in accordance with the origin rules for that preference, or having undergone 'sufficient work or processing'; and

(3) have been transported direct from the preference country or groups of countries to the EC.

Some of the most important preferences are goods from the Generalised System of Preferences (GSP).

From 1 January 2014, the GSP is to be fundamentally overhauled as many of the beneficiary countries have been developing their own economies.

The renewed GSP scheme focuses preferences exclusively on those countries most in need – least developed countries and other poor economies with no other preferential channels to access the EU market.

The changes will apply to goods entering into free circulation on or after 1 January 2014.

Once implemented, the scheme will continue to apply for a period of ten years except for the special arrangement for the least-developed countries, which will be open-ended.

Under the new scheme, the status of countries will be revised continuously. When a country no longer fulfils the criteria to be a beneficiary, it will exit the beneficiary list following a transition period of at least one year.

The current preferences under Council Regulation (EC) No. 732/2008, as extended by Regulation (EU) No. 512/2011 ceased on 31 December 2013.

There will be just 87 beneficiaries of the new GSP scheme. This has been reduced from 176 beneficiaries under the previous regulation which will provide greater benefit for countries most in need.

Forty-nine least-developed countries will continue to receive duty-free access (see Annex IV of 154/2013).

Thirty-eight 'low income' and 'lower middle income' countries, as classified by the World Bank, will receive tariff reductions (on 'sensitive' products) or zero tariffs (for 'non-sensitive') under the general arrangements (see Annex V for list of products included in the general arrangement).

Thirty-five of these 38 countries can receive full duty-free access under GSP+ if they ratify and implement certain international conventions.

Thirty-three overseas countries and territories of the EU or other developed countries will no longer be eligible.

A further 54 countries will remain eligible but will no longer benefit. These consist of:

Eight 'high income' and 12 'upper middle income' countries as listed by the World Bank, and

Thirty-four countries that have already been granted EU preferences through other bilateral agreements or autonomous arrangements.

The list of beneficiary countries of the general arrangement which applies from 1 January 2014 is contained in Annex II of Regulation 978/2012.

The access to preference rules, however, must be obeyed and there is an updated version of PN 830 (December 2011) and PN 828 (August 2013) that gives details.

For some goods, the availability of preferential rates is restricted by tariff quota or ceilings, or is limited to a certain period of the year. If these restrictions apply, further information will be found in the tariff and from HMRC either at the port of entry or from the CHIEF Notice Boards.

Some countries are eligible for preferential treatment under two separate arrangements. Other non-preferential duty reliefs may also be available, for example 'customs duty suspensions'. Importers are entitled to enter the goods at the most advantageous rate for which they are eligible and for which appropriate valid documents are held.

Preferential arrangements do not affect the liability to anti-dumping duties.

The customs authorities may check goods which are imported under preference. Where any of these checks fail to show that the goods qualified for the preference claimed, the importer is required to pay duty at the full non-preferential rate, and Community legislation allows for the collection of back-duty (but not interest) for a period of up to three years after the goods have been imported. To ensure against the possibility, many importers now include a clause in the contracts with the supplier allowing them to recover duty from the supplier if it transpires that the goods that they bought in good faith did not comply with the origin rules for which a certificate has been granted.

Legislation: Reg 2913/92, art. 22–27, 220, Legislation detailing revisions to the GSP was published on 31 October 2012 in Regulation (EU) No. 978/2012 (PDF 1.69MB) (Official Journal L303/2013); PNs 839 and 828

9550 Licences

Most goods can be imported into the EC without the need for a specific import licence and are covered by the 'open general import licence' (OGIL). However, for certain imports, a licence must be applied for to a competent EC authority. In the UK, this is the Department for Business, Innovation and Skills (BIS). In most cases, restricted goods already in free circulation within the EC do not require a further licence to import into the UK.

Import licences are required for various reasons. These are mainly:

(1) to protect certain UK or EC industries;

(2) to implement internationally agreed policies designed to stabilise markets and encourage the practice of free trade;

(3) for surveillance purposes, i.e. to provide information about trends in imports of sensitive goods; and

(4) in the interests of public health and safety.

9560 Tariff quotas (TQs)

Tariff quotas are a form of EC preference under which limited amounts of certain goods may be admitted to free circulation at a reduced or nil rate of customs duty, and/or charges under the Common Agricultural Policy (CAP) of the EC. The limit can be expressed in units of rate, volume, quantity or value.

Quotas are set for the whole of the EC and claims are granted on a first come, first served basis. Quotas are controlled entirely by the European Commission.

Quotas that are not expected to exhaust quickly are termed 'open' and valid claims to quota relief can be accepted without security for duty.

New quotas are ones which are likely to be exhausted within a short period of time and are termed 'critical' status.

Goods eligible for quotas that have become critical, or for open quotas which have been taken up to the extent that they become critical, may be released only against security for full duty. When a quota is exhausted, that information is sent electronically to the customs authorities, after which the full rate of duty must be paid.

Some quotas are restricted to goods from particular countries or groups of countries. In this case, importers must produce the appropriate certificate of origin or movement certificate to qualify and benefit from the nil or reduced rate.

Certain quotas can be expected to exhaust within a few days of opening, and these are called 'banded' quotas. To give fair and equal treatment, all valid claims lodged before a deadline previously announced by the EC are considered to have been presented simultaneously. If the volume of claims made within that banding period exceeds the quota available, allocation of the relief is then made on a pro rata basis.

Quota relief must be formally claimed and belated claims against a quota that has been exhausted, will not be entertained by HMRC.

Goods eligible for quota relief are individually described and coded in the tariff and can be identified by the abbreviation 'TQ' in column 3 of the schedule. Even if all initial indications of availability are there, the importer must still make further enquiries with HMRC immediately prior to actual import to ensure that the quota is still open.

9570   The Common Agricultural Policy of the EC

Certain basic and processed products in the agricultural sector are subject, not only to customs duties, but also to other charges under the Common Agricultural Policy (CAP) of the EC. The purpose of CAP charges is to protect EC produced goods by increasing entry prices, so that non-EC goods come in line with the generally higher prices in the EC. The rates are changed annually and are published in the tariff. Additional safeguard measures and charges may also be imposed in exceptional circumstances to give extra protection to EC production.

The CAP charge regime is administered by the Intervention Board.

9580   Duty reliefs

Changes to customs procedures with economic impact (CPEI)

CPEI are becoming 'Special Procedures' made up of:

- processing – inward processing (IP) and outward processing (OP);
- specific use – temporary admission (TA) and end use;
- transit – external and internal transit;
- storage – customs warehousing and free zones.

Other indirect taxes

Most Special Procedures will be subject to some form of transition. All current special procedures authorisations will need to become UCC authorisations by 1 May 2019.

The following CPEI (special procedures) will be unavailable:

- free zone type II;
- customs warehouse type D;
- PCC;
- IP drawback system.

In addition, the following changes will be introduced:

- a financial guarantee will be a mandatory requirement for most special procedures authorisations;
- the need to re-export IP goods will be removed;
- compensatory interest will be abolished;
- remote retail sales will be allowed from a customs warehouse.

Temporary admission

Certain goods may be imported into the community without payment of import duty or VAT, provided they are exported after only a temporary period of use in the EC (usually up to 24 months).

The Implementing Regulations contain a list of items that can be imported under this relief.

These include:

- goods for art exhibitions;
- personal goods;
- means of transport (lorries); and
- pallets and packaging.

Normally, an authorisation is required, but an oral declaration at importation may be permitted.

Legislation: UCC, art. 250, Imp. Reg. art. 322

Other material: Notice 3001

Customs warehousing

Customs warehousing is a popular relief that allows goods imported into the EU to be stored in a tax-free 'buffer zone' and customs duties and import VAT will not be payable whilst the goods are in the warehouse. Public Notice 3001 gives the detail.

The warehouses can either be physical premises or computer-based.

Under the new UCC, Type D (physical warehouse premises, where the customs value is fixed when the good enter the warehouse) is no longer permitted.

Like all the special procedures, CW will need authorisation from HMRC (on form SP2). In order to hold a special procedures authorisation, you will be required to meet the following criteria:

* be financially solvent;

* have a good history of compliance;

* maintain adequate records appropriate to the procedure you wish to claim;

* have an EORI number if established in the EU.

A guarantee for Import VAT will be required when:

* the economic operator is not established in the EU;

* the guarantee is part of an authorisation involving more than one member state;

* an authorisation by declaration is being used;

* non-compliance is identified.

Legislation: UCC, art. 240, Del. Reg. article 161

Other material: PN 3001 (June 2016 edn)

Inward processing (IP)

You can use inward processing (IP) to get relief from customs duty and import VAT on goods that are imported from outside the EU to be processed, and then exported outside the EU or released for free circulation in the EU. Excise duty is also suspended when goods are entered into IP.

You will have to pay duties once the goods have been processed if they are released into free circulation. The duties you will pay can be based on the value of the goods at import, or the value of the final product – see art. 85 and 86(3) of the Union Customs Code.

IP authorisation

In order to be eligible for duty relief under IP, you need to be authorised.

Full authorisation

Use full authorisation if you are a regular user of IP. You should apply at least one month before importing using form SP3.

Authorisation by declaration

Authorisation by declaration is suited to traders importing goods occasionally to IP and carrying out all processing in the UK. You should only use this method if you intend to import no more than three times in a calendar year.

It lets you enter goods into IP without making a prior application for authorisation. You use the relevant customs procedure codes on your customs declaration (form C88) and place indicators in box 44. You will also need to complete a Bill of Discharge for each entry.

You cannot use an authorisation by declaration to import goods listed under chapter 93 and 97 of the Trade Tariff, or over £500,000 in value.

The economic test

The economic test applies to specific goods. In order to get IP authorisation on these goods, you will need to provide evidence showing why you cannot use EU-produced goods instead. The full list of goods is in Annex 71-02 of the *Commission Delegated Regulation* 2015/2446.

Under the new UCC, IP drawback is no longer permitted.

Processing under customs control (PCC) is no longer available. Traders with PCC authorisations will need to migrate to IP.

Outward processing relief (OPR)

Normally, when goods are exported outside the EC they lose 'Community status', and duty must be paid on their full value at reimportation. 'Outward processing relief' (OPR) is a trade facilitation measure available for the reimportation of Community goods which have been exported outside the EC for process (very often to take advantage of lower labour rates) or repair.

The amount of duty relief available on the re-imported product or 'compensating product' will depend on the type of process the goods underwent while outside the EC, and the duty rate applicable to the goods originally exported outside the Community.

A similar relief called the 'standard exchange system' (SES) is available for goods sent to the EC as replacements for faulty goods sent outside the EC.

If goods are repaired or replaced free of charge, there is total relief from import duties provided that evidence is submitted to HMRC to support this claim, for example, a guarantee or warranty document.

If goods are repaired or replaced in return for payment, the import duties are calculated on the cost of the repair or replacement plus any freight and insurance charges made for the return of the repaired goods or replacements. However, this is conditional on the cost not being influenced by any relationship between the exporter and the processor.

For all other processes, the duty relief is calculated by deducting the import duty, which would have been payable on the exported goods if they had been imported at the same time and from the same country as the compensating product, from the import duty due on the full customs value of the compensating product. This is known as the duty differential method (art. 151, Code).

There is an alternative 'cost of operations method' which normally gives the importer a better result (art. 591, IP).

With the exception of goods held under IPR, exported goods must be Community goods, that is, they must have originated in the Community or if originally imported from outside the member states, all customs duty must have been paid. Their export must not result in any refund or remission of import duties or refunds or other financial benefits under the CAP.

Except for replacements imported under the SES, it must be possible to identify the exported goods in the imported compensating products. The compensating products must also be reimported within time limits specified in the authorisation granted by Customs.

Legislation: UCC, art. 259

Other material: Notice 3001

Returned goods relief (RGR)

Goods exported from the EC can, in certain circumstances, be re-imported with total or partial relief from import duty, charges under the CAP, excise duty and VAT. The rules for the relief vary according to the category of tax involved. Where relief is sought for more than one category, the rules applicable to each must be satisfied.

This commonly used relief is used for goods exported outside the EC which are rejected by the buyer and it is also used for goods such as cranes, which are used outside the EC on construction projects and then reimported afterwards.

There is a general three-year time-limit on the goods being re-imported.

Returned goods relief (RGR) does not apply to goods temporarily exported outside the EC for process. Outward processing relief (OPR) should be used instead. However, if goods are exported for the process or repair and this does not take place, RGR can be used on re-import if the goods return unaltered.

HMRC have published Notice 236 (April 2014) *Customs: Importing returned goods free of duty and tax.*

Legislation: UCC, art. 203, Imp. Reg. art. 253

End-use

End-use relief is designed to assist certain industries and trades in the EC by allowing a nil or reduced rate of duty on goods imported from non-EC countries provided those goods are put to a prescribed use. The relief is common to all EC member states.

There are a number of areas of the economy that benefit from end-use relief. These include:

* shipwork goods;
* continental shelf relief (oil rigs and parts);
* military aircraft; and
* civil aircraft.

Legislation: UCC, art. 254

Website: www.gov.uk/guidance/end-use-relief

Personal reliefs

There are a number of personal reliefs that are available to individuals in certain circumstances which allow relief from duty and/or VAT.

These include:

(1) relief for persons entering the EC from a third country for their personal property. The property can be imported duty free provided the person has been normally resident in a third country for at least 12 months, and the property has been in the person's possession for at least six months. The property may not be alcohol or tobacco products;

(2) relief on wedding gifts under £800 in value;

(3) relief for honorary decorations and awards;

(4) relief for inherited goods.

There are also personal reliefs for special visitors. These are designed to give relief from customs and excise duty to goods imported by either:

(1) diplomats; or

(2) serving members of visiting forces.

The reliefs cover motor vehicles, alcohol and tobacco products.

Legislation: Regulation 918/83; Regulation (EEC) No. 186/2009 articles 17–20, and the *Customs and Excise Duties (Personal Reliefs for Goods Permanently Imported) Order* 1992

9590 Duty-free stores

Duty-free stores sell goods which will be used, consumed or sold on ships and aircraft leaving the UK for third country destinations. These goods include, fuel, foodstuffs and spare parts.

These goods are stored under a modified form of customs warehousing, the details of which are in the relevant customs notice.

The ship or aircraft must be 'entitled' to this procedure.

For an aircraft, this means it must be departing on a flight to a country outside the UK.

For a ship, this means that it must be:

(1) at least 40 tons net registered tonnage and departing on a voyage outside the UK;

(2) at least 40 tons departing to certain sea areas; or

(3) yachts less than 40 tons departing on a voyage to a destination south of Brest or north of the Eider.

A warehouse keeper must not allow goods to be removed from the warehouse unless the ship or aircraft is entitled to receive them.

The shipper or agent ordering the goods must give a written statement to confirm entitlement.

Other Material: Customs Notice 3001

9610 Free zones

A free zone is an enclosed area in which non-Community goods are treated for the purposes of import duties as being outside the Customs territory of the Community. The administration of free zones is governed by EC regulations. They are rarely used in the EC.

In the UK, the detailed rules which govern the operation of free zones are in the *Free Zone Regulations* 1984 (SI 1984/1177).

Customs duty, import VAT and other import charges are not due until the goods are released for free circulation. This allows goods to be handled or processed without payment of duty or VAT.

Free zones are operated by free zone managers and not HMRC, but HMRC's approval is still required to operate within a free zone. Under the UCC, there will only be one free zone in the UK – the Isle of Man.

Legislation: Union Customs Code (UCC) art. 243–249; Guidance – Public Notice 3001 (July 2016)

9615 Authorised Economic Operators (AEOs)

Following the 9/11 attacks, the USA brought pressure on other trading blocks to police the supply chains of goods moving round the world.

As a result, the EC has implemented the concept of the Authorised Economic Operator (AEO), which gives a certain status and credibility to importers and exporters in the EC.

The advantages to taxpayers who adopt these provisions are: increased security and safety and the benefit of simplifications.

It is not mandatory to become an AEO unless you wish to be authorised for:

- moving goods in TS between different member states;

- centralised clearance (to be introduced at a later date);

- waiver of the presentation of goods requirement when making declarations in your records – Entry in Declarants Records (EIDR);

- self-assessment (to be introduced at a later date);

- deferment accounts – reduced guarantees for customs duties payable.

Economic operator registration and identification (EORI)

From 1 May 2016, there are no changes to the EORI process. It is a requirement for all economic operators (such as businesses) involved in international trade to be registered and to have an EORI number.

You will need to have an EORI number to be able to apply for any customs authorisations, approvals or decisions.

Legislation: Regulation 952/2013   (UCC),   art. 38;   Implementing Regulation 2015/2446 art. 24–35

Excise duties

9650   Introduction to excise duties

Historically, excise duties have been charged on certain home produced goods, such as beer duty which is the oldest excise duty. Excise duties are now charged on a wide range of goods and services. Unlike VAT, excise duty is chargeable on the production or importation, rather than sale. Excise duty falls into the following categories:

- *Alcohol*: beer and spirits are taxed according to their alcoholic content, whereas wine, made wine, cider and perry are all subject to specific (i.e. by volume) taxes;

- *Gambling*: Machine Games Duty is levied on machines provided for play. Bingo Duty, Lottery, General Betting and Pools duties are ad valorem taxes. Gaming duty is a banded, premises based tax on casino profits;

- *Tobacco*: duties on tobacco are aimed at both raising revenue and to support the government's health objective. The duty is charged on the finished product, for cigars, hand-rolling tobacco and other smoking and chewing tobacco, the charge is specific (per kg) whereas for cigarettes there is an additional ad valorem component; and

- *Mineral and heating oils (fuels duties)*: duties are levied for the purpose of revenue-raising, and protecting the environment with a particular focus on reducing emissions of greenhouse gases.

The holding and movement of excise goods within the EC by the use of excise warehousing is dealt with at 9740.

9655   New rules for some gambling from 1 December 2014

From 1 December 2014, HMRC changed the rules for remote gaming duty (RGD), general betting duty (GBD) and pool betting duty (PBD).

- RGD applies to remote gambling, for example, casinos and bingo played through the internet.
- GBD covers more general betting such as fixed-odds betting and pool bets on horse and dog racing.
- PBD applies to pool betting (other than on horse and dog racing) and non-fixed-odds betting.

Premises based betting and the treatment of spread betting will be unaffected except for some administrative changes.

The new rules affect:

- the remote gambling industry who offer remote betting and gaming to UK consumers from outside the UK; and
- UK land-based betting business such as high street betting shops.

Land-based gaming sector businesses such as casinos and bingo halls will not be affected by these new rules unless they offer remote betting or gaming.

From 1 December 2014, general betting duty (GBD) is charged on a bookmaker's profits in the following situations:

- general bets or pool bets on horse racing or dog racing made with a bookmaker by a customer who is present in a betting shop regardless of where the customer usually lives;
- general bets or pool bets on horse racing or dog racing made with a bookmaker, not in a UK betting shop, by a UK person regardless of where in the world the bookmaker is located;
- spread bets that is betting on the outcome of financial or non-financial fluctuations of an index, made with a bookmaker who is in the UK.

This is in line with the Government's reform of GBD, Pool Betting Duty (PBD) and Remote Gaming Duty (RGD) so that these duties apply on a 'place of consumption' basis. In other words, remote gambling operators are to pay UK gambling duty on their gross gambling profits from UK customers no matter where in the world the operators are located.

The main implications of the reform of GBD are for remote bookmakers based outside the UK who take bets from UK customers over the internet, etc. These remote bookmakers will become liable to GBD for the first time. Bookmakers taking bets solely in betting shops in the UK and those offering spread betting from the UK will see minimal change but there will be some differences in the way the duty is administered.

HMRC have published the *General Betting, Pool Betting and Remote Gaming Duties (Registration, Records and Agents) Regulations* 2014 (SI 2014/2257).

9660   General betting duty (GBD)

Scope of the duty

General betting duty is an excise duty and is levied on all:

- off-course bets made with a UK bookmaker (for example in a high street bookmaker);

- financial and other spread bets made with a UK bookmaker; and

- pool betting on horse and dog races.

On-course bets are not subject to general betting duty on horse and dog races. All other on-course bets are subject to GBD.

Rates of duty

The rate of general betting duty depends on the type of bet and is applied to the bookmaker's net stake receipts. The net stake receipts represent the difference between the total amount of money received (i.e. stake receipt) and the total amount paid out (i.e. winnings) in an accounting period (i.e. in effect gross profits). An accounting period is normally a calendar month but HMRC may designate another period.

GBD is charged at 15% of the net stake receipts for that period.

For spread bets made with a bookmaker, the amount of general betting duty charged in an accounting period will be:

- in respect of financial spread bets, 3% of the net stake receipts from those bets for that period; and

- in respect of other spread bets, 10% of the net stake receipts from those bets for that period.

Spread betting involves betting on the outcome of an event based on a points spread. Gamblers can buy at the top or sell at the bottom of the spread, with winnings or losses calculated by multiplying the unit staked by the difference between the actual result and the buying or selling price.

Internet betting has become very popular and attempts have been made by HMRC to raise revenue from the activities. One of these is through person to person (P2P) betting websites, where a person can bet with another. This is known in BGDA 1981 as a betting exchange.

Legislation: BGDA 1981, s. 1ff.; *General Betting Duty Regulations* 1987 (SI 1987/1963)

Other Material: Public Notice 451 (now withdrawn) and Public Notice 451a (April 2016 edn)

9670   Pool betting duty

Scope of the duty

Pool betting duty applies to bets made by pool betting with a UK-based promoter. This duty classically covers the 'Pools'. Most pool betting is liable to pool betting duty, but certain types of pool betting are currently liable to general betting duty, for example, any pool betting through the Tote's facilities and pool betting through a totalisator on an event that is taking place on that day at the track where the totalisator is situated (see 9660 above). This means that pool betting on horse racing or dog racing that is not made through the facilities described above, is liable to pool betting duty. All pool betting on dog racing or horse racing falls within the general betting duty provisions when the promoter or the totalisator is based in the UK. All other pool betting, where the promoter or totalisator is based in the UK, falls within the pool betting duty provisions.

From 1 December 2014, pool betting duty (PBD) will be charged on a bookmaker's profits in the following situations:

- pool bets (other than those on horse racing or dog racing) made with a bookmaker by a customer who is present in a betting shop regardless of where the customer usually lives; and

- pool bets (other than those on horse racing or dog racing) made with a bookmaker, not in a UK betting shop, by a UK person regardless of where in the world the bookmaker is located.

This is in line with the Government's reform of PBD, General Betting Duty (GBD) and Remote Gaming Duty (RGD) so that these duties apply on a 'place of consumption' basis. In other words, remote gambling operators are to pay UK gambling duty on their gross gambling profits from UK customers no matter where in the world the operators are located.

There is a new Public Notice (PN 147a) (April 2016) that covers this.

The main implications of the reform of PBD are for remote bookmakers based outside the UK who take pool bets from UK customers over the internet, etc. These remote bookmakers will become liable to PBD for the first time (or GBD if the pool bets are on horse racing or dog racing). Bookmakers taking pool bets solely in betting shops in the UK will see minimal change but there will be some differences in the way the duty is administered.

Registration

A permit issued by HMRC is required to carry on a pool betting or fixed odds coupon betting business.

Rates of duty

The current rate of pool betting duty is 15% of gross profits (also known as net pool betting receipts) calculated as stakes plus expenses and profits less winnings paid out. It is payable by the promoter of the betting.

Record-keeping requirements

Pools promoters are required to keep records to enable the calculation of the duty, in particular an excise duty account must be maintained. Agents for fixed odds coupon bookmakers are required to keep a record of the money collected and copies of returns and other information given to the bookmaker. Coupons must be retained for at least two months and other records for at least four years.

Legislation: *Betting and Gaming Duties Act* 1981, s. 6ff.

Other Material: Public Notice 147 (September 2010 edn) and Notice 147a (April 2016 edn)

9680   Bingo duty

Scope of the duty

Bingo duty is levied on the playing of bingo in the UK, unless it is subject to one or more of the exemptions in BGDA 1981, Sch. 3.

These exemptions are: domestic bingo, small scale bingo and non-profit making bingo.

Bingo duty is charged on a person's bingo profits. The rate of duty is 10% of a person's profits derived from providing bingo in an accounting period.

Other indirect taxes

Legislation in *Finance Act* 2014 reduces the rate of bingo duty from 20% to 10%. In addition, the amendment to the bingo duty exemption provision, affecting adult gaming centres, simply updates the legislation and maintains the scope of the relief. The rate reduction has effect for bingo duty accounting periods beginning on or after 30 June 2014.

The legislation defines a person's bingo promotion profits as the difference between the amount he receives from providing bingo and the amount he pays out as prizes in any accounting period.

An accounting period runs from the first Monday of a calendar month until midnight of the Sunday before the first Monday of the next calendar month. Where payments that allow players to play bingo fall due to a person in an accounting period, for the purposes of bingo duty, he has bingo receipts for that period. These payments would include bingo card fees, but not admission fees (unless they carry a right to play).

Registration

Commercial bingo promoters must give their local HMRC advice centre at least 14 days' notice of their intention to operate a bingo club and complete a duty registration form.

Record-keeping requirements

Commercial records must be kept, including a bingo duty account, a summary account for use in completing the return and a stock account of bingo cards and tickets. Entries must be made in the accounting records within 48 hours of the end of the week. All records must be retained for at least four years.

Enforcement

HMRC officers have powers to enter premises where bingo is played or on which they have reasonable cause to suspect it has been or will be played. Officers may remain on those premises when they are being used for bingo or there is reasonable cause to suspect they will be used. They may:

- require information to be provided by any manager, promoter or player and for any card or document used in playing the game to be produced;
- direct which books, records and accounts shall be kept;
- require the production of any books, records and accounts including business bank accounts and trading accounts which relate to or appear to relate to the business; or

- specify any other information which they require, and estimate the amount of duty due where books, records and accounts are not kept or are incomplete or inaccurate.

Legislation: *Betting and Gaming Duties Act* 1981, s. 17ff.; *Bingo Duty Regulations* 2003 (SI 2003/2503); FA 2009

Other Material: Public Notice 457 (January 2016 edn)

9690 Gaming duty

Scope of the duty

Gaming duty is levied on casino games and equal chance gaming. The games are not specifically listed but they will include roulette, blackjack and various forms of poker.

Any person who is:

- the holder of a gaming licence;

- a provider of premises used for dutiable gaming; or

- concerned on the management or organisation of a dutiable gaming on unlicensed premises,

must register, account for pay over gaming duty.

Rates of duty

The duty is based on the 'gross gaming yield' (GGY) (essentially gross profits). This consists of the total value of the value of the stakes, minus players' winnings, on games in which the house is banker, and participation charges, or 'table money', exclusive of VAT, on games in which the bank is shared by players.

It is accounted for in six-month periods, usually beginning on 1 April and 1 October. Two returns are made in each six-month periods:

- After the first three months, a return is completed and a payment on account made.

- At the end of the six month accounting period, the gaming duty for the whole six month period is calculated. The amount of any payment made on account for the first three months of the period should be deducted from the total amount due and any balance paid. Current rates for accounting periods starting on or after 1 April 2016 are as follows:

Part of gross gaming yield	Rate (%)
The first £2,370,500	15
The next £1,634,000	20
The next £2,861,500	30
The next £6,040,000	40
The remainder	50

Record-keeping requirements

The gaming Board of Great Britain has produced a booklet *The Accounting Guide for Gaming Clubs* which provides guidance regarding accounts, procedures and documentation.

Legislation: FA 1997, s. 10ff.; FA 2016, s. 152; *Gaming Duty Regulations* 1997 (SI 1997/2196)

Other material: Public Notice 453 (January 2016 edn)

9695 Remote gaming duty

Remote gaming duty attempts to levy duty on playing a game of chance for a prize by the use of remote communication – for example, the internet, telephone or television.

Some of the leading players are established in places like Gibraltar, so they may or may not co-operate with this duty.

The rate of duty is 15% of a person's remote gaming profits (in effect, gross profits).

Remote gambling tax reform – as announced in Budget 2012, legislation has been introduced in *Finance Act* 2014 to make all UK facing remote gambling operators liable to UK gambling taxes on the gambling profits generated from UK customers, no matter where in the world the operator itself is located. Following consultation, the legislation has been revised to take account of consultation responses and to provide for transitional arrangements. These changes will have effect from 1 December 2014.

Legislation: BGDA 1981, s. 26Aff.; *Remote Gaming Regulations* 2007 (SI 2007/2192)

Other material: PN 455, *Remote Gaming* Duty (April 2010 edn) and PN 455a (January 2016 edn)

9700 Machine Games Duty (MGD)

Scope of the duty

MGD is a duty of excise which is charged on playing 'dutiable machine games' in the UK. Not all machine games are dutiable.

A machine game is a game played on a machine for a prize. A machine game is 'dutiable' (and subject to MGD) if at least one of the prizes that can be won is, or includes, cash to a value greater than the cost to play once.

The following are examples of dutiable machine games:

• games played on a gaming machine; and

• games of skill, or games combining chance and skill, played on a machine for a cash prize which exceeds the cost to play the game once. Games along these lines include quizzes and tests of coordination or manual dexterity.

The machines on which dutiable machine games may be played can be in a particular location (e.g. a pier) or on portable devices such as a handheld 'tablet'.

MGD is not due on any machine game that only offers non-cash prizes.

If a machine game offers both cash and non-cash prizes it is the size of the cash prize that determines whether or not MGD is due.

Example

In order to play a 'pusher' (sometimes called a 'penny falls machine'), the player inserts a 10p piece. The cost to play is therefore 10p. The action of the machine on the inserted 10p may cause one or several 10p pieces to fall into the prize hopper. This means that there is a cash prize on offer which is more than the cost to play so there is a liability to MGD. The pusher game remains liable to MGD even if non-cash prizes (for example, key rings) are placed in the machine (in addition to the 10p pieces) and may be pushed out as prizes (taken from PN 452 (July 2016 edn)).

Registration

If someone holds a relevant licence or permit for the premises, then it is that person who should register. Relevant licences and permits are listed below.

Other indirect taxes

In Great Britain:

- premises licence for gambling activities under the *Gambling Act* 2005;
- family entertainment centre gaming machine permit;
- club gaming permit;
- club machine permit;
- prize gaming permit;
- the *Licensing (England and Wales) Act* 2003 premises licence for on-sales of alcohol and the equivalent under the *Licensing (Scotland) Act* 2005. However, in the case of a tenanted pub, where the alcohol licence is held by someone other than the tenant, the tenant will nevertheless be the registrable person for MGD;
- club premises certificate granted under the *Licensing Act* 2003, Pt. 3.

In Northern Ireland:

- registration certificate including a club registration certificate;
- bookmaking office licence;
- bingo club licence;
- amusement permit;
- licence allowing the serving of alcohol (but only if a licence permit or certificate listed above is not held for the same premises).

(*Finance Act* 2012, Sch. 24, para. 22)

Rates of duty

MGD is charged on a taxable person's total net takings in an accounting period.

Net takings are takings less payouts.

There are three rates of duty for MGD:

- lower rate 5% – for machines where the maximum cost per game (the 'maximum stake') is 20p, and the cash prize is £10 or less. These will be called 'Type 1' machines;
- standard rate 20% – applies to machines where the highest charge to play a game can be more than 20p but not more than £5, or the highest cash prize for a game is higher than £10. These will be called 'Type 2' machines;

- higher rate 25% – applies to machines that are not Type 1 or 2 machines. In effect, any machine where it can cost more than £5 to play a game.

Returns and payment

MGD runs on three calendar month accounting periods (although non-standard accounting periods are accepted by HMRC). The returns may be submitted either online (encouraged by HMRC) or by paper.

The returns must be submitted within 30 days of the end of the accounting period. Payment must be within the same one-month period.

MGD is paid electronically by:

- Direct Debit – Variable Payment and Single Payment Plans;
- Bacs Direct Credit;
- Faster Payments by online or telephone banking; and
- CHAPS.

There are penalties for late payment, but HMRC have accepted that the introduction of MGD has caused problems, especially for smaller operators. HMRC have also encountered some system issues which have confused some customers and made it more difficult for them to comply.

Exceptionally, therefore, HMRC have decided not to apply penalties for the late submission of the first returns. This only applies to these penalties.

Legislation: FA 2012, Sch. 24; *Machine Games Duty Regulations* 2012 (SI 2012/2500)

Other Material: Public Notice 452 (July 2016 edn)

9710 Alcoholic liquor duties

Scope of the duties

Alcoholic liquors comprise:

- spirits;
- beer;
- wine;
- made-wine; and
- cider.

Other indirect taxes

Spirits

Before producing spirits, application for approval of the plant and process to be used must be made to HMRC and a distiller's licence must be obtained from HMRC. In general, HMRC will not license manufacturers with stills of less than 1,800 litres capacity, although smaller stills may be allowed for, say, heritage centres and universities for research.

Spirits are made from ethyl alcohol and ethyl alcohol is produced in the EC for many purposes. It is only when it is drinkable (potable) that it is dutied as an alcoholic liquor.

Registration

All manufacturing operations must be approved by HMRC and carried out in distillation periods agreed with them. At the end of each quarter, a return for each class of spirit produced must be submitted to HMRC.

Rates of duty

The rates from 21 March 2016 are as follows:

Description	Rates from 21 March 2016
Spirits[1]	£27.66 per litre of pure alcohol @ temperature of 20°C
Beer[2]	£18.37 per hectolitre for every 1% of alcohol by volume and in proportion for any smaller quantity
Fortified wine and made-wine[3] [4] (sparkling or still) of an alcoholic strength >22%	£27.66 per litre of pure alcohol
Spirits-based 'coolers'[6]	£27.66 per litre of pure alcohol
Fortified wine and made-wine[3] [4] (sparkling or still) of an alcoholic strength >15% and not >22%	£370.41 per hectolitre
Sparkling wine and made-wine[3][4] of an alcoholic strength 8.5% and above, but not >15%	£355.87 per hectolitre
Sparkling wine and made-wine[3][4] of an alcoholic strength of >5.5% and <8.5%	£268.99 per hectolitre
Still wine and made-wine[3][4] of an alcoholic strength >5.5% and not >15%	£277.84 per hectolitre

Description	Rates from 21 March 2016
Wine, made wine, spiritous and mixed drinks made from cider/perry base >4% and not >5.5%	£117.72 per hectolitre
Wine, made wine, spiritous and mixed drinks made from cider/perry base >1.2% and not >4%	£85.60 per hectolitre
Sparkling cider[5] or perry of an alcoholic strength >5.5% and <8.5%	£268.99 per hectolitre
1.2% and n/e 5.5%	£38.87 per hectolitre
Still cider[5] or perry of an alcoholic strength of >7.5% and <8.5%	£58.75 per hectolitre
Still cider[5] or perry of an alcoholic strength >1.2% and not >7.5%	£38.87 per hectolitre

[1] 'Spirits' means spirits of any description which are of a strength exceeding 1.2%, any such mixture, compound or preparation made with spirits as is of a strength exceeding 1.2% or liquors contained with any spirits, in any mixture which is of a strength exceeding 1.2%, but does not include methylated spirits.

[2] 'Beer' includes ale, porter, stout and any other description of beer and any liquor which is sold as beer or as a substitute for beer, and which is of an alcoholic strength exceeding 0.5% but does not include black beer, the worts of which before fermentation were of a specific gravity of 1200° or more. The black beer exemption has gone from 1 April 2013, so it is subject to duty like all other beers.

Lower strength beer (>1.2% and n/e 2.8%) has a reduced rate of duty (£8.10) and high strength beer (>7.5%) an extra £5.48 in addition to the normal beer rate.

[3] 'Wine' means any liquor obtained from the alcoholic fermentation of fresh grapes or the must of fresh grapes, whether or not the liquor is fortified with spirits or flavoured with aromatic extracts.

[4] 'Made-wine' means any liquor obtained from the alcoholic fermentation of any substance, but does not include wine, beer, black beer, spirits or cider.

[5] 'Cider' means cider (or perry) of a strength of less than 8.5% of alcohol by volume at 20°C, obtained from the fermentation of apple or pear juice without the addition at any time of any alcoholic liquor or of any liquor or substance which communicates colour or flavour other than such as the commissioners may allow as appearing to them to be necessary to make cider (or perry).

[6] Spirits-based drinks not exceeding 5.5% alcohol by volume ('coolers') used to be taxed as made-wine. From 28 April 2002, they are taxed as spirits.

Inward Processing Relief (IPR)

Individual grain whisky distillers may apply for approval under IPR to allow the levy-free importation of maize, high diastatic barley and high diastatic malted barley for use in the production of grain whisky and spirits for re-exportation as such or as blended whisky. HMRC's authorisation is required and certain conditions in respect of importation and exportation procedures and reporting requirements must be met. Such cereals for use in the production of gin or vodka for export may also qualify for IPR relief.

Record-keeping requirements

Records of spirit producing activities, including details of fermentations, distillations and deliveries to warehouse must be maintained. Also, all business records relating to stock, handling, purchases, sales, imports and exports must be maintained.

Any taking of account of spirits must be entered into the distiller's business records immediately before the account is taken. HMRC may require notice to be given of an intention to take the account.

Spirits must be removed to an approved warehouse immediately after details of the spirits account have been entered in the business records, or any standing time imposed by HMRC has elapsed.

Beer

Beer includes ale, porter, stout and any liquor which is branded or sold as a beer.

Reduced rate for small breweries

There is a reduced rate of beer duty for small breweries. The reduction is 50% where production is less than 5,000 hectolitres per year. Where production is between 5,000 and 30,000 hectolitres per year, the rate is found by applying the formula:

$$\% \text{ of duty payable} = \frac{\text{annual production} - 2,500}{\text{annual production}}$$

There is a detailed regime surrounding this relief. It can be found in the *Alcoholic Liquor Duties Act* 1979, s. 36A–36H.

Wine and made-wine

Wine is made from the alcoholic fermentation of fresh grapes and made-wine is made from the alcoholic fermentation of any substance other than fresh grapes (for example country wines made from damsons, etc.). The duty rates for wine are in ALDA 1979, Sch. 1 and are amended as appropriate by the Finance Act each year.

Made wine is also a category that drinks that don't fall into other categories fall into as a default. For example, cider is defined as being made from apples and with a strength not exceeding 8.55% abv. So *cider above* that strength has to be made wine.

Cider

Cider (which includes perry) is made from fermenting apples (or pears). To be cider, the alcoholic strength (ABV) must be between 1.2% and 8.5%. Any fermented apple juice with an ABV outside this range will not be dutied as cider.

9715 Due diligence – tackling alcohol fraud

On 1 November 2014, HMRC introduced a due diligence requirement for businesses in the alcohol sector. It will be a condition of trading that businesses undertake reasonable, appropriate checks on their customers, suppliers and supply chains and have robust procedures to reduce risks of trading in illicit goods. According to HMRC, this is crucial to help identify fraud and prevent illicit alcoholic drinks entering the market place, which costs the UK taxpayer an estimated £1bn p.a.

This will apply to all businesses dealing in alcoholic drinks which are approved or registered by HMRC, including:

- breweries trading under duty suspension;
- registered excise warehouse keepers;
- registered owners of goods (within an excise warehouse);
- registered duty representatives;
- registered commercial importers;
- temporary registered consignees;
- registered consignees;
- registered consignors.

This condition will also apply to businesses wholesaling alcoholic drinks upon introduction of the Alcohol Wholesaler Registration Scheme from 2016.

From 1 November 2014, it will be a condition of an approval that traders must:

- objectively assess the risks of alcohol duty fraud within the supply chains in which they operate;
- put in place reasonable and proportionate checks in day to day trading to identify transactions that may lead to fraud or involve goods on which duty may have been evaded;
- have procedures in place to take timely and effective mitigating action where a risk of fraud is identified;
- document the checks the trader intends to carry out and have appropriate management governance in place to ensure that these are, and continue to be, carried out as intended.

Failure to carry out due diligence

Failing to consider fraud risks, undertake due diligence checks or respond to clear indications of fraud could lead to civil penalties and ultimately to revocation of excise approvals and licences.

Inadequate due diligence may lead to fraud, or expose businesses to receiving and holding illicit/non-duty paid alcoholic drinks for which there are also serious penalties including:

- the holder may be liable for the duty;
- the goods may be seized;
- a wrong doing penalty of up to 100% of the excise duty due may be applied;
- criminal prosecution;
- 'naming and shaming' as a deliberate tax defaulter by HMRC.

9716   Alcohol wholesaler registration scheme (AWRS)

A new registration scheme (AWRS) for wholesalers of alcohol is being introduced from 1 January 2016 (the scheme was originally due to be launched from 1 October 2015 but was subsequently postponed).

Existing alcohol wholesalers or start-ups before 1 April 2016 will need to apply online for registration between 1 January 2016 and 31 March 2016.

From 1 April 2017, trade buyers who buy their alcohol from UK wholesalers for resale will need to make sure that these wholesalers are approved by HMRC. The check will be made using an online look up service, and using this to check the validity of wholesalers will form part of these businesses' 'due diligence' processes.

From April 2017, it will become an offence for a retailer to buy alcohol from an unregistered wholesaler (unless they are buying direct from abroad or from another retailer who makes incidental wholesale sales).

The Government says that alcohol duty fraud costs UK taxpayers an estimated £1bn each year through smuggling or diversion, exploiting the European Union-wide duty suspension arrangements. Illicit alcohol typically works its way into legitimate supply chains at the point of wholesale.

The new AWRS is designed to introduce effective control at the point in alcohol supply chains most vulnerable to organised criminal attack.

There are around 20,000 alcohol wholesalers in the UK. All alcohol wholesalers will need to demonstrate they are 'fit and proper' and have their supply chains tested to make sure they are legitimate before being approved to operate in the sector, and entered onto a register.

Retailers will be required to purchase alcohol only from registered wholesalers and will be able to check whether their suppliers are registered on an online look-up facility. This will provide businesses with more certainty of the legitimacy of who they are trading with. It will also remove the excuse of ignorance for any business who might take the risk of dealing in illicit alcohol.

HMRC will have new powers to deal with any wholesaler not registered quickly and effectively. Any alcohol goods found in the premises of unregistered businesses will be liable for seizure – whether or not the duty has been paid. Those involved will also be liable to penalties. In addition, any retailer purchasing from an unregistered wholesaler will be liable to penalties.

More information about the scheme will be available once the draft legislation is published later this year.

Legislation: *Alcoholic Liquor Duties Act* 1979; *Wine and Made Wine Regulations* 1989 (SI 1989/1356); *Cider and Perry Regulations* 1989 (SI 1989/1355); *Spirits Regulations* 1991 (SI 1991/2564); *Beer Regulations* 1993 (SI 1993/1228); *Wholesaling of Controlled Liquor Regulations* 2015 (SI 2015/1516)

Other Material: Notices 226 *Beer Duty* (August 2016 edn); PN 162 *Cider production* (October 2016); PN 163 *Wine production* (September 2016) have also been upgraded; Notice 2002 *The Alcohol Wholesaler Registration Scheme* (July 2016)

9720 Tobacco products

Scope of the duty

The following are all liable to tobacco products duty if manufactured wholly or partly from tobacco or any substance used as a substitute for tobacco, but does not include herbal smoking products:

- cigarettes;
- cigars;
- hand-rolling tobacco;
- other smoking tobacco (pipe tobacco); and
- chewing tobacco.

Other indirect taxes

Registration

Any premises in which tobacco products are manufactured must be registered. Application for registration must be made to the local HMRC advice centre. HMRC will also register stores adjoining factories to enable duty-free storage of products, as well as remote storage premises, subject to certain conditions being met.

Removals and warehousing

All tobacco products manufactured in the registered factory must normally be removed to the registered store immediately after manufacture. They cannot be removed from the registered store before duty has been accounted for or secured and removal documentation has been prepared and issued or deposited.

Tobacco products can be removed to home use in the UK on payment of the duty.

They can also be removed free of duty for certain specified purposes, including, exportation, consignment to another EU Member State, sale in duty-free shops, transfer to other registered stores, transfer to other registered factories for further manufacture or transfer to a UK excise warehouse. HMRC require documentary procedures to be followed and all tobacco products will remain potentially liable to tobacco products duty until HMRC are satisfied that the products have been satisfactorily accounted for, supported by documentary evidence.

Importation

Imported tobacco products can be removed either in a finished state or for further manufacture to registered premises direct from the place of importation or via an excise warehouse, without payment of tobacco products duty subject to meeting HMRC's requirements. Any customs duty, payable on the imported product will need to be paid, unless customs warehouse approval is held in respect of the registered premises.

Rates of duty

The current rates of duty from 16 March 2016 are as follows:

Description	Rate
cigarettes[1]	16.5% of the retail price[2] plus £196.42 per thousand cigarettes
cigars[3]	£245.01 per kg[4]
hand-rolling tobacco[5]	£198.10 per kg
other smoking tobacco (eg pipe tobacco)	£107.71 per kg
chewing tobacco	£107.71 per kg

(1) 'Cigarette' means any roll of tobacco capable of being smoked as it is and not falling within any of the descriptions of a cigar. Any cigarette more than 9 cm long (excluding any filter or mouthpiece) will be treated as if each 9 cm or part thereof were a separate cigarette.

(2) The retail price is defined as the higher of:

(i) the recommended retail selling price in the UK of cigarettes of that description; and
(ii) the highest retail price shown at that time on the packaging of the cigarettes in question.

Where there is no such price recommended or shown, the retail price will be taken as the highest price at which cigarettes of that brand are normally sold by retail at that time in the UK.

(3) 'Cigar' means any cigar capable of being smoked as it is and which is either:

(a) a roll of tobacco with an outer wrapper of natural tobacco;
(b) a roll of tobacco containing predominantly broken or threshed leaf, with a binder of reconstituted tobacco and with an outer wrapper which is of reconstituted tobacco having the normal colour of a cigar and which is fitted spirally; or
(c) a roll of tobacco containing predominantly broken or threshed leaf with an outer wrapper of reconstituted tobacco having the normal colour of a cigar; and having a weight exclusive of any detachable filter or mouthpiece, of not less than 2.3 g; and having a circumference over at least one-third of its length of not less than 34 mm.

(4) The weight for duty is the total weight of the cigar, which may however, exclude any detachable filter or mouthpiece.

(5) 'Hand-rolling tobacco' means tobacco which is sold or advertised by the importer or manufacturer as suitable for making into cigarettes; or which is of a kind used for making into cigarettes; or of which more than 25% by weight of the tobacco particles have a width of less than 1mm.

In the emergency Budget in June 2010, the Chancellor announced that the law on long cigarettes would be slightly amended, so that from 1 January 2011, cigarettes longer than 8cm will be treated as two cigarettes (down from 9 cm) (TPDA 1979, s. 4).

Credits

A duty credit on products returned from UK customers to registered tobacco premises will be allowed if the products have been recycled, repackaged, or destroyed by a method acceptable to HMRC and are of a net weight of at least 1kg. Credit will also be allowed on products previously removed to duty-paid storage but not delivered to customers, provided they are returned to the registered premises for recycling, repackaging, or destruction. The terms 'recycling' and 'repackaging' are specifically defined by HMRC.

Duty can be reclaimed on imported tobacco products returned by an overseas supplier for recycling or repackaging, or disposal by a method acceptable to HMRC, providing the claim is made by the person who imported or removed the products from warehouse and paid the duty, the products were imported for sale and their net weight is at least 1kg.

Record-keeping requirements

A high standard of control on goods, persons and vehicles entering and leaving the registered premises must be maintained.

Records of all materials received, used in manufacture and disposed of, and resulting refuse and its disposal, giving details of quantity, description and date, must be maintained.

A production account of the products made in the factory must be raised as soon as the products are put in a state suitable for removal from the factory or are packed for delivery. For each tobacco product, the production account must show the quantity produced, the type, size and brand of the retail pack and the date of production and entry into the account.

A daily declaration of the total quantity of products manufactured (the production return) must be completed and submitted to HMRC, usually by noon of the following day.

A materials reconciliation account must be maintained to reconcile materials received against products manufactured.

A stock account must be maintained for products received into the registered store, operated on therein and removed.

Enforcement

Failure to comply with HMRC's requirements could result in civil penalties being imposed and cancellation of the registration.

Legislation: *Tobacco Products Duty Act* 1979; FA 2016, s. 154; *Revenue Traders (Accounts and Records) Regulations* 1992 (SI 1992/3150); *Tobacco Products Regulations* 2001 (SI 2001/1712); *Tobacco Products (Description of Products) Order* 2003 (SI 2003/1471)

9730   Hydrocarbon oil duties

Scope of the duty

Historically, excise duties were charged on hydrocarbon oils, but times have changed and new forms of energy are now on the market. There is a European framework for this and generically, the products are referred to as 'energy products'. These include biofuels and electricity. In the UK, the law in the *Hydrocarbon Oils Duties Act* 1979, still taxes oils and biofuels, but the tax on electricity is climate change levy (CCL) (see 10020). Carbon floor pricing has been incorporated into CCL in 2013.

All hydrocarbon oil is liable to excise duty at a full or rebated (i.e. reduced – which can be reduced down to zero) rate. Hydrocarbon Oil means petroleum oils, coal tar, and oils produced from coal, shale, peat or any other bituminous substance, and all liquid hydrocarbons, but does not include such hydrocarbons as bituminous or asphaltic substances as are:

(1) Solid or semi-solid at a temperature of 15°C; or

(2) Gaseous at a temperature of 15°C and under a pressure of 1013.25 millibars.

Rates of duty

Excise duty rates on hydrocarbon oils are specific, and calculated per standard litre, that is litres at 15°C.

In Budgets 2013 and 2014, the Government cancelled the planned fuel duty increases that were scheduled for September 2013 and 2014 respectively. The Chancellor continued the freeze on fuel duty in Budget 2015 and again in Budget 2016, such that fuel duty will now remain unchanged until at least 2017.

The categories and rates are:

	Duty rate per litre (£) From 23 March 2011
Unleaded petrol	0.5795
Heavy Oil	0.5795

	Duty rate per litre (£) From 23 March 2011
Light oil (other than unleaded petrol or aviation gasoline)	0.6767

	Duty rate per litre (£) From 23 March 2011
Aviation gasoline (Avgas)	0.3770

	Duty rate per litre (£) From 23 March 2011
Light oil delivered to an approved person for use as furnace fuel	0.1070
Marked gas oil	0.1114
Fuel oil	0.1070

	Duty rate per litre (£) From 23 March 2011
Heavy oil other than fuel oil, gas oil or kerosene used as fuel	0.1070
Kerosene to be used as motor fuel off-road or in an 'excepted vehicle' (red diesel)	0.1114
Biodiesel for non-road use	0.1114
Biodiesel blended with gas oil for non road use	0.1114

	Duty rate per litre (£) From 23 March 2011
Biodiesel	0.5795
Bioethanol	0.5795

	Duty rate per kg (£) From 23 March 2011
Road fuel natural gas (NG), including biogas	0.2470
Road fuel gas other than NG – e.g. liquefied petroleum gas (LPG)	0.3161

Finance Act 2016, Sch. 17 introduces a new duty of £0.079 per litre on Aqua Methanol, from 14 November 2016.

Excise Notice 75 – Fuel for road vehicles has been updated (September 2015).

HMRC have also issued a revised Notice 263 on marine fuels, which may qualify for relief in some circumstances.

Secondary legislation has been made to introduce a duty relief scheme for retailers of fuel in the Inner and Outer Hebrides, the Northern Isles, the islands in the Clyde and the Isles of Scilly. Registered retailers within these areas will be entitled to claim 5 pence per litre (ppl) relief on fuel purchased after 1 January 2012. Sixty days after registration, from 1 March for those registered on 1 January, the retailers will be required to reduce the price of fuel they sell by an equivalent amount to the relief claimed, to benefit consumers in the areas concerned.

HMRC have now published an updated notice (PN 7001) which gives the details.

Policy objective

The price of fuel on the Scottish islands is on average 10ppl, and on the Scilly Isles 25ppl, more than in other parts of the UK, mainly as a result of higher transport and distribution costs. The 5ppl relief will offer some help to consumers in the areas concerned, who are faced with the high costs of petrol and diesel.

The control environment for oils

Duty evasion is an important area of concern for HMRC and they have implemented several controls over the years to deal with this. These include the Tied Oils Scheme and the Registered Dealers in Controlled Oils Scheme (RDCO). There is a new notice on the RDCO scheme (PN 192 (January 2016)).

The use of red diesel (aka marked gas oil) in certain situations has been controversial – for example using red diesel in tractors on the road over long distances and using tractors to grit rural roads in the winter. Another area of uncertainty has been the use of red diesel in private pleasure craft in UK waters. HMRC released HMRC Brief 09/12 that assists boat owners' practical understanding of the mechanics of this. Notice 554 has been amended.

Legislation: The Energy Products Directive (Dir. 2003/96); *Hydrocarbon Oil Duties Act* 1979, s. 6ff., Sch. 1 (for excepted vehicles); FA 2010; The *Hydrocarbon Oil and Biofuels (Road Fuel in Defined Areas) (Reliefs) Regulations* 2011 (SI 2011/2935)

Other Material: Excise Notice 75: Fuel for road vehicles (September 2015); Public Notice 192 (January 2016); Motor and Heating Fuels Notice 179 has been updated (August 2015). It now contains guidance on recent legal and technical changes, and new contact details; Public Notice 2001 (Rural Fuel Duty Relief – October 2015); Public Notice 554 (November 2014); Notice 263 – Marine Fuels Relief (May 2016)

9740 Excise warehousing

Overview

Excise warehousing is quite different to customs warehousing. They both do different things: customs warehousing shelters goods against customs duties and import VAT; and excise warehousing shelters goods against excise duties and import VAT. It is possible to have a single building that can be both a customs warehouse and an excise warehouse.

Excise warehousing is central to the EC Holding and Movements regime, by which excise goods such as wine and spirits can move in duty suspension across EC boundaries. Duty only becomes due when the goods are removed from the regime.

Other indirect taxes

There are three types of excise warehouse:

- general storage and distribution warehouses (GSD);
- trade facility warehouses; and
- distillers' warehouses (ALDA 1979, s. 15).

This distinction between GSDs and trade facility warehouses is not in the law, but is in one of the main public notices (Public Notice 196 (January 2016)).

Approval of warehouses

To obtain HMRC's approval to operate an excise warehouse certain conditions must be met. Furthermore, each type has its own additional qualifying criteria. The most common type of warehouse in use is the general storage and distribution warehouse. To qualify for approval for such, there must be either a minimum potential duty liability of £500,000 on average stockholdings, or a minimum potential duty liability of £2m on annual throughput.

A computerised list of all UK authorised warehousekeepers, tax warehouses and Registered Consignees (see 9750) is available from HMRC. They are also able to confirm details of such traders operating in other EC member states.

Access and security

Access to any part of the warehouse must be offered to HMRC officers at all reasonable times.

Financial guarantees are required to cover intra-EC movements of excise goods. Financial security may also be required as a condition of the warehouse approval or for UK movements. Premises must be physically secure.

What goods can be warehoused

Goods liable to excise duty can be warehoused, subject to meeting any additional conditions in respect of particular products, such as hydrocarbon oil or tobacco products.

UK-manufactured tobacco products can only be stored in an excise warehouse if they are intended for export, shipment as stores, or for visiting forces, embassies or duty-free shops, unless it also has approval as registered tobacco premises.

Record-keeping requirements

Stock accounts are required to be maintained in respect of all receipts into and deliveries from the warehouse. Computer records may be used, providing hard copy or visual interrogation facilities are available to HMRC. All information in stock accounts must be permanent and legible. They must provide:

- a full description of the goods;
- their location within the warehouse;
- their duty status and evidence of duty payment;
- details of the owner of the goods and whether they have been sold whilst in the warehouse; and
- the means to identify all goods by reference to their stock number.

A certified summary stock return may be required by HMRC on either a monthly or quarterly basis. Separate returns are required for:

- UK-produced whisky and plain spirits;
- other spirits;
- wine, made-wine, cider/perry and beer; and
- tobacco products.

An annual return of all whisky movements is also required by HMRC.

Receipts of goods

On receipt of goods into the warehouse, the warehousekeeper must carry out physical checks on the load and issue a certificate of receipt. HMRC require certain documentary procedures to be followed depending on the location from which the goods have been consigned.

All goods received must be recorded in the warehouse stock account.

Goods may be delivered duty-free from a warehouse for use as ship's stores by following HMRC's documentary procedures.

Movement of goods in the warehouse

All goods must be marked and stored in clearly identified locations in the warehouse in order that they can be readily identified from the stock account.

Any movements of goods within the warehouse must be recorded on the stock account.

Other indirect taxes

A satisfactory inventory checking system, agreed by HMRC, must be in place to enable stock verifications. Stocktaking must take place annually for all goods other than bulk, which must be verified monthly.

Processing allowable in the warehouse

In contrast to customs warehouses, where only low-level operations are permitted, a wide range of operations are permitted in excise warehouses.

Operations necessary for the preservation, sale, shipment or disposal of the goods are normally allowed.

Furthermore, other operations are allowed, depending on the specific type of goods concerned. For example, bottled goods can be relabelled and repacked, whilst goods in casks, drums or vats can be bottled. The only operation allowed on tobacco products is repacking of retail packs.

All operations must be monitored and account taken immediately prior to and after each operation, as well as meeting other HMRC requirements.

Removal of goods from warehouses

Home use (i.e. to the UK market)

In order to remove goods from the warehouse to home use, the warehouse keeper must first write them off from the stock account. Commercial documents are required to identify the goods, their stock rotation number, the consignee and the type of transaction. A list of all home-use deliveries must be completed daily and show details of each delivery.

Excise duty is paid either by cash, banker's draft or guaranteed cheque before the goods leave the warehouse, or under duty deferment arrangements.

Rather than accounting for removals on a daily basis, warehouse keepers can apply to schedule their removals whereby they can submit twice-monthly schedules.

UK inter-warehouse removals

Excise goods can be removed to another excise warehouse without payment of the duty. From 1 January 2011, these movements are within the EMCS (see below) (see Public Notice 197).

Intra-EC movements

In order to transfer excise goods between approved warehouses in different EU member states, a guarantee needs to be provided to cover the suspended excise duty.

From 1 April 2010, a new paperless control system (The Excise Movement and Control System (EMCS)) replaces the old paper-based AAD system for intra Member State movement.

The Excise Movement and Control System (EMCS)

The EMCS is an electronic system for monitoring and controlling movements of duty-suspended goods across the EC.

From 1 January 2011, the electronic administrative document (eAD) replaces the old paper AAD (Accompanying Administrative Document). The EMCS generates an Administrative Reference Code (ARC) that uniquely identifies the movement.

The EMCS covers both intra UK movements and intra EC movements. The movements need guarantees to cover the duty at stake. If the electronic system is not working, a fallback paper system is available.

On 15 October 2012, the next stage of EMCS will be launched. The next stage of EMCS introduces a range of changes:

- new messages to alert serious incidents and/or discrepancies with movements;

- anew manual closure message;

- removal of transport mode restrictions when splitting movements of energy products;

- registered consignors will be able to cancel eADs.

Export

Excise duty is not liable on goods exported from the EC. However, commercial evidence of export must be held by the warehouse keeper in order to discharge his duty liability.

Ship's stores

Goods may be delivered duty free from the warehouse for use as ship's stores by following HMRC's documentary procedures.

Losses and deficiencies

Losses and deficiencies of warehoused goods are not chargeable with duty, providing it can be proved that they were due to natural causes or accidents. All losses must be recorded in the appropriate stock account and investigated. Losses can sometimes be offset against surpluses, providing they can be shown to be related and the offset can be justified.

Legislation: Directive 2008/118; CEMA 1979, s. 92 and 94; ALDA 1979, s. 15; *Excise Warehousing (Etc) Regulations* 1988 (SI 1988/809); *Excise Duties (Deferred Payment) Regulations* 1992 (SI 1992/3152); *Beer Regulations* 1993 (SI 1993/1228); *Excise Goods (Holding, Movement, and Duty Point) Regulations* 2010 (HMDP) (SI 2010/593)

Other Material: PN 196 (January 2016) and PN 197 (September 2016) (These are very important public notices.)

9750   Registered consignees (formerly registered excise dealers (REDs))

From 1 April 2010, the concept of the REDs is gone. Instead, a new person is created – a 'Registered Consignee', who still has some of the characteristics of the REDs, but the regime has been modified.

Registered consignees are revenue traders who are approved by HMRC to obtain excise goods commercially from other EC Member States duty free. A registered consignee (just like the older REDS that it replaced) is an alternative procedure to the full excise warehousing procedure.

The difference is that a registered consignee may not hold or consign excise goods received in duty suspension, so duty (subject to deferment) is triggered on arrival.

Like excise warehouse keepers, the new registered consignor/consignee system will need to use the EMCS (Excise Movement and Control System).

There is a 'watered down' version of a registered consignee, called the temporary registered consignee (TRC).

Legislation: HMDP 2010 (SI 2010/593)

Other Material: HMRC have published revised versions of PN 197 (Excise goods: receipts into and removal from an excise warehouse of excise goods), 203A (Registered Consignees) and 204A (Temporary Registered Consignees) to reflect FS2.1 changes to EMCS

Air passenger duty

9760   Introduction to air passenger duty

APD is a specific duty of excise, under the care and management of HMRC, levied on civil airlines and other aircraft operators on their carriage of passengers on flights from airports in the UK. The airlines invariably pass on the duty to the passengers.

- From 1 April 2015, the number of Air Passenger Duty (APD) destination bands was reduced to two by merging the former bands B, C and D, and the higher rates that apply to aircraft with an authorised take-off weight of 20 tonnes or more and with fewer than 19 seats were set at six times the reduced rates.

- To this end, HMRC published a revised Excise Notice 550 Air Passenger Duty – published February 2015.

The Government announced that APD rates would increase with inflation from April 2016.

APD rates from 1 April 2016

Destination Bands and distance from London (miles)	Reduced rate: (for travel in the lowest class of travel available on the aircraft)	Standard rate: (for travel in any other class of travel)	Higher rate: (for travel in aircraft of 20 tonnes or more equipped to carry fewer than 19 passengers)
Band A (0 to 2,000 miles)	£13	£26	£78
Band B (over 2,000 miles)	£73	£146	£438

Previous APD rates from 1 April 2015

Destination Bands and distance from London (miles)	Reduced rate: (for travel in the lowest class of travel available on the aircraft)	Standard rate: (for travel in any other class of travel)	Higher rate: (for travel in aircraft of 20 tonnes or more equipped to carry fewer than 19 passengers)
Band A (0 to 2,000 miles)	£13	£26	£78
Band B (over 2,000 miles)	£71	£142	£426

From 1 May 2015, children who are under the age of 12 years on the date of the flight, and in the lowest class of travel, are not chargeable passengers. Children 12 years and over, or travelling in any other class, are chargeable passengers and APD is due.

From 1 March 2016, children who are under the age of 16 years on the date of the flight, and in the lowest class of travel, are not chargeable passengers. Children 16 years and over, or travelling in any other class, are chargeable passengers and APD is due.

APD rates for flights originating in Northern Ireland

No APD is paid on direct long-haul flights departing from airports in Northern Ireland. A flight is a 'direct long-haul flight' when:

- the passenger's journey begins from an airport in Northern Ireland;
- the first part of the journey is to a destination outside Band A;
- that part of the journey is direct and does not connect elsewhere beforehand.

APD rates for flights originating in Northern Ireland from 1 April 2016

Destination Bands and distance from London (miles)	Rates from 1 April 2016 (reduced/standard/higher)	
	Direct	Indirect
Band A (0 to 2,000 miles)	£13/£26/£78	£13/£26/£78
Band B (over 2,000 miles)	£0/£0/£0	£74/£146/£438

APD rates for flights originating in Northern Ireland from 1 April 2015

Destination Bands and distance from London (miles)	Rates from 1 April 2015 (reduced/standard/higher)	
	Direct	Indirect
Band A (0 to 2,000 miles)	£13/£26/£78	£13/£26/£78
Band B (over 2,000 miles)	£0/£0/£0	£71/£142/£426

Legislation: FA 1994, s. 30; FA 2009 and FA 2010; FA 1994, s. 28ff; FA 2016, s. 149; *APD Regulations* 1994 (SI 1994/1738)

Other Material: Guidance Rates and allowances: Excise Duty – APD 6 April 2015; Public Notice 550: *Air Passenger Duty* (February 2015 edn)

9770   Persons liable for the duty

Aircraft operators are required to register for the tax with HMRC. Aircraft operators without permanent establishments in the UK are required to appoint a UK fiscal representative to ensure the principal's compliance, and to stand jointly and severally liable with them in regard to the tax.

Finance Act 1998, s. 15 introduced a measure to address problems faced by foreign airlines looking for fiscal representation in the UK. Airlines are able to appoint a representative whose sole responsibility is to keep tax records and accounts, without being liable for duty debts. Airlines using this facility need to provide security to HMRC to cover any duty they have to pay.

HMRC have the power, after reasonable notice, to require that an aircraft operator or fiscal representative provide appropriate security for the payment of the duty. Additionally, after the service of notice, a non-resident aircraft operator's handling agent can be made jointly and severally liable in regard to the tax due from the aircraft operator.

Legislation: *Air Passenger Duty Regulations* 1994 (SI 1994/1738)

Other   Material: HMRC   Notice 550:   *Air   Passenger   Duty* (February 2015 edn)

9780   Administration

Aircraft operators registered for APD, or their fiscal representatives, are required to keep the duty accounts.

The *Aircraft Operators (Accounts and Records) Regulations* 1994 require that every operator keeps and retains an APD account which includes for each accounting period:

(a) the amount of duty payable;

(b) any adjustment;

(c) the adjusted duty payable;

(d) amounts paid, date and means of payment;

(e) the numbers of passengers carried at the lower rate and at the higher rate of APD;

(f) the numbers of passengers not chargeable by category for each of the exemptions; and

(g) Isle of Man passengers exempted.

Operators using a special accounting scheme (see below) are required instead of (e) above to record their calculation of the amount due, and additionally they are required to keep a copy of the scheme they are using, and any surveys necessary in establishing their calculations.

Returns and payment of the duty

Aircraft operators are required to file monthly returns with HMRC by the 22nd of the following month. The return shows the total number of passengers carried from UK airports, the number chargeable at the lower rate and the number chargeable at the higher rate. Then, by use of the appropriate rates, the duty is calculated and reported on the return.

Other indirect taxes

Payment of the duty must be made either by the 29th of the following month when payment is by direct debit/credit transfer, or otherwise by the 22nd of the following month.

Special accounting schemes

HMRC have the discretion to prepare a scheme for an aircraft operator to calculate the extent of the connected flight, return journey, and any other of the exemptions from duty and of any consequent adjustments between the rates of APD to be applied, where there are, or would be, difficulties in obtaining or recording the information otherwise required in regard to the duty. At the heart of the complexity in determining APD liabilities for passengers is the connected-flights feature in the tax.

Connected flights

Many air passengers reach their destinations after a series of two or more flights in which they may have had to get from one intermediate airport to another, as well as having had to change aircraft. If such carriage is not to be taxed differently from single non-stop carriage from origin to destination, then mechanisms to connect separate intermediate flights in a journey are required.

Two rules are set out in the regulations by which successive flights can be connected so as to provide exemption for passengers transferring between flights within certain specified time-limits, and to identify, within these same limits, each passenger's final place of destination for determining which APD rate should apply.

The 'Case A rule' (domestic connections)

The Case A rule requires that the scheduled departure time of a UK domestic flight must be within six hours of the scheduled time of arrival of the preceding flight (extended for flights arriving after 1,700 hours overnight, or for early morning arrivals before 0400 hours, to a departure time no later than 1,000 hours) for the two flights to be treated as connected.

A flight from a particular airport cannot be connected using the Case A rule to a flight destined for this same (domestic) airport.

The 'Case B rule' (international connections)

The Case B rule requires that the scheduled departure time of an international flight must be within 24 hours of the scheduled time of arrival of the preceding flight for the two flights to be treated as connected.

A flight from an airport in a particular country cannot be connected using the Case B rule to a flight destined for an airport in this same country. This latter sustains the charging of APD on passengers, mainly businessmen and women, who are flying into the UK and returning all within 24 hours.

Worked examples

The following examples show how the tax works differently for two different passengers sitting on the single class morning flight from London's Gatwick airport to Newcastle.

Example – Passenger one

The first passenger has boarded this flight after arriving at London's Heathrow airport at the scheduled arrival time of 0645 on a flight from New York. His ticket shows Newcastle as his final destination on a trip from the USA. No APD is due on his departure from Gatwick since the connected flight exemption applies. The requirements of the Case A rule are met, since they do not demand that the connection is made at the same airport.

Example – Passenger two

The second passenger is returning home to Newcastle after a trip to London. She flew down on a flight to Heathrow airport two days earlier. Even though she has a 'return' ticket, APD will be due at the lower rate of £13 on her departure from Gatwick.

Upgrades

If passengers are upgraded from one class of travel to another and:

- the upgrade has been provided at no extra cost to the passenger;

- the agreement for carriage does not include the possibility of an upgrade; and

- there has been no change in the agreement for carriage,

a reduced rate of APD applies to those passengers.

If the possibility of an upgrade at no extra cost has not been previously advertised or offered to the passenger prior to the decision to upgrade them, HMRC would not consider the agreement for carriage to have been changed.

> **Example**
>
> If passengers are upgraded because they:
>
> - buy additional services on board unconnected with premium seats, for example, book an emergency exit seat or buy a bottle of champagne;
>
> - were the earliest to book; or
>
> - are on a package holiday,
>
> then they will still be liable to a reduced rate of APD providing the conditions set out above are met.

The class of travel in a seat with a seat pitch in excess of 1.016 metres (40 inches) is regarded as standard class travel.

Legislation: *Aircraft Operators (Accounts and Records) Regulations* 1994 (SI 1994/1737); *Air Passenger Duty Regulations* 1994 (SI 1994/1738); *Air Passenger Duty (Connected Flights) Order* 1994 (SI 1994/1824)

Other Material: HMRC Notice 550: *Air Passenger Duty* (February 2015 edn)

Insurance premium tax

9800 Introduction to insurance premium tax

IPT is a tax on premiums where the risk covered is in the UK, unless the risk is on one of the excepted items.

It is a tax payable by the insurers on gross premiums, although clearly the insurer will seek to pass it on to the insured.

In common with VAT, insurers account to HMRC on a quarterly basis for all tax charged, which is either on a 'cash receipts' basis or as an alternative, a 'written premium' basis. There is no right of recovery of the tax by either the insurer or the insured.

There are two rates of IPT: the standard rate of 9.5% on 'normal' insurance such as car and home insurance and a higher rate of 20% on certain insurance such as car insurance sold with cars and insurance sold with white goods such as refrigerators.

From 1 November 2015, the standard rate of IPT was increased from 6% to 9.5%.

All premiums received by insurers using the IPT cash accounting scheme from this date will be levied at 9.5%.

For insurers using the special accounting scheme, there is a four-month concessionary period beginning on 1 November 2015 and ending on 29 February 2016, during which premiums received that relate to policies entered into before 1 November 2015 will continue to be liable to IPT at 6%.

From 1 March 2016, all premiums received by insurers are taxed at the new rate of 9.5%, regardless of when the policy was entered into.

In the March 2016 Budget, the Chancellor announced that the standard rate of IPT will increase from 9.5% to 10% on 1 October 2016.

Example

Motor premium liable to the higher rate

A motor dealer has an associated insurance agent. Insurance is promoted as an optional add-on with every vehicle sold, and customers are encouraged to take out policies with the dealer's associated company. The majority of the agent's business is made up of such sales. This motor insurance arranged by the insurance agent would be regarded as 'connected' to the sale of the motor vehicles by the associated dealer and would be liable to the higher rate.

Example

Motor premium not liable to the higher rate

A motor dealer has an associated insurance agent, but this agent operates completely independently and from a different site. No attempt is made by the motor dealer to promote the insurance arranged by this agent, and the car dealer's customers buy their insurance from a range of outlets. The insurance agent is under no obligation to ask customers where they purchased the vehicle that they are insuring, in order to identify those purchased from the associated dealer. The motor insurance arranged by the insurance agent is not liable to the higher rate of IPT even if, coincidentally, it should occasionally be sold to customers of the associated motor dealer.

Example

Examples of premiums liable to the higher rate

- Someone buys an extended warranty from an electrical retailer for a washing machine that they already own.

- Someone renews their extended warranty for a washing machine directly with the insurer and the insurer passes a commission to the store that sold the original policy.

- A customer buying a video player via mail order completes an application form which was enclosed with the equipment by the manufacturer; the form is sent back directly to the insurer who passes a commission back to the manufacturer.

> **Example**
>
> Some roadside assistance insurance (for example AA, RAC cover) is supplied to travellers who intend to take their vehicle with them. This is regarded as insurance relating to a motor vehicle risk, not to a travel risk, so it will generally not be liable to the higher rate of IPT (although higher rate would apply if supplied by a 'motor dealer').

Legislation: FA 1994, s. 48ff.; FA 2016, s. 141; *Insurance Premium Tax Regulations* 1994 (SI 1994/1774)

Other Material: HMRC Reference: Notice IPT 1: *Insurance Premium Tax* (October 2016 edn)

9810 The scope of the tax

The essential point of the IPT legislation is that all insurance contracts which cover UK risks are taxable, except those falling within certain specified exemptions.

These exemptions are within FA 1994, Sch. 7A and include:

- reinsurance;

- the motorbility scheme;

- commercial ships and aircraft; and

- risks outside the UK.

Thus, if a business is receiving insurance premiums in relation to taxable insurance contracts, then that business is engaged in a taxable business for IPT purposes.

IPT is therefore due on premiums received under taxable insurance contracts. IPT does not apply to contracts which are entered into by insurers which are not contracts of insurance. In this regard, some contracts are treated as insurance business for regulatory purposes but these are outside the scope of IPT. These include contracts for fidelity, performance, administration, bail or customs' bonds.

The IPT definition of 'premium' includes payments received by, or on behalf of, an insurer for a right to require the insurer to provide cover under a taxable contract of insurance.

Legislation: FA 1994, Sch. 7A

Other Material: Public Notice IPT1 (February 2016 edn)

9820   Apportionment

Finance Act 1994, s. 70(1) says that all insurance contracts are prima facie taxable, unless they are specifically exempt under Sch. 7A.

If a contract contains both taxable and exempt portions, then the insurer is required to apportion that contract on a just and reasonable basis.

This is an important issue, especially as FA 1997 introduced 'higher rate' as well as 'standard rate' levels of IPT.

If the insurance cover is split into separate policies to avoid the need to apportion, each separate policy must be valued on an open market value basis and must ignore the inter-related nature of the two policies.

Where more than one insurer is involved in providing cover under a co-insurance arrangement, then it is the lead insurer who will normally decide on the apportionment and, having done so, must retain records on how the apportionment was done, for inspection by Customs.

Legislation: FA 1994, s. 69 and Sch. 7A

9830   Registration

Liability to register

A person who receives, as insurer, premiums (and in some limited cases this can include fees) in the course of a taxable business and is not already registered for IPT, is liable to be registered. There is no minimum registration threshold as there is for VAT (FA 1994 s. 53(1)).

Additionally, anyone forming the intention of receiving premiums in the course of a taxable business must register such intention with HMRC (s. 53(2)).

Where a person is liable to be registered by virtue of s. 53(1) above, the Commissioners can register them with effect from the time when they begin to receive premiums in the course of the business concerned.

A person who is under an obligation to notify HMRC is required to do so in writing within 30 days.

Taxable intermediaries

Finance Act 1997 introduced some anti-avoidance measures for IPT in areas where insurance was provided with goods and services subject to VAT. This was to prevent 'value shifting' from goods or services with a (then) 17.5% rate of VAT to insurance which was exempt for VAT purposes and had only a (then) 2.5% rate of IPT thereon.

This is discussed in detail below (see 9850) but for the purposes of this section, FA 1997 introduced the concept of a 'taxable intermediary' (see 9860). From Royal Assent of FA 1997 (19 March 1997), anyone falling within this concept is required to register and account for IPT on the charging of an insurance fee with certain goods and services set out in FA 1994, Sch. 6A.

Thus a person who is a taxable intermediary and is not registered for IPT is liable to be registered (FA 1994, s. 53AA(1)).

A person who becomes liable to be registered under FA 1994, s. 53AA(1) above, will be registered from the time he begins to charge taxable intermediary's fees in the course of the business concerned.

Failure to notify liability to register

A person who forms the intention of either receiving premiums as an insurer or charging taxable intermediary's fees and fails to inform HMRC, may be liable to a penalty. For a liability arising before 1 April 2010, this was 5% of the relevant tax (subject to a minimum penalty of £250). For a liability arising on or after 1 April 2010, this is between 30% and 100% of the potential lost revenue, depending on the circumstances.

This is subject to a defence of a reasonable excuse for the failure to notify.

If a person is convicted of an offence or is charged with a penalty in respect of dishonesty, a penalty under Sch. 7, para. 14 will not arise.

Legislation: FA 1994, s. 53(1), (2), 53AA(1), Sch. 6A, Sch. 7, para. 14, FA 2010 (now superseded by Sch. 41, FA 2010)

9840   Method of accounting

Accounting periods

Finance Act 1994 provides that a registrable person must account for IPT by reference to accounting periods determined under the regulations.

A normal accounting period is three months, as it is for VAT, although the regulations provide for non-standard accounting periods if that is helpful to the registrable person.

At the end of each accounting period, the registrable person completes an IPT return and returns it to HMRC by the due date, which is the last day of the next month following the end of the accounting period.

Tax points

Like VAT, the tax point is the date which triggers the liability to IPT and determines the accounting period in respect of which the tax must be paid. The tax point will depend on which accounting method is used.

Accounting methods

There are two methods of accounting for IPT, and the registrable person may choose which method he wishes to adopt.

They are:

(1)   The 'cash receipt' method; and

(2)   The optional special 'written premium' basis.

The 'cash receipt' method

Like cash accounting for VAT, this is based on the receipt of cash. A tax point is triggered when taxable premiums or insurance based fees by taxable intermediaries are received, or received on their behalf.

The 'written premium' basis

Under this accounting method, the tax point is the date that an entry is made in the accounts showing the premium or fee due (this is the written premium date). A registrable person must use this method for at least 12 months.

Under the written premium scheme, there is a choice of tax points and a registrable person may choose which best suits him.

(1)   The registrable person may account for IPT on the date on which the premium is due to him. For example, an entry in the registrable person's books on 18 November showing a premium due on 31 October will give rise to a tax point on 31 October.

(2)   The registrable person may, as an alternative, account for IPT by using the date he enters the premium in his books.

So using the example above, the entry on 18 November will trigger a tax point on 18 November.

Whichever method is adopted, there are anti-avoidance rules for preventing unnecessary delay in bringing the tax to account.

Anti-avoidance

HMRC normally expect to see a premium written within 90 days of the tax point that would apply under the cash receipt method. HMRC will apply a number of tests and would expect to see a premium written in the same accounting period on the earliest of:

(1) 14 days of notification of receipt of premium by the broker or other intermediary;

(2) 14 days of notification by the broker or other intermediary of commencement of cover;

(3) 14 days of receipt of the premium by the insurer;

(4) 30 days of commencement of cover.

Legislation: FA 1994, s. 54; *Insurance Premium Tax Regulations* 1994 (SI 1994/1774), reg. 2, 12, 23, 26

Other Material: Public Notice IPT 1: *Insurance Premium Tax* (October 2016 edn)

9850 The selective higher rate of IPT

Finance Act 1997 introduced a selective higher rate of IPT to attack VAT planning schemes which indulged in 'value shifting' from goods and services subject to the standard rate of VAT to associated insurance which is exempt for VAT purposes.

Thus, the sales price of the standard rated VAT goods and services was artificially lowered, and the price of the exempt insurance element was artificially raised, leading to a 'leakage' of VAT revenue for the Treasury.

Accordingly, FA 1994 now provides that a premium received under a taxable insurance contract by an insurer is liable to tax at the higher rate if it falls within one or more of the paragraphs in FA 1994, Pt. II of Sch. 6A.

These are essentially:

- extended warranties insurance sold with cars and motorbikes (unless it's given free to the insured person);

- extended warranty insurance sold with household goods (unless it's given free to the insured person); and

- travel insurance.

The higher rate of IPT is 20% from January 2011.

Legislation: FA 1994, Sch. 6A

9860 Taxable intermediaries

Having introduced the selective higher rate, discussed in 9850, HMRC then deemed it necessary to plan for avoidance and introduced advance anti-avoidance measures in FA 1997.

These were designed to beat planning schemes by which the value of the insurance itself is artificially lowered (thus lowering the exposure higher rate IPT) and instead charge a 'fee' to arrange the insurance which avoids IPT. These fees are liable to IPT at the higher rate when they are charged in connection with a higher rate insurance contract.

9870 Administration

Record keeping

As with VAT, there is a general duty on registrable persons to keep records. Regulation 16 of the IPT Regulations requires every registrable person to keep the following records:

(1) his business and accounting records;

(2) policy documents cover notes, endorsements and similar documents and copies of such documents that are issued by him;

(3) copies of all invoices, renewal notices and similar documents issued by him;

(4) all credit or debit notes or other documents received by him which show an increase or decrease in the amount of any premium and copies of such documents that are issued by him; and

(5) such other records as the commissioners may specify in a notice published by them and not withdrawn by them.

Every registrable person must keep the above records for six years.

Records may be kept in hard copy, microfilm or microfiche, providing that copies can be easily produced and there are adequate facilities for HMRC to view them when required.

Records may also be kept on magnetic tape or disc, providing they can readily be accessed and understood by HMRC. The registrable persons should obtain agreement before starting to use any method of information storage other than hard copy.

Legislation: FA 1994, Sch. 7, para. 1; *Insurance Premium Tax Regulations* 1994 (SI 1994/1774) reg. 16

Other Material: HMRC Notice IPT 1: *Insurance Premium Tax* (October 2016 edn)

9880   Tax representatives

Appointing a tax representative

If an insurer, or a taxable intermediary, has no fixed establishment in the UK, but nevertheless covers risks (or intends to cover risks) sited in the UK, then that person is still liable to account for IPT.

Until FA 2008, *Finance Act* 1994, s. 57 provided that such a person must appoint a tax representative in the UK and request HMRC approval of the same. The representative could be a company or an individual. From 2008, the overseas insurer may deal directly with HMRC.

Rights and duties of a tax representative

Finance Act 1994, s. 58 set out the rights and duties of a tax representative.

The representative was entitled to act on the insurers' or taxable intermediary's behalf for the purpose of IPT.

The representative secured the insurer's or taxable intermediary's compliance with the IPT legislation and was jointly and severally liable.

Finance Act 2008 repealed these provisions, so now an overseas insurer will not have to have a tax representative in the UK and if they do, the representative will not be jointly and severally liable for any debt.

Legislation: *Insurance Companies Act* 1982, s. 10; FA 1994; FA 2008; *Insurance Premium Tax Regulations* 1994 (SI 1994/1774), reg. 34, 35

Other Material: HMRC Notice IPT1 (October 2016 edn)

9890   Penalties

The IPT legislation provides for two avenues to punish wrongdoing in IPT, criminal proceedings and civil penalties. By far the majority of penalties will be civil penalties. These are part of the cross-tax penalty regime that was enacted in FA 2007, FA 2008 and FA 2009.

9900   Effects of IPT: practical situations

Arrangements for brokers and agents

The main issues arising in relation to brokers and agents regarding IPT are:

- how to deal with policies sold through an intermediary where the insurer does not know the final selling price of that policy;

- whether amounts received by the intermediary as remuneration are part of the chargeable amount upon which insurers must account for IPT; and

- whether amounts received by intermediaries as remuneration are part of the chargeable amount upon which the intermediary must account for IPT at the higher rate.

Fees and commissions

Whether or not amounts received by a broker or intermediary for arranging taxable insurance contracts are included in the sum upon which the insurer accounts for IPT, depends upon the contract under which payment is received and the rate at which IPT applies to the contract of insurance.

Net premiums for contracts liable to IPT at the standard rate

Where an intermediary makes any additional charge in relation to an insurance contract that is taxable at the normal rate of IPT and this is done under a separate contract to the contract of insurance, these charges are not liable to IPT and should not be included in the intermediary's notification of the premium to the insurer for the purposes of IPT.

The main principle is that IPT is chargeable on the premium, which is defined as any payment under the insurance contract between the insurer(s) and the insured(s). The amount on which the insurer accounts for IPT includes commission paid to or retained by the broker, if the commission is part of the payment due to the insurer under the contract of insurance. The following examples assume that any commission paid to or retained by the broker is due to the insurer under the contract of insurance and also that the contract is taxable at the standard rather than the higher rate of IPT:

- The broker retains all commission due to him from the insurer and also charges the insured a fee, under a separate contract to the contract of insurance. The existence of both the fee contract and fee is disclosed in writing to the insured. The insurer accounts for IPT on the gross premium, inclusive of commission. The fee (because it is charged under a different contract) is not liable to IPT.

- The broker pays over to the insured a share of the broker's commission (thus indirectly reducing the cost of the insurance for the insured party). IPT remains due on the gross premium, which includes the entire amount of the commission.

- The broker pays over to the insured all of the commission due to the broker, thus heavily discounting the insurance. IPT is due on the gross premium, which includes the entire amount of commission.

Other indirect taxes

- The broker pays over to the insured all of the commission due to the broker, and charges the insured a smaller fee under a separate contract the existence of both contract and fee being disclosed in writing to the insured. IPT is due on the gross premium, which includes the entire amount of the commission. The fee is not liable to IPT.

The above arrangements reflect the underlying contracts and are not, in any way, affected by the name given to any charges made (for example, 'fee', 'commission', and 'discount').

Net premium for contracts liable to IPT at the higher rate

Where a taxable intermediary makes any additional charge in relation to an insurance contract that is liable to IPT at the higher rate, this additional charge forms part of the premium for IPT purposes. This is still the case even if this additional charge is not due under the contract of insurance. The taxable intermediary must account for the IPT based on this separate chargeable amount, which is separate to the chargeable amount on which the insurer must account for IPT.

Estimated premiums

If a taxable insurance contract is sold through a broker or intermediary and the final selling price of the insurance is unknown, the gross premium may be estimated. Estimation should be based on a representative sample of the final selling prices charged by the intermediary.

Arrangements for Lloyd's

Lloyd's is a very old and established insurance market and it has its own special working practices.

Registration

The IPT Regulations allow that where taxable business is carried out by underwriting members of Lloyd's, the syndicate rather than the individual members may be registered for IPT.

Any change in syndicate members will not affect the registration.

Responsibility for IPT

The regulations provide that compliance for IPT is the joint and several responsibility of both the underwriting members and the managing agent.

Lloyd's acting as representative

Where a syndicate which is registered for IPT has elected to account for IPT under the special accounting scheme (the written premium scheme), then the syndicate may make an election in writing that Lloyd's shall act as its representative in accounting for IPT.

In these circumstances, Lloyd's is also jointly and severally liable for the IPT with the syndicate and the managing agent.

Groups of companies

The IPT legislation provides for companies which satisfy the 'control' requirements to be treated as a group for IPT purposes.

The legislation is virtually a mirror of the VAT group legislation, and provides that the group of companies may make an application to be treated as a group for IPT purposes.

The group may only consist of companies, and each member must have an established place of business in the UK or be resident in the UK.

Two or more companies are eligible to be a group if one of them controls the other, or one person or partnership controls them both. Control means effectively 51% of the votes.

A group is treated as being in existence from the beginning of an agreed IPT accounting period. One group member is treated as being the representative member.

HMRC may not refuse an application unless it appears necessary for the protection of the revenue.

The representative member is the group member whose name is on the IPT return.

In law, all the business of the group is treated as being carried out by the representative member, which is treated as either the insurer or a taxable intermediary. All members of the group are jointly and severally liable for tax due from the representative member. However, unlike in the case of VAT grouping, supplies of insurance between members of an IPT group are subject to IPT.

Warranties and extended warranties

A warranty is commonly given by a manufacturer or vendor of goods. The warranty is an undertaking that if the goods are faulty the provider of the goods will replace them without charge.

This type of warranty is not insurance and is not therefore subject to IPT.

If, however, the supplier takes out insurance cover against this replacement, the related premium is taxable but not at the higher rate.

If the warranty is an extended warranty (often called mechanical breakdown insurance (MBI)), and, in return for a premium, the insurer will replace the goods in the event of breakdown that premium is subject to IPT and may be caught by the selective higher rate rules.

Legislation: FA 1994, s. 63, 64; *Insurance Premium Tax Regulations* 1994 (SI 1994/1774), reg. 8 and 9(3)

Landfill tax

9950   Introduction to landfill tax

Landfill tax is designed as a tax on waste disposal at landfill sites, in part, at least, as an incentive to reduce waste and to encourage alternative methods of dealing with waste such as recycling it. Thus in part it was billed, on introduction, as an environmentally friendly tax that would help protect the environment.

Landfill tax is charged on disposal of waste made at landfill sites and the time at which the waste is landfilled is the basic tax point for the tax.

The tax is chargeable by weight and there are two rates:

	From 1 April 2016	From 1 April 2017	From 1 April 2018
Standard rate per tonne	£84.40	£86.10	£88.95
Lower rate per tonne	£2.65	£2.70	£2.80

The tax falls on the landfill site operator who becomes liable to pay the tax, although where possible the operator will clearly seek to pass the tax on to people using the landfill site.

The lower rate of landfill tax is on 'qualifying material' within the *Qualifying Material Order* 2011. The list is selected on various criteria including greenhouse gas emission and low polluting potential.

HMRC have published guidance on the application of the lower rate of landfill tax. Following recent consultation with representatives of the waste management industry and other stakeholders, this advice clarifies matters relating to HMRC Briefs 15/12 and 18/12.

Where a disposal to landfill contains both active and inactive materials, tax is due on the whole load at the standard rate. However, as long as it does not lead to any potential for pollution, you may ignore the presence of an incidental amount of active waste in a mainly inactive load, and treat the whole load as taxable at the lower rate.

Example

HMRC would accept the following as qualifying for the lower rate:

- a load of bricks, stone and concrete from the demolition of a building that has small pieces of wood in it and small quantities of plaster attached to bricks as it would have not been feasible for a contractor to separate them;

- a load of soil that contains small quantities of grass;

- inactive waste such as mineral dust packaged in polythene bags for disposal; and

- a load of soil and stone from street works containing tarmac would qualify but a load of tarmac containing soil and stone would not.

Previously, waste from cleaning up contaminated land disposed of by landfill was exempt from landfill tax. However, this exemption is being phased out and applications for landfill tax exemption certificates will not be accepted by HMRC on or after 1 December 2008. Anyone in possession of a valid exemption certificate will have until 31 March 2012 to dispose of their waste if they wish to benefit from the exemption. All certificates issued under the scheme will cease to be valid on or after 1 April 2012 and disposals to landfill of waste from cleaning up contaminated land made on or after that date will be liable to landfill tax at the appropriate rate.

Liability is extended to landfill tax operators who are not the holders of the waste management licence for their sites. Such an operator will become liable with the licence holder for any landfill tax incurred on waste disposals at the site.

HMRC guidance on landfill tax is contained in public notice LFT 1 (December 2015 edn).

Legislation: FA 1996, s. 39–71, Sch. 5; FA 2010; *Landfill Tax (Material From Contaminated Land) (Phasing Out of Exemption) Order* 2008 (SI 2008/2669); *Landfill Tax Regulations* 1996 (SI 1996/1527); *Landfill Tax (Qualifying Material) Order* 2011 (SI 2011/1017); *Landfill Tax (Contaminated Land) Order* 1996 (SI 1996/1529)

Other Material: HMRC Reference: Notice LFT1 (May 2012 edn); HMRC Brief 15/12 and 18/12. Landfill tax – an update on the draft guidance (September 2013).

9960   Scope of the tax

Landfill tax is charged on a 'taxable disposal'. A disposal is a 'taxable disposal' if:

(a)   it is a disposal of material as waste;

(b)   it is made by way of landfill;

(c)   it is made at a landfill site; and

(d)   it is made on or after 1 October 1996.

The *Landfill Tax (Prescribed Landfill Site Activities) Order* 2009 (SI 2009/1929) took effect from 1 September 2009. The Order prescribes seven uses of material on a landfill site which will be subject to landfill tax. It also provides that material is taxable if certain requirements for notification, designation of information areas, provision of information or keeping of records are not complied with.

This change in the legislation took place because of the defeat in the Court of Appeal of HMRC in the Waste Recycling Group Limited case in 2008 which rules that material received and used on a landfill site is not taxable. HMRC changed the law to ensure that material used (for example in building cells to contain waste) is now taxable.

There are a number of exemptions from landfill tax. These are:

- material removed from dredging inland waterways and harbours;

- mining and quarrying waste;

- material from the reclamation of land (up to 2012);

- filling of quarries; and

- waste from visiting forces.

These exemptions are within FA 1994 and are explained in some detail in the public notice, LFT1.

Legislation: FA 1996, s. 40(1), s. 65A

Other Material: Public Notice LFT1 (May 2012 edn)

9970   Registration

A person who carries out taxable activities and is not registered for LFT is liable to be registered.

Additionally, a person who at any time forms the intention of carrying out taxable activities and is not registered must notify the commissioners of his intention.

Where a person ceases to have the intention of carrying out taxable activities he is required to notify the commissioners of that fact.

Taxable activities are the making of taxable disposals in respect of which he is liable to pay tax. Taxable disposals are defined in FA 1996, s. 40 (see 9960).

A person liable to be registered shall notify the commissioners within 30 days of either forming, or continuing to have, the intention of carrying out taxable activities. Notification shall be on the form(s) specified in the *Landfill Tax Regulations* 1996 (SI 1996/1527), reg. 4.

Changes in registration particulars shall be notified to the commissioners within 30 days of the change. This is designed to help HMRC keep its records up to date.

Legislation: FA 1996, s. 47 and 69; *Landfill Tax Regulations* 1996 (SI 1996/1527), reg. 4 and 5

9980   Accounting for the tax

The landfill tax return

Once registered, a registrable person is required to submit a landfill tax return (form LT 100). This will normally be for three months and it is due by the last day of the month following the end of the accounting period.

Tax point

The tax point is the time at which the liability to account for the tax falls. There are two tax points:

(1)   the disposal tax point – this is the date on which the waste was disposed of to landfill; and

(2)   the invoice date tax point.

The legislation concerning landfill tax provides that if a landfill operator wishes, he can use as an alternative to the disposal tax point, the date on which a landfill tax invoice is issued. This must normally be within 14 days of the disposal tax point although a longer period (to allow for monthly invoicing) may be negotiated with HMRC.

If a landfill site operator chooses the invoice date tax point, then he must issue a landfill invoice, which must contain the details laid out in *Landfill Tax Regulations* 1996 (SI 1996/1527), reg. 37.

Other indirect taxes

These include:

- an identifying number;
- invoice date;
- date of disposal;
- name, address and landfill tax registration number of the operator;
- weight and description of waste disposed of;
- the rate of tax applied to each disposal; and
- the total amount payable on the invoice.

It is not necessary to show the amount of landfill tax on the disposal but if it is shown, then the invoice must also contain a statement that the amount is not recoverable as VAT input tax.

If the operator wishes, he may issue a combined VAT and LFT tax invoice. The VAT must be applied to the full invoiced amount including LFT.

It is important to note that a tax point is NOT created (as it is in VAT) by the earlier issue of an invoice or the receipt of payment. A tax point can never arise before the date of disposal.

Correction of errors

In common with VAT and insurance premium tax, LFT contains a mechanism by which errors below a de minimis threshold may be corrected on the next LFT return. This threshold is £10,000, but this can increase to £50,000 in some circumstances. Errors above that amount are treated on a 'voluntary disclosure' basis.

Records

The LFT legislation requires a registrable person to keep records to provide an audit trail for Customs to follow. The records which a landfill operator must keep are:

(1) the landfill tax account;

(2) invoices;

(3) credit and debit notes;

(4) bad debt relief account; and

(5) other records such as business and accounting records including analyses of waste.

These records must normally be kept for six years. However, bad debt records only need to be kept for five years.

Legislation: *Landfill Tax Regulations* 1996 (SI 1996/1527), reg. 16, 37; *Landfill Tax (Amendment) Regulations* 2009 (SI 2009/1930)

9990   Credit

There are conditions under which a landfill site operator has accounted for LFT and then because of a change in circumstances needs to claim credit in respect of the LFT already paid. There are three circumstances in which this can happen:

(1) permanent removal;

(2) bad debt relief; and

(3) environmental bodies credit scheme.

The maximum credit that landfill site operators may claim against their annual landfill tax liability, for contributions made to bodies with objects concerned with the environment, is 6.2% of his relevant tax liability (from 1 April 2011).

Legislation: *Landfill Tax Regulations* 1996 (SI 1996/1527)

Cases: *Waste Recycling Group Ltd v R & C Commrs* [2008] EWCA Civ 849; [2008] BTC 8,076

10000   Assessments, penalties and interest

Power to assess

The LFT legislation provides that where a person has failed to make LFT returns, or failed to keep documents necessary to verify returns, or failed to afford facilities necessary to verify returns, or it appears to the commissioners that its submitted returns are incorrect or incomplete, then they may assess the amount of tax due from him to the best of their judgment and notify him accordingly.

There are two types of assessment arising from the legislation:

(1) an assessment in respect of the tax itself; and

(2) an assessment in respect of interest and penalties.

An assessment shall not be made more than two years after the end of the relevant accounting period, or one year after 'evidence of facts', sufficient in the commissioner's opinion to justify the making of the assessment, comes to their knowledge. In any event is subject to an overall time-limit of four years from 1 April 2010 (for careless behaviour) and 20 years for deliberate behaviour.

Interest

Interest on under-declared tax

Where an assessment has been raised for under-declared tax, the commissioners may also assess for interest which runs from the due date (one month after the end of an accounting period) to the day before 'the relevant day'.

The relevant day is the earlier of:

(a) the day on which the assessment is notified to the person; or

(b) the day on which the additional amount is paid.

The rate of interest is set by the *Air Passenger Duty and Other Indirect Taxes (Interest Rate) Regulations* 1998 (SI 1998/1461).

Interest on unpaid tax

The LFT legislation also provides for interest to run on unpaid tax on LFT returns. This interest runs from the due date until the date before that on which the tax is paid.

The interest charge is subject to mitigation by either the commissioners or, on appeal by a tribunal. A 'reasonable excuse' is a factor which may well influence the amount of mitigation.

Interest payable by the commissioners

Where, due to an error on the part of the commissioners, LFT is overpaid by a registrable person, interest will lie in favour of the 'taxpayer'.

Penalties

The LFT legislation provides (in common with the VAT and IPT legislation) two ways of punishing 'wrongdoing':

(1) criminal penalties; or

(2) civil penalties.

Criminal penalties

If a person is found guilty of an offence, he will be subject to the criminal penalties laid out in FA 1996, Sch. 5, Pt. IV.

These are:

(a) on summary conviction (in a magistrates' court) a fine of £5,000 or of three times the amount of tax, whichever is the greater and/or up to six months in prison; and

(b) on conviction on indictment, an unlimited fine and/or up to seven years in prison.

Criminal penalties are only likely to be sought in extreme cases and/or for habitual offenders.

Civil penalties

Most offences will be dealt with under the civil procedures.

The main civil penalties are as follows.

(a) *Evasion*

The civil evasion penalty regime has been repealed and landfill tax is now under the general penalties for errors regime introduced in April 2009 and extended to environmental taxes in 2010.

(b) *Registration*

A person who fails to notify the commissioners of his liability to register is liable to a penalty of 5% of the tax (subject to a £250 minimum).

(c) *Breach of regulations*

Where the legislation requires compliance and that person fails to comply (such as a duty to produce records) that person will be liable to a fine of £250.

In the case of documents, further non-compliance can result in a further fine of £20 per day for each day of non-compliance.

Mitigation and reasonable excuse

Where a person is liable to a civil penalty, the commissioners, or on appeal a tribunal, can reduce the penalty as they think fit (including reducing it to nil).

Where a person satisfies the commissioners, or on an appeal a tribunal, that a 'reasonable excuse' exists, that may be taken into account in determining the level of mitigation. It is important to note that there is one major difference in this area between LFT and VAT. In VAT, all of the civil penalties are subject to a 'reasonable excuse' which is an all or nothing defence but only certain penalties are subject to mitigation. In the LFT legislation, the draftsman has taken a different approach which is outlined above.

Legislation: FA 1996, s. 50 and Sch. 5, para. 33, Pt. V, VI, Sch. 40; FA 2008

Other Material: Public Notice LFT 1 (October 2012 edn)

10010 Review and appeals

A review and appeal procedure for LFT is available to taxpayers who are in dispute with HMRC.

LFT is now subject to the revised review and appeal procedures from 1 April 2009.

If HMRC issue a 'decision' (often an assessment), HMRC are bound to tell the taxpayer that he has the following choice:

- have the decision reviewed; or
- appeal the decision.

If the taxpayer accepts the offer of a review within 30 days, then HMRC will be bound to review it and inform the taxpayer within 45 days of the conclusions of the review.

The review will either:

- uphold;
- vary; or
- cancel the decision.

After the conclusions of the review have been notified to the taxpayer, the taxpayer will still have 30 days to appeal.

If the taxpayer does not wish to have the decision reviewed, then he may go straight to an appeal within 30 days, providing the matter is an appealable matter under FA 1996, s. 54 (most matters are appealable).

Legislation: FA 1996, s. 54–57

Climate change levy

10020 Climate change levy: supplies

As part of its liabilities toward the Kyoto agreement and the Copenhagen Climate Summit, climate change levy (CCL) is levied on supplies of electricity, gas and coal to industry, commerce, agriculture and the public sector for their business use of light, heat and power. In other words, the CCL is levied on supplies of 'taxable commodities' for business use. The CCL is not levied on supplies of taxable commodities for non-business use, such as domestic use or use by a charity to the extent it is for non-business purposes.

The carbon price support (CPS) mechanism for addressing carbon pricing has been enacted through the CCL legislation from 1 April 2013. This introduces a new imposition of CCL on supplies of fossil fuels to electricity generators. This means that CCL will now be in the supply chain at the beginning rather than just as a one-stage levy when the supplies are made to the final customer.

The CPS mechanism is designed to provide an incentive to invest in low-carbon power generation by providing greater support and certainty to the carbon price in the UK's electricity generation sector.

Supplies of coal, gas and liquefied petroleum gas (LPG) used in most forms of electricity generation would become liable to newly created Carbon Price Support (CPS rates of climate change levy (CCL), which would be different from the main CCL rates levied on consumers' use of these commodities (and electricity). The amount of fuel duty reclaimable on oil used in electricity generation would be adjusted to establish new CPS rates of fuel duty.

Supplies by utilities and producers of taxable commodities for their own use and not for production are deemed to be self-supplies for CCL purposes. However, in general, no CCL is levied on taxable supplies made by a utility or producer of taxable commodities to another utility or other such producer; the aim is to prevent CCL being charged twice on the same commodity.

Generally, the CCL will be added to the consumer's energy costs by inclusion on the invoice issued by the supplier. Due to the exemption for non-business use, residential consumers should not see the CCL on their energy bills.

Climate change levy is levied on taxable supplies of taxable commodities. These are supplies of taxable commodities that arc not *excluded*, *exempt* or *outside the scope* of CCL.

Taxable commodities comprise:

- electricity;
- gas that is in a gaseous state and is of a kind normally supplied by a gas utility;
- petroleum gas, or other gaseous hydrocarbon, in a liquid state; coal and lignite; and
- coke, semi-coke, of coal or lignite; petroleum coke.

Other indirect taxes

Taxable commodities do not include hydrocarbon oils, steam, heat, road fuel gases and any waste containing taxable commodities.

An *excluded* supply is a supply for domestic use, or for non-business use by a charity. Where a supply is for domestic use and business use, or for business and non-business use by a charity, then an apportionment of the mixed supply is required. If the percentage attributable to non-business use is 60% or more then the whole of the mixed supply shall be deemed to be an excluded supply; accordingly CCL is not then charged on any part of the mixed supply.

Certain small supplies are deemed to be always for domestic use. For example:

- supplies of coal or coke not exceeding one tonne when held out for sale as domestic fuel;

- supplies of gas or petroleum gas, in a gaseous state, through pipelines to the buildings concerned at a rate not exceeding 4,397kWh per month;

- supplies of liquid petroleum gas in cylinders weighing less than 50kg each, either made through the delivery of 20 or less cylinders, or, where in excess of this number, the liquid petroleum gas is not intended for resale;

- supplies of liquid petroleum gas made other than by delivering cylinders where the recipient does not have the capacity to store more than two tonnes;

- metered supplies of electricity where the supply to the building was not exceeding the rate of 1,000kWh per month in total; and

- unmetered supplies of electricity where the supply to the building was not exceeding the rate of 1,000kWh per month in total.

The following are *exempt* supplies:

(a) supplies of taxable commodities, other than electricity and gas in a gaseous state, for burning outside of the UK (i.e. mainly LPG and solid fuels);

(b) supplies of gas by a gas utility for burning in the province of Northern Ireland;

(c) supplies of taxable commodities for burning (or consuming in the case of electricity) to propel:

(i) a train for transporting passengers or freight; or

(ii) other vehicles for transporting passengers,

or to provide light and heat in:

    (i)   a train and railway carriages for transporting passengers and freight;

    (ii)   other vehicles for transporting passengers; or

    (iii)   a ship for transporting freight when part of its journey entails going outside of the UK territorial waters;

(d)   supplies to produce taxable commodities other than electricity;

(e)   certain supplies, other than self-supplies, to produce electricity in a generating station which is neither a fully exempt nor a partly exempt combined heat and power (CHP) station;

(f)   supplies, other than self-supplies, from a partly exempt CHP;

(g)   self-supplies by electricity producers;

(h)   supplies not used as fuel;

(i)   electricity generated from renewable sources (RSE); and

(j)   electricity generated from good quality combined heat and power.

From 1 August 2015, electricity generated from renewable sources is no longer eligible for the CCL exemption for RSE when supplied under a renewable source contract.

Electricity utilities that have accumulated RSE and renewable LECs relating to RSE that was generated before 1 August 2015 may continue to allocate these to renewable source contracts for a transitional period commencing on 1 August 2015. Such supplies can be exempted from CCL.

The Government has said that it is costly to support RSE and that there are better ways of doing it, especially as some of the exemption applies RSE from other countries.

Legislation: FA 2000, Pt. II

Other Material: Public Notice CCL1 (April 2016 edn); Public Notice CCL1/2: Combined heat and power schemes (June 2014 edn); Public Notice CCL1/3 (November 2015 edn); CCL1/4: Electricity from renewable sources (October 2015); HMRC have also published PN CCL1/6 – a Guide to the Carbon Price Floor (April 2015)

10025   Rates of CCL

CCL – main rates	From 1 April 2016	From 1 April 2017	From 1 April 2018
Electricity (£ per kWh)	0.00559	0.00568	0.00583
Natural gas (£ per kWh)	0.00195	0.00198	0.00203
LPG (£ per kg)	0.01251	0.01272	0.01304
Any other taxable commodity	0.01526	0.01551	0.01591

The carbon price support (CPS) rates of CCL which apply to taxable commodities (other than electricity) used in the generation of electricity, following the introduction of the carbon price floor on 1 April 2013. Details about the carbon price floor and the carbon price support rates of CCL are set out in Notice CCL1/6 *A guide to the carbon price floor*.

The CPS rates are designed to reflect a carbon price equivalent of £18.08 per tonne from 1 April 2015.

A reduced rate levy will apply in circumstances where the taxable commodities are used efficiently and in an environment-friendly way, at 35% of the above full rates from 1 April 2011. For the reduced rate to apply, a Climate Change Agreement (CCA) with the Secretary of State for Energy and Climate Change needs to be in place.

These agreements, which are negotiated at sector level, will set targets for energy efficiency and milestone targets will be set every two years.

Legislation: FA 2000, Sch. 6, para. 42; FA 2008; *Climate Change Levy (General) Regulations* 2001 (SI 2001/838); FA 2010

Other Material: Public Notice CCL 1 (April 2016 edn); CCL1/1 (registration) Public Notice CCL1/3 (reliefs) (November 2015 edn)

Aggregates levy

10040   Aggregates levy: general

Aggregates levy (AL) was introduced to combat the environmental damage done by quarrying operations, many of which take place in the most beautiful parts of the UK. The aggregates levy is administered by HMRC.

The levy is on the commercial exploitation of aggregates and is at a flat rate of £2 per tonne for both 2015 and 2016.

There are a number of exemptions.

The application of the levy was challenged under state aid provisions and, in August 2013, the UK was notified of the EU Commission's decision to open a formal state aid investigation into certain exemptions from the levy. The Government at the time was obliged to suspend these exemptions (in some cases partially so that the material was only taxable when used as aggregate) pending the outcome of the investigation. The suspension took effect from 1 April 2014.

In March 2015, the Commission concluded its investigation and decided that the aggregates levy as a whole and the exemptions under investigation were lawful, with the exception of part of the shale exemption.

Legislation was introduced in F(No. 2)A 2015, s. 48 to repeal FA 2014, s. 94 and make certain consequential changes in relation to shale. As a result, the following materials will once again be exempt from the levy regardless of their use:

- clay, coal, lignite and slate;

- spoil from the separation of coal, lignite and slate from other rock after extraction;

- spoil, waste or other by-products (not including the overburden) from china clay and ball clay extraction or separation;

- other industrial minerals, namely: anhydrite; ball clay; barites; china clay; feldspar; fireclay; fluorspar; fuller's earth; gems and semi-precious stones; gypsum; any metal or the ore of any metal; muscovite; perlite; potash; pumice; rock phosphates; sodium chloride; talc and vermiculite;

- spoil from the separation of the above industrial minerals from other rock after extraction;

- material that is mainly but not wholly the spoil, waste or other by-product of any industrial combustion process or the smelting or refining of metal.

The legislation will provide that shale is not an exempt material. However, shale that is extracted as by-product of the extraction of some other untaxed materials (e.g. coal) will be exempt as spoil from the separation of rocks after extraction; and shale used in ceramic processes (such a brick-making) will continue to be a relieved industrial process and therefore not subject to tax. Similarly, shale used with limestone in the production of cement will continue to be an exempt process and therefore not subject to tax.

The legislation will provide for a new exempt process for shale that is used for a purpose other than construction purposes.

Details of the Commission's decision and the implications for businesses affected were set out in HMRC Brief 6/15 issued on 27 March 2015.

A standard charge of £2.00 per tonne of taxable material currently applies to the commercial extraction or importation of taxable aggregate in the UK or its territorial waters. This rate was due to rise to £2.10 per tonne from 1 April 2012, but has been deferred. It remains at £2 per tonne for 2015 and 2016.

This will avoid putting additional pressure on the aggregates industry in Northern Ireland, following the suspension of the aggregates levy credit scheme.

In addition, FA 2015 has introduced a tax credit for aggregates imported into Northern Ireland.

There are a number of events that have to occur before a charge to aggregates levy arises. The type of aggregate and its intended usage are the main factors. It is 'commercial exploitation' which renders the aggregate liable to the levy. There are, to all intents and purposes, four limbs to the definition:

(1) if the aggregate is removed from a site;

(2) if the aggregate becomes the subject of a contract;

(3) if it is used for construction services; and

(4) if it is mixed with another substance other than water.

Aggregate for the purposes of the levy means rock, gravel or sand, and substances that are incorporated in the rock, gravel or sand or are naturally mixed with it. The definition includes rock that has not been through an industrial crushing process. However, not all of this material is taxable. All commercially exploited aggregate is taxable unless exempted. Consistent with the aim of reflecting the environmental cost of quarrying and mining, recycled aggregate is exempted from aggregates levy. Aggregate that is, or is derived from, material which has already been subjected to the levy is not taxable (thereby avoiding double taxation). Aggregate commercially exploited before the commencement date is outside the scope of the levy.

All commercially exploited aggregate is deemed to be taxable unless specifically exempted. The exemptions are conferred on the grounds of 'quality' or the primary purpose for its extraction. For example, aggregate will be exempt if it is extracted as a by-product of another venture. Such by-products may arise from excavating the foundations of any building site, dredging a watercourse or maintaining a road. There is also a 'china and ball clay exemption', whereby the waste or spoil of the processes of extracting or separating such materials is exempt (but not any aggregate contained in the overburden).

In addition to extraction being exempt under these headings, aggregate may also be exempt if:

- it has at any time been used for construction purposes – i.e. it is recycled rubble;

- it is, or it is from, aggregate which has already been subjected to the aggregates levy; or

- it was removed from the originating site before the commencement date of the aggregates levy.

The levy does not apply to other quarried or mined products such as coal, clay, shale and slate, metals and metal ores, gemstones or semi precious stones and industrial minerals.

Aggregate may also be exempt from the levy as a result of processes which are applied to it. The method of exploiting the aggregate may fall into the relevant definition of 'commercial exploitation' and the aggregate may fail to fall into an exempted type; nonetheless, a process applied to the aggregate may allow it to qualify for an exemption. In this regard, it should be noted that an intention to perform this process is insufficient. It is the process itself not the connection with a particular industry which gains the exception. So aggregate may be exempt if it is produced from the cutting of any rock to produce dimension stone ('stone with one or more flat surfaces'), or is produced by a relevant substance having been extracted or separated, or alternatively if it is from the production of lime or cement from limestone or a similar substance.

In addition, if aggregate is exploited in order to extract certain, specified substances then it is also exempt. The substances include flint, gypsum, potash, metals and ores of metals, gems and semi precious stones and the clay mentioned above. The list is clearly intended to be exhaustive as it fails to include a term such as 'and any other such substance', and variation of the list is stated to be by statutory order.

Aggregate removed from the ground along the line, or proposed line, of any railway, tramway or monorail for the purposes of improving, maintaining or constructing it, is exempt from the levy, providing the aggregate was not removed for the purpose of extracting the aggregate.

In *C & E Commrs v East Midlands Aggregates Ltd* [2004] EWHC 856 (Ch); [2004] BTC 8,107, the High Court upheld a decision of the VAT and Duties Tribunal that the removal of certain aggregate in order to lay the foundations for a lorry park and the drainage system servicing a new warehouse would be exempt from aggregates levy.

The levy is administered by a register, kept by HMRC of all those liable to account for aggregates levy. The returns and payments are to be filed periodically, and HMRC have the powers to make regulations governing factors such as the frequency of return periods.

Non-resident taxpayers (essentially importers) are mandated to appoint tax representatives for the purposes of provisions under the Act. Powers for security for the levy, recovery and interest are also available to HMRC. Credits and repayments of any overpaid levy are dealt with in essentially the same way as other indirect taxes, while the criminal and civil penalties and remedies laid down are based on existing provisions. Also akin to the landfill tax and climate change levy legislation, provision is made for aggregates levy groups, whereby members are jointly and severally liable for aggregates levy due from other group members in the same way as for VAT grouping.

The review and appeal procedure for aggregates levy is essentially the same for the other indirect taxes from 1 April 2009.

For rates of aggregates levy and associated interest rates, see Key Data.

Legislation: FA 2001, Pt. 2

Other Material: Public Notice AGL 1 (August 2015 edn)

Council tax and business rates

10050   Council tax (domestic rates)

Council tax is a property tax. It is payable in respect of residential (i.e. domestic) property. Council tax was introduced on 1 April 1993. It is a local tax insofar as the tax is collected and retained by local authorities and the rate is fixed by them. However, it is not a true local tax as local authorities have no control over the structure of the tax or the detailed rules which impose liabilities – although they do have limited discretion in some areas. Furthermore, in recent years, the Government has imposed a cap or limitation on the level of council tax imposed by some local authorities.

Local authority spending is largely financed by grants from the central government. These are, however, largely earmarked to cover the provision of specific services, in particular education and housing which, together with social services, make up the bulk of local authority expenditure. Council tax and business rates are the main source of finance for the provision of discretionary local authority services.

Legislation: *Local Government Finance Act 1992*

10060   Business rates (non-domestic rates)

Business rating is similar to a property tax. It is payable on non-domestic property (and some mixed use property). The tax payable in respect of an individual property is based on its rateable value and this is given by the Valuation Office Agency (VOA). This is, broadly speaking, its rental value on a letting from year to year, on the assumption that the tenant is responsible for all usual tenant's rates and tax and the cost of repairs and insurance and any other expenses necessary to maintain the building in a state to command that rent.

Rateable values are updated every five years. The most recent revaluation was in 2010 and some transitional arrangements were implemented in order to help small properties (those with a rateable value below £25,500 in London and £18,000 elsewhere).

Business rates are charged by using a multiplier on the rateable value. In England (outside of London), the multiplier for 2014–15 was 48.2p and in the 2015–16 was 49.3p.

The small business multiplier was 47.1p for 2014–15 and was 48p for 2015–16.

In Budget 2016, the Chancellor announced that from April 2017, small businesses that occupy property with a rateable value of £12,000 or less will pay no business rates.

Currently, this 100% relief is available if you're a business that occupies a property (e.g. a shop or office) with a value of £6,000 or less.

There will be a tapered rate of relief on properties worth up to £15,000. This means that 600,000 businesses will pay no rates.

Stamp duty

10100   Introduction to stamp duty

Stamp duties are imposed by Act of Parliament on certain documents (or technically 'instruments'). Historically, they have been very important, but the FA 2003 changes essentially reduce them to charges on instruments relating to share transfers.

The rate of stamp duty charged on instruments relating to stocks and securities is 0.5%.

Legal background

Stamp duty is in the main governed by the *Stamp Duties Management Act* 1891 (SDMA 1891) (which is mainly administrative) and the *Stamp Act* 1891 (SA 1891) (which imposes the charges). Both these Acts have been amended by subsequent Finance Acts and in particular by FA 1999 which modernised the basis of the charge and the interest and penalty regime. *Finance Act* 2003 completely overhauled the legislation and introduced Stamp Duty Land Tax (SDLT) for land transactions, with effect from 1 December 2003.

Jurisdiction

The *Stamp Act* 1891, s. 14(4) is regarded as laying down the jurisdiction rule for stamp duty. It covers documents:

- executed in the UK; or

- not executed in the UK, but relating to any property situated in or to any matter or thing done or to be done in the UK.

United Kingdom means England, Wales, Scotland and Northern Ireland. It excludes the Channel Islands and the Isle of Man.

Scope of stamp duty prior to 1 December 2003

Stamp duty is paid by paying for a stamp, and affixing the stamp to the document. It follows that stamp duty is a tax on documents, not on transactions (e.g. unlike VAT). Consequently, if a transaction can be carried out orally, or by conduct, there is no duty.

However, 'instrument', the technical word for document, is very widely defined in SA 1891, as including 'every written document'. For example, an oral contract for the sale of goods, followed by the physical transfer of the goods by delivery attracts no duty. But if the parties effected the transfer of goods by means of an instrument, the same transaction would be chargeable to duty.

Documents will attract stamp duty if they fall under the heads of charge, and may attract ad valorem or fixed amounts of duty. In addition, there are special charging rules relating to bearer instruments and to unit trusts and open-ended investment companies. There are, though, numerous exemptions and reliefs.

Stamp duty is abolished except on instruments relating to stock or marketable securities with effect from 1 December 2003. So, effectively, it is only chargeable on paper transactions of share transfers at 0.5% of the value. Most shares are traded electronically and stamp duty is not chargeable.

Legislation: SDMA 1891; SA 1891; FA 1999, Sch. 13, para. 3 ; FA 2003, s. 125

Stamp duty reserve tax

10150 Introduction to stamp duty reserve tax

Stamp duty reserve tax (SDRT) is a tax of relatively recent origin. In essence, it taxes transactions on the London Stock Exchange, that are not subject to the 0.5% stamp tax, because they are not stampable at that stage to stamp duty. SDRT is, in effect, a substitute stamp duty to capture tax on these transactions.

It was introduced by FA 1986. SDRT is allied to, but is not part of, stamp duty. It is a separate tax enforceable by assessment and not by stamping of instruments. SDRT is not concerned with instruments as such, but rather with agreements to transfer chargeable securities for a consideration in money, or money's worth.

It was introduced to cover circumstances where shares were sold but no stamp duty was payable, as there was no instrument of transfer which could be charged to stamp duty. For example, the purchase and resale of securities within a stock exchange account period, the purchase of renounceable letters of allotment or the purchase of shares registered in the name of a nominee acting for the seller and purchaser. Such cases are, of course, outside the *Stamp Act* 1891, s. 59, which charges certain contracts as if they were conveyances on sale, since it excepts '... agreement(s) for the sale of ... marketable securities...'

Legislation: SA 1891, s. 59; FA 1986, s. 86

10160 The principal charge

Chargeable transactions

The principal charge is found in FA 1986, s. 87. Subsection (1) provides that:

> 'This section applies where a person (A) agrees with another person (B) to transfer chargeable securities (whether or not to B) for consideration in money or money's worth.'

Accordingly, for a charge to SDRT to arise, there must be:

(1) an agreement between A and B;

(2) a transfer (whether to B or not);

(3) chargeable securities; and

(4) consideration in money or money's worth,

unless either stamp duty is paid or the instrument would be exempt from stamp duty.

By FA 1986, s. 91, the person liable for SDRT charged under s. 87, is the transferee (B). However, it is usually collected and paid, not by B, but by intermediaries in the securities market, called 'accountable persons'. The collection and administration of the tax is discussed in more detail below.

The rate of tax is 0.5% (FA 1986, s. 87(6)), although a special rate of 1.5% may apply where 'deposits' are involved or shares are put into a 'clearance service system' (see s. 93 and s. 96).

The principal charge gives rise to certain questions of definition which are considered below.

What constitutes an 'agreement'?

For a charge to SDRT to arise, the legislation requires (inter alia) an '... agreement between A and B'. The identity of B is important since B is liable for the tax. However, the legislation provides only that A and B must be persons. This can result in theoretical difficulties, especially where there are intermediaries.

An 'agreement' would certainly include a contract (i.e. an agreement enforceable at law). However, it is not clear whether the agreement *must* be enforceable at law. The agreement does not need to be in writing, so it may be an oral agreement. It may be constituted under UK law or the law of a country other than the UK. The charge can arise even if the agreement has not been completed. The making of the agreement can be sufficient for a charge to arise. The agreement may be conditional. If it is, the charge does not arise until the day on which the condition is satisfied or, if there is more than one condition, when the final condition is satisfied (FA 1986, s. 87(3)(a)).

What kinds of transactions represent a 'transfer'?

General

The agreement must be one to 'transfer' chargeable securities. This presupposes that the chargeable securities are in issue, and so can be assigned or transferred. Accordingly, an agreement to issue shares would not fall within the principal charge under FA 1986, s. 87 since it is not an agreement to transfer chargeable securities.

Transactions involving onward sales of chargeable securities (sub-sales)

A charge can arise in the situation where A agrees to sell to B, and B agrees to sell on to C. Normally, the transfer would be direct from A to C.

Thus, C pays stamps duty on the transfer to C. However, this only franks the transfer to C. The agreement to sell, i.e. transfer between A and B, is not franked and a SDRT charge arises. Careful analysis is needed where such a transaction is envisaged.

Definition of chargeable securities

The Stamp Office comments that in broad terms:

> 'Chargeable securities include stocks, shares and rights to stocks and shares in a UK company or in those shares of a foreign company which are kept on a register in the UK. Most categories of loan stock are not chargeable securities.'

What is meant by the term 'for consideration in money or money's worth'?

Broadly, the first question is what is the quid pro quo for the securities? The second question is whether it constitutes 'consideration in money or money's worth'. This expression is not defined by FA 1986 but it is clearly wider than its stamp duty equivalent. It has been described 'as being a way of expressing the price or consideration given for property where property is acquired in return for something other than money, such as services or other property where the price or consideration which the acquirer gives for the property has got to be turned into money before it can be expressed in terms of money' (*Secretan v Hart* (1969) 45 TC 701 at p. 705H per Buckley J).

It is important to identify the whole consideration given for the securities. This is not always easy where collateral contracts form part of the consideration. Identification of the consideration is of practical significance for B who is liable for the tax.

Once the consideration is ascertained, s. 87(7) makes provision for its valuation.

Legislation: FA 1986, s. 84, 87, 91, 93, 96, 97B, 99

Cases: *Secretan v Hart* (1969) 45 TC 701; *Eastham (HMIT) v Leigh London & Provincial Properties Ltd* (1971) 46 TC 687; *IR Commrs v Ufitec* [1977] 3 All ER 924

10170 Other charges

Stamp duty reserve tax also applies to depositary receipts and clearance services.

Legislation: FA 1986, s. 93–97

10180 Repayment of SDRT and cancellation of the charge to SDRT

The s. 87 charge to SDRT is relieved by s. 92 if an instrument is executed and duly stamped within six years, and the instrument transfers to B, or his nominee, all the chargeable securities to which the agreement relates (s. 92(1A), (1B)). The effect of s. 92 is to cancel the charge to SDRT, or if the tax has been paid, to provide for its repayment with interest if a repayment claim is made within six years of the date the charge to tax arose (see s. 87(3)).

Legislation: FA 1986, s. 87, 87(7A), 88, 92 and 92(1A), (1B)

10190 Administration

Finance Act 1986, s. 98 permits the Treasury to make regulations as to the administration, assessment, collection and recovery of SDRT. The Treasury is also given power to apply provisions of the *Taxes Management Act* 1970, with such modifications as they think fit.

HGV road user levy

10250 Introduction of HGV Road User Levy

The Government has introduced a road user levy for heavy goods vehicles, 12 tonnes or more, aimed at ensuring these vehicles make a contribution to the wear and tear of the UK road network. This levy was introduced by the *HGV Road User Levy Act* 2013 and began on 1 April 2014.

The UK law is based on the EC legislation for energy products: Dir 2003/96

UK-registered vehicles

From 1 April 2014, UK-registered vehicles will pay levy costs at the same time and in the same transaction as vehicle excise duty (VED) with payments collected by the DVLA.

VED has been reduced and, consequently, over 90% of HGVs will not see costs rise. The VED changes were announced by the Chancellor in the March 2013 Budget and have been made in FA 2014.

Non-UK registered vehicles

Vehicles registered abroad must make levy payments before entering the UK (including Northern Ireland) and can be paid by day, week, month or year and discounts are available for longer levy periods.

Online payment of the HGV road user levy for operators completing journeys on UK roads is available now and also offers a 'registered account' and a 'pay and go' purchasing option.

'Pay and go' purchasing can also be completed:

* by telephone;

* at a limited number of point of sale terminals on ferries and truck stops.

Legislation: *HGV Road User Levy Act* 2013

Vehicle excise duty

10260   Introduction to vehicle excise duty (VED)

At the moment, VED is based on the CO_2 emissions of the car.

The current VED structure, based on CO_2 bands, was introduced in 2001 when average UK new car emissions were 178g CO_2/km. The Band A threshold of 100g CO_2/km below which cars pay no VED was introduced in 2003 when average new car emissions were 173g CO_2/km.

Since then, to meet EU emissions targets, average new car emissions have fallen to 125g CO_2/km. This means that an increasingly large number of ordinary cars now fall into the zero- or lower-rated VED bands.

In the July 2015 Budget, the Government announced that a new VED banding system for cars registered on or after 1 April 2017 will be introduced, which is designed to reward only the cleanest cars.

First year rates (FYRs) of VED will vary according to the CO_2 emissions of the vehicle. A flat standard rate (SR) of £140 will apply in all subsequent years, except for zero-emission cars for which the SR will be £0.

Cars with a list price above £40,000 will attract a supplement of £310 on their SR for the first five years in which a SR is paid.

All cars first registered before 1 April 2017 will remain in the current VED system, which will not change.

Dealing with HMRC

KEY POINTS

- The information and inspection powers in *Finance Act* 2008 enable HMRC to check a person's tax position at any time without opening an enquiry. Practitioners need a working knowledge of the provisions in order to advise clients how to respond (see 11900ff.).

- Under the former penalty regime, the practitioner was often only able to influence the abatement for co-operation. Under the current penalty regime, a pro-active practitioner can do significantly more to limit the impact of penalties (see 12000ff.).

- Appropriate use of the white space section of a tax return (or a note in a computation) can reduce the risk of an enquiry. It can also limit the risk of a discovery by HMRC (see 12410ff.).

- Practitioners need to understand the implications of the radical changes to the appeals process from 1 April 2009 including the introduction of a statute-based internal review of HMRC decisions, the Alternative Dispute Resolution process (see 12625) and the replacement of the General and Special Commissioners with the First-tier Tribunal and Upper Tribunal. There are significant opportunities here for practitioners to best serve their clients' interests (see 12600ff.).

The harmonisation of tax administration

11000   Introduction

The period since the merger in April 2005 of the Inland Revenue and HM Customs and Excise to form HM Revenue & Customs (HMRC) has been one of enormous change. On top of the resulting cultural and organisational changes within the department, there have been radical legislative changes in relation to HMRC powers, penalties and the appeals process.

The organisational changes have included the introduction of enquiries covering both the direct and indirect tax affairs of a business at the same time. They have also brought a new vocabulary. HMRC speak of interventions and compliance checks. For simplicity, the general term 'enquiry' is used in this commentary to describe any situation where HMRC employ its statutory powers to review a person's tax affairs.

The relevant legislative changes are described in detail elsewhere but for convenience, the key changes are briefly summarised below. The cross-references shown below lead to the detailed sections which refer to the relevant legislation.

Tax Reporter: ¶180-000ff.

11005   Penalty regime for errors

A unified penalty regime applies for errors in returns in relation to all the main taxes. Originally, this applied to income tax, corporation tax, capital gains tax, value added tax, the construction industry scheme, employers' PAYE and National Insurance contributions. In relation to these taxes, penalties under the current regime are chargeable in respect of inaccuracies in returns or documents for return periods starting on or after 1 April 2008 where the due date for filing is on or after 1 April 2009 (see 12001).

Since 1 April 2010, the current penalty regime also applies to all excise duties, environmental taxes, inheritance tax, insurance premium tax, stamp duties and petroleum revenue tax.

The current regime includes a statutory basis for the abatement of penalties and significantly changes the basis of penalty calculation.

Tax Reporter: ¶184-650ff.

11010   Enquiry window

Where tax returns are submitted in advance of the statutory filing date, the normal enquiry window for individuals, partnerships and trusts closes 12 months after the filing of the return with effect for returns for the 2007–08 tax year (previously, the enquiry window expired 12 months following the statutory filing deadline (i.e. 31 January) irrespective of when the return was filed. The same change applies to company returns in respect of accounting periods ending after 31 March 2008 except in relation to companies that are members of a group that is not treated as a small group within the Companies Act definition.

This change overcomes the previous concern that early filing served only to extend HMRC's enquiry window. However, the significance of the closure of the window is somewhat reduced by the inspection and information powers (see 11900ff.).

Tax Reporter: ¶185-600ff.

11015   Penalty regime for failures

As just noted, penalties for errors in returns are dealt with at 12001ff. Separate provisions apply to a failure to notify (see 12120ff.). Current provisions apply to a failure occurring on or after 1 April 2010 in relation to income tax, corporation tax, CGT, Class 2 and 4 NICs, VAT, excise duties, environmental taxes and insurance premium tax.

Tax Reporter: ¶184-650ff.

11020   Record keeping requirement

Since 1 April 2009, HMRC have had powers to specify the records to be kept by particular types of business. In addition, HMRC have issued additional non-statutory guidance on the types of records that businesses are expected to maintain to satisfy the statutory requirements (see 12405ff.).

Tax Reporter: ¶181-900ff.

11025   HMRC information and inspection powers

Since 1 April 2009, HMRC have had revised statutory information and inspection powers. The current information powers replace the previous powers and can be used at any time to demand information or documents reasonably required to check a person's tax position – their use is not restricted to carrying out an enquiry into a return. The current inspection powers give HMRC the power to enter businesses premises at any time to inspect the statutory records, the business premises and business assets. These current provisions mean that HMRC can start enquiring into a person's tax position at any time, whether before or after the submission of a return (see 11100 and 11900ff.).

Tax Reporter: ¶186-550ff.

11030   Time limits for assessments and claims

Since 1 April 2010, four-year time limits have applied both for assessments by HMRC and claims by a taxpayer.

Tax Reporter: ¶184-275 and ¶191-585

11035   Late filing and late payment penalties

From 6 April 2011, current penalty provisions apply in relation to the late filing of a return (see 12201ff.). From the same date, the application of current penalty provisions in relation to the late payment of tax was extended (see 12207).

Tax Reporter: ¶181-325 and ¶184-650

Information and inspection powers

Introduction

11900   Information and inspection powers – introduction

HMRC's powers to require the provision of information are mainly contained in FA 2008, Sch. 36. The current information powers include:

- the requirement to make available information and documents that are legally required to be maintained, including business records;

- giving HMRC access to business assets and premises;

- the requirement for those whose tax position is being checked (taxpayer notices) to produce supplementary information and documents; and

- the requirement for third parties to produce documents or provide information (third party notices) about named taxpayers.

Tax Reporter: ¶186-550ff.

11902   Relevant taxes

The current powers first applied from 1 April 2009 but only in relation to income tax, CGT, corporation tax, VAT, NICs and any defined relevant foreign tax. Their application was extended from 1 April 2010 to insurance premium tax, inheritance tax, stamp duty land tax, stamp duty reserve tax, petroleum revenue tax, aggregates levy, climate change levy and landfill tax.

Tax Reporter: ¶186-550ff.

Information powers

11910   Information powers

The powers enable HMRC to issue a formal notice to a taxpayer (a taxpayer notice) requiring them to provide information and documents reasonably required to check their tax position. There does not have to be an open enquiry except where a return has been submitted and the enquiry window is still open. The items will usually be requested informally in the first instance.

There is an important distinction in the application of the powers as between matters which are and are not part of a business's statutory records. That term is loosely defined by FA 2008 but precisely what forms part of a particular client's statutory records will depend on the client's circumstances. For example, if he or she is a sole trader or partner, they will need to keep (amongst other things) the records specified in TMA 1970.

There is no right of appeal against a notice requiring the provision of statutory records. By contrast, there is a right of appeal against a notice requiring the provision of supplementary information and documents if the taxpayer does not agree that they are reasonably required.

The officer can issue as many information notices as necessary throughout the course of an enquiry. It would be normal for an informal request for the information to be made in each case.

Legislation: TMA 1970, s. 12B; FA 2008, Sch. 36, Pt. 1 and para. 62

Cases: *PML Accounting Ltd* [2015] TC 04612; *Alvi* [2016] TC 04989; *Cherian* [2016] TC 05085

Other Material: HMRC *Compliance Manual* CH 21150; GOV.UK website: www.gov.uk/government/publications/keeping-records-for-business-what-you-need-to-know

Tax Reporter: ¶186-550ff.

11911 Private records

HMRC can use their information powers to request private records, including bank and building society statements, paying-in slips and details of property or other assets. The information or documents requested must, however, be reasonably required for checking the taxpayer's tax position. HMRC consider that reasonable equates to 'fair and sensible' in the circumstances. Whether a request is reasonable is, therefore, dependent on the circumstances in each case.

As private records do not form part of the statutory records they are supplementary information. There is, therefore, a right of appeal against a notice requiring them. The onus will be on the officer to satisfy the tribunal that the information is reasonably required.

When requesting private records, HMRC acknowledge the need to take account of:

- the cost – for example the cost of obtaining duplicate bank statements; and

- the taxpayer's right to privacy – the officer must be able to demonstrate that seeing the private records is an effective way of checking the person's liability to tax and that it will cause the minimum necessary intrusion into their private lives.

As a practical point, clients should always be advised to operate a separate business bank account so that they cannot be required to immediately produce their private records at the start of an enquiry.

Other Material: HMRC *Compliance Handbook* CH 22180; *Enquiry Manual* EM1561

Tax Reporter: ¶186-550ff.

11912   Restrictions on taxpayer notices

Finance Act 2008, Sch. 36, Pt. 4 includes a range of restrictions on the requirement to provide or produce information or documents. In summary, a person cannot be required to provide or produce:

- a document that is not in his or her possession or power;

- information relating to the conduct of a pending tax appeal;

- journalistic material in the possession of the person who acquired or created it;

- personal records concerning the health, spiritual or welfare counselling or assistance in respect of an individual but note that provision is made for the editing out of such information from general records;

- documents more than six years old unless the notice is given by or with the agreement of an 'authorised officer';

- information for the purpose of checking the tax position of someone who died more than four years before the date of the notice;

- information or any part of a document that attracts legal professional privilege;

- subject to significant limitations, information held by that person in connection with his or her performance of a statutory audit or documentation created by him or her or on his or her behalf in connection with that function (note that under the pre-April 2009 regime, HMRC accepted that the comparable provision applied where the client chose to have an audit to statutory standard despite no statutory requirement or where the audit was a requirement of his or her professional body (see *Statement of Practice* SP 5/90); and

- again subject to significant limitations, information held by a tax adviser about 'relevant communications' or documents belonging to the tax adviser, which are communications between the tax adviser and his or her client or any other tax adviser of the client (but note that the same communications in the hands of your client are not protected).

The restrictions and limitations can be applied in an appropriately selective manner where some information is and some is not protected.

Legislation: FA 2008, Sch. 36, Pt. 4, para. 18–28

Other Material: *Statement of Practice* SP 5/90

Tax Reporter: ¶186-550ff.

11913   Taxpayer notices following tax return

The legislation specifies restriction of HMRC's powers where a return has been made in respect of the relevant chargeable period but in reality the provision means that an information notice may be issued to a taxpayer notwithstanding that he or she has made a tax return in respect of the relevant chargeable period in any of the following circumstances:

- there is an open enquiry;
- an HMRC officer has reason to suspect that circumstances would permit the making of a discovery assessment; or
- the notice is given for the purpose of obtaining any information or document that is also required for the purpose of checking that person's VAT, PAYE or CIS position.

Legislation: FA 2008, Sch. 36, para. 21

Tax Reporter: ¶186-550ff.

11914   Third party notices

HMRC's powers under FA 2008 extend to obtaining information and documents from third parties. The purpose of a third party notice is the same as that for a taxpayer notice; the information or document has to be reasonably required for the purpose of checking the tax position of the relevant person.

There are additional constraints upon the issue of a third party notice. Except in relation to information that forms part of any person's statutory records and relates to the supply of goods or services (or certain imports), a third party notice can only be issued with either the agreement of the taxpayer or the approval of the tribunal.

The National Crime Agency is also entitled to apply to the tribunal for permission to issue a third party information notice where it has taken over all the 'general Revenue functions' in relation to a taxpayer pursuant to PCA 2002, s. 317 (*National Crime Agency, ex parte a taxpayer*).

Finance Act 2011 includes detailed provisions on HMRC's power to obtain data from third parties. These provisions take effect from 1 April 2012.

Legislation: FA 2008, Sch. 36, para. 3; FA 2011, Sch. 23

Cases: *PML Accounting Ltd* [2015] TC 04612; *Re an application by R & C Commrs* [2015] TC 04649; *National Crime Agency, ex parte a taxpayer* [2016] TC 05191

Tax Reporter: ¶186-550ff.

11915   Client confidentiality

HMRC will not accept that a legal or professional adviser's duty of confidentiality towards their client is sufficient reason for not complying with a taxpayer notice addressed to themselves for the purpose of checking their own tax position.

Other Material: HMRC *Compliance Handbook* CH22300

Tax Reporter: ¶186-550ff.

11916   Medical records

The information powers in FA 2008, Sch. 36 cannot be used to obtain medical records. Where the records mix both medical and financial information, HMRC take the view that they can be requested but that a request for patient's records (or other records containing patient information) should only be made if:

- there is reason to believe that fees have been omitted from the return because the records examination shows weaknesses that may have led to an understatement of fees;

- it has been established that the patient record cards are prime income records; and

- the patient record cards are the most effective way of working out the true amount of liability.

Legislation: FA 2008, Sch. 36, para. 19(2)

Tax Reporter: ¶186-550ff.

11917 Legal professional privilege

Common law, the *Data Protection Act* 1998, the *Human Rights Act* 1998 and FA 2008, Sch. 36, para. 23 give protection to legally privileged documents. HMRC cannot obtain any documents in respect of which the legal professional is entitled to legal professional privilege. Where privilege is claimed in respect of information relating to a client of the professional or another third party, there is a strong presumption in favour of the privacy of the information.

Legislation: FA 2008, Sch. 36, para. 23

Other Material: HMRC *Compliance Handbook* CH22240ff.

Tax Reporter: ¶186-700

11918 Penalties for non-compliance with information notices

As noted, an informal request will normally be made for information before HMRC considers issuing a formal notice. If the informal request does not allow sufficient time, the practitioner can request an extension. However, if the officer does not consider that there is a good reason for such a request, they may issue a formal notice as soon as the time limit in the informal request has expired.

If the time-limit set in a formal notice is too short, the practitioner should contact the officer as soon as it is clear that more time is needed. Delay in contacting the officer could lead to complications and possibly the imposition of a penalty for delay. When considering any eventual penalties, the issue of a formal notice could have implications for the subsequent consideration of the quality of the taxpayer's disclosure.

If the officer refuses to accept that more time is needed, a subsequent appeal against the notice or a penalty for non-compliance can be made to the tribunal on the grounds that the officer allowed insufficient time. In such a situation, a clear file note should be made of the conversation in which the refusal was made in order that this can be produced in evidence.

If a taxpayer or third party fails to comply with a notice requiring the provision of information or the production of a document, HMRC may impose an initial penalty of £300 and a daily penalty of up to £60 until the notice is complied with. Before doing so, the officer should try to contact the taxpayer to find out why the notice has not been complied with and, if necessary, agree more time. They should also explain that a penalty will be charged if they do not comply with the notice.

If the failure continues for more than 30 days beginning with the date of the assessment of a daily penalty, HMRC can apply to the tribunal for an increased daily penalty to be imposed. Before making such an application, HMRC must warn the person concerned that such an application might be made. In determining the amount of any such increased daily penalty, the tribunal must consider the likely cost of complying with the information notice and any benefits (to that person or any other) of not complying with it. The penalty awarded by the tribunal cannot exceed £1,000 for each day starting with the applicable day. These provisions took effect from 1 April 2012.

R & C Commrs v Tager (Personal Representatives of the Estate of Tager (deceased)) was the first case in which a tribunal considered an application by HMRC for the imposition of a 'tax-related penalty' under FA 2008, Sch. 36, para. 50, for failure to comply with an information notice. The tribunal determined that the starting point for each penalty was 100% of the tax at stake and imposed a penalty of £1.17m representing 100% of the inheritance tax at stake (as calculated by HMRC) with no mitigation and a further penalty of £75,000 representing 100% of the income tax at stake (£80,549) with mitigation of a modest rounding down only.

No penalty should be imposed while the appeal period is still open or if an appeal has been made against the notice and the appeal is still open.

In addition to any non-compliance penalty, failure to comply with an information notice may limit the practitioner's scope to argue for a reduction of any penalty charged in respect of any inaccuracies found in a return.

Legislation: FA 2007, Sch. 24, para. 9; FA 2008, Sch. 36, para. 39 and 40; FA 2011, Sch. 24

Cases: *R & C Commrs v Tager (Personal Representatives of the Estate of Tager (deceased))* [2015] BTC 509; *PML Accounting Ltd* [2015] TC 04612; *Doshi* [2016] TC 04813; *Spring Capital Ltd* [2016] TC 05007; *Cherian* [2016] TC 05085

Other Material: HMRC *Compliance Handbook* CH26220

Tax Reporter: ¶187-075

11919   Tribunal approval

HMRC can seek advance approval of the tribunal for an information notice. There is no right of appeal against a taxpayer notice that has been approved by the tribunal.

If HMRC want to inspect documents and business premises at the same time, they can ask the tribunal for their approval for both the inspection visit and the taxpayer notice.

Legislation: FA 2008, Sch. 36, para. 29(3)

Case: *Taxpayer* [2016] TC 05116

Other Material: HMRC *Compliance Handbook* CH24100ff.

Tax Reporter: ¶186-550ff.

Inspection powers

11920   Inspection powers

Finance Act 2008, Sch. 36 contains powers that enable HMRC to inspect business premises, business assets and statutory records.

Between 2011 and 2015, increased significance was placed on inspections by HMRC as part of the Business Records Checks initiative (see 12407).

The powers must be used reasonably and proportionately and can only be used to inspect *business* premises, not premises that are used wholly for residential purposes. However, the premises must be used wholly for residential purposes to be exempt from the powers. If they are used only partly for business purposes, then they are partially subject to HMRC's inspection powers.

There are safeguards built into the legislation that are intended to ensure that the use of the powers is reasonable and proportionate. Over and above such safeguards, HMRC must take care not to breach a taxpayer's right to privacy under the Human Rights Act.

Tax Reporter: ¶186-850ff.

11921   Business premises, business assets and business documents – definitions

Business premises are defined in relation to a person as premises that an HMRC officer has reason to believe are used in connection with the carrying on of a business by or on behalf of that person. Premises are given an extended definition to include any means of transport.

Business assets are defined as assets that an HMRC officer has reason to believe are owned, leased or used in connection with the carrying on of business by any person.

Business documents are defined as documents that relate to the carrying on of a business by any person and that form part of any person's statutory records. Statutory records are themselves defined in FA 2008, Sch. 36, para. 62 but precisely what forms part of your particular client's statutory records will depend on the client's circumstances. For example, if he or she is a sole trader or partner, he or she will need to keep (amongst other things) the records specified in TMA 1970, s. 12B.

Legislation: FA 2008, Sch. 36, para. 10, 58 and 62

Tax Reporter: ¶186-850ff.

11922 Why visits will be made

Situations where a visit to premises is more likely include those where an HMRC officer considers it necessary in order to:

- inspect the business records on site (not restricted to those of the enquiry period);
- inspect the business assets, for example to check the stock held;
- detect people operating in the black economy;
- collect evidence of suspected deliberate understatements; or
- to carry out credibility checks.

Before an inspection visit is made, the risk should have been identified and a note made by the HMRC officer of why it is best addressed by way of a visit instead of calling for documents and information. The timing of the visit should be reasonable and the officer must be able to show that the compliance check is reasonable and proportionate so that the conditions of the *Human Rights Act* 1998, s. 8(2) are satisfied.

The officer should be told if there is a good reason why the business premises should not be visited. This might be due to lack of space, disruption caused to the operation of the business or the adverse affect on customers. The officer may then arrange to see the business records at an HMRC office or the premises of the practitioner or perhaps at a different time.

Tax Reporter: ¶186-850ff.

11923 Visits arranged or with notice

Visits can be announced or unannounced. Announced visits will usually be made by prior arrangement, following an informal request for information and an inspection of the business records and premises. If the taxpayer refuses an informal request for a visit, the officer can arrange a visit by issuing a formal notice. Examples of the various formal notices are included in HMRC's *Compliance Handbook*.

When an announced visit is arranged (whether by agreement or by formal notice), the taxpayer will be notified of the date and time of the visit, the name of the visiting officer and the records that are to be inspected. They will also be sent the Fact Sheet on visits explaining relevant rights and responsibilities.

If the visit is arranged by way of a formal notice rather than by agreement, the officer will probably also issue a notice requiring that the records should be produced at the business premises whether or not they are normally kept there.

Although a visit arranged with the taxpayer's agreement might be made with less than seven days notice, if it has not been possible to reach agreement on the time of the visit, the officer must give at least seven days notice (whether in writing or otherwise) unless a shorter period is approved by an authorised officer.

An officer may seek advance approval for an inspection by the tribunal (see 11925) even where the taxpayer is to be notified in advance. There is no right of appeal against a notice of an inspection visit but only in relation to a tribunal-approved visit is there a penalty for obstructing a visit.

Legislation: FA 2008, Sch. 36, para. 10–13

Other material: CC/FS3

Tax Reporter: ¶186-850ff.

11924   Unannounced visits

If the nature of the risk requires it, HMRC may carry out an unannounced visit, without giving any notice of the intended visit. No unannounced visit should be carried out unless it has been approved by an authorised officer. An authorised officer is a senior officer authorised for the purpose of the legislation.

If an officer believes that their inspection may be obstructed they can, with the approval of an Authorised Officer, apply to the tribunal for their approval to a visit (see 11425). There is no right of appeal against a notice of an inspection visit but only in relation to a tribunal-approved visit is there a penalty for obstructing a visit.

As with announced visits, unannounced visits must be made at a reasonable time and the occupier of the premises must at the start of the visit be given written notice of the inspection together with the relevant factsheet on unannounced visits (CC/FS4 or CC/FS5 if tribunal-approved). The officer will then explain the reason for the visit and how they intend to carry it out.

If the taxpayer is present, the officer must advise them of their right to ask their agent to be present but need not delay the start of the inspection to await their arrival. Clients should be advised that if an officer makes an unannounced visit, they should ask to see the tribunal's authorisation for the visit. The client does not have to allow access to the premises. Only if the tribunal's authorisation has been obtained will HMRC be able to assess a £300 obstruction penalty (see 11925). Otherwise, there is no risk of a penalty and it will be sufficient to agree a more convenient date and time for the officer to call back.

Legislation: FA 2008, Sch. 36, para. 10–13

Other Material: HMRC *Compliance Handbook* CH25520

Tax Reporter: ¶186-850ff.

11925   Visits authorised by tribunal

A penalty can be imposed on a taxpayer who obstructs a visit that has been approved by the tribunal. The initial penalty is a fixed £300 and there can additionally be daily penalties of up to £60 for each day on which the obstruction continues. There is no right of appeal against a tribunal authorised visit.

At the same time as seeking the tribunal's approval for the inspection visit, the officer will probably also seek approval for a taxpayer notice to make the records available at the premises. By obtaining the tribunal's approval, the officer ensures that no appeal can be made against any requirements in the information notice.

Legislation: FA 2008, Sch. 36, para. 10–13, 39

Tax Reporter: ¶186-850ff.

11926   Private residences

HMRC do not have the power to inspect premises that are used *wholly* as a private residence but they can do so if invited to do so by the taxpayer. If the premises are used partly for business and partly as a private residence, HMRC can only inspect the parts used for the business.

HMRC's departmental instructions advise officers, 'Wherever practicable you should avoid inspecting at premises that are also a person's home. You will normally be able to find an alternative location such as at an agent's premises or an HMRC office'. Practitioners may wish to remind officers of this if the advice is overlooked.

It is the view of HMRC that they can inspect a private residence if:

- the business is run from the home;

- business assets are stored at the home;

- business records are kept at the home;

- the business accounts include a claim for 'use of home as office'; or

- a home is registered as the principal place of business for VAT.

HMRC accept that storing records at home because there is nowhere else to keep them is not sufficient to allow them to inspect the private residence unless invited to do so.

Example

A dental surgery is run from the dentist's home. The officer can inspect the offices and waiting rooms and any consulting rooms that are not in use. The inspection cannot be extended into any areas that are used solely as a private residence.

Legislation: FA 2008, Sch. 36, para. 10(2)

Other Material: HMRC *Compliance Handbook* CH25220, CH25240

Tax Reporter: ¶186-850ff.

11927   Record-keeping obligations

Practitioners can help to strengthen their clients' position in the event of an enquiry or a business records inspection by advising on the maintenance of adequate business records. This advice will also ensure that clients are not penalised for failing to comply with the record-keeping obligations imposed by TMA 1970.

HMRC conducted a programme of live Business Records Checks every year between 2011 and 2015 under the Business Records Check (BRC) initiative (see 12407).

HMRC have published a range of Fact Sheets and online tools to help businesses understand their record-keeping obligations. The website locations of some of these are shown below.

Further commentary on record-keeping obligations is included in the consideration of tax returns and record keeping (see 12400ff.).

Legislation: TMA 1970, s. 12B(5)

Other Material: www.gov.uk/keeping-your-pay-tax-records

Tax Reporter: ¶181-900

11928   The visit itself

At the start (or in advance) of the visit, the officer will give the taxpayer a copy of the Fact Sheet on visits and explain what will happen during the visit. These sheets are on the HMRC website. The officer may indicate that they would like to discuss the records with the person who keeps them. They can only do this with the agreement of the taxpayer.

The taxpayer has the right to refuse to allow the officer to enter the premises. However, unless the taxpayer agrees to a visit at a later date, the officer will consider asking the tribunal for approval for the inspection. If the tribunal has approved the inspection, the taxpayer can be penalised for obstructing the visit unless there is a reasonable excuse such as illness. The penalty for obstructing an inspection that has been approved by the tribunal is a fixed £300 plus a daily penalty of up to £60.

There is no statutory definition of what inspection involves. Some guidance on the point is included in HMRC's Compliance Handbook.

The officer should not mark the records that are inspected in any way, even to indicate that they have been checked. Goods or assets can, however, be marked to show that they have been inspected, although the officer must not damage them when doing so.

The officer can record the information obtained in the course of the inspection and can take copies of the documents inspected or make extracts from them, if necessary by removing them from the premises. If a written receipt for any documents removed is not offered, the taxpayer can request one.

Documents removed by an officer should not be retained longer than necessary. If any are lost or damaged, the taxpayer is entitled to compensation.

Legislation: FA 2008, Sch. 36, para. 10–17

Other Material: HMRC *Compliance Handbook* CH25140 and CH25160; GOV.UK website www.gov.uk/government/collections/hm-revenue-and-customs-leaflets-factsheets-and-booklets#compliance-checks-factsheets-general-information

Tax Reporter: ¶186-850ff.

Other information powers

11930   Data gathering powers

In addition to the information powers explained above which are commonly used to obtain information in the course of an enquiry, there are other, less commonly used powers. These include the data-gathering powers within FA 2011, Sch. 23, which provides a framework of powers for HMRC to obtain third-party data from a range of specified data-holders, subject to appeal, with penalties for non-compliance.

Following consultation, *Finance Act* 2016 extends HMRC's data-gathering powers in FA 2011, Sch. 23 to include providers of electronic stored-value payment services and business intermediaries 15 September 2016 (Royal Assent).

Schedule 23 provides for an initial penalty of £300 for failure to comply with a data-holder notice and provisions by which increased daily penalties can be approved and assessed if a data-holder does not comply with a data information notice request. *Finance Act* 2016 amends Sch. 23 (with effect from 15 September 2016 (Royal Assent)) to clarify the administration of the increased daily penalty and to increase the amount of the maximum daily penalty from £60 to £1,000. The amendments provide that the tribunal will decide whether an increased daily penalty is allowed, determine the new maximum amount of such a penalty and the date from which it can be applied, although the process for assessing the increased penalty remains with HMRC.

Legislation: TMA 1970, s. 20A–20D; FA 2011, Sch. 23

Tax Reporter: ¶187-095ff.

11932   Powers to obtain information about certain tax advantages and publish state aid information

Finance Act 2016 introduces new powers to enable HMRC to collect information on certain state aids for the purpose of complying with EU obligations in relation to state aids granted through tax advantages, with effect from 15 September 2016 (Royal Assent). HMRC may determine that claims for a tax advantage specified must include (or be accompanied by) such information, presented in such form, as the determination may specify.

The specified tax advantages are:

* enhanced capital allowances (business premises renovation allowances, zero-emission goods vehicle allowances and expenditure on plant and machinery for use in designated assisted areas (enhanced capital allowances for enterprise zones));

- creative tax reliefs (film tax relief, television tax relief, theatre tax relief and orchestra tax relief);

- research and development reliefs (relief for SMEs: cost of research and development incurred by SME and vaccine research relief).

HMRC may also issue an information notice requiring information in respect of specified tax advantages (as follows):

- reduced rate of climate change levy payable in respect of a reduced rate supply (for supplies covered by climate change agreement);

- relief granted to investors in a company under the enterprise investment scheme;

- relief granted to investors in a venture capital trust under the venture capital trust scheme.

Finance Act 2016 further introduces new powers to enable HMRC to publish and disclose information on certain state aids.

Legislation: FA 2016, s. 180–183 and Sch. 24

Penalties

12000   General introduction

Within the context of an enquiry, a liability to penalties can arise in various circumstances. The main provisions relate to:

- incorrect returns and documents (see 12001ff.);

- failure to notify liability (see 12120ff.); and

- late filing and payment (see 12200ff.).

In addition, a penalty can arise in relation to record-keeping obligations (see 12407).

Finance Acts of 2007, 2008 and 2009 introduced radical changes in both the application and calculation of penalties. The same 'behaviour-based' principles of calculation now apply to most taxes. The current rules apply standard percentages of the potential lost revenue to determine the penalty for three distinct categories of behaviour and then provide specific reductions to reflect the extent of disclosure during the enquiry. The former rules left much more discretion to HMRC, although the department tried to work to a standard practice.

As the current provisions only apply from their relevant introduction dates, the former provisions continue to apply up to the cut-off dates. If a client has possibly incurred penalties in relation to years that straddle the cut-off dates, the practitioner needs to be familiar with the mechanics of calculation under both regimes. As the current penalties focus heavily on the behaviour that caused the under-declaration of tax liability, the penalty loadings can vary between 0% (innocent error) to 100% (deliberate and concealed error with no reduction for disclosure) of the under-declared tax. In situations involving offshore matters, penalties under the current regime can since 6 April 2011 be as high as 200%. Under the former regime, penalty loadings tended to bunch in a narrower and lower banding.

In certain circumstances, the names of 'deliberate defaulters' can be published by HMRC. Lists are published quarterly. The list was last updated on 14 September 2016 and is available at the link below.

Finance Act 2016 makes changes to the naming provisions in FA 2009, s. 94, so that where there is an inaccuracy in a taxpayer's document, or failure to notify which relates to offshore matters or offshore transfers, only full, unprompted disclosures will be outside the scope of the provisions. Section 94 is also amended to allow the naming of certain people who have benefited from the inaccuracy or failure. The amendments come into force on a day appointed by regulations made by the Treasury.

HMRC will also monitor the tax affairs of people who deliberately get them wrong, known as serious defaulters. These include people who have been charged a penalty because of their deliberate behaviour.

Consultation

On 17 September 2015, HMRC published a summary of responses to a consultation entitled 'HMRC Penalties: a discussion document' which ran from 2 February 2015 to 11 May 2015. The summary of responses provides that HMRC propose to issue firstly a further consultation document on proposals for a new penalty scheme for late filing and late payment and then a document on inaccuracy penalties. If ministers ultimately decide to proceed to legislation, the draft legislation would be consulted on, with the earliest possible date for legislation being Finance Bill 2017.

The discussion document and response are available at www.gov.uk/government/uploads/system/uploads/attachment_data/file/461357/HMRC_Penalties_a_Discussion_Document_-_Summary_of_Responses.pdf.

Other Material: HMRC publication of deliberate defaulters: www.gov.uk/government/publications/publishing-details-of-deliberate-tax-defaulters-pddd#history; CC/FS13; CC/FS14; CC/FS15

Legislation: FA 2009, s. 94

Tax Reporter: ¶181-325; ¶184-650ff.

Incorrect returns and documents

12001 Penalties for incorrect returns for periods commencing on or after 1 April 2008

As part of the unification of the administrative provisions for direct and indirect taxes, FA 2007, Sch. 24 introduced a completely new legislative framework for the imposition of penalties in relation to Penalties for Errors.

The provisions initially applied in relation to Income Tax, CGT, Corporation Tax, PAYE, Class 1 and Class 4 NICs, the Construction Industry Scheme and VAT in respect of any return for a period commencing on or after 1 April 2008 that is completed on or after 1 April 2009.

Example

A submits her 2008–09 tax return in June 2009. On the same day, she also submits her 2007–08 tax return late. If both returns contained errors, the current provisions would apply to the 2008–09 return but the former provisions would apply to the 2007–2008 return.

The Sch. 24 provisions were then extended to documents in respect of:

- Insurance Premium Tax;

- Inheritance Tax;

- Stamp Duty Land Tax;

- Stamp Duty Reserve Tax;

- Petroleum Revenue Tax;

- Excise Duties including:

  - Aggregates Levy;

  - Climate Change Levy;

  - Landfill Tax;

  - Air Passenger Duty;

  - Alcoholic Liquor Duties;

  - Tobacco Product Duty;

  - Hydrocarbon Oil Duties;

  - General Betting Duty;

  - Pool Betting Duty;

  - Bingo Duty;

  - Lottery Duty;

- Gaming Duty and Remote Gaming Duty;
- Warehouse Keepers; and
- Registered Excise Dealers and Shippers.

The current regime applies to the extended range of taxes in respect of documents for periods commencing on or after 1 April 2009 and due on or after 1 April 2010.

Where the period under enquiry involves earlier years that fall within the former regime and later years that are within the current regime, the practitioner will need to be familiar with the provisions of both regimes. For both the HMRC officer and the practitioner, there is a risk that the distinct concepts of one regime will incorrectly be applied to years governed by the other regime.

The current provisions are examined first in this commentary (see 12002ff.) before the former provisions (see 12050ff.).

Other material: CC/FS7a

Tax Reporter: ¶184-850

12002   Penalties for errors

The current penalty regime provisions in relation to errors in returns and documents are contained in FA 2007, Sch. 24. The main elements of the penalty regime are that:

- it applies to incorrect returns for both direct and indirect taxes;

- it provides different levels of penalties for each of three different 'behaviours';

- the standard penalty can be reduced by reference to the quality of any disclosure made to HMRC;

- the statutory minimum is lower for an unprompted disclosure than for a prompted disclosure;

- the penalty cannot be reduced below the statutory minimum unless there are special circumstances;

- HMRC have the power to suspend penalties.

Overall, the current regime provisions respond to HMRC's view that penalties had become inappropriately low under the former regime as a result of excessive abatement. The fixing of statutory maximum and minimum amounts for the penalty by reference to the different 'behaviours' results in a much wider (and generally higher) range of penalties.

HMRC have published a video and transcript of a presentation 'Penalties for inaccuracies in documents and returns'. This can be accessed via the GOV.UK website. It should not be regarded as the last word on the subject but it provides a useful summary.

Cases: *Fab Cleaning Management Ltd* [2016] TC 04824; *Atkinson* [2016] TC 05141

Other material: GOV.UK website: www.gov.uk/government/news/webinars-e-learning-and-videos-if-youre-a-tax-agent-or-adviser

Tax Reporter: ¶184-850

12003   Behaviours

Different standard levels of penalty are set for each of three different classes of behaviour. The three identified behaviours are:

- careless action;

- deliberate but not concealed action; and

- deliberate and concealed action.

For commentary on each behaviour, see 12005ff.

Tax Reporter: ¶184-850

12004   Mistake

Where an error results from a genuine mistake despite the taxpayer having taken reasonable care to complete the return correctly, no penalty arises unless there was an unreasonable delay in notifying HMRC once the error had been identified by the taxpayer. The legislation does not specify that no penalty arises in the case of a genuine mistake; it simply specifies what penalties do arise where the taxpayer's action was careless or deliberate.

HMRC's *Compliance Handbook* provides the following illustrations of when an inaccuracy might arise despite reasonable care:

- a reasonably arguable view of situations that is subsequently not upheld;

- an arithmetical or transposition inaccuracy that is not so large either in absolute terms or relative to overall liability, as to produce an obviously odd result or be picked up by a quality check;

- following advice from HMRC that later proves to be wrong, provided that all the details and circumstances were given when the advice was sought;

- acting on advice from a competent adviser which proves to be wrong despite the fact that the adviser was given a full set of accurate facts (see *Compliance Handbook* CH 84530); and

- accepting and using information from another person where it is not possible to check that the information is accurate and complete.

HMRC also provide specific practical examples (see *Compliance Handbook* CH 81131).

Other Material: HMRC *Compliance Handbook* CH81130 and 81131

Tax Reporter: ¶184-850

12005   Careless action

An inaccuracy in a document given to HMRC is careless if the inaccuracy is due to a failure to take reasonable care. Although the range of penalties is defined by reference to the nature of the action, they apply equally where the 'action' involved an omission – for example, the non-disclosure on a tax return of a source of income.

The current regime provides for a maximum statutory penalty of 30% of the revenue lost for understatements due to a failure to take reasonable care. The maximum reduction in the penalty for a disclosure (see 12020ff.) that was completely unprompted could reduce this to a statutory minimum penalty of nil. By contrast, the minimum statutory penalty for a prompted disclosure of an understatement due to a failure to take reasonable care is 15% of the revenue lost. These differences in the level of penalty explain why it is so important for the practitioner to advise the client fully concerning the benefits of disclosure.

As a penalty arises where there is a failure to take reasonable care, it is important to establish what constitutes reasonable care. Under the former regime, the equivalent of failure to take reasonable care was 'negligent conduct'. It is generally accepted that the change in terminology has not changed the test.

In relation to negligent conduct, HMRC have long relied on the definition identified in the 1856 case of *Blyth v Birmingham Waterworks Co* when it was said:

> 'Negligence is the omission to do something which a reasonable man, guided upon those considerations which ordinarily regulate the conduct of human affairs, would do, or doing something which a prudent and reasonable man would not do. The defendants might be liable for negligence, if, unintentionally, they omitted to do that which a prudent and reasonable person would have done, or did that which a person taking reasonable care would not have done.'

However, HMRC do not interpret this to impose the same test of reasonableness on all taxpayers. The department's *Compliance Handbook* clarifies the point as follows:

'Every person must take reasonable care, but "reasonable care" cannot be identified without consideration of the particular person's abilities and circumstances. HMRC recognises the wide range of abilities and circumstances of those persons completing returns or claims.

So whilst each person has a responsibility to take reasonable care, what is necessary for each person to discharge that responsibility has to be viewed in the light of that person's abilities and circumstances.

For example, we do not expect the same level of knowledge or expertise from a self-employed un-represented individual as we do from a large multinational company. We would expect a higher degree of care to be taken over large and complex matters than simple straightforward ones.'

HMRC's guidance to its officers includes the following (in summarised form from *Compliance Handbook* 81140):

- repeated inaccuracies may indicate a lack of reasonable care but repetition does not necessarily indicate a failure;

- an action cannot be careless if the taxpayer intended the inaccuracy – that is deliberate; and

- people do make mistakes. We do not expect perfection. Has the person taken the care and attention that a reasonable person would in similar circumstances.

Practical examples of careless inaccuracy are included in HMRC's *Compliance Handbook*.

Previous editions of HMRC publications included the following additional examples of what constituted a failure to take reasonable care:

- omitting items from a return (too many, or too large relative to overall liability, to suggest that they are simply mistakes);

- failing to notify a new source of income in time, where the person could reasonably be expected to have known liability arose;

- failing to bring to HMRC's attention a mistake or misinterpretation which is identified by the taxpayer, whether made by HMRC or the taxpayer, and which is significant in relation to overall liability;

- making arithmetical errors (too many, or too large, relative to the overall liability, to suggest they are simply isolated mistakes);

- mis-classifying items of income or expenditure without giving the matter adequate consideration or, if the amounts and complexity warrant it, taking professional advice;

- keeping books and records that are incomplete in some respects;

- not having appropriate accounting systems in place, including to ensure items are captured in the correct return period (failure over a sustained period may however be an indication of *deliberate* understatement);

- omitting occasional items of income or gains;

- having insufficient quality control and not checking the work of others;

- applying PAYE wrongly occasionally or to an unusual item without checking on the correct treatment; and

- failing to check a return is consistent with underlying records.

HMRC publish a range of 'toolkits' that are intended to help reduce errors in returns and which are updated annually. A list of these is available on the HMRC website.

Legislation: FA 2007, Sch. 24, para. 3(1), 4(1), 10(1) and 10(2)

Cases: *Patel* [2015] TC 04617; *Blackman* [2016] TC 05218

Other Material: HMRC *Compliance Handbook* CH81120ff., 81140, 81145; GOV.UK website: www.gov.uk/government/collections/tax-agents-toolkits

Tax Reporter: ¶184-850

12010 Deliberate but not concealed inaccuracy

If the inaccuracy in a return given to HMRC is deliberate but does not involve any arrangements to conceal the inaccuracy, it is described by the legislation as 'deliberate but not concealed'. The maximum statutory penalty for deliberate understatements without concealment will be 70% of the lost revenue. The penalty for an unprompted disclosure can be reduced to no less than 20% of the lost revenue and for a prompted disclosure the statutory minimum penalty will be 35% of the lost revenue. Disclosure is discussed at 12020ff. and, as already noted, these differences in the level of penalty make it essential for the practitioner to advise the client fully concerning the benefits of disclosure.

A deliberate inaccuracy occurs when a person knowingly and intentionally gives HMRC an inaccurate document but does nothing by way of covering their tracks. HMRC's examples of actions that constitute deliberate but not concealed behaviour include:

- systematically paying wages without accounting for operating PAYE;

- knowingly failing to record all sales, especially where there is a pattern to the under-recording, such as omitting all transactions with a particular customer or at a particular time of the week, month or year;

- deliberately describing transactions inaccurately or in a way likely to mislead;

- giving a VAT return to HMRC that includes a figure of net VAT due that is too low because the person does not have the cash at that time to pay the full amount, and later telling HMRC the true figure when they have the funds to pay;

- claiming a deduction for personal expenses of such a size or frequency that the inaccuracy must have been known;

- deliberately not making any attempt to ensure that money withdrawn for personal use from a limited company is treated correctly for tax purposes; and

- deliberately omitting a known asset from an inheritance tax account (rather than making enquiries about its value) on the basis that the asset can be included in a corrective account later.

Practical examples illustrating these points are included in HMRC's *Compliance Handbook*.

Practitioners will appreciate that by asserting that behaviour is deliberate rather than merely careless, HMRC can not only seek higher penalties but can also bring a greater number of earlier years into account in the enquiry (because of the differing time limits for assessment).

Although it would be unusual for actions that did not involve concealment to form the basis of an HMRC prosecution, practitioners need to be alert to the possibility. HMRC's *Compliance Handbook* states in the context of deliberate but unconcealed actions:

> 'Although the penalties for deliberate inaccuracies are civil monetary penalties, we also have a criminal investigation policy and will refer the most serious cases for consideration of criminal proceedings where appropriate.'

Legislation: FA 2007, Sch. 24, para. 3(1)(b), 4(1)(b), 10(1) and 10(2); TMA 1970, s. 36

Other Material: HMRC *Compliance Handbook* CH81150 and 81151

Tax Reporter: ¶184-850

12015   Deliberate and concealed inaccuracy

The most serious behaviour dealt with under FA 2007, Sch. 24 is that involving deliberate and concealed action. This carries a maximum penalty of 100% of the lost revenue unless there is an overseas aspect (in which case see 12024). Where the disclosure is unprompted, the minimum statutory penalty will be 30% of the lost revenue. The minimum statutory penalty for a prompted disclosure of a deliberate understatement with concealment will be 50% of the tax lost. This demonstrates why HMRC are expecting to recover significantly higher levels of penalty under the current regime. Penalties as high as 50% would have been very unusual under the former regime.

The key additional element in this class of behaviour is of course the concealment. Unusually, the legislation includes an example of the type of behaviour involved. It says '(for example, submitting false evidence in support of an inaccurate figure)'.

HMRC have traditionally been very hesitant to use the word 'fraud' but practitioners will recognise that ingredient in most of the examples given by HMRC. These include:

- creating false invoices to support inaccurate figures in a return;

- backdating or postdating contracts or invoices;

- creating false minutes of meetings or minutes of fictitious meetings;

- destroying books and records so that they are not available;

- systematically diverting takings into undisclosed bank accounts and covering the traces;

- invoice routing, for example, the purported sale or purchase of goods through a tax haven company (with no activity undertaken by that company even though contracts exist showing the contrary) leaving profits untaxed in that company;

- creating sales records that deliberately understate the value of the goods sold, the balance of the full price being paid separately to the person;

- describing expenditure in the business records in such a way as to make it appear to be business related when it is in fact private (possibly with the supplier agreeing to change the description on the relevant invoices); and

- altering genuine purchase invoices to inflate their value.

Finally, practitioners need to note that deliberate and concealed action must stand the greatest risk of being considered by HMRC for prosecution. The warning included in the *Compliance Handbook* is:

'Although the penalties for deliberate inaccuracies are civil monetary penalties, we also have a criminal investigation policy and will refer the most serious cases for consideration of criminal proceedings where appropriate.'

Legislation: FA 2007, Sch. 24, para. 3(1)(c), 4(1)(c), 10(5) and 10(6); TMA 1970, s. 36

Other Material: HMRC *Compliance Handbook* CH81160 and 81161

Tax Reporter: ¶184-850

12020 Reduction of penalty for disclosure

A core concept of the current regime is the statutory standardisation of penalties by reference to the behaviours that resulted in the inaccuracy in the return or document. That, however, could not work satisfactorily without an incentive on a taxpayer to work to rectify any identified underpayment. This is addressed in the legislation by a structured discounting of the standard penalty by reference to the extent of disclosure provided by the taxpayer. The potential impact of disclosure is summarised in the key data tables.

The tables demonstrate the importance of the practitioner's role both in seeking to have the behaviour classified as favourably as possible and ensuring that their client is recognised to have disclosed to the maximum extent. Nothing can be done to change the history of an inaccuracy but the practitioner can substantially help to reduce the penalty consequences.

Legislation: FA 2007, Sch. 24, para. 3, 4 and 10

Tax Reporter: ¶184-850

12021 Unprompted disclosure

As shown by the key data tables, the legislation rewards an unprompted disclosure more generously than a prompted disclosure. A disclosure is prompted unless it meets the statutory definition of an unprompted disclosure. FA 2007, Sch. 24, para. 9(2) reads:

> 'Disclosure is 'unprompted' if made at a time when the person making it has no reason to believe that HMRC have discovered or are about to discover the inaccuracy, the supply of false information or withholding of information, or the under assessment.'

It will be noted that the legislation refers to the person 'having no reason to believe' rather than their 'believing'. This means that what the person actually believed is not the test but rather what the facts gave them reason to believe.

Other Material: HMRC *Compliance Handbook* CH82420 and CH82421

Tax Reporter: ¶184-850

12022 The elements of disclosure

The legislation identifies three elements to the disclosure of an inaccuracy:

- telling HMRC about it;

- giving HMRC reasonable help in quantifying it; and

- allowing HMRC access to records to ensure it is fully corrected.

HMRC describe the three elements slightly differently as telling, helping and giving but the meaning in each case appears to follow the statutory framework. HMRC's *Compliance Handbook* identifies ingredients within each element as follows:

Telling includes:

- admitting the inaccuracy;

- disclosing the inaccuracy in full; and

- explaining how and why the inaccuracy arose.

Helping includes:

- giving reasonable help in quantifying the inaccuracy;

- positive assistance as opposed to passive acceptance or obstruction;

- actively engaging in the work to accurately quantify the inaccuracies; and

- volunteering any information relevant to the disclosure.

Giving includes:

- responding positively to requests for information and documents;

- allowing access to business and other records and documents; and

- doing more than simply complying with requests for information.

Whilst these ingredients are not specifically identified in the legislation, they provide a useful checklist for the practitioner. If a client satisfies all these tests in relation to their disclosure, they should be in line to achieve the maximum possible reduction in any penalty.

Legislation: FA 2007, Sch. 24, para. 9

Other Material: HMRC *Compliance Handbook* CH82430ff.

Tax Reporter: ¶184-850

12023   The quality of disclosure

The legislation requires penalties to be reduced by reference to the quality of the disclosure. The only statutory guidance on the meaning of that term is that 'quality includes timing, nature and extent'. Given that the legislation identifies three elements to disclosure (see 12022), it would be surprising if the quality of disclosure was not determined significantly by reference to those factors. However, the legislation provides no guidance as to relative weighting as between those three elements. Neither does it indicate the relationship of timing, nature and extent to the three elements.

HMRC guidance assumes, not unreasonably, that the legislation requires consideration of the timing, nature and extent of the three elements of disclosure. One point to make here is that the statutory definition of quality is an inclusive rather than an exhaustive one. It is difficult to think of an example where any other factor might be significant but, in such a case, practitioners should not feel limited by the definition.

What is less helpful is HMRC's assumption that the three elements of disclosure need to be given relative weightings. HMRC's manuals put forward the following as guidelines:

- telling – 30%;

- helping – 40%; and

- giving access – 30%.

Despite the manual wording being written in terms of guidance, other HMRC material, including that provided to practitioners at workshops in the Spring of 2011 referred to these reductions without distinguishing their basis from the statutory provisions set out in paragraph 10. The resulting impression was that this was the only way to determine the quality of the disclosure.

HMRC's approach is to assess the taxpayer's disclosure score for each of the three elements against their guideline allocations in order to determine the percentage of the available statutory reduction for disclosure that should be given.

Example 1

After an initial denial, a person admitted that their return was inaccurate and provided the information needed to calculate the tax lost, but with some delays. The quality of the disclosure might be determined as:

	Possible reduction	Actual reduction
Telling	30%	15%
Helping	40%	30%
Giving access	30%	25%
Quality of disclosure	100%	70%

HMRC's *Compliance Handbook* notes that there will be cases where the circumstances are such that little in the way of telling, helping and access is needed to establish the reasons for the person giving an inaccurate document and the amount of any additional tax due. The guidance to officers in this situation reads: 'You should allow the full reduction for those elements of the disclosure that are not required.'

If the inaccuracy in question arose from deliberate but not concealed action, the statutory penalty banding would be between a maximum of 70% (para. 4(1)(b) with no reduction for disclosure) and a minimum of 35% (para. 10(4) for full but prompted disclosure). Applying HMRC's 70% calculation of the quality of the disclosure to the difference of 35% between the maximum and minimum statutory penalty levels would mean that a reduction of 24.5% (being 70% of 35%) should be made. Thus the penalty loading based on HMRC's approach should be (70 − 24.5) = 45.5%. A detailed explanation of the penalty calculation is set out in 12025.

In answer to the charge that this was producing a much higher penalty that would have been the case under the former regime, HMRC's response would doubtless be that the current regime was imposed by Parliament for that very purpose and that the taxpayer could have secured a 35% penalty loading if they had made a full disclosure after prompting or a penalty as low as 20% if they had made an unprompted full disclosure. HMRC could reasonably argue that such a 20% level might in fact be lower than would have applied under the former regime.

As the percentage calculation of the quality of a disclosure is only based on HMRC guidance, practitioners should be prepared to challenge the calculation if it produces a level of penalty which appears high in all the circumstances.

Legislation: FA 2007, Sch. 24, para. 9, 10

Other Material: HMRC *Compliance Handbook* CH82430ff.

Tax Reporter: ¶184-850

12024   Penalties relating to overseas matters

Since 6 April 2011, a higher level of penalties can be charged in cases where the inaccuracy in a return or document relates to certain offshore income, gains or assets. These special overseas provisions apply in relevant circumstances in relation to documents given to HMRC and assessments issued by HMRC in relation to a tax period commencing after 5 April 2011.

The general Sch. 24 penalty provisions continue to apply to domestic matters and where the offshore matter concerns a jurisdiction which automatically exchanges information with the UK. The target of the higher penalties is where the offshore inaccuracy involves a jurisdiction which has less tax transparency. Such jurisdictions are classified as category 2 or category 3 territories.

The special offshore provisions applied initially to income tax and CGT in respect of offshore matters. *Finance Act* 2015, however, extended the provisions to include inheritance tax and offshore transfers, with effect from 6 April 2016 (SI 2016/456).

Thus, in order to be within the scope of the higher penalty charge (as amended by FA 2015), the inaccuracy in question must:

- relate to an offshore matter or offshore transfer;
- relate to income tax, CGT or inheritance tax; and
- involve a category 2 or category 3 territory.

Category 1 and category 3 territories are defined. Category 2 territories are all other jurisdictions (apart from the UK itself).

Where an inaccuracy involves a category 1 jurisdiction (or the UK), it is referred to as a category 1 inaccuracy. The penalties applying are those that apply to domestic inaccuracies. Category 2 and category 3 inaccuracies are similarly defined by reference to the categorisation of the jurisdiction. It is only the category 2 and 3 inaccuracies that attract the higher penalties.

The penalty levels for a category 2 inaccuracy are all set at one and a half times the penalties for a category 1 inaccuracy.

The penalty levels for a category 3 inaccuracy are all set at twice the penalties for a category 1 inaccuracy.

An inaccuracy involves an offshore matter if it results in a potential loss of revenue that is charged on or by reference to income arising from a source in a territory outside the UK, assets situated or held in a territory outside the UK, activities carried on wholly or mainly in a territory outside the UK, or anything having effect as if it were income, assets or activities of a kind described above.

The concept of an 'offshore transfer' is separate from the existing concept of 'offshore matter' and applies for inaccuracies which are deliberate and result in a potential loss of revenue, the tax at stake is income tax, capital gains tax or inheritance tax, and either the income (income tax) or the proceeds of disposal (capital gains tax) are received in a territory outside the UK, or transferred before the filing date to a territory outside the UK or the assets (inheritance tax) are transferred before the filing date to a territory outside the UK.

Finance Act 2015 also updates the territory classification system to reflect the new Common Reporting Standard (CRP) by creating four (instead of three) levels of penalty, with the existing lowest level applying to territories that adopt automatic exchange of information under the CRP (territories to be reclassified in a new statutory instrument).

The new category of penalty, 'penalty 0', will apply to penalties for inaccuracies (under FA 2007, Sch. 24), failures to notify (under FA 2008, Sch. 41) and failures to make returns (under FA 2009, Sch. 55). The new category of penalty will carry the lowest level of penalty equivalent to those currently in category 1 (i.e. 30%, 70% and 100%) and the penalty percentages for category 1 penalties will be increased to 37.5%, 87.5% and 125% respectively. The intention is that only overseas territories making information exchange arrangements with the UK that meet the new Common Reporting Standard will fall into category 0, however, it is envisaged that most or all territories currently in category 1 will, over time, make arrangements so as to fall within category 0. The provisions are to take effect from a date to be appointed by Treasury order.

Finance Act 2016 increases minimum penalties (after mitigation) for inaccuracies, failure to notify a charge to tax or failure to deliver a return, where the penalty relates to an offshore matter or transfer. For the increased penalties to apply, the behaviour that led to the penalty must have been deliberate or deliberate and concealed. The new provisions will come into force on a day appointed by regulations.

Finance Act 2016 further amends the provisions for reducing penalties for deliberate offshore inaccuracies by introducing a new requirement for a taxpayer to provide HMRC with 'additional information', in addition to that which is already requirement to make a full disclosure of the inaccuracy.

Legislation: FA 2007, Sch. 24, para. 4A–4D; FA 2010, s. 35 and Sch. 10; FA 2015, Sch. 21; SI 2011/975

Other Material: A list of Category 1 and Category 2 territories is at www. hmrc.gov.uk/manuals/chmanual/attachments/CH73214_table2.pdf; CC/ FS17

Tax Reporter: ¶184-850

12025 Calculating the penalty

The stages for calculating the amount of the penalty are as follows:

(1) identify the behaviour leading to the inaccuracy;

(2) establish whether the disclosure was prompted or unprompted;

(3) identify the maximum (a) and the minimum (b) penalty;

(4) deduct the minimum penalty from the maximum penalty to work out the maximum permitted reduction in percentage terms for disclosure (c): $c = a - b$;

(5) work out the percentage reduction for the quality of the disclosure (d);

(6) apply the percentage reduction for the quality of the disclosure to the maximum permitted reduction for disclosure to work out the actual reduction percentage for disclosure (e): $e = d \times c$;

(7) deduct the actual reduction percentage from the maximum penalty percentage to work out the penalty percentage (f): $f = a - e$;

(8) apply the penalty percentage to the potential lost revenue (PLR) to work out the amount of the penalty: amount of the penalty = PLR × f.

Example

A person made an unprompted disclosure of an inaccuracy that was deliberate but without concealment. The PLR is £43,000. The quality of the disclosure justifies a reduction for disclosure of 75%:

(1) The failure was deliberate but without concealment and the disclosure was unprompted.

(2) The maximum penalty is 70% and the minimum 20%.

(3) The maximum permitted deduction for disclosure is 50% (70% − 20%).

(4) The reduction for the quality of the disclosure has been determined as 75%.

(5) The actual reduction percentage for disclosure is 37.5% (50% × 75%).

(6) The penalty percentage is 32.5% (70% − 37.5%).

(7) The penalty is £13,975 (PLR £43,000 × 32.5%).

Special provisions apply where there are multiple errors that require correcting which result from different levels of culpable behaviour.

Legislation: FA 2007 Sch. 24, para. 3, 5–10

Other Material: HMRC *Compliance Handbook* CH82000ff.

Tax Reporter: ¶184-850

12026 Special reduction

The legislation provides for HMRC to reduce a penalty for special circumstances. The legislation does not define what constitutes special circumstances but does specifically exclude inability to pay and the compensation of potential loss by another taxpayer's potential overpayment. HMRC manuals unsurprisingly indicate that the provision will be used sparingly.

If the officer does not apply any special reduction, the taxpayer can appeal to the tribunal against that decision. However, the tribunal can only substitute its own decision for that of the HMRC officer if the officer's decision process was flawed. It cannot simply override the officer's conclusion.

Two tribunal decisions, *Hardy* and *White*, demonstrate that a tribunal may take a more generous view of what constitutes special circumstances than HMRC.

Cases: *Hardy* [2011] TC 01435; *White* [2012] TC 02050

Tax Reporter: ¶184-850

12027 Suspension of penalties

The 2007 legislation introduced a completely new concept: the suspension of all or part of a penalty. The provision can only apply where the behaviour giving rise to the inaccuracy is careless. Suspension cannot apply if the inaccuracy was deliberate. The penalty can be suspended wholly or in part for up to two years. This approach may be applied, for example, in the case where defective accounting systems had led to the understatement.

It is for the HMRC officer to decide whether it is appropriate to suspend a penalty. Where the penalty is to be suspended, the officer must notify the taxpayer:

- what part of any penalty is to be suspended;
- the period of suspension (not exceeding two years); or
- the conditions of suspension that must be complied with.

If at the end of the period of suspension the taxpayer can demonstrate that the conditions have been complied with, the penalty is cancelled.

The suspension will end sooner if a further incorrect return has been received in which case the suspended penalty would immediately become payable.

The onus will be on the taxpayer to demonstrate that they have met the conditions and they may be required to provide access to HMRC to check the position themselves.

If the officer does not suspend all or part of a penalty, the taxpayer can appeal to the tribunal against that decision. The taxpayer can also appeal to the tribunal against the suspension conditions. However, in either case, the tribunal can only substitute its own decision for that of the HMRC officer if the officer's decision process was flawed. It cannot simply override the officer's conclusion.

In marked contrast with these penalties for incorrect returns, there is no provision for suspension of penalties in respect of record keeping (see 12407).

In appropriate cases, practitioners should be prepared to challenge the non-suspension of penalties. In such cases, it will always be sensible to identify what conditions might reasonably be imposed to give HMRC the required confidence that careless inaccuracies can be reduced. There is apocryphal evidence both of some substantial penalties being suspended where appropriate conditions were suggested by practitioners and situations where the possibility of suspension had not been considered at all.

In its *Small Business Tax Review* published at the end of February 2012, the Office of Tax Simplification added its voice on the issue. It commented:

> 'Penalty rules include the option of suspended penalties for careless errors provided that conditions for improvement can be agreed with the taxpayer. These provide an excellent tool for encouraging businesses to get things right in the future.
>
> The OTS has found evidence that HMRC officers are not always following their guidance and look for reasons not to suspend penalties, rather than seeking conditions for agreement to suspend. We understand that by around April 2012 all HMRC staff will have attended training in this area which it is hoped will resolve this issue.'

Legislation: FA 2007, Sch. 24, para. 14, 15

Cases: *Patel* [2015] TC 04617; *Steady* [2016] TC 05225

Other Material: HMRC *Compliance Handbook* CH83100ff.; CC/FS10

Tax Reporter: ¶184-850

12028   Matters relating to companies

As with income tax, the FA 2007 penalty regime applies to any company return that is both for a period commencing on or after 1 April 2008 and completed on or after 1 April 2009. As well as the general penalty provisions, there are some that only affect companies. These are designed to combat:

- the avoidance of a penalty through using group relief; and

- deliberate understatements of company profits by an officer of the company.

Group relief

The legislation prevents groups of companies using group relief to avoid a penalty being charged where profits have been understated in a group company. Under the former provisions, the following scenario was possible in respect of group companies A, B and C.

- Company A declares profits of £500,000 but has understated them by £500,000 so that a penalty should be due.

- Company B has correctly declared profit of £2m.

- Company C, has losses of £1m, and had originally surrendered £500,000 to Company A and £500,000 to Company B.

- Had companies A, B and C been divisions of one company, it would have declared a profit of £1.5m which would have been increased to £2m and a penalty would be calculated using the £500,000 understatement.

- The surrender is amended to surrender the full loss of £1m to Company A so that Company B will pay tax on additional £500,000 but Company A now has no liability on which a penalty can be charged.

The former penalty regime accordingly gave a group an advantage over a single company competitor. The current legislation counters any advantage from such reallocation of group relief.

Penalties for company and partnership officers

The current penalty regime aligns the company penalty position for direct taxes with the existing VAT provision. Part or all of any company penalty can be charged on an officer of the company (for example, a director or company secretary) if the inaccuracy resulted from the deliberate act of that officer. This change is aimed at preventing the avoidance of a penalty by owner-managed companies putting their company into liquidation and then restarting as a new entity – phoenixism.

The same provision extends to a member of an LLP. Separate provisions apply in relation to a partner's responsibility for errors in a partnership return.

Legislation: FA 2007, Sch. 24, para. 5, 19 and 20

Other Material: HMRC *Compliance Handbook* CH84600

Tax Reporter: ¶184-850

12029   Error attributable to third party

A third party can be liable to a penalty if they deliberately supply false information to (or withhold information from) a taxpayer with the intention that the taxpayer gives HMRC a document containing an inaccuracy. A penalty can be charged under this provision even if the taxpayer themselves is liable to a penalty in respect of the same inaccuracy.

This type of situation requires particularly careful handling by a practitioner as there can be significant complications.

Legislation: FA 2007, Sch. 24, para. 1A

Other Material: HMRC *Compliance Handbook* CH81165

Tax Reporter: ¶184-850

12030   Penalties and the Human Rights Act

Penalties charged under the *Taxes Management Act* 1970 can be categorised as criminal or civil for the purposes of the *Human Rights Act* 1998 (HRA). The taxpayer will have the protection of the HRA if a penalty is categorised as criminal but not if it is categorised as civil. The scope of criminality in this context is wider than might generally be thought to be the case and may encompass penalties not categorised as criminal by the state.

HMRC Factsheet CC/FS9 explains the rights provided by the European Convention on Human Rights, art. 6 (the right not to self-incriminate or the right to silence) which applies to certain penalties. Under art. 6, taxpayers have the right not to answer HMRC's questions but must provide us with such information or documents that already exist, if HMRC have a legal right to ask for them.

Other material: CC/FS9

Tax Reporter: ¶184-675

12040   Deceased persons

Following a period of some uncertainty as to HMRC's ability to charge penalties on personal representatives in respect of inaccuracies in returns submitted by the person prior to the date of death the position was clarified by *Finance Act* 2007.

The position is summarised as follows:

- no penalty can be charged on personal representatives in respect of an inaccuracy in a return that was submitted by the deceased in their lifetime;

- additional tax assessments may however be issued in such circumstances. Assessments must be raised as soon as possible after the inaccuracy is discovered and within the statutory time limits;

- any penalty that was charged to a taxpayer during their lifetime and which remains unpaid on their death is a liability of the estate and enforceable against the personal representatives;

- if a penalty charged prior to a person's death is under appeal at the time of their death, HMRC's instructions to officers is that discussions to conclude any appeal must continue with personal representatives;

- if a personal representative of the deceased has submitted an incorrect document to HMRC in connection with the administration of a deceased's estate, the personal representative may be liable to a penalty in the normal way.

Other Material: *Enquiry Manual* EM1395

Tax Reporter: ¶184-650

12050   Penalties for incorrect returns for periods commencing before 1 April 2008 (the former regime)

The current penalty regime in relation to inaccuracies in a return or document was introduced by *Finance Act* 2007 for returns for periods commencing on or after 1 April 2008 and with a filing date of 1 April 2009 or later (see 12002ff.). However, the former penalty regime continues to apply for returns for periods commencing before 1 April 2008. The following commentary and the commentary on abatement in 12060 describe the penalty regime as it applies to returns for periods commencing before 1 April 2008 with a filing date on or before 31 March 2009. A normal personal tax return for the 2007–08 tax year is accordingly dealt with under the former regime rules.

This section refers to the provisions for income tax and capital gains tax. Comparable provisions applied for corporation tax. There were separate provisions under the former regime for VAT. As noted in 12001, the current provisions have applied to an extended range of taxes since 1 April 2010 in relation to periods commencing on or after 1 April 2009.

An incorrect return is a return which self assesses the amount of tax in a figure which is not that finally found to be due. Not every incorrect return leads to a penalty being charged however. If the error is innocent, as opposed to being as a result of fraudulent or negligent conduct, there can be no penalty. None of these terms is defined by statute but if an incorrect return is made other than as a result of fraudulent or negligent conduct, it will be incorrect as a result of innocent error. Note, however, that if such an innocent error is not remedied without unreasonable delay, the legislation treats the error as arising from negligent conduct. This is the parallel of a provision in the current regime (see 12004).

The categorisation of certain tax penalties as a criminal charge for the purposes of article 6 of the European Convention on Human Rights (*King v Walden*) has led HMRC to issue revised guidance to its staff on what can be said about the abatement of penalties.

Legislation: TMA 1970, s. 95 and 97

Case: *King v Walden* [2001] BTC 170

Other Material: HMRC *Enquiry Manual* EM4801ff.; CC/FS15

Tax Reporter: ¶184-875

12051 Fraudulent conduct under the former regime

Under the former regime legislation, there are very few practical distinctions between the consequences arising from something done fraudulently and something done negligently. The time limits for assessing are no shorter for negligence than fraud and there is a common tax-based maximum 100% penalty for both types of conduct. As a result, it was very rarely necessary for the Inland Revenue (as it then was) to assert that the relevant behaviour was anything more than negligent. One notable exception following the merger of the departments was where the same conduct had resulted in an error for both direct and VAT purposes and there was a risk that the VAT penalty might be vulnerable if the direct tax offence was only seen as negligence.

This statutory lumping together of fraud and negligence under the former regime means in practical terms that an HMRC officer only has to establish negligence in order to be able to recover penalties. Whilst HMRC's instructions include a detailed commentary on what constitutes fraud, this commentary accordingly focuses on what constitutes negligence.

Legislation: TMA 1970, s. 36 (pre-FA 2007 version) and 95

Case: *Bayliss* [2016] TC 05251

Other Material: HMRC *Enquiry Manual* EM5105ff.

Tax Reporter: ¶184-875

12052 Negligent conduct under the former regime

Under the former regime, the penalty in respect of an incorrect return requires the delivery of the return to have been made negligently. For all practical purposes, there is no significant difference between an action (or omission) that constitutes negligent conduct under the former regime and something that amounts under the current regime to careless behaviour. The reader is accordingly referred to 12005 above for commentary on careless behaviour. The penalty consequences that arise under the two regimes are very distinct but the underlying cause of the error is the same in relation to both negligent conduct and careless behaviour.

What the practitioner needs to appreciate is that an HMRC officer may well be reluctant to use the word 'fraud' and be content to describe something as negligent for the purposes of the former regime but wish to assert that the same behaviour is deliberate rather than careless for the purpose of the current regime (in order to impose the higher penalties that apply for deliberate behaviour). In an enquiry involving years in both former and current regimes, this may lead to some interesting points on appeal to the tribunal.

Legislation: TMA 1970, s. 95, 95A; FA 1998, Sch. 18, para. 20

Case: *Bayliss* [2016] TC 05251

Other Material: HMRC *Enquiry Manual* EM5125

Tax Reporter: ¶184-875

12060 Abatement of the penalty for periods commencing before 1 April 2008

The former penalty regime starts with a maximum tax-based penalty amount of 100%. As noted, the legislation makes no distinction here between negligent and fraudulent conduct. The legislation empowers an authorised officer to make a determination imposing a penalty and setting it at such an amount as, in their opinion, is correct or appropriate. It is this power that enables an officer to impose a penalty at less than the statutory maximum.

Practitioners (and historically HMRC) refer to the resulting reduction in penalties as 'mitigation'. However, HMRC refer to the officer's power as one of abatement. The department reserves the term 'mitigation' to the way it is used in TMA 1970, s. 103.

Under the former regime provisions, HMRC recognise three factors as contributing to the appropriate abatement. The presence or absence of these factors determines the extent to which penalties are abated from their maximum limit of 100% of the additional tax. The three factors are:

- disclosure;

- co-operation; or

- seriousness (previously referred to as size and gravity).

HMRC's long-standing guidance to their officers is that abatement from the maximum limit should be:

- between zero and 20% (exceptionally 30%) for disclosure;

- between zero and 40% for co-operation; and

- between zero and 40% by reference to seriousness.

Each of the three factors is considered below.

Legislation: TMA 1970, s. 100

Other Material: HMRC *Enquiry Manual* EM6065

Tax Reporter: ¶184-875

12061 Disclosure under the former regime

A disclosure of irregularities does not have to be detailed and quantified to qualify for abatement. A disclosure in general terms which identifies all the areas of irregularity and indicates the approximate amounts involved may suffice. HMRC's manuals indicate that what is required is a disclosure of irregularities or an admission that the returns or accounts have been wrong. What will constitute a full disclosure will vary between cases. It will for example, in some but not all cases need to include a description of the manner in which the irregularities arose. The manuals advise officers that disclosure involves positive, voluntary and useful contributions to their knowledge of the irregularities.

The timing of disclosure can significantly affect its impact. The same statement made very usefully at an early stage in the enquiry could if made much later do little more than confirm what the officer had already established.

To earn the 20% abatement, the taxpayer must make an immediate full disclosure when first challenged. At the other extreme, the person who continues to deny any irregularity until the conclusion of the enquiry will earn no abatement for disclosure. There are various degrees of disclosure falling within these extremes and the level of abatement is a matter for negotiation between the practitioner and the officer.

The normal maximum 20% abatement for disclosure can be increased to 30% for a spontaneous and complete disclosure where in the words of HMRC's *Enquiry Manual* 'the taxpayer has no reason to fear early discovery'. It is unclear why HMRC have included the word 'early' although informally within the department reference was made to the challenge 'walking up the garden path' which also identified the immediacy. Apart from a possible distinction on this timing point, there is for practical purposes no significant difference between this test and the statutory definition for 'unprompted' disclosure under the current regime (see 12021).

Other Material: HMRC *Enquiry Manual* EM6070ff.

Tax Reporter: ¶184-875

12062   Co-operation under the former regime

The abatement for co-operation, which can be up to 40%, is given to reward the taxpayer's willing co-operation to enable the errors on the return to be corrected. The factors taken into account in assessing the amount of abatement include the speed of response when providing information and whether there has been any deliberate obstruction of HMRC's enquiries.

Co-operation is difficult to measure. HMRC's manual indicates that one approach is to compare the time that could have been taken with the actual time elapsed and the co-operation that might have been expected with what was actually given.

HMRC's *Enquiry Manual* recognises that:

- a complex enquiry will inevitably take longer to settle;
- the length of the enquiry period often depends as much on the officer as the taxpayer;

- age, health and availability may need considering; and
- factors influencing an officer's view of the level of co-operation given may include:
  - general delay, prevarication and procrastination;
  - concealment of assets, piecemeal disclosures, and truthfulness;
  - willingness to attend meetings;
  - number of occasions formal information powers used;
  - necessity for making discovery assessments or jeopardy amendments or closure notices;
  - persistence in uncorroborated stories of gifts, cash hoards, betting wins, etc.;
  - necessity to have the liabilities determined by the tribunal;
  - irregularities continuing during the course of the enquiry; and
  - payments on account.

Officers are advised that a genuine disagreement over the interpretation of a set of facts or the statute is not a lack of co-operation. Neither is an appeal for assistance from a third party, including the local MP or seeking a closure notice unless such action involved deliberate obstruction and/ or clear evidence of attempts to mislead such third parties. Under the former regime, abatement for co-operation is often the only aspect of the penalty calculation that the practitioner can influence. Practitioners should therefore do everything they can to avoid the assertion that they have failed to maximise the abatement for co-operation, or indeed jeopardised any abatement, through delays in their office.

A threat to reduce the abatement for co-operation for a failure to attend an interview is one of the ways in which HMRC might try to force a meeting even though they have no legal right to insist that a meeting takes place. If the taxpayer has good reason for not agreeing to be interviewed, this pressure should be resisted (see 11510).

A failure to provide information without the need for a formal notice would be viewed as obstructive. If a practitioner cannot provide information within the time given by the officer, it is important to seek to agree a sensible revised timetable and thus help to preserve the maximum abatement for co-operation.

Other Material: HMRC *Enquiry Manual* EM6075

Tax Reporter: ¶184-875

12063   Seriousness under the former regime

The abatement for seriousness cannot be affected by the taxpayer's response to HMRC's enquiries. It depends entirely on the historical factors of the amount of tax at risk and the seriousness of the offence.

Thus, a settlement involving a very large amount of tax lost due to the taxpayer's negligent or fraudulent conduct over a long period will earn less abatement than the case of a small amount of the tax lost due to negligent conduct over a short period.

Maximum abatement would be earned where the omissions were less than the limit for re-opening earlier years (see 11700) and there was no more than negligent conduct on the part of the taxpayer.

HMRC's civil investigation of fraud specialists who deal with the most serious cases involving fraud will normally allow abatement for seriousness of 15%. Abatement of any less than that in a local office enquiry would therefore be surprising.

Other Material: HMRC *Enquiry Manual* EM6080

Tax Reporter: ¶184-875

12064   Overall penalty calculation under the former regime

Once the three individual factors have been considered by the officer, they will normally contact the practitioner and indicate the overall level of penalty that they would expect to be included in a letter of offer. They will normally be prepared to justify their suggestion by reference to the three factors. There is some limited scope for negotiation at this stage. Often it will be appropriate at that stage for the practitioner to simply listen and explain that they will need to take instructions but much must depend on the chemistry of the relationship that has developed over the enquiry between the officer and the practitioner. The important thing is for the practitioner to consider the penalties without being under pressure. Ideally, they should formulate their own view before any discussion with the officer.

If the level of penalty can be agreed, it will be calculated and built into the letter of offer, assuming that the officer is inviting that approach. Even if it not possible to agree on an appropriate level of penalty, the taxpayer can present the officer with a letter of offer. The letter is exactly what it says – an offer. In order for it to be legally binding, it needs to be freely made without duress. If the offer is 'sub-standard', the officer will probably need to submit it to a more senior officer. In doing so, the officer will make recommendations as to whether it should nevertheless be accepted. The practitioner can assist the client's case by ensuring that reasons for the level of offer are spelt out in a covering letter. The reasoning should follow HMRC's own approach to the quantification of penalties. There may then be a period of negotiation.

If the client's offer is eventually accepted by HMRC, payment of the settlement figure will proceed on a contractual basis. If agreement cannot be reached, the officer would make formal penalty determinations. These could then be appealed. To avoid the risk of formally determined penalties being pitched at a higher level than those discussed with the officer, it is useful for the practitioner to ensure that written reference is made to those previously discussed levels. There appears to be a growing acceptance within HMRC that the levels put forward in informal discussion should be adhered to in any formal determination. This is logical as the relevant factors will not have changed. Not agreeing to a particular level of penalty should not be seen as involving any lack of co-operation.

The HMRC manuals include examples of penalty calculations in various scenarios. These demonstrate the somewhat inconsistent and bizarre results that can emerge. It remains to be seen whether the current regime (see 12002) produces generally more logical and appropriate penalties.

Other Material: HMRC *Enquiry Manual* EM6085ff.

Tax Reporter: ¶184-875

Failure to notify

12120   Introduction

TMA 1970 imposes an obligation on an individual who is chargeable to income tax or CGT and who has not been notified of a requirement for a tax return to notify HMRC that they are chargeable. Sensible exceptions are made to remove that obligation where the individual's income will be properly taxed without the need for a return, for example where the whole of someone's income is subject to PAYE. Comparable provisions apply for corporation tax purposes. Penalties apply if a person fails to provide such notification within the specified time. This commentary first considers the penalties arising under the current unified regime for failures occurring on or after 1 April 2010. It then notes the different provisions that applied if the failure occurred before that date (see ¶12150ff.).

The provisions of *Finance Act* 2008 relating to failure to notify chargeability (along with a wide range of other types of failure) apply where the act of failure occurred on or after 1 April 2010.

In order to know whether the current or former regime provisions apply, the practitioner needs to identify the date on which the failure occurred.

For example, in an income tax case, TMA 1970, s. 7(1) imposes an obligation on a taxpayer to notify chargeability within six months of the end of the tax year. In relation to the tax year 2008/09, that would require notification no later than 5 October 2009. If notification was delayed beyond that date, the failure would have occurred on 6 October 2009. As that predated 1 April 2010, the former rather than the current provisions would apply to that failure.

Tax Reporter: ¶181-325ff.

12121 Failure to notify from 1 April 2010 – introduction

The current provisions impose tax-geared penalties for a failure to notify that occurred on or after 1 April 2010 where that failure resulted in a loss of tax. This means the first time that the current penalties can apply is:

- the 2009–10 tax year for income tax, capitals gain tax and Class 4 NICs; and

- accounting periods ending on or after 31 March 2010 for corporation tax.

The amount of any penalty is determined by the nature of the behaviour that resulted in the failure. As with the penalties for inaccuracies in returns, a failure that was deliberate incurs a higher penalty than one that was not and the highest level of penalty is imposed where there was concealment. If there was a reasonable excuse for the failure, there may be no penalty liability.

Tax Reporter: ¶181-325ff.

12122 Occurrence of failure

The occurrence of a failure is normally not in dispute. Either notification was or was not given within the permitted statutory period. In relation to income tax and CGT, that period is six months from the end of the relevant tax year. For corporation tax, it is 12 months from the end of the accounting period. A detailed list of all the failures and other actions within the provision is set out in FA 2008, Sch. 41, para. 1. Whenever a practitioner is notifying HMRC of chargeability on behalf of a client within the statutory period, it is essential to preserve a record that evidences the action. Whenever possible, dated confirmation should be obtained of the notification.

If the failure resulted in no loss of tax, there can be no penalty.

Legislation: TMA 1970, s. 7; FA 1998, Sch. 18, para. 2; FA 2008, Sch. 41, para. 1, 6

Tax Reporter: ¶181-325ff.

12123   Reasonable excuse

The legislation recognises that there may be a reasonable excuse for a failure. Where that is the case, no penalty arises. This cannot, however, apply if the failure was deliberate. To avoid a penalty, the taxpayer has to satisfy HMRC or (on appeal) the tribunal that there was a reasonable excuse for the failure.

Statute specifically indicates that:

- a lack of funds is not a reasonable excuse;
- there are only limited circumstances where reliance on someone else could constitute a reasonable excuse; and
- once the excuse has ceased, the failure must be remedied without unreasonable delay.

HMRC see 'reasonable excuse' as an exceptional and unforeseeable event (or a combination of such events) that is beyond the person's control. Bereavement and serious illness are likely to be viewed sympathetically. By contrast, thinking that it would be too difficult to have to prepare a return, pressure of work, lack of information, and ignorance of basic (as distinct from complex) tax law are unlikely to cut much ice. HMRC's Compliance Handbook advises officers that:

- the onus is on the taxpayer to demonstrate reasonable excuse;
- the taxpayer's explanation must be carefully considered taking into account all the circumstances and available information;
- if the excuse is reasonable, it must be accepted;
- any request for evidence must be reasonable and proportionate and pay proper regard to Human Rights Act procedures;
- if the excuse is not considered reasonable, the taxpayer must be told and given the opportunity to provide further argument and/or evidence; and
- if the excuse is rejected, the letter notifying the person of that decision must also advise them of their appeal and review rights.

Legislation: FA 2008, Sch. 41, para. 20

Other Material: HMRC *Compliance Handbook* CH71580, 75100ff.

Tax Reporter: ¶181-325ff.

12124   Nature of failure

The legislation distinguishes between three types of behaviour:

- deliberate and concealed failure;
- deliberate but not concealed failure; and
- non-deliberate failures.

The legislation does not elaborate on what constitutes deliberate behaviour or concealment. This absence of definition of deliberate failure does not help to identify when a non-deliberate failure occurs but it would seem that (in the absence of reasonable excuse) the simple absence of notification (regardless of the taxpayer's state of mind or knowledge) is all that is required for the failure to incur a penalty.

Legislation: FA 2008, Sch. 41, para. 6

Other Material: HMRC *Compliance Handbook* CH72100

Tax Reporter: ¶181-325ff.

12125   Deliberate failure

HMRC advise its officers that a failure to notify is deliberate if the person:

- knows that they are required to give notification; and
- is able to do so; but
- chooses not to do so.

HMRC's *Compliance Handbook* indicates that the failure can be deliberate in an indirect manner and gives the example of a person deliberately failing to keep the records necessary to know when a notification would be required.

A failure will be deliberate if the person knows that they should have notified HMRC but chose not to. A person might for example know that the turnover of their business has reached the threshold for VAT registration but decide not to notify HMRC. Their failure would be deliberate. However, provided they took no steps to conceal their failure, it would not be 'deliberate with concealment'.

Another example of a deliberate failure without concealment is where a person works as an employee but then decides to do some freelance work in the evenings and at weekends. If they do not receive a tax return and take no steps to conceal their failure to notify HMRC of their self-employment, their failure will be deliberate but without concealment.

Other Material: HMRC *Compliance Handbook* CH72160ff.

Tax Reporter: ¶181-325ff.

12126 Deliberate failure with concealment

HMRC's *Compliance Handbook* emphasises that concealing the fact that a notification should be given is the most serious level of evasion. Examples of concealment are indicated to include:

- creating false evidence of a non-taxable source to explain undisclosed taxable income;

- creating false stock records;

- creating false invoices to support inaccurate figures of turnover;

- backdating or postdating contracts or invoices;

- destroying books and records so that they should not be available;

- creating sales records that deliberately understate the value of the goods sold, the balance of the full price being paid separately to the person; and

- concealing excise goods on which the duty has not been paid or deferred with 'innocent' goods.

The handbook also warns that HMRC would in the most serious cases consider criminal proceedings rather than the civil tax penalties.

HMRC take the view that the act of concealment can occur after the act of failure. The two things do not need to occur at the same time. Some of the HMRC examples demonstrate that the line between failure to notify and making an inaccurate return can be a fine one. In practice, HMRC are probably much less likely to assert that a failure is concealed than simply deliberate.

Other Material: HMRC *Compliance Handbook* CH72120ff.

Tax Reporter: ¶181-325ff.

12127 Non-deliberate failure

Unless HMRC can show that, on the balance of probabilities, the failure was deliberate (either with or without concealment), it will be a non-deliberate failure. It will be appreciated, however, that whether the failure was deliberate is dependent on the taxpayer's state of knowledge and mind. No action of any kind is required. This makes it essential for the practitioner to establish so far as possible what was (or was not) in the mind of their client.

Other Material: HMRC *Compliance Handbook* CH72200ff.

Tax Reporter: ¶181-325ff.

12128 Disclosure

The standard penalties can be reduced by disclosure (see key data tables). The legislation defining disclosure is very similar to that for inaccuracies in returns (see 12020ff.) with the same distinction between unprompted and prompted disclosure.

HMRC adopt the same non-statutory basis of allocating percentage reductions for three elements of disclosure as it does in relation to penalties for inaccuracies (see 12023). Thus the available statutory reduction for disclosure is assumed by HMRC (without statutory authority) to be attributable to the three elements of disclosure as follows:

* telling – 30%;

* helping – 40%; and

* giving access – 30%.

For more detailed commentary on this point (in relation to inaccuracies), see 12023.

Legislation: FA 2008, Sch. 41, para. 12

Other Material: HMRC *Compliance Handbook* CH73100ff. and CH73220ff.

Tax Reporter: ¶181-325ff.

12129 Calculation of penalties for failure to notify from 1 April 2010

The relationship between the nature of the failure, the elements and quality of the disclosure and the level of penalty is similar (but not identical) to that for inaccuracies in returns (see 12002 for detailed commentary).

The standard penalties by reference to the class of behaviour are again 100%, 70% and 30% of the potential lost revenue (PLR). The calculation of PLR is explained with examples in some detail in relation to the various relevant taxes in HMRC's Compliance Handbook at CH72600 onwards.

Where the failure relates to an income tax or CGT matter with an overseas element and the failure occurs on or after 6 April 2011, the standard penalties are increased by multiples of 1.5 or 2.0 where the failure involves a category 2 or a category 3 territory respectively (see 12024).

The concept of an offshore transfer is included from 6 April 2016 (SI 2016/456) by FA 2015.

A failure involves an 'offshore matter' if it results in a potential loss of revenue that is charged on or by reference to income arising from a source in a territory outside the UK, assets situated or held in a territory outside the UK, activities carried on wholly or mainly in a territory outside the UK, or anything having effect as if it were income, assets or activities of a kind described above.

The concept of an 'offshore transfer' is separate from the concept of 'offshore matter' and applies for failures which are deliberate and result in a potential loss of revenue, the tax at stake is income tax or capital gains tax and either the income (income tax) or proceeds of disposal (capital gains tax) are received in a territory outside the UK, or transferred before the calculation date to a territory outside the UK.

In line with the amendments made to FA 2007, Sch. 24 and FA 2009, Sch. 55 (see 12024 and 12202), FA 2015 also introduces a new category of offshore territory, category 0, for the purposes of Sch. 41 penalties. Category 0 will carry the lowest level of penalty, equivalent to those currently in category 1 and the penalties in category 1 will be increased from 100% to 125%, from 70% to 87.5% and from 30% to 37.5%. The amendments are due to take effect from a date to be appointed by Treasury order.

Finance Act 2016 provides increased maximum and minimum penalty rates (after mitigation) for failures involving an offshore matter or offshore transfer. *Finance Act* 2016 also introduces a new requirement for failures involving an offshore transfer, or an offshore matter with deliberate behaviour, requiring the taxpayer to provide 'additional information' to HMRC in order to receive the maximum penalty reduction.

Unlike the position in relation to penalties for inaccuracies, no provision is made for the attribution of the lost tax where there are multiple failures involving different behaviours.

The main difference from the inaccuracy penalties is in relation to the 'other' (i.e. non-deliberate) failures. Here the legislation distinguishes between a failure that is disclosed less than 12 months after the time tax first became unpaid by reason of the failure and one disclosed later by allowing a greater reduction for early disclosure.

The resulting penalty loadings are summarised in the key data tables.

The point at which a penalty lies between the standard (undiscounted) level for the type of behaviour and the reduced level permitted by statute in any particular case will depend on the quality of disclosure. Given the substantial differences between the standard and the minimum penalties, it is essential that the practitioner does everything possible to ensure both that the behaviour is correctly classified and that maximum reduction is earned for disclosure. The client needs to appreciate the importance of the disclosure reduction from the very beginning of the enquiry.

Legislation: FA 2008, Sch. 41, para. 6

Other Material: HMRC *Compliance Handbook* CH72000ff., 72600ff.; CC/FS11; CC/FS17

Tax Reporter: ¶181-325ff.

12130   Penalty calculation steps

HMRC's approach to the calculation of a failure to notify penalty is as follows:

- Calculate the percentage for the quality of the disclosure (a), following the guidance at CH73220.

- Having established the behaviour and whether the disclosure was prompted or unprompted, identify:

  - the maximum penalty (b); and

  - the minimum penalty (c).

- Calculate the maximum disclosure reduction (d), where (d) = (b) − (c).

- Calculate the actual reduction percentage for disclosure (e) by multiplying the maximum disclosure reduction (d) by the percentage for the quality of the disclosure (a).

- Calculate the penalty percentage (f) by deducting the actual reduction percentage for disclosure (e) from the penalty maximum (b).

- To arrive at the amount of the penalty to be charged (g), apply the penalty percentage (f) to the potential lost revenue (PLR) calculated in line with CH 72620.

- The penalty should be rounded down to the next £1.

Other Material: HMRC *Compliance Handbook* CH73500ff.

Tax Reporter: ¶181-325ff.

12150   Failure to notify prior to 1 April 2010 (former rules)

Although FA 2008 introduced a current penalty regime for failures to notify, it did not change the underlying statutory obligations to notify. Broadly speaking, the former penalty regime for failure to notify follows the same principles that apply in respect of inaccuracies under the former regime (see 12050ff.).

The former provisions impose tax-geared penalties for a failure to notify that occurred on or before 31 March 2010 where that failure resulted in a loss of tax. If there was a reasonable excuse for the failure, there may be no penalty liability.

Legislation: TMA 1970, s. 7(8); FA 1998, Sch. 18, para. 2(3)

Other material: CC/FS15

Tax Reporter: ¶181-325ff.

12151　Occurrence of failure (former rules)

The occurrence of a failure is normally not in dispute. Either notification was or was not given within the permitted statutory period. In relation to income tax and CGT, that period is six months from the end of the relevant tax year. For corporation tax, it is 12 months from the end of the accounting period. Whenever a practitioner is notifying HMRC of chargeability on behalf of a client within the statutory period, it is essential to preserve a record that evidences the action. Whenever possible, dated confirmation should be obtained of the notification. If the failure resulted in no loss of tax, there can be no penalty.

Legislation: TMA 1970, s. 7; FA 1998, Sch. 18, para. 2

Tax Reporter: ¶181-325ff.

12152　Reasonable excuse (former rules)

The legislation recognises that there may be a reasonable excuse for a failure. Where that is the case, no penalty arises. Reasonable excuse is not given the same prominence in the former legislation, simply being referred to in the interpretation section of TMA 1970 without any statutory definition. The underlying principle is, however, identical to that already described in relation to the current regime (see 12123). HMRC and (on appeal) the tribunal may accordingly see the more clearly defined current regime as providing useful guidance.

HMRC see 'reasonable excuse' as an exceptional and unforeseeable event (or a combination of such events) that is beyond the person's control. Bereavement and serious illness are likely to be viewed sympathetically. By contrast, thinking that it would be too difficult to prepare a return, pressure of work, lack of information, failure of HMRC to send a reminder and ignorance of basic (as distinct from complex) tax law are unlikely to cut much ice.

The former regime provisions operate in the same way as the current in relation to the obligation to remedy the failure 'without unreasonable delay'. A practitioner should therefore notify HMRC as soon as they become aware of any failure.

Legislation: FA 2008, Sch. 41, para. 20

Other Material: HMRC *Enquiry Manual* EM5152

Tax Reporter: ¶181-325ff.

12153   Nature of failure (former rules)

Apart from the situations where there was a reasonable excuse for the failure, the former regime provisions do not focus on the cause or nature of the failure. There is accordingly no attempt to classify the act as negligent or fraudulent. Neither is any distinction made for failures that are disclosed within one year of the original date of the related tax liability (as there is under the current regime). However, factors such as the period of the failure, its recurrence and the taxpayer's stated or assumed state of mind can have a significant influence on the resulting penalty level.

Tax Reporter: ¶181-325ff.

12154   Abatement of penalty for failure (former rules)

The starting point for the calculation of the tax-geared penalties for failure under the former regime is the amount of tax that was underpaid as a result of the failure. In considering what penalty might be appropriate in any particular case, HMRC exercise their powers of abatement by applying the department's percentage discounts for disclosure, co-operation and seriousness. These are discussed in detail in the commentary on penalties for inaccuracies under the former regime (see 12060).

Legislation: TMA 1970, s. 7(8); FA 1998, Sch. 18, para. 2(3)

Tax Reporter: ¶181-325ff.

12155   Negotiation of penalties (former rules)

Once HMRC have formed a view on the appropriate level of penalties for a failure to notify, the negotiating process follows very closely that described in relation to penalties for inaccuracies under the former regime (see 12064).

Tax Reporter: ¶181-325ff.

12156   Special provision regarding companies (former rules)

For accounting periods ending no later than 31 March 2010, there is a separate penalty provision if a company fails to notify HMRC that it is within the charge to corporation tax. The initial penalty is an amount up to £300 with subsequent daily penalties of up to £60 for each subsequent day.

Legislation: FA 2004, s. 55

Tax Reporter: ¶181-325ff.

Late filing and payment

12200   Personal tax late filing and payment

Finance Act 2009 introduced the current penalty provisions for personal taxpayers in relation both to late filing and late payment of tax. The former provisions have continuing relevance so practitioners have to understand both the current and the former provisions. This section of commentary is set out as follows:

- late filing of tax return for 2010–11 and later years – 12201ff.;
- late filing of tax return for 2009–10 and earlier years – 12206;
- late payment of tax for 2010–11 and later years – 12207; and
- late payment of tax for 2009–2010 and earlier years – 12208.

Separate provisions apply in relation to corporation tax (see 12210ff.).

Tax Reporter: ¶181-325ff.

12201   Penalty for late filing of tax return for 2010–11 and later years

The current penalty regime for late returns introduced by FA 2009 applies where a filing deadline is missed in respect of a self-assessment return for 2010–11 or any later year. The normal deadline will have been missed in the case of a paper return if it is filed on or after 1 November immediately following the end of the relevant tax year or in the case of an online return if it is filed on or after the corresponding 1 February.

The penalty builds up in stages as follows:

- an immediate penalty of £100;
- following the issue of a notice by HMRC, a daily penalty of £10 for each day that the failure continues for a period of up to 90 days

commencing with the date specified in the notice – that date must not be earlier than the end of the period of three months after the filing date;

- a further penalty of the greater of £300 and 5% of the liability shown in the return is payable if both:

  - the return is still outstanding six months after the filing date; and

  - there would have been a liability to tax shown in the return (but in this scenario the 5% penalty is replaced by the higher 'relevant percentage' penalty if, by failing to make a return, the taxpayer deliberately withholds information which would enable or assist HMRC to assess their liability to tax with the penalty depending on the category of the information withheld (see 12202)).

Legislation: FA 2009, Sch. 55, para. 1–6

Case: *Donaldson v R & C Commrs* [2016] BTC 28

Tax Reporter: ¶181-500

12202   Tax-geared relevant percentage payable after 12 months

The relevant percentage is determined by:

- whether the withholding of information was:

  - deliberate; or

  - deliberate with concealment;

- which of the territorial categories the liability related to; and

- the quality of any disclosure.

The nature of the behaviour (deliberate or deliberate with concealment) is defined as for penalties for inaccuracies (see 12010 and 12015).

The three territorial categories are the same as those used in the other penalty provisions under FA 2007, Sch. 24 and FA 2008, Sch. 41 (see 12024 and 12129). *Finance Act* 2015 extends the higher penalties to inheritance tax and introduces a new category of offshore territory, category 0, which will carry the lowest level of penalty, equivalent to those currently in category 1, with penalties in category 1 being increased from 70% to 87.5% and from 100% to 125%. The amendments will take effect from a date to be appointed by Treasury order.

Finance Act 2015 also introduces the concept of an 'offshore transfer', with effect from 6 April 2016 (SI 2016/456) (but only in respect of income tax and capital gains tax) which is separate from the existing concept of 'offshore matter' for failures which involve deliberately withholding information which would enable or assist HMRC to assess liability to income tax, capital gains tax (and in due course, inheritance tax) and either the income (income tax) or the proceeds of disposal (capital gains tax) are received in a territory outside the UK, or transferred before the relevant date to a territory outside the UK (and in due course, the assets (inheritance tax) are transferred before the relevant date to a territory outside the UK).

Finance Act 2016 provides for increased maximum and minimum penalty rates (after mitigation) for failures involving an offshore matter or offshore transfer. *Finance Act* 2016 also makes further amendments so that failures involving an offshore transfer, or an offshore matter with deliberate behaviour, require the taxpayer to provide 'additional information' to HMRC in order to receive the maximum penalty reduction.

The quality of disclosure is determined as for penalties for inaccuracies (see 12020–12023). Given that the taxpayer has failed to submit a tax return, it is difficult to see how any disclosure would be 'unprompted' unless there was also a failure to notify chargeability. There is provision to prevent the same act resulting in penalties being payable under more than one offence.

The standard relevant percentage chargeable for category 1 is 100% of the tax if the withholding of information is deliberate and concealed but 70% if the withholding was deliberate but not concealed. For category 2 and 3, those standard percentages are increased to 150% and 200% respectively for deliberate and concealed withholding and 105% and 140% respectively for deliberate but not concealed withholding.

Special provisions to enable HMRC to determine the amount of any penalty in advance of the submission of the outstanding return. The amount of tax is determined to the best of HMRC's information and belief.

Legislation: FA 2009, Sch. 55, para. 1–6 and 24

Other material: CC/FS17; CC/FS18a

Tax Reporter: ¶181-500

12203   Reduction for disclosure

Reductions for disclosure may be given where the taxpayer discloses 'relevant information', which has been withheld by a failure to make a return. 'Disclosure' has the same meaning as for the current inaccuracy penalties (see 12020–12023). The reduction is greater for unprompted disclosure than prompted disclosure. Again these terms have the same meaning as for the current inaccuracy penalties. See Key Data for penalty reduction tables.

The potential size of the penalties make it essential for the practitioner to work for maximum reduction for disclosure from the time of their first becoming aware of their client's exposure to penalties. Where appropriate, specialist advice should be sought.

Legislation: FA 2009, Sch. 55, para. 14 and 15

Tax Reporter: ¶181-450

12204 Appeals

There is a right of appeal against both a decision by HMRC to impose a failure-related penalty and the amount of any such penalty.

A person is not required to pay a penalty before an appeal against the assessment of the penalty is determined.

Legislation: FA 2009, Sch. 55, para. 20

Tax Reporter: ¶188-800ff.

12205 Reasonable excuse

No penalty is chargeable if the taxpayer satisfies HMRC or (on appeal) the tribunal that there is a reasonable excuse for the failure and that the failure was rectified as soon as the excuse came to an end.

There are two situations laid down by statute which are not reasonable excuses. These are:

- lack of funds – unless this is due to unforeseen events outside the person's control; and

- reliance on another person – unless the person can show they took reasonable care to make sure the other person completed what they were asked to do.

Legislation: FA 2009, Sch. 55, para. 23

Cases: *Kaivani* [2015] TC 04620; *Porter* [2016] TC 05156

Tax Reporter: ¶181-540

12206 Penalty for late filing of tax return for 2009–10 and earlier years (former rules)

For failures before April 2011 in relation to 2009–10 or earlier years, the penalty stages are as follows:

- there is a fixed penalty of £100 for failing to comply with a notice to make a tax return by the filing date;

- there is a further fixed penalty of £100 if the failure extends beyond six months after the filing date but this does not apply if HMRC have already applied to the tribunal before that date for daily penalties;

- upon application by HMRC, the tribunal may make a direction for further penalties not exceeding £60 a day from the date of notice of the direction but no daily penalty can be imposed by the tribunal if the failure to make the return has already been remedied; and

- where the failure to make a return extends beyond the anniversary of the filing date and there would have been a liability to tax shown in the return, the taxpayer is automatically (without any application to the tribunal) liable to a tax-geared penalty up to the amount of tax which would have been shown.

Reasonable excuse

No penalty would arise if the taxpayer had reasonable excuse for the failure to make their return on time provided they remedied the failure as soon as the excuse ceased to exist. Reasonable excuse in the context of 'former regime' penalties is discussed at 12152.

Reduction of fixed penalties

Where the taxpayer can show that the liability to tax is less than the fixed penalties incurred, then any penalty is limited to the amount of tax due. However, this does not apply to daily penalties imposed by the tribunal.

Abatement of tax-geared penalty

In arriving at the appropriate level of the tax-geared penalty, HMRC would follow the same abatement procedure as discussed in the context of inaccurate tax returns (see 12060ff.).

Appeals

The taxpayer may appeal to the tribunal against a penalty. The tribunal can only confirm or set aside a fixed penalty but it can confirm, set aside, increase or decrease a tax-geared penalty.

In order to try and clear the decks of these former regime late filing situations by higher rate taxpayers, HMRC conducted a campaign that ended on 2 October 2012.

Legislation: TMA 1970, s. 8, 93, 100(1), 118(2)

Other Material: HMRC *Enquiry Manual* EM4560ff.

Tax Reporter: ¶181-530

12207   Late payment of tax for 2010–11 and later years

Finance Act 2009 introduced the current penalty regime for late payments of tax. It applies from 6 April 2011 to an amount of tax which:

- is payable in relation to the tax year 2010–11 or any subsequent tax year; and

- is specified in the table contained in the legislation.

In relation to income tax and CGT, the current late payment penalty provisions apply to tax payable:

- under self-assessment;

- as a result of an HMRC determination;

- because it has not been postponed;

- as a result of an amendment or correction to a return; or

- under an assessment.

Amount of the penalty

The longer the delay in making payment, the greater the penalty. The penalties are cumulative, so if, for example, payment is more than six months late, the first two penalties shown in the table below may be charged.

Length of delay	Penalty
Thirty days	5% of the tax unpaid at that date
Six months (see below)	A further 5% of the tax unpaid at that date
Twelve months (see below)	A further 5% of the tax unpaid at that date

Timing

The legislation stipulates that the first 5% penalty arises if the tax has not been paid 30 days after the due date and imposes the subsequent penalties five and 11 months after the date the first penalty was incurred. For tax payable on 31 January, the latest day for payment to avoid incurring the penalty is 1 March in a leap year or 2 March in any other year (being the 30th day following the due date of 31 January). The first penalty is accordingly raised on 2 or 3 March, which constitutes the penalty date. The succeeding penalties arise on any amount not paid at five and 11 months after that date, with the second penalty being issued on 2 or 3 August and third on 2 or 3 February the following year. Those dates are slightly later than six and 12 months after the due date.

Appeal

A taxpayer can appeal to the tribunal against either the imposition of a late payment penalty or its amount. If the appeal is against the imposition, the tribunal can either affirm or cancel HMRC's decision. If the appeal is against the amount, the tribunal can either affirm HMRC's decision or substitute it in any amount that could have been imposed by HMRC.

Other provisions

HMRC are empowered to charge lower penalties if there are special circumstances.

Where a time-to-pay arrangement has been negotiated with HMRC and its terms are being honoured, these late payment penalty provisions do not apply. This makes it important for the practitioner to ensure that any such arrangement is strictly adhered to by their client.

Reasonable excuse provisions apply.

Legislation: FA 2009, Sch. 56

Cases: *Duffy* [2013] TC 02795; *Finch* [2015] TC 04734; *Porter* [2016] TC 05156

Other Material: HMRC *Compliance Handbook* CH155000ff.

Tax Reporter: ¶184-650ff.

12208   Late payment of tax for 2009–10 and earlier years

The current penalty regime applies only from 6 April 2011 to late payments of tax for the tax year 2010–11 or any subsequent tax year. For late payments before that date, the former surcharge regime continues to apply.

A surcharge arises where any income tax or CGT is still unpaid more than 28 days after the due date. The surcharge is 5% of that unpaid tax. Where tax remains unpaid more than six months after the due date, a further 5% surcharge arises.

Surcharges are imposed by notices served on the taxpayer stating the date of issue and the time limit for an appeal. The surcharge itself carries interest from 30 days after the date of the notice until payment.

Appeals may be made within 30 days from the date of issue of the surcharge notice. The tribunal may set aside the surcharge if they consider that the taxpayer has a 'reasonable excuse' for not paying the tax throughout the period of default, but inability to pay the tax can never be regarded as a reasonable excuse.

A surcharge can only be imposed if the taxpayer was still in default at the time of the notice. In *McMullan*, the tribunal decided that a taxpayer was not liable to a surcharge for failure to pay tax since he was not in default on the relevant dates.

In *Rowland v R & C Commrs*, a special commissioner found that a taxpayer had a 'reasonable excuse' for not paying tax on the due date where she had relied on the advice of reputable specialist accountants in connection with a complex matter and been advised that she only had to pay a lower amount.

By contrast, the tribunal held in *Clarke* that the taxpayer was liable for the surcharge imposed by HMRC because he had no reasonable excuse for not paying the tax due. Reliance upon his accountant in complying with the tax regime did not assist the taxpayer, who had ultimate responsibility to ensure that his personal tax return was completed correctly. Furthermore, inability to pay was specifically excluded as a reasonable excuse.

The relationship between inability to pay and reasonable excuse is not necessarily as clear cut as HMRC assert. There have been tribunal cases where an exceptional and unpredictable inability to pay has been considered to provide reasonable excuse. See, for example, the 2009 case of *Mutch*.

Legislation: TMA 1970, s. 59A, 59B

Cases: *Rowland v R & C Commrs* (2006) Sp C 548; *Mutch* [2009] TC 00232 *McMullan* [2010] TC 00305; *Clarke* [2010] TC 00603

Tax Reporter: ¶184-650ff.

12210 Corporation tax late filing and payment

Finance Act 2009 penalty provisions in respect of late filing and tax payment extend to corporation tax with effect from the relevant commencement dates. The former provisions have continuing relevance so practitioners have to understand both the current and the former provisions. This section of commentary is set out as follows:

- late filing of corporation tax return after the commencement date (12211);

- late filing of corporation tax return prior to the commencement date (12212);

- late payment of corporation tax for periods commencing on or after the commencement date (12215);

- late payment of corporation tax for periods commencing before the commencement date (12218).

Tax Reporter: ¶184-650ff.

12211 Late filing of corporation tax return after the commencement date

The provisions of FA 2009, Sch. 55 extend to corporation tax but do not apply until the commencement date which has yet to be announced.

Legislation: FA 2009, Sch. 55

Tax Reporter: ¶184-650ff.

12212 Late filing of corporation tax return prior to the commencement date

For returns for accounting periods that fall before the commencement date, the former provisions continue to apply. Under those provisions, where a company has had a notice to make a return and fails to deliver it by the filing date, it becomes liable to a flat-rate penalty of:

- £100, if it is delivered within three months of the filing date;

- £200, if it is delivered after three months of the filing date;

- £500, if it is delivered within three months of the filing date but the returns for the two immediately previous consecutive accounting periods were also late; and

- £1,000, if it is delivered after three months of the filing date but the returns for the two immediately previous consecutive accounting periods were also late.

Where the delay continues, a tax-geared penalty becomes payable as follows:

- 10% of the unpaid tax where the return is delivered more than 18 months but no more than 24 months after the end of the accounting period;

- 20% of the unpaid tax where the return is delivered more than 24 months after the end of the accounting period.

The reasonable excuse provisions apply but are interpreted very strictly. The flat-rate penalty can be reduced by HMRC but there is no provision for relaxation of the tax-geared penalty.

Both flat-rate and tax-geared penalty notices are issued automatically without warning shortly after the date the penalty has been incurred.

Local HMRC offices have the power to stop automatic notices being issued where they are felt to be inappropriate (for example, where a return has not been made because the company has a reasonable excuse for not doing so).

Under the automatic notification system, it is imperative that companies inform HMRC of a change of an accounting date leading to a period of account of more than 12 months. Early notification of a long period of account (and hence a delayed filing date for the return) will prevent unnecessary issue of penalty notices and the inconvenience of such incorrect notices.

Legislation: TMA 1970, s. 118(2); FA 1998, Sch. 18, para. 14, 17 and 18

Other Material: HMRC *Company Tax Manual* CTM94005ff. and 94140ff.

Tax Reporter: ¶184-650ff.

12215 Late payment of corporation tax after the commencement date

FA 2009 penalty regime relating to late payment of tax applies to corporation tax from the commencement date (yet to be announced).

Legislation: FA 2009, Sch. 56

Tax Reporter: ¶184-650ff.

12218 Late payment of corporation tax for periods before the commencement date

Until the FA 2009 provisions apply, there is no penalty provision in relation to late payment of corporation tax. Interest liabilities do, however, apply.

Tax Reporter: ¶184-650ff.

Offshore penalties

12250 Offshore asset moves

Finance Act 2015, Sch. 21 provides for a new penalty, with effect in relation to relevant offshore asset moves occurring on or after 26 March 2015, for income tax, capital gains tax and inheritance tax where assets are moved from a 'specified territory' to a 'non-specified territory' and the main, or one of main purposes, of the movement is to prevent the discovery of a loss of revenue by HMRC.

The new penalty is an additional penalty which can only be levied once a penalty has already been levied for 'deliberate failure' under:

- FA 2007, Sch. 24, para. 1 (penalty for error in taxpayer's document) (see 12010ff.);

- FA 2008, Sch. 41, para. 1 (penalty for failure to notify) (see 12125ff.); or

- FA 2009, Sch. 55, para. 6 (penalty for failures to make return, etc. where failure continues after 12 months) (see 12202).

The amount of the penalty is 50% of the amount of the original penalty.

The time limits for HMRC to assess the penalty are the same as those applying to the relevant original penalty. Payment must be made before the expiry of 30 days beginning on the day of notification. Procedurally, the penalty is treated in the same way as a tax assessment and may be enforced in the same way. An amendment must be made to the amount of penalty if the original penalty is amended (up or down). HMRC's decision to impose a penalty under this Schedule may be appealed and either affirmed or cancelled by a tribunal.

Territories are specified by SI 2015/866.

Legislation: FA 2015, Sch. 21; SI 2015/866

Tax Reporter: ¶181-400; ¶181-500; ¶184-850

12252 Asset based penalties for offshore inaccuracies and failures

Finance Act 2016 introduces a new asset-based penalty, which may be charged on taxpayers who have been charged a penalty for deliberate offshore inaccuracies and failures, with effect from a day to be appointed by statutory instrument.

An asset-based penalty will be payable by a person where one or more standard offshore tax penalties have been imposed on that person in relation to a tax year and the potential lost revenue (PLR) threshold has been met in relation to that tax year. A standard offshore tax penalty is a penalty imposed under FA 2007, Sch. 24, para. 1 (see 12024); FA 2008, Sch. 41, para. 1 (see 12129) or FA 2009, Sch. 55, para. 6 (see 12202) in respect of a person's deliberate action or failure involving an offshore matter or an offshore transfer, where the tax at stake is inheritance tax, capital gains tax or asset-based income tax.

The PLR threshold is reached where the offshore potential lost revenue in relation to a tax year exceeds £25,000.

The standard amount of the asset-based penalty will be the lower of 10% of the value of the relevant asset or ten times of the amount of the offshore PLR relevant to the penalty.

The standard amount of the asset-based penalty will be reduced where the person liable to the penalty does all of the following: discloses the inaccuracy or failure giving rise to the relevant standard offshore penalty, provides HMRC with a reasonable valuation of the asset and provides HMRC with further information or access to records required for valuation purposes. The amount of the reduction depends upon the degree of cooperation provided. Minimum penalty tables will be published by regulations.

Legislation: FA 2016, s. 165 and Sch. 22

12255 Penalties for enablers of offshore tax evasion or non-compliance

Finance Act 2016 introduces new penalties for deliberate enablers of offshore tax evasion, or non-compliance, including a new financial penalty, and a new power to publish information about the enabler. The penalties will be applicable in relation to income tax, capital gains tax and inheritance tax. The new Schedule will come into force on a day appointed by the Treasury in regulations.

Two conditions need to be met for the penalty to be payable:

(1) that an enabler has enabled another person to evade tax offshore and they knew at the time that their actions enabled or were likely to enable that evasion; and

(2) either:

  (a) in the case of offshore tax evasion or non-compliance consisting of the commission of a relevant offence (cheating the public revenue, fraudulent evasion of income tax (TMA 1970,

s. 106A) or failure to comply with TMA 1970, s. 7 or 8 (TMA 1970, s. 106B–106D), the evader has been convicted of the offence and that conviction is final; or

(b) in the case of offshore tax evasion or non-compliance consisting of conduct that makes the evader liable to a relevant penalty (under FA 2007, Sch. 24, para. 1; FA 2008, Sch. 41, para. 1; FA 2009, Sch. 55, para. 6 or FA 2015, Sch. 21, para. 1) the penalty has been assessed and notified and the penalty is final or a contract has been made between the HMRC and the evader under which HMRC undertake not to assess the penalty or (if it has been assessed) not to take proceedings to recover it.

The penalty is either:

(i) the greater of 100% of the potential lost revenue (FA 2016, Sch. 20, para. 3(1)) or £3,000; or

(ii) where the evader is liable for a penalty under FA 2015, Sch. 21, para. 1, the greater of 50% of the potential lost revenue in relation to the original tax non-compliance (the potential lost revenue under FA 2007, Sch. 24, FA 2008, Sch. 41 or FA 2009, Sch. 55) or £3,000 (FA 2016, Sch. 20, para. 3(2)).

Penalties are subject to reduction for disclosure:

(i) to the higher of 10% of the potential lost revenue or £1,000 for unprompted disclosure or assistance; or

(ii) the higher of 30% of the potential lost revenue or £3,000 for prompted disclosure or assistance.

HMRC may also reduce the penalty (or stay the penalty or agree to a compromise in relation to penalty proceedings) for 'special circumstances' which does not include ability to pay or the fact that a potential loss of revenue from one taxpayer is balanced by a potential overpayment by another.

Where a person is liable for a penalty under *Finance Act* 2016, Sch. 20 and the potential lost revenue exceeds £25,000, HMRC may publish information about the person. HMRC may also publish information if the person has been found to have incurred five or more penalties under *Finance Act* 2016, Sch. 20 in any five-year period.

Legislation: FA 2016, s. 162 and Sch. 20

Other material: www.gov.uk/government/publications/ten-things-about-offshore-assets-and-income/ten-things-about-offshore-assets-and-income

12260   Offences relating to offshore income, assets and activities

Finance Act 2016 introduces a new criminal offence which does not require the need to prove intent for failing to declare taxable offshore income and gains, through an amendment to TMA 1970. The offences will apply for the purposes of income tax and capital gains tax, where a person has failed to properly declare offshore income or gains in accordance with TMA 1970, s. 7 and 8 leading to a loss of tax over a threshold amount which will be defined in regulations and will be on a per tax year basis (but must be not less than £25,000). The provisions will come into force on a day to be appointed by statutory instrument.

The offence is a strict liability offence, which is a criminal offence where it is not necessary for the court to ascertain the state of mind of the defendant before convicting because Parliament has determined that the state of mind (the 'mens rea' of the defendant has no bearing on whether they should be liable to a criminal sanction).

Legislation: TMA 1970, s. 106B–106H (as inserted by FA 2016, s. 166)

Other material: www.gov.uk/government/publications/ten-things-about-offshore-assets-and-income/ten-things-about-offshore-assets-and-income

Tax Reporter: ¶195-100

Other matters

12300   Outline

A key element to the relationship with HMRC and to the basis for HMRC Enquiries is a taxpayer's statutory obligation to make tax returns and keep records. This is considered in 12400ff.

In assisting a client with the preparation of a return, a practitioner often needs to consider what if any additional information needs to be disclosed. This can be an important element in protecting a client from an enquiry. Commentary on this is at 12410ff. Commentary is also included on the statutory obligation to disclose the marketing and use of tax avoidance schemes (see 12421) and the obligations imposed on practitioners in relation to suspected money laundering (see 12425ff.).

Whilst the respective obligations and rights that govern the relationship between a taxpayer and HMRC are defined by statute, the legislation provides no guidance on the quality as distinct from the mechanics of the relationship. The HMRC charter is an attempt to fill this gap (see 12430). Human relationships can, in the nature of things, go wrong. Taxpayers have a range of statutory and non-statutory routes through which to seek remedies. These are summarised in 12440. Regardless of the efforts of taxpayers (with their advisers) and HMRC officers, there will inevitably be matters on which agreement cannot be reached. The review procedure operated by HMRC and the independent tribunal system provide the mechanism for resolving such matters. Commentary on both is included at 12600ff.

Tax Reporter: ¶180-000ff.

Tax returns and record keeping

12400   Tax returns – correspondence with clients

Taxpayers are obliged to take reasonable care in completing their returns and, as we have seen elsewhere in this manual, there are penalties for failing to do so. That obligation may in some situations be discharged by relying on a competent adviser but HMRC would normally resist that conclusion except in relation to a complex matter. A taxpayer cannot usually avoid penalties for errors or omissions by blaming their accountant. It is important that the client appreciates that even though their agent has prepared the return, the responsibility for its accuracy and completeness remains with them personally.

When sending a tax return or computation to a client for approval, it is essential for the practitioner to:

- make clear which year it relates to;

- seek clarification on any points of uncertainty;

- highlight any assumptions or estimates that have been made and ask the client whether these are appropriate;

- ask the client to review it carefully to ensure that it is complete and correct;

- ask the client to check in particular that all sources of income (including any new sources) have been included, that all allowances to which they are entitled have been claimed and that full details of all capital gains are included.

It is also sensible to attach copies of any additional information that will accompany the return when it is submitted. This ensures that the client is aware of any proposed disclosures.

The use of appropriate standard form letters both for requesting the information required for the preparation of a return and for sending the return to the client for approval is encouraged by the professional institutes as this reduces the risk of any misunderstanding.

Tax Reporter: ¶180-000ff.

12401 Use of estimates

There is nothing to stop a taxpayer using estimates in their self-assessment calculations and there is no statutory requirement to disclose where estimates have been used. This is confirmed by HMRC's own leaflet *How to fill in your Tax Return* which states:

'If you consider your estimates to be reliable, for example, some private proportions of business expenses, there is no need to draw attention to them.'

However, if a figure on the face of the return is estimated, it is usually sensible to indicate this fact in the 'Additional Information' box (or computation) and to tick the box indicating that estimates have been used. If figures in the client's business accounts are estimated, consideration should be given as to whether either an individual item, or the aggregate of estimated items, is a material figure in the context of the accounts. If it is not, there may be no point in disclosing it if it is a genuine and properly considered estimate but it is sensible for practitioners to assume that disclosure of all estimates is required until they are satisfied otherwise. An estimate of a material figure should always be disclosed. If it is not and the return is selected for enquiry, the client runs the risk of HMRC questioning whether the return can be said to be correct. Also, HMRC could seek to use what they regarded as a non-disclosure to make a discovery at a later date (see 11370).

Other Material: HMRC Leaflet SA150 (2014)

Tax Reporter: ¶180-000ff.

12402 Valuations, exceptional items and disregarding HMRC guidance

There is generally no statutory duty to disclose the use of a valuation but it will almost inevitably be appropriate for the practitioner to do so.

The decision in *Langham (HMIT) v Veltema* meant that, where a self-assessment depends on a valuation, HMRC can raise a discovery assessment if they successfully dispute the accuracy of that valuation. This decision led to uncertainty for taxpayers as to whether the risk of an enquiry disappeared at the end of the enquiry period. Guidance was therefore developed by HMRC in consultation with representative bodies to help taxpayers achieve finality for most practical purposes. This resulted in the publication of the Statement of Practice SP01/06. In summary, this clarifies the position in three types of situation, namely:

- the use of valuations;
- the treatment of exceptional items; and
- not following HMRC guidance.

Legislation: TMA 1970, s. 29(6)

Case: *Langham (HMIT) v Veltema* [2004] BTC 156

Other Material: HMRC Statement of Practice SP1/06 *Self-assessment: Finality and Discovery*

Tax Reporter: ¶180-000ff.

12403   Use of provisional figures

HMRC interpret case law as requiring provisional figures to be disclosed and they include a box on the personal self-assessment return to be ticked if provisional figures are included. If this is not done, HMRC might view it as an attempt to mislead and consider the imposition a penalty. Where provisional figures are used, an explanation should be included in the 'Additional Information' (white space) box or computation.

HMRC accept that they cannot send back a return as incomplete where provisional figures are included even if the white space box has not been completed. However, returns with provisional figures are routinely selected for enquiry and HMRC may seek to impose a penalty where the use of a provisional figure was considered unjustified.

Whenever a provisional figure has to be used in a return, the practitioner should ensure that a diary note or other system is used to ensure that a final figure is provided as promptly as possible. If information is required from the client, they should be left in no doubt of the urgent need for the information.

Tax Reporter: ¶180-000ff.; ¶180-150

12404   Unification of legislation

Prior to the introduction of the FA 2008 provisions, the records that had to be kept for tax purposes differed across taxes. Thus:

- for income tax, CGT and corporation tax, taxpayers had to keep whatever records were required to make a correct and complete return or claim;

- for PAYE and NIC, employers had to maintain and produce for inspection the records specified by the legislation; and

- for VAT, taxable persons had to keep business and accounting records and HMRC published detailed guidance on how that requirement was interpreted.

Finance Act 2008 includes provisions for aligning the record keeping obligations for income tax, CGT, corporation tax and VAT. The approach is to:

- specify in primary legislation (statute) the basic record keeping requirement for tax purposes;

- expand on that basic requirement with more detailed requirements in secondary legislation (statutory instruments and regulations).

As previously, the record keeping requirements will be more specific in relation to VAT, PAYE and NICs and there will be more non-statutory guidance on what records HMRC are likely to regard as meeting the requirements of the primary and secondary legislation.

The general approach of HMRC remains that taxpayers are entitled to decide what records they need to keep based on their own particular circumstances, subject to the need to satisfy the general legislation and comply with any special rules. HMRC do, however, provide a significant volume of non-statutory guidance including its Toolkits (see 12005). There is no obligation to follow such guidance but if a taxpayer chooses to ignore that guidance without adopting appropriate record systems and an error occurs, HMRC might seek to assert that this demonstrated a lack of care. The discovery of such an error could occur either in the course of an enquiry or as a result of a 'live' inspection of business records as part of the HMRC's Business Record Checks (see 12407).

There are financial penalties for not keeping the records required by statute (see 12407).

HMRC have yet to use its secondary legislation powers to extend the statutory record keeping requirements. It is thought likely that this may at some stage be used to impose an obligation to retain such items as:

- diaries/appointment books;

- year planners;

- copies of quotations given to customers; or

- work sheets used to prepare invoices.

None of these are specifically required to be kept by the TMA 1970 provisions.

HMRC's increasing focus on business records (including its Business Record Checks) will put additional pressure on many businesses. There is an opportunity here for practitioners to help clients avoid enquiries by offering clients additional services such as:

- reviewing existing records to advise on required improvements;
- providing or arranging book keeping service;
- conducting unannounced inspections of records; and
- arranging archiving facilities or off-site storage.

Legislation: FA 2008, Sch. 37

Other Material: Guidance on record keeping can be found on the GOV.UK website at www.gov.uk/keeping-your-pay-tax-records

Tax Reporter: ¶180-000ff.

12405   Record keeping obligation

Whenever a person has an obligation to make a self-assessment return, they have a related obligation to retain the supporting documents. There is a general statutory duty to keep the records they need to make and deliver a correct and complete return for the tax year or period.

In addition, there are more specific record keeping requirements for people carrying on a trade (including the letting of property), profession or business alone or in partnership and for companies. They must keep:

- records of all receipts and expenses in the course of the trade, profession or business, or company activities;
- records of the matters in respect of which those receipts and expenditure take place; and
- records of all sales and purchases made in the course of any trade involving dealing in goods.

HMRC have powers under FA 2008, Sch. 37 to make regulations specifying in detail what records must be kept. As of July 2012, no such regulations had been made.

To be able to advise clients on the appropriate records to keep for their particular business, a practitioner will need a full understanding of the business. This is likely to involve a similar process to that followed by HMRC. The practitioner should therefore establish:

- what goods or services are provided;
- who are the suppliers and what are their terms;

- who are the customers and what terms are they given;
- what is the pattern of trade, weekly and annually;
- what is the normal pattern of stock holding;
- how any wastage is incurred;
- the role of each person who works in the business; and
- how employees are remunerated and if with bonuses how these are calculated.

Once the practitioner understands the operation of the business, they can identify the records that need to be maintained.

CCH Business Focus helps practitioners to gain a full understanding of various types of business and provides background information on operating practices, likely activities and the records, including any non-financial records, that can be expected to be kept to run the business.

A limited company and a limited liability partnership (LLP) must also keep the accounting records specified in the *Companies Act* 2006. Compliance with those provisions will largely satisfy the Corporation Tax requirements but the company's transfer pricing record obligations also need to be met. There is no specific provision concerning transfer pricing records so the general statutory obligation applies.

The requirement for a taxpayer to keep the records which enable a return to be completed or a claim to be made can normally be satisfied by taking copies of the information or recording it in the business books, and such copies are admissible in evidence before the tribunal. There are, however exceptions to this. These are specifically identified in TMA 1970, s. 12B(4A).

In advance of their campaign from the autumn of 2011 to improve the quality of record keeping by businesses, HMRC published guidance in a variety of forms on what it regards as satisfactory record keeping. Internet links are provided by HMRC to these products. None of these have statutory force but HMRC can be expected to argue that failure to meet the suggested criteria may constitute carelessness. Penalties could then be charged (see 12406).

In April 2012, HMRC announced the launch by software companies of mobile 'apps' for small businesses with turnovers below the VAT threshold.

Once an information notice has been issued to a person by HMRC (or even if an officer has simply indicated that the documents concerned are likely to be the subject of an information notice), the person must not conceal, destroy or otherwise dispose of a document. The normal sanction for a breach of this provision is the £300 fixed penalty for failure to comply with an information notice. However, if the notice had been approved by the tribunal (or if the officer had indicated an intention to seek such approval), the subsequent concealment or destruction constitutes a criminal offence. A person guilty of the offence is liable on indictment to imprisonment for a term not exceeding two years or to a fine, or to both.

Concealment of documents could additionally mean that HMRC were able to assert that the error or failure was deliberate and concealed. This could involve a very substantial increase in the penalties sought.

Legislation: TMA 1970, s. 12B; FA 1998, Sch. 18, para. 21; FA 2008, Sch. 36, para. 39, 42, 43, 53–55

Other Material: HMRC *Compliance Handbook* CH10000ff., 11100ff., 11200ff.; www.gov.uk/keeping-your-pay-tax-records; www.hmrc.gov.uk/softwaredevelopers/mobile-apps/record-keeping.htm

Tax Reporter: ¶181-900ff.

12406   Record keeping retention periods

In relation to income tax returns, the length of retention period depends on whether the person is carrying on a trade (including property letting), profession or business. If they are, the related records must be retained until the fifth anniversary of the 31 January following the particular tax year. If they are not carrying on any such activity, the records only need to be kept until the second 31 January following the tax year. In relation to corporation tax, the retention period runs to the sixth anniversary of the end of the accounting period.

Where a notice requiring a return is issued late, the retention period is extended to the later of the date when any enquiry window is closed or the date when any enquiry into the return is completed. Separate provisions apply to records supporting claims which are not included in a return.

Notwithstanding the length of the statutory periods, the practitioner may well consider it advisable to recommend a longer period of retention. In the event of any subsequent enquiry, the availability of the records can make a significant difference. Where the client does not have the necessary storage space, consideration could be given to the use of electronic copying or off-site archiving.

Legislation: TMA 1970, s. 12B(2), Sch. 1A, para. 2A

Tax Reporter: ¶181-900

12407   Record keeping penalties and business record checks

HMRC have an absolute right to inspect statutory records (see ¶11910).

Failure to comply with the record keeping requirements attracts a maximum penalty of £3,000. In practice, it has been extremely unusual for HMRC to impose such a separate penalty. In the context of enquiry cases, HMRC practice has been to simply take the record keeping compliance into account in considering the appropriate penalty loading under another provision such as for an inaccuracy in a return. Failure to keep the required records is likely to be regarded by a tribunal as evidence of carelessness if it gives rise to an inaccuracy in a return.

It is important to note that there is no provision for a record keeping penalty to be suspended. Thus, a penalty can be imposed for an inaccuracy in the records even if it is one which the practitioner would have identified and corrected in the process of preparing the business accounts and tax return. This makes it important for the practitioner to ensure that they have advised clients of weaknesses in their record keeping and of the corrective measures that are required. If in the course of preparing the annual accounts it becomes clear to the practitioner that there are deficiencies in a client's records, the client should be advised of:

- the nature of the errors;
- the action required to correct systems and records;
- HMRC's increasing vigilance in relation to record keeping obligations;
- the risk of penalties; and
- the possibility that record keeping failures could lead to a full enquiry.

HMRC publish various record-keeping products for the self-employed, sole traders and small businesses, including factsheets and online tools. Links to these are shown below. None of these has statutory authority but HMRC are likely to regard a taxpayer's failure to consider this advice or take other appropriate advice to indicate possible carelessness. A practitioner can do a lot to help a client to avoid that exposure by ensuring that the records are satisfactory. There is an important marketing opportunity for practitioners here. Clients may require persuasion that the cost of keeping their records in a satisfactory state is a sound investment. If HMRC start charging penalties of up to £3,000 for record keeping failures, that attitude may change.

Business records checks

In October 2015, HMRC announced that its Business Records Checks (BRC) initiative was being brought to a close, with immediate effect. As far as checks that had already been initiated, HMRC stated:

'For customers this means:

- If they have received an initial letter from HMRC, they will still go through the phone questionnaire and will be advised whether, or not, a visit is to be arranged. HMRC will also provide a link for customers to obtain help and support on keeping business records from the HMRC internet site.

- If customers have been advised that a visit is required and has still to be arranged, the visit will be booked shortly.

- Where a visit has been booked or customers are awaiting a follow up visit then these will still continue.'

HMRC's Business Records Check (BRC) programme started following an announcement by HMRC that it intended to make 50,000 live checks of business records every year from 2011 onwards indicating that the department expected to be making much greater use of the record-keeping penalty provisions in future. Whereas a penalty was only likely to arise previously after the related return had been submitted, the new HMRC approach meant that penalties could be imposed where the records were found to be unsatisfactory even before the submission of the related tax return.

HMRC's Business Records Checks (BRC) programme underwent a number of changes. Following the expression of substantial opposition by practitioners, the original target of 50,000 checks every year was scaled back to 20,000. In February 2012, HMRC suspended the programme and relaunched it with a 'revamped approach' later in the year. In November 2013, HMRC acknowledged that the new approach was producing too many false positives which meant that HMRC staff time was being unnecessarily committed to visiting businesses whose records were acceptable. HMRC then piloted the new approach in the Edinburgh, Glasgow, Leeds, Bradford and Stockport areas and, in other areas, switched the emphasis to an educational approach.

As part of the announcement that initiative was being brought to a close, HMRC stated that:

'BRC has positively encouraged businesses to keep better records, including updating them more frequently. As a result, most customers with inadequate records who have received follow up visits have improved their record-keeping to an acceptable standard. However, we have found that we were contacting more compliant customers than expected, because it has proved more difficult than originally anticipated to select those customers who would benefit from a visit.

HMRC remains committed to helping businesses to keep better records, and the BRC initiative has helped us better understand the risks and pressures that businesses face with record keeping. Using what we have learnt from BRC we are working to design a better approach to embed best practice into our routine compliance checks. We will continue to support businesses through our online learning packages and the investment we are making into digital tax accounts which will mean businesses can easily interface with HMRC from their own accounting software.'

Legislation: TMA 1970, s. 12B(5)

Case: *Seafield General Store & Post Office* [2010] TC 00333

Other Material: HMRC and related websites: www.gov.uk/government/publications/keeping-records-for-business-what-you-need-to-know; www.gov.uk/record-keeping-checks-on-your-business; www.gov.uk/government/uploads/system/uploads/attachment_data/file/377656/rk-bk1.pdf; www.gov.uk/running-a-limited-company/directors-responsibilities

Tax Reporter: ¶181-900

Disclosure

12410   Disclosure – introduction

The word 'disclosure' is used in two very different contexts within taxation. In the context of enquiries, it is used to describe the provision of information to HMRC as part of the admission of an error or failure. We have seen that such disclosure, particularly if unprompted, can significantly reduce the resulting penalties (see 12020ff.).

In the current section of this manual, it has a wholly different meaning and purpose. It refers to the provision of information in or with a tax return or computation in order to ensure that HMRC are given a proper understanding of an item in the return or computation. Aspects of this are considered separately in relation to the use of estimates, valuations and provisional figures (see 12401ff.). The purpose of this type of disclosure is to fulfil the taxpayer's obligation to properly describe matters and, in so doing, to radically curtail HMRC's opportunity to subsequently make a discovery.

Clients have an obligation under self-assessment to submit tax returns which, to the best of their knowledge and belief, are correct and complete. The HMRC officer has the power to enquire into returns to check that taxpayers have fulfilled that obligation.

A major benefit of disclosure for taxpayers is the concept of finality. If a return has not been selected for enquiry within (normally) 12 months of filing, HMRC cannot subsequently open that year unless they can make a 'discovery' (see 11370ff.). Disclosure limits the circumstances in which HMRC can displace the finality of a self-assessment and make a discovery assessment.

Legislation: FA 2008, Sch. 39, para. 7; *Finance Act 2008, Schedule 39 (Appointed Day, Transitional Provision and Savings) Order* 2009 (SI 2009/403); TMA 1970, s. 29(6), (7)

Case: *Sokoya* [2009] TC 00125

Tax Reporter: ¶180-000ff.

12411   Disclosure – benefits

From 1 April 2010, if HMRC discover that tax has been lost they can make an assessment to recover the tax lost at any time up to four years from the end of the year of assessment, with extended periods of six or 20 years respectively if careless or deliberate behaviour was involved. However, HMRC cannot base a discovery on information that has previously been made available to them before the enquiry window closed if the HMRC officer could have been reasonably expected, on the basis of that information, to be aware of the under-assessment.

In the majority of cases where a return is selected for enquiry, it will be for an 'aspect' enquiry. In these aspect cases, the HMRC officer will be focusing on specific entries in the return, and not enquiring into the whole return. The risk of an aspect enquiry can be reduced by the practitioner identifying areas where a word of explanation in the Additional Information (white-space) box on the return or computation might help the reviewing officer understand an unusual feature that might otherwise prompt an enquiry. This might for example be the case where relevant information was volunteered to explain a significant change in the results of a business.

Given that an aspect enquiry can develop into a full enquiry, anticipation and disclosure by the practitioner of the explanations that an officer might require could in some cases prevent a time-consuming enquiry. Appropriate disclosure could also well make a difference in how HMRC or, on appeal, the tribunal viewed the actions of a taxpayer and thus impact the time-limits for assessment and the level of any penalty.

The guidelines of the professional institutes indicate that a policy of full disclosure should be adopted. That does not of itself require the use of the Additional Information section of the return but if a practitioner considers what if any additional information they would require if they were the HMRC officer reviewing the return, they are likely to be meeting the guidelines.

In May 2012, HMRC published guidance on its approach to potential IR35 situations. This included an undertaking that voluntary disclosure of a contract for review by HMRC's IR35 team could assist the early closure of a subsequent review within the following three years.

Tax Reporter: ¶180-000ff.

12412   Disclosure – prevention of discovery

A key purpose of volunteering information with a return is to prevent or reduce the scope that HMRC have for making a discovery (see 11370).

The disclosure of information that might debar discovery is only regarded as made available to HMRC if it is:

(1)   information that is contained in the taxpayer's self-assessment tax return (or in a claim outside the return) for that year (or either of the two previous years) or in any accounts, statements or documents accompanying the return (or claim);

(2)   information contained in any document, accounts or particulars produced to HMRC for the purpose of its enquiries into the return (or into the claim);

(3)   other information, the existence and relevance of which could reasonably be expected to be inferred by HMRC from information within (1) or (2); and

(4)   other information, the existence and relevance of which is notified in writing by the taxpayer to HMRC.

Where the taxpayer is a partner, information contained in the partnership return and accompanying statements is similarly protected.

It is important to note the distinction that the legislation makes between the first two and the second two situations. Information within (1) and (2) above is automatically within the protection of disclosure if its relevance to the return or enquiry should be obvious to the HMRC officer. By contrast information within (3) has to satisfy the additional test of reasonable inference and information within (4) is only protected if the taxpayer makes it clear:

•   the return to which it applies; and

•   the relevance of the information to that return.

In relation to (2), it is worth noting that when HMRC close an enquiry, the taxpayer has finality for that year. HMRC have only one bite at the cherry and can only reopen that year by reference to new information subsequently coming into their possession.

In relation to all four situations, there is of course a question mark over the extent to which an HMRC officer could have been reasonably expected to be aware of the significance of the information. HMRC's view is that if the taxpayer specifically pointed out the relevance of the information to their tax position, that would prevent such a question arising. That is undoubtedly correct. But it is also undoubtedly correct that there are many categories of information where it is obvious that it is relevant to the taxpayer's tax position.

HMRC do not seriously question that an officer ought to know that accounts and computations, CGT computations and many other documents accompanying a return will contain information that is likely to be relevant to the taxpayer's self-assessment. Accordingly, such information is automatically protected. But if, for instance, a 96-page sale agreement is sent with the return, an officer probably could not reasonably be expected to be aware of something tucked away on p. 85 that cast doubts on the tax treatment adopted.

However, most tribunals are likely to decide that the officer could reasonably be expected to realise that the sale agreement was sent with the return because it had a relevance to the taxpayer's liability. A reasonable officer, confronted with the 96 pages, could be expected at least to realise that the identity of the vendor, the amount of the consideration, and possibly the identity of the purchaser was relevant information, even if he could not be expected to study the agreement fully just in case there was something else important to the tax position, and thus be aware of the few lines on p. 85 that the taxpayer or their adviser thought were pertinent to the tax treatment.

As a rule of thumb, the practitioner should consider drawing attention to the relevance of information if that relevance is not immediately apparent. Consideration of some of the practical issues of disclosure is included below (see 12413).

Tax Reporter: ¶184-310

12413   Disclosure – practical considerations

Practitioners have differing views on how much supporting information should be sent as a matter of course with tax returns. What is much more important is to consider on a case-by-case basis whether the volunteering of additional information is likely to protect the client from the risk of enquiry or discovery.

Disclosure may mean attaching a document to the return. It may mean attaching a statement explaining an entry. It may mean putting a note in the white space on the return or in the computation. If anything is attached to a return, a note detailing the attachments should be entered in the white space as the enclosures are likely to be separated from the return when it is processed by HMRC. The reference in the white space will make the officer aware that additional information has been provided.

Consideration should be given as to whether to disclose appropriate information without reference to the client, or whether this should be agreed with the client first. Many clients will leave this decision to their tax adviser, and in this situation, the position should be made clear in the initial engagement letter, for example, by reference to a policy of full disclosure. However, ethical issues and responsibilities exist in relation to disclosure and it is important that these factors are also given careful consideration. This has added significance when something being volunteered also has a bearing on the tax affairs of a third party.

The rules for corporation tax self-assessment are broadly the same as for income tax. The most significant differences are that accounts must be sent with a corporation tax self-assessment (CTSA) return and that there is no equivalent in a corporation tax return of the white-space box. The advent from April 2011 of XBRL tagging of company accounts and computations has two implications for enquiries:

- the codified presentation of information for all companies will enable HMRC's IT systems to carry out more sophisticated risk assessments (see 11220); and

- the inconvenience of creating attachments to accompany the returns may discourage the disclosure of relevant information.

The corporation tax return no longer contains an optional page for directors' remuneration. Many practitioners, nevertheless, provide an analysis within the corporation tax computation as a matter of course HMRC frequently try to tie in remuneration shown in a company's accounts with the returns of the individual directors. Voluntary provision of the information removes one possible reason for the opening of an enquiry.

Legislation: TMA 1970, s. 29

Case: *Freeman* [2013] TC 02885

Other Material: HMRC *Enquiry Manual* EM3260ff.

Tax Reporter: ¶180-225

Tax avoidance

12420   General Anti-Abuse Rule (GAAR)

In December 2010, the Government asked Graham Aaronson QC to lead a study that would consider whether there should be a general anti-avoidance rule for the UK. Graham Aaronson assembled a study group of tax experts which published its Report on 21 November 2011. This set out a recommendation to the Government for the introduction into the UK tax system of a narrowly focused general anti-abuse rule targeted at abusive tax avoidance schemes. In Budget 2012, the Government announced that it accepted the broad recommendation of that Report and *Finance Act* 2013 introduced the GAAR (with effect from 17 July 2013) largely based on the principles developed in the GAAR Study Group Report but with some material differences reflecting the results of the formal consultation process.

The primary objective of the GAAR is to deter taxpayers from entering into abusive arrangements, and to deter would-be promoters from promoting such arrangements. If a taxpayer is undeterred, and goes ahead with an abusive arrangement, then the GAAR operates so as to counteract the abusive tax advantage which he or she is trying to achieve. The counteraction that the GAAR permits will be a tax adjustment which is just and reasonable in all the circumstances. The appropriate tax adjustment is not necessarily the one that raises the most tax.

The GAAR legislation requires counteraction of the abusive tax arrangement to be initiated by an official who has been specifically designated for this purpose by HMRC. The procedure for applying the GAAR to any arrangement requires that the proposed application of the GAAR should be put before an advisory panel of experts, independent of HMRC, who will give their opinion (or opinions if they are not unanimous) as to whether the arrangements in question constitute a reasonable course of action.

Finance Act 2016 introduces changes to the GAAR procedure so that a GAAR Advisory Panel opinion will enable counteraction of the equivalent arrangements by other uses and to enable a provisional counteraction by HMRC within assessing time limits, with effect from 15 September 2016 (Royal Assent) but with effect in relation to tax arrangements entered into at any time, whether before, on or after that date.

The GAAR has effect in relation to any arrangements which are entered into on or after 17 July 2013 in respect of: income tax; capital gains tax; inheritance tax; corporation tax (and any amount chargeable as if it were corporation tax or treated as if it were corporation tax (i.e. controlled foreign company (CFC) charge, the bank levy, the oil supplementary charge and tonnage tax)); petroleum revenue tax; stamp duty land tax; the annual tax on enveloped dwellings, and from 13 March 2014 in respect of National Insurance contributions.

GAAR penalty

Finance Act 2016 introduces a new penalty for all cases successfully counteracted under the GAAR. A penalty of 60% of the counteracted tax will be charged whenever a taxpayer submits to HMRC a return or other document on the basis that a tax advantage arises from the tax arrangements where all or part of that tax advantage is later counteracted under the GAAR. The new penalty will apply to tax arrangements entered into on or after 15 September 2016 (Royal Assent).

Legislation: FA 2013, Pt. 5

Tax Reporter: ¶187-850ff.

12421   Disclosure of Tax Avoidance Schemes

The Disclosure of Tax Avoidance Schemes (DOTAS) provisions were introduced in 2004 to provide an early warning system for HMRC and thereby enable the department to take retaliatory action to protect the public purse.

The legislation has been amended a number of times with further changes by *Finance Act* 2015.

For the practitioner, the provisions governing the promotion of schemes is likely to be of most relevance when advising a client on the risks of using a particular structure for a transaction. The knowledge that a scheme has already been disclosed to HMRC provides no guarantee that HMRC accept that it works or will not seek to introduce legislation to counter the apparent advantages. Conversely, knowledge that something that appears to require disclosure has not been disclosed may put the practitioner on notice of a significant risk for their client.

The main burden of the legislation falls upon scheme promoters. Where, however, there is no obligation on a promoter, for example, where the promoter is not based in the UK or where a scheme was developed by its user, the obligation to notify can pass to the scheme user. Some sections of tax returns require specific reference to the use of a scheme and the disclosure of its official reference number.

Finance Act 2015 includes further measures, with effect from 26 March 2015, to strengthen the regime by: changing the information that employers must provide to employees and to HMRC in relation to avoidance involving their employees; providing HMRC with a power to identify users of undisclosed avoidance schemes, increasing the penalty for users who do not comply with their reporting requirements under DOTAS and introducing protection for those wishing to voluntarily provide information about potential failures to comply with the DOTAS. It also introduces a requirement, under which promoters of tax avoidance schemes must notify HMRC of relevant changes to notified schemes and provides for HMRC to publish information about promoters and schemes that are notified under the regime.

There are specific penalties for failure to comply with the reporting requirements.

Consideration of DOTAS obligations is a specialist subject on which practitioners may well wish to seek expert advice.

In October 2015, HMRC published a factsheet for promoters, intermediaries such as tax agents or independent financial advisers and users of tax avoidance schemes entitled 'Ten things about disclosing a tax avoidance scheme' (see link below).

Legislation: TMA 1970, s. 98C; FA 2004, Pt. 7; SI 2015/948

Other Material: HMRC guidance: www.gov.uk/government/uploads/ system/uploads/attachment_data/file/341960/dotas-guidance.pdf; www.gov.uk/forms-to-disclose-tax-avoidance-schemes; www.gov.uk/ government/publications/ten-things-about-disclosing-a-tax-avoidance-scheme/ten-things-about-disclosing-a-tax-avoidance-scheme

Tax Reporter: ¶192-110ff.

12422   Follower notices

Finance Act 2014 introduced a new regime to tackle behaviour by taxpayers involved in tax avoidance schemes, primarily schemes marketed to a large number of taxpayers, with effect from 17 July 2014.

Often, the same scheme will be marketed but with small variations. When a judicial decision is handed down by the court or tribunal that potentially resolves a large number of cases, many taxpayers with the same or similar arrangements agree to settle, but some do not. They argue that the small differences in the arrangements mean that the decision cannot apply to them. Follower notices are intended to address this behaviour by giving taxpayers who are 'followers' a clear choice between settling their issue with HMRC in line with the other judicial ruling, or continuing their dispute with the risk of a penalty.

Follower notices can be issued to taxpayers who have used an avoidance scheme which has been shown in another taxpayer's litigation to be ineffective. The notice tells the taxpayer they may be liable to a penalty of up to 50% of the tax in dispute (subject to reduction for co-operation (see Factsheet CC/FS30a for reduction tables) and a minimum penalty of 10%) if they do not amend their return or settle their dispute.

HMRC may give a follower notice to a person (P) if all of the conditions (A) to (D) are met.

Condition A:
  (i)   There must be an enquiry in progress into a tax return or claim made by a person for any of the six relevant taxes mentioned above.
  (ii) There must be a live appeal to HMRC or the tribunal.

Condition B:

> The return, claim or appeal must be made on the basis that particular tax arrangements lead to tax advantages.

Condition C:

> HMRC are of the opinion that there is a relevant judicial ruling.

Condition D:

> No previous follower notice has been given to the same person in the same circumstances.

In addition, any follower notice must be given within 12 months of the later of the date the claim, return or appeal was received or the date the relevant judicial ruling was made.

Legislation: FA 2014, Pt. 4

Other Material: CC/FS25a; CC/FS25b; CC/FS30a; HMRC guidance – Follower notices and accelerated payments is available at www.gov.uk/ government/publications/follower-notices-and-accelerated-payments

Tax Reporter: ¶192-762ff.

12423 Accelerated payment notices

Alongside the follower notice rules introduced by *Finance Act* 2014 (see 12422) are the accelerated payment rules which will require recipients of a follower notice to pay the disputed tax to HMRC if they decide to continue with the dispute (i.e. they do not amend their return or claim or otherwise settle their dispute as requested by the follower notice).

Accelerated payments apply to annual tax on enveloped dwellings, capital gains tax, corporation tax, Class 4 National Insurance contributions, income tax (self assessment), inheritance tax, PAYE income tax and National Insurance contributions and stamp duty land tax.

Accelerated payments will also apply to avoidance arrangements which are within the Disclosure of Tax Avoidance Schemes (DOTAS) rules or are issued with a counteraction notice under the General Anti-Abuse Rule (GAAR).

The intention behind the rules is to ensure that tax in dispute will sit with Exchequer rather than the taxpayer as otherwise, taxpayers who self-assess can claim a tax advantage from an avoidance scheme and hold the money in dispute while the dispute is resolved. Repayments claimed can already be retained so that the disputed tax rests with HMRC until the dispute is resolved and the accelerated payment rules bring the vast majority of remaining tax avoidance cases into line with this position.

An accelerated payment notice (APN) may be issued to taxpayers who have used an avoidance scheme and where three conditions are met.

Condition A:

There is an open enquiry into a tax return for one of the relevant taxes; or that there is an appeal to HMRC or the First-tier Tribunal which is pending.

Condition B:

The disputed return, claim or appeal is made on the basis that a particular tax advantage results from particular arrangements.

Condition C:

That either:

(a) HMRC have issued a Follower Notice in respect of the same return, claim or appeal by reason of the exact same tax advantage and arrangements as in Condition B;

(b) the tax arrangements are 'DOTAS arrangements';

(c) a GAAR Counteraction Notice has been issued (independently or at the same time as a Follower Notice) and at least two members of the GAAR panel decided that it was not reasonable to enter into the said tax arrangements.

The APN tells the taxpayer they must pay the specified amount which equates to the tax in dispute as a result of their use of the avoidance scheme. Payment is due within 90 days and although the taxpayer may make representations to HMRC if they disagree with the notice, there is no right of appeal.

From 26 March 2015, accelerated payment notices are extended to include amounts that might otherwise be surrendered by way of group relief. Previously, where a company had losses or certain other amounts that derive from arrangements that meet the criteria, an APN might not require it to pay over any amounts because there might be no actual tax to pay when the dispute is resolved (due to the existence of losses). However, the company could surrender some or all of the amounts by way of group relief enabling the cash timing benefit to be obtained by other companies in the group. The amendments by FA 2015 prevents such amounts from being surrendered and claimed while the dispute is in progress so the relevant cash amount remains with the Exchequer during the dispute.

Penalties will be charged where payment is not made in full by the due date as follows:

- 5% of the amount still owed if payment is not made on or before the due date;

- further 5% of the amount still owed after the end of the period of five months beginning with the first penalty day; and

- further 5% of the amount still owed after the end of the period of 11 months beginning with the penalty day.

On 13 September 2015, HMRC published a factsheet *Ten things about Accelerated Payment Notices (APNs)* which is available at www.gov.uk/ government/publications/ten-things-about-accelerated-payment-notices/ ten-things-about-accelerated-payment-notices.

Legislation: FA 2014, Pt. 4

Cases: *R (on the application of Sword Services Ltd) v R & C Commrs* [2015] BTC 40; *R (on the application of Aston) v R & C Commrs* [2016] BTC 1; *Walapu v R & C Commrs* [2016] BTC 14

Other material: CC/FS24; CC/FS26; HMRC guidance – Follower notices and accelerated payments is available at www.gov.uk/government/ publications/follower-notices-and-accelerated-payments

Tax Reporter: ¶192-762ff.

12424 Promoters of tax avoidance schemes

Building on the existing regime for the disclosure of tax avoidance schemes, *Finance Act* 2014, Pt. 5 introduced new rules that apply to promoters of tax avoidance schemes and which aim to deter the development and use of avoidance schemes by influencing the behaviour of promoters, their intermediaries and clients.

In broad outline, the provisions define promoters of tax avoidance schemes, identify when they have triggered 'threshold' conditions targeting specified behaviours and provide for a 'conduct' notice to be applied to those promoters. Those who fail to comply with a conduct notice may be issued with a 'monitoring' notice, which requires pre-approval by a tribunal. Names of promoters subject to monitoring notices will be published by HMRC, including details of how the conduct notice was breached, and the promoter will be required to publish its monitored status to clients. Information requirements will apply to monitored promoters, and intermediaries and clients of monitored promoters.

The threshold conditions include: deliberate tax defaulters; breach of the banking code of practices; dishonest tax agents; non-compliance with DOTAS; criminal offences; opinion notice of GAAR advisory panel; disciplinary action by a professional body; disciplinary action by a regulated authority; failure to comply with information notices; restrictive contractual terms (promoters who contractually restrict the other parties from disclosing information) and continuing to promote certain arrangements once a stop notice has been issued.

Finance Act 2015 introduced further legislation, with effect from 26 March 2015, to allow HMRC to issue conduct notices to a broader rate of connected persons under the common control of a promoter of a tax avoidance scheme; to provide that the three-year time limit for issuing notices to promoters who have failed to disclose avoidance schemes to HMRC applies from the date the failure is established and to ensure that the threshold conditions take account of decisions by independent bodies in matters of all relevant forms of professional misconduct.

Finance Act 2016 introduces a new threshold, with effect from 15 September 2016 (Royal Assent), intended to tackle the behaviour of promoters who promote a series of avoidance schemes that do not work. Where a promoter meets any of the conditions specified, an authorised officer must consider whether to issue a conduct notice. The conditions are:

(1) there have been three relevant defeats (new FA 2014, Sch. 34A) of a promoter's promoted arrangements in the preceding three years;

(2) a promoter has been given a defeat notice in respect of one defeat in the preceding three years (new FA 2014, s. 241A) and there have been two further defeats while that notice had effect;

(3) a promoter has been given a defeat notice in respect of two defeats in the preceding three years and there is a further defeat while that notice had effect.

Legislation: FA 2014, s. 234–283 (Pt. 5) and Sch. 34–36; SI 2015/549; SI 2015/945

Tax Reporter: ¶192-770ff.

12424A Serial tax avoiders

Finance Act 2016 introduces a new regime of warnings and escalating sanctions for those who persistently engage in tax avoidance schemes which HMRC defeat. Following the first defeat of a tax avoidance scheme, HMRC will place the taxpayer on a warning that the use of any avoidance schemes in the following five years which HMRC defeat, will result in a penalty being issued, based on the amount of the understated tax. That penalty will be 20% of the amount of tax understated or overclaimed for the first defeat of a scheme used during a warning period, 40% for the second such defeat and 60% for any subsequent defeats.

If HMRC defeat three tax avoidance schemes while the taxpayer is on a warning, the taxpayer's details can be published. If three avoidance schemes which exploit reliefs are used while under warning and HMRC defeat them, the taxpayer will be denied further benefits of reliefs until the warning period expires. The regime has effect in relation to relevant defeats incurred after 15 September 2016 (Royal Assent) but disregarding defeats incurred before 6 April 2017 in relation to arrangements entered into before 15 September 2016 and disregarding also defeats incurred on or after 6 April 2017 where the arrangements were entered into before 15 September 2016 and before 6 April 2017 full disclosure is made to HMRC or HMRC are notified of an intention to make full disclosure.

Legislation: FA 2016, s. 159 and Sch. 18

Money laundering

12425   Money laundering – introduction

Within the wider context of disclosure, special considerations apply in respect of money laundering. Here, the obligations are on the practitioner and not the client.

Practitioners need to be fully aware of the requirements of the anti-money laundering provisions of the *Proceeds of Crime Act* 2002 and the *Money Laundering Regulations* 2003. These provisions originally came into effect on 1 March 2004 and apply to any knowledge or suspicion of money laundering that arises after that date.

From 1 October 2008, all firms involved in providing tax advice must be supervised in respect of money laundering compliance either by a recognised supervisory authority or by HMRC. The latter alternative is unlikely to be particularly attractive to practitioners. Failure to comply with the registration requirement carries the potential of a fine or two years imprisonment or both.

The regulations are subject to regular amendment. Practitioners are therefore strongly recommended to consult the website either of their regulatory body or HMRC to ensure that any guidance to which they refer is the most recent version.

What follows in this section of this manual is not intended to provide comprehensive advice on a practitioner's anti-money laundering obligations.

Tax Reporter: ¶196-600ff.

12426 What is money laundering?

Money laundering is specifically defined by the legislation. It occurs when someone:

- conceals, disguises, converts, transfers or removes (from the UK) criminal property;

- enters into or is concerned in an arrangement which they know or suspect facilitates the acquisition, retention, use or control of criminal property by or on behalf of another person; or

- acquires, uses or has possession of criminal property and they know or suspect that the property constitutes or represents a benefit from criminal conduct.

There is thus a requirement for both an act and a state of mind.

Tax evasion is itself criminal conduct, so criminal property includes the proceeds of tax evasion, no matter how small the amount – there is no de minimis limit. Examples of what constitutes money laundering in the field of taxation include:

- deliberately understating profits;

- deliberately overstating expenses;

- failing to notify HMRC, once it comes to light, of an innocent or careless error which led to a loss of tax; or

- failing to notify HMRC of an over-repayment of tax when the repayment is know to be excessive.

A moment's reflection on the above may help practitioners appreciate why they may need to report a suspected money laundering activity.

Tax Reporter: ¶196-650; ¶196-900

12427 Reporting requirements

If, in the course of their professional activities, a practitioner suspects or ought to have suspected that someone has been involved in money laundering, a report must be made by the Money Laundering Reporting Officer (MLRO) to the National Crime Agency (NCA) (formerly the Serious Organised Crime Agency (SOCA)) as soon as possible. The practitioner does not require evidence in support of the suspicion, nor is it necessary to be sure that a criminal offence has been committed – a report has to be made if the practitioner merely suspects money laundering.

The obligation to make a report is a personal one. It does not matter that the practitioner thinks that someone else has made a report and nor is the obligation to make a report affected by the known willingness of HMRC to seek a civil settlement in the case.

It is an offence under the legislation for the practitioner to tell someone that it is known or suspected that a report is to be, or has been made to NCA. It is also an offence to tell anyone else if doing so will prejudice any investigation which is made as a result of NCA receiving the report.

Tax Reporter: ¶196-600ff.

12428 Defences and exemptions

The legislation recognises that some situations require exceptional treatment. Special provision is accordingly made in relation to Overseas Offences and Professional Privilege.

Overseas offences

Under the original legislation, it was irrelevant whether the particular act which produced the proceeds was lawful in the overseas country where it took place. It was sufficient that the act would have been a criminal offence had it taken place in the United Kingdom.

Under amendments to the *Proceeds of Crime Act* 2002 made in 2006, a defence to the money laundering offences in that Act was introduced. Subject to certain exceptions, the defence applies where:

- a person knows or believes on reasonable grounds that the acts which produced the proceeds took place in a particular country overseas and the acts were lawful in that country; and

- the act generating the proceeds would not be punishable in the United Kingdom by a maximum sentence of more than twelve months imprisonment.

Professional Privilege

A mandatory exemption from reporting knowledge or suspicion of money laundering that came to a person in privileged circumstances was originally available only to lawyers. The legislation was amended so that, with effect from 21 February 2006, the exemption was extended to accountants, auditors and tax advisers who are members of appropriate professional bodies.

This means that knowledge or suspicion of money laundering that comes from information received when providing legal advice and acting in respect of litigation does not have to be reported to NCA unless the services provided will be used in the furtherance of a criminal purpose.

However, the exemption only applies in the narrow circumstances stipulated. The examples included in the guidance of where privilege does apply do not address the situation of an existing HMRC enquiry or an intended unprompted disclosure. Privilege does not extend to the general provision of tax advice and is therefore of very limited relevance for most practitioners.

The professional privilege exemption applies only to reports of money laundering required under the *Proceeds of Crime Act* 2002; it does not apply to the reporting requirement under the *Terrorism Act* 2000.

Tax Reporter: ¶196-775

12429   Steps required

Practitioners are required to take certain steps to comply with the money laundering regulations. They must:

- be registered with a recognised supervisory authority or HMRC;
- appoint a money laundering reporting officer to receive reports from colleagues and make reports to NCA;
- train principals and staff in the requirements of the legislation so they know how to check the identity of clients and can recognise and report money laundering;
- verify the identity of new clients; and
- establish internal procedures to detect and deter money laundering.

The CCAB guidance that has been approved by the Treasury for accountants and tax advisers can be found on the CCAB website. It is also accessible through the websites of many of the recognised supervisory bodies (the professional institutes and associations).

Legislation: *Proceeds of Crime Act* 2002; *Money Laundering Regulations* 2007 (SI 2007/2157)

Other Material: HMRC guidance: www.gov.uk/money-laundering-regulations-introduction

Tax Reporter: ¶196-600ff.

Taxpayers' charter and remedies

12430 Taxpayers charter

HMRC are required by statute to maintain a Charter. The current Charter, entitled *Your Charter*, sets out standards of behaviours and values for HMRC to aim at when dealing with taxpayers and others. The legislation also requires the Commissioners for HMRC to report annually on how well HMRC is doing in meeting Charter standards.

The summary included in the four-page leaflet reads:

'Your rights

What you can expect from us:

(1)   Respect you

(2)   Help and support you to get things right

(3)   Treat you as honest

(4)   Treat you even-handedly

(5)   Be professional and act with integrity

(6)   Tackle people who deliberately break the rules and challenge those who bend the rules

(7)   Protect your information and respect your privacy

(8)   Accept that someone else can represent you

(9)   Do all we can to keep the cost of dealing with us as low as possible

Your obligations

What we expect from you:

(1)   Be honest

(2)   Respect our staff

(3)   Take care to get things right'

The full version expands upon the summary and is worth studying periodically. Amid a range of predictable and worthy aspirations, there are some more interesting commitments. For example, within 'Treat you even-handedly' is 'consider any financial difficulties you may be having'; within 'Be professional and act with integrity', we find 'make sure that you are dealt with by people who have the right level of expertise' and within 'Protect your information and respect your privacy' HMRC promise to 'give you the information we hold about you when you ask for it, as long as the law lets us'.

Less helpfully, 'Tackle people who deliberately break the rules and challenge those who bend the rules' demonstrates how HMRC tend to minimise the distinction between tax evasion and tax avoidance. The expanded version explains rather vaguely that this means distinguishing 'between legitimately trying to pay the lowest amount and bending the rules through tax avoidance'.

Under Expectation 4, is a commitment to 'explain what you can do if you disagree with our decisions or want to make a complaint'. In practice, the options for a taxpayer are those summarised in 12440.

Legislation: *Commissioners for Revenue and Customs Act* 2005, s. 16A

Other Material: GOV.UK website – www.gov.uk/government/publications/ your-charter

Tax Reporter: ¶193-310

12440   Remedies when things go wrong

There are defined channels for making a complaint about the way HMRC have dealt with a matter including unreasonable delays, mistakes and how HMRC staff have behaved. These are:

- to complain to HMRC; either the person who has been dealing with the matter, one of the HMRC helplines or a customer service adviser;

- to complain to the Adjudicator if a complaint has been made to HMRC and the taxpayer is not satisfied with the response; and

- to ask their MP to raise a complaint with the Parliamentary and Health Service Ombudsman (as an alternative to the Adjudicator) or to ask their MP to raise their complaint with ministers.

Complaints in respect of income tax (self-assessment and PAYE) may be made online using the form at www.gov.uk/guidance/complain-to-hm-revenue-and-customs.

Further guidance 'How to complain to HMRC about the service you've received, and how your complaint will be dealt with' is available on GOV.UK website.

A separate guide is available on 'How to complain about serious misconduct by HMRC staff and how your complaint will be dealt with'. Serious misconduct includes assault leading to death or serious injury; corruption; fraud; and unauthorised disclosure of customer information. HMRC consider serious misconduct by members of its staff to be criminal or near criminal behaviour and the Independent Police Complaints Commission (IPCC) oversees the way HMRC deal with these complaints.

When the disagreement is not about the way in which a matter has been or is being handled but about the actual decision reached by HMRC, the route to resolution is likely to be through the review and appeal procedures (see 12600ff.).

Other Material: GOV.UK website – www.gov.uk/complain-to-hm-revenue-and-customs;   www.gov.uk/complain-about-serious-misconduct-by-hm-revenue-and-customs-staff; Factsheet C/FS – www.gov.uk/government/publications/putting-things-right-how-to-complain-factsheet-cfs

Tax Reporter: ¶193-410

Reviews, appeals and applications

12600   Introduction

The tax appeals system changed radically from 1 April 2009. The key features of the current regime are as follows:

- the replacement of the General Commissioners, Special Commissioners, VAT and Duties Tribunals by the First-tier Tribunal (Tax Chamber);

- the introduction of a statutory internal review procedure as a preliminary to an appeal;

- the removal in relation to direct tax cases from HMRC of the administrative responsibility of bringing an appeal to hearing;

- the replacement of the High Court's functions in tax appeals by the Upper Tribunal; and

- appeal hearings are (at least in theory) normally in public.

It is probably in relation to the functions of the former General Commissioners that things have changed most, certainly from the perspective of the practitioner. The General Commissioners had done sterling unpaid work in providing accessible justice on tax matters and many practitioners had some historic experience of attending a commissioners' hearing, even if only to request an appeal adjournment back in the days before self-assessment. By contrast, the current system can appear much more formal, remote and potentially expensive. The reality, fortunately, is refreshingly different and all practitioners need to have an understanding of the appeal and review procedures. The subsequent paragraphs outline the current regime in the following order:

- overview of the tribunal system 12610;

- HMRC's internal review procedure 12620ff.;

- alternative dispute resolution 12625;

- notification of appeal to the tribunal 12630ff.;

- tribunal procedures before the hearing 12640ff.;

- tribunal procedures at the hearing 12650ff.;

- notice of Tribunal Decision 12660ff.;

- tribunal practicalities 12670; and

- other applications to the tribunal 12680.

Practitioners may also find it helpful to refer to the July 2011 updated version of HMRC's Litigation and Settlements Strategy for which a website link is provided below.

Appeals in Scotland: The Scottish Tribunals

On 1 April 2015, the First-tier Tribunal for Scotland and Upper Tribunal for Scotland were constituted having been established by the *Tribunals (Scotland) Act* 2014 and the *Revenue Scotland and Tax Powers Act* 2014. The Scottish Tribunals operate in parallel with the existing tribunals exercising functions in relation to devolved taxes.

Legislation: *Tribunals Courts and Enforcement Act* 2007; FA 2008, s. 124; *Tribunals (Scotland) Act* 2014; *Revenue Scotland and Tax Powers Act* 2014; *Transfer of Tribunal Functions and Revenue and Customs Appeal Order* 2009 (SI 2009/56)

Other Material: www.gov.uk/government/publications/litigation-and-settlement-strategy-lss; www.justice.gov.uk/tribunals/tax; www.justice.gov.uk/tribunals/tax-and-chancery-upper-tribunal; www.scotland.gov.uk/Topics/Justice/policies/civil-courts/tribunal-system/Tribunals

Tax Reporter: ¶188-800ff.

12610 Overview of the tribunal system

As part of the general restructuring of all tribunals in the United Kingdom, that relating to the tax system involved the introduction of two different tribunals into the tax litigation process. These two tribunals are known as:

- the First-tier Tribunal Tax Chamber, often referred to as the First-tier Tribunal; and

- the Upper Tribunal.

The people hearing cases in the First-tier Tribunal are referred to as judges or other members (collectively, referred to as 'members'), depending on their qualifications. The presiding member will usually, but not necessarily, be a judge. A judge may be either full-time or part-time. Their background and experience vary significantly but all have the professional skills to enable them to conduct the hearing. Where the presiding member is not a judge, they will nevertheless have had the required training to conduct the hearing. There will usually be one other member of the tribunal. They are likely to be either someone with a professional background in taxation or with substantial experience in other tribunals. Practitioners can therefore have confidence in the professionalism, competence and relevant experience of the tribunal.

Unlike meetings of the General Commissioners, but more like the former VAT and Duties Tribunals, the tribunal hearings are at regional centres. The accommodation facilities at these centres vary between locations from the barely acceptable to the excellent. There is a presumption that all appeal hearings (but not certain application hearings) are open to the public. The tribunal may agree to hear matters in private but there is a strong presumption that justice should be seen to be done. In practice, there is very rarely any member of the public present at a hearing but the presumption of a public hearing does for example enable family and friends to attend. Despite the public hearing concept, there is (unlike matters in the High Court) no advance public listing of matters coming to hearing.

The vast majority of tax cases will be first heard by the First-tier Tribunal Tax Chamber. Note, however, that appeals against decisions in relation to tax credits are heard by the First-tier Tribunal (Social Security and Child Support). Appeals from the decisions of the First-tier Tribunal are made to the Upper Tribunal (Tax and Chancery Chamber). The Upper Tribunal effectively has the same status as the High Court itself. Appeals from the Upper Tribunal go direct to the Court of Appeal (in England and Wales and in Northern Ireland) or the Court of Session (in Scotland). The ultimate appeal is to the Supreme Court.

One of the intended changes under the current appeal system is to give taxpayers a greater control over the listing of their appeal for hearing, particularly in direct tax cases. Historically, HMRC were effectively in control of when and whether an appeal came to hearing. That simplified matters for taxpayers (as it removed one level of bureaucracy from them), but it resulted in the perception of a closeness between the tax authorities and the appeal commissioners. Under the current tribunal system, the administrative aspects in preparation for a hearing are undertaken by the tribunal's own administrative officers.

There is presently no charge for taking cases to the First-tier Tribunal or Upper Tribunal, however, plans to introduce such fees were set out as part of a wider consultation on court and tribunal fees which closed on 15 September 2015.

The consultation is available at consult.justice.gov.uk/digital-communications/ further-fees-proposal-consultation/supporting_documents/Government%20 response%20to%20consultation%20on%20enhanced%20fees%20 and%20consultation%20on%20further%20fees%20proposals%20web.pdf.

Legislation: TCEA 2007, s. 3, 11 and 25

Tax Reporter: ¶188-950ff.

12620 HMRC's internal review procedure – introduction

In order to avoid the tribunal administrative system becoming involved in matters when there is still a reasonable prospect of the matter being resolved without resorting to formal litigation, the current appeals system gives statutory recognition to the merit of an internal review by HMRC as a preliminary step. As part of this, it introduces a mechanism to prevent HMRC from delaying a case being brought to hearing.

There are some remaining distinctions between the system as between direct and indirect tax matters but the common points in relation to any appeal-able decision are that:

- the appeal is initially notified in writing to HMRC;

- the taxpayer can request (or accept HMRC's offer of) a review of the decision;

- the taxpayer may (following the outcome of any such review) notify the appeal direct to the tribunal.

Whichever approach is taken, it does not prevent the parties from settling the dispute by mutual agreement prior to an appeal hearing by the tribunal.

In March 2012, HMRC released a short video *Resolving Disputes – Reviews & Appeals*. This provides a brief explanation of the mechanics of appeals and reviews and the approach of HMRC.

Other Material: HMRC *Appeals Reviews & Tribunals Guidance* ARTG1030ff. and 2000ff.

Tax Reporter: ¶189-200ff.

12621 HMRC's internal review procedure – mechanics

The necessary legislation to link the review process to the appeal procedure is contained in TMA 1970. The basic mechanisms introduced are not complex but the legislation is not as clearly written as it might have been. The essential concepts are as follows:

- an appeal against an HMRC decision needs to be made to HMRC within 30 days;
- if HMRC offer a review, the offer must:
  - include HMRC's view of the matter in question;
  - give the taxpayer 30 days (starting with the date stated on HMRC's offer of a review) to accept the offer of a review;
- if HMRC do not offer a review but the taxpayer requests one, HMRC must set out their initial view of the matter within 30 days of their receipt of the request for the review (or such longer period as is reasonable) thus putting the taxpayer in the same situation as if HMRC had offered a review;
- HMRC must notify the taxpayer of their conclusions of the review and their reasoning within a 45-day period (unless the parties agree a different timescale) with that 45-day period running:
  - in a case where the taxpayer requested the review, from the day on which HMRC notified the taxpayer of their initial view of the matter; and
  - in a case where the taxpayer accepted HMRC's offer of a review, from the day on which HMRC received the acceptance of the offer;
- a review cannot be requested by the taxpayer or offered by HMRC (and HMRC cannot be required to conduct a review) if:
  - the taxpayer has already requested a review in relation to the matter;
  - HMRC have already offered a review in relation to the matter; or
  - the taxpayer has already notified the First-tier Tribunal of the appeal;
- following the notification by HMRC to the taxpayer of the outcome of a review:
  - the review decision is deemed to constitute a final agreement on the matter but;
  - the taxpayer has 30 days in which to notify the tribunal of the appeal and thereby displace that deemed finality;
- if HMRC fail to give the conclusions of their review within the 45-day (or longer agreed) period, their original decision is deemed to stand in the same way as if the review had formally upheld the original decision, so that the taxpayer then has 30 days in which to notify the tribunal of the appeal and thereby displace that deemed finality; and

- if the taxpayer declines the offer of a review, they have 30 days from the date of the offer to notify their appeal to the tribunal, failing which the decision is final unless the tribunal agree to admit a late appeal.

Other Material: HMRC *Appeals Reviews & Tribunals Guidance* ARTG1030ff. and 2000ff.

Tax Reporter: ¶189-200ff.

12622   HMRC's internal review procedure – practical implications

It is essential for the practitioner to pay careful attention to the relevant time-limits as their client's interest might otherwise be prejudiced. The operation of a simple log or diary reminder could be useful.

The deemed finality provisions can appear to be somewhat draconian. Their purpose, however, is to ensure that momentum is not lost. HMRC cannot stall by simply refusing to make a decision; the taxpayer cannot prevaricate by re-opening discussion with HMRC.

Practitioners may need to consider the likely timing of any review decision in order to avoid the possibility of a review decision arriving (or being deemed to have arrived) when they or their client were away for any extended period.

Other Material: HMRC *Appeals Reviews & Tribunals Guidance* ARTG1030ff. and 2000ff.

Tax Reporter: ¶189-200ff.

12623   Nature of HMRC's internal review

The nature and extent of the review will depend on what appears to be appropriate to HMRC in the particular circumstances. However, HMRC must bear in mind the steps taken by HMRC in first deciding the matter and any steps taken by any person seeking to resolve the disagreement.

The review must also take into account any representations made by the taxpayer, provided that they are made sufficiently early to give HMRC a reasonable opportunity to consider them. To avoid difficulties with this hurdle, it is strongly recommended that the representations be included in the request for a review (or the acceptance of the offer of the review).

HMRC's Appeals Reviews & Tribunals Guidance indicates that the 'review will be carried out by a review officer, who is, in most cases, outside the direct line management chain of the decision maker and was not involved in making the decision.' There is no statutory provision stipulating who should or should not conduct a review.

Statute recognises three possible outcomes of a review. The original HMRC decision can be upheld, varied or cancelled.

Experience suggests that the quality of the review can be variable.

HMRC publish statistics about the outcome of reviews (see website reference below). They require a word of explanation. Many of the occasions where the review resulted in a decision in favour of the taxpayer concerned penalties that were imposed automatically. In these cases, the taxpayer's request for a review, typically on the grounds of reasonable excuse, results in the first intervention within HMRC of a human-being so the level of decisions in favour of the taxpayer is unsurprising.

Legislation: TMA 1970, s. 49E

Other Material: HMRC *Appeals Reviews & Tribunals Guidance* ARTG1030ff. and 2000ff.; Factsheet: HMRC1 *HMRC decisions – what you can do if you disagree*

Tax Reporter: ¶189-200ff.

12625   Alternative Dispute Resolution

ADR became generally available to SMEs and individuals from September 2013, providing an alternative way of dealing with a tax dispute with HMRC where dealings with HMRC have stopped making progress. ADR aims to help resolve disputes or get agreements on which issues need to be taken for a legal ruling. ADR does not affect a taxpayers' right to appeal or to ask for a statutory review.

ADR provides the option of having someone who has not been involved in the dispute to work with the agent and HMRC officer and act as a neutral third party mediator. They do not take over responsibility for the dispute but help both sides explore disputes through meetings and telephone conversations.

The facilitator's functions are 'to help all the parties reach a shared and full understanding of the disputed facts and arguments' and 'to help explain what each side is trying to say to the other'. Both functions could prove useful in the context of an enquiry.

Disputes not suitable for ADR include disputes about payments, fixed penalties on the grounds of reasonable excuse, tax credits, PAYE coding, HMRC delays in using information, cases being dealt with by HMRC's criminal investigators or default surcharges.

The GOV.UK website includes an online application form to request consideration of a case for the ADR process. To protect legal rights an appeal or request for statutory review should be made in addition to a request for ADR. ADR can also be requested before HMRC have made a decision.

Other Material: GOV.UK website: www.gov.uk/tax-disputes-alternative-dispute-resolution-adr; CC/FS21

Tax Reporter: ¶188-875

12630   Notification of appeal to the tribunal

The introduction of the review mechanism necessitates a duplication of the notification of an appeal. Notice is first given to HMRC (see 12620ff.). It is the notification to the tribunal that will usually require more consideration by the practitioner. It may be appropriate to seek specialist advice. The time limits and grounds for appeal are two of the most important points to keep in mind.

Other material: Factsheet: HMRC1 *HMRC decisions – what you can do if you disagree*

Tax Reporter: ¶189-175ff.

12631   Time-limits for notifying appeal to the tribunal

The time-limit for notifying the tribunal of the appeal will depend on whether and how the parties involved the review procedure. The obvious alternative scenarios are considered below:

- if a review has been concluded, the taxpayer must notify the tribunal of the appeal within a 30-day period of the decision notice;

- if HMRC have failed to notify their review decision within the 45-day (or longer agreed) period, the taxpayer may notify the tribunal of the appeal at any time between:

  - the conclusion of the review period (usually 45 days); and

  - the 30th day following HMRC giving the formal notice that no decision has been reached;

- if, in a direct tax cases, no review is either offered or requested when a written appeal is made to HMRC, the parties are able to continue to discuss matters until such time as the taxpayer either requests a review or applies directly to the tribunal or HMRC formally offers a review. This enables the parties to explore the possibility for a settlement without any external time pressure at the same time as giving both some protection against delay by the other party.

If the taxpayer is late in notifying the First-tier Tribunal of the appeal, the appeal may only proceed with the permission of the tribunal.

Once the tribunal has been notified of the appeal, the tribunal will decide the matter in question.

Legislation: TMA 1970, s. 49B–49E, 49G and 49H

Cases: *Patrick* [2015] TC 04666; *Odunlami* [2016] TC 04786; *Ashraf* [2016] TC 05206; *Martin* [2016] TC 05221

Tax Reporter: ¶189-175ff.

12632 Form of appeal to the tribunal

An appeal to the tribunal should be notified in accordance with the tribunal's procedures. Form TS-TaxAp1 should be used. This can be downloaded from the Tax Tribunal section of the Ministry of Justice website.

Notices of appeal should specify the grounds of appeal. If the appeal is eventually heard by the tribunal, further or different grounds not originally specified in the notice may be taken into consideration, provided that the tribunal is content that their omission was not wilful or unreasonable. Where detailed reasons have been set out in support of an HMRC decision, it is advisable to specify briefly every point that the taxpayer may wish to contest at the hearing.

Other Material: Ministry of Justice website: www.justice.gov.uk/guidance/courts-and-tribunals/tribunals/tax/appeals.htm

Tax Reporter: ¶189-175ff.

12640 Tribunal procedures before the hearing

In order to streamline the tribunal's handling of cases, they will be allocated to one of four categories when the tribunal receives a notice of appeal, application notice or notice of reference:

- default paper cases;
- basic cases;
- standard cases; and
- complex cases.

The initial allocation of a case is not final. Either on its own initiative or upon an application of a party, the tribunal may reallocate a case to a different category by giving a further direction.

Tax Reporter: ¶189-175ff.

12641   Default paper cases

A default paper case will usually be decided by a single judge or member without any hearing.

This category applies to appeals against:

- fixed penalties for late filing of tax returns;
- fixed penalties for late filing of employer returns (P35s);
- fixed penalties for late filing of returns under the Construction Industry Scheme;
- Class 2 NICs late notification penalties;
- income tax surcharges (for late payment of tax under self-assessment); and
- applications by HMRC for the imposition of daily penalties in relation to late self-assessment tax returns.

Such cases may (upon request by any party) be dealt with at a hearing.

Tax Reporter: ¶189-175ff.

12642   Basic cases

Basic cases are those which will usually be decided after a hearing, but with minimal exchange of documents beforehand. The basic case category applies to appeals against:

- tax-geared penalties for late filing of tax returns;
- most tax-geared penalties for incorrect returns (but not where the penalty is for deliberate and concealed action, nor where there is also an appeal against the assessment itself);
- mitigation and reasonable excuse appeals against indirect tax penalties;
- appeals against CIS gross payment status decisions; and
- appeals against information notices.

The basic case category also applies to:

- applications for permission to make a late appeal;
- postponement applications (where HMRC refuse); and
- closure notice applications.

Tax Reporter: ¶189-175ff.

12643 Standard cases

Standard cases are those which will usually be decided after a hearing and which may require more detailed case management. That might for example include directions as to what and when documents need to be exchanged between parties. This is the likely category if a matter is within neither the Default Paper nor Basic category. In relation to enquiry cases, this would be the usual categorisation where the appeal concerned the quantification of any omitted tax liability.

Tax Reporter: ¶189-175ff.

12644 Complex cases

An appeal will only be allocated to the Complex category if it satisfies at least one of three criteria, namely:

* it will require lengthy or complex evidence or a lengthy hearing;

* it involves a complex or important principle of law; or

* it involves a large financial sum.

Either party to any appeal can request its reclassification but reclassification to Complex would require satisfaction of one or more of the above criteria.

A Complex appeal differs from a Standard appeal in that:

* the tribunal has full costs jurisdiction (although the taxpayer (only) can opt to exclude the costs regime); and

* there is potential for transfer of the hearing to the Upper Tribunal (although this requires the consent of the President of the tribunal and is unlikely to be done unless the case involved difficult points of law and little or no dispute of fact). MTIC (missing trader) and similar cases fall into this category.

Case: *Drummond v R & C Commrs* [2016] BVC 517

Tax Reporter: ¶189-175ff.

12650 Tribunal procedure at the hearing

This commentary is not intended as a summary of formal legal procedure. Rather, it is intended to help the practitioner and their client prepare for the hearing.

One of the key features of the General Commissioners' meetings was their ability to move readily between a more formal and a more informal approach as the need arose. This helped the unrepresented taxpayer or the inexperienced adviser to be able to present their case without undue emphasis upon formal considerations. The intention is that this characteristic should be retained at least for Basic cases and where the taxpayer is unrepresented.

Where a practitioner is involved in presenting a case, there will inevitably be somewhat greater formality, for example, because the taxpayer is likely to be called as a witness and there needs to be an clear procedure for taking evidence, cross-examining and re-examining.

The tribunal members will inevitably be seated in the room when the parties are called in by the clerk. It is normal for the tribunal panel to greet the parties and their representatives (Good morning, etc). Formal bows would not generally be expected. It is normal for all witnesses to be called into the room at the same time as the appellant and HMRC.

The normal form of address to the judge or a member during the hearing is 'Madam' or 'Sir' as appropriate although any polite and respectful form of address is likely to be acceptable. The tribunal does not stand on ceremony.

HMRC's case will almost inevitably be presented by someone other than the officer who has previously dealt with the matter under appeal. Typically, the HMRC presenter will be a member of a Regional Appeals Unit. The practitioner may have had contact with them in preparation for the hearing. Individual styles differ considerably. Some are much more at ease than others when presenting. Their standard approach is typified by thoroughness rather than flair, often with repetition of the key factors that favour their position. It is not an exciting style but it serves its purpose and practitioners could do a lot worse than follow the example.

The standard running order is that of:

- appellant (taxpayer);
- respondent (HMRC); and
- appellant summary (in which no new material should be introduced).

However, there can be some flexibility and the tribunal would for example probably accept the appellant's request for HMRC to open by first setting out the background to the appeal if that is what the appellant wants. Practitioners should carefully consider the implications of this. One difficulty is that it can result in HMRC getting two opportunities to present their case. An alternative if the practitioner wishes to open but to do so on more comfortable ground, might be to prepare a statement of agreed facts with HMRC and to use that to introduce the case. That can then lead easily into the areas which are in dispute.

The tribunal panel may ask questions of clarification during the presentation of the appellant's case by the practitioner but if the matter is being conducted more formally, questions would normally be raised at the end of the presentation. If replying at an earlier stage might destroy the practitioner's line of thought rather than clarify matters, it would be acceptable to explain that the point will be clarified at a later stage.

Witnesses may be asked (or permitted) by the tribunal to give evidence on oath (or to make an affirmation). If any witness is asked to do so by the tribunal, the tribunal will make the same request of all witnesses. The appellant must be permitted to give evidence on his own account even if they are not prepared to give evidence on oath or affirmation but the tribunal will explain to them that such evidence will carry less weight than anything said by a witness who has been sworn.

After the taxpayer (and any other witness for the appellant) has been 'examined' by their own representative, HMRC have the opportunity to cross-examine. The practitioner needs to be particularly attentive here in order to identify any points that may need to be clarified by re-examination of the client (or witness).

When HMRC presents its case, the practitioner needs to be making a careful note of anything that potentially damages their client's case so that it can if possible be challenged in the appellant's summing up. When cross-examining an HMRC witness (typically the officer who made the decision that is under appeal), the practitioner's questions are likely to need to be a mixture of open and closed questions. Closed questions may be more effective but their significance may need to be drawn out in the summing up.

After the HMRC presentation has concluded, the appellant (through their representative) has the final word. No new material or arguments can be introduced at this stage (doing so gives HMRC the right of reply). This is the practitioner's opportunity to:

- counter points made by the HMRC presenter;

- comment on the evidence given by any HMRC witness, highlighting any weaknesses and inconsistencies;

- emphasise the positive points brought out in the evidence of any witness for the appellant and any clarification already brought out in re-examination; and

- succinctly restate the arguments as to why the tribunal should find in favour of the appellant and not be persuaded by any arguments put by HMRC.

Tax Reporter: ¶189-175ff.

12660   Notice of tribunal decision

After the appellant's summary, the tribunal will either ask the parties to retire from the room to enable consideration of the case or indicate that the decision will instead be issued at a later date. If the decision can be given on the day, it will be given orally and followed up with a written decision notice. If the decision cannot be given on the day, the parties will be dismissed and advised that a written decision will follow. In either case, the hearing will be followed within 28 days by a decision notice in one of three forms:

- if the parties so agree, a simple statement of the decision without any reasons; or
- if the parties do not so agree, either:
  - a summary of the findings of fact and reasons for the decision; or
  - full written findings of fact and reasons for the decision.

Unless full written findings are provided with the decision notice, any party to the appeal may within 28 days of the decision notice request such a full decision. The tribunal then has a further 28 days in which to issue the full decision. Either party may within 56 days of the full decision notice apply to the tribunal for permission to appeal against the decision.

Tax Reporter: ¶189-175ff.

12670   Tribunal hearing practicalities

Experience suggests that practitioners may wish to note the following practical points:

- Where a number of cases are to be heard by the tribunal on the same day, some of them are likely to have been listed for the same time of day. It may be tactical to arrive early and ask the Clerk to the tribunal if there is any chance of being heard early (ideally with an appropriate reason for the request such as travel arrangements, domestic commitments, etc.). It will of course be for the tribunal to decide on the order of cases and priority is likely to be given to those which are expected to take the least time but if the Clerk mentions that they have received a request and gives the reason it may be considered.

- Waiting-room accommodation at tribunal venues varies significantly in quality. There will normally be provision of separate rooms for the parties but this cannot be guaranteed. Even where there are separate rooms, it is best to assume that they are not soundproof.

- The tribunal members need to take extensive notes of what is being said during a hearing. It is very helpful if the speed of delivery takes account of this. A useful maxim is 'watch the pen'.

- When the client is called to give evidence, the practitioner should ensure that it is their client who is providing the key facts which the practitioner wishes the tribunal to accept in support of the appeal. 'Open' questions encouraging the client to explain things in their own words are therefore much more useful than closed questions that only enable the client to reply with 'Yes' or 'No'.

- The practitioner needs to ensure that their client understands that HMRC's cross-examination of the client is the time when the tribunal will be most closely observing the appellant. Differences between their manner and demeanour under cross-examination from when they were giving evidence in chief may influence the tribunal's impression of the reliability of their evidence. A direct, courteous and open style is usually the most appropriate.

- As hearings are normally open to the public (see 12610), there can be no objection to a practitioner being accompanied by a note taker. Ideally, the tribunal administration team should be notified in advance so that the seating arrangement enables the note-taker to sit with the practitioner.

- Presenting to a tribunal is within the capabilities of most practitioners but the preparation can be daunting and time-consuming for someone without experience. It may be appropriate to involve expert assistance either for some mentoring or to actually present the case.

Tax Reporter: ¶189-175ff.

12680   Other applications to the Tribunal

In addition to appeals against HMRC decisions, the First-tier Tribunal also hears:

- applications from HMRC including those relating to:

  - first and third party information notices (see 11914);

  - approval for an HMRC inspection;

  - daily penalties where there has been a continuing failure to make a tax return;

  - proceedings for penalties under TMA 1970, s. 100C;

  - certain referrals of clearance applications.

- applications from taxpayers including those relating to:
  - the closure of an enquiry;
  - a late review in relation to a restoration decision;
  - late notice of a direct or indirect tax appeal to HMRC or the tribunal;
  - approval of a hardship request after refusal by HMRC;
  - apportionment of market value;
  - postponement request following HMRC refusal.
- joint applications from the parties for a determination of any question in connection with the subject-matter of an enquiry (see 12685).

Other Material: HMRC *Appeals Reviews & Tribunals Guidance* ARTG7510ff.

Tax Reporter: ¶189-175ff.

12685   Joint application for determination of any question

It is worth mentioning one rarely used facility that could in an appropriate case provide a constructive solution to a situation. In the course of an enquiry, it is possible for the parties to jointly apply to the tribunal for a binding determination of 'any question arising in connection with the subject-matter of an enquiry'.

The lack of any significant use of the facility may well indicate that the parties involved in an enquiry are much more likely to agree that they cannot agree than to agree to a procedure that would enable them to resolve the point conclusively. If, however, there is a significant technical point at issue or if the direction in which an enquiry was to go turned substantially on the interpretation of a particular situation, the provision could well give a cost-effective and relatively swift solution.

Tactically, a practitioner might consider proposing a joint application to the tribunal to HMRC on an point that was proving intractable and holding up progress with other aspects of an enquiry. If HMRC agreed, it would provide such a solution; if they did not, the suggestion could be referred to in passing if the matter eventually came to appeal and used to demonstrate the positive manner in which the matter had been addressed by the taxpayer and practitioner.

Legislation: TMA 1970, s. 28ZA–28ZE

Other Material: HMRC *Appeals Reviews & Tribunals Guidance* ARTG7555

Tax Reporter: ¶189-175ff.

HMRC enquiries

12700   Introduction

HMRC have over time used various descriptions for the process of reviewing returns. Their current terminology is normally 'compliance check'. Practitioners, by contrast, normally refer to enquiries or investigations. In this work, the word 'enquiry' is used to cover all relevant situations without distinction between aspect and full enquiries.

What follows is a very brief summary of some of the key matters that practitioners may need to consider in the context of an enquiry. For more detailed guidance, please see CCH *Practical Enquiries Manual.*

The extent and seriousness of enquiries varies enormously and the practitioner's response must vary accordingly. Some matters can be delegated within a practice; others may need to be referred to a specialist. But there are common themes and these are summarised in the following paragraphs.

Tax Reporter: ¶185-600ff.

12710   Statutory framework for enquiries

The statutory basis for income tax enquiries is in TMA 1970, comparable corporation tax provisions are in Sch. 18 of FA 1998. They detail amongst other things the statutory enquiry window and the discovery provisions.

An enquiry notice has to be in writing and delivered to the taxpayer before the time limit expires.

HMRC should send a copy of the notice to the agent. To be valid, the taxpayer must receive the enquiry notice by midnight on the last date of the period during which it can be issued.

HMRC have an absolute right to make enquiries into a return. They do not have to demonstrate grounds for dissatisfaction.

HMRC normally open an enquiry with an informal request for information. There is no obligation to comply with this but a refusal is likely to prompt HMRC to use their formal information powers (see 11900ff.). It may also adversely impact the possibility of reducing penalties (see 12020ff.).

Under the FA 2008 powers, a person's tax position can (with some limitations) be reviewed before or after a return has been submitted.

Since 1 April 2010, the normal time limit for making an assessment is four years from the end of the tax year in question. Where the loss has been brought about carelessly, the time limit is six years from the end of the tax year; where the loss has been brought about deliberately, it is 20 years.

Since 2013–14, HMRC have adopted a Single Compliance Process (SCP) within which the majority of small and medium enterprise business compliance checks are undertaken, catering for both single tax and cross-tax enquiries. SCP does not apply to Local Compliance Fraud cases (worked under Code of Practice 9 or the Contractual Disclosure Facility), certain types of avoidance work and work carried out by specialist 'Alcohol' teams. It does, however, share the same legal basis as all enquiries. Further information is available on the GOV.UK website.

Cases: *Tinkler* [2016] TC 04960; *Mabbutt* [2016] TC 05075

Other Material: GOV.UK website: www.gov.uk/tax-compliance-checks and www.gov.uk/compliance-checks-an-overview-for-agents-and-advisers; CC/FS1a; CC/FS1b

Tax Reporter: ¶185-600ff.

12720   Selection for enquiry

Selection for enquiry is made either on a random basis or by risk assessment. Practitioners should never assume that an enquiry has been opened on a random basis. Relatively few such enquiries are opened.

The first stage of the selection is automated using sophisticated computer facilities to identify the existence of risk factors. In a business context, the core risk indicators include the following:

- type of business;
- poor trading results;
- inadequate drawings;
- unexplained capital accretions;
- poor compliance; and
- third party information.

After the automated process, an investigating officer conducts a critical review of all the information to determine whether an enquiry should be opened and, if so, how it should be approached.

Where there are unusual features in a return or accounts, a vigilant practitioner can sometimes help their client to avoid an enquiry by providing an appropriate explanation in the return's white space or in notes to a computation. The explanation would be considered in the critical review.

Tax Reporter: ¶185-600ff.

12730   Working an enquiry

Once an officer has opened an enquiry, its progress to conclusion will depend on a wide range of variables including such diverse matters as:

- the confidence and competence of both the officer and the practitioner;
- the credibility of the client;
- the chemistry of the parties;
- the client's previous tax history;
- the nature and quality of any information held by HMRC;
- the reliability of the client's records;
- the availability of evidence to assist the quantification of undeclared liability;
- the nature and quality of any disclosures by the client;
- the underlying reason for any previous under-recognition of profits or gains;
- the means of the client to fund any underpayments of tax;
- the possibility of suspension of penalties; and
- the existence of fee protection insurance.

In any particular enquiry, the interaction of the above factors (and others) makes it impossible to predict how it will develop and be resolved. They also make it impossible in the context of this publication to provide any detailed guidance as to how the officer might 'work' the enquiry. Practitioners will find more guidance in CCH *Practical Enquiries Manual*.

Where the enquiry relates to a business, the officer is likely to want to meet the taxpayer. The officer has no right to insist on either the taxpayer or their representative attending an interview but a refusal to meet could impact the reduction for disclosure if any under-declaration is found.

If the practitioner agrees to a meeting, they need to:

- establish, if possible, HMRC's agenda for the meeting;
- explain to their client in advance the likely style of the meeting;
- prepare for the meeting;
- ensure that any necessary disclosures are volunteered first thing in the meeting;
- emphasise as appropriate that there was no lack of care or deliberate action;

- focus on factors which can reduce liabilities;

- keep a record of evidence of disclosure and/or special circumstances;

- ensure that their own contributions are conducive towards a resolution of matters;

- be alert to the possibility of misunderstanding and intervene to clarify as necessary;

- ensure that estimates are not understood as facts;

- take notes at the meeting (including of their own contributions);

- request a copy of HMRC's notes;

- indicate that it is not their practice's policy to recommend clients to sign such notes;

- promise to provide information after relevant checking; and

- ensure that their client remains calm and comfortable (water, comfort breaks, etc.).

After the meeting, the practitioner should:

- briefly discuss the outcome with their client;

- identify all points that need following up;

- provide any promised information as quickly as possible;

- review HMRC's notes of the meeting and draw attention to any required amendments;

- advise HMRC of relevant points that have emerged since the meeting; and

- identify steps to assist the early closure of the enquiry.

Where the officer undertakes a review of records, the purpose is to establish their reliability. Can the records be 'broken'? Before records are provided to the officer, the practitioner should:

- review the records to ensure that they understand them;

- identify any relevant weaknesses and consider how these might be overcome;

- offer appropriate explanations to HMRC on significant matters; and

- identify factors that might usefully overcome any minor weaknesses.

If the officer considers that the records have been broken, they may embark on a business economics exercise. CCH *Practical Enquiries Manual* includes commentary on HMRC's approach.

Tax Reporter: ¶185-600ff.

12740   Reopening earlier years

Once HMRC have established that there are omitted profits in the year under enquiry, they are entitled (subject to the four, six and twenty year provisions) to raise assessments for earlier years. In doing so, they will rely on the 'presumption of continuity' established in *Jonas v Bamford*. The onus of proof is with the taxpayer to show that any such assessments for the earlier years are excessive. This means that the practitioner would have to rebut the presumption by (for example) providing evidence of a change in circumstances which supported the conclusion that it was unlikely on the balance of probabilities that the error identified in the later year applied equally (or at all) to the earlier year or years.

If the presumption of continuity applies, adjustments may be required in earlier years. The officer may propose scaling back the omissions or perhaps the adjusted level of drawings in the enquiry year by applying the Retail Price Index or applying the adjusted gross profit rate to the earlier years.

The practitioner may be able to demonstrate that:

* there were exceptional circumstances in the enquiry year;

* there were different circumstances in some or all of the earlier years;

* changes in the business needed to be recognised; and

* additional reliefs were available in some or all of the years.

Case: *Jonas v Bamford (HMIT)* (1973) 51 TC 1

Tax Reporter: ¶185-600ff.

12750   Conclusion of enquiry

At the end of an enquiry that has identified under-declared income or gains, matters will be finalised in one of two ways. Either the officer will follow the formal statutory basis of issuing a closure notice and any necessary assessments or they can invite the taxpayer to offer a contractual settlement. Whichever alternative is adopted should make no difference to the financial impact on the taxpayer as the constituent elements of tax, penalties (see 12000ff.) and interest are the same in both cases. There are, however, significant practical differences between the two.

The statutory basis involves the issue by an officer of a closure notice together as appropriate with any assessments and penalty determinations. The closure notice will state the conclusions reached as a result of the enquiry and the adjustments required to the self-assessment return. Where appropriate, an amended self-assessment will be issued. Any appeal against the closure notice has to be made within 30 days.

The contractual settlement procedure:

- HMRC advising the taxpayer of what they consider their available statutory sanctions to be in terms of:
  - raising or amending assessments;
  - making a formal penalty determination;
  - charging interest on unpaid tax;
- the taxpayer signing a Letter of Offer under which they:
  - admit that the tax liabilities, penalties and interest have arisen wholly or in part due to them failing to meet their obligations;
  - offer to pay a monetary sum within a specified time period in consideration of HMRC agreeing not to enforce its formal sanctions;
- HMRC accepting the Letter of Offer;
- HMRC being able to enforce the contractual debt without having to prove their statutory entitlement.

The main practical differences between formal closure procedures and a contractual settlement are that under the latter:

- there are no grounds for appeal against the tax, penalty and interest liabilities;
- time to pay provisions can be included;
- the amounts of tax, penalties and interest are necessarily finalised at the same time; and
- both parties have greater certainty that matters have been finalised.

Before concluding an enquiry, the officer will normally ask for a statement of assets and liabilities and a certificate of full disclosure. The former could be formally required; the latter cannot, but refusal to provide it might lead to the enquiry being extended.

Consultation

At Autumn Statement 2014, the Government announced a consultation on a proposal to introduce a new power, enabling HMRC to achieve early resolution and closure of one or more aspects of a tax enquiry whilst leaving other aspects open. The summary of responses was published on 28 September 2015 and is available at www.gov.uk/government/uploads/system/uploads/attachment_data/file/464066/Tax_enquiries_closure_rules_-_summary_of_responses_-_28_september.pdf. Legislation has yet to be published.

For more guidance on enquiries, please refer to CCH *Practical Enquiries Manual*.

Case: *Nichols* [2016] TC 04942

Tax Reporter: ¶185-600ff.

Case Table

1821

Legislation Finding List

Individual Savings Account Regulations 1998

Inheritance (Provision for Family and Dependants) Act 1975

Inheritance Tax (Delivery of Accounts) (Excepted Estates) (Amendment) regulations SI2011/214

Inheritance Tax (Delivery Of Accounts) (Excepted Estates) Regulations 2004

Inheritance Tax (Delivery Of Accounts) (Excepted Settlements) Regulations 2008

Inheritance Tax (Delivery Of Accounts) (Excepted Transfers And Excepted Terminations) Regulations 2008

Inheritance Tax (Double Charges Relief) Regulations 1987

Inheritance Tax Avoidance Schemes (Prescribed Descriptions Of Arrangements) Regulations 2011

Insolvency Act 1986

Insurance Premium Tax Regulations 1994

Index to Concessions and Statements

Index

1861

Index

Index

Index

Index

Index

Index

Index

Index

Index

Index